BIOLOGY
and
MANAGEMENT
of the
CERVIDAE

A Conference Held at the Conservation and Research Center

NATIONAL ZOOLOGICAL PARK
SMITHSONIAN INSTITUTION

Front Royal, Virginia
August 1–5, 1982

RESEARCH SYMPOSIA OF THE
NATIONAL ZOOLOGICAL PARK

BIOLOGY
and
MANAGEMENT
of the
CERVIDAE

Christen M. Wemmer, Editor

SMITHSONIAN INSTITUTION PRESS
Washington, D.C.   London

© 1987 by Smithsonian Institution

Library of Congress Cataloging-in-Publication Data

Biology and management of the Cervidae.
(Research Symposia of the National Zoological Park)
   Bibliography: p.
   1. Cervidae—Congresses. 2. Wildlife management—
Congresses. I. Wemmer, Christen M. II. Series.
QL737.U55B5626   1987   599.73'57   86-600124
ISBN 0-87474-981-6 (pbk.)
ISBN 0-87474-980-8

British Library Cataloguing-in-Publication Data is
available.

∞The paper used in this publication meets the
minimum requirements of the American National
Standard for Permanence of Paper for Printed Library
Materials Z39.48-1984.

Typesetter: The Composing Room of Michigan, Inc.

Contents

Contents

Contents

Contributors

Sumaryoto Atmosoedirdjo
Directorate of Nature Conservation
Jl. Ir. H. Juanda 9
Bogor, Indonesia

Cyrille Barrette
Biology Department
Laval University
Québec, Canada G1K 7P4

Hansjörg Blankenhorn
Federal Game Commissioner
Federal Forestry Office
Laupenstrasse 20
Berne, Switzerland

Raleigh A. Blouch
World Wildlife Fund Indonesia Program
P.O. Box 133
Bogor, Indonesia

Wm.V. Branan
Florida Defenders of the Environment
102 West Third Avenue
Tallahassee, Florida 32303

A.R. Bray
Winchmore Irrigation Research Station
Ministry of Agriculture and Fisheries
Private Bag
Ashburton, New Zealand

T.H. Clutton-Brock
Large Animal Research Group
Department of Zoology
Cambridge, England

A.B. Bubenik
10 Stornoway Crescent
Ontario, Canada L3T 3X7

G.A. BUBENIK
Department of Zoology
University of Guelph
Ontario, Canada L3T 3X7

FRED L. BUNNELL
Faculty of Forestry
University of British Colombia
Vancouver, British Columia V6T 1W5

M. BUSH
Animal Health Department
National Zoological Park
Smithsonian Institution
Washington, DC 20009

RONALD K. CHESSER
Department of Biological Sciences
The Museum, Texas Tech University
Lubbock, Texas 79409

EUGENE J. DEGAYNER
3856 Denali
Ketchikan, Alaska 99901

ERIC DINERSTEIN
SI/Nepal Terai Ecology Project
American Embassy (GSO)
Kathmandu, Nepal

K.R. DREW
Invermay Agriculture Research Center
Ministry of Agriculture and Fisheries
Private Bag
Mosgiel, New Zealand

JOHN F. EISENBERG
The Florida State Museum
University of Florida
Gainesville, Florida 32611

WILLIAM D. ELDRIDGE
United States Department of the Interior
Fish and Wildlife Service
1011 E. Tudor Road
Anchorage, Alaska 99503

P. FENNESSY
Invermay Agricultural Research Center
Ministry of Agriculture and Fisheries
Private Bay
Mosgiel, New Zealand

THOMAS J. FOOSE
AAZPA Conservation Coordinator
ISIS Office
Minnesota Zoological Garden
Apple Valley, Minnesota 55124

HANS FRÄDRICH
Zoologischer Garten Berlin
Hardenbergplatz 8
D-1000 Berline 30
West Germany

ALBERT W. FRANZMANN
Alaska Department of Fish and Game
Moose Research Center
P.O. Box 3150
Soldotna, Alaska 99669

G. GEIGER
Swiss Ornithological Station
Sempach, Switzerland

VALERIUS GEIST
Faculty of Environmental Design
University of Calgary
Calgary, Alberta T24 1N4
Canada

MICHAEL J.B. GREEN
Conservation Monitoring Center
219(C) Huntingdon Road
Cambridge CB3 ODL
England

COLIN P. GROVES
Department of Prehistory and Anthropology
Australian National University
P.O. Box 4
Canberra, A.C.T. 2600
Australia

PETER GRUBB
35 Downhills Park Road
London N17 6PE
England

W.J. HAMILTON
Hill Farming Research Organization
Glensaugh Research Station
Laurencekirk
Scotland AB3 1HB

JOHN E. JACKSON
Instituto Nacional de Tecnologia Agropecuario
Estación Experimental Agropecuaria San Luis
Casille de Dorreo N17
5730 Villa Mercedes
San Luis, Argentina

Christine M. Janis
Department of Biology and Medicine
Brown University
Providence, Rhode Island 02912

Peter A. Jordan
Department of Fisheries and Wildlife
University of Minnesota
St. Paul, Minnesota 55108

R.N.B. Kay
Rowett Research Institute
Bucksburn
Aberdeen AB2 95B
Scotland

R.W. Kelly
Invermay Agricultural Research Center
Ministry of Agriculture and Fisheries
Private Bag
Mosgiel, New Zealand

Andrzej Krzywińsky
Institute of Genetics and Animal Breeding
Polish Academy of Sciences
Popielno
12-222 Wejsuny
Poland

Alfredo Langguth
Instituto Nacional de Tecnologia Agropecuario
Estación Experimental Agropecuaria San Luis
Casille de Dorreo N17
5730 Villa Mercedes
San Luis, Argentina

Adrian M. Lister
Department of Zoology
Downing Street
Cambridge CB2 3EJ
England

Andrew S.I. Loudon
Institute of Zoology
The Zoological Society of London
Regent's Park
London NW1 4R4
England

R.L. Marchinton
School of Forest Services
University of Georgia
Athens, Georgia

Claude Martin
World Wildlife Fund - Switzerland
Postfach
8037 Zürich
Switzerland

Dale R. McCullough
Department of Forestry and Resource Management
145 Mulford Hall
University of California, Berkeley
Berkeley, California 94720

Mark MacNamara
Milestone Genetics Inc.
11 Park Avenue
Ardsley, New York 10502

Juan R. Merkt
Concord Field Station
Harvard University
Old Causeway Road
Bedford, Massachusetts 01730

Frank Miller
Canadian Wildlife Service
Western and Northern Region
#1000,9942–108 Street
Edmonton, Alberta, T5K 2J5
Canada

Hemanta R. Mishra
King Mahendra Trust for Nature Conservation
National Park Building
P.O. Box 3712
Babar Mahal
Kathmandu, Nepal

G.H. Moore
Invermay Agricultural Research Center
Ministry of Agriculture and Fisheries
Private Bag
Mosgiel, New Zealand

Dietland Muller-Schwarze
College of Environmental Science and Forestry
State University of New York
Syracuse, New York 13210

Choompol Ngampongsai
Department of Conservation
Kasetsart University
Bangkok 10900
Thailand

Olav T. Oftedal
Department of Zoological Research
National Zoological Park
Washington, DC 20008

Katherine I. O'Rourke
Department of Veterinary Microbiology and
Pathology
Washington State University
Pullman, Washington 99164

Nicholas V. Pacheco
Corporacion Nacional Forestal
Correo Entre Lagos
Casilla 22
Osorno, Chile

Kenneth J. Raedeke
College of Forest Resources AR-10
University of Washington
Seattle, Washington 98195

Kent H. Redford
Florida State Museum
University of Florida
Gainesville, Florida 32611

Charles T. Robbins
Wildlife Biology Program
Washington State University
Pullman, Washington 99164

R.M.F.S. Sadleir
Ecology Division
Department of Scientific and Industrial Research
Private Bag
Lower Hutt
New Zealand

Charles Schwartz
Alaska Department of Fish and Game
Moose Research Center
P.O. Box 3150
Soldotna, Alaska 99669

Kathleen M. Scott
Department of Biological Sciences (Zoology Unit)
Rutgers University
Box 1059
Piscataway, New Jersey 08854

U.S. Seal
Bldg. 49, Room 207
Veterans Administration Medical Center
54th Street & 48th Ave., S.
Minneapolis, Minnesota 55417

Michael H. Smith
Savannah River Ecology Laboratory
Drawer E
Aiken, South Carolina 29801

Richard Taber
College of Forest Resources AR-10
University of Washington
Seattle, Washington 98195

Dennis Turner
Ethology and Wildlife Research
Institute of Zoology
University of Zürich
Zürich, Switzerland

Chris Wemmer
Conservation and Research Center
National Zoological Park
Front Royal, Virginia 22630

Danny C. Wharton
New York Zoological Society
Bronx Park
Bronx, New York 10460

Don Wilson
National Fish and Wildlife Laboratory
National Museum of Natural History
Washington, DC 20560

Erhard Ueckermann
Forschungstelle für Jagdkunde und Wildschaden-
verhütung des Landes
Nordrhein - Westfalen
Forsthaus Hordt,
5300 Bonn 3

Preface

The need for a review of cervid biology became evident to me in the late 1970s when I became involved in behavioral studies of captive deer and had the opportunity to undertake some cursory investigations of deer in South Asia. Though the comparative literature was growing at the time, there were few reviews of any aspect of cervid biology. In the course of travels I also became aware of a number of deer research studies in developing countries which for various reasons had not yet reached the printed page. The rather tenuous future of many of these species made it apparent that management of endangered deer and their habitats is a requisite for their continued survival. Thus the symposium was conceived to address three specific areas: biological reviews, field studies of exotic deer, and the management of selected species and related topics. This was perhaps an overly ambitious undertaking; a full conference could have been convened on any of the general headings. But symposia are also social events, and the idea of bringing together the prime stags and the spikers promised, among other things, good theatre. The usual barriers of zoogeography and peer affiliation soon gave way to a lively discourse and productive exchange of ideas and information. There was also no shortage of cervid display.

An urgency to publish the proceedings is a feature of most symposia, and in this regard the present symposium was no exception. In spite of my well-intentioned promises I found it impossible to complete the editing in a timely fashion, and a 14-month stint as acting director of the National Zoo further delayed the product. Being familiar with the pre-publication review systems of professional journals, I still do not see how a large volume can be carefully and quickly edited. But lest that should sound like an excuse let me apologize one last time for the delay and acknowledge the robust forebearance of my colleagues.

For their guidance, support, and encouragement I would like to thank Dr. Theodore H. Reed and John F. Eisenberg. Jack Williams and Mary McComas were indispensable to organizing the conference, and Charmaine Moberly and Barbara Atwood assisted with many of the details. Charmaine Moberly deserves special recognition as the one who painstakingly typed all the manuscripts; she saw the syposium through to the end even after she left the zoo for more tranquil if not greener pastures, and still kindly maintains that the 1000 pages of typescript had nothing to do with the change. Charmaine's replacement, Laura Walker, was extremely responsive in attending to the many repeated editorial changes and last-minute details. Michael Stüwe on the other hand never allowed the dimension of the undertaking to lose perspective or to escape me, and volunteered needed assistance as computer-jockey in preparing word-processing copy. Ingvar Matthiasson and Warren Cutler carefully restored, improved, or re-sketched marginal illustrations. Mary Frances Bell deserves special thanks for her careful reading of the manuscript and assistance in standardizing format. Kay Kenyon cheerfully performed indispensable service by providing full citations of innumerable bibliographic references. Lastly, I owe thanks to all those who gave their time to review manuscripts in their field of specialty: Theodore H. Grand, Robert J. Emry, Peter Grubb, Joseph Leinders, Olaf Oftedal, Kent Redford, Kathleen Scott, Michael Stüwe, and David Webb, and David Wildt.

Chris Wemmer
Conservation and Research Center
National Zoological Park
Front Royal, Virginia 22630

Part I

Review Papers and Theoretical Issues

KATHLEEN M. SCOTT
and
CHRISTINE M. JANIS
Department of Biological Sciences (Zoology)
Rutgers University
Box 1059 Piscataway, New Jersey 08854

Newnham College and Department of Zoology
Cambridge University
Cambridge, England

Phylogenetic Relationships of the Cervidae, and the Case for a Superfamily "Cervoidea"

ABSTRACT

This paper reviews the phylogenetic position of the Cervidae within the ruminant Artiodactyla and the various ideas about which families of ruminant artiodactyls should be placed with the Cervidae in a superfamily Cervoidea. We also suggest a new classification of "cervoids". The Suborder Ruminantia can be divided into two infraorders, the Tragulina and the Pecora. The Tragulina are considered to include the living family Tragulidae and the fossil families Hypertragulidae and Leptomerycidae. The Protoceratidae and the Amphimerycidae are placed in the Tylopoda. We follow Webb and Taylor (1980) in placing the Gelocidae in the Pecora. The Pecora also include the families Cervidae, Dromomerycidae, Antilocapridae, Giraffidae, Bovidae, and Moschidae. The living genus *Moschus* and a number of fossil genera are placed in the family Moschidae, rather than in the Cervidae. The Palaeomerycidae is regarded as a polyphyletic group, and most genera can be assigned to other families; those that cannot are best regarded as Pecora, *incertae sedis*.

The characters that have been used in allying these families at the suprafamilial level are also reviewed. The frontal appendages of all ruminants are not necessarily homologous and should not be used to ally those families possessing them as more closely related to each other than to any of the hornless ruminants. Leinders and Heintz (1980) have considered two characters to be derived for the superfamily Cervoidea: a double lacrimal orifice and a closed metatarsal gully. However, both characters are variable in at least some taxa, making them difficult to interpret, and both have arisen independently in some taxa, suggesting that they should not be assumed to be homologous wherever present. These appear to be the best characters now available for assessing relationships of the cervoid taxa. Using these characters we suggest that Dromomerycidae and the antilocaprine antilocaprids should be considered cervoids. Moschids have a single lacrimal orifice, but may be regarded as the sister group of the other cervoids on the basis of the metatarsal gully. Merycodontine antilocaprids have a single orifice and the metatarsal gully is highly variable. We question their inclusion in the Antilocapridae but a detailed consideration of their position is not given. The position of the giraffids is problematical, but there is no evidence to ally them to the Cervidae.

Introduction

The Cervidae is a family in the order Artiodactyla, included in the infraorder Pecora of the suborder Ruminantia. The ruminant Artiodactyla are a diverse and complex group, and the phylogenetic position of the Cervidae within this assemblage has been the subject of some controversy. We will review the relationships which have been postulated amongst the ruminant artiodactyls, and the characters which have been used in assigning relationships among these families, with special attention to the origin and relationships of the Cervidae, and the groups which have been allied with them at the suprafamilial level.

Artiodactyls first appear in the early Eocene, characterized by two osteological features: an astragalus of a unique shape (deeply grooved and pulley-like on both proximal and distal surfaces) and paraxonic foot structure, in which the axis of foot symmetry passes between the third and fourth digits. In more derived artiodactyls the weight is borne by the third and fourth digits alone, the first digit is lost, and the second and fifth digits are variably reduced or lost entirely.

The earliest artiodactyls are grouped as a basal assemblage of "palaeodonts". Later artiodactyls (first appearing in the late Eocene) are divided into three suborders: the Suina (including pigs, peccaries, hippos, and several extinct families); the Tylopoda (including camels and several extinct families); and the Ruminantia. The Ruminantia are further subdivided into the Infraorder Tragulina (small hornless forms including living tragulids or chevrotains, and a number of extinct forms) and the Infraorder Pecora (larger forms that usually possess horns or other cranial appendages, including superfamilial groupings of bovoids, cervoids, and giraffoids).

The superfamily Cervoidea of the infraorder Pecora includes the family Cervidae, plus a number of extinct and living families which have been allied with the antlered deer. The family Cervidae as commonly used includes the subfamilies Muntiacinae (muntjacs), Hydropotinae (Chinese water deer), Cervinae (most Old World cervids plus the New World red deer), and Odocoileinae (most New World cervids and the European roe deer). The musk deer (*Moschus* species) are sometimes included in the family Cervidae, although their systematic position is open to debate. The families that have been included with the Cervidae in the superfamily Cervoidea have varied greatly according to different authors over the past century. We here review the different positions and suggest our definition of the "Cervoidea".

The Phylogeny of the Ruminantia

The Position of the Ruminantia within the Artiodactyla

The Ruminantia is the only suborder of the Artiodactyla distinguished by a uniquely derived character (autapomorphy), and thus appears to be the only natural group within the order. Ruminants are distinguished by the fusion of the cuboid and navicular bones in the tarsus, and fossil artiodactyls with this distinguishing character first appear in the late Eocene (Colbert, 1941; Webb and Taylor, 1980). Living members of the Ruminantia have a compartmentalized stomach which serves as a chamber for fermentation of cellulose by symbiotic microorganisms, and also chew the cud. They possess an incisiform lower canine, and replace the upper incisors by a horny pad.

The suborder Ruminantia is generally more closely allied with the Suborder Tylopoda than with the Suborder Suina (e. g. Webb and Taylor, 1980) although alternative views exist (e. g. Gazin, 1955). The Tylopoda resemble the Ruminantia in the elongate limbs and reduced side toes, and in their selenodont molars. Selenodont molars have the cusps united into lophs in a characteristic double crescent shape running longitudinally across both buccal and lingual portions of the molars. The primitive molar morphology in Artiodactyla, seen in the palaeodonts, is bunodont; that is, molars with distinct individual cusps. In living ungulates bunodont teeth are correlated with an omnivorous or frugivorous diet. Members of the Suina usually retain the bunodont condition, in contrast to the selenodont molars of the Ruminantia and Tylopoda, and it is partly on this basis that the latter two suborders are allied. Selenodont molars have also evolved in parallel in the extinct suine family Anthracotheriidae.

Webb and Taylor (1980) assign the Ruminantia to the Neoselenodontia, which unites them with the family Camelidae and the extinct family Protoceratidae among the tylopods. Characters uniting this monophyletic assemblage include the loss or reduction of the upper incisors, fusion of the ectocuneiform and mesocuneiform in the carpus, loss of the paraconule in the upper molars, and the presence of a "ruminant" type of digestive physiology (inferred in the Protoceratidae). The stomach of living camelids clearly evolved largely in parallel with the stomach of the Ruminantia, as it differs in general shape and morphology, and has three chambers, rather than four as in the Ruminantia. However, embryological studies suggest that the initial ontogenetic development of the forestomach is similar in the two groups, and that they may well be derived from a common ancestor with this initial enlargement of the forestomach (Langer, 1974). In addition, both types of "ruminants" chew the cud. Hippos and peccaries also have an enlarged forestomach in conjunction with forestomach fermentation, but the ontogenetic development of the forestomach is different (Langer, 1974), and these "ruminating" suines do not regurgitate the food.

Whilst the common features of Tylopoda and Ruminantia may unite them at a higher ordinal level, Webb and Taylor (1980) pointed out that no autapomorphic characters unite the tylopods as a whole, although Protoceratidae and Camelidae do share some derived features. Tylopods represent an assemblage of selenodont artiodactyls that are excluded from the Ruminantia by the absence of the fusion of the cuboid and navicular bones in the tarsus.

Subdivisions within the Suborder Ruminantia

Simpson (1945) followed the original classification of Flower (1883) in using the suborders Tylopoda and Ruminantia, with the Ruminantia divided into the infraorders Tragulina and Pecora. The Pecora are then divided into the Cervoidea, the Giraffoidea, and the Bovoidea. This terminology is preferred by current authors (e. g. Webb and Taylor, 1980). Stirton (1944) used the term "Ruminantia" to include the Tylopoda and the Ruminantia (*sensu* Simpson), terming this latter group the "Pecora". He then divided his infraorder Pecora into three superfamilies: Traguloidea (chevrotains and primitive pecorans without frontal appendages), Cervoidea (including deer and giraffes), and Bovoidea (including bovids and antilocaprids). This classification has been followed by Romer (1966). However, Stirton himself stated that these three superfamilies were not of equal rank, and the Traguloidea represented a taxonomic rank equal to the Cervoidea plus the Bovoidea. This corresponds to the classification used by Simpson (1945), which

would thus appear to represent a more natural taxonomic grouping.

The division of the more advanced Pecora into two basic groups, cervoids and bovoids, has been followed by numerous authors, but the taxa included in these groups have varied. The Cervoidea as used by Romer (1966) included the families Palaeomerycidae, Cervidae, and Giraffidae, while the Bovoidea included the Bovidae and Antilocapridae. Both Matthew (1934) and Hamilton (1978a) allied the giraffids with the bovids in a superfamily Bovoidea. Although most authors ally the Antilocapridae with the Bovidae at either the superfamilial or familial level, Leinders and Heintz (1980) include them in the Cervoidea. Some authors (e. g. Simpson, 1945; Crusafont, 1961; Viret, 1961) consider giraffids to be an independent radiation within the Ruminantia, and have erected a third superfamily Giraffoidea (including Giraffidae plus a number of fossil forms) within the infraorder Pecora. Interpretation of the characters used to subdivide the Pecora has also varied. Pilgrim (1941) groups giraffes and cervids because they lack the keratin sheath of bovids and antilocaprids, and because they both have low-crowned (brachyodont) cheek teeth. On the other hand, Matthew (1934) and Hamilton (1978a) both group the giraffes with the bovids based on similarities in horn development, and Matthew was also influenced by the similar elongation of the limbs and the loss of the lateral digits in both.

Classification of groups within the Pecora has thus been the subject of much controversy, as is the origin of the infraorder. Most authorities agree that the ancestry of the Cervoidea and the Bovoidea lies within the Tragulina, but the ancestral group is uncertain. The next part of this paper will review the definitions of the families of the Tragulina and Pecora and the characters which have been used in defining possible interrelationships of the families.

Families of the Ruminantia

Infraorder Tragulina

TRAGULIDAE

The family Tragulidae, with three surviving genera, *Tragulus*, *Mosciola*, and *Hyemoschus*, is representative of the general morphological characteristics of the Infraorder Tragulina. Present day tragulids, also known as chevrotains or mouse deer, are small animals (2–15 kg) found in the Old World tropical forests. The family first appears in the Miocene of Eurasia and Africa. Tragulids lack any kind of antlers or horns, but both sexes possess large canine tusks which are considerably larger in the males. The subdivisions of the stomach are less complex than living Pecora (see Kay, this volume). The limbs are considerably less specialized than those of other Pecora. Both fore–and hindlimbs are functionally two-toed, but lateral toes and slender lateral metapodials are present. Although the third and fourth metapodials are fused in the hindlimb in both genera, in the forelimb they are separate in *Hyemoschus* and partially fused in *Tragulus*. The fibula, as in higher ruminants, is incomplete, with proximal and distal rudiments fused to the tibia. Distal keels of the metapodials are found only on the ventral (posterior) surface, in contrast to the higher pecorans in which they continue onto the dorsal surface. Specialized features (autapomorphies) of the family include the posterior extension of the palatine bones, a reduced postglenoid process, and a large cancellous auditory bulla. Although tragulids resemble higher ruminants in possessing a complete postorbital bar, it appears to have been formed differently in this family than in other ruminants, being composed primarily of the jugal as opposed to the frontals (Webb and Taylor, 1980).

OTHER TRAGULOIDS

Although the Tragulidae are clearly primitive ruminants which provide an indication of the general level of organization of the Tragulina, they are specialized in many ways and do not adequately reflect the diversity of the group. The infraorder Tragulina (*sensu* Webb and Taylor, 1980) also includes two extinct families, the Hypertragulidae and the Leptomerycidae. All species included in the Tragulina are hornless and of small body size. Leptomerycids lack the large canine in the male that characterizes hypertragulids, tragulids and the other hornless members of the Pecora (*sensu* Webb and Taylor, 1980). Hypertragulids and leptomerycids both have a caniniform lower first premolar, a specialization absent in tragulids and higher ruminants.

Hypertragulids (Figure 1) are known from the late Eocene through the early Miocene of North America. They are the most primitive of the families of the Ruminantia, as they lack both the fusion of the magnum and trapezoid in the carpus and the confluence of the jugular foramen and posterior lacerate foramen in the basicranial regions, which are features present in all the other families. Other primitive features of the Hypertragulidae include an incomplete postorbital bar, unfused third and fourth metapodials, presence of complete (though reduced) second and fifth digits, a vestigial first digit in the carpus, and a fibula that is reduced in width over the primitive artiodactyl condition but still has a complete shaft (Webb and Taylor, 1980).

The Leptomerycidae (Figure 1) are known from the

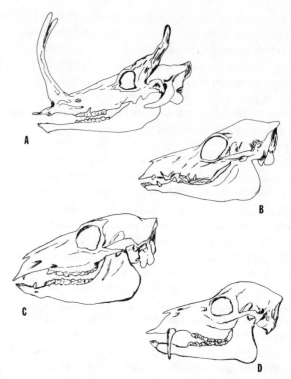

Figure 1. Tylopoda and hornless Ruminants. A, *Synthetoceras*, a horned North American tylopod; B, *Hypertragulus* (Hypertragulidae); C, *Leptomeryx* (Leptomerycidae); D, *Blastomeryx* (Moschidae). (After Frick, 1937).

Oligocene and Miocene of North America and Eurasia. They differ from the Hypertragulidae and resemble more advanced ruminants in a number of features of the carpus and basicranium. They also appear to be more advanced than the Tragulidae, as they share a number of derived features with higher ruminants. These include restriction of the mastoid to the occipital region of the cranium, details of premolar and tarsal morphology, and a postorbital bar composed primarily of the frontal bone (Webb and Taylor, 1980). In the limbs the fibula is incomplete, the first metapodial is lost, and the second and fifth metapodials are reduced, though usually complete. In *Archaeomeryx*, a Mongolian Eocene genus, metapodials three and four are separate in both the fore- and hindlimbs. However, in the later North American genus *Leptomeryx*, the third and fourth metatarsals are fused and metatarsals two and five are reduced to proximal rudiments (Webb and Taylor, 1980).

Protoceratids have been considered traguloids by many authors (e. g. Simpson, 1945; Romer, 1966). Protoceratids were an exclusively North American group of small to medium-sized animals spanning the Late Eocene to the Early Pliocene. They resemble

Scott and Janis

cervoid ruminants in general body proportions, and possess paired, bony, non-deciduous frontal horns in the males only. Later genera also possessed a single, median, forked nasal horn in the males (Figure 1). However, Webb and Taylor (1980) point out that they lack the derived ruminant character of fusion of the cuboid and navicular in the tarsus. Patton and Taylor (1973) demonstrated that protoceratids can be placed within the Tylopoda. Moreover, they share derived characters with Camelidae which support the idea that they are the sister group of this family (Webb and Taylor, 1980). Their superficial resemblance to the Ruminantia, especially with regard to the evolution of sexually dimorphic bony horns, appears to have developed in parallel (Janis, 1982).

Amphimerycidae were considered tragulids by Simpson (1945). They are small animals from the Eocene and Oligocene of Europe, and were considered members of the Ruminantia because of a questionably referred fused cubonavicular bone (see discussion in

Webb and Taylor, 1980). They were removed from the Ruminantia by Viret (1961), and this view has been upheld by subsequent authors. Romer (1966) places them in the superfamily Anoplotherioidea in the Tylopoda.

The relationships of the traguloid groups to the higher pecora and amongst themselves have been the subject of much disagreement. Pilgrim (1947) and Matthew (1934) considered *Archaeomeryx* closest to the ancestry of the Pecora. Simpson (1945) and Webb and Taylor (1980) place *Gelocus* nearest the families of higher ruminants: as Webb and Taylor (1980) point out (see next section), the Gelocidae should be included in the Pecora. Most authors agree in placing the living Tragulidae some distance from the ancestry of the Pecora. Although the Tragulidae are the closest living relatives of the higher Pecora, they are actually quite distantly related to them. The placement of traguloid and primitive pecoran groups as given by Webb and Taylor (1980) is shown in Table 1.

Table 1. Classification of the Ruminantia by various authors, with special attention to the composition of the "Palaeomerycidae" and the "Cervoidea"

Genus	Subfamily	Family	Superfamily	Infraorder
I. Simpson (1945)				
		Amphimerycidae[a]	AMPHIMERYCOIDEA	
		Hypertragulidae[e]		
		(& leptomerycids[e])	HYPERTRAGULOIDEA	TRAGULINA
		Protoceratidae[f]		
		Tragulidae[ab]	TRAGULOIDEA	
		Gelocidae[a]		
Palaeomeryx[a]				
Dremotherium[a]				
Amphitragulus[a]				
Blastomeryx[e]	Palaeomerycinae			
Parablastomeryx[e]				
Machaeomeryx[e]				
Longirostromeryx[e]				
Dromomeryx[f]		Cervidae	CERVOIDEA	
Rakomeryx[f]				
Matthewmeryx[f]				
Barbouromeryx[f]				
Bouromeryx[f]				
Procranioceras[f]	Dromomerycinae			
Cranioceras[f]				
Yumaceras[f]				
Pediomeryx[f]				

Key to superscripts: a, fossil Eurasian hornless genera; b, living Eurasian hornless genera; c, fossil Eurasian horned genera; d, fossil African horned genera; e, fossil North American hornless genera; f, fossil North American horned genera; g, living North American horned genera; h, fossil African hornless genera

Table 1. (cont.)

Genus	Subfamily	Family	Superfamily	Infraorder
Aletomeryx[f] *Sinclairomeryx*[f] *Moschus*[b] cervids	Muntiacinae Cervinae Odocoileinae (& *Hydropotes*[b])			PECORA
Lagomeryx[c] *Procervulus*[c] *Climacoceras*[d]		Lagomerycidae	GIRAFFOIDEA	
giraffes		Giraffidae		
antilocaprids	Merycodontinae Antilocaprinae	Antilocapridae	BOVOIDEA	
bovids (& *Propalaeomeryx*[d])		Bovidae		

II. Stirton (1945)

Genus	Subfamily	Family	Superfamily	Infraorder
			TRAGULOIDEA	
Palaeomeryx[a] *Dremotherium*[a] *Amphitragulus*[a] blastomerycids[e] *Lagomeryx*[c] *Procervulus*[c] *Climacoceras*[d]	Palaeomerycinae	Palaeomerycidae	CERVOIDEA	PECORA
dromomerycids[f]	Dromomerycinae			
Moschus[b]		Moschidae		
cervids	Cervulinae Cervinae	Cervidae		
giraffids		Giraffidae		
antilocaprids	Merycodontinae Antilocaprinae	Antilocapridae	BOVOIDEA	
bovids		Bovidae		

III. Viret & Crusafont (in Pivateau, 1961)

Genus	Subfamily	Family	Superfamily	Infraorder
		Hypertragulidae[e] (& leptomerycids[e]) Protoceratidae[f]	HYPERTRAGULOIDEA	TRAGULINA
		Tragulidae[ab] Gelocidae[a]	TRAGULOIDEA	
Palaeomeryx[a] *Dremotherium*[a] *Amphitragulus*[a]	Palaeomerycinae		CERVOIDEA	
blastomerycids[e]	Blastomerycinae			
Procervulus[c] *Lagomeryx*[c] *Climacoceras*[d]	Lagomerycinae	Cervidae		
Moschus[b]	Moschinae			

Table 1. (cont.)

Genus	Subfamily	Family	Superfamily	Infraorder
cervids	Muntjacinae Pliocervinae Cervinae			PECORA
dromomerycids[f] (& *Triceromeryx*[c])		Dromomerycidae	GIRAFFOIDEA	
giraffes		Giraffidae		
antilocaprids	Merycodontinae[f] Antilocaprinae[fg]	Antilocapridae	BOVOIDEA	
bovids		Bovidae		

IV. Romer (1966)

Genus	Subfamily	Family	Superfamily	Infraorder
		Hypertragulidae[e] (& leptomerycids[e]) Protoceratidae[f] Tragulidae[ab] Gelocidae[a]	TRAGULOIDEA	
Palaeomeryx[a] *Dremotherium*[a] *Amphitragulus*[a] blastomerycids[e] *Procervulus*[c] *Climacoceras*[d] *Walangania*[h] dromomerycids[f]		Palaeomerycidae	CERVOIDEA	PECORA
Moschus[b] cervids		Cervidae		
giraffids *Triceromeryx*[c] *Prolibytherium*[d]		Giraffidae		
antilocaprids[fg] bovids (& *Propalaeomeryx*[d])		Antilocapridae Bovidae	BOVOIDEA	

V. Current Literature View
(incorporating Hamilton, 1978 and Webb and Taylor, 1980)

Genus	Subfamily	Family	Superfamily	Infraorder
		Hypertragulidae[e] Tragulidae[ab] Leptomerycidae[ae]		TRAGULINA
		Gelocidae[ae]		
Dremotherium[a] *Amphitragulus*[a] blastomerycids[e] *Moschus*[b]		Moschidae		MOSCHINA
Palaeomeryx[a] *Procervulus*[c] *Lagomeryx*[c] *Propalaeomeryx*[d] *Prolibytherium*[d]	*incertae sedis*			PECORA

Table 1. (cont.)

Genus	Subfamily	Family	Superfamily	Infraorder
cervids	Hydropotinae[b] Muntiacinae Cervinae Odocoilinae	Cervidae	CERVOIDEA	EUPECORA
dromomerycids[f]	Dromomerycinae	Dromomerycidae ?		
Triceromeryx[c] *Climacoceras*[d] *Canthumeryx*[d] giraffes		Giraffidae	GIRAFFOIDEA	
antilocaprids	Antilocaprinae[fg] Merycodontinae[f]	Antilocapridae	BOVOIDEA	
walanganids bovids		Bovidae		

VI. Proposed View

    (this paper, including Janis & Lister, in press; Leinders, in press; Leinders and Heintz, 1980)

Genus	Subfamily	Family	Superfamily	Infraorder
		Hypertragulidae[e] Tragulidae[ab] Leptomerycidae[ae] "Gelocidae"[ae]		TRAGULINA
Walangania[h] *Palaeomeryx*[a] *Lagomeryx*[c] *Procervulus*[c] *Triceromeryx*[c] *Prolibytherium*[d] *Propalaeoryx*[d]	*incertae sedis*			PECORA
Dremotherium[a] *Amphitragulus*[a] blastomerycids[e] *Moschus*[b]		Moschidae		
merycodontines[f] antilocaprines[fg]	Merycodontinae Antilocaprinae } ?	Antilocapridae		
dromomerycids[f] hoplitomerycids cervids		Dromomerycidae Hoplitomerycids Cervidae	CERVOIDEA	
Climacoceras[d] *Canthumeryx*[d] giraffes (incl. sivatheres)		Giraffidae	?"BOVOIDEA"	
bovids		Bovidae		

Infraorder Pecora

GELOCIDAE

The Gelocidae are a group of small, hornless ruminants known from the Oligocene and Miocene of Eurasia and North America. They include the Eurasian Oligocene genera *Gelocus, Lophiomeryx, Eumeryx,* and *Prodremotherium* (Viret, 1961) and the North American late Miocene genus *Pseudoceras* (S. D. Webb, ms.). Poorly known Asian Eocene genera that were assigned to the Gelocidae by Simpson (1945), such as *Cryptomeryx,* may be better included somewhere within the Tragulina (Webb and Taylor, 1980). The Gelocidae traditionally have been placed in the Tragulina or Traguloidea (e. g. Romer, 1966), presumably because of their superficial resemblance to members of the infraorder in the small body size, enlarged upper canines, and the absence of horns. However, Webb and Taylor (1980) suggest that the Gelocidae belong in the Pecora, as their most primitive family, as they share a number of derived characters with the other pecoran families. These include the loss of the stapedial artery and the reduction of the subarcuate fossa in the basicranium, bifurcation of the paraconid in the lower premolars, forelimbs nearly equal in length to the hindlimbs, loss of the trapezium in the carpus, and a compact, parallel-sided astragalus.

The family Gelocidae appears to be an assemblage of primitive hornless pecorans and we can find no unique character that unites the included genera as a monophyletic group. Webb and Taylor (1980) state that the posteriorly displaced protocone of the upper third molar is a synapomorphy of gelocids. However, we have also observed this character in *Bachitherium,* clearly a leptomerycid as defined by Webb and Taylor (1980). (Viret classified *Bachitherium* as a leptomerycid, but his "Leptomerycidae" includes the Hypertragulidae and Leptomerycidae of Webb and Taylor.) As the ancestry of the ruminant families must be within the Oligocene and Eurasian pecora, it seems likely that further work will result in the assignation of the various "gelocid" genera to a basal position within some other pecoran family. However, such considerations are beyond the scope of this paper.

MOSCHIDAE

The living musk deer, *Moschus,* is usually classified within the family Cervidae in classifications that include living species only, but *Moschus* lacks many of the derived characters of living cervids. A number of authors, beginning with Gray (1821), and including Brooke (1878), Bubenik (1966) and Groves and Grubb (this volume), have suggested that *Moschus* should be placed in its own family, the Moschidae. Webb and Taylor (1980) expanded the Moschidae to include such fossil genera as the North American Miocene blastomerycids *Parablastomeryx, Blastomeryx, Longirostromeryx, Machairomeryx,* and the European Oligocene and Miocene *Dremotherium* and *Amphitragulus.* Although *Moschus* superficially resembles living deer, its inclusion in a separate family with at least the blastomerycids seems to be justified. These genera retain primitive ruminant characters such as small to medium body size, large canines in the males, and the absence of cranial appendages. The moschids and blastomerycids also possess a number of autapomorphies such as a laterally enclosed subcentral tympanohyal in the basicranium, and upper canines specialized over the traguloid condition in being sabre-like, and set loosely in enlarged alveoli. Although we include *Dremotherium* and *Amphitragulus* with the moschids in this paper, work in progress may result in the separation of one or both of these genera from this group.

However, while the Moschidae appear to form a natural group, the relationship of this group to the other Pecora is unclear. Webb and Taylor (1980) unite moschids with gelocids as the Moschina within the Pecora (with the other pecoran families forming the Eupecora), but do not state any synapomorphic characters that specifically unite the two families (see Table 1). Moschids share a number of derived features with higher pecorans which make them more advanced than the gelocids. These include a large suprameatal fissure in the basicranium, loss of the lower first premolar, triangular upper second and third premolars, anteriorly projecting and flattened metaconid on the lower fourth premolar, fusion of third and fourth metacarpals, and presence of complete second and fifth metapodials.

Webb and Taylor (1980) exclude the moschids from the Eupecora largely on the absence of cranial appendages. As discussed below, cranial appendages in higher ruminants have evolved more than once, and thus do not constitute a derived character for the group. Absence of this character thus does not constitute a good basis for placing the moschids in a sister group relationship to the horned Pecora. The only other features which distinguish moschids from horned ruminants are the retention of a subarcuate fossa on the endocranial side of the petrosal and the retention of a median branch of the carotid artery. Further study of fossil pecorans will be necessary to determine whether the loss of these features is synapomorphic or occurred in parallel in the higher pecoran families. Table 1 shows how ideas on the systematic position of the Moschidae have changed since 1944 and the genera included in a familial level grouping with the genus *Moschus.*

The family "Palaeomerycidae" has traditionally been used to include a number of Tertiary ruminants, both horned and hornless, that were not easily assignable to one of the living pecoran families (e. g. Stirton, 1944; Romer, 1966). The concept of the family "Palaeomerycidae" as a basal higher pecoran family has been refuted by Hamilton (1978b) who pointed out that most members can be assigned to existing pecoran families. Unfortunately, the type genus *Palaeomeryx*, a ubiquitous medium-to-large-sized ruminant of the Miocene of Eurasia and Africa, does not appear to be clearly assignable to any existing family. Although Ginsberg and Heintz (1966) claim that *Palaeomeryx* had a giraffid-like ossicone, there is no firm evidence that cranial appendages are associated with this genus. The metatarsal gully of European *Palaeomeryx* is closed, but the condition of the lacrimal foramen is unknown. The African *"Palaeomeryx"* may be synonymous with the giraffid *Canthumeryx* (J. Leinders, pers. comm.).

Of the other genera originally assigned to this family, the American hornless blastomerycids and the Eurasian hornless genera *Dremotherium* and *Amphitragulus* have been assigned to the Moschidae (Webb and Taylor, 1980), and Hamilton (1978a) pointed out that the Miocene African genera *Climacoceras* and *Canthumeryx* share the bilobed lower canine which is an autapomorphic condition of the Giraffoidea. Simpson (1945) considered that the Asian genera *Procervulus* and *Lagomeryx*, which are poorly known forms with branched, non-deciduous cranial appendages, also belong in the Giraffoidea. Despite the fact that their cranial appendages show resemblances to the branching, non-deciduous horns of *Climacoceras*, their taxonomic position must be considered uncertain until their anterior dentition is known. Certain other genera formerly placed in the "Palaeomerycidae" are of uncertain affinities, and are best regarded as Pecora *incertae sedis* until more material is available for study. These include *Prolibytherium* and *Propalaeoryx* (Hamilton, 1978b) and *Triceromeryx* (Janis and Lister, 1985). The final group of ruminants formerly classed as palaeomerycids is the North American dromomerycids. These were recognized as a separate assemblage by Stirton (1944) and placed in the subfamily Dromomerycinae within the Palaeomerycidae. However, with the abandonment of the concept of the family Palaeomerycidae, there is good reason to assign them to their own family Dromomerycidae, as they appear to form a monophyletic assemblage (Hamilton, 1978a). (Table 1 shows how the genera included in the palaeomerycid assemblage have varied with different authors since 1945, and to which other pecoran families these genera have been assigned.)

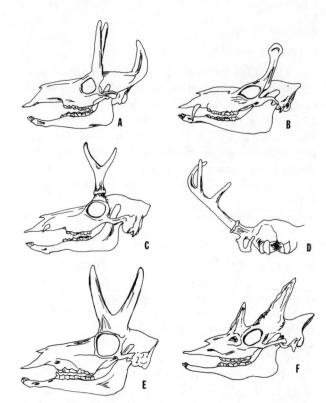

Figure 2. Representative "horned" pecorans. A, *Cranioceras* (Dromomerycidae); B, *Aletomeryx* (Dromomerycidae); C, *Meryceros* (Antilocapridae, Merycodontinae); D, "horn" of *Ramoceros* (Antilocapridae, Merycodontinae), posterior view; E, *Stockoceros* (Antilocapridae, Antilocaprinae); F, *Giraffokeryx* (Giraffidae). A-E after Frick (1937), E after Romer (1966).

DROMOMERYCIDAE

Dromomerycids are known from the Miocene of North America, and ranged in size from that of a roe deer to that of a large red deer. They presumably radiated from an immigrant Eurasian genus in the early Miocene, as the endemic ruminants of North America (hypertragulids and leptomerycids) possess derived features that would debar them from the ancestry of the pecoran families. The males of all known dromomerycid genera bear paired supraorbital horns which were unbranched, non-deciduous, and were probably skin-covered, at least in the earlier genera. In the genus *Aletomeryx* (Figure 2) small horns are also found in the female. In some later genera, such as *Dromomeryx*, the rugosity of these horns suggests a certain amount of keratinous thickening, especially at the base of the horn, but there is no evidence for a fully developed bovine-like sheath. Webb (1983) united one subfamily, the Cranioceratinae, on the basis of a third, median occipital horn (Figure 2). Frick (1937) restored the horns of dromomerycids with deciduous keratin tips, which he assumed allied them with the cervids, but there is no evidence for such features (Webb, 1983). The horns of dromomerycids were probably derived independently from those of other pecorans (Janis, 1982). Dromomerycids had relatively short limbs, short necks, and low-crowned cheek teeth, and most genera displayed a lengthening of the posterior part of the skull, a feature seen in present day ruminants that browse at high levels, such as the okapi (*Okapia johnstoni*) and the gerenuk (*Litocranius walleri*). (Table 1 shows the changing ideas as to the systematic position of the dromomerycids since 1945.)

CERVIDAE

Cervids first appeared in the early Miocene of Eurasia, and have been a predominately Eurasian and northern group. They have never been found in Africa south of the Sahara, and did not appear in North or South America until the Late Pliocene. The most immediately obvious features of the Cervidae are the deciduous antlers in males of all genera and in which (except both sexes of *Rangifer*, although an antlerless exception (*Hydropotes*) has always been noted. Brooke's (1878) diagnosis of the Cervidae is still perhaps the best available. He states: 'deer may therefore for the present be characterized as Pecora having two orifices to the lacrimal duct, situated on or inside the orbit, lacrimal fossae, an anteorbital vacuity, cutting off the lacrimal from articulation with the nasals, the first molar brachyodont, the parieto-squamosal suture nearer the upper than the lower border of the temporal fossa, and the placenta with few cotyledons' (Brook, 1878, p. 885). To this definition should be added the absence of a gall bladder (Flower, 1875) and the presence of the closed metatarsal gully (Leinders and Heintz, 1980). Deer usually have brachyodont cheek teeth, short necks, and lack extreme elongation of the metapodials. Exceptions to these generalities exist; for example, Pere David's deer (*Elaphurus*) have relatively hypsodont cheek teeth, and the roe deer has elongated legs.

GIRAFFIDAE

Giraffids first appeared in the early Miocene of Africa. They are a predominately African group, though also found in Eurasia until recent times. Living giraffids have simple, unbranched, skin-covered, non-deciduous postorbital ossicones present in both sexes in *Giraffa* and in the males alone of *Okapia*, and have relatively elongated metapodials with the loss of the lateral digits. Like cervids they retain brachyodont cheek teeth. The diversity of ossicone forms is greater in fossil genera (see Figure 2) with supraorbital branching ossicones in *Climacoceras* and palmate os-

sicones in sivatheres. Various fossil groups have been allied with the giraffes in superfamily Giraffoidea (see Table 1). The Giraffoidea of Hamilton (1973; 1978a), whom we have followed in this paper, is characterized by the autapomorphic possession of a bilobed lower canine.

BOVIDAE

Bovidae first appeared in the early Miocene of Africa and Eurasia, and were widespread in these continents during the Tertiary. They first appeared in North America during the Late Miocene, but unlike cervids never migrated to South America. Bovids are characterized by the presence of unbranched, non-deciduous supraorbital or postorbital horns, consisting of a bony core that may or may not have internal sinuses, covered by a hollow, keratinized sheath (Gentry, 1978). Horns are present only in the males in some genera and in both sexes in others. Many bovid genera have highly hypsodont cheek teeth and elongated metapodials with the loss of the lateral digits, but these characters are not diagnostic of the family. There appears to be no morphological feature uniting the bovid tribes other than the possession of a similar type of horn.

A Miocene African group of small-bodied, hypsodont pecorans, the walanganids, have been placed in the Bovidae (Hamilton, 1973). However, these animals are poorly known, except for isolated cheek teeth; no horn material has ever been found in association with them. Apart from the possession of hypsodont teeth there seems to be little reason to link them with the Bovidae. We prefer to consider this group Pecora *incertae sedis* until further material is available to determine their relationships.

ANTILOCAPRIDAE

Antilocaprids are an exclusively North American family of ruminants that first appeared in the early Miocene, presumably as Eurasian immigrants, and survive at the present time as the pronghorn, *Antilocapra americana*. This reduced present day diversity belies their past success and radiation. Antilocaprids are divided into two subfamilies (Frick, 1937), the small-sized merycodontines, which were present only during the Miocene, and the larger antilocaprines, which first appeared in the late Miocene, and reached the peak of their diversity during the Plio-Pleistocene. Antilocaprids are characterized by small to medium body size, hypsodont cheek teeth, and elongated metapodials with the loss of the lateral digits. *Antilocapra* possess a non-deciduous, unbranched bony horn core, covered by a deciduous, branched keratin sheath in males and females. Fossil antilocaprines (Figure 2) have a great diversity of forked or spiralled horn cores and in at least some antilocarpid genera females were hornless. The deciduous or non-deciduous nature of the keratinous covering in fossil genera is equivocal.

Merycodontines (Figure 2) resembled antilocarpines in the possession of horn cores that were non-deciduous and supraorbital in position. In other respects they were not similar structures. Merycodontine horns were rounded in cross-section (as opposed to the flattened, ovoid cross-section of antilocaprine horn cores), were invariably branched or forked, and were present in males only. Despite their definite non-deciduous nature (Voorhies, 1969; R.D. Guthrie, pers. comm.) one or more structures resembling cervid-like burrs were often seen on the base or lower mid-shaft of merycodontine horns, but are never seen in fossil antilocaprines (see Figure 2). The morphology of the horn surfaces does not support the idea that they were covered by a deciduous sheath, but rather that they were skin-covered or naked (R.D. Guthrie, pers. comm.).

The Position of the Cervidae within the Pecora

Relationships among higher Pecora have traditionally been inferred from supposed homologies between the frontal appendages of the different groups. Most modern cervids can be distinguished from all modern bovids and giraffids by the presence of deciduous, branching antlers, but as this character is an autapomorphy of the family it is of little assistance in determining the ancestry of the Cervidae among the Ruminantia, or of determining which other pecoran families may be closely related to the Cervidae. Central to these issues are two questions: first, are the cranial appendages of pecorans homologous, and are they of value in allying families at the suprafamilial level; and, second, what morphological characters, other than cranial appendages, can be used to unite other pecoran families with the Cervidae in the formation of a superorder "Cervoidea".

Antlers and the classification of the Cervidae

The presence of cranial appendages was originally assumed to characterize the Pecora. Pilgrim (1941; 1947) considered that the skin-covered ossicones of giraffes were representative of the primitive horned condition, from which the pedicles of cervids and the horn cores of bovids and antilocaprids could be derived. This idea is also implied, although not specifically stated, by Webb and Taylor (1980), in their separation of moschids and gelocids from the "Eupecora" based on the absence of cranial appendages, despite the fact that as the traguloid ancestors of the Pecora lacked horns or antlers, the primitive condition for both the Pecora and the "Eupecora" must be the absence of

cranial appendages. Central to this notion is the underlying assumption that cranial appendages in ruminant artiodactyls evolved only once, and that all of the types of cranial appendages were derived from a common ancestor with simple ossicones. However, a number of lines of evidence suggest that cranial appendages have evolved independently at least twice, and may have evolved in parallel within each pecoran family.

Consideration of the antlerless Chinese water deer (*Hydropotes inermis*) clearly suggests that antlers at least have arisen independently. Forbes (1882) and Garrod (1877) present strong evidence that *Hydropotes* does indeed belong in the Cervidae and it appears to lack the derived characters Webb and Taylor (1980) cite for the Moschidae, so that it cannot be assigned to this family. If the lack of antlers in *Hydropotes* is primitive it suggests that antlers at least arose independently. Hamilton (1978b) discusses the affinities of *Hydropotes* and concludes that it forms a monophyletic group with the Cervidae, but branches off before the evolution of antlers. Stirton (1944), Simpson (1945), and Flerov (1953) imply by their placement of the genus that it is secondarily antlerless. Hamilton (1978b) also mentions the possibility that *Hydropotes* may have secondarily lost its antlers, but notes that there is no evidence to support this, as have other authors (e. g. Groves and Grubb, this volume). Until evidence can be presented that *Hydropotes* has secondarily lost its antlers it must be regarded as primitively antlerless.

Horns and antlers appear to be non-homologous in their development, providing further evidence that they evolved independently. Antlers are an outgrowth of the frontal bone, whereas bovid horns and giraffid ossicones are initially dermal elements that fuse with the frontal or parietal bone (Frechkop, 1955; Bubenik, 1966). This implies that the two types of cranial appendages arose independently. However, similar developmental histories are not sufficient to prove homology between types of cranial appendages, as there are only a limited number of ways to produce a bony cranial appendage: as an outgrowth of one or more cranial bones or as a separate ossification center which later fuses with a cranial bone. Janis (1982) has suggested ecological and behavioral reasons as to why independent lineages of ruminant artiodactyls may have undergone strong selective pressure to develop sexually dimorphic cranial appendages. In light of the limited ways to produce bony appendages this strongly suggests that mere presence or superficial similarity of cranial appendages should be used only with caution in allying ruminant groups (see discussion by Leinders, 1984). Similarities of structural detail and development may still, of course, indicate homology.

Independent acquisition of bony horns can be documented in other groups of artiodactyls. Bony horns similar in form to those of Ruminantia are present in the family Protoceratidae. This family is excluded from the Ruminantia by the lack of the cubo-navicular fusion in the tarsus, and, on other characters, seems to be the sister group of the Camelidae (Webb and Taylor, 1980). The horns in this family must therefore have evolved independently of those of ruminants. Additional evidence for independent evolution of cranial appendages comes from a new genus, *Hoplitomeryx*, from the Miocene of Italy which Leinders (1984) places in a new family, the Hoplitomerycidae. The associated cranial and postcranial material of this animal, which is about the size of a roe deer, show a number of features which ally it with the cervoids. However, the cranial appendages appear to be similar to those of bovids; they are unbranched (although four "horns" are present, as in the four-horned antelope *Tetracerus*), apparently non-deciduous, and are marked by deep grooves suggesting the presence of a bovid-like permanent keratin sheath. As this animal is clearly cervid related on other morphological criteria and yet it is difficult to imagine the derivation of this type of appendage from a typical cervid antler, this animal probably represents another example of the independent acquisition of cranial appendages within the Pecora.

Validity of "Cervoid" Characters in Assessing Phylogenetic Relationships

Leinders and Heintz (1980) assert that the cervid characters of double lacrimal orifice and closed metatarsal gully (see Figure 3) are derived conditions within the Pecora, and hence can be used to ascertain the inclusion of other Pecoran families with the Cervidae as a monophyletic assemblage of "Cervoidea". They point out that *Antilocapra americana* shares these features with the cervids, and hence antilocaprids can be included in the Cervoidea. On this basis the dromomerycids should also be included, as they all possess these diagnostic characters. Leinders and Heintz (1980) admit to some difficulty over the positioning of the musk deer, *Moschus*, which has a closed metatarsal gully and a single lacrimal orifice. They conclude that *Moschus* belongs in the Cervoidea, but is more distantly related to the antlered deer and *Hydropotes* than are the antilocaprids. However, there are problems with the use of both these characters in assessing phylogenetic relationships, and with the positioning of the family Antilocapridae within the Cervoidea.

In the first instance, the double lacrimal foramen evidently evolved more than once, since it is present in two tribes of the Bovidae, the Bovini and the Trag-

LACRIMAL ORIFICE

SINGLE, INSIDE ORBIT   DOUBLE, ON ORBITAL RIM

ANTERIOR SURFACE OF THE METATARSAL

FUSED

UNFUSED   CLOSED GULLY   OPEN GULLY

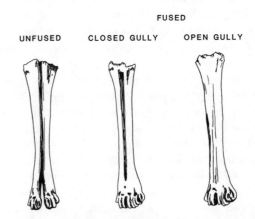

Figure 3. Character states of cervoid and non-cervoid ruminant artiodactyls. Top, comparison of lacrimal orifice states. The single orifice inside the rim of the orbit is typical of tragulids, moschids, gelocids, giraffids, most bovids, and merycodontine antilocaprids. The double orifice on the rim of the orbit is typical of cervids, dromomerycids, antilocaprine antilocaprids, and tragelaphine and bovine bovids. Bottom, comparison of the anterior surface of the metatarsals. The unfused condition is typical of most tragulids. The closed gully shows the high fusion typical of cervids, dromomerycids, and antilocaprine antelopes (the fused gully of tragulids, gelocids, moschids, and merycodontine antilocaprids, when present, is placed more distally). The open gully is typical of giraffids, bovids, most merycodontines, and some moschids.

elaphini, and has also appeared independently in the Suidae (Figure 3). Thus this character cannot be assumed to be homologous when it appears in isolation, although it may be useful if used as part of a suite of defining characters.

Additionally, the condition of the lacrimal orifices can be variable within species. In the genus *Antilocapra* about 20% of specimens in the American Museum of Natural History collections have a single orifice while in *Moschus* about 25% have a double foramen (Janis and Scott, unpublished data), although according to Leinders and Heintz (1980) the opposite condition for each genus is supposed to be invariably the case. The state of this character should thus be regarded with caution, especially in fossil groups where it may be known from only one or a few specimens. Neither should the state in a single species or genus be assumed to apply to the entire family.

Interpretation of the metatarsal gully is problematical on several levels (see Figure 3). The possession of a closed metatarsal gully is assumed to be a derived state within the Pecora, with an open gully being the primitive condition (Leinders and Heintz, 1980). This is supported by the fact that *Gelocus*, the earliest known pecoran, appears to have an open gully, based on material referred to *Gelocus communis* from Le Puy. However, the referral is not positive and this interpretation should not be regarded as final. The metapodials in all fossil traguloids are unfused and the fusion in present day *Tragulus* and *Hyemoschus* appears to have occured independently of the fusion in pecorans. It therefore seems possible that the primitive condition for ruminants is for the metatarsals to be unfused, with the closed or open gully representing independent methods in both ontogeny and phylogeny of forming a cannon bone in the hind foot (Figure 3). Whether in this case the methods of metatarsal fusion can be taken as a good autapomorphy remains open to debate. However, the cervid type of closed gully seems to be quite unique, as the other artiodactyls that fuse the metatarsals to form a cannon bone, the tylopod camels, form an open gully. This suggests that the closed gulley might be taken as a synapomorphy to unite the cervoid lineages that possess it. However, the living tragulid *Hyemoschus* forms a closed gully when the metatarsals fuse in older animals. In *Tragulus* the gully does not close when the metatarsals fuse, indicating that the fusion in *Hyemoschus* is independent. The ontogeny of the closed bridge is also different in *Hyemoschus* and cervids. This suggests that the method and details of formation of the closed gully should also be taken into account in drawing homologies.

Interpretation of the metatarsal gully can also be problematical because much postcranial material of fossil ungulates is referred rather than associated. The bridge closing the gully may be thin and in some worn material it is difficult to ascertain its condition. Although the state of the metatarsal gully is fixed in living species of pecorans, and is not related to variables such as habitat preference, the presence of the gully appears to be variable in some fossil moschids such as *Blastomeryx*, within certain populations of *Dremotherium* and *Amphitragulus*, and within the merycodontine antilocaprids. Although some of the variation may result from incorrect referrals, it appears that at least some of the variation is real (Janis and Scott, in prep.). The method of closure of the gully in those genera in which it is closed, and the appearence of the gully in some later genera in which it is open, suggests that in merycodontines a closed gully may have become open secondarily. The possibility of variation in this character needs to be more fully investigated.

Inclusion of Other Pecoran Families in the Cervoidea

Although a number of uncertainties exist about the usefulness of the metatarsal gully and the double lacrimal orifice, they appear to be the best characters currently available for assessing cervoid relationships, especially since characters of the cranial appendages are of limited value. Various combinations of the Moschidae, Dromomerycidae, Giraffidae, and Antilocapridae have been allied with the Cervidae in a superfamily Cervoidea. In the section that follows we have evaluated these relationships based on the characters of the lacrimal orifice and metatarsal gully, and assuming parallel evolution of cranial appendages.

The presence of the metatarsal gully could be used to unite the moschids with the cervids, forming a sister group relationship to all cervoids with both the metatarsal gully and double lacrimal foramina. This would agree with the viewpoint of Leinders and Heintz (1980), and contrast with that of Webb and Taylor (1980), who place the moschids as the sister group to all higher Pecora. However, if parallel evolution of cranial appendages is accepted then this viewpoint should pose no problem. The characters that unite fossil and recent moschids are autapomorphies of the group and need not exclude them from a position as the sister group of the other Cervoidea.

A more serious problem with this interpretation is the fact that a North American "gelocid", *Pseudoceras*, has a closed metatarsal gully (Webb, ms.), as does the Eurasian gelocid *Eumeryx* (authors' personal observation). Since the metatarsals in *Gelocus* apparently have an open gully, the presence of the closed gully in *Pseudoceras* could be interpreted in three ways, with differing implications for cervoid relationships. First, *Pseudoceras* and/or *Eumeryx* may be early immigrant offshoots of the moschid lineage, rather than "true" gelocids. Second, the cervoids (including moschids) may have split off from the other pecoran lineages within the level of the Gelocidae, with the presence of a closed metatarsal gully in some gelocids linking them with the ancestry of the Cervoidea. This would mean that the Cervidae are much more distantly related to the other families of living pecorans than was previously thought. Third, the presence of a closed gully in *Pseudoceras* and *Eumeryx* may represent an independent acquisition of this character in parallel

Scott and Janis

with other cervoids, in which case the value of the character is thrown into doubt. Careful examination of the variability of this character in the fossil pecorans in the Miocene of North America and Eurasia and of the relationships within the "Gelocidae" is needed to establish the relative likelihood of these various possibilities, and is the subject of work in preparation by the authors.

The placement of the family Antilocapridae within the pecora is perhaps the most problematical issue of all the familial relationships. Antilocapridae traditionally have been allied with the Bovidae on the basis of the horn cores, especially by workers familiar only with the living species. Like bovids, *Antilocapra* has a hollow, bony, unbranched horn core, covered by a keratinous sheath. However, unlike the bovid condition, the sheath in *Antilocapra* is forked, and is shed and regrown annually. O'Gara and Matson (1975) placed *Antilocapra* in the Bovidae on the basis of these similarities and other characters which they cite as indicative of close relationship. However, some of these characters, i.e. presence of a gall bladder, are primitive and are not valid for assessing relationship. Characters such as hypsodont dentition and elongation of the metapodials with concurrent loss of lateral digits have also been used to ally antilocaprids and bovids (e. g. Matthew, 1904; Pilgrim, 1941) but such characters have evolved in parallel a number of times in ungulates, and should not be used to infer taxonomic relationship. O'Gara and Matson (1975) also link *Antilocapra* with the Bovidae on the basis of the single lacrimal foramen. Even if this assessment of the character state in *Antilocapra* were correct, this is the primitive condition for pecorans, and so cannot be used to ally the two families. But in fact this character was interpreted erroneously; although it is variable, 80% of the *Antilocapra* examined by the authors had double foramina. Leinders and Heintz (1980) point out that *Antilocapra* shares not only this character with the Cervidae, but also the closed metatarsal gully (see also Leinders, 1979), and on this basis they relate it to the Cervidae, a position also accepted by Groves and Grubb (this volume). (See Figure 4 for a summary of the views of different authors of the interrelationships of the living pecoran families.)

Based on the characteristics of the living *Antilocapra* the Antilocapridae would thus be regarded as a separate radiation from a basal "cervoid" stock, which developed horn cores and keratin sheaths independently of cervid antler development (and, of course, bovid horn development). However, it should be noted that there is some question as to whether the fossil merycodontine antilocaprids form a monophyletic assemblage with the antilocaprine antilocaprids. Merycodontines and antilocaprines have traditionally

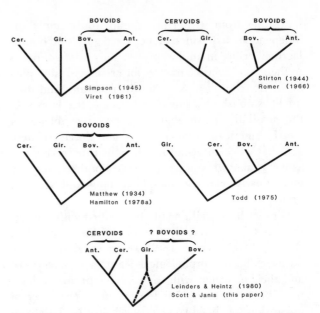

Figure 4. Five views of pecoran relationships, including living families only.

been united by the supraorbital position of the horn cores, hypsodont dentition, elongated metapodials, prominent tubular orbits, and other cranial details. Some authors have been influenced by the suitability of the geographical and stratigraphic position of the merycodontines for this group to be ancestral to the antilocaprines (Matthew, 1904; Frick, 1937). However, many of these features are paralleled by open habitat bovids, such as gazelles, and may not specifically unite these two groups of North American ruminants. Apart from these features, there appear to be no good characters linking the antilocaprid subfamilies. Although they both show supraorbital horn position, as opposed to the postorbital horns of bovids, cervids, and giraffids, supraorbital horns are also found in dromomerycids and in the giraffoid *Climacoceras*, and the type of horn in the subfamilies of Antilocapridae appears to be quite different in nature. Merycodontines differ from antilocaprines in the possession of a single lacrimal orifice, the variability of the presence of a metatarsal gully, and the possession of horns which, although non-deciduous (Voorhies, 1969) were branched and apparently naked or covered by skin rather than a keratin sheath (R. D. Guthrie, pers. comm.). A more comprehensive discussion of the taxonomic relationships of the North American ruminants is in preparation by the authors, and is beyond the scope of this paper.

If it is assumed that the merycodontine antilocaprids form a monophyletic assemblage with the antilocaprine antilocaprids, the derivation of the antilocaprines from within this group would imply the independent acquisition of the closed gully and double lacrimal orifice in antilocaprines. This casts doubts as to their validity as characters for use in assessing phylogenetic relationships within the pecorans, and their use in establishing a superfamily Cervoidea. However, the possibility exists that these two assemblages of North American ruminants are not closely related, and that while antilocaprines may be true cervoids, of as yet unknown ancestry, merycodontines may be more closely related to moschids (Janis and Scott, in prep.)

Giraffes have traditionally been allied with the cervids in the superfamily Cervoidea (Simpson, 1945; Romer, 1966; Thenius, 1979). However, giraffes share no specialized morphological features with cervids, and their inclusion with the cervids appears to have been based primarily on the primitive character of possession of brachyodont cheek teeth. Frechkop (1955) and Hamilton (1978a) both regard the formation of a horn or ossicone from a dermal ossicone as a shared derived character linking giraffes with bovids. However, this may not be a valid character. Horns certainly have evolved more than once and may have evolved in parallel a number of times. If there are only two methods of horn development available (i. e. outgrowth from the frontal bone or fusion of a dermal ossicone), then similarity of horn growth cannot be used as conclusive evidence of phylogenetic relationship. Other resemblances between giraffids and bovids are either characters primitive for the Pecora, such as presence of a gall bladder and a single lacrimal foramen (and possibly an open metatarsal gully), or are characters that might well have evolved in parallel, such as the lengthening of the metapodials and the concommitant loss of the lateral digits.

Todd (1975) presented chromosomal evidence to place the Giraffidae as the sister group to all the other horned pecora. He bases this placement on the presence of an X-autosome translocation-fusion which he considers to be shared by cervids, bovids and antilocaprids, but not by giraffids. If Todd's assumptions are correct, and the X-autosome-translocation-fusion is a synapomorphy for these groups, it would indicate that the giraffids diverged from the basal pecoran stock before the other higher Pecora. However, the character is present in only one or two living cervids (*Muntiacus muntjac* and possibly *Elaphodus cephalophus*) and in species of *Gazella*. It is not found in *Hydropotes*, which is presumably a more primitive cervid than *Muntiacus*, nor in *Boselaphus*, arguably the most primitive living bovid. More important, however, is the fact that there is no evidence that the autosome which is fused to the x-chromosome is the same one in the Antilopini as in *Muntiacus*. In fact, banding studies of the two subspecies of *Muntiacus muntjac* which have been karyotyped (*M. m. vaginalis* and *M. m. grandicornis*) show that the autosome fused to the x-chromosome is *not* the same one in the two subspecies (Wurster and Aitkin, 1972). This suggests that the system arose independently in the two subspecies of *M. muntjac*. Although banding studies have not been done in *Gazella*, the autosome translocation system cannot be simultaneously homologous to both systems in muntjacs. The x-autosome translocation system must have arisen independently more than once within the Pecora, and thus cannot be used as a synapomorphy to unite the Cervidae with the Bovidae and relegate the Giraffidae to the position of sister group to all the other Pecora. Figure 4 summarizes the views of different authors on the interrelationships among the living families of the Pecora.

Summary

Table 1 shows our suggested revised classification of ruminant artiodactyls, as evidenced by currently available fossil material, including a superfamily "Cervoidea". *Hydropotes* should clearly be placed as the sister group of the antlered deer, and included within the Cervidae. We have followed Hamilton (1978a) and others in recognizing the dromomerycids as a separate family Dromomerycidae and we place it within the Cervoidea on the basis of the state of the lacrimal orifice and the metatarsal gully, although the value of these characters in phylogenetic reconstruction is still subject to further investigation. They appear to be a separate radiation from the cervoid stock, which developed cranial appendages independently. The position of such anomalous cervoid groups as the Hoplitomerycidae within the Cervoidea is impossible to determine at present, and we follow Leinders (1984) in placing it in its own family within the Cervoidea. Many of the features that ally *Hydropotes* with other cervids are those of soft anatomy, and it is impossible to know where to place fossil genera with respect to the Hydropotinae in the Cervoidea.

The position of the Antilocapridae is more problematical. We include them among the Cervoidea in Figure 4, with some misgivings, on the basis of the characters of *Antilocapra*, and leave the placement of the merycodontines unresolved. Certainly *Antilocapra* appears to share more derived features with cervids than with bovids, but the possibility of independent acquisition of characters cannot be overlooked. Finally, we place the Moschidae at the base of the Cervoidea, as the sister group to the other cervoids, on the assumption that the closed metatarsal gully is a valid character for determining this relationship (as per Leinders and Heintz, 1980). The possibility of independent acquisition of this character by some

Scott and Janis

gelocids, or the splitting off of the Cervoidea from the other higher pecoran groups within the gelocids (in which case the family Gelocidae would be a paraphyletic assemblage and an alternative classification of this group would have to be adopted) remains the subject of further investigation of geographically scattered, poorly preserved and equivocally identified material.

With regard to the positioning of the Cervoidea within the Ruminantia, there seems to be no good reason to ally them either with giraffids (as per Stirton, 1944; Romer, 1966) or with bovids (as per Todd, 1975). Cervoids are probably best considered as an early independent offshoot from amongst the Oligocene Pecora, and some of the genera currently included in the Gelocidae may be assignable to a basal cervoid stock. The question of interrelationships of giraffids and bovids, to form a superfamily Bovoidea, is not really an issue for this paper. We feel that cervids, bovids and giraffids are best regarded, for the time being, as an unresolved trichotomy. While some of the features shared by giraffids and bovids, such as the open metatarsal gully and the formation of horns from dermal ossicones, may be valid synapomorphies uniting the two families, it is impossible to be certain of this on the basis of present evidence. Alternatively, giraffids might be the sister group to a grouping within the Pecora of the bovids and the cervids, as advocated by Todd (although not for the reason he states). At any rate, there is no positive evidence to support the long held tenet that giraffids are more closely related to cervids than to bovids amongst the pecoran families. Amongst the living families of ruminant artiodactyls, we consider that only the Moschidae and the Antilocapridae should be united with the Cervidae in a superfamily Cervoidea.

Acknowledgments

We are grateful to A. Lister, P. Grubb, J. Leinders, S. D. Webb, A. Gentry, M. Pickford, and D. Guthrie for comments and discussions of ruminant relationships. We would also like to thank R. Tedford for access to the collections of the American Museum of Natural History. Scott was supported by a grant from the Rutgers University Research Council and Janis was supported by a research fellowship from Newnham College, and is indebted to the Department of Zoology for the use of facilities.

Literature Cited

Brooke, V.
1878.   On the classification of the Cervidae, with a synopsis of the existing species. *Proceedings of the Zoological Society of London*, 1878:833–928.

Bubenik, A. B.
1966.   *Das Geweih*. Verlag, Hamburg & Berlin: P. Parey.

Colbert, E. H.
1941.   The osteology and relationships of *Archaeomeryx*, an ancestral ruminant. *American Museum Novitates*, 1135:1–24.

Crusafont, M.
1961.   Giraffoidea. In *Traite de Paleontologie*, Tome 6., edited by J. Piveteau, pp. 1022–1037. Paris: Masson et Cie.

Flerov, C.
1952.   Musk deer and deer. *Fauna of the USSR. Mammals*, Volume 1, No. 2. Moscow: Academy of Science of the USSR.

Flower, W. H.
1883.   On the arrangement of the orders and families of existing Mammalia. *Proceedings of the Zoological Society of London*, 1883:178–186.

Forbes, W. A.
1882.   Supplementary notes on the anatomy of the Chinese water deer (*Hydropotes inermis*). *Proceedings of the Zoological Society of London*, 1882:636–638.

Frechkop, S.
1955.   Ruminantia. In *Traite de Paleontologie*, Tome 6., edited by J. Piveteau, pp. 569–667. Paris: Masson et Cie.

Frick, C.
1937.   Horned Ruminants of North America. *Bulletin of the American Museum of Natural History*, 69:1–669.

Garrod, A. H.
1877.   Notes on the anatomy of the Chinese water deer (*Hydropotes inermis*). *Proceedings of the Zoological Society of London*, 1877:789–793.

Gazin, C. L.
1955.   A review of upper Eocene Artiodactyla of North America. *Smithsonian Miscellaneous Collections*, 128(8), 96 pp.

Gentry, A. W.
1978.   Bovidae. In *Evolution of African Mammals*, edited by V. I. Maglio and H. B. S. Cooke, pp. 540–572. Cambridge: Harvard University Press.

Ginsberg, L., and E. Heintz.
1966.   Sur les affinities du genre *Paleomeryx*. *Comptes Rendus Academie des Sciences, Paris*, 262:979–982.

Gray, J. E.
1821.   On the natural arrangement of vertebrate mammals. *London Medical Repository*, 15(pt 1):296–310.

Hamilton, W. R.
1973.   On the lower miocene ruminants of Gebel Zelten, Libya. *Bulletin of the British Museum of Natural History (Geology)*, 21:75–150.

1978a.   Fossil giraffes from the Miocene of Africa and a revision of the phylogeny of the Giraffoidea. *Philosophical*

Transactions Royal Society of London. Series B. Biological Sciences, 282:165–229.

1978b. Cervidae and Paleomerycidae. In *Evolution of African Mammals,* edited by V. I. Maglio and H. B. S. Cooke, pp. 540-572. Cambridge: Harvard University Press.

Janis, C.
1982. Evolution of horns in ungulates: ecology and paleoecology. *Biological Review,* 57:261–318.

Janis, C., and A. E. Lister
1985. The use of the morphology of the lower fourth premolar as a taxonomic character in the Ruminantia (Mammalia, Artiodactyla) and the systematic position of *Triceromeryx. Journal of Paleontology,* 59(2):403–410.

Kowalevsky, V.
1876. Osteologie des *Gelocus aymardi.* Paleontographia, new series 4:145–162.

Langer, P.
1974. Stomach evolution in the Artiodactyla. *Mammalia,* 38:295–314.

Leinders, J. J. M.
1979. On the osteology and function of the digits in some ruminants, and their bearing on taxonomy. *Zeitschrift für Saügetierkunde,* 44:305–318.

1984. Hoplitomerycidae nov. fam. (Ruminantia, Mammalia) from Neogene fissure fillings in Gargano (Italy), Part I: The cranial osteology of *Hoplitomeryx* gen. nov. and a discussion on the classification of pecoran families. *Scripta Geologica,* 70:1–68.

Leinders, J. J. M., and E. Heintz
1980. The configuration of the lacrimal orifice in pecorans and tragulids (Artiodactyla; Mammalia) and its significance for the distinction between Bovidae and Cervidae. *Beaufortia,* 30:155–160.

Matthew, W. D.
1904. A complete skeleton of *Merycodus. Bulletin of the American Museum of Natural History,* 20:101–129.

1934. A phylogenetic chart of the Artiodactyla. *Journal of Mammalogy,* 15:207–209.

O'Gara, B. W., and G. Matson
1975. Growth and casting of horns by pronghorns and exfoliation of horns by bovids. *Journal of Mammalogy,* 56:829–846.

Patton, T. H., and B. E. Taylor
1973. The Protoceratidae (Mammalia, Tylopoda, Protoceratidae) and the systematics of the Protoceratidae. *Bulletin of the American Museum of Natural History,* 150:347–414.

Pilgrim, G. E.
1941. The dispersal of the Artiodactyla. *Biological Review,* 16:155–158.

1947. The evolution of the buffalos, oxen, sheep, and goats. *Journal of the Linnaean Society of London,* 41(279):272–286.

Romer, A. S.
1966. *Vertebrate Paleontology.* Chicago: University of Chicago Press.

Simpson, G. G.
1945. Principles of classification and a classification of mammals. *Bulletin of the American Museum of Natural History,* 85:1–350.

Stirton, R. A.
1944. Comments on the relationships of the Palaeomerycidae. *American Journal of Science,* 242:633–655.

Taylor, B. E., and S. D. Webb
1976. Miocene Leptomerycidae (Artiodactyla, Ruminantia) and their relationships. *American Museum Novitates,* no. 2596:1–22.

Thenius, E.
1979. *Phylogeny der Mammalia.* Berlin: Walter Gruyter & Co.

Todd, N. B.
1975. Chromosomal mechanisms in the evolution of artiodactyls. *Paleobiology,* 1(2):175–188.

Viret, J.
1961. Artiodactyla. In *Evolution of African Mammals,* edited by V. I. Maglio and H. B. S. Cooke, pp. 540–572. Cambridge: Harvard University Press.

Voorhies, M. R.
1969. Taphonomy and population dynamics of an early Pliocene vertebrate fauna, Knox County, Nebraska. *Contributions to Geology, Special Papers, no. 1.* Wyoming: University of Wyoming Press.

Webb, S. D.
1983. A new species of *Pediomeryx* from the late Miocene of Florida, and its relationships within the subfamily Cranioceratinae (Ruminantia: Dromomerycidae). *Journal of Mammalogy,* 64(2):261–276.

(ms). A revision of the Pseudoceratinae (Artiodactyla; Ruminantia) from the late Miocene of North America.

Webb, S. D., and B. E. Taylor
1980. The phylogeny of hornless ruminants and a description of the cranium of *Archaeomeryx. Bulletin of the American Museum of Natural History,* 167:121–157.

D. Wurster, and R.J. Aitken
1972. Muntjac chromosomes: a new karyotype of *Muntiacus muntjac. Experimentia,* 28:972–973.

COLIN P. GROVES
and
PETER GRUBB
Department of Prehistory and Anthropology
Australian National University
P.O. Box 4
Canberra, A.C.T. 2600
Australia

35 Downhills Park Road
London N17 6PE

Relationships of Living Deer

ABSTRACT

In this paper we review the species of living deer and their interrelationships. Morphological characters useful in classifying deer are summarized: There has been much convergence in the evolution of derived characters, which inhibits reliable cladistic analysis. However, karyotype and morphology provide independent assessments of phylogenetic relationships which, broadly, are in agreement. We conclude that plesiometacarpal deer, but not telemetacarpal deer, are monophyletic. *Moschus* is excluded from the Cervidae. Within the latter, the reindeer is related to the genera endemic to America and together they form the Odocoileini. With the moose (Alcini) they constitute a clade, of which the roe deer (Capreolini) are the sister group. These three tribes make up the subfamily Odocoileinae or antlered telemetacarpal deer. Their sister group, the plesiometacarpal deer (Cervinae), includes tribes Muntiacini (muntjac and tufted deer) and Cervini ("typical" deer). The subfamily Hydropotinae (the antlerless Chinese water deer) is the sister group of the antlered deer. The classification is provisional pending better knowledge of fossil cervids. Cladistic relationships within the Cervini and Odocoileini are still uncertain.

Living deer are provisionally considered to include five species of Moschidae and 40 of Cervidae. There are more species of musk deer, roe, muntjac, and rusa than is generally admitted. A number of nominal deer species are made up of semispecies: Some of these may prove to be full species. There are too many subspecies recognized, particularly in *Mazama* and *Odocoileus*, but poorly founded subspecies also occur in *Alces*, *Capreolus*, and *Cervus*. The species most in need of systematic revision is the sika, *C. nippon*, in China. Its genetic integrity has been questioned, and the morphology of wild populations is poorly known. Translocated deer populations also have hardly been studied, though some have attained subspecies status. We conclude that systematic knowledge of living deer is very far from being complete.

Introduction

The living chevrotains and deer form an assemblage of ruminants with a wide variation in size and morphology, from a mouse deer at 1 kg to the moose at 600 kg. The group is monophyletic, and through its extinct relatives has given rise to the rest of the Pecora, the giraffes, pronghorn, antelopes, and other bovids.

In this paper we will draw attention to the present state of knowledge of deer systematics. Two principle fields for study are involved—geographic variation, distribution, and reproductive integrity of populations; and phylogenetic relationships between taxa. We cannot solve all outstanding problems here, but we shall emphasize the uncertainties which impede our further understanding of deer evolution.

The systematic study of deer has tended to stagnate. There are several reasons for this. Few biologists have been interested in the scientific evaluation of ungulate systematics, yet large numbers of species and subspecies have been uncritically described. Ungulates, even though regarded as well known or familiar mammals, are not well represented in scientific collections. This is particularly true for deer, and not only because many species of deer are found in relatively poorly explored parts of the world. For example, Banfield (1961) had to obtain new material to complete his study of caribou systematics, even though collections of North American mammals are the most representative in the world. We have been struck by the dearth of postcranial material, unworn dentitions, juvenile skins, and adequate series of many species in museum collections, and especially of rare species from zoos, which should eventually have been available for preservation when they died.

A third problem is that deer populations have been managed, translocated, and artificially selected, especially in Europe and China, but also throughout Malesia. Populations apparently distinct enough phenetically to be regarded as subspecies have nevertheless differentiated only subsequent to human intervention. Names of taxonomic and nomenclatural significance possibly are certainly based on such populations are listed in Table 1. The biological status of these populations is often uncertain. It is possible that some of the names are based on strictly phenotypic

Table 1. Important scientific names of deer possibly or certainly based on translocated animals, or on captives of uncertain provenance

Cervus dama Linnaeus, 1758 (Sweden).

C. mariannus Desmarest, 1822 (Guam)

C. timorensis de Blainville, 1822 (Timor)

C. peronii G. Cuvier, 1825 (Timor; = *C. timorensis*)

C. moluccensis Quoy and Gaimard, 1830 (Buru; = *C. timorensis*)

C. pseudaxis Gervais, 1841 ("Java deer" but almost certainly obtained in Vietnam; = *C. nippon*)

C. kuhlii Muller and Schlegel, 1844 (Bawean Island)

Axis oryzus Kelaart, 1852 (Ceylon; = *A. porcinus*)

C. hortulorum Swinhoe, 1864 (Garden of the Summer Palace, Pekin; = *C. nippon*)

Elaphurus davidianus Milne Edwards, 1866 (same locality)

C. mandarinus Milne Edwards, 1871 (same locality; = *C. nippon*)

Hyelaphus calamianensis Heude, 1888 (Calamian Islands)

Sikelaphus soloensis Heude, 1894 (Sulu Islands; = *C. nippon*)

Hippelaphus floresianus Heude, 1896 (Flores; = *C. timorensis*)

H. sumbavanus Heude, 1896 (Sumba; = *C. timorensis*)

H. macassaricus Heude, 1896 (Sulawesi; = *C. timorensis*)

H. menadensis Heude, 1896 (Sulawesi; = *C. timorensis*)

H. buruensis Heude, 1896 (Buru; = *C. timorensis*)

H. hoevellianus Heude, 1896 (Buru; = *C. timorensis*)

C. (Rusa) tavistocki Lydekker, 1900 (locality ?; = *C. timorensis*)

C. (Rusa) unicolor boninensis Lydekker, 1905 (Bonin Island; = *C. mariannus*)

Sika nippon keramae Kuroda, 1924 (Kerama Island, Riu Kiu Islands)

Rusa timorensis djonga Van Bemmel, 1946 (Pulau Muna, Sulawesi)

and hence potentially temporary variation. The capacity for rapid and conspicuous change in deer populations through environmental improvement or deterioration is well known, but its relevance to the geographic variation of undisturbed native deer has not been evaluated.

Phylogenetic relationships, too, have been hard to determine, because workers have tended to study fossil or recent material independently, using different morphological characters. To infer phylogenetic relationships, neontologists have relied on very few characters indeed. Formal classifications of deer have been inadequate, yet through repetition have become regarded as unquestioned primary sources of knowledge.

Groves and Grubb

Methods

Our study is based on a review of the literature, our own investigations into the systematics of some species, and a general examination of bones, teeth, and skins of all recognised living species of deer in museum collections.

The following abbreviations are used:

A and P	anterior and posterior antler branches (Figure 4)
C	canine
CBL	condylobasal length of skull
GL	greatest length of skull
HBL	head and body length
I	incisor
2N	diploid number (of chromosomes)
PM	premolar
SH	shoulder height

The Determination of Phylogenetic Relationships among Deer

When attempting to reconstruct the phylogenetic history of organisms, a principle aim is to define clades within the group being studied. Clades are single lineages inclusive of their descendents and are hence both monophyletic and holophyletic. Through speciation, lineages branch, generating nested sets of successively lower-order branches, each of which is a clade. Members of clades may share character states which are derived with respect to their condition in organisms that are excluded from the clade. Hence the identification of shared-derived (synapomorphic) character-states should help to define clades. Shared-primitive (symplesiomorphic) characters are not necessarily indicative of relationship because by definition they are also possessed by organisms outside the clade being studied.

Formal classifications of deer have not distinguished polyphyletic, paraphyletic, and holophyletic taxa, and have been dependent on single characters. On the basis of either the condition of the lateral metacarpal rudiments (Brooke, 1878) or the presence or absence of a vomerine nasal septum (Carette, 1922) deer have been classified into two main groups. The classifications of Simpson (1945) and Flerov (1952) respectively are refined versions of these two arrangements. Simpson's "Odocoileinae" was paraphyletic, as it included antlerless deer, but not all presumably derivative antlered species. Flerov's "Cervinae" was frankly polyphyletic, as on his own admission species included within it had originated independently from his "Muntiacinae". Azzaroli (1953), querying the evidence for Simpson's classification, recognized seven subfamilies in the Cervidae, from which he excluded

Moschus: Hydropotinae, Capreolinae, Alcinae, Odocoileinae, Rangiferinae, Muntiacinae, and Cervinae. We believe that there is evidence for a more hierarchical arrangement and classify the deer and deer-like mammals as follows:

Infraorder Tragulina, Superfamily Traguloidea:
    Tragulidae (*Hyemoschus, Moschiola, Tragulus*)
Infraorder Pecora, Superfamily Cervoidea:
    Moschidae (*Moschus*)
    Antilocapridae (*Antilocapra*)
    Cervidae
        Hydropotinae (*Hydropotes*)
        Odocoileinae
            Capreolini (*Capreolus*)
            Alcini (*Alces*)
            Odocoileini—the neocervines (*Pudu, Mazama, Hippocamelus, Blastocerus, Ozotoceros = Blastoceros, Ocodoileus*—hereinafter collectively referred to as the New World deer—and *Rangifer*)
        Cervinae
            Muntiacini (*Muntiacus, Elaphodus*)
            Cervini (*Dama; Axis* including *Hyelaphus, Cervus* including *Rusa, Rucervus,* and *Przewalskium* and *Elaphurus*)

Morphological Features Used in Determining Cervid Affinities

Evidence in support of this classification comes from the examination of cervid morphological characters, many of which have already been used in attempting to classify them or deduce their phylogenetic interrelationships.

FUSED MEDIAN METACARPALS

The third and fourth metapodials are fused to form a cannon bone in all living ruminants except the water chevrotain (*Hyemoschus aquaticus*), where the median metacarpals remain unfused, and the fused metatarsals retain a deep groove between them. This condition is either an evolutionary reversal, or the primitive condition for the Ruminantia. If the latter is the case, then either the other living tragulids (*Moschiola, Tragulus*) have acquired cannon bones independently of the Pecora, or they form a clade with the latter. But since the extinct Leptomerycidae and Gelocidae had separate median metacarpals, and since on the basis of a cladistic analysis involving numerous skeletal characters, these families are regarded as forming a clade with the Moschidae and the horned Pecora (Webb and Taylor, 1980), the convergence hypothesis seems the more probable.

The metacarpals of the second and fifth digits are complete in tragulids, but are retained only in part, or are absent in living deer. In most species, with the exception of the Muntiacini and Cervini, the distal segments of these bones are present, articulating with the phalanges, and separate proximal rudiments are absent (at least in *Capreolus*). This is the telemetacarpal condition (Brooke, 1878). Flerov (1952) stated that there are both proximal and distal rudiments in the neocervines, but this is not the case at least in *Pudu* and *Mazama* (Hershkovitz, 1982).

In the Muntiacini and Cervini, there are no distal segments of the lateral metacarpals, but small proximal rudiments are usually present (at least in *Cervus elaphus*). This is the plesiometacarpal condition. Garrod (1876) could find no trace of the lateral metacarpals in *Elaphodus*, where there are no lateral phalanges either, though small lateral hooves are retained. In *Muntiacus*, the proximal splints are quite long. Flerov (1952) says that distal rudiments sometimes occur, though other authors have not reported these, and there are no lateral phalangeal bones. The lateral hooves are even smaller than in *Elaphodus*, reduced to small round button-shaped structures placed close together above the pasterns.

Pliocene Asian antlered deer (*Cervocerus*, syn. *Cervavitus*, *Damacerus*) retained complete lateral metacarpals (Alexejew, 1915; Azzaroli, 1953; Teilhard de Chardin and Trassaert, 1937) indicating that the telemetacarpal condition had been acquired independently by the much more primitive and antlerless *Moschus* and *Hydropotes*, probably independently of each other, and that the condition is not symplesiomorphic for modern deer.

Simpson (1945) and Flerov (1952) included these Pliocene deer within their respective concepts of a subfamily Cervinae, from which the muntjacs were excluded. Since *Cervocerus* already had three-tined antlers, the implication was that the two-tined muntjacs were not involved in this clade, and that the plesiometacarpal condition is not synapomorphic for the living Muntiacini and Cervini, which must have acquired the condition independently.

But the western Asian *Cervocerus* was in many respects a most primitive antlered deer (Alexejew, 1915). Its lateral metacarpals were not only complete, but also articulated with the lateral phalanges, it possessed *Paleaomeryx* and protoconal folds on its molars, its cheek teeth were very barchyodont, and it had canines as large as those of muntjacs, and a very prominent lacrimal pit. Except for its rather unusual three-tined antlers, it had the morphology to be expected of an ancestor of all modern antlered deer, including the Muntiacini.

The Chinese *"Cervocerus"* (Zdansky, 1925; Teilhard de Chardin and Trassaert, 1937) had complete lateral metacarpals which, however, narrowed distally and did not articulate with the phalanges, hence presaging the plesiometacarpal state, and was dentally less primitive. Azzaroli (1953), who noted that this deer requires a new scientific name, thought it could be ancestral to the Cervini. The principal reason for excluding this deer from the ancestry of the Muntiacini as well would seem to be the advanced, three tined antlers, as compared with the simpler ones of muntjac. But like the western Asian *Cervocerus*, the Chinese cervocerine need not be a direct ancestor, and could have acquired its antler form independently of the modern Cervini. There is insufficient reason, then, for excluding the hypothesis that plesiometacarpal deer represent a monophyletic lineage.

With the exception of Flerov's (1952) allusions, there appears to be no evidence for deer retaining both proximal and distal splints of the lateral metacarpals, and there is no need to assume that this was the condition (which would have been identified as "telemetacarpal") from which plesiometacarpal deer evolved. It seems most parsimonious to assume that plesiometacarpal and antlered telemetacarpal deer originated independently from the holometacarpal state shown by *Cervocerus*, and each on only one occasion.

METATARSAL BRIDGE

The gully running down the front surface of the metatarsus is covered over by bone at its distal end in *Moschus*, *Hydropotes*, antlered cervids, and *Antilocapra* (and *Blastomeryx*: Matthew, 1908) but not in other living pecorans, and is presumed to be a synapomorphic character (Heintz, 1963; Leinders, 1979).

TARSAL BONES

Pudu, *Muntiacus*, and *Elaphodus* are unique among deer in that the cubonavicular and external and median cuneiform are fused into a single bone (Hershkovitz, 1982). According to Garrod (1876), the internal cuneiform is also fused in *Elaphodus*. It has generally been accepted that the occurrence of this derived character in Old World and New World deer (also found in tragulids) is the result of convergence.

PALAEOMERYX FOLD AND PROTOCONAL FOLD

These are, respectively, a labial fold of the protoconid, and a lingual fold of the protocone, present in most Miocene deer, but lost in most modern species. The terminology used here follows Heintz (1970).

Flerov (1952) recognized the *Palaeomeryx* fold in the moose (*Alces*), though we have not detected it in the

Groves and Grubb

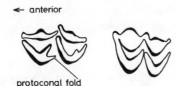

Figure 1. Worn enamel surfaces of right upper molars of *Mazama americana* and *Axis porcinus*, showing the position of the protoconal fold in the former, and its absence in the latter.

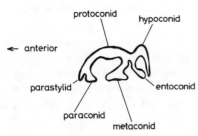

Figure 2. Worn enamel surface of right PM$_4$ in *Axis axis* showing the relative positions of the conids and parastylid.

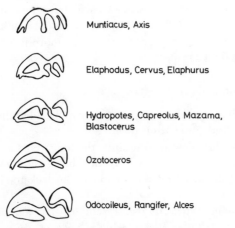

Figure 3. Worn enamel surfaces of right PM$_4$ showing successive stages of molarization among deer.

molars of specimens we have examined, either of this species (see also Heintz and Poplin, 1981) or of any other extant deer.

Heintz (1970) indicated that the protoconal fold has tended to be retained later in Phylogeny than the *Palaeomeryx* fold. It gives a characteristic trilobed wear pattern to the protocone (Figure 1). The protoconal fold is clearly evident in the upper molars of moose, but not in any other extant Old World deer. Among the neocervines, however, it is present in *Mazama, Pudu, Odocoileus,* and *Blastocerus* (Frechkop, 1965). The fold is absent in *Ozotoceros, Hippocamelus,* and *Rangifer,* though in recently erupted molars of *Ozotoceros,* a trace of the fold can be present at the top of the crown. It has presumably been lost independently in the plesiometacarpal deer and *Capreolus.*

MOLARIZATION OF PREMOLARS

PM$_4$ is molarized to some extent in most modern deer, with the posterior part (entoconid plus hypoconid) relatively large, and often with a long, blade-like metaconid (Figure 2). In *Muntiacus,* the metaconid does not usually form a longitudinal loph, and the posterior part of the tooth is relatively small. In *Axis,* the metaconid is more clearly developed as a discrete conid, while in *Cervus, Elaphurus, Dama,* and *Elaphodus* it is longer, and with wear contacts and fuses with the paraconid (or sometimes the parastylid). *Moschus, Hydropotes, Pudu, Mazama, Blastocerus, Ozotoceros,* and *Capreolus* have progressed further: The metaconid has become detached from the protoconid, but the posterior wing of the latter which formerly connected the two conids is still evident, though all trace of it has often been lost in *Ozotoceros.* Molarization has advanced furthest in *Odocoileus, Rangifer,* and *Alces,* where a very characteristic diagonal loph forms through the union of protoconid with entoconid, the metaconid and hypoconid being relatively detached (Figure 3).

PM$_3$ is not usually so molarized as PM$_4$: Only in *Alces* and *Rangifer* does it approach a selenodont condition with a diagonal fusion of crests somewhat similar to that in PM$_4$.

Molarization appears to have accelerated in the Odocoileinae relative to the Cervinae, and the progressive condition of PM$_4$ in *Moschus, Hydropotes,* and *Elaphodus* has presumably arisen independently in each case.

UPPER CANINES

Large canines are found in the tragulids, *Moschus* and *Hydropotes* (where they are long and sabre-like), and the Muntiacini (where they are relatively shorter). Again this would appear to be a symplesiomorphic character for the Ruminantia.

Small canines are (usually?) present in *Hippocamelus*, *antisensis*, *Rangifer*, *Cervus (Rusa) unicolor*, *C.(R.) alfredi*, *C.(R.) timorensis*, *C. (Przewalskium)*, *C. (Rucervus) eldi*, *C. (Cervus)*, and *Elaphurus*. They are absent in sufficient proportions of individuals for this to be noted in museum collections, in *H. bisulcus*, *Ozotoceros*, *Mazama*, *C. (Rucervus) duvauceli*, and *C. (Rusa) mariannus*, and are virtually always absent in *Capreolus*, *Alces*, *Blastocerus*, *Odocoileus*, *Dama*, and *Axis*.

The two groups of deer with small canines (Cervini and Odocoileinae) have presumably evolved independently from deer with large muntjak-like canines, and canines must have been lost independently on several occasions.

INCISIFORM MANDIBULAR DENTITION

Three conditions of these teeth can be recognized, relating to their relative size: a) Primitive type: In the tragulids, *Hydropotes*, the Muntiacini, *Mazama*, *Dama*, *Axis*, *Cervus (Rusa) mariannus*, and *C. (Cervus) nippon*, the first incisor is broad and the remaining teeth are narrow. In the smaller species, the crowns of the latter are very narrow, no wider than the roots, and crowded together. In the species of Cervini, these teeth are a little broader, but still narrower than the first incisor, which in *Axis* and *Dama* is exceptionally broad relative to crown height.

Since this disparity between median and lateral incisiform crown breadth is also found in many of the small bovids, it is likely to be symplesiomorphic for the Ruminantia as a whole. b) Intermediate type: In *Capreolus* and *Ozotoceros*, there are three size grades in the teeth, the crown of I_2 being intermediate in width between the broad I_1 and the narrow I_3 and C. c) Advanced type: In *Moschus*, *Pudu*, *Hippocamelus*, *Blastocerus*, *Odocoileus*, *Rangifer*, most *Cervus* species, *Elaphurus*, and *Alces*, the crowns are all of about the same width, or decrease a little in width gradually from I_1 to C. The detailed form of the crowns varies, suggesting that the condition has arisen more than once.

LACRIMAL DUCTS

Moschus and the tragulids (and *Dremotherium*: Sigogneau, 1968) have a single lacrimal duct orifice, while *Hydropotes*, the antlered cervids, and *Antilocapra* have a double orifice on the orbit rim (Leinders and Heintz 1980), presumed to be a synapomorphic character.

BENDING OF THE BASICRANIUM

Meunier (1964) has shown that the basicranium in deer may be straight or lordotic. The first condition appears to be primitive, as it occurs in *Tragulus* and *Moschus*, and the second derived. The neocervines

tend towards lordosis, but variation in the character is continuous and discrete character states are not recognized.

VOMERINE SEPTUM OF THE POSTERIOR NARES

Among living deer, this character is found only in *Rangifer* and the New World deer. It is a derived feature, and no evidence that it has evolved on more than one occasion has been presented.

AUDITORY BULLAE

The bullae are cancellous internally in tragulids as in non-ruminant artiodactyls, and hollow in cervids and other pecorans. They are large and inflated in *Hydropotes*, *Axis (Hyelaphus)*, and *C. (Cervus) nippon*. They are slightly less inflated in *A. (Axis)* and *C. (Rucervus)*, and much less inflated, or not inflated at all in other deer. Inflation of the bulla may be a symplesiomorphic character for the Cervini.

FREQUENCY OF MOLT

Dobroruka (1975) noted that some deer have a single annual molt (*Alces*, *Hydropotes*), while others have two molts (*Muntiacus*, *Capreolus*, *Cervus*). The North American populations of *Odocoileus* also have two annual molts (Cowan, 1936). Evidently, the double molt condition cannot be regarded as a synapomorphic character for the Cervidae.

SPOTTED PELAGE

Several types of colour pattern can be identified in fawns, and some adult deer:
a) Tragulid type: In tragulids, the light spots are distributed across the body in vertical lines, and there are white gular stripes extending down the neck and along the flanks.
b) *Moschus* type: *Moschus* resembles *Tragulus* in the presence of gular stripes which, however, do not extend beyond the neck. The spots on the body differ, as they are arranged in longitudinal lines. There is a pair of well separated dorsal lines of spots and ventral to this, two to three curved lines of spots, with additional spots on the haunches. There is also usually an ochraceus median dorsal stripe.
c) *Capreolus* type: In *Hydropotes*, *Muntiacus*, *Capreolus*, *Mazama*, *Pudu puda*, *Ozotoceros*, and *Odocoileus*, there are no gular stripes or pale median dorsal stripe, but the spots are distributed as in *Moschus*, so that the most dorsal lines of spots are separated by a broad median unspotted band. *Capreolus* has more haunch spots than the others. The linear arrangement of flank spots breaks down in *Odocoileus*, only the lowermost ones forming a line. The spotting pattern is never retained

Groves and Grubb

in the adult in this group. The disposition of spots may be symplesiomorphic for the Moschidae plus Cervidae, with the loss of gular stripes synapomorphic for the latter.

d) *Cervus* type: Here the paired dorsal lines of spots are very close to each other, often edging a narrow dark dorsal stripe; while among the other spots, only those on the lower flanks form lines, much as in *Odocoileus*. This spotting pattern is present in juveniles and adults of *Dama, Axis (Axis), Cervus (Rusa) alfredi, C. (Cervus) nippon* (not always in adult winter pelage); in fawns of *Axis (Hyelaphus), C. (Rucervus)* and *C. (elaphus)*, where it may be retained in the adult summer pelage at least in some races; and in juveniles only of *Elaphurus*. The pattern is reduced to the paired dorsal lines of spots, with a few spots also on the fore and hind-quarters, in *C. (Rusa) unicolor* and *C. (R.) timorensis* (Chasen, 1925; van Bemmel, 1949).

The presence of spots in adults may be a secondary condition, synapomorphic for the Cervini, for no other true deer are spotted as adults, and the character may then have been lost again in several lineages within the group. Close spacing of the dorsal lines of spots could be synapomorphic for the Cervini.

e) In *Alces, Rangifer, Blastocerus, Hippocamelus, Pudu mephistopheles,* and *C. (Rusa) mariannus* (Sheridan, 1967; Donal, 1971), the spotting pattern is absent, a derived state that has arisen on several occasions. The coloration of juvenile *Elaphodus* and *C. (Przewalskium)* has not been described.

INTERDIGITAL WEB AND INTERDIGITAL GLANDS

The third and fourth digits are not bound together by a web of skin in tragulids, and there is consequently no place for interdigital glands. *Moschus* also has no interdigital glands, but the digits are connected at the "heels", as in the Cervidae.

Glandular areas are present in the forefeet of *Odocoileus* (Cowan, 1936), *Mazama, Pudu,* and *Hippocamelus* (where they are very small: Hershkovitz, 1958), and in *Dama* alone among Old World deer.

Glandular pockets are more common in the hind foot. They are particularly long and deep, communicating with the interdigital space, in *Hydropotes, Muntiacus, Pudu,* and *Dama*. In *Axis* they demarcated from the interdigital space. The gland pouches are similar but shallower in *Mazama, Odocoileus, Ozotoceros, Blastocerus, Hippocamelus, Rangifer, Capreolus,* and *Alces*. They are absent, and the interdigital web is naked in *Cervus,* including *C. alfredi* (contra Lydekker, 1915), and *Elaphurus*.

Foot glands might appear to be a synapomorphic character for the pecorans, other than *Moschus,* that has been secondarily lost within the Cervini, but see the next paragraph.

PREORBITAL GLANDS

These are absent in tragulids and *Moschus,* and present in all Cervidae except *Pudu mephistopheles* and *Capreolus*. As these glands are also found in bovids, they are perhaps synapomorphic for the pecorans and have become secondarily absent in the two cases cited. However, if the Cervoidea is a true clade, either *Moschus* has also secondarily lost the face glands (and foot glands), or they have been acquired by the Cervidae independently from the Bovidae.

METATARSAL GLANDS

Metatarsal glands are absent in tragulids, *Moschus, Hydropotes, Pudu, Blastocerus, Mazama rufina* (Hershkovitz, 1958), and apparently *Muntiacus*. Distinct areas of secretion, and glandular tufts can be present in other *Mazama* species, and in *Hippocamelus,* while secretory areas only can be present in *Ozotoceros* (Hershkovitz, 1958), and in *Elaphodus* (Garrod 1876). Distinct gland tufts, and therefore active glandular areas, are recorded from *Capreolus, Alces, Cervini* (though not *C. duvauceli*) and *Odocoileus*. Special metatarsal areas of secretion could be symplesiomorphic for the antlered cervids, but a metatarsal tuft might have evolved independently in the Odocoileinae and Cervini.

TARSAL GLANDS AND RUB-URINATING BEHAVIOR

Tarsal glands are present in *Mazama, Hippocamelus, Ozotoceros, Blastocerus, Odocoileus, Rangifer,* and *Alces*. They are usually associated with thick tufts of hair, but these are rudimentary in *Mazama,* and absent in *Alces* (Geist, 1966). Deer with tarsal glands may urinate normally, or with a special stance so that urine washes onto the hocks, which are rubbed together. This behavior, "urine marking" (Geist, 1966) or "rub-urinating" (Muller-Schwarze, 1971) has been recorded in moose (Geist 1963, 1966), mule deer (Browman and Hudson, 1957; Geist, 1966; Muller-Schwarze, 1971), white-tailed deer (Moore and Marchinton, 1974), and reindeer (Espmark, 1964; Lent, 1965), and may occur in all deer with tarsal glands. Rub-urinating has not been recorded from strictly Old World genera, and among American deer, it does not occur in wapiti (*Cervus elaphus*) (Geist, 1966). It is such a distinctive behavior pattern that one is inclined to assume that it has evolved only once.

OTHER SKIN GLANDS

These include inter-ramal (*Tragulus* sensu stricto), mental and frontal (*Muntiacus*), inguinal (*Hydropotes*), and preputial glands (*Moschus,* and also *Dama*: Chapman and Chapman, 1975). Most of these glands are

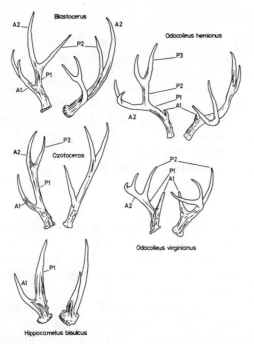

Figure 4. Antlers of American odocoileine deer, showing the equivalence of antler branches in different genera, and the contrast in structure of the first branch between *Ococoileus* and the others. The terminology of antler branches is that of Pocock (1935), in which at each dichotomous fork, anterior (A) and posterior (P) branches are distinguished.

1978) and so they are not synapomorphic structures for the higher Pecora. Deer antlers tend to fork dichotomously as they grow, and Pocock (1933) used this observation to identify the "homologies" of antler branches, including single tines. His nomenclature is shown in Figures 4,5, and 6. Even if antlers of different species share similar patterns of branching, however, they may have evolved independently from more simple ones, so that their tines are not truly homologous. Evidently, antler characters must be used with caution in suggesting phylogenetic relationships.

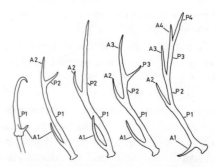

Figure 5. Anterior views of right antlers of plesiometacarpal deer (schematic, not to scale) illustrating stages of increasing complexity of branching, from (left to right) *Muntiacus muntjak, Axis porcinus, Cervus timorensis, C. nippon*, to *C. albirostris*. As the antler becomes more complex in the series (not a phylogeny), the small postero-internal terminal tine repeatedly enlarges and then branches. Naming of antler branches follows Pocock (1933).

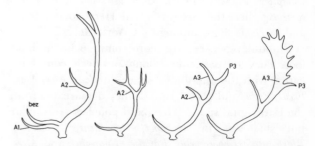

Figure 6. Lateral views of right antlers of Cervini (schematic, not to scale) showing modifications of patterns illustrated in Figure 5. Left to right, they are *Cervus elaphus affinis* (with supernumerary or bez tine), *C. duvauceli* (with branching of second anterior tine, A2), young *Dama dama*, and adult of the same species (to show that the palmated part of the antler forms mainly from the third anterior antler branch, A3).

probably unique specialisations. Preputial glands are also recorded in some small bovids (Ansell, 1969) and conceivably represent a synapomorphic character for early pecorans which was soon lost in most lineages; the glands in the fallow deer are quite different and are probably of independent origin. Vestibular nasal glands are known only for *Blastocerus* and *Ozotoceros* (Jacob and von Lehmann, 1976; Langguth and Jackson, 1980) but have not been searched for in other deer. Forehead glands (Atkeson and Marchinton, 1982) and tail glands (Muller-Schwarze et al., 1977) occur in several species of deer, but their distribution through the family is still poorly known. See Muller-Schwarze (this volume) for more information on this topic.

ANTLERS

Horn-like organs probably originated in deer independently from giraffoids and bovoids (Hamilton,

Groves and Grubb

Table 2. Karyotypes of tragulids and deer

Species and reference ("Atlas" is Hsu and Benirschke, 1967–1976)	Diploid number	Metacentric and submetacentric autosomes	Acrocentric autosomes	Number of autosome arms
I. Tragulids, with a submetacentric X chromosome				
Tragulus javanicus (Yong, 1973)				
T. napu (Todd, 1975	32	30	0	60
II. Cervids with an acrocentric X chromosome				
Hydropotes inermis (Atlas, 1973; 7:345)				
Mazama gouazoubira (Neitzel, 1982)	70	0	68	68
M. gouazoubira X *M.* sp. (Neitzel, 1982)	63/64	2	59/60	63/64
M. sp. (by inference)	58	4	52	60
Dama dama (Atlas, 1967; 1:41)				
Axis (Hyelaphus) porcinus (Atlas, 1977; 10:498)				
Cervus (Cervus) elaphus (Atlas, 1969; 3:134; Wang and Du, 1982a)				
Elaphurus davidianus (Atlas, 1971; 5:241)	68	2	64	68
C. (C.) nippon cf. *nippon* (Wang and Du, 1982a)				
C. (C.) n. yesoensis (Makino and Muramoto, 1966)	68	2	64	68
C. (C.) nippon cf. *nippon* (Gustavson and Sundt, 1968)	67	3	62	68
C. (C.) nippon cf. *nippon* X *C. (C.) n. yesoensis* (Miyake et al., 1982)	65	5	58	68
	66	4	60	68
	67	3	62	68
	68	2	64	68
C. (C.) nippon, Woburn "Manchurian" herd (Gustavson and Sundt, 1969)	64	6	56	68
	65	5	58	68
	66	4	60	68
	67	3	62	68
	68	2	64	68
C. (Przewalskium) albirostris (Wang et al., 1982)				
Axis (A.) axis (Atlas, 1974; 8:390)	66	4	60	68
C. (Rusa) mariannus (Atlas, 1973; 7:344)	65	5	58	68
	64	6	56	68
C. (R.) unicolor "dejeani" (i.e. *cambojensis*; Wang and Du, 1982b)	62	8	52	68
C. (R.) unicolor subsp. (Neitzel, 1982)				
C. (R.) timorensis (Neitzel, 1982; Wang and Du, 1982a)	60	10	48	68
C. (R.) u. unicolor (Chandra et al., 1967)				
C. (Rucervus) eldi (Neitzel, 1982)	58	12	44	68
C. (R.) duvauceli (Atlas, 1968; 2:87; Neitzel, 1982)	56	14	40	68
Elaphodus cephalophus, female; single X chromosome ? (Shi, 1981)	47	2	44	48
Muntiacus reevesi (Atlas, 1968; 2:88)	46	0	44	44
M. feai (Neitzel, in lit.)	13	—	—	—
III. Cervids with X-autosome chromosome complex and additional Y chromosome in male				
Muntiacus muntjak (*muntjak* group, female; Wurster and Aitken, 1972)	8	4	2	10
M. muntjak (*vaginalis* group; Atlas, 1971; 6:291)	6/7	4	0	8

Table 2. (cont.)

Species and reference ("Atlas" is Hsu and Benirschke, 1967–1976)	Diploid number	Metacentric and submetacentric autosomes	Acrocentric autosomes	Number of autosome arms
IV. Cervids with a metacentric or submetacentric X chromosome				
Capreolus capreolus (Atlas, 1968; 2:86)	70	0	68	68
C. pygargus (Sokolov et al., 1978)	74	0	72	72
C. pygargus (Neitzel, 1979)	80	0	78	78
Pudu puda (Atlas, 1975; 9:438)				
Mazama americana subsp. (Taylor et al., 1969; Jorge and Benirschke, 1977)				
Odocoileus virginianus (Atlas, 1967; 1:43)				
O. hemionus (Atlas, 1967; 1:42)				
Rangifer tarandus (Atlas, 1969; 3:135)				
Alces alces (*americana* group; Atlas, 1969; 3:133)	70	2	66	70
Pudu mephistopheles (Neitzel, 1969)	69	3	64	70
Alces a. alces (Gustavson and Sundt, 1968)				
Ozotoceros bezoarticus (Neitzel, 1982)	68	4	62	70
Blastocerus dichotomus (Neitzel, 1982)	66	6	58	70
Mazama americana temama (Atlas, 1976; 10:499; Jorge and Benirschke, 1977)	50	20	28	68

During development, the first set of antlers in most deer is a pair of unbranched "spikes", but the earliest known antlered deer (*Dicrocerus* and allies) had forked antlers, so the spikes of *Pudu, Mazama, Elaphodus,* and *Muntiacus atherodes* probably represent a secondary condition.

KARYOTYPE

A major contribution to our understanding of cervid karyotypes has been made by Neitzel (1979, 1982), whose phylogenetic interpretations follow those of Taylor et al. (1969) and largely supersede the conclusions of Todd (1975) and Wang and Du (1982b).

The divergence of cervid and tragulid karyotypes awaits study, as their chromosomes have not been homologized (Neitzel, 1982). Deer show considerable interspecific variation in chromosome number. The primitive karyotype of cervids (Neitzel, 1982) consists of 70 chromosomes, with 68 acrocentric autosomes and an acrocentric X chromosome, and is retained appropriately by *Hydropotes inermis* (but also by *Mazama gouazoubira*). All antlered telemetacarpal deer examined (Table 2), with the exception of *M. gouazoubira* and possibly an undetermined species of brocket, have a metacentric X chromosome, which would seem to be synapomorphic for the group.

Alces and the neocervines all have a pericentric inversion of an autosome, increasing the number of autosome arms from 68 to 70. This might be a synapomorphy, but *Mazama* is again exceptional. One specimen of *M. americana* is reported to have 70 autosome arms but others have the primitive number of 68 (Table 2).

No member of the Cervini examined has more than 66 autosomes and Neitzel (1982) has confirmed that at least *Dama dama, Cervus elaphus, C. unicolor, C. eldi,* and *C. duvauceli* share a homologous fusion of two chromosomes, reducing the number of autosomes from the primitive figure of 68. This is evidently a synapomorphy of the group. Whether this fusion is shared by the Muntiacini cannot be determined, as that group of deer have a karyotype strongly altered by another process, tandem fusion. One species has autosomes fused with the X chromosome. Otherwise Cervini and Muntiacini resemble *Hydropotes* in their acrocentric X chromosome.

Alces alces, Mazama americana, and *Muntiacus muntjak* show regional variation in the number of chromosome arms and/or the proportion which are centrically fused. In the latter two species, karyotypic differences between populations are so great that one wonders if more than a single species is involved in each case. *Capreolus pygargus, Cervus unicolor, C. mariannus, C. nippon,* and probably *Pudu mephistopheles* and *C. duvauceli* (Neitzel, 1979) exhibit polymorphism in the proportion of centric fusions.

Apart from the uncertain position of *Mazama,* the

Groves and Grubb

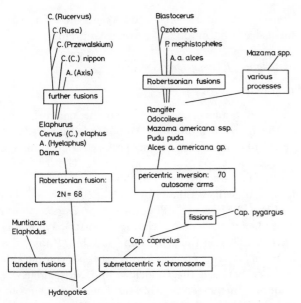

Figure 7. Dendrogram of possible phylogeny of cervid karyotypes.

pattern of karyotypic evolution in deer seems to be relatively clear (Figure 7). Parallel reductions in the diploid number in various lineages can be explained mostly by successive Robertsonian fusions, while *Capreolus pygargus* has probably undergone fission of autosomes.

VISCERA

The gall bladder is present in tragulids, *Moschus*, *Antilocapra*, bovids, and some giraffids, but is absent in *Hydropotes* and antlered cervids. This absence is probably a derived character of the Cervidae, independently acquired also by giraffids.

The tragulids have a diffuse placenta, but it is cotyledonous in *Moschus* (Garrod, 1877b) and the other advanced pecorans.

The stomach is three-chambered in tragulids, and four-chambered in *Moschus* (Flower, 1875; Garrod, 1877a) and other pecorans, by the addition of the omasum (psalterium).

Phylogenetic Conclusions

For most of the morphological characters which we have reviewed, it appears that derived conditions have arisen more than once from ancestral states. No phylogeny could be compatable with their all being synapomorphic. The phylogeny which we propose (Figure 8) therefore aims to be the most parsimonious that could be constructed on available evidence, and it attempts to make the least demanding assumptions concerning the convergence of derived characters. Our interpretation of the divergence of clades leading to the origin of the Cervidae follows Heintz (1970),

Leinders (1979), and Leinders and Heintz (1980). The horned pecorans are not thought to represent a clade, as assumed by Webb and Taylor (1980), and *Moschus* is brought close to the Cervidae than envisaged by these authors or by Flerov (1952). We cannot place the Giraffidae and Bovidae exactly. [See Scott and Janis (this volume) for additional views of cervid affinities.]

Cladistic relationships among the antlered deer require more discussion. Matthew (1908) postulated that the New World deer had originated from hornless blastomerycines, an assumption requiring that the evolution of deciduous antlers, the loss of the gall bladder, the telemetacarpal condition, the reduction in the size of the upper canine, and the appearance of preorbital and pedal glands, had all arisen independently in New World and Old World deer. Matthew's view was accepted uncritically by Flerov (1952), but has not usually been supported (Simpson, 1945; Hershkovitz, 1982). The apparent need for the hypothesis is in any case not based on morphology but on biogeography—other than moose and caribou, no fossils indicative of a dispersal of telemetacarpal deer between Asia and America are known. We consider the hypothesis that antlered telemetacarpal deer all represent a clade quite well founded, though not without its problems, and reject Matthew's (1908) thesis.

Rangifer resembles the New World deer in the vomerine septum, the number of autosome arms, and syndrome of urine-rubbing involving tarsal glands. It seems very improbable that these characters could represent coincident convergences, as they are so un-

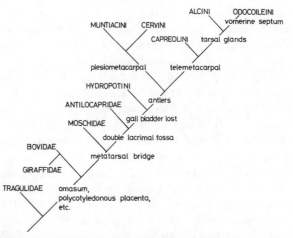

Figure 8. Cladogram expressing phylogenetic relationships between living cervids and other Ruminantia, with some important autapomorphic characters indicated. The assumption that Giraffidae and Bovidae form a clade is speculative.

related functionally. A phylogenetic relationship should be seriously considered, and on the basis of the vomer character, it has already been accepted (Carette, 1922; Flerov, 1952; Hershkovitz, 1982). Since the neocervines might be paraphyletic if *Rangifer* is excluded, the latter is not assigned to a tribe of its own.

Alces resembles the neocervines in the number of autosome arms, and in the urine-rubbing behavior, but it does not possess the vomerine septum. As *Alces* and related genera are not known as fossils in America before the Rancholabrean (Kurtén and Anderson, 1980), it seems a reasonable hypothesis to assume that alcines and neocervines represent vicarious sister-groups of a single clade. The taxon ancestral to both lineages could have colonized American in the Lower Pliocene. No more than one species need have been involved. If of moderate size and living in an environment not conducive to fossilization, it would have left no fossil record.

With this interpretation of relations between *Alces* and the neocervines, either *Mazama* species would have reverted to primitive characters of the X chromosome and number of autosome arms (Table 2), or the derived states would have been acquired independently by New World deer. We adopt the former conjecture provisionally, appreciating its ad hoc nature.

There can be little doubt that antlered and non-antlered telemetacarpal deer do not form a hylophyletic clade, but antlered deer could well have evolved the telemetacarpal condition only once. *Capreolus* would therefore form a sister-group to *Alces* plus the neocervines which had not acquired the autosomal pericentric inversion and urine-rubbing characters of these taxa. The submetacentric condition of the X chromosome could be a derived character uniquely shared by antlered telemetacarpal deer.

We have assumed that the plesiometacarpal condition is synapomorphic, and hence that modern Muntiacini and Cervini form a clade. Extinct *Megaceros, Croizetocerus,* and *Eucladoceurus* belong to the clade, as they are also plesiometacarpal (Reynolds, 1929; Heintz, 1970). *Muntiacus* and *Elaphodus* share derived characters of fused tarsal bones, loss of phalanges, and considerable non-Robertsonian reduction in chromosome number. The Cervini are not well defined by shared-derived character states, though the pattern of the juvenile pelage is probably an example.

Our classification is based on the systematic conclusions listed above, and actually agrees with that of Simpson (1945) as modified by Ellerman and Morrison-Scott (1951) (*Hydropotes* given subfamily rank) and Groves (1974) (Muntiacini assigned to the Cervinae), except that *Rangifer* is associated in the same tribe as the New World genera. A classification based more rigorously on a cladogram of extant cervid rela-

tionships would not take into account the affinities of fossil deer and in any case would be premature.

Systematics of Living Deer Species

TRAGULIDAE

The chevrotains or mouse-deer are the most primitive of the living Ruminantia (Webb and Taylor, 1980). Different opinions have been expressed concerning the interrelationships of the living species. Gentry (1978) states "There seems every likelihood that *Tragulus* and *Hyemoschus* will eventually be sunk in *Dorcatherium*" (an Old World Miocene to Pliocene genus; *Tragulus* would nevertheless have nomenclatural priority). Webb and Taylor (1980) on the other hand say that "Major differences between *Tragulus* and *Hyemoschus*, comparable to those between the Gelocidae and Moschidae, for example, further emphasize the long distinct evolutionary history of the Tragulidae." We sympathize with Gentry's opinion, for on the basis of external characters (Pocock, 1919) and the form of the skull (Flerov, 1931), the Indian mouse deer is clearly intermediate between the African *Hyemoschus* and the southeast Asian *Tragulus* sensu stricto. It should not be included in the latter taxon, but assigned to a separate genus, *Moschiola*. Observations on the morphology of *Tragulus* sensu lato should be checked to see whether they really apply to both the Asiatic taxa.

Hyemoschus aquaticus is the water chevrotain of the African tropical high forest belt. The metapodials are short, the median metacarpals remain unfused, and the fused metatarsals retain a deep groove between them.

Moschiola meminna of southern India and Sri Lanka has completely fused median metacarpals and metatarsals, but in color pattern and skull form is close to *Hyemoschus*.

Tragulus sensu stricto includes the common Southeast Asian mouse deer. The unusual form of the skull may be derivative, and the genus also differs from the other tragulids in its dentition, the presence of an inter-ramal gland, a lateral appendage to the penis, and a bare area on the pasterns. Gular stripes are retained, but the body color is uniform, not spotted as in the other genera. *T. napu* (formerly termed *T. javanicus*) is much the larger of the two species, duller in color, and with lengthened toes. *T. javanicus* (former *T. kanchil*) is small, brighter in color, and with short toes. Both species range widely in mainland Southeast Asia and Sundaland. Only *T. javanicus* occurs on Java, and only *T. napu* ranges as far as Balabac in the Philippines. Mouse deer occur on many small or very small Indonesian islands and show much geographic variation (Miller, 1909). On the smallest islets, only one or other of the two species occurs.

Groves and Grubb

MOSCHIDAE

The musk deer are now excluded from the Cervidae (Flerov, 1952; Webb and Taylor, 1980). They therefore become the only living members of the Moschidae, a group which may include the Dremotheriidae of Ginsburg and Heintz (1966) and Hamilton (1973). There are at least three species of musk deer, whose diagnostic characters of the skeleton, pelage, and ecology are discussed by Flerov (1952), Kao (1963), Groves (1976), and Grubb (1982). Recently, two more species have been distinguished.

Moschus chrysogaster is usually called *M. sifanicus,* but the name *chrysogaster* was originally applied to individuals of the same species and has priority (Grubb, 1982). *M. chrysogaster* occurs in the Alpine zone of the eastern and southern edge of the Tibetan Plateau, extending onto the southern side of the Himalayas. It is the largest of the musk deer, with a characteristic long-snouted skull. The pelage is a pale speckled yellow brown in color, with yellow-tipped ears and a broad whitish band down the throat. These last two features are sometimes absent in north Indian populations which apparently bridge the gap between nominate *chrysogaster* and a newly described subspecies, *cupreus,* from Kashmir (Grubb, 1982).

M. leucogaster is recognized as a separate species by Cai and Feng (1981) under the name *chrysogaster.* Its pelage is melanized, dark brown to black, with localization of agouti-banded hairs and no neck stripes. It is smaller than the previous species, of which P.G. thinks it is a subspecies; C.P.G. considers it to represent *M. berezovskii.* It is recorded reliably only from Sikkim, Bhutan, intervening parts of Chinese Tibet, and Nepal (Groves, 1976, 1980; Cai and Feng, 1981; Grubb, 1982).

M. fuscus has just been described by Li (1981) from the Salween Valley in Yunnan, and is also the species in north Burma. It is like the dark Nepalese musk deer but is even more melanized. Pale phaeomelanin banding of the hairs is completely absent and there are no light-colored markings at all. The status of *fuscus* is puzzling: In pelage, it seems most like *leucogaster,* but it is smaller, within the size range of *berezovskii* with which it apparently occurs.

M. berezovskii is found in wooded areas of western China, marginally sympatric with *M. chrysogaster,* from the Sichuan mountains to the southeast coast and into northern Vietnam. The population of Vietnam north to Guangsi (*M. b. caobangis* Dao 1977) is regarded as a small-sized subspecies (Groves 1980). *M. berezovskii* is the smallest species, dark brown but finely speckled all over with buff, with two whitish stripes down the neck and black ear tips.

M. moschiferus of Siberia, northern China, and Korea is a large species with more specialized limb anatomy than the other musk deer, including much longer metapodials (Flerov, 1952), a more complicated juvenile pattern of stripes as well as spots which are often retained in adulthood, softer pelage, and a pair of white throat stripes as in *M. berezovskii.*

ANTILOCAPRIDAE

The prongbuck (*Antilocapra americana*) has recently been assigned to the Bovidae (O'Gara and Matson, 1975), but Leinders (1979) and Leinders and Heintz (1980) indicate that it is more probably a cervoid.

CERVIDAE: HYDROPOTINAE

Hydropotes is a true deer but a primitive one in its large laniary canines and the absence of antlers. *Dremotherium* of the European Lower Miocene may lie near the ancestry of *Hydropotes* (Sigogneau, 1968; Hamilton, 1978). Flerov (1950) derived *Hydropotes* from the ancestry of the Muntiacini, therefore implying that it was secondarily antlerless, but there is little to be said for this view.

The Chinese water deer (*H. inermis*) is the only species. The Chinese and Korean populations have been classed as different subspecies (Howell, 1929). Flerov (1952) has suggested that the curious form of the anterior dentary is an adaptation towards feeding on submerged water plants, but his explanation is not very clear and he did not account for the pinched-in form of the premaxillae which could seem to be part of the same functional complex.

CERVIDAE: ODOCOILEINAE: CAPREOLINI

Only a single species of roe deer has been recognized by many authors, but von Lehmann (1958, 1960) has drawn attention to the considerable differences between the western *capreolus* group and the eastern *pygargus* group of subspecies. The karyotypes are also very different (Table 2). Stubbe and Bruholz (1979) have hybridized representatives of these two groups and found that male hybrids are sterile, while females are fertile. The hybrids moreover show hybrid vigor, being at four to five months already larger than their dams. Coupled with the morphological evidence, this would seem to be sufficient grounds for considering that two species are involved, *C. capreolus* of Europe and the Middle East, and *C. pygargus* of Siberia and China.

The European roe (*C. capreolus*) is the smaller of the two (HBL 100–136 cm, SH 75–91.5 cm, GL 190–216 mm—sexes combined). It is grey-brown to pale grey in winter, red-brown or dark brown in summer. The antlers are close together at the base, short (25–30 cm long), directed up, and little tuberculated. The skull is broad at the orbits with a compressed muzzle, and very small bullae. It is widely distributed in Western Europe as far east as Byelorussia and the Crimea, perhaps as far as the Volga. It is also found in Asia Minor, Transcaucasia, Palestine, northern Iraq, and northern Iran. The species probably has several distinguishable races: Harrison (1968) recognized a very pale Kurdistan race, *coxi*, geographically isolated around the Tigris headwaters, and a Turkish race, *armenius*. Von Lehmann (1960) listed in addition European subspecies *capreolus*, *transsylvanicus*, *canus*, and *whittali* but without diagnosing them.

The Siberian roe (*C. pygargus*) is larger (HBL 115–151 cm, SH 77–100 cm. GL 207–253 mm—sexes and races combined). It is grey to red in winter with a creamy or red-creamy belly, and reddish in summer. The antlers are widely separate at the base, slant upward, are long (38 cm or more), and strongly tuberculated. The skull is narrow, long-faced, broadened over the canines, and with large bullae (Flerov, 1952; Heptner et al., 1961).

C. pygargus ranges to the Soviet Far East and Korea, Sichuan, Gansu, the Central Asian Mountains, and west at least to the Volga. According to Heptner et al. (1961) it is known from the right bank of the Volga and from the lower Don, so that it might be marginally sympatric with *C. capreolus*. A thorough description of the ecology of the two species where they meet, and of their precise dispersion, would be most desirable. *C. pygargus* also occurs on the northern flank of the Caucasus.

As many as five subspecies may be recognized (Flerov, 1952; Heptner et al.; 1961):

1) *C. pygargus pygargus* is distributed, from the Urals and perhaps from still further west, to Transbaikalia and northwestern Mongolia. Dimensions for the sexes combined are HBL 119–151 cm, SH 80–100 cm, GL 215–253 mm. Color is grey with belly creamy in winter, but redder in summer. Antlers are strongly lyrate.

2) *C. p. caucasicus* is not recognized by Flerov (1952) and Heptner et al. (1961) admit that the differences between it and the nominate race are unclear. It is found geographically isolated on the northern slopes of the Caucasus, and contrasts markedly with the roe of the southern flank which belongs to *C. capreolus*. Skull length (GL 216–238) is in the lower end of the range for the nominate race, but outside the range (GL 184–213) for the Transcaucasian form of the European roe.

3) *C. p. tianschanicus* is another subspecies, of similar dimensions (GL218–238 mm), not recognized by Flerov and not clearly distinguished from the nominate race. It is restricted to the slopes of the Tianshan range.

4) *C. p. bedfordi* of the Soviet Far East, Korea, and Manchuria south to Shansi (type locality) is rather distinctive. It is somewhat small in size (HBL about 122 cm, GL 211–236 cm—sexes combined), ochery-red to grey-red in winter, with a red-tinted rump patch and underside, and bright red in summer.

5) *C. p. melanotis*, the race of Gansu (type locality) and Sichuan, is still smaller (GL 207–223 mm). Engelmann (1939) gives some body dimensions (HBL 115–129 cm, SH 77–81 cm). It is red in summer and grey to red-grey in winter. Engelmann's measurements suggest that the antlers are smaller than those of other races, somewhat closer together, and less lyrate. Allen (1930) regarded *melanotis* as a synonym of *bedfordi*; the type localities are relatively close.

CERVIDAE: ODOCOILEINAE: ALCINI

There is only one living species of elk or moose (*Alces alces*), but the European/West Siberian and the East Siberian/American populations are highly distinctive (Flerov, 1952), really ranking as semispecies. It would be interesting to investigate the border area between the two to examine how far reproductive isolation might have progressed. The western form is uniform brown in color over the body and neck; the muzzle is pale; the haunches, lower flanks, belly and upper segments of the limbs are darker than the back and neck, grading with the latter. The lower segments and posterior surfaces of the limbs tend to be whitish. There is little seasonal change in color. The nose is not greatly humped, and the bare spot at its tip, between the nostrils, is elliptical. The rostrum is relatively shorter, with proportionally longer nasal processes of the premaxillae; and the diploid number is 68. However, in the eastern (including North American) races, the black throat, inter-ramal region, and lower parts of the body contrast strongly with the grey-brown upper part of the flanks and neck. But the legs are light brown on their lower segments and posterior surfaces. There is a distinct seasonal change in color: colors are most vivid in August, becoming lighter and more contrasty in winter and spring. The muzzle is greatly swollen, and the bare spot at its tip is pear-shaped or T-shaped, while the rostrum is relatively longer, but with proportionally shorter nasal processes of the premaxillae. The diploid number is 70.

Within the western form, Flerov (1952) discriminated the living *Alces alces alces*, widespread from Europe to the Yenisei River, and *A. a. caucasicus* from the Circassian foothills. The latter became extinct at the beginning of the last century, and is known only from its skull and antlers; the skull was smaller and differed in minor features from that of the nominate race, and the antlers were weak and not palmated.

Within the eastern form, Flerov (1952) recognized no separate subspecies: for him, all East Siberian and North American moose were *A. a. americana*. Peterson

Groves and Grubb

(1952) and Heptner et al. (1962) did, however, recognize a number of subspecies. For Siberia, the latter authors distinguished *A. a. pfizenmayeri*, from most of Siberia east of the Yenisei, and *A. a. cameloides* from the Amur drainage north to the Stanovoi mountains and the upper Lena River. The latter is much smaller, with shorter muzzle, shorter legs usually rather light in color, and weak, unpalmated antlers, contrasting markedly with the massive broadly palmate antlers of the more widespread race. Recently, Chernyavskyi and Zheleznov (1982) have separated the very large moose of eastern Siberia (Indigirka to Anadyr basins) from *A. a. pfizenmayeri* as a new subspecies, *A. a. buturlini*. Ranges of GL for bulls are 560–575 (5 *cameloides*), 569–620 (11 *pfizenmayer*), and 578–668 mm (14 *buturlini*).

For North America, Peterson (1952) distinguished subspecies *gigas* (Alaska), *andersoni* (Western and Central Canada), *shirasi* (Rockies), and *americana* (Eastern Canada). He thought that each race diverged in its own glacial refuge. *A. a. gigas* is very big (GL 582–686 mm in 22 bulls), the largest subspecies, and blackish with a rusty-brown "saddle", not unlike *pfizenmayeri* but less grey on the back. The other races are smaller (GL 559–660 mm in 78 bulls). *Andersoni* is more rusty brown in color, *americana* deeper brown with a reduced saddle, while *shirasi* has a pale brownish saddle. These differences and the reported skull characters are not very striking, and it seems that much geographic variation in American moose is clinal. Youngman (1975) considers *andersoni* an intergrade population, connecting *gigas* with the other forms and not worthy of subspecific rank. He agrees that *gigas* was formerly confined to a Beringian refuge. But at that time did it form a population continuous with *burturlini?* The naming of this new subspecies raises questions about the validity of described races of east Siberian and American moose which cannot be resolved here.

CERVIDAE: ODOCOILEINAE: ODOCOILEINI

Phylogenetic relationships within the endemic New World genera have yet to be evaluated. As discussed earlier, the spike-antlered genera (*Mazama* and *Pudu*) may be derived from species with forked antlers. Haltenorth (1963) included *Pudu* within *Mazama*, while Hershkovitz (1982) separated *Pudu* tribally from the other genera and regarded it as the most primitive of the neocervines. But it has several specializations, and we believe that some of its supposed primitive characters are actually derivative. We keep *Mazama* and *Pudu* apart provisionally.

Different opinions have been expressed concerning affinities among the branch-antlered genera. Neitzel (1982) suggested that *Odocoileus*, *Ozotoceros*, and

Blastocerus form a clade, as they share derived karyotypic characters which are not present in the other neocervine she studies, *Mazama gouazoubira*. However, the derived characters are apparently also shared by *Pudu*, and in part by other *Mazama* species (Table 2), so are not sufficient evidence that *Odocoileus* forms a clade among the neocervines with *Ozotoceros* and *Blastocerus*. Hershkovitz (1972, 1982) has indeed suggested that *Odocoileus* is not immediately related to these genera, a view partly supported by the form of the antler. In *Hippocamelus*, *Blastocerus*, and *Ozotoceros*, the first anterior antler branch lies in front of the first posterior branch, and all branching is more or less in the same plane. But in *Odocoileus*, the pattern is different. The first anterior antler branch, or *brow tine* (A1; Figure 4) sticks up vertically and lies anteromedially, while the first posterior branch, which continues the beam, is situated postero-externally and then curves outwards and upwards, then forwards and inwards, branching at least twice. In the smallest members of the genus, the South American races of *O. virginianus*, the anterior tine is relatively large, suggesting that it is not an adventitious snag but a true antler branch. It is relatively smaller in North American populations of this species, and tends to be much reduced or absent in *O. hemionus*, where P2 and A2 both fork. The result is an antler superficially with the same branching pattern as that of *Blastocerus*, but the two are not homologous tine for tine (Pocock, 1933; Figure 4).

The karyotype of *Hippocamelus* is unknown, but *Ozotoceros* and *Blastocerus* share two homologous Robertsonian fusions of autosomes recorded from no other deer (Neitzel, 1982), and this is suggestive evidence that they at least form a clade. Flerov (1952) had anticipated this result, for he placed them in the same subgenus. If their sharing of vestibular nasal glands is unique, this is further evidence for a relationship. But we think they are too different in other respects to be regarded as congeneric before the phylogeny of the neocervines is reassessed. Sharing of derived characters does not give a clear cladistic picture of relationships within the group as yet.

PUDU

The pudu are the smallest deer. Though similar to *Mazama*, they differ in the fusion of cubonavicular and cuneiform bones, the relatively broader lateral incisiform teeth, and the more primitive pedal glands. The genus has just been revised very thoroughly by Hershkovitz (1982). *P. mephistopheles* is the more primitive species of Colombia, Equador, and Peru. *P. puda* (sic—Hershkovitz shows that this is the original spelling) occurs in Chile and neighboring parts of Argentina. Of the characters which Hershkovitz considers to be primitive in the genus, we suggest the following may actually be derived: broadened lateral incisiform teeth; absence of tarsal and metatarsal tufts and glands; unspotted fawn of *P. mephistopheles*.

MAZAMA

These are relatively small or very small deer with simple spike-like, unbranched antlers, very short tails, no or rudimentary tarsal glands, a long deep cleft for posterior interdigital glands, and basicranial lordosis. *Mazama* has been reviewed by Allen (1915), Tate (1939), and Cabrera (1960). *M. americana* (red brocket) is a widely distributed species ranging from southern Mexico to northern Argentina. Tate (1939) excluded smaller reddish brockets of Central America from the *americana* group. Their very distinct karyotype (Table 2) may indicate that they represent a separate species, for which the name would be *M. temama. M. gouazoubira* (brown brocket) has a more restricted distribution and does not occur in Central America, except perhaps as the form *permira* of Isla San Jose off Panama (Hall, 1981). These two species are broadly sympatric and range up to about 2000 m in the Andes. The other species of brocket occur at higher altitudes, 3–4000 m. *M. rufina* (rufous brocket) of the mountains of Venezuela and Ecuador is much smaller than the two lowland brockets. The status of a supposed lowland subspecies *nana* of Brazil, Argentina, and Paraguay (Cabrera, 1960) requires clarification. Haltenorth (1963) separated *bricenii* from *rufina* as a species to include *M. chunyi*. But topotypes of *rufina* in the British Museum are extremely similar to *bricenii*, while *M. chunyi* of Bolivia and Peru is quite distinct and still smaller than *M. rufina*. Hershkovitz (1959) noted the resemblances of *M. chunyi* to *Pudu,* but regarded them as superficial.

HIPPOCAMELUS

These are larger deer, but with relatively short limbs, rather narrow ears, simple forked antlers, and large uninvaginated face glands. Juveniles are unspotted. The skull base is straight, and there are several derived dental characters (no protoconal folds, broad incisiform crowns, reduced molar styles). *H. antisensis*, the taruca of Peru, Ecuador, Bolivia, and northern Argentina is the smaller of the two montane species. It is pale-colored, with a dark V-mark on the forehead, and when fleeing displays a large light rump patch (J. Merkt, pers. com.). *H. bisulcus*, the huemal, occurs along the cordillera of Chile and Argentina. It is the largest South American deer after *Blastocerus dichotomus,* and differs from *H. antisensis* in its dark color, short premaxillae, and truncated nasals. Apparently no distinct rump patch is evident (McNamara, pers. com.). Hershkovitz (1982) surmised that the huemal

originated from a taruca-like ancestor, paralleling the relationship between the species of *Pudu*.

OZOTOCEROS

The pampas deer (*O. bezoarticus*), a specialized grass feeder of Brazil, Uruguay, and Argentine, has been divided into three subspecies (Cabrera, 1943) whose status should perhaps be re-evaluated. Derivative characters include the absence of forefoot glands, no protoconal folds, the most hypsodont cheek teeth among South American deer, the advanced molarization of PM_4, and intermediate condition of the incisiform crowns. The juvenile is spotted as in *Mazama* and like that genus and *Blastocerus*, the tail is short and bushy. There are no metatarsal tufts and metatarsal glands are usually not present (Hershkovitz, 1958), but adults often retain upper canines. The face glands are well developed and there is lordosis of the basicranium, while the antlers are usually three-pointed. With its narrow ears, absence of black muzzle markings, pale eye ring and labial marks, and relatively small size, the pampas deer looks very different from the related marsh deer.

BLASTOCERUS

A monotypic species of Brazil, Bolivia, Paraguay, Argentina, and formerly Uruguay, the marsh deer (*B. dichotomus*) is the largest South American cervid. Its red color, very broad ears, and black muzzle and shank markings are distinctive. It agrees with *Odocoileus* in its broad incisiform teeth, the absence of canines, the shape of the ears, and the retention of protoconal folds, but similarities in the form of the antlers are superficial (Figure 4). It differs from *Odocoileus* and resembles *Ozotoceros* in that the tail is shorter and more bushy and the face glands are more developed. The important similarities in karyology and nasal glands have already been mentioned. It differs from the other branch-antlered genera in the straight basicranium and the unspotted pelage of the young. Metatarsal glands and tufts are absent, again a distinction from *Odocoileus*. From the karyological evidence, Haltenorth (1963) was creating a polyphyletic taxon in placing *Blastocerus* in the same subgenus as *Odocoileus*.

ODOCOILEUS

The genus is characterized by the form of the antlers, with their relatively long and curved beams, the relatively long, evenly haired tail, very small face glands, the presence of tarsal and anterior and posterior interdigital glands, very strongly molarized PM_4, basicranial lordosis, somewhat enlarged auditory

Groves and Grubb

bullae, rather extensive ethmoid fissures, and the presence of spots in the young. While some of these characters recall the pampas and marsh deer, it is not clear what the cladistic relationship between *Odocoileus* and these taxa might be. There is the possibility that as a group, they are polyphyletic, *Odocoileus* having originated independently from a fork-antlered ancestor. Pending further studies, we have not amalgamated *Ozotoceros* and *Blastocerus* with *Odocoileus*.

O. virginianus, the white-tailed deer, has an extensive distribution from the savannas of northern South America and the northern Andes to southern Canada. Systematics has been reviewed by Kellogg (1956) and Hershkovitz (1948) who recognized 37 subspecies. There is considerable geographic variation in size. The North American subspecies are the largest: The maximum condylobasal length of the largest males recorded from each race of Canada and most of the U.S. was 287–322 mm (Kellogg, 1956). For subspecies of the U.S. Caribbean coast, the range was 275–292 mm. Small insular subspecies of Georgia and South Carolina had values of 251–273 mm, with 240 mm for the Florida Key deer (*O. v. clavium*). For Mexico and Central America, the range was much lower, 224–254 mm. There is also variation in the metatarsal gland and tuft which are usually present in northern Mexico and further north, but usually absent from Oaxaca and southward (Hershkovitz, 1958; Quay, 1971). Hershkovitz (1958) distinguished lowland South American races with a "permanent summer" pelage from highland races with a "permanent winter" pelage.

Much geographic variation in the white-tailed deer is probably clinal. However, we think there is sufficient evidence to recognize two subspecies groups, the tropical *cariacou* group, usually with no metatarsal glands or tuft, and smaller in size, and the temperate *virginianus* group, usually with a metatarsal gland and tuft, and significantly larger is size, except for some insular populations. Davis and Lukens (1958) have already suggested that the Central American populations may be specifically distinct from *O. virginianus*.

O. hemionus is clearly divided into two semispecies, the black-tailed deer (*columbianus* subspecies-group) and the mule deer (*hemionus* group), which meet along the western edge of the Rockies and interbreed or narrowly intergrade along a very extensive front, fully described by Cowan (1936, 1956). The black-tailed deer is more like the allopatric white-tailed deer in morphology: It is the less similar mule deer which is sympatric with the latter. The mule deer also extends over a much wider range of habitats, and in its antlers and pelage is the most derived taxon in the genus. As a species, *O. hemionus* also differs from *O. virginianus* in

its more molarized premolars and specialized tarsal gland hairs (Muller-Schwarze et al., 1977).

RANGIFER

It has been supposed that the caribou is of Asiatic or perhaps Beringian origin (Kurtén and Anderson, 1980), and possibly related to the Wisconsin Glacial *Rangifer fricki* of North America (Flerov, 1952). Banfield (1961) regarded *fricki* as a palaeosubspecies of *R. tarandus* but it is now known to be a short limbed deer with three-tined antlers, and has been assigned to a monotypic genus *Navahoceros* (Kurtén and Anderson, 1980), possibly related to *Agalmoceros* of Equador and Bolivia, another extinct deer with short metapodials (Hoffstetter, 1952). A further possible relative of *Rangifer* is the Patagonian Pleistocene deer *Morenelaphus brachyceros* (Lydekker, 1898; Frick, 1937; Flerov, 1952). The antlers of *Morenelaphus* are unlike those of any living South American deer but resemble *Rangifer* antlers in their length and the presence of palmate brown and distal tines. The beam is relatively much longer, however, and the distal palmate antler-branch is very short, while there is an additional anterior tine between the two palmate ones, so the homology is not certain. However, no other potential relative of *Rangifer* has been identified, and it is possible that caribou evolved from a *Morenelaphus*-like ancestor and reached North America from Patagonia along the cordillera. Other North American temperate or boreal species of South American origin include the extinct dire wolf (*Canis dirus*) and the porcupine *Erethizon dorsatum* (Kurtén and Anderson, 1980).

Banfield (1961) has revised the genus *Rangifer,* recognizing a single species with nine subspecies, and Siivonen (1975), Nieminen (1980) and Espmark (1981) have reconsidered the European wild and domestic populations. Three distinct semispecies or subspecies groups of reindeer can be distinguished (Banfield, 1963)—the woodland *caribou* group, the tundra *tarandus* group, and the Arctic Island *pearyi* group. The first two range across the Holarctic and the third is restricted to arctic Canada and Greenland. It is not clear whether the Spitzbergen reindeer (*R. tarandus platyrhynchus*) belongs with the tundra or with the Arctic Island group. Unaware of Banfield's study, Michurin (1965) described *R. t. taimyrensis* from the Taimyr Peninsula, western Siberia. From the description, it would appear to be no more than a deme with certain average distinguishing features, not recognizable as a subspecies.

Tundra reindeer interbreed or intergrade with woodland populations, but there are also areas where they are seasonally sympatric outside the breeding season, and geographically segregated so as to be reproductively isolated during the arctic summer. The zone of intergradation running from Alaska through the Yukon to British Columbia is extensive and of considerable interest, since it probably dates only from postglacial times. Banfield (1961) interpreted most of the Alaskan populations as intergrades between the tundra races *R. t. groenlandicus* (Canadian Arctic) and *R. t. granti* (Alaskan Peninsula) on the one hand, and the woodland caribou *R. t. caribou* on the other. Yet in his discussion, he makes it apparent that some supposed intergrade populations were identical with typical *granti*, others with typical *groenlandicus*, while certain adjacent populations assigned to *caribou* showed some tundra reindeer characters. Therefore a fuller investigation of this zone is probably desirable before a more definitive taxonomic allocation of populations can be made.

Representatives of the tundra and Arctic Island groups (*R. t. groenlandicus, R. t. pearyi*) intergrade on Banks Island and Victoria Island in the Canadian Arctic, but both subspecies apparently coexist without interbreeding even during the reproductive season on Queen Elizabeth Island (Manning, 1960; Manning and Macpherson, 1961; Thomas and Everson, 1982).

The phylogenetic relationships between the semispecies of reindeer and caribou have hardly been investigated. The *pearyi* group is presumably derived from tundra reindeer which were stranded in a Pearyland glacial refuge (Macpherson, 1965). Either the tundra or the woodland form could be ancestral to the other, but which? Most Pleistocene records of reindeer in Europe, and certainly those for Britain, are of tundra reindeer (Reynolds, 1933). But one might expect that adaptations for a tundra existence would be derivative, and that by analogy with other boreal ungulates where the more northerly species are more specialized, caribou were primitively forest animals.

CERVINAE: MUNTIACINI: ELAPHODUS

Cranially, the tufted deer (*E. cephalophus*) is very different from the muntjacs—the muzzle is short but very broad, and the lacrimal pit is extremely large, larger than the orbit, so that the lacrimal bone extends further forward, almost closing the ethmoid fissure; the pedicles do not extend as bony ridges along the frontals and are short and thin; the antlers are extremely small; and PM$_4$ is more molarized, with a large metaconid.

Four subspecies have been described: the nominate *cephalophus* (Sichuan); *ichangensis* (Ichang); *fociensis* (Fukien); and *michianus* (Zhejiang). The British Museum has the types or other material from these four areas, as well as a specimen from the Myitkyina district, northern Burma. Preliminary studies suggest

that no subspecies should be recognized and that geographical variation is probably clinal.

MUNTIACUS

Except for the frontal ridges, which are peculiar to the genus, the general form of the skull in *Munticaus* is more like that of *Axis (Hyelaphus)* than *Elaphodus*. It would be interesting to know whether this resemblance is more than superficial, and how the living muntiacines might be related to the various rather poorly known fossil genera of muntjac-like deer.

The number of species of *Muntiacus* is not certain. Five are currently recognized. Suspicions that two species of muntjac live sympatrically on Borneo have recently been substantiated (Groves and Grubb, 1982). In addition to *M. muntjak*, a yellower endemic species (*M. atherodes*) occurs throughout the island and is of particular interest because of the very small spike antlers which are normally never shed.

The Chinese muntjac, *M. reevesi*, is smaller, more compactly built and of a duller color than *M. muntjak*, but otherwise similar. Its chromosome complement (2N = 46) is not grossly reduced however (Table 2). The two species may overlap in distribution in southern China (Sokolov, 1957). *M. reevesi* is individually variable, but there is little or no geographic variation on the mainland (Allen, 1930). From our research, only the Taiwan form, *micrurus*, seems distinguishable. It is significantly smaller, and the ear-backs are red rather than yellow.

Fea's muntjac (*M. feai*), always a poorly known species, has recently been briefly reviewed by Grubb (1977), who for the first time described the skull. So far, eleven museum specimens have been traced, from southern Tibet and China, to the Burma-Thailand border. Frädrich (1981) has described a living example and Ngampongsai (pers. comm.) has noted other captive specimens. Its karyotype (2N = 13; Neitzel, in lit.) is intermediate between *M. reevesi* and *M. muntjak*.

The only specimen of *M. rooseveltorum* known hails from Laos and was described as intermediate between *M. muntjak* and *M. reevesi*, but with curiously hypertrophied mental gland tufts (Osgood, 1932). It has not been compared with *M. feai*, however, and similar gland tufts are also found in some specimens of *M. muntjak*.

For over a century, only five specimens of the hairy-fronted muntjac (*M. crinifrons*) had been recorded, but recently the species has become well known (Sheng and Lu, 1980). It appears to be relatively common, living in a restricted range in eastern China, in the provinces of Zhejiang, Jiangxi, and Anhui, in steep mountain forest at about 1000 m. In the same region, *M. reevesi* lives in the lowlands and tufted deer at intermediate altitudes. Brief descriptions and measurements have been published by Sheng and Lu, and it will be useful to see photographs of the living animal and to determine the karyotype.

The last species, the red or "Indian" muntjac (*M. muntjak*), is relatively large with particularly large antlers and long robust pedicles. There is considerable geographical variation in colour and size. The Indonesian populations (revised by van Bemmel, 1952) and those of Malaya form the nominate *muntjak* group of subspecies. They are deep mahogany red, with dark brown limbs and a diploid chromosome complement of eight in the female, nine in the male (Table 2). The populations of Burma, Yunnan, Indochina, the Indian peninsula and Sri Lanka are yellower with little or no dark color on the limbs and constitute the *vaginalis* subspecies group. The chromosome number is the lowest among mammals, six in the female, six or seven in the male. The X chromosomes are fused to different autosomes in each subspecies group (Wurster and Aitkin, 1972), and White (1978) maintains that such a karyotypic difference would be incompatible with hybrid fertility. Consequently, a species boundary might well exist, perhaps at the Isthmus of Kra, by analogy with other Oriental fauna. The northern populations would be known as *M. vaginalis*.

There is much homology in G-banding of the chromosomes of *M. reevesi* and *M. (muntjak) vaginalis*, the karyotype of the latter being derivable by tandem translocation from that of the former (Shi et al., 1980; Neitzel, 1982), but spermatogenesis in the male hybrid is arrested at early prophase (Shi and Pathak, 1981).

CERVINAE: CERVINI

The Cervini have antlers with at least three tines. The species which most resembles muntjac in the form of its antlers is the hog deer, *Axis (Hyelaphus) porcinus* (Flerov, 1952), where the pedicel is long, in line with the antler beam, and in the frontal plane; the brow tine is erect and makes an acute angle with the beam; and the postero-internal tines (P2) bend in and back, rather as the posterior tines of muntjac curl inwards at the tip.

Cervini with three point antlers may show various modifications on the hog deer plan, but can be classified into two groups according to the proportions of the terminal fork (Teilhard de Chardin and Piveteau, 1980; Teilhard de Chardin and Trassaert, 1937). Either the antero=external terminal tine (A2) is longer than the postero-internal one (P2) and in line with beam, as in the hog deer; or the postero-internal tine becomes the larger and is deflected upwards and backwards, taking over the course of the beam (Figure 5). This derived condition presages a four point antler, where the enlarged branch (P2) will fork once more and initially will again have the postero-internal terminal tine (this time P3) relatively small: It would have to enlarge before further branching were to occur.

It is therefore possible to arrange antlers in a series from more primitive to more derived types, but each derivative state could have arisen on more than one occasion.

In some Cervini, there are divergent trends in antler branching: *Dama* and *Cervus (Rucervus)* resemble *Rangifer* or *Megaceros* in switching branch dominance from the posterior dichotomous fork to the anterior one as the antlers grow. *Elaphurus* has the anterior branch dominant from the start. And *Cervus (Cervus) elaphus* has evolved a large supernumerary tine, the bez, between A1 and A2 (brow and trez), perhaps as an elaboration of a snag like those of *C. (Rucervus) eldi* or *Axis axis* (Figure 6).

In attempting a reconstruction of the phylogeny of the Cervini, a cladistic approach has to rely on characters other than the antlers, though few appropriate ones are yet available. The structure of the feet may provide one guideline. The fallow deer (*Dama*) combines a primitive condition of the foot glands with several other primitive features, but also some distinctive specializations. It may be regarded as the sister taxon to the rest of the living Cervini, presumed to form a clade in that they have derived pedal characters—either more advanced pouch-shaped foot glands, and in the hind feet alone (*Axis*), or no foot glands at all, with the interdigital skin naked (*Cervus, Elaphurus*).

For more detailed relationships, the karyotype provides some clues. The Cervini share a homologous pair of metacentric autosomes (Neitzel, 1982). In addition, *C. (Rusa) unicolor*, *C. (Rucervus) eldi*, and *C. (Rucervus) duvauceli* share four other homologous Robertsonian fusions (Neitzel, 1979). There would seem to be little doubt that *Rusa* and *Rucervus* at least form a clade within *Cervus*. However, not all *C. (Rusa) unicolor* share all these fusions, nor does the closely related *C. (Rusa) mariannus* (Table 2). Polymorphism for the number of fusions, so far inadequately disclosed, could account for this apparent discrepancy. Neitzel (1969) indeed records a *C. (Rucervus) duvauceli* which was heterozygous for two fusions that are homozygous in other species with otherwise a less specialised karyotype. The situation is complex and further studies are awaited before definitive phylogenetic conclusions can be drawn.

Axis axis, C. (Cervus) nippon, C. (Przewalskium) albirostris, C. (Rusa) mariannus, and *C. (Rusa) timorensis* also have supernumerary Robertsonian fusions but their homologies are not yet known. From morphological evidence, it seems likely that *Axis axis* and *C. (Cervus) nippon* at least derived their fusions, whether by the joining of homologous chromosomes or not, independently from *Rusa* and *Rucervus*.

DAMA

The fallow deer have antlers of a strongly modified four-tine form. It is clear from the ontogeny and from specimens where the antlers are not palmate, that a switch in branch-dominance occurs at the third dichotomy, so that A3 forms the "palm". P3 is much smaller and often incorporated into the latter (Figure 6). The Pleistocene *Dama clactoniana* is supposedly ancestral to the extant species, but the antlers were differently formed, with a supplementary tine between A2 and the palm (Sickenberg, 1965). The extinct Chinese *Dama sericus* (Teilhard de Chardin and Trassaert, 1937) is probably related to *Megaceros*. *"Cervus" nestii*, a European Villafranchian deer with simple four-tine antlers is a putative ancestor for *Dama* (Azzaroli, 1948).

Fallow deer have primitive characters of spotted pelage, no mane, long tail, foot glands in the forefeet as well as in the hind feet, broad central incisors, and brachyodont cheek teeth with almost no trace of basal pillars. But the bullae are not inflated, and there are usually no canines. Fallow deer also have some rather distinctive morphological features that set them apart from other Cervini—the large functional preputial glands with prominent gland-tuft, the hypertrophied larynx, nasals which are shortened medially but have lateral projections extending forward to meet the premaxillae, distinctive antlers, and distinctive markings, with a light strip placed higher up the flank than in other spotted deer.

The post-glacial refuge or refuges of *Dama dama dama* and therefore its "natural" distribution have still not been determined (Chapman and Chapman, 1975), but it has been dispersed artificially over an immense area of the world (Chapman and Chapman, 1980). Work by Miss J. Pemberton (University of Reading) has demonstrated a remarkable uniformity at many genetic loci in the introduced British populations, which may reflect the small size of the source population.

Although the Mesopotamian fallow deer is superficially very similar to the common species, its antlers are most peculiar, with a flattened proximate section of the beam, very reduced brow tine, and narrow distal palmate region often represented only by back-pointing tines (Haltenorth, 1959). It formerly ranged from Lebanon to Iran, and had been introduced to Cyprus, where remains from archaeological sites suggest that it may have been domesticated (Zeuner, 1958). We treat it as a subspecies, *D. d. mesopotamica*.

AXIS (HYELAPHUS)

The hog deer has been regarded as the most primitive of the Cervini (Flerov, 1952). In size and proportions it is similar to *Muntiacus*, and its antlers are of a primitive form. It differs in details of the juvenile spotting pattern, absence of canines, swollen auditory bullae, and much reduced lacrimal pit, with the ethmoid fissure closer to the orbit, characters mostly typical of the Cervini.

The hog deer ranges from northern India through Burma and Thailand to Indo-China. Western and eastern subspecies (*A. porcinus porcinus* and *A. p. annamiticus*) are usually recognized but have not been critically compared. The hog deer also occurs on Sri Lanka, where it may have been introduced, and Pocock (1943a) considered this population represented a further subspecies, *A. p. oryzus*. *"Rusa" oppenoorthi* of the Javanese Plio-Pleistocene was apparently a representative of the hog deer (von Koenigswalk, 1933), and deer referred to *Axis* were present on Palawan in the late Pleistocene (Fox, 1979), though perhaps they were rusas. The Bawean deer, *A. kuhli* (on Bawean Island between Java and Borneo), and the Calamian deer, *A. calamianensis* (Calamian Islands, north of Palawan, Philippines), are similar to the hog deer. Their origin could be interpreted in two ways. Either they originated from hog deer that were introduced by human agency, perhaps by traders from India, within the last 2000 years, as may be the case with *A. p. "oryzus";* or they are peripheral populations of an otherwise extinct Sundaland representative of the hog deer, a descendent of *A. oppenoorthi*. Both *A. kuhli* and *A. calamianensis* may have survived the inundation of the Sunda Shelf and the spread of forests at the end of one of the Quaternary glaciations. Both Bawean, near the mouth of the eastern drainage of former Sundaland, and the Palawan group of islands, are separated from the rest of the Sunda Shelf by relatively deep water, and would not have been part of Sundaland except briefly at times of extreme sea-level lowering. This could explain why they survived in these two places, while in the rest of Sundaland hyelaphine deer were replaced by rusas.

Indo-Chinese hog deer appear to be brighter in color than Indian populations, more streaked and less speckled because of the broader pale bands towards the tips of the body hairs. But we have seen few specimens. Bawean deer are in Surabaya and Singapore zoos, and C.P.G. briefly studied specimens in the museums of Bogor and Amsterdam. Calamian deer are in Howletts Zoo, England (Shave, 1980) and there are

Groves and Grubb

specimens in the Field Museum, Chicago (Sanborn, 1952, and examined by P.G.). As far as our data go, the differences between the Indian hog deer and the insular forms are consistent (Table 3). A few other differences appear between the Bawean and Calamian deer, noticeably the very wide spread of the antlers of the former, but the variation within the hog deer seems to encompass them both. Comparing the photographs published by Shave (1980) with photographs in the literature and taken by C.P.G. of the other two species, we have the impression that the Calamian deer is longer-legged and more slender than the others and is probably a valid species. *A. kuhli* differs much less from *A. porcinus* but the straighter antlers, the less contrasting dorsum/flank tones, the more contrasting hair bands, and the bushier tail do appear to be consistent distinctions. Provisionally we retain it as a species.

Table 3. Characters of three species of *Axis* (*Hyelaphus*); measurements in mm

	A. porcinus	A. kuhlii	A. calamianensis
GL (males)	225–241	213–234	204–239
Antler length	306–444	306–480	205–313
Burr to brow tine origin	48–66	57	35–43
Antler shape from side	well curved	straighter	well curved
Terminal tine in relation to tip of beam	shorter, acute angle	shorter, points back	longer, acute angle
Dark back contrasts with fawn flanks	yes	no	no
Dark shafts of hairs contrast with light tip	somewhat	much	less
Inner haunches	white	white	buffy
Muzzle	black	black	white
White inside ears and at roots	not much	not much	much—bases all white
Legs	as body	as body	much darker
Dark mat on forehead	yes	yes	no
Tail	not bushy	bushy	bushy

AXIS (AXIS)

The chital, *Axis axis* (reviewed by Pocock, 1943a), differs from the hog deer in its larger size and different proportions, in retaining the full spotting pattern in the adult, and in skull features (broadened paroccipital processes, long nasals, different shape of the ethmoid fissure, and smaller bullae). It also has a derived karyotype, and its antlers are modified from the primitive three-point pattern: They are very long, A2 is hypertrophied, long and straight; P2 is relatively larger than in the hog deer, deflected towards A2, subparallel to it and not directed backwards; the brow-tine/beam angle is obtuse, not acute; the antlers describe a lyrate rather than a V-shaped outline; and snags are often present near or on the brow tine. There are long hairs at the distal end of the preorbital gland which are normally folded inwards and enclosed in its slit-like opening. When the gland is everted, the hairs are rolled outwards, forming an oily tuft at the end of the gland pouch (Graf and Nichols, 1967), presumably facilitating scent dissemination. All these derivative characters suggest that the chital may not be as phylogenetically close to the hog deer as is often implied, but do not preclude the genus *Axis* from being holophyletic.

The chital is naturally restricted to the Indian Peninsula and Sri Lanka, but formerly occurred as far east as Java (von Koenigswald, 1933) where it was part of the Trinil and Djetis faunas, and there was a closely related species in Japan (Otsuka, 1967). Other fossil deer referred to the genus or subgenus *Axis* have not been conclusively shown to resemble *A. axis* rather than three-point antlered deer generally.

CERVUS

A clade composed of *Cervus* and *Elaphurus* includes the Cervini with derived characters—large size; coarse pelage unspotted in adults; a mane of long hairs at least in males; short tail; prominent rump patch; all incisiform teeth with broad crowns; small auditory bullae; hypsodonty, with basal pillars and prominent styles and columns on molars; large metaconid on PM$_4$. But not all species within *Cervus* have all of even these few derived character states. *C. alfredi* and *C. nippon* have spotted adult pelage, and narrower lateral incisiform teeth; *C. mariannus* has the latter feature and together with *C. alfredi* and some races of *C. unicolor*, a primitive three-point antler, albeit with some apparently derived features; *C. duvauceli*, *C. schomburgki*, *C. eldi*, and particularly *C. nippon* retain swollen auditory bullae. *C. elaphus* and *C. nippon* have more brachyodont teeth than the others. Most species do not have an enlarged rump patch or a greatly shortened tail. We recognize four species-groups, treated here as subgenera, based on phenetic distinctiveness, morphoclinal continuity, and shared derived characters. From the karyological evidence discussed earlier, subgenera *Rusa*, *Rucervus*, and perhaps *Przewalskium* form a sister group to the subgenus *Cervus*. *Elaphurus* does not clearly share unique derived characters with only one species-group of *Cervus*, so in turn is assumed to represent the sister group of that genus.

During the rut, male *Cervus* and *Elaphurus* spray urine onto the belly and forequarters (McCullough, 1969), possibly a synapomorphic behavioral pattern, for it is not recorded in *Axis* or *Dama*. In the latter genus, only the preputial brush becomes impregnated with urine and glandular secretions (Chapman and Chapman, 1975).

CERVUS (RUSA)

The rusas and sambar are characterized by having robust, rugose antlers with a long erect brow tine, very deep lacrimal pits, reduced auditory bullae, and dark eumelanic pelage. They vary considerably in size, but all species are allopatric and form a morphocline.

Cervus alfredi may be the most primitive rusa. It retains spots even in the adult pelage and the hair is noticeably soft. It replaces the next species on the Visayas Islands in the Philippine archipelago. *C. mariannus* (revised by Grubb and Groves, 1982) is another relatively small species, found on Mindanao, Basilan, Luzon, and Mindoro. As its name implies, it was first described from the Marianna Islands, where it was introduced in precolonial times. It has also been introduced to the Caroline Islands, and may be the species that is or was present on Bonin. Of the four subspecies, the montane *C. m. nigellus* (synonym *apoensis*) was formerly regarded as a separate species (Sanborn, 1952). *C. mariannus* resembles *C. alfredi* in its very small ears and closed-up ethmoid fissures, but it has coarser pelage without spots and a broader skull.

A third species, the sambar or rusa, *C. unicolor*, has a much wider distribution. It varies geographically in dimensions but is always outside the size range of the smaller *C. mariannus* and has very large, broad ears; broad incisiform teeth, and a different karyotype (Table 2). Pocock (1942a, 1943b) and van Bemmel (1949) have revised the systematics of the species. The smaller sized races include *brookei* (Borneo), *equinus* (Malay Peninsula, Sumatra, introduced on the Mentawei Islands), and *swinhoei* (Taiwan). Populations in Indo-China, southern China, and Burma are larger with relatively longer antlers and should be recognized as a separate subspecies, *cambojensis*. The sambar —the nominate subspecies of the Indian subcontinent and Sri Lanka—has a more derived antler form and is larger again. Pocock's (1943b) separation of *niger* (India) from *unicolor* (Sri Lanka) was based on scant evidence of a size difference, and is not followed here.

The Javanese rusa or Timor deer, *C. timorensis* (revised by van Bemmel, 1949), has broad ears like *C. unicolor* but its pelage is even coarser than in other rusines, and its antlers are of a more advanced three-point form, with P2 larger than A1, almost continuous with the beam, and parallel with its fellow (Figure 5).

The late appearance of *C. timorensis* in prehistoric deposits in both Sulawesi (Hooijer, 1950) and Timor (Glover, 1970) carries with it the strong implication, already predictable from zoogeographical considerations, that it had been introduced to these islands through human agency. It is likely that the Timor deer was originally confined to Java and Bali though it could well have reached the western Lesser Sundas (Nusatenggara) by swimming. Fossil antlers resembling those of *C. unicolor equinus* are known from Java (von Koenigswald, 1933); so the biogeography of rusine deer was probably complicated.

Van Bemmel (1949) distinguished several subspecies of *C. timorensis* from the Wallacean region. They are based on substantial samples, so there seems no reason to question the reality of the distinctions he makes, and they therefore provide interesting evidence for rapid evolution. The Javanese rusa was also introduced to Borneo, where it was said to exist sympatrically with *C. unicolor brookei* (van Bemmel, 1949), but the records are based on observations made in the last century and the present state of affairs has not been recorded. The two species could probably coexist as they have different ecological requirements and different social behavior. They have both been introduced into southeastern Australia, where their ecological segregation should be investigated. Bentley (1978) said that they had hybridized in the past in Victoria, but gave no evidence.

The Javanese rusa is the only living cervine with an advanced three–point antler (Figure 5). Fossil taxa also possessing this trait include *C. philisi* of the European late Pliocene to early Pleistocene (Heintz, 1970). *C. philisi* resembled the Javanese rusa in the general form of the antlers, including the primitive acute angle between the long brow tine and the beam, and its dentition was similar. Critical comparisons between the two species have yet to be made. Other deer with advanced three–point antlers are unlikely to be related: *C. punjabensis* (Padri, middle Siwaliks) had a smaller brow tine branching obtusely from the beam, a flattened fork, and no basal pillars on the molars (Brown, 1926). *Axis shansius* (lower Pleistocene, Shansi, China) was described as somewhat brachyodont, while in the antlers, P2 branches posteriorly to A2; the brow tine originates relatively high above the burr (Teilhard de Chardin and Trassaert, 1937). This spe-

Groves and Grubb

cies may represent a variant or growth stage of "*Dama*" *sericus* of the same deposits, and both resemble specimens of *Arvernoceros ardei* (Heintz, 1970).

CERVUS (RUCERVUS)

The rucervine deer (reviewed by Pocock, 1943c) are unique among the Cervini in that the trez tine (A2) normally branches (Figure 6). The antlers are unlikely to have been derived from the robust relatively straight *Rusa* type. More probably they evolved from a slender form intermediate in appearance between the antlers of chital and hog deer, with primitive characters of the fork, yet with advanced obtuse brow-tine/beam angle. Unlike most *Rusa* species, the rucervines all retain a spotted pattern in juveniles and in the adult dry season coat, slender antlers, and large auditory bullae. They differ also in derived characters—the branching of A2, the more flexed skull, the more hypsodont teeth with bigger molar columns and more prominent styles and pillars, and the smaller canines, if present at all. Flerov (1952) included *Rucervus* in *Rusa* but did not explicitly account for this taxonomic allocation. The karyological evidence of course suggests that *Rucervus* is at least a sister group of *Rusa*, but further data are required. Hypsodonty could be a feature shared with the common ancestor, but the dentition of the smaller rusas has not been closely examined, and the more specialized condition of *Rucervus* teeth results from an evolutionary trend (Azzaroli, 1954) which may have been independent from a similar one among rusas.

Cervus eldi, the thamin or brow-antlered deer, has antlers more like those of *Axis axis* than *C. unicolor*. They are slender, lyrate, with a very obtuse brow-tine/beam angle, and have a tendency to form supernumerary snags on the brow tine or brow-beam junction. But P2 is very short and unbranched; the pedicels are parallel; the antlers are rugose; the brow tine, beam, and A2 form a continuous curve; the supernumerary snags are larger, more frequent than in the chital, and often symmetrical; and A2 may branch into very short tines or be somewhat palmate. *C. eldi* also differs from the allied *C. duvauceli* in having a deep lacrimal pit, like *Rusa*, and a metatarsal tuft, but usually lacks the black muzzle band.

The nominate race is restricted to the Logtak Lake in Manipur, where it lives in the phumdi, masses of floating vegetation, on which it walks with its modified digits: The hoofs are elongated and spreading, with bare, cornified skin on the backs of the pasterns. In 1977, a wild population of 18 was counted, an increase of four over the 1975 census. Fortunately, there were 49 in captivity, in eight Indian zoos, where it is breeding well (Ranjitsinh, 1978). The other races,

with unspecialized digits, live in forested country further east in Burma, Thailand, Vietnam, Laos, and southern China including Hainan. They are *C. e. thamin* and *C. e. siamensis*, separated by rather minor antler differences (Pocock, 1943c).

The swamp deer or barasingha (*C. duvauceli*) is a floodplain species with digits usually modified as in *C. e. eldi*, though south of the Ganges it is adapted to an environment of dry meadow and woodland. Subspecies are *branderi*, the hard-ground form, formerly widespread in Madhya Pradesh, now restricted to Kanha National Park; *duvauceli* of western Nepal and neighboring parts of Uttar Pradesh, India; and a newly recognized form (Groves, 1982), *ranjitsinhi*, from Assam, and formerly also northern Bengal.

C. duvauceli differs from *C. eldi* in a number of respects: Its antlers are smooth; supernumerary snags are rare; the brow-tine/beam angle, though obtuse, is never so extreme; the beam is much straighter; A2, though continuing the line of the beam, is subequal to P2 and both are usually branched. The swamp deer retains the black muzzle band, but has a shallow lacrimal pit, apparently no metatarsal tuft, and canines are often absent. At first sight it may not seem especially close phenetically to *C. eldi*, but antlers with thamin-like curvature are known (Pocock, 1933); the branching pattern of the antlers, and the hypsodont, strongly ridged cheek teeth, are characteristic of both; and the two species have similar ecological propensities.

Schomburgk's deer (*C. schomburgki*), formerly of the Chao Phraya floodplain of southern Thailand, has been extinct since 1939. It was similar to *C. duvauceli*, but the antler beam is greatly shortened and the tines correspondingly elongated. The beam divides equally to form branches A2 and P2, which in turn branch again, leading to the species-characteristic candelabra of tines. The brow tine is branched in nearly a tenth of cases (Boonsong and McNeely, 1977), and the skull is broader than in the swamp deer.

CERVUS (PRZEWALSKIUM)

The only species, the white-lipped or Thorold's deer, *C. albirostris*, is said to be of rusine origin (Flerov, 1952). From the karyotype (Table 2), the white-lipped deer could be the sister group of both *Rusa* and *Rucervus*. The chromosome complement is identical to that of *Axis axis*, but the homologies of Robertsonian fusions are not known. Its morphology is very distinctive. The skull, particularly the facial part, is exceptionally broad; the nasal bones have broad, blunt lateral projections at their proximal ends; and the teeth are not very hypsodont. The pelage is very long and dense, yet without underwool; the hairs are thick and pithy; and there is no mane, but the hair on the withers is reversed. Antlers are five-point and are slender, smooth, and flattened. The brow tine is short and branches obtusely from the beam. The lanceolate ears are unlike those of any *Rusa* or *Rucervus*. Flerov (1952) saw resemblances between *C. timorensis* and *C. albirostris* in the white throat and the form of the antlers, but the similarities are superficial: The white markings are better defined in *albirostris* and extend round the muzzle. That *timorensis* is advanced for a six-pointer is no indication that it is particularly related to a 10-pointer. The antlers of the Timor deer are quite different in other respects—rugose, thicker, more cylindrical, with erect brow tine—and the extinct *C. punjabensis* with its rather flattened fork and downbent brow tine is a more probable relative. A Chinese Pleistocene deer, "*Epirusa*" *hilzheimeri,* was thought to be related to *C. albirostris,* but Flerov (1952) did not state which features of the skull resemble the latter, and the original illustration (Zdansky, 1925) indicates none.

The white-lipped deer, with its stout limbs and short, robust hoofs, is adapted to high-altitude as in the eastern part of the Tibetan plateau and Sichuan highlands, where it is stratified above *C. unicolor cambojensis* (Engelmann, 1939).

CERVUS SENSU STRICTO

Like members of the subgenus *Rusa,* deer of this group span a great range of form and size, from the primitive spotted sika to the advanced wapiti, one of the largest deer. Dentally, they are surprisingly primitive, brachyodont, with very small basal pillars, poorly marked styles, and no columns. But the antlers are of an advanced form, normally with at least four tines. As in the case of *Rusa,* this group of deer is considered to be a clade not so much because of unique shared derived characters, but because of the morphoclinal continuity between phenetic extremes. Only two species are extant.

CERVUS NIPPON

The sika is the more primitive member of the group. It has an acute brow-tine/beam angle; long pedicels; tine P3 smaller than A3 and usually turned in away from the beam; large inflated bullae; narrow lateral incisiform teeth; spotted pattern retained in the adult; and a long tail. As indicated in previous discussions of the cervid morphology, these are primitive character states for the Cervini, which are modified in the more specialized *C. elaphus.*

A very large number of names have been given to sika deer, mainly by Père Pierre-Marie Heude, yet the geographic variation of the species is very poorly understood, and we have seen very few specimens.

Groves and Smeenk (1978) have revised the subspecies of the main Japanese Islands. Here we will list tentatively valid subspecies in an attempt to indicate geographical trends in variation:

A) Southern, brightly colored races

1) *C. n. taiouanus* of Taiwan is probably extinct in the wild. It resembles Chinese rather than Japanese populations in its pelage, having only a small white rump patch and lacking a frontal chevron (Heude, 1884). The color is a rather bright orange-brown, spotted with white at all seasons; the tail is long and black above; and the underside is light fawn, with no white on it, though there are large white marks on chest and lower throat.

2) *C. n. pseudaxis* is the earliest name for specimens from Vietnam (Delacour, 1931; Glover, 1956) and *kopschi* of southeastern China, south of the lower Yangtze, is probably synonymous. These deer tend to be small in size (HBL 1320 mm, CBL 300 mm), brightly colored, chestnut to fawn in summer, gray-fawn or brown-fawn to nearly black in winter, with large, well-spaced spots in summer which nearly disappear in winter and never extend to the shoulder and neck. The dorsal stripe is dark, often black, and the ear is very white inside.

Cervus cyclorhinus and *C. hyemalis* were names given by Heude to two sika from Shantung Province, having pale facial chevrons like Japanese races. They would seem to have been like the more southerly type in color, or more fawn in winter, and spotted in both seasons. They might have represented a distinguishable race, though Sowerby (1917) stated that wild deer had been exterminated long ago in Shantung, and that Heude's specimens were of captive stock of uncertain origin.

A sika deer described from the Imperial Hunting Park outside Peking as *Cervus hortulorum* or *C. mandarinus* was not at all like specimens recorded from the wild in northern China. It was a small deer (HBL 1480 mm, CBL 304 mm), light red in summer, grey in winter, well-spotted in both seasons, and with a distinct dorsal stripe. Such descriptions tally better with a southern race. Glover (1956) stated that the Park deer were likely to have come from a hybrid stock of many different Chinese populations. It is no less likely that they represented a carefully preserved pure-bred stock of unknown origin, or were the result of selective breeding. *Hortulorum* has been widely used as a name for the Ussuri sika (for example, Lydekker 1915) but it should perhaps be sunk into the synonymy of *pseudaxis.*

3) *C. n. soloensis* is recorded from Jolo in the Sulu Archipelago, south of the Philippines. How sika deer got there is not known. Heude (1894) described the

Groves and Grubb

form as being brilliant fawn in summer, paler in winter; black on the tail; a red-brown dorsal stripe; a white rump patch with black borders; spotted at all seasons. The antlers were described as complex, multi-tined, "elaphine" in tine number, but "sikine" in shape, with P3 internal in position instead of posterior and perpendicular.

B) Larger Northern Races

4) *C. n. sichuanicus* has recently been described by Guo et al. (1978) from Sichuan. It is a large form (HBL 1700 mm), less spotted than *pseudaxis*, with a white chin and with white at the ear-base as well as inside. These white head-marks are the distinguishing characters of *C. n. swinhoei* Glover 1956 (preoccupied by *C. unicolor swinhoei* Sclater, 1862) based on the description of a "big stag" seen by Swinhoe at Amoy in 1864.

5) *C. n. mantchuricus*: The north Chinese sika are described as medium sized to large deer. Sowerby (1918) gave some dimensions of a Shansi stag (HBL 1525 mm, CBL 322 mm), apparently a much smaller animal than Ussuri stags (HBL 1680-1800 mm, according to Heptner et al. 1961). *Mantchuricus* would be the earliest name for the deer of Ussuriland, Manchuria, and Korea. If the more southerly deer of Shansi are consistently smaller, the name *grassianus* Heude, 1884, would apply to them. The color of these northern sika is red-fawn to foxy-red in summer, dark grey-brown to brown-maroon in winter, spotted in summer with small white spots extending onto the neck and often fusing into rows on the flanks, but only vaguely spotted or not spotted at all in winter. A dorsal stripe is only vaguely marked, the throat is pale yellow grey, and the tail is black (Shansi) or red with black hairs (Ussuri).

6) *C. n. yesoensis* is the grey Hokkaido race (with CBL up to 305 mm). The Hokkaido mammal fauna lacks Japanese endemic species and is more affiliated to that of mainland Asia. Imaizumi (1970) indicates this is true for sika deer as well.

C) Japanese Races

These are among the smallest, with large disc-shaped rump patches intruding onto the sides and base of the tail, and very dark winter pelage.

7) *C. n. nippon* is the relatively small form of southern Honshu, Kyushu, Shikoku, the Goto Islands, Yakushima, and Mageshima.

8) *C. n. aplodontus* is the larger northern Honshu race.

9) *C. n. keramae* from the Kerama group, Ryukyu Islands, is now very rare. It is very small, dark in color, unspotted, with apparently a very long trez tine. Kuroda (1924) mentions a supposition that deer are not indigenous to these islands, but were introduced from Satsuma in medieval times, in which case we have another example of rapid evolution in deer.

10) *C. n. pulchellus* from Tsushima is medium-sized with a long basal segment to the antlers, and a dull ochraceous or tawny-olive coloration with whitish throat and abdomen. Imaizumi (1970) described this as a full species, and divided the other races of *C. nippon* between three species, but this is not justifiable (Groves and Smeenk, 1978).

Sika and wapiti (*Cervus elaphus xanthopygus*) hybridize in the Soviet Far East (Flerov, 1952; Heptner et al., 1961), but the ecological context of hybridization is not fully known. Hybridization between red deer and introduced Japanese sika occurs in northern England and the Wicklow Mountains, Ireland (Lowe and Gardiner, 1975), and in Czechoslovakia (Bartos and Zirovnicky, 1981), but not in Killarney, Ireland, where they have shared the same range since the 19th century (Harrington, 1973). A sika stag is unlikely to be allowed to serve red deer hinds by the larger red stags. But studies of captive animals by R. Harrington (pers. comm.) suggest that sika hinds may actually prefer to mate with red stags or hybrids. If the stag is too large, he may injure the hind during copulation, even causing her eventual death. Hybridization, then, is unlikely to be free, but it is not clear why it has occurred in one context but not in another. Lowe and Gardiner (1975) suggest that red deer hybridize more readily with mainland sika than with Japanese stock, but the evidence is hardly adequate. Possibly, under field conditions there are ethological and ecological barriers to interbreeding that have not yet been identified.

Serological studies of many captive populations of "mainland" sika showed that they carry genes of unidentified elaphine deer (R. Harrington, pers. comm.). There is therefore the possibility that in eastern Asia, hybridization is leading to genetic infiltration of sika by *Cervus elaphus*, even if hybridization is less frequent than in Britain. But it should be emphasized that the genealogy and purity of these captive stocks is not known: They could have acquired red deer or wapiti genes in captivity rather than in the wild. Wild-caught mainland sika have not yet been examined serologically, and there is little phenetic indication that wild Chinese sika generally carry wapiti genes, for they do not show intermediate characters of the pelage or antlers.

Bartos and Zirovnicky (1981) speculate that the true karyotype of Japanese sika is 2N = 66, compared with 68 for *C. elaphus*, and that chromosomal polymorphism in the former is an indication of genetic introgression by the latter. This could only give a range of diploid numbers of 66, 67, or 68: Records of 64 and 65, based on the Woburn "Manchurian" herd (Gustavson and Sundt, 1969), might be due to hybridization with other species. However, observations of Japanese sika karyotypes (Table 2) cast doubt on this hypothesis by suggesting that sika are naturally polymorphic for two Robertsonian fusions of autosomes.

Lowe and Gardiner (1975), Bartos and Zirovnicky (1981), and Harrington (pers. comm.) develop a further proposition, however. Because intergrades between red deer and Japanese sika often closely resemble mainland sika, they conclude that the latter may have originated from the interbreeding of imported Japanese sika and native wapiti by Chinese deer farmers. Presumably, some of these stocks became feral and dispersed into areas where deer were not kept in captivity, differentiating rapidly into several geographic variants.

Red-deer/sika hybrids, wapiti/sika hybrids, and mainland sika have still to be critically compared, and if sika and elaphine deer are related as proposed below, we should in any case expect hybridization to produce a phenotype closely similar to a phylogenetic intermediate. Apart from these considerations, the hypothesis that mainland sika are not native and are of hybrid origin is vitiated by the extensive fossil record of the sika in China from the Middle Pliocene to Recent (Young, 1932; Teilhard de Chardin and Young, 1936). It is sometimes the commonest animal in deposits and was a contemporary of Pekin man at Choukoutien (Zhoukoudien).

Nevertheless, we cannot totally discard the very interesting proposition that a large and socially dominant species may genetically invade and swamp a smaller allied species. Batchelor and McLennan (1977) record just this phenomenon, which they term one-way hybridization, where red deer and socially dominant wapiti interbreed in Fjordland, New Zealand. There is clearly a call for very careful examination of the history and morphology of all captive sika stocks, and for serological examination of wild populations, not to mention the preservation of voucher specimens or at least good photographic records. The conservation of the mainland sika genome is clearly a matter for concern.

A sika-like deer was probably the ancestor of *Cervus elaphus*: In the Villafranchian of Europe a number of mammals of eastern Asiatic affinity occurred, among them a large deer *C. perrieri* that combines the characters of the two extant species. The antlers were large, with a flexed beam, but P3 lies posteriorly to A3 in a sikine position, and there is no bez tine (Heintz, 1970).

CERVUS ELAPHUS

The elaphine deer are larger or very much larger than sika, usually unspotted as adults, and with a super-

numerary tine (the bez) above the brow tine. They show strong geographical variation over their extensive distribution. The elaphine deer of Asia and European Russia were revised by Bobrinskoy and Flerov (1934), who recognized three principal species, *C. elaphus* (Europe), *C. affinis* (Central Asia), and *C. canadensis* (Siberia, China, and North America). Two further species were considered valid—*C. yarkandensis* (presumably because its antlers combined *elaphus* and *affinis* characters), and *C. wallichi* (which combined *affinis* and *canadensis* characters). However, several of the subspecies placed by Bobrinskoy and Flerov in their major species are also intermediate in morphology so it is preferable to consider all elaphine deer as a single species. The Russian authors' main divisions can be taken to be semispecies or subspecies groups, with both *yarkandensis* and *wallichi* subsumed into the *affinis* group, which for reasons of nomenclatural priority must take the name *wallichi*.

THE NOMINATE ELAPHUS GROUP (RED DEER)

These are reddish deer with dark antlers, which in mature stags often terminate in a crown or cup of three or more tines. The occipital condyles of stags are relatively small. The rump patch is narrow, bisected by the broad dark tail, with the reddish suffused upper part darker than the lower (not uniform as in wapiti or Bukhara deer). There is a tendency for some populations to retain spots in the adult summer pelage. In many individuals and some populations, there is no bez tine or third tine to the fork. Geist (1971) takes the view that this is the ancestral condition within the group, and coupled with the spottedness of adults, an indication that the red deer is the most primitive representative of the elaphine deer. But in our opinion, these antler features are secondary for red deer, occurring in populations that have responded phenotypically, perhaps even genotypically to poor foraging conditions. Late Pleistocene red deer had complicated antlers, with bez and crown well developed (Reynolds, 1933; Lister, this volume).

Geographical variation in European red deer is unlikely to have represented a primary cline, as populations are likely to have dispersed over the continent from more than one direction since the last glaciation. The true pattern of geographic variation may now be obscured by local extinction, restocking and other management activities, but nevertheless requires a more objective and comprehensive systematic revision than it has yet received.

Lowe and Gardiner (1974) examined the skulls of hinds from European populations and showed extensive overlap in dimensions. Flerov (1952) treated all European populations except for some Mediterranean

Groves and Grubb

ones, as a single subspecies. Other authors have regarded eastern European red deer as related to, even consubspecific with, red deer of the near east (Lydekker, 1898, 1915; Geist, 1971; Dobroruka, 1960). Geist contends that there are two main groups of continental red deer—western and eastern.

Relative to the eastern group, the western deer are smaller and said to have less "supernumerary" tines: The bez tine is less common, shorter than the brow, and more primitive in position (though we query this last statement). Geist (1971) proposed that these western deer had dispersed from a west European glacial refuge. In a study of Norwegian deer, Ingebrigtsen (1923) found deer from inland areas to be larger (average GL for stags 391 mm), while on Hitra island and some of the coastal areas, the means were much lower (Hitra, 364 mm; Aalfot, 372 mm). While strict application of the "75%" rule would demand that the small insular populations be separated as a subspecies, there are intermediate populations and the subspecies would seem in any case to be polytopic. Decline in the condition of the animals may also be involved. In a more extensive study, Ahlen (1965) concluded that the smaller and geographically isolated Norwegian red deer was subspecifically separable from the Swedish and Danish populations, but he examined only Scandinavian deer and other populations have yet to be studied using his methods.

Following these results and the work of Lowe and Gardiner (1974), we suggest that only one subspecies of red deer be recognized for western Europe, *C. e. elaphus* (syn. *scoticus, hippelaphus, atlanticus, bolivari*).

Flerov (1952) indicated that red deer in the Carpathians and Caucasus are larger than those in western Europe, and red-grey in color with indistinct light spots, though he retained them within his broad concept of *C. e. elaphus*. Dobroruka (1960) considered the characters of these large eastern deer sufficiently constant to warrant their recognition as a distinct subspecies, *C. e. montanus* (syn. *brauneri*), characterized additionally by the lack of a mane and the absence of a dark mark on the rump patch. Their range would begin in the eastern Carpathians. The skull measurements recorded by Matschie (in Ingebrigtsen, 1923) also seem to separate an eastern from a western form: Stags from the Baltic coast were larger (GL 455–490 mm), those from other parts of Germany smaller (GL 380–415). Geist (1971) referred the larger red deer to his eastern group. They were regarded as more diverse than the western populations, with an admixture of shou if not wapiti characters. They have supernumerary tines and occasionally an enlarged fourth tine (A3) like a wapiti. The rump patch was said to be more like that of the Bokhara than the Barbary deer, and may be fringed with dark hair on its lower part,

and the mane (*contra* Dobroruka) is generally better developed. They may have originated from a Pleistocene refuge in Russia.

We suggest the larger eastern European deer extending not only from the Carpathians but also the Baltic coast, and as far as the Crimea, should be termed *C. e. montanus*. Published data are ambiguous as to where *montanus* should be regarded as giving way to the equally large form from still further east, *C. e. maral*. Dobroruka (1960) and Lydekker (1898, 1915) among others considered that the latter ranges northwest to the Carpathians, while Flerov (1952) restricted its distribution to Turkey, the Caucasus, and Kurdistan. *C. e. maral* is brown-red in winter, lighter in summer, with a small rump patch like that of the nominate race, but poorly outlined in darker tones; and a narrower skull, with muzzle breadth about 50% of muzzle length. A two-tine fork appears to be relatively frequent even in the antlers of mature stags, perhaps evidence of a transition towards the next race to the east, *C. e. bactrianus*. Barclay (1934) referred to supposed wapiti-like characters in the Caucasus population, some of which, however, are also shared by the shou group. In some heads, the fourth tine (A3) is very large, with the next tine of the crown placed posteriorly rather than mesially to it. This feature is indeed suggestive of wapiti rather than shou or other red deer, and genetic introgression from wapiti dispersing from the east could have occurred (Geist, 1971). Fossil elaphine deer are known from what is presently a gap between the natural distributions of red deer and wapiti (Heptner et al., 1961) but their affinities do not appear to have been ascertained: They might have been hybrids.

The deer of Sardinia, Corsica, North Africa, and southern Spain in the Guadalquivir basin have been lumped together by Flerov (1952) as a subspecies *C. e. corsicanus*, which has relatively small, simple antlers with three to four tines; often no bez tine or crown; dark brown, sometimes blackish color; and spotting in the adult. Specimens of this nominal polytopic subspecies are very scarce and it is rare and endangered throughout its range, already extinct on Corsica (Krumbiegel, 1982). We are unable to say whether Flerov was right to recognize it as a single subspecies. The African population, the Barbary stag, has been regarded as the most primitive of the red deer, a "western sika" (Geist, 1971). The antlers are thin with relatively short tines, the bez tine is usually absent, and the brow tine can be very short (Kock and Schomber, 1961; Meyer, 1972), paralleling the condition in the Persian fallow deer. Nevertheless, a three-tine crown can occur. This is in contrast to sika deer, which have robust tines and very exceptionally form a crown. As the Barbary stag is more like other red deer in coloration, it appears to us more probable that it has originated from populations in which there has been selection for size reduction in relation to changes in forage quality.

THE WALLICHI OR ACORONATE GROUP (SHOU AND RELATIVES)

Deer of this group are poorly known either as wild animals or museum specimens, and the surviving populations are very localized. They are neither "red deer" nor "wapiti" and tend to be forgotten by those who still consider the elaphine deer to be represented by two species. So it is not always appreciated that they are the nuclear part of *Cervus elaphus*, the primitive form from which both red deer and wapiti have evolved, connecting them morphoclinally through the extinct *C. perrieri* to *C. nippon*. Under the form *acoronatus*, they are the first representatives of *C. elaphus* to appear in the fossil record (early middle Pleistocene–Kurtén, 1968), and they still retain primitive characters of simple antlers, speckled agouti pelage, and in most races a small rump patch. The antlers are particularly characteristic. The beam terminates in two tines which are directed inwards, P3 lying mesially to A3, and are of similar dimensions. Usually no crown or cup is formed.

Two subspecies stand apart from the rest, and might be regarded equally as primitive red deer. *C. e. bacrinus*, the Bukharan stag, of the Syr Darya and Amu Darya valleys ranging up into northern Afghanistan, is dull light grey in winter, fawn brown in summer. The legs and neck are darker than the body, at least in the winter coat of stags (Mohr, 1955); the rump patch resembles that of red deer, but the tail is wholly dark. There is rarely a third tine at the end of the beam, forming a crown. Bukharan deer are relatively small, like *C. e. elaphus*. Separated from the last by the Tienshan mountains is the Yarkand stag (*C. e. yarkandensis*) which ranges along the whole of the Tarim basin in Sinkiang. It is usually regarded as a very distinct subspecies, and Bobrinskoy and Flerov (1934) originally treated it as a distinct species, but it is similar to *bactrianus* in color and in the relatively straight antler beam. The principle differences are, firstly, that the rump patch is larger, reddish white with no dark stripe bisecting it and no black edging, and secondly, there is usually a crown of three to five tines, though not formed in quite the same way as in true red deer (*C. e. elaphus*). The Yarkand stag has rarely been seen since the early part of this century, though there were specimens in the Prague zoo in the 1960s.

The deer of the southern and eastern flanks of the Tibetan Plateau form a distinct group, with a variable rump patch, dull earthy color, and large antlers which bend or angle markedly inwards. Flerov (1952) puts them all, with the exception of *wallichi*, into a single race, but it is apparent from his earlier paper (Bobrinskoy and Flerov, 1934) that he had seen no material from the Himalayas. Pocock (1942b) carefully compared the Himalayan populations and recognized three taxa as valid. *C. e. hanglu* is a little smaller than the other two (SH of stags 122–132 cm), with a small rump patch edged with dark brown. It is the hangul of the Vale of Kashmir. *C. e. wallichi*, the next race to the east, is known with certainty from only two specimens from the upper Tsangpo valley. It is larger (SH about 130 cm), with a very large white rump patch. The difference between the rump patches of *hanglu* and *wallichi* are so great that Bobrinskoy and Flerov (1934) were led to regard the latter as a full species. But our studies suggest it is even more closely related to the next subspecies than Pocock (1942b) admitted. Caughley (1970) has outlined its probable former range in the valleys north of Nepal. It may now be extinct. The third Himalayan race, the shou (*C. e. affinis*) is very large (SH 132–152 cm), but with a rump patch more like that of the hangul. Ludlow (1959) has reviewed its distribution in Bhutan and neighboring parts of Tibet. It still survives (Anon., 1982).

The remaining two members of the group are found on the eastern flank of the Tibetan highlands, *C. e. macneilli* in Sichuan and south to Yunnan, and *C. e. kansuensis* in Gansu. The former, made better known from the descriptions of Engelmann (1939), is brownish to silvery grey, paler on the flanks, and speckled agouti. The legs are paler than the body and the rump patch is very small, white, with a bisecting line which varies from very broad to rather thin and vague, and has a black-brown upper edging. The throat mane is weak or absent. Engelmann's photographs show antlers of a range of morphological types, from shou-like to wapiti-like. The subspecies is about the same size as the hanglu (SH 120–140 cm). *C. e. kansuensis* is said to have the legs darker than the body, and a larger rump patch with a narrower dividing band. It may lie within the range of variation of *macneilli*. Specimens from Shansi suggest that there is intergradation with the wapiti *C. e. xanthopygus*.

Geist (1971) adopted a different position to our own on the *wallichi* group. He distinguished two subgroups, a "northern" one (*bactrianus, wallichi, yarkandensis*) with large wapiti-like rump patch and short tail of the same light color; and a southern group (*affinis* including *hanglu* and *macneilli*) with a small sika-like rump patch circled by a black band, and a broad, long and dark tail. It is possible that the possession of a large rump patch results from former hybridization with wapiti, but *wallichi* is phenetically and geographically much closer to *affinis* than to *bactrianus* or *yarkandensis*, and as

Groves and Grubb

discussed above, we consider *hanglu* and *macneilli* to be valid subspecies.

Geist (1971) postulated that deer of the *wallichi* group resulted from an eastward dispersion of early elaphine deer intergrading with sika-like forms in the Sinohimalayan region, and so generating the present diversity of the group. It appears that this hypothesis is required because the *wallichi* group cannot be regarded as ancestral to the *elaphus* group, as the latter lack the massive occipital condyles, large rump patch, and short stubby condition of the tail.

But the last two features are not true of all the shou group, and condyle size is allometrically related to body size. We consider that the balance of evidence favors the views expressed earlier in this section.

THE CANADENSIS GROUP (WAPITI OR ELK)

The wapiti are the largest members of the species, with characteristic antlers: The "fifth" tine (P3) is placed posteriorly and not mesially in relation to the "fourth" (A3) and usually is itself branched in a parasagittal plane. The fourth tine is very long and erect, and the distal part of the antler, which is rather pale colored as a whole, is somewhat flattened. The rump patch is always very large.

The first race, *C. e. alashanicus*, is known from only two specimens collected by Przewalsky on the Alashan Ridge, and is of uncertain status. Haltenorth (1963) regarded it as a synonym of *kansuensis*. It is grey-brown, paler on the flanks, unspeckled, with legs and body the same color. The rump patch is very large, brownish white, divided by a broad but indistinct line, and has no dark edging. Shoulder height of a stag is 130 cm. The only known antlers are not typical for wapiti—they have four tines with a simple terminal fork (Bobrinskoy and Flerov, 1934).

The next subspecies, *C. e. xanthopygus*, is dark grey-brown, again unspeckled, with legs paler than body. The rump patch is very large, reddish, narrowly divided by a dark line. In summer, it merges with the color of the back. *Xanthopygus* is a primitive wapiti (Geist, 1971): The body color is uniform, the antlers are relatively small with slender tines, the fourth tine is not large, dimensions are smaller than in typical wapiti (SH 145–150 cm, and CBL 390–435, in stags), and during the rut this race does not bugle. It is found in the Soviet Far East and Manchuria.

All other wapiti, except provisionally for *merriami* and *nannodes* of the United States, were united by Flerov (1952) in *C. e. canadensis*, making it a polytopic Asian-American subspecies. They all share several features—large size (SH up to 163 cm, CBL to 456 mm); less red color but rump patch with orange tones; dark underparts, legs, neck, and head; and large

mane. Asian and American wapiti have rarely been critically compared, and most authors have recognized the populations as taxonomically distinct. Flerov (1952) admitted that Asian wapiti are somewhat darker, with more elongated skull (muzzle breadth 53–57% of muzzle length, versus 55–63% in American deer). Heptner et al. (1961) even divided the Asian wapiti into two races, admitting, however, that they are dubiously distinct from each other: *C. e. sibiricus* from the Altai, Sayan, and Baikal regions is light grey-brown or yellow-brown in winter, brownish-cinnamon in summer, while *C. e. songaricus* from the Tienshan mountains and Dzungarian Alatau is said to be darker with some minor skull differences. But in a paper that was much less radical than Flerov's (1952) later contribution, Bobrinskoy and Flerov (1934) nevertheless regarded *songaricus* merely as a synonym of *sibiricus*, after examining listed museum specimens. In the most recent comment on this subject, Geist (1971) has returned to Flerov's (1952) opinion of the consubspecificity of *sibiricus* and *canadensis*, after seeing live animals of both forms.

A number of races of wapiti have been described for North America. They have never been reviewed as a whole, though McCullough (1969) came closest to this, comparing the described forms *nannodes* (southern California coast), *roosevelti* (north California to Washington State), and *nelsoni* (Rocky Mountains). The first of these would seem to be distinct: It is smaller than the others (CBL of stags averaging 416 and 423 in two populations); lighter in color; with more inflated bullae; and small antlers with arched beam and tines, tending towards palmation in large specimens. The other two are considerably darker and larger (CBL averages 452 mm in *roosevelti* and 470 mm in *nelsoni*, but the standard deviations overlap widely). The antlers are large in both, but tend to be longer and wider apart in *nelsoni*, shorter and heavier and more upwardly directed in *roosevelti*. Judging from descriptions it seems doubtful whether these two would be consistently recognizable, and their relationship to *C. e. canadensis* needs to be investigated. This nominal subspecies, formerly of central and eastern North America, is described as being lighter colored with long, lightly built antlers.*

The final race described from America is the poorly known *C. e. merriami*, from Arizona and New Mexico, which is now extinct. Anderson and Barlow (1978) found it very doubtfully distinct on the limited evi-

*Since completion of this manuscript Schonewald-Cox et al. (1985) reported significant differences between populations of *roosevelti* and between *roosevelti* and *nannodes* on the basis of Principal Component Analysis (Ed.).

dence available. It is marginally larger than other races, but even on the most distinct measurement (breadth across the premaxillae) the standard deviations overlap widely. The antlers are very big, sometimes with only a single brow tine. The color is said to have been paler than in *roosevelti*, with more reddish head and legs, and darker nose.

We accept *nannodes* as valid but think that the other North American races should all be lumped as *C. e. canadensis*.

ELAPHURUS

The milu or Père David's deer (*E. davidianus*) has many distinctive morphological features (Flerov, 1952), making it phenetically very unlike the other Cervini. Some of its characteristics reflect adaptation to a diet of reeds and grasses in a flood plain habitat, but others are of obscure functional significance.

The main beam of the antler is equivalent to branch A1 (Pocock, 1912, 1923, 1933) arising in primitive position at an acute angle to the pedicel, indeed in line with it. *E. (Elaphuroides) bifurcatus* from Nihowan and the very similar *E. (E.) shikamai* represent an extinct and more primitive group in which A1 is relatively much shorter but erect and branched, P1 is very long, branches from A1 at about 90°, and forms the beam, and the antler forks relatively lower down (Otsuka, 1972; Otsuka and Hasewaga, 1976). These authors and Teilhard de Chardin and Piveteau (1930) suggested that there might be a relationship between the fossil milu and the Villafranchian *Arvernocerus ardei* which, however, is also considered to be an early megacreine (Heintz, 1970).

Tsao (1975) recorded Holocene subfossils of the milu near Shanghai; previous records were always north of the Yangtze. *E. menzesianus* of the Middle Pleistocene of Anyang was identified with the modern species. Cao (1978) brought the list of subfossil localities to 64: A few records are from just south of the Yangtze; he concluded that Père David's deer became extinct as a wild animal at the end of, or after, the Han Dynasty (220 AD)—no other large mammal has such a long history of conservation.

Swinhoe brought two skins of fawns from Hainan in the 1860s, accessioned in the British Museum collections in 1870 as *Cervus eldi*, but recently identified as *Elaphurus* (Dobroruka, 1970). Thomas (1904) noted a sketch of Père David's deer made on Hainan and thought to be based on captive animals. It looks as if *Elaphurus* may have survived on Hainan only a little over a century ago, but whether it was the last remnant of the wild population, or feral, or imported is not yet apparent.

Table 4.   Species of deer and the countries to which they have been introduced where they are said to still maintain feral populations (Banerji, 1956; Bentley, 1978; Chapman and Chapman, 1980; Corbet, 1978; Haltenorth, 1963; Presnel, 1958; Olrog and Lucero, 1980; Roberts, 1968); occurrences listed in Table 1 not included

Hydropotes inermis: Britain, France.

Muntiacus reevesi: Britain, France.

M. muntjak: Texas.

Odocoileus virginianus: Finland, New Zealand.

O. hemionus: Hawaiian Islands (black-tailed deer), Argentina (mule deer).

Rangifer tarandus (domestic): South Georgia, Greenland, Alaska, Canada.

Dama dama: South Africa, Australia, Wakaya (Fiji Islands), U.S.A., Argentina, Chile, Peru, Uruguay, Leeward Islands, most European nations.

Axis (Hyelaphus) porcinus: Australia, Maryland (U.S.A.).

A. (Axis) axis: Hawaiian Islands, New Guinea, Australia, Brazil, Argentina, Yugoslavia, U.S.A., Andaman Islands.

Cervus (Rusa) mariannus: Caroline Islands.

C. (R.) unicolor: Australia, New Zealand, U.S.A.

C. (R.) timorensis moluccensis: Aru Islands, New Guinea.

C. (R.) t. timorensis: Borneo (?), Amboina, Sulawesi, Mauritius, Anjouan (Comoro Islands), Madagascar.

C. (R.) t. ssp.: Friday and Prince of Wales Islands (Queensland, Australia), Australian mainland, New Caledonia and from there to New Zealand.

C. (Rucervus) duvauceli: Texas.

C. (Cervus) nippon nippon: Britain, Ireland, U.S.A., Madagascar, Denmark, France, Germany, Czechoslovakia.

C. (C.) n. mantchuricus: Azerbaijan (U.S.S.R.).

C. (C.) n. taiouanus: Oshima Island (Japan).

C. (C.) elaphus elaphus: Bioko (?), Morocco, U.S.A., Argentina, Chile, Australia, New Zealand.

C. (C.) e. canadensis: New Zealand, Ural Moutains ("*sibiricus*")

SUBSPECIES AND INTRODUCED POPULATIONS OF DEER

The scientific discovery of deer populations involved the description of new species and subspecies, and the continued recognition of subspecies has become a rough-and-ready way of noting infraspecific geographic variation. Some nominal subspecies will prove invalid, as they are actually based on non-geographic variation in populations, or lie within the range of variation

Groves and Grubb

of subspecies which had been described earlier. Some may be indicators of morphologically distinctive populations, which nevertheless will eventually prove to be parts of clines. Others are even more provisional, in that there is insufficient museum material for one to arrive at definite conclusions concerning their status. Finally, some subspecies constitute populations naturally isolated geographically, morphologically discrete, and in some cases, verging on species status. But until geographic variation in deer is more comprehensively described, and our knowledge continually updated, numerous subspecific names will remain in currency, especially in *Odocoileus* and *Mazama*. New systematic reviews are time consuming and costly, but unless they are completed, we will have little idea of what biological diversity there is to conserve, and where conservation priorities should lie.

Identifiable regional variation in deer may be below the level where it would be recognized taxonomically (Lowe and Gardiner, 1974; Rees, 1969, 1970). Rees' study suggests that this variation can arise relatively quickly on a geological time-scale, and subspecies based on populations translocated within prehistorical or early historical time (Table 1) suggest the same phenomenon. It is often forgotten that there is also a very large stock of "evolutionary experiments" awaiting examination, in the form of deer populations introduced into new environments within recent historical times (Table 4). The nominal taxonomic position of these populations, their morphological characteristics, and the extent to which they may have evolved since their introduction occurred, all deserve examinations.

Final Comments

In the context of this symposium, systematists should determine how best their interests may contribute to the conservation of deer. What, exactly, are we trying to conserve? What fraction of a species' genotype can we realistically hope to maintain for the future, and how may our efforts unwittingly exert new selective pressures upon it? How should translocations and reintroductions be managed with these problems in mind? Is it realistic to aim for the conservation of each subspecies, when many are notional concepts? Alternatively, should interpretations of geographical variation other than those of the taxonomist be taken into account?

The principal goals of conservation are not divorced from those of pure science—far from it. In the case of deer, the most interesting scientific problems as often as not coincide with the most urgent conservation issues, including the conservation of hybrid zones or areas of parapatric contact between deer taxa. We draw attention to the following topics in taking leave of the very broad field of cervid systematic biology, and recommend them as areas for intensive and urgent study:

1) Investigation of taxa whose systematics are particularly complex and whose survival status is precarious, especially *Cervus mariannus*, *C. alfredi*, and *C. calamianensis* in the Philippines, and *C. nippon* in continental Asia.

2) Determination of the origin, history, karyology, and serology of non-Japanese sika in zoo collections with a view to enhancing our knowledge of possible genetic introgression from *C. elaphus*, and determining whether they represent samples of natural, wild populations.

3) Re-evaluation of zones of intergradation between populations of *Rangifer* and *Odocoileus*, primary field investigations of contact zones in *Alces* and *Capreolus*, and between karyotypically distinct populations in *Muntiacus* and *Mazama*.

4) Investigation of the status and morphology of musk deer throughout the Himalayas, especially in relation to species limits and possible ecological segregation of species.

5) Preservation of study material of less common species of deer. We strongly exhort all those who have access to culled specimens, natural kills, or dead zoo animals to ensure that material is preserved in accessible permanent scientific collections—skulls, antlers, whole skeletons, skins and glands and organs, all well documented, are still urgently needed for academic study, but also provide a monitoring of possible phenotypic and genotypic alteration to wild and captive stocks.

Acknowledgments

We are grateful to H. Frädrich, V. Geist, C. Janis, A. Lister, K. Scott, and C. Wemmer for discussions on cervid relationships. P.G. is particularly grateful to C. Wemmer and the F.O.N.Z. for funds allowing him to attend the Symposium. We also thank museum curators, more fully acknowledged in our other papers on deer systematics, for permission to examine specimens in their care.

Literature Cited

Ahlen, I.
1965. Studies on the red deer, *Cervus elaphus* L., in Scandinavia II. Taxonomy and osteology of prehistoric and recent populations. *Viltrevy,* 3:39–176.

Alexejew, A.
1915.   *Animaux fossiles du Village Novo-Elisavetovka Odessa.* Odessa: Typographia 'Tiechnek' Iekaterenenskaya (in Russian).

Allen, G.M.
1930.   Pigs and deer from the Asiatic Expeditions. *American Museum Novitates*, 430:1–19.

Allen, J.A.
1915.   Notes on American deer of the genus *Mazama. Bulletin of the American Museum of Natural History*, 34:521–553.

Anderson, S., and R. Barlow
1978.   Taxonomic status of *Cervus elaphus merriami* (Cervidae). *Southwestern Naturalist*, 23:63–70.

Anonymous
1982.   Not extinct after all. *Species Survival Commission Newsletter* N.S., 1:19.

Ansel, W.F.H.
1969.   Addenda and corrigenda to "Mammals of Northern Rhodesia." No. 3. *Pudu*, 5:1–48.

Atkeson, T.D., and R.L. Marchinton
1982.   Forehead glands in white-tailed deer. *Journal of Mammalogy*, 63:613–617.

Azzaroli, A.
1948.   I cervi fossili della Toscana con particolare riguardo alle specie villafranchiane. *Paleontographica Italica*, 43:45–81.

1953.   The deer of the Weybourn Crag and Forest Bed, Norfolk. *Bulletin of the British Museum of Natural History and Geology*, 2:1–96.

1954.   Critical observations upon Siwalik deer. *Proceedings of the Linnean Society of London*, 165:75–83.

Banerji, J.
1956.   Wild animals in the Andaman Islands. *Journal of the Bombay Natural History Society*, 53:256.

Banfield, A.W.F.
1961.   A revision of the reindeer and caribou, genus *Rangifer. Bulletin of the National Museum of Canada*, 177:1–137.

1963.   The post-glacial dispersal of American caribou. *Proceedings of the XVI Congress of Zoology, Washington*, 206 pp.

Barclay, E.N.
1934.   The red deer of the Caucasus. *Proceedings of the Zoological Society of London*, pp. 789–798.

Bartos, L., and J. Zirovnicky
1981.   Hybridization between red and sika deer. II. Phenotype analysis. *Zoologischer Anzeiger*, 207:271–287.

Batcheler, C.L., and M.J. McLennan
1977.   Craniometric study of allometry, adaptation and hybridism of red deer (*Cervus elaphus scoticus*, L.) and wapiti. *New Zealand Ecological Society*, 24:57-75.

Bemmel, A.C.V. van
1949.   Revision of the rusine deer in the Indo-Australian Archipelago. *Treubia*, 20:191–262.

1952.   Contribution to the knowledge of the genera *Muntiacus* and *Arctogalidia* in the Indo-Australian archipelago (Mammalia, Cervidae and Viverridae). *Beaufortia*, 16:1–50.

Bentley, A.
1978.   *An introduction to the deer of Australia with special reference to Victoria.* Second edition, Hurstbridge, Victoria: Ray Manning for Printing Associates.

Bobrinskoy, N., and K. Flerov
1934.   Materials for systematics of deer of the subgenus *Cervus. Archives of the Museum of Zoology, University of Moscow*, 1:13–41 (in Russian).

Boonsong, L., and J.A. McNeely
1977.   *Mammals of Thailand.* Bangkok: Association for the Conservation of Wildlife.

Brooke, V.
1878.   On the classification of the Cervidae, with a synopsis of the existing species. *Proceedings of the Zoological Society of London*, pp. 883–928.

Browman, L.G., and P. Hudson
1957.   Observations on the behavior of penned mule deer. *Journal of Mammalogy*, 38:247–253.

Brown, B.
1926.   A new deer from the Siwaliks. *American Museum Novitates*, 242:1–6.

Cabrera, A.
1943.   Sobre la sistematica del venado y su variacion individual y geografica. *Revista Museo de La Plata* (N.S.), 3(Zoology):5–41.

1960.   Catalogo de los mamiferos de America del Sur. II. *Revista del Museo Argentino Ciencias Naturales "Bernardino Rivadavia"*, 4:309–732.

Cai Gui-Quan, and Feng Zuo-Jian
1981.   On the occurrence of the Himalayan musk-deer (*Moschus chrysogaster*) in China and an approach to the systematics of the genus Moschus. *Acta Zootaxonomica Sinica*, 6:106–110 (in Chinese).

Cao Keqing
1978.   On the time of extinction of the wild mi-deer in China. *Acta Zootaxonomica Sinica*, 24:289–291 (in Chinese).

Carette, E.
1922.   Cervidos actuales y fosiles de Sud America. Revision de las formas extinguidas pampeanas. *Revista Museo de La Plata*, 26:292–472.

Caughley, G.
1970.   *Cevus elaphus* in southern Tibet. *Journal of Mammalogy*, 51:611–614.

Groves and Grubb

Chandra, H.S., D.A. Hungerford, and J. Wagner
1967. Chromosomes of five artiodactyl mammals. *Chromosoma*, 21:211–220.

Chapman, D.I., and N.G. Chapman
1975. *Fallow deer: their history, distribution and biology*. Lavenham, England: Terence Dalton Ltd.

Chapman, N.G., and D.I. Chapman
1980. The distribution of fallow deer: a worldwide review. *Mammalian Review*, 10:61–138.

Chasen, F.N.
1925. On the colour-pattern of the young Malay Rusa (*Cervus unicolor equinus*). *Journal of the Malay Branch of the Royal Asiatic Society*, 3:89–91.

Chernyavskyi, F.B., and N.K. Zheleznov
1982. On the distribution and taxonomy of the European elk (*Alces alces* L.) in the north-eastern Siberia. *Byulleten Moskoskogo Obshchestva Ispytatelei Prirody*, 87:25-32.

Corbet, G.B.
1978. *The mammals of the Palaearctic Region: a taxonomic review*. London: British Museum (Natural History).

Cowan, I. McT.
1936. Distribution and variation in deer (genus *Odocoileus*) of the Pacific coastal region of North America. *California Fish and Game*, 22:155–246.

1956. What and where are the mule and black-tailed deer? In *The deer of North America. The white-tailed, mule, and black-tailed deer, genus Odocoileus. Their history and management*, edited by W.P. Taylor, pp. 335–359. Harrisburg and Washington, D.C.: Stackpole Company and Wildlife Management Institute.

Dao Van Tien
1977. Sur quelques rares mammifères au Nord du Vietnam. *Mitteilungen aus dem Zoologischen Museum in Berlin*, 53:325–330.

Davis, W.B., and P.W. Lukens
1958. Mammals of the Mexican State of Guerrero, exclusive of Chiroptera and Rodentia. *Journal of Mammalogy*, 39:347–367.

Delacour, J.
1931. Le cerf pseudaxis. *La Terre et la Vie*, 1:373–375.

Dobroruka, L.J.
1960. Der Karpatenhirsch, *Cervus elaphus montanus* Botezat 1903. *Zoologischer Anzeiger*, 165:481–483.

1970. To the supposed formerly occurrence of the David's deer, *Elaphurus davidianus* Milne-Edwards, 1866, in Hainan. *Mammalia*, 34:162–164.

1975. Verlauf des Haarwechsels bei einigen Hirschen. II. (Artiodactyla: Cervidae). *Vestnik Ceskoslovenske Spolecnosti Zoologicke*, 39:94–103.

Dolan, J.M.
1971. Deer . . . the successful invaders. *Zoonooz*, 44(10):4–15.

Ellerman, J. R., and T. C. S. Morrison-Scott
1951. *Checklist of Palaearctic and Indian mammals 1758 to 1946*. London: British Museum (Natural History).

Engelmann, C.
1939. Über die Grossäuger Szetschwans, Simongs und Osttibets. *Zeitschrift für Säugetierkunde*, 13:1–76.

Espmark, Y.
1964. Rutting behaviour in reindeer (*Rangifer tarandus* L.). *Animal Behaviour*, 12:159–163.

1981. Taxonomic notes on the Swedish domestic reindeer, genus *Rangifer*. *Zoologica Scripta*, 10:155–159.

Flerov, C.
1931. On the generic characters of the Family Tragulidae (Mammalia, Artiodactyla). *Comptes Rendus de Academie des Sciences U.S.S.R.*, pp. 75–79.

1950. Morphology and ecology of cervines in process of evolution. *Material of the Quaternary Period of the U.S.S.R., Academy of Sciences of the U.S.S.R.*, Moscow Part 2, pp. 50–69 (in Russian).

1952. *Musk deer and deer. Fauna of U.S.S.R., Mammals*, vol. 1, no. 2. Moscow: Academy of Sciences of the U.S.S.R. (translated through Israel Program for Scientific Translation, 1960).

Flower, W.H.
1875. On the structure and affinities of the musk-deer (*Moschus moschiferus* Linn.). *Proceedings of the Zoological Society of London*, pp. 159–190.

Fox, R.B.
1979. The Tabon caves. *Monograph of the National Museum of Manila*, 1:1–197.

Frädrich, H.
1981. Ein schopftragender Muntjac. *Bongo*, Berlin, 5:57–60.

Frechkop, S.
1965. Notes sur les mammifères. LII. Au sujet d'un caractere dentaire des Cervides. *Bulletin Institut Royal des Sciences Naturelle de Belgique*, 41(25):1–10.

Frick, C.
1937. Horned ruminants of North America. *Bulletin of the American Museum of Natural History*, 69:1–669.

Garrod, A.H.
1876. On the Chinese deer named *Lophotragus michianus* by Mr. Swinhow. *Proceedings of the Zoological Society of London*, pp. 757–765.

1877a. Notes on the visceral anatomy and osteology of the ruminants with a suggestion regarding a method of expressing the relation of species by means of formulae. *Proceedings of the Zoological Society of London*, pp. 1–18.

1877b. Notes on the anatomy of the musk deer (*Moschus moschiferus*). *Proceedings of the Zoological Society of London*, pp. 287–292.

Geist, V.

1963. On the behaviour of the North American moose (*Alces alces andersoni*, Peterson, 1950) in British Columbia. *Behaviour*, 20:377–416.

1966. Ethological observations on some North American cervids. *Zoologische Beiträge* (N.F.), 12:219–250.

1971. The relation of social evolution and dispersal in ungulates during the Pleistocene, with emphasis on the Old World deer and the genus *Bison*. *Quaternary Research*, 1:285–315.

Gentry, A.W.

1978. Tragulidae and Camelidae. *Evolution of African mammals*, edited by V.J. Maglio and H.B.S. Cooke, pp. 536-539. Cambridge and London: Harvard University Press.

Ginsburg, L., and E. Heintz

1966. Sur les affinités du genre *Palaeomeryx* (Ruminant du Miocene europeen). *Comptes Rendus des Seances Academie des Sciences*, 262(D), no. 9:979–982.

Glover, I.

1970. *Excavations in Timor*. Ph.D. dissertation, Australian National University.

Glover, R.

1956. Notes on the sika deer. *Journal of Mammalogy*, 37:99–105.

Graf, W., and L. Nichols

1967. The axis deer in Hawaii. *Journal of the Bombay Natural History Society*, 63:629–734.

Groves, C.P.

1974. A note on the systematic position of the muntjac (Artiodactyla, Cervidae). *Zeitschrift für Säugetierkunde*, 39:369–372.

1976. The taxonomy of *Moschus* (Mammalia, Artiodactyla) with particular reference to the Indian Region. *Journal of the Bombay Natural History Society*, 72:662–782.

1980. A further note on *Moschus*. *Journal of the Bombay Natural History Society*, 77:130–133.1982. Geographic variation in the barasingha or swamp deer (Cervus düvaüceli). Journal of the Bombay Natural History Society, 79:620-629.

Groves, C.P., and P. Grubb

1982. The species of muntjac (genus *Muntiacus*) in Borneo: unrecognised sympatry in tropical deer. *Zoologische Mededelingen (Leiden)*, 56:203–216.

Groves, C.P., and C. Smeenk

1978. On the type material of *Cervus nippon* Temminck, 1836; with a revision of Sika deer from the main Japanese islands. *Zoologische Mededelingen (Leiden)*, 53:11–28.

Grubb, P.

1977. Notes on a rare deer, *Muntiacus feai*. Annali des Museo Civico di Storia Naturale "Giacomo Doria", 81:202–207.

1982. The systematics of Sino-Himalayan musk deer (*Moschus*) with particular reference to the species described by B.H. Hodgson. *Säugetierkundliche Mitteilungen*, 30:127–135.

Grubb, P., and C.P. Groves

1982. Notes on the taxonomy of the deer (Mammalia, Cervidae) of the Philippines. *Zoologischer Anzeiger*, 210:119–144.

Guo Zhuopu, Chen Enyu, and Wang Youzhi

1978. A new subspecies of sika deer from Sichuan - *Cervus nippon sichuanicus* subsp. nov. *Acta Zoologica Sinica*, 24:187–192 (in Chinese).

Gustavson, I., and C.O. Sundt

1968. Karyotypes of five species of deer (*Alces alces* L., *Cervus elaphus* L., *Cervus nippon nippon* Temm., and *Dama dama* L.). *Hereditas*, 60:233–248.

1969. Three polymorphic systems of centric fusion type in a population of Manchurian sika deer (*Cervus nippon hortulorum* Swinhoe). *Chromosoma*, 28:245–254.

Hall, E.R.

1981. *The mammals of North America* (2nd ed.). New York: Wiley.

Haltenorth, T.

1959. Beitrag zur Kenntnis des Mesopotamischen Damhirsches—*Cervus (Dama) mesopotamicus* Brooke, 1875—und zur Stammes- und Verbreitungeschichte der Damhirsche allgemein. *Säugetierkundliche Mitteilungen*, 7:1–89.1963. 1. Teil: Die Klassification der Säugetiere: 18. Ordnung Paarhufer, Artiodactyla Owen, 1848. *Handbuch der Zoologie*, Berlin, 8(32):1–167.

Hamilton, W.R.

1973. The lower Miocene mammals of Gebel Zelten, Libya. *Bulletin of the British Museum of Natural History and Geology*, 21:76–150.

1978. Cervidae and Palaeomerycidae. *Evolution of African mammals*, edited by V.J. Maglio and H.B.S. Cooke, pp. 496-508. Cambridge and London: Harvard University Press.

Harrington, R.

1973. Hybridisation among deer and its implications for conservation. *Irish Forester*, 30:64–78.

Harrison, D.L.

1968. *The mammals of Arabia*. Vol. II., London: Benn.

Heintz, E.

1963. Les caractééres distinctifs entre metatarses de Cervidae et Bovidae actuels et fossiles. *Mammalia*, 27:200–209.

1970. Les cervides villafranchiens de France et d'Espagne. *Memoires. Museum National d'Histoire Naturelle Paris (Sci. Terre)*, 22(1):1–303, 22(2):1–206.

Groves and Grubb

Heintz, E., and F. Poplin
1981. *Alces carnutorum* (Langel, 1862) du Pleistocene de Saint-Prest (France). Systematique et evolution des Alcines (Cervidae, Mammalia). *Auartarpalaeontologie,* 4:105–122.

Heptner, V.G., A.A. Nasimovitsch, and A.G. Bannikov
1961. *Die Säugetiere der Sowjetunion,* Bd. I. *Paarhufer und Unpaarhufer.* Jena: G. Fischer.

Hershkovitz, P.
1948. The technical name of the Virginia deer with a list of the South American forms. *Proceedings of the Biological Society of Washington,* 61:41–48.

1958. The metatarsal glands in white-tailed deer and related forms of the Neotropical region. *Mammalia,* 22:537–546.

1959. A new species of South American brocket, genus *Mazama* (Cervidae). *Proceedings of the Biological Society of Washington,* 72:45–54.

1972. The recent mammals of the Neotropical region: a zoogeographic and ecological review. *Evolution, mammals and southern continents,* edited by A. Keast, F.C. Erk, and B. Glass, pp. 311-431. Albany: State University of New York Press.

1982. Neotropical deer (Cervidae). Part 1. Pudus, genus *Pudu* Gray. *Fieldiana Zoology, N.S.,* No. 11, 86 pp.

Heude, P.-M.
1884. Catalogue des cerfs tachetés (sikas) du Mussée de Zi-Ka-Wei, ou notes preparatoires a la monographie de ce groupe. *Mémoires concernant l'Histoire naturelle de l'Empire Chinois,* 1:1–12.

1888. Études sur les ruminants de l'Asie orientale. Cerfs des Philippines et de l'Indo-Chine. *Mémoires concernant l'Histoire naturelle de l'Empire Chinois,* 2:1–64.

1894. Catalogue revisé des cerfs tachetés (sika) de la Chine Centrale. *Mémoires concernant l'Histoire naturelle de l'Empire Chinois,* 2:146–163.

Hoffstetter, R.
1952. Les mammifères Pléistocenes de la République de l'Equateur. *Memoires Societe Geologique de France,* 66:1–391.

Hooijer, D.A.
1950. Man and other mammals from Toalian sites in South-Western Celebes. *Verhandelingen der Koninklijke Nederlandse Akademie van Wetenschappen. Afdeling Natuurkunde,* 46(2):1–158.

Howell, A.B.
1929. Mammals from China in the collections of the United States National Museum. *Proceedings of the United States National Museum,* 75:1–82.

Hsu, T.C., and K. Benirschke
1967– *An atlas of mammalian chromosomes.* New York:
1976. Springer-Verlag.

Imaizumi, Y.
1970. Description of a new species of *Cervus* from the Tsushima Islands, Japan, with a revision of the subgenus *Sika* based on clinal analysis. *Bulletin of the National Science Museum of Tokyo,* 13:185–194.

Ingebrigtsen, O.
1923. Das norwegische Rotwild (*Cervus elaphus* L.). Eine kraniometrische Untersuchung. *Bergens Museum Aarbok,* 7:1–262.

Jacob, J., and E. von Lehmann
1976. Bemerkungen zu einer Nasendrüse des Sumpfhirsches, *Odocoileus (Dorcelaphus) dichotomus* (Illiger, 1811). *Säugetierkundliche Mitteilungen,* 24:151–156.

Jorge, W., and K. Benirschke
1977. Centromeric heterochromatin and G-banding of the red brocket-deer, *Mazama americana temama* (Cervoidea, Artiodactyla) with a non-Robertsonian translocation. *Cytologia,* 42:711–721.

Kao Yueh-Ting
1963. Taxonomic notes on the Chinese musk-deer. *Acta Zoologica Sinica,* 15:479–488 (in Chinese).

Kellogg, R.
1956. What and where are the whitetails? *The deer of North America. The white-tailed, mule and black-tailed deer, genus Odocoileus. Their history and management,* edited by W.P. Taylor, pp. 31-55. Harrisburg and Washington, D.C.: Stackpole Co. and Wildlife Management Institute.

Kock, D., and H.W. Schomber
1961. Beitrag zur Kenntnis des Verbreitung und des Bestandes des Atlashirsches (*Cervus elaphus barbarus*) sowie eine Bemerkung zu seiner Geweihausbildung. *Säugetierkundliche Mitteilungen,* 9:51–54.

Koenigswald, G.H.R. von
1933. Beitrag zur Kenntnis der fossilen Wirbeltiere Javas. I. *Wetenschappelijke Mededelingen. Dienst van de Mijnbouw in Nederlandsch Oost-Indie.* Weltevreden. 23:1-127.

Krumbiegel, I.
1982. Der Korsika-Rothirsch (*Cervus elaphus corsicanus,* Erxleben 1777) und sein biotop. *Säugetierkundliche Mitteilungen,* 30:281–286.

Kuroda, N.
1924. *On new mammals from the Riukiu Islands.* Tokyo: published by the author.

Kurtén, B.
1968. *Pleistocene mammals of Europe.* London: Weidenfeld and Nicolson.

Kurtén, B., and E. Anderson
1980. *Pleistocene mammals of North America.* New York: Columbia University Press.

Langguth, A., and J. Jackson
1980.   Cutaneous scent glands in pampas deer *Blastoceros bezoarticus* (L., 1758). *Zeitschrift für Säugetierkunde*, 45:82–90.

Lehmann, E. von
1958.   Chevreuils d'Asie et d'Europe. Contribution a l'etude du genre *Capreolus. Mammalia*, 22:262–270.

1960.   Entstehung und Auswirkung der Kontakzone zwischen dem Europäischen und Siberischen Reh. *Säugetierkundliche Mitteilingen*, 8:97–102.

Leinders, J.J.M.
1979.   On the osteology and function of the digits of some ruminants and their bearing on Taxonomy. *Zeitschrift für Säugetierkunde*, 44:305–318.

Leinders, J.J.M., and E. Heintz
1980.   The configuration of the lacrimal orifices in pecorans and tragulids (Artiodactyla, Mammalia) and its significance for the distinction between Bovidae and Cervidae. *Beaufortia*, 30:155–162.

Lent, P.C.
1965.   Rutting behaviour in a barren-ground caribou population. *Animal Behaviour*, 13:259–264.

Lister, A.
This   Diversity and evolution of antler forms in Quater-
volume.nary deer.

Li Zhi-Xiang
1981.   On a new species of musk-deer from China. *Zoological Research*, Kunming, 2:157–161 (in Chinese).

Lowe, V.P.W., and A.W. Gardiner
1974.   A re-examination of the subspecies of red deer (*Cervus elaphus*) with particular reference to the stocks in Britain. *Journal of Zoology*, 174:185–201.

1975.   Hybridization between red deer (*Cervus elaphus*) and sika deer (*Cervus nippon*) with particular reference to stocks in N.W. England. *Journal of Zoology*, 177:553–566.

Ludlow, F.
1959.   The shou or "Sikkim stag". *Journal of the Bombay Natural History Society*, 56:626–627.

Lydekker, R.
1898.   *The deer of all lands. A history of the family Cervidae living and extinct.* London: Rowland Ward.

1915.   *Catalogue of the ungulate mammals in the British Museum (Natural History).* Volume IV. London: British Museum.

Macpherson, A.H.
1965.   The origin of diversity in mammals of the Canadian Arctic Tundra. *Systematic Zoology*, 14:153–173.

Makino, S., and J. Muramoto
1966.   The chromosomes of the deer (*Cervus yesoensis* Heude). *Mammalian Chromosomes Newsletter*. 22:197.

Manning, T.H.
1960.   The relationship of the Peary and barren ground caribou. *Arctic Institute of North America Technical Paper*, 4:1–52.

Manning, T.H., and A.H. Macpherson
1961.   A biological investigation of Prince of Wales Island, N.W.T. *Transactions of the Royal Canadian Institute*, 33:116–239.

Matthew, W.D.
1908.   Osteology of *Blastomeryx* and phylogeny of the American Cervidae. *Bulletin of the American Museum or Natural History*, 24:535–562.

McCullough, D.R.
1969.   The Tule elk. Its history, behavior and ecology. *University of California, Publications in Zoology*, 88:1–190.

Meunier, K.
1964.   Die Knickungsverhaltnisse des Cervidenschadels mit Bemerkungen zur Systematik. *Zoologischer Anzeiger*, 172:184–216.

Meyer, P.
1972.   Zur Biologie und Ökologie des Atlashirsches *Cervus elaphus barbarus*, 1833. *Zeitschrift für Säugetierkunde*, 37:101–116.

Michurin, L.N.
1965.   On some morphological peculiarities of reindeer on the Taimyr Peninsula. *Zoologischeskii Zhurnal*, 44:1396–1404 (in Russian).

Miller, G.S.
1909.   The mouse deer of the Rhio-Linga archipelago: a study of specific differentiation under uniform environment. *Proceedings of the United States National Museum*, 37:1–9.

Miyake, Y.-I., H. Kanagwa, and M. Kosuge
1982.   Chromosomal polymorphism in interspecific hybrids of deer between *Cervus nippon nippon* and *C. yesoensis* Hende (sic). *Proceedings. Japan Academy. Series B. Physical and Biological Sciences*, 58 B:93–96.

Mohr, E.
1955.   *Cervus canadensis bactrianus* Lydekker 1900 und der "Hagenbeck-Hirsch" im Stellinger Tierpark. *Zoologische Garten, Leipzig*, 21:44–58.

Moore, W.G., and R.C. Marchinton
1974.   Marking behavior and its social function in white tailed deer. In *The behavior of ungulates and its relation to management*, edited by V. Geist and F. Walther, pp. 447-456. Morges: I.U.C.N.

Muller-Schwarze, D.
1971.   Pheromones in black-tailed deer (*Odocoileus hemionus columbianus*). *Animal Behaviour*, 19:141–152.

Muller-Schwarze, D., W.B. Quay, and A. Brundin
1977.   The caudal gland in reindeer (*Rangifer tarandus* L.): its behavioral role, histology, and chemistry. *Journal of Chemical Ecology*, 3:591–601.

Groves and Grubb

Muller-Schwarze, D., N.J. Volkman, and K.F. Zemanek
1977. Osmetrichia: specialized scent hair in black-tailed deer. *Journal of Ultrastructure Research*, 59:223–230.

Neitzel, H.
1979. Chromosomen evolution in der Familie der Hirsche (Cervidae). *Bongo*, Berlin, 3:27–38.

1982. *Karyotypen evolution und deren Bedeutung für den Speciationprozess der Cerviden (Cervidae; Artiodactyla; Mammalia)*. Inaugural dissertation, Freien Universität, Berlin.

Nieminen, M.
1980. Evolution and taxonomy of the genus *Rangifer* in northern Europe. In *Proceedings of the 2nd International Reindeer/Caribou Symposium*, pp. 379-391. Røros, Norway, 1979, edited by E. Reimers, E. Gaare, and S. Skjenneberg. Trondheim: Direktoratet for vilt og ferskvannsfisk.

O'Gara, B.W., and G. Matson
1975. Growth and casting of horns by pronghorns and exfoliation of horns by bovids. *Journal of Mammalogy*, 56:829–846.

Olrog, C.C., and M.M. Lucero
1980. *Guia de los mammiferos Argentinos*. Tucuman: Ministero de cultura y education.

Osgood, W.H.
1932. Mammals of the Kelley-Roosevelts and Delacour Asiatic Expeditions. *Fieldiana Zoology*, 18:193–339.

Otsuka, H.
1967. Pleistocene vertebrate fauna from the Kuchinotsu Group of West Kyushu. Part 2. *Memoirs, Faculty of Science, Kyushu Univversity. Series D, Geology*, 18:277–312.

1972. *Elaphurus shikamai* Otsuka (Pleistocene cervid) from the Akarbi Formation of the Osaka Group, Japan, with special reference to the Genus *Elaphurus*. *Bulletin National Science Museum*, 15:197–210.

Otsuka, H., and Y. Hasewaga
1976. On a new species of *Elaphurus* (cervid, mammal) from Akushima City, Tokyo. *Bulletin National Science Museum, Tokyo (Geology and Palaeontology)*, 2(3):139–144.

Peterson, R.C.
1952. A review of the living representatives of the genus *Alces*. *Contributions of the Royal Ontario Museum, Zoology and Palaeontology*, 34:1–30.

1955. *North American Moose*. Toronto: University of Toronto Press.

Pocock, R. I.
1910. On the specialised cutaneous glands of ruminants. *Proceedings of the Zoological Society of London*, pp. 840–986.

1912. On antler-growth in the Cervidae, with special reference to *Elaphurus* and *Odocoileus (Dorcelaphus)*. *Proceedings of the Zoological Society of London*, pp. 773–783.

1919. On the external characters of existing chevrotains. *Proceedings of the Zoological Society of London*, pp. 1–11.

1923. On the external characters of *Elaphurus, Hydropotes, Pudu* and other Cervidae. *Proceedings of the Zoological Society of London*, pp. 181–207.

1933. The homologies between the branches of the antlers of the Cervidae based on the theory of dichotomous growth. *Proceedings of the Zoological Society of London*, pp. 377–406.

1942a. The skull characters of some of the forms of Sambar (*Rusa*) occurring to the east of the Bay of Bengal. Part 1. *Annals and Magazine of Natural History*, (11)9:516–625.

1942b. The larger deer of British India. *Journal of the Bombay Natural History Society*, 43:298–317.

1943a. The larger deer of British India. Part IV. The chital (*Axis*) and the hog-deer (*Hyelaphus*). *Journal of the Bombay Natural History Society*, 44:169–178.

1943b. The larger deer of British India. Part III. The sambar (*Rusa*). *Journal of the Bombay Natural History Society*, 44:27–36.

1943c. The larger deer of British India. Part II. *Journal of the Bombay Natural History Society*, 43:553–572.

Presnall, C.C.
1958. The present state of exotic mammals in the United States. *Journal of Wildlife Management*, 22:45–50.

Quay, W.B.
1971. Geographic variation in the metatarsal "gland" of the white-tailed deer (*Odocoileus virginianus*). *Journal of Mammalogy*, 1–11.

Ranjitsinh, M.K.
1978. The Manipur brow-antlered deer (*Cervus eldi eldi*)— a case history. In *Proceedings of the Working Meeting of the Deer Specialist Group of the Survival Service Commission*, International Union for the Conservation of Nature, pp. 26–37.

Rees, J.W.
1969. Morphologic variation in the cranium and mandible of the white-tailed deer (*Odocoileus virginianus*): a comparative study of geographical and four biological distances. *Journal of Morphology*, 128:95–112.

1970. A multivariate morphometric analysis of divergence in skull morphology among geographically continuous and isolated groups of white-tailed deer (*Odocoileus virginianus*) in Michigan. *Evolution*, 24:220–229.

Reynolds, S.H.
1929. The giant deer. *A Monograph of the British Pleistocene Mammalia*, 3(3):1–58. London: The Paleontographical Society.

1933. The red deer, reindeer, and roe. *A Monograph of the British Pleistocene Mammalia*, 3(4):1–46. London: The Paleontographical Society.

Roberts, G.
1968. *Game animals in New Zealand*. Wellington: A.H. and A.W. Reed.

Sanborn, C.C.
1952. Philippine Zoological Expedition 1946–1947. Mammals. *Fieldiana Zoology*, 33:89–158.

Sclater, P.L.
1862. Note on the deer of Formosa. *Proceedings of the Zoological Society of London*, pp. 150–152.

Schonewald - Cox, C., J.W. Bayless, and J. Schonewald
1985. Cranial morphometry of Pacific coast elk (Cervus elaphus). *Journal of Mammalogy*, 66:63-74.

Scott, K.M., and C.M. Janis
This volume. Phylogenetic relationships of the Cervidae, and the case for a superfamily "Cervoidea".

Shave, J.
1980. Calamian deer. *Help*, 3:14–15.

Sheng Helin, and Lu Hogee
1980. Current studies on the rare Chinese black muntjac. *Journal of Natural History*, 14:803–807.

Sheridan, B.W.
1967. Carabaos and deer from Guam. *Zoonooz*, 40(4):4–8.

Shi Liming
1981. Unique cytogenetic characteristics of a tufted deer, *Elaphodus cephalophus. Mammalian Chromosomes Newsletter*, 22:47–50.

Shi Liming, and S. Pathak
1981. Gametogenesis in a male Indian muntjac X Chinese muntjac hybrid. *Cytogenetics Cell Genetics*, 30:152–156.

Shi Liming, Ye Yingying, and Duan Xingsheng
1980. Comparative cytogenetic studies on the red muntjac, Chinese muntjac and their F1 hybrids. *Cytogenetics Cell Genetics*, 26:22–27.

Sickenberg, O.
1965. *Dama clactoniana* (Falc.) in der Mittelterasse der Rhume=Leine bei Edesheim (Landkreis Northeim). *Geologisches Jahrbuch*, 83:353–396.

Sigogneau, D.
1968. Le genre *Dremotherium* (Cervoidea): anatomie du crane, denture et montage endocranien. *Annales de Paleontologie Vertebres*, 54:39–64.

Siivonen, L.
1975. New results on the history and taxonomy of the mountain, forest and domestic reindeer in northern Europe. *Occasional Publications. Institute of Marine Science, College, Alaska, No. 1 (Special Publication)*, pp. 33–40.

Simpson, G.G.
1945. The principles of classification and a classification of mammals. *Bulletin of the American Museum of Natural History*, 85:1–350.

Sokolov, I.I.
1957. On the Artiodactyla-fauna in the southern part of Yunnan-province (China). *Zoologischeskii Zhurnal*, 36:1750–1760 (in Russian).

Sokolov, V.E., V.N. Orlow, G.A. Chudinovskaya, and A.A. Danilkin
1978. Differences in chromosomes between two subspecies, *Capreolus capreolus capreolus* L. and *C.c. pygargus* Pall. *Zoologischeskii Zhurnal*, 57:1109–1112 (in Russian).

Sowerby, A. de C.
1917. On Heude's collection of pigs, sika, serows and goral in the Sikawei Museum, Shanghai. *Proceedings of the Zoological Society of London*, pp. 7–26.

1918. Notes upon the sika-deer of North China. *Annals and Magazine of Natural History*, (9)2:119–122.

Stubbe, G., and Z. Bruholz
1979. Experiments on crossing the roe and tartarian deers *Capreolus c. capreolus* L. (1758) X *C.c. pygargus* Pall. (1771). *Zoologischeskii Zhurnal*, 58:1398–1403 (in Russian).

Tate, G.H.H.
1939. The mammals of the Guianan region. *Bulletin of the American Museum of Natural History*, 76:151-229.

Taylor, K.M., D.A. Hungerford, and R.L. Snyder
1969. Artiodactyl mammals: their chromosome cytology in relation to patterns of evolution. In *Comparative mammalian cytogenetics*, edited by K. Benirschke, pp. 346-356. New York: Springer Verlag.

Teilhard de Chardin, P., and J. Piveteau
1930. Les mammifères fossiles de Nihowan (Chine). *Annales de Paleontologie*, 19:1–134.

Teilhard de Chardin, P., and M. Trassaert
1937. The Pliocene Camelidae, Giraffidae and Cervidae of South Eastern Shansi. *Palaeontologia Sinica, Series C, N.S.*, 1:1–56.

Teilhard de Chardin, P., and C.C. Young
1936. On the mammalian remains from the archaeological site of Anyang. *Palaeontologie Sinica, Series C*, 12(1):1–61.

Thomas, D.C., and P. Everson
1982. Geographic variation in caribou on the Canadian arctic islands. *Canadian Journal of Zoology*, 60:2442–2454.

Thomas, O.
1904. Exhibition of, on behalf of the President, a sketch by a Chinese artist of Père David's deer from Hainan. *Proceedings of the Zoological Society of London*, Part 2:83.

Groves and Grubb

Todd, N.B.
1975.   Chromosomal mechanisms in the evolution of ar-
        tiodactyls. *Palaeobiology*, 1:175–188.

Tsao Ke-Ching
1975.   The discovery of holocene *Elaphurus davidianus* sub-
        fossils near Shanghai and their palaeogeographical
        distribution in China. *Vertebrata Palasiatica*, 13:48–57
        (in Chinese).

Wang Zongren, and Du Ruofu
1932a. Karyotypes of four species of deer. *Acta Zoologica
        Sinica*, 28:35–40 (in Chinese).

1982b. Evolution of karyotype of the genus *Cervus*. *Acta Ge-
        netica Sinica*, 9:24–31 (in Chinese).

Wang Zongren, Du Ruofu, Xu Juanhua, and Che Qicheng
1982.   Karyotype, C-banding and G-banding pattern of
        white-lipped deer (*Cervus albirostris* Przewalski). *Acta
        Zoologica Sinica*, 28:250–255 (in Chinese).

Webb, S.D., and B.E. Taylor
1980.   The phylogeny of hornless ruminants and a descrip-
        tion of the cranium of *Archaeomeryx*. *Bulletin of the
        American Museum of Natural History*, 167:117–158.

White, M.J.D.
1978.   *Modes of speciation*. San Francisco: Freeman and Co.

Wurster, D.H., and N.B. Aitken
1972.   Muntjac chromosomes: a new karyotype for *Mun-
        tiacus muntjak*. *Experientia*, 28:972–973.

Yong, H.S.
1973.   Complete Robertsonian fusion in the Malaysian
        leser mouse deer (*Tragulus javanicus*). *Experientia*,
        29:266–367.

Young, C.C.
1932.   On the Artiodactyla from the *Sinanthropus* site at
        Choukoutien. *Palaeontologia Sinica, Series C*, 8(2):1–
        100.

Youngman, P.M.
1975.   Mammals of the Yukon Territory. *National Museum of
        Natural Sciences. Publications Zoology*, Ottawa, 10:1–
        192.

Zdansky, O.
1925.   Fossile Hirsche Chinas. *Palaeontologia Sinica, Series C*,
        2(3):1–94.

Zeuner, F.E.
1958.   Animal remains from a late Bronze Age sanctuary
        on Cyprus, and the problem of the domestication of
        fallow deer. *Journal of the Palaeontology Society of India*,
        3:131–135.

JOHN F. EISENBERG
The Florida State Museum
University of Florida
Gainesville, Florida

The Evolutionary History of the Cervidae with Special Reference to the South American Radiation

ABSTRACT   The origin of the Cervidae is still somewhat obscure; however, it is now apparent that the adaptive radiation of true deer probably began in Eurasia. By the time of the Pliocene, deer were present in North America; and at the completion of the land bridge between North America and South America, deer entered the southern continent and began a dramatic adaptive radiation. Since bovids were not present in South America, the deer radiated to fill a number of grazing and browsing niches that would be occupied by bovids on the more contiguous continental landmasses. The small deer of the genera *Pudu* and *Mazama* are probably secondarily small, deriving from an ancestral form that was larger and had a more complex antler.

Cervid Origins and Radiation

The reconstruction of the evolutionary history of any group is dependent upon an adequate fossil record. Given the gaps that exist in the record, one is often led to speculate upon the history of a group by looking at contemporary forms. Conversely, armed with some knowledge of the fossil record, it is possible to look at extant species and make an educated guess as to the most probable sequence of evolutionary change. Ungulates traditionally are viewed as springing from an omnivore precursor that gave rise on the one hand to carnivores and on the other hand to a radiation that became more and more specialized for feeding on plants. Ungulate adaptive radiation commenced in the Eocene and the earliest forms were adapted to browsing niches in forests. These early ungulates began to rely more upon early detection of predators and speed than on overt offensive anti-predator action. Thus, we view our "proto-ungulate" as a browser that also utilized fruits, and became more cursorial in its locomotor adaptation. By losing toes, it became digitigrade and underwent intensive selection with respect to its dental and digestive apparatus to more efficiently process green plant parts into a digestible feeding substrate. At some point in time our Eocene herbivore stock diverged to produce the contemporary Perissodactyla and the Artiodactyla. Our attention is focused on this latter group, and in particular, the contemporary Cervidae.

The early history of cervid evolution in North America is somewhat obscure. It is known that in the Oligocene of Asia *Eumeryx* existed and was very similar in morphology to the present-day musk deer of the family Moschidae. Something like *Eumeryx* probably gave rise in the Miocene to moschid genera as *Dremotherium* of Europe and *Blastomeryx* of North America. During the early Miocene in Eurasia one finds the first records of ruminants that have bony outgrowths on the frontal bone. Some species have permanent horns but others clearly had deciduate antlers. Those with permanent horns are referable to the Palaeomerycidae. Their North American counterparts are called the Dromomerycidae. Frick (1937) placed the Dromomerycines within the Cervidae, but Webb (1983) demonstrates the horns were not deciduate and refers them to their own family. The first true deer with deciduous antlers born on an elongated projection from the frontal bone appear as *Dicrocerus* and *Procervulus* in the Miocene of Eurasia. There is no record of antlered forms in North America until the early Pliocene when they must have entered from Eurasia.

Looking at the fossil record one can speculate upon what an early cervid might have been like. It was certainly small in stature; it probably had more than one young. It did not bear antlers. It was a browser, adapted to a mixed feeding strategy in tropical forests; and, indeed, might have looked something like the contemporary mouse deer (Family Tragulidae) or the musk deer *Moschus*. Ralls, et al. (1975) documented the behavior of captive *Tragulus napu,* and in their article they speculate upon the degree of sexual dimorphism shown between males and females. Males have large canine teeth, which they use rather effectively when contesting among themselves over access to estrous females. Within the contemporary Cervidae, competition among males for females has apparently been an important selective force because in most cervids sexual dimorphism is demonstrable with respect to male weapons. In what we believe to be the more conservative species within the family, males bear large canines that are presumably employed in contesting among themselves for access among females. At least in some of these tusk-bearing species dermal shields have evolved as protective adaptations (Dubost and Terrade, 1970; Wemmer, 1982).

In contemporary musk deer (family Moschidae), the males bear large canines that are probably employed in fights to determine priority of access to females. The Hydropotinae of the Cervidae contains a single extant species, *Hydropotes inermis*, and the males bear enormous canines that certainly serve in intraspecific combat. Within the Muntiacinae (=Cervulinae) we see not only the possession of large canines on the part of males but a bony structure on the head that bears a deciduous antler. Thus, at one or several points in time, the ancestral deer evolved a bony, deciduous excrescence on the head employed by males in combat for access to females. With the continued evolution of antlers the canine declined in importance.

For the purpose of this discussion, I prefer to divide the deer into the classical subfamilies. I realize that in most recent revisions this is not done but I feel there is good reason to maintain subfamilial status for certain genera. In Corbet and Hill (1980), the musk deer have been raised to their own familial level, Moschidae; this concurs with Webb and Taylor (1980) and Groves and Grubb (this volume). I then consider the subfamilies of the Cervidae as follows: Muntiacinae for the muntjacs; Cervinae for the true deer; Hydropotinae for the water deer; Odocoilenae for the American deer and *Capreolus*. The taxonomic categories Rangiferinae for the caribou and reindeer, and Alcinae for the moose *Alces* are provisionally retained.

The modern deer are characterized by a set of morphological features that include the following: They are artiodactyls with two functional toes on each foot; there are two tarsals (III and IV), while carpals III and IV are fused. Within the family, residual toes on the fore and hind foot representing digits two and five may be retained. All species have a four chambered stomach and generally possess a facial gland anterior to the eye. Most members possess well developed pedal glands between the toes of the fore and/or the hind feed and metatarsal glands on the hind legs. A tail gland is present and well developed in some species. Only in the musk deer, *Moschus* (which is not a true cervid), is an abdominal gland present in the male, which elaborates a secretion apparently used in marking territories. The topic of cutaneous glands and funtion is discussed by Muller-Schwarze (this volume).

The upper incisors are lost and in many members of the family the upper canine is missing. The upper canine is retained in a reduced size in *Cervus elaphus* and *Elaphurus davidianus* for example, but is a moderately large sized tooth in the genera *Elaphodus* and *Muntiacus*. Canines are extremely large in the genera *Moschus* and *Hydropotes*. Males of both of these latter two genera do not develop antlers. Antlers are present in the males of other species of the Cervidae and are carried by females only in the genus *Rangifer*. Tail reduction reaches its extreme expression in *Capreolus* and *Hydropotes*. In most northern, boreal forms, the antlers are shed annually. In smaller, tropical deer precise annual shedding is not always the case, and antlers may be carried for slightly more than one year. This is especially true of those deer that have simplified antlers reduced to spikes or, at the most, two prongs.

This unique structure, the antler, differs from the true horn of a bovid in that it is shed periodically and renewed. I believe that the primitive antler form was something like that shown by a muntjac and it was forked. A forked antler probably enables combatants to catch one another's antlers and hold themselves locked together in such a way that minimal damage can be done (Geist, 1966). Although forked antlers are highly efficient in catching an opponent, they are also subject to stress, fracture and breakage; thus I believe that natural selection favored a nearly annual change of this weapon.

The family Moschidae, together with the cervid Muntiacinae, and Hydropotinae retain conservative morphological features. The Cervinae are typical true deer showing many apomorph characters and the Rangiferinae and Alcinae appear most recently in the fossil record and have many derived characters.

The Cervinae presents us with an array of genera and subgenera. The fallow deer typically are conserved in the genus *Dama* and exhibit the only palmate antlers within this subfamily. The genus *Axis* was erected for the species *Axis axis* and *A. porcinus* but are closely allied with the subgenus *Cervus (Rusa)* which includes *C. unicolor, C. timorensis, C. mariannus,*

and *C. alfredi*. These latter five species are deer bearing only three tines on their antlers and are broadly distributed through south India and southeast Asia, having colonized the Sunda Islands and the Philippines. The subgenus *Cervus (Rucervus)* includes *C. duvauceli, C. schomburgki,* and *C. eldi,* all of southeast Asia. *Cervus nippon* and related subspecies, together with the *Cervus elaphus* complex, represent the true deer and it is with these forms that most of our behavior and ecology data have been developed. The genus *Elaphurus,* now preserved only in the captive state, typically occupied the riverine habitats of central China.

There are several species among contemporary forms that exhibit conservative features. As noted previously, *Hydropotes* or the Chinese water deer does not have antlers, but males have enlarged canines. They are small in stature and the females have typically two or more young. *Hydropotes* may in fact be carrying forward into present time conservative morphological features rather than reacquired characters that approximate an ancestral condition. Yet we know it is possible for selection to favor a morphotype that resembles an ancestral condition when a reduction in body size has taken place. This is most clearly shown when one examines the radiation of the deer in South America.

Adaptive Radiation of South American Cervids

By the early Pliocene true cervids are identifiable in North America (Webb, 1983). It is presumed that these forms entered South America over the Pliocene land bridge, thereafter to differentiate rapidly into the genera which we observe today. It is customary to group all South American deer together with the North American genus *Odocoileus* and the European *Capreolus* into the subfamily Odocoileinae. This is a rather unified morphological group frequently showing a loss of the upper canine and all showing a telemetacarpal fore foot. The odocoileines share this character with the musk deer, Chinese water deer, moose, and reindeer.

The South American forms include eleven species grouped into six genera. The genus *Odocoileus* ranges from southern Canada to Brazil. It is generally agreed that a single species is present in South America, *Odocoileus virginianus*. In northern South America, it can occur at reduced densities in multistratal evergreen rain forests. It reaches its highest density, however, in the Llanos of Venezuela and Colombia where it occupies a mixed browsing/grazing niche never far from permanent water.

To the south of the Amazon, *Odocoileus virginianus* is replaced by two species, the pampas deer, *Ozotoceros*

Eisenberg

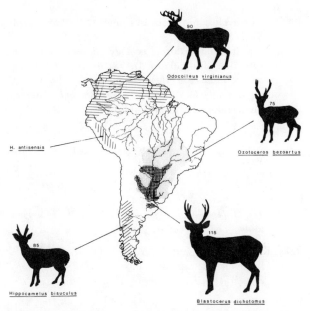

Figure 1. Distribution of the larger deer in South America. The more open areas of Brazil, Uruguay, and Argentina were formerly occupied by the pampas deer, *Ozotoceros*. The swamp deer, *Blastocerus*, occupied the riverine areas of the Rio Paragua, Parana and their tributaries. *Hippocamelus* is typically a high altitude form. Numbers refer to average shoulder heights in centimeters. (Modified from Hershkovitz, 1982.)

bezoarticus, and marsh deer, *Blastocerus dichotomus*. The pampas deer occupies the cerrado, chaco and pampas habitat characterized by reduction in tree cover and large areas of grassland. Herd size in the pampas deer is characteristically small, consisting of does and young offspring, but as many as 8 to 12 individuals are seen grazing in small herds (see Jackson and Langguth, and Redford, this volume). *Blastocerus*, the marsh deer, formerly occupied more rivering habitats along the Rio Parana, the Rio Paraguay and their tributaries (Figure 1).

The genus *Hippocamelus*, divisible into two species, occupies montane habitats in Chile, Argentina, Peru, and Ecuador. This is a stocky deer with body proportions more reminiscent of a mountain sheep than a deer and indeed appears to occupy the sheep niche. It is well to bear in mind that South America is a land without bovids and when the odocoileine deer first entered South America they did not encounter any other modern ruminant forms with the exception of the camelids. Thus, in the brief span from a late Pliocene entry to the present time, the deer have radiated to fill niches that in the more contiguous continental landmasses would be occupied by bovids.

The genera *Mazama* and *Pudu* occupy forest browsing niches in a manner comparable to that shown by

the forest duikers in Africa and the muntjacs of Asia. *Mazama* is divisible into four species; two, *M. rufina* and *M. chunyi*, are rather small (38–44 cm shoulder height). *Mazama gouazoubira* and *M. americana* range from 61–71 cm at the shoulder. The two species of *Pudu*, *P. mephistophiles* and *P. puda*, are very reduced in size and represent the extreme in size reduction, probably secondarily acquired (Figure 2). Hershkovitz (1982) has summarized the existing data concerning life history and morphology of the genus *Pudu*.

While much is still speculative, it is known with some certainty that deer entered South America in the late Pliocene. These early New World cervids most certainly had antlers and were of an intermediate body size. The genera *Pudu* and *Mazama* have spike antlers and no enlarged canine. These spike antlers may not be a conservative character but rather may have evolved in conjunction with selection for a smaller body size. The fact that canines are lacking in the

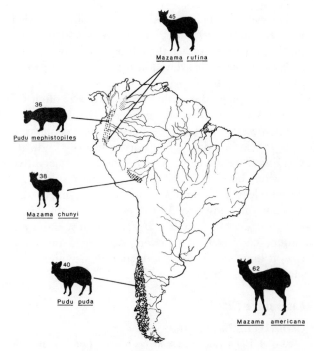

Figure 2. Distribution of the dwarf deer species. *Mazama chunyi*, *M. rufina*, *Pudu puda*, and *P. mephistophiles* are drawn to scale. The numbers indicate shoulder height in centimeters. The smaller deer are probably allopatric. The distribution of *M. rufina* in southern Brazil is not shown pending further study of the presumed *M. rufina* material. *M. americana* is shown to indicate relative size. *M. americana* is distributed at low altitudes from Veracruz, Mexico, to northern Argentina. Over much of its range in South America, the smaller *M. gouazoubira*, or brown brocket, occurs; but they are separated according to microhabitat preferences. (Modified from Hershkovitz, 1982.)

male brocket and pudu implies that canines were absent in their ancestors and that more complicated antlers may have been carried.

Within the genus *Mazama* the four named species exhibit a great range in size: The species *M. chunyi* is as small as *Pudu mephistophiles*. The exact process of selection for small body size is not well understood but one could speculate that adaptation to dense highland forests might have favored a small stature.

It is worth noting that both species of *Pudu* and the two dwarf species of *Mazama* occupy rather restricted habitats in the temperate forests and foothills of the Andes. One might speculate that the rapid evolution of such small forms adapted to dense montane forests could have occurred during the formation of habitat refugia during cycles of Pleistocene glaciation. The creation of "insular-like habitats" during periods of glacial maxima deriving from the vastly reduced rainfall over many parts of South America has generated testable hypotheses concerning adaptive radiation in butterflies, birds, and mammals (Muller, 1973). Perhaps the dwarf races of brockets and pudu evolved during such habitat fragmentation (Hershkovitz, 1982).

The evolution of large body size in ruminants is tied with adaptation to more open habitats and to more localized grazing rather than browsing habits. That larger body size has evolved in the tropics is not to be disputed (e.g., *Blastoceros*). But it is also true, as Geist (1974) has pointed out, that large body size often accompanies adaptation to a periglacial habitus.

The possession of spike antlers by some contemporary species of deer does not necessarily indicate carrying forward into present time a conservative character, but rather spikes may be the result of reduced selection for large antlers accompanying overall reduction in body size. As a rule of thumb, the larger species of cervids have the largest and most elaborate antlers; conversely, if selection favors a smaller body size, it may equally favor reduction in size and complexity of the antler.

Literature Cited

Corbet, G.B., and J.E. Hill
1980.   *A World List of Mammalian Species*. London: British Museum (Natural History).

Dubost, G., and R. Terrade
1970.   La transformation de la peau des Tragulidae en bouclier protecteur. *Mammalia*, 34:505–513.

Frick, C.
1937.   Horned ruminants of North America. *Bulletin of the American Museum of Natural History*, LXIX: xxvii + 669pp.

Geist, V.
1966.   The evolution of horn-like organs. *Behaviour*, 27(3–4): 175–215.
1974.   On the relationship of ecology and behavior in the evolution of ungulates. In *The Behavior of Ungulates and its Relation to Management*, Vol. I, edited by V. Geist and F. Walther, pp. 235–247. Morges, Switzerland: I.U.C.N. Publications.

Hershkovitz, P.
1982.   Neotropical Deer (Cervidae). Part I. Pudus, Genus *Pudu* Gray. *Fieldiana* (Zoology), New Series No. 11: 86 pp.

Muller, P.
1973.   *The Dispersal Centers for Vertebrates in the Neotropical Realm*. The Hague: W. Junk.

Ralls, K., C. Barasch, and K. Minkowski
1975.   Behavior of captive mouse deer, *Tragulus napu*. *Zeitschrift für Tierpsychologie*, 37:356–378.

Webb, S.D.
1983.   A new species of *Pediomeryx* from the late Miocene of Florida and its relationships within the subfamily Cranioceratinae (Ruminantia: Dromomerycidae). *Journal of Mammalogy*, 64:261–276.

Webb, S.D., and B.E. Taylor
1980.   The phylogeny of hornless ruminants and a description of the cranium of Archaeomeryx. *Bulletin of the American Museum of Natural History*, 167(3):117–158.

Wemmer, C.
1982.   The dermal shield of the lesser mouse deer. *Malayan Nature Journal*, 36:137–139.

KATHLEEN M. SCOTT
Department of Biological Sciences (Zoology Unit)
Rutgers University
Box 1059
Piscataway, New Jersey 08854

Allometry and Habitat-related Adaptations in the Postcranial Skeleton of Cervidae

ABSTRACT

Interspecific variation in the limb dimensions of Cervidae can be separated into two major categories: regular allometric changes correlated with increasing size, and deviations from regular scaling related to particular habitats or locomotor styles. Most dimensions of the skeleton are highly correlated with body weight. Lengths of radius, metacarpal, tibia, and metatarsal have the lowest R-square values. Limb lengths generally scale against body weight with negative allometry, diameters, and areas with positive allometry. Exponents for most relationships of forelimb bones are higher than those of the hindlimb; that is, as body weight increases forelimb bones decrease in length more slowly and increase in thickness more rapidly than do hindlimb bones. Cervids are neither geometrically nor elastically similar: exponents for most relationships lie between elastic and geometric values. Differences in scaling between cervids and Bovidae are in part a consequence of the difference in size range between the two families.

Departures from regular allometric trends in limb lengths were analysed by scaling the length of each limb bone against femur length, and calculating the difference between the actual and the expected length. Small cervids living in dense forest tend to have moderate length or markedly shortened limbs while *Hydropotes* has elongate limb segments. Most cervids weighing between 40–100 kg have elongate segments. These species are specialized for rapid, highly maneuverable locomotion and for clearing obstacles. Cervids larger than 100 kg generally have shortened limb segments. In large cervids, as in large ungulates generally, specializations for speed may not be as important as in smaller cervids.

Introduction

The species in the family Cervidae differ markedly in general body form: some species appear to be relatively long-legged, some short-legged, some have relatively longer hind legs, while in other species the limbs appear more equal in length. Cervids also span a wide range of body sizes, live in different habitats, and display a number of different behaviors. The question can than be posed, are differences in body form a consequence solely of body size, or solely of habitat, or some combination of these and perhaps other factors. This study examines the dimensions of the postcranial skeleton of Cervidae with several objectives. First, the scaling relationships of skeletal dimensions and body weights will be determined for the complete size range of the family to identify those dimensional changes which are dictated by increasing body weight. Second, the mechanical and physical properties of the locomotor system that govern such changes will be evaluated. Third, this study will determine whether deviations from regular scaling related to habitat occur and, if so, the nature and direction of these changes.

The family Cervidae is an excellent group in which to examine allometric changes and to test predictions which have been made about scaling in ungulates, most of which have been based on studies of Bovidae. Cervids span a sufficiently wide size range, from approximately ten to 500 kg, to allow an accurate determination of scaling relationships; however, the range is narrower than it is in bovids. Although their habitats differ, cervids appear to inhabit a narrower range of habitats than do Bovidae. Thus, scaling results for cervids can be contrasted to the well-studied scaling relationships of bovids to answer several interesting questions. First, can theories of scaling be generalized throughout the ungulates? Second, does the size range of the group being studied affect scaling relationships or results? Third, is the apparently wider range of habitats of bovids reflected in wider deviations from regular allometry in this group than in Cervidae?

Scaling Relationships

In any series of related animal species which span a large size range, the geometry of the skeletal system will differ among species of different sizes. As size increases, the dimensions of the supporting skeletal system must change to maintain functional equivalence as the load placed upon the skeleton changes.

Such allometric changes are widespread throughout the animal kingdom; cases of isometry, or no change in shape as size increases, are rare (Gould, 1966). Allometric changes required by increasing size can be separated from those changes related to adaptations to particular habitats or modes of locomotion (Gould, 1975). Groups of related species with similar demands of habitat would be expected to show fewer deviations from regular allometric scaling than groups in which large differences in habitat occur.

In a series of related animals of different sizes skeletal dimensions may change in one of three ways as size increases. Dimensions may maintain the same relationships to each other, so that the shape of the skeleton does not change. This is geometric similarity or isometry. Maintenance of geometric similarity indicates that the same mechanical system is adequate for the size range of the family. Skeletal dimensions may increase more rapidly than increasing body weight; such positive allometry results in larger animals with relatively longer or thicker legs than smaller species. Lastly, dimensions may increase more slowly than body weight, so that limbs become relatively shorter or more slender in larger animals. The dimensional relationships which result if a series of species maintained geometric similarity have been used to make some predictions about the kinds of scaling relationships which might be expected. In a geometrically similar series of species, limb lengths and diameters would scale as body weight to the .33 power, and areas as body weight to the .67 power. Since the weight bearing ability of bone, or its compressive strength, depends on its cross-sectional area, this means that larger animals would have relatively less weight-bearing ability than smaller animals. Obviously, these relationships imply an upper size limit for a geometrically similar series of animals. This leads to the prediction that cross-sectional area would increase more rapidly with body weight than would geometric relationships. This is in fact the case in a variety of animal groups, although cross-sectional area never scales directly as body weight (Gould, 1966). The relationships of geometric scaling do not predict any other relationships for scaling of limb lengths and diameters.

Only a single theory of scaling relationships has been proposed which predicts all dimensional changes within the skeleton. This is the elastic similarity hypothesis (McMahon, 1973, 1975a, 1975b, 1976, 1977). McMahon proposed that in a series of animals the dimensions of the skeleton would change in such a way that the animals would maintain the same elastic resistance to bending. Bending moments are created in any tall, slender column (such as the long bones of a limb) which is loaded eccentrically, that is, in which the load is not centered directly over the column at all times. In such a column subjected to bending, tensile stresses are created on one side of the column and compressive stresses on the other. Bone has a much higher resistance to compressive stress than to tensile stress. Thus, fracturing is often initiated on the side of a bone which is undergoing tensile stress, and compressive fractures are quite rare (Burstein et al., 1967; Curry, in Wainwright et al., 1976). Experimental evidence from studies on sheep indicates that long bones are subjected to bending stresses during normal locomotion (Lanyon and Baggott, 1976; Lanyon and Bourn, 1979). Lanyon (1980) also found that bending moments during growth are necessary for the attainment of normal bone size and shape in rats. Resistance to bending stresses must be an important factor in defining skeletal dimensions. If it is the only factor, elastic scaling theory predicts that all long bone lengths would scale as body weight to the .25 power, all diameters as body weight to the .375 power, all areas as body weight to the .75 power, and all lengths as diameters to the .67 power.

Studies of interspecific scaling relationships in ungulates have largely been devoted to testing these predictions. McMahon (1975a) partially tested his theory by determining the length to diameter scaling relationships for a number of ungulates of the orders Artiodactyla and Perissodactyla. He found that members of the family Bovidae scaled at close to elastic predictions, and that the Artiodactyla as a whole gave the next best fit. More inclusive taxonomic groups gave poorer fits to elastic predictions. His results for cervids were particularly interesting: cervids deviated farther from elastic predictions than bovids. If elastic similarity were important in determining skeletal dimensions, elastic predictions would be expected to apply equally to bovids and cervids. McMahon's study only considered length to diameter relationships and does not give full information on scaling relationships. Lister (in lit.) has scaled McMahon's data on lengths and diameters against published body weights; his results indicate that scaling relationships of cervids are closer to geometric similarity than to elastic similarity.

Studies on other ungulate groups have concentrated mainly on the Bovidae. Alexander (1977) found good agreement with elastic predictions in seven species of bovids for relationships of length and diameters to body weight. However, I (in press) found poorer agreement with elastic theory when 108 species of bovids were analysed for scaling relationships of lengths, diameters, and areas with body weights. Although resistance to bending appears to be an important factor in determining proportions of the bovid skeleton, bovids do not scale so as to maintain elastic similarity; that is, other factors must also be important in determining bovid skeletal dimensions. Elastic scaling does not apply to mixed groups of ungulates and other mammals, either: Alexander et al. (1979) calculated scaling relationships of lengths and body weights for a "shrew to elephant" curve and found poor agreement with elastic theory.

Gaits and Adaptive Differences

The basic locomotor morphology of cervids is a type generally characterized as cursorial; the morphology of cursorial adaptations has been described by Hildebrand (1959, 1962) and Smith and Savage (1956), among others. More detailed analyses of cervid locomotor systems and locomotion are rare. Gambaryan (1974) presents the most complete analysis of gaits and skeletal proportions, but for only a few species (*C. nippon, Cap. capreolus, R. tarandus*). Howell (1944) presented limb ratios for several species of cervids. However, his ratios are problematical since they do not take into account the size of the animal, and also because for Artiodactyla he notes that he could not always distinguish between metacarpals and metatarsals. Muybridge (1899) published photographic locomotory sequences of several cervids, and Gambaryan (1974) includes tracings of the gallop in two species of cervids. Dagg and de Vos (1968) included four species of cervids in their analysis of pecoran gaits. Several cervids are included in Hildebrand's gait analyses (1977) although he does not discuss cervid adaptations specifically.

Many authors (Hildebrand, 1959, 1962; Smith and Savage, 1956; Howell, 1944) have associated longer limb segments with more rapid locomotion. Specializations for high speed locomotion in the form of longer limb segments thus would be expected in ungulates which depend on speed to escape predation, especially in open country. Species which depend on the cover provided by brush, tall grass, or forest, and may only run a short distance before seeking cover would be expected to show less elongate limb segments; this group will be highly variable depending on the exact habits and habitats of the species. Species for which delivery of power at the foot is more important than speed should show the most shortened distal segments (Scott, 1979). These general factors will be modified by other considerations. Dagg and de Vos (1968) point out that substrate type will affect locomotion; animals living on yielding substrate would be expected to show fewer specializations for speed. Special feeding adaptations may also be reflected in limb morphology; the elongate limbs of the giraffe, a high level browser, are the most obvious example of this. Species depending on crypsis or those which move in thick brush, may, on the other hand, have shorter limbs. ost of these types of modifications have been described for bovids (Scott, 1979). This paper will present a preliminary analysis of some types of modifications seen in cervids and speculate on the functional basis for these differences.

Many cervids live in habitats that provide at least some cover, and most species which graze in the open avoid coming out in full daylight. Most cervids do not depend on speed over distances in open places to escape predation. Cervids would therefore not be expected to show the extreme modifications of gazelles (Scott, 1979) or *Antilocapra*. Neither do any cervids occupy the types of cliff habitats which many bovids of the tribes Caprini and Rupicaprini do. The extremely shortened distal segments seen in these species would not be expected to find parallels among the cervids. In the Pecora, cervids would be expected to show moderate to somewhat elongate distal limb segments.

Some limb modificaions in cervids may be related to locomotor differences, especially the number and duration of the suspended phases in the gallop. In a galloping animal there are two phases in the stride when the animal may leave the ground completely. These phases are important since they increase the length of the stride. The two points during which suspended phases can occur are the gathered suspension which follows the step of the leading forefoot, and the extended suspension, which is pushed off by the leading hindfoot or both hindfeet more or less simultaneously. Hildebrand (1977) states that deer have only one suspended phase during the gallop, the extended suspension. Since the cervids he looked at were *Hydropotes, Muntiacus,* and *O. hemionus* this may be typical for many smaller cervids. However, Dagg and de Vos (1968) report a short gathered suspension for *O. virginianus.* Gambaryan (1974) also reports two suspended phases for *Capreolus.* Data from both Gambaryan (1974) and Dagg and de Vos (1968) indicate that the extended suspension phase is longer in small cervids than in small bovids, while the gathered phase is less important. Larger bovids, equids, and apparently larger cervids have only a single, gathered suspension phase in their stride (Gambaryan, 1974; Dagg and de Vos, 1968). These differences in use of fore- or hindlimbs to launch a phase of extension may be reflected in skeletal differences. Hildebrand (1977) also reports that mule deer use the pronk, a gait in which all four feet strike the ground simultaneously. Although many ungulates use this gait at times, very few use it as a mode of progression over any distances. Although such gait differences may also be reflected in

the skeletal system too little is known about gaits in cervids to fully analyze these possibilities.

This study will describe the general patterns of deviation from regular scaling in limb lengths and suggest probable reasons for some of the differences. These discussions will be general, rather than a species by species account, for several reasons. Good data on preferred habitat are not available for all species and for many cervid species, preferred habitats vary geographically. I did not have sufficient specimens available to compare subspecific differences, so that individuals of a species were lumped. Although this gives a general idea as to the modifications of a species, comparisons between species are premature for some cervids. Differences in morphology may not depend simply on habitat but on strategies of predator escape, and on gait and locomotor behaviors. Interpretations of morphology of introduced species, or those which may have changed habitats or behavior due to human interference are difficult. Species found in one habitat today may retain adaptations to former habitats. Lastly, cervid long bone lengths are quite variable, more so than bovids, and where sample sizes are small I cannot be confident that some species by species differences are real.

Materials and Methods

Measurements were taken on 183 specimens belonging to 27 species of Cervidae. The specimens used are from the collections of the American Museum of Natural History, the U. S. National Museum of Natural History, the Museum of Comparative Zoology, Harvard University, the Field Museum of Natural History, the Peabody Museum of Natural History, Yale University, and the Museum of Vertebrate Zoology, University of California (Berkeley). A list of specimens measured and the raw data are available from the author. The number of specimens measured and the species examined are listed in Appendix I. All specimens were adult individuals (as indicated by completion of epiphyseal fusion) collected in the wild which showed no sign of gross deformity. Zoo specimens were included only for *Elaphurus davidianus* and *Dama dama*, for which no other specimens were available. All measurements of long bone lengths were taken to the nearest 0.1 cm using a GPM anthropometer; all other measurements were made to the nearest 0.01 cm with a dial caliper.

Length measurements were taken on each long bone (humerus, radius, metacarpal, femur, tibia, and metatarsal). These measurements were chosen to represent the greatest length between articular surfaces. The diameters of each bone were measured at mid-

Scott

Table 1. Scaling relationships of limb lengths and body weight for Cervidae. Exponents for Bovidae weighing less than 500 kg are given in parentheses. The confidence intervals of the exponent are expressed as exponent ± confidence interval. The right-hand column indicates whether the elastic (E) and geometric (G) exponents, respectively, lie within the confidence interval of the experimental exponent.

	Exponent	*Constant*	*R-Square*	*E/G*
Forelimb	.314 ± .058 (.277 ± .017)	14.4	.910	no/yes
Humerus	.277 ± .042 (.283 ± .016)	5.7	.916	yes/no
Radius	.326 ± .060 (.304 ± .017)	4.9	.898	no/yes
Metacarpal	.339 ± .082 (.241 ± .035)	4.1	.851	yes/yes
Hindlimb	.277 ± .049 (.247 ± .014)	22.2	.908	yes/no
Femur	.276 ± .044 (.277 ± .014)	7.5	.938	yes/no
Tibia	.261 ± .052 (.243 ± .014)	8.9	.894	yes/no
Metatarsal	.300 ± .067 (.213 ± .029)	5.8	.861	yes/yes

shaft in both the transverse and antero-posterior directions. These diameters were used to calculate the area of the bone at midshaft. Area was calculated as though the cross section of the bone were an ellipse with major and minor axes equal to the two diameters. This does not give an exact estimate since it does not take into account the size of the marrow cavity, and it should be regarded as an indication of relative amount of bone between the species studied.

Allometric equations of the form $y = mx^b$ were fitted to these data by performing a least squares analysis on logarithmic transformations of the data using the procedure GLM in the Statistical Analysis Systems libraries (SAS). Calculations of 95% confidence intervals of the exponents were as described in Simpson et al. (1960). The exponents (b), constants (m), and R-square values are given in Tables 1 and 3–5. Sample plots of some relationships are given in Figures 1–3, 5, and 6. Regressions of length versus diameter were calculated based on the individual specimens. For regressions involving body weight the arithmetic mean of each measurement for all specimens measured was used. Sexually dimorphic species and those in which subspecies varied by more than about 15% in body weight were separated by sex or subspecies.

For most species body weights used were average values of the male or female reported in the literature. In some cases museum specimens and zoo records provided supplemental weights. As many weight records as possible were collected for each species, and estimates for each species were based on these. The major sources of body weights used were Corbet and Southern (1977), Ward (1896), Allen (1940), Tate (1947), Burt and Grossenheider (1964); Medway

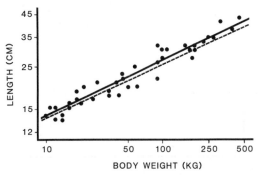

Figure 1. Femur length plotted against body weight on logarithmic coordinates. Solid line is the regression line for Cervidae, dashed line for Bovidae.

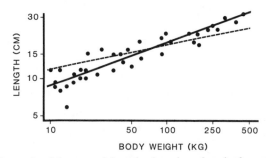

Figure 2. Metacarpal length plotted against body weight on logarithmic coordinates. Solid line is regression line for Cervidae, dashed line for Bovidae.

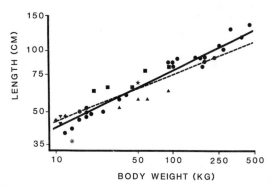

Figure 3. Hindlimb length plotted against body weight on logarithmic coordinates. Solid line is regression line for Cervidae, dashed line is regression line for Bovidae. Certain species are identified as follows: ▼ = *Moschus berezovskii*; ♦ = *Hydropotes*; ⊛ = *Pudu*; ★ = *Antilocapra*; ▲ = *Axis porcinus* and *A. axis*; ■ = *C. nippon, Capreolus, O. virginianus, O. hemionus*.

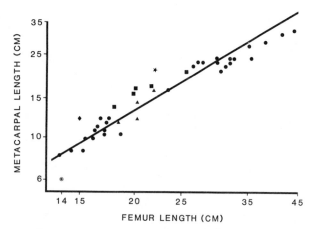

Figure 4. Metacarpal length plotted against femur length on logarithmic coordinates. Certain species are identified as follows: ● = *Hydropotes*; ⊛ = *Pudu*; ★ = *Antilocapra*; ▲ = *Axis porcinus* and *A. axis*; ■ = *C. nippon, Capreolus, O. virginianus, O. hemionus*.

(1969), Walker (1968), Dollman and Burlace (1935), Whitehead (1972), and Grzimek (1972). The weights given in some of these sources must be used with caution. The weights reported by big game hunters are usually weights of record males; for bovids these were found to overestimate the weight of an average male by about 10% (Scott, 1979). Where these were the only weights available they were adjusted accordingly. The same caution must be applied to body weights given in Walker (1968) since many of his weights are taken directly from sources such as Rowland Ward's Records of Big Game (Dollman and Burlace, 1935).

In order to compare deviations from regular scaling in species of different sizes limb bone lengths were transformed into dimensionless variables in the following manner. This method has been used by Emerson and Radinsky (1980) and Radinsky (1981a, 1981b, 1982) to study skull morphology in carnivores, and is described in greater detail there. All long bone lengths were transformed to logarithms (base 10) and humerus, radius, metacarpal, tibia and metatarsal lengths were scaled against femur length (Figure 4). Reduced major axis equations were calculated for each of these relationships; these are of the form $\log y = b \log X + \log m$, where 'x' represents femur length. The values of b, log m, and the correlation coefficients between the variables are given in Appendix II. Femur length was chosen as a standard because, of the limb bones, it scales most closely with body weight and at about the same exponents for most Pecora, so that results between groups are comparable. Body weights are too inexact to use in this context for many ungulate species. Reduced major axis was used in these calculations because neither element could be considered dependent. The equations were used to calculate predicted bone lengths for each species. Dimensionless variables representing deviations from the regression lines were computed by dividing the actual length by the predicted length for each bone (Table 2). Values greater than 1.00 indicate that the bone is longer than predicted; values less than 1.00 indicate that the bone is shorter than predicted. (Compare variables in Table 2 with deviations of the identified species in Figure 4.)

Results and Discussion

Scaling Relationships of Limb Lengths

The scaling relationships for total limb lengths and individual limb bones with body weights are given in Table 1, and several of the relationships are illustrated in Figures 1–3. The differences in scaling relationships between the two limbs are striking. The forelimb and most of its individual elements scale with slight negative allometry at exponents close to isometry. The

Table 2. Mean (± SD) of transformed limb length variables

Species	Humerus	Radius	Metacarpal	Tibia	Metatarsal
Small Cervids, Moderate to Elongate Limbs					
Hyd. inermis	0.932 ± .003	1.099 ± .028	1.298 ± .125	1.069 ± .041	1.095 ± .090
Moschus	1.089 ± .048	1.063 ± .041	1.018 ± .028	1.117 ± .028	1.053 ± .076
Maz. americana	1.005 ± .012	1.035 ± .018	1.108 ± .065	1.019 ± .038	1.096 ± .043
Maz. gouazoubira	.0990 ± .022	1.003 ± .034	1.060 ± .039	1.004 ± .261	1.051 ± .054
M. reevsi	0.999 ± .016	1.000 ± .028	0.985 ± .053	0.975 ± .018	1.017 ± .032
Small Cervids, Short Limbs					
M. muntjak	0.980 ± .030	1.002 ± .08	0.991 ± .076	0.985 ± .037	0.962 ± .032
E. cephalophus	1.006 ± .021	0.939 ± .023	0.888 ± .025	0.992 ± .024	0.914 ± .025
Pudu pudu	1.079	0.889	0.735	0.911	0.787
P. mephistophiles	1.151 ± .028	0.977 ± .024	0.712 ± .008	0.961 ± .001	0.828 ± .024
Medium-Sized Cervids, Elongate Limbs					
Cap. capreolus	1.037 ± .013	1.165 ± .038	1.267 ± .062	1.103 ± .033	1.188 ± .059
C. nippon	0.993 ± .011	1.090 ± .020	1.214 ± .041	1.033 ± .009	1.122 ± .025
O. hemionus	1.030 ± .026	1.082 ± .039	1.104 ± .043	1.048 ± .027	1.147 ± .038
O. virginianus	0.991 ± .019	1.079 ± .010	1.167 ± .158	1.032 ± .048	1.140 ± .138
Ozot. bezoarticus	1.014 ± .370	1.107 ± .111	1.239 ± .116	1.023 ± .043	1.112 ± .103
Axis axis	0.979 ± .009	1.014 ± .043	1.085 ± .075	0.980 ± .026	1.007 ± .032
C. timorensis	0.981 ± .003	1.005 ± .002	1.021 ± .004	0.964 ± .033	0.930 ± .007
C. eldi	0.960	1.018	1.136	1.008	1.012
Medium Cervids, Moderate or Short Limbs					
Axis porcinus	0.962 ± .025	0.959 ± .038	0.968 ± .042	0.988 ± .012	0.906 ± .028
B. dichotomus	0.974 ± .004	0.996 ± .030	1.048 ± .054	1.005 ± .007	0.987 ± .037
Large Cervids, Short Limbs					
C. elephas	1.030 ± .015	0.998 ± .039	0.922 ± .062	0.998 ± .013	0.948 ± .043
C. unicolor	0.967 ± .019	0.891 ± .021	0.882 ± .034	0.935 ± .005	0.864 ± .020
C. duvauceli	0.941 ± .015	0.965 ± .025	0.937 ± .028	0.959 ± .015	0.871 ± .019
Elaphurus	0.964 ± .009	0.960 ± .017	0.966 ± .032	0.966 ± .015	0.928 ± .022
Alces alces	1.112 ± .024	1.040 ± .032	0.862 ± .025	1.000 ± .020	0.950 ± .023
R. tarandus	1.046 ± .037	1.108 ± .027	0.855 ± .040	0.997 ± .026	1.024 ± .054

hindlimb and its individual elements scale with marked negative allometry, and at exponents close to the predictions of elastic theory. The exponents for humerus, total hindlimb, femur, and tibia do not differ significantly from elastic predictions. The exponents for total forelimb, ulna, and radius do not differ significantly from isometry. The exponents for metacarpal and metatarsal do not differ significantly from either elastic predictions or isometry. The confidence intervals for these two bones are larger than those for the other limb bones; metapodials vary more relative to body weight than do other long bones. This is also reflected in the lower R-square values for these bones.

Within each limb the proximal bones (humerus and femur) show the highest R-square values, and these values decrease from proximal to distal. Two questions of particular interest arise from these results: first, why are there differences in exponents between the fore- and hindlimbs and, second, why is body weight more highly correlated with lengths of proximal than distal bones.

The differences in scaling between the forelimb and the hindlimb cannot be explained simply. Cervids are obviously not a simple geometric series, nor are they an elastic series: if elastic theory were correct it should apply to both the fore- and hindlimbs equally.

Hindlimb lengths increase more slowly with increasing body size than do forelimb lengths. Cervids are not unique in this respect; bovids show the same differences, although they are less marked (Scott, in press). I have suggested that in bovids this may be related to the shifting emphases on the two limbs during locomotion. In small bovids both the leading forefoot and the leading hindfoot push off a suspended phase, while in large bovids only the forelimb propels a suspended phase (Hildebrand, 1977; Gambaryan, 1974). In cervids the contrast in emphasis is greater with small cervids having only an extended suspension, or a long extended and short gathered suspension, while large cervids have only a gathered suspension (Hildebrand, 1977; Gambaryan, 1974; Dagg and de Vos, 1968). I believe that as ungulates become larger the length of the forelimb is maximized to maintain the greatest possible thrust for the pushoff into the suspended phase while the hindlimb can become relatively shorter. Conversely, in small ungulates the hindlimb is relatively longer to achieve maximum thrust for the extended suspension. There is some evidence that in smaller bovids hindlimb musculature is more massive relative to body weight while in larger bovids forelimb musculature is relatively more massive (Smith and Ledger, 1965; T. Grand, pers. comm.), but data are not available for cervids. I believe that this tendency to emphasize forelimb as size increases is a general one in ungulates, and accounts for the differences in scaling relationships of limb lengths between fore- and hindlimbs. This difference is more marked in cervids than in bovids, probably because of the greater emphasis placed on hindlimb-powered extended flight in small cervids.

All of the exponents of length to body weight relationships in cervids are higher than those of bovids. That is, limb lengths do not decrease as rapidly relative to body size in cervids as they do in bovids, so that cervids appear to be close to a geometric series in many dimensions. (Compare bovid and cervid regression lines in Figures 1–3.) These differences are in part an artifact of the size range of living species in the two families. If the length to body weight scaling relationships of bovids are recalculated omitting species weighing more than 500 kg, so that the size range conforms more closely to that of cervids, the exponents are higher and closer to the cervid values. Most of the bovids larger than 500 kg are in the tribe Bovini, and these species differ from other bovids in a number of respects (Scott, 1979, in press). All of their limb segments are short relative to body weight; this results in lower exponents for the entire group. Although the bovid and cervid exponents still differ when Bovini are omitted from the bovid regressions, the exponents of humerus, radius, femur, and tibia have overlapping

confidence intervals. Metapodial scaling relationships still differ, with bovid exponents being much lower, and consequently total fore- and hindlimb exponents are still lower for bovids.

In cervids, as in bovids, metapodial lengths are more variable than are proximal limb elements (compare Figures 1 and 2), but the metapodials of Bovidae are more variable at any given body size than are those of cervids. Metapodial length in Bovidae is related to habitat: species which live on open plains, and which depend on speed to outrun predators, have relatively long metapodials, and species living in mountainous habitats have extremely shortened metapodials, as do the Bovini. Species living in forested areas or open hilly country show metapodials of intermediate lengths (Scott, 1979, in press). Although cervids do show variation in limb segment length related to habitat, the range of habitats in which cervids are found is not as varied as that of bovids. No cervid species are found in the cliff habitats utilized by many Rupicaprini and Caprini, nor are cervids found in open arid areas or living exclusively in open, short grasslands. As a result, some of the more extreme modifications seen in bovid metapodials are not seen in cervids. The scaling relationships of cervid metapodials are therefore different from those of bovids; the absence of species with extremely shortened metapodials probably explains the higher exponents in cervids as opposed to bovids.

In both bovids and cervids proximal bone lengths are almost entirely determined by body weight while distal limb elements vary to a greater degree at a given body weight. Much of this variation can be related to differences in habitat and locomotion. However, this difference in variability raises the question: why should proximal bones vary less? I have suggested reasons why proximal bones show less variation in bovids (Scott, in press); these reasons apply equally to Cervidae. In any animal the bulk of the body mass will be associated with the trunk, and much of this will be locomotor musculature. This is pronounced in ungulates, since the limb musculature is proximally placed, with very little musculature associated with distal parts of the limb. Variation in proximal bones must be constrained by the mass of musculature which originates and inserts on these bones. These constraints would not apply to more distal bones, especially the metapodials; dimensions of these bones are more free to vary.

McMahon (pers. comm.) has suggested that proximal bones should conform more closely to elastic predictions because the greatest bending moments would be set up in the proximal part of a limb. However, this would only be true if limbs functioned as a single unit. Since limbs are jointed each bone must be loaded individually, and this cannot explain the closer conformity of proximal bones to elastic predictions. Alexander (1977) proposed that angulation of bones would affect the magnitude of the bending moments set up in the bone, with larger bending moments in more horizontal bones. This may in part explain the closer conformity of proximal bones with elastic scaling.

Deviations from Allometric Scaling: Habitat Differences

SMALL CERVIDS

The smaller cervids can be divided into three groups: those in which limb elements are about 1.00, or only slightly elongated or shortened, those with markedly elongate limb segments, and those with markedly shortened limb segments (Table 1 and Fig. 4). The first group includes *Moschus berezovskii*, *Mazama gouazoubira* and *Muntiacus reevesi*. *Mazama americana* and *Moschus moschiferus* show moderately elongate limbs. *Hydropotes* is the only small cervid with markedly elongate limbs. *Muntiacus muntjak*, *Elaphodus*, and *Pudu* show marked shortening of elements, *Pudu* most strongly so. All of these small cervids except *Hydropotes* live in areas of fairly dense thicket or bush (Whitehead, 1972; Walker, 1968). *Hydropotes* is found mostly in areas of tall grasses and reeds (Whitehead, 1972). Although such a habitat serves as cover for an animal the size of *Hydropotes*, the greater openness of the terrain probably places a greater premium on speed. Heavy undergrowth is not an environment in which speed is at a premium, nor is it even useful. Shortened limbs and a "low profile" would allow animals to move more easily through brush, and probably make them less noticeable. Interestingly, this same shortening of the limbs is seen in the duikers (*Cephalophus*) (Scott, 1979). The species of *Mazama* available to me have somewhat longer limbs than the muntjacs; the bush duiker (*Sylvicapra*) shows similar elongation compared to *Cephalophus* (Scott, 1979). However, from the information available at this time I am unable to say whether differences in habitat or locomotion can account for this difference.

Both species of *Moschus* show a particularly interesting modification in the elongation of the tibia, although it is more marked in *M. moschiferus*. Musk deer, like many other small cervids, give the appearance of being higher in the rump than at the withers. Elongation of the hindlimb, especially the tibia, is characteristic of some primitive artiodactyls, tragulids, and some small forest-living bovids (Scott, 1979). I believe that this basic morphology is a primitive one for small, forest-living artiodactyls, which has been retained in *Moschus*. However, *Moschus* has longer limb segments generally than tragulids and the fossil species.

It should be noted that the general impression that small cervids have hindlimbs relatively longer than forelimbs, as compared to large cervids, is correct (Figure 3). However, this difference is not indicated in these variables, which only reflect variance around regular scaling relationships. It is reflected in the scaling relationships, the more negative exponent for the hindlimb indicating that the hindlimb is relatively longer in smaller cervids, while the forelimb stays more nearly the same length in small versus large cervids.

The relatively longer hindlimb in small cervids is expected because the extended phase of suspension comprises a high percentage of the stride in small cervids (Dagg and de Vos, 1968; Gambaryan, 1974). Gambaryan and Dagg and de Vos have also suggested that in ungulates living in areas with many obstacles a gallop with a long extended phase is ideally suited for clearing obstacles. Many small cervids may use a rapid bounding gait as a means of maneuvering in undergrowth. The elongate hindlimb in *Moschus* (Figure 3) and in some primitive ungulates suggests that this may be a primitive pattern of locomotion. From this basic morphology some cervids have shortened limbs as an alternative strategy for moving through heavy undergrowth. In *Hydropotes* it is interesting that most elongation is in the forelimb, which produces limbs more nearly equal in length. Clearing obstacles (and thus emphasis on the hindlimb) is probably less important in this species.

MEDIUM TO LARGE CERVIDS

Among the medium to large cervids two basic patterns emerge (Table 2). Most cervids weighing more than about 100 kg have limb segments which are about 1.00 or shorter. *Alces* basically fits with this group excepting that the humerus is elongate and the radius and tibia slightly so. Cervids weighing less than about 100 kg tend to have all segments elongated, with the greatest degree of elongation in the metacarpal. *Rangifer* shows a unique pattern with most limb elements about 1.00, but with marked elongation of the radius.

Most of the medium-sized cervids have elongate limbs and are probably specialized for a bounding gait with a long extended suspension which is suitable for clearing obstacles and highly maneuverable. This correlates well with the evidence of Dagg and de Vos (1968) and Gambaryan (1974) that the extended suspension is of long duration in smaller cervids, as opposed to small bovids and large cervids. Many cervids in this grouping live in open woodland areas, and many also graze in the open. Thus it is not surprising that they should show modifications for rapid locomotion. This may be an adaptive type which is only open to smaller cervids, however. In larger species the energy required to raise the center of mass in this kind of gait may make it inefficient.

Two smaller cervids which might be expected to show elongate limbs according to my suggestions in fact have shortened limb segments. These are *Blastocerus*, which has limb variables about 1.00 as do larger cervids, and *Axis porcinus* which has quite short distal limb elements. *Blastocerus* lives in marshy areas. Dagg and de Vos (1968) have pointed out that species living on yielding substrate are unlikely to be specialized for rapid locomotion, since any fast gait would have phases where only one foot at a time would touch the ground and the feet would sink into the substrate. Swamp living species would thus be expected to have shorter limb segments than similarly sized related species. *C. duvauceli* also has shortened distal segments, although not as markedly so for their size range.

Hog deer are found in areas of tall grass on alluvial plains, and might not be expected to show such markedly shortened limbs. This may, however, be an alternative strategy for living in tall grasses analogous to that suggested for *Pudu* in dense undergrowth. That is, shorter stature may decrease the chances of the animals being seen. These species have adopted the strategy of maximizing concealment rather than speed to avoid predators (C. Wemmer, pers. comm.).

The larger cervids do not have elongated limbs and some species show quite marked reduction in segment lengths. These species definitely place greater emphasis on the gathered suspension than on the extended suspension (Gambaryan, 1974; Dagg and de Vos, 1968), but I found little else on gait in these species. I would expect them to use a gallop with less vertical displacement than do smaller cervids. Dagg and de Vos (1968) also state that the large cervids they studied prefer the trot to the gallop when not closely pursued. The trot is a more stable and less tiring gait than the gallop. Dagg and de Vos also point out that large cervids may not depend on speed to escape predation as much as do small cervids. They cite Mech's (1966) study which showed that moose on Isle Royale were more successful in countering a wolf attack if they stood their ground than if they fled. This is probably true to some extent for all large as opposed to small ungulates. In this group of larger species then, limbs are not elongated for rapid locomotion.

Alces is the largest cervid and although it shares many aspects of limb segment length with the larger cervid group the humerus and radius do differ in being elongate. Elongation of proximal as opposed to distal segments results in increased power at the foot

rather than increased speed. This could be related to the frequency with which moose swim and move on swampy ground. Elongation of the radius combined with only moderate elongation of the metacarpal is also characteristic of some bovids (especially Alcelaphini and Hippotragini) and camelids (Scott, 1979; unpublished data). Radius elongation may occur in place of metacarpal elongation since less stress would be placed on this bone than on the metacarpal. Even if there is selection for increased power related to swimming or moving on soft substrate in this species it cannot be to the advantage of a browser to shorten the limbs too much, and the proportions which exist may be a compromise.

Rangifer also has an elongated radius and shortened metacarpal, but a slightly elongate metatarsal. The forelimb proportions are similar to those of alcelaphine bovids. In alcelaphines this may be a mechanism for lengthening the forelimb, which pushes off the single suspended phase in these species (Scott, 1979, in press). Again, the distal metacarpal, with less surrounding muscle, is probably more subject to increased stress, so that it is more advantageous to elongate the radius. Although *Rangifer* has a short extended flight it does place more emphasis on the gathered suspension phase. For this reason it may be advantageous to have one bone of the forelimb elongate, but since there is also an extended flight, the metatarsal is still slightly elongate.

Scaling of Diameters and Areas with Body Weights

The scaling relationships of transverse and anteroposterior diameters vary from marked positive allometry to slightly negative allometry (Table 3, Fig. 5). The exponents of forelimb bones are higher than those of hindlimb bones. Although the forelimb bones scale at exponents consistently closer to elastic predictions, and hindlimb bones at closer to geometric, most of the exponents do not differ significantly from either elastic or geometric predictions. Only two exponents show significant differences, humerus antero-posterior diameter from geometric predictions and tibia anteroposterior diameter from elastic predictions. Since these are the only two exponents which differ significantly from either set of predictions they have little meaning in terms of the scaling relationships of these dimensions as a whole. The scaling relationships of areas follow a similar pattern to those of diameters. The forelimb bones scale with positive allometry, at close to elastic predictions, while those of the hindlimb scale with positive allometry but are closer to isometry, except the tibia, which scales with nega-

Table 3. Scaling relationships of anteroposterior diameter, transverse diameter, and area at midshaft to body weight, as in Table 1

	Exponent	Constant	R-Square	E/G
Antero-Posterior Diameters				
Humerus	.3787 ± .054	.480	.961	yes/no
Radius	.3589 ± .056	.312	.909	yes/yes
Metacarpal	.3811 ± .064	.304	.946	yes/yes
Femur	.3501 ± .051	.513	.941	yes/yes
Tibia	.2934 ± .063	.570	.890	no/yes
Metatarsal	.3584 ± .057	.401	.935	yes/yes
Transverse Diameters				
Humerus	.3849 ± .053	.388	.952	yes/yes
Radius	.3801 ± .054	.466	.947	yes/yes
Metacarpal	.3388 ± .046	.422	.920	yes/yes
Femur	.3355 ± .052	.512	.952	yes/yes
Tibia	.3526 ± .054	.510	.964	yes/yes
Metatarsal	.3280 ± .045	.428	.938	yes/yes
Midshaft Areas				
Humerus	.7644 ± .105	.146	.960	yes/yes
Radius	.7398 ± .184	.114	.941	yes/yes
Metacarpal	.7206 ± .106	.101	.948	yes/yes
Femur	.6836 ± .101	.206	.952	yes/yes
Tibia	.6466 ± .114	.228	.952	yes/yes
Metatarsal	.6872 ± .134	.134	.942	yes/yes

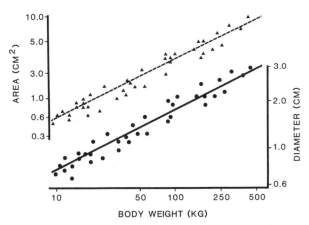

Figure 5. Area (upper curve) and antero-posterior diameter (lower curve) of metacarpal plotted against body weight on logarithmic coordinates (not to same vertical scale).

tive allometry. Cervids are thus neither geometrically nor elastically similar in these dimensions.

Areas also show slightly less variability than do diameters; transverse and antero-posterior diameters may deviate more from regular scaling in some species than do areas. Maintenance of a particular mass of bone at the midshaft appears to be more critical than whether this bone is arranged in the antero-posterior or transverse direction. This close association between area and body weight intuitively suggests that compressive strength, which is proportional to area, may be the critical factor determining midshaft areas. However, if compressive strength alone were critical, area might be expected to scale directly as body weight; otherwise large animals would maintain a smaller margin of safety than small animals. Increasing the area of bone also increases its resistance to bending, and many of the exponents do suggest that areas scale at approximately elastic predictions. I believe that elastic factors are important in determining scaling relationships. The evidence that most fractures are initiated by bending is strong, and it is elastic resistance which counters bending forces. Long bones must maintain both sufficient resistance to bending and to compression to remain intact. Whatever the relative importance of these two factors, long bones of cervids do not increase in thickness as rapidly as would be expected. The fact that resistance to bending is important does not mean that a series of related ungulate species should be expected to scale elastically.

Other factors not considered by McMahon (1973, 1975a) may account for the fact that bone thicknesses do not increase as rapidly with increasing size as might be predicted. Alexander (1977) suggested for bovids that deviations from elastic scaling may result from different angulations of bones. Maximum bending moments are set up in bones which are loaded in the horizontal position; the humerus would most closely meet this requirement, and it does scale at close to elastic predictions. Alexander also found that in larger bovids the angles between the hindlimb bones decreased as size increases. On this basis he predicted that exponents of 0.362 should be found for elastically scaling bovid hindlimb diameters, and this would give an exponent of 0.724 for areas. These values are closer to those he obtained and those given here for cervids, but they are too close to both elastic and geometric predictions to be tested.

Alexander et al. (1977) and Alexander et al. (1979) point out that large ungulates run with larger duty factors than small ones. This means that each foot remains on the ground longer and consequently that each foot is loaded with a smaller multiple of body weight. They state that stresses in the limbs of large and small animals are approximately equal. As bovids increase in size, loading during locomotion thus does not increase in direct proportion to body weight. This would mean that bones would not have to increase in area as rapidly as does body weight in order to have equal resistance to either compressive or bending forces. If these findings apply to small versus large ungulates generally this might explain why scaling relationships of areas generally are more negative than expected. Maloiy et al. (1979) have suggested that these factors negate elastic scaling theory entirely.

For bovids I suggested that changing distribution of body mass could account for differences between fore- and hindlimb thicknesses (Scott, in press). That is, as bovids become larger the muscle mass of the hindlimb decreases more rapidly relative to body weight than does mass of the forequarter. Cervid scaling relationships follow a similar pattern, and this suggests that distribution of mass in cervids may follow a similar pattern. However, data are not yet available to test this suggestion.

The greater amount of variation seen in diameters is interesting in several respects. McMahon (1973; 1975a) originally proposed that it is maintenance of the length to diameter relationship which is important in maintaining elastic resistance to bending. He stated that major forces in locomotion would be directed in the antero-posterior direction. However, this assumption is based on studies of animals walking or running in a straight line on a treadmill. In a galloping ungulate, especially one which is turning frequently, bending stresses must also be set up in the transverse plane, so that this dimension should scale according to elastic predictions. However, it is possible that in certain modes of locomotion greater stresses may be generated in one plane or the other. In bovids, for instance, species which live in mountainous terrain (for example, *Oreamnos americanus*) show transversely expanded and flattened metapodials. I believe that these are associated with greater lateral forces generated in

these habitats by the uneven stresses created during climbing. Plains-living species tend to have very rounded metapodials. There may be other adaptive reasons for changes in the dimensions of metapodials. In some cervids the deep flexor tendon has muscular tissue associated with it. Grand (pers. comm.) has observed that this musculature is well developed in *Muntiacus* and I have observed moderate amounts in *Rangifer*. The metapodials of many of the smaller cervids are flattened, perhaps to allow more surface area for this musculature to take origin. In *Rangifer* the metapodials are rounded but with a deep groove on the posterior surface in which the flexor tendons lie. On the other hand, the long-legged *Capreolus* shows the rounded metapodials typical of more speed adapted species (i. e., gazelles, genus *Gazella*). Such adaptive differences may account for the greater variability in diameters as opposed to areas.

Scaling of Length and Diameter

The results of the scaling relationships of length with diameter provide an important test of the elastic theory (McMahon, 1973). For all long bones, length scales against diameter with negative allometry, that is, with exponents less than one (Table 4). However, all of the exponents are higher than those predicted by elastic theory: as diameter increases bone lengths increase less than would be predicted if cervids scale geometrically, but more than if they scaled elastically. The length to diameter relationships of all long bones show high R-square values, with metapodials showing slightly lower values. These are interesting contrasts to results obtained for bovids, especially for distal bones. Although the scaling relationships of length to diameter for humerus and femur are similar, for all other bones the cervid exponents are much higher. In addition, the distal bones of bovids show a much greater degree of variation than do those of cervids; R-square values for length to diameter relationships of bovid metacarpals and metatarsals are 0.65 and 0.78, respectively, compared to 0.917 and 0.931, for cervids.

It is apparent that as cervids increase in size their limbs become thicker relative to length, although not as rapidly as elastic criteria predict, and not as rapidly as found in bovids. There are several reasons why diameters may scale so close to isometry in cervids. For example, small cervids have shorter, thicker metacarpals on the average than bovids of the same size (compare regression lines on Fig. 6). Although the slope of the cervid line is steeper, for all but the smallest cervids the length of a bone for a given diameter will not differ greatly for cervids and bovids weighing from approximately 30 to 500 kg. The apparent near isometry of the length to diameter relationships of cer-

Table 4. Scaling relationships of length to diameter, as in Table 1

	Exponent	Constant	R-Square	E/G
Humerus	.7375 ± .002	9.8	.960	yes/no
Radius	.8662 ± .004	14.4	.929	no/no
Metacarpal	.8976 ± .006	11.7	.917	no/no
Femur	.7668 ± .002	13.1	.962	yes/no
Tibia	.8169 ± .002	15.5	.920	no/no
Metatarsal	.8366 ± .004	12.4	.931	no/no

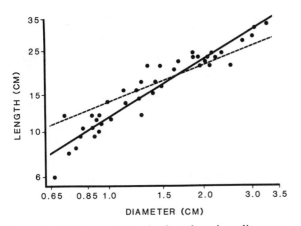

Figure 6. Metacarpal length plotted against diameter on logarithmic coordinates. Solid line is the regression for Cervidae, dashed line for Bovidae.

vids is thus partly an artifact related to the relatively short, thick metacarpals of small cervids. Humerus and femur length to diameter relationships are very similar in bovids and cervids; in both families large species have relatively longer or more slender bones than would be expected. I have also suggested for bovids that bending moments may be countered in other ways in proximal bones (Scott, 1985). Proximal bones are surrounded by musculature which inserts and takes origin there. Bending moments may be reduced by the pull of opposing sets of muscles, though not completely offset by the pull of musculature (Lanyon, 1980).

Summary and Conclusions

If a series of related species scales geometrically, they maintain the same relative dimensions of the locomotor system, but they are not mechanically equivalent. In order to maintain mechanical equivalence, deviations from isometry must occur. In the locomotor system the ability to support increasing mass and load on the limbs must determine mechanical equivalence, at least in part. The smaller the range of sizes, the smaller the deviations which will be necessary to maintain equivalence as size increases. Over a wider size range scaling relationships would thus be expected to show greater deviations from isometry, than over a small size range. Species in the family Cervidae do show deviations from geometric similarity as size increases. Lengths of hindlimb bones scale with marked negative allometry, while the bones of the forelimb scale with only slight negative allometry. Diameters and midshaft areas of forelimb bones scale with marked positive allometry while those of the hindlimb show slight positive allometry (with the exception of the tibia). All length to diameter scaling relationships show negative allometry, that is, bones become shorter

relative to their diameter as diameter increases. Most of the scaling relationships differ from elastic predictions: bones are longer or more slender than predicted by elastic theory.

In smaller cervid species, then, the hindlimb is relatively longer than in larger cervids. The forelimb is also relatively longer in small cervids, but only slightly so; the forelimb is much closer to geometric similarity than the hindlimb. Limb bones also become relatively thicker as size increases; bones of the forelimb increase in thickness more rapidly than those of the hindlimb. I believe that these scaling differences are related, at least in part, to locomotor differences between small and large cervids. In the gallop of small cervids the extended suspension phase forms a major part of the stride (Gambaryan, 1974; Dagg and de Vos, 1968) and in some species this may be the only suspended phase (Hildebrand, 1977). In the gallop of medium cervids both extended phases are present, but the extended suspension is longer in duration. In large cervids the extended suspension becomes less important and is not present in the largest species. As several authors (Gambaryan, 1974; Dagg and de Vos, 1968) have pointed out, the extended flight is well-suited for clearing obstacles, as would be encountered in forest environments. The emphasis on the hindlimb in the cervid gallop may have arisen in small, forest-living cervids. As cervids become larger, the emphasis shifts from hindlimb to the forelimb-powered gathered suspension. This is a common trend in large ungulates and is probably related to the energetic cost of launching a heavy body into a bound off of the hindlegs. In bovids there is some evidence that the mass of musculature shifts forward. Although data are not available for cervids, if this were the case it would explain the more rapid increase in thickness of forelimb bones as size increases.

Cervid scaling relationships differ from those of bovids in several respects. Most cervid exponents are higher than those of bovids: that is, cervids are closer to being geometrically similar, probably in part because they span a smaller size range for which a given mechanical design is sufficient with only small deviations necessary to maintain mechanical equivalence. This is supported by the fact that regressions for bovids based on only species with body weights less than 500 kilograms are much closer to those of cervids than for the entire family Bovidae. In bovids the differential in scaling between the fore- and hindlimbs is not as extreme, although the same trends are present. In the gallop of small bovids the extended suspension is of shorter duration than in small cervids, and the two suspended phases are of more nearly equal importance. Consequently there is not as great a differential between the lengths of the two limbs.

Cervids, like bovids, do not form an elastic series, but elastic resistance to bending is probably a factor in determining dimensions since fractures are usually initiated by bending moments. As species increase in size bending moments on their limbs increase. These increased moments can be countered either by increasing the thickness of limbs or by decreasing the length of limb elements. Elastic theory maintains that so long as the appropriate relationship between the two dimensions is maintained the limb will have sufficient resistance to bending. However, while elastic scaling is possible in engineering terms, in a large ungulate it would create a very heavy distal limb element that would be energetically expensive to move. Increasing speed is probably not important to large ungulates: their size is a defense against many predators. Thus shortening distal limb segments is probably a more mechanically efficient solution to increased bending moments in large ungulates.

Limb lengths, especially of distal elements, show the largest deviations from regular scaling relationships, and I have suggested that much of this variation is related to differences in habitat and locomotor habits. Small cervids can be divided generally into two groups, species with moderate to short limbs living in heavy cover, and longer legged species living in more open areas. Medium-sized cervids tend to have elongate limbs and probably have emphasized fairly rapid locomotion with a long extended suspension phase for clearing obstacles. Larger cervids have shorter limb segments, and probably place more emphasis on gathered suspension. Speed is probably less important for large cervids. Swamp-living species also have shorter metapodials than expected for their size. Cervids show less variation in limb elements than do bovids. The range of habitats in cervids is narrower; this probably is responsible for the difference. Although the deviations from regular scaling and their relationships to habitat and locomotor habits have only been discussed generally the basic patterns of morphological distinction are clear. As more data on habitat, behavior, and especially gait become available, these outlines can be fleshed out into a more comprehensive picture of cervid morphology.

Acknowledgments

I would like to thank T. Grand, C. Janis, K. Kranz, A. Lister, L. Marcus, and L. Radinsky for advice and assistance in various forms. I am grateful to the curators of the collections I visited for access to the specimens. This study was supported by a grant from the Rutgers Research Council.

Literature Cited

Alexander, R. McN.
1977.   Allometry of the limbs of antelopes (Bovidae). *Journal of Zoology*, London, 183:125–146.

Alexander, R. McN., A. S. Jayes, G. M. O. Maloiy and E. M. Wathuta
1979.   Allometry of limb bones of mammals from shrews (*Sorex*) to elephant (*Loxodonta*). *Journal of Zoology*, London, 198:305–314.

Alexander, R. McN., V. A. Langman, and A. S. Jayes
1977.   Fast locomotion of some African ungulates. *Journal of Zoology*, London, 183:291–300.

Alexander, R. McN., G. M. O. Maloiy, B. Hunter, A. S. Jayes, and J. Nturibi
1979.   Mechanical stresses in fast locomotion of buffalo (*Syncerus caffer*) and elephant (*Loxodonta africana*). *Journal of Zoology*, London, 189:135–144.

Allen, G. M.
1940.   *The Mammals of China and Mongolia*. New York: American Museum of Natural History.

Burstein, A.H., J.D. Currey, V.H. Frankel, and D.T. Reilly
1972   The ultimate properties of bone tissue: the effects of yielding. *Journal of Biomechanics*, 5:35–44.

Burt, W. H., and R. P. Grossenheider
1964.   *A Field Guide to the Mammals*. Boston: Houghton Mifflin Company.

Corbet, G., and H. N. Southern
1977.   *The Handbook of British Mammals*, 2nd ed. Oxford: Blackwell Scientific Publications.

Dagg, A. I., and A. de Vos
1968.   Fast gaits of pecoran species. *Journal of Zoology*, London, 155:499–506.

Dollman, G., and J. B. Burlace
1935.   *Rowland Ward's Records of Big Game. African and Asiatic Sections*. 10th ed. London: Rowland Ward Limited.

Emerson, S. B., and L. B. Radinsky
1980.   Functional analysis of sabertooth cranial morphology. *Paleobiology*, 6:295–312.

Gambaryan, P. P.
1974.   *How Mammals Run*. New York: Halstead Press.

Gould, S.J.
1966.   Allometry and size in ontogeny and phylogeny. *Biological Review*, 41:87–640.

1975.   On the scaling of tooth size in mammals. *American Zoologist*, 15:351–362.

Grzimek, B.
1972.   *Animal Life Encyclopedia. Vol. 13 (Mammals IV)*. New York: Van Nostrand Reinhold Company.

Hildebrand, M.
1959.   Motions of the running cheetah and horse. *Journal of Mammalogy*, 40:481–495.

1962.   Walking, running, and jumping. *American Zoologist,* 2:151–155.

1977.   Analysis of asymmetrical gaits. *Journal of Mammalogy,* 58(2):131–156.

Howell, A. B.
1944.   *Speed in Animals.* New York: Hafner Publishing Company.

Lanyon, L. E.
1980.   The influence of function on the development of bone curvature. An experimental study on the rat tibia. *Journal of Zoology,* London, 192:457–466.

Lanyon, L. E., and D. G. Baggott
1976.   Mechanical function as an influence on the structure and form of bone. *Journal of Bone Joint Surgery,* 58-B:436–443.

Lanyon, L. E., and S. Bourn
1979.   The influence of mechanical function on the development and remodelling of the tibia. An experimental study in sheep. *Journal of Bone Joint Surgery,* 61-A:263–273.

Maloiy, G. M. O., R. McN. Alexander, R. Njau and A. S. Jayes
1979.   Allometry of the legs of running birds. *Journal of Zoology,* London, 187:161–167.

McMahon, T.
1973.   Size and shape in biology. *Science,* 179:1201–1204.

1975a. Allometry and biomechanics: limb bones in adult ungulates. *American Naturalist,* 109(969):547–563.

1975b. Using body size to understand the structural design of animals: quadrupedal locomotion. *Journal of Applied Physiology,* 39(4):6 19–627.

1976.   Tree structures: deducing the principles of mechanical design. *Journal of Theoretical Biology,* 59:443–466.

1977.   Scaling quadrupedal galloping: Frequencies, Stresses and joint angles. In *Scale Effects in Animal Locomotion,* edited by T. J. Pedley, pp. 143–150. New York: Academic Press.

Mech, L. D.
1966.   The wolves of Isle Royale. *Fauna of the National Parks U. S., Fauna Series No. 7.*

Medway, G. G.-H.
1969.   *The Wild Mammals of Malaya.* London: Oxford University Press.

Muybridge, E.
1899.   *Animals in Motion.* London: Chapman and Hall, Ltd. (Republished with minor changes, 1957, edited by L. S. Brown. New York: Dover Publishing Company.)

Radinsky, L.
1981a. Evolution of skull shape in carnivores. 1. Representative modern carnivores. *Biological Journal of the Linnean Society,* 15(4):369–388.

1981b. Evolution of skull shape in carnivores. 2. Additional modern carnivores. *Biological Journal of the Linnean Society,* 16:337–355.

1982.   Evolution of skull shape in carnivores. 3. The origin and early radiation of the modern carnivore families. *Paleobiology,* 8: 177–195.

Scott, K. M.
1979.   Adaptation and allometry in bovid postcranial proportions. Unpublished Ph.D. dissertation, Yale University, New Haven.

1985.   Allometric trends and locomotor adaptations in the Bovidae. *Bulletin of the American Museum of Natural History,* 179:197–288.

Simpson, G. G., A. Roe, and R. C. Lewontin
1960.   *Quantitative Zoology.* New York: Harcourt, Brace and World, Inc.

Smith, J. M., and L. C. Savage
1956.   Some locomotory adaptations in mammals. *Journal of the Linnean Society, Zoology,* 42:603–622.

Smith, N. S., and H. P. Ledger
1965.   A method for predicting live weight from dissected leg weight. *Journal of Wildlife Management,* 29:504–511.

Tate, C. H.
1947.   *Mammals of the Pacific World.* New York: McMillen Publishers.

Wainwright, S. A., W. D. Biggs, J. D. Currey, and J. M. Gosline
1967.   *Mechanical Design in Organisms.* New York: John Wiley and Sons.

Walker, E. P.
1968.   *Mammals of the World, 2nd ed.* Baltimore: The Johns Hopkins University Press.

Ward, R.
1896.   *Records of Big Game.* London: Rowland Ward and Company, Ltd.

Whitehead, G. K.
1972.   *Deer of the World.* London: Constable.

Appendix I. Species of the family Cervidae included in this study, with number of specimens measured and body weights used in the regression analyses. Species which are nondimorphic or in which the degree of dimorphism is small are indicated by 'ND' under female weight. Specimen numbers followed by (Z) are zoo specimens; (P) indicates partial specimens.

Species	Weight		Number
	Male	*Female*	
Moschus moschiferus	11	ND	10
Muntiacus muntjak			
M. m. bancanus	19	ND	1
M. m. grandicornis	36	ND	3
M. m. moschatus	25	ND	2
M. m. muntjak	25	ND	1
M. m. pleiharicus	16	ND	6
Muntiacus reevsi	14	12	8
Elaphodus cephalophus	18	ND	13
Dama dama	67	44	1 (Z)
Axis axis	90	60	4
Axis porcinus	50	35	2
Cervus unicolor			
C. u. brookei	121	91	1
C. u. dejeani	???	?	1
C. u. equinus	215	162	2
C. u. francianus	???	?	1
C. u. niger	270	?	1
Cervus timorensis	118	?	1
Cervus duvauceli	230	?	1
Cervus eldi	100	64	1
Cervus nippon	64	41	4
Cervus elephas			
C. e. canadensis	400	250	11
C. e. cashmirensis	200	?	1
C. e. corsicanus	?	?	1
C. e. hispanicus	250	?	1
C. e. hanglu	200	?	2
C. e. nannodes	?	?	2
C. e. scoticus	180	125	1
Elaphurus davidianus	190	ND	7 (Z)
Odocoileus hemionus	91	57	16
Odocoileus virginianus	68	45	14
Mazama americana	29	ND	4
Mazama gouazoubira	18	ND	7
Hippocamelus bisulcus	???	55	1 (P)
Blastocerus dichotomus	100	?	2
Ozotoceros bezoarticus	40	35	2
Pudu pudu	13.5	ND	1
Pudu mephistophiles			2

Appendix I. (cont.)

Species	Weight		Number
	Male	*Female*	
Alces alces	450	318	14
Rangifer tarandus	179	110	12
Hydropotes inermis	12	10	2
Capreolus capreolus	27	21	16

Appendix II. Reduced major axis equations used to compute limb variables.

Bone	b	$\log a$	Correlation Coefficient
Humerus	0.9966	−0.1193	.9895
Radius	1.2240	−0.4133	.9795
Metacarpal	1.3840	−0.6777	.9454
Tibia	0.9986	−0.0452	.9800
Metatarsal	1.1890	−0.3314	.9461

Scott

ADRIAN M. LISTER
Department of Zoology
Downing Street
Cambridge CB2 3EJ
England

Diversity and Evolution of Antler Form in Quaternary Deer

ABSTRACT

The antlers of each of the thirty or so known species of cervid from the European Quaternary are described and illustrated. An enormous diversity of antler structure is revealed, and the size, complexity and general "gestalt" of species' antlers are correlated to their adaptive requirements. There nonetheless remains a high diversity of form within adaptively similar categories of deer: antler form is an extreme example of "multiple solutions to similar requirements"

A detailed examination of selected fossil lineages through the Middle and Upper Pleistocene provides examples of antler evolution at the species level. In the elk lineage there was a reduction in length of the antler beam relative to body size; in the red deer the bez tine was gradually reduced, and a "crown" evolved at the top of the antler. Selective explanations for these transitions can be postulated in terms of changing habitat or social behaviour.

The possible roles of micro-evolution and "quantum" change in creating antler diversity are discussed. One possibility is that all levels of diversity are explicable by accumulated micro-evolution. Another is that basic structural types arise in larger steps whose direction contains a stochastic component, but that these are subsequently "refined" by micro-evolution.

Introduction

The Quaternary is the most recent geological period, extending from ca. 2 million years ago to the present. Many hundreds of dated horizons within the Quaternary of Europe have yielded fossil mammal faunas. These demonstrate considerable faunal changes through time (see e.g., Stuart (1982) for the British Isles). Throughout the Quaternary sequence, Cervidae were consistently one of the dominant large-mammal groups, although the species composition of the cervid fauna was constantly changing. Described species include many which are now extinct, others which were the ancestors of present-day species, and extant species occurring as fossils from the later phases of the Quaternary.

A considerable proportion of research on Quaternary cervids has been devoted to antler remains, which are often abundant as fossils and are generally the most taxonomically diagnostic elements. Antlers, characteristic of the Cervidae, are a pair of bony outgrowths of the skull which are periodically shed and a new set regrown. In contrast to the relative conservatism of other skeletal elements amongst cervid species, antlers display a great variety of form and tendency to evolve. This diversity is achieved by variation in the size, direction and curvature of the beam, in the number, position and form of the branches (tines), in the cross-sectional shape of the beam and tines (especially the provision of areas of flattening or palmation), and in the nature of superficial ornamentation (Figure 1).

In the present paper, I hope firstly to illustrate the diversity of cervid species and their antler form in the European Quaternary (plus a few species from the uppermost Pliocene), reflecting active radiation prior to and during that period. Subsequently I want to focus on some examples of individual species lineages, where evolution of antler form can be followed in detail. Finally, some tentative ideas on the pattern and process of antler evolution will be discussed.

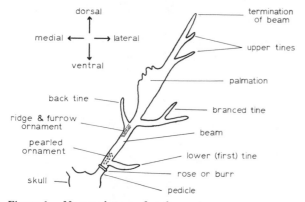

Figure 1.   Nomenclature of antler parts.

Table 1.   Quaternary Time Scale

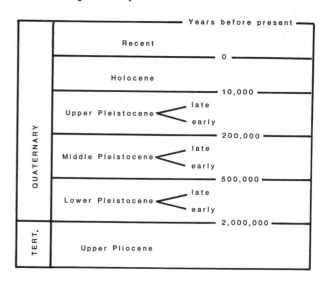

I shall be restricting my comments almost entirely to European fossils. A reasonably detailed stratigraphic sequence has been worked out for the European Quaternary, which enables faunal and evolutionary changes to be traced. Further interesting cervid species occur across Asia, and should ultimately be included in a broader study of Eurasian Quaternary Cervidae. However, this is severely limited at present by the practical problems of comparative research across Eurasia as a whole, as well as by the primitive state of geological correlation over this very large area. In Table 1, a simplified, general time-scale for the Quaternary of Europe is presented for reference. More detailed stratigraphies exist in particular areas, e.g. Britain (Mitchell, Penny, Shotton and West, 1973) and the Netherlands (Zagwijn, 1975). At present, however, only the broad stratigraphic units of Table 1 will allow species found in different parts of Europe to be included in a single scheme. Note that the Plio-Pleistocene boundary is variably placed between 2.7 m.y. and 1.8 m.y. according to different authors, and that the other absolute dates are also tentative.

Diversity of Antler Form in Quaternary Deer

The following inventory includes most if not all valid species described to date from the European Quaternary. Descriptions are based in most cases on my own observation and study of the primary material, in consultation with published sources.

Because of space limitation, and because my basic aim is to illustrate diversity of form, I shall be limiting taxonomic and stratigraphic details to the essentials. Fuller details can be found in the references given. For each species I give an indication of body size on the scale small–medium–large (roughly as Recent European *Capreolus–Cervus–Alces*); the contour length of a typical mature antler; a rough stratigraphical range as currently evidenced; geographical provenance in the case of insular species; and the most recent and/or complete reference(s) in which further information may be found. This is followed by a brief, illustrated description of the adult antler morphology. Note that these descriptions are not intended as full diagnoses of the species of given genera, which are based on skeletal as well as antler characters; also that imperfection of fossil material means that descriptions of some species are incomplete, most often as regards the orientation of the antler with respect to the skull, and the morphology of the distal parts.

Some comments on the problems of defining and recognising fossil deer species, and consequently of assessing species diversity, should be made at this point. The high intraspecific variability of antler form between age-classes, adult individuals, and populations is well-known from present-day species. This, in combination with the frequent lack of large fossil samples, and the rather typological approach of many palaeontologists in the past, has resulted in excessive subdivision of fossil material into genera, species and subspecies. Thus, many more nominal species than those listed here can be found in the literature. More recent workers, however, have paid due attention to these factors, and I believe that the inventory given here is a realistic, if anything minimal, listing of species diversity. Thus, for example, Heintz (1970) was able to show that several putative Lower Pleistocene species were in fact based on various young antler stages of *Croizetoceros ramosus,* and were therefore synonymous with the latter; Kahlke (1956a) showed that numerous nominal Middle Pleistocene species were no more than individual variants of *Megaceros verticornis.* I have not given synonymy lists, as these can be found in the references cited.

I have arranged the species by tribe and genus, but the tribes are not grouped further since their relationships and higher-level classification are in most cases unclear. Subspecies are included only when they show interesting, statistically well-established differences of form.

Tribe Megacerini

Genus *Megaceros* OWEN (early Middle to late Upper Pleistocene). Nomenclature within the tribe Megacerini has been much debated: see Azzaroli (1978–79) for details. Here the simple policy of the latter author in referring all species to the genus *Megaceros* will be followed.

Megaceros giganteus (BLUMENBACH) (late Middle to Upper Pleistocene).

M. g. hiberniae (POHLIG) (large; 120 cm; Upper Pleistocene; Reynolds (1929), Mitchell & Parkes

(1949), Gould (1974)). Figure 2a. Beam turns outwards above rose to lie more or less horizontally for the rest of its length. Brow tine, directly above rose, is bifurcated and/or flattened, often into a broad horizontal palmation. Second tine about half-way along beam anteriorly; back tine a little further along; beam then expands into a broad, flattened palmation bordered by several rather long tines, mostly on its anterior edge. Ridged ornament on proximal part of beam, smooth on palmation.

M. g. antecedens (BERCKHEMER) (large; 100 cm; late Middle Pleistocene; Berckhemer (1941)). Figure 2b. As for *M. g. hiberniae,* except that brow tine expanded into a circular horizontal plate, back tine subsumed within palmation, and palmation somewhat more laterally compressed and upwardly directed.

Megaceros savini (DAWKINS) (medium-large; 120 cm; early Middle Pleistocene; Azzaroli (1953), Kahlke (1956a)). Figure 2c. Beam very long and thin, of flattened section but unpalamated. Very characteristic broadly palmated basal tine whose base, of triangular section, is set directly above the rose but angled obliquely to it. Long, thin second and third tines anteriorly, and back tine posteriorly, then terminal point or fork. Beam turns dorsally in region of back tine. Smooth surface.

Megaceros verticornis (DAWKINS) (large; 100 cm; early Middle Pleistocene; Kahlke (1956a), Azzaroli (1953, 1978–79)). Figure 2d. Beam turns outward from rose to lie almost horizontally in its lower half, then turns sharply upward, forming a right angle, so that its upper half is vertical. Very characteristic first tine, of round section, springs some centimetres from the rose on the antero-internal side of the beam, and turns gradually through an arc to be directed antero-laterally. Just before the upward turn of the beam is the flattened second tine, and on the 'elbow' of the turn a back tine. Upper (vertical) part of beam broadens into a flat palmation which may bear some short tines or offers. In some specimens this palmation is absent (e.g. *M. v. dendroceros:* Ambrosetti (1967)); in others an additional small lower tine occurs below and lateral to the normal "first" tine. Mild ridge-and-furrow ornament on beam.

Megaceros solilhacus (ROBERT) (large; 100 cm; early Middle Pleistocene; Azzaroli (1978–79)). Figure 2e. Related to *M. verticornis,* with large, pointed spade-shaped palmation in upper half.

Megaceros dawkinsi (NEWTON) (medium; 60 cm; early Middle Pleistocene; Azzaroli (1953, 1978–79)). Figure 2f. Beam departs at a rather acute angle from rose, and is often thinner than the pedicle. Lower tine absent or a small basal knob; one or two strong, laterally-flattened, downwardly-directed anterior tines half-way along beam, and a back tine posteriorly; distal palmation of beam which has already begun at the

Figure 2. Antlers of European Quaternary cervid species. L.Pl. = Lower Pleistocene, M.Pl. = Middle Pleistocene, U.Pl. = Upper Pleistocene; e = early, l = late.

a. *Megaceros giganteus hiberniae* POHLIG. Skull and antlers in anterior view. From original photograph of specimen in Senckenberg Museum. l.U.Pl., Ireland.

b. *Megaceros giganteus antecedens* BERCKHEMER. Skull and antlers in anterior view. From Berckhemer (1941, Figure 1). l. M.Pl., Steinheim, Germany.

c. *Megaceros savini* (DAWKINS). Skull and antlers in an-terior view. From Kahlke (1956a, Taf. 15). e.M.Pl., Süssenborn, Germany.

d. *Megaceros verticornis* (DAWKINS). Skull and antlers in antero-lateral view. From Azzaroli (1953) e.M.Pl., Pakefield, England.

e. *Megaceros solilhacus* ROBERT. Left antler, internal view. From Azzaroli (1978–79, Figure 4). e.M.Pl., Solil-hac, France.

f. *Megaceros dawkinsi* (NEWTON). Reconstruction of antlers in antero-lateral view. From Azzaroli (1953). Based on e.M.Pl. specimens from Norfolk, England.

Lister

g. *Megaceros pachyosteus* (YOUNG). Skull and right antler in lateral view. From Pei (1934, Figure 2). l.M.Pl., Choukou'tien, China.

h. *Megaceros cazioti* (DEPERET). Skull and right antler in lateral view. From Caloi and Malatesta (1974, Figure 38). l.U.Pl., Sardinia, Italy.

i. *Candiacervus cerigensis* KUSS. Lateral view of shed antler. From Kuss (1975, Pl.III, Figure f). l.U.Pl., Karpathos, Greece.

j. *Megaceros cretensis* (SIMONELLI). Lateral view of shed antler. From`Azzaroli (1961). l.U.Pl., Crete, Greece.

k. *Eucladoceros dicranios* (NESTI). Skull and antlers in antero-dorsal view. After Pohlig (1982). l.L.Pl., Val d'Arno, Italy.

l. *Eucladoceros senezensis* (DEPERET). Skull and antlers in anterior view. From Heintz (1970, Pl.XI, Figure 1a). l.L.Pl., Senéze, France.

m. *Eucladoceros tetraceros* (DAWKINS). Left shed antler, lateral view. From original photograph of specimen in British Museum (Natural History). l.L.Pl., Peyrolles, France.

n. *Eucladoceros catenoides* (NESTI). Right shed antler, lateral view. From Kunst (1937, Figure 1a). l.L.Pl., Tegelen, Netherlands.

o. *Eucladoceros falconeri* (DAWKINS). Right shed antler in antero-medial view (tines broken off). From Dawkins (1868, Pl.XVIII, Figure 9). e.L.Pl., Norfolk, England.

p. *"Euctenoceros" mediterraneus* BONIFAY. Lateral view of shed antler (base and first tine only). From Bonifay (1969, Figure 3). l.M.Pl., Lunel-Viel, France.

q. *Dama dama dama* (L.). Left antler, medial view. From original photograph of specimen in British Museum (Natural History). Recent, England.

r. *Dama dama mesopotamica* (BROOKE). Left antler, medial view. From original photograph of specimen in the University Museum of Zoology, Cambridge. Recent, Iran.

s. *Rangifer tarandus* (L.). Left antler, medial view. From original photograph of specimen in British Museum (Natural History). Recent, Scandinavia.

t. *"Cervus" cusanus* CROIZET AND JOBERT. Right antler, lateral view. From Heintz (1970, Pl.I, Figure 5). U. Pliocene, Etouaires, France.

u. *Capreolus capreolus* (L.). Skull and antlers in antero-lateral view. From original photograph of specimen in the University Museum of Zoology, Cambridge. Recent, England.

v. *Croizetoceros ramosus* (CROIZET AND JOBERT). Right antler, medial view. From Heintz (1970, Pl.V, Figure 5a). U. Pliocene, Etouaires, France.

w. *Arvernoceros ardei* (CROIZET AND JOBERT). Left antler, lateral view. From Heintz (1970, Pl.XVIII, Figure 1). U. Pliocene, Etouaires, France.

x. *Cervus pardinensis* CROIZET AND JOBERT. Left antler in internal view. From original photograph of specimen in Museum National d'Histoire Naturelle, Paris. U. Pliocene, Etouaires, France.

y. *Cervus philisi* SCHAUB. Right antler, medial view. From Heintz (1970, Pl.IX, Figure 1). l.L.Pl., Senéze, France.

z. *Cervus perrieri* CROIZET AND JOBERT. Left antler in antero-medial view. From Heintz (1970, Pl.IV, Figure 1). U. Pliocene, Etouaires, France.

a'. *Cervus elaphus acoronatus* BENINDE. Right antler in anterior view. From Kahlke (1959, Figure 11). e.M.Pl., Mosbach, Germany.

b'. *Cervus elaphus acoronatus* BENINDE. Top tines, ante-

rior view. From Kahlke (1959, Figure 11). e.M.Pl., Mosbach, Germany.

c'. *Cervus elaphus elaphus* L. Right antler in antero-medial view. From original photograph of specimen in British Museum (Natural History). e.U.Pl.

d'. *Cervus elaphus elaphus* L. Right antler, lateral view. From Lyneborg (1971, Figure 114). Recent, Sweden.

e'. *Alces gallicus* (AZZAROLI). Skull and antlers in posterior view. From Azzaroli (1952). e.M.Pl., Senéze, France.

f'. *Alces latrifrons* JOHNSON. Left and right antlers in anterior view. From Hennig (1952). e.M.Pl., Goldhöfer sands, Germany.

g'. *Alces alces* (L.). Skull and antlers in dorsal view. From Egorov (1967). Recent, Siberia.

level of these tines. Ornament weak.

Megaceros pachyosteus (YOUNG) (medium-large; 80 cm; late Middle Pleistocene, China; Young (1932), Kahlke & Hu (1958)). Figure 2g.

Megaceros yabei (SHIKAMA) (medium-large; 100 cm; Upper Pleistocene, Japan; Shikama and Okafuji (1958)). Although they are from outside the European range, I am taking the liberty of illustrating one of these two species of *Megaceros* from the Far East which show extraordinary developments of the megacerine form. Probably related to *M. giganteus*, they are characterized by enormous, tranversely-palmated spade-shaped brow tines; a long, horizontal beam without "second tine" but leading to a large palmation from which spring a back tine and several terminal tines.

Megaceros cazioti (DEPERET) (small-medium; 80 cm; Upper Pleistocene of Corsica and Sardinia; Caloi and Malatesta (1974)). Figure 2h. Dorso-laterally directed, S-shaped beam. First tine, several centimeters above rose, is cylindrical and ventrally-directed. Second tine, half-way up beam, is short and internally-directed. On main bend of beam is a short back tine; above this, beam flattens into a narrow palmation with rows of short tines ("digitations") on its anterior and posterior borders.

Megaceros cretensis (SIMONELLI) (small; 30 cm; ?late Middle—late Upper Pleistocene, Crete; Malatesta (1980)). Figure 2j. Small, possibly degenerate antlers. Rose very large and sharply angled with respect to pedicle and beam. Tine, several cm above rose, is rather short and antero-dorsally directed. Beam then flattens into a narrow palmation before terminating. Only very occasionally does it bear a second tine, in the plane of the first and rather flattened. Strong ridge-and-furrow ornament.

Megaceros calabriae (BONFIGLIO) (small; ?60 cm; Upper Pleistocene, S.W. Italy; Bonfiglio (1978)). Beams turns horizontally as in *M. giganteus*, and is directed postero-laterally. Basal tine, resting directly on rose, is long, subcylindrical and directed`anteriorly. Second anterior tine, half-way along beam, is somewhat flattened; this is followed by a flattened back tine and then a digitated palmation.

Megaceros messinae (POHLIG) (small; ?40 cm; Upper Pleistocene, Sicily; Caloi (1973)). Poorly known. Basal tine, and broad, probably horizontal palmation. Possibly a scaled-down version of *M. giganteus*.

cf. Tribe Cervini

Genus *Eucladoceros* (FALCONER) (=*Euctenoceros* TROUESSART) ("comb-antlered" deer) (early to late Lower Pleistocene). Many forms have been described; their taxonomy is still rather confused (see Heintz, 1970: Table 75). The following is a minimal estimate of the valid species.

Eucladoceros senezensis (DEPERET)—*E. tetraceros* (DAWKINS) lineage (medium-large; 90 cm; early–late Lower Pleistocene; Heintz (1970)). Figure 2l and m. Beam and tines narrow, smooth, and of roundish or somewhat flattened section. Beam strongly posteriorly inflected at level of first tine. The latter inserted antero-laterally on beam close above rose, then usually three more tines, subequal in length and inserted antero-medially on beam, before the terminal point of the beam. Tines curved medially in *E. senezensis*, straighter in the later *E. tetraceros*.

Eucladoceros sedgwicki (FALCONER) & *E. dicranios* (NESTI) (probably equivalent) (large; 120 cm; ?early–late Lower Pleistocene; Azzaroli (1953), Heintz (1970)). Figure 2k. Beam and tines stout and flattened. First tine inserted anterolaterally 10–15 cm above rose, then 2–3 subsequent tines inserted more medially. Each tine, and terminal section of beam, subdivided into 2, 3 or 4 branches.

Eucladoceros ctenoides (NESTI) and *E. tegulensis* (DUBOIS) (probably equivalent) (large; 75 cm; ?early–late Lower Pleistocene; Kunst (1937)). Figure 2n. Similar to *E. tetraceros* but beam and tines much stouter and with moderate ridge-and-furrow ornament. Beam and tines of oval but not flattened section.

Eucladoceros falconeri (DAWKINS) (medium; 40 cm; early Lower Pleistocene; Azzaroli (1953)). Figure 2o. Beam and tines of oval or somewhat flattened section. First tine inserted anterolaterally a few cm above burr. Second tine short, third tine stronger and flattened; both second and third tines inserted medial to first tine. Smooth surface.

"Euctenoceros" mediterraneus (BONIFAY) (medium; ?60 cm; late Middle Pleistocene; Bonifay (1969)). Figure 2p. The referral of this recently-discovered species to the eucladocerines must be regarded as provisional. Pedicle, and hence beam, diverge widely from midline of skull. Beam thin and round in section. First tine departs gradually from anterolateral side of beam a little above rose, forming an acute or right angle with the beam, and is very long, thin and slightly sinuous.

Beam continues without further tines for a long distance, before being broken off in all known specimens, so the existence and nature of higher tines is unknown. Mild ridge-and-furrow ornament.

Tribe Cervini

Genus *Dama* (FRISCH) (early Middle Pleistocene–Recent).

Dama dama (L.) (medium; 70 cm; early Middle Pleistocene–Recent; Haltenorth (1959), Leonardi & Petronio (1976)).

D. d. dama (L.) (Upper Pleistocene–Recent). Figure 2q. Beam departs rather laterally from rose. First tine, cylindrical, springs directly above rose and is directed antero-ventrally. Second tine half-way along beam, then back tine as beam turns more dorsally, then a broad, thin, sagitally-aligned palmation with short tines springing from its posterior border.

D. d. clactoniana (NEWTON) (Middle Pleistocene). As for *D. d. dama*, but with an additional third anterior tine above the second, and a narrower palmation.

(N. B. *D. d. mesopotamica* (BROOKE) of the Near East (Figure 2r) differs from *D. d. dama* in that the brow tine is reduced, the second tine is flattened, and the palmation forms at the apex of the beam only.)

Genus *Cervus* L. (Middle Pliocene–Recent).

Cervus pardinensis (CROIZET & JOBERT)–*Cervus philisi* (SCHAUB)–*Cervus perolensis* (BRAVARD) lineage (small to medium; 60 cm; Upper Pliocene–late Lower Pleistocene; Heintz (1970)). Figure 2x and y.

C. pardinensis (Upper Pliocene). Beam, dorso-laterally oriented, more or less straight and of round section. First tine, short and stout, diverges gradually from beam a short distance above rose, forming an angle of approximately 70 degrees. At the insertion of this tine the beam is convex medially, concave laterally. Second tine half-way up beam and forming an angle of around 40 degrees with it. Both tines anterior and of round section. Somewhat pearled ridge-and-furrow ornament.

C. philisi (early Lower Pleistocene). Similar to *C. pardinensis* but with longer first tine.

C. pardinensis (late Lower Pleistocene). Poorly known.

Cervus perrieri (CROIZET & JOBERT) (medium; 80 cm; Upper Pliocene; Heintz (1970)). Figure 2z. Beam rather straight and dorsally-directed, round or slightly oval in section. Three simple tines, of subcircular section, are placed anteriorly on the beam: the first, just above the rose, at approximately 90 degrees to the beam; the second, one half to, two-thirds up the beam, somewhat more acute; the third, near top of beam, forming a symmetrical 45 degree fork with the beam end. Mild ridge-and-furrow ornament, slightly pearled. Possible the form nearest the ancestry of *C. elaphus* (red deer).

Cervus elaphus L. (medium to large; 90 cm; early Middle Pleistocene to Recent; Beninde (1937), Ahlén (1965)). Figure 2a′,b′,c′,d′. Two basal tines anteriorly, the second (bez) above and somewhat lateral to the first (brow); third (trez) tine anterior and half-way up the beam; simple fork or many-pointed "crown" at top of beam. Pearled ornament. See further, Evolution of Antler Form within Lineages, below.

Tribe Rangiferini

Genus *Rangifer* (L.) (early Middle Pleistocene–Recent).

Rangifer tarandus (L.) (medium; 90 cm; early Middle Pleistocene–Recent; Spiess (1979)). Figure 2s. Beam, smooth and of round or oval section, is directed postero-laterally in its lower part, but turns through a large arc so that its end points anteriorly. One, or often two, lower tines are variably laterally-flattened into palmations with terminal points. Further tines are rather variable but usually include a back tine mid-way along the beam, and further back tines springing from the upper part of the beam, which often becomes flattened into a narrow palmation.

Cf. Tribe Capreolini

"*Cervus*" *cusanus* (CROIZET & JOBERT) (small; 30 cm; Upper Pliocene; Heintz (1970)). Figure 2t. Antler short and transversely flattened, with 3–5 points aligned in the antero-posterior plane. First tine half-way up beam on anterior side; second tine above it on posterior side. Second tine and end of beam may be forked in old individuals. Strong ridged ornament. Similar in form to *Capreolus*, to which it might be ancestral. Attribution of *Cervus* is dubious.

Tribe Capreolini

Genus *Capreolus* (HAMILTON SMITH) (early Middle Pleistocene–Recent).

Capreolus capreolus (L.) (small; 25 cm; early Middle Pleistocene–Recent; Azzaroli (1953), Stuart (1982)). Figure 2u. Antlers simple, vertical, and heavily pearled. Most usually three points: an anterior tine well up the beam, a second tine posteriorly, and the termination of the beam.

Tribe Alcini

Genus *Alces* (GRAY) (late Lower Pleistocene–Recent). Pedicle departs horizontally from skull. Beam continues in lateral direction, without lower tines, and then expands into a broad terminal palmation bordered by numerous tines. Strong ridged and/or pearled ornament.

A. gallicus (AZZAROLI) (medium; 90 cm; late Lower Pleistocene; Azzaroli (1952)). Figure 2e . Beam up to palmation is very long and thin.

A. latifrons (JOHNSON) (large; 100 cm; early Middle Pleistocene; Kahlke (1956a & 1959)). Figure 2f . Beam up to palmation is long but stout.

A. alces (L.) (large; 60 cm; Upper Pleistocene–Recent; Szymczyk (1973)). Figure 2g′. Beam up to palmation is short and stout. See further, Section III below.

Tribe incertae sedis

Genus *Candiacervus* (KUSS) (?late Middle–Upper Pleistocene, E. Mediterranean islands; Kuss (1975)). *Candiacervus cerigensis* (KUSS) (small; 30 cm) Figure 2i; and *C. pigadiensis* (KUSS) (small–medium; 40 cm). Rose steeply angled; beam vertical except at tip where it turns posteriorly. Lower third of beam naked of tines; on the upper two-thirds three or four short tines are equally spaced on the anterior side of the beam. Beam and tines of round or oval section, and with a strong ridge-and-furrow ornament.

Genus *Croizetoceros* (HEINTZ) (Upper Pliocene–late Lower Pleistocene)

Croizetoceros ramosus (CROIZET & JOBERT) (small-medium; 60 cm; Upper Pliocene–late Lower Pleistocene; Heintz (1970)). Figure 2v. Beams rather divergent from skull, and lyre-shaped. Beam of rather compressed, piriform section. All tines are on anterior side of beam and oriented in antero-posterior plane, and all are curved upwards. First tine several cm above rose. Second tine simple or branched, and longer than first. Then a series of one to four more tines, decreasing in size toward the apex of the beam.

Genus *Arvernoceros* (HEINTZ) (Upper Pliocene)

Arvernoceros ardei (CROIZET & JOBERT) (medium; 60 cm; Upper Pliocene; Heintz (1970)). Figure 2w. First tine, anteriorly placed some distance above rose, usually has a small branch. Beam turns strongly toward the posterior at level of first tine, and then proceeds, long, straight, of circular section and without further tines, until its terminal part where a palmation with up to three forwardly directed points is formed. Moderate ridge-and-furrow ornament.

Discussion

The above account shows that approximately thirty distinct species of Cervidae occurred in Europe during the past two million years. A summary list, showing stratigraphic ranges, is given in Table 2. Approximately one-fifth of the described species are endemic island forms, which probably evolved from isolated populations of mainland species (Azzaroli, 1961). Of the mainland forms themselves, it can be seen from Table 2 that approximately half a dozen species oc-

Table 2.   Stratigraphic range of European Quaternary cervid species

	Upper Pliocene	Early Lower Pleistocene	Late Lower Pleistocene	Early Middle Pleistocene	Late Middle Pleistocene	Early Upper Pleistocene	Late Upper Pleistocene	Recent
Mainland Species								
Cervus elaphus				x	x	x	x	x
Dama dama				x	x	x	x	x
Capreolus capreolus				x	x	x	x	x
Megaceros giganteus					x	x	x	
Megaceros verticornis				x				
Megaceros dawkinsi				x				
Megaceros savini				x				
Alces alces							x	x
Alces latifrons				x				
Alces gallicus			x					
Eucladoceros senezensis & E. tetraceros		x	x					
Eucladoceros ctenoides & E. tegulensis		?	x					
Eucladoceros sedgwicki & E. dicranios		?	x					
Eucladoceros falconeri		x						
Cervus perolensis/ Cervus philsi/ Cervus pardinensis	x		x	x				
Croizetoceros ramosus	x	x	x					
Arvernoceros ardei	x							
Cervus perrieri	x							
"Cervus" cusanus	x							
Island Species								
Megaceros cazioti							x	
Megaceros cretensis						x	x	
Megaceros messinae							x	
Megaceros calabriae							x	
Candiacervus cerigensis & C. pigadiensis							x	

curred on mainland Europe during any one of the main stratigraphic divisions used here. Although the species present during a particular division were not necessarily all sympatric nor even always exactly chronosynchronous, detailed examination of site records [see, e.g., Heintz (1970), Stuart (1982)] suggests that in the majority of cases there was at least some degree of spatio-temporal overlap between the half-dozen or so species.

As might be expected on grounds of resource partitioning, each stratigraphic division generally contains both small, medium and large species. The most striking observation, however, is the extraordinary range of antler form which occurred over the sequence as a whole. The beam may be upright or horizontal, straight or curved, narrow or flattened or palmated; and similarly each species has a characteristic set of tines of particular position and form, with each tine short or long, narrow or palmated, directed forward or outward or upward; and so on.

The range of shape is not, of course, infinite, and a comparative study would allow categorization of the forms and yield insights into constraints. An explication of the diversity and of its limits must invoke adaptive aspects of ecology and behaviour, mechanical and physiological contraints, the legacy of inheritance, and an element of chance. This will be discussed further (see Evolution of Antler Form within Lineages, below).

Evolution of Antler Form within Lineages

The phylogenetic relationships between the different cervid genera described above, and even between the species within each genus, are in most cases not well known. Some sequences of species do, however, appear to form an approximate ancestor-descendent series, i.e. they are more or less on a direct line of descent. By focussing on the changes undergone by such a sequence, or by a single species during its history, the evolutionary development of a particular antler form can be investigated. Examples include the *Cervus pardinensis, C. philisi, C. perolensis* lineage, and that of *Croizetoceros ramosus*, for both of which antler evolution has been described by Heintz (1970). Here I have selected two other examples for illustration: the red deer (*Cervus elaphus*) through its Middle and Upper Pleistocene history in Western Europe; and the three successive species of the elk lineage (*Alces* spp.) from the late Lower Pleistocene to the Recent.

Before describing these antler sequences, a note on the problems of detecting evolutionary change in antler form is necessary. The notorious individual variation to which antlers within a population are subject, due both to yearly development and to differ-

ences between individuals of the same age-class, must constantly be borne in mind when interpreting differences between fossil samples. Firstly, it is essential to have a sufficient sample-size of antlers from each population or species to be compared, so that common underlying basic features can be separated from the individual variation which overlies them. Secondly, the sequence of yearly development must be taken into account. A comparison between second-year heads of one species and sixth-year heads of another could lead to very misleading conclusions about evolutionary change. It is not generally possible to give a precise age-class to a fossil antler; but with a reasonable sample of antlers of various ages one can often reconstruct a general sequence of head development, with the pricket at one end and the most fully formed mature antlers at the other (see, e.g., Heintz, 1970, for examples). Valid comparisons are then possible between two populations, both in terms of the actual sequence of antler development in each population, and, most usually, by comparing the most mature heads of each population. The latter provide a fixed point for assessment and comparison of size and form, since they represent the fullest expression of the genotypic and environmental forces acting on each population. They are usually well-represented in fossil samples, both because the developmental plateau lasts several years, and because strong antlers are most easily preserved as fossils. Thirdly, true evolutionary change (i.e., with a genetic basis) should if possible be separated from environmentally induced change such as stunting of antlers due to poor feeding. The latter is usually recognizable by its effects on other parts of the skeleton, and by its tendency to shift the strength of the antler as a whole, and perhaps the ages at which successive stages of development occur, rather than the actual form of the antler stages themselves. Finally, if at all possible, samples from various fossil localities in each time sector should be examined, so that evolutionary trends in the species as a whole can be separated from inter-population variation, so well known from the occurrence of local idiosyncrasies of antler structure in present-day species. This is not to say that such inter-site variation is not of interest: indeed, it may play an important role in the evolution of the species as a whole.

The Elk: Length of the Antler Beam

It is very likely on stratigraphical and anatomical grounds that the European elks *Alces gallicus* (Lower Pleistocene), *Alces latifrons* (Middle Pleistocene), and *Alces alces* (Upper Pleistocene) form a more-or-less direct line of descent. The differences in antler proportions between these species represent a most striking evolutionary transition. The basic alcine antler form is present in all three species: a horizontal, laterally directed beam terminating in a broad, digitated palmation. But the relative length of the beam has undergone drastic change. The form of the palmation may also have changed (Kahlke, 1956a), but as this is difficult to quantify and as the palmation is in any case usually broken in fossil specimens, this aspect will be omitted here and only the proportions of the beam considered.

Alces gallicus *to* Alces latifrons

Both Lower and Middle Pleistocene *Alces* species are characterized by very long antler beams, in comparison with the Upper Pleistocene *A. alces*. See Figure 2, e′–g′. The type skeleton of *A. gallicus* from the late Lower Pleistocene of Senèze, France (Figure 2e′) is the largest known specimen of the species, clearly representing a fully grown adult animal. The length of each antler beam (measured from the rose to the beginning of the palmation) is 60 cm; the total antler-span, with palmations restored, was approximately 2.4m (Azzaroli, 1952, and personal measurements). In a sample of *A. gallicus* from the English late Lower Pleistocene locality of East Runton, a range of age stages are represented, with the largest antlers comparable to the Senèze specimen, approx. 50 cm from rose to palmation (Lister, unpub. data).

Turning to *A. latifrons*, the large sample of approximately 30 measurable antlers from the early Middle Pleistocene locality of Mosbach, Germany (Kahlke, 1959) may be cited, covering the whole range from young to fully mature antlers. Several skulls with both antlers are preserved; these indicate complete antler spans of 2–2.5 m, as in the type of *A. gallicus*. Actual beam lengths from rose to palmation may be somewhat reduced relative to *A. gallicus*: most mature specimens measure around 40 cm, although a few reach 50 cm. Similar dimensions are found in *A. latifrons* samples from other sites (e.g., Kahlke, 1956a and b; Figure 2f′).

But this apparent lack of change, or slight reduction in length, between *A. gallicus* and *A. latifrons*, must be viewed in the light of the great difference in body size between the two species. Abundant skeletal material shows that whereas *A. gallicus* was an elk of very small size, *A. latifrons* was very large, exceeding even the Recent *A. alces* in size (Azzaroli, 1953). Measurement of teeth and bones shows *A. latifrons* to have been approximately 1.5 times larger in linear dimensions than *A. gallicus* (Lister, unpub. data). *A. gallicus* stood perhaps 1.3 m at the shoulder (Azzaroli, 1952), comparable to a Recent European red deer. In *A. latifrons* this figure was perhaps 2.2 m. Thus the apparent constancy or slight reduction of antler beam length from *A. gallicus* to *A. latifrons* can be seen in relative terms as a

very marked reduction of beam length in relation to body size. If *A. latifrons* had been simply scaled up isometrically from *A. gallicus*, its antlers would have had a span of 1.5×2.4 m = 3.6 m, or even more if the positive allometry of antler size with body size normal between cervid species (Gould, 1974) is allowed. Selection against such monstrously large antlers may well have been the cause of the relative reduction in beam length between *A. gallicus* and *A. latifrons*, at a time when (unknown) selective forces were bringing about great increase in body size. Selective pressure would have been provided by the great energy requirement for growth, weight to be borne by the skull, and adverse effects on maneuverability.

Notes: (i) Samples of both *Alces gallicus* and *A. latifrons* include a range of young antler stages which in each species are isometrically scaled-down versions of the mature ones. Thus the difference in beam proportioning between the species was consistent along the series of antler development. Nonetheless it is conceivable that there might have been a difference in the rate (in terms of absolute age) at which the developmental plateau of mature antlers was reached. This cannot be tested, since the young stages cannot be aged to their precise year, but only placed in approximate order.

(ii) The larger body and skull size of *A. latifrons* is reflected in a greater diameter of the pedicle, and hence of the antler beam, at any given beam length, than in *A. gallicus*. Thus the reduced beam length/body size ratio in *A. latifrons* is reflected in a reduced ratio of beam length/diameter.

Alces latifrons *to* Alces alces

In mature antlers of recent European *Alces alces*, the length of the beam from rose to palmation rarely exceeds 20 cm (see e.g. data in Erdbrink, 1954), and the total antler span is rarely greater than 1.2 m. This represents a very marked decrease in beam length from *A. latifrons*, only a very small part of which could be accounted for by the approximately 10–15% linear reduction of body size from *A. latifrons* to *A. alces* (Lister, unpub. data). In other words, there has been a second decrease in relative antler length in the alcine lineage; this time, because body size has not itself increased, resulting in a very marked decrease in *absolute* length. And since pedicle diameter, following body and skull size, is somewhat lower at any corresponding point in the age sequence than in *A. latifrons*, the reduction in beam length/body size ratio again results in a lower beam length/diameter ratio at any point in the age sequence.

For the *A. latifrons*–*A. alces* transition, changes in the known habitat of the species provide a clue to the cause of the reduction in antler length. *A. latifrons* inhabited grassy, herbaceous, rather open habitats (Kahlke, 1959; Sher, 1974), whereas the living *A. alces* is an inhabitant of coniferous forests, chiefly the taiga. Long, outstretched antlers may have been ideal display organs in an open environment, but in a forest they would impede movement (Soergel, 1918).

*The Red Deer (*Cervus elaphus *L.): Strength of the Bez Tine*

In Recent European red deer, the second (bez) tine nearly always appears one or two years later than the first (brow), and in older antlers is almost always the weaker of the two (see Figure 2d'). Beninde (1937) noted, however, that in Middle Pleistocene fossils of the species, the bez was often as strong as, and sometimes even stronger than, the brow. In this section I attempt to chart this change in detail.

The 'strength' of a tine is a resultant of its length and girth. In many fossil antlers the ends of the tines are broken off, so that girth at the base of the tine is the only feasible measure of tine strength. Here I have measured brow and bez tine strength as the circumference of each tine at its base, using a small flexible tape. In Figure 3a I have plotted the basal circumference of brow and bez tines against one another for samples of antlers from two Holocene deposits in England: a sample of 45 antlers from the eary Holocene of Star Carr (ca. 9500 BP), and one of 37 antlers from the Cambridgeshire Fens (7000–3000 BP). In this plot, specimens towards the top and right of the scatter tend to be larger and older antlers, whereas those towards the bottom and left are smaller and younger ones.

A few antlers (lying on the diagonal line) have brow and bez tines of equal strength; in all the others the bez is weaker than the brow (points below the line), as in Recent red deer. (Note that the absence of a tine is plotted as zero circumference.)

In Figure 3b are plotted antlers from numerous British Pleistocene localities. The sites, grouped into four stratigraphic categories, are:—Early Middle Pleistocene: West Runton, Trimingham, Pakefield, Bacton, Overstrand, Sidestrand, Happisburgh; Late Middle Pleistocene: Clacton, Hoxne, Swanscombe; Upper Pleistocene: Ilford, Crayford, Stutton, Brundon, Trafalgar Square, Brentford, Westminster, Pall Mall, Acton, Barrington, Barnwell Abbey, Tornewton Cave, Easton Torrs. Information on these localities may be found in Sutcliffe (1960), Stuart (1982), and references therein.

Note that the scatters of all three Pleistocene stratigraphic groups are displaced relative to the Holocene samples of Figure 4a, with many specimens having a bez tine of strength equal to or greater than the brow tine. This appears to be most pronounced for the early Middle Pleistocene sample.

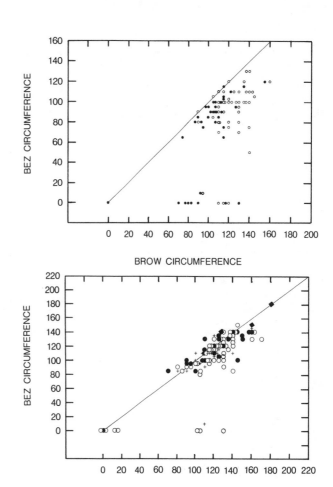

Figure 3. Relative circumference of brow and bez tines in *C. elaphus* antlers. The diagonal line designates equal circumference of brow and bez tines. *Upper graph:* Holocene samples (open and closed circles). *Lower graph:* Pleistocene samples; closed circles = early Middle Pleistocene, crosses = late Middle Pleistocene, open circles = Upper Pleistocene.

It may next be determined whether this shift in relative size was due to decrease of the bez tine, or to increase of the brow tine, or to a combination of the two. In Figures 4a and 5, brow circumference and bez circumference are plotted separately against beam circumference at the base of the antler, for the early Middle Pleistocene and Star Carr Holocene samples. (N.B. Basal beam circumference is an index of the general size of the basal part of the antler, and is roughly proportional both to the age and size of the animal (see, e.g., Hattemer and Dreschler, 1976). It therefore acts as a suitable abscissa against which to view the development, with size and age in a population, of a particular antler structure, and to compare the size and form of that structure between populations, since the age and size composition of the samples are thereby taken into account. Points to the left of the scatter are small, young individuals; points to the right, large, older ones.)

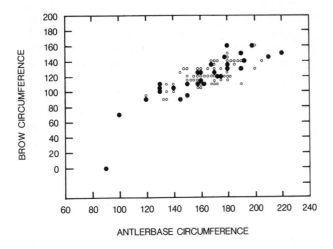

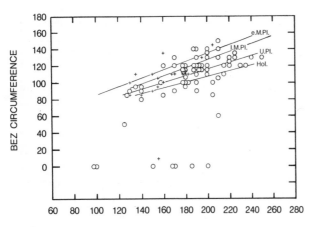

Figure 4. Bez tine circumference of *C. elaphus* antlers. Symbols as in Figure 3. Regression lines for each of the four samples are shown in the lower graph.

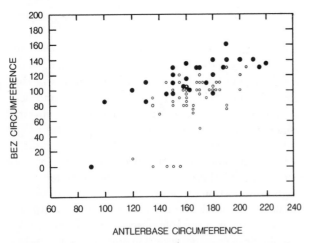

Figure 5. Brow tine circumference of *C. elaphus* antlers. Symbols as in Figure 3.

In Figure 5, the scatters coincide, showing that brow tine strength does not differ between the early Middle Pleistocene and Holocene samples. In Figure 4a, on the other hand, there is a clear displacement of scatters, with the early Middle Pleistocene antlers possessing a stronger bez tine than the Holocene ones at any given antler base size. Thus the change in relative strength of the two tines seems due to reduction of the bez rather than to increase of the brow.

In Figure 4b, the bez tines of the two samples of intermediate age are plotted. Superimposed are their least squares regression lines, and those of the early Middle Pleistocene and Holocene samples of Figure 4a; specimens whose bez tine is vestigial or absent were excluded from calculations of regressions. It can be seen that there was a directional, step-by-step reduction in strength of the bez tine from early Middle Pleistocene to late Middle Pleistocene to Upper Pleistocene to Holocene. T-testing for difference in elevation of the regression lines shows the trend to be statistically significant (Figure 6).

This result is somewhat crude in that the various sites contributing to each stratigraphic grouping are not all of exactly the same age. Thus there may have been changes in bez strength *within* each stratigraphic group which are not revealed by this analysis. However, the individual site samples available to us at present are not large enough to test for this.

Although the above analysis has been based on tine circumferences only, my observations of those Pleistocene antlers in which the bez is more or less fully preserved suggest that basal circumference does reflect overall tine size, and that the Pleistocene bez tines of greater circumference were larger and stronger in general. An example is shown in Figure 2c′.

The reason for this apparent decline in strength of the bez tine through the Quaternary history of *C. elaphus* is difficult to deduce. In the possession of a bez tine, *C. elaphus* is alone amongst deer of similar antler form (chiefly other species of *Cervus:* cf. Section "Diversity of Antler Form in Quartenary Deer" above). In Recent *C. elaphus* stags, the bez tine acts along with the brow tine to protect the eyes and face during fights, and sometimes to anchor the antler in the ground to help the stag hold its ground. Reduction of this tine might reflect a change in fighting technique, or conceivably in the method of display. Alternatively, it is possible that the change may not have been selected for *per se*, but have occurred by genetic drift or as a corollary (e.g., by pleiotropy) of some other change.

The Red Deer: Origin of the "Crown"

Above the brow and bez tines, *C. elaphus* possesses a third tine about halfway up the beam, and then two or more 'top tines' at the end of the beam. In living East

Lister

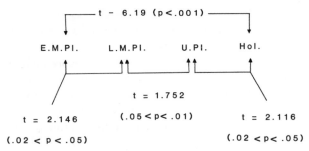

Figure 6. Results of t-tests of y-displacement of regression lines $(\bar{x} + \bar{x}_1/2)$ for bez tine data of different stratigraphic categories presented in Figure 4.

Asian populations of the species, there are generally only two top tines, forming a simple fork, or if further points are present, they all lie in the same plane (Flerov, 1952). The living red deer of Europe, however, and to a lesser degree those of Western Asia, characteristically possess in mature individuals a "crown" in which three or more top tines are arranged in a complex, three-dimensional structure of variable form (Figure 2c',d').

The question of the evolutionary origin of the "crown" has evoked considerable interest, especially since in the early Middle Pleistocene, European red deer appear inherently to have lacked a crown (Beninde, 1937; Kahlke, 1956a and b). The best-known such 'acoronate' fossil population is that of Mosbach, Germany. The large sample of antlers from this site includes many which clearly belonged to mature animals in their prime (seen from their size and stoutness, the fact that they are the strongest in a large sample, and from features of attached skulls). Yet in the vast majority of specimens, there are only two top tines, forming a stout, simple fork transverse to the long axis of the body (Beninde, 1937; Figure 2a'). (The very few exceptions will be discussed below.) Similarly, in the smaller samples from other early Middle Pleistocene localities, the antler always ends in a simple fork and a crown never forms (e.g. Mauer: Beninde (1937) and personal observations: Boigtstedt: Kahlke (1956b); Süssenborn: Kahlke (1956a)).

In fossil red deer from late Middle Pleistocene localities, by contrast, a well-formed, cup-like crown of up to six points is generally present. Examples include Steinheim, Germany (Beninde, 1937), and Swanscombe, England (Lister, 1986). And in all subsequent Upper Pleistocene and Holocene samples up to the present day, the crown is preserved. It therefore appears that the crown originated in Europe between the early Middle Pleistocene of Mosbach, Mauer, etc. (ca. 500,000–400,000 BP), and the late Middle Pleistocene of Steinheim and Swanscombe (ca. 300,000–200,000

BP). A lack of well-dated samples of intermediate age prohibits us at present from further investigation of the transition. Some of the specimens from Mosbach and Mauer are, however, themselves of interest in possibly showing the beginnings of crown evolution (Beninde, 1937; Kleinschmidt, 1938). In a very few antlertops from these sites, representing perhaps 10% of the sample, a small third point is present between the two main points of the terminal fork. An example is shown in Figure 2b'. Whether these specimens were simply variants not connected to the subsequent development of a crown, or whether they were indeed a first step in direct ancestry of later crown evolution as Beninde (1937) believed, is not known.

The selective explanation for the origin of the crown probably lies in its role in fighting and/or display. The latter may have been the more important, since the crowns rarely come into play when stags lock antlers (Clutton-Brock, et al., 1979). It is an interesting fact that the crown, from its presumed Middle Pleistocene origin in Europe or Western Asia, has spread only minimally into populations further east. (Indeed, Kahlke (1959) noted that antler tops of *C. elaphus* from China today are quite similar to the acronate ones of the European early Middle Pleistocene.) This might be explained by the breaks of distribution, and hence of gene flow, seen in red deer across Asia at the present day; however, these breaks may be of fairly recent origin (Flerov, 1952).

Discussion

It is thus possible to demonstrate antler evolution within species, and through successions of species, and in some cases to suggest plausible adaptive explanations for the changes. In the case of the elk, the postulated selective forces were first mechanical (control of antler size) and then habitat-related (prevention of interference). In the case of the red deer (crown and bez tine), they were concerned with social behavior, particularly display and fighting. There may perhaps have been a functional connection between the reduction of the bez and the development of the crown in red deer, since both contribute to a distal shift of mass of the antler as a whole.

Only for the *C. elaphus* bez tine, which shows a stepwise transition across four levels, can we state with some confidence that our evolutionary sequence was a "gradual" one. In the elk sequence, we have three successive samples such that in the two steps between them the antlers evolve in the same direction. This sampling is still rather coarse, and samples of intermediate ages would be of great interest. For the *C. elaphus* crown, we have essentially witnessed a simple transition from one level to another, although the earlier population gives a possible hint of the initiation of this transition. In none of these examples can we be certain whether we are witnessing evolution *in situ,* or waves of already-evolved new types entering Western Europe from elsewhere.

General Discussion

Earlier in this paper, the large number of European Quaternary cervid species was illustrated, each with its peculiar antler form. Subsequently, evolutionary change of antler form within species or genus lineages was demonstrated. I wish now to discuss these two aspects and their interrelationships.

Looking first at the diversity of antler form certain generalizations can be made. There is fairly good correlation of antler size with body size, and the most elaborate antlers tend to occur mostly among the larger species. The tendency for horizontally outspread antlers is also commonest amongst larger forms. Such correlations have their bases in the general categorization of adaptive strategy, seen amongst deer species at the present day (see Chaplin, 1975; Barrette, 1977; Clutton-Brock, et al., 1980). Thus, small solitary forest-dwelling species tend to have small, weapon-like antlers; larger, gregarious species, with more pronounced social competition, have relatively larger and more complex antlers, usually with an array of medium-sized points which can be directed forward to engage the opponent in a test of strength and skill. Clutton-Brock, et al. (1980) have suggested that the allometric increase of antler size and complexity with body size (see also Gould, 1974, Figure 1) is due primarily to a correlation with polygamy and the intensity of inter-male competition, rather than with body size *per se.* In turn, these features also correlate with the trend from more closed to more open habitats (Geist, this volume). Thus differences in social structure, behavior and habitat may account for the residual variation in antler size and complexity seen between species of similar body size. The relatively large and complex antlers of *Megaceros cazioti* (Figure 2h), compared to those of other "small" species, provide an example of such variation. Geist (1971 and this volume) has invoked a historical perspective, suggesting that antler size and complexity may in some species reflect past dispersal history, large antlers having evolved at a time of immigration into vacant areas of high-quality habitat which favored rapid growth and early reproduction.

In some living species, antlers are used not only in actual fights, but also in "display", during both male-female and male-male interactions (e.g. Lincoln, 1972). Areas of palmation, for example, are utilized in this way in species such as *Dama dama* (Geist, 1971 and

this volume; Gould, 1974). In the Pleistocene fauna, several of the antler types may be envisaged as having had a display role in part. The horizontally outstretched, palmated antlers of *Alces latifrons* and *Megaceros giganteus* have been regarded as a solution to the requirements of a large, open-ground form with social behavior dominated by ritual display (Coope, 1973). The "display" usage has been interpreted as aiding status assessment between males (including "bluffing": Geist, this volume), and/or mate choice by females. Fisher (1930) suggested that female choice might sometimes result in "runaway selection" which could produce great elaboration of male social structures; see West-Eberhard (1983) for discussion. On the other hand, some authors have questioned the evidence for mate choice or status assessment based on antler size and structure (Clutton-Brock, et al., 1980, 1982); this would imply that the display role was not an important selective force on antler form. Further evidence is required on these questions.

The physical nature of the habitat may also influence antler form. For example, in forest-dwelling species the antlers are likely to be streamlined so that they do not impede movement, whereas on more open ground this constraint is lifted and more outspread antlers are possible (Bubenik, 1973). This may account for Geist's observation (this volume) that deer living in dense vegetation tend to have their main antler mass more proximally placed, whereas distal antler mass is usually found in more open-country forms. Geist also suggests that radial branching, in which the tines divide secondarily, is common in deer living in swamps, bogs and fens, but it is unknown whether this correlation has adaptive significance or is fortuitous.

In these ways, inter-species differences in the size, degree of elaboration, and overall "gestalt" of antlers are explicable in terms of the different ecological niches and social behavior of the species. Yet it is hard to believe that the enormous variety of detailed ways in which antlers are elaborated can fully be accounted for by differences in social structure, behavior and habitat. Take, for example, the antlers of the three species *Eucladoceros dicranios* (Figure 2k) *Megaceros savini* (Figure 2c) and *Megaceros verticornis* (Figure 2d). All are the highly elaborated antlers of large cervids, and yet each is quite differently constructed, both in the general pattern of tines and palmation, and in details such as the form of the brow tine. Although these differences may well have been associated with certain differences in display and fighting behavior, I do not believe that they need imply correspondingly important differences in the habitat or sociobiology of the species. As Geist (1971) states: "it may be that palmation or the sprouting of tines in a brushlike form are simply alternatives to the same type of selection". Simpson (1949, pp 165–168) invoked the concept of "multiple solutions to similar requirements" in this vein, and adduced the variety of antelope horns as an example. See also Geist (1966), and especially West-Eberhard (1983), on the diversity of "social structures" in various animal groups. Given the framework of antler size and general "gestalt" suitable for the ecology and behavior of a cervid species, and provided the antler form is recognizable to conspecifics and developmentally feasible, a range of possible structures would probably have been acceptable for many species; and hence it seems likely that a considerable contingent element may have operated in the production of the diversity of antler form.

A new antler structure would become established in a population by the essentially neo-Darwinian process of an individual variant becoming population-characteristic, by natural selection and/or because it arose in a small isolate or founder population. Antlers are a "special case" simply in their unusually high capacity for producing variants, and in the variety of forms which would be acceptable for a given adaptive requirement.

In addition to adaptive functional constraints, the range of possibilities for a species will always be constrained to a greater or lesser extent by developmental factors and the legacy of inheritance. In some genera or subfamilies, certain aspects of form are strongly conserved between species. In the genus *Eucladoceros*, for example, all the species may be viewed as variants on a common theme which was presumably established in the common ancestor of the group and became genetically entrenched. Again, there may have been a considerable contingent element in the original establishment of this basic framework (e.g., the eucladocerine arrangement of first tine antero-lateral, succeeding tines anterior). Other taxa, such as *Megaceros*, were less constrained, and produced a wide variety of forms.

Geist (1971, Figure 6; this volume, Figure 2) classified various living and fossil deer species according to the number of points in their basic antler plan and whether they were elaborated by the addition of supernumerary points or palmation. It should be remembered that the columns in Geist's figure illustrate different grades of antler complexity but not actual phyletic sequences. While it is true that the process of cervid evolution has included the appearance of successively more elaborated antler types, this has happened in parallel in many different lineages and, most pertinent to the present argument, in many different ways. Thus a "five-point" antler, for example, has

been achieved in various species, with quite different antler configurations. Examples of this can easily be found from Figure 2 of the present paper, as well as from Geist's (1971) Figure 6, and Pocock's (1933) review of antler forms in living cervid species.

Even to rather specific functional needs there have been divergent solutions. For example, a guard against damage to the head during fights is provided by "brow" tines in many species (e.g. *Cervus*, *Rangifer*), by expanded burrs in others (e.g. *Capreolus*), and by the inward curvature of the main beams in others (e.g. *Odocoileus*) (Bubenik, 1973). The tines engaged during fights are in *Cervus* spp. on the anterior side of the beam, in *Odocoileus* spp. on the posterior side, but because of the different curvature of the beam in the two groups, the points in each case come to point forwards when the head is lowered. These various functional aspects cannot be considered separately: the nature of the defensive guard, attacking points, and areas of display value, together form a functional whole in each species. But the nature of that whole may vary widely between species of relatively similar size and ecology.

Finally, the various secondary uses to which antlers are put, should be mentioned. These include such activities as preparing wallows in the ground, picking up brushy twigs for added ornamentation, and knocking fruit from trees (Chapman, 1975). Parallel usages are seen in a wide range of living deer species, with a variety of antler forms. One rather species-specific example has recently been described for living *Elaphurus davidianus* (Pere David's deer) by Wemmer, et al. (1983). The long backwardly directed branch of this species' antler is used to plaster the body with mud in hot weather. Such activities might in some instances exert a selective force on antler form. However, there are as yet no documented examples of this, and it would seem unlikely that such factors are responsible in a major way for the diversity of antler structure.

Turning now to the evolutionary transitions such as those in red deer and elk illustrated above, and also those described for other species by other authors (e.g. Heintz, 1970), we may note that they are all in a sense "micro-evolutionary": they entail morphological change, but always within the basic framework of antler form ("Bauplan") of the species or lineage, without fundamentally altering that framework. In the case of *Cervus elaphus*, the evolution of the crown and of the bez tine modify the detailed form of the antler, but do not greatly affect its overall "gestalt." In the case of the reduction in length of the beam in the *Alces* lineage, the fundamental structural plan of the antler has again remained constant, but in this case a simple change of proportion has in fact brought the alcine antler into a new category of "gestalt." Thus micro-evolution can effect changes both of detail and "gestalt," the latter not necessarily requiring change of fundamental structure ("Bauplan").

The possibility of such micro-evolutionary refinement explains how, even with the variety of antler types between species of similar adaptive requirements, each can still be well-adapted to those requirements.

But how were the more major differences of structure themselves achieved? A first possibility is that it was simply by gradual accumulation of the sort of micro-evolutionary changes seen in the red deer and elk lineages. A continuous sequence of such transitions could in theory account for any postulated evolutionary path between species of quite different form. We do not possess sequences of fossils which show transitions between species of substantially differing form, but this may be due to the considerable gaps in our fossil record, which if filled up, might demonstrate such changes. For example, our "late Lower Pleistocene" and "early Middle Pleistocene" deposits are probably separated by several hundred thousand years, so that the apparently sudden "turnover" of cervid species, which occurred between these levels (see Table 2), does not necessarily negate the possibility that some of the "new" species had in fact evolved gradually from some of the known "old" ones, despite the lack of obvious morphological continuity between them. More fossil material of intermediate ages is required.

On the other hand, it is possible that micro-evolution does indeed occur only within an already laid-down basic structure, but that the major structural features themselves originate in rather larger evolutionary steps which can allow a considerable element of novelty to be incorporated provided the antler form as a whole passes the selective test of being within the adaptive and developmental constraints discussed above. One may envisage a model in which a new basic form of antler arises, relatively rapidly, in such an event, and this is then followed by micro-evolution *within* the basic form, to modify and "refine" it according to the adaptive role of antlers in the species. The observed phenomena of great diversity of basic form on the one hand, and micro-evolution within these forms on the other, would then reflect a certain dichotomy in the processes involved. The concept of larger steps for the origin of major structural types, recalls the "punctuation" events envisaged by Eldredge and Gould (1972). However, I am here mentioning them as a possibility not in consequence of a general model, but because of the particular attributes of cervid antlers, namely their great capacity for producing variants, and their observed exceptional diversity of

form within adaptively similar categories of species. Nor would the intervening periods be simply "equilibria" (periods of evolutionary stasis), but rather, phases of micro-evolutionary modification. It is an unfortunate fact that the possible occurrence of larger, perhaps rapid evolutionary steps is by definition difficult to pick up in the fossil record, so their existence remains speculative.

The diversification of species requires not only morphological change, but also reproductive isolation. Antlers could play a significant role here, since a new antler form might contribute to the species-specific mate recognition system, and thus help in the reproductive isolation of a new species. (This is not to say that the antler divergence was actually selected as a species isolation mechanism: see West-Eberhard, 1983). In other cases, it is quite possible that speciation could occur without major change in antler form, but that the latter would occur subsequently.

There may have been no general rules: the extent to which "quantum" or micro-evolutionary mechanisms were involved in creating the different types, and whether they were associated with speciation, no doubt varied from one lineage to another.

There is a great need for detailed comparative studies of the precise ways in which living species with different antler forms use those antlers, and hence of the ways in which the major and minor features of antler form may be specifically adaptive. We may then be able to deduce how the antlers of fossil species were being used, and how the complementary forces of chance on the one hand, and adaptive control of form on the other, combine in the creation of diversity.

Acknowledgments

I thank the following persons for access to collections in their care: Dr. A. J. Sutcliffe and Dr. J. Jewell (British Museum (Natural History)); Dr. K. A. Joysey (University Museum of Zoology, Cambridge); Mr. B. McWilliams (Norwich Castle Museum); Prof. E. Heintz (Museum National d'Histoire Naturelle); Monsieur Prieur (University of Lyon I); Dr. O. Neuffer (Naturhistorisches Museum, Mainz); Prof. K.-D. Adam (Stuttgart). Drs. A. J. Stuart, T. H. Clutton-Brock and A. W. Gentry kindly read the draft manuscript. Financial support was provided by Gonville and Caius College, the German Academic Exchange Service, and the Royal Society of London.

Literature Cited

Ahlén, I.
1965. Studies on the red deer, *Cervus elaphus* L., in Scandinavia. *Viltrevy*, 3:1–376.

Lister

Ambrosetti, P.
1967.   Cromerian fauna of the Rome area. *Quaternaria*, 9:267–284.

Azzaroli, A.
1952.   L'Alce di Senèze. *Palaeontographica italica*, 47:133–141.
1953.   The deer of the Weybourne Crag and Forest Bed of Norfolk. *Bulletin of the British Museum Natural History*, (A. Geology), 2:3–96.
1961.   Il nanismo nei cervi insulari. *Palaeontographica italica*, 56:1–32.
1978–   Critical remarks on some Giant Deer (genus *Mega-*
1979.   *ceros* Owen) from the Pleistocene of Europe. *Palaeontographica italica*, 71:5–16.

Barrette, C.
1977.   Fighting behaviour of muntjacs and the evolution of antlers. *Evolution*, 31:169–176.

Beninde, J.
1937.   Über die Edelhirschformen von Mosbach, Mauer and Steinheim a.d. Mürr. *Paläontologische Zeitschrift*, Berlin, 19:79–116.

Berckhemer, F.
1941.   Über die Riesenhirschfunde von Steinheim a.d. Mürr. *Jahresheft des Vereins für vaterlandische Naturkunde in Württemburg*, 96:63–88.

Bonfiglio, L.
1978.   Resti di Cervide (Megacero) dell' Eutirreniano di Bovetto (RC). *Quaternaria*, 20:87–108.

Bonifay, M.-F.
1969.   Les grands mammifères découverts sur le sol de la cabane acheuléene du Lazaret. *Mémoires de la Société Préhistorique Francaise*, 7:59–73.

Bubenik, A.
1973.   Hypothesis concerning the morphogenesis in moose antlers. Canadian Ministry of Natural Resources Contribution No. 74–2. *Proceedings of the 9th North American Moose Conference and Workshop, Quebec City*, pp. 195–231.

Caloi, L.
1973.   Cranio di *Megaceros giganteus* (BLUM.) nel Museo del Servicia Geologica d'Italia. *Bollettino della Societá Geologica Italiana*, 93:195–226.

Caloi, L., and A. Malatesta
1974.   Il Cervo Pleistocenico di Sardegna. *Memorie dell Ístituto Italiano di Paleontologia Umana*, 2:162–247.

Chaplin, R.E.
1975.   *Deer.* Poole, Dorset: Blandford Press.

Chapman, D.I.
1975.   Antlers—bones of contention. *Mammal Review*, 5:121–172.

Clutton-Brock, T.H., S.D. Albon, R.M. Gibson, and F.E. Guinness
1979.   The logical stag: adaptive aspects of fighting in red deer (*Cervus elaphus* L.). *Animal Behaviour*, 27:211–225.

Clutton-Brock, T.H., S.D. Albon, and P.H. Harvey
1980.   Antlers, body size and breeding group size in the Cervidae. *Nature*, 285:565–567.

Clutton-Brock, T.H., F.E. Guinness, and S.D. Albon
1982.   *Red deer: behaviour and ecology of two sexes.* Chicago: University of Chicago Press.

Coope, G.R.
1973.   The ancient world of *Megaceros*. *Deer*, 2:974–977.

Eldredge, N., and S.J. Gould
1972.   Punctuated equilibria: an alternative to phyletic gradualism. In *Models in Paleobiology*, edited by T.J.M. Schopf, pp. 82–115. San Francisco: Freeman, Cooper & Co.

Erdbrink, D.P.
1954.   On one of the oldest known remains of the common elk, *Alces alces* L., found recently in the Netherlands. *Geologie en Mijnbouw* (N.S.), 16:301–309.

Flerov, K.K.
1952.   *Musk deer and deer. In Fauna of the USSR. Mammals.* Volume 1, No. 2. Jerusalem: Israel Program for Scientific Translation.

Geist, V.
1966.   The evolution of horn-like organs. *Behaviour*, 27:175–214.
1971.   The relation of social evolution and dispersal in ungulates during the Pleistocene, with emphasis on the Old World deer and the genus *Bison*. *Quaternary Research*, 1:283–315.

This   On the evolution of optical signals in deer: a pre-
volume liminary analysis.

Gould, S.J.
1974.   The origin and function of "bizarre" structures: antler size and skull size in the "Irish Elk" *Megaloceros giganteus*. *Evolution*, 28:191–220.

Haltenorth, T.
1959.   Beitrag zur Kenntnis des Mesopotamischen Damhirsches—*Cervus (Dama) mesopotamicus* Brooke, 1875—und zur Stammes-und Verbreitungsgeschichte der Damhirsche allgemein. *Säugetierkundliche Mitteilungen*, 7:1–54.

Hattemer, H.H., and H. Dreschler
1976.   Rosenstock- und Geweihmerkmale von Harz-Hirschen und ihr Zusammenhang mit dem Alter. *Zeitschrift für Jagdwissenschaft*, 22:36–50.

Heintz, E.
1970.   Les cervidés villafranchiens de France et d'Espagne. *Mémoires du Museum nationale d'Histoire naturelle Série C.*, 22:1–303.

Kahlke, H.-D.

1956a. *Die Cervidenreste aus den altpleistozänen Ilmkiesen von Süssenborn bei Weimer.* Berlin: Akademis-Verlag.

1956b. Die Cervidenreste aus den altpleistozänen Tonen von Voigtstedt bei Sangerhausen. Teil I: Die Schädel, Geweihe und Gehorne. *Abhandlungen der Akademie der Wissenschaften zu Berlin, Klasse für Chemie, Geologie und Biologie,* 156:9, 51 pp.

1959. Die Cervidenreste aus den altpleistozänen Sanden von Mosbach (Biebrich-Wiesbaden). *Abhandlungen der Akademie der Wissenschaften zu Berlin, Klasse für Chemie, Geologie und Biologie,* 7:1–75.

Kahlke, H.-D., and Hu Changkang

1958. On the distribution of *Megaceros* in China. *Vertebrata palasiatica,* 1:273–283.

Kleinschmidt, O.

1938. Was ist *Cervus benindei? Falco,* Leipzig, 34.

Kunst, C.E.

1937. *Die Niederlandischen Pleistozänen Hirsche.* Leiden. 126 pp.

Kuss, S.E.

1975. Die Pleistozänen Hirsche der ostmediterränean Inseln Kreta, Kasos, Karpathos und Rhodos (Griechenland). *Bericht der Naturforschenden Gesellschaft zu Freiburg in Breisgau,* 65:25–79.

Leonardi, G., and C. Petronio

1976. The fallow deer of European Pleistocene. *Geologica Romana,* 15:1–67.

Lincoln, G.A.

1972. The role of antlers in the behaviour of red deer. *Journal of Experimental Zoology,* 182:233–250.

Lister, A.M.

1986. New results on deer from Swanscombe, and the stratigraphic significance of deer in the Middle and Upper Pleistocene of Europe. *Journal of Archaeological Science,* 13(4):319–338.

Lyneborg, L.

1971. *Mammals in colour.* London: Blandford Press.

Malatesta, A.

1980. Dwarf deer and other late Pleistocene fauna of the Simonelli Cave in Crete. *Problemi Attuali di Scienza di Cultura,* 249:1–128.

Mitchell, G.F., and H.M. Parkes

1949. The giant deer in Ireland. *Proceedings of the Royal Irish Academy,* 52B:291–314.

Mitchell, G.F., L.F. Penny, F.W. Shotton, and R.G. West

1973. A correlation of Quaternary deposits in the British Isles. *Geological Society of London Special Report 4.*

Pocock, R.I.

1933. The homologies between the branches of the antlers of the Cervidae based on the theory of dichotomous growth. *Proceedings of the Zoological Society of London,* 377–406.

Reynolds, S.H.

1929. The British Pleistocene Mammalia. Vol. III, Part III. *The Giant Deer.* London: Palaeontographical Society.

Sher, A.V.

1974. Pleistocene mammals and stratigraphy of the far North-east U.S.S.R. and North America. II. Description of Pleistocene mammal remains. *International Geological Review,* 16:1–206.

Shikama, T., and G. Okafuji

1958. Quaternary cave and fissure deposits in Akiyosi District, Yamaguti prefecture. *Science Reports of the Yokohama National University, Section II,* 7:43–103.

Simpson, G.G.

1949. *The meaning of evolution.* New York: Mentor Book New American Library.

Soergel, W.

1918. Das Kieslager von Süssenborn bei Weimar. *Monographien zur Steinbruch Industrie,* 5, Berlin.

Spiess, A.E.

1979. *Reindeer and Caribou Hunters: An Archaeological Study.* London: Academic Press.

Stuart, A.J.

1982. *Pleistocene Vertebrates in the British Isles.* London: Longman.

Sutcliffe, A.J.

1960. Joint Mitnor Cave, Buckfastleigh. *Transactions and Proceedings of the Torquay Natural History Society,* 13:1–26.

Szymczyk, W.

1973. Occurrence of elk, *Alces alces* (L.) in the Holocene of Europe. *Przeglad Zoologiczny,* 17:89–94.

Wemmer, C., L. Collins, B. Beck, and B. Rettberg

1983. The Ethogram. In *The Biology and Management of an Extinct Species. Pere David's Deer,* edited by B.B. Beck and C.M. Wemmer, Chapter 9, pp. 91–125. New Jersey: Noyes Publications.

West-Eberhard, M.J.

1983. Sexual selection, social competition, and speciation. *Quarterly Review of Biology,* 58:155–183.

Young, C.C.

1932. On the Artiodactyla from the *Sinanthropus* site at Choukou'tien. *Palaeontologi a Sinica* (c), 8:1–100.

Zagwijn, W.H.

1975. Variations in the climate as shown by pollen analysis, especially in the Lower Pleistocene of Europe. In *Ice Ages Ancient and Modern,* edited by Wright, A.E. and F. Mosely, pp. 137–152. *Geological Journal Special Issue no. 6.*

G.A. BUBENIK
and
A.B. BUBENIK
Department of Zoology
University of Guelph
Guelph, Ontario

10 Stornoway Crescent
Thornhill, Ontario

Recent Advances in Studies of Antler Development and Neuroendocrine Regulation of the Antler Cycle

ABSTRACT

The cervid antler is a physiologically unique tissue, but the process of antlerogenesis is still only partially understood. This paper is a brief review of recent advances for the study of critical periods of antler induction, neural control of antler form, and photoperiodic and hormonal of the antler cycle. The chronology of antler development beginning at the end of the first trimester of pregnancy is given, and the role of nerves and androgens is discussed. The origin and evolution of antlers from the pseudocervicorn condition is hypothesized on the basis of similarity to the antlers of castrated male deer, pseudoantlers of female deer, and other findings. The effects of hormones are discussed as they relate to antler growth, mineralization, and shedding, and evidence is presented that implicates prolactin and throidal hormones in the indirect control of antlerogensis. Future investigations of antler regulation should focus on the interaction between receptors, nerves, and hormones.

Introduction

Classical neuroendocrinology describes the role of nerves in the secretion of neurotransmitters releasing hormones or endorphins and other less closely grouped neuropeptides (Harris, 1948; Guillemin, 1978; Powell and Skrabanek, 1979). Progress of this branch of neuroendocrinology overshadowed the other part of this science occupied with a direct role of nerves on body tissues depending on hormonal stimulation for proper function. A typical example of this so called "trophic" influence is the compensatory hypertrophy of the endocrine organs after unilateral removal of the testis, ovary or adrenal gland. Such hypertrophy was attributed to a purely hormonal mechanism. However, more recent evidence indicates that a direct link exists between endocrine organs and the corresponding centers of the brain (Gerendai and Halasz, 1981). This direct link between the brain and the peripheral organs might not be limited only to the endocrine glands, but might also exist elsewhere. Unlike other paired organs the antlers have several advantages for neuroendocrine studies: they are easily accessible and their deciduous, photoperiodically controlled nature allows artificial monitoring of the cycle. In contrast to other bones, the growth of antler tissue is more dynamic (up to 2 cm/day) and it experiences within about 4–5 months all stages of bone development, ossification and mineralization. Growing antlers respond readily to external and internal stimuli with the unique advantage being independent control mechanisms, so that in the same individual in the same time one antler can serve as experimental, the other as control organ (Bubenik, A., 1966; Bubenik, G., 1983a).

Critical Periods of Antler Ontogeny

Except for the genus *Rangifer* (reindeer and caribou) the possession of antlers seems to be a unique feature of male deer. However, the ability to grow antlers is present in both sexes. It is only the special endocrine milieu in males during a few critical periods of their lives that enables them to regularly produce this unique bony organ.

The first such period is approximately at the end of the first trimester of fetal life. At that time, the fetal testes increase production of testosterone, which leads to masculinization of external genitalia and the development of the primordial pedicles (the protuberances of the frontal bone which in adult life provides a nonrenewable base for the antlers) (Lincoln, 1973). There is no direct evidence in deer that the brain centers involved in endocrine activity of the male are masculinized at that time. However, overwhelming evidence from other species indicates that such process

(observed in numerous laboratory animals including domestic ruminants) (Neumann et al., 1970) takes place also in male deer during the early fetal stage.

After this early androgenization phase, antler development ceases and recommences after a few months of postnatal life when a renewal of androgenesis in the prepubertal testes is observed. In well nourished and high ranking males of the *Odocoileinae* pedicle growth is terminated at the age of 4–5 months by petrification of its tip, converting it into the first antlers which range from knob size to a few centimeters in length. Pedicle growth in *Cervinae* however is slow during the first year of life. It accelerates the second spring, and depending on the species the antlers can attain a length of 15–65 centimeters. Thereafter in both subfamilies, all subsequent antlers begin to grow in the spring, except the roe deer (*Capreolus*) which grows the antlers in the winter.

The Role of Nerves and Androgens in Antlerogenesis

Experimental and observational evidence from nature indicates that the development of pedicles and the subsequent growth of antlers requires the formation of a pathway between the so called "inductive" periosteum of the frontal bone and the brain trophic centers (Bubenik, G. 1983a). The formation of the pathway usually requires a certain amount of androgen. Therefore, if the second androgenization phase is missed (as in males castrated early postnatally) the pedicles or antlers will never develop (Tachezy, 1956). However, as experimental evidence and cases from nature revealed, the induction of antler growth in fertile females can be induced only by strong neurogenic stimulation (i.e., trauma to inductive periosteum) (Jaczewski and Krzywinska, 1974; Jaczewski, 1976, 1983; Jaczewski et al., 1975; Bubenik, G., et al., 1982a). Once the first set of antlers has grown, the tissues which first give rise to them (i.e., the inductive periosteum, the underlying bone, or the covering dermal tissues) can be totally removed surgically or destroyed by chemicals and still, after healing such enormous wounds, the antler growth process will start again somewhere in the region supplied by nerve fibers which connect to the proper brain center (Bubenik, A. and Pavlansky, 1965; Robbins and Koger, 1981). On the other hand, if such destruction takes place before the pathway is established, no growth of antlers will occur in male deer (Hartwig and Schrudde, 1974; Robbins and Koger, 1981). A similar lack of antler growth was observed in some male deer maintained on a very marginal diet (Lincoln and Fletcher, 1976). This failure to grow antlers is probably due to improper androgenization during postnatal

Bubenik and Bubenik

periods as it is known that malnutrition delays the maturation of the pituitary-gonadal axis (Lincoln, 1971). On the other hand recent data indicate that emotional and endocrine status may be more crucial for antler development than nutritional conditions (Bartos and Hyánek, 1983; Bubenik, A., 1966, 1983a; Pfandl, 1977). When the first set of antlers are induced, the subsequent cycles probably require very little androgenic stimulation (as seen in bucks castrated in later life or in does with artificially induced antlerogenesis (Tachezy, 1956; Jaczewski, et al., 1975; Jaczewski, 1976; Bubenik, G., et al., 1982a). However, the fact that certain androgens are essential for proper function of centers involved in antler growth has been documented in castrates. The rate of antler growth in castrated white-tailed bucks steadily diminishes every subsequent year after gonadectomy, and after 3 years is only about 30% of the growth rate of intact bucks. However, when complete mineralization of antlers was achieved in two castrates by exogenous application of testosterone cypionate (Upjohn Corp. Don Mills, Ontario) (100 mg, 2× a week for 2 week periods), antler growth in the following year increased by more than 200 and 300%, respectively. In addition, the shape of the antlers resembled the species specific pattern, an occurrence not observed in non-treated castrates (Bubenik, G., 1983a) (Figures 1,2).

We assume that treatment by testosterone sensitized the appropriate androgen receptors in the CNS or the target organ and therefore, even when the treatment was discontinued, the low amount of extragonadal androgens in castrates (mostly of adrenal origin) was sufficient to stimulate the rapid growth of antlers displaying species specific pattern. In addition, traumatic stimulation of nerves around the wound created by casting the mineralized antlers, might have contributed to stimulation of antler growth in a way similar to trauma induced antler growth in a doe (Bubenik, G., et al., 1982a). That surgical trauma might be "remembered" in CNS centers has been numerously documented. The engram of this so called "trophic memory" (Bubenik, A. and Pavlansky, 1965) can stimulate rapid antler growth months or years after injury (Bubenik, G., et al., 1982a). Lately, emotional trauma (loss of rank) has been connected with dramatic reduction of antler growth in the *next* antler cycle (Bartos and Hyánek, 1983), thus also implicating a possible mechanism of trophic memory.

The Neural Control of Antler Shape

Some preliminary evidence exists that species specific patterns of antler growth require intact nerve connections. When sensitive nerves supplying growing antlers were cut, the shape of antlers changed

Figure 1. White-tailed buck Beta, castrated in 1977. Photo taken in June 1981, after four years of continuous antler growth. End parts of beams and points (usually no longer than 5 cm) damaged in winter were regularly separated in the spring.

Figure 2. The same buck photographed in June 1982, after complete mineralization and casting was achieved in the fall of 1981 following i.m. administration of testosterone. Compare the shape of antlers and intensity of growth.

Figure 3. (a) Malformation of antlers in the buck whose antler nerves were electrically stimulated in the *previous* antler growth period.

(b) Normal antler growth in control white-tailed buck.

(Wislocki and Singer, 1946). If growth of bony tissue was induced in atypical places (like cannon bone) by transplantation of "inductive" periosteum from the tip of the pedicle, the shape of this "pseudo-antler" never resembled the species specific pattern (Hartwig and Schrudde, 1974; R. Goss, pers. comm.). On the other hand, electrical stimulation of nerves supplying growing antlers in the mule deer resulted in an alteration of the species-specific pattern (Lake et al., 1979). Electrical stimulation of antler nerves in white-tailed deer induced antler growth in a mirror image of the normal pattern (Figure 3a,b). Similar examples of atypical antler growth are known from the hunting literature, e.g., moose antlers in red deer, red deer antlers in moose or red deer antlers in sambar (Bubenik, A., 1966) (Figure 4).

The Function and Evolution of Antlers

These examples of unusual development of antlers might help to elucidate the evolution of these bony organisms in cervids. Contrary to the hypothesis of Geist (1974; 1978) that antlers developed primarily as

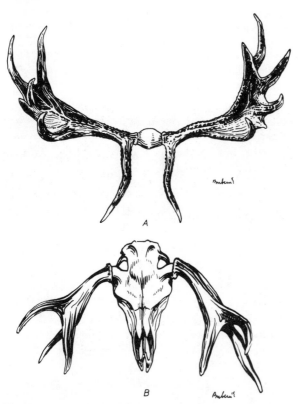

Figure 4. Atypical growth of antlers. (a) Palmative, moose-like antlers in red deer and (b) deer-like antlers with "royals" in moose.

Figure 5. Tertiary Pseudocervicorn Protuberantia of: 1) *Stephanocemas*, 2) *Merycodus*, 3) *Dicroceros*, and 4) *Procervulus*.

　　　　　　　　　　　　　　　　Bubenik and Bubenik

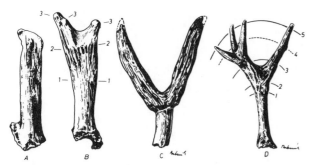

Figure 6. Perennial growth of pseudocervicorns in *Dicroceros elegans*; numbers indicate seasonal enlargements.

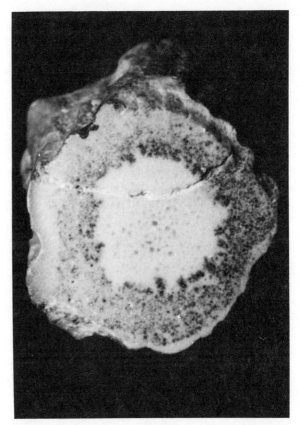

Figure 7. Centrifugal mineralization in *Dicroceros* from Sansan—Villafranchien—France.

Figure 8. Microstructure of the beam of *Merycodus*.

weapons for inflicting painful superficial injury, our studies (Bubenik, A., 1966; 1983a) lead to the conclusion that antlers evolved because of more general social effects. We believe antlers serve as the most sophisticated accentuation of the head pole (Portmann, 1960) and that their development is linked to species specific gestures not present in other pecorans.

The primitive predecessors of antlers known as pseudocervicorns (Frick, 1937) were found in the middle Miocene in the cervid merycodonts of North America (Figure 5) and dicrocerids and lagomeryds of Eurasia (Bubenik, A., 1983b). Pedicles of all pseudocervicorns were true apophyses, bony protuberances located on the *crista orbitalis*. They were permanent or temporary perennial organs, which most probably exhibited periods of growth leading to an increase in diameter and length with each successive cycle (Figure 6). This continuing growth was made possible by slow, centrifugal mineralization (Figure 7) of the core and the cortex, and the development of a fine microstructure of osteons (Figure 8). The slow progress of calcification in some antlers grown in today's cervids is due to relative hypogonadism or low sensitivity of receptors to androgens (Bubenik, G., et al., 1974). Similar factors might also have been responsible for the slow mineralization of pseudocervicorns in merycodonts.

The microstructure of the pseudocervicorn appendices is in many ways similar to pseudoantlers of a castrated male or antlered female deer. These pseudoantlers are also perennial, relatively fragile, and, because of their structure, are not suitable as a weapon (Bubenik, G., et al., 1974, 1975; Bubenik, G., 1983a). Because of an almost total lack of broken pseudocervicorn protuberances exhibiting any process of healing (which would indicate that they were broken in a fight), we assume that these organs were also not used in sparring. Another factor which might

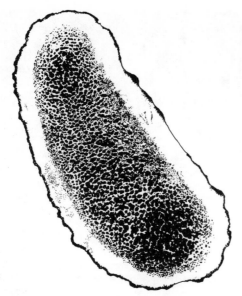

Figure 9. Compact cortex with spongious bone core in red deer.

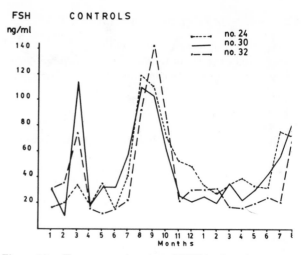

Figure 10. Two seasonal cycles of FSH in three intact mature white-tailed bucks. Note the similarity in timing and range of FSH levels. The fall peak is obvious in both years. The spring peak was missed in the second cycle.

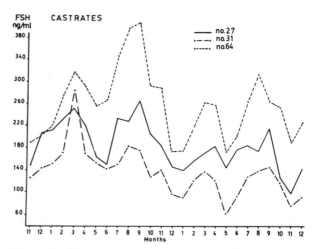

Figure 11. Two seasonal cycles of FSH in three castrated mature white-tailed deer. Note the diversity in individual levels, which are 2–4 × higher than similar values in controls. Both the spring and the fall peaks (coinciding with equinoxes) are well detected.

have prevented the use of pseudocervicorns as weapons would be a highly sensitive innervation of their skin. Deer antler velvet is extremely well supplied with sensitive nerve endings (Vacek, 1955) and the animals avoid any contact with hard objects. On the other hand, traumatic stimulation to perennially growing antlers is unavoidable and often leads to dramatic changes in pattern and intensity of antler growth (Bubenik, G., et al., 1982a). Therefore, we might assume that the traumatic stimulation of sensory nerves in pseudocervicorns operated via the trophic centers in CNS (Bubenik, A. and Pavlansky, 1965) and facilitated further development and ramification of these organs as long as the tissue remained alive. We hypothesize that because the permanent irritation of pseudocervicorn protuberances became counterproductive in the long run, a solution was found in the modification of the bony structure (i.e., formation of compact bone cortex and spongy bone core) (Figure 9) and annually enforced petrification of bony tissues. In today's cervids, antlers are highly sensitive to the mineralizing effect of androgens (Bubenik, G., et al., 1974). The conversion of perennial pseudocervicorns into deciduous antlers might have been caused either by a relatively large increase of testosterone levels in deer which became seasonal breeders, or by an increase in sensitivity to circulating androgen levels. In addition, with rising androgen levels, trophic centers in the CNS or other parts of the nervous system might have been stimulated, as it is known that testosterone can act as a potentiator of neural transmission (Kendric and Drewett, 1979).

It is not yet clear if pseudocervicorn protuberances of North American merycodonts were true predecessors of antlers as no intermediate developmental stages between them and modern antler-bearers were found. In contrast, the dicrocerids of Eurasia show two different types of appendices. Those of the Middle Miocene (Sansan-France, about ± 18 million years ago) have typical pseudocervicorn protuberances but those from Upper-Middle-Miocene (Göriach-Austria) have typical true antlers (Bubenik, A. 1962).

Bubenik and Bubenik

Photoperiodic Control of the Antler Cycle

As mentioned above, the first antler development in juvenile males starts in the fall, but subsequent cycles begin in the spring. It is assumed that shifting photoperiodicity is a common denominator which triggers antlerogenesis.

The changes of light and dark periods are registered in the pineal gland which responds to the onset of darkness by massive secretion of the hormone melatonin (M) (Bubenik, G., et al., 1978). The removal of the pineal gland in deer results in a shortening of the antler cycle and the premature molt of the coat (Brown et al., 1978). The result of our latest experiment indicates that similar changes can also be achieved by oral administration of melatonin (5 mg/day—Sigma Inc. Saint Louis, U.S.A.); M was given in gelatinous capsules a few hours before the onset of darkness, in order to simulate the shortening of the photoperiod. The treatment of two white-tailed bucks started on May 4; 7 weeks later (June 22) antler growth ceased completely, velvet became dry and the summer coat started to change into the winter one. In addition, the bucks displayed aggressive behavior. The velvet was shed on July 6 and 22 respectively (2 months ahead of time) and the pelage change was completed on July 20 (Bubenik, G., 1983).

As demonstrated by Goss (1976), the start of the antler cycle can be initiated by both the lengthening, as well as the shortening, of the photoperiod. Correspondingly, plasma levels of gonadotropins also fluctuate according to an alteration of photoperiodicity. Both LH and FSH increase around the spring and fall equinoxes (Bubenik, G., et al., 1982b). However, the spring increase in control animals is probably of a very short duration and was detected infrequently because sampling was only once a month (Figure 10). In castrates (Figure 11) the gonadotropin levels are not only higher, but also correlate better with photoperiodicity. It is hypothesized that in intact male deer, the sharp increase of estrogen levels in plasma observed in the spring (Bubenik, G., et al., 1979) induces a fast reduction of gonadotropins and thus diminishes the chance of a second stimulation during the time unsuitable for reproduction. The data also indicate the greater variability in individual levels of gonadotropins detected in plasma of castrates (Figure 11). On the other hand, the individual hormonal levels of intact animals are similar in amplitude (Figure 10), but unlike the levels in castrates, the synchronization with photoperiodicity is less perfect. The difference in seasonal rhythmicity of gonadotropins in castrates as compared to intact bucks might be due not only to the drastic reduction in levels of sexual steroid, but also to change in seasonal levels of other hormones. Almost

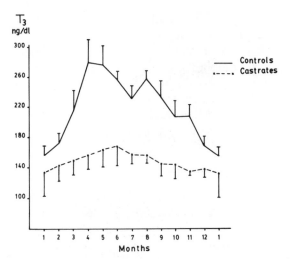

Figure 12. Seasonal levels of triiodo-L-thyronine (T_3) in intact and castrated white-tailed deer. Castration abolished spring increase of T_3.

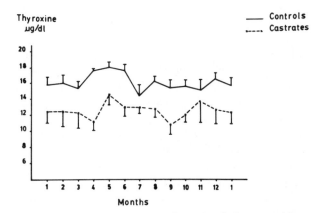

Figure 13. Seasonal levels of thyroxine in intact and castrated mature male white-tailed deer. Castration did not change the pattern of secretion, but reduced the average levels significantly.

complete abolition of circannual rhythm of thriiodo-L-thyronine (T_3) (Figure 12) as well as significant reduction of L-thyroxine (T_4) levels (Figure 13) was detected in castrates.

The Role of Thyroidal Hormones

However, none of the above mentioned hormones seems to be directly involved in the development or maturation of antlers. Despite earlier reports on the dramatic increase of antler formation after the administration of T_4 to infantile bucks (Lebedinsky, 1939; Bruhin, 1953) the treatment of adult deer with T_4 had no effect on antler growth (Bruhin, 1953). The results of our recent studies confirmed Bruhin's observation. Twice a week administration of 0.5 mg of L-thyroxine (sodium salt) either orally (Armour Pharmaceutical Comp., Phoenix) or intramuscularly (Flint Lab., Malton) had no dramatic effect on the production of antler bone tissues. On the other hand, the deer treated with intramuscular doses of T_4 changed their coat about twice as fast as the control bucks and developed an unusually shiny hair coat. In addition they became very excitable (Bubenik, G. and Smith, 1985).

The Role of Prolactin

The reduction of peak spring levels of prolactin by 95% (caused by i.m. administration of bromocriptine) did not influence the speed of antler growth. However, the drastic decrease of plasma prolactin levels was associated with a very early rise in testosterone levels (Figure 14). This caused a very early mineralization of antlers, shedding of velvet and initiated premature rutting behavior. On the other hand, when bromocriptine was used in combination with the antiandrogen cyproterone acetate (CA), the antler growth continued until the CA treatment ceased (Bubenik, G., 1983b).

These observations indicate that changes in seasonal levels of some hormones (e.g., prolactin, thyroidal hormones or others) which are not directly linked to antlerogenesis might influence this process indirectly. The process may be permissive, by blocking feedback mechanisms, or by action on receptors at the target organ level. Therefore, castration not only drastically reduces the level of circulating androgens, but also changes the circannual rhythm of metabolic activity, molt, immunobiologic resistance, etc. (Morris and Bubenik, G., 1982).

It is fairly well established that androgens are the most important hormones involved in the development and mineralization of the normal antlers (Bubenik, G. et al., 1975; Morris and Bubenik, G., 1983). Photoperiodically controlled antlerogenesis begins during the period characterized by minimal levels of testosterone in the blood. At this time, when the amount of androgens begins to rise, the antlers are usually fully developed and ready to be completely mineralized. The completion of hardening of antler bone precedes the rutting season by several weeks during which testosterone levels increase further. The first sign of rapid calcification is the drying of the velvet. It is believed that during later developmental stages antlers are supplied by blood mostly from the velvet arteries. Therefore the death of the velvet (caused by calcification of the arterial wall and almost complete occlusion) will cause the death of the entire antler. However, some reports indicate that the core of the antlers can survive the death and shedding of the velvet (Acharjyo and Bubenik, A., 1983; Bubenik,

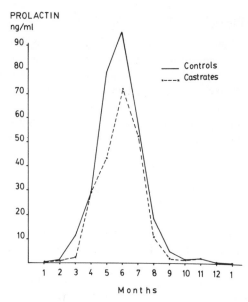

Figure 14. Seasonal levels of prolactin in intact and castrated mature male white-tailed deer. The slightly lower peak levels in castrates were not significantly different from control values.

1983b). In our latest research we observed a dramatic increase in levels of alkaline phosphatase (AP) in plasma of a buck which was treated with antiandrogen cyproterone acetate (CA) at the time its velvet started to peel off. The elevation of AP to levels observed only during periods of maximal antler growth indicates that CA revived the bone-building process which survived the interruption of the blood supply from the velvet. The levels of AP were high as long as CA was administered (in total 8 weeks), despite the fact that the antlers appeared dead (Bubenik, G., unpub. obs.). The portion of antlers which most probably survived the loss of the velvet would be the coronet and areas proximal to it. Cutting off of large antlers just above the coronet a few days after velvet shedding will still result in a light bleeding from the coronetal blood vessels (Bubenik, G., unpub. obs.).

Maintenance of the connection between the dead tissues of the antler and the living tissue of the pedicle is possible only during the period of high androgen levels in plasma. As soon as the testosterone levels decrease to a certain point (which seems to be very close to the level causing shedding of velvet) the narrow bridge of bony tissue between pedicle and coronet is resorbed and the antler is cast. The process of antler separation has been studied in detail (Wislocki and Waldo, 1953). However, the mechanism behind this connection between living and dead bone, which is unique in mammalian species, is still unknown.

Bubenik and Bubenik

Conclusion

As has been shown by numerous studies, antlerogenesis is a unique phenomenon, but many aspects of the process are still unknown. Research on antlers can open new ways to explore fundamental questions on the regulation of tissue development, interactions between target organs and the CNS, trophic function of neurons, regeneration of organs and other physiological processes which are high on the list of neuro-hormonal research.

In order to elucidate some of these questions, future antler research should concentrate on the function and properties of inductive periosteum, investigate the interactions between receptors, nerves and hormones in antler tissue, and to try to pinpoint the so far hypothetical centers regulating of growth processes of the peripheral appendages.

Acknowledgments

The authors would like to thank Mrs. Mary Bubenik, Mr. Peter Smith and Miss Bonnie Parker for their excellent technical and clerical assistance.

Literature Cited

Acharjyo, L.N., and A.B. Bubenik
1983. The structural peculiarities of antler bone in general *Axis, Rusa,* and *Rucervus*. In *Antler Development in Cervidae*, edited by R.D. Brown, pp. 195–209. Kingsville, Texas: Caesar Klebert Wildlife Research Institute.

Bartos, L., and J. Hyánek
1983. Social position in the red deer stag II, the relationship with developed antlers. In *Antler Development in Cervidae*, edited by R.D. Brown, pp. 463–466. Kingsville, Texas: Caesar Kleberg Wildlife Research Institute.

Brown, R.D., Kavanaugh, J.F., and Cowan, R.L.
1978. Effect of pinealectomy on seasonal androgen titers, antler growth and feed uptake in white-tailed deer. *Journal of Animal Science,* 47(2):435–440.

Bruhin, H.
1953. Zur Biologie der Stirnaufsatze bei Huftieren. *Physiologie Comparative et Oecologie, B, III:* 63–127.

Bubenik, A.B.
1962. Geweihmorphogenese im Lichte der neurohumoralen Forschung. *Symposium Thierologicum, CSAV Brno,* 1960:59–66.

Bubenik, A.B.
1966. *Das Geweih.* Hamburg: Paul Parey.

Bubenik, A.B.
1983a. The behavioral aspects of antlerogenesis. In *Antler Development in Cervidae*, edited by R.D. Brown, pp. 389–449. Kingsville, Texas: Caesar Kleberg Wildlife Research Institute.

1983b. Taxonomy of Pecora in relation to morphophysiology of their cranial appendices. In *Antler Development in Cervidae*, edited by R.D. Brown, pp. 163–185. Kingsville, Texas: Caesar Kleberg Wildlife Research Institute.

Bubenik, A.B., and R. Pavlansky
1965. Trophic responses to trauma in growing antlers. *Journal of Experimental Zoology,* 159:289–302.

Bubenik, G.A.
1983a. The endocrine regulation of the antler cycle. In *Antler Development in Cervidae*, edited by R.D. Brown, pp. 73–107. Kingsville, Texas: Caesar Kleberg Wildlife Research Institute.

Bubenik, G.A.
1983b. Shift of seasonal cycle in white-tailed deer by oral administration of melatonin. *Journal of Experimental Zoology,* 225:155–156.

Bubenik, G.A., and J. Smith
In press. The effect of thyroxine (T_4) administration on plasma levels of tri-iodothyronine (T_3) and T_4 in male white-tailed deer. *Comparative Biochemistry and Physiology 83A.*

Bubenik, G.A., G.M. Brown, A.B. Bubenik, and L.J. Grota
1974. Immunohistological localization of testosterone in the growing antler of the white-tailed deer (*Odocoileus virginianus*). *Calcified Tissue Research,* 14(2):121–130.

Bubenik, G.A., A.B. Bubenik, G.M. Brown, and D.A. Wilson
1975. The role of sex hormones in the growth of antler bone tissue. I. Endocrine and metabolic effects on the growth and mineralization of the antler bone. *Journal of Experimental Zoology,* 194(2):349–358.

Bubenik, G.A., R.A. Purtill, G.M. Brown, and L.J. Grota
1978. Melatonin in the retina and the Harderian gland. Ontogeny, diurnal variations and melatonin treatment. *Experimental Eye Research,* 27:323–334.

Bubenik, G.A., A.B. Bubenik, and J. Zamecnik
1979. The development of circannual rhythm of estradiol in plasma of white-tailed deer (*Odocoileus virginianus*). *Comparative Biochemical Physiology,* 62A: 869–872.

Bubenik, G.A., A.B. Bubenik, E.D. Stevens, and A.G. Binnington
1982a. The effect of neurogenic stimulation on the development and growth of bony tissues. *Journal of Experimental Zoology,* 219:205–216.

Bubenik, G.A., J.M. Morris, D. Schams, and A. Claus
1982b. Photoperiodic control of deer reproduction. The circannual levels of LH, FSH and testosterone in normal and castrated male white-tailed deer. *Canadian Journal of Physiological Pharmacology,* 60:788–793.

Frick, C.
1937. Horned ruminants of North America. *Bulletin of the American Museum of Natural History,* 69:669 pp.

Geist, V.
1974.   On fighting strategies in animal combat. *Nature*, 250:354.

Geist, V.
1978.   On weapons, combat and ecology. In *Aggression, dominance and individual spacing*, edited by L. Kramer, P. Pliner and T. Alloway, pp.1–30. Plenum Publishing Corporation.

Gerendai, I., and B. Halasz
1981.   Participation of a pure neuronal mechanism in the control of gonadal functions. *Andrologia*, 13(4):275–283.

Goss, R.J.
1976.   Photoperiodic control of antler cycles in deer. III. Decreasing versus increasing day lengths. *Journal of Experimental Zoology*, 197(3):307–320.

Guillemin, R.
1978.   Biochemical and physiological correlates of hypothalamic peptides. The new endocrinology of the neuron. *Research Publications of Association for Research of Nervous Mental Disorders*, 56:155–194.

Harris, G.W.
1948.   Neural control of the pituitary gland. *Physiological Review*, 28:137–139.

Hartwig, H., and Schrudde, J.
1974.   Experimentelle Untersuchungen zur Bildung der primaren Stirnauswuchse beim Reh. (*Capreolus capreolus* L.). *Zeitschrift für Jagdwissenschaft*, 20:1–13.

Jaczewski, Z.
1976.   The induction of antler growth in female red deer. *Bulletin de L'Academie Polonaise des Science*, 21(1):61–65.

Jaczewski, Z.
1983.   The artificial induction of antler growth in deer. In *Antler Development in Cervidae*, edited by R.D. Brown, pp. 143–162. Kingsville, Texas: Caesar Kleberg Wildlife Research Institute.

Jaczewski, Z., and K. Krzywinska
1974.   The induction of antler growth in a red deer male castrated before puberty by traumatization of the pedicle. *Bulletin de l'Academie Polonaise des Sciences*, 22:67–72.

Jaczewski, Z., T. Doboszynska, and A. Krzywinski
1975.   The induction of antler growth by amputation of the pedicle in red deer (*Cervus elaphus* L.) males castrated before puberty. *Folia Biologica*, 24(3):299–307.

Kendric, K.M., and R.F. Drewett
1979.   Testosterone reduces refractory period of a stria terminalis. *Science*, 204:877–879.

Lake, F.T., B.C. Solomon, R.W. Davis, N. Pace, and J.R. Morgan
1979.   Bioelectric potentials associated with the growing deer antlers. *Clinical Orthopaedic Related Research*, 142:237–243.

Lebedinsky, N.G.
1939.   Beschleunigung der Geweihmorphogenese beim Reh (*Capreolus capreolus* L.) durch das Schilddrüsenhormon. *Acta Biologica Latvica*, 9:125–134.

Lincoln, G.A.
1971.   The seasonal reproductive changes in the red deer stag (*Cervus elaphus*). *Journal of Zoology* 163:105–123.

Lincoln, G.A.
1973.   Appearance of antler pedicles in early foetal life in red deer. *Journal of Embryology and Experimental Morphology*, 29:431–437.

Lincoln, G.A., and T.J. Fletcher
1976.   Induction of antler growth in a congenitally polled scottish red deer stag. *Journal of Experimental Zoology*, 195:247–262.

Morris, J.M., and G.A. Bubenik
1982.   Seasonal levels of minerals, enzymes, nutrients and metabolic products in plasma of intact and castrated male white-tailed deer (*Odocoileus virginianus*). *Comparative Biochemistry of Physiology*, 74(1):21–28.

1983.   The effects of androgens on the development of antler bone. In *Antler Development in Cervidae*, edited by R.D. Brown, pp. 123–141. Kingsville, Texas: Caesar Kleberg Wildlife Research Institute.

Neumann, F., R. von Berswordt-Wallrabe, W. Elger, H. Steinbeck, J.D. Hahn, and M. Kramer
1970.   Aspects of androgen-dependent events as studied by antiandrogens. *Recent Progress in Hormone Research*, 26:338–410.

Pfandl, E.
1977.   Ergebnisse aus den Achentaler Forschungsrevieren. *Jagd in Tirol*, 29(10):10–14.

Portman, A.
1960.   *Die Tiergestalt*. Basel: Franz Reinhardt.

Powell, D., and P. Skrabanek
1979.   Brain and gut. *Clinics in Endocrinology and Metabolism*, 8(2):299–312.

Robbins, C.T., and L.M. Koger
1981.   Prevention and stimulation of antler growth by injections of calcium chloride. *Journal of Wildlife Management*, 45(3):733–735.

Tachezy, R.
1956.   Über den Einfluss der Sexual Hormone auf das Geweihwachstum der Cerviden. *Säugetierkundliche Mitteilungen*, 4:103–112.

Vacek, Z.
1955.   Inervace lyci rostoucich parohu u Cervidu. [The innervation of the velvet of growing antlers of the Cervidae]. *Ceskoslovenska Morfologie*, 3(3):249–264.

Wislocki, G.B., and M. Singer

1946.   The occurrence and the function of nerves in the
        growing antlers of deer. *Canadian Journal of Physiologi-
        cal Pharmacology,* 60:788–793. *Journal of Comparative
        Neurology,* 85:1–19.

Wislocki, C.B., and M. Waldo

1953.   Further observations on the histological changes as-
        sociated with the shedding of the antlers of the
        white-tailed deer (*Odocoileus virginianus borealis*). *Ana-
        tomical Record,* 117(3):353–375

T.H. CLUTTON-BROCK
Large Animal Research Group
Department of Zoology
Cambridge
England

Sexual Selection in the Cervidae

ABSTRACT

Among cervids, as in many other vertebrate groups, sexual dimorphism is most pronounced in polygynous species. The usual explanation of this trend is that polygyny is associated with an increase in the extent to which male breeding success varies.

Measures of variation in lifetime breeding success have only recently become available for vertebrates. Studies show that variation in success in males and females calculated over short portions of the lifespan does not necessarily reflect variation in lifetime success. While variation in success is greater among males than females in polygynous species, it can vary as widely in males of some monogamous animals as in polygynous ones.

However, it is not the extent to which male success varies (either in absolute terms or relative to variation in female success) that will determine the development of sexual dimorphism, but the comparative effects of particular traits on breeding success in males and females. Dimorphism is probably related to polygyny because the factors affecting breeding success in the two sexes are more similar in monogamous species than in polygynous ones.

The ruminants are eminently polygamous, and they present sexual differences more frequently than any other group of mammals; this holds good especially in their weapons, but also in other characteristics. (Charles Darwin, 1871)

Sexual Dimorphism and Polygyny

As Charles Darwin himself noted (1871), an association between polygyny and the development of sexual dimorphism is found in many different groups of animals. For example, among primates, sex differences in body size are most highly developed in polygynous species (Clutton-Brock et al., 1977) and so, too, is male weaponry (Harvey et al., 1978). Primary sexual characters are also related to the nature of the breeding system: the males of primate species that typically live in groups including more than one adult male have relatively larger testes than monogamous or harem forming species—presumably because sperm competition is likely to be important where several males may mate with the same female during the course of a single estrous period (Harcourt et al., 1981).

Similar relationships between polygyny and the development of primary and secondary sexual characters are found among ungulates (Alexander et al., 1979), though studies of their breeding behavior are more limited. Among the Cervidae, species that are typically seen singly or in small groups during the breeding season and where males presumably cannot monopolize breeding access to large numbers of females (such as *Hydropotes*, *Mazama* and *Muntiacus* spp.) commonly show little size dimorphism (Figure 1), while differences between the sexes are most pronounced in species where females congregate in large herds which males can defend, as in *Rangifer* and most *Cervus* species. The size of male antlers is also greatest in species belonging to the latter group (Figure 2) and so, too, is testis size: fallow deer, reindeer, red deer, sika and wapiti have larger testes relative to their body weight than muntjac, roe deer, white-tailed deer, mule deer and moose (Figure 3).

These sex differences in morphology and physiology may have important consequences for the population dynamics and ecology of males and females. Theoretical studies of sexual selection show that, in polygynous species, traits which confer an important advantage in direct competition for mates are likely to develop in males to a point at which their costs—usually to the individual's survival—balance their benefits (Lande, 1980). As theory predicts, adolescent and adult males are more likely to die during periods of food shortage than females of the same age in several dimorphic species (Klein, 1968; Robinette, et al., 1957; Grubb, 1974) and populations close to carrying capacity commonly show female-biased adult sex ratios (Cowan, 1950; Clutton-Brock et al., 1982). Though sex differences in dispersal (see Greenwood, 1980) may contribute to this trend, they cannot satisfactorily account for it since male-biased mortality oc-

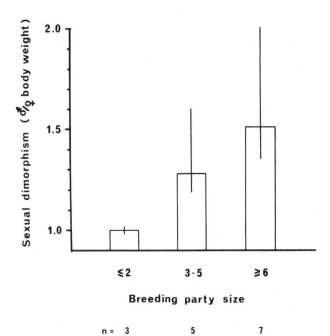

Figure 1. Mean body weight dimorphism (male/female weight) for different species of cervids allocated to three categories on the basis of the size of parties in the breeding season (from Clutton-Brock et al., 1982). A: *Muntiacus*; *Mazama* spp.; *Hydropotes inermis*. B: *Capreolus capreolus*; *Alces alces*; *Cervus unicolor*; *Odocoileus hemionus*; *O. virginianus*. C: *Cervus canadensis*; *Dama dama*; *Axis axis*; *Cervus duvauceli*; *Rangifer tarandus*; *Cervus elaphus*. (Vertical lines show ranges).

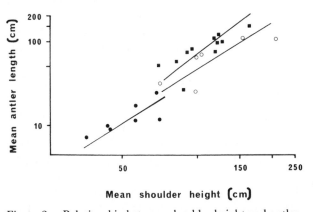

Figure 2. Relationship between shoulder height and antler length in different cervid species (from Clutton-Brock et al., 1980). (Closed circles, *Muntiacus muntjac, M. reevesi, Axis kuhlii, Mazama americana, M. gouazoubira, M. rufina, Pudu puda*. Open circles, *Cervus unicolor; Odocoileus hemionus, O. virginianus, Capreolus capreolus, Alces alces, Hippocamelus bisulcus*. Squares: *Dama dama, Axis axis, Axis porcinus, Cervus duvauceli, C. elaphus, C. canadensis, C. eldi, C. nippon, Elaphurus davidianus, Rangifer tarandus, Hippocamelus antisensis*).

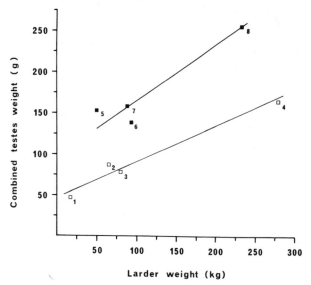

Figure 3.   Testes weight† during the summer months plotted on larder weight* for different cervids (from Clutton-Brock et al., 1982). 1. *Capreolus capreolus* (Short and Mann, 1966; Bramley, 1970); 2. *Odocoileus virginianus* (Mirarchi et al., 1977); 3. *O. hemionus* (Anderson et al., 1974); 4. *Alces alces* (Peek, 1962); 5. *Dama dama* (Chaplin and White, 1972); 6. *Rangifer tarandus* (Leader-Williams, 1979); 7. *Cervus elaphus* (Mitchell et al., 1976); 8. *Cervus canadensis* (Flook, 1970).

curs both before and after the dispersal phase (Clutton-Brock et al., 1982) and can be demonstrated under controlled conditions (Widdowson, 1976). Nor can the 'unguarded' X chromosome of male mammals provide a satisfactory explanation (Myers, 1978), for juvenile and mature males show higher mortality than females in a number of bird species where females are the heterogametic sex (Latham, 1947; Howe, 1977).

While dimorphism and polygyny are commonly related to each other, there are many exceptions to the general trend (Ralls, 1977). Among the cervids, moose are more dimorphic than might be expected on the basis of their breeding systems (Peterson, 1955; Geist, 1963), while Siberian roe deer are less dimorphic (Whitehead, 1972). In other ungulate groups, there are polygynous species which show little sexual dimorphism, like Burchell's zebra (Klingel, 1972) as well as territorial species where females are larger than males, including chevrotains, duikers and dik-diks (Ralls, 1976).

The reason that is usually given for the association between polygyny and sexual dimorphism is that breeding success varies more widely among males in

†includes epididymides.

*this is approximately 70-75% of live weight.

polygynous species, leading to more intense competition for access to mates and stronger sexual selection on males (Clutton-Brock et al., 1977; Alexander et al., 1979; Harvey and Mace, 1982). However, few studies have yet attempted to measure the extent to which breeding success varies or the intensity of direct competition within both sexes. The following sections describe some of the practical problems faced by any attempt to measure the intensity of sexual selection, review field studies of vertebrates which have measured the extent to which reproductive success varies between individuals, and suggest an alternative explanation of the association between polygyny and dimorphism.

Measures of Variation in Male Breeding Success

Two kinds of measures of variation in male breeding success are in use as estimates of the strength of sexual selection. The first expresses variation in breeding success among males relative to variation in female success: for example, Ralls (1977) argues that "the intensity of intrasexual selection in a species should be proportional to the ratio of the lifetime number of offspring sired by a highly successful male compared to the number born by a highly successful female in her lifetime." Similarly Payne (1979) suggests that the extent to which variance in breeding success differs between the sexes is important.

The second type of measure expresses variance in male success relative to the *success of the average male*. Several different indices are in use (Howard, 1979; Payne, 1979) but the most convenient is variance in breeding success divided by the square of mean breeding success (Wade, 1979; Wade and Arnold, 1980; Arnold and Wade, 1984)—a measure derived from Crow's (1958) index of the intensity of selection, $I = V/W^2$ where V is variance in fitness between individuals and $\bar{W}$ is the fitness of the average individual.

The first of these two measures has the disadvantage that it can be affected either by the extent to which male success varies or by the extent to which female success varies. Since the aim of calculating such measures is usually to make comparisons between the sexes or between populations (Wade and Arnold, 1980; Clutton-Brock, 1983) it is preferable to adopt the latter approach, calculating variance relative to mean success separately for both sexes where necessary (Wade and Arnold, 1980).

This still leaves two important questions unanswered. First, over what time period should variation in breeding success be calculated? In practice, variation in breeding success is often calculated at a single point in time (e.g., McCauley and Wade, 1980), on a particular day (Lincoln and Guinness, 1977) or over a single breeding season (Howard, 1979). However, since it is on individual differences in *lifetime* breeding success that selection will usually operate (Falconer, 1960; Maynard Smith, 1969; Cavalli-Sforza and Bodmer, 1961) measures calculated over shorter periods are only valid in so far as they reflect variation in lifetime success.

Even variation in lifetime success may not always be sufficient if the average reproductive success of offspring born into large families is lower than those of offspring born into small families (Clutton-Brock et al., 1982). However, in practice, the number of offspring that an individual produces during its lifetime is usually likely to provide an estimate of the number of its descendants in the next generation, even where offspring born into large families show lower breeding success than those born into small ones. For example, even in the red deer population of Rhum where belonging to a large family depresses the breeding success of individuals (Clutton-Brock et al., 1983) there is still a positive correlation between the number of daughters that a hind produces and the number of granddaughters surviving at her death (Figure 4).

Second, should measures of the intensity of sexual selection be based on variance in breeding success overall, or only on that portion of variance arising as a consequence of differences in mate number and quality? The question concerns the basic distinction between sexual and natural selection (Mayr, 1972; Halliday, 1978). Originally, Darwin distinguished sexual from natural selection on the grounds that sexual selection depends "not on a struggle for existence in relation to other organic beings or to external conditions, but on a struggle between the individuals of one sex, generally the males, for the possession of the other sex. The result is not death to the unsuccessful competitior but few or no offspring."

However, though Darwin's distinction is clear enough in theory, it is often difficult to draw in practice. Competition for resources of all kinds is usually most intense between members of the same sex and it is now generally recognized that differences in reproductive success (rather than in survival) are the principal cause of natural selection (Huxley, 1942; Maynard Smith, 1958). The distinction is further blurred by cases where variation in reproductive success is a consequence of differences in survival induced by sexually dimorphic traits—should these be regarded as forms of natural or sexual selection?

As a result, operational definitions of sexual selection rarely attempt to distinguish between the different causes of variance in breeding success, though in polygynous breeding systems differences in mate number are usually the most important source of variation in male success (Bateman, 1948; Wade, 1979;

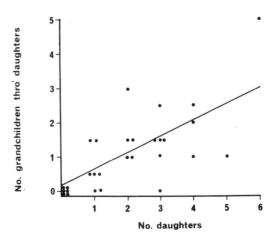

Figure 4. The number of grand daughters of 29 mature hinds plotted against the number of daughters each animal produced over a ten year period. Data from the red deer population of the North Block of Rhum (Clutton-Brock et al., 1982).

Wade and Arnold, 1980). Where the aim is to estimate the potential rate of evolution in males and females, total variance is clearly the appropriate measure but where it is to compare the relative importance of different factors affecting reproductive success, it will be necessary to partition the overall variance into different components (see Arnold and Wade, 1984). In some cases, a straight comparison between the effects of differences in survival and mate number may be all that is required, but in others it will be desirable to subdivide these two categories further and to examine how more specific differences—such as age at first breeding, mate's age, clutch size, offspring mortality, juvenile and adult mortality—contribute to variation in lifetime success (Arnold and Wade, 1984).

One additional point concerning the relationship between variation in breeding success and selection intensity must be emphasized. While measures of the extent to which breeding success varies are commonly referred to as measures of the intensity of selection, this is only the case where differences are fully heritable—which is rarely the case (Maynard Smith, 1958). In fact, variation in breeding success measures the *potential* intensity of selection, and most functional arguments rely on the assumption that non-heritable (or partly heritable) differences in phenotypic characteristics have the same effects on breeding success as similar differences which are inherited.

Practical Problems

Though it is relatively easy to decide how the potential intensity of sexual selection should be estimated, collecting the relevant data poses a variety of problems, especially in long-lived and highly mobile animals like cervids. If females can be recognized and observed consistently, variation in their breeding success can be measured accurately (Guinness et al., 1978)—though it is important to remember that individual differences in offspring survival may be a more important cause of differences in breeding success than variation in fecundity (Clutton-Brock et al., 1982).

Measuring male success is inevitably fraught with problems. In particular, in many polygynous ungulates, younger males often avoid competing directly with larger or older animals and adopt a policy of surreptitious fertilization or kleptogamy (Gibson and Guinness, 1980; Wirtz, 1982) while females are more likely to move between harems around the time of conception (Clutton-Brock et al., 1982). As a result, it is often difficult to be sure that breeding males fertilize all the females in the groups they guard. While no one has yet vasectomized breeding males and examined whether or not their females fail to conceive (or conceive late) similar experiments with red-winged blackbirds show that females guarded by vasectomized males can still lay fertile eggs (Bray et al., 1975). The use of genetic markers provides a promising method of checking paternity estimates (McCracken and Bradbury, 1977) though it is not yet widely used in studies of breeding success in deer.

However, it is important to keep these problems in perspective. If the structure of the mating system is such that the proportion of successful copulations achieved by "thieves" is low relative to the proportion achieved by harem-holders, these errors are likely to have a comparatively minor effect on measures of variation in male success. In contrast, sampling biases may be a far more important cause of major errors in estimating variation in breeding success than is yet appreciated.

While most estimates of variation in breeding success in vertebrates rely on observations made over a part of the individual's lifespan, it is on differences in *lifetime* success that selection will operate. Unfortunately, there are several reasons why estimates of variation in short-term success may either under- or over-estimate variation in lifetime success. First, the reproductive success of breeding males often varies from day to day—for example, in the red deer of Rhum, stags which hold harems in one place on one day may lose them the following day because the wind has changed. As a result of short-term changes of this kind, variation in success calculated within days often over-estimates variation calculated over a longer period (Table 1). Similar effects may also occur between breeding seasons and may cause variation in seasonal success to over-estimate variation in lifetime success (Clutton-Brock, 1982).

Table 1. Variation in number of hinds held by all red deer stags ≥ 1 year old (from Clutton-Brock, 1983)

October	6	11	17	23	29	Season[1]
$\bar{X}$	.74	1.30	1.03	.82	.80	24.02
$\dfrac{\sigma^2}{\bar{X}^2}$	12.31	6.68	6.03	7.08	7.48	3.49
N	61	71	64	68	65	68

[1]Calculations based on number of hind/days held by different individuals over the whole breeding season

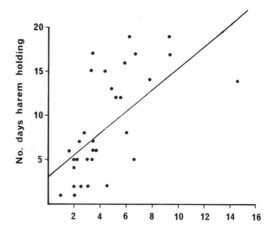

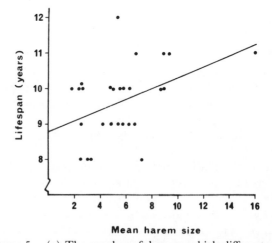

Figure 5. (a) The number of days on which different red deer stags on Rhum held harems in one breeding season plotted against the mean of hinds ≥1 year old in their harems. (b) The number of years in which the same sample of stags held harems plotted against mean harem size during October (from Clutton-Brock, 1983).

T.H. Clutton-Brock

Second, if individuals that are particularly successful during a portion of the breeding season are likely to cease breeding earlier than those that are less successful, variation in success within days will systematically over-estimate variation within seasons. Similarly, if individuals that are particularly successful during their peak period are likely to die earlier than those that expend less effort, variation in seasonal success will over-estimate variation in lifetime success. There is evidence that successful reproduction depresses survival in mountain sheep rams (Geist, 1971), but in several other animals the trend runs in the *opposite* direction and the effective breeding lifespans of successful males are *longer* than those of less successful individuals (Figure 5). Such trends presumably occur because differences in individual quality (Clutton-Brock and Harvey, 1979) affect both breeding success and survival and this relationship obscures any effects of breeding on survival, which may still be considerable (Partridge and Farquhar, 1981). Under these circumstances, variation in success within seasons will tend to *under-estimate* variation in lifetime success.

A third problem arises where the breeding success of males is related to their age. Where age exerts an important effect on success (Geist, 1971) variation within seasons calculated across animals of different ages is likely to over-estimate variation in lifetime success. For example, in red deer stags, fighting ability changes with age (Clutton-Brock et al., 1979) and, as a result, breeding success is strongly age related (Figure 6), with the result that variation in breeding suc-

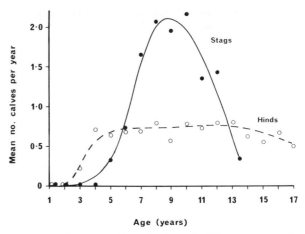

Figure 6. Mean number of calves sired/born per year by red deer hinds and stags of different ages in the North Block of Rhum (from Clutton-Brock et al., 1983).

cess calculated within years across all animals that have reached sexual maturity grossly over-estimates variation in breeding success within cohorts or across the lifespan (Table 2). It is important to notice that this effect also causes variation in male success to be over-estimated relative to variation in female success, which is less strongly age-dependent.

Fourth, estimates of variation in success will be affected by the sample of males included. A recurrent problem in field studies of sexual selection is that field observers commonly record the reproductive success only of actively breeding males since unsuccessful in-

Table 2. Variation in number of calves sired (a) calculated across all male red deer $\geq$ 1 year old present in each of seven breeding seasons and (b) across stags of the same age within breeding seasons. Variation in lifetime success calculated across all individuals reaching breeding age (5 years) is also shown (LRS).

(a)

	Year						
	1974	1975	1976	1977	1978	1979	1980
$\bar{X}$	0.857	1.130	0.884	0.654	0.725	0.825	0.725
$\frac{\sigma^2}{\bar{X}^2}$	3.090	2.108	4.762	6.126	8.072	3.624	3.293
N	46	56	69	78	91	61	68

(b)	1–4	5	6	7	8	9	10	11	12	13+	LRS
$\bar{X}$	0	0.32	0.72	1.65	2.07	1.95	2.17	1.35	1.43	0.33	10.15
$\frac{\sigma^2}{\bar{X}^2}$	—	7.21	2.17	1.61	1.02	1.22	1.35	0.71	2.26	2.25	1.22
N		28	29	41	28	19	12	10	7	8	28

Table 3. Variation in harem size calculated (a) across all red deer stags ≥ 5 years old on different days in the October rut, (b) across only those holding harems.

(a) October	6	11	17	23	29	Season
$\bar{X}$	1.364	2.359	1.806	1.697	1.625	43.730
$\dfrac{\sigma^2}{\bar{X}^2}$	6.279	3.249	3.047	2.962	3.219	1.491
N	33	39	36	33	32	37

(b) October	6	11	17	23	29	Season
$\bar{X}$	4.09	7.08	5.00	4.31	3.71	50.875
$\dfrac{\sigma^2}{\bar{X}^2}$	1.499	0.421	0.467	0.569	0.863	1.138
N	11	13	13	13	14	32

dividuals are often less visible—and may be dead! As a result, the extent of variation in reproductive success may be under-estimated: for example, variation in the number of females held by all red deer stags over 5 years holding harems in our study area on the Isle of Rhum is consistently smaller than variation calculated across *all stags* over 5 years old (Table 3). Even if lifetime success is used, estimates of variation in success can be strongly affected by the sample of animals included. For example, one may calculate the extent to which lifetime success varies among all males conceived; among all males born; among those surviving the neonatal period; among those reaching sexual maturity; among those breeding at least once —and the sample used is likely to have a considerable effect on the effect to which reproductive success varies (Table 4).

None of these four biases are likely to be consistent across the two sexes: all four are more likely to affect estimates of variation in success among males than

Table 4. Variation in lifetime breeding success (based on number of offspring surviving to 1 year old) calculated for different samples of red deer stags on Rhum.

All males born	1.681
All those surviving to 1 year old	1.202
All those surviving to 5 years old	1.202
All those fathering ≥ 1 calves	0.959

females and are consequently likely to influence relative values for the two sexes as well as absolute ones. Moreover, all four biases are more likely to be important in polygynous species than in monogamous ones.

For example, age is likely to have a stronger effect on the success of males than on that of females in many polygynous vertebrates (Wiley, 1974; Clutton-Brock et al., 1983) and short-term measures of variation in male success such as the breeding sex ratio will tend to over-estimate the extent of variation in male success, both in absolute terms and relative to variation in female success. Short-term measures of male success are also likely to over-estimate the extent of variation in polygynous species compared to monogamous ones, where the effective breeding lifespans of males is often longer (Wiley, 1974; Clutton-Brock et al., 1982).

Polygyny and Variation in Male Success

Unfortunately, studies of the extent to which lifetime reproductive success varies are scarce. Among the Cervidae, estimates are so far available only for red deer and we know particularly little about the smaller, less polygynous species. However, lifetime breeding success has recently been measured in several monogamous birds (McGregor et al., 1981), including one with a lifespan comparable to that of red deer, the kittiwake, *Rissa tridactyla* (Coulson, 1966, 1968; Coulson and Thomas, pers. comm.; Wooler and Coulson, 1977) and these data provide some basis for examining the assumption that polygyny is associated with a substantial increase in the extent to which male breeding success varies.

T.H. Clutton-Brock

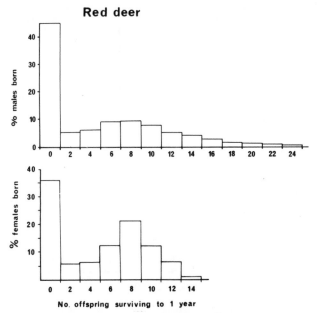

Red deer

Figure 7. Variation in lifetime breeding success (calculated in terms of the number of offspring surviving to one year old) among red deer hinds and stags on the Isle of Rhum (from Clutton-Brock et al., 1983).

In red deer, lifetime breeding success varies considerably more widely among males than females (Figure 7, Table 5): the most successful stags born leave over 25 surviving offspring while the most successful hinds leave no more than fourteen. The difference between the sexes is more pronounced if calculations are restricted to all individuals reaching breeding age (3 for hinds, 5 for stags) and is absent in kittiwakes (Table 5).

However, variation in lifetime breeding success is little greater in red deer stags than in male kittiwakes: in fact, if all individuals born/hatched are included it

Table 5. Variation in lifetime reproductive success for red deer and kittiwakes based on number of surviving offspring. (a) Figures calculated for all individuals born/hatched. (b) Figures calculated for all individuals reaching breeding age. Sample sizes in brackets (from Clutton-Brock, 1983).

		♂		♀	
Red deer	(a)	1.681	(11)	1.065	(42)
	(b)	1.202	(9)	0.354	(30)
Kittiwake	(a)	1.976	(367)	1.896	(417)
	(b)	0.826	(220)	0.691	(250)

is slightly greater in male kittiwakes! Clearly, the comparison is far from ideal since there are important differences in life histories between the two species (Clutton-Brock, 1983), but it serves to emphasize that male success in monogamous breeding systems can vary as widely as in polygynous ones though this may not always be the case.

Nor is it clear that the intensity of direct competition between males is always most intense in polygynous species. The available data are inadequate to allow the frequency of either wounding or fighting to be compared between monogamous and polygynous cervids—or between monogamous and polygynous species in any other vertebrate group. While dangerous fights certainly occur between males in many polygynous mammals (Geist, 1971; Clutton-Brock et al., 1979), they also occur in monogamous species (Kleiman, 1977; P. Moehlmann, pers. comm.; Barrette, 1977). While variation in male success in monogamous species may be caused principally by differences in mate or territory quality whereas differences in mate number are probably the principal cause of variation in polygynous species (Wade, 1979; Clutton-Brock et al., 1982), monogamous males might be expected to compete as intensely for the best mates or territories as do polygynous ones for the biggest harems. Where this is not the case, it may be because males cannot identify the breeding potential of young females or because female choice pre-empts male competition rather than because variation in success is slight among males.

Polygyny and Dimorphism

This raises the question of why it is that polygyny and sexual dimorphism are related to each other *at all*. To understand both this relationship and the exceptions to it, it is necessary to rid ourselves of the assumption that there is any direct relationship between sexual dimorphism and the extent of variation in male breeding success. It is the *effects* of a particular phenotypic trait on breeding success in males and females that will determine the extent to which the development of the trait will differ between the sexes (Price, 1970; Lande, 1980; Clutton-Brock, 1983). For example, while size dimorphism will develop where male success varies more widely than female success and a given increment in size has the same effect on a female as on a male (Figure 8), it will also develop if variation in breeding success is the same in both sexes (Figure 8) or is greater among females (Figure 9) if body size has a stronger effect on the success of males. Conversely, monomorphism in size is likely to be found where body size has a similar effect on the breeding success of both sexes whether or not variation in breeding success differs between the sexes.

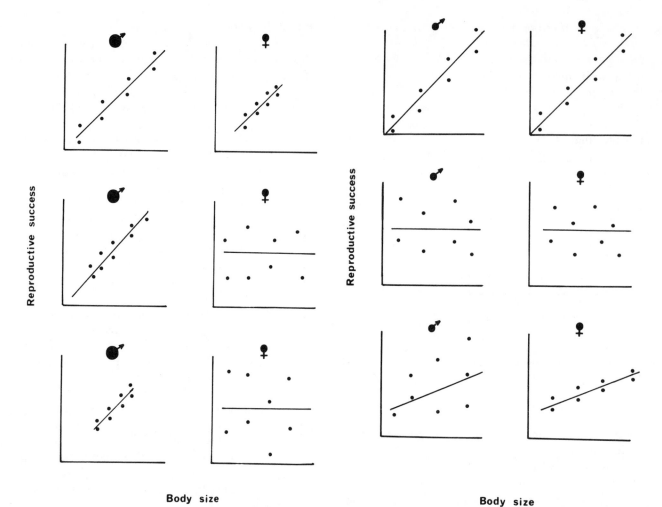

Figure 8. Three hypothetical relationships between body size and reproductive success likely to lead to the evolution of sexual dimorphism.

Figure 9. Three hypothetical relationships between body size and reproductive success unlikely to lead to the evolution of sexual dimorphism.

The common association between polygyny and dimorphism probably occurs not because male breeding success varies more widely in polygynous species but because the factors affecting breeding success in males and females are likely to be more different in polygynous species and more similar in monogamous ones. For example, the factors affecting lifetime breeding success in male and female red deer differ widely (Clutton-Brock et al., 1983). Among females reaching breeding age, the most important determinants of success are differences in lifespan and in calf survival; individual differences in the number of offspring born per year are relatively unimportant. In contrast, among males reaching breeding age, neither lifespan nor calf survival have an important effect on lifetime success, which is principally determined by the average number of hinds fertilized per year (Clutton-Brock et al., 1982). The ultimate factors affecting breeding success also differ between the sexes. Among red deer hinds, breeding success depends on the

quality of the individual's home range and the number of relatives with which she shares it, while her dominance, size and fighting ability do not appear to be important. In contrast, neither home range quality nor group size has an obvious effect on the breeding success of stags, which depends principally on their fighting ability, body size and (as a result of its effect on adult size) early growth rates (Clutton-Brock et al., 1982). Though we do not yet have similar data for any monogamous or territorial species, it is reasonable to suppose that the factors limiting breeding success in males and females are more similar.

This emphasis on the importance of understanding the factors affecting breeding success in males and females is important because it forces us to ask specific comparative questions (Clutton-Brock, 1983). Does male body size have a stronger effect on male success in moose than in roe deer? Do female reindeer have antlers (unlike any other cervid) because their dominance in winter herds exerts a more important influ-

T.H. Clutton-Brock

ence on their breeding success? Does body size have a lesser effect on male success among equids than among cervids and bovids because the former fight by biting their opponents in the neck and hocks rather than by pushing contests?

Moreover, where we observe physiological differences between males and females which do not have a function that is immediately obvious, this approach encourages us to deliberate carefully before dismissing them as non-adaptive. For example, in red deer, as well as in many other dimorphic mammals (Glucksman, 1974), young males lay down less body fat than females (Table 6). This difference is commonly dismissed as a side effect of the action of androgens in males, but it may also have an important functional significance. In red deer, and probably in many other animals where male success depends on adult size, early growth rates have an important effect on the eventual breeding success of males (Clutton-Brock et al., 1982). Consequently, it would not be surprising if, in males, selection had favoured increased allocation of resources to skeletal and muscular growth instead of laying down body fat to assure survival during periods of food shortage. This prompts the question of whether, in vertebrates showing reversed sexual dimorphism, young *females* lay down less body fat than young males. Recent research shows that this is the case in at least one such species, the European sparrow-hawk (I. Newton, pers. comm.).

Thus, if we wish to understand the evolution of sexual differences among the Cervidae, we need to investigate the contrasting forms of competition among males and females and the factors determining breeding success in each sex. In Trivers' (1972) terms, we need to treat males and females as if they were two different species united only because it is the availability of females that limits the breeding success of males.

Table 6. Kidney fat indices of male and female red deer of different ages shot at Glen Feshie, Inverness-shire (from Mitchell, Staines & Welch, 1977)

| | Age (years) | | | |
	0.5	1	2	3
Males	1.5	1.5	1.9	3.6
Females	1.6	2.0	3.5	3.8
N males	26	38	49	67
N females	24	36	47	51

Acknowledgments

I would like to thank Paul Harvey, Peter O'Donald, John Maynard Smith, Linda Partridge, Marion Petrie, Maurice Gosling, Meg McVey, Steve Albon, Dafila Scott and Glenn Iason for comments, criticism and stimulating suggestions as well as my collaborators in the Rhum red deer project (Fiona Guinness, Steve Albon, Glenn Iason, Callon Duck) for collecting and processing the red deer data. Rhum is a National Nature Reserve; and I am grateful to the Nature Conservancy Council for access to its deer population.

Literature Cited

Alexander, R.D., J.L Hoogland, R.D. Howard, M. Noonan, and P.W. Sherman
1979. Sexual dimorphism, and breeding systems in pinnipeds, ungulates, primates and humans. In *Evolutionary Biology and Human Social Behavior, an Anthropolgical Perspective*, edited by N.A. Chagnon and W. Irons, pp. 402–604. Massachusetts: Duxbury Press.

Anderson, A.E., D.E. Medin, and D.C. Bowden
1974. Growth and morphometry of the carcass, selected bones, organs and glands of mule deer. *Wildlife Monographs*, 39:1–122.

Arnold, S.J., and M.J. Wade
1984. On the measurement of natural and sexual selection in field and laboratory populations. *Evolution*, 38:709–734, 2 parts.

Barrette, C.
1977. Some aspects of the behaviour of muntjacs in Wilpattu National Park. *Mammalia*, 41(1):1–29.

Bateman, A.J.
1948. Intrasexual selection in *Drosophila. Heredity*, 2:349–368.

Bramley, P.S.
1970. Territoriality and reproductive behaviour of roe deer. *Journal of Reproduction and Fertility* Supplement 11:43–70.

Bray, O.E., J.S. Kennelly, and J.J. Guarino
1975. Fertility of eggs produced on territories of vasectomized red-winged blackbirds. *Wilson Bulletin*, 87:187–195.

Cavalli-Sforza, L.L., and W.F. Bodmer
1961. *The Genetics of Human Populations*. San Francisco: Freeman.

Chaplin, R.E., and R.W.G. White
1972. The influence of age and season on the activity of the testes and epidiymides of the fallow deer, *Dama dama. Journal of Reproduction and Fertility*, 30:361–369.

Clutton-Brock, T.H.
1982. The function of antlers. *Behaviour*, 79:108–125.
1983. Selection in relation to sex. In *Evolution from Mole-*

cules to Men, edited by D.S. Bendall, pp. 457-481. Cambridge: Cambridge University Press.

Clutton-Brock, T.H., and P.H. Harvey
1979.   Comparison and adaptation. *Proceedings of the Royal Society of London, Series B*, 207:547–565.

Clutton-Brock, T.H., S.D. Albon, and P.H. Harvey
1980.   Antlers, body size and breeding systems in the Cervidae. *Nature*, 285:565–567.

Clutton-Brock. T.H., F.E. Guinness, and S.D. Albon
1982.   *Red Deer: The Behavior and Ecology of Two Sexes.* Chicago: Chicago University Press.

Clutton-Brock. T.H., P.H. Harvey, and B. Rudder
1977.   Sexual dimorphism, socionomic sex ratio and body weight in primates. *Nature*, 269:797–800.

Clutton-Brock. T.H., S.D. Albon, R.M. Gibson, and F.E. Guinness
1979.   The logical stag: adaptive aspects of fighting in red deer (*Cervus elaphus* L.). *Animal Behaviour*, 27:211–225.

Clutton-Brock, T.H., F.E. Guinness, and S.D. Albon
1983.   The costs of reproduction to red deer hinds. *Journal of Animal Ecology*, 52:367–383.

Coulson, J.C.
1966.   The influence of the pair bond and age on the breeding biology of the kittiwake gull *Rissa tridactyla. Journal of Animal Ecology*, 35:269–279.

Coulson, J.C.
1968.   Differences in the quality of birds nesting in the centre and on the edge of a colony. *Nature* 217:478–499.

Cowan, I.McT.
1950.   Some vital statistics of big game on over-stocked mountain range. *Transactions of the North American Wildlife Conference*, 15:581–588.

Crow, J.F.
1958.   Some possibilities for measuring selection intensities in man. *Human Biology*, 30:1–13.

Darwin, C.
1871.   *The Descent of Man and Selection in Relation to Sex.* London: Murray.

Falconer, D.S.
1960.   *Introduction to Quantitative Genetics.* New York: Ronald Press.

Flook, D.R.
1970.   A study of sex differential in the survival of wapiti. *Canadian Wildlife Service Report Series* No. 11, 71 pp.

Geist, V.
1963.   On the behaviour of the North American moose (*Alces alces andersoni* Peterson 1950) in British Columbia. *Behaviour*, 20:175–214.

Geist, V.
1971.   *Mountain Sheep: a Study in Behavior and Evolution.* Chicago: Chicago University Press.

Gibson, R.M., and F.E. Guinness
1980.   Behavioural factors affecting male reproductive success in red deer (*Cervus elaphus* L.). *Animal Behaviour*, 28:1163–1174.

Glucksman, A.
1974.   Sexual dimorphism in mammals. *Biological Review*, 49:423–475.

Greenwood, P.J.
1980.   Mating systems, philopatry and dispersal in birds and mammals. *Animal Behaviour*, 28:1140–1162.

Grubb, P.
1974.   Population dynamics of the Soay sheep. In *Island Survivors: the Ecology of the Soay Sheep of St. Kilda*, edited by P.A. Jewell, C. Milner and J.M. Boyd, pp. 242–272. London: Athlone Press.

Guinness, F.E., S.D. Albon, and T.H. Clutton-Brock
1978.   Factors affecting reproduction in red deer (*Cervus elaphus* L.). *Journal of Reproduction and Fertility*, 54:325–334.

Halliday, T.R.
1978.   Sexual selection and mate choice. In *Behavioural Ecology: an Evolutionary Approach*, edited by J.R. Krebs and N.B. Davies, pp. 180–213. Oxford: Blackwells.

Harcourt, A.H., P.H. Harvey, S.G. Larson, and R.V. Short
1981.   Testes weight, body weight and breeding system in primates. *Nature*, 293:55–56.

Harvey, P.H., M.J. Kavanagh, and T.H. Clutton-Brock
1978.   Sexual dimorphism in primate teeth. *Journal of Zoology*, 186:475–485.

Harvey, P.H., and G.M. Mace
1982.   Comparisons between taxa and adaptive trends: problems of methodology. In *Current Problems in Sociobiology*, edited by King's College Sociobiology Group, pp. 343–362. Cambridge: Cambridge University Press.

Howard, R.D.
1979.   Estimating reproductive success in natural populations. *American Naturalist*, 114:221–231.

Howe, H.
1977.   Nestling sex ratio adjustment among common grackles. *Science*, 198:744–746.

Huxley, J.S.
1942.   *Evolution, the Modern Synthesis.* London: Allen and Unwin.

Kleiman, D.G.
1977.   Monogamy in mammals. *Quarterly Review of Biology*, 52:39–69.

Klein, D.R.
1968.   The introduction, increase and crash of reindeer on St. Mathew Island. *Journal of Wildlife Management*, 32:350–367.

T.H. Clutton-Brock

Klingel, H.
1972. Social behaviour of African Equidae. *Zoologica Africana*, 7:175–185.

Lande, R.
1980. Sexual dimorphism, sexual selection, and adaptation in polygenic characters. *Evolution*, 34:292–305.

Latham, R.M.
1947. Differential ability of male and female game birds to withstand starvation and climatic extremes. *Journal of Wildlife Management*, 11:139-149.

Leader-Williams, N.
1979. Age-related changes in the testicular and antler cycles of reindeer, *Rangifer tarandus*. *Journal of Reproduction and Fertility*, 57:117–126.

Lincoln, G.A., and F.E. Guinness
1977. Sexual selection in a herd of red deer. In *Reproduction and Evolution*, edited by J.H. Calby and C.H. Tyndale-Biscoe, pp. 33–39. Canberra: Australian Academy of Sciences.

McCauley, D.E., and M.J. Wade
1980. Female choice and the mating structure of a natural population of the soldier beetle *Chaulignathus pennsylvanicus*. *Evolution*, 32:771–775.

McCracken, G.F., and J.W. Bradbury
1977. Paternity and genetic heterogeneity in the polygynous bat, *Phyllostomus hastatus*. *Science*, 198:303–306.

McGregor, P.K., J.R. Krebs, and C.M. Perrins
1981. Song repertoires and lifetime reproductive success in the great tit, *Parus major*. *American Naturalist*, 118:149–159.

Maynard Smith, J.
1958. *The Theory of Evolution*. Harmondsworth: Penguin Books.

1969. The status of neo-Darwinism. In *Towards a Theoretical Biology*, edited by C.H. Waddington, Volume 2, pp. 82–89. Edinburgh: Edinburgh University Press.

Mayr, E.
1972. Sexual selection and natural selection. In *Sexual Selection and the Descent of Man*, edited by B.A. Campbell, pp. 88–104. London: Heinemann.

Mirarchi, R.E., P.F. Scanlon, and R.L. Kirkpatrick
1977. Annual changes in spermatozoan production and associated organs of white-tailed deer. *Journal of Wildlife Management*, 41(1):92–99.

Mitchell, B., D. McCowan, and I.A. Nicholson
1976. Annual cycles of body weight and condition in Scottish red deer, *Cervus elaphus*. *Journal of Zoology* 180:107–127.

Mitchell, B., B.W. Staines, and D. Welch
1977. *Ecology of Red Deer: a Research Review relevant to their Management*. Cambridge: Institute of Terrestrial Ecology.

Myers, J.H.
1978. Sex ratio adjustment under food stress: maximization of quality or numbers of offspring? *American Naturalist*, 112:381–388.

Partridge, L., and M. Farquhar
1981. Sexual activity reduces lifespan of male fruitflies. *Nature*, 294:580–582.

Payne, R.B.
1979. Sexual selection and intersexual differences in variance of breeding success. *American Naturalist*, 114:447–452.

Peek, J.M.
1962. Studies of moose in the Gravelly and Snowcrest Mountains. *Journal of Wildlife Management*, 26:360–365.

Peterson, R.L.
1955. *North American Moose*. Toronto: University of Toronto Press.

Price, G.R.
1970. Selection and covariance. *Nature*, 227:520–521.

Ralls, K.
1976. Mammals in which the female is larger than the male. *Quarterly Review of Biology*, 51:245.

1977. Sexual dimorphism in mammals: avian models and unanswered questions. *American Naturalist*, 111:917–938.

Robinette, W.L., J.S. Gashwiler, J.B. Low, and D.A. Jones
1957. Differential mortality by sex and age among mule deer. *Journal of Wildlife Management*, 21:1–16.

Short, R.B., and T. Mann
1966. The sexual cycle of a seasonally breeding mammal, the roebuck (*Capreolus capreolus*). *Journal of Reproduction and Fertility*, 12:337–351.

Trivers, R.L.
1972. Parental investment and sexual selection. In *Sexual Selection and the Descent of Man 1871–1971*, edited by B. Campbell, pp. 136–179. Chicago: Aldine-Atherton.

Wade, M.J.
1979. Sexual selection and variance in reproductive success. *American Naturalist*, 114:742–746.

Wade, M.J., and S.J. Arnold
1980. The intensity of sexual selection in relation to male sexual behaviour, female choice, and sperm precedence. *Animal Behaviour*, 28:446–461.

Whitehead, G.K.
1972. *Deer of the World*. London: Constance.

Widdowson, E.M.
1976. The response of the sexes to nutritional stress. *Proceedings of the Nutrition Society*, 35:1175–1176.

Wiley, R.H.
1974. Evolution of social organisation and life history patterns among grouse. *Quarterly Review of Biology*, 49:201–227.

Wirtz, P.
1982.   Territory holders, satellite males and bachelor males
        in a high density population of waterbuck (*Kobus
        ellipsiprymnus*) and their associations with con-
        specifics. *Zeitschrift für Tierpsychologie*, 58:277–300.

Wooler, R.D., and J.C. Coulson
1977.   Factors affecting the age at first breeding of the kit-
        tiwake *Rissa tridactyla*. *Ibis*, 119:339–349.

T.H. Clutton-Brock

R.M.F.S. SADLEIR
Ecology Division
Department of Scientific and Industrial Research
Private Bag
Lower Hutt
New Zealand

Reproduction of Female Cervids

ABSTRACT   Although the age at first ovulation varies considerably between cervid species, and inside cervid populations, the ovulation rates of adult females do not vary greatly between populations. There is evidence of ovarian activity before the estrus of conception in many species. *Muntiacus* spp. show post-parturition ovulation and several cervid species can ovulate while lactating. Breeding seasons are described, as are the effects of age and physiological condition on the timing of conception. Several species have infrequent but persistent records of conceptions "out-of-season". Gestation lengths and litter sizes are reviewed. Cervid populations have high pregnancy rates with little prenatal mortality. Milk yields and durations of lactation are reviewed.

Introduction

The reproductive pattern of any species is largely the result of its body size and the environmental factors acting upon it. Some components of mammalian reproduction such as gestation length, size at birth, and the number of young born are closely related to body weight (Millar, 1981), and cervid species follow the same trends shown for a variety of mammals. Although cervids are found in habitats ranging from equatorial jungles to the high Arctic, far more is known of the biology of temperate and northern species than of tropical species. In temperate climates severe winter nutritional deficiencies have resulted in very similar reproductive timing of cervids living there. Observations on species such as *Odocoileus virginianus*, which has a wide latitudinal range in North and South America, and the introduced populations of *Cervus elaphus* in the milder winters in parts of New Zealand, suggest that some cervid species retain sufficient reproductive plasticity to alter their temperate zone patterns.

This review will describe the variation in patterns of reproduction in female cervids. It will not cover details of reproductive behavior nor some recently published material on endocrinology. Emphasis has been placed on more recent papers and on discussion of apparent anomalies in the published information. Taxonomic limits of the Cervidae follow Groves and Grubb (this volume), but a small amount of information on *Moschus* (Family Moschidae) is included.

Table 1.   Age at first ovulation within the Cervidae

Usually under 12 months	Usually 12–24 months	Over 24 months
Ax. axis[1]	A. alces[7]	C. duvauceli[13]
H. inermis[2]	Cap. capreolus[2(14)]	C. timorensis[5]
M. muntjac[3]	D. dama[2,8]	
M. reevesi[4]	C. elaphus[9(15)]	
Mos. moschiferus[5]	C. eldi[5]	
O. virginianus[6]	C. nippon[2(16)]	
	C. unicolor[10(15)]	
	O. hemionus[11(17)]	
	R. tarandus[12(18)]	

1. Graf and Nichols, 1966; 2. Chapman, 1974; 3. Barrette, 1977; 4. Sheng and Wang, 1976; 5. Asdell, 1964; 6. Haugen, 1975; Hesselton and Jackson, 1974; Nixon, 1971; 7. Simkin, 1974; 8. Chapman and Chapman, 1975; 9. Clutton-Brock et al., 1982; 10. Acharjyo and Misra, 1971; 11. Robinette and Gashwiler, 1950; 12. Kelsall, 1968; Dauphine, 1976; 13. Schaller, 1967; ( ): observations of early puberty under 12 months of age under special circumstances; 14. Wandeler, 1975; 15. Daniel, 1963; 16. Chapman and Horwood, 1968; 17. Mueller and Sadleir, 1979; 18. Palmer, 1934.

Age at First Ovulation

Females of most deer species ovulate for the first time either when under 12 months of age or between 12 and 24 months (Table 1). Generally the smaller species reach puberty earlier, but this pattern is confused because seasonal breeding affects the time to the first breeding opportunity. The age at first ovulation varies considerably between populations and years in a number of species. This has been reviewed for *C. elaphus* (Clutton-Brock et al., 1982), *A. alces* (Schladweiler and Stevens, 1973; Simkin, 1974), and *R. tarandus* (Dauphine, 1976). It can be of considerable importance in population recruitment. For example, in most *O. virginianus* populations a large, though variable, proportion of fawns ovulate and conceive (Ramsey et al., 1979), but in certain populations no fawns ovulated (in pens, Pennsylvania; Woolf and Harder, 1979; in the wild, Montana; Mundinger, 1981). *C. elaphus* appears to be particularly variable in the proportion of yearlings which ovulate (15–100%: Brna, 1969; 0–17%: Follis and Spillet, 1974; 0–41%: Hamilton and Blaxter, 1980; 30–70%: Lowe, 1969; 54%: Morrison, 1960a; 0–26%: Smith, 1974; 0–50%: Wegge, 1975). This can be related to varying captive *C. elaphus*. The ovulation rate in any year class is directly related to the body weight at estrus. Recently Thomas (1982) noted that pregnancy rates in yearling *R. tarandus* were related to fat reserves.

Extra nutrition probably causes exceptionally early puberty in a number of species (Table 1) in pens or with access to high quality pasture, due apparently to an early achievement of necessary body weight (Hamilton and Blaxter, 1980; Mueller and Sadleir, 1979).

Variation in Reproductive Rate with Age

After puberty almost all adult female cervids ovulate every year. In *O. virginianus* in Iowa 77% of fawns, 87% of yearlings and over 92% of older females had ovulated (Haugen, 1975). In *R. tarandus*, no calves but 57% of yearlings, 80% of 2–year olds and 100% of older females ovulated (Dauphine, 1976). Conception rates, pregnancy rates, and birth rates show similar patterns with age in three separate studies of *C. elaphus* (Figure 1). However, females in this species live long enough to undergo a decline in fertility. In *R. tarandus* (Dauphine, 1976), females were sampled up to 15 years of age but only in small numbers after 10 years. There was no indication of a decline in fertility with age and the full potential fertility was not reached (Figure 2). Studies on *O. virginianus* (Haugen, 1975) and *O. hemionus* (Robinette et al., 1955; Salwasser et al., 1978) did not adequately sample the older age classes to allow comment on this aspect.

R.M.F.S. Sadleir

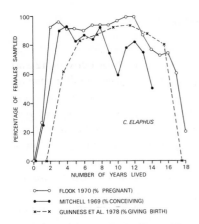

Figure 1. Change in fertility with age in three populations of *C. elaphus*.

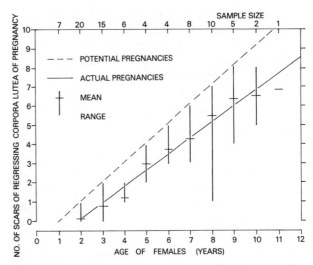

Figure 2. Comparison of potential and actual pregnancies with age in *R. tarandus* (redrawn from Figure 22 in Dauphiné (1976)).

Table 2. Age related differences in mean number of embryos per pregnant doe in three cervid species

	Cap. capreolus	*O. virginianus*			*O. hemionus*		
Reference	1	2	3	4	5	6	7
Age in years							
>1	—	1.21	0	0	0	0	0
1	1.00	1.96	1.26	1.54	0.78	1.30	1.33
2	2.33	2.00	1.50	1.57	1.33	1.74	1.68
3		2.25*	1.77	1.65			1.53
4	2.35		1.75				1.85*
5			1.75*	2.00	1.75	1.80	
6	2.14						
7							
8	1.88			1.22	1.19*	1.81*	
9							
10				1.00*			

*includes older age classes

1. Borg, 1970; 2. Haugen, 1975; 3. Mundinger, 1981; 4. Severinghaus and Cheatum, 1956; 5. Robinette and Gashwiler, 1950; 6. Robinette et al., 1955; 7. Salwasser et al., 1978.

In potentially ditokous species the embryo rate increases with age (Table 2) and then may decline in old age.

Estrus and Ovulation

By far the majority of cervid species are polyestrous (Table 3); only *C. duvauceli* is clearly stated to be monestrous (Panwar, 1978; Schaller, 1967; Martin, 1975). *Cap. capreolus* is probably monestrous. The duration of estrus is known for only a few species (Table 3) and only in *C. elaphus* is there good information on the length of the estrous cycle. Even in species as well known as *O. virginianus*, *O. hemionus* and *R. tarandus* there is considerable confusion in the literature on this point, which may reflect irregularity in cycle length.

In some cervids there is considerable ovarian activity before the first overt estrus. Follicular cycles, well before first estrus, have been reported in *A. alces* (Markgren, 1969), *O. virginianus* (Harder and Moorhead, 1980) and *O. hemionus* (Thomas and Cowan, 1975). In both species of *Odocoileus* the first ovulation rarely results in a pregnancy although ova can be fertilised. At less than 14 days (*O. virginianus*, Harder and Moorhead, 1980), or 8 to 9 days later (*O. hemionus*, Thomas and Cowan, 1975) there is a second ovulation at which almost every female conceives and a corpus luteum of pregnancy is formed. Using data from back-dated embryos Edwards and Ritcey (1958) suggested that a similar phenomenon may occur in *A. alces*.

In other ungulates ovulation can take place with no overt behavioral estrus before the first observable estrus. Such "silent heats" can only be detected by sequential observations of behavior coupled with hormonal assays, laparoscopy or subsequent histological examination of autopsy material. Simkin (1974) suggested that one third of *A. alces* in a Canadian study showed silent heats, but Markgren (1969) found very few silent heats in the same species in Sweden. Similar suggestions of silent heat, based on autopsy material only, have been made for *O. hemionus* (Thomas and Cowan, 1975), *O. virginianus* (Harder and Moorhead, 1980) and *R. tarandus* (Bergerud, 1975). In Scotland, Guinness et al. (1971), using progesterone assays, found no evidence of silent heats in *C. elaphus*. However, work in New Zealand on *C. elaphus* showed that 16% of hinds 2 years of age or older autopsied before the main rut had active corpora lutea, which suggests early ovulation (Kelley and Challies, 1978). These observations have been further supported by the results from ovarian examination (by laparoscopy) at weekly intervals about the onset of the breeding season in 30 hinds joined with one stag (R. Kelly, pers. comm.). Eleven hinds had a corpus luteum on 13 April, yet the first hind was not mated

Table 3. Estrus and estrous cycles in cervids

		Length of estrus	*Length of estrous cycle (days)*
A. alces	polyestrous[1,2]	—	25–30[1,2]
Ax. axis	polyestrous[3]	—	27–30[4]
D. dama	polyestrous[5,6,7,8]*	—	24–26[5,7,8]
C. duvauceli	monestrous[9]	—	—
C. elaphus	polyestrous[10]	1 day[11,12]	18.3 ± 1.7[11]**
		2 days[12,13]	17.5 ± 1.9[14]
C. nippon	polyestrous[6,24]	—	—
M. muntjac	polyestrous[15]	about 2 days[15]	14–21[15]
M. reevesi	—	—	14–15[16]
O. hemionus	polyestrous[17]	—	22–29[17]
O. virginianus	polyestrous[18]	39.9 ± 2.4 hrs[19]	28[18]
R. tarandus	polyestrous[20,21]	50 hours[22]	24[23]

*incorrectly stated in Asdell (1964) as monestrous

**excludes some very short (7–9 day) and very long (34–59 day) cycles

1. Markgren, 1969; 2. Edwards and Ritcey, 1958; 3. Asdell, 1964; 4. Graf and Nichols, 1966; 5. Baker, 1973; 6. Chapman, 1974; 7. Chapman and Chapman, 1975; 8. O'Bryan, 1978; 9. Panwar, 1978; 10. Clutton-Brock et al., 1982; 11. Guinness et al., 1971; 12. Krzywinski, and Jaczewski, 1978; 13. Morrison, 1960b; 14. Lincoln et al., 1970; 15. Barrette, 1977; 16. Yahner, 1979; 17. Thomas and Cowan, 1975; 18. Cheatum and Morton, 1946; 19. Verme and Ozoga, 1981; 20. Dauphine, 1976; 21. McEwan and Whitehead, 1972; 22. Bergerud, 1974; 23. Bergerud, 1975; 24. Haensel, 1980.

R.M.F.S. Sadleir

until 15 April (based on mating records and calving dates). Additionally, 5 or 6 hinds that conceived or were mated before laparoscopy on 22 April had a corpus luteum before their date of conception or mating. This information strongly suggests that *C. elaphus* also has ovulations well before conception in many females.

Cervid species differ as to whether or not accessory corpora lutea are found during pregnancy. Dauphine (1976) reports no accessory corpora lutea in *R. tarandus*, and in *A. alces* (Markgren, 1969), *D. dama* (Armstrong et al., 1969) and *Cap. capreolus* (Chapman and Chapman, 1971) they are very rare. They are fairly frequent in *C. nippon* (Chapman and Chapman, 1971) and *M. reevesi* (Chapman and Dansie, 1970) and very frequent in *C. elaphus*:

79% of sample—Scotland (Douglas, 1966)
52% of sample—Scotland (Guinness et al., 1971)
66% of sample—USA (Halazan and Buechner, 1956)
59% of sample—New Zealand (Kelly and Challies, 1978)

A post-partum ovulation (i.e. occurring within a few days of parturition) has been reported for captive *M. muntjac* (Barrette, 1977; Chaplin and Dangerfield, 1973) and captive *M. reevesi* (Chaplin and Harrison, 1971; Chapman and Dansie, 1970; Dubost, 1971). Post-partum estrus is reported for captive *B. dichotomus* (Frädrich, 1973). *M. reevesi* shows post-partum estrus also in wild populations (Sheng and Wang, 1976) while *M. crinifrons* (Sheng and Lu, 1981) and *Maz. americana* (Gardner, 1971) may do so. Several species can ovulate while lactating, e.g. *Cap. capreolus* (Short and Hay, 1966; Prior, 1968), *Ax. axis* (Graf and Nichols, 1966), *O. hemionus* (Sadleir, 1980a) and *O. virginianus* (Scanlon et al., 1976). This process is reviewed for a variety of mammals by Lamming (1978). No conceptions occur in lactating *C. duvauceli* (Martin, 1975). Although *O. virginianus* in northern latitudes does not exhibit a post-partum estrus, a study by Brokx (1972) of a population at 8° north latitude suggested that females ovulate throughout the year and may ovulate within a few weeks after parturition.

A description of estrus behavior in cervids is outside the scope of this review, but it is interesting that copulation has been described in detail in only three species. *C. elaphus* in Scotland copulates repeatedly during estrus in captivity, but the stag is reported to keep his hind legs on the ground at ejaculation (Guinness et al., 1971). In North America the stag was described as jumping off the ground at ejaculation (Struhsaker, 1967) and this is also reported in New Zealand *C. elaphus* (G.H. Moore, pers. comm.) and in *O. hemionus* (C.C. Mueller, pers. comm.). Hirth (1977) saw 4 cop-

ulations in *O. virginianus* lasting from 6 to 20 seconds (see also Warren et al., 1978) while in *R. tarandus* the mean copulation length was 7 seconds with a maximum of 15 seconds (Bergerud, 1974).

Breeding Seasons

The length of breeding and timing is recorded in reasonable detail for 12 species of cervids. I have found no references to the times of breeding in *M. feai*, *M. rooseveltorum*, *C. albirostris*, *C. schomburgki*, *B. dichotomus*, *Maz. chunyi*, *Maz. gouazoubira*, *Maz. rufina*, or *P. mephistophiles*. For the following species there is either extremely limited or equivocal information about breeding in the wild which I have chosen not to review here. They are referred to primarily by Whitehead (1972) and by other authors where indicated: *C. duvauceli* (Schaller, 1967; Martin, 1975), *C. eldi* (Desai and Malhotra, 1978), *C. nippon* (Davidson, 1976), *Ax. kuhli* (Blouch and Atmosoedirdjo, 1978; Bentley, 1978), *C. timorensis*, *C. unicolor* (Schaller, 1967; Bentley, 1978), *Mos. moschiferus*, *Maz. americana* (Gardner, 1971; Branan and Marchinton, this volume), *Hyd. inermis*, *H. bisulcus*, *H. antisensis* (Roe and Rees, 1976), *Ozot. bezoarticus*, *P. puda* and *E. cephalophus*.

Length of breeding season

Breeding for five species, as judged by the spread of births or observed rutting behavior, may take place throughout the year: these include three species of muntjak, *M. muntjac* (Barrette, 1977; Dubost, 1971), *M. reevesi* (Sheng and Wang, 1976), *M. crinifrons* (Sheng and Lu, 1981), and *Ax. axis* (Graf and Nichols, 1966; Schaller, 1967). However, Sharatchandra and Gadgil (1975) report that *Ax. axis* only ruts from April to August in South Karnataka, India, and De and Spillett (1966) report rutting from February to May in Uttar Pradesh, India. As *Elaph. davidianus* no longer occurs in the wild its original breeding season is unknown, but it is reported in British parks to mate from June to September (Short and Hay, 1966) and in the Bronx Zoo (New York) to mate in June and July (Schaller and Hamer, 1978).

The remaining 8 species of cervids have well documented breeding seasons (Table 4). *O. virginianus* has the widest latitudinal range (52°N to 15°S) and breeds seasonally in the United States and Canada but continuously, or over much longer periods, closer to the equator. I have found no references to the pattern of breeding of the species on the mainland between 28°N and 8°N where it would be of great interest to know over how many months fawns were produced. In 6 species calving in temperate regions is extremely synchronized (Dauphine and McClure, 1974), especially in *R. tarandus* (Table 5). Bergerud (1975), reporting on

Table 4. Season of ovulation (in which a majority of adult ♀ ♀ in the population ovulate within a period of less than a month)

A. alces	(September, October)	Edwards and Ritcey, 1958; Markgren, 1969; Serafinski, 1969.
Cap. capreolus	(July, August)	Lincoln and Guinness, 1982; Prior, 1968; Borg, 1970; Wandeler, 1975.
D. dama	(October, November)	Asher et al., 1981*; Baker, 1973*; Chapman and Chapman, 1975; O'Bryan, 1978*.
C. elaphus	(September–October)	Boyd, 1978; Caughley, 1971*; Fletcher, 1974; Flook, 1970; Guinness et al., 1978; Mitchell and Lincoln, 1974; Morrison et al., 1959; Smith, 1974*.
C. nippon	(September–November)	Yevtushevsky, 1974; Miura, 1980.
O. hemionus	(November, December)	Anderson et al., 1970; Jordan and Vohs, 1976; Robinette and Gashwiler, 1950; Salwasser and Holl, 1979; Thomas and Cowan, 1975.
O. virginianus	(November, December)**	Dunbar, 1976; Harder and Moorhead, 1980; Harris, 1982*; Jackson and Hesselton, 1973; McGinnes and Downing, 1977; Nixon, 1971.
R. tarandus	(October)	Bergerud, 1975; Dauphine and McClure, 1974; Desmeules and Simard, 1970; Leader-Williams, 1980*.

*Southern Hemisphere (transposed 6 months)
**Also reported breeding: all year round in Venezuela (Brokx, 1972) and Virgin Islands (Webb and Nellis, 1981); over seven months in Colombia (Blouch, 1983); six months or longer in Suriname (Branan and Marchinton, 1983).

Table 5. Synchrony of conception in various cervid species

A. alces	85% of ♀ ♀ conceived in 10 days	Edwards and Ritcey, 1958
"	89% " " " " 14 "	Serafinski, 1969
D. dama	83% " " " " 18 "	Asher et al., 1981
C. elaphus	75% " " " " 15 "	Boyd, 1978
Elaph. davidianus	75% " " " " 21 "	Schaller and Hamer, 1978
O. virginianus	90% " " " " 19 "	Harder and Moorhead, 1980
O. hemionus	69% " " " " 21 "	Salwasser and Holl, 1979
"	95% " " " " 20 "	Hudson and Browman, 1959
R. tarandus	80% " " " " 11 "	Dauphine and McClure, 1974

R.M.F.S. Sadleir

a 6-year study, found that 90% of calves each year were born within a period of 8 to 16 days. This population in Newfoundland and others in Alaska and Northwest Territory were found on open plains or tundra; whereas, in a forest population in Northern Quebec, calves were born over a 30-day period. In view of the work of Estes (1976) on wildebeest birth synchronization in relation to predation and aggregation of social units, it would be worth studying the relationship between predation, cover at the birth site, and birth synchrony in a variety of cervid species.

Annual Timing

In several species, investigated in detail over a sequence of years, it appears that there is very little difference in the range and median dates of conception between years in the same population. This was noted for *A. alces* (Markgren, 1969), *C. elaphus* (Guinness et al., 1978a; Mitchell and Lincoln, 1974), *O. virginianus* (McGinnes and Downing, 1977; Nixon, 1971) and *R. tarandus* (Bergerud, 1975). There is some evidence of a latitudinal effect, suggesting a photoperiodic control mechanism. *O. hemionus* mate in December and January in New Mexico (34°N, Anderson et al., 1970), 15 November to 19 December in California (37°N, Salwasser and Holl, 1979), late November in Oregon (44°N, Jordan and Vohs, 1976) and mid-November in British Columbia (49°N, Thomas and Cowan, 1975). Similarly the breeding season is transposed by six months in the Southern Hemisphere (see references in Table 4, especially Caughley, 1971; also Sadleir, 1969). Certain other observations suggest that the latitude effect can be modified by local conditions: (A) calving in zoos by *C. elaphus* from 41°N to 57°N at essentially the same median date (Fletcher, 1974); (B) three populations of *R. tarandus* at similar latitudes in southern Norway with consistent median calving dates over several years of 5 May, 12 May and 28 May (Holthe, 1975); (C) *C. elaphus* in Glen Feshie, Scotland, having a median calving date of 19 October while on Rhum it was 10 days earlier (Mitchell and Lincoln, 1974); (D) the interesting observation in Fiordland, New Zealand (Caughley, 1971; Batcheler and McLennan, 1977), that *C. elaphus* (wapiti) from North America calve some two weeks earlier than *C. elaphus* (red deer) from Britain although this could be related to gestation length differences (see below); (E) observations in Canada that at similar latitudes the main conception period of *R. tarandus* (reindeer) is early September with calving in late April, whereas *R. tarandus* (caribou) conceive some six weeks later with calving in mid June (McEwan and Whitehead, 1972); or (F) *C. nippon* mating in a Japanese park (Lat. 34°N) primarily in October and November (Miura, 1980) and

in a transplanted population in Cherkass province, USSR (west of the Black Sea, 43°N) from September to November (Yevtushevsky, 1974) whereas in Berlin Zoo (53°N) mating in this species takes place at the strange time of July and August (Haensel, 1980).

The timing of conception is also afffected by the age and physiological condition of females in the population. In a detailed study of *O. virginianus* Jackson and Hesselton (1973) showed that the mean conception date of does at least 2½ years old was 22 November and of 1½ year old does was 21 November, but fawns conceived considerably later with a mean date of 6 December. A similar effect was documented by Nixon (1971). In other cervids young of the year very rarely breed, but I have found no published evidence, other than a suggestion by Smith (1974) for *C. elaphus* in New Zealand, that first-time breeders in the wild (i.e. at 1½ or 2½ years of age) conceive later than older does. However, in captivity *C. elaphus* hinds of 3 years or older showed a calving onset of 10 November to 23 November (over 3 years) compared with 4–9 December for 2 year olds in New Zealand (G.H. Moore, pers. comm.). Captive *O. hemionus* fawns which conceived did so at similar times to older does (Mueller and Sadleir, 1979). In *C. elaphus* in Scotland there is clear evidence that milk hinds conceive about a week later than yeld hinds (Mitchell and Lincoln, 1974; Clutton-Brock et al., 1982) which suggests that the metabolic strain of lactation can delay ovulation. It is possible that female *R. tarandus* may fail to breed in seasons that follow a full lactation because of the metabolic stress (Preobrazhenskii, 1961; Dauphine, 1976; Thomas, 1982). Nutritional changes may also explain the observations of H. Ellenberg (pers. comm.) that between 1930 and 1969 the birth season of *Cap. capreolus* advanced by 7 to 10 days in central Europe. This trend has not continued into the past decade.

Conception Out of Regular Season.

In most cervid species studied there is evidence, from the birth distribution, that a few females do not conceive in their first estrous cycles but conceive at their second, third or later estrus. The birth distributions for captive *O. hemionus* in my own studies are fairly typical (Figure 3). Although the mean birth date was 12 June, 12% of births were recorded after the end of June. A similar pattern was noted for *C. nippon* by Miura (1980).

There are a number of conception dates, usually based on sightings of newborn young or back-dated from fetus measurements, which are well outside the usual range (Figure 4). These "outliers" are sufficiently frequent in cervids to suggest that some females retain the ability, perhaps due to variation in photoperiodic response, or because their ovaries are not totally

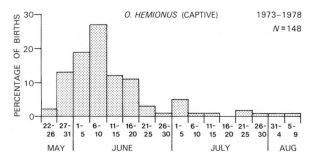

Figure 3. Birth distribution of black–tailed deer (*O. hemionus*) in captivity (British Columbia).

quiescent during the anestrous period, to ovulate at times well away from normal. There appears to have been only one study of calf mortality in relation to this phenomenon. In habitat with very little cover, Guinness and co-workers (1978) were able to locate a large proportion of the carcasses of *C. elaphus* calves on Rhum. They found that, whereas summer mortality did not depend on which quartile of the birth season calves were born into, calves born in the last quartile had a much higher probability of death in the next

winter, and calves born in the first quartile had significantly lower mortality than those born later.

The season of conception of *Cap. capreolus* (i.e. July and August) is so different from that of other cervids that it has provoked interest as to whether females *can* conceive in autumn in this species. There are many anecdotal reports of a "false rut" in October (Prior, 1968; Corbet, 1966). In Sweden Borg (1970) dissected two fawn does, on 3 September and 19 November, and found developing follicles which he suggests would have ovulated in November/December. In another study (Borg, 1962) a 12 month old roe was killed in early June with a large fetus close to term. Either this female ovulated and conceived when 2 or 3 months old, which seems unlikely, or it had conceived around December. There are two reports of "no delay" in *Cap. capreolus*. Prior (1968) noted a doe shot in December with a fully developed fetus and Renfree (1978) a female which mated in August and gave birth in January.

There are two reports of exceptional parturitions in *O. virginianus*. Hesselton and Van Dyke (1969) reported twin fawns born two days apart; while, in a really remarkable observation, Bartmann (1971) reported that a doe in a German zoo gave birth to a singleton on 9 June 1969, to twins on 27 June 1970 and

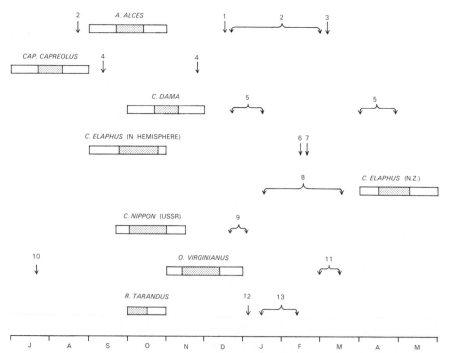

Figure 4. "Out-of-season" conceptions (bar indicates usual season of conception with most conceptions inside shaded portion). 1. Coady, 1974; 2. Markgren, 1969; 3. Maehlum, 1981; 4. Borg, 1970; 5. Armstrong et al., 1969; 6. Wishart, 1981; 7. Batchelor, 1965; 8. Smith, 1974; 9. Yevtushevsky, 1974; 10. Hall and Hall, 1980; 11. Harwell and Barron, 1975; 12. Desmueles and Simard, 1970; 13. Holthe, 1975.

R.M.F.S. Sadleir

Table 6. Gestation periods in Cervidae

Species	N	$\bar{x}$ (days)	Range (days)	Reference
A. alces	?	?	227–239	Serafinski, 1969
	19	236	226–244	Skuncke, 1949
Cap. capreolus	?	?	294	Prior, 1968
Ax. axis			229	Graf and Nichols, 1966
Ax. kuhli		8 months		Whitehead, 1972
D. dama	?	229	—	Chapman and Chapman, 1975
	11	229	225–234	Prell, 1938
C. duvauceli	?	—	240–250	Schaller, 1967
C. elaphus (Red)	9	234		Prell, 1938
	?	236 ♂♂		Clutton-Brock et al., 1981
	?	234 ♀♀		
	3*	233	231–235	Krzywinski and Jaczewski, 1978
	13	231	223–238	Guinness et al., 1971
C. elaphus (N.Z. wapiti-type)	3	246	240–254	G.H. Moore, (pers.comm.)
C. eldi	5	—	236–244	Desai and Malhotra, 1978
	3	242	240–244	Blakeslee et al., 1979
C. nippon	11	222		Prell, 1938
	12	221	214–225	Haensel, 1980
	?	—	226–230	Miura, 1980
C. unicolor		8 months		Schaller, 1967
O. virginianus	9	202	197–207**	Haugen and Davenport, 1950
	55	202	196–213	Verme, 1969
O. hemionus	5	204	199–207	Golley, 1957
R. tarandus (caribou)	15	216		McEwan and Whitehead, 1972
(reindeer)	7	208		
R. tarandus (caribou)	4	229	227–230	Bergerud, 1975
(reindeer)	79	227	210–238	Schmitt, 1936
M. muntjac**	?	?	224–238	Dubost, 1971
M. reevesi***	4	216	213–219	Barrette, 1977
	4	214	209–220	Chaplin and Dangerfield, 1973
	1		217	Yahner, 1979
Mos. moschiferus		160		Gupta and Jain, 1980
Maz. americana		about 225		Thomas, 1975
Hyd. inermis		about 170		Chaplin and Dangerfield, 1973
			180–210	Chapman, 1974
Elaph. davidianus		10 months		Whitehead, 1972
		250		Kenneth, 1947
	?		285–300	Schaller and Hamer, 1978

*based on artificial insemination

**one length of 222 days omitted

***assumes conception at the post-partum estrus

then to a single fawn on 9 September 1970 (74 days later). All fawns were normal and lived. Split parturition phenomena have been reviewed for other mammalian species by Vandeplassche (1969).

Gestation Lengths

Gestation periods in mammals are directly related to adult size (Western, 1979). Millar (1981) has reviewed the relationships for a large range of mammals (including 6 cervid species) and has produced predictive equations using body weight and litter size as dependent variables. He suggests that gestation periods may be determined by structural and physiological constraints related to placental type and physiology and, through birth weight, to pelvic canal size. Placental morphology of several cervids has been described by Hamilton et al. (1946).

It is remarkable that, even in species as well studied as some of the cervids, there still remains either little, or somewhat confusing, data on gestation periods (Table 6). For example Smith (1974), using references I have not been able to sight (Blunt, 1962; Hepworth, 1966), cites gestation lengths of 250, 246, 247 and 250 days for *C. elaphus* (wapiti) and also uses the somewhat questionable gestation of 247 days given by Morrison et al. (1959) for the same species. On the basis of these and other figures, Smith (1974) suggested that wapiti gestation periods may exceed red deer gestation periods by about 16 days. Three separate papers, each 3 decades apart, quote exactly the same range for wapiti gestation—249 to 262 days (Lantz, 1910; Rust, 1946; and Boyd, 1978). The latter two authors did not give their source, and in the original paper no information is given as to how this range was determined! Three accurately determined gestations (observed mating to calving) from New Zealand are given in Table 6.

There is considerable difference in the lengths of gestation cited for *R. tarandus* (Table 6). This is more confused by the observations of Gensch (1969) who recorded two cows whose maximum gestation periods were 200 and 210 days. Krog et al. (1980) suggest that embryonic development time may vary to ensure synchrony of calving. Asdell (1964) quotes a highly unlikely gestation for *C. duvauceli* of 340 to 350 days! This originated from Zuckerman (1953) who quoted the same range by misquoting Kenneth (1947), who actually gave two single observations, not a range, of 240 and 250 days. Asdell (1964) also gives a considerable range of gestation (249–284 days) for *C. timorensis*, but it is difficult to determine the source of this information. There is also some doubt as to the true gestation length of Pere David's deer (*Elaph. davidianus*), and Frädrich (1983) suggests a somewhat unlikely gestation length of 271 days for *B. dichotomus*.

Number of Young

The following species of cervid regularly produce only a single offspring: *D. dama* (Baker, 1973; O'Bryan, 1978), *C. duvauceli* (Schaller, 1967; Martin, 1975), *C. elaphus* (Clutton-Brock et al., 1982), *C. eldi* (Whitehead, 1972), *Ax. axis* (Blouch and Atmosoedirdjo, 1978), *C. nippon* (Haensel, 1980), *C. unicolor* (Schaller, 1967), *R. tarandus* (Dauphine, 1976), *M. muntjac* (Barrette, 1977), *M. reevesi* (Sheng and Wang, 1976), *M. crinifrons* (Sheng and Lu, 1980, 1981), *Maz. americana* (Thomas, 1975) and *Elaph. davidianus* (Asdell, 1964). There are, however, some interesting exceptions among these species. Chapman and Chapman (1975) reported two pairs of twins in 270 births in *D. dama*, and Schaller (1967) noted 1 twin in 347 births in zoos of *Ax. axis*. Haensel (1980) reported 1 set of twins in 83 births of *C. nippon*. There are repeated observations (see Guinness and Fletcher, 1971) of rare twinning in *C. elaphus*, and larger samples show this is consistent:

0.2% twins (N = 1690) : Kittams, 1953
0.2% twins (N = 1186) : Flook, 1970
0.6% twins (N = 1106) : Greer, 1968
1.2% twins (N = 875) : Kroning and Vorreyer, 1957
2.0% twins (N = 976) : Brna, 1969

The complete lack of any records of triplets in this species strongly suggests that a Poisson distribution does not represent litter size. In many years of field experience Nowosad (1973) reported only 3 pairs of *R. tarandus* twins, while Shoesmith (1976) shot one cow with twin fetuses and McEwan (1971) had one cow produce twins in captivity. Like Barrette (1977), Chapman and Dansie (1970) noted only 1 fawn in tracts of *M. muntjac* and, interestingly, in 90% of cows the embryos were located in the right uterine horn.

Casual reports on a small group of species describe "one, occasionally two" young: *Mos. moschiferus* (Gupta and Jain, 1980) and Whitehead's (1972) descriptions of *H. bisulcus*, *P. puda* and *E. cephalophus*. Of 18 fetuses of *Maz. americana*, only 2 were twins (Branan and Marchinton, this volume). In discussing the remaining multiparous species (Table 7) I have not considered the many papers which refer to mean corpora lutea counts or to mean fetus counts per doe because these conceal important information, i.e. the proportions of females with 1, 2 or 3 young. In *A. alces* the proportion of females with twins varies considerably between different populations (Edwards and Ritcey, 1958; Hauge and Keith, 1981). Schladweiler and Stevens (1973) reviewed five North American studies where the twinning rate varied from 11% to 29%. In Poland, Serafinski (1969) described three forest areas where the percentages of females with twin calves were 14%, 45% and 49%.

Table 7. Litter size in multiparous cervids

Species	Percentage					Source	Reference
	N	1	2	3	4		
A. alces	307	61	39	0*	—	C.L.	Markgren, 1969
"	6271			0.9	0.2	Young	Ling, 1974
Cap. capreolus	362	16	50	33	1	fetus	Borg, 1970
"	152	13	62	22	3	C.L.	Prusiate et al., 1976
O. virginianus	126	24	66	9	0.7	fetus, yearlings	Nixon, 1971
"	210	10	79	10	1.0	fetus, adults**	
O. hemionus	135	37	59	3	1	fetus	Nellis, 1968
"	102	31	64	5	—	fetus	Salwasser et al., 1978
"	486***	37	62	1	—	fetus	Robinette and Gashwiler, 1950

*one female with 2 CL and 3 fetuses
**one female had 5 fetuses
***data for several previous studies combined

Field observations of cows with twins following may be due to calf adoption. Murie (1934) noted that there were no wolves on Isle Royale, Michigan, where moose populations were high and some animals were in poor condition. Only 2% of females had twins. In Mech's (1966) study wolves were present, the population was reduced and 38% of females had twin calves. A set of triplets was seen in 1974 (Moll and Moll, 1976). In a large study in Estonia, Ling (1974) noted that under favourable conditions 1.89% of cows autopsied had 3 corpora lutea and 0.19% of cows had quadruplet fetuses. Unfortunately it is not possible to work out the exact sample sizes from his paper.

There is evidence that in *Cap. capreolus* the proportion of females ovulating 2, 3, and 4 ova depends on nutrition, and Loudon (this volume) has shown a clear relationship between ovulation rate, body weight and the nature of the forest habitat. Prior (1968) discusses Swedish observations of this species which were fed in large pens over winters before 1939 when some females produced 3 or 4 young. With reduced feed in the early 1940s, almost all does produced 1 or 2 young. Chapman and Chapman (1971) reviewed several British populations in which 65–100% of females produced twins, but noted a population on poor nutrition in Inverness shire where only 27% produced twins.

Although *O. virginianus* usually gives birth to 2 fawns over most of its range, in Venezuela (Brokx, 1972), Colombia (Blouch, 1983) and New Zealand (Harris, 1982) twins are very rare indeed.

A number of papers show a relatively constant frequency of litter size in *O. hemionus* (Table 7). In my studies of a penned population, of 72 parturitions 32% were of 1 fawn, 67% were of twins and 1% was of triplets. A set of quadruplets was born some years later in the same group of black-tailed deer, but all died within 2 days. Sears and Browman (1955) show a doe with 4 fetuses, and Nellis et al. (1976) found an *O. hemionus* doe with 5 corpora lutea and 5 fetuses.

Perhaps the most interesting cervid in this regard is the Chinese water deer (*Hyd. inermis*). Whitehead (1972) and Walker (1975) say that 2 to 3 fawns are common and up to 6 have been recorded, but this is queried by Dobroruka (1970) who reviewed information from zoos and the published literature. He notes that more than 4 young per birth have not been recorded in zoos and that, although there are literature reports of up to 8 young, all records above 4 are from fetuses *in utero*. He suggests that many of the fawns in these larger litters would have died before or immediately after birth.

Why do a very few females in many cervid populations occasionally produce exceptionally large litters? Because of their size and relative visibility immediately after birth, compared with the more cryptic rodents and carnivores, this phenomenon will be more easily documented in cervids and other artiodactyls. While large litters may reflect exceptional ovulation rates due to high levels of nutrition, there are still sufficient observations to suggest that large litters occur at very low but persistent frequencies. This may be a genetically conservative mechanism to allow the species, should its environment change, to increase fecundity fairly quickly. Inability to do this may close off a future option. Interestingly, domesticated *R. tarandus* do *not* show an increased level of twinning com-

Table 8. Pregnancy rates in cervid populations

Species	N	Percentage of adult females pregnant	Source	Reference
A. alces	—	76	autopsy	Edwards and Ritcey, 1958
	—	72	birth	Hauge and Keith, 1981
	37	86	autopsy	Markgren, 1969
	—*	76–90	autopsy	Schladweiler and Stevens, 1973
Cap. capreolus	206	96	autopsy	Prusaite et al., 1976
Ax. axis	152	85	autopsy	Graf and Nichols, 1966
D. dama	94	95	autopsy	Armstrong et al., 1969
	191	73	birth	Asher et al., 1981
	70	91	autopsy	Baker, 1973
	—	96	birth	Chapman and Chapman, 1975
C. elaphus	1012	93	autopsy	Flook, 1970
	731	71	birth in captivity	Hamilton and Blaxter, 1980
	2072	80	autopsy	Kittams, 1953
O. virginianus	1004	92	autopsy	Hesselton and Jackson, 1974
	127	96	autopsy	Mundinger, 1981
O. hemionus	101	88	autopsy	Robinette and Gashwiler, 1950
R. tarandus	280	90	autopsy	Dauphine, 1976
	—	90	autopsy	Leader-Williams, 1980
	—	90	autopsy	Parker, 1981

*data from several North American studies

pared with wild animals. Geist (1974) has suggested that the ability to twin in *A. alces* allows the species to realize a larger reproductive potential in successional stages of "burn-habitats": he compares this species with *R. tarandus* for which fires, in contrast, reduce carrying capacity.

Pregnancy Rates

In a variety of cervids, if yearlings and other submature females are excluded, there is a high pregnancy rate (Table 8), but not all adult females become pregnant. As with ovulation rate, the proportion which actually become pregnant is affected by nutrition. For example, in a detailed review of *C. elaphus* populations, Smith (1974) concluded that when less than 80% of hinds are pregnant nutrition is poor. Greer (1968) claimed that the pregnancy rate varied inversely with density, and Guinness et al. (1978) showed that 82% of milk hinds compared to 96% of yeld hinds gave birth. Similarly Dauphine (1976) noted that barren *R. tarandus* cows had higher pregnancy rates in the subsequent year than cows that were previously pregnant, and Thomas (1982) clearly demonstrated that pregnancy rates in the same species were directly correlated with fat reserves.

Prenatal Mortality

There are many ways of measuring prenatal mortality—the commonest being to compare the number of ovulations per female, as indicated by corpora lutea counts, with the number of live fetuses. There are only a limited number of studies of prenatal mortality in cervids. Markgren (1969) stated that about 19% of ova were lost in Swedish populations of *A. alces* but considered that this was an overestimate due to the age distribution of his sample. For *D. dama*, Chapman and Chapman (1975) estimated up to 10% prenatal mortality, but their method was questionable.

There are far better estimates for *Odocoileus*. In a four year study involving 331 autopsies Barron and Harwell (1973) found a 14% difference between the corpora lutea and fetus counts in *O. virginianus*. Hesselton and Jackson (1974), using data from large samples of the same species, found that prenatal mortality ranged consistently from 7% to 10% in different years despite differences in age and condition of does. Nixon (1971) reported 9% prenatal mortality in yearlings (N = 179) and 12% for 2½ years or older does (N = 215). The most detailed study of prenatal mortality in any cervid is that for *O. hemionus* by Robinette et al. (1955);

R.M.F.S. Sadleir

1 corpus luteum (N = 128)— 0% ova loss
2 corpora lutea (N = 329)—10% ova loss
3 corpora lutea (N = 22)—32% ova loss
4 corpora lutea (N =   2)—50% ova loss
5 corpora lutea (N =   1)—60% ova loss

Although the sample sizes with corpora lutea of 3 or more are necessarily small it is interesting that the loss of ova restores the fetal rate to 2 per doe.

While reviewing the literature I have found only two references to post-implantation mortality and embryonic death or resorption. A macerated fetus was seen in the uterus of a *Cap. capreolus* doe (Heidemann, 1974). Salwasser et al. (1978) reported one resorption in a sample of 102 *O. hemionus*. During my studies of this species in Canada, serial X-rays of pregnant females showed one case of internal resorption in mid pregnancy with no external sign. A second female died just after the normal birth season and the post mortem examination revealed a macerated fetus *in utero*.

The case of *Cap. capreolus* is a special one because of delayed implantation (Short and Hay, 1966; Renfree, 1978; Aitken, 1981). Borg (1970) reported a 9.4% prenatal mortality (N = 362) in Sweden, but this cannot be considered normal as his sample came from carcasses submitted for veterinary examination. In a more representative Swiss study, Wandeler (1975) noted a 1.5% embryo loss before implantation in January and a 1% loss thereafter. These data show that the very long gestation, unique among cervids, has little or no detrimental effect on uterine survival.

It would thus seem that pregnancy in cervids is generally a period of very little mortality of embryos. Almost all females that conceive subsequently give birth. Thus corpora lutea counts are a good indication of subsequent fecundity.

Parturition and Birth Weights

Descriptions of diurnal patterns of parturition and maternal behavior at that time have been published for several cervids: *Cap. capreolus* (Bubenik, 1965), *D. dama* (Chapman and Chapman, 1975; Meier, 1973), *C. elaphus* (Arman, 1974; Bubenik, 1965), *C. nippon* (Sato et al., 1981), *O. virginianus* (Haugen and Davenport, 1950; Michael, 1964; Townsend and Bailey, 1975) and *O. hemionus* (Halford and Alldredge, 1975). With two exceptions there appear to be no references in the literature to difficulties in parturition resulting in mortality of doe and/or fawn. Miller (1970) describes four cases of *O. hemionus* does in late pregnancy having accidents yet giving birth to healthy fawns. During nearly a decade of management of some hundreds of *C. elaphus* on Invermay research station in New Zealand no parturitional deaths have been seen (G.H. Moore,

pers. comm.). However, Yevtushevsky (1974) describes two female *C. nippon* dying during parturition. In studies on *R. tarandus* populations in Newfoundland and South Georgia (Bergerud, 1971; Leader-Williams, 1980) there is frequent mention of parturitional death which forms a measurable component of the overall adult mortality. C. Wemmer (pers. comm.) noted parturitional difficulties in a young *C. eldi* doe in captivity who had twin fetuses, both dead.

Birth weights, fetal growth and neonatal growth in cervids and other ungulates have been exhaustively reviewed by Robbins and Robbins (1979).

Lactation

Lactation, as a physiological production process, is partially scaled to the species' body size. Several reviewers (Payne and Wheeler, 1968; Linzell, 1972; Hanwell and Peaker, 1977; Robbins and Robbins, 1979) have shown that milk yield and energy content are related to body weight over a range of mammals, but unfortunately they have only compared maximum daily yield to weight. There is little information on the total milk yield of lactations. Blaxter (1971) found a positive relationship between the duration of lactation and maternal weight but, as Millar (1981) pointed out, this is not a strong pattern, and should be re-evaluated because of the variation in lactation length to be described below.

The composition of cervid milk has been discussed by Jenness (1974) but mostly from small samples taken at different stages of lactation. Peaker (1977) has emphasized the dangers involved in interspecies comparison of milk qualities because the method of collection can alter the proportion of nutritive components. There are only a few studies where milk composition has been reported at different stages of lactation and where the milk was collected by constant methods throughout lactation: *C. elaphus* (Arman et al., 1974; Krzywinski et al., 1980; Robbins et al., 1981), *O. hemionus* (Mueller and Sadlier, 1977), *R. tarandus* (Luick et al., 1974). These papers show considerable variation between species and individuals of a species, particularly in the pattern of changes in fat and sugar concentration. Robbins et al. (1983) have given a detailed comparison of the composition of cervid milks.

Similarly, in the small number of species which have been studied, there is considerable variation in the milk yield curves between individuals as lactation progresses. Robbins and Robbins (1979, p. 108) stated that "Peak milk production estimates are quite important since the rest of the milk production values can be predicted based upon the general shape of the lactation curves in mammals". This statement is definitely not supported by the yield curves of Robbins et al.

(1981) for *C. elaphus* in the United States and compared with those of Arman et al. (1974) for the same species in Scotland or with data for *O. hemionus* (Sadleir, 1980a) or with the data of Robbins and Moen (1975) for *O. virginianus*. In *C. elaphus* the type and amount of food available has recently been shown to greatly influence the milk yield curve (Loudon et al., 1983).

The duration of lactation in cervids is known accurately in only a few species and again shows considerable variation. Captive *O. hemionus* varied in lactation duration from 84 days (Sadleir, 1980a, b) to 238 days (Mueller and Sadleir, 1977). Sudden reductions in the fat content of milk of the three does in the later study occurred at 145, 163 and 177 days which suggest that lactation normally ceases about November or December.

In *Cap. capreolus*, lactation can continue to December in the wild (Borg, 1970) which is a long duration of 8 months. In *C. nippon* (Miura, 1980) most does lactated for 6 months but some for up to 11 months. Lactation in *D. dama* is variable. Chapman and Chapman (1975) noted that, although some females were dry in October, others lactated till January and four into March. Jackson (1977) gave the following figures:

Jan 1–5	9 of 10 females lactating
Jan 16–31	10 of 16 females lactating
February	1 of 17 females lactating
April/May	0 of 5 females lactating

In *C. elaphus*, Clutton-Brock et al. (1982) described the weaning pattern of calves and noted very considerable differences in the duration of lactation between hinds of two types. Hinds which became pregnant in October were last observed suckling their previous calves in November or December (N = 72 observations), whereas hinds which did not conceive in October suckled their previous calves until the next June or July (N = 36 observations). Krzywinski et al. (1980) claim that barren hinds will continue to lactate for 2 years.

The calves of *C. elaphus* hinds on a hill pasture (poorer nutrition) suckled much more frequently than the calves of hinds on a grass pasture (Loudon et al., 1983), although the milk yields of hinds on hill pasture were considerably lower than those of hinds on grass. Interestingly, the plasma prolactin levels of the hill pasture hinds were elevated so these authors suggest that the lactational infertility may be greatly affected by the suckling frequency which in turn is dependent on the role of maternal nutrition in milk yield.

It is interesting to note Smith's (1974) comparison of the duration of lactation in *C. elaphus* in New Zealand with that in North America and Britain. The British pattern has already been described, but in North America very few calves suckle after January. Under the more even climate of Fiordland in New Zealand, 10% of pregnant hinds suckled their previous calf until 1 or 2 months before birth, as did 41% of barren hinds. Nutritional conditions in southern New Zealand may be so good that a few female *C. elaphus* can acutally suckle young through till late pregnancy. This is very unusual for *C. elaphus* and for cervids generally. However, the milk yield towards the end of these long lactations will probably be very low (Sadleir, 1980b).

In *O. virginianus* Brokx (1972) suggests that lactation proceeds for 5 months in a continuously breeding population in Venezuela. In more northern latitudes Scanlon and Urbston (1978) and Woolf and Harder (1979) have noted that this species lactates until December and then stops fairly suddenly.

The cessation of lactation is difficult to document accurately, and some durations described—while representing physiological actuality—are probably rare in the wild. Captive studies, where fawn mortality is reduced to a minimum and there is a forced proximity of mother and young, are suspect. There is a considerable need for more studies of natural populations where the proportion of adult females lactating is documented as the season progresses.

Cross suckling (i.e. the suckling of non-filial calves in the wild) has only been reported in *C. elaphus*. Clutton-Brock et al. (1982) report that hinds rarely suckle calves that are not their own and then, if they do, they are usually calves of close relatives. No cervid species are mentioned in a review of cross suckling by Walser (1977).

Conclusions

In temperate zones cervids are large in body size and are characteristically fall breeders with one or two young born in early or mid summer. Once past the immediately post-pubertal years, almost every female conceives every year and then gives birth. There are only two major phases of the reproductive patterns in these species which vary to any degree between season and habitat—the age at first conception and the proportion of females in the population which conceive and give birth to twins. There is considerable variation in the age of initial conception in many cervid populations which, dependent on their age structure, may have a considerable effect on recruitment. In contrast, the twinning rate is very low and nearly constant in populations of *R. tarandus*, *C. elaphus* and other large cervids, whereas in the largest cervid, *A. alces*, twinning is highly variable between populations and years. The variation in twinning rates is relatively constrained in both *Odocoileus* species.

Cap. capreolus is the only small cervid living in tem-

R.M.F.S. Sadleir

perate northern areas. To be consistent with the body size/gestation length relationship shown by other mammals (Millar, 1981), this species should have a gestation length of around 130 days. Instead there is a pre-implantation gestation of 5 months and a post-implantation gestation of 5 months. Delayed implantation has thus permitted this small cervid to live in northern habitats.

Much less is known of the biology of tropical and sub-tropical cervids. They show a wide range of sizes, but these species are generally smaller than those in temperate zones. Breeding is less seasonal and a post-parturition estrus is more common so that pregnancy and lactation may frequently overlap. Because most tropical habitats are relatively consistent in their climates and therefore in their food supply, I predict that members of these species will reach puberty at a relatively constant age, with little variability in ovulation rates between seasons, and with little synchrony of estrus.

The South American cervids are relatively small but occupy a wide latitudinal and altitudinal range. Thus most species live in highly seasonal habitats. I hope that populations of these species, many of which are endangered, will survive and be studied so as to determine their special patterns of reproduction. They are probably seasonal breeders with variable reproductive patterns. The attainment of puberty and the ovulation rate per female (or more likely, the proportion of females ovulating at any time) at each breeding season may fluctuate considerably between years.

This review of reproduction in cervids has shown that, although much is known about certain species, there are considerable gaps in our understanding of the basic parameters for most species. Only when these are closed will it be possible to establish the range of adaptive variations available to each species to respond to changes in habitat or population structure. The major evolutionary question remains: which individuals contribute to the next generation and under what conditions do they accomplish that contribution? The outstanding study of Clutton-Brock et al. (1982) shows that our knowledge of at least one cervid species is more advanced here than for almost any other wild mammal. Most of the progeny in the herd of *C. elaphus* are sired by a very few stags—a pattern that has great evolutionary implications. It is to be hoped that studies at similar depth will be carried out on other cervids to determine whether or not such a relationship is widespread in the family.

Acknowledgments

I thank R. Kelly and G.H. Moore (Invermay Agricultural Research Centre, Mosgiel, New Zealand) for permission to quote unpublished information, and T. Clutton-Brock, S. Albon and F. Guinness for access to the MS of their recently published book. T. Dauphine gave permission for the use of Figure 2. I am very grateful to the Friends of the National Zoo and the Department of Scientific and Industrial Research for travel funds to attend the conference. J. Flux helped with translations of German material. I thank J. Flux, J. Gibb and A. Pritchard for their comments on this paper in preparation. I thank P. Scanlon for drawing my attention to the Vandeplassche reference.

Literature Cited

Archarjyo, L.N., and R. Misra
1971.   Age of sexual maturity of three species of wild animals in captivity. *Journal of the Bombay Natural History Society*, 68:446.

Aitken, R.J.
1981.   Aspects of delayed implantation in the roe deer *Capreolus capreolus*. *Journal of Reproduction and Fertility* Suppl., 29:83–95.

Anderson, A.E., W.A. Snyder, and G.W. Brown
1970.   Indices of reproduction and survival in female mule deer Guadalupe Mountains, New Mexico. *Southwestern Naturalist*, 15:29–36.

Arman, P.
1974.   A note on parturition and maternal behaviour in captive red deer (*Cervus elaphus* L.). *Journal of Reproduction and Fertility*, 37:87–90.

Arman, P., N.B. Kay, E.D. Goodall, and G.A.M. Sharman
1974.   The composition and yield of milk from captive red deer (*Cervus elaphus* L.). *Journal of Reproduction and Fertility*, 37:67–84.

Armstrong, N.G., R.E. Chaplin, D.I. Chaplin, and B. Smith
1969.   Observations on the reproduction of female wild and park fallow deer in South England. *Journal of Zoology*, 158:27–37.

Asdell, S.A.
1964.   *Patterns of Mammalian Reproduction* (2nd Edition). London: Constable & Co.

Asher, G.W., L.J. Howell, R. Ellison, and M. Langridge
1981.   Fallow deer: Fawning season and fawn deaths. AgLink (1/3000/9/81). *Ministry of Agriculture and Fisheries New Zealand*. 2 pp.

Baker, K.
1973.   *Reproductive biology of fallow deer (Dama dama) in the Blue Mountains of New Zealand*. MSc. Thesis, University of Otago, Dunedin.

Barrette, C.
1977.   Some aspects of the behaviour of muntjacs in Wilpattu National Park. *Mammalia*, 41:1–34.

Barron, J.C., and W.F. Harwell
1973. Fertilization rates of South Texas deer. *Journal of Wildlife Management*, 37:179–182.

Bartmann, W.
1971. Superfetation beim Virginia-Hirsch. (*Odocoileus virginianus* Zimmerman 1780)? *Zeitschrift für Säugetierkunde*, 36:200–201.

Batcheler, C.L., and M.J. McLennan
1977. Craniometric study of allometry adaptation and hybridism of red deer *Cervus elaphus scoticus* and wapiti *Cervus elaphus nelsoni* in Fiordland, New Zealand. *Proceedings of the New Zealand Ecological Society*, 24:57–75.

Batchelor, R.F.
1965. The Roosevelt elk in Alaska. Job Completion Report, Federal Aid Project No. W-6-R-6. Alaska Dept. Fish and Game. 37 pp. (reference not seen as quoted in Smith, 1974)

Bentley, A.
1978. *An Introduction to the Deer of Australia*. Hurstbridge, Victoria: Printing Association.

Bergerud, A.T.
1971. The population dynamics of Newfoundland caribou. *Wildlife Monograph*, 25: 55 pp.
1974. Rutting behaviour of Newfoundland caribou. In *The behaviour of ungulates and its relation to management*, edited by V. Geist and F. Walther, pp. 395–435. IUCN Publication No. 24, Volume 1.

1975. The reproductive season of Newfoundcaribou. *Canadian Journal of Zoology*, 53:1213–1221.

Blakeslee, C.K., C.G. Rice, and K. Ralls
1979. Behaviour and reproduction of captive brow-antlered deer *Cervus eldi thamin* (Thomas 1918). *Säugetierkundliche Mitteilungen*, 27:114–127.

Blaxter, K.L.
1971. The comparative biology of lactation. In *Lactation*, edited by I.R. Falconer, pp. 51–69. London: Butterworths.

Blouch, R.A.
This Reproductive seasonality of the white-tailed deer on volume the Colombian Llanos.

Blouch, R.A., and S. Atmosoedirdjo
1978. Preliminary report on the status of the Bawean deer (*Axis kuhli*). *Proceedings of the Working Meeting of the Deer Specialist Group of the Survival Service Commission*, International Union for the Conservation of Nature, pp. 49–55.

Blunt, F.M.
1962. General study on breeding habits, gestation, lactation and young of big game animals. Job Completion Report, Federal Aid Project No. W-69-R-H. Sybille Game Research Station, Wyoming Game

and Fish Comm. pp. 20–23. (Reference not seen – as quoted in Smith 1974)

Borg, K.
1962. Draktighet has ettarigt rodjur. *Svenska Jagarforb. Tidskr.*, 100: 464.
1970. On mortality and reproduction of roe deer in Sweden during the period 1947–1969. *Viltrevy*, 7:121–149.

Boyd, R.J.
1978. American elk. In *Big Game of North America*, edited by L. Schmidt and D.L. Gilbert, pp. 11–20. Harrisburg, Pennsylvania: Stackpole Co.

Branan, W.V., and R.L. Marchinton
This Reproductive ecology of white-tailed and red volume brocket deer in Suriname.

Brna, J.
1969. Fertility of hinds and post natal mortality of young red deer *Cervus elaphus* in Belje. *Jelen*, 8:69–72. (Reference not seen Biol. Abst. 1970, 88032.)

Brokx, P.A.
1972. Ovarian composition and aspects of the reproductive physiology of Venezuelan white-tailed deer (*Odocoileus virginianus gymnotis*). *Journal of Mammalogy*, 53:760–773.

Bubenik, A.B.
1965. Beitrag zur Geburtskunde und zu den Mutter-Kind-Beziehungen des Reh- (*Capreolus capreolus* L.) und Rotwildes (*Cervus elaphus* L.). *Zeitschrift für Säugetierkunde*, 30:65–128.

Caughley, G.
1971. The season of birth for northern hemisphere ungulates in New Zealand. *Mammalia*, 35:204–220.

Chaplin, R.E., and G. Dangerfield
1973. Breeding records of Muntjac deer (*Muntiacus reevesi*) in captivity. *Journal of Zoology*, 170:150–151.

Chaplin, R.E., and R.J. Harrison
1971. The uterus, ovaries, and placenta of the Chinese muntjac deer (*Muntiacus reevesi*). *Journal of Anatomy*, 110:147.

Chapman, D.I.
1974. Reproductive physiology in relation to deer management. *Mammal Review*, 4:61–74.

Chapman, D.I., and N.G. Chapman
1971. Further observations on the incidence of twins in roe deer *Capreolus capreolus*. *Journal of Zoology*, 165:505–509.

1975. *Fallow deer*. Lavenham: Terence Dalton Ltd.

Chapman, D.I., and O. Dansie
1970. Reproduction and fetal development in female muntjac deer *Muntiacus reevesi*. *Mammalia*, 34:303–319.

Chapman, D.I., and M.T. Horwood
1968.   Pregnancy in a Sika deer calf, *Cervus nippon*. *Journal of Zoology*, 155:227–228.

Cheatum, E.L., and G.H. Morton
1946.   Breeding season of white-tailed deer in New York. *Journal of Wildlife Management*, 10:249–263.

Clutton-Brock, T.H., S.D. Albon, and F.E. Guinness
1981.   Parental investment in male and female offspring in polygynous mammals. *Nature*, 289:487–498.

Clutton-Brock, T.H., F.E. Guinness, and S.D. Albon
1982.   *Red Deer: Behavior and Ecology of Two Sexes*. Chicago: University of Chicago Press.

Coady, J.
1974.   Late pregnancy of moose in Alaska. *Journal of Wildlife Management*, 38:571–572.

Corbet, G.B.
1966.   *The Terrestrial Mammals of Western Europe*. London: G.T. Foulis.

Daniel, M.J.
1963.   Early fertility of red deer hinds in New Zealand. *Nature*, 200: 380.

Dauphiné, T.C.
1976.   Biology of the Kaminuriak population of barren ground caribou. Part 4. Growth, reproduction and energy reserves. *Canadian Wildlife Service Report Series* No. 18.

Dauphine, T.C., and R.L. McClure
1974.   Synchronous mating in Canadian barren-ground caribou. *Journal of Wildlife Management*, 38:54–66.

Davidson, M.M.
1976.   Season of parturition and fawning percentages of Sika deer *Cervus nippon* in New Zealand. *New Zealand Journal of Forestry Science*, 5:355–357.

De, R.C., and J.J. Spillett
1966.   A study of the chital or spotted deer in Corbett National Park, Uttar Pradesh. *Journal of the Bombay Natural History Society*, 63:576–598.

Desai, J.H., and A.K. Malhotra
1978.   The Manipur brow-antlered deer *Cervus eldii eldii*, its status and breeding in captivity. *International Zoo Yearbook*, 18:235–236.

Desmeules, P., and B. Simard
1970.   Dates of calving in northern Quebec caribou *Rangifer tarandus*. *Naturaliste canadien*, 97:61–66.

Dobroruka, L.J.
1970.   Fecundity of the Chinese water deer *Hydropotes inermis* Swinhoe 1870. *Mammalia*, 34:161–162.

Douglas, M.J.W.
1966.   Occurrence of accessory corpora lutea in red deer *Cervus elaphus*. *Journal of Mammalogy*, 47:152–153.

Dubost, C.
1971.   Observations ethologique sur le Muntjak (*Muntiacus munjak* Zimmerman 1780 et *M. reevesi* Ogilby 1839) en captivite et semi-liberte. *Zeitschrift für Tierpsychologie*, 28:387–427.

Dunbar, M.R.
1976.   Breeding season of white-tailed deer in Eastern Oklahoma. *Proceedings of the Oklahoma Academy of Science*, 56:24–25

Edwards, R.Y., and R.W. Ritcey
1958.   Reproduction in a moose population. *Journal of Wildlife Management*, 22:261–268.

Estes, R.D.
1976.   The significance of breeding synchrony of the wildebeest. *East African Wildlife Journal*, 14:135–152.

Fletcher, T.J.
1974.   The timing of reproduction in red deer *Cervus elaphus* in relation to latitude. *Journal of Zoology*, 172:363–367.

Flook, D.R.
1970.   Causes and implications of an observed sex differential in the survival of wapiti. *Canadian Wildlife Service Report Series* No. 11: 71 pp.

Follis, R.B., and J.J. Spillett
1974.   Winter pregnancy rates and subsequent cow/calf ratios in elk. *Journal of Wildlife Management*, 38:789–791.

Frädrich, H.
This   The husbandry of tropical and temperate cervids in
volume the West Berlin Zoo.

Gardner, A.L.
1971.   Postpartum estrus in a red brocket deer *Mazama americana* from Peru. *Journal of Mammalogy*, 52:623–624.

Geist, V.
1974.   On the evolution of reproductive potential in moose. *Naturaliste canadien*, 101:527–537.

Gensch, W.
1969.   A remarkably short gestation period of *Rangifer tarandus*. *Zoologische Garten*, 37:150–151.

Golley, F.B.
1957.   An appraisal of ovarian analyses in determining reproductive performance of black-tailed deer. *Journal of Wildlife Management*, 21:62–65.

Graf, W., and L. Nichols
1966.   The axis deer in Hawaii. *Journal of the Bombay Natural History Society*, 63:629–734.

Greer, K.R.
1968.   Special collections Yellowstone elk study 1967–1968. Job Completion Report, Federal Aid Project No. W-83-R-11. 26 pp. (Reference not seen as quoted in Smith 1974).

Groves, C, and P. Grubbs
This   Relationships of Living Deer.
volume

Guinness, F.E., S.D. Albon, and T.H. Clutton-Brock
1978a. Factors affecting reproduction in red deer hinds on Rhum. *Journal of Reproduction and Fertility*, 54:325–334.

Guinness, F.E., T.H. Clutton-Brock, and S.D. Albon
1978b. Factors affecting calf mortality in red deer (*Cervus elaphus* L.). *Journal of Animal Ecology*, 47:817–832.

Guinness, F.E., and J. Fletcher
1971. First ever recorded incidence of twins born to a red deer hind in Britain. *Deer*, Journal of the British Deer Society, 2:680–682.

Guinness, F.E., R.M. Gibson, and T.H. Clutton-Brock
1978. Calving times of red deer (*Cervus elaphus* L.) on Rhum. *Journal of Zoology*, 184:105–114.

Guinness, F.E., G.A. Lincoln, and R.V. Short
1971. The reproductive cycle of the female red deer *Cervus elaphus* L. *Journal of Reproduction and Fertility*, 27:427–438.

Gupta, M.P., and M.S. Jain
1980. Experience in breeding of musk deer for the production of musk. *Indian Forester, 106:357–362.*

Haensel, J.
1980. Zur Biologie der Vietnam-Sikas (*Cervus nippon pseudaxis* Eydoux & Souleyet, 1838) Untersuchungen an der Zuchtgruppe im Tierpark Berlin. *Milu, Berlin, 5:69–99.*

Halazon, G.C., and H.K. Buechner
1956. Post conception ovulation in elk. *Transactions of the North American Wildlife Conference*, 21:545–554.

Halford, D.K., and A.W. Alldredge
1975. Behavior associated with parturition in captive Rocky Mountain mule deer. *Journal of Mammalogy*, 56:520–522.

Hall, M.H., and E.C. Hall
1980. An early-born fawn in New York. *New York Fish and Game Journal*, 27: 103.

Hamilton, W.J., and K.L. Blaxter
1980. Reproduction in farmed red deer. 1. Hind and stag fertility. *Journal of Agricultural Science*, 95:261–273.

Hamilton, W.J., R.J. Harrison, and B.A. Young
1946. Aspects of placentation in certain Cervidae. *Journal of Anatomy*, 94:1–33.

Hanwell, A., and M. Peaker
1977. Physiological effects of lactation on the mother. *Symposium of the Zoological Society of London*, 41:297–312.

Harder, J.D., and D.L. Moorhead
1980. Development of corpora lutea and plasma progesterone levels associated with the onset of the breeding season in white-tailed deer *Odocoileus virginianus. Biology of Reproduction*, 22:185–191.

Harris, L.
1982. White-tailed deer in New Zealand. *New Zealand Wildlife*, Suppl., 8:1–12.

Harwell, W.F., and J.C. Barron
1975. The breeding season of the white-tailed deer in Southern Texas. *Texas Journal of Science*, 26:417–420.

Hauge, T.M., and L.B. Keith
1981. Dynamics of moose populations in Northeastern Alberta. *Journal of Wildlife Management*, 45:573–597.

Haugen, A.O.
1975. Reproductive performance of white-tailed deer in Iowa. *Journal of Mammalogy*, 56:151–159.

Haugen, A.O., and L.A. Davenport
1950. Breeding records of white-tail deer in the Upper Peninsula of Michigan. *Journal of Wildlife Management*, 14:290–298.

Heidemann, G.
1974. Fruckttod beim Reh. *Zeitschrift für Jagdwissenschaft*, 20:159–161.

Hepworth, W.G.
1966. General study on breeding habits, gestation, lactation and young of big game animals. Job Completion Report, Federal Aid Project No. FW-3-R-13. Sybille Game Research Station, Wyoming Game and Fish Commission, pp. 1–4. (Reference not seen as quoted in Smith 1974.)

Hesselton, W.T., and L.W. Jackson
1974. Reproductive rates of white-tailed deer in New York State. *New York Fish and Game Journal*, 21:135–152.

Hesselton, W.T., and E. Van Dyke
1969. Twin fawns born two days apart. *New York Fish and Game Journal*, 16:261.

Hirth, D.H.
1977. Social behaviour of white-tailed deer in relation to habitat. *Wildlife Monograph*, 53: 55 pp.

Holthe, V.
1975. Calving season in different populations of wild reindeer in South Norway. *Biological Papers of the University of Alaska, Special Report*, 1:194–198.

Hudson, P., and L.G. Browman
1959. Embryonic and fetal development of the mule deer. *Journal of Wildlife Management*, 23:295–304.

Jackson, J.
1977. The duration of lactation in New Forest fallow deer (*Dama dama*). *Journal of Zoology*, 183:542–543.

Jackson, L.W., and W.T. Hesselton
1973. Breeding and parturition date of white-tailed deer in New York. *New York Fish and Game Journal*, 20:40–47.

Jenness, R.
1974. The composition of milk. In *Lactation: a comprehensive treatise*. Volume III, edited by B.L. Larson and V.R. Smith, pp. 3–107. New York/London: Academic Press.

Jordan, J.W., and P.A. Vohs
1976. Natality of black-tailed deer in McDonald State Forest, Oregon. *Northwest Science*, 51:108–113.

Kelsall, J.P.
1968. *The migratory barren-ground caribou of Canada*. Ottawa: Queens Printer.

Kelly, R.W., and C.N. Challies
1978. Incidence of ovulation before the onset of the rut and during pregnancy in red deer hinds. *New Zealand Journal of Zoology*, 5:817–819.

Kenneth, J.H.
1947. *Gestation periods*. Edinburgh: Imperial Bureau of Animal Breeding and Genetics.

Kittams, W.H.
1953. Reproduction of Yellowstone elk. *Journal of Wildlife Management*, 17:177–184.

Krog, J., M. Wika, and P. Savalov
1980. The development of the foetus of the Norwegian reindeer. In *Proceedings of the 2nd International Reindeer/Caribou Symposium, Roros, Norway*, edited by E. Reimers, E. Gaare, and S. Skjenneberg, pp. 306–310. Direktoratet for vilt og Fersk-vannsfisk, Trondheim.

Korning, F., and F. Vorreyer
1957. Untersuchungen über Vermehrungsraten und körpergewichte beim weiblichen Rotwild. *Zeitschrift für Jagdwissemscjaft*, 4:145–153. (Reference not seen – as quoted in Smith 1974.)

Krzywinski, A., and Z. Jaczewski
1978. Observations on the artificial breeding of red deer. *Symposium of the Zoological Society of London*, 43:271–287.

Krzywinski, A., K. Krzywinska, J. Kisza, A. Roskosz, and A. Kruk
1980. Milk composition, lactation and the artificial rearing of red deer. *Acta Theriologica*, 25:341–347.

Lamming, G.E.
1978. Reproduction during lactation. In *Control of Ovulation*, edited by D.B. Crighton, N.B Haynes, G.R. Foxcroft and G.E. Lamming, pp. 335–353. London/Boston: Butterworths.

Lantz, D.E.
1910. Raising deer and other large game animals in the United States. *United States Department of Agriculture Biological Survey Bulletin*, 36.

Leader-Williams, N.
1980. Population dynamics and mortality of reindeer introduced into South Georgia. *Journal of Wildlife Management*, 44:640–657.

Lincoln, G.A., and F.E. Guinness
1972. Effect of altered photoperiod on delayed implantation and moulting in roe deer. *Journal of Reproduction and Fertility*, 31:455–457.

Loncoln, G.A., R.W. Youngson, and R.V. Short
1970. The social and sexual behaviour of the red deer stag. *Journal of Reproduction and Fertility* Suppl., 11:71–103.

Ling, H.J.
1974. Multifetation of females and population productivity in elks. *Byulletin Moskovskogo Obshches TVA Ispytatelei Prirody Otdel Biologicheskii*, 79:5–14.

Linzell, J.L.
1972. Milk yield, energy loss in milk, and mammary gland weight in different species. *Dairy Science Abstract*, 34:351–360.

Loudon, A.S.I.
This The influence of forest habitat structure on growth, volume body size, and reproduction in roe deer.

Loudon, A.S.I., A.S. McNeilly, and J.A. Milne
1983. Nutrition and lactational control of fertility in red deer. *Nature*, 302:145-147.

Lowe, V.P.W.
1969. Population dynamics of the red deer (*Cervus elaphus* L.) on Rhum. *Journal of Animal Ecology*, 38:425–457.

Luick, J.R., R.G. White, A.M. Gau, and R. Jenness
1974. Compositional changes in the milk secreted by grazing reindeer. l. Gross composition and ash. *Journal of Dairy Science*, 57:1325–1333.

Maehlum, J.
1981. Elgkalv in Januar. *Fauna*, 34:131.

Markgren, G.
1969. Reproduction of moose in Sweden. *Viltrevy*, 6:127–299.

Martin, C.
1975. Status and ecology of the Barasingha (*Cervus duvauceli branderi*) in Kanha National Park (India). Ph.D. Thesis, University of Zurich, Zurich.

McEwan, E.H.
1971. Twinning in caribou. *Journal of Mammalogy*, 52:479.

McEwan, E.H., and P.E. Whitehead
1972. Reproduction in female reindeer and caribou. *Canadian Journal of Zoology*, 50:43–46.

McGinnes, B.S., and R.L. Downing
1977. Factors affecting the peak of white-tailed deer fawning in Virginia. *Journal of Wildlife Management*, 41:715–719.

Mech, L.D.
1966. The wolves of Isle Royale. *Fauna of the National Parks of the U.S.*, 7:1–210.

Meier, E.
1973. Beiträge zur Geburt des Damwildes (*Cervus dama* L.). *Zeitschrift für Säugetierkunde*, 38:348–373.

Michael, E.D.
1964. Birth of white-tailed deer fawns. *Journal of Wildlife Management*, 28:171–173.

Millar, J.S.
1981. Pre-partum reproductive characteristics of eutherian mammals. *Evolution*, 35:1149–1163.

Miller, F.L.
1970. Accidents to parturient black-tailed deer. *American Midland Naturalist*, 83:303–304.

Mithcell, B., and G.A. Lincoln
1974. Conception dates in relation to age and condition in two populations of red deer in Scotland. *Journal of Zoology*, 171:141–152.

Miura, S.
1980. Annual seasonal activities of Nara deer, 11: Concentrating on the birth season. *Survey Report on Nara deer, Akira Dasuga Society* 1979:87–94.

Moll, D., and B.K. Moll
1976. Moose triplets on Isle Royale. *Transactions of the Illinois State Academy of Science*, 69:151.

Morrison, J.A.
1960a. Ovarian characteristics in elk of known breeding history. *Journal of Wildlife Management*, 24:297–307.

1960b. Characteristics of estrus in captive elk. *Behaviour*, 24:84–92.

Morrison, J.A., C.E. Trainer, and P.L. Wright
1959. Breeding season in elk as determined by known-age embryos. *Journal of Wildlife Management*, 23:27–34.

Mueller, C.C., and R.M.F.S. Sadleir
1977. Changes in the nutrient composition of milk of black-tailed deer during lactation. *Journal of Mammalogy*, 58:421–423.

1979. Age at first conception in black-tailed deer. *Biology of Reproduction*, 21:1099–1104.

Mundinger, J.G.
1981. White-tailed deer reproductive biology in the Swan Valley, Montana. *Journal of Wildlife Management*, 45:132–139.

Murie, A.
1934. The moose of Isle Royale. *Miscellaneous Publications, Museum of Zoology, University of Michigan*, 25: 44 pp.

Nellis, C.H.
1968. Productivity of mule deer on the National Bison Range, Montana. *Journal of Wildlife Management*, 32:344–349.

Nellis, C.H., J.L. Thiessen, and C.A. Prentice
1976. Pregnant fawn and quintuplet mule deer. *Journal of Wildlife Management*, 40:795–796.

Nixon, M.
1971. Productivity of white-tailed deer in Ohio. *Ohio Journal of Science*, 71:217–225.

Nowosad, R.F.
1973. Twinning in reindeer. *Journal of Mammalogy*, 54:781.

O'Bryan, D.J.
1978. The Koetong fallow deer project. In *An introduction to the deer of Australia*, edited by A. Bentley, pp. 304–342. Hurstbridge, Victoria: Printing Association.

Palmer, L.J.
1934. Raising reindeer in Alaska. *United States Department of Agriculture Miscellaneous Publications*, 207: 41 pp. (Reference not seen as quoted in Leader-Williams 1980.)

Panwar, H.S.
1978. Decline and restoration success of the central Indian barasingha (*Cervus duvauceli branderi*). *Proceedings of the Working Meeting of the Deer Specialist Group of the Survival Service Commission*, International Union for the Conservation of Nature, pp. 143–158.

Parker, G.R.
1981. Physical and reproductive characteristics of an expanding woodland caribou population (*Rangifer tarandus caribou*) in Northern Labrador. *Canadian Journal of Zoology*, 59:1929–1940.

Payne, P.R., and E.F. Wheeler
1968. Comparative nutrition in pregnancy and lactation. *Proceedings of the Nutrition Society, Cambridge*, 27:128–138.

Peaker, M.
1977. The aqueous phase of milk: ion and water transport. *Symposium of the Zoological Society of London*, 41:113–134.

Preobrazhensii, B.V.
1961. Management and breeding reindeer. In *Reindeer husbandry*, edited by P.S. Zhigunov. (Translated from Russian: U.S. Dept. of Commerce, Springfield, VA., USA) (Reference not seen as quoted in Geist 1974.)

Prell, H.
1938. The gestation of native game animals. *Tharandter Forstliches Jahrbuch*, 89:696–701.

Prior, R.
1968. *The roe deer of Cranborne Chase: an ecological survey.* New York/Toronto: Oxford University Press.

Prusaite, J., A. Blazys, and R. Baleisis
1976. Intensity of breeding and fecundity of the European roe deer in Lithuania. *Lietuvos T.S.R. Mokslu Akademijos Darbai Serija C. Biologijos Mokslai (ser C)*, 3:105–110.

Ramsey, P.R., J.C. Avise, M.H. Smith, and D.F. Urbston
1979. Biochemical variation and genetic heterogeneity in South Carolina deer populations. *Journal of Wildlife Management*, 43:136–142.

Robbins, C.T., and A. Moen
1975. Milk composition and weight gain of white-tailed deer. *Journal of Wildlife Management*, 39:355–360.

R.M.F.S. Sadleir

Robbins, C.T., R. Podbielanchik-Norman, D.L. Wilson, and E.D. Moult
1981.   Growth and nutrient consumption of elk calves compared to other ungulate species. *Journal of Wildlife Management*, 45:172–186.

Robbins, C.T., O.T. Oftedal, and K.I. O'Rourke
This   Lactation, early nutrition, and hand-rearing of wild
volume ungulates with special reference to deer.

Robbins, C.T., and B.L. Robbins
1979.   Fetal and neonatal growth patterns and maternal reproductive effort in ungulates and subungulates. *American Naturalist*, 114:110–116.

Robinette, W.L., and J.S. Gashwiler
1950.   Breeding season, productivity and fawning period of the mule deer in Utah. *Journal of Wildlife Management*, 14:457–469.

Robinette, W.L., J.S. Gashwiler, D.A. Jones, and H.S. Crane
1955.   Fertility of mule deer in Utah. *Journal of Wildlife Management*, 19:115–136.

Roe, N.A., and W.E. Rees
1976.   Preliminary observations of the Taruca (*Hippocamelus antisensis*: Cervidae) in southern Peru. *Journal of Mammalogy*, 57:722–730.

Renfree, M.B.
1978.   Embryonic diapause in mammals a developmental strategy. In *Dormancy and Developmental Arrest*, edited by M.E. Clutter, pp. 1–46. New York/San Francisco/London: Academic Press.

Rust, H.J.
1946.   Mammals of Northern Idaho. *Journal of Mammalogy*, 27:308–327.

Sadleir, R.M.F.S.
1969.   *The ecology of reproduction in wild and domestic animals.* London: Methuen.
1980a. Milk yield of black-tailed deer. *Journal of Wildlife Management*, 44:472–478.
1980b. Energy and protein intake in relation to growth of suckling black-tailed deer fawns. *Canadian Journal of Zoology*, 58:1347–1354.

Salwasser, H., and S.A. Holl
1979.   Estimating fetus age and breeding and fawning period in the North Kings River deer herd. *California Fish and Game*, 65:159–165.

Salwasser, H., S.A. Holl, and G.A. Ashcraft
1978.   Fawn production and survival in the North Kings River deer herd. *California Fish and Game*, 64:38–52.

Sato, T, T. Tango, and R. Haga
1981.   Parturitional symptoms, parturition and neonatal behaviors of Sika deer (*Cervus nippon yesoensis* Heude). *Research Bulletin, Obihiro University*, 12:149–157.

Scanlon, P.F., W.F. Murphy, and D.F. Urbston
1976.   Initiation of pregnancy in lactating white-tailed deer. *Journal of Wildlife Management*, 40:373–374.

Scanlon, P.F., and D.F. Urbston
1978.   Persistence of lactation in white-tailed deer. *Journal of Wildlife Management*, 42:196–197.

Schaller, G.B.
1967.   *The Deer and the Tiger*. Chicago/London: University of Chicago Press.

Schaller, G.B., and A. Hamer
1978.   Rutting behaviour of Pere David's deer, *Elaphurus davidianus*. *Zoologische Garten*, 48:1–15.

Schladweiler, P., and D.R. Stevens
1973.   Reproduction of Shiras moose in Montana. *Journal of Wildlife Management*, 37:535–544.

Schmitt, E.V.
1936.   A determination of the period of gestation of domestic reindeer. *Sov. Reindeer Ind. Arc-. Inst. USSR, Leningrad.*, 8:35–43. (Reference not seen as quoted by McEwan and Whitehead 1972.)

Sears, H.S., and L.G. Browman
1955.   Quadruplets in mule deer. *Anatomical Record*, 122:355–340.

Serafinski, W.
1969.   Reproduction and dynamics of moose *Alces alces* population in Kampinos National Park. *Ekologia Polska, Seria A*, 17:709–718.

Severinghaus, C.W., and E.L. Cheatum
1956.   Life and times of the white-tailed deer. In *Deer of North America*, edited by E.P. Taylor, pp. 57–186. Washington: Stackpole and Wildlife Management Inst.

Sharatchandra, H.C., and M. Gadgil
1975.   A year of Bandipur. *Journal of the Bombay Natural History Society*, 72:623–647.

Sheng H., and H. Lu
1980.   Current studies on the rare Chinese black muntjac. *Journal of Natural History*, 14:803–807.
1981.   Reproduction of the Chinese black muntjac (*Muntiacus crinifrons* Sclater). *Acta Theriologica Sinica.*, 1:14–18.

Sheng, H., and P. Wang
1976.   The ecology and utilization of the Reeves Muntjac (*Muntiacus reevesi* Ogilby). *Journal of Zoology*, Peking, 1:39–40.

Shoesmith, M.W.
1976.   Twin fetuses in woodland caribou. *Canadian Field-Naturalist*, 90:498–499.

Short, R.V., and M.F. Hay
1966.   Delayed implantation in the roe deer *(Capreolus capreolus)*. *Symposium of the Zoological Society of London*, 15:173–194.

Simkin, D.W.
1974.   Reproduction and productivity of moose. *Naturaliste canadien*, 101:517–526.

Skuncke, W.
1949.   *Algen studien, jakt och vard*. Stockholm: Norsteds.

Smith, M.C.T.
1974.   *Biology and management of the Wapiti (Cervus elaphus nelsoni) of Fiordland, New Zealand*. Wellington, New Zealand: New Zealand Deerstalkers Association.

Struhsaker, T.T.
1967.   Behaviour of elk (*Cervus canadensis*) during the rut. *Zeitschrift für Tierpsychologie*, 24:80–114.

Thomas, D.C., and I.McT. Cowan
1975.   The pattern of reproduction in female Columbian black-tailed deer (*Odocoileus hemionus columbianus*). *Journal of Reproduction and Fertility*, 44:261–272.

Thomas, D.C.
1982.   The relationship between fertility and fat reserves of Peary caribou. *Canadian Journal of Zoology*, 60:597–602.

Thomas, W.D.
1975.   Observations on captive brockets. *International Zoo Yearbook*, 15:77–78.

Townsend, T.W., and E.D. Bailey
1975.   Parturitional, early maternal and neonatal behavior in penned white-tailed deer. *Journal of Mammalogy*, 56:347–362.

Vandeplassche, M.
1969.   The physiological explanation of split parturition in the pig and other mammalian species. *Annals of Endocrinology*, 30:328–341.

Verme, L.J.
1969.   Reproductive patterns of white-tailed deer related to nutritional plane. *Journal of Wildlife Management*, 33:881–887.

Verme, L.J., and J.J. Ozoga
1981.   Sex ratio of white-tailed deer and the estrous cycle. *Journal of Wildlife Management*, 45:710–715.

Walker, E.P.
1975.   *Mammals of the World*. 3rd edition. Baltimore: Johns Hopkins Press.

Walser, M.S.
1977.   Maternal behaviour in mammals. *Symposium of the Zoological Society of London*, 41:313–331.

Wandeler, A.I.
1975.   Die Fortpflangungsleistung des Rehs (*Capreolus capreolus* L.) im Berner Mittelland. *Jahrbuch Naturhistorischen Museums der Stadt Bern*, 5 (1972–1974): 245–301.

Warren, R.J., R.W. Vogelsang, R.L. Kirkpatrick, and P.F. Scanlon
1978.   Reproductive behaviour of captive white-tailed deer. *Animal Behaviour*, 26:179–183.

Webb, J.W., and D.W. Nellis
1981.   Reproductive cycle of white-tailed deer of St. Croix, Virgin Islands. *Journal of Wildlife Management*, 45:253–258.

Wegge, P.
1975.   Reproduction and early calf mortality in Norwegian red deer. *Journal of Wildlife Management*, 39:92–100.

Western, D.
1979.   Size, life history and ecology in mammals. *African Journal of Ecology*, 17:185–204.

Whitehead, G.K.
1972.   *Deer of the World*. London: Constable.

Wishart, W.D.
1981.   January conception in an elk in Alberta. *Journal of Wildlife Management*, 45:544.

Woolf, A., and J.D. Harder
1979.   Population dynamics of a captive white-tailed deer herd with emphasis on reproduction and mortality. *Wildlife Monograph*, 67: 53 pp.

Yahner, R.H.
1979.   Temporal patterns in male mating behaviour of captive Reeves muntjac *Muntiacus reevesi*. *Journal of Mammalogy*, 60:560–567.

Yevtushevsky, N.N.
1974.   Reproduction of spotted deer (*Cervus nippon hortulorum* SW.) under conditions of the Middle Dnipro area. *Vestnik Zoologii*, 4:23–28.

Zuckerman, S.
1953.   The breeding seasons of mammals in captivity. *Proceedings of the Zoological Society of London*, 122:827–950.

FRED L. BUNNELL
Faculty of Forestry
University of British Columbia,
Vancouver, B.C.   V6T 1W5

Reproductive Tactics of Cervidae and Their Relationships to Habitat

ABSTRACT

Data from 155 populations of the family Cervidae are reviewed and expressed in terms of simple models relating reproduction and mortality. Birth weights (BW) of Cervidae are related to the dam's metabolic weight (BW = 0.077 $M^{0.98}$ for singletons; BW = 0.41 $M^{0.66}$ for twins; M = maternal weight, kg). Monotocous species are generally grazers or mixed feeders and invest proportionately more in their young than do polytocous species bearing singletons. Species having postpartum estrus or poorly synchronized birth seasons occur in stable habitats and invest less in individual young. Twinning is very nearly confined to unstable habitats or early seral stages and involves an additional female investment of 40%. The average juvenile mortality rate among *Rangifer* is 76% over the first year, primarily to predation. *Rangifer* populations are relatively free of nutritional controls on reproduction and adult mortalities are among the lowest within the Cervidae. *Cervus canadensis* is more immune to early predation by virtue of the largest birth weights among Cervidae. One consequence of the greater female investment of *Cervus* in newborn young is greater nutritional control on reproduction and alternate year reproduction on poor ranges. Polytocous species are less susceptible to predation because of their high reproductive rates. Effects of poor nutrition or inclement weather are multiplicative—they alter both mortality and reproduction. Because influences are multiplicative, relatively small changes in forage quality can reduce reproduction of polytocous species to the level that it cannot match predation.

Introduction

This paper is an attempt at synthesis. One of the finest syntheses of cervid populations is Bergerud's (1980) treatment of *Rangifer*. Bergerud expressed his rationale succinctly; I paraphrase: because the scientific method is largely deductive we hypothesize from the general to the specific. The plurality-of-causes approach is self-defeating because it provides no further insight and an *a posteriori* catalog of causes becomes descriptive and untestable. My major objective has been to extract general patterns, the first step in deduction. Given that objective, data from more than 175 cervid populations were reviewed. I subsequently chose to restrict discussion to those species for which considerable data were available; statistical treatment was limited to 155 populations. Using the general patterns described, I have addressed broad hypotheses. Given the sparsity of data for some species and topics, not all hypotheses are unequivocably testable and the treatment of those remains descriptive.

The treatment concentrates on reproduction but considers how birth rates and death rates are related in selected taxa. Although dispersal undoubtedly influences the growth rates of some cervid populations (Bunnell and Harestad, 1983), the role of dispersal is ignored because data are too sparse to permit useful interspecific analyses. Therefore this review is limited to examination of birth and death rates, and three elements of habitat: food, weather, and predation. Unless otherwise stated, all statistical treatments employ $P < 0.05$, and standard error (SE) is the measurement of variation. Taxonomy follows Groves and Grubb (this volume). For most species, analyses of pregnancy rates acknowledge only embryos or fawns as evidence of pregnancy; thus, many studies employing ovarian analyses are not incorporated. I begin by examining potential habitat-related differences between monotocous and polytocous species. Selected representatives of the two groups are then examined in terms of the apparent control exerted by the three broad habitat components—food, weather, and predation.

I ask an indulgence of the reader: that he refer to Appendix I for specific references for those figures or tables collating more than 10 studies. Captions and footnotes would otherwise be extensive.

Single Versus Multiple Births

The ability or inability to produce more than one young places initial constraints on a species' reproductive tactics. Some species (e.g. *Elaphurus davidianus* and *M. reevesi*) are probably physically incapable of carrying more than one fetus because only the right horn of the uterus is developed. In other species the uterus is structurally capable of carrying twins, but usually only one ovum ripens. They are monotocous. I have defined monotocous species as those in which the reported incidence of multiple births is less than 5% (Table 1). Because the ability to produce multiple births appears sharply defined, the categorization of most genera is straightforward. In monotocous taxa for which ample data exist (e.g. *C. elaphus canadensis, C. e. elaphus, D. dama, R. tarandus*) the incidence of multiple births is less than 0.1%. Data are sparse for other taxa and some *C. nippon* subspecies may twin more frequently than 5% (see also Sadleir, this volume).

Polytocous species tend to be browsers (*Alces* and *Odocoileus*) or mixed feeders (*Capreolus, Moschus*). Only *Hyd. inermis* is preferentially a grazer. The reverse is true of monotocous species; most are preferentially grazers, the others are generally mixed feeders (Table 1). It is possible that the browsing habit with its greater likelihood of obtaining succulent, high-protein, low-fiber forage encourages multiple births. The monotocous taxa in Table 1 that are most suspect of multiple births (*C. nippon* and *Mazama*) tend to have browsing food habits. There are few other differences apparent between the two groups. Weights of adult females in both groups span a considerable range; from 6 to 260 kg in monotocous species (*Pudu* to *C. e. canadensis*), from 10 to >400 kg in polytocous species (*Hydropotes* to *Alces*). Females of most taxa weigh less than 55 kg and most taxa are monotocous (15 our of

Table 1. Distribution of single and multiple births among Cervidae

Monotocous[a]		Polytocous	
Pudu	M/B[b]	*Moschus*	M
Mazama	B	*Hydropotes*	G
Hippocamelus	M/B	*Capreolus*	M
Blastocerus	G	*Alces*	B
Ozotoceros	G	*Odocoileus*	B
Rangifer	M		
Elaphodus	B?		
Muntiacus	M		
Dama	G		
Axis	G		
Cervus	G/M[c]		
Elaphurus	G		

[a]Considered monotocous if frequency of twin births < 5%
[b]Predominant foraging pattern: B = browser, G = grazer, M = mixed
[c]Most *Cervus* preferentially grazers, *C. nippon* one exception

20 species treated). In only one polytocous species (*Alces*) do females regularly exceed 75 kg; females of five monotocous species exceed 75 kg (*C. e. canadensis, C. e. elaphus, C. unicolor, Elaphurus, Rangifer*).

Whereas polytocous species can also increase their litter size, monotocous species have only three options available to enhance their reproductive rate: 1) reproduce younger, 2) decrease the inter-breeding interval, and/or 3) enhance the survivorship of the single young.

Bigger is not necessarily better in terms of immediate survival. Initial mortality rates of young deer follow a bimodal pattern with respect to weight. Both the smallest and the very largest young experience greater rates of mortality. The former generally as a result of thermoregulatory difficulties or inability to reach the teats, the latter as a result of dystocia. My interpretation of published birth weights and subsequent mortality is that few fetuses attain the size that dystocia is a problem, even though it occurs occasionally (e.g. *Elaph. davidianus*, Whitehead, 1950; *R. tarandus* (reindeer), Baskin, 1970; *R. tarandus* (caribou), Bergerud, 1971). There is more evidence that the smaller neonates of some cervid species experience greater mortality rates (e.g., Skunke, 1949; Heptner and Nasimovitch, 1968; Preobrazhenskii, 1968; Thorne et al., 1976). These observations and others relating the dam's nutritional status to birth weight (e.g. Verme, 1965; Thorne et al., 1976; Clutton-Brock et al., 1982) suggest that natural selection acts on dams, particularly of monotocous species, to produce neonates of large birth weight.

Several workers have examined relationships between maternal and neonatal weights of mammals (Leitch et al., 1959; Robbins and Robbins, 1979; Tuomi, 1980; Bunnell, 1982). The approach here differs from earlier treatments in three ways: 1) whenever possible only female birth weights were treated; 2) singletons and twin births were treated independently; and 3) female weights were generally taken from the same population from non-parturient females near time of conception. These strictures eliminated some data from consideration, but the material retained includes 55 estimates from 24 cervid taxa (Figure 1, Appendix I).

Both Leitch et al. (1959) and Robbins and Robbins (1979) obtained relationships of the form $y = ax^b$, between birth weight (BW) and maternal weight (M). For monotocous cervid species, using data of Figure 1, I found the relationship:

$$BW = 0.077\ m^{0.98} \qquad (1)$$
$$(n = 29, \underline{r}^2 = 0.95)$$

The exponent differs insignificantly from 1.0, and use of the linear relationship is statistically justified:

$$BW = 0.299 + 0.068\ M \qquad (2)$$
$$(n = 29, \underline{r}^2 = 0.92)$$

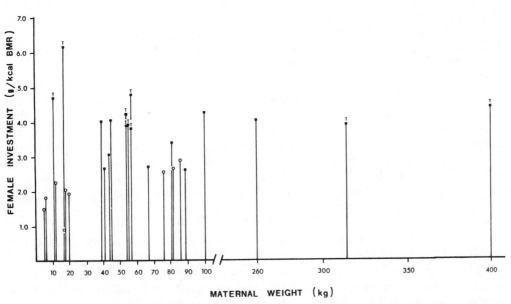

Figure 1. Female investment in young (g neonate weight/ BMR of dam) as a function of average maternal weight in Cervidae. Open circles represent species in stable habitats, solid squares represent species from unstable habitats, T represents computation for twin births in polytocous species.

The relationship for polytocous species differs in form between singleton and twin births (x̄ litter size in *Hyd. inermes*):

Singletons $\quad BW = 0.081\ M^{0.89}$ (3)
$\qquad\qquad\qquad (n = 14,\ \underline{r}^2 = 0.90)$
Twins $\qquad BW = 0.41\ M^{0.66}$ (4)
$\qquad\qquad\qquad (n = 11,\ \underline{r}^2 = 0.98)$

Several points emerge. First, the exponent for polytocous taxa bearing singletons does not differ significantly from linearity, but exceeds 0.75 ($P < 0.05$). However, the relationship for polytocous individuals making the greater investment (twins) departs significantly from linearity but not from a function of maternal metabolic weight. Second, the amplitude of the curve for twins is not double that of singletons. The difference results partly because the maternal weight is usually larger for dams bearing twins. Furthermore, the weight of twin births is approximately 1.8 times that of singletons. Third, the relationship for polytocous taxa bearing twins departs significantly from linearity whereas that of monotocous species does not. Other than for twinning polytocous taxa, we reject the hypothesis that birth weight is a function of maternal metabolic weight.

Relationships are clearer if we treat other features of the species ecology and utilize other measurements. Birth weight as a proportion of maternal weight is not particularly revealing because potential relationships with metabolic weight exist and because about 75% of birth weights across taxa are in the range of 6 to 10% of maternal weight. It is departures from potential underlying metabolic relationships that are most revealing. The relationship with metabolic weight can be incorporated by considering g neonatal biomass per kcal maternal BMR($70W^{0.75}$), termed 'female investment' by Bunnell (1982). One broad hypothesis in that taxa in more stable environments show a lower female investment.

Maz. americana and *M. reevesi* undergo postpartum estrus (Gardner, 1971; Chapman and Dansie, 1970). Data of Hick (1969) indicate that *P. puda* can give birth three times within 20 months, and its breeding in zoos shows no marked seasonality (Chaplin, 1977). Although the proportions of maternal weights represented by *Pudu*, *Mazama*, and *Muntiacus* neonate weights do not differ from other monotocous species (0.071 vs 0.074), the female investment differs greatly, 1.86 g/kcal BMR compared to 3.32 g/kcal BMR. Reproductive tactics of species showing short inter-birth intervals seem to be: invest little but invest often.

Habitats of *Pudu*, *Muntiacus* and *Mazama*, together with *Rangifer*, are relatively more stable than those of the other species considered. On average, neonates of species in stable habitats represent 6.7 ± 0.5% of the maternal weight and a female investment of 2.15 g/kcal BMR. Comparable values for species in less stable habitats are 8.9 ± 0.6% and 3.72 g/kcal BMR (Figure 1). Within less stable habitats, those species twinning invest more than monotocous species (4.13 compared to 3.47 g/kcal BMR). Of the species in stable habitats, *R. tarandus* makes the greatest female investment (2.66 ± 0.09, n = 4). It is the only species within that group exhibiting highly synchronized reproduction.

Some generalities can be extracted from these comparisons of female investment expressed as birth weights. Twinning is almost always confined to species in unstable habitats or early seral stages. Browsers are more likely to be polytocous; grazers or mixed feeders are more likely to be monotocous, as are species in which the dam weighs > 75 kg. Individual birth weights of twins are generally less than 15% smaller than singletons. That observation reveals part of the reason why multiple births are not prevalent in larger taxa (dystocia), and underscores the significant maternal contribution when twinning (Figure 1). Among larger Cervidae, apparently only the largest (*Alces*) is big enough to bear twins, given the apparent selection pressure to produce large young (Figure 1). For a somewhat different interpretation see Geist (1974). Selective pressure for large birth weights to maternal weight up to about 100 kg (Equations 2 and 3).

Monotocous species that have not shortened the interbirth interval to < 1 year invest more in individual young than do polytocous species in singletons. Those species showing the lowest female investment at birth also show a shorter inter-birth interval such that the female investment over several years roughly equals that of species investing more in individual young. These species are generally small, secretive, and occur in more stable habitats (Figure 1). Beyond this point, tactics of the two groups differ. Monotocous species can do little more than lower the age of first reproduction to increase reproductive rates, but polytocous species can also increase litter size. To evaluate further potential influences of habitat it is useful to consider the most sensitive features of reproduction, or those showing the greatest variability.

Monotocous Species

The reproductive feature exhibiting the greatest variability (as measured by the coefficient of variation) is the proportion of yearling females pregnant (Table 2). Adult animals, which I considered 3.5 years and older, exhibit the least variability, and 2-year-olds are intermediate. For the three species yielding sufficient data to evaluate variation, C.V.'s for percentages of yearlings pregnant were 0.65, 0.89, and 0.96 (Table 2).

Bunnell

Table 2. Variation in age-specific pregnancy rate within and among populations of monotocous Cervidae

Species	Number of populations or years	Age class[a] (years)	Percent pregnant $\bar{x}$	SD	CV	Range
Among populations						
Cervus e. canadensis	13	1.5	19.3	12.5	0.65	0–48
	4	2.5	65.8	24.7	0.38	33–92
	8	3.5–7.5	91.3	6.8	0.07	81–98
Cervus e. elaphus	6	1.5	32.2	30.9	0.96	0–88
	4	2.5	82.3	9.4	0.12	69–91
	4	3.5–7.5	90.0	2.8	0.03	88–94
Rangifer tarandus	4	1.5	14.7	13.1	0.89	2–33
	5	2.5	64.8	24.2	0.37	48–100
	6	3.5+	87.0	9.3	0.11	78–100
	8	2.5+	82.5	8.5	0.10	73–100
Among years, same population						
C. e. canadensis	7	1.5	13.9	12.5	0.90	0–34
C. e. elaphus	3	1.5	54.5	20.4	0.37	31–70[b]
R. tarandus	11	2.5+	82.0	6.0	0.07	72–92
	3	1.5+	69.3	4.7	0.07	64–73

[a] at conception
[b] variation among three 2- to 5-year periods; degree of variation thus reduced

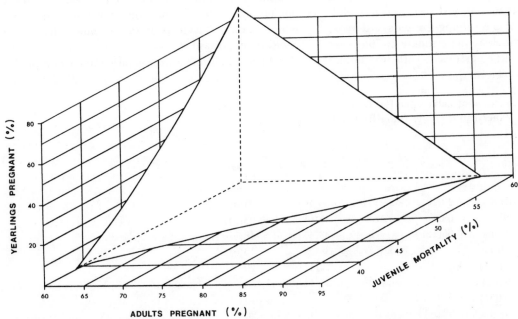

Figure 2. The proportion of yearlings that must give birth just to balance the population ($r_o = 0.0$) as a function of first year mortality and adult pregnancy rates in monotocous species (other assumptions in text).

To evaluate what influence this variation has on population growth we must consider how many yearlings are present to breed (juvenile mortality) and the pregnancy rate of older females. Relationships between these three population characteristics are illustrated in Figure 2. The example illustrated assumes a 1 : 1 sex ratio at birth and annual mortality rates from the first to second birthday of 30%, and 25% thereafter. Higher rates would raise the entire surface. The worst case illustrated combines a 60% adult pregnancy rate with 60% juvenile mortality (birth to first birthday). Under those conditions about 84% of the yearlings would have to give birth to balance the population (Figure 2). As either juvenile mortality decreases or adult pregnancy rates increase, the proportion of breeding yearlings necessary to balance the population decreases (non-linearly for changes in mortality, linearly for changes in adults pregnant under a given mortality regime). I consider the implications of Figure 2 for *Cervus* and *Rangifer,* two genera for which data are sufficient to permit effective comparison.

RANGIFER

Treatment concentrates on North American studies because much of the European and Soviet literature is derived from domesticated or semi-domesticated herds. Mortality over the first year, particularly the first six months, is remarkably high (on average 76%, Table 3). Values beyond about two months of age in Table 3 overestimate mortality slightly because adult females are then off the calving grounds and more likely to die. Nevertheless, the estimate of 76% over the first year is in close agreement with two studies

excluded from the calculations of Table 3. Bergerud (1971) and Parker (1972) provided estimates of 76% (males only) and 78% respectively. I am aware of no records of wild caribou calves becoming pregnant and giving birth as yearlings although reindeer can and do. Rather, the data suggest that only 15% of wild yearlings conceive to give birth at age 2 years (Table 2). Among *Rangifer,* natural adult mortality is unusually low compared to other Cervidae. Published estimates of annual mortality range from 5 to 13%: 5% in the Canadian Northwest Territories (Kelsall, 1968), 5–6% in the Nelchina herd of Alaska (Skoog, 1968), 6% in Labrador (Bergerud, 1967), 6% in Newfoundland (Bergerud, 1971), and 7–13% for eight North American herds reviewed by Bergerud (1983). These estimates are for both sexes. Some studies suggest that adult mortality is lower among females than among males (Bergerud, 1971; Miller, 1974).

The data of Tables 2 and 3 and the relationships of Figure 2 reveal three broad points about features of *Rangifer* habitat that may be governing population growth. First, relatively small reductions in adult survivorship will be critical. Second, given the already high pregnancy rates of adults, reductions in first-year mortality below about 60% are almost essential for a population to increase rapidly. Third, adult pregnancy rates can decrease little before the population will decline. The first two points suggest that predation rates could be critical among *Rangifer* populations, and that hypothesis is testable. The second and third points suggest that if range quality can improve pregnancy rates, or survivorship of the young, then it too could be important.

All herds in Table 3 were exposed to natural preda-

Table 3. Changes in ratios of calves per 100 females (≥2.5-years-old) with age of calf in North American *Rangifer* (modified and extended from Bergerud 1980: Fig. 2)

	Birth	1 month	2 months	5–6 months	1 year
Nelchina	86(1)	49(10)	34(3)	36(16)	24(4)
Western Arctic	91(1)	69(6)	53(6)	43(6)	23(9)
Forty-mile		66(12)		33(4)	18(5)
Porcupine	86(2)		52(6)	39(2)	15(6)
Interior, Nfld.	84(11)			22(11)	20[b]
Avalon Peninsula				51(11)	
Kaminuriak	69(3)[a]	31[b]			15[b]
Weighted x̄	84.9	69.6	48.8	36.9	20.1
SE	±0.49	±1.7	±2.0	±1.4	±0.8

[a]includes yearlings, based on uteri sampled by McEwan (1963)
[b]converted to calves/100 cows from mortality rates and calves/100 cows at birth, not included in weighted x̄

Bunnell

Table 4. Changes in calf survivorship of *Rangifer* as a result of predator control (data of Bergerud 1971, 1980)

	Apparent survivorship to 6 months of age (%)		
Predator control	Avalon herd	Nelchina herd	Interior herd
No	85	24	16.3 (85)[a]
Yes	27	5	2.7 (49)

[a]bracketed values are survivorship over the first month

tion during the periods for which data are reported. In two areas, Nelchina and Interior herds, predators were controlled (Table 4). The major predator within the range of the Avalong and Interior herds was *Lynx canadensis*, wolves (*Canis lupus*) were the major predator on the Nelchina herd. Responses to predator control were dramatic, and there is ample evidence that predation of some sort frequently governs the rate of population growth (Figure 3). Comprehensive reviews by Bergerud (1980, 1983) strongly suggest that hunting and natural mortality tend to be more additive than compensatory. The effects of man's predation are particularly dramatic when added to normal wolf predation. Wolves were the major predator in 17 of the 19 populations experiencing hunting harvests > 5%, and lynx were the major predators in the remaining two (Figure 3). 'Normal' predators of Figure 3 represent $\geq$ 1 wolf/256 km^2 if both *Alces* and *Rangifer* are prey and $\geq$ wolf/512 km^2 if *Rangifer* is the only big game, prey species. Herds experiencing normal predation usually

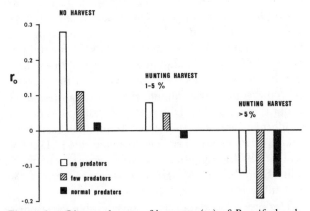

Figure 3. Observed rates of increase (r_o) of *Rangifer* herds subject to different rates of hunter harvest and different predator densities (modified and extended from Bergerud, 1980: Table 4).

lose 50% of their calves in the first six months (Table 3; Miller and Broughton, 1974; Bergerud, 1980, 1983).

Herds without predators frequently experience little mortality by the time calves are 6 months old (Table 4) and increase rapidly in population size (Figure 3, no harvest). Five of the six unharvested herds were confined to islands. The eruptions of the St. George, St. Paul, St. Matthews, and South Georgia herds are well documented (Scheffer, 1951; Klein, 1968; Leader-Williams, 1980a; Leader-Williams, 1980a; Leader-Williams and Payner, 1980). It is noteworthy that the mean value of r_o (0.28 $\pm$ 0.02) for this group closely approximates the value of r_{max} for a herd of caribou (0.30) calculated by Bergerud (1983). Together these observations strongly implicate natural predation on calves as a major factor regulating caribou populations.

It is obvious that additional predation by man can have a profound effect (Figure 3). Three of the four *Rangifer* herds contributing to the case 'hunting harvest > 5%: no predators' in Figure 3 are from Norway (Hardangervidda, Rondane, and Snohetta herds). Lynx are present, but there is little predation. The decline in the herds for the period when hunting harvest exceeded 5% is primarily attributable to harvest by man. One potential effect of man's harvest of *Rangifer*, which does not form harems, is the modification of the sex ratio to the extent that some females fail to conceive and pregnancy rates are reduced. I evaluated this concept by regressing pregnancy rates (P) on the number of adult males per 100 adult females (SR) in the preceding fall. Data used were those of Bergerud (1971), Reimers (1975), and Leader-Williams (1980a). Slope of the regression differs significantly from zero, but the standard error is large:

$$P = 46.5 + 0.83 \text{ SR} \qquad (5)$$
$$(n = 17, \underline{r} = 0.69, Sy.x = 14.01)$$

Equation 5 suggests that adult sex ratios lower than 50 males per 100 females would lead to pregnancy rates less than those commonly observed (Table 2). At sex ratios below about 30:100, adult pregnancy rates should decline sufficiently to affect population growth adversely (Figure 2).

It is less clear how inclement weather during calving or winter may regulate *Rangifer* populations. The effects could be mediated primarily through thermoregulation and thus are potentially a function of the dam's nutritional status and effects of that status on birth weight or lactation. Thermogenesis is well developed at birth and metabolic rate can be increased up to five times resting metabolism in response to cold, wind, and wetting. *Rangifer* apparently can withstand ambient temperatures as low as $-52°C$ with no apparent increase in heat production beyond resting rates (Hart et al., 1961). We do know that significant losses occur in cohorts born following a severe winter (Kelsall, 1968; Bos, 1975), but we have few field observations to indicate whether calves were aborted or stillborn, or lived to confront a poor spring or an undernourished, poorly lactating mother. McEwan et al. (1965) noted that a transient lowering of body temperature may occur in undernourished, young caribou. Bergerud (1971) found a 34% difference in birth weight between years which correlated with the preceding winter's snowfall ($r^2 = 0.45$), but not at all with mortality over the next month ($r^2 = 0.014$). Similarly, Espmark (1980) found that imposed undernutrition of captive, pregnant female reindeer had no apparent detrimental effects upon their calves; all calves survived their first summer.

Despite studies on a great variety of North American *Rangifer* herds there are no unequivocal relationships evident between birth weight and subsequent survivorship or between adult nutritional status and birth weight or pregnancy rate. The lack of relationship between birth weight and survivorship is not surprising if predation in indeed the major factor governing calf mortality, but the lack of evidence of nutritional effects mediated through the dam is unexpected given European and Soviet observations. There is sparse evidence that in both wild and domestic reindeer herds age of first reproduction is a function of female growth rate, suggesting nutritional control (Preobrazhenskii, 1968; Klein and White, 1978). In herds in which calves conceived, yearling conception rates were lowered. Indirect evidence of some alternate-year breeding in North American herds is presented later (Table 7).

The history of the reindeer introduced to St. Matthews Island illustrates the apparent lack of nutritional control. The 29 animals introduced in 1944 increased to 6000 by 1963 (from a density of 0.08 to 18 reindeer/km²), and then 'crashed' in the winter of 1963–64 to only 42 animals in 1965 (Klein, 1968). Until the crash the animals exhibited no appreciable decrease in reproductive rate and survivors of the crash continued to ovulate. If this incident identifies a remarkable degree of independence between reproduction and food supply, we are left with no explanation of the apparent variations in pregnancy rates (Table 2). We do, however, observe a number of features suggesting a common adaptation to meliorate juvenile mortality through predation. These include: 'follower' behavior (*sensu* Lent, 1974) permitting extensive movements of mother and young in large aggregations during early infancy; relatively large female investment considering its stable habitat (Figure 1); high fat and protein content of milk permitting rapid early growth rates (Table 5); and social facilitation during breeding (Baskin, 1970; Henshaw, 1970) which encourages a tightly synchronized birth season (Bergerud, 1961, 1975; Dauphiné and McClure, 1974) and provides the potential for predator swamping (e.g., Estes, 1981).

Cervus elaphus canadensis and *C. e. elaphus*

Because *Cervus e. canadensis* calves are initially 'hiders', methods using early calf/cow ratios are not possible before July when cows with calves leave seclusion to form cow/calf groups. Thus fewer estimates of early mortality exist than do for *Rangifer*. Taber et al. (1982) estimated first month mortalities ranging from 25 to 50% dependent on the severity of the preceding winter. Potential reasons are evident in data of Thorne et al. (1976). They found that among *C. e. canadensis* weight change in the dam during pregnancy was correlated with both birth weight of the calf and calf growth rate to four weeks ($r = 0.61$, $P < 0.01$ for both). Calves born to dams losing >15% of their weight experienced greater mortality over the first month (42%, 5/12) than those born to dams experiencing < 10% weight loss or weight gain (4%, 1/24) (see also Figure 7). Clutton-Brock et al., (1982) noted that *C. e. elaphus* calves that died early had lower birth weights, and suggested that birth weight was influenced by the mother's weight and condition in the spring. Severe winters could encourage weight loss in cows thereby increasing subsequent calf mortality.

Schlegel (1976) fitted radio-transmitters to 53 calves < 1 week old and documented that 34 (64%) succumbed to predation within the first 2-3 weeks before cows aggregated and predation almost ceased. Major predators in Schlegel's study area were black bear (*Ursus americanus*, 28 kills) and cougar (*Felis concolor*, 6 kills). Where wolves are common it is less likely that a sharp cessation of predation would occur. The estimate of early mortality provided by Flook (1970) in Figure 4 is based on proportion of females pregnant compared to proportion of females lactating at 6-months post parturition. For females conceiving at age 2-years and older, I compute an apparent calf mortality rate of 35% to age 6-months. Using data of Schoen (1977) to calculate probable births, the apparent mortality of elk calves from birth to the August calf/cow counts was about 27% (over a period of about three months). Differences in calf/cow ratios in California between July and August suggest 16% March (data of Schwartz and Mitchell, 1945). Data of Knight (1970) suggest lower rates of apparent mortality from July to March in a Montana herd, 14% and 18%.

The preceding data reveal considerable variability, but suggest that early mortality is normally much less than in *Rangifer*, while adult mortality is much greater (7-40%; Figure 4). Kimball and Wolf (1980) provided

Bunnell

Table 5. Natural history features of selected cervid genera

Feature	Genus			
	Rangifer	*Cervus*	*Odocoileus*	*Alces*
Female birth weight (kg)	5–6	6[a] 12–18[b]	2.5–4	9–16
female investment (g/kcal)	2.6–2.9	2.6–3.4[a] 3.2–4.0[b]	3.8–4.8	3.8–4.4
Approximate milk composition—near peak				
lactation % fats	18	7–10	8–12	6–10
% protein	11	6–7	6–9	8–10
kcal/day	2100–3800	2100	1450	2200–6600[e]
Time to double birth weight (d)	15–16	13–28[c]	9–18[c]	21–28[c]
Neonate behavior	follower	hider, 3–4 d[a] 18–20 d[b]	hider, 21–28 d	hider,[d] 3–4 d
Juvenile mortality	high, 76%	variable, 8–40%	variable, 11–71%	variable, 10–67%
Adult mortality	low, 7–13%	moderate, 7–40%	high, 25–59%	variable, 7–24% (probably greater under heavy hunting)
Predation	significant on young, especially wolves	variable, wolves less common on current range	can be high, rarely controlling	can be high, rarely evidence of control
Nutritional control	little effect on conception, generally annual breeding	lengthens lactation, alternate year breeding, impact through calf weight and survival	governs age of first reproduction and litter size	influences age of first reproduction and litter size
Abiotic control	can be strong, but rarely important	primarily through snow depth, thus nutrition	significant winter kill not uncommon	serious winter kill not uncommon, females may be undernourished affecting calf crop

[a] *C.e. elaphus*

[b] *C.e. canadensis*

[c] growth is compensatory, smaller young grow more rapidly than larger young

[d] *Alces* young are not 'typical' hiders, but do approximate the characteristics for a hider proposed by Lent (1974) for a short period

[e] yields generated by hand-milking

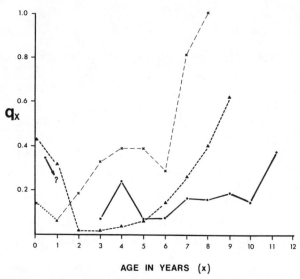

Figure 4. Age-specific mortality rates of *Cervus e. canadensis* and *C. e. elaphus*. Data of Lowe (1969) --**x**--, first year mortality using time-specific calculations, the remainder are dynamic calculations; Flook (1970) --▲--; and Caughley (1971) —•—.

a further estimate of adult female survivorship of 0.74 (26% mortality). In part, the greater adult mortality among *Cervus* is due to human harvest. That is particularly true for data of Lowe (Figure 4).

Pregnancy rates of adult female *Cervus e. canadensis* and *C. e. elaphus* center around 90%, but 2.5-year-old females conceive less frequently (Table 2). The specific surface of Figure 2 relating reproduction and mortality is broadly applicable and suggests that at juvenile mortality rates much beyond 40% some yearlings must conceive to maintain the population at a constant level. Because juvenile mortalities are commonly less than 40%, and some yearlings do conceive, we expect *Cervus* populations to show positive growth rates more often than do *Rangifer*. Peek et al. (1982) reviewed the status of elk herds in 16 states and provinces in North America. Herds were increasing in nine, stable in six, and decreasing in only two. The *C. e. elaphus* populations included in Table 2 were increasing.

Major empirical distinctions between *Rangifer* and the *Cervus* taxa treated are summarized in Table 5. Available evidence suggests that *C. e. canadensis* has moderated the potential effects of predation on the young by investing heavily in the initial birth weight. Newborn of *C. e. canadensis* weigh more than singleton moose (*A. alces*); young of *C. unicolor* may be equally large (14.4 kg). Both *Rangifer* and *C. elaphus* subspp. form mother-young aggregations following birth, and both demonstrate rapid initial growth rates (Table 5). That of *Rangifer* is likely faster, a product of milk richer in fats, protein, and total energy (Table 5, see

also Robbins et al., this volume). Growth rate appears compensatory in *Cervus*, the largest neonates showed the slowest growth rates, and weights differed little after four weeks (Thorne et al., 1976). Generally, by four weeks *C. e. canadensis* calves weigh 40–45 kg, while *Rangifer* calves weigh less than 15 kg (*C. e. elaphus* may weigh only 11–12 kg, Youngson, 1970). One consequence of the relatively larger female investment by *Cervus* is that nutritional control is more evident—both in birth weight of the young and their subsequent survival (Clutton-Brock et al., 1982; Thorne et al., 1976; Figure 7), and in alternate year reproduction (Figure 5).

After 2.5 years of age when most red deer on Rhum conceive, the proportion of females breeding in any age class declines gradually towards 0.5, suggesting that many females are breeding and nursing young in alternate years (Figure 5; see also Clutton-Brock et al., 1982: 84). On better range in New Zealand the proportion nursing rather than breeding is smaller, but the zig-zag pattern (Figure 5) suggests a small proportion are still engaging in alternate year reproduction (possibly those animals conceiving as yearlings). Conversely, there is only sparse evidence of alternate year breeding in old reindeer populations (Klein and White, 1978). It apparently occurs only on the best ranges when some females conceive as calves and a proportion (< 10%) forego breeding the following year.

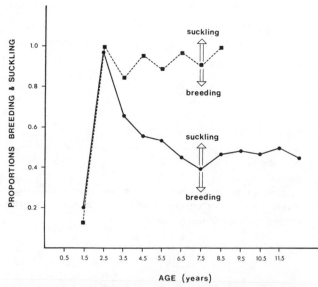

Figure 5. Age-specific proportions of females breeding as opposed to suckling last year's calves for two *Cervus elaphus* populations. Calculated from data of Lowe (1969) from Rhum (•—•) and Caughley (1971) from New Zealand (■----■). Proportion 'suckling' on Rhum also includes yeld hinds that failed to ovulate in the breeding season following calving.

Table 6. **Variations in reproductive features among populations of polytocous Cervidae**

Species	Number of populations	Reproductive feature	Percent pregnant or twinning			
			$\bar{x}$	SD	CV	Range
Alces alces	5	Pregnant, 1.5 years	13.7	19.3	1.41	(0–46)
	7	Pregnant, ≥2.5 years	79.4	12.0	0.15	(60–93)
	13	Twinning, age unspecified	16.8	8.7	0.52	(0–33)
Odocoileus hemionus	9	Pregnant, 1.5 years	59.7	22.5	0.38	(20–85)
	12	Pregnant, ≥2.5 years	96.4	3.7	0.04	(88–100)
	19	Twinning[a], age unspecified	61.4	8.5	0.14	(42–70)
Odocoileus virgianus	14	Pregnant, 0.5 years	18.0	12.8	0.75	(0–39)
	6	Pregnant, 1.5 years	73.0	13.4	0.18	(55–84)
	9	Pregnant, 2.5 years	87.9	7.6	0.09	(78–98)
	4	Pregnant, ≥2.5 years	78.7	5.7	0.07	(73–88)
	13	embryos/female[a], 0.5 years	0.50	0.46	0.92	(0–1.26)
	6	embryos/female[a], 1.5 years	1.55	0.29	0.19	(1.29–1.70)
	17	embryos/female[a], ≥1.5 years	1.51	0.33	0.22	(0.98–2.23)

[a]includes triplets

Rangifer's reproductive tactics appear to have reduced the likelihood of nutritional control, but those of at least some *Cervus* taxa have not. An additional result is that, while *Rangifer* survivorship may be much reduced during rare and unusually severe winters or springs, elk populations show more frequent responses to weather conditions. As one example, I examined a 10-year period using data of Townsend (1957) for the Gallatin elk herd. Regression of percent winter mortality (%M, all animals) against total snowfall (S, cm) yields:

$$\%\mathrm{M} = -6.98 + 0.32\,(\mathrm{S}) \qquad (6)$$
$$(\underline{r} = 0.62, \underline{P} < 0.03)$$

During that 10-year period, four winters had sufficient snowfall to increase the mortality rate of all age classes an average of six-fold over that experienced in the six milder winters. In no case did the population growth rate exceed 16%.

In summary, the mechanism most commonly controlling population growth in *Rangifer* is juvenile mortality (predation); in *Cervus* it is yearling or adult pregnancy rates (nutrition directly or mediated by abiotic effects). Nelson and Peek (1982) provided an alternative analysis of population regulation in *Cervus* which attained the same conclusion.

Polytocous Species

Treatment is concentrated on two genera, *Alces* in which adult females commonly weigh 300 to 400 kg and *Odocoileus* in which adult females weigh 35 to 55 kg depending on species (smaller subspecies exist). There is a weak tendency for adult pregnancy rates to be lower than in monotocous species (cf Tables 2 and 6). Pregnancy rates of lower age classes show the greatest variability. Proportions twinning or mean numbers of embryos/female show moderate variability in older females, and proportions of adults pregnant are relatively constant (Table 6). Environmental effects on reproductive features should be manifest first in the youngest age classes, secondarily in the mean litter size of adults.

The proportions of yearlings that must birth successfully to maintain $r_o = 0$ are summarized from the model of Figure 2 as linear relationships versus adult (≥ 2.5 years) pregnancy rates (Figure 6a). At adult pregnancy rates of 80% or greater, younger animals need not reproduce unless juvenile mortality exceeds 40%. When juvenile mortality exceeds 40%, monotocous taxa must increase yearling pregnancy rates to maintain a stable population; polytocous taxa can increase litter size with the same effect. The specific case illustrated (Figure 6b) assumes a pregnancy rate of 85% among females 2.5-years and older, a second year mortality of 30%, and 25% annual mortality thereafter. At 60% juvenile mortality about 100% of the yearlings would have to reproduce successfully were the species monotocous, but if 40% of the adults could twin the requirement from the yearlings would decline to zero (Figure 6b).

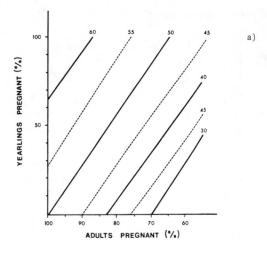

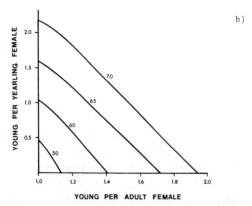

Figure 6. a) Isoclines of the proportion of yearling females which must give birth to balance population growth as a function of adult pregnancy rate (%). Numbers for each isocline are the rates of juvenile mortality (%).
b) Effect of adult twinning rates on the contribution from yearling females necessary to balance population growth. Numbers by each isocline are juvenile mortality rates.

My computations from a variety of age structures provided by government management agencies for hunted *Odocoileus* species yield a range in apparent mortality from 29 to 55% for adult males ($\bar{x} = 43.2 \pm 1.3\%$, n = 22) and 25 to 59% for adult females ($\bar{x} = 32.1 \pm 1.4\%$, n = 22). The higher male mortality has less effect on population growth rate than does female mortality, but would shift the isoclines of Figure 6b slightly, and non-linearly, to the right. Because many polytocous species both breed frequently as yearlings and have multiple births (Table 6), juvenile and yearling mortality must be high before predation can exert significant control (Figure 6b). It is precisely for these

reasons that many polytocous species are major game animals. I found fewer appropriate data for *Cap. capreolus;* that which I examined suggests a similar low likelihood of control by predation. Careful reading of Chaplin (1977) suggests high perinatal mortality exists (most of which does not appear due to predation) among increasing populations of *Hydropotes* in England.

These observations do not suggest that insignificant amounts of predation occur, but that polytocous species are seldom limited by natural predation. Connolly (1981) reviewed 19 case history studies of predation on *O. hemionus* subspecies. In 10 of 19 studies predators exerted a detectable effect on fawn survival; coyotes (*Canis latrans*) and wolves had the most pronounced effects. In six studies survivorship was much more closely associated with range conditions and nutrition; in three the results were equivocal. Several patterns emerge from Connolly's review and related literature. First, predators on many ranges kill substantial numbers of *Odocoileus* spp. and moose. Of 47 radio-collared *Alces* calves in Alaska, 23 (49%) were killed by predators, primarily black bear, and a total of 27 (57%) died over the first two months postpartum (Franzmann et al., 1980). Second, in no case has predation by coyotes or cougar (*Felis concolor*) been documented as the principal reason for population decline. Wolves have decimated local populations of both *O. h. columbianus* (Merriam, 1964; Bunnell and Jones, 1982), and *O. virginianus* (Mech and Karns, 1977). Thus, most instances of low fawn survival have not been associated unequivocably with predation. Of the 10 studies reviewed by Connolly (1981) documenting an increase in fawn survival following predator control, only one provided an increase in numbers of deer taken by hunters. In that instance, where coyotes were controlled in Utah, Robinette et al. (1977) estimates that a minimum of 25 coyotes were killed to 'save' 83 fawns of which a small portion may have been passed on to hunters. Fourth, as with *Rangifer,* the bulk of the evidence suggests that natural and human-induced mortality is frequently additive, not compensatory. Fifth, there is evidence suggesting that nutrition is more often limiting.

The two broad factors, nutrition and predation, are not clearly separable. Poor nutrition may predispose animals to predation, or reduce reproduction to levels such that it cannot match predation rates. Where winter habitat is sparse deer can be concentrated and made more vulnerable to predation (Jones and Bunnell, 1982). Although predators can reduce fawn survivorship significantly, the highest rates of fawn mortality (60 to 70+%) have been associated with severe weather conditions, drought or long-lasting, deep snowfall (Anderson et al., 1974; Hines, 1975; Jones

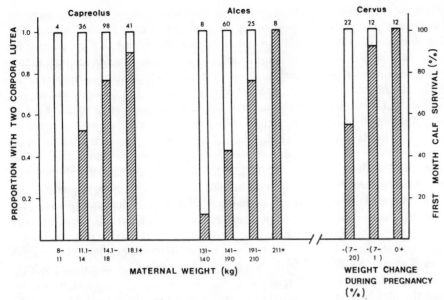

Figure 7. Influences of maternal weight on reproduction and early survivorship in selected Cervidae. Calculated from data of Chaplin (1977:151) for *Capreolus*, Markgren (1969: 221) for *Alces*, dressed weights; Thorne et al. (1976: 331, 332) for *Cervus*.

and Bunnell, 1982). Unlike predation, effects of severe abiotic conditions are multiplicative. They not only increase mortality directly, but also influence all reproductive features: age of first reproduction, conception rates, and litter size. The topic has been reviewed elsewhere (Dasmann, 1971; Klein, 1969), and I present only a reanalysis of one aspect, the effect of maternal body weight on production or survival of young. Data of Figure 7 are not confounded by effects of age (all are adult or in the same age class), with the possible exception of the smallest weight-class for *Capreolus*. The apparent influence of nutrition on reproductive performance is evident.

Nutritional effects likely produce the correlations between reproductive parameters evident in Table 7. Mean litter size in *Odocoileus* increases with the proportion of adults pregnant. Mean litter size of yearlings increases with increasing litter size of adults (*O. hemionus*). Proportions of yearlings and older animals pregnant are positively correlated (*O. virginianus*). The apparent lack of relationships with *Alces* may result from small sample sizes. When data of Markgren (1969) (which represent ovulation rather than pregnancy rates) are treated, the proportion of yearlings breeding is positively correlated with adult ovulation rate ($r = 0.73$, $P \leq 0.01$).

Proportions of pregnant *C. e. canadensis* 1.5- and 2.5-year-olds were strongly correlated with proportions of pregnant adults, suggesting nutritional control as noted earlier. The relationship is less evident among

Table 7. Correlation coefficient (r) among reproductive measurements of different age classes for six cervid species

Monotocous species		$p_{2.5}$[a]	$p_{3.5+}$		
C.e. canadensis	$p_{1.5}$	0.20	0.91*		
C.e. elaphus	$p_{1.5}$	0.70	0.42		
Rangifer	$p_{1.5}$	0.03	0.50		
C.e. canadensis	$p_{2.5}$		0.99**		
C.e. elaphus	$p_{2.5}$		0.50		
Rangifer	$p_{2.5}$		−0.96*		

Polytocous species		$p_{2.5}$	$p_{2.5+}$	$LS_{0.5}$[b]	$LS_{2.5+}$
O. virginianus	$p_{0.5}$	−0.53	0.28	0.34	0.51
A. alces	$p_{1.5}$		0.26	n.d.	0.26
O. hemionus	$p_{1.5}$		0.20	0.55	0.47
O. virginianus	$p_{1.5}$		0.71*	n.d.	n.d.
A. alces	$p_{2.5+}$			n.d.	0.33
O. hemionus	$p_{2.5+}$			0.21	0.59*
O. virginianus	$p_{2.5+}$			0.56	0.86**
O. virginianus	$L_{0.5}$				0.32
O. hemionus	$L_{1.5}$				0.68*

[a]p_i refers to the proportion pregnant in age class i
[b]LS_i refers to the litter size of age class i
[c]n.d. indicates insufficient data to compute the correlation
*significant at $p \leq 0.05$; ** significant at $p \leq 0.01$

C. e. elaphus, possibly because of alternate year breeding. The correlation between *Rangifer* age groups is strongly negative, also representing evidence of alternate year breeding. The same is true of *O. virginianus* which may conceive as fawns, and forego reproduction the following year (Table 7). To a limited extent early breeding in *Odocoileus* species is balanced by failure to breed the subsequent year. That apparently is less true of *Rangifer* giving birth as 3-year-olds (Table 2).

The high reproductive potential of polytocous species makes them relatively immune from control by predation. However, the multiplicative effects of nutritional influences, whether mediated by abiotic phenomena or not, can lower the reproductive potential rapidly (Figure 6b, Table 7). Bishop and Rausch (1974) documented several instances of abiotic conditions increasing mortality through malnutrition among *Alces* in Alaska. As expected the likelihood of nutritional or abiotic control is greater in species exhibiting greater female investment (Table 5). That is particularly true of *Odocoileus* in which the milk is somewhat richer and early growth rates more rapid than in either *Alces* or *Cervus*. We expect similar relationships in *Capreolus*, given their high female investment, and find that the relationship holds (Figure 7; see also Bubenik, 1959; Eiberle, 1963; Klein and Strandgaard, 1972; Sägasser, 1966). Within polytocous species, tactics for dealing with predation differ between *Odocoileus* and *Alces*. *Alces* dams are large enough to be effective defenders of their young and the hiding phase is short (Table 5). The young are likely less vulnerable when following the dam, than when hiding alone. *Odocoileus* is much smaller and the hiding phase is among the longest within the Cervidae (Table 5). It is also long for *Capreolus* (2-3 weeks, Kurt, 1968).

In summary, the potential for population control by juvenile mortality or predation is frequently present in polytocous species, but it is usually over-ridden by the high reproductive rate. That is particularly evident in data of Ozoga and Verme (1982): a captive herd of *O. virginianus* experiencing a mean juvenile mortality rate of 33.7% over an 11-year-period, also exhibited a mean rate of increase of 40.4%.

Summary

Given the variability of cervid habitats and the potential number of reproductive components that can be modified (e.g., Table 5), it is not surprising that cervid reproductive tactics are diverse and do not segregate neatly into discrete classes. For example, birth weights are not a simple function of maternal metabolic weight. Rather, monotocous species are generally grazers or mixed feeders (less nutritious forage than browsers) and invest proportionately more in their young than do polytocous species bearing singletons. Similarly, species in more stable habitats invest less in individual neonates, but invest more often (especially if they are mixed feeders or browsers).

The relationships between reproductive tactics and habitat have implications to management. *Rangifer* frequently encounter only one major, natural predator (usually wolves) and their tactics are concentrated on reducing the potential impact of that predation on their young. One result is that small reductions in adult survivorship are critical (Figure 2), and the addition of human-induced mortality can quickly produce negative growth rates (Figure 3). *Cervus* species, which also are monotocous, frequently encounter more than one major, natural predator. Their tactics differ, in part by the production of proportionately larger young that are hiders. The greater female investment in young increases the probability of nutritional control, either directly (range condition) or mediated by abiotic conditions (Figures 5 and 7).

Polytocous species (Table 1) are also particularly susceptible to nutritional or abiotic influences, because both litter size (Figure 7) and proportion of females conceiving (Table 7) can be affected. Because such species are capable of producing more young per capita, they are less likely to be limited to predation than is *Rangifer*. Unfortunately, the relationships do not consistently produce the single, upper equilibrium in population numbers proposed by Caughley (1976) and McCullough (1979) and idealized by managers as carrying capacity. There are two major reasons. First, predation still may be a major mortality factor influencing population growth rates. Second, influences of nutrition are multiplicative, influencing both mortality and reproduction. As a result, an equilibrium density induced by nutritional control is more poorly defined and elusive than that induced by control by predators. When both predators and nutrition or weather are combined, multiple equilibria are possible and we expect polytocous species in particular to undergo major fluctuations (e.g., Peterson and Page, 1983). It appears that 'carrying capacity' is a Holy Grail for deer managers—highly desirable, frustratingly elusive, and of questionable authenticity. One major reason is the influence of habitat on reproductive tactics.

Literature Cited

Ables, E.D.
No date. Introduction. In *The Axis Deer in Texas*, edited by E.D. Ables, pp. 7–23. College Station, Texas: Kleberg studies in natural resources., Department of Wildlife and Fisheries Sciences, Texas A. and M. University.

Altmann, M.
1963.   Naturalistic studies of maternal care of moose and elk. In *Maternal behavior in mammals*, edited by H.L. Rheingold, pp. 233–253. New York: Academic Press.

Anderson, A.E.
1981.   Morphological and physiological characteristics. In *Mule and black-tailed deer of North America*, edited by O.C. Wallmo, pp. 27–97. Lincoln, Nebraska: University of Nebraska Press.

Anderson, F.M., G.E. Connolly, A.N. Halter, and W.M. Longhurst
1974.   A computer simulation study of deer in Mendocino County, California. *Agricultural Experimental Station Technical Bulletin* No. 130. Corvallis: Oregon State University.

Arman, P., R.N.B. Kay, E.D. Goodall, and G.A.M. Sharman
1974.   The composition and yield of milk from captive red deer (*Cervus elaphus* L.). *Journal of Reproduction and Fertility*, 37:67–84.

Arnold, D.A., and L.J. Verme
1963.   Ten years' observations of an enclosed deer herd in northern [sic] Michigan. *Transactions of the North American Wildlife Conference*, 28:423–430.

Barrette, C.
1975.   *Social behaviour of Muntjak.* Ph.D. Thesis, Alberta: University of Calgary.

Bannikov, A.G., S.K. Ustinov, and P.N. Lobanov
1978.   The musk deer *Moschus moschiferus* in USSR. Morges, Switzerland: unpubl. report of the IUCN.

Baskin, L.M.
1970.   [*Reindeer ecology and behaviour*] Institute for evaluation of morphology and ecology of animals, USSR Academy of Science, Moscow. (in Russian. Unpublished English translation by Foreign Language Division, Ottawa, Canada: Department of State)

Bennetsen, E.
1976.   Sikavildtet (*Cervus nippon*) i Danmark. *Danske Vultundersogelser*, No. 25.

Bergerud, A.T.
1961.   *Reproduction of Newfoundland caribou.* M.Sc. Thesis, University of Wisconsin.

1967.   Management of Labrador caribou. *Journal of Wildlife Management*, 31:621–642.

1971.   The population dynamics of Newfoundland caribou. *Wildlife Monograph*, No. 25.

1975.   The reproductive season of Newfoundland caribou. *Canadian Journal of Zoology*, 53:1213–1221.

1978.   *The status and management of caribou in British Columbia.* Victoria, British Columbia: B.C. Fish and Wildlife Branch Report.

1980.   A review of the population dynamics of caribou and wild reindeer in North America. In *Proceedings of the Second International Reindeer/caribou Symposium*, edited by E. Reimers, E. Gaar, and S. Skjenneberg, pp. 556–581. Trondheim: Direktoratet for Vilt og Ferskvannsfisk.

1983.   The natural population control of caribou. In *Proceedings of a Symposium on Natural Regulation of Wildlife Populations*, edited by F.L. Bunnell, D.S. Eastman, and J.M. Peek, pp. 14–61. Moscow, Idaho: Forest and Wildlife Range Experiment Station.

Bergerud, A.T., and H.E. Butler
1978.   *Life history studies of caribou in Spatsizi Wilderness Park.* Victoria, British Columbia: British Columbia Parks Branch Report.

Bischoff, A.I.
1958.   Productivity in some California deer herds. *California Fish and Game*, 44:253–359.

Bishop, R.H., and R.A. Rausch
1974.   Moose fluctuations in Alaska, 1950–1972. *Naturaliste canadian*, 101:559–593.

Bos, G.N.
1974.   Nelchina and Mentasa caribou reports. Juneau, Alaska: Alaska Deptartment of Fish and Game.

1975.   A partial analysis of the current population status of the Nelchina caribou herd. In *Proceedings of the First International Reindeer/Caribou Symposium*, edited by J.R. Luick; P.C. Lent; D.R. Klein; and R.G. White, pp. 170–180. Biological Papers of the University of Alaska, Special Report No. 1.

Brown, E.R.
1961.   The black-tailed deer of western Washington. *Biological Bulletin* No. 13. Olympia: Washington Deptartment of Game.

Brüggemann, J., U. Drescher-Kaden, and K. Walser-Karst
1973.   Die Zusammensentzung der Rotwildmilch. 1. Mitteilung: Der Rohnahrstoffgehalt (Rohfett, Rohprotein, Lactose, and Rohasche). *Zeitschrift für Tierphysiologie, Tierernährung, und Futtermittelkunde*, 31:227–238.

Bubenik, A.B.
1959.   Ein Beitrag zum Problem der Rehwildgehege. *Deutsche Jäger-Zeitung*, 25:555.

1965.   Beitrag zur Geburtskunde und zu den Mutter-kind - Beziehungen des Reh - (*Capreolus capreolus* L.) und Rotwildes (*Cervus elaphus* L.). *Zeitschrift für Säugetierkunde*, 30:65–128.

Buechner, H.K., and C.V. Swanson
1955.   Increased natality resulting from lowered population density among elk in southeastern Washington. *Transactions of the North American Wildlife Conference*, 20:560–567.

Bunnell, F.L.
1982.   The lambing period of mountain sheep: synthesis, hypotheses, and tests. *Canadian Journal of Zoology*, 60:1–14.

Bunnell, F.L., and G.W. Jones
In   Black-tailed deer and old-growth forests—a syn-
press. thesis. *Perspectives*.

Bunnell, F.L., and A.S. Harestad
1983.   Dispersal and dispersion of black-tailed deer—models and observations. *Journal of Mammalogy*, 64(2):201–209.

Calef, G.W.
1979.   *The population status of caribou in the Northwest Territories*. Yellowknife: Progress Report of the Northwest Territory Wildlife Service.

1980.   Status of *Rangifer* in Canada. II Status of *Rangifer* in the Northwest Territories. In *Proceedings of the Second International Reindeer/caribou Symposium*, edited by E. Reimers, E. Gaare, and S. Skjenneberg, pp. 754-759. Trondheim: Direktoratet for Vilt og Ferskvannsfisk.

Calef, G.W., and P.C. Heard
1980.   The status of three tundra wintering caribou herds in northeastern mainland Northwest Territories. In *Proceedings of the Second International Reindeer/caribou Symposium*, edited by E. Reimers, E. Gaare, and S. Skjenneberg, pp. 582–594. Trondheim: Direktoratet for Vilt og Ferskvannsfisk.

Caughley, G.
1971.   Demography, fat reserves and body size of a population of red deer *Cervus elaphus* in New Zealand. *Mammalia*, 35:369–383.
1976.   Wildlife management and the dynamics of ungulate populations. In *Applied Biology Volume I*, edited by T.H. Coaker, pp. 183–246. London: Academic Press.

Chaplin, R.E.
1977.   *Deer*. Dorset: Blandford Press.

Chapman, D.I.
1974.   Reproductive physiology in relation to deer management. *Mammal Review*, 4:61–74.

Chapman, D., and N. Chapman
1975.   *Fallow deer. Their history, distribution and biology.* Suffolk: Terrence Dalton Ltd.

Chapman, D.I., and O. Dansie
1970.   Reproduction and foetal development in female muntjac deer (*Muntiacus reevesi* Ogilby). *Mammalia*, 34:303–319.

Chattin, J.E.
1948.   Breeding season and productivity in the Interstate deer herd. *California Fish and Game*, 34:25–31.

Cheatum. E.L., and J.E. Gabb
1952.   Productivity of north Yellowstone elk as indicated by ovary analysis. *Proceedings of the Western Association of State Game and Fish Commissioners*, 32:174–177.

Cheatum, E.L., and C.W. Severinghaus
1950.   Variations in fertility of white-tailed deer related to range conditions. *Transactions of the North American Wildlife Conference*, 15:170–190.

Clutton-Brock, T.H., F.E. Guinness, and S.D. Albon
1982.   *Red deer, behavior and ecology of two sexes*. Chicago: University of Chicago Press.

Connolly, G.E.
1981.   Limiting factors and population regulation. In *Mule and black-tailed deer of North America*, edited by O.C. Wallmo, pp, 245–285. Lincoln, Nebraska: University of Nebraska Press.

Cowan, I.McT., and A.J. Wood
1955.   The growth rate of the black-tailed deer (*Odocoileus hemionus columbianus*). *Journal of Wildlife Management*, 19:331–336.

Dansie, O.
1977.   Genus *Muntiacus*. In *The handbook of British mammals*, edited by G.B. Corbett and H.N. Southern, pp. 447–451. Oxford: Blackwell Scientific Publications.

Darling, F.F.
1937.   *A herd of red deer: a study in animal behaviour*. London: Oxford University Press.

Dasmann, W.P.
1971.   *If deer are to survive*. Harrisburg: Stackpole Books.

Dauphiné, T.C.
1976.   Biology of the Kaminuriak population of the barren-ground caribou Part 4. Growth, reproduction and energy reserves. *Canadian Wildlife Service Report Series*, No. 38.

Dauphiné, Jr., T.C., and R.L. McClure
1974.   Synchronous mating in barren-ground caribou. *Journal of Wildlife Management*, 38:54–66.

Davidson, M.M.
1976.   Season of parturition and fawning percentages of Sika deer (*Cervus nippon*) in New Zealand. *New Zealand Journal of Forestry Science*, 5:355–357.

Davis, J.L.
1978a. *Sex and age composition of the Porcupine caribou herd*. Juneau: Alaska Department of Fish and Game.

1978b. History and current status of Alaska Caribou herds. In *Parameters of caribou population ecology in Alaska*, edited by D.R. Klein and R.G. White, pp. 1–8. Biological Papers of the University of Alaska, Special Report No. 3.

Davis, J.L., R. Shideler, and R.E. Le Resche
1978.   *Fortymile caribou herd studies*. Juneau: Alaska Department of Fish and Game.

Davis, J.L., and P. Valkenburg
1978.   *Western Arctic caribou herd studies.* Juneau: Alaska
        Department of Fish and Game, Federal Aid to Wild-
        life Restoration Project W-17-18 and W-17-9.

Davis, J.L., P. Valkenburg, and H.V. Reynolds
1980.   Population dynamics of Alaska's western Arctic
        herd. In *Proceedings of the Second International Reindeer/
        caribou Symposium*, edited by E. Reimers, E. Gaare,
        and S. Skenneberg, pp. 595–604. Trondheim: Direk-
        toratet for Vilt og Ferskvannsfisk.

Denniston, R.H. II
1951.   Ecology, behavior and population dynamics of the
        Wyoming or Rocky Mountain moose, *Alces alces
        shirasi. Zoologica*, 41:105–118.

desMoules, R., and J.M. Brassard
1963.   *Inventaive preliminaire du caribou Rangifer tarandus
        caribou d'un secteur de la cote-Nord et du secteur centre de
        Ungava.* Quebec Department Fish and Game.

Dodds, D.G.
1959.   Feeding and growth of a captive moose calf. *Journal
        of Wildlife Management*, 23:231–232.

Edwards, R.Y., and R.W. Ritcey
1958.   Reproduction in a moose population. *Journal of Wild-
        life Management*, 22:261–268.

Egorov, O.V.
1967.   *Wild ungulates of Yakutia.* Jerusalem, Israel Program
        for Scientific Translations.

Eiberle, K.
1963.   Futtereigenschaften und Wildverbiss. *Schweizerische
        Zeitschrift für Forstwesen*, 114:10.

Eisenberg, J.F.
1981.   *The mammalian radiations. An analysis of trends in evolu-
        tion, adaptation, and behavior.* Chicago: Univ. of
        Chicago Press.

Espmark, Y.
1980.   Effects of maternal pre-partum undernutrition on
        early mother-calf relationships in reindeer. In *Pro-
        ceedings of the Second International Reindeer/caribou Sym-
        osium*, edited by E. Reimers, E. Gaare, and S. Skjen-
        neberg, pp. 485–496. Trondheim: Direktoratet for
        Vilt og Ferskvannsfisk.

Estes, R.D.
1981.   The survival value of synchronized calving in the
        wildebeest. *National Geographic Society Research Reports*,
        13:211–213.

Flook, D.R.
1970.   A study of sex differential in the survival of wapiti.
        Canadian Wildlife Service Report Series No. 11.

Follis, T.B., and J.J. Spillet
1974.   Winter pregnancy rates and subsequent cow/calf
        ratios in elk. *Journal of Wildlife Management*, 38:789–
        791.

Franzmann, A.W.
1981.   *Alces alces. Mammalian Species*, No. 154.

Franzmann, A.W., and C.C. Schwartz
1979.   *Kenai Peninsula moose calf mortality study.* Juneau: Alas-
        ka Department of Fish and Game. P-R Proj. Final
        Report.

Franzmann, A.W., R.E. Le Resche, R.A. Rausch, and J.L.
Oldemeyer
1978.   Alaskan moose measurements and weights and
        measurement-weight relationships. *Canadian Journal
        of Zoology*, 56:298–306.

Franzmann, A.W., C.C. Schwartz, and R.O. Peterson
1980.   Moose calf mortality in summer on the Kenai Penin-
        sula, Alaska. *Journal of Wildlife Management*, 44:764–
        768.

Gardner, A.L.
1971.   Postpartum estrus in a red brocket deer, *Mazama
        americana*, from Peru. *Journal of Mammalogy*, 52:623–
        624.

Gee, E.P.
1960.   Report on the status of the brow-antlered deer of
        Manipur (India): October–November 1959 and
        March 1960. *Journal of the Bombay Natural History So-
        ciety*, 57:597–617.

Geist, V.
1974.   On the evolution of reproductive potential in moose.
        Naturaliste canadien, 101:527–537.

1981.   Behavior: adaptive strategies in mule deer. In *Mule
        and black-tailed deer of North America*, edited by O.C.
        Wallmo, pp. 157–223. Lincoln, Nebraska: Univer-
        sity of Nebraska Press.

Gill, R.B.
1972.   *Productivity studies of mule deer in Middle Park, Colorado.*
        Paper presented at Annual Mule Deer Workshop,
        Elko, Nevada.

Golley, F.B.
1957.   Gestation period, breeding and fawning behavior of
        Columbian black-tailed deer. *Journal of Mammalogy*,
        38:116–120.

Graf, W., and L. Nichols, Jr.
1966.   The axis deer in Hawaii. *Journal of the Bombay Natural
        History Society*, 63:629–734.

Greer, K.R.
1965.   Collections from Gallatin elk post season, 1964–65.
        Job Completion Report, Project No. W-83-R-8. Helena:
        Montana Department of Fish and Game.

1966.   Fertility rates of the northern Yellowstone elk popu-
        lations. *Proceedings of the Western Association of Fish and
        Game Commissioners*, 46:123–128.

1968.   Special collection–Yellowstone elk study, 1967–1968.
        Job Completion Report, Proj. No. W-83-R-11. Helena:
        Montana, Department of Fish and Game.

Haber, G.C.
1977.   *Socio-ecological dynamics of wolves and prey in a subarctic ecosystem*. Ph.D. Thesis. Vancouver: University of British Columbia.

Hagen, H.L.
1951.   Composition of deer milk. *California Fish and Game*, 37:217–218.

Hancock, N.V.
1957.   A preliminary report of elk reproduction in Utah with special reference to precociousness in the yearling female. *Proceedings of the Western Association of State Game and Fish Commissioners*, 37:195–197.

Harlow, R.F.
1974.   Reproductive rates in white-tailed deer in Florida. *Quarterly Journal of Florida Academy of Sciences*, 35:165–170.

Harper, J.A.
1971.   *Ecology of Roosevelt elk*. Portland: Oregon State Game Commission. P-R Report W-59-R.

Harper, J.A., J.H. Harn, W.W. Bentley, and C.F. Yocom
1967.   The status and ecology of the Roosevelt elk in California. *Wildlife Monographs*, No. 16.

Harris, R.A., and K.R. Duff
1970.   *Wild deer in Britain*. Newton Abbot: David and Charles

Hart, J.S., O. Heroux, W.H. Cottle, and C.A. Mills
1961.   The influence of climate on metabolic and thermal responses of infant caribou. *Canadian Journal of Zoology*, 39:845–56.

Hatter, J.
1950.   *The moose of central British Columbia*. Ph.D. Thesis. Pullman: Washington State University.

Haugen, A.O.
1975.   Reproductive performance of white-tailed deer in Iowa. *Journal of Mammalogy*, 56:151–159.

Haugen, A.O., and L.A. Davenport
1950.   Breeding records of white-tailed deer in the upper peninsula of Michigan. *Journal of Wildlife Management*, 14:290–295.

Hemming, J.E.
1971.   The distribution and movement patterns of caribou in Alaska. *Wildlife Technical Bulletin* No. 1. Juneau: Alaska Department of Fish and Game.

Henshaw, J.
1970.   Consequences of travel in the rutting of reindeer and caribou (*Rangifer tarandus*). *Animal Behavior*, 18:256–258.

Heptner, W.G., and A.A. Nasimovich
1968.   *Der Elch*. Die Neue Brehm-Bücherei No. 386. Wittenberg: A. Ziemsen Verlag.

Heptner, W.G., A.A. Nasimovich, and N.P. Naumov
1966.   *Die Säugetiere der Sowjetunion. Band I. Paarhufer und Unparrhufer*. Jena: VEB Gustav Fischer Verlag.

Hershkovitch, P.
1982.   *Neotropical deer (Cervidae) Part 1, Pudus, Genus Pudu Gray*. Fieldiana Zoology, New Series, No. 11.

Hesselton, W.T., and L.W. Jackson
1974.   Reproductive rates of white-tailed deer in New York State. *New York Fish and Game Journal*, 21:135–152.

Hick, U.
1969.   Successful breeding of a pudu (*Pudu pudu*) at Cologne Zoo. *International Zoo Yearbook*, 9:110–112.

Hines, W.W.
1975.   *Black-tailed deer behaviour and population dynamics in the Tillamook burn, Oregon*. Portland: Wildlife Commission, Wildlife Research Report Number 5.

Holleman, D.F., J.R. Luick, and R.G. White
1971.   Transfer of radiocesium in milk from reindeer cow and calf. In *Radionucleides in ecosystems*, edited by D.J. Nelson, Vol. 1, *Third National Symposium on Radioecology*, pp. 76–80. Oak Ridge, Tennessee: U.S. Atomic Energy Commission.

Horwood, M.T.
1971.   *Sika deer research—2nd. Progress report*. London: Nature Conservation Council.

Houston, D.B.
1968.   The Shiras moose in Jackson Hole, Wyoming. *Technical Bulletin of the Grand Teton Natural History Association*, No. 1.

Hudson, P.
1959.   Fetal recoveries in mule deer. *Journal of Wildlife Management*, 23:234–235.

Irvine, C.
1976.   *Population size of the Alaska Peninsula caribou herd*. Juneau: Final Report, Federal Aid to Wildlife Restoration Project Report W-17-7 and 8, Job 3, 17R.

Jenness, R., and R.E. Sloan
1970.   The composition of milk of various species: a review. *Dairy Science Abstracts*, 32:599.

Jensen, W., and W.L. Robinette
1955.   A high reproductive rate for Rocky Mountain mule deer. *Journal of Wildlife Management*, 19:503.

Johns, P.E., R. Baccus, M.N. Manlove, J.E. Pinder, III, and M.H. Smith
1977.   Reproductive patterns, productivity and genetic variability in adjacent white-tailed deer populations. *Proceedings of the Annual Conference of the Southeastern Association of Fish and Wildlife Agencies*, 31:167–172.

Johnson, D.E.
1951.   The biology of the elk calf, *Cervus canadensis nelsoni*. *Journal of Wildlife Management*, 15:396–410.

Jones, G.W., and F.L. Bunnell
In   Response of black-tailed deer to winters of different
press. severity on northern Vancouver Island. *Perspectives*.

Jordan, J.W., and P.A. Vohs, Jr.
1976.   Natality of black-tailed deer in McDonald State Forest, Oregon. *Northwest Science*, 59:108–113.

Julander, O., W.L. Robinette, and D.A. Jones
1961.   Relation of summer range condition to mule deer herd productivity. *Journal of Wildlife Management*, 25:54–60.

Juniper, I.
1977.   Summary of recent research on caribou in the Quebec-Labrador Peninsula. In *The First Quebec-Labrador Caribou Conference*, pp. 42–55. Ottawa: Department of Indian and Northern Affairs.

Kelsall, J.P.
1968.   The migratory barren-ground caribou of Canada. *Canadian Wildlife Service Monograph*, No. 3:1–340.

Kimball, J.F., and M.L. Wolfe
1980.   Continuing studies of the demographics of a northern Utah elk population. In *North American elk: ecology, behavior and management*, edited by M.S. Boyce and L.D. Hayden-Wing, pp. 20–28. Laramie: University of Wyoming.

Kitts, W.D., I.McT. Cowan, J. Bandy, and A.J. Wood
1956.   The immediate post-natal growth in the Columbian black-tailed deer in relation to the composition of the milk of the doe. *Journal of Wildlife Management*, 20:212–214.

Klein, D.R.
1968.   The introduction, increase and crash of reindeer on St. Matthew Island. *Journal of Wildlife Management*, 32:350–367.

1969.   Food selection by North American deer and their response to over-utilization of preferred plant species. In *Animal populations in relation to their food resources*, edited by A. Watson, pp. 25–44. Oxford: Blackwell Scientific Publications.

Klein, D.R., and H. Strandgaard.
1972.   Factors affecting growth and body size of roe deer. *Journal of Wildlife Management*, 36:64–79.

Klein, D.R., and R.G. White
1978.   Parameters of caribou population ecology in Alaska. *Biological Papers of the University of Alaska, Special Report*, No. 3.

Knight, R.R.
1970.   The Sun River elk herd. *Wildlife Monograph*, No. 23.

1973.   Calf:cow ratios in the Lochsa elk herd. In *Proceedings of the Biennial Conferences of Western States Elk Workshop*, pp. 90–91. Bozeman: Montana.

Knorre, E.P., and E.K. Knorre
1956.   [Size and seasonal changes in live weights of moose]. (in Russian) *Zoologicheskii Zhurnal*, 35:1229–1237.

Krebs, C.J., and I.McT. Cowan
1962.   Growth studies of reindeer fawns. *Canadian Journal of Zoology*, 40:863–869.

Kurt, F.
1968.   *Das Socialverhalten des Rehes. Eines Feldstudie.* Berlin: Paul Parey-Verlag.

Laukhart, J.B.
1948.   Black-tailed deer in western Washington. *Proceedings of the Western Association of State Game and Fish Commissioners*, 28:152–161.

Leader-Williams, N.
1980a. Population dynamics and mortality of reindeer introduced into South Georgia. *Journal of Wildlife Management*, 44:640–657.

1980b. Population ecology of reindeer on South Georgia. In *Proceedings of the Second International Reindeer/caribou Symposium*, edited by E. Reimers, E. Gaare, and S. Skjenneberg, pp. 664–676. Trondheim: Direktoratet for Vilt og Ferskvannsfisk.

Leader-Williams, N., and M.R. Payne
1980.   Status of *Rangifer* on South Georgia. In *Proceedings of the 2nd International Reindeer/caribou Symposium*, edited by E. Reimers, E. Gaare, and S. Skjenneberg, pp. 786–789. Trondheim: Direktoratet for Vilt og Ferskvannsfisk.

Leitch, I., F.E. Hutten, and W.Z. Billewicz
1959.   The maternal and neonatal weights of some mammalia. *Proceedings of the Zoological Society of London*, 133:11–28.

Lent, P.C.
1974.   Mother-infant relationships in ungulates. In *The behaviour of ungulates and its relationship to management*, edited by V. Geist and F. Walther, pp. 14–55. IUCN Publication, New Series No. 24.

Lower, V.P.W.
1969.   Population dynamics of the red deer (*Cervus elaphus* L.) on Rhum. *Journal of Animal Ecology*, 38:425–457.

Luick, J.R., R.G. White, A.M. Gau, and R. Jenness
1974.   Compositional changes in the milk secreted by grazing reindeer. I. Gross composition and ash. *Journal of Dairy Science*, 57:1325.

Luttich, S.
1977.   *Census and composition of the George River caribou herd on the Hebran calving range, 5–9 June 1975 and 3–8 June 1976.* St. John's: Newfoundland Wildlife Division of Progress Report Number 76c-10a.

Mansell, W.D.
1974.   Productivity of white-tailed deer on the Bruce Peninsula, Ontario. *Journal of Wildlife Management*, 38:808–814.

Markgren, G.
1969.   Reproduction of moose in Sweden. *Viltrevy*, No. 6:127–285.

McCullough, D.R.

1969. *The Tule elk: its history, behavior and ecology.* Berkeley: University of California Press.

1979. *The George Reserve Deer Herd.* Ann Arbor: University of Michigan Press.

McEwan, E.H.

1963. *Reproduction of barren-ground caribou, Rangifer tarandus groenlandicus (Linnaeus) with relation to migration.* Ph.D. Thesis. Montreal: McGill University.

1968. Growth and development of the barren-ground caribou (*Rangifer tarandus*). *Canadian Journal of Zoology,* 46:1023–29.

McEwan, E.H., A.J. Wood, and H.C. Nordan

1965. Body temperature of barren-ground caribou. *Canadian Journal of Zoology,* 43:683–687.

McKean, J.W.

1947. Interstate deer herd study. *Proceedings of the Western Association of Game and Fish Commissioners,* 27:110–115.

Medin, D.E.

1976. *Modelling the dynamics of a Colorado mule deer population.* Ph.D. Thesis. Fort Collins: Colorado State University.

Mech, L.D., and P.D. Karns

1977. *Role of the wolf in a deer decline in the Superior National Forest.* USDA Forest Service Research Paper NC-148.

Merriam, H.R.

1964. The wolves of Coronation Island. *Proceedings of the Alaska Science Conference,* 15:27–32.

Miller, F.L.

1974. Biology of the Kaminuriak population of barren-ground caribou. Part 2. Dentition as an indication of age and sex; composition and socialization of the population. *Canadian Wildlife Service Report Series,* No. 31.

Miller, F.L., and E. Broughton

1974. Calf mortality on the calving ground of Kaminuriak caribou. *Canadian Wildlife Service Report Series,* No. 26.

Mitchell, B.

1969. The potential output of meat as estimated from natural and park populations of red deer. In *The husbanding of deer,* edited by M.M. Bannerman and K.L. Blaxter, pp. 16–27. Aberdeen, Scotland: Highlands and Islands Development Board and the Rowett Research Institute.

1971. The weights of new-born to one-day-old red deer calves in Scottish moorland habitats. *Journal of Zoology,* 164:250–254.

Moisan, G.

1952. Investigation on moose populations. In *General Report of the Ministers of Game and Fisheries,* pp. 25–43. Quebec: Department of Fish and Game.

Moran, R.J.

1973. *The Rocky Mountain elk in Michigan.* Wildlife Division, Research and Development Report No. 267. Lansing: Michigan, Department of Natural Resources.

Mueller, C.C.

1977. *An investigation of precocious puberty in female black-tailed deer (Odocoileus hemionus columbianus).* Ph.D. Thesis, Burnaby, British Columbia: Simon Fraser University.

Mueller, C.C., and R.M.F.S. Sadleir

1977. Changes in the nutrient composition of milk of black-tailed deer during lactation. *Journal of Mammalogy,* 58:421–423.

Murie, A.

1934. *The moose of Isle Royale.* University of Michigan, Miscellaneous Publications of the Museum of Zoology, No. 25.

1944. *The wolves of Mount McKinley.* U.S. National Park Service, Fauna Series No. 5.

Murie, O.J.

1951. *The elk of North America.* Harrisburg: Stackpole Company.

Nellis, C.H.

1968. Productivity of mule deer on the National Bison Range, Montana. *Journal of Wildlife Management,* 32:344–349.

Nelson, L.J., and J.M. Peek

1982. Effect of survival and fecundity on rate of increase of elk. *Journal of Wildlife Management,* 46:535–540.

Ozoga, J.J., and L.J. Verme

1982. Physical and reproductive characteristics of a supplementally-fed white-tailed deer herd. *Journal of Wildlife Management,* 46:281–301.

Parker, G.R.

1972. Biology of the Kaminuriak population of the barren-ground caribou. Part I. Total numbers, mortality, recruitment, and seasonal distribution. *Canadian Wildlife Service Report Series,* No. 20.

Peek, J.M.

1962. Studies of moose in the Gravelly and Snowcrest Mountains, Montana. *Journal of Wildlife Management,* 26:360–365.

Peek, J.M., R.J. Pederson, and J.W. Thomas

1982. The future of elk and elk hunting. In *Elk of North America. Ecology and Management,* edited by J.W. Thomas and D.E. Toweill, pp. 599–625. Harrisburg: Stackpole Books.

Peterson, R.L.

1955. *North American moose.* Toronto: University of Toronto Press.

Peterson, R.O., and R.E. Page

1983. Wolf-moose fluctuations at Isle Royale National Park, Michigan, U.S.A., *Acta Zoologica Fennica,* 174:251–253.

Bunnell

Pimlott, D.H.
1959. Reproduction and productivity of Newfoundland moose. *Journal of Wildlife Management,* 23:381–401.

Preobrazhenskii, B.V.
1968. Management and breeding of reindeer. In *Reindeer husbandry,* edited by P.S. Zhigunov, pp. 78–128. Washington, D.C.: Israel Program for Scientific Translations.

Rausch, R.A., and A. Bratlie
1965. Annual assessments of moose calf production and mortality in south–central Alaska. *Proceedings of the Western Association of State Game and Fish Commissioners,* 45:140–146.

Reimers, E.
1975. Age and sex structure in a hunted population of reindeer in Norway. In *Proceedings of the First International Reindeer/caribou Symposium,* edited by J.K. Luick, P.D. Lent, D.R. Klein, and R.G. White, pp. 181–188. Biological Papers of the University of Alaska, Special Report No. 1.

Ritcey, R.W.
1955. *Abundance and fall distribution of caribou in Wells Gray Park.* Victoria: British Columbia Department of Recreation and Conservation.

Ritcey, R.W., and D.J. Low
1975. *Caribou census, 1975.* Kamloops, British Columbia: B.C. Fish and Wildlife Report.

Robbins, C.T., and A.N. Moen
1975. Milk consumption and weight gain of white-tailed deer. *Journal of Wildlife Management,* 39:355–360.

Robbins, C.T., and B.L. Robbins
1979. Fetal and neonatal growth patterns and maternal reproductive effort in ungulates and subungulates. *American Naturalist,* 114:101–116.

Robinette, W.L., C.H. Bauer, R.E. Pilmore, and C.E. Knittle
1973. Effects of nutritional change on captive mule deer. *Journal of Wildlife Management,* 37:312–326.

Robinette, W.L., and J.S. Gashwiler
1950. Breeding season, productivity, and fawning period of the mule deer in Utah. *Journal of Wildlife Management,* 14:457–469.

Robinette, W.L., J.S. Gashwiler, J.B. Low, and D.A. Jones
1955. Differential mortality by sex and age among mule deer. *Journal of Wildlife Management,* 21:1–16.

Robinette, W.L., N.V. Hancock, and D.A. Jones
1977. *The Oak Creek mule deer herd in Utah.* Resource Publication 77-15. Salt Lake City: Utah Division of Wildlife.

Robinette, W.L., and O.A. Olsen
1944. Studies of the productivity of mule deer in central Utah. *Transactions of the North American Wildlife Conference,* 9:156–161.

Sägesser, H.
1966. Über den Einfluss des Standortes auf das Gewicht des Rehwildes (*Capreolus c. capreolus* [Linne 1758]). *Zeitschrift für Jagdwissenschaft,* 12:54–62.

Sankhala, K.S., and J.H. Desai
1971. Reproductive behaviour of the brow-antlered deer. *Journal of the Bombay Natural History Society,* 67:561–565.

Scheffer, V.C.
1951. The rise and fall of a reindeer herd. *Scientific Monthly,* 73:356–362.

Schlegel, M.
1976. Factors affecting calf elk survival in north-central Idaho—a progress report. *Proceedings of the Western Association of State Game and Fish Commissioners,* 56:342–355.

Schoen, J.W.
1977. *The ecological distribution and biology of wapiti, Cervus elaphus nelsoni, in the Cedar River watershed, Washington* Ph.D. Thesis. Seattle: University of Washington.

Schwartz, J.E., and G.E. Mitchell
1945. Roosevelt elk on the Olympic Peninsula, Washington. *Journal of Wildlife Management,* 9:295–319.

Sears, H.S.
1955. *Certain aspects of the reproductive physiology of the female mule deer.* M.S. Thesis. Missoula: Montana State University.

Sears, H.S., and L.G. Browman
1955. Quadruplets in mule deer. *Anatomical Record,* 122:335–340.

Severinghaus, C.W., and E.L. Cheatum
1956. Life and times of the white-tailed deer. In *The deer of North America,* edited by W.P. Taylor, pp. 57–186. Harrisburg: Stackpole Co.

Sexton, J.J.
1976. Survey-inventory progress report, Adak Island. In *Annual report of survey-inventory activities, Part III, Caribou, brown bear, polar bear, and black bears,* edited by D.E. Knight, pp. 8–12. Juneau: Alaska Department of Fish and Game.

Silver, H.
1961. Deer milk compared with substitute milk for fawns. *Journal of Wildlife Management,* 25:66–70.

Simkin, D.W.
1965a. Reproduction and productivity of moose in Northwestern Ontario. *Journal of Wildlife Management,* 29:740–750.

1965b. A preliminary report of the woodland caribou study in Ontario. *Ontario Department of Lands and Forests Section, Report,* 59.

Skoog, R.O.
1968. *Ecology of the caribou (Rangifer tarandus granti) in Alaska.* Ph.D. Thesis. Berkeley: University of California.

Skuncke, F.
1949.   *Algen*. Stockholm: P.A. Norstedt and Soners.

Spencer, D.L., and E.F. Chatelain
1953.   Progress in the management of moose in south-central Alaska. *Transactions of the North American Wildlife Conference*, 18:539–552.

Stringham, S.F.
1974.   Mother-infant relations in moose. *Naturaliste canadien*, 101:325–369.

Sunquist, M.E.
1981.   *The social organization of tigers (Panthera tigris) in Royal Chitwan National Park, Nepal, Smithsonian Contributions to Zoology, No. 336:1–98.*

Taber, R.D., K. Raedeke, and D.A. McCaughran
1982.   Population characteristics. In *Elk of North America. Ecology and Management*, edited by J.W. Thomas and D.E. Toweill, pp. 279–298. Harrisburg: Stackpole Books.

Tamang, K.M.
1982.   *The status of the tiger Panthera tigris tigris and its impact on principal prey populations in The Royal Chitawan National Park, Nepal*. Ph.D. Thesis, Lansing: Michigan State University.

Teer, J.G., J.W. Thomas, and E.A. Walker
1965.   Ecology and management of white-tailed deer in the Llano Basin of Texas. *Wildlife Monograph*, Number 15.

Thomas, D.C.
1970.   *The ovary, reproduction, and productivity of female Columbian black-tailed deer*. Ph.D. Thesis. Vancouver: University of British Columbia.

Thomas, W.D.
1975.   Observations on captive brockets. *International Zoo Yearbook*, 15:77–78.

Thomson, B.R.
1977.   *The behaviour of wild reindeer in Norway*. Ph.D. Thesis. Edinburgh, Scotland: University of Edinburgh.

Thorne, E.T., R.E. Dean, and W.G. Hepworth
1976.   Nutrition during gestation in relation to successful reproduction in elk. *Journal of Wildlife Management*, 40:330–335.

Tolman, C.D.
1950.   Productivity of mule deer in Colorado. *Transactions of the North American Wildlife Conference*, 17:482–496.

Townsend, J.E.
1957.   Game management aspects of the Gallatin elk herd in Montana. *Proceedings of the Western Association State of Game and Fish Commissioners*, 37:207–210.

Trainer, C.E.
1971.   *The relationship of physical condition and fertility of female Roosevelt elk (Cervus canadensis roosevelti) in Oregon*. M.Sc. Thesis. Corvallis: Oregon State University.

Tuomi, J.
1980.   Mammalian reproductive strategies: a generalized relation of litter size to body size. *Oecologia*, 45:39–44.

Ullrey, D.E., W.G. Youatt, H.E. Johnson, L.D. Fay, B.L. Schoepke, and W.T. Magee
1971.   A basal diet for deer nutrition research. *Journal of Wildlife Management*, 35:57–62.

Valentincic, S.I.
1958.   Beitrag zur Kenntis der Reproduktionserscheinungen beim Rotwild. *Zeitschrift für Jagdwissenschaft*, 4:105–130.

Vanoli, T.
1967.   Beobachtungen an Pudus. *Säugetierkundliche Mitteilungen*, 15:155–163.

Verme, L.J.
1963.   Effect of nutrition on growth of white-tailed deer fawns. *Transactions of the North American Wildlife Conference*, 28:431–443.

Verme, L.J.
1965.   Reproduction studies on penned white-tailed deer. *Journal of Wildlife Management*, 20:74–79.

White, R.G., F.L. Bunnell, E. Gaare, T. Skogland, and B. Hubert
1981.   Ungulates on arctic ranges. In *Tundra ecosystems: a comparative analysis*, edited by L.C. Bliss, O.W. Heal, and J.J. Moore, pp. 397–482. Cambridge: Cambridge University Press.

Whitehead, G.K.
1950.   *Deer and their management in deer parks of Great Britain and Ireland*. London: Country Life Ltd.

1972.   *Deer of the world*. London: Constable and Co.

Wright, B.S.
1956.   *The moose of New Brunswick*. Report to the Minister Lands and Mines. Fredericton: New Brunswick.

Wyett, W., and G. Keesey
1978.   *Faunal investigations in Pukaskwa National Park*. Unpublished Report, Pukaskwa National Park, Marathon, Ontario.

Yazan, Y., and Y. Knorre
1964.   Domesticating elk in a Russian National Park. *Oryx*, 7:301–304.

Youatt, W.G., L.J. Verme, and D.E. Ullrey
1965.   Composition of milk and blood in nursing white-tailed does and blood composition of their fawns. *Journal of Wildlife Management*, 29:79–84.

Youngson, R.W.
1970.   Rearing red deer calves in captivity. *Journal of Wildlife Management*, 34:467–470.

Appendix 1. Literature used to derive values in Figures and Tables.

Figure 1. Mean values illustrated are my calculations from data of *Alces*: Heptner et al. (1966), Knorre and Knorre (1956), Skuncke (1949); *Axis*: Ables (no date), Graf and Nichols (1966), Sunquist (1981), Tamang (1982); *Capreolus*: Chaplin (1977), Egorov (1967); *Cervus elaphus canadensis (nelsoni)*: Flook (1970), Johnson (1951), Thorne et al. (1982), Mitchell (1969, 1971); *C.e. nannodes*: McCullough (1969); *C. eldi*: Gee (1960), Sankhala and Desai (1971) - adult male weights converted to female assuming sexual dimorphism as in *C. elaphus* and *C. nippon*; *C. nippon*: Bennetsen (1976), Davidson (1976), Harris and Duff (1970), Heptner et al. (1966), Horwood (1971); *C. timorensis*: Whitehead (1950); *C. unicolor*: Eisenberg (1981), Sunquist (1981), Tamang (1982); *Dama*: Chapman and Chapman (1975); *Elaphurus*: Wemmer pers comm.; Whitehead (1950); *Hydropotes*: Chaplin (1977), Whitehead (1950); *Mazama americana* and *gouazoubira*: Eisenberg (1981), Thomas (1975); *Moschus sibiricus*: Bannikov et al. (1977), Heptner et al. (1966); *Muntiacus muntjak*: Barrette (1975), Eisenberg (1981); *M. reevesi*: Chaplin (1977), Dansie (1977); *Odocoileus hemionus columbianus*: Cowan and Wood (1955), Golley (1957), Mueller (1977); *O.h. hemionus*: Robinette et al. (1973); *O. virginianus*: Haugen and Davenport (1950), Severinghaus and Cheatum (1956), Ullrey et al. (1971), Verme (1963); *Pudu puda*: Eisenberg (1981), Hershkovitz (1982), Hick (1969), Vanoli (1967); *P. mephistophiles*: Eisenberg (1981); *Rangifer*: Kelsall (1968), Krebs and Cowan (1962), McEwan (1968).

Figure 3. Calculated from data of Bergerud (1967, 1971, 1978, 1980, 1983), Calef (1979, 1980), Calef and Heard (1980), Davis (1978a and b), Davis et al. (1978, 1980), des Meules and Brassard (1963), Haber (1977), Hemming (1971), Irvine (1976), Juniper (1977), Klein (1968), Leader-Williams (1980b), Luttich (1977), Parker (1972), Reimers (1975), Ritcey (1955), Ritcey and Low (1975), Scheffer (1951), Sexton (1976), Skoog (1968), Thomson (1977), Wyett and Keesey (1978).

Table 2. Calculated from data of *C.e. canadensis*: Buechner and Swanson (1955), Cheatum and Gabb (19520, Flook (1970), Follis and Spillett (1974), Gree (1965, 1966, 1968), Hancock (1957), Harper (1971), Harper et al. (1967), Knight (1970, 1973), Moran (1973), Murie (1951), Trainer (1971); *C.e. elaphus*: Caughley (1971), Chapman (1974), Lowe (1969), Mitchell (1969), Valentinic (1958); *Rangifer*: Bergerud (1971, 1980), Bergerud and Butler (1978), Bos (1974), Dauphiné (1976), Davis and Valkenburg (1978), Leader-Williams (1980b), Simkin (1965b), Skoog (1968).

Table 3. Calculated from data of Bergerud (1971, 1980), Dauphiné (1976), Davis (1978a), Davis and Valkenburg (1978), Davis et al. (1978), McEwan (1973), Miller and Broughton (1974).

Table 5. Female investment and growth rates calculated from data of Figure 1; some mortality rates from data of Tables 3 and 4 and Figure 4; other mortality references cited in text. Additional sources were – *Alces*: Bishop and Rausch (1974), Denniston (1951), Dodds (1959), Franzman et al. (1978), Jenness and Sloan (1970), Lent (1974), Peek (1962), Stringham (1974), Yazan and Knorre (1964); *Cervus*: Altmann (1963), Brüggerman et al. (1973), Bubenik (1965), Darling (1937), Youngson (1970); *Odocoileus*: Bunnell (un-published), Geist (1981), Hagen (1951), Kitts et al. (1956), Mueller and Sadleir (1977), Robbins and Moen (1975), Silver (1961), Youatt et al. (1965); *Rangifer*: Holleman et al. (1971), Lent (1974), Luick et al. (1974), White et al. (1981).

Table 6. Calculated from data of *Alces*: Edwards and Ritcey (1958), Franzmann et al. (1976, in Franzman, 1981), Franzmann and Schwartz (1979), Hatter (1950), Houston (1968), McDowell and Moy (1942, in Peterson, 1955), Moisan (1952), Murie (1934, 1944), Peek (1962), Peterson (1955), Pimlott (1959), Rausch and Bratlie (1965), Simkin (1965a), Spencer and Chatelain (1953), Wright (1956); *O. hemionus*: Anderson (1981), Bischoff (1958), Brown (1961), Chattin (1948), Gill (1972), Hudson (1959), Jensen and Robinette (1955), Jordan and Vohs (1976), Julander et al. (1961), Laukhart (1948), McKean (1947), Medin (1976), Nellis (1968), Reed and Pojar (1977, in Anderson, 1981), Robinette and Gashwiler (1950), Robinette and Olson (1944), Robinette et al. (1955, 1977), Sears (1955), Sears and Browman (1955), Thomas (1970), Tolman (1950); *O. virginianus*: Arnold and Verme (1963), Cheatum and Severinghaus (1950), Harlow (1974), Haugen (1975), Hesselton and Jackson (1974), Johns et al. (1977), Mansell (1974), Teer et al. (1965).

Table 7. Calculated from data of Tables 2 and 6.

RONALD K. CHESSER
and
MICHAEL H. SMITH
Department of Biological Sciences
The Museum, Texas Tech University
Lubbock, Texas 79409

Savannah River Ecology Laboratory
Drawer E
Aiken, South Carolina 29801

Relationship of Genetic Variation to Growth and Reproduction in the White-tailed Deer

ABSTRACT

Genetic variation of seven polymorphic loci was assessed by starch-gel electrophoresis for 2455 white-tailed deer from the Savannah River Plant. Does with relatively high levels of heterozygosity (at 2, 3, and 4 of the seven loci) had significantly higher rates of twinning than females with lower levels of heterozygosity. Rate of post-natal growth to maturity was significantly faster for deer of both sexes with relatively low heterozygosity, but highly heterozygous deer attained larger overall body size. Heterozygosity was also significantly associated with conception times with highly heterozygous does breeding later than homozygous does. The kidney fat index was significantly higher in does carrying twins than for those with single offspring at the time of conception. However, does with twins lost their fat reserves significantly faster during gestation than does carrying single offspring. Deer with different levels of heterozygosity appear to have different strategies by which they maximize their fitness.

Chesser and Smith

Introduction

Growth and reproductive rates are perhaps the most important life history characteristics determining the fitness of an individual. The strong interdependence of these rates (Hirth, 1977; Ozoga, 1972; Cothran et al., 1983) necessitates the joint analysis of the dynamics of growth and productivity as they relate to the relative success of individual animals. Rapid growth rates may lead to early maturity and high lifetime productivity by shortening the generation time (Cole, 1954; Case, 1978). Litter size influences the growth rate of the offspring (Cothran et al., 1983). Large female body size allows the production of greater numbers of offspring per breeding period than small female body size (Falconer, 1960; Millar, 1977; Nixon, 1971). Large body size in males is an important determinant of social status and breeding success in deer (Hirth, 1977). Fitness is largely determined by an optimization of energetics such that the atainment of a critical body size is realized early in life and it is often enhanced by maximizing body size.

Genetic variability has been documented as an important determinant for the expression of characteristics necessary for reproductive success. Heterozygosity has been found to be positively associated with factors such as overall body size (Koehn et al., 1973; Boyer, 1974; Garten, 1976; Smith and Chesser, 1981; Cothran et al., 1983), growth rates (Singh and Zouros, 1978; Cothran et al., 1983), number of offspring produced (Smith et al., 1975; Johns et al., 1977), social dominance (Baker and Fox, 1978), aggressiveness and exploratory behavior (Garten, 1976, 1977), and developmental stability (Mitton, 1978; Soulé, 1979). In white-tailed deer (*Odocoileus virginianus*) heterozygosity is associated with fetal growth (Cothran et al., 1983), reproduction (Johns et al., 1977), survivorship (Chesser et al., 1982b), antler development, and adult body size (Smith et al., 1983). This list of partial fitness characters (Lewontin, 1974) which are positively associated with genetic variability documents the important role of genetic variability on the expression of phenotypic attributes.

The effects associated with heterozygosity are often complex and the possible selective advantages cannot allways be interpreted clearly. When the effects of number of *in utero* offspring are statistically accounted for, highly heterozygous deer fetuses grow significantly faster than their more homozygous counterparts (Cothran et al., 1983). However, single fetuses tend to be produced by homozygous does (Johns et al., 1977) and in reality grow faster than more heterozygous twin fetuses (Cothran et al., 1983). Maternal heterozygosity is also associated with fetal growth in addition to fetal heterozygosity and number. Although heterozygosity appears to bestow a growth ad-vantage within each category of single and twin fetuses, the overall selective value of heterozygosity is still subject to question. Growth rate must have a constraint on its upper level imposed by the natural history of the animal. Additionally, if highly heterozygous animals are always more fit, selection would result in populations with high numbers of individuals with very high levels of heterozygosity. Thus, selective compensation for the homozygous types must be present in white-tailed deer populations because heterozygosity is not high and is within the range expected for mammals (Ramsey et al., 1979; Nevo, 1978. Further studies aimed at the investigation of genetic correlates of fitness characters at all life history stages of deer are needed to document the realized fitness of white-tailed deer with different levels of genetic variation.

In this study we investigate the associations of genetic variation to the rate of post-natal growth and asymptotic body weight of white-tailed deer of both sexes. Because of the strong influence of reproductive, and body condition of deer on growth and vice versa (Cothran et al., 1983), we also investigate potential genetic correlates for these variables.

Materials and Methods

A total of 2455 white-tailed deer were collected during public hunts on the U.S. Department of Energy's Savannah River Plant (SRP) near Aiken, South Carolina, during the years 1974–1977. Deer of both sexes and any age were collected from two regions on the SRP designated as swamp and upland (Urbston 1967). Individual deer were weighed to the nearest pound and age was determined by the pattern of tooth wear and eruption (Severinghaus, 1949). Kidneys and perineal fat were collected and weighed to the nearest gram to calculate the kidney fat index (KFI; weight of kidney fat divided by kidney weight multiplied times 100; Riney, 1955), a good predictor of total body fat (Finger et al., 1981). Liver and blood samples were taken for subsequent electrophoretic analysis.

Electrophoretic procedures followed those of Manlove et al. (1976) for seven polymorphic loci: beta hemoglobin, esterase—2, glutamate oxalate transaminase—2, malate dehydrogenase—1, phosphoglucomutase—2, sorbitol dehydrogenase–1, and transferrin. The phenotype for each of these loci was determined for each individual. Heterozygosity for an individual deer was calculated as the number of loci which were heterozygous for the seven polymorphic loci. The heterozygosity classes included in subsequent analyses were 0, 1, 2, 3, 4, and 5 or more (5+) except for the growth analyses in which the classes were 0, 1, 2, 3, and 4+. These heterozygosity classes

Table 1. Values for sample size (N), mean number of fetuses per female and standard error (S.E.), variance in number of offspring, and conception date (with November 1 as day 304) are given for white-tailed deer with different numbers of heterozygous loci out of seven loci studied on the Savannah River Plant.

Heterozygosity	N	Mean number of fetuses (S.E.)	Variance	Conception* Date
0	13	1.46 (0.144)	0.26	315.8
1	53	1.70 (0.064)	0.21	311.9
2	68	1.85 (0.043)	0.13	313.3
3	61	1.85 (0.046)	0.13	319.6
4	38	1.84 (0.060)	0.14	326.3
5+	14	1.71 (0.15)	0.22	327.9

*Values are least squares means adjusted for age.

were necessary to maintain adequate sample sizes in each age genetic category for data analysis.

Fetuses were taken from pregnant does and the size and number recorded. Length of pregnancy was calculated from the size of the fetuses by the method of Armstrong (1950). Conception date was calculated by subtracting the estimated length of pregnancy from the day of collection (January 1 as day 1). For does collected after 1 January but which conceived in the previous year, the collection day number was added to 365 before the conception date was calculated.

Growth rates of deer were analyzed using the von Bertalanffy growth curve (c.f. Allen, 1966). Other growth curve models, e.g., Gompertz, logistic, and Richard's (Richards, 1959; Timon and Eisen, 1969), were also run, but the von Bertalanffy gave results with consistently smaller standard errors. Rates of growth to the asymptote and asymptotic values were estimated. Standard errors of these values were obtained for each sex and heterozygosity category. One-way and two-way analyses of variance were used to investigate the relationships among conception dates, KFI, body weight, number of fetuses, and age. In some instances analyses of covariance and least squares means were used to statistically account for the effects of some variables. Conception dates were transformed by logarithims (base 10) to comply to normal distributions. The relationship between the length of pregnancy and KFI was analyzed by linear regression for females carrying twin versus single offspring. All data analyses were performed using the Statistical Analysis System (Barr et al., 1979). Statistical significance was accepted at the $P = 0.05$ level.

Results

A significant relationship between the number of fetuses per pregnant doe and the number of hetero-

Table 2. Statistics for von Bertalanffy growth curves for male and female white-tailed deer from the Savannah River Plant. Values for rate of growth to the asymptotic body weight and body weight at 4 years of age for males and 3 years of age for females are given with 95% confidence intervals for deer with different numbers of heterozygous loci out of seven loci studied.

Sex Heterozygosity		Rate of Asymptote	Asymptotic Weight (Kg)	Estimated Weight at 3 Years (female) or 4 Years (male)
Male	0	0.989 ± 0.08	73.56 ± 2.13	75.9 ± 2.3
	1	0.951 ± 0.04	74.77 ± 1.86	77.3 ± 2.1
	2	0.830 ± 0.04	78.22 ± 0.91	82.4 ± 1.8
	3	0.913 ± 0.07	75.52 ± 1.93	79.5 ± 1.9
	4±	0.786 ± 0.09	76.03 ± 2.57	80.9 ± 2.0
	overall	0.871 ± 0.07	76.22 ± 1.36	79.7 ± 2.8
Females	0	1.720 ± 0.10	48.38 ± 2.01	51.4 ± 1.6
	1	1.605 ± 0.09	48.05 ± 1.98	49.6 ± 1.4
	2	1.354 ± 0.10	49.03 ± 1.26	55.5 ± 1.2
	3	1.313 ± 0.11	48.42 ± 1.87	52.0 ± 1.2
	4±	1.396 ± 0.13	48.41 ± 1.10	54.0 ± 1.5
	overall	1.399 ± 0.10	48.23 ± 1.92	52.1 ± 2.1

Chesser and Smith

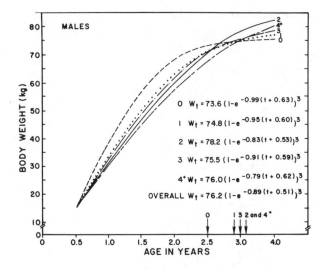

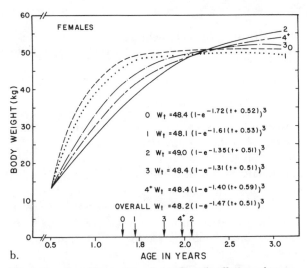

Figure 1.   Growth curves and von Bertalanffy growth equations for male (a) and female (b) white-tailed deer from the Savannah River Plant. Growth parameters are presented for deer which were heterozygous at 0, 1, 2, 3, and 4 or more loci of seven loci studied. The ages at which the asymptotic date was reached for deer of each heterozygosity category are indicated by the arrows on the ordinate.

zygous loci was found (Table 1). Deer heterozygous at two, three and four of the seven polymorphic loci had significantly greater numbers of fetuses than does heterozygous for zero, one and five or more (5+) loci. Variance of the number of offspring per doe was lowest for the high levels of heterozygosity (except for deer with 5+ heterozygous loci). Thus, deer with high heterozygosity values had greater numbers of fetuses per pregnancy and lower variance in their offspring number.

Post-natal growth rates of both male and female white-tailed deer with low levels of heterozygosity (zero and one heterozygous locus) were significantly higher than for deer with high (two, three, and four or

more) heterozygosity (Table 2). Deer with the fastest growth rates usually had lower asymptotic body weights than those with slow rates of growth. However, this trend was significant only for males in that deer with two heterozygous loci had significantly higher asymptotic body size than those with zero or one.

Deer with low heterozygosity levels attained their adult body weights at an earlier age than other deer (Figures 1a, 1b). The disparities of the age at which adult body weight is attained among deer with different heterozygosity values were most pronounced in females (Figure 1b). Homozygous deer may mature earlier and possibly breed at an earlier age than more genetically variable deer.

Deer carrying twin offspring had significantly higher KFI's at the time of conception than did does with only single fetuses ($P<0.01$; analysis only included pregnant does collected between October 15 and November 15). However, loss of body fat reserves declined significantly faster during the gestation period for does with twins than for does carrying a single embryo (Figure 2). This loss of fat reserves, apparently due to energy demands of pregnancy, resulted in significantly lower KFI at the time of birth (≈ 210 days) for does with twins than for does with single offspring (Figure 2). Relatively slow growth rates of the highly heterozygous deer may be due to the lower maternal investments that females are able to bestow on each individual fawn, as they tend to have twins. The difference in energy reserves between does with single fawns and those having twins probably increases in the post-partum period because energy demands during lactation are greater than those of gestation (Moen, 1978).

Conception dates of does may be influenced by several factors. Females with high levels of heterozygosity tended to conceive relatively late in the breeding season (Table 1). Values for the kidney fat index (KFI) were also positively associated with conception time ($P=0.056$). This result was somewhat surprising because deer in better body condition might be expected to breed earlier than those with lower energy reserves. However, significant first order interactions of KFI and body weight and KFI and the number of fetuses indicated that conception date probably varied as a function of the product of these variables. When body weight was statistically accounted for, the association of KFI and conception date became negative. Hence, larger females tended to breed earlier than smaller does, but does with twins bred later than those with single offspring. Thus, recovery of body condition for the high energy demands of earlier lactation appears to be important in controlling conception times for female white-tailed deer.

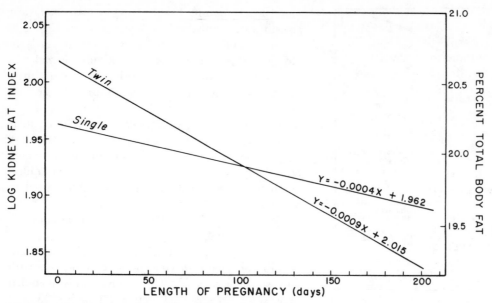

Figure 2. Linear regressions of loss of kidney fat during gestation periods for female white-tailed deer carrying single or twin offspring on the Savannah River Plant. Slopes, intercepts, and estimated KFI at conception were significantly different for the twin and single classes. The R^2 values for the twin and single regressions were 0.26 and 0.06, respectively.

Discussion

Post-natal growth, reproductive rates, and timing of reproduction in SRP white-tailed deer are associated with the level of heterozygosity. Whereas the positive relationship between heterozygosity and the number of fetuses for pregnant does seems relatively simple, the influences of genetic variability on growth and conception dates is more complex. These complexities deserve examination because of their implications for the realized fitness of deer and their probable effects on ultimate productivity.

Deer with low heterozygosity grew significantly faster and attained adult body sizes at earlier age than more heterozygous individuals (Table 2, Figure 1a, 1b). Deer which mature earlier may also breed at an earlier age than slower maturing deer (c.f., Lack, 1968; Ricklefs, 1967, 1968, 1976; Case, 1978). Early reproduction shortens the generation time and insures greater genetic representation of the fast growing deer (c.f., Cole, 1954). For example, given two types of deer which both live for four years: the first type has only single offspring but is able to breed in the first year, the second type always has twins but delays reproduction until its second year; assuming that their offspring have the same breeding schedule of their mothers, a 1 : 1 sex ratio, and no mortality, then after ten breeding periods (years), starting with one deer of each type, the deer bearing single offspring would be represented by 644 deer whereas the offspring of the twinning deer would number only 385. White-tailed deer do not behave in a manner which meets the re-

quirements of such an extreme model as that depicted, but the example demonstrates how early reproduction alone may markedly alter the fitness of individuals. Sufficient details are not known concerning natality and mortality in deer to build such a model at this time. However, the growth rates suggest that the relative fitness of fast growing deer (homozygotes) could be relatively high under some conditions.

The number of fetuses a female carries has a strong influence on the growth rate of the offspring (Cothran et al., 1983) but not on their ultimate size (this study). The number of fetuses per female is significantly smaller for highly homozygous deer (Table 1). The *in utero* growth rate of single offspring is significantly faster than that for twins (Cothran et al., 1983). Since maternal heterozygosity is highly correlated with offspring heterozygosity (Cothran et al., 1983), the relatively homozygous deer were most likely a single fetus in utero. However, high heterozygosity consistently resulted in deer of larger ultimate body size than did homozygosity. It appears that the greater early maternal investments bestowed on single offspring compared to that for twins enhanced their early growth rate, but subsequent accumulation of body mass is less than for more heterozygous deer.

Large body size may be selectively advantageous for white-tailed deer. Females with large body size may have larger and greater numbers of offspring per reproductive period (Millar, 1977) and suffer fewer natal mortalities (Knowlton, 1964, 1968; White, 1966;

Cook et al., 1971; Clutton-Brock et al., 1982). Large males are more likely to be socially dominant and thus able to control mates (Hirth, 1977; Ozoga, 1972). Therefore, the benefits bestowed by faster growth to more homozygous deer are not the same as those of greater ultimate growth for highly heterozygous deer. The relative success of either of these strategies compared to the other is dependent on the extant conditions. Age structures, sex ratios, and reproductive parameters are variable in different parts of the SRP deer herd during the same year, as well as over years (Dapson et al., 1979; Chesser et al., 1982b). These population characteristics along with density and local environmental differences could determine which strategy is optimal for individual deer at any one time. Therefore, it seems likely that the relative advantages of faster growth or larger ultimate body size change through time and space with a dynamic balance resulting from current evolutionary processes.

Body condition, as measured by the KFI, is strongly associated with reproductive parameters in white-tailed deer. Reproductive activities appear to be the major influence on the loss of energy reserves in SRP white-tailed deer. Total body fat declines rapidly for female deer during periods of gestation and lactation, and for males during the rut period (Johns et al., 1984). Does carrying twin fetuses had significantly larger KFI's than those with single fetuses early in the reproductive season (October 15–November 15), but lose these reserves faster as the pregnancy proceeds (P<0.01; Figure 2). Large males lose body fat faster during the rut than younger males as a result of reproductive related activities (Brooks, 1978; Johns et al., 1982). Relative energy demands for reproduction are high for southern deer even though forage availability and climate is not as severe as in northern latitudes (Harlow et al., 1979).

Reproductive effort varies greatly as a function of whether the female produces single or twin offspring. Millar (1977) has defined reproductive effort (RE) in terms of the body weight of the mother (MW), body weight of the offspring at the time of weaning (WW) and the number of offspring (N) such that $RE=N.WW^{0.75} (MW^{0.75})^{-1}$. RE is the relative increase in energy costs for reproductive activities and parental investment above those of maintenance metabolism. Reproductive efforts for does that raise either single or twin fawns to a weaning weight of 25 kg (an approximate average for the SRP [Moore, 1972]) have very different RE values depending on their body weight (Figure 3). Does with lower body weights may not be capable of meeting the energy demands of routine body maintenance in addition to supplying energy to twin offspring. As previously suggested, it may be that does with low body weight may be the result of

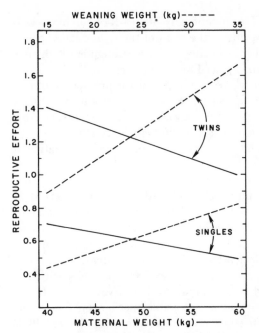

Figure 3. Values of reproductive effort necessary (a) for does of different body weights to rear fawns (either singles or twins) to a weaning weight of 25 kg (solid lines and lower abscissa), and, (b) for mothers with a body weight of 50 kg to rear fawns (either singles or twins) to various weaning weights (dashed lines and upper abscissa). Equations for calculating reproductive effort are from Millar (1977).

lower metabolic efficiency. The relative energy demands of carrying twin offspring are much less for larger females. Highly heterozygous does do in fact have significantly larger body sizes for each age class (Cothran et al., 1983). Thus, the differences in ultimate body sizes of female deer with high twinning rate may be adaptive.

Perhaps more important, in terms of fitness, than maternal body weight is the weight of the offspring at the time of weaning. A large fawn may have an advantage in terms of survival during times of harsh climate (Lack, 1968; Ricklefs, 1967, 1968, 1976; Case, 1978; Clutton-Brock et al., 1982) and may better compete for vital resources. In the case of female offspring, large body size may increase the chances of early reproduction. The differences of reproductive effort necessary for a 50 kg doe (approximate average for SRP [Moore, 1972]) to rear twin offspring to an equivalent weight of single offspring are very large (Figure 3). Not only are absolute energy demands different for mothers of single and twin offspring but relative energy costs are changing rapidly as the weaning weight increases from 15 to 35 kg. As the weaning weight of the offspring increases, the relative energy needed to successfully raise twins increases at a more rapid rate than that to produce single offspring of the same weight. The significantly higher KFI for mothers of twin offspring at the onset of the reproductive period is probably associated with the subsequent high energy demands placed on the mother.

The energy requirement for the production of twin offspring far surpasses that for producing singles. These differences in energy requirements strongly suggest that the rate and/or efficiency at which energy is assimilated for the deer may differ in relation to their reproductive performance. Almost all does of reproductive age on the SRP are pregnant at the end of the breeding season (Johns et al., 1977). Thus, all adult females must rebuild their energy reserves after their previous offspring are weaned, to be ready for the subsequent reproductive season. Highly heterozygous deer, which have high twinning rates, may be able to ingest or assimilate energy more efficiently and have higher KFI's than the homozygous deer. Berger (1976) presented a possible mechanism for greater metabolic efficiency for heterozyotes. Berger (1976) hypothesizes that heterozygosity reduces the energy required to maintain and synthesize molecules important to primary metabolic pathways. Hence, greater metabolic efficiency for routine maintenance requirements will provide additional energy reserves for reproduction and growth. Another plausible hypothesis is that the level of heterozygosity is reflective of the level of outbreeding with heterozygotes having little inbreeding depression (Falconer, 1960; Lerner, 1954). The latter hypothesis is contingent upon a highly subdivided population (Wright, 1978). The SRP deer herd is subdivided into several genetic subunits (Manlove et al., 1976; Ramsey et al., 1979; Chesser et al., 1982b) as are populations of many large, highly mobile ungulates (Chesser et al., 1982a; Gyllensten et al., 1980; Ryman et al., 1977, 1980).

Accumulation of energy reserves and improvement of body condition after parturition are important not only for investments to the survival and growth of fawns, but also to reproductive readiness in the subsequent breeding season (Clutton-Brock et al., 1982). In red deer the birth date of calves is related to the mother's condition during rut (Clutton-Brock et al., 1982). Similarly, body condition (KFI) is inversely related to conception dates in white-tailed deer. Late breeding deer (November 15–24; Table 1) have relatively high heterozygosity and tend to have twins. Recovery of body condition after high energy demands associated with twins is probably an important determinant of reproductive timing. Late breeding and, thus, late birth dates may result in high mortality of offspring due to either harsh environment or poor nutritive condition of the mother (cf., Guinness et al., 1971; Mitchell and Lincoln, 1973; Clutton-Brock et al., 1982). Data are not available regarding the severity of mortality for white-tailed deer fawns born at different times on the SRP, but late breeding may be associated with early weaning of fawns. However, the complex interactions of genetics, body condition, growth, age at sexual maturity, numbers of offspring, and timing of reproduction are not "random events, but represent short- and long-term feedback systems whose balancing capabilities determine species survival" (Robbins and Robbins, 1979) and individual reproductive success.

White-tailed deer with different levels of genetic variability appear to have alternative strategies by which their fitness may be realized. There are several dichotomies in regard to methods of attaining reproductive success in highly heterozygous and homozygous individuals: (1) Highly heterozygous deer have greater numbers of offspring per female for each breeding period, but highly homozygous deer seem to have shorter generation times. (2) Highly heterozygous deer attain larger body sizes, but highly homozygous deer have faster growth rates and may attain adult body sizes earlier. (3) Highly heterozygous deer have faster in utero growth rates for single and twin fetuses, but single fetuses which tend to be highly homozygous grow faster than twin fetuses. (4) Highly heterozygous deer may have more offspring under stable population conditions, but highly homozygous deer may be able to bestow greater parental investments to their individual offspring, and, thus, insure greater competitive potential for their offspring. (5) Highly heterozygous deer are in better body condition at the times of conception, but highly homozygous deer breed earlier than heterozygous deer and may increase the chances of survival of their offspring. Thus, it is evident that highly heterozygous and highly homozygous deer may be differentially successful under a variety of populations and environmental conditions. More studies concerning reproductive capabilities, particularly for males in conjunction with genetic variation, demography, and habitat, are needed to accurately assess the dynamics of white-tailed deer populations.

Acknowledgments

This research was supported by contract DE-AC09-76SR00819 between the University of Georgia's Institute of Ecology and the U.S. Department of Energy. Other groups cooperated in conducting this research including the employees of E.I. du Pont de Nemours Company and the U.S. Forest Service at the SRP, and the South Carolina Wildlife and Marine Resources Department who granted permission to conduct the research. Special thanks are extended to I.L. Brisbin, Jr., E.G. Cothran, P.E. Johns, and M.C. Wooten and our colleagues at the Savannah River

Chesser and Smith

Ecology Laboratory who contributed their labor and ideas toward the completion of this work. We also thank C. Wemmer and members of the National Zoological Park for the opportunity and funds to participate in the Cervid Biology and Management conference.

Literature Cited

Allen, K.R.
1966. A method of fitting growth curves of the von Bertalanffy type to observed data. *Journal of the Fisheries Research Board of Canada*, 23:163–179.

Armstrong, R.A.
1950. Fetal development of the northern white-tailed deer (*Odocoileus virginianus borealis* Miller). *American Midland Naturalist*, 43:650–666.

Baker, M.C., and S.F. Fox
1978. Dominance, survival and enzyme polymorphism in dark-eyed Juncos, *Junco hyemalis*. *Evolution*, 32:697–711.

Barr, A.J., J.H. Goodnight, J.P. Sall, and J.T. Helwig
1979. *A User's Guide to SAS-79*. Raleigh, N.C.: SAS Institute Inc.

Berger, E.
1976. Heterosis and the maintenance of enzyme polymorphism. *American Naturalist*, 110:823–839.

Boyer, J.F.
1974. Clinal and size dependent variation at the Lap locus in *Mytilus edulis*. *Biological Bulletin*, 147:535–549.

Brooks, P.M.
1978. Relationship between body condition and age, growth, reproduction and social status in impala, and its application to management. *South African Journal of Wildlife Research*, 8:151–157.

Case, T.J.
1978. On the evolution and adaptive significance of postnatal growth rates in the terrestrial vertebrates. *Quarterly Review of Biology*, 53:243–282.

Chesser, R.K., C. Reuterwall, and N. Ryman
1982a. Genetic variation of the Scandinavian moose (*Alces alces*) over short geographic distances. *Oikos*, 39:125–130.

Chesser, R.K., M.H. Smith, P.E. Johns, M.N. Manlove, D.O. Straney, and R. Baccus
1982b. Spatial, temporal, and age-dependent heterozygosity of beta hemoglobin in the white-tailed deer. *Journal of Wildlife Management*, 46:983–990.

Clutton-Brock, T.H., F.E. Guinness, and S.D. Albon
1982. *Red Deer. Behavior and Ecology of Two Sexes*. Chicago: University of Chicago Press.

Cole, L.C.
1954. The population consequences of life history phenomena. *Quarterly Review of Biology*, 29:103–137.

Cook, R.S., M. White, D.O. Trainer, and W.C. Glazener
1971. Mortality of young white-tailed deer fawns in South Texas. *Journal of Wildlife Management*, 35:47–56.

Cothran, E.G., R.K. Chesser, M.H. Smith, and P.E. Johns
1983. Influences of genetic variability and maternal factors on fetal growth in white-tailed deer. *Evolution*, 37:282–291.

Dapson, R.W., P.R. Ramsey, M.H. Smith, and D.F. Urbston
1979. Demographic differences in contiguous populations of white-tailed deer. *Journal of Wildlife Management*, 43:889–898.

Falconer, D.S.
1960. *Introduction to Quantitative Genetics*. New York: Ronald Press.

Finger, S.E., I.L. Brisbin, Jr., M.H. Smith, and D.F. Urbston
1981. Kidney fat as a predicator of body condition in white-tailed deer. *Journal of Wildlife Management*, 45:964–968.

Garten, C.T., Jr.
1976. Relationships between aggressive behavior and genic heterozygosity in the oldfield mouse, *Peromyscus polionotus*. *Evolution*, 30:59–72.

Garten, C.T., Jr.
1977. Relationships between exploratory behavior and genic heterozygosity in the oldfield mouse. *Animal Behaviour*, 25:328–332.

Guinness, F.E., G.A. Lincoln, and R.V. Short
1971. The reproductive cycle of the female red deer (*Cervus elaphus L.*). *Journal of Reproduction and Fertility*, 27:427–438.

Gyllensten, U., C. Teutenwall, N. Ryman, and G. Stahl
1980. Geographical variation of transferrin allele frequencies in three deer. *Hereditas*, 92:237–241.

Harlow, R.F., D.F. Urbston, and J.G. Williams, Jr.
1979. Forages eaten by deer in two habitats at the Savannah River Plant. USDA Forest Service Research Note S.E., 275 pp.

Hirth, D.H.
1977. Social behavior of white-tailed deer in relation to habitat. *Wildlife Monograph* 41:6–55.

Johns, P.E., R. Baccus, N.M. Manlove, J.E. Pinder III, and M.H. Smith
1977. Reproductive patterns, productivity and genic variability in adjacent white-tailed deer populations. *Proceedings of the Annual Conference of the Southeastern Association of Game and Fish Wildlife Agencies*, 31:167–172.

Johns, P.E., M.H. Smith, and R.K. Chesser
1984. Annual cycles of the kidney fat index in a Southeastern white-tailed deer herd. *Journal of Wildlife Management*. 48:969–973.

Johns, P.E., M.H. Smith, E.G. Cothran, and R.K. Chesser
1982. Fat levels in male white-tailed deer during the breeding season. *Proceedings of the Annual Conference of the Southeastern Association of Game and Fish Wildlife Agencies,* 36:454–462.

Knowlton, F.F.
1964. Aspects of coyote predation in South Texas with special reference to white-tailed deer. Ph.D. Thesis. Lafayette, Indiana: Purdue University.

Knowlton, F.F.
1968. Coyote predation as a factor in management of antelope in fenced pastures. Biennial Antelope Status Workshop Proceedings, 3:65–74.

Koehn, R.K., F.J. Turano, and J.B. Mitton
1973. Population genetics of marine pelecypods. II. Genetic differences in microhabitats of *Modiolus demissus. Evolution,* 31:526–537.

Lack, D.
1968. *Ecological Adaptations for Breeding in Birds.* London: Methuen.

Lerner, I.M.
1954. *Genetic Hoemostasis.* London: Oliver and Boyd.

Lewontin, R.C.
1974. *The Genetic Basis of Evolutionary Change.* New York: Columbia University.

Manlove, N.M., M.H. Smith, H.O. Hillestad, S.E. Fuller, P.E. Johns, and D.O. Straney
1976. Genetic subdivision in a herd of white-tailed deer as demonstrated by spatial shifts in gene frequencies. *Proceedings of the Annual Conference of the Southeastern Association of Game and Fish Wildlife Agencies,* 30:487–492.

Millar, I.S.
1977. Adaptive features of mammalian reproduction. *Evolution,* 31:370–386.

Mitton. J.B.
1978. Relationship between heterozygosity for enzyme loci and variation of morphological characters in natural populations. *Nature,* 273:661–662.

Mitchell, B., and G.A. Lincoln
1973. Conception dates in relation to age and condition in two populations of red deer in Scotland. *Journal of Zoology,* 171:141–152.

Moen, A.N.
1978. Seasonal changes in heart rates, activity, metabolism, and forage intake of white-tailed deer. *Journal of Wildlife Management,* 42:715–738.

Moore, G.
1972. White-tailed deer research project. Annual Progress Report, South Carolina Wildlife Marine Resources Department, 18 pp.

Nevo, E.
1978. Genetic variation in natural populations: patterns and theory. *Theoretical Population Biology,* 13:121–177.

Nixon, C.M.
1971. Productivity of white-tailed deer in Ohio. *Ohio Journal of Science,* 71:218–225.

Ozoga, J.J.
1972. Aggressive behavior of white-tailed deer at winter cuttings. *Journal of Wildlife Management,* 36:861–868.

Ramsey, P.R., J.C. Avise, M.H. Smith, and D.F. Urbston
1979. Biochemical variations and genetic heterogeneity in South Carolina Deer populations. *Journal of Wildlife Management,* 43:136–142.

Richards, F.J.
1959. A flexible growth function for empirical use. *Journal of Experimental Botany,* 10:290–300.

Ricklefs, R.E.
1967. A graphical method of fitting equations to growth curves. *Ecology,* 48:978–983.

1968. Patterns of growth in birds. *Ibis,* 110:419–451.

Ricklefs, R.E.
1976. Growth rates of birds in the humid new world tropics. *Ibis,* 118:179–207.

Riney, T.
1955. Evaluating condition of free-ranging red deer with special reference to New Zealand. *New Zealand Journal of Science and Technology,* 36:429–463.

Robbins, C.T., and B.L. Robbins
1979. Fetal and neonatal reproductive effort in ungulates and subungulates. *American Naturalist,* 114:101–116.

Ryman, N., G. Beckman, G. Bruun-Peterson, and C. Reuterwall
1977. Variability of red cell enzymes and genetic implications of management policies in Scandinavian moose (*Alces alces*). *Hereditas,* 85:157–162.

Ryman, N., C. Reuterwall, K. Nygren, and T. Nygren
1980. Genetic variation and differentiation in Scandinavian moose (*Alces alces*): Are large mammals monomorphic? *Evolution,* 34:1037–1049.

Severinghaus, C.W.
1949. Tooth development and wear as criteria for age in white-tailed deer. *Journal of Wildlife Management,* 13:195–216.

Singh, S.M., and E. Zouros
1978. Genetic variation associated with growth rate in the American oyster (*Crassostrea virginica*). *Evolution,* 32:342–353.

Smith, M.H., C.T. Garten, and P.R. Ramsey
1975. Genetic heterozygosity and population dynamics in small mammals. In *Isozymes IV, Genetics and Evolution,*

edited by C.L. Markert, pp. 85–102. New York: Academic Press.

Smith, M.H., R.K. Chesser, E.G. Cothran, and P.E. Johns
1982. Genetic variability and antler growth in a natural population of white-tailed deer. In *Antler Development in Cervidae*, edited by R.D. Brown, pp. 365–387. Kingsville, Texas: Caesar Kleberg Wildlife Research Institute, Texas A&I University.

Soulé, M.E.
1979. Heterozygosity and developmental stability: another look. *Evolution*, 33:396–401.

Timon, V.M., and E.J. Eisen
1969. Comparisons of growth curves of mice selected and unselected for postweaning gain. *Theoretical and Applied Genetics*, 39:345–351.

Urbston, D.F.
1967. Herd dynamics of a pioneer-like deer population. *Proceedings of the Annual Conference of the Southeastern Association of Game and Fish Wildlife Agencies*, 21:42–50.

White, M.
1966. Population ecology of some white-tailed deer in South Texas. Ph.D. Thesis. Lafayette, Indiana: Purdue University.

Wright, S.
1978. *Evolution and the Genetics of Populations*. Vol. 4. *Variability within and among Natural Populations*. Chicago: University of Chicago Press.

EUGENE J. DEGAYNER
and
PETER A. JORDAN

Department of Fisheries and Wildlife
University of Minnesota
St. Paul, Minnesota 55108

Skewed Fetal Sex Ratios in White-tailed Deer: Evidence and Evolutionary Speculations

ABSTRACT

Male/female ratios of fetuses from two populations of white-tailed deer (*Odocoileus virginianus*) were examined relative to age and weight of the pregnant does. In does bearing twins, the common litter size in the study region, those ≥ 4.5 year conceived more than 50% females, while those ≤ 3.5 year conceived more males. We develop the hypothesis that dominant females within matriarchies promote their fitness by producing daughters, because later they can influence the ability of these daughters to control good-quality fawning habitat. Mothers do not have similar abilities to influence the reproductive success of their sons. Consequently subordinate does, which include the youngest breeders and those in non-matriarchal, marginal circumstances, are more likely to bear males. This permits them to counter the over-production of females by dominant females. Also, since male offspring are likely to disperse outside their maternal region in search of good habitat, at maturity they will be equitably competing for mates, and their success will not be seriously affected by their early maternal environment. We discuss the adaptiveness of these strategies for habitats that are either stable or changing, a dual circumstance characteristic of much of the species' natural range.

It had been shown by others that timing of breeding relative to onset of estrus will sequentially skew fetal sex ratio in both directions. Given three conditions that probably do exist—a matriarchal social organization, a synchronous estrus among adult members of a matriarchy, and an exercise of mate preference among does of a matriarchy—the timing mechanism can account for the sex skewing we observed. To fit our data, the model also requires that age be a good predictor of dominance; we offer indirect evidence to support this.

Introduction

An evasive issue in the analysis of evolutionary strategies is whether selective advantages accrue from disproportionate production of one sex over the other. Charnov (1982) summarized the extensive evidence for the adaptiveness of differential sex production in various animal taxa; for mammals, however, he concluded that, despite numerous hypotheses and suggestive reports, no convincing example of an adaptive strategy had been shown. The question in mammals was also thoroughly examined by Clutton-Brock and Albon (1982). It is generally accepted that natural selection imparts greater fitness to parents who (a) produce the sex in short supply so that, within the population as a whole, investment between the sexes is balanced (Fisher, 1930); and who (b) specialize in one sex if, relative to other parents, they are more efficient in producing that sex (Trivers and Willard, 1973). Among mammals, a group often examined for skewed sex production is the Cervidae.

Sex Ratios in Cervids

There is much variation among cervids in body size, habitat preference, predation pressure, and social interactions including mating systems. Just because a given sex-ratio strategy is adaptive to the life history of one deer species, it is not necessarily so for another's. Therefore, we hypothesize that no single strategy will be found throughout the Cervidae. Trivers and Willard (1973) predicted that in caribou (*Rangifer tarandus*) the more robust cows should bear more males because that sex is the more expensive to produce. This hypothesis is considered an important evolutionary contribution (Charnov, 1982), despite the absence of data for testing it (Myers, 1978). Clutton-Brock et al. (1982) reported that in red deer (*Cervus elaphus*) males were the more expensive sex to produce up to the time of weaning. At the time of this writing, however, those workers had not published data showing that males were being produced less frequently than females to equalize investment nor that the most robust red deer hinds were specializing in sons. Recently, however, Clutton-Brock, et al., 1986 presented new evidence showing that dominant hinds produce more males than females. In contrast, for white-tailed deer (*Odocoileus virginianus*) McCullough (1979) hypothesized that females living in good habitat should produce predominantly females, because such mothers are able to aid their daughters' access to good breeding habitat. Females in poor habitat correspondingly should produce sons, because these offspring can

disperse to better habitats and/or may achieve dominance at a later time when, with possible vegetation changes, local habitats become more favorable. Although working extensively with white-tailed deer, McCullough did not provide convincing data to corroborate this hypothesis. He did find, however, that fetal sex ratios appeared to shift in favor of males as population density approached carrying capacity. Our studies of the same species gave results that tend to support a number of McCullough's speculations and conclusions.

Natural History and Adaptive Strategies in the White-tailed Deer

The white-tailed deer is considered an early-succession (vegetation) species, adapted to exploit temporally favorable patches in spatially heterogeneous environments (Severinghaus and Cheatum, 1956). Females aggregate in socially discrete, matriarchal groups which most likely comprise most or all mature-female descendants of the oldest individual present (Hawkins and Klimstra, 1970; Ozoga et al., 1982). This individual, by virtue of her seniority and her ability to survive and to produce surviving daughters, is probably the matriarch and hence the socially dominant member. Immature males disperse from their maternal group and join discrete male groups which are organized in a linear dominance hierarchy. Actually, some of the largest males may participate in several of these bachelor groups (Brown, 1974). Hawkins and Klimstra (1970) found that reproducing males do not necessarily overlap the region of their mothers' clan, but tend rather to disperse beyond. This suggests a mechanism for genetic dispersal as well as for discovering those favorable habitat patches where female reproductive success should be relatively high.

Ozoga et al. (1982), working with whitetails within a 2.6 km² enclosure, reported that dominant females occupied the superior breeding habitat. These females, at the time of parturition, also vigorously defended their fawning grounds against incursion of other deer. Fawning grounds selected by new mothers tended to be closer to their own mothers' than to fawning areas of adjacent clans. Nelson and Mech (1978), studying seasonal migration of whitetails in northern Minnesota, showed that among related females there was a consistent, inter-generation tradition of returning to the family fawning area. Manlove et al. (1976) showed that genetically distinct subgroups of whitetails remain spatially segregated while actively competing for control of space. Thus it appears that successful matriarchal clans dominate access to certain patches of habitat, and that allocations within these patches are most influenced by the matriach and other high-ranking females. Because the type of fawning habitat preferred by whitetails is generally patchy in distribution, a basis for competition exists. Maximizing the probability of a scarce patch being occupied by successive generations of one's own lineage should certainly be evolutionarily adaptive. The matriarch that controls a good patch would favor her gene line by assisting her daughters in controlling part of that patch for raising her grandchildren. The matriarch can accomplish this by exclusion of other deer and/or by demonstrating through maternal example how best to use local security and forage resources. Such a strategy is best pursued with a surfeit of daughters. Were dominant females to specialize in sons, someone else's daughters would occupy the local good fawning habitat for propagating their genes.

For whitetails, we hypothesize that maternal influence on male reproductive success is more a function of where the mother lives than of her age, weight, or social status. This is in sharp contrast to the case made for caribou (Trivers and Willard, 1973) and for red deer (Clutton-Brock et al, 1982); however, these two species appear far less adapted to hetergeneous and changing habitats than are whitetails. Given that maternal investment is adequate, other variables, i.e. predation, weather, and forage resources, probably have more influence on relative reproductive success among males than do pre- or post-natal maternal contributions. Although reproductive success varies more widely in males than in females, in a matriarchal society that portion of the variation attributable to maternal contribution alone may not be as great for sons as it is for daughters (Altmann, 1980). Simpson and Simpson (1982) suggest that dominant rhesus monkeys (*Macaca mulatta*) enhance their fitness by producing a surplus of daughters who in turn "inherit" their mothers' dominance.

Subordinate mothers, because they would be disadvantaged in placing daughters—according to the model we propose, should increase their fitness through disproportionate production of sons. Although these mothers have no special strategy for increasing the future reproductive potential of their sons, the chance that their male offspring will achieve reproductive success should be more competitively equitable than it is for their daughters. Furthermore, if dominant mothers are over-producing females, then the subordinates should favor their own fitness by a compensatory over-production of sons (Fisher, 1930).

A Mechanism for Skewing Fetal Sex

A major challenge in proposing a sex-selective strategy is to identify an inherited physiological mechanism that adaptively skews sex either at fertilization or during gestation. To fit evolutionary theory, such a mechanism must consistently skew sex to favor the parents' fitness. Recently for white-tailed deer, experiments by Verme and Ozoga (1981) showed that timing of copulation relative to the onset of estrus apparently influences sex determination. They reported that does being bred relatively early in estrus (13–24 hr) produced few (14.3%) males, while does bred later (49–95 hr) produced 80.8% males. This strongly suggests a mechanism that could have arisen from or been maintained by adaptive selection. It also is a mechanism that could consistently respond to changing social circumstances which in turn are related to variations in the environment or in the social status of individuals.

If sex determination is adaptively influenced through timing of copulation relative to onset of estrus, then a couple of conditions appear necessary to produce consistent results relative to the social position of females. To begin with, the adaptive hypothesis discussed here is applicable primarily to an equilibrium circumstance—where a matriarch has maintained control over a suitable patch of fawning habitat for many generations and is consistently exhibiting good reproductive success; and where density is prevented from exceeding carrying capacity, most likely by natural predation or an equivalent hunting harvest. Implications of varying habitat quality or of nonequilibrium densities are treated in the discussion. Skewing of sex ratios under these latter circumstances, while differing in pattern from the equilibrium case, appear explainable in accord with the copulation-timing mechanism.

In the established matriarchy, estrus among all but the youngest of reproducing females should be synchronous; also the availability or acceptability of breeding males should be limited so that all females of the group cannot be bred at the same time. Sheep, goats, (Sadleir, 1969), and possibly white-tailed deer (P. Karns, pers. comm.) display synchrony, the Whitten effect; it is believed this is induced by pheromones in male urine (Sadleir, 1969). For whitetails we suggest that synchrony may be mediated in females by olfactory stimulation from urine deposited in scrapes by males during the rut (Moore and Marchington, 1974).

A male hierarchy is established early in the rut before the onset of courtship activities. Males intensely court females prior to estrus (Brown and Hirth, 1979). As estrus approaches, brief pair bonds are formed, and the pairs become isolated from other deer until after copulation. If a dominant female and a subordinant female come into estrus together, it seems likely the dominant female will displace the subordinant to assure prompt copulation. It appears that does preselect their mates. This would be related to the prior establishment of a male hierarchy and an intense pre-

DeGayner and Jordan

estrus courtship. If so, then subordinate does are more likely to delay copulation than to seek out or accept a subordinate male in order to copulate immediately. One can speculate on the adaptiveness of this. The female programmed to produce sons should enhance her fitness by choosing the most competitively successful male to father these sons. In their copulation-timing experiment, Verme and Ozoga (1980) observed that some does, presumably in estrus, refused to copulate, suggesting a courtship requirement and/or a preference for certain males.

If dominant males are preventing subordinant males from mating (Brown, 1974), and females of a clan reach estrus synchronously, and females choose to be bred by the local dominant male, then not all females can be bred at the same time. Length of delay for a subordinate doe would most likely be a function of refractory time in the dominant male. Lambiase et al. (1972) provided evidence that white-tailed bucks are relatively limited in frequency of fertile ejaculations; they concluded, however, that bucks are probably capable of "at least one successful mating daily." Delays of 12–70 hours are long enough to cause sex differentiation but short enough to permit one buck to successfully fertilize several synchronous does within a single estrous period.

Testing of the Sex Ratio Hypothesis

From necropsies of white-tailed deer during the season of gestation, we were able to relate number and sex of fetuses to age and weight of the does. The results were analyzed to test our hypotheses on differential production of sexes. We then discuss the evolutionary and ecological implications of our findings.

Study Areas and Deer Populations

Deer were collected within the metropolitan region of St. Paul, Minnesota, latitude 45° 0′ N and elevation 254 m. Annual precipitation averages 74.7 cm, and snowfall averages 104 cm. Temperature minima are Dec −11.7°, Jan −16.0°, and Feb −11.7°C; maxima are Jul 28.0° and Aug 27.1°C.

The Twin Cities Army Ammunition Plant, "The Arsenal," is a 1025-ha tract with controlled access. It is enclosed by a 2-m fence which essentially restricts movement of deer except for an occasional animal jumping over the fence or going through one of several gates open during business hours. Despite the lack of total isolation, strong evidence from previous studies (Keenlyne, 1976; Jordan, unpub. rep.) indicates that the population has behaved as though it was insular. Deer occupy some 660 ha of undeveloped land. Terrain is flat to slightly hilly and includes 60 ha of wetlands that are traversed by deer only when waters are

frozen. Vegetation comprises patches of oak (*Quercus* sp), open grasslands, and lowland shrub with scattered aspens (*Populus tremuloides*), cottonwoods (*P. deltoides*), and willows (*Salix* sp). Wetlands are dominated by cattails (*Typha* sp).

From an unstable peak population of nearly 400 animals in 1968, the Arsenal herd was reduced by shooting to a low of 11 by January 1972 (Keenlyne, 1976). Each winter 1976–1983, when the ground was evenly snow-covered, we searched the Arsenal thoroughly from a helicopter to count all deer. The population had remained low until 1976 or 1977; then it started to increase rapidly. In January 1978, 64 were counted, and we estimated 70 were present. During 1978–79, 59 animals were removed by shooting: 19 adult females, 13 adult males, 9 yearlings, and 18 fawns. In January 1982 the aerial count was 110, and we probably missed no more than 5. Specimens for this study were removed from the Arsenal after the 1982 count.

We were not measuring forage supply or feeding habits of the Arsenal deer, so there was no quantitative estimate of carrying capacity relative to numbers present. However, thorough necropsies of deer collected during 1978–79 showed the herd was in good to excellent health and reproductive output (DeGayner and Jordan, in prep.). As evident from the fetal data reported here, pregnancy rates from the fall 1981 breeding season were relatively high. Subsequently, however, early 1982 witnessed an unusually severe winter. By March most adult males had died, and fawns were weak and dying. The fetal numbers and sex ratios we report, however, should reflect only the breeding season. Although we did not count corpora lutea to check for subsequent *in utero* loss, pregnant does were not approaching the level of malnutrition at which fetal losses can be expected.

The second sample of deer was from North Oaks, an affluent residential community 3 km east of the Arsenal. No barriers to movement existed there. The herd comprised both year-round residents and migrants moving in for winter from adjacent farms and abandoned farmland. Vegetation within and adjacent to the widely spaced residential dwellings provided good winter habitat for deer—better than at the Arsenal due to greater cover and greater diversity of woody species. Various conifers planted around homes were eaten; in some years localized tree felling provided tops that are highly preferred forage; and some home owners put out corn, a nutritious winter feed for deer. Deer removals were part of a program to reduce excessive numbers in this suburban setting (Jordan and DeGayner, in prep). Land area within the village was 1870 ha, but deer were confined mainly to 1300 ha or less. We counted deer here in early or mid winter from a helicopter as at the Arsenal; annual best estimates ranged from 300 to 350 for 1978, 1979, and 1980.

Methods

Deer were collected by shooting (Moore et al., 1977); some at North Oaks were first trapped (Clover, 1956) and then shot in the trap. In field shooting at North Oaks, our first priority was to take dominant females; criteria for identifying them were their relative size plus their observed social interactions (Hawkins and Klimstra, 1970). At the Arsenal, essentially all females > 0.5 yr old were removed in order to examine the entire interacting set. All collecting was later than 10 January by which time fetuses are of macroscopic size and sex is clearly evident. Carcasses were moved to a building and weighed (live wt. less a blood loss of < 0.5 kg), eviscerated (field dressed), and reweighed (dressed wt.). Age was estimated from counts of incisor annuli (Gilbert, 1966); age reported here is years at the previous breeding season (Nov). Measures of fat deposits were taken as indices of health and nutritional status (DeGayner and Jordan, in prep). Intact reproductive tracts were removed within 2–3 hr of death and prevented from freezing. Fetuses were weighed (0.1 g) and were sexed from external genitalia.

Results

During 3 winters at North Oaks and 1 at the Arsenal, 235 fetuses were recovered from 144 does 11/2 years and older. Frequencies among litter sizes from the entire sample were as follows: none, 2%; singles, 35%; twins, 59%; and triplets, 3%. We did remove nearly all reproducing does from the Arsenal; probably no more than 4 and more likely only 2 remained after 2 mo of collecting.

Because litter size may be a confounding factor in an analysis for sex correlates—as suggested for mule deer (*Odocoileus hemionus*) (Robinette et al., 1973), white-tailed deer (Verme, 1969), and wood rate (*Neotoma floridana*) (McClure, 1981)—we analyzed separately within each litter-size set. Twin litters provided the largest sample (n=85); in this region whitetails ≥ 1.5 yrs in average to good condition most frequently produce litters of two (Harder, 1980).

Among all does with twins, those 1.5–3.5 years old produced more than 50% males; and those ≥ 4.5 years old produced more than 50% females (Figure 1).

To explore more carefully the relationship between fetal sex ratios and factors such as age and weight of the doe and time and place of sampling, it is convenient to fit statistical models that can "explain" the variation in sex ratio as a function of these variables. An appropriate technique is linear logistic regression in which a particular function, the proportion of

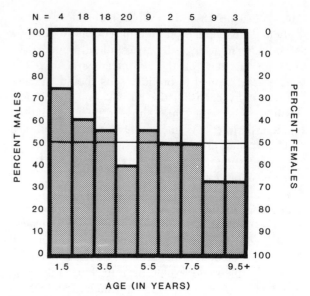

Figure 1.   Fetal sex-ratio in twin litters according to age of doe in the pooled sample.

females, is modeled as a linear function of the predictor variables. The technique is similar to multiple linear regression, except that we use the fact that errors are binomially rather than normally distributed in computing estimates and tests (Cox, 1970; Fienberg, 1980; McCullagh and Nelder, 1983).

Briefly, if π is the expected proportion of females borne by a doe, then $(1 - \pi)/\pi$ is the usual sex ratio of males to females, and the linear logistic model posits that

$$\log 1 = \pi/\pi = b_o t \text{ (linear function of predictors).} \quad (1)$$

For example, using age as a predictor, for all n=85 does with twins, we get the fitted model (via maximum likelihood)

$$\log 1 = \pi/\pi = 0.79 - 0.16 \text{ (age),} \quad (2)$$

so that the fitted log of the sex ratio (of males to females) is seen to decrease with the age of the doe. A formal test of significance–a test of the coefficient for age equal to zero, implying constant sex ratio for all ages of does–uses the likelihood ratio test, often called partial G^2. For our data, partial $G^2 = 5.10$, which, when compared to the chi-squared distribution with 1 d.f., gives a (two sided) P value < .02. This suggests that the relative proportion of female fetuses increased with the age of the doe. Substituting $\pi = 0.5$ into (1) and solving for age gives the age at which the sex ratio is estimated to be 1 : 1. Since log (.5/.5) = 0, we get: 0.79/0.16 = 4.9 yr. Thus, does older than 5 years tended to have more than 50% female offspring. The fitted logistic curve

= 1/ [1+exp(.79–.16 age)] for all ages is shown in Figure 2. This predicts that the proportion of female

DeGayner and Jordan

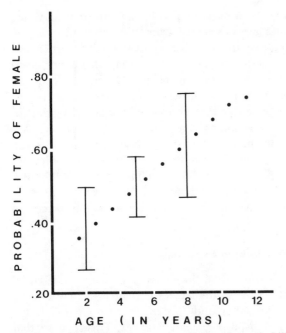

Figure 2.   Fitted logistic curve predicting the probability of female offspring in twin litters according to age of doe in the pooled sample.

Table 1.   Analysis by linear logistic regression of relationships between fetal sex and three independent variables—age of doe, weight of doe, and site and/or year of collection (="samples"). Derivation and interpretation of partial G^2 values are explained in the text.

	Twin Fetuses			Single Fetuses		
	df	G^2	p-value*	df	G^2	p-value*
Comparing four samples, with age as a predictor	6	10.0	>0.1			
Comparing four samples, with weight as a predictor	6	9.7	>0.1			
Four samples pooled, age as a predictor	1	5.1	<0.02	1	0.5	>0.5
Four samples pooled, weight as a predictor	1	2.1	>0.3	1	0.4	>0.5
Four samples pooled, age adjusted for weight	1	3.5	>0.1	1	0.2	>0.5
Four samples pooled, weight adjusted for age	1	0.4	>0.4	1	0.1	>0.5

*All are two-tailed tests. For the 1 d.f. tests, one-tailed tests, with half the shown p-value, are possible if the alternative hypothesis posits that the proportion of female fetuses increases with age and weight.

offspring is only 0.37 for 1.5 year-old does while it is 0.71 for 10.5-year olds.

Similar model fitting was done with age and weight as predictors (both singly and in combination), and separate models were fitted for each of the four samples (Table 1). The results showed: (1) There were no significant differences between samples, hence pooling of the four categories was appropriate. (2) The proportion of female fetuses appeared to increase significantly with age of the doe. This relationship was weaker but still evident when the effect of age was adjusted for the weight of the doe. (3) There was no clear relationship between proportion of females and weight of the doe, whether or not we adjusted for age.

The analysis described above was repeated for litters of one (Table 1). Here we found no evidence that sex ratio varied with age or with weight of the doe (Figure 3). Precise estimation was restricted by a relatively poor representation in the sample of does > 4.5 yrs old bearing only one fetus.

Elsewhere we are reporting (DeGayner and Jordan, in prep.) that the relative weights of male vs. female fetuses in sets of mixed-sex twins varies with age of the doe. Most of the pregnant does were collected during the mid trimester of gestation, from 20 January to 1 April; fetus weights averaged 342 g (SD = 207, range = 18–826). In does ≤ 3.5 yrs, the male was heavier; in does ≥ 4.5 yrs, the female was heavier. Statistical analysis indicated that fetal weight by sex was not associated with the does' weight; rather the does' age alone was the significant predictor.

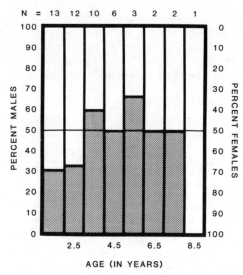

Figure 3. Fetal sex-ratio in single-fetus litters according to age of doe in the pooled sample.

Discussion

Our primary hypothesis was that, because dominant does have a territorial-like control over favorable fawning habitat patches, and because they can favor their daughters' gaining access to such patches, these does will maximize their fitness by producing more daughters than sons. Also, because dominant does do not have a similar ability to contribute to the reproductive success of their sons, subordinate does, unable to compete equitably in aiding their daughters, will maximize their fitness by a compensatory specialization in males. Qualitative and quantitative evidence from pregnant white-tailed does in Minnesota indicated these deer exhibit two forms of age-specific differential investment. Older does tended to have more female fetuses; and, when bearing mixed-sex twins, they tended to invest more heavily in females. In younger females these tendencies were directly reversed as though selection in their case was favoring an equally distinct but oppositely directed strategy.

Social Rank and Age—An Assumption

Our hypothesis was based on social rank being the operative factor. We believe that within an interactive group of reproducing white-tailed does, age is a consistent predictor of social position. Townsend and Bailey (1981) found in a set of penned whitetails that they had classified only as fawns, yearlings, and adults, that females rank was positively related to age. Unlike males, female rank was not affected by weight

changes. It is likely that within a matriarchy all young females are descended from the oldest member; in such a case this member ought to be the most experienced and successful of her group in holding good habitat and in rearing fawns (Ozoga et al., 1982). When the matriarch dies or for some reason leaves, dominance should pass to her oldest surviving daughter. Correspondingly, does that do not reproduce successfully, hence do not have surviving daughters and grand-daughters, would not, as they grow older, remain part of a matriarchy. Thus we believe the association here between age and fetal-sex trends can be interpreted as an association between dominance and fetal sex.

Dual Selective Pressures

Our finding that, in mixed-sex twins, differential weight between the fetuses is related to the mothers' age (DeGayner and Jordan, in prep.) parallels the trend of disproportionate fetal sex. This suggests that selection has been shaping more than one mechanism; if so, it further indicates the critical importance to the fitness of dominant females of having daughters. It again suggests a strategy directly opposite the one proposed by Trivers and Willard (1973) and supported by Clutton-Brock and Albon (1982) and Clutton-Brock et al. (1986). The older, more capable does are not only biased against specializing in males, the more expensive sex, but furthermore, if they conceive a mixed-sex pair, they contribute somewhat more to the female's development in utero than to the male's.

Litters of One Not Applicable

In single-fetus litters we did not find a significant relationship between the age or weight of does and the sex of their offspring. Among the youngest producers, singles are common. In contrast to our results, Robinette et al. (1955) for mule deer and McDowell (1959) for whitetails reported that first offspring were skewed towards males. In our study, does that carried singles weighed significantly less (P < 0.05) than those with twins. Typically, deer of this region that carry but one fetus are either young, hence primiparous, or are subnormal in health or body size (Verme, 1969). Thus lack of similar age-related patterns between those with singles vs. those with twins may reflect the latter not participating within synchronous sets of females competing for dominant males. Older females with singles may well not be members of matriarchies; they may be living in marginal habitats and breeding opportunistically with subordinate or outcast males. Fawn and yearling does may be within matriarchies, but are breeding at a different time; subadult breeders tend to ovulate later than adults. Also, nutritionally stressed

DeGayner and Jordan

does come into estrus later than normal does (Verme, 1969), and hence would not be ovulating synchronously with others even if they are part of a matriarchy.

Verme (1969) found from experiments with captive deer that the nutritional status of a doe in the breeding season influenced fetal sex ratios; poor nutrition skewed conceptions towards males. At first glance, this response by itself appears an unlikely product of natural selection, particularly since deer populations tend to experience year-to-year variations in food resources. A basic characteristic of any optimal strategy within a population is its compatibility with the relative frequency of other strategies within the same population (Maynard-Smith, 1976). If a population on an excellent nutritional plane was producing 50% females, there would be an adaptive advantage for some individuals to cheat and produce males (Fisher, 1930). For one subset of the population to be selected to produce one sex, there should be a countering tendency and advantage for another subset to produce the opposite sex. It is unlikely a doe can assess her body condition relative to the rest of the herd, particularly at the time of breeding when all does are generally fat (Verme and Ozoga, 1980; Monson et al., 1974; DeGayner and Jordan, in prep.). Therefore nutrition or robustness alone seems an unlikely regulator for an evolutionarily stable strategy. Our studies failed to find live weight of the doe to be a reliable predictor of sex ratio in either single or twin litters, or of the fetal male/female weight ratio in mixed-sex twins. Litter size is related to nutrition (Morton and Cheatum, 1946; Verme, 1965, 1967, 1969; Ransom, 1967). We failed to find a skewing towards males or females in single litters, although single litters in adult does presumably indicate subnormal nutrition. Thus, we have little reason to suspect that nutrition has a proximal effect on sex ratio.

Balancing Early Mortality in Males

Our sample probably did not include an adequate subset of animals that were as nutritionally stressed as Verme's population (1969), and even he was hesitant to draw firm conclusions due to the small size of his sample. One can, however, speculate that the effect Verme reports represents an evolutionarily stable strategy in accord with Fisher's (1930) predicted balanced investment between the two sexes. As maternal condition in mule deer does declines, mortality in prebreeding male offspring tends to exceed that in female offsrping (Robinette et al., 1955; Steigers and Flinders, 1980). Thus if younger does do produce a preponderance of males (Verme and Ozoga, 1980; McCullough, 1979), these males may have a far lower

survivorship in dense populations (Ozoga et al., 1982). Hence they would constitute a "cheap" sex to rear because parental investment would frequently be terminated early.

Male versus Female Strategies

From an evolutionary perspective, one should contrast the strategies of adult males with those of adult females. The latter specialize by maintaining control of localized patches of preferred fawning habitat, while males travel widely in search of sites where high-quality habitat presumably enhances success of their progeny. In this dichotomy, our proposed mechanism for differential sex determination would operate as follows: If habitat is poor, regardless of local density, production of males would rise because the ratio of breeding males to females is relatively low; hence, average delay between onset of ovulation and mating should increase. In good habitat, which attracts males, the higher ratio of males would correspondingly raise production of females. In a sense, this suggests male abundance is a bioassay of environmental quality. The adaptive advantages of this dichotomy follow the lines discussed above: In good habitat, individuals who invest immediately in daughters are most fit because overall production and survival of every female born will be high in the immediate future; in poor habitat local prospects are poor, so investment should favor the sex which moves out in search of better habitat or at least can afford to wait 4–6 years (approximate age of first mating success in males) until conditions might improve. In mule deer (Robinette et al., 1955) and in white-tailed deer (McCullough, 1979), adult male density in poor habitats relative to that of females was lower due both to dispersal and to disproportionately higher mortality.

Selection Under Stable versus Changing Environments

The evolutionary strategy we propose for white-tailed deer could well have arisen under a combination of stable and unstable environmental circumstances which are together typical for the species' range as a whole. In order for election to have adapted this species for long-term occupation of habitat patches by matriarchal lineages, suitable habitats themselves must have been stable for periods spanning many generations of deer. At the same time, white-tailed deer respond by rapidly increasing their local density when vegetational disturbances convert habitats of poor quality (e.g. mature forests) to high-quality mosaics of varied vegetation. It is not possible today to quantitatively reconstruct the frequency of forest disturbance or the degree of stability of favorable vegetational configurations that were common during the pre-Columbian millenia within the species' original distribution. Qualitatively, however, we have good evidence that in much of their range lightning or aboriginal caused fire was common in many forest types. There is also good evidence that in many regions ecotones or local mosaics of herb, shrub, and forest were stable over many decades. Support for these statements appears in a recent set of reviews of Holocene and Pleistocene plant communities (Wright, 1983).

In the foregoing discussion of differential strategies between the sexes, we suggested how the female is prepared to optimally exploit stable habitats, to the benefit of her fitness, while simultaneously the male is adapted to opportunistically exploit changing habitats. Thus, dual mechanisms are present within the genome of a single clan. Such an ecologically versatile adaptation may well contribute to *Odocoileus virginianus* being the most widely distributed of cervids and probably the most numerous species among the Cervidae, as well as its being a deer highly resilient to massive habitat alterations and to exploitations by man.

Further Research

If nothing else, our hypothesis suggests the need to analyze interactions among familial ties, social rank, habitat quality, and fetal sex ratios in the white-tailed deer. The best study setting would be an enclosed, free-living group that could be intensively observed to document social and spatial patterns in relation to reproductive success over many years. Experimental manipulations would be critical for hypothesis testing.

Acknowledgments

S. Weisberg provided statistical and editorial assistance. D. McCullough and E. Charnov reviewed the manuscript and made helpful suggestions. We wish to express thanks to T. Donney, L. Mason, S. Posner, S. Fitzgerald, J. Stewart, and particularly J. Pertz for their excellent field assistance. M. Thessing, Minn. Dept. of Natural Resources; O. Mobley, U.S. Army; N. Rozycki, North Oaks Village; and R. Peterson, Spring Hill Farm, North Oaks, all provided vital logistical support. We thank B. DeGayner for field assistance and manuscript preparation. This project was funded in part by the Minnesota Agricultural Experiment Station.

Literature Cited

Altmann, J.
1980. *Baboon Mothers and Infants*. Cambridge: Harvard University Press.

Brown, B.A.
1974. Social organization in male groups of white-tailed deer. In *The behaviour of ungulates and its relation to management*, edited by V. Geist and F. Walther, pp. 436–446, Volume 1. IUCN Publ. New Series 24.

Brown, B.A., and D.H. Hirth
1979. Breeding behavior in white-tailed deer. In *Proceedings of the First Welder Wildlife Foundation Symposium*, edited by D.L. Drawe, pp. 83–95. Sinton, Texas.

Charnov, E.L.
1982. *The Theory of Sex Allocation*. Princeton University Press.

Clover, M.R.
1956. Single-gate deer trap. *California Fish and Game*, 42:199–201.

Clutton-Brock, T.H., and S.D. Albon
1982. Parental investment in male and female offsrping in mammals. In *Current Problems in Sociobiology*, edited by Kings College Sociobiology Group, pp. 223–248. Cambridge University Press.

Clutton-Brock, T.H., F.E. Guinness, and S.D. Albon
1982. *Red deer: Behavior and ecology of two sexes*. Chicago: University of Chicago Press.

Clutton-Brock, T.H., S.D. Albon, and F.E. Guinness
1986. Great expectations: dominance, breeding success and offspring sex ratios. *Animal Behaviour*, 34:460–471.

Cox, D.R.
1970. *The analysis of binary data*. London, Methuen.

Dapson, R.W., P.R. Ramsey, M.H. Smith, and D.F. Urbston
1979. Demographic differences in contiguous populations of white-tailed deer. *Journal of Wildlife Management*, 43:889–898.

Fienberg, S.E.
1980. *The Analysis of Cross-classified Categorical Data*. Cambridge: MIT Press.

Fisher, R.A.
1930. *The genetical theory of natural selection*. Oxford: Clarendon.

Gilbert, F.F.
1966. Aging white-tailed deer by annuli in the cementum of the first incisor. *Journal of Wildlife Management*, 30:200-202.

Harder, J.D.
1980. Reproduction of white-tailed deer in the North Central United States. In *White-tailed deer population management in the North Central States. North Central Section*, edited by R.L. Hine and S. Nehls, pp. 23–35. The Wildlife Society, Wisconsin Division of Natural Resources, Madison.

Hawkins, R.E., and W.D. Klimstra
1970. A preliminary study of the social organization of

DeGayner and Jordan

white-tailed deer. *Journal of Wildlife Management*, 34:407–419.

Hirth, D.H., and D.R. McCullough
1977. Evolution of alarm signals in ungulates with special reference to white-tailed deer. *American Naturalist*, 111:31–42.

Keenlyne, K.D.
1976. *Population Dynamics of the Twin Cities Arsenal Deer Herd.* Unpublished Ph.D. thesis. University of Minnesota.

Lambiase, J.T., R.P. Mann, and J.S. Lindzey
1972. Aspects of Reproductive Physiology. *Journal of Wildlife Management*, 36(3):868–875.

Manlove, M.N., M.H. Smith, H.O. Hillestad, S.E. Fuller, P.E. Johns, and D.O. Straney
1977. Genetic subdivision in a herd of white-tailed deer as demonstrated by spatial shifts in gene frequencies. *Proceedings of the Annual Conference of the Southeastern Association of Fish and Wildlife Agencies*, 30:487–492.

Maynard-Smith, J.
1976. Evolution and the theory of games. *American Scientist*, 64:41–45.

McClure, P.A.
1981. Sex-biased litter reduction in food-restricted wood rats (*Neotoma floridana*). *Science*, 211:1058–1060.

McCullough, D.R.
1979. *The George Reserve Deer Herd: population ecology of a K-selected species.* Ann Arbor: University of Michigan Press.

McCullagh P., and J.A. Nelder
1983. *Generalized linear models.* New York: Chapman-Hall.

McDowell, R.D.
1959. Relationship of maternal age to prenatal sex ratios in white-tailed deer. Northeast Section, Wildlife Society, Oglebay Park, W.Va. mimeo. 6 pp.

Monson, R.A., W.B. Stone, B.L. Weber, and F.J. Spadero
1974. Comparison of Riney and total kidney fat techniques for evaluating the physical condition of white-tailed deer. *New York Fish and Game Journal*, 21:67–72.

Moore, W.G., W.E. Mahan, and L.O. Rogers
1977. Selectively collecting white-tailed deer. *Wildlife Society Bulletin*, 5:131–134.

Moore, W.G., and R.L. Marchinton
1974. Marking behavior and its social function in white-tailed deer. *The Behavior of Ungulates and its Relation to Management*, edited by V. Geist and F. Walther, pp. 447–456. IUCN Publ. new series 24.

Morton, G.H., and E.L. Cheatum
1946. Regional differences in breeding potential of white-tailed deer in New York. *Journal of Wildlife Management*, 10:242–248.

Myers, J.H.
1978. Sex ratio adjustment under food stress: maximization of quality or numbers of offspring? *American Naturalist*, 112:381–388.

Nelson, M.E., and L.D. Mech
1981. Deer social organization and wolf predation in northeastern Minnesota. *Wildlife Monograph 77*, 53 pp.

Ozoga, J.J., L.J. Verme, and C.S. Bienz
1982. Parturition behavior and territoriality in white-tailed deer: impact on neonatal mortality. *Journal of Wildlife Management*, 46:1–11.

Ransom, A.B.
1967. Reproductive biology of white-tailed deer in Manitoba. *Journal of Wildlife Management*, 31:114–123.

Robinette, W.L., J.S. Gashwiler, D.A. Jones, and H.S. Crane
1955. Fertility of mule deer in Utah. *Journal of Wildlife Management*, 19:115–136.

Robinette, W.L., C.H. Baer, R.E. Pillmore, and C.E. Knettle
1973. Effects of nutritional change on captive mule deer. *Journal of Wildlife Management*, 37:312–326.

Sadleir, R.M.F.S.
1969. *The Ecology of Reproduction in Wild and Domestic Mammals.* London, Methuen.

Severinghaus, C.W., and E.L. Cheatum
1956. Life and times of the white-tailed deer. *The deer of North America*, edited by W.P. Taylor, pp. 57–186. Harrisburg, Stackpole.

Simpson, M.J.A., and A.E. Simpson
1982. Birth sex ratios and social rank in rhesus monkey mothers. *Nature*, 300:440–441.

Steigers, W.D., and J.T. Flinders
1980. Mortality and movements of mule deer fawns in Washington. *Journal of Wildlife Management*, 44:381–388.

Townsend, T.W., and E.D. Bailey
1981. Effects of age, sex and weight on social rank in penned white-tailed deer. *American Midland Naturalist*, 106:92–101.

Trivers, R.L., and D.E. Willard
1973. Natural selection of parental ability to vary the sex ratio. *Science*, 179:90–92.

Verme, L.J.
1965. Reproduction studies on penned white-tailed deer. *Journal of Wildlife Management*, 29:74–79.

1967. Influence of experimental diets on white-tailed deer reproduction. *Transactions of the North American Wildlife and Natural Resources Conference*, 32:405–420.

1969.   Reproductive patterns of white-tailed deer related to nutritional plane. *Journal of Wildlife Management,* 33:881–887.

1981.   Sex ratio of white-tailed deer and the estrus cycle. *Journal of Wildlife Management,* 45:710–715.

Verme, L.J., and J.J. Ozoga
1980.   Effects of diet on growth and lipogenesis in deer fawns. *Journal of Wildlife Management,* 44:315–324.

Werren, J.H., and E.L. Charnov
1978.   Facultative sex ratios and population dynamics. *Nature,* 272:349–350.

Wright, H.E., Jr. (ed).
1983.   *The Late Quaternary Environments of the United States,* 2 Volumes. Minneapolis: Univ. Minnesota Press.

DeGayner and Jordan

CHRIS WEMMER
and
DON E. WILSON
Conservation & Research Center
National Zoological Park
Front Royal, Va. 22630

National Fish & Wildlife Service
National Museum of Natural History
Washington, D.C. 20540

Cervid Brain Size and Natural History

Introduction

The search for life history correlates of mammalian brain size has been a recent development in investigations of brain evolution (Eisenberg and Wilson, 1978, 1981; Eisenberg, 1981; Clutton-Brock and Harvey, 1980, Mace et al., 1981). Other earlier studies demonstrate the size of the neocortex shows a strong positive correlation with the degree of encephalization (Edinger, 1948; Radinsky, 1969; Pirlot and Stephan, 1970). The more recent studies have focused on non-ungulate orders, and have revealed that a complex of factors broadly related to feeding and reproduction explain much of the variation in relative brain size.

There have been numerous studies of ungulate brain structure and size (Krueg, 1878; Herre, 1936; Rose, 1942; Edinger, 1948; Lunau, 1956; Herre and Thiede, 1965; Oboussier and Schliemann, 1966; Kruska, 1970, 1973; Ronnefeld, 1970; Jerison, 1971; Oboussier, 1970, 1971), but few have dealt with the cervid brain, and no efforts have dwelled on ecological and behavioral relationships to brain size or structure. This paper investigates several hypotheses of brain size and habitus in species of deer (Cervidae) and musk deer (Moschidae).

Methods

The National Museum of Natural History was the source of specimens for this study. Intact skulls of adult specimens of both sexes were used for morphometric data (Appendix I), with adulthood being defined by a full complement of non-deciduous cheek teeth. The geographic origin of specimens was known in all but a few cases of transplanted, park, or zoo populations, i.e. *Axis axis, Elaphurus davidianus, Cervus duvauceli*, and *C. nippon*. We analyzed data separately for subspecies of differing body size (e.g., *Cervus unicolor, Odocoileus virginianus*, and *O. hemionus*). Most skulls were measured to the nearest 0.1 mm with a 300 mm vernier calipers. Larger crania were measured with an anthropomometer to the nearest 0.5 mm.

Condylobasal length, the greatest length from the occipital condyles to the tip of the pre-maxillary bone, was used as a reference dimension because corresponding head and body lengths were not available for a majority of specimens. This decision was based on the desire to relate brain size to the actual body size of the specimen. The alternative, using mean values of body size from published literature (e.g. body weight, head and body length, or shoulder height) was deemed less than satisfactory because of variance between biologists and methods, or because of variance related to age of the samples or time of year data were collected. Rationale favoring skull length as a refer-

ence dimension are discussed in detail by Gould (1974).

Cranial foramina and in some cases small openings due to damage were filled with clay, and the crania were then filled with 4 mm glass beads. After tapping the brain case additional beads were added until the volume was packed to maximum capacity at the level of the foramen magnum. The beads were then poured into a beaker and weighed on an electronic balance. The weight of the beads was converted to volume using an empirically derived calibration curve. Encephalization indices (EI) were calculated for each species according to the following equation:

$$EI = \frac{\log 10 \; observed \; cranial \; volume}{A \; \log 10 \; condylobasal \; length \, + \, B}$$

where A = slope, and B = y - intercept. Dimorphism indices were calculated by dividing the mean condylobasal length of females by that of males using a larger sample size than used for calculating cranial volume (Appendix I). Appendix II lists taxa which are referenced by numbers in the figures.

Results

The correlation coefficient between log 10 transformations of brain volume and condylobasal length of each sex of the 38 taxa was 0.95, and the linear relationship was y = −2.28 + 1.8367x (Figure 1). There was no significant difference between mean male and female EIs for species where data were available for both sexes (females = 1.004, males = 0.994, t = 1.321, d.f. = 60, P > .05). To eliminate the effects of sexual dimorphism we have used only female data for subsequent analyses.

Systematic and Zoogeographic Comparisons

Do the primary cervid lineages differ significantly in degree of encephalization? To test this hypothesis we compared members of the Telemetacarpalia (all Odocoileinae) with the Plesiometacarpalia (Cervinae, Muntiacinae and Moschidae), and found a significant difference with higher EIs in the Plesiometacarpalia (means = 1.01 versus 0.98, t = 2.444, d.f. = 30, P = .021, Figure 2). When only the Cervinae and Odocoileinae were compared an even greater difference was found in mean EIs (1.02 versus 0.98, t = 3.023, d.f. = 26, P = .006, Figure 3). Thus the Muntiacinae and Moschidae tend to reduce the difference in the mean EIs between the Telemetacarpalia and the Plesiometacarpalia. We inferred from this result that body size is a confounding factor, and computed mean EIs of the Odocoileinae and Cervinae after

Wemmer and Wilson

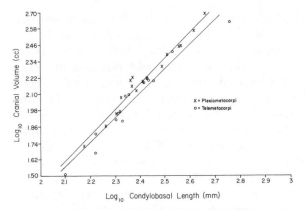

Figure 1. The relationship of cranial volume to condylobasal length in 31 cervid taxa treating the sexes separately (y = −2.28 + 1.8367x, r² = .95).

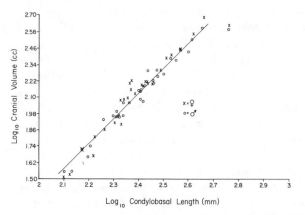

Figure 2. The relationship between cranial volume and condylobasal length in the Plesiometacarpi and the Telemetacarpi (y = −2.1819 + 1.7866x, r² = .94).

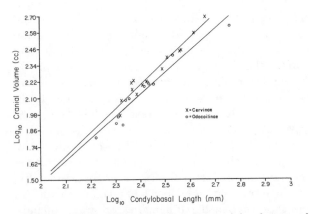

Figure 3. The relationship between cranial volume and condylobasal length in the Cervinae (sans Muntiacinae, and *Hydropotes*, y = −1.9582 + 1.7285x, r² = .946) and the Odocoileinae (sans *Pudu* spp., y = −1.7315 + 1.6055x, r² = .938).

deleting values for small species (i.e. those with CBLs < 200 mm). The difference between the means was reduced (1.009 versus 0.985), but still significantly different (t = 2.222, d.f. = 23, P = .036).

Next, we tested the EIs between South American and North American Odocoileinae, and found a significant difference (t = 2.99, d.f. = 8, P < .02). However, when the small bodied pudus were removed from the comparison, the difference was no longer apparent (t = .276, d.f. = 10, P > .05).

The Effects of Body Size

To compare cervids of differing body size we defined small species as those having condylobasal lengths < 200 mm, and large cervids as those with condylobasal lengths > 300 mm. Medium-size deer were all those with condylobasal lengths within the two limits (>200 and <300 mm). Analysis of variance indicated significant differences (F = 3.623, P = .039), with the smallest EIs occurring in the small cervids (mean = 0.973), moderate EIs occurring in large cervids (mean = 0.997), and the highest EIs occurring in medium-size cervids (mean = 1.01). Small and large cervids did not differ significantly in mean EIs (t = 1.961, d.f. = 12, P > .05), nor did medium and large cervids (t = 0.657, d.f. = 24, P > .05). However, small cervids had a significantly lower mean EI than medium-size deer (t = 2.777, d.f. = 22, P < .02). The relationship between EI and body size approximates a parabolic distribution with the relatively small brained but large bodied *Alces* clearly contributing to the shape of the curve (Figure 4).

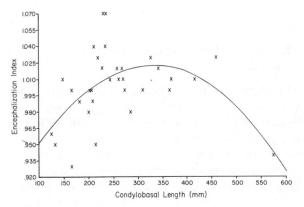

Figure 4. The relationship between encephalization index and condylobasal length in 32 cervid taxa (y = .874 + .001x + x², r² = .33).

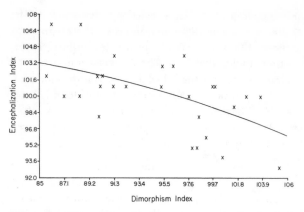

Figure 5. The relationship between encephalization index and dimorphism index in 29 cervid taxa (y = 1.32 − .003x, r^2 = .316).

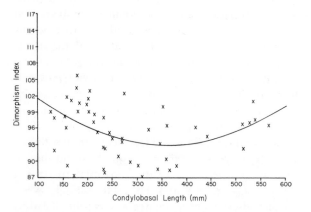

Figure 6. The relationship between dimorphism index and condylobasal length in 50 cervid taxa (y = 109.515 − .092x + x^2, r^2 = .17).

The Effects of Habitat and Life History Characters

The range of body size dimorphism exhibited by the Cervidae is a consequence of differences in sexual selection, and reflects mating systems, and degree of polygyny. EI is greatest in those species in which males are the larger sex, and it decreases as the disparity diminishes and continues decreasing as the body size ratio reverses with females being the larger sex (Figure 5). This is also evident when the dimorphism index is regressed against female condylobasal length (Figure 6): the parabolic model fits the data best (y = 109.515 − 0.0927x + x^2) with the lowest dimorphism indices occurring in species in the middle body size range.

To test the hypothesis that relative brain size is a function of degree of polygyny we categorized species into two groups on the basis of relative size of the testes. Clutton-Brock et al. (1982) demonstrated that species forming "large breeding groups that vary in membership from day to day" have relatively larger testes than those which defend breeding territories or exhibit successive tending bonds with single females. The criterion used to categorize species was the ratio of maximum testis size based on the literature or unpublished data to mean condylobasal length; the ratio was > .40 for species with large testes , while those with values < .35 were classified as having small testes. Regression analysis showed that species with large testes had larger EIs than species with small testes (Figure 7), however a t-test of these limited data yielded an insignificant difference (mean of large testes species = 1.028, small testes species = .99, t = 1.926, d.f. = 8, P = .09).

Sexual dimorphism on the other hand is measurable in a much larger sample of species and also is a function of mating system. Three groups were defined: species with DIs > 100, > 95 <100, and < 95. Here a significant difference was found between mean EIs (F = 3.118, d.f. = 3, 28, P = .042). Tukey's HSD test at P = .05 revealed a significant difference in means only between small (mean EI= .973) and medium size taxa (mean EI = 1.01).

Length of gestation is a reflection of basal metabolic rate and maternal investment, and could bear a relation to EI. When EI is plotted against gestation period the pattern of data points is best approximated by a parabolic model: relatively lower EIs are distributed at the ends of the gestation range, and there is more spread in EIs of species having mid-range gestations (Figure 8). We examined the relationship of EI to neonatal weight to further explore the question, while assuming that weight at birth indicates degree of development, and that species giving birth to large young should invest relatively shorter periods to maternal care. It is again seen that the highest EIs tend to be those species in the middle range of neonatal weights, while species having lower EIs lie at both ends of the spectrum of neonatal weights (Figure 9). No significant difference however was found in a comparison of EIs between monotocous (mean = 1.008) and ditocous (mean = .983) taxa (t = 1.396, d.f. = 29, P = .161).

Lastly, we hypothesized that EI would mirror differences in behavior and ecology broadly embodied in habitat selection. Specifically, we predicted that EIs would average larger in open habitats (grasslands and marshes) than in closed habitats (forests, scrublands, and thickets), and this was confirmed by regression analysis (Figure 10). While the two groups are not discrete, the slopes are distinct, and a comparison of means yielded a significant difference (closed habitat mean = .985, open habitat mean = 1.009, t = 2.222,

Wemmer and Wilson

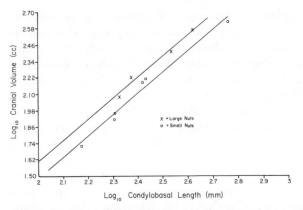

Figure 7. The relationship between cranial volume and condylobasal length in species having large testes (spp 9, 13, 15, 36) and species having small testes (spp 6, 7, 25, 27, 35, 37). Refer to Appendix I for identification of species.

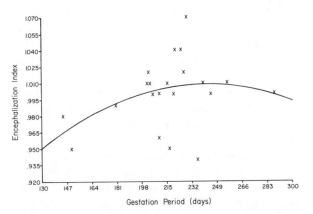

Figure 8. The relationship of encephalization index to gestation period in 21 cervid taxa ($y = .737 + .002x + x^2$, $r^2 = .144$).

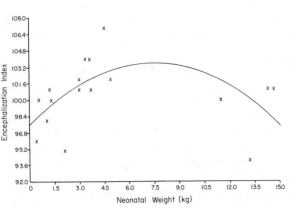

Figure 9. The relationship between encephalization index and neonatal weight in 17 cervid taxa ($y = .9752 + .0162x - .0011x^2$, $r^2 = .261$).

d.f. $= 24$, $P = .036$). We attempted to refine the analysis by categorizing species as open habitat dwellers (prairies, deserts), ecotone species, and forest, woodland, or thicket dwellers. The differences in mean EI however were not significant ($F = 3.111$, d.f. $= 2, 29$, $P = .06$). Future refinements in the definition of habitat use might further clarify the pattern.

Discussion

The relationship between brain size and body size can be examined in a number of ways to elucidate why certain species are peripheral to the main pattern resulting from regression analysis (see Figure 1). In general, species that fall above the line in Figure 1 have brains that are larger than would be predicted for their body size, and those that fall below the line have smaller brains than would be predicted by body size alone. Furthermore, females tend to have larger brains than males, as demonstrated by Eisenberg (1981) for a large number of mammalian taxa. The complete data set is useful for determining the overall pattern for the group, but individual subsets allow the testing of more specific hypotheses.

Taxonomic distinctions are a logical second step for sub-dividing the data set. If the current systematic arrangement truly reflects the evolutionary history of the group, we might expect differences in brain size between the two major lineages. Muntjaks have brain sizes only slightly below the average for the Cervidae, and their relatively small body size probably accounts for this (Appendix I). Smaller species tend to fall be-

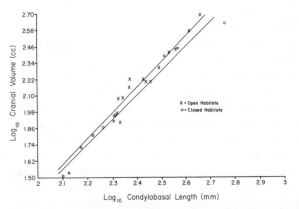

Figure 10. The relationship between cranial volume and condylobasal length in cervid taxa inhabiting closed habitats ($y = -2.1754 + 1.7816x$, $r^2 = .984$), and open habitats ($y = -2.3362 + 1.8737x$, $r^2 = .927$). Refer to Appendix I for closed habitat species: 5-8, 18, 19, 32-35, 37; and open habitat species: 9-13, 15, 17, 23, 24, 26, 29, 30, 31, 36.

low the regression line for the complete data set, suggesting that the relationship is non-linear at the extremes.

There is a significant difference in brain size between the two major cervid lineages (Figure 2). The Plesiometacarpi have brains sufficiently large to fall above the regression line for the Telemetacarpi. Similarly, all but one taxon of the Telemetacarpi have brain sizes that plot below the regression line for the Plesiometacarpi. The single exception is *Odocoileus virginianus couesi*, an insular desert subspecies of the American southwest which may have retained the larger brain of larger bodied ancestral forms.

A comparison of the Cervinae and Odocoileinae shows similar differences when the smaller muntjaks (Muntiacinae) are deleted (Figure 3). In this comparison, all Odocoileinae fall below the regression line for the Cervinae, and all but one species of Cervinae fall above the regression line for the Odocoileinae. The exception again is a small bodied form, *Axis porcinus*. In fact, it is the smallest member of the Cervinae that we examined and the only one with a female encephalization index below 1.00 (Appendix I). Unlike the example above however, *Axis porcinus* is believed to be primitively small, rather than secondarily dwarfed (Groves and Grubb, this volume). These findings conflict with the statement of Geist (1981) and attributed to Kruska (1970) that New World deer have relatively large brains. The opposite situation seems to hold true.

Parabolic regression equations fit most of the curves as well or better than do linear ones. An extreme example is seen in Figure 4 where *Alces alces*, the largest member of the family also exhibits one of the lowest encephalization indices. In plotting encephalization indices against condylobasal length, there is no reason to expect a positive linear relationship, because the encephalization index contains body size in the denominator. The general pattern is greater similarity in the EI's of small and large bodied deer, and disparity in EI's between these two size classes and medium-size deer.

The relationship between brain size and degree of sexual dimorphism is striking (Figure 5). As with many other relationships between brain size and various biological attributes, surely this is one of correlation rather than causation. Allowing the assumption that large brain size is indicative of a particular adaptive zone, many of these correlations may become less enigmatic. If a major progressive evolutionary pathway among cervids has been towards increased degree of polygyny, then perhaps sexually dimorphic forms with males larger than females represent one extreme of this pathway. In these forms, large brain size may be a correlate of a suite of selective pressures refining this habitus. Deviations from this life style in the direction of monomorphism or species with females larger than males may represent specialization outside of the mainstream of cervid evolution. Small solitary forest-dwelling species such as the muntjaks are an example.

If we can show that medium size species tend to have larger brains than smaller or larger species, and that male biased sexually dimorphic species have larger brains than those tending toward monomorphism, then it should come as no surprise that medium size species are generally sexually dimorphic with males being the larger sex (Figure 6). This is reassuring support for the contention that large brained cervids are representative of a major adaptive zone characterized by animals that are medium size, and social systems that select for larger body size in males.

Data on testes size, although not statistically significant, are suggestive (Figure 7). The fact that species with large testes tend to have larger brains than similar size species with small testes fits the pattern we have alluded to. Clutton-Brock et al. (1982) have demonstrated that those species with larger testes fit what we are calling the major or progressive adaptive zone of the cervids.

Length of gestation may approximate a normal distribution within almost any taxonomic unit. One expects the majority of forms to have a modal gestation length relative to body size, and forms with much longer or shorter periods to have evolved under selective regimes differing from the majority. A correlative hypothesis in the current context would be for larger brained forms to fit the modal pattern of gestation length, which they do indeed (Figure 8).

A similar pattern might be argued for the distribution of neonatal birth weights, and once again the brain size data support the hypothesis that the modal animals will have the largest brain size (Figure 9). The tails of the distribution of neonatal birth weights may represent species that are in a sense taking an evolutionary gamble on concentrating maternal care either pre- or postnatally, rather than opting for the compromise, which should afford maximum adaptability. Robbins and Robbins (1979) have demonstrated that among small ungulates (i.e., < 100 kg) there is considerable variance in the relationship of birth weight and average maternal weight. Our data indicate that large brained taxa most often have medium-size rather than large or small neonates.

If our hypothesis is correct – that large brain size is related to a broad adaptive complex of life history and morphological characters – then we should be able to relate brain size to habitat type, as this variable in itself is a good predictor of ecological traits (Jarman, 1974). The sexually dimorphic polygynous species

Wemmer and Wilson

representing the cervid evolutionary "fast lane" tend to live in open grasslands, marshes, or prairie ecotone, rather than forests and thickets. As expected, species in those open habitats tend to have larger brains than similar size species living in forested or closed habitats (Figure 10).

In summary then, relatively large brains are correlated with species of medium body size, strongly male biased sexual dimorphism, large testes, medium length gestation periods, medium neonatal birth weights, and life in relatively open habitats. This description fits a variety of species that may be thought of as occupying a major cervid adaptive zone consisting of seasonally group forming species, with polygynous mating systems, and probably a greater dependence on visual communication patterns than have progressive taxa such as small solitary forest deer, or progressive but deviant lineages such as moose.

Literature Cited

Clutton-Brock, T. and P. Harvey
1980.   Primates, brains and ecology. *Journal of Zoology*, 190:309-324.

Edinger, T.
1948.   Evolution of the horse brain. *Geological Society of America*, Memoir 25, 177 pp.

Eisenberg, J. F.
1981.   *The mammalian radiations*. Chicago: University of Chicago Press.

Eisenberg, J. F. and D. E. Wilson
1978.   Relative brain size and feeding strategies in the Chiroptera. *Evolution*, 32:740-751.

1981.   Relative brain size and demographic strategies in didelphid marsupials. *American Naturalist*, 118:1-15.

Geist, V.
1981.   Behavior: adaptive strategies in mule deer. In *Mule and black-tailed deer of North America*, edited by O. C. Wallmo, pp. 157-223. Lincoln: University of Nebraska Press.

Gould, S. J.
1974.   The origin and function of "bizarre" structures: antler size and skull size in the "Irish elk", *Megaloceros giganteus*. *Evolution*, 28:191-220.

Herre, W.
1936.   Untersuchungen an Hirnen von Wild- und Hausschweinen. *Verhandlungen der Deutschen Zoologischen Gesellschaft Freiburg*, 1936:200-211.

Herre, W., and U. Thiede
1965.   Studien an Gehirnen südamerikanischer Tylopoden. *Zoologisches Jahrbuch Analien*. 82:155-176.

Jarman, P.J.
1974.   Social organisation of antelopes in relation to their ecology. *Behaviour* 48:215-267.

Jerison, H.
1971.   Quantitative analysis of the evolution of the camelid brain. *American Naturalist*, 105:227-239.

Krueg, J.
1878.   Über die Furchung der Grosshirnrinde der Ungulaten. *Zeitschrift für wissenschaftlichen Zoologie*, 31:297-345.

Kruska, D.
1970.   Über die Evolution des Gehirns in der Ordnung Artiodactyla Owen, 1848, insbesondere der Teilordnung Suina Gray, 1868. *Zeitschrift für Säugetierkunde*, 35:214-238.

1973.   Cerebralisation, Hirnevolution und domestikationsbedingte Hirngrössenänderungen innerhalb der Ordnung Perissodactyla Owen, 1848 und in Vergleich mit der Ordnung Artiodactyla Owen, 1848. *Zeitschrift für zoologische Systematik und Evolutionsforschung*, 11:81-103.

Lunau, H.
1956.   Vergleichend metrische Untersuchungen am Allocortex von Wild- und Hausschweinen. *Anatomisches Anzeiger*, 62:673-698.

Mace, G., P.H. Harvey, and T.H. Clutton-Brock
1981.   Brain size and ecology in small mammals. *Journal of Zoology*, 193:333-354.

Oboussier, H.
1970.   Beiträge zur Kenntnis der Alcelaphini (Bovidae–Mammalia) unter besonderer Berücksichtigung von Hirn und Hypophyse. Ergebnisse der Forschungsreise in Afrika (1959-1967). *Morphologische Jahrbuch*, 114:393-435.

1971.   Quantitative und morphologische Studien am Hirn der Bovidae, ein Beitrag zur Kenntnis der Phylogenie. *Gegenbaurs morphologisches Jahrbuch*, 117:162-168.

Oboussier, H., and H. Schliemann
1966.   Hirn-Körpergewichtbeziehungen bei Boviden. *Zeitschrift für Säugetierkunde*, 31:464-471.

Pirlot, O. and H. Stephan
1970.   Encephalization in Chiroptera. *Canadian Journal of Zoology*, 48:433-444.

Radinsky, L.
1969.   Outlines of canid and felid brain evolution. *Annals of the New York Academy of Sciences*, 167:277-288.

Robbins, C.T., and B.L. Robbins
1979.   Fetal and neonatal growth patterns and maternal reproductive effort in ungulates and subungulates. *American Naturalist*, 114:101–116.

Ronnefeld, U.
1970.   Morphologische und quantitative Neocortexuntersuchungen bei Boviden, ein Beitrag zur Phylogenie dieser Familie. I. Formen mittlerer Körpergrösse (25 kg bis 75 kg). *Gegenbaurs morphologisches Jahrbuch*, 115:161-230.

Appendix I. Brain volumes, condylobasal lengths (CBL), encephalization and dimorphism indices of 34 cervid and moschid taxa. Encephalization indices were computed separately for males (A=1.787, B=−2.174) and females (A=1.9015, B=−2.422) (see Methods section). Dimorphism indices are based on larger samples than used for brain volume and EI determinations

Species			Brain volume (cc)	CBL (mm)	Enceph. index	Dimorphis index
Alces alces gigas	f		425.7	576.7	0.93	100.5
			388.5–447.2	570.0–580.0		
			3	3		
	m		397.0	574.0		0.94
			357.9–434.8	528.0–601.0		
			3	3		
Axis axis	f		145.2	235.0	1.04	91.3
	m		143.9	257.5		1.01
			142.6–145.2	241.0–274.0		
			2	2		
Axis porcinus	f		93.5	209.0	0.99	
Blastocerus dichotomus	f		159.4	286.3	0.98	90
			158.0–160.7	282.0–290.5		
			2	2		
	m		187.8	318		0.99
			186.5–189.1	310–326		
			2	2		
Capreolus capreolus	f		82.2	201.4	0.98	98.5
			51.9–100.6	195.6–209.7		
			3	3		
	m		99.7	204.5		1.02
			95.3–104.3	199.5–208.4		
			3	3		
Cervus duvauceli	f		202.7	310.0	1.00	87.1
	m		237.3	356.0		1.00
Cervus elaphus nelsoni	f		371.6	417.3	1.00	92.3
			344.0–393.7	413.0–424.0		
			3	3		
	m		407.6	452.0		1.02
			382.9–432.5	420.0–479.0		
			3	3		
Cervus eldi thamin	m		161.1	289.5		1.00
			153.1–169.2	285.0–294.0		
			2	2		
Cervus nippon subsp.	f		120.4	212.0	1.04	97.2
			118.2–124.8	210.0–216.0		
			3	3		
	m		115.7	218.0		1.03
Cervus nippon hortulorum	f		156.8	258.8	1.01	
			155.7–157.9	255.8–262.2		
			2	2		
Cervus timorensis	f		165.0	268.3	1.01	89.9
			155.2–171.2	266.0–270.0		
			3	3		
	m		201.5	298.5		1.02
			197.3–205.7	295.0–302.0		
			2	2		

Species			Brain volume (cc)	CBL (mm)	Enceph. index	Dimorphis index
Cervus unicolor brookei	f		248.5	326.0	1.02	96.3
			227.6–264.7	320.0–338.0		
			3	3		
		m	244.8	338.7		1.02
			208.1–269.5	319.0–364.0		
			3	3		
Cervus unicolor equinus	f		284.9	369.0	1.00	99.7
			280.4–289.4	368.0–370.0		
			2	2		
		m	284.4	370		1.02
			249.8–348.9	353.0–396.0		
			3	3		
Cervus unicolor francianus	f		134.2	244.0	1.00	95.3
			121.8–146.6	237.0–251.0		
			2	2		
		m	122.7	256.0		0.98
Cervus unicolor mariannus		m	140.7	255.3		1.01
			126.2–149.7	254.0–256.0		
			3	3		
Cervus unicolor philippensis	f		161.3	232.0	1.06	88.5
		m	117.9	262.0		0.96
Dama dama	f		167.4	235.7	1.06	86
			162.8–170.3	233.0–237.0		
			3	3		
		m	199.0	274.0		1.05
Elaphodus cephalophus	f		73.6	184.0	0.99	101.5
			67.4–79.7	177.0–191.0		
			2	2		
		m	86.6	181.3		1.04
			82.1–91.3	178.0–187.0		
			3	3		
Elaphurus davidianus	f		278.8	365.0	1.00	88.4
		m	335.6	413.0		1.01
			328.8–344.4	407.0–420.0		
			3	3		
Hippocamelus bisulcus	f		160.0	274.0	1.00	102.5
			159.6–160.3	267.0–281.0		
			2	2		
		m	153.9	267.3		1.01
			144.2–166.5	264–273		
			3	3		
Hydropotes inermis	f		46.8	165.9	0.93	105.3
			45.5–48.1	164.6–167.3		
			2	2		
		m	46.0	157.6		0.95
			41.6–51.1	140.3–173.5		
			3	3		

Species			Brain volume (cc)	CBL (mm)	Enceph. index	Dimorphis index
Mazama americana sheila	f		91.8	205.2	0.99	97.6
			84.4–101.8	199.0–209.6		
			4	4		
	m		90.6	210.3	0.99	
			79.2–96.3	192.0–288.0		
			4	4		
Mazama gouazoubira subsp.	f		64.6	166.7	1.00	103.7
			58.6–69.3	161.0–171.0		
			3	3		
	m		55.2	160.7	0.99	
			50.1–62.2	157–164		
			3	3		
Megaceros hibernicus	f		489.1	460.0	1.02	
Moschus moschiferus	f		34.3	132.7	0.95	97.9
			32.5–36.2	129.4–136.0		
			2	2		
	m		36.0	135.5	0.95	
			34.9–37.1	135.4–135.5		
			2	2		
Muntiacus muntjac	f		91.0	202.8	1.00	102.5
			83.1–95.1	190.0–214.0		
			3	3		
	m		92.3	197.9	1.02	
			77.6–106.9	193.8–202.8		
			3	3		
Muntiacus reevesi	f		52.5	149.0	1.01	99.9
			41.2–59.7	133.2–159.0		
			3.00	3.00		
	m		51.9	149.1	1.00	
			45.4–55.4	142.4–156.0		
			3	3		
Odocoileus hemionus hemionus	f		164.1	270.6	1.01	90.1
			145.9–186.3	266.8–273.6		
			3	3		
	m		179.9	300.3	1.00	
			178.1–182.7	291.1–312.4		
			3	3		
Odocoileus hemionus columbianus	f		125.5	227.5	1.02	90.3
			116.7–134.7	218.5–234.3		
			3	3		
	m		141.8	251.9	1.02	
			127.8–152.2	250.1–253.6		
			3	3		
Odocoileus virginianus borealis	f		154.4	262.4	1.01	91.2
			148.4–161.5	246.0–271.9		
			3	3		
	m		170.9	287.7	1.01	
			166.3–173.2	277.3–295.2		
			3	3		

Appendix I. (cont.)

Species			Brain volume (cc)	CBL (mm)	Enceph. index	Dimorphis index
Odocoileus virginianus couesi	f		122.3	219.8	1.03	95.4
			118.6–127.3	207.5–229.3		
			3	3		
	m		115.6	230.4	1.01	
			109.3–122.5	228–231.9		
			3	3		
Ozotocerus bezoarticus	f		80.2	214.0	0.95	98.3
			78.8–81.6			
			2.0			
	m		93.0	217.7	0.98	
			90.4–94.6	212.0–221.0		
			3	3		
Pudu mephistopheles	f		32.6	125.4	0.97	99.1
	m		35.9	126.6	0.98	
Rangifer tarandus caribou	f		259.9	341.7	1.01	85.6
			241.1–271.5	323.0–366.0		

Appendix II.   Code used for referencing taxa referred to in statistical analyses.

Numerical Code	Taxa	Numerical Code	Taxa
5	Moschus moschiferus	23	Elaphurus davidianus
6	Muntiacus muntjac	24	Megaceros hibernicus
7	Muntiacus reevesi	25	Odocoileus virginianus borealis
8	Elaphodus cephalophus	26	Odocoileus virginianus couesi
9	Dama dama	27	Odocoileus hemionus hemionus
10	Axis axis	28	Odocoileus hemionus columbianus
11	Axis porcinus	29	Ozotoceros bezoarticus
12	Cervus duvauceli	30	Blastocerus dichotomus
13	Cervus elaphus nelsoni	31	Hippocamelus bisulcus
15	Cervus nippon	32	Mazama americana sheila
16	Cervus nippon hortulorum	33	Mazama gouazoubira subspp
17	Cervus timorensis	34	Pudu mephistopheles
18	Cervus unicolor brookei	35	Alces alces gigas
19	Cervus unicolor equinus	36	Rangifer tarandus caribou
20	Cervus unicolor francianus	37	Capreolus capreolus subspp
22	Cervus unicolor philippensis	38	Hydropotes inermis

CYRILLE BARRETTE
Biology Department
Laval University
Québec, Canada G1K 7P4

The Comparative Behavior and Ecology of Chevrotains, Musk Deer, and Morphologically Conservative Deer

ABSTRACT

The 8 genera (19 species) considered here are small (1.5 to 25 kg) forest-living Cervidae (muntjacs, tufted deer, water deer) Moschidae (musk deer of Asia) brocket deer, and pudus of Asia and South America, and Tragulidae (chevrotains of Asia and Africa). Published field studies are available for only 3 species: the African chevrotain (*Hyemoschus aquaticus*), the Siberian musk deer (*Moschus sibiricus*) and the Sri Lankan muntjac (*Muntiacus muntjak*). From minimal data and numerous anecdotal and widely dispersed published observations these are all strict forest ruminants, which feed on rich bits of vegetation (fruits, buds, leaves, lichens). They live a solitary yet social life, are probably non-territorial yet sedentary on a limited home range (15 to 50 ha), and are polygynous with a litter size of one in most cases (2 for *Moschus* and *Hydropotes*), and a gestation of 5 to 7 months followed by a post-partum estrus in at least 4 species (*Tragulus napu, M. reevesi, M. muntjak, Mazama americana*). This seemingly clear and complete image of life history characteristics is in fact a gross over-simplification of the ecology and behavior of a group of animals where each species is unique and apparently very adaptable. More field studies are greatly needed both to provide a sound basis for understanding the evolution of artiodactyls, and for conservation and management purposes.

Introduction

Reviewing our knowledge of the behavior and ecology of tragulids and small deer is a legitimate and highly desirable objective. However interesting and useful such a review would be, it can hardly be complete at the present time, because we are far from having the necessary information to make sound intra- or inter-specific comparisons. In spite of that I have three purposes here. First, it is important to stress that paucity of information. I will also identify two unfortunate consequences that follow from our very limited knowledge of these fascinating animals.

My second purpose is to summarize what little is known. I am aware that my summary is incomplete as I will present only published information. In a few years as evidenced by some of the papers in this symposium one will be in a better position to review the subject, and that is very encouraging. Also, some of the literature I have seen is in Russian or Chinese, two languages that I cannot read, and there are probably many additional published and unpublished documents in those languages I am unaware of because they are inaccessible to the literature retrieval systems I used (*Bio-Abstract, Zoological Record, Bulletin Signalitique*). Fortunately, many important works in the field happen to be in French, one language I do know. One recommendation I may make here would be for someone to solicit papers in English from Russian, Chinese and French researchers that would review their vast knowledge of the subject (particularly the muntjacs, musk deer and water deer).

My third and last purpose is to indicate, on the basis of what is known, what kind of research I feel should be done in the future.

This is a somewhat negative paper which criticizes the literature and underscores how little is known, but I think that it is a useful exercise, and I am convinced it is necessary. I hope my criticisms will be seen for what they are: above all, an appeal for much needed research.

Selection of Species

I will be talking about the chevrotains (3 species of Asian *Tragulus*, and the single species of African *Hyemoschus*), the musk deer (there are 5 described species of *Moschus*), and "morphologically conservative deer". I did not choose the latter expression, but it accurately describes the muntjacs (4 species of *Muntiacus*), tufted deer (*Elaphodus cephalophus*), Chinese water deer (*Hydropotes inermis*), and South American brocket deer (4 species of *Mazama*) and pudus (2 species of *Pudu*). That is a total of 19 species belonging to 8 genera in two families. It may look like an odd mixture, but based on the limited available informa-

Figure 1. *T. memmina* in Wilpattu National Park, Sri Lanka.

tion, all these species have enough in common to be considered together. I have excluded the roe deer (*Capreolus capreolus*), even though on the basis of body size it could have been included. My reasons are rather arbitrary. On the one hand, its geographical range is so vast (from Spain to Korea, and from Iran to Norway) that the best comparisons could be made within the species itself. The other reason is that so much more is known of the roe deer that it would be difficult to compare it with the other species in a balanced manner. I therefore take it that "morphologically conservative" means first and foremost "small", that is, less than 25 kg. There is nothing magical about that upper limit either; it too is rather arbitrary. "Morphologically conservative" does not necessarily refer to primitiveness; though all such species share small body size with certain fossil forms, some may be secondarily small. This is probably the case for South American brocket and pudu, and the key deer (*O. virginianus floridanus*). Their small size is presumably a recent specialization and not a retained primitive character.

Finally, being interested in ecology rather than phylogeny, I will not compare ethograms. Dubost (1971, 1975, 1978, 1980) has done some revealing comparisons of that nature among cervids, tragulids and bovids, concentrating mainly on small forms exhibiting what Geist (1971) has called the "Duiker syndrome", and to which belong all the species concerned here (Figure 1).

Summary of Available Knowledge

This will be a critical assessment of what is known of the behavioral ecology of tragulids and small deer. When appropriate, I will identify and challenge unsupported published claims. I want to stress that I am not criticizing authors; all of them are justly respected researchers. I only want to expose and oppose the publication of statements where suppositions are very hard to distinguish from facts. Also I fully realize the difficulties in obtaining reliable information on any of these species. I therefore apologize if any of my comments incidentally devalue the commendable efforts made by many authors to study such secretive animals in the field.

Body Size

All species considered here (hereafter called "Small Solitary Forest Deer" or SSFD) are small compared to most cervids. I found reliable data on adult body weights of adults of both sexes for only seven species: *T. javanicus* (Nordin, 1978), *T. memmina* (Phillips, 1935), *H. aquaticus* (Dubost, 1978), *Moschus moschiferus* (Egorov, 1967), *M. muntjak* (Phillips, 1935), *M. crinifrons* (Sheng and Lu, 1980), and *Hydropotes inermis* (Whitehead, 1950, in Bunnell, this volume). In addition, Chapman and Dansie (1970) gave weights for nineteen female *M. reevesi* in England (Figure 2). I have presented in Figure 2 weights for all other species of SSFD, taken from sources where authors either simply gave approximate values or cited someone else who gave no indication of having weighed specimens (e.g. Whitehead, 1972; Walker, 1975; Haltenorth, 1963). One indication of the difficulty of finding reliable information on this rather simple and important subject is found in Sunquist (1981). He cites two authors giving 12 and 17 kg respectively as the average weight of *Muntiacus muntjak* in Royal Chitawan National Park in Nepal. But in his table 26 he gives the weight of one female at 20 kg and that on one male at 25 kg, for animals he actually weighed in the same Park.

In addition to measures of body weight, one can also find approximate values on body length and shoulder height, as well as some reliable skull measurements. For the latter, see Groves (1975) on *Moschus moschiferus*, Grubb (1976-77) on *Muntiacus muntjak* and *M. reevesi*, Sheng and Lu (1980) on *M. crinifrons*, and van Bemmel (1952) on many sub-species of *M. muntjak*.

One first comment on body size is that although all species are small, they are far from being the same size: *T. javanicus* is tiny at 1.5 kg, compared to *T. memmina* (4 kg) and *T. napu* (6 kg). In turn all three are rather small compared to the African chevrotain (11 kg). Similar differences are found in the genus *Muntiacus*: from *M. reevesi* at some 12 kg to *M. crinifrons* at 23 kg, and some races of *M. muntjak* on Java weighing about 32 kg (Hoogerwerf, 1970). The same is true of *Moschus*: metacarpal length varies from 82-89 mm in

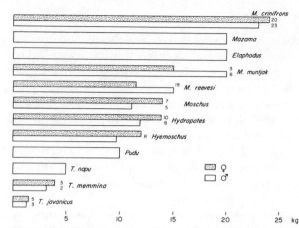

Figure 2. Body weight and sexual dimorphism of most SSFD. Figures indicate sample sizes when known. (For *Hyemoschus*, it is unknown but I consider the measures to be reliable (R).)

M. berezovskii to "not less than 126 mm" in *M. sibiricus sibiricus* (Flerov, 1952). Such three-fold differences in body weight in these groups cannot be ignored when discussing ecology. To do so would be to regard the size difference between mule deer (*Odocoileus hemionus*) and wapiti (*Cervus elaphus canadensis*) as negligible, in spite of the three-fold difference one finds here as well.

A second comment concerns sexual dimorphism. For the seven species mentioned earlier for which there are reliable data one finds that females are heavier than males in *T. javanicus*, *T. memmina*, *Hyd. inermis*, *Mos. moschiferus* and *Hyemoschus*, as well as marginally so in *M. crinifrons* (Figure 1). This agrees with Ralls' (1976, 1977) findings that in small artiodactyls (i.e. tragulids and duikers (*Cephalophus*)), females are larger than males. On the other hand, in *M. reevesi* and *M. muntjak*, females seem to be smaller than males. Going from *T. javanicus* to *M. muntjak* one sees a reversal in dimorphism from females to males being the larger sex. The exception to this apparently general trend (*M. crinifrons*) may be partly explained by the fact that a female muntjac is almost continually pregnant and her full term fetus represents a high proportion of her body weight (about 1 kg for female *M. reevesi* averaging 12 kg, Chapman and Dansie, 1970). Therefore, the weight of the fetus may account for larger females in *M. crinifrons*, where the intersexual difference of one kg is small (Dansie, 1970).

Egorov (1967) and Feer (1979) did consider this problem. Feer found female *Neotragus batesi* to be heavier than males (2.8 ± 0.4 kg, n = 30, versus 2.2 ± 0.2, n = 26), even when females close to parturition were discarded from his computations. The same seems to be true for *Mos. moschiferus* as Egerov (1967, p. 31)

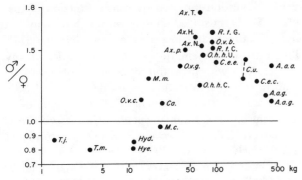

Figure 3.   Body weight dimorphism in some tragulids and cervids. Only species for which I could find reliable primary literature were included. *A. a. a.* = *Alces alces americana*, Peterson (1974); *A. a. g.* = *Alces alces gigas*, Franzmann et al. (1978); *Ax.*H. = *Axis axis* in Hawaii, Ables (1977); *Ax.*N. = *Axis axis* in Nepal, Sunquist (1981); *Ax.*T. = *Axis axis* in Texas, Ables (1977); *Ax.p.* = *Axis porcinus*, M. Sunquist (1981); *Ca.* = *Capreolus capreolus*, Ellenberg (1978); *C. e. c.* = *Cervus elaphus canadensis*, Flook (1970); *C. e. e.* = *Cervus elaphus elaphus*, Mitchell et al (1976); *C. u.* = *Cervus unicolor*, Sunquist (1981): the lower point is on the basis a minimum weight of 227 kg (the upper limit of Sunquist's scale), the higher point considers 250 kg, a likely average weight for males (Sunquist, pers. comm.); *Hyd.* = *Hydropotes inermis*, Corbet and Southern (1977) and Whitehead (1950) both cited in Bunnell (this volume); *Hye.* = *Hyemoschus aquaticus*, Dubost (1978); *M. c.* = *Muntiacus crinifrons*, Sheng and Lu (1980); *M. m.* = *Muntiacus muntjak*, Phillips (1935); *O. h. h.*C. = *Odocoileus hemionus hemionus* in Colorado, Anderson et al (1974); *O. h. h.*U. = *Odocoileus hemionus hemionus* in Utah, Robinette et al. (1977); *O. v. b.* = *Odocoileus virginianus borealis*, Huot (1973); *O. v. c.* = *Odocoileus virginianus clavium*, R.P. Allen (1952); *O. v. g.* = *Odocoileus virginianus gymnotis*, Brokx (1972); *R. t.* = *Rangifer tarandus* in Canada, McEwan (1968); *R. t.*G. = *Rangifer tarandus* on South Georgia Island, Leader-Williams (1980); *T. j.* = *Tragulus javanicus*, Nordin (1978); *T. m.* = *Tragulus memmina*, Phillips (1935). The body weight of females includes the uterus and its contents. This clearly affects dimorphism, particularly in smaller species (see Robbins and Robbins, 1979). The value for *Moshus moshiferus* is the same as *Hye.* (see Table 1).

explicitly states that the larger weight of females "is not explained by the gravidity of females". More generally, whenever seasonal variations in weight are large one should define for each species or population the appropriate time to weigh animals. The importance of this is illustrated by the difference between *O. h. hemionus* in Utah and *O. h. hemionus* in Colorado seen in Figure 3. In the first case all males were weighed in October, before significant weight loses brought about by the rut and the winter (x̄ = 84 kg, n = 698), whereas in Colorado, males were collected throughout the year (x̄ = 74 kg, n = 51).

Weight dimorphism may not be the most important feature of SSFD. They are dimorphic in another more striking way, namely tusks or antlers. It appears that

below a certain body size sexual selection produces dimorphism only in body size, but beyond that critical size, bioenergetic or other ecological constraints bring about additional expressions of sexual selection such as antlers. At least one fact supports this contention. The most pronounced weight dimorphism in a cervid is found neither in the largest genus (*Alces*), nor in the most polygynous one (*Cervus*), but in *Axis axis* and *Rangifer tarandus* (Figure 3). On the other hand, it is in the largest genera that one finds by far the largest antlers (*Alces* and *Cervus elaphus*) (Clutton-Brock et al., 1977, 1980).

Habitat Use, Activity, Food Habits and Population Density

The word "forest" in SSFD simply means a closed or visually obstructive, or physically congested habitat (Dubost, 1979). Beyond that common character, the forests where SSFD are found can be vastly different, e.g. from *Hyemoschus* living in equatorial forests in Africa (Dubost, 1978), to *Moschus* in coniferous forests at the Arctic circle of the USSR (Bannikov et al., 1978). Even within the same species and over a short distance, the word "forest" can mean very diverse habitats, e.g. muntjacs in Sri Lanka are found from "semi-evergreen scrub forests" (Dittus, 1977) at sea level, to "montane rain forests" at 2000 m altitude, some 100 km away (Phillips, 1935). These are two strikingly different habitats, yet they are two places where *M. muntjak malabaricus* live and thrive, an impressive demonstration of adaptability.

Two generalities emerge: first, to know the types of habitats where SSFD live one only needs to know the geographical range of the species and the types of forest found there. Secondly, there seems to be something about open habitats that repel SSFD. This is one aspect of SSFD behavior that is consistently reported by casual observers and confirmed by all systematic studies; these animals very seldom break cover and then with extreme care, and for short periods only (Barrette, 1977a). This is presumably the primary anti-predator tactic of such small and rather defenseless animals (see Eisenberg and McKay, 1974). This is clearly confirmed by Feer's (1979) work on the pygmy antelope (*Neotragus batesi*), which shows that at night animals frequent forest cover where the vegetation is significantly lower and less dense than during the day.

Being limited to forest cover has two consequences. First, all SSFD are extremely difficult to observe, and this is why so little is known of their behavior and ecology. Secondly, seeing them almost never in the open, and very seldom in the forest, most writers have concluded that SSFD are nocturnal. The only reliable study of activity of a SSFD in nature is that on *Hyemoschus* by Dubost (1975). He studied animals kept in enclosures erected in the natural habitat of the species, and showed that his animals were very active at night. Although his daytime observations were not as systematic as those he made at night, it seems clear that *Hyemoschus* is nocturnal. For all other species there is no information available, only unsupported claims. Dubost (1975, p. 413) claims for instance that *Tragulus memmina* "ne se déplace que la nuit dans la nature" (travels only at night in nature), citing Eisenberg and Lockhart (1972) in support of that affirmation. Yet the latter, in their very useful and stimulating work present no evidence whatsoever to that effect. They revealingly state " . . . we contacted only eighteen mouse deer in the course of our operations . . . (14 months of field work) . . . . Since the animal is nocturnal in its habits and quite secretive, we were unable to determine the age and sex of the specimens . . ." (Eisenberg and Lockhart, 1972, p. 52). I think Hoogerwerf's (1970, p. 359) opinion on the activity rhythm of *Tragulus javanicus* in nature is more reasonable, and could apply to most SSFD: "Although the kanchil is also active at night . . . the species is not an expressly nocturnal animal. There are numerous daytime observations in which in most cases the impression was gained that browsing individuals were concerned, not ones which had been disturbed in their rest". This is clearly the case for the ecologically similar pygmy antelope which" . . . contrary to a generally held opinion is both nocturnal and diurnal" (Feer, 1979, p. 180). In addition, one species of small forest ruminant, the blue duiker (*Cephalophus monticola*) was found to be "strictly diurnal" (Dubost, 1980). Waser (1975a) found the bushbuck (*Tragelaphus scriptus*), a 50 kg solitary forest bovid to be both nocturnal and diurnal, as did Yahner (1980) with captive Reeve's muntjacs.

Many predictions on food habits of SSFD can be made on the basis of their consistent occurrence in forested habitats, their small body size and the fact that they all are ruminants. These three characters are best seen as constraints that set limits to what the animal can eat and, consequently, how many can live per unit area, and also the character of their social life (see Western, 1979).

Jarman (1974) has made a very useful analysis of African bovids, drawing some revealing correlations between body size, food habits, habitat use and social organization. (See Brown et al., 1978, and Prothero and Sereno, 1982, for a similar line of arguments applied to nectar feeding birds and Miocene dwarf rhinoceroses respectively.) Jarman's approach can be readily applied to cervids and tragulids. Because of their small size and the associated high metabolic rate, and the limited capacity for speeding up the rate

of food ingestion imposed by rumen function (Janis, 1976), SSFD must feed on food with high protein and energy content, and low fiber content (Geist, 1974). There are no systematic food habits studies of any species dealt with here, but all available observations confirm this generalization. Musk deer in the USSR eat primarily arboreal lichens (62% of volume of 16 stomach contents: Bannikov et al., 1978), *Hyemoschus* is a frugivore (68.7% dry weight of stomach contents: Gauthier-Hion et al., 1980) *Muntiacus muntjak* eat fruits, buds and fresh leaves, both in Sri Lanka (Barrette, 1977a), and Java (Hoogerwerf, 1970), and so does *M. reevesi* in England (Jackson et al., 1977). Similar food habits were reported by Feer (1979) for the 2.5 kg folivorous pygmy antelope, (analysis of 128 stomach contents), by Dubost (1980) for the 5 kg frugivorous blue duiker, (78.5% dry weight of stomach contents, see also Gauthier-Hion et al., 1980), and by Wilson (1966) in his excellent work on the common duiker, *Sylvicapra grimmia*, in which he analysed 191 stomach contents. From this, one can say that forest ruminants are neither grazers nor browsers (Hofmann and Stewart, 1972), but nibblers: searching and eating the small rich bits on the forest floor or on saplings within their reach. Since much of their food is fallen from the forest canopy, either freely or as a result of primates' foraging activities, SSFD are functionally arboreal. This is an important point to consider when estimating the availability and spatial distribution of their food. Such food items are dispersed on a small scale (a few m²) compared to grasses for instance (Jarman, 1974). But on a larger scale (a few ha or the animal's home range), the available food in the form of a few fruiting trees for instance is clumped (Dittus, 1977) and occurs in unpredictable places.

The fact that such rich food is much less abundant than more fibrous vegetation like grass or browse, used by larger herbivores, probably explains in a large measure the low density of any population of SSFD (see Bourlière, 1973–1975; Jarman, 1974). Except for temporary aggregations where animals may gather at a localized resource (a water hole, a fruiting tree or a lichen-loaded fallen conifer) densities are usually below 10/km². On the basis of the few attempted estimations, normal densities are as follows: *Moschus sibiricus*: from 0.2 to 7 (Bannikov et al., 1978), *Hyemoschus*: from 8 to 28 (Dubost, 1978), *Muntiacus muntjak*: from 0.5 to 7 (Pfeffer, 1969; Hoogerwerf, 1970; Eisenberg and Lockhart, 1972; Barrette, 1977a; Seidensticker, 1976; Eisenberg and Seidensticker, 1976; Dinerstein, 1980).

Home Range and Territoriality

It is extremely difficult to map and measure the home range of SSFD. This is made evident by how difficult it can be to do it even for the territory of an open habitat antelope (Walther, 1978). The only successful attempts on SSFD are those of Dubost (1978) on *Hyemoschus* (also see his work on the blue duiker, Dubost, 1980). His results confirm what all authors familiar with tragulids and small forest deer have said: these are extremely sedentary animals, an individual apparently spending its entire life in a very restricted area (Hoogerwerf, 1970; Barrette, 1977a). (On the other hand Bannikov et al. (1978) reported that in the musk deer, home range size is from 150 to 300 ha.) On the basis of tracking (2 females) and numerous recaptures of marked animals (31 females, and 14 males), Dubost (1978) gives 14 and 28 ha as the mean home range size of female and male *Hyemoschus* respectively. Since SSFD live in low densities, (< 10 adults/km²), in habitats where food is usually available in one form (fruits) or another (fresh leaves) (Hladik and Hladik, 1972), and consume relatively small absolute quantities of food, intra or interspecific competition for food is probably infrequent (Fleming, 1979). The subject of home range size is therefore relatively unimportant.

Whether such an area, or a portion of it, is defended as a territory, however, is an important matter in our understanding of the evolution of the social behavior of all small solitary forest ruminants (see Jarman, 1974; Estes, 1974). Dubost's (1978) results on *Hyemoschus* in that respect are by far the best available. He categorically concluded that the African chevrotain is not territorial, thus confirming a hypothesis I had presented before (Barrette, 1977a) that, on the basis of their food distribution, most small forest ruminants should not be territorial. Feer (1979) found no evidence of territoriality in the pygmy antelope either, even though, as he himself points out, these animals use scent marking, and like-sex adults are very seldom seen together (Feer, 1979). On the other hand, Dubost (1980) found some minimal evidence of territoriality in the blue duiker. In this case, the seasonal home range (an individual living on a given area for 3–4 months) coincides with what Dubost calls a territory. There clearly is a problem of definition here, in addition to the obvious difficulties in mapping the territory of a small cryptic animal living over several hectares of forest. What can be said at the moment is that not one species of SSFD has been demonstrated to be territorial anywhere near as convincingly as Bramley (1970) has shown the roe deer to be (Waser, 1981; Mitani and Rodman, 1979).

My justification for discussing territoriality at such length is that this particular aspect of the behavioral ecology is where numerous authors have used more imagination and oversimplifications than facts. While most authors have merely mentioned that small forest ruminants are territorial, at least three have not only stated it as fact but made it the basis for their reconstruction of the evolution of social organization in the

artiodactyls. Two of these were dealing with bovids (Estes, 1974; Jarman, 1974) and one with tragulids and South Asian deer (Kurt, 1978). The latter states: 'Territoriality in deer is best represented in the Muntjac . . ." (Kurt, 1978), but offers support neither from the literature nor from his own observations. I think one cannot ignore such unsupported statements, but must expose them as such. I am not saying that Kurt and others are wrong; some populations of some species of SSFD could very well be territorial. I simply say that we do not know, and that there are good reasons to predict that most of them are not (Barrette, 1977a). Identifying a species as territorial often colors one's interpretations of subsequent observations in a counterproductive way. Owen-Smith (1977) did recognize the paucity of information on small forest ungulates and consequently refrained from speculating on their behavior in his very useful and sound review of territoriality in ungulates.

Social Organization and Mating System

Information on social organization is relatively abundant and reliable: when one sees a single deer, one can be reasonably sure that the animal *is* alone (but not absolutely so: see Aldrich-Blake, 1970). The social organization of all SSFD is simple and minimal: the only groups are courting pairs, mother and offspring, or a male accompanying the latter group. Two adults of the same sex are very seldom seen together, and then they are engaged in a fight or an aggressive pursuit (see Barrette, 1977a; Dubost, 1978; and Dunbar and Dunbar, 1979). A high proportion of the animals seen in nature are alone: 64% (n = 1005) in *M. muntjak* (Barrette, 1977a), 100% (n = 37) in *T. memmina* (Eisenberg and Lockhart, 1972; pers. obs.); "usually solitary" in *T. javanicus* (Hoogerwerf, 1970).

Four is the maximum group size apparently ever recorded for any species. The same is true for small solitary forest bovids (e.g., Esser, 1980; Dubost, 1980; Dunbar and Dunbar, 1979; Waser, 1975b). The duration of any association between two individuals is difficult to establish. It is also difficult to interpret the social relationship of two individuals seen together. In other words an animal may be seen alone, and spend most of its life alone, but still be an active member of a group, having established relationships without close and constant proximity (see Underwood, 1982). What this means is that the word "solitary" may describe part of the social life of a small solitary forest ruminant, but by no means is it a complete and accurate, or even useful, description (see Barrette, 1977a; Waser, 1975b; and Dubost, 1980). This is particularly evident in the fact that olfactory communication (e.g. scent marking) is very important in most species of SSFD. Muntjacs for instance have the largest preorbital glands among ungulates, and are the only one to have frontal glands as well (Barrette, 1976); in addition both male and female *M. reevesi* have paraurethral glands (Dansie and Williams, 1973) that probably play a role in marking with urine (Barrette, 1977b). The musk deer is another striking example, with the ventral musk gland and caudal glands, present in males only, being used extensively for marking (Sokolov and Prikhodko, 1979). One last example will suffice to show the strong development of scent organs in the SSFD: male *Hyemoschus* have a chin gland used in marking objects, as well as a preputial gland; in addition, both sexes have a highly developed anal gland (Dubost, 1975), indicating that animals mark directly with glandular secretions, and use them to mark both their urine and feces.

Given the presumed importance of olfactory communication in SSFD, the word solitary is therefore rather misleading since it refers to *sightings*. Given the thick habitats they live in, and that most sightings are short (58% of 338 sightings of muntjacs in the forest were shorter than 60 seconds, Barrette, 1977a), what one sees as a lone animal may often be a member of a loose group held together by scent. The word solitary should therefore be limited to what one sees and should not be extended to what it may mean to the animals, until one knows more about it.

SSFD are presumably polygynous. Dubost's (1970) description of the mating system of captive *M. reevesi* living in a large (6.6 ha) enclosure in France, and his work on wild *Hyemoschus* (Dubost, 1978) is probably a valid model for most species in the wild. A male patrols a home range larger than and overlapping those of several females, and associates with a given female for the duration of her sexual receptivity. Therefore, contrary to what others have supposed (e.g. Bigalke, 1974), small solitary forest ruminants are probably not monogamous. The few bovid species that live in pairs seem to be monogamous, and are probably territorial, but they are ecotone species, found in rather open savanna-like habitats (e.g. *Madoqua kirki*, Hendrichs and Hendrichs, 1971; *Ourebia ourebi*, Monfort and Monfort, 1974; Esser, 1980).

The blue duiker is the one forest species where monogamy and territoriality seem to be found (Dubost, 1980). Unfortunately too little is known of tragulids and small cervids in the wild to do any more than predict, on the basis of a few data and theory (Kleiman, 1977), that most are likely to be polygynous. This is partly supported by the very large testes of *M. muntjak* (Barrette, 1977a: Figure 4), possibly an indication of a high copulatory frequency (see Harcourt et al., 1981b; and Short, 1979, for a similar argument applied to primates).

Reproduction

In most species of SSFD the litter size is one (Table 1). An exception is the musk deer for which Bannikov et al. (1978) report the mean litter size to be 1.82 (n = 119 litters: 38% = 1, 52% = 2, 10% = 3). The Chinese water deer is also an exception, being widely reported to have normal litters of 4 to 7 (Walker, 1975; Whitehead, 1972; Haltenorth, 1963). This is probably an exaggeration apparently based on G.M. Allen's 1938–1940 report of litters of 6 and 7 found in two females. On the basis of 45 fawns born in captivity, Crandall (1964, p. 562) states that "most births have been of twins, with occasional singles and 2 or 3 sets of triplets, but not more". This is both more likely, and remarkably similar to the musk deer, as reported above.

The length of gestation is known only for three species: *T. napu* (155 days: Davis, 1965), *M. reevesi* (215 days: Chaplin and Dangerfield, 1974; Barrette, 1977a) and *M. muntjak* (224 days: Dubost, 1971). Information on gestation for most species of SSFD can be found in the literature (Table 1), but it is impossible to know how such information was established, or how reliably.

Females of four species are known to have a post-partum estrus, mating taking place from 1 to 5 days after parturition: *Mazama americana* (Gardner, 1971), *Muntiacus reevesi* (Barrette, 1977a; Chaplin and Dangerfield, 1974), *M. muntjak* (Dubost, 1971), and *Tragulus napu* (Davis, 1965). There apparently is no post-partum estrus in *Hyemoschus* (Dubost, 1968a, 1978) (and the same is true for the blue duiker, von Ketelhodt, 1977). It is not known for all other species of SSFD, but I agree with Lent (1974, p. 42) that it " . . . may be far more widespread than has been reported, especially in the smaller 'primitive tropical forest ungulates . . . ". This adaptation allows a female to have up to two fawns a year (given a gestation of five to seven months and a litter size of one), when she otherwise could have at most slightly more than one (given a lactation anestrus of 3 to 5 months). When climatic and cyclical food abundance patterns do not impose seasonal reproduction, post-partum estrus should therefore be expected. It should for instance be found in all *Tragulus* as well as in *Muntiacus* in the equatorial part of their range, but not in the temperate regions where reproduction is reportedly seasonal (see Barrette, 1977a; Wharton, this volume). Some confirmation of this hypothesis is found in northern musk deer where a post-partum estrus is apparently not found and animals rut in December and give birth in May, after a gestation of 185 days (Bannikov et al., 1978). Of course, if a female is to take advantage of her post–

Table 1. Behavioral ecology of tragulids and small deer

Species	Weight (kg)		Gestation (days)	Litter Size	Postpartum estrus
Tragulus javanicus	♂ =	1.30 (n = 3)[1]		1 (n = 21)[2]	?
	♀ =	1.46 (n = 5)[1]		2 (n = 2)[2]	
Tragulus napu[3]	♂ =	5.8 (n = 1)	155(n = 7)	1 (n = 8)	Yes
	♀ =	5.9 (n = 1)			
Hyemoschus aquaticus	♂ =	9.7 (n = ?)[4]	180(?)[5]	1(? *) (n = 48)[5]	No[5](?)
	♀ =	12.0 (n = ?)[4]			
Muntiacus muntjak	♂ =	20 (n = 6)[6]	224[7]	1 (n = 166)[8]	Yes
	♀ =	15 (n = 3)[6]			
M. reevesi	♂ =	15[9]	215[8,11]	1 (n = 97)[8]	Yes[8,11]
	♀ =	11.6 (n = 19)[10]			
Moschus sibiricus	♂ =	15[15]	185[13]	1.82 (n = 119)[13]	No[13]
	♀ =	12[12]			
Hydropotes inermis	♂ =	11.8 (n = 8)[19]	170[11]	1, 2, 3[15]	?
	♀ =	13.8 (n = 10)			
Mazama americana		20[16]	225[16]	1 (n = 9)[16]	Yes[17]
Mazama gouazoubira[20]	♂ =	10 (n = 1)	206	1 (n = 17)	?
	♀ =	17 (n = 1)			
Pudu puda		10[14,21]	211(n = 5)[21]	1 (n = 28)[18,21]	?

[1]: Nordin 1978, [2]: Hoogerwerf 1970, [3]: Davis 1965, [4]: Dubost 1978, [5]: Dubost 1968a, [6]: Phillips 1935, [7]: Dubost 1971, [8]: Barrette 1977a, [9]: Dansie 1970, [10]: Chapman and Dansie 1970, [11]: Chaplin and Dangerfield 1974, [12]: Green 1978, [13]: Bannikov et al 1978, [14]: Whitehead 1972, [15]: Crandall 1964, [16]: Thomas 1975, [17]: Gardner 1971, [18]: Vanoli 1967, [19]: Whitehead 1950, cited in Bunnell (this symp.), [20]: Frädrich 1974, [21]: Hershkovitz 1982.
*Nowhere does Dubost (1968, 1975, 1978) say that the litter size is 1, but it is suggested by many passages.

partum estrus in any season, she needs a rutting male in the vicinity. Given the very low densities under which these animals live, that would be unlikely if males were in non-reproductive state like other cervids while their antlers are in velvet (about three months each year for muntjacs). As if by design, males can breed even with their antlers in velvet in at least two species of muntjacs (*M. muntjak* and *M. reevesi*: Barrette, 1977a), in the brown brocket (*Mazama gouazoubira*: Frädrich, 1974), as well as in the hog deer (Miller, 1975).

Hyemoschus would thus contradict the above prediction. But Dubost's writings on the subject are not quite as categorical as one would wish; he states (1968a, p. 52): "A female is pregnant for about six months, then nurses her young for two to three months, without apparently being inseminated during that time"; and (1978, p. 52): "Given a gestation lasting from six to nine months and nursing from three to six months accompanied by a lactational anestrus, each sexually mature female can theoretically give birth to one young each year". It is not clear whether these are suppositions or observations.

Also, in at least one muntjac (*M. reevesi*), in addition to post-partum estrus one finds unilateral implantation (Chapman and Dansie, 1969). The same is found in another artiodactyl with post–partum estrus *Adenota kob thomasi*: Morrison and Buechner, 1971. This suggests a hormonal control of ovulation and lactation similar to that of some marsupials (see Renfree, 1981).

Consequences of Knowing So Little

I can identify two consequences of our very limited knowledge on the ecology and behavior of tragulids and small deer. First, it is tempting to assume we know more than we do about SSFD. This is unfortunate because it creates and perpetuates a double-edged notion about SSFD: the notion that one has an adequate knowledge of the behavior and ecology of SSFD, and that all species exhibiting that "adaptive syndrome" are sufficiently similar.

At best, such a notion, by covering holes in our knowledge with suppositions disguised as facts, is not bound to encourage further research. At worst it is a one way avenue to groundless and sterile speculations.

That probably sounds too harsh a criticism, but unfortunately it is deserved. As the examples show, numerous authors have made general statements on one species or a group of species where on examination of the sources apparent facts evaporate.

The second consequence has to do with the evolution of ungulates. I think everyone will agree that if any extant artiodactyl is close to what the first representatives of the order were in the Eocene (Rose, 1982), these must be among the SSF ruminants. The skeleton and dentition of tragulids and muntjacs are very much like those of Miocene ungulates. If social behavior and mating can be inferred from morphology, then extant SSFD are very good living models for understanding the ecology of ancestral forms. It is therefore unfortunate that we know so little of the ecology and behavior of these "living fossils".

As "living fossils" SSFD possess some of the constraints (e.g. small body size, and the possession of a rumen) which shaped their own behavioral adaptations, as well as those of larger and more recent species. Once one has recognized these characters as historical constraints, one can begin to tease apart cause and effect in the gordian knot of correlations that we can see in extant species (i.e. between body size, food habits, social organization, sexual dimorphism, mating system, population density, reproduction strategy, etc., Jarman, 1974). Martin and May (1981) refer to morphological "anchor points" which must be considered to understand behavioral adaptations. Given these "anchor points" one can then move beyond correlations for example by deducing consequences of body size and the possession of a rumen for instance, and then measuring how the animal deals with those consequences (see Brown et al., 1978). Primary and secondary consequences also need to be distinguished. An ambiguous or casual use of language can obscure distinctions and hinder understanding.

An example may clarify this last point. In a recent popular account on the social behavior of mule deer, Kucera (1982, p. 51) states: "Open habitats . . . make living in groups advantageous for many animals." This is not wrong, but it is incomplete. Such "advantages" are only secondary consequences of living in open habitats. First of all, for some reason, the animal lives in an open habitat; this *allows* group living (Barrette, 1977a; Jarman, 1974). Then, secondarily, given a life in open habitats, group-living becomes advantageous: group living, merely permitted by the open habitat, becomes an "exaptation" (Gould and Vbra, 1982) to predation pressure for instance (i.e., selfish herd effect, dilution of risk, greater vigilance for the whole group, reduced individual vigilance: Hamilton, 1971; Bertram, 1980; Elgar and Catterall, 1981). That is how open habitats make group-living advan-

tageous. Therefore, what Kucera says is very reasonable, but it is not formulated clearly with regard to cause and effect.

Conclusion

"Most adaptive explanations . . . are founded initially on comparison" (Clutton-Brock and Harvey (1979, p. 547). Differences are of course what one looks for in making comparisons in order to understand adaptation or function. But since adaptation is most often a matter of fine tuning, or delicate adjustments to environmental conditions, one is more likely to understand function or adaptation when comparing organisms that have a lot in common, but show some subtle differences. I see two consequences to these rather simplified theoretical considerations in respect to SSFD. First, it is probably more fruitful to compare the Javan muntjac for instance to the pygmy antelope than to the musk deer. Being two cervids is probably less important than being two ecologically similar species, even belonging to different families or even orders (Dubost, 1968b). The ecology of the equatorial muntjac is so vastly different from that of the musk deer at the arctic circle as to make comparisons between them only minimally useful. In other words, in attempting to understand the ecology and behavior of tragulids and "morphologically conservative deer" one should make full use of what is known on all duiker-like ruminants (Geist, 1971), as I have attempted here.

The second consequence is that adaptations are best understood when comparing populations of the same species: Here the organisms being compared have everything in common, except that they live in different places and different ecological conditions. That is probably the closest one can come to an ideal experimental situation in nature. There is no problem in finding within a species the variability needed to make comparisons. As seen before, one needs only look at the geographical range of most species of SSFD to realize the wide range of ecological conditions they live in, and therefore their great adaptability. My point here is that it is in studying such intraspecific (or inter-population) adaptability that one is most likely to understand a species' behavioral adaptations to its environment (e.g. MacDonald, 1979; Armitage, 1977; Monfort-Braham, 1975; Kruuk, 1972; Barash, 1973). What one sees then is "adaptation in action" rather than the end product of a long and complex history of successive past adaptations interacting with past morphologies in unknown ecological conditions.

One consequence of the preceding is that conclusions cannot be made about a species' typical ecology and behavior on the basis of studying only one population over a short time (i.e. 1 or 2 years). Harcourt et al. (1981a) have stressed this most cogently concerning the gorilla. The more wide ranging a species, the more adaptable it is likely to be, and the more "atypical" is a study of one population likely to be. This makes any generalizations about the species (and the more so to all SSFD) vulnerable to falsification by a lot of exceptions. But that is only an apparent misfortune; the little that one may loose in immediate description of a species, one is likely to compensate for in deep understanding of how it actually interacts with its environment. As Peter Waser (1975b, p. 34) has said of the bushbuck, much of the interest of the animal " . . . may lie in its adaptability to different habitat types, and the variations which may exist in their social organization". That is certainly true for most species of small solitary forest ruminants, which live in numerous habitat types, over a wide range, and representing what most envision as the primitive artiodactyls' niche (Geist, 1971, 1974; Jarman, 1974; Estes, 1974). These species exhibit a great plasticity and a great capacity to adapt.

All this leads to an obvious conclusion: the future effort, resources and imagination that may be devoted to studying SSFD could be most effectively executed by the same person studying the same things in two or more populations of a given species, and by being attentive to subtle behavioral differences between populations, rather than looking for a single typical set of adaptations for the species. Otherwise, one is not likely to do much more than confirm the general and gross characters that are already known (like small solitary forest ruminants), and that tell us very little of the richness of a species' adaptations or of its capacity to endure diverse conditions.

Literature Cited

Ables, E.D.
1977.   Introduction, In *The Axis deer in Texas*, edited by E.D. Ables, pp. 7–23. College Station, Texas: Kleberg studies in natural resources, Department of Wildlife and Fisheries Sciences, Texas A. and M. University.

Aldrich-Blake, F.P.G.
1970.   Problems of social structure in forest monkeys. In *Social behaviour in birds and mammals*, edited by J. H. Crook, pp. 79–101. New York: Academic Press.

Allen, G.M.
1938–   *The mammals of China and Mongolia.* New York: Ameri-
1940.   can Museum of Natural History.

Allen, R.P.
1952.   The Key deer: a challenge from the past. *Audubon Magazine*, 54(2):76–81.

Anderson, A.E., D.E. Medin, and D.C. Bowden
1974.   Growth and morphometry of the carcass, selected bones, organs and glands of mule deer. *Wildlife Monograph* No. 39.

Armitage, K.B.
1977.   Social variety in the yellow-bellied marmot: A population-behavioral system. *Animal Behaviour*, 25:585–593.

Bannikov, A.G., S.K. Ustinov, and P.N. Lobanov
1978.   The Musk deer *Moschus moschiferus* in USSR. Unpublished report of the IUCN, Morges. 51 pp.

Barash, D.P.
1973.   Social variety in the yellow-bellied marmot (*Marmota flaviventris*). *Animal Behaviour*, 21:579–584.

Barrette, C.
1976.   Musculature of facial scent glands in the muntjac. *Journal of Anatomy*, 122:61–66.

1977a. Some aspects of the behaviour of muntjacs in Wilpattu National Park. *Mammalia*, 41:1–34.

Barrette, C.
1977b. Scent-marking in captive muntjacs, *Muntiacus reevesi*. *Animal Behaviour*, 25:536–541.

Bertram, B.C.
1980.   Vigilance and group size in the ostriches. *Animal Behaviour*, 28:278–286.

Bigalke, R.C.
1974.   Ungulate behaviour and management, with special reference to husbandry of wild ungulates on South African ranches. In *The behaviour of Ungulates and its relation to management*, edited by V. Geist and F. Walther, pp. 830–852. IUCN, N.S. No. 24.: Morges.

Bourlière, F.
1973.   The comparative ecology of rain forest mammals in Africa and tropical America: some introductory remarks. In *Tropical forest ecosystems in Africa and South America: A comparative review*, edited by B.J. Meggers, E.S. Ayensu, and W.D. Duckworth, pp. 279–292. Washington: Smithsonian Institution Press.

Bourlière. F.
1975.   Mammals, small and large: the ecological implications of size. In *Small mammals: their productivity and population dynamics*, edited by F.B.Golley, K. Petrusewicz, and L. Ryszkowski, pp. 1–8. Cambridge: Cambridge University Press.

Bramley, P.S.
1970.   Territoriality and reproductive behaviour of roe deer. *Journal of Reproductive Fertility Supplement*, 11:43–70.

Brokx, P.A.J.
1972.   *A study of the biology of Venezuelan white-tailed deer (Odocoileus virginianus gymnotis), with a hypothesis on the origin of South American cervids.* M.Sc. thesis, Ontario: University of Waterloo.

Brown, J.H., W.A. Calder III, and A. Kodric-Brown
1978. Correlates and consequences of body size in nectar-feeding birds. *American Zoologist*, 18:687–700.

Chaplin, R.E., and G. Dangerfield
1974. Breeding records of muntjac deer (*Muntiacus reevesi*) in captivity. *Journal of Zoology*, 170:150–151.

Chapman, D.I., and O. Dansie
1969. Unilateral implantation in muntjac deer. *Journal of Zoology*, 159:534–536.

1970. Reproduction and foetal development in female muntjac deer (*Muntiacus reevesi* Ogilby). *Mammalia*, 34:303–319.

Clutton-Brock, T.H., S.D. Albon, and P.H. Harvey
1980. Antlers, body size and breeding group size in the Cervidae. *Nature*, 285:565–566.

Clutton-Brock, T.H., and P.H. Harvey
1979. Comparison and adaptation. *Proceedings of the Royal Society of London, Section B (Biological Sciences)*, 205:547–565.

Clutton-Brock, T.H., P.H. Harvey, and B. Rudder
1977. Sexual dimorphism socionomic sex ratio and body weight in primates. *Nature*, 269:797–800.

Crandall, L.S.
1964. *Management of wild mammals in captivity.* Chicago: University of Chicago Press.

Dansie, O.
1970. *Muntjac.* Leeds: British Deer Society.

Dansie, O., and J. Williams
1973. Paraurethral glands in Reeves muntjac deer, *Muntiacus reevesi. Journal of Zoology*, 171:469–470.

Davis, J.A.
1965. A preliminary report of the reproductive behavior of the small Malayan chevrotain, *Tragulus javanicus*, at New York Zoo. *International Zoo Yearbook*, 5:42–44. (It is in fact *T. napu*: see *International Zoo Yearbook*, 7: 405.)

Dinerstein, E.
1980. An ecological survey of the Royal Karnali-Bardia Wildlife reserve, Nepal. Part III : Ungulate populations. *Biological Conservation*, 18:5–38.

Dittus, W.P.J.
1977. The ecology of semi-evergreen forest community in Sri Lanka. *Biotropica*, 9:268–286.

Dubost, G.
1968a. Le rythme annuel de reproduction du chevrotain aquatique, *Hyemoschus aquaticus* Ogilby, dans le secteur forestier du nord-est du Gabon. In *Cycles génitaux saisonniers de mammifères sauvages*, edited by R. Canivenc, pp. 51–65. Paris: Masson.

1968b. Les niches écologiques des forêts tropicales sudaméricaines et africaines, sources de convergences remarquables entre rongeurs et artiodactyles. *Terre et Vie*, 22:3–28.

1970. L'organisation spatiale et sociale de *Muntiacus reevesi* Ogilby 1839 en semi-liberté. *Mammalia*, 34:331–355.

1971. Observations éthologiques sur le Muntjac (*Muntiacus muntjak* et *M. reevesi*) en captivité et semi-liberté. *Zeitschrift für Tierpsychologie*, 28:387–427.

1975. Le comportement du chevrotain africain, *Hyemoschus aquaticus* (Artiodactyla, Ruminantia). Sa signification écologique et phylogénétique. *Zeitschrift für Tierpsychologie*, 37:403–501.

1978. Un aperçu sur l'écologie du chevrotain africain, *Hyemoschus aquaticus* Ogilby, Artiodactyle Tragulidé. *Mammalia*, 42:1–62.

1979. The size of African forest artiodactyls as determined by the vegetation structure. *African Journal of Ecology*, 17:1–17.

1980. L'écologie et la vie sociale du Céphalophe bleu (*Cephalophus monticola* Thunberg), petit ruminant forestier africain. *Zeitschrift für Tierpsychologie*, 54:205–266.

Dunbar, R.I.M., and E.P. Dunbar
1979. Observations on the social organization of common duiker in Ethiopia. *African Journal of Ecology*, 17:249–252.

Egorov, O.V.
1967. *Wild ungulates of Yakutia.* Israel Program for Scientific Translations, Washington D.C.: United States Department of Interior and National Science Foundation.

Eisenberg, J.F., and M. Lockhart
1972. An ecological reconnaissance of Wilpattu National Park, Ceylon. *Smithsonian Contributions to Zoology*, 101:1–118.

Eisenberg, J.F., and G.M. McKay
1974. Comparison of ungulate adaptations in the New World and Old World tropical forests, with special reference to Ceylon and the rainforests of Central America. In *The behaviour of Ungulates and its relation to management*, edited by V. Geist and F. Walther, pp. 585–602. IUCN, New Series No. 24. Morges.

Eisenberg, J.F., and J. Seidensticker
1976. Ungulates in Southern Asia: a consideration of biomass estimates for selected habitats. *Biological Conservation*, 10:298–308.

Elgar, M.A., and C.P. Catterall
1981. Flocking and predator surveillance in house sparrow: test of an hypothesis. *Animal Behaviour*, 29:868–872.

Ellenberg, H.
1978. Zur Populationsökologie des Rehes (*Capreolus capreolus* L., Cervidae) in Mitteleuropa. *Spixiana*, Supplement No. 2:1–211.

Esser, J.D.

1980.   Grouping pattern of ungulates in Benoue National Park and adjacent areas, Northern Cameroon. *Spixiana*, 3:179–191.

Estes, R.D.

1974.   Social organization of the African Bovidae. In *The behaviour of Ungulates and its relation to management*, edited by V. Geist and F. Walther, pp. 166–205. IUCN, N.S. No. 24. Morges.

Feer, F.

1979.   Observations écologiques sur le Néotraque de Bates (*Neotragus batesi* de Winton, 1903, Artiodactyle, Ruminant, Bovidé) du Nord-est du Gabon. *Terre et Vie*, 33:159–239.

Fleming, T.H.

1979.   Do tropical frugivores compete for food? *American Zoologist*, 19:1157–1172.

Flerov, K.K.

1952.   *Fauna of the U.S.S.R. Mammals–Musk Deer and Deer* (Vol. 1, no. 2) Moscow, Academy of Sciences of the USSR. Israel Program for Scientific Translations.

Flook, D.R.

1970.   A study of sex differential in the survival of Wapiti. *Canadian Wildlife Service Report series* No. 11.

Frädrich, H.

1974.   Notizen über seltener gehaltene Cerviden Teil 1. *Zoologische Garten*, 44:189–200.

Franzman, A.W., R.E. LeResche, R.A. Rausch, and J.L. Oldemeyer

1978.   Alaskan moose measurements and weights and measurement- weight relationships. *Canadian Journal of Zoology*, 56:298–306.

Gardner, A.L.

1971.   Postpartum estrus in a red brocket deer, *Mazama americana*, from Peru. *Journal of Mammalogy*, 42:623–624.

Gauthier-Hion, A., L.H. Emmons, and G. Dubost

1980.   A comparison of the diets of three major groups of primary consumers of Gabon (Primates, Squirrels and Ruminants). *Oecologia*, 45:182–189.

Geist, V.

1971.   The relation of social evolution and dispersal in ungulates during the Pleistocene, with emphasis on the Old World Deer and the genus *Bison*. *Quarternary Research*, 1:285–315.

1974.   On the relationship of social evolution and ecology in ungulates. *American Zoologist*, 14:205–220.

Gould, S.J., and E.S. Vbra

1982.   Exaptation, a missing term in the science of form. *Paleobiology*, 8:4–15.

Green, M.J.B.

1978.   Himalayan musk deer (*Moschus moschiferus moschiferus*). In *Proceedings of a Working Meeting of the Deer Specialist Group of the Survival Service Commission*, pp. 56-64. Morges, Switzerland: International Union for the Conservation of Nature.

Groves, C.P.

1975.   The taxonomy of *Moschus* (Mammalia, Artiodactyla), with particular reference to the Indian region. *Journal of the Bombay Natural History Society*, 72:662–676.

Grubb, P.

1976   Notes on a rare deer, *Muntiacus feai*. *Annali del Museo*
–77.   *Civico di Storia Naturale 'Giacomo Doria'*, 81:202–207.

Haltenorth, T.

1963.   Klassifikation der Säugetiere: Artiodactyla. *Handbuch der Zoologie*, Band 8, Leiferung 32; 1(18):1–167.

Hamilton, W.D.

1971.   Geometry for the selfish herd. *Journal of Theoretical Biology*, 31:295—311.

Harcourt, A.H., D. Fossey, and J. Sabater-Pi

1981a.   Demography of *Gorilla gorilla*. *Journal of Zoology*, 195:215-233.

Harcourt, A.H., P.H.H. Harvey, S.G. Larson, and R.V. Short

1981b.   Testis weight, body weight and breeding system in primates. *Nature*, 293:55–57.

Hendrichs, H., and V. Hendrichs

1971.   *Dikdik und Elefanten*. München: Piper and Company.

Hershkovitz, P.

1982.   Neotropical deer (Cervidae). Part I. Pudus, genus *Pudu* Gray. *Fieldiana, Zoology*, N.S., No. 11.

Hladik, C.M., and A. Hladik

1972.   Disponibiltiés alimentaires et domaines vitaux des Primates á Ceylan. *La Terrre et la Vie*, 26:149–215.

Hofmann, R.R., and D.R.M. Stewart

1972.   Grazer or browser: a classification based on the stomach structure and feeding habits of East-African ruminants. *Mammalia*, 36:226–240.

Hoogerwerf, A.

1970.   *Udjung Kulon, the land of the last Javan Rhinoceros*. Leiden: E.J. Brill.

Huot, J.

1973.   Le cerf de Virginie au Québec. Service Faune Québec. Bulletin Number 17.

Jackson, J.E., D.I. Chapman, and O. Dansie

1977.   A note on the food of muntjac deer (*Muntiacus reevesi*). *Journal of Zoology*, 183:546–548.

Janis, C.

1976.   The evolutionary strategy of the Equidae and the origins of rumen and cecal digestion. *Evolution*, 30:757–774.

Jarman, P.J.

1974.   The social organization of antelope in relation to their ecology. *Behaviour*, 48:215–267.

Ketelhodt, H.F. von
1977. The lambing interval of the blue duiker, *Cephalophus monticola* Gray, in captivity, with observations on its breeding and care. *South African Journal of Wildlife Research*, 7:41–43.

Kleiman, D.G.
1977. Monogamy in mammals. Quarterly Review of Biology, 52:39–69.

Kruuk, H.
1972. *The spotted hyena: a study of predation and social behavior.* Chicago: University of Chicago Press.

Kucera, T.E.
1982. How mule deer mate in Texas. *Natural History,* 91(6):50–57.

Kurt, F.
1978. Socio-ecological organization and aspects of management in South Asian deer. *Proceedings of a Working Meeting of the Deer Specialist Group of the Survival Service Commission,* International Union for the Conservation of Nature, Morges, Switzerland. pp. 219–239.

Leader-Williams, N.
1980. Population ecology of Reindeer on South-Georgia. In *Proceedings of the Second International Reindeer/ Caribou Symposium,* edited by E. Reimers, E. Gaare, and S. Skenneberg, pp. 664–676. Trondheim: Direktoratet for Vilt og Ferskvannsfisk.

Lent, P.C.
1974. Mother-infant relationships in Ungulates. In *The behaviour of Ungulates and its relation to management,* edited by V. Geist and F. Walther, pp. 14–55. IUCN N.S. No. 24. Morges.

MacDonald, D.W.
1979. The flexible social system of the golden jackal, *Canis aureus. Behavioral Ecology and Sociobiology,* 5:17–38.

Martin, R.D., and R.M. May
1981. Outward signs of breeding. *Nature,* 293:7–9.

McEwan, E.H.
1968. Growth and development of the barren-ground caribou. II. Postnatal growth rates. *Canadian Journal of Zoology,* 46:1023–1029.

Miller, R.
1975. Notes on the behaviour of hog deer in an enclosure. *Natural History Bulletin of the Siam Society,* 26:105–131.

Mitani, J.C., and P.S. Rodman
1979. Territoriality: The relation of ranging pattern and home range size to defendability, with an analysis of territoriality among primate species. *Behavioral Ecology and Sociobiology,* 5:241–251.

Mitchell, B., D. McCowan, and J.A. Nicholson
1976. Annual cycles of body weight and condition in Scottish red deer, *Cervus elaphus. Journal of Zoology,* 180:107–127.

Monfort, A., and N. Monfort
1974. Notes sur l'écologie et le comportement des Oribis (*Ourebia ourebi* Zimmerman 1783). *Terre et Vie,* 28:169–208.

Monfort-Braham, N.
1975. Variation dans la structure sociale du topi, *Damaliscus korrigum* Ogilby, au Parc National de l'Akagera, Rwanda. *Zeitschrift für Tierpsychologie,* 39:332–364.

Morrison, J.A., and H.K. Buechner
1971. Reproductive phenomena during the post partum-preconception interval in the Uganda Kob. *Journal of Reproduction and Fertility,* 26:307–317.

Nordin, M.
1978. Voluntary food intake and digestion by the lesser mouse deer. *Journal of Wildlife Management,* 42:185–187.

Owen-Smith, N.
1977. On territoriality in ungulates and an evolutionary model. *Quarterly Review of Biology,* 51:1–52.

Peterson, R.L.
1974. A review of the general life history of moose. *Naturaliste canadien,* 101:9–21.

Pfeffer, P.
1969. Considérations sur l'écologie des forêts claires du Cambodge oriental. *Terre et Vie,* 23:3–24.

Phillips, W.W.A.
1935. *Manual of the mammals of Ceylon.* London: Dulau and Company, Ltd.

Prothero, D.R., and P.C. Sereno
1982. Allometry and paleoecology of middle Miocene dwarf rhinoceroses from the Texas Gulf coastal plain. *Paleobiology,* 8:16–30.

Ralls, K.
1976. Mammals in which females are larger than males. *Quarterly Review of Biology,* 51:245–276.

1977. Sexual dimorphism in mammals: avian models and unanswered questions. *American Naturalist,* 111:917–938.

Renfree, M.B.
1981. Marsupials: alternative mammals. *Nature,* 293:100–101.

Robbins, C.T., and B.L. Robbins
1979. Fetal and neonatal growth patterns and maternal reproductive effort in ungulates and subungulates. *American Naturalist,* 114:101–116.

Robinette, W.L., N.V. Hancock, and D.A. Jones
1977. *The Oak Creek mule deer herd in Utah.* Resource Publication 77–15. Salt Lake City: Utah Division of Wildlife.

Rose, K.D.
1982.   Skeleton of *Diacodexis*, oldest known Artiodactyl. *Science*, 216:621–623.

Seidensticker, J.
1976.   Ungulate populations in Chitawan Valley, Nepal. *Biological Conservation*, 10:183–210.

Sheng, H., and H. Lu
1980.   Current studies on the rare Chinese black muntjac. *Journal of Natural History*, 14:803–807.

Short, R.V.
1979.   Sexual selection and its component parts, somatic and genital selection, as illustrated by man and the great apes. *Advances in the Study of Behavior*, 9:131–158.

Sokolov, V.E., and V.I. Prikhodko
1979.   Marking of territory by caudal gland of male musk deer. *Doklady Biological Sciences*, 246:894–897.

Sunquist, M.E.
1981.   The social organization of tigers (*Panthera tigris*) in Royal Chitawan National Park, Nepal. *Smithsonian Contributions to Zoology*, 336:1–98.

Thomas, W.D.
1975.   Observations on captive brockets. *International Zoo Yearbook*, 15:77–78.

Underwood, R.
1982.   Seasonal changes in African ungulate groups. *Journal of Zoology*, 196:191–205.

van Bemmel, A.C.V.
1952.   Contribution to the knowledge of the genera *Muntiacus* and *Arctogalidia* in the Indo-Australian archipelago. *Beaufortia*, 16:1–50.

Vanoli, T.
1967.   Beobachtungen an Pudus. *Säugetierkundliche Mitteilungen*, 15:155–163.

Walker, E.P.
1975.   *Mammals of the World*. 3rd ed. Vol. 2. Baltimore: Johns Hopkins University Press.

Walther, F.R.
1978.   Mapping the structure of the marking system of a territory of the Thomson's gazelle. *East African Wildlife Journal*, 16:167–176.

Waser, P.
1975a. Diurnal and nocturnal strategies of the bushbuck *Tragelaphus scriptus* (Pallas). *East African Wildlife Journal*, 13:49–63.

1975b. Spatial associations and social interactions in a "solitary" ungulate: the bushbuck *Tragelaphus scriptus* (Pallas). *Zeitschrift für Tierpsychologie*, 37:24–36.

1981.   Sociability or territorial defense? The influence of resource renewal. *Behavioral Ecology and Sociobiology*, 8:231–237.

Western, D.
1979.   Size, life history and ecology in mammals. *African Journal of Ecology*, 17:185–204.

Whitehead, G.K.
1972.   *Deer of the World*. London: Constable.

Wilson, V.J.
1966.   Notes on the food and feeding habits of the common duiker, *Sylvicapra grimmia* in Eastern Zambia. *Arnoldia*, 2(14):1–19.

Yahner, R.H.
1980.   Time budgets in captive Reeve's muntjacs (*Muntiacus reevesi*). *Applied Animal Ethology*, 6:277–284.

R.N.B. KAY
Rowett Research Institute
Bucksburn
Aberdeen AB2 9SB
Scotland

The Comparative Anatomy and Physiology of Digestion in Tragulids and Cervids and Its Relation to Food Intake

ABSTRACT

The digestive anatomy and physiology of deer is reviewed in relation to nutrition. The tragulids, though not strictly deer, are of interest in that they retain characteristics that seem primitive, as do the true deer, and show how the ruminant mode of digestion can be practiced by a very small animal. Digestive function in the cervids is next considered, starting with the teeth. Animals must adapt to annual cycles of climate and forage growth by readily changing from diets that are plentiful and rich to those that are scarce and poor. Deer show a pattern of adaptations, cued by day length, that include a remarkable seasonal cycle of metabolism, growth and apetite. Ruminants can be classified, according to their feeding habits and gut anatomy, as concentrate selectors, roughage eaters, or adaptable intermediate forms. Deer belong mainly to the selectors and the adaptable category.

The nature of ruminal fermentation in deer depends on their diet and resembles that seen in farm ruminants given comparable foods. However, deer tend to digest dry matter and fiber rather less well than sheep or cattle, evidently as the result of the more rapid passage of food through their gut. In some species the large intestine is well developed, perhaps compensating for incomplete digestion of food in the rumen.

Many of the larger species of deer are now being subjected to domestication, and this will encourage the advance in our understanding of the biology of these attractive animals.

Introduction

The success of deer as ruminants is second only to that of the bovids. Deer account for 41 of the 176 species of the Ruminantia (Morris, 1965), and they range in size from the 6 kg pudu (*Pudu mephistophiles*) to the 700 kg moose (*Alces alces*). They occupy habitats as diverse as tundra and tropical forest, mountain and reed bed, consuming forages as unusual as lichens and swamp plants.

Many deer are well able to adapt to changes of diet and food intake and so are fitted to areas showing sharp seasonal cycles in the quality and availability of forage. Species taken into captivity and the red deer (*Cervus elaphus*), rusa deer (*C. timorensis*), sika (*C. nippon*) and fallow (*Dama dama*) now being domesticated as farm animals have shown that they can thrive when confined almost wholly to grass diets. On the whole, however, wild deer have tended to be rather conservative, preferring the forests and browsing habits of the early ruminants and leaving the grass plains that developed subsequently to be exploited largely by the bovids. Arid areas are also shunned by most deer. Experiments on red deer given a hay diet with restricted amounts of drinking water showed that their appetites began to fall earlier and more seriously than sheep on the same regimen, and that the deer were unable to concentrate their urine or dessicate their feces as effectively as the sheep when both had lost 10–15% of body weight (Maloiy, 1968).

Tragulidae

While the tragulids are not at all closely related to the cervids, they provide an instructive introduction to a study of deer. Not only do they also retain many primitive characteristics and habits, but these little forest creatures show how a ruminant may tackle the demanding nutritional requirements of a small animal. The smallest of them all is the lesser Malay mouse deer (*Tragulus javanicus*) which has been carefully studied in captivity by Nordin and his colleagues in Kuala Lumpur.

The lesser mouse deer is a solitary, nocturnal animal, feeding on nutritious but widely dispersed fruit, leaves and shoots. In captivity the deer were given diets of peanuts, beans, fruit, kangkong leaves and maize (Nordin, 1978a). They spent only a short time ruminating these rich, low-fiber diets (52–73 min/d); the digestibility of dry matter (DM) was high 90.8–92.4 g/100 g), and the time during which a dose of chromic oxide was retained in the gut was short (42.7–45.0 h). In another experiment (Nordin, 1978b) the voluntary intake of a diet of peanuts and kangkong leaves was 33.4 g DM daily, and DM digestibility was 87.9 g/100 g. This was enough to maintain body weight in animals weighing about 1.4 kg. Assuming the digestible energy content of the diet's organic matter to be 2.4 kcal/g, Nordin (1978b) calculated digestible energy intake to average 59.8 kcal/d or 45.6 kcal/kg metabolic body weight ($kg^{0.75}$) daily. Such a surprisingly low value, viewed alongside rather low plasma values for thyroid hormones (Kamis, 1980), might indicate that the mouse deer has a low metabolic rate, thus avoiding the need for a high food intake that is the rule for small mammals with fasting metabolic rates near to the mean value of 70 $kcal/kg^{.75}$ (Kleiber, 1981). However, the metabolizable energy content of peanuts (digestible energy less the energy content of urine and methane) is about 5.04 kcal/g (ADAS, 1976). If the peanuts component of the diet is given a more realistic value of 5.8 kcal digestible energy/g DM, the food intake of the mouse deer will have provided some 127 kcal/d or 91 $kcal/kg^{.75}$, more nearly approaching the value of about 1.5 times fasting metabolic rate expected in penned mammals maintaining body weight. This would imply that, like other small ruminants, the mouse deer has high energy requirements/kg body weight, which must be met by selection of a very digestible diet allowing rapid fermentation and swift passage through the gut.

The stomach of mouse deer shows a number of supposedly primitive features. The rumen is S-shaped, the dorso-caudal sac being inconspicuous while the ventro-caudal sac is very large. Rumen pillars are poorly developed, and so may do little to selectively prolong the retention of fiber. The omasum is absent, or nearly so, a very small portion of the anterior end of the abomasum being all that could possibly be regarded as the rudiment or vestige of a omasum (M. Nordin, pers. comm.).

The other three species of tragulids are considerably heavier than *T. javanicus* weighing about 4–8 kg. They are therefore in the weight range of the smallest of the cervids (*P. mephistophiles*) and bovids (the dik-dik, *Madoqua* spp, and the suni, *Nesotragus moschatus*).

Cervidae

Before discussing the function of the gastrointestinal tract it is appropriate to briefly consider the teeth. The dental formula of the cervids is: incisors $^{0}/_{3}$, canines $^{1}/_{1}$, premolars $^{3}/_{3}$, molars $^{3}/_{3}$. As in the bovids the three lower incisors and the incisiform canine bite against the anterior edge of the dental pad. The upper canine, absent in bovids, is present in many deer. In some smaller species with little or no antler growth, such as the musk deer (*Moschus moschiferus*), this canine grows into a long tusk, especially in the male, that proves an effective weapon. I can find no report of the tusk being used to obtain food, and even when it does not project from the mouth, as in red deer, it seems badly placed,

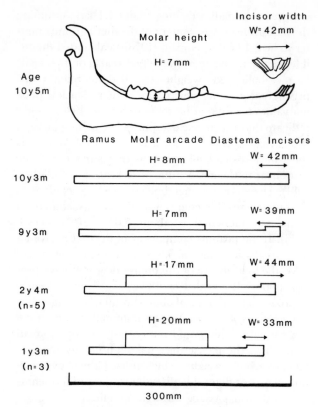

Figure 1. Changes with age in the mandible and teeth of red deer stags (dimensions taken from x-ray film).

opposite the toothless diastema of the mandible, to be of much use in chewing.

In red deer the permanent teeth have usually all erupted by the age of 27 months, when the animal is little more than half grown. Their sequence of eruption, their subsequent wear and annual rings in the dental cement can conveniently be used to age the animal (Lowe, 1967; Mitchell, 1967). After 2 years of age, as shown in Figure 1, there is no extension of the length of the molar arcade or of the width of the incisor arcade; if anything, these dimensions decrease slightly as the crowns of the teeth wear down. However, food intake nears its upper limit at an even earlier stage of growth, and the decreasing requirement for growth balances the increasing maintenance requirement as the animal approaches its mature size. Thus no increase in mastication is needed after the deer is half grown. None the less, growth of the mandible continues until the animal is about 6 years old leading to lengthening of the diastema and of the ramus of the jaw. As a consequence, although bite width does not increase with age, the length of the mouth and the gape of the jaw during feeding do increase. This conceivably allows the deer to take in

more food at each bite, but at the expense of selection for the most nutritious parts of the plant.

The stags whose teeth are illustrated in Figure 1 were from the experimental deer farm at Glensaugh in Scotland, and had grazed natural hill vegetation, mainly heather and grass, supplemented with some hay in winter. Their teeth were in excellent condition and showed no sign of the shedding of incisor teeth ("broken mouth") that is a serious problem among the sheep at Glensaugh. However, about two-thirds of the crowns of the molars had worn away by 10 years of age, and it seems likely that further wear will soon lead to dental problems. The teeth of wild red deer in Scotland also are usually healthy and are subject to a similar rate of wear. The greater frequency of tooth abnormality and disease found in wild red deer dying of natural causes than in those that are shot suggests that tooth disease contributes significantly to mortality (Mitchell, McCowan and Parish, 1971). A similar conclusion was reached by Leader-Williams (1980) in a study of the dental abnormalities that are prevalent among the reindeer (*Rangifer tarandus*) of South Georgia.

Food Intake and Season

Digestive function depends not only on the anatomy and physiology of the gut but also on the quality and quantity of food that is consumed. The quality depends on what the deer selects from the food available and the quantity, provided there is no serious shortage of forage, on its appetite.

Deer living in tropical and subtropical regions are not likely to have to deal with marked seasonal changes in their food supply, since they are mainly animals of forest and thicket and avoid seriously arid regions. Deer of higher latitudes, however, must adapt to the annual cycle of climate and consequent changes in the quality and availability of their forage. Most species, using day length as their cue, time the breeding season so that the young are born in early summer; as a result the nutritional requirements of late pregnancy, lactation, early calf growth, antler growth and improvement in condition before the rut, can all be met when good food is plentiful. The roe deer (*Capreolus capreolus*) also practices delayed implantation to achieve this end. Many deer molt and grow coats appropriate to the season.

The annual cycle of plant growth and dormancy is associated with clear changes in foraging behavior, sometimes with movement from one habitat to another as in the migration of caribou from open tundra to forest at the onset of winter. It is also associated with a seasonal variation in body weight, of as much as 30%, much of it due to the deposition of fat reserves

R.N.B. Kay

during summer and their mobilization during the rut or during late winter, as is seen in red deer whether wild (Mitchell et al., 1976) or farmed (Blaxter et al., 1974; Moore and Brown, 1977). Such effects have been reported also in mule deer (*Ococoileus hemionus*) (Wood et al., 1962; Bandy et al., 1970), white-tailed deer (*O. virginianus*) (Cowan and Long, 1962) reindeer (McEwan and Whitehead, 1970), moose (Gasaway and Coady, 1974) and roe deer (Drożdż et al., 1975). In many cases as in white-tailed deer (Cowan and Long, 1962) and in red deer (Kay, 1979), the changes in body weight and food intake are not a passive consequence of food availability for they are seen also in penned animals receiving a standard diet to appetite throughout the year. As with reproductive cycles, day length serves as the entraining stimulus of this growth and appetite cycle (Kay, 1979).

A number of hormonal and metabolic changes, including in white-tailed deer a decline in fasting metabolic rate and maintenance requirement during winter (Silver et al., 1969; Holter et al., 1977), are linked to the growth and reproductive cycles to form a complex and deep-rooted physiological adaptation to the annual cycle of abundance and scarcity of food. In many breeds of farm animals, this adaptation seems to have been reduced by selection for year-round productivity (reproduction, growth potential and wool production). In white-tailed deer Moen (1978) has integrated information on metabolism, heart rate and activity into the wider concept of an annual cycle of "ecological metabolism".

Stomach Anatomy

In 1973 Hofmann published his stimulating morphological study of the stomachs of 28 of the ruminants of East Africa. The species were divided into three major groups, according to feeding habit and stomach anatomy: the concentrate selectors, mainly browsers, the bulk and roughage eaters, mainly grazers, and an intermediate group notable for ability to adapt to seasonally changing pasture and to the nutritional opportunities of a varied habitat. By 1979 the list of species so classified could be considerably enlarged (Kay et al., 1980); a number of deer were now included, though none appeared to be wholeheartedly grazing animals.

Recently Hofmann (1982) has again reviewed the position. He emphasizes that each feeding group contains both small and large animals, though the very smallest species will not be able to meet their high energy requirements from a coarse roughage diet. Among the cervids the concentrate selectors include both the largest, the moose, as well as small deer such as muntjac (*Muntiacus* spp.) and roe. Many of the trop-ical and subtropical deer, to judge by their forest or riverine habitat and their preference for fruit and nuts, succulent browse and young grass, are concentrate selectors though detailed anatomical studies have yet to be made. Forest deer of temperate and boreal regions such as white-tailed deer are clearly established in this group. The roe is a characteristic concentrate selector, with large salivary glands, a small and evenly papillated rumen with poorly developed pillars that allow homogeneous distribution and rapid egress of fibrous matter, a small omasum with a few laminae and a small abomasum (Hofmann, 1982). Other species of deer belong to the intermediate and adaptable group. These include the many preferring the mixed habitat of the forest edge, such as fallow, sika and red deer. They have relatively smaller salivary glands (Kay et al., 1980), and their stomach, as typified by the Roosevelt elk (*C. canadensis*) (Church and Hines, 1978), shows well developed ruminal compartments divided by strong pillars, papillae that are longest in the ventral parts of the compartments indicating non-homogeneous distribution of digesta, and a proportionately larger omasum and abomasum than is seen in roe. Roe, fallow and red deer provide a well-graded sequence of stomach anatomy, digestive function and dietary habit from concentrate selector to intermediate feeder with some characteristics of a grazer (Prins and Geelen, 1971; Nagy and Regelin, 1975; Hofmann, et al., 1976; Drescher-Kaden, 1976). Studies by White and his colleagues on Alaskan reindeer and caribou indicate they are also intermediate feeders with a preference for forbs, deciduous shrubs such as willow, and lichens (White and Trudell, 1980); they must also adapt to a sharp alternation of summer and winter diets. A characteristically high bite rate relative to cattle and sheep, and a small bite size were thought to facilitate forage selection (Trudell and White, 1981).

While to some extent adaptations of the digestive tract to diet must have a genetic basis, fitting each species to a more or less restrictive range of dietary niches and so encouraging complementary feeding habits, it is also evident that the gut readily adapts anatomically and functionally to the nature of the diet that the animal chooses or is constrained to eat. Careful controlled feeding experiments are needed to distinguish between the two forms of adaptation.

Digestion of Food in the Reticulo-Rumen

Many authors have studied fermentation rate and fermentation products in the rumen contents of wild deer, using both in vivo and in vitro methods. Fermentation rate, pH and the concentrations and proportions of volatile fatty acids depend on the intake and digestibility of food, though fermentation may also be inhibited by the presence of secondary compounds in the vegetation such as tannins or essential oils (Oh et al., 1968). The rumen microbial population of different species of deer reflects feeding habit. White-tailed deer living in forests in Texas have a rich diet for much of the year, forbs being important in spring, mushrooms in summer and acorns in autumn, and at these times there was a fairly close acetate:propionate ratio, 2 : 1, in their rumen content, typical of a concentrate diet, whereas in winter the ratio lengthens to 4 : 1 (Short, 1971). The nutritious diet selected by roe deer also results in a close acetate : propionate ratio, associated with high amylolytic activity, low pH and a scarcity or absence of ciliate protozoa; the rumen contents of less-selective red deer are characterised by a more divergent acetate : propionate ratio, high cellulolytic activity, high pH and a numerous and varied population of ciliates, while fallow deer occupy an intermediate position (Brüggemann et al., 1965; Prins and Geelen, 1971).

Reindeer eating lichens in winter have a plentiful population of ciliates. In feeding trials on reindeer Jacobsen and Skjenneberg (1976) showed that the digestibility of the organic matter of lichens was high, 74.9%, despite the low nitrogen content of this peculiar diet, and was depressed by addition of supplements of cereals or meals. Like domestic ruminants, caribou (Wales et al., 1975) and white-tailed deer (Robbins et al., 1974) have been shown to be able to recycle a large proportion of the urea they produce to the gut, so supplementing the ammonia available for rumen microbial growth and activity when dietary nitrogen is in short supply. The rumen microbes of reindeer evidently adapt specifically to the unusual forages consumed, for when studying the digestion of lichens or mosses in vitro it was found that greater digestibility was achieved when inocula of rumen contents were taken from animals receiving the appropriate diet (Trudell et al., 1980). Hobson and his colleagues (Hobson et al., 1976a, b) found that sheep, red deer and reindeer grazing Scottish hills but consuming different diets had differing rumen microbial populations and digestive characteristics. However, in a comparison of digestion in penned rumen-fistulated sheep and red deer fed identical diets of hay or dried grass, Maloiy and Kay (1971) found that rumen pH and the concentrations of volatile fatty acids and ammonia differed between diets but were closely similar in the two ruminant species.

Thus in species that do not differ very greatly in size or feeding habit, such as sheep and red deer, the rumen digestive process depends more on the food consumed than on the anatomical and physiological peculiarities of their digestive tracts. Between animals of

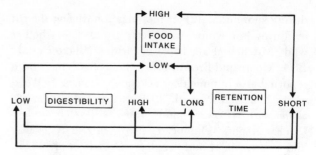

Figure 2.   Relationships between the intake, retention time and digestibility of food in the ruminant gut.

more disparate size and habit, animal factors are likely to create greater differences in the nature and duration of ruminal digestion of standard diets, though the evidence for this emerges from studies of the bovids rather than the cervids (Kay et al., 1980). Rumen fermentative digestion and its end-products are dependent on rumen pH, which in turn is buffered by the secretion of alkaline saliva supported by selective absorption of VFA in their acid form, while the extent to which fiber is digested is affected not only by the acid-sensitive cellulolytic flora but also by the time rumen contents are retained for digestion. In concentrate selectors such as roe deer salivary glands are larger than in grazing animals (Kay et al., 1980), and so provide the additional buffering capacity and promote the more rapid fluid turnover required for efficient digestion of their rich diet, while rumen papillae are better developed and more uniformly distributed, so increasing absorptive area (Hofmann, 1982).

Retention of Food Residues in the Gut

Retention in the capacious forestomach accounts for much of the characteristically long time that food is retained in the digestive tract of ruminants. Cellulose and hemicellulose are much more resistant to fermentation than sugars or starch and so the digestibility of fiber depends not only on the activity of cellulolytic microbes and on how well the fiber has been pulped during feeding and rumination but also on the length of time the fiber is held in the rumen. Coarse food or roughage tends to be confined in the rumen by the rumen pillars and reticulo-rumen fold, continually kneaded and turned by rumen contractions until it is reduced by maceration and microbial attack to a particle size that can be carried through the reticulo-omasal orifice in the rapid flow of fluid passing to the omasum and abomasum. The succulent, easily digested food consumed by the concentrate selectors, on the other hand, passes rapidly through the fore-

R.N.B. Kay

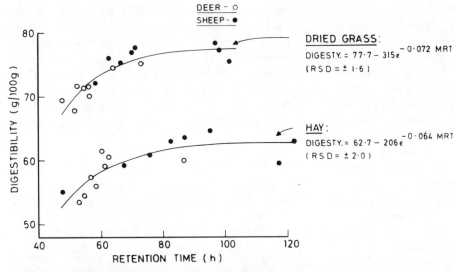

Figure 3. Relationship between mean retention time and dry matter digestibility for diets of dried grass and hay given to female sheep and red deer at controlled levels.

stomach giving much less opportunity for digestion of fiber (Kay et al., 1980).

The relationships between food intake, retention time and digestibility at any particular rumen volume are summarized in Figure 2. If food intake is increased, retention time must fall and with it digestibility. Conversely if retention time is shortened, as by more vigorous propulsion, by reduction in anatomical structures delaying the flow of fibre, or by ingestion of a rapidly degraded or finely macerated diet, food intake may increase. An increase in rumen capacity will give an added dimension to these relationships, allowing greater food intake without a corresponding reduction in retention time and digestibility, but this will add to the burden the animal must carry.

In controlled feeding trials it has been shown that both in white-tailed deer (Short, 1963) and in red deer (Maloiy and Kay, 1971), standard diets are less well digested in deer than in cattle or sheep, and that this is associated with more rapid passage of food through the gut (Mautz and Petrides, 1971; Kay and Goodall, 1976; Milne, et al., 1978). In Kay and Goodall's experiment (1976), the digestibility of dry matter and of cellulose in roughage diets was about 5 percentage units less in red deer than in sheep; however, the relationship between digestibility and retention time did not differ between the two species (Figure 3), suggesting that food retention was indeed the principal factor accounting for the differences in digestibility. Similar results were obtained by Milne et al. (1978) who compared voluntary intake, digestibility and retention time in red deer and sheep given standard diets of

dried grass, moorland grasses or heather harvested in late summer. The intake of the moorland vegetation by the deer was about twice that of the sheep, on a body weight (kg^0.75) basis. A sharp increase in intake was seen between January and April, especially in the deer. Curiously this was not accompanied by any consistent decline in digestibility, suggesting that a compensatory enlargement of the gut may have occurred between winter and spring.

Ruminal contractions in white-tailed deer (Dziuk, Fashingbauer and Idstrom, 1963) and in red deer (Maloiy, 1968) resemble those recorded in sheep and cattle but tend to be more frequent. The swift passage of food residues in deer may thus be due in part to more active propulsive movements though more efficient maceration or reduced resistance to fiber flow may also be concerned. Although a reduction in digestibility is obviously disadvantageous in itself, rapid elimination of food residues enables an animal to consume large amounts of poorer quality food when the need arises, increased intake more than compensating for decreased digestibility. Besides, rapid flow may be associated with over-riding benefits such as an increased passage of undegraded dietary protein to the abomasum and intestine.

Intestinal Digestion

In his recent review Hofmann (1982) extends his comparison of ruminants having selective or unselective feeding habits to include consideration of the anatomy of the intestines. In concentrate selectors such as the roe deer the small intestine tends to be relatively short

(70–73% of total intestine length) and the large intestine is quite capacious (about one tenth the volume of the reticulo-rumen). The large intestine thus provides for fermentation of some of the fiber that readily escapes ruminal digestion in this group. Roughage eaters show the reverse tendencies, the small intestine accounting for 81–82% of total intestine length and the large intestine having but one thirtieth of the volume of the reticulo-rumen. Mule deer (*O. hemionus*) are not concentrate selectors by this definition for Allo et al. (1973) found that the weight and fermentation product of the contents of the large intestine resembled that found in sheep, amounting to only about 5% of that of the reticulo-rumen contents. Reindeer with their unusual habits prove difficult to fit into this pattern. While they are certainly not concentrate selectors, the large intestine is exceptionally long, forming 34–40% of total intestine length in animals from Norway and Svalbard (Staaland et al., 1979). The diet of these reindeer includes large amounts of moss of low digestibility, and the authors suggest the great size of the large intestine will encourage more complete digestion of the poor diet and will also allow more complete absorption of water and salts.

No review of the function and anatomy of the digestive tract of deer is complete without mention of the curious case of the missing gall bladder. It has been known since the time of Aristotle that, in common with an assortment of other animals, deer lack a gall bladder. However, though the closely related giraffe (*Giraffa camelopardis*) shares this characteristic, musk deer (*Moschus moschiferus*) do not (Walker, 1964). As Thomas Browne (1650) pointed out at some length, after correcting Aristotle's list, it does not follow that because deer have no gall bladder they do not produce bile. As far as is known the bile secreted by the otherwise apparently normal biliary system plays its full digestive and excretory roles.

Domestication of Deer

In northern regions, nomadic tribes of man have for millenia had an almost symbiotic relationship with the reindeer, but other cervids were regarded rather as animals of the chase. Now, all of a sudden, there has been a remarkable upsurge of interest in the possibility of exploiting deer as meat producing animals. Père David's deer (*Elaphurus davidianus*) should perhaps be regarded as a long-domesticated species. Foremost among those heading for new domestication is the red deer (Blaxter et al., 1974; Drew, 1976; Kay, 1981), but others proving amenable to intensive management are fallow, sika, rusa and wapiti (*C. e. canadensis*). Some deer, such as the moose (Yazan and Knorre, 1964), are managed essentially in their wild

state so as to gain most benefit from their adaptation to their natural habitat in a low cost system. Others, such as the red deer, are now farmed on improved pastures where they must prove their worth in competition with conventional domestic animals. These developing husbandry practices will both require and provoke rapid advances in our knowledge of the biology and productive potential of many species of deer.

Literature Cited

Agricultural Development and Advisory Service
1976. *Nutrient Allowances and Composition of Feedingstuffs for Ruminants.* ADAS Advisory Paper No. 11. London: Ministry of Agriculture, Fisheries and Food.

Allo, A.A., J.H. Oh, W.M. Longhurst, and G.E. Connolly
1973. VFA production in the digestive systems of deer and sheep. *Journal of Wildlife Management,* 37:202–211.

Bandy, P.J., I.McT. Cowan, and A.J. Wood
1970. Comparative growth in four races of black-tailed deer (*Odocoileus hemionus*). I. Growth in body weight. *Canadian Journal of Zoology,* 48:1401–1410.

Blaxter, K.L., R.N.B. Kay, G.A.M. Sharman, J.M.M. Cunningham, and W.J. Hamilton
1974. *Farming the Red Deer.* Edinburgh: Her Majesty's Stationery Office.

Browne, T.
1650. *Pseudodoxia Epidemica: or Enquiries into very many Received Tenets and commonly Presumed Truths.* London: A. Miller.

Brüggeman, J., D. Giesecke, and K. Kärst
1965. Untersuchungen am Pansinhalt van Reh- und Rotwild. *Transactions of the Congress of the International Union of Game Biologists,* 6:139–144.

Church, D.C., and W.H. Hines
1978. Ruminoreticular characteristics of elk. *Journal of Wildlife Management,* 42:654–659.

Cowan, R.L., and T.A. Long
1962. Studies on antler growth and nutrition of white-tailed deer. Paper 107, Pennsylvania Cooperative Wildlife Research Unit, University Park, Pennsylvania.

Drescher-Kaden, U.
1976. Untersuchungen am Verdauungstrakt von Reh, Damhirsch und Mufflon. *Zeitschrift für Jagdwissenschaft,* 22:184–190.

Drew, K.R.
1976. The farming of red deer in New Zealand. *World Review of Animal Production,* 12:49–60.

Drożdż, A., J. Weiner, Z. Gebczyńska, and M. Krasińka
1975. Some bioenergetic parameters of wild ruminants. *Polish Ecological Studies,* 1:85–101.

R.N.B. Kay

Dziuk, H.E., B.A. Fashingbauer, and J.M. Idstrom
1963.   Ruminoreticular pressure patterns in fistulated white-tailed deer. *American Journal of Veterinary Research*, 24:772–783.

Gasaway, W.G., and J.W. Coady
1974.   Review of energy requirements and rumen fermentation in moose and other ruminants. *Naturaliste Canadien*, 101:227–262.

Hobson, P.N., S.O. Mann, and R. Summers
1976a. Rumen function in red deer, hill sheep and reindeer in the Scottish Highlands. *Proceedings of the Royal Society of Edinburgh, Section B, Natural Environment*, 75:181–198.

Hofmann, R.R.
1973.   *The Ruminant Stomach*. East African Monographs in Biology, 2. Nairobi: East African Literature Bureau.

1983.   Adaptive changes of gastric and intestional morphology in response to different fibre content in ruminant diets. In *Fibre in Human and Animal Nutrition*, edited by G. Wallace and L. Bell. The Royal Society of New Zealand. Bulletin 20.

Hofmann, R.R., G. Geiger, and R. König
1976.   Vergleichend-anatomische Untersuchungen an der Vormagenschleimhaut von Rehwild (*Capreolus capreolus*) und Rotwild (*Cervus elaphus*). *Zeitschrift für Säugetierkunde*, 41:167–193.

Holter, J.B., W.E. Urban, and H.H. Hayes
1977.   Nutrition of northern white-tailed deer throughout the year. *Journal of Animal Science*, 45:365–376.

Jacobsen, E., and S. Skjenneberg
1976.   Digestibility of lichen and supplemental feed for reindeer. *Forskning og Forsoek i Landbruket*, 27:287–305.

Kamis, A.B.
1980.   Acclimation of mousedeer (*Tragulus javanicus*) to hot temperature: changes in thyroid activity. *Comparative Biochemistry and Physiology*, 67A:517–518.

Kay, R.N.B.
1979.   Seasonal changes of appetite in deer and sheep. *Agricultural Research Council Research Review*, 5:13–15.

1981.   The productive potential of domesticated red deer. *Tep. Rowett Institute*, 37:125–134.

Kay, R.N.B., W.V. Engelhardt, and R.G. White
1980.   The digestive physiology of wild ruminants. In *Digestive Physiology and Metabolism in Ruminants*, edited by Y. Ruckebusch and P. Thivend, pp. 743–761. Lancaster, England: MTP Press.

Kay, R.N.B., and E.D. Goodall
1976.   The intake, digestibility and retention time of roughage diets by red deer (*Cervus elaphus*) and sheep. *Proceedings of the Nutrition Society*, 35:98A.

Kleiber, M.
1961.   *The Fire of Life*. New York: Wiley.

Leader-Williams, N.
1980.   Dental abnormalities and mandibular swellings in South Georgia reindeer. *Journal of Comparative Pathology*, 90:315–330.

Lowe, V.P.W.
1967.   Teeth as indicators of age with special reference to red deer (*Cervus elaphus*) of known age from Rhum. *Journal of Zoology*, 152:137–153.

Maloiy, G.M.O., and R.N.B. Kay
1971.   A comparison of digestion in red deer and sheep under controlled conditions. *Quarterly Journal Experimental Physiology*, 56:257–266.

Mautz, W.W., and G.A. Petrides
1971.   Food passage rate in the white-tailed deer. *Journal of Wildlife Management*, 35:723–731.

McEwan, E.H., and P.E. Whitehead
1970.   Seasonal change in the energy and nitrogen intake in reindeer and caribou. *Canadian Journal of Zoology*, 48:905–913.

Milne, J.A., J.C. MacRae, A.M. Spence, and S. Wilson
1978.   A comparison of the voluntary intake and digestion of a range of forages at different times of the year by the sheep and the red deer (*Cervus elaphus*). *British Journal of Nutrition*, 40:347–357.

Mitchell, B.
1967.   Growth layers in dental cement for determining the age of red deer (*Cervus elaphus* L.). *Journal of Animal Ecology*, 36:279–293.

Mitchell, B., D. McCowan, and I.A. Nicholson
1976.   Annual cycles of body weight and condition in Scottish red deer, *Cervus elaphus*. *Journal of Zoology*, 180:107–127.

Mitchell, B., D. McCowan, and T. Parish
1971.   Some characteristics of natural mortality among wild Scottish red deer (*Cervus elaphus* L.). In *Proceedings of the International Congress of Game Biologists*, 10:437–450.

Moen, A.N.
1978.   Seasonal changes in heart rates, activity, metabolism, and forage intake of white-tailed deer. *Journal of Wildlife Management*, 42:715–738.

Moore, G.H., and C.G. Brown
1977.   Growth performance in farmed red deer. *New Zealand Agricultural Science*, 11:175–178.

Morris, D.
1965.   *The Mammals*. London: Hodder & Stoughton.

Nagy, J.G., and W.L. Regelin
1975.   Comparison of digestive organ size of three deer species. *Journal of Wildlife Management*, 39:621–624.

Nordin, M.
1978a. Nutritional physiology and behaviour of the lesser mousedeer. In *Symposium on Animal Population: Wildlife Management, 1978, Bogor, Indonesia*.

1978b. Voluntary food intake and digestion by the lesser mousedeer. *J. Wildlife Management*, 42:185–187.

Oh, H.K., M.B. Jones, and W.M. Longhurst
1968. Comparison of rumen microbial inhibition resulting from various essential oils isolated from relatively unpalatable plant species. *Applied Microbiology*, 16:39–44.

Prins, R.A., and M.J.H. Geelen
1971. Rumen characteristics of red deer, fallow deer and roe deer. *Journal of Wildlife Management*, 35:673–680.

Robbins, C.T., R.L. Prior, A.N. Moen, and W.J. Visek
1974. Nitrogen metabolism of white-tailed deer. *Journal of Animal Science*, 38:187–191.

Short, H.L.
1963. Rumen fermentations and energy relationships in white-tailed deer. *Journal of Wildlife Management*, 27:184–195.
1971. Forage digestibility and diet of deer on southern upland range. *Journal of Wildlife Management*, 35:698–706.

Silver, H., N.F. Colovos, J.B. Holter, and H.H. Hayes
1969. Fasting metabolism of white-tailed deer. *Journal of Wildlife Management*, 33:490–498.

Staaland, H., E. Jacobsen, and R.G. White
1979. Comparison of the digestive tract in Svalbard and Norwegian reindeer. *Arctic Alpine Research*, 11:457–466.

Trudell, J., and R.G. White
1981. The effect of forage structure and availability on food intake, biting rate, bite size and daily eating time of reindeer. *Journal of Applied Ecology*, 18:63–81.

Trudell, J., R.G. White, E. Jacobsen, H. Staaland, K. Ekern, K. Kildemo, and E. Gaare
1980. Comparison of some factors affecting the in vitro digestibility estimate of reindeer forages. In *Proceedings of the 2nd International Reindeer/Caribou Symposium, Røros, Norway, 1979*, edited by E. Reimers, E. Gaare, and S. Skjenneberg, pp. 262–273. Diretoratet for vilt og ferskvannsfisk, Trondheim.

Wales, R.A., L.P. Milligan, and E.H. McEwan
1975. Urea recycling in caribou, cattle and sheep. In *Proceedings of the 1st International Reindeer and Caribou Symposium, Fairbanks, Alaska*, edited by J.R. Luick et al. pp. 297–305. Biological Papers of the University of Alaska, Special Report No. 1.

Walker, E.P.
1964. *Mammals of the World*. Baltimore: Johns Hopkins Press.

White, R.G., and J. Trudell
1980. Habitat preference and forage consumption by reindeer and caribou near Atkasook, Alaska. *Arctic Alpine Research*, 12:511–529.

Wood, A.J., I.McT. Cowan, and H.C. Nordan
1962. Periodicity of growth in ungulates as shown by deer of the genus *Odocoileus*. *Canadian Journal of Zoology*, 40:593–603.

Yazan, Y., and E.P. Knorre
1964. Domesticating elk in a Russian National Park. *Oryx*, 7:301–304.

DIETLAND MULLER-SCHWARZE
College of Environmental Sciences and Forestry
State University of New York
Syracuse, New York 13210

Evolution of Cervid Olfactory Communication

ABSTRACT   This paper reviews the use of glandular secretions, urine, and feces in cervid communicatory repertoires, and then discusses evolutionary trends in cervid olfactory communication. Most scent glands in deer contain both sebaceous and apocrine glandular elements associated with hair follicles. Indirect chemical communication via scent marks require lipid keeper substances that are provided by sebaceous glands (e.g. the antorbital gland), while direct, air borne inter-individual odors are often of the suboriferous that is produced by apocrine glands (e.g. metatarsal and caudal glands). For the most part, cervid scent glands are localized on the hindlegs, head, and anogenital and tail region. Forest and swamp dwelling species have an average of three scent glands, while open habitat species have an average of five glands. The number of scent glands is also greater in deer from arid versus humid climates. The number of chemical communication patterns is not necessarily greater in group living versus solitary living deer. Instead, different social needs favor the use of different signals, and hence different odor sources such as glands, urine, or feces.

Introduction

There is no doubt that deer have a keen sense of smell, of which the first applied ethologists, the prehistoric hunters, must have been only too aware. Cervids use their sense of smell not only in food selection, sensing predators, and recognizing their own bedding sites, but also and particularly in many intraspecific contexts. These include a) *general social interactions* such as tracking other individuals, or recognizing group members; b) *agonistic behavior* with olfactory threats such as rub-urinating, or scent marking objects with secretions from head or tail and urine, often accompanied by head or antler thrashing, or pawing; c) *sexual behavior*: ground sniffing, sniffing and licking urine on the ground or as it is voided, Flehmen, anogenital sniffing and licking; d) *maternal behavior*: sniffing and licking the newborn, maternal recognition of the fawn by its tail odor; and e) *alarm*: alerting group members with glandular odors, such as the metatarsal secretion in *O. hemionus columbianus*, or possibly interdigital secretion in *Capreolus* (Kurt, 1964, 1966), or *Rangifer* (Lent, 1966).

Chemical communication includes all chemical senses, notably olfaction, taste, and the vomeronasal organ, and the sources of chemical signals in deer are urine, a variety of skin glands, feces, saliva, and birth fluids. This review will concentrate on the better known patterns of chemical communication with glandular secretions and urine.

As in other mammals, the typical cervid scent gland consists of sebaceous glands and apocrine glands, both associated with hair follicles. One or the other type of gland may dominate a particular organ. Apocrine glands produce airborne odors as in metatarsal and caudal organs, while sebaceous glands provide materials for marking the substrate (example: antorbital gland organ). There are arrector pili muscles that function in discharging secretion, and hair, usually in tufts that accumulate secretion and assist in application to the substrate. There may be specialized scent hairs (osmetrichia). Most of the skin glands are located on the head, anogenital/tail region, and the hindlegs. The chemistry of glandular secretions and behaviorally active urine constituents has been investigated in only a few species, notably *O. hemionus*, *O. virginianus*, and *Rangifer*.

In the first part of this paper taxonomic groups will be reviewed; in the second, the discussion, taxa will be compared and trends pointed out. By necessity, this second part will be rather speculative and is intended to stimulate future research.

Taxonomic Groups

Moschus

The two main skin glands in the musk deer (*Moschus*) are the ventral and the caudal glands. The ventral gland of the male is the source of the musk, a precious commodity. The main odoriferous compound is muscone, a macrocyclic ketone with 16 carbon members (Ruzicka, 1926). The exact function of the musk is unknown at the present time. Techniques have been developed to "milk" the gland for its secretion (Mukti Shresta, pers. comm.), and efforts are being made to farm musk deer for musk production (Gupta and Jain, 1980).

The caudal gland extends from the rump into the tail (Pocock, 1910); Schaffer, 1940). Musk deer back up to an object and rub the tail on it for marking (Frädrich, 1966; Sokolov, 1979).

The front feet have interdigital glands, while the hind feet do not (Pocock, 1910).

Muntiacus

The two dominant glands in the muntjacs (genus *Muntiacus*) are the antorbital and frontal glands (pers. obs., Dubost, 1971). In *Muntiacus muntjak* and *M. reevesi* both sexes mark the ground with their frontal and antorbital glands. The males also mark trees by first cutting the bark with their lower incisors, and then rubbing the antler bases (Dubost, 1971). Conspecifics are also marked with the facial glands (Barrette, 1975, 1977). Muntjacs are able to evert their antorbital gland similar to *Axis porcinus*. They possess a peculiar semicircular sphincter muscle below the gland that enables them to evert the glandular pouch (Barrette, 1976, 1977). North American cervids, such as *O. hemionus*, *O. virginianus*, *C. e. canadensis*, and *A. alces* do not have this unique muscle. They can merely open, but not evert the gland (Barrette, 1976, 1977). For *M. muntiac*, Pocock (1910) described interdigital glands only on the hind feet.

Hydropotes

Hydropotes, the Chinese water deer, is the only cervid for which inguinal glands have been described. The pair of inguinal glands is located outside the mammae (Pocock, 1923). There is a small antorbital gland. The interdigital gland is developed only in the hindfoot as a "glandular depression" (Pocock, 1923), rather than a pouch. There are no tarsal and metatarsal glands (Pocock, 1923). Pocock was so struck by the anatomical peculiarities of *Hydropotes* that he proposed to place this species in a separate subfamily, Hydropotinae, within the Cervidae.

Cervus

Cervus e. elaphus (red deer) and *C. e. canadensis* (wapiti) are well investigated species, but olfactory communication has not been found to be very elaborate or important. This is in keeping with the general rule that larger ungulate species rely less on olfactory com-

Muller-Schwarze

munication (see *Elaphurus* and *Alces*). Instead, vocal communication plays an important role.

Urine is an important source of odor during the rut. *Cervus* males maintain rutting pits into which they urinate and in which they paw and wallow. Thus, urine is distributed over most of the body of the male. Furthermore, rutting males urinate onto their abdomen, brisket, and neck mane, thus soaking themselves with a strong odor. McCullough (1969) has suggested that one communicative function may be that the male marks the female with his mane and abdomen during mating. Thus, a signal would be available to other males that this particular doe has been bred already.

Cervus elaphus has been thoroughly searched for skin glands. This species possesses antorbital, infracaudal, circumcaudal (Frankenberger, 1957), metatarsal, and interdigital glands. The ultrastructure of interdigital glands was investigated by Sokolov and Stepanova (1980).

Cervus eldi, the brow-antlered, or Eld's deer, marks trees with the antorbital gland (Muller-Schwarze, 1975; Blakeslee et al., 1979).

Rusa

The sambar, *Cervus* (=*Rusa*) *unicolor* has large antorbital glands and possesses metatarsal glands. Interdigital glands are not discernible (Pocock, 1910).

Axis

The spotted deer (or chital), *A. axis*, and hog deer *A. porcinus*, of South Asia have both well developed antorbital, interdigital and metatarsal glands. The chital as a highly social species of open country, and the hog deer as a more solitary inhabitant of dense grass jungle deserve more studies of their social behavior and communication. *A. axis* marks vegetation with the antorbital glands (Schaller, 1967). The antorbital

Figure 1. Antorbital gland of male *Axis axis*, with short bristles protruding. Kathmandu Zoo, Nepal; April 1982.

gland of the male has stiff hair that at times can be seen protruding from the cavity like a stiff paint brush (Figure 1).

Dama dama

Fallow deer are more visually oriented, and their olfactory display repertoire is not as elaborate as in other cervids. Bucks in the rut urinate on sites they have pawed on the ground. They also spray themselves on their abdomen. The antlers are raked through these soaked areas, and then thrashed on the ground. The urine of rutting bucks has a potent odor, possibly due to preputial secretion (Heidemann, 1973). Seasonal changes of the prepuce of the fallow deer have been described by Kennaugh et al., 1977).

Elaphurus

Elaphurus davidianus, Pere David's deer, as a large species fits the described trend of the importance of olfactory communication being inversely related to body size. The only well developed gland is the antorbital gland. There are no interdigital or caudal glands (Wemmer, 1983). Pocock (1910, 1923) found no tarsal gland, and a metatarsal gland in one museum skin (sex not given), but not in a female carcass. The bucks with urine spray their bodies and wallow during the rut developing a strong odor. Urine may be the source, but this needs to be confirmed (Wemmer, 1983).

Elaphodus

Both sexes of the tufted deer (*Elaphodus cephalophus*) have well developed antorbital glands, slightly developed metatarsal glands without a hair tuft, and interdigital glands on the hind feet (Pocock, 1910).

Odocoileus

The smaller *O. hemionus columbianus* (black-tailed deer) has more elaborate chemical communication than the larger forms *O. h. hemionus* (mule deer) and *O. virginianus* (white-tailed deer).

Black-tailed deer (*O. h. columbianus*)

At birth, the fawn is smelled and licked by its mother. She eats the birth membranes and licks all birth fluid off the ground. Even a dead born fawn is licked for hours. Soon after birth the mother recognizes her fawn olfactorily. From then on it is recognized by smelling the anal/caudal region. On the first day many of our hand-raised fawns had a noticeable odor to their metatarsal glands, especially when held or disturbed. When about one week old, fawns rub their hocks together and urinate over them when left alone. This chemical distress signal attracts the mother or even other females in the same pen (Muller-Schwarze, 1971).

The fawn is not selective in its following response until about one week old. That odor plays a role is evident from experiments with scented dummies. Given a choice a fawn prefers to stay with and suckle a dummy that bears the scent it experienced during the first two weeks of life (Muller-Schwarze and Muller-Schwarze, 1971; Muller-Schwarze, 1979).

Flehmen occurs during the rut, and less often to estrous does. It is a response to *all* types of urine (male, estrous and anestrous female, fawns of both sexes) if given out of context, i.e., in a glass bowl (Altieri and Muller-Schwarze, 1980). Males start to exhibit the Flehmen response to female urine before they are two months old (first observation: 53 days of age; Muller-Schwarze, 1971). Deprivation of female urine during the first two years of life does not result in measurable development differences, such as growth of body or antlers, neck swelling, or subsequent Flehmen to female urine (Muller-Schwarze and Altieri, pers. obs.).

Behavior tests with fractionated urine showed that the active principle that releases Flehmen is water-soluble, of low volatility, not readily extractable with organic solvents, and between 200 and 12,000 daltons in molecular weight (Crump et al., 1984).

Urine is not only an important social stimulus for determination of estrus by mature bucks, but also as a threat between members of the same sex, especially males. In captivity two males stand parallel to each other, at a distance of 3 to 5 m, rub their hocks, and urinate over them. Thereupon they do not approach closer, and a fight is averted. "Rub-urination" is particularly frequent during the rut, when captive bucks may perform it at intervals of about 5 minutes.

Skin glands are used as follows: forehead and antorbital glands deposit material on wooden objects during forehead rubbing and antler thrashing. Subordinate males smell these scent marks of dominant males, but do not forehead-rub in turn (Muller-Schwarze, 1972). Only the combined secretions of antorbital and forehead glands provide informaion on age class of the marking buck (Volkman, 1981; Volkman et al., 1978).

The tarsal gland produces sebum that is mixed with urine to form the "tarsal scent" (Muller-Schwarze et al., 1978b). The main odoriferous component is cis-r-hydroxydodec-6-enoic acid lactone (Brownlee et al., 1968). It is contained in large amounts in urine of both sexes (Muller-Schwarze et al., 1978b) and has been synthesized (Ravid et al., 1978; Pirkle and Adams, 1979). It is transferred to the tarsal hair tuft during rub-urination (Figure 2). To hold sebum and "scent" the tarsal hair tuft has specialized scent hairs, "osmetrichia" (Muller-Schwarze et al., 1977b) with large

Figure 2.   Male *O. hemionus columbianus* rub-urinating during the rut. He is guarding an estrous female (on left) against the observer, positioning himself in between. Green Canyon Field Station, Utah State University.

spaces under the cuticular scales. The tarsal scent carries information for individual recognition, as strangers are sniffed at the tarsal tuft, and fawns smell their mother's hock when following.

The metatarsal gland consists primarily of greatly enlarged apocrine glands and discharges a strong odor that is reminiscent of garlic or skunk. The odor is released when deer are alerted, chased, cornered, or brought into strange surroundings. Both sexes discharge the odor, fawns have it from their first days on, and there is no noticeable seasonal variation in odor or secretion (Muller-Schwarze, 1971). Experimental exposure to metatarsal secretion of conspecifics increases alertness in females (Muller-Schwarze, 1980; Porter, 1982; Muller-Schwarze et al., in press). Considerable effort at chemical identification of the biologically active principle has been unsuccessful to date.

The caudal glands of fawns are sniffed during recognition by the mother (Figure 3).

Interdigital glands are equally developed on fore- and hindfeet. There is little behavioral evidence for their use, except that deep footprints in mud are occasionally sniffed.

The histology of the skin glands to *O. hemionus columbianus* has been described by Quay and Muller-Schwarze (1970), and those in *O. h. hemionus* by Quay and Muller-Schwarze (1971).

White-tailed deer *(O. virginianus)*

The white-tailed deer has the same skin glands as the black-tailed deer (Quay, 1959), except that the metatarsal gland is very small compared to the former. It does not have the strong smell of black-tailed deer, and efforts to demonstrate responses to metatarsal se-

Figure 3. Female *O. hemionus columbianus* smells one of her fawns at the tail, the decisive step in individual recognition. Green Canyon Field Station, Utah State University.

cretion have been unsuccessful thus far (Muller-Schwarze and Volkman, 1977). During the rut the white-tailed deer maintains rubs on small tree trunks and scrapes in the ground (DeVos, 1967; Kile and Marchinton, 1977).

Rangifer

In caribou and reindeer (*Rangifer tarandus*) the tail and hindfoot interdigital glands are highly developed (Quay, 1955; Muller-Schwarze et al., 1977a). They also have antorbital and tarsal glands, and lack metatarsal glands. Small glands have been found scattered about the skin of the flanks (Kallquist and Mossing, 1977).

The antorbital gland is opened during threats between bulls and is also rubbed on trees during antler thrashing episodes (Muller-Schwarze et al., 1979). It is the only skin gland in reindeer that shows seasonal and sexual variation. It is most active during the pre-rut period of September, when both the area of the apocrine glands and the diameter of their tubuli are largest (Mossing and Kallquist, 1981). At this time secretion first appears at the anterior portion of the gland when testosterone concentration in the blood starts to increase drastically (Mossing and Damber, 1981).

The tarsal gland of caribou is the least developed gland and also behaviorally less important (Muller-Schwarze et al., 1979). Volatile components identified in the tarsal secretion are the aldehydes *n*-heptanal, *n*-octanal, *n*-nonanal, and *n*-decanal: the alcohols *n*-dodecanol, *n*-tetradecanol, and *n*-hexadecanol; and the hydrocarbon *n*-heptadecane (Andersson et al., 1975).

The interdigital gland of the hindfoot is well developed. Non-rutting forest reindeer in Sweden smelled experimental tracks made from interdigital secretion more often if the donor was of the same sex as the responding animal (Muller-Schwarze et al., 1978a). The concentration of three ketones in the secretion of the interdigital gland varies with the season: 6-methyl-2-heptanone, 7-methyl-3-octanone, and 7-meth-

yl-1-octen-3-one (Brundin and Andersson, 1979). There are also fatty acids. Of these, captive reindeer sniffed isovaleric and isobutyric acid more often than blanks and pivalic acid, an isomer of isovaleric acid that is not found in interdigital secretion (Brundin et al., 1978). Reindeer rub the interdigital glands of the hindfeet on their growing antlers. The Lapps call this behavior "antler-making" and believe it to be essential for normal antler growth. This "hindleg-head contact" (HHC) is particularly frequent in midday during bouts of grooming behavior (Muller-Schwarze et al., 1979).

The caudal gland in *Rangifer* was first described from museum skins (Lewin and Stelfox, 1967) for caribou. It consists of sebaceous and sudoriferous glands, with the latter more developed. Mothers smell their calves at the tail before accepting them, and bulls smell cows at their tails (Muller-Schwarze et al., 1977a, 1979). Volatile constituents of the caudal secretion are the aldehydes *n*-heptanal, *n*-octanal, *n*-nonanal, and *n*-decanal, and the short chain acids cetic acid, propionic acid, isokbutyric acid, *n*-butyric acid, isovaleric acid, and methylbutyric acid. It is not known which of these compounds are behaviorally active, nor their precise behavioral effects.

Rutting bulls urinate on their hindlegs and rub them together ("rub-urinating"). The hindlegs are held in such a position that the urine soaks the lower portion and the interdigital glands (Espmark, 1964; Muller-Schwarze et al., 1979). This is in contrast to *Odocoileus* where the urine during rub-urination runs over the tarsal glands on the hocks. Fittingly, the interdigital gland is highly developed in *Rangifer*, and the tarsal gland of less significance while the reverse is true for *Odocoileus*.

Capreolus

The roebuck has a forehead gland patch that was first described by Schumacher (1936). It is used to mark branches of trees during the rut in July/August (Kurt, 1968). The organ metabolizes testosterone best in June and July, and reaches its metabolic minimum in December (Johnson and Leask, 1977).

The interdigital gland of the hindfoot is kicked against the ground by bucks during the so-called "Hinterlaufschlagen" (Kurt, 1968). Conspecifics avoid or flee from experimentally placed interdigital secretion of mature bucks (Kurt, 1966, 1968).

Ozotoceros

Ozotoceros bezoarticus, the pampas deer, possesses antorbital and tarsal glands, but no metatarsal gland (Schaffer, 1940). Langguth and Jackson (1980) described interdigital glands on the hindfoot, and for the first time a vestibular nasal gland in both sexes. It is composed of sebaceous glands.

Blastocerus

Blastocerus, the South American swamp deer, also has a nasal gland in addition to antorbital and tarsal glands (Jacob and Lehmann, 1976a). The chemical composition of the nonvoltaile (wax ester) constituents was investigated by Jacob and Lehmann (1976b).

Mazama

In the brockets the size of the antorbital gland (AOG) varies from species to species. In the two larger species *Maz. americana* and *Maz. gouazoubira* the AOG is small or missing, while it is medium-sized in the small grey dwarf brocket (*Maz. bricenii*) and large in the lesser brocket (or bororo), *Maz. nana*. Thus, there is a tendency for larger AOGs in the smaller forms. This may be correlated with habitat since the smaller species live in more dense cover.

Maz. americana marks vegetation with the antler base and paws the ground (Krieg, in Grzimek, 1972). The AOG is also used during marking (Volkman and Ralls, 1973).

The tarsal gland is "represented by a small tuft of hair" (Pocock, 1923); interdigital glands are developed on all four feet (Pocock, 1923). Brockets lack a metatarsal gland.

Alces

The moose (*Alces alces*) has well developed antorbital, tarsal and metatarsal glands. A peculiar "throat gland" at the base of the hair tuft ("beard") on the throat has been described (v. Wangenheim, in Schaffer, 1940). Bubenik et al (1980) found *o*-cresol in tarsal gland secretion of Ontario moose, especially females, but no behavior effects were observed.

Pudu

In *Pudu mephistophiles* the antorbital gland is an "inconspicuous pouch opening about ½ cm in diameter", as observed in preserved or tanned skin (Hershkovitz, 1982). Pocock (1923) described it as a "comparatively small and shallow pouch". Tarsal and metatarsal glands, "if present, are not evident on dry or tanned skin" (Hershkovitz, 1982). They are absent according to Pocock (1923). The interdigital glands on all feet are "contained within shallow, interdigital, trough-like skin fold" (Hershkovitz, 1982).

The antorbital gland of *Pudu puda* is "large, the opening wide, conspicuously displayed" (Hershkovitz, 1982). Tarsal and metatarsal glands are "not evident

in available material" (Hershkovitz, 1982), while the interdigital glands of the forefoot are "contained in deep trough or pocket, of hindfoot in well-defined pouch" (Hershkovitz, 1982). Pocock (1923) considered the interdigital glands in *Pudu puda* the most primitive type of hoof glands in the cervids. Based on extensive measurements, Hershkovitz (1982) considers *P. mephistophiles* of the northern Andes primitive, while the southern Chilean-Argentine *P. puda* is derived.

Hippocamelus

The huemul has well developed antorbital glands, tarsal glands, but no metatarsal or interdigital glands (Pocock, 1910; Schaffer, 1940).

Localized defecation

Only the small, more primitive forms *Moschus*, *Muntiacus*, and *Mazama* maintain dung piles. Among the larger forms they have been observed in Eld's deer (C. Wemmer, pers. comm.). Fawns however may defecate on a specific site. Captive, hand-raised *O. hemionus columbianus* usually had two to three dung piles where they defecated and urinated (pers. obs.). Thus, dung piling appears to be correlated with small body size (Eld's deer is an exception) and a constant, restricted home range, and not with the habitat as such, as for instance forest or dense cover.

Use of Urine

The Cervinae spray urine on their body, notably abdomen and mane, while the Odocoileinae rub-urinate, i.e. rub their hindlegs together and urinate over them. The urine can be focussed on the hock (tarsal gland), as in *Odocoileus*, or on the toes (interdigital gland) as in *Rangifer*.

It is possible that the tendency to develop manes in the Cervinae is correlated with self-enurination, while the tarsal tufts of *Odocoileus* are specialized structures for rub-urinating. This would be in addition to selection pressures to develop and maintain these regions of long hair as visual signals, and possibly (or originally) for thermoregulation.

As like in most ungulates and many other mammals, Flehmen (lip curl) is an important male response to female urine in deer (Henderson et al., 1980).

Discussion

The approximately 53 species of deer are well suited for comparison, as their rate of evolution (0.17) has been estimated to be slower than that of mammals on the average (0.20). For comparison, the values for the Bovidae and Muridae are 0.21 and 0.29, respectively

Muller-Schwarze

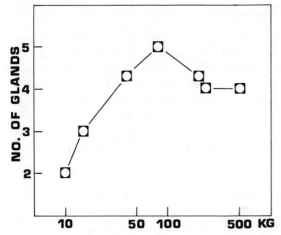

Figure 4. Relationship between body weight in kg (abscissa) and number of skin glands (ordinate). Each point represents one or more deer species.

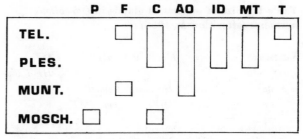

Figure 5. Presence of glands in the four cervid taxa: *Moschus, Muntiacus,* Plesiometacarpalia, and Telemetacarpalia. Glands: Ventral (V), forehead (F), caudal (C), antorbital (AO), interdigital (ID), metatarsal (MT), tarsal (T).

(Stanley, 1975). The encephalization quotient (EQ) is at the mammalian average which is 1.00. The EQ for *O. virginianus* is 1.055, and that for *C. e. canadensis* 0.902 (Eisenberg, 1981) (see Wemmer and Wilson, this volume).

Trends Within the Cervid Family

Advanced features of deer species are increased body and antler size, complexity of antlers, decrease in number of young, loss of spots, larger social groups, colonization of more open habitat (correlated with body size and sociality), more complex social organization and communication (correlated with increased group sizes), and ability to cope with varying habitats (seasonal physical and vegetation changes, or seasonal migration between different habitats).

There is a taxonomic trend from two major scent glands in *Moschus* and the muntjacs to an average of three in the Plesiometacarpalia and four in the Telemetacarpalia (Figure 4). Given the evolutionary trend for body size to increase it follows that olfactory communication, as expressed by the number of major scent glands, is not as important in larger cervids; or at least it does not increase any further from medium size to large species, such as *Cervus, Elaphurus,* and *Alces.* This is paralleled in the bovids: olfactory communication is less important in species such as kudu and oryx, than in smaller species such as the gazelles or dikdiks.

There are two major taxonomic lines of scent communication. The Plesiometacarpalia use urine on their body and in rutting pits or scrapes, and have no tarsal glands. The Telemetacarpalia have tarsal glands, and use urine during rub-urinating (Figure 5). Hershkovitz (1958) stated that "the metatarsal

glands proper are, apparently, of little or no taxonomic importance within the Odocoileini". This absence of consistent taxonomic trends renders this group more interesting in the search for ecological factors that favor expression of metatarsal glands independently of taxonomic relationships.

Interspecific Differences

O. virginianus varies geographically with regard to presence or size of its metatarsal gland (Hershkovitz, 1958; Quay, 1971). The gland is more pronounced in the north of the species' range. It is greater in the north, and more individuals possess the gland (Quay, 1971). Quay concluded that there are two "geographic divisions": in the north the organ is always well developed, and in the south (from the southwestern United States to Central and South America) the gland is only sporadically present, and then only of small size. He found no correlation with sex or climate.

Using Hershkovitz' (1958) qualitative data, I assign a value of 0 to absence of the metatarsal gland from any specimens, 1 to poorly developed glands, and 2 to well developed glands. The degree of definition of the metatarsal gland then decreases from an average 1.43 in northern and central Mexico to 0.13 in the area between southern Mexico (Chiapas) and Panama. In that range, metatarsal glands were found only in Guatemala specimens. Finally, from Columbia to Peru the value increased again to 0.61. Here metatarsal glands were found in three out of four geographical areas.

What factor is operating in the North that favors well-developed metatarsal glands? In Central and South America this influence appears relaxed, resulting in only sporadic occurrence of the gland. One

Table 1. Size of metatarsal glands in *Odocoileus hemionus* (after Cowan, 1956)

Subspecies (from North to South)	Length (in inches)			$\dfrac{MT}{HF}$ Ratio
	Body	Hindfoot (HF)	Metatarsal gland (MT)	
O. h. sitkensis	61	17.3	1.8	0.10
O. h. columbianus	58	17.5	2.0	0.11
O. h. californicus	62	18.0	3.5	0.19
O. h. fuliginatus	57	17.5	3.0	0.17
O. h. peninsulae	60	16.0	3.5	0.22
Inland:				
O. h. hemionus	70	22.0	4.5	0.21
O. h. eremicus	67	19.5	5.0	0.27

possible correlation is between the degree of development of the metatarsal gland and the aridity of the region. Annual rainfall increases south to the Central American isthmus, and then decreases again into South America. Also, mule and black-tailed deer with their well developed metatarsal gland live in arid conditions, while the humid climate white-tailed deer has a poorly developed gland, for which a communicatory function has not yet been found. Furthermore, this correlation has been suggested for other mammals, too. The gerbil (genus *Tatera*) of arid northern India has a ventral gland, while the species of the humid South has none (M. Alexander, pers. comm.). In *O. hemionus* a tenuous North-South gradient can also be detected. The metatarsal gland in the northernmost subspecies *O. h. sitkensis* is smallest (4.4 cm long), while it is largest in the southernmost form, *O. h. eremicus* (12.5 cm long) (Cowan, 1956). When related to body length, the ratio of metatarsal gland length to body length is 0.10 in *sitkensis*, and 0.27 in *eremicus*. Other forms are intermediate, although not in a consistent, straight gradient (Table 1). Humidity increases evaporation of volatile compounds from surfaces, as water molecules compete with odor molecules for surface sites (Regnier and Goodwin, 1977).

Behavioral Specificity

Rocky Mountain mule deer (*O. h. hemionus*) and black-tailed deer (*O. h. columbianus*) each respond more strongly to their own tarsal scent than to that of the other subspecies (Muller-Schwarze and Muller-Schwarze, 1975).

Social Organization

How does chemical communication of solitary species differ from that of species living in larger social groups, whether they be closed or open? Solitary species usually mark their territory or home range with antorbital, frontal or caudal secretion, urine and dung piles, while social species employ direct interaction to determine individual identity, social rank, reproductive status, or state of alertness. There is not necessarily an increase of the number of patterns of chemical communication from solitary to social species. Instead, different social needs will favor the use of different signals, and hence, different odor sources, such as glands or urine. More complex social groups require more elaborate communication in general, regardless of sensory modality involved. Therefore, chemical communication is expected to be more differentiated and refined when compared to the simpler needs of solitary species for territorial defense and sexual attraction (Table 2). Indirect chemical communication via scent marks requires lipid keeper substances that are provided by sebaceous glands, while direct, airborne interindividual odors are often of the sudoriferous type that is produced by apocrine glands. If individual odors are due to different ratios in the same mixture of chemical compounds, one would expect more complex chemical signals in more social species than in solitary ones, where simple signals would suffice to identify species, sex, and perhaps age or reproductive status.

Ecological Considerations

HABITAT

Forest dwelling is the basic pattern of ecological adaptation in deer. Grassland, tundra, or alpine species are considered derived and should therefore show deviations from the conservtive deer pattern of olfactory communication. As long as our knowledge of chemical communication is uneven between species, and even

Table 2. Social group sizes and number of scent glands

Category of social group size	No. of species or genera	Average no. of skin glands
0 (Solitary)	3	3.3
0.5–1	8	2.6
1.5–2	3	3.5
3	2	5.0
4	1	5.0

Muller-Schwarze

very limited for the better investigated species, the rather crude measure of number of major scent gland organs has to be used for taxonomic comparisons. The oldest deer fossils are from the lower Oligocene of Asia, where the greatest diversity exists even today. Therefore, the Asian forest deer can be taken as a basis for ecological comparisons.

Habitat and number of major scent gland organs are difficult to correlate for many species because some live in mixed habitats (*Axis axis*, *Capreolus*), others migrate between open and forested areas (*Rangifer*), while still others experience climatic extremes of hot summers and cold winters with deep snow (*Odocoileus hemionus*). On the other hand, some jungle grass forms, such as *Axis porcinus* live in cover as dense as or denser than forest. Forest and swamp deer have the lowest average number of scent gland organs (3), and these live in more open habitat the most (5; Table 3). However in open habitat, deer like bovids, are more social.

Flehmen in *O. virginianus* was not only more frequent than in *O. h. columbianus* but occurred more often in response to urine on the ground (Table 4). This can be interpreted as an adaptation to forest habitat in white-tailed deer, while black-tailed deer in their more open habitat are able to interact more directly.

CLIMATE

Fourteen forms living in humid climates average 3.4 major scent glands while six species from arid areas average 4.2.

There is no correlation with climate zones. Tropical deer average 3.2 glands, subtropical forms 3.4, temperate zone species 3.25, and polar/alpine ones 3.67. This slight trend may be due more to the tendency to

Table 3. Habitat and number of major skin glands

Habitat	Average no. of glands	N	Typical species
Swamp Forest	2	3	*Elaphurus*, *Blastocerus*
	3	4	*O. virginianus*, *Cervus*
Forest-Grass	3	2	*Capreolus*
Grass Jungle	4	1	*Ax. porcinus*
Forest-Open	4	2	*Ax. axis*
Forest-Bush (Chapparal)	4.5	2	*O. hemionus*
Tundra, Grassland	5	2	*Rangifer*, *Ozotoceros*

Table 4. Flehmen in captive penned black- and white-tailed deer during 20 hours of observation

Behavior	O. hemionus columbianus	O. virginianus
No. of Flehmen observed	89	138
No. of ground Flehmen (%)	49 (55)	121 (87.7)
Flehmen to urinating female (%)	40 (44.9)	17 (12.3)
No. of female urinations	79	42
% of female urinations resulting in Flehmen	50.6	40.5
Flehmen per male hour	2.1	4.3
Rate of ground Flehmen per urination	0.6	2.9

have more glands in open (tundra, alpine) habitats than in dense cover, such as tropical forests.

In summary, we find more scent glands and expect more elaborate chemical communication in a cervid species if it:

a. is of medium body size,
b. lives in social groups,
c. lives in an arid climate, and
d. inhabits a varied or more open habitat.

However, appreciation of the significance of chemical communication of any species can only be based on thorough experimental studies of behavior. For most of the cervid species we are far from this goal, and this discussion can do no more than provide inspired suggestions for future work. In any discussion of chemical communication the other senses should not be ignored, as different taxa emphasize different sensory modalities. In the genus *Odocoileus*, for instance, the white-tailed deer (*O. virginianus*) uses a conspicuous visual signal, tail-flagging, when alarmed, while mule deer (*O. hemionus*), have a less conspicuous tail, do not wag it laterally, and appear to rely more on the odor or metatarsal secretion in alarm situations. In any one species, multisensory control of behavior has to be kept in mind: "A good nose is requisite also, to smell out work for the other senses" (Shakespeare, The Winter's Tale, iv, 4).

Literature Cited

Altieri, R., and D. Muller-Schwarze
1980. Seasonal changes in Flehmen to constant stimuli. *Journal of Chemical Ecology*, 6:905-909.

Andersson, G., K. Andersson, A. Brundin, and C. Rappe
1975. Volatile compounds from the tarsal gland of rein-

deer (*Rangifer tarandus*). *Journal of Chemical Ecology*, 1:275-281.

Barrette, C.
1975. Social behaviour of muntjac. Ph.D. Dissertation, University of Calgary.

1976. Musculature of facial scent glands in the muntjac. *Journal of Anatomy*, 122(1):61-66.

1977. Scent-marking in captive muntjacs, *Muntiacus reevesi*. *Animal Behaviour*, 25:536-541.

Blakeslee, C. K., C. G. Rice, and K. Ralls
1979. Behavior and reproduction of captive brow-antlered deer, *Cervus eldi thamin* (Thomas, 1918). *Säugetierkunde Mitteilungen*, 40:114-127.

Brownlee, R. G., R. M. Silverstein, D. Muller-Schwarze, and A. G. Singer
1968. Isolation, identification and function of the chief component of the male tarsal scent in black-tailed deer. *Nature*, 221:284-285.

Brundin, A., and G. Andersson
1979. Seasonal variation in three ketones in the interdigital secretion of reindeer (*Rangifer tarandus*). *Journal of Chemical Ecology*, 5:881-889.

Brundin, A., G. Andersson, K. Andersson, T. Mossing, and M. L. Kallquist
1978. Short-chain aliphatic acids in the interdigital gland secretions of reindeer (*Rangifer tarandus* L.), and their discrimination by reindeer. *Journal of Chemical Ecology*, 4:613-622.

Bubenik, A. B., M. Dombalagian, J. W. Wheeler, and O. Williams
1980. The role of the tarsal glands in the olfactory communication of the Ontario moose. In *Chemical Signals*, edited by D. Muller-Schwarze and R. M. Silverstein, pp. 415. New York: Plenum.

Cowan, I. McT.
1956. What and where are the mule and black-tailed deer? In *The Deer of North America*, edited by W. P. Taylor, pp. 335-359. Harrisburg: Stackpole, and Washington, D.C.: Wildlife Management Institute.

Crump, D., A. A. Swigar, J. R. West, R. M. Silverstein, D. Muller-Schwarze, and R. Altieri
1984. Urine fractions that release Flehmen in black-tailed deer, *Odocoileus hemionus columbionus*. *Journal of Chemical Ecology*, 10:203-215.

DeVos, A.
1967. Rubbing of conifers by white-tailed deer in successive years. *Journal of Mammalogy*, 48:146-147.

Dubost, G.
1971. Observations ethologiques sur le Muntjak (*Muntiacus muntjak*) Zimmermann 1780 et *M. reevesi* Ogilby 1839 en captivite et semi-liberte. *Zeitschrift für Tierpsychologie*, 28:387-427.

Eisenberg, J. F.
1981. *The Mammalian Radiations*. Chicago: University of Chicago Press.

Espmark, Y.
1964. Rutting behaviour in reindeer (*Rangifer tarandus* L.). *Animal Behaviour*, 12:159-163.

Frädrich, H.
1966. Einige Verhaltensbeobachtungen am Moschustier (*Moschus moschiferus* L.). *Der Zoologische Garten*, 33:65-78.

Frankenberger, Z.
1957. Circumanal and circumgenital glands of our Cervidae. *Zeitschrift Morphologische Verhandlungen*, 3:255-256.

Grzimek, B.
1972. *Grzimek's Animal Encyclopedia*. Vol. 13. New York: Van Nostrand Rheinhold Company.

Gupta, M. P., and M. S. Jain
1980. Experience in breeding of musk deer for the production of musk. *Indian Forester*, 106(5):357-362.

Heidemann, G.
1973. Zur Biologie des Damwildes (*Cervus dama* Linne 1758). *Mammalia depicta* 9, 95 pp. Hamburg: Paul Parey.

Henderson, J., R. Altieri, and D. Muller-Schwarze
1980. The annual cycle of Flehmen in black-tailed deer (*Odocoileus hemionus columbianus*). *Journal of Chemical Ecology*, 6:537-547.

Hershkovitz, P.
1958. The metatarsal glands in white-tailed deer and related forms of the Neotropical Region. *Mammalia*, 22:537-546.

1982. Neotropical deer (Cervidae). Part I. Pudus, Genus *Pudu* Gray. *Fieldiana Zoology New Series*, No. 11. *Field Museum of Natural History*, Publication 1330, 86 pp.

Jacob, J., and E. von Lehmann
1976a. Bemerkungen zu einer Nasendruse des Sumpfhirsches, *Odocoileus (Dorcelaphus) dichotomus* (Illiger). *Zeitschrift für Naturforschung*, 31c:496-498.

Johnson, E., and J.T.S. Leask
1976b. Chemical composition of the nasal gland secretion from the marsh deer *Odocoileus (Dorcelaphus) dichotomus* (Illiger). *Zeitschrift für Naturforschung*, 31c:496-498.

1977. Metabolism of testosterone by forehead skin of the roebuck (*Capreolus capreolus*). *Journal of Endocrinology*, 75:363-372.

Kallquist, C., and T. Mossing
1977. The distribution of sudoriferous glands in the hairy skin of reindeer (*Rangifer tarandus* L.). *Acta Zoologica*, 58:65-68.

Kennaugh, J. H., D. I. Chapman, and N. G. Chapman
1977.   Seasonal changes in the prepuce of adult fallow deer (*Dama dama*) and its probable function as a scent organ. *Journal of Zoology*, 183:301-310.

Kile, T. L., and R. L. Marchinton
1977.   White-tailed deer rubs and scrapes. Spatial, temporal and physical characteristics and social role. *American Midland Naturalist*, 97:257-266.

Kurt, F.
1964.   Zur Rolle des Geruchs im Verhalten des Rehwildes. *Verhandlungen der Schweizerischen Naturforschenden Gesellschaft in Zürich*, 144:140-142.

1966.   Feldbeobachtungen und Versuche uber das Revierverhalten der Rehböcke (*Capreolus capreolus* L.). *Revue Suisse de Zoologie*, 73:408-421.

1968.   Das Sozialverhalten des Rehes *Capreolus Capreolus* L. Eine Feldstudie. *Mammalia depicta*, 4:102 pp. Hamburg: Paul Parey.

Langguth, A., and J. Jackson
1980.   Cutaneous scent glands in Pampas deer *Blastoceros bezoarticus* (L., 1758). *Zeitschrift für Säugetierkunde*, 45:82-90.

Lent, P.
1966.   Calving and related social behavior in the barrenground caribou. *Zeitschrift für Tierpsychologie*, 6:701-756.

Lewin, V., and J. G. Stelfox
1967.   Functional anatomy of the tail gland and associated behavior in woodland caribou. *Canadian Field Naturalist*, 81:63-66.

McCullough, D. R.
1969.   *The Tule elk. Its history, behavior and ecology.* Berkeley: University of California Press.

Mossing, T., and J. E. Damber
1981.   Rutting behavior and androgen variation in reindeer (*Rangifer tarandus* L.). *Journal of Chemical Ecology*, 7:377-389.

Mossing T., and L. Kallquist
1981.   Variation in cutaneous glandular structures in reindeer (*Rangifer tarandus*). *Journal of Mammalogy*, 62:606-612.

Muller-Schwarze, D.
1971.   Pheromones in black-tailed deer. *Animal Behaviour*, 19:141-152.

1972.   Social significance of forehead rubbing in black-tailed deer. *Animal Behaviour*, 20:788-797.

1975.   A note on the use of the antorbital gland in marking by Eld's deer. *Applied Animal Ethology*, 1:301-303.

1977.   Complex mammalian behavior and bioassay in the field. In *Chemical Signals in Vertebrates*, edited by D. Muller-Schwarze and M. M. Mozell, pp. 413-433. New York: Plenum.

1979.   Flehmen in the context of mammalian urine communication. In *Chemical Ecology: Odour Communication in Mammals*, edited by F. Ritter, pp. 85-93. North Holland: Elsevier.

1980.   Chemical signals in alarm behavior of deer. In *Chemical Signals*, edited by D. Muller-Schwarze and R. M. Silverstein. pp. 39-51. New York: Plenum.

Muller-Schwarze, D., and C. Muller-Schwarze
1971.   Olfactory imprinting in a precocial mammal. *Nature*, 229:55-56.

1975.   Subspecies specificity of response to a mammalian social odor. *Journal of Chemical Ecology*, 1:125-131.

Muller-Schwarze, D., and N. Volkman
1977.   Responses of white-tailed and black-tailed deer (Genus *Odocoileus*) to metatarsal gland secretions (Abstract). Annual Meeting of the Animal Behavior Society, Pennsylvania State University, June 1977.

Muller-Schwarze, D., W. B. Quay, and A. Brundin
1977a.   The caudal gland in reindeer (*Rangifer tarandus* L.): Its behavioral role, histology, and chemistry. *Journal of Chemical Ecology*, 3:591-601.

Muller-Schwarze, D., N. J. Volkman, and K. Zemanek
1977b.   Osmetrichia: Specialized scent hairs in black-tailed deer. *Journal of Ultrastructure Research*, 59:223-230.

Muller-Schwarze, D., L. Kallquist, and T. Mossing
1979.   Social behavior and chemical communication in reindeer (*Rangifer t. tarandus* L.). *Journal of Chemical Ecology*, 5:438-517.

Muller-Schwarze, D., L. Kallquist, T. Mossing, A. Brundin, and G. Andersoon
1978a.   Responses of reindeer to interdigital secretions of conspecifics. *Journal of Chemical Ecology*, 4(3):325-335.

Muller-Schwarze, D., U. Ravid, A. Claesson, A. G. Singer, R. M. Silverstein, C. Muller-Schwarze, N. J. Volkman, K. F. Zemanek, and R. G. Butler
1978b.   The deer lactone. Source, chemical properties, and responses by black-tailed deer. *Journal of Chemical Ecology*, 4:247-256.

Muller-Schwarze, D., R. Altieri, and N. Porter
1984.   An alert odor of glandular origin in black-tailed deer, *Odocoileus hemionus columbianus*. *Journal of Chemical Ecology*, 10:1707-1730.

Pirkle, W. H., and P. E. Adams
1979.   Broad-spectrum synthesis of enantiomerically pure lactones. Part 1. *Journal of Organic Chemistry*, 44:2169-2175.

Pocock, R. I.
1910.   On the specialized cutaneous glands of ruminants. *Proceedings of the Zoological Society of London*. 1910, No. 62, 84-985.

1923. On the external characters of *Elaphurus, Hydropotes, Pudu,* and other Cervidae. *Proceedings of the Zoological Society of London.* 1923, No. 13, 181-207.

Porter, N.
1982. Responses of black-tailed deer (*Odocoileus hemionus columbianus*) to metatarsal secretion. M.S. thesis, State University of New York, Syracuse.

Quay, W. B.
1955. Histology and cytochemistry of skin gland areas in the Caribou, *Rangifer. Journal of Mammalogy,* 36:187-201.

1959. Microscopic structure and variation in the cutaneous glands of the deer, *Odocoileus virginiaus. Journal of Mammalogy,* 40:114-128.

1971. Geographical variation in the metatarsal "gland" of the white-tailed deer (*Odocoileus virginianus*). *Journal of Mammalogy,* 52:1-11.

Quay, W. B.
1971. Relations of age and sex to integumentary glandular regions in Rocky Mountain mule deer (*Odocoileus hemionus heionus*). *Journal of Mammalogy,* 52:670-685.

Quay, W. B., and D. Muller-Schwarze
1970. Functional histology of integumentary glandular regions in black-tailed deer (*Odocoileus hemionus columbianus*). *Journal of Mammalogy,* 51:675-694.

Ravid, U., R. M. Silverstein, and L. R. Smith
1978. Synthesis of the enantiomers of 4 substituted gamma lactones with known absolute configuration. *Tetrahedron,* 34:1449-1452.

Regnier, F. E., and M. Goodwin
1977. On the chemical and environmental modulation of pheromone release from vertebrate scent marks. In *Chemical Signals in Vertebrates,* edited by D. Muller-Schwarze and M. M. Mozell, pp. 115-133. New York: Plenum.

Ruzicka, L.
1926. Zur Kenntnis des Kohlenstoffrings. VII. Über die Konstitution des Muskons. *Helvetica Chimica Acta,* 9:715.

Schaffer, J.
1940. *Die Hautdrüsenorgane der Säugetiere.* Berlin: Urban and Schwarzenberg.

Schaller, G. B.
1967. *The deer and the tiger.* Chicago: University of Chicago Press.

Schumacher, S.
1936. Das Stirnorgan des Rehbockes (*Capreolus capreolus capreolus* L.), ein bisher unbekanntes Duftorgan. *Zeitschrift für Mikroskopisch-Anatomische. Forschung,* 39:215-230.

Sokolov, V. E.
1979. Marking of territory by caudal gland of male musk deer (*Moschus moschiferus* L.). *Proceedings of the Academy of Science of the USSR,* 246:894-897.

Sokolov, V. E., and L. V. Stepanova
1980. Ultrastructural organization of the interdigital gland of the elk. *Doklady Akademii Nauk SSSR,* 250(2):451-453.

Sokolov, V. E., Prikhod'ko, V. I., and V. M. Smilin
1980. Poses and demonstrations in behavior of *Moschus moschiferus. Zoologischeskii Zhurnal,* 59:1884.

Stanley, S. M.
1975. A theory of evolution above the species level. *Proceedings of the National Academy of Science,* 72:646-650.

Volkman, N. J.
1981. Some aspects of olfactory communication of black-tailed and white-tailed deer: Responses to forehead, antorbital, and metatarsal secretions. M.S. thesis, State University of New York, Syracuse.

Volkman, N., and K. Ralls
1973. Scent marking in the red brocket, *Mazama americana. Zoologica,* 58(2):55-56.

Volkman, N., K. Zemanek, and D. Muller-Schwarze
1978. Antorbital and forehead secretions of black-tailed deer: their role in age-class recognition. *Animal Behaviour,* 26:1098-1106.

Wemmer, C.
1983. Systematic position and anatomical traits. In *Biology and Management of an Extinct Species, Pere David's Deer,* edited by B. Beck and C. Wemmer, pp. 15-25. Park Ridge, New Jersey: Noyes Publication.

VALERIUS GEIST
The University of Calgary
Faculty of Environmental Design
Calgary, Alberta T2N 1N4, Canada

On the Evolution of Optical Signals in Deer: A Preliminary Analysis

ABSTRACT

The evolution of optical signals in deer is closely tied to the speciation process. Contrasting body marking and showy redundant behavior, often accompanied by strong vocal and olfactory signals characterizes the species that evolved into strongly seasonal, open landscapes. Forest forms opted for uniform, much less conspicuous exteriors and noticeably less showy behavior. There is a progression in ornateness from tropical resource defenders to "grotesque giants" of high latitudes and altitudes. In this, deer parallel other mammalian Ice Age lineages. The evolution of the Ice Age mammals is one of enhancement of social organs and a broadening of ecological adaptations; by contrast tropical forms retain old, late Tertiary body forms but are ecologically specialized. Despite great differences in appearance even within a lineage of closely related species, the social signals remain surprisingly conservative. The evolution of social organs in the speciation process following dispersal is discussed.

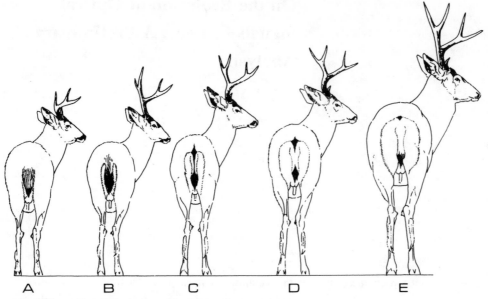

Figure 1. Altitudinal cline in mule deer (*Odocoileus hemionus*), beginning at sea level in wet forests (A. *O.h. sitkensis*), leading on to dry coastal mountains (B. *O.h. columbianus*), to the west slopes of the Sierras (C. *O.h. californicus*), to the east slopes of the high Sierras (D. *O.h. inyoensis*), and to the mule deer (E. *O.h. hemionus*) of the Rocky Mountains. Note changes in body size, antler configurations, tail and rump patch shape, and size of metatarsal gland (after Cowan, 1936).

Introduction

The question how optical signals evolved in the Cervidae cannot be answered simply, nor securely. Not only is the subject beset by complexity, difficulties in methodology and the procurement of data, and the frequent need to cross different disciplinary boundaries, but it is also subject to the controversies surrounding speciation. The evolution of optical signals in large mammals, ultimately, is tied to the speciation process (Geist, 1971a, b). However, even a cursory examination of cervids indicates that there may be as many as five different kinds of deer species, and by implication five different types of speciation processes. In addition, the subject of speciation is in considerable turmoil currently, as the Neo-Darwinian synthesis is questioned and old doubts are resurrected (Goldschmidt, 1940; Waddington, 1957, 1975; Eldridge and Gould, 1972; Grassé, 1973; Lovtrup, 1977, 1981; Gould and Eldridge, 1978; Geist, 1978a; White, 1978; Stanley, 1979; Balon, 1981).

I shall briefly review some of my earlier work (Geist, 1971a, b; 1974a, b; 1978a, b; 1983, in press), but also update information relevant to how optical signals evolve.

The Phenomenon to be Explained

A number of lineages of large mammals change in clinal fashion in external appearance with latitude or altitude. The shape of social organs (horns or antlers, rump patch and tail configurations, coloration, hair and shade patterns, sexual dimorphism, skin glands, but also vocal repetoires) changes geographically, as illustrated for black-tailed deer (*Odocoileus hemionus*) (Figure 1). However, this relationship is not consistent in that there are species with far-flung geographic distributions lacking noticeable changes in social organs. An example is the mule deer (*O. hemionus hemionus*): while there is an altitudinal cline from the most primitive to the most advanced subspecies, the terminal subspecies, the mule deer occupies a range from the central Yukon to northern Mexico. So far, no clinal change in antlers, or rump patch shape, etc. is discernible across this large range of latitudes. When clinal change in social organs does and does not occur, both situations must be explained.

The nature of clinal changes in external appearance, both latitudinally and altitudinally, can also be studied in the Old World deer (tribe Cervini). Species and subspecies change with increasing seasonality and lower winter temperatures in such a fashion as to become increasingly ornate in coloration and antler structure, and, generally, large in body size. The end forms in this type of evolutionary progression are "grotesque giants" in extreme environments; terminal species in subalpine and subarctic environments may be remarkably convergent, as illustrated by wapiti (*Cervus elaphus canadensis*) and the white-lipped deer (*Cervus (Przewalskium) albirostris*) (Figure 2). One also finds convergent changes in Old and New World deer geographically, e.g., moose (*Alces alces*), red deer (*C. elaphus*) and roe deer (*Capreolus*) change in social organs geographically in the same direction, so that primitive is found with primitive, advanced with advanced (Geist, in press). One finds that the geographic gradient from warm to cold climates is roughly paralleled by the mid-Tertiary to Pleistocene time gradient in deer evolution (Figure 3). The primitive-advanced axis parallels also an ecological gradient from tropical forests, to warm savannah, to temperate forest and savannah, to subarctic steppe, tundra, and periglacial environments, alpine and arctic. It also approximates ontogenetic development.

Body size appears to track the *duration* of the seasonal productivity pulse, as suggested by Guthrie (1984) and Geist (in press), but not the *height* of the pulse (Margalef, 1963). Consequently, latitudinally body size varies curvilinearly (Figure 4), not linearly as suggested by Bergman's rule. Since deer are very sensitive to nutrition in their morphological development (Vogt, 1936, 1948, 1951), and since body dimensions in mammals vary allometrically with size as animal science enshrined in the "centripetal theory of growth" (Hammond, 1960; but see also Ingebristen, 1923; Beninde, 1937; Gottschlich, 1965), considerable variation in size and shape can occur geographically for purely

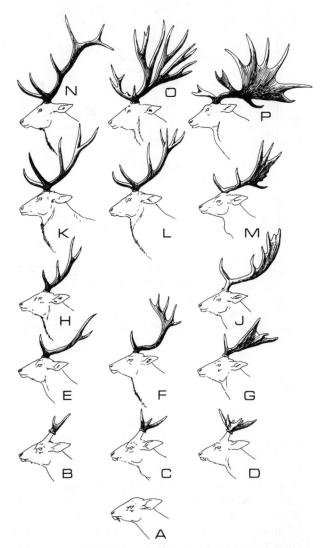

Figure 3. The evolution of Old World deer from the Mid-Tertiary to the Pleistocene, roughly corresponding with their latitudinal evolution. Deer with small antlers are of tropical (mid-Tertiary) origin, those with the most ornate antlers are found in cold climates (Pleistocene). Old World deer can be arranged in order of antler complexity, beginning with deer of a two-pronged stage and terminating with six-pronged deer. Also, each antler plan can be usually found in three versions, the simple, the supernumerary tined and the palmate. (A) antlerless tusked deer of early Tertiary times, (B) *Eustylocerus* (mid-Miocene), (C) *Dicrocerus*) (early Miocene), (D) *Stephanocemas* (mid Miocene), (E) *Axis* (early Pliocene), (F) *Rucervus*, (6) *Cervavitas* (early Pliocene), (H) *Cervus* (late Pliocene), (J) *Aoglochis* (Villafranchian), (K) *Cervus elaphus acoronatus* (Pleistocene), (L) *C.elaphus hippelaphus* (late Pleistocene), (M) *Dama dama* (mid-Pleistocene Riano fallow deer), (N) wapiti (*C.elaphus canadensis*) (late Pleistocene), (O) *Eucladoceros* (Villafranchian), (P) *Megaceros giganteus* (late Pleistocene). (After Thenius and Hofer, 1960; Kurtén, 1968; Kurtén and Anderson, 1980; Gramova, 1962; from Geist, 1971b, modified).

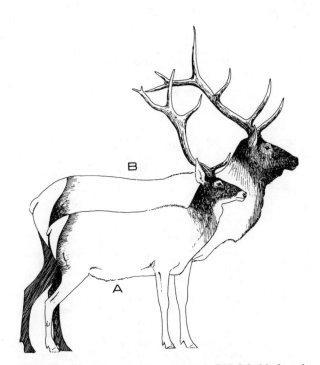

Figure 2. Convergence in unrelated Old World deer in latitudinal and altitudinal evolution. The white-lipped deer (A) exemplifies the latter, the wapiti (B) the former. Note similarities in antler and rump patch shape and size.

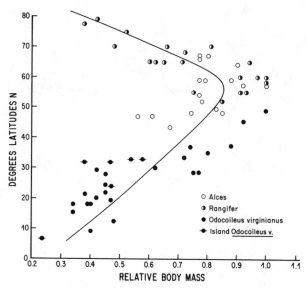

Figure 4. Because the annual productivity pulse varies curvilinearly with latitude (see Geist, in press), so does body size. Relative body mass expresses the small bodied forms as a fraction of the heaviest. Data for New World deer only.

body and antler mass than deer from upland habitats. A cursory examination indicates that "marsh deer" in the Old and New World are all relatively large deer with relatively large antlers (see Appendix I), but data for critical comparison are still lacking.

The changes in social organs that are of concern here are based on hereditary factors with complete "penetrance". That is, they express themselves phenotypically, irrespective of the individual's environment. Mule deer remain recognizable as mule deer even in zoos, because of canalized hereditary factors. Antlers are weakly canalized and show size related changes in shape and branching with nutrition, they lose symmetry with illness and age, and assume juvenile or paedomorphic proportions at small body size, no matter how old their bearer. They appear to be rigidly expressed by genes, as are rump patch and tail configurations, hairy coat and color patterns, the relative size of skin glands, and rutting vocalizations of the males.

While lineages progressing in evolution into increasingly colder climates change progressively in so-

non-genetic reasons. Beninde (1937) concluded for red deer that, if transplanted, they assume the morphology and appearance typical of the phenotype of deer in the region the deer are transplanted to. His conclusions were recently vindicated by the experimental work of James (1983). The same genotype can, depending on the environment it encounters, generate a great range of phenotypes as discussed in detail in Geist 1978 (pp. 116-144). It is also a phenomenon well known in fishes (Balon, 1981, 1985; Noakes and Balon, 1982).

Antlers are social organs that are highly sensitive to nutrition and health (Goss, 1983). Genetic differences can only be detected when these organs are grown to maximum size; only the antlers of "trophy" males have taxonomic significance. Antler mass changes with the latitude and habitat occupied by deer. It is smallest in tropical forest dwellers, and largest in steppe or tundra forms from cold climates. There is a large jump in antler mass between forest and open landscapes (savannah or steppe) (Geist, in press) (Figure 5).

It appears *a priori* that some of the latitudinal or altitudinal differences in maximum antler mass may be due to a longer period of productivity (the "productivity pulse") between low and temperature latitudes. Therefore, rivers running from high mountains to tropical low lands should carry there a seasonal pulse via flood waters and fertilizing silt, so that tropical deer living in riparian habitat should have a larger

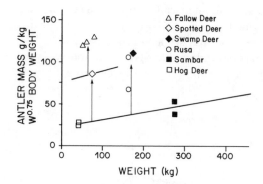

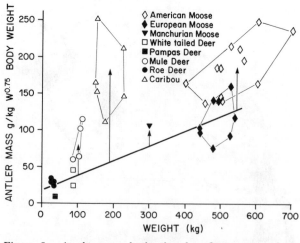

Figure 5. At the same body size deer from savannah or open landscapes carry almost twice the antler mass of deer from forests at the same latitude; an additional increase in antler mass takes place with latitude. This is exemplified by a sample of Old World deer (A), and by New World deer (B) (Geist, in press).

Geist

Figure 6. Two- and three-pronged Old World deer from India, representing a within-latitude radiation of ecologically diverse deer of a similar body plan. Note the long tails, lack of rump patch, absence or scarceness of neck mane, as well as simple antler plan, (A) *Muntiacus muntjac*, (B) *Axis porcinus*, (C) *Axis axis*, (D) *Cervus (Rucervus) duvauceli*, (E) *Cervus unicolor* (to scale) (Geist, 1983).

cial organs, lineages within a latitude, such as tropical Old World deer, retain the basic body plan, but change in ecological adaptations (Figure 6). Here, the "three-pronged" deer can be seen in a great diversity of ecological niches. Primitive body plans are tied to warm climate, but primitive giants can be highly specialized to the ecological conditions of the tropics while giants in the arctic can have advanced social body plans, but be ecologically adapted as generalists. Clearly, species differ greatly both between latitudes and within a latitude, and must have arisen differently. Also different are the *paedomorphic dwarfs* arising within lineages (Geist, unpublished data), the dwarfed island forms of large mammals (Azzaroli, 1982), and species arising from hybridization.

Here, we must note that lineages, evolving into increasingly colder climates, give rise to allopatric populations, while those evolving within a latitude give rise to sympatric populations. Consequently, latitudinal/altitudinal speciation is likely to be subject to disturbance by hydridization when allopatric branches meet. Continental sika deer (*C. nippon*) according to chromosonal studies (Bartos and Zirovnicky, 1981) may well have hydridized with red deer. Sika deer and red deer, placed together by human hands do interbreed (Kiddie, 1962; Harrington, 1973; Lowe and Gardiner, 1975), and they appear to interbreed in native populations as well (Heptner et al., 1961).

From some of the foregone points, one can make a number of deductions: if body and antler size vary with the duration of the productivity pulse, be it latitudinally, altitudinally, or with riparian communities, then antler and body size reflect the quality, quantity, and availability in space and time of forage resources. If so,

- species and populations from fertile soils will have better developed bodies and antlers, since deer require a feed high in minerals to fulfill the demands of antler growth (Vogt, 1948).

- periglacial ecosystems, due to the availability of fertile rock dust (loess), water and sunlight are favorable to deer that require a large intake of minerals for antler growth (see Geist, 1978a, pp. 196–207).

- deer are expected to survive better in the rejuvenated, nutrient rich Pleistocene landscapes, than on leached, nutrient poor soils and continents.

The foregoing indicates that between-regional differences in antler size and shape may have no evolutionary significance. However, between-individual differences within a population may reflect more than the differences in the quality of the occupied habitat. It may also reflect the abilities of males to find, procure, and process forage resources, and can thus serve as an index of males' resource procuring abilities. If so, annual size of horn-like organs of males should covary with the annual reproductive success of the

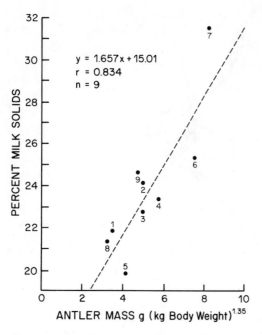

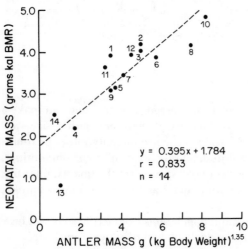

Figure 7. (A) Antler mass is correlated with percentage of milk solids, (1. *Odocoileus virginianus*, 2. *O. hemionus*, 3. *Capreolus capreolus*, 4. *Cervus elaphus elaphus*, 5. *C. elaphus canadensis*, 6. *Dama dama*, 7. *Rangifer tarandus*, 8. *Alces alces alces*, 9. *A. alces americana*.) (B) Antler mass is correlated with the amount of neonatal investment by the female. (1. *Odocoileus virginianus*, 2. *O. hemionus*, 3. *Capreolus capreolus*, 4. *Muntiacus reevesi*, 5. *Cervus nippon*, 6. *C. elaphus elaphus*, 7. *C. e. canadensis*, 8. *Dama dama*, 9. *Axis axis*, 10. *Rangifer tarandus*, 11. *Alces alces alces*, 12. *A. alces gigas*, 13. *Mazama sp.*, 14. *Pudu puda*.

females. For Dall's sheep (*Ovis dalli dalli*) this relationship was indeed found by Bunnell (1978).

One can now deduce that where neonates must rapidly grow to "survivable" size – such as in highly cursorial species that depend on speedy, enduring flight for security (Gambaryan, 1974) – the female must spare relatively more resources from her own growth and maintenance towards neonatal growth and milk production. If so, females should select mates with large horn-like organs, and males should have special behaviors emphasizing horn-like organs in courtship. Conversely, where there is no need for rapid postnatal growth, such as in species with a hider syndrome, there is no need for large neonates or a high production of milk. Here males can compete by force for access to females. Here it pays to shunt nutrients towards body growth, so that the males increase annually in body size but have small horn-like organs. All these predictions can indeed be verified: relative antler mass in deer correlates with the relative size of the neonates, and the percentage of solids in the milk (Figure 7). Large antlered deer such as American-type moose plateau in body mass, whereas the bulls of small antlered European-type moose continue

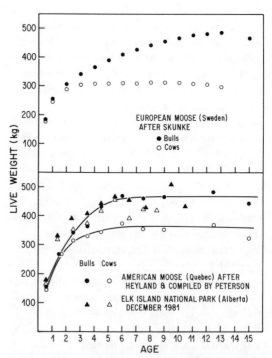

Figure 8. A comparison of body growth in small-antlered moose (European-West Siberian type, upper) and large-antlered moose (American type, lower). The small-antlered bulls show continual body growth with age, while the large-antlered American moose reach a plateau in body growth (data for upper and lower graphs from Peterson, 1955, 1974).

to increase in body mass with age (Figure 8). The deer with the highest relative antler mass, the caribou (*Rangifer*) and fallow deer (*Dama*) (Appendix 1), have very conspicuous antler displays in courtship. Whether females indeed prefer large over small antlered males in these two species requires experimental testing; in red deer the experimental evidence is not conclusive (see Clutton-Brock, 1982), but neither does *Cervus* possess a conspicuous antler display in courtship. Indirect evidence thus suggests that classical sexual selection as envisioned by Darwin (1888) may indeed be taking place in deer.

The foregoing indicated that antler mass may be a function of an anti-predator strategy of the neonate. Antler size and shape can be readily related to two broad classes of life strategies (Geist, 1978a, b): defenders of material resources, as opposed to plains dwellers that compete by scramble, but join into gregareousness as an anti-predator strategy (Wilson, 1975).

Species which defend material resources on a seasonal or year round territory are characterized by weapons that function to maximize surface damage, and which are virtually limited to that one function. The most common weapons are stiletto-like antlers, horns, or tusks. This strategy generates a syndrome of interlocking adaptations in morphology, social behavior, and ecology as described elsewhere (Geist, 1974a; 1978a, b). The weapon is of the type illustrated by the antlers of *Mazama*.

Gregariousness as an antipredator strategy selects for weapons and behavior in which injury is replaced by subjugation by force (as in wrestling). Horn-like organs function not only as weapons, but are used as shields to parry attacks (Geist, 1966) and as grappling organs (Walther, 1958) that allow the locking of opponents and full-strength wrestling arrangements. I described the logic of this weapon system elsewhere in detail (Geist, 1978a, pp. 79-80; 1978b). Branching of deer antlers and the evolution of complex sparring rituals (Geist, 1981, 1982) are logical additions to the morphology of such antlers and their use.

An additional dichotomy is possible granted the existence of complex horn-like organs: on one hand are forms which expend surplus energy defending breeding territories. The territory is their rank symbol and social mechanism for breeding. Due to the high costs of defence they show definitive growth, small horn-like organs, and very small fat reserves.

On the other hand mating may take place within a hierarchial rank system. In this case the surplus nutrients are expended on growing a larger body. The males enlarge year by year, resulting in undetermined growth. Horn-like organs serve strictly as grappling and locking organs and shields. Nutrients in excess of body growth can however be put into larger horn-like organs, and these can thus signal the attainment of large body size, as well as success in finding and procuring forage. The hierarchial breeding system is thus the point of departure for large horn-like organs via sexual selection under the narrow conditions of cursorialism, as explained earlier.

If it is granted that evolving in areas of prolonged pulses of seasonal productivity generates the geographic clines in social organs, then it is logical to expect that evolving in the opposite direction, namely into a shorter seasonal pulse (such as in colonizing from south to north, or from a time of abundance into a time of scarcity) should lead to the obverse. When species colonize southern from northern latitudes we expect dwarfing in body and antler size, but a retention of the typical coat pattern. There is also the possibility that a species at minimum phenotypic size will somehow give rise to paedomorphic dwarfs. That is, there may be a reversal to ancestral features in social organs, a "reversal" of evolution. Cervids colonizing South America from North America are therefore expected not only to stay primitive, but to regress via paedomorphic speciation to secondarily primitive forms. One thus expects symmetry in latitudinal-altitudinal speciation.

This leaves unexplained the *process* by which social organs increase in size and complexity with geographic dispersal along the gradient of an increasing productivity pulse. How is it possible that tissues, which in primitive species are expressed only under conditions of superabundant material resources are progressively fixed in genetic expression? How are hypermorphs generated? We must look now at several problems inherent to social organs and visual communication.

The Picture Plane

Social organs in ungulates are organized in what artists refer to as *picture planes*, as if each hair tassel, pigment spot, demarcation line as well as the antlers and the conspicuous rear-pole of the animal are arranged to catch and guide the attention of the onlooker. As I discussed elsewhere (Geist, 1978a), a logical picture plane arises during the dominance displays in ruminants, in which the markings are arranged as if to maximize the movement of the onlooker's eye across the full size of the picture plane; even optical illusions in the service of such a purpose can be identified. Individual elements of this picture plane can be understood from physiological investigations of processes of perception. There appears to be a "biology of art", rooted in common perception processes of mammals. Some quantifiable relationships in cervid external appearance can be tackled tentatively.

Figure 9. The accentuation of head and tail pole is illustrated by *Cervus unicolor equina* (A) and *Cervus (Rusa) timorensis* (B). With a relative increase in antler size goes an enlargement of the tail and an increase in the size of the neck mane.

Symmetry of head and tail pole

This symmetry was long ago pointed out by Portmann (1959). That is, visual changes in the head and tail poles of animals occur simultaneously. As antlers increase in size and complexity the tail and rump patch change so that either the tail becomes longer, or the rump patch enlarges while the tail shrinks. For instance, according to Hoogerwerf (1970) in the forest-dwelling *Cervus unicolor equina* the average skull length was 333.2 mm (n=11), antler length 450 mm (n=14), and tail length 236 mm (n=12). The comparable figures for the *Cervus timorensis* are 274 mm (n=15), 824 mm (n=15) and 217 mm (n=14). Thus *C. timorensis*, grew 0.79 mm of tail/millimeter of skull, and in *C. unicolor equina* the relationship is 0.71 (Figure 9). The relative tail length is thus 1.12 times greater in *C. timorensis*, and its silhouette is $(1.12)^2 = 1.25$ times greater. In a similar vein, *C. timorensis* grew 2.2 times as long an antler, relatively, and increased the silhouette $(2.2)^2 = 4.9$ times. Using photos of Pere David's stags, measuring relative antler lengths compared to face length and comparing it to sambar stags, I obtained an identical relationship. That is, the Pere David's stag grows about 2.2 times the linear dimension of antlers compared to sambar, while its tail is about 1.25 times as long as that of sambar. The increase in antler versus tail silhouette in both cases is

thus $(2.2)^2 = 3.1$ times. Clearly, the head poles of the animal increase in silhouette size, and thus conspicuousness, at a faster rate than the rear pole. In the *Cervus* species, *timorensis* also grows a larger neck mane than *equina*, just as the American type moose increases not only in antler size over the European one, but also in the size of the bell, and the ornateness of its body (Geist, in press).

A 68 kg hog deer (*Axis porcinus*) grows antlers about 60 cm in length, with a basal diameter of 3.0 cm and a weight of 600 g. Sambar (*C. unicolor*) carry antlers of the same plan that are virtually isometric in linear dimensions compared to the hog deer. For a 272 kg sambar we expect an antler length of 95.2 cm, and a basal diameter of 4.8 cm. According to Whitehead (1972) large sambar antlers measure about 100 cm in length, with a basal diameter of 4.8 cm; they weigh about 3.6 kg. The hog deer produces about 25 g (Wt kg) $^{0.75}$ of antler mass, but the sambar, to grow antlers of relatively the same length must produce 54 g (Wt kg) $^{0.75}$, or twice as much per unit of metabolic weight. The weight of antlers thus increases exponentially with body size. The weight of large hog deer and sambar antlers is approximated however by 2.0 grams (Wt kg) $^{1.35}$ which is the exponent I used throughout. Thus if sambar are derived from a hog deer like ancestor, they apparently maintained *visual constancy* in antlers. Why this should be so is not at all apparent. At 25 g (Wt kg) $^{0.75}$ a 272 kg sambar would carry antlers weighting 1.67 kg with a length of 74 cm, which is not much short of one meter and costs half as much.

Mysteries in Coat Patterning and Color

How rump patches or body colors evolve in cervids is still a mystery. Rump patches co-vary with antler size in some lineages; in cold climate species tail size appears to follow Allen's rule while rump patches expand; conversely, tails become more densely furred in the absence of rump patch development. In plains dwellers rump patches are usually fixed; in forest forms they are subject to flaring, that is, to allow the animal to hide, or to expose the rear pole. In roe deer from Europe the nominal subspecies has no rump patch in its summer coat, but does have one in its winter coat. However, in a relict subspecies in Spain the rump patch is well developed summer and winter (Meunier, 1983) as is the case in the Siberian roe deer.

Body color is mysterious, although Hamilton's (1973) discourse on coloration has shed at least some light on this subject. *A priori* considerations indicate that body color should serve not only in thermoregulation, the main focus of Hamilton's (1973) ideas, but also in security and social life.

A cursory review of large mammals indicates that species which either regularly confront predators, or which defend material resources against conspecifics, are usually dark in color. In particular those body parts are dark which form the picture plan seen by predators during confrontation. In nuptial colors male ungulates often retain a dark face (compared to females) although in related sympatric species males may have antithetical facial markings. Mule deer, which live sympatrically with white-tailed deer, have light faces in the males, white-tailed deer have dark faces; wapiti are dark faced, but red deer stags are light faced against a dark mane, as are Pere David's stags. Although red deer from Europe or Pere David's deer today are not in contact with wapiti, they may well have been in times of glacial advances since wapiti-like red deer were then found in Europe (Kurtén, 1968; Lister, 1984).

Paedomorphic coloration, that is the retention of the juvenile coat, is found in a number of deer, such as the axis, sika, fallow deer and several island forms of the genus *Cervus* (subgenus *Rusa*); it appears to be associated with gregariousness. In some species the nuptial coat of the male tends to become dark, overlying the spotted "juvenile coat" of the adult. Again, darkness of body or face appears to be linked to aggressive behavior.

The hypothesis that species confronting predators are likely to be dark predicts that dark-bodied forms are more likely among large than small-bodied species. Hamilton's theory predicts that if a species is faced concomitantly with a high workload, and a high solar heat load when ambient temperatures are high, then the species will evolve a reflective surface on its body to reflect solar heat. This predicts that not only desert forms are expected to be light, but also those species in temperate zones which rut during late summer and early autumn.

Since large rutting males of moose, elk, or *Megaceros* probably lose or lost 20-25 percent of their body weight in 25-35 days of rutting, their average daily heat production must jump at least three-fold; exertion increases heat production 15-20 fold (Brody, 1945). Considering the combined needs to deter predators and to shed heat, it can be predicted that those body parts facing predators will be dark, and those facing the sun will be light. That is, the species will likely feature a "reflective shield", being light on top and dark on the bottom. We find such light saddles in species that crossed the Beringian plains to North America. These plains were apparently fairly open, dry habitats with low shrubs and a few, probably well-shaped spruce trees, much as one still finds in much of Alaska and the Yukon. Note the light-colored saddle on the species during the summer and early fall rut: wapiti, moose, bison, musk oxen—as well as the brown bear of the interior, the grizzly—all have this color pattern. Caribou and thin horn sheep do not have saddles, but neither ruts during hot weather; nor does the forest dwelling coastal brown bear have the light saddle. Hamilton's theory correctly predicted a light back in *Megaceros* as is now apparent from cave paintings in the upper Paleolithic (Meroc and Mazet, 1953; Ulenhaut, 1959; R.D. Guthrie, pers. comm.). *Megaceros* must have rutted in the first two weeks of August, assuming it bore young in June and had a gestation period typical of Old World deer (Geist, unpublished data).

Social Behavior Patterns

Great changes have occurred in the external appearance of deer, but their signals of communication have changed modestly at most. The dominance display of the muntjac (Barrette, 1977) is very similar to that of hog-, axis-, Eld's-, swamp deer and sambar, so that homology is most likely (Figure 10). Moose, caribou, and white-tailed deer have little resemblance in external appearance, but their social signals are remarkably similar, implying common decent. Hofer (1972) pointed out that evolution of social signals was likely to be slow since neural structure of recognition

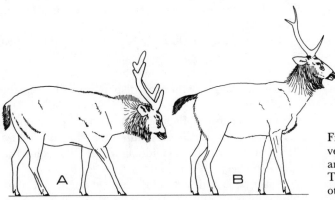

Figure 10. Dominance display of *Cervus unicolor* when in velvet (A) and in hard antlers (B). The display in velvet antlers is reminiscent of that of *Odocoileus*, *Alces* and *Rangifer*. The display in hard antlers is virtually identical to that in other three-pronged Old World deer.

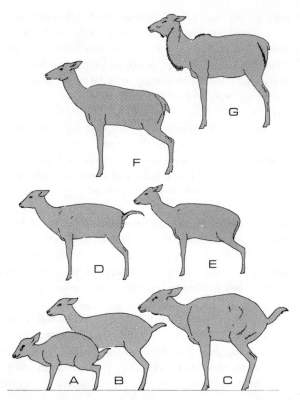

Figure 11. The female urination posture in Old World deer changes latitudinally with species. Primitive tropical deer urinate in a crouched posture; advanced deer crouch less or not at all. (A) *Muntiacus*, (B) *Axis axis*, (C) *Cervus unicolor*, (D) *Cervus nippon*, (E) *Dama dama*, (F) *C. elaphus canadensis*.

and of sending a signal had to change in unison. There are, however, some signals that change in line with the morphological clines discussed earlier.

The urination posture of Old World deer parallels the changes in latitudinal evolution, in that the urine-crouch so typical of primitive forms is lost with latitudinal dispersion (Figure 11). In the temperate zones, *Cervus, Dama,* and *Elaphurus* adopt a distinctly different courtship strategy than do the primitive forms. The tropical three-pronged Cervini tend to fixate on and defend individual estrous females, much as do New World deer irrespective of evolutionary position. In the temperate zones, the tending bond gives way to an advertisement strategy, the logic of which I discussed in detail for wapiti (Geist, 1982). This advertisement strategy leads to mandatory harem formation. A harem, collected and watched over by the male, generates in the male a conflict between herding and courtship approaches, a conflict solved in the same manner by *Cervus* and *Dama*. Herding is an aggressive act, dangerous to the female, from which the female escapes, usually by returning to the harem. Courtship must convey the opposite information, en-

ticing the female to stay. The herding displays of *Cervus* and *Dama* appear to be modified forms of the dominance displays of the primitive, three-pronged deer. The courtship approach in *Cervus* is the antithesis of the herding display; in *Dama* it is a new palm-waving display, not found in any other species of deer (Figure 12). The dominance display in *Cervus* is the parallel march, quite different in execution from the dominance display of the three-pronged deer. The dominance display of *Dama* also has lost the stiffness and, similar to *Cervus*, has become a parallel marching display, although the fallow deer holds his head noticeably higher than red deer or wapiti. In striking convergence, the Pere David's deer female does not squat while urinating, although the spotted calves still squat acting like primitive deer; the rutting stag roars, has a parallel march prior to combat, and a courtship approach with alternate antler turning, reminiscent of *Dama* but without vocalizations and quite slow in execution; the male also uses the low-stretch, like a primitive Old World deer (Wemmer et al., 1983).

Primitive three-pronged Old World deer have some superficial similarities to New World deer in their social signals. They have an expressive low-stretch approach in courtship which virtually hides the antlers; the submissive postures are similar, and the dominance displays of Old Word deer in velvet are similar to those of New World deer, in or out of velvet (Figure 10). These similarities may be due to convergence, since most New World deer and tropical Old World deer are closely tied to forest or cover, and thus carry small antlers.

In the New World deer (=Telemetacarpi) *Capreolus* departs in some of its signals from other New World deer due to its territorial strategy, but the "scrape" of *Capreolus, Alces,* and *Odocoileus virginianus* appears to be a homologous behavior. In the latter species it may serve in attracting females (Marchinton and Hirth, 1984). In *O. hemionus* the "scrape" is missing, apparently an antithetical solution to contacts with its ancestral form, *O. virginianus*. In these two species which are very closely related, the courtship behavior, but not the aggressive behavior, is greatly antithetical (Geist, 1981).

In *Rangifer* as in *Dama*, the species with the largest relative antler mass in New and Old World deer respectively, there is a showy antler display in both courtship and dominance display, missing in the small-antlered deer. In American moose, there is also a noticeable antler display though not as pronounced as in *Rangifer*. In *Dama* small-antlered males follow large-antlered males (Heidemann, 1973) much as in bighorn sheep (Geist, 1971a).

Sparring is highly developed in *Odocoileus* and quite different from any I saw in Old World deer (Geist,

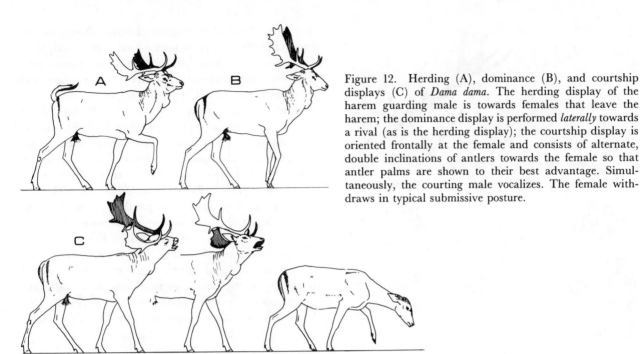

Figure 12. Herding (A), dominance (B), and courtship displays (C) of *Dama dama*. The herding display of the harem guarding male is towards females that leave the harem; the dominance display is performed *laterally* towards a rival (as is the herding display); the courtship display is oriented frontally at the female and consists of alternate, double inclinations of antlers towards the female so that antler palms are shown to their best advantage. Simultaneously, the courting male vocalizes. The female withdraws in typical submissive posture.

1981; 1982). It may function to establish bonds between males of unequal size in *Odocoileus*, which then share the costs of guarding females and reproduction, with the latter slanted greatly in favor of the dominant. In Old World deer all sparring partners acted as if equals; that is, their behavior was symmetrical, but asymmetrical in *Odocoileus* where one partner signalled inferiority, the other dominance.

Evolution of Novelty

It was shown earlier that, despite variation in morphology, coloration, and behavior, there are common trends in the geographic dispersion of Old and New World deer, as well as in other Ice Age mammals. We are faced with exploring a progression from primitive, tropical, resource defending forms to deer of new body and antler plans, often growing into giants in Pleistocene environments.

I shall here review briefly the explanation of this type of evolutionary progression, while being silent on other modes of speciation. The latitudinal/altitudinal model of speciation can be explained as follows (for details see Geist, 1978a, 1983).

(1) The first step towards the evolution of new form is dispersal into a large area of unoccupied habitat with a *superabundance of resources*. Dispersal must be into an enlarging productivity pulse. If these two conditions are not met, there will be no speciation.

(2) Deer can form extremes in phenotype depend-

ing on the availability of material resources for ontogenetic development. Environmental paedomorphic dwarfs are one extreme—that is, efficiency phenotypes characterized by slow growth, small adult body size, underdevelopment of tissues of low growth priority, low reproductive output, low levels of social behavior, low behavioral vigor, but fairly long life expectancy—except under extreme conditions. These are termed *maintenance phenotypes*. At the opposite end of resource availability are *dispersal phenotypes*, in every respect the opposite, being luxurious in growth, behavior and reproduction (Figure 13) (Geist, 1978a; pp. 116-144).

(3) During explosive colonization of unoccupied habitat, abundant material resources act as a stimulant to develop—over three to four generations (Vogt, 1948, 1951)—the full-fledged dispersal phenotype.

(4) The large size of the males and frequent social interactions put great physical stresses on the weapons and body of the males. Since they have grown to the genetic limits of body size, and sturdiness, their genetic potential for sturdiness has been actualized. Now natural selection can rapidly select for males having sturdier weapons.

Since large body size is adaptive in winning contests, and since genetic capability for body size is fully exposed, natural selection can also rapidly select for large size.

(5) If the males grow completely to their maximal genetic body size, differences in their individual abil-

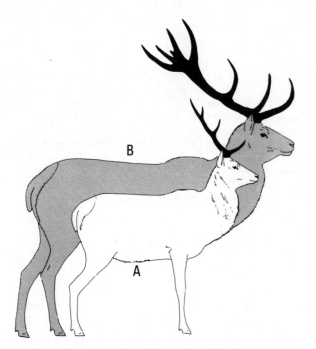

Figure 13. Maintenance (A) and dispersal phenotype (B) in red deer. Extremes in resource availability for ontogenetic development produce extremes in phenotype development (after Ingebristen, 1923; Beninde, 1937; Vogt, 1948).

ities to procure resources can be expressed only via tissues of low growth priority, such as antlers.

From a male's perspective, to maximize reproduction during the colonization stage, a large neonate and high milk production are highly adaptive. Both of these factors in cervids are correlated with antler mass (Figure 7). This suggests that during pulses of exceptionally high reproduction antlers may be subject to classic Darwinian sexual selection.

(6) During colonization, and rapid selection for body and antler size, we expect a strong founder effect, and the production of many "phenodeviants", coupled with a relaxation of selection on all maintenance phenotype features (competition is for mates, not material resources). Great variation is expected to arise in phenotypes. Since genetic limits to body size do exist, increases in body size depend on chromosonal rearrangement of alleles, not on mutant alleles. This implies that there will be chromosonal evolution in parallel with morphological and behavioral changes.

(7) With colonization completed, and resources stripped to the maintenance level, the foregoing process reverses, while *efficiency selection* on the maintenance phenotype begins to fine-tune the new form. This halts further social evolution. The size of the body and of tissues of low growth priority shrinks, but

not to the level of the ancestral form. Over geologic time, efficiency selection is expected to trim body size, and cause improvements in the organs of food procurement and processing as the new form becomes ever more capable of reproduction of lower costs to maintenance and growth. Followed to its logical extreme, efficiency selection probably generates the island dwarfs in the absence of predation. Social strategy probably changes from "forceful acquisition" of rank to "negotiation via display"; social displays are cheap bioenergetically (MacArthur et al., 1982). In this context I point to the parallel changes in the antlers of red deer, fallow deer, giant deer and moose over the late Pleistocene. In all four lineages antlers change from a simple structure with long, very sturdy tines to one of distal enlargement of antlers via radial branching of the tines, as in *Dama*, *Alces* and giant deer with additional palmation as well (Figure 14). While the animals become dwarfed (excepting *Mega-*

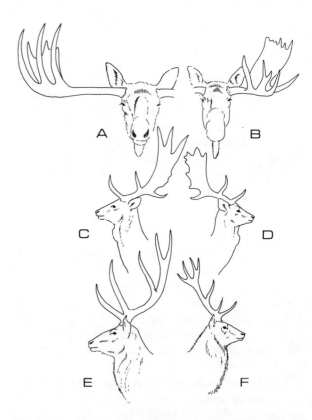

Figure 14. Compared to their ancestors from the mid-Pleistocene, recent species of *Alces*, *Dama dama*, and *Cervus elaphus* are not only smaller, but also feature antlers that are distally more complex. (A) *Alces (Cervalces) latifrons*, (B) *Alces alces gigas*, (C) *Dama dama clactonia*, (D) *Dama dama dama*, (E) *C. elaphus acoronatus*, (F) *C. elaphus hippelaphus*. Mid-Pleistocene forms were characterized by massively beamed and tined antlers, rather than supernumerary tines or enlarged palmation. (after Kurtén, 1968; Beninde, 1937; Lister, 1984; Azzaroli, 1981; Heintz and Poplin, 1981).

ceros) to their current body sizes, the antlers become more complex, as if enhancing displays.

Some Conclusions

The foregoing is a brief sketch of earlier work, but with some changes in points 4 and 6. This theory predicts a pulse of rapid speciation, followed by a very long phase of fine tuning, irrespective of ups and downs in body size. It implies that evolution is confined to extreme conditions only, and thus rare despite ongoing natural selection; the "fine tuning" period is not "stasis", but due to efficiency selection, a long period of gradual change. Above all, it explains how social evolution occurs, that is, as a consequence of conditions during explosive colonization irrespective of ecological adaptations. It indicates that social organs evolve in pulses, in part as a function of dispersal and colonization, in part under the influences of maintenance conditions. Some social organs, such as antlers, change greatly in form and size with resource availability, and in symmetry with the health of their bearer. However, this function appears to be important mainly if there is a premium on neonatal body size and post-natal growth. Very short, sharp spikes - as in *Mazama* - are weapons of resource defenders, probably of little importance in signaling. Where a lineage evolves progressively *into* an increasing productivity pulse, body size and ornateness increase; the obverse should produce opposite results, that is, the evolution of paedomorphic forms. However, in the process of dwarfing one does not expect increased complexity, but a simplification of social organs or no change at all. Therefore, species that dispersed towards the equator, or which retained gene flow over a

large area, are not expected to have changed in social characteristics.

The lineage of greatest evolutionary change among deer was that of the Pleistocene megacerines (Figure 15). *Megaceros giganteus* was highly cursorial (Geist, unpublished data), and that was the reason for its enormous antlers. We suspect that cursorialism was associated with large, follower-type young, and ready mobility, much as in the Alcelaphines which also showed a high rate of speciation in their history (Vrba, 1980). The white-tailed deer and roe deer, the "generalists" with hiding as an antipredator strategy, are long-lived, but have not greatly speciated. This is much as Vrba (1980) noted for the impala, whose young are also hiders. The probable reason for the difference in speciation rates appears to rest with the antipredator strategy: cursorialism under high predation pressure will drive phenotypes to the "dispersal phenotype" extreme, creating vigorous roamers that probe continually every opportunity for dispersal, increasing the chance for diversification. Hiders, however, will be confined more and more the harder the predation pressure. Consequently, they are more likely to live at the maintenance phenotype end of the spectrum, a condition not conducive to speciation.

Gregariousness and ornateness tend to go hand-in-hand, of which *Axis axis* is a modest example, and the highly gregarious *Rangifer* (the most cursorial of extant deer, Gambaryan, 1974) is a better one. Wapiti, more cursorial than red deer, are also more ornate. As to *Megaceros*, cave paintings indicate a light deer with strong external markings (Figure 15). Enlargement of antlers is also associated with a noticeable change in the behavior of courting or displaying males. Antlers in such forms are not held rigidly, but are tilted in rhythm with walking or with courtship movements. It is as if males enhance the visibility of their already conspicuous antlers with conspicuous, redundant movements. All in all, the subject of visual displays is complex, and much in need of careful, comparative investigations.

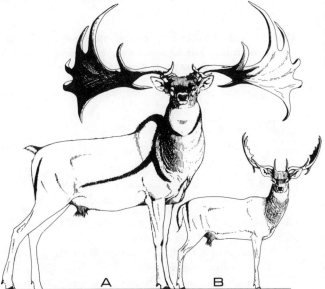

Figure 15. Two megacerines, the extinct periglacial *Megaceros giganteus* (A) and the extant *Dama dama* from warm-temperate climates. The giant deer appeared to have been a strikingly marked species as can be deciphered from upper Paleolithic cave paintings (Meroc and Mazet, 1953; R.D. Guthrie, personal communication).

Literature Cited

Anderson, A.E., and D.E. Medin
1969.   Antler morphology in a Colorado mule deer population. *Journal of Wildlife Management*, 33:520–533.

Azzaroli, A.
1981.   On the quaternary and recent cervid genera *Alces, Cervalces, Libralces*. *Bullettino della Societa Paleontologica Italiana*, 20, pp. 147-154.
1982.   Insularity and its effects on terrestrial vertebrates: evolutionary and biogeographic aspects. In *Paleontology, Essential of Historical Geology*, edited by Ju E.M. Gallitelle, pp. 193-213. Italy: S.T.E.M. Mucchi Modena.

Balon, E.K.
1981.   Saltatory process and altricial to precocial forms in the ontogeny of fishes. *American Zoologist*, 21:573-596.
1985.   *Early life history of fishes*. Hingham, Massachusetts: Dr. W. Junk Publishers.

Barrette, C.
1977.   The social behaviour of captive muntjacs (*Muntjacus reveesi*) (Ogilby 1839). *Zeitschrift für Tierpsychologie*, 43:188-213.

Bartos, L. and J. Zirounicky
1981.   Hybridization between red and sika deer II. Phenotype analysis. *Zoologischer Anzeiger*, 207:271-287.

Beninde, J.
1937.   *Zur Naturgeschichte des Rothirsches*. Leipzig: P. Schops.

Blood, D.A., and A.L. Lovaas
1974.   Measurement and weight relationships in Manitoba elk. *Journal of Wildlife Management*, 30:135–140.

Brody, S.
1945.   *Bioenergetics and Growth*. New York: Reinhold.

Bunnell, F.L.
1978.   Horn growth and population quality in Dall sheep. *Journal of Wildlife Management*, 42:764-775.

Clutton-Brock, T.H.
1982.   The function of antlers. *Behaviour*, 79:108-125.

Cowan, J. McT.
1936.   Distribution and variation in deer (Genus *Odocoileus*) of the Pacific coast region of North America. *California Fish and Game*, 22:155-246.

Darwin, C.
1888.   *The decent of man and selection in relation to sex*. London: John Murray.

Eldridge, N. and S.J. Gould.
1972.   Puntuated Equilibria. An Alternative to phyletic gradualism. In *Models in Paleobiology*, edited by T.J.M. Schopf, pp. 82-115. San Francisco:

Flook, D.R.
1970.   Causes and implications of an observed sex differential in the survival of wapiti. *Canadian Wildlife Service Report*, Series 11, 71 pp. Freeman, Cooper, and Company.

Frevert, W.
1977.   *Rominten*. München: BLV Verlagsgesellschaft.

Gambaryan, P.P.
1974.   *How mammals run*. New York: John Wiley and Sons.

Geist, V.
1966.   The evolution of hornlike organs. *Behaviour*, 27:175–215.
1971a.   *Mountain Sheep*. Chicago: University of Chicago Press.
1971b.   On the relation of social evolution and dispersal in ungulates during the Pleistocene, with emphasis on the Old World deer and the genus *Bison*. *Quaternary Research*, 1:283-315.
1974a.   On the relationship of ecology and behaviour in the evolution of ungulates: theoretical considerations. In *The Behaviour of Ungulates and Its Relationship to Management*, edited by V. Geist, and F. Walther, 2 Volumes, pp. 235-246. Morges: I.U.C.N.
1974b.   On the relation of social evolution and ecology in ungulates. *American Zoologist*, 14:250-220.
1978a.   *Life Strategies, Human Evolution, Environmental Design*. New York: Springer Verlag.
1978b.   On weapons, combat, and ecology. In *Aggression, Dominance, and Individual Spacing*, edited by L. Krames, P. Pliner, and T. Alloway, pp. 1-30. New York: Plenum Press.
1981.   On the reproductive strategies in ungulates and some problems of adaptation. In *Systematics and Euduhonony Biology*, edited by G.G.E. Scudder and J.L. Reveal, pp. 111-132. Pittsburgh: Carnegie-Mellon University.
1982.   Adaptive behavioural strategies. Chapter 2 in *Elk of North America*, edited by J.W. Thomas and D.E. Toweill, pp. 219-277. Harrisburg, Pennsylvania: Stackpole Books.
1983.   On the evolution of Ice Age mammals and its significance to an understanding of speciation. *Association of South Eastern Biologists Bulletin*, 30:109-133.
(in press).   On the evolution and adaptations of *Alces*. *Viltrevy.*

Goldschmidt, R.
1940.   *The Material Basis of Evolution*. New Haven: Yale University Press.

Goss, R.J.
1983.   *Deer Antlers*. New York: Academic Press.

Gottschlich, H.J.
1965.   Biotop and Wuchsform—eine craniometrish- allometrische Studie an europaischen Populationen von *Cervus elaphus*. Beiträge zur Jagd und Wildforschung. IV. *Deutsche Akademie der Landwirtschaftswissenschaften*, Berlin DDR. pp. 83-101.

Gould, S.J.
1974. The origin and function of bizarre, structures, antler size, and skull size in the Irish elk, *Megaloceros giganteus*. *Evolution*, 28:191–220.

Gould, S.J., and N. Eldridge.
1978. Punctuated equilibria. The tempo and mode of evolution reconsidered. *Paleobiology*, 3:115-151.

Gramova, V.I.
1962. Fundamentals of Paleontology, Vol. 8. In *Mammals*. (Translated from Russian). Smithsonian Institution and National Science Foundation. Springfield: Clearinghouse.

Grassé, P.P.
1973. *Evolution of Living Organisms*. (English translation, 1977). New York: Academic Press.

Guthrie, R.D.
1984. Mosaics, allochemics and nutrients. An ecological theory of late Pleistocene megafaunal extinctions. In *Quaternary Extinctions*, edited by P.S. Martin and R.G. Klein, pp. 259-298. Tucson: University of Arizona Press.

Hamilton, W.J. III
1973. *Life's Colour Code*. New York: McGraw-Hill.

Hammond, J.
1960. *Farm Animals*. London: Arnold.

Harrington, R.
1973. Hybridisation among deer and its implication for conservation. *Institute of Forestry*, 30:64-78.

Heidemann, G.
1973. Zur Biologie des Damwildes (*Cervus Dama* Linne 1758). *Mammalia Depicta*. Berlin: P. Parey.

Heintz, E., and F. Poplin
1981. *Alces carnutorum* (Laugel, 1862) du Pleistocene de Saint-Prest (France) Systematique et evolution des Aleines (Cervidae, Mammalia). *Quartarpalaontologic*, 4:105-122.

Heptner, V.G., A.A. Nasimovic, and A.G. Bannikov
1961. *Die Säugetiere der Sowjetunion*. Vol. 1. *Paarhuffer und Unpaarhufer*. Jenda: VEB Gustav Fisher Verlag.

Herre, W.
1956. *Rentiere*. Neue Brehm Bucherei. No. 180 Wittenberg Lutherstadt: A. Ziemsen Verlag.

Hofer, H.
1972. Prolegomena primatologiae. In *Die Sonderstellung des Menschen*, edited by H. Hofer and G. Altner, pp. 113-148. Stuttgart: Fischer.

Hoogerwerf, A.
1970. *Udjung Kulon. The Land of the Last Javan Rhinoceros*. Leiden: E.J. Brill.

Ingebristen, O.
1923. Das Norwegische Rotwild. Eine kraniometrische Untersuchung. *Bergens Museum, Aarbok. Naturvideusk.* No. 7, pp. 242.

James, F.C.
1983. Environmental components of morphological differentiation in birds. *Science*, 211:184-186.

Kiessling, W.
1913. *Der Rothirsch und seine Jagd*. Neudamm: J. Neuman.

Kiddie, D.G.
1962. *The sika deer (Cervus nippon)*. Wellington: New Zealand Forest Service.

Koppy, W. von
1926. *Jagderlebnisse in Norwegen*. Neudamm: J. Neuman.

Kramer, H.
1963. *Elchwald*. Munich. Bayerisches Landwirtschaftsverlag.

Kurtén, B.
1968. *Pleistocene Mammals of Europe*. London: Weidenfeld and Nicolson.

Kurtén, B. and E. Anderson
1980. *Pleistocene Mammals of North America*. New York: Columbia University Press.

Linke, W.
1957. *Der Rothirsch*. Die Neue Brehm-Bucherei, No. 129. Wittenberg Lutherstadt: A. Ziemsen Verlag.

Lister, A.
1984. Evolutionary and ecological origins of British deer. *Proceedings of the Royal Society of Edinburgh*, 82B:205-229.

Lovtrup, S.
1981. Introduction to evolutionary epigenetics. In *Evolution Today*, edited by G.G.E. Scudder and J.L. Reveal, pp. 139-144. Proceedings of the Second International Congress on Systematics and Evolutionary Biology.

1977. *The Phylogeny of Vertebrata*. London: J. Wiley and Sons.

Lowe, V.P.W., and A.S. Gardiner
1975. Hybridisation between red deer (*Cervus elaphus*) and sika deer (*C. nippon*) with particular reference to stocks in N.W. England. *Journal of Zoology*, 177:553-566.

MacArthur, R.A., V. Geist, and R.H. Johnson
1982. Physiological correlates of social behavior in bighorn sheep: a field study using electrocardiogram telemetry. *Journal of Zoology*, 196:401-405.

Marchinton, R.L., and D.H. Hirth
1984. Behavior (Chapter 6). In *White-tailed Deer*, edited by L.K. Halls, pp. 129-168. Harrisburg: Stackpole.

Margalef, R.
1963. On certain unifying principles in ecology. *American Naturalist*, 97:357–374.

McCullough, D.
1982. Antler characteristics of George Reserve whie-tailed deer. *Journal of Wildlife Management.*, 46:821–826.

Mehlitz, S., and A.. Siefert
1974. Zur Körper- und Geweihentwicklung des Damwildes *Cervus (Dama) dama L. Beiträge sur Jagd- und Wildforschung*, 8:49–74.

Meroc, L., and J. Mazet
1953. Les peintures de la grotte de Cougnac (Lot). *Anthropologie* 57:490-494.

Meunier, K.
1983. Das Spanisch Reh. In *Wildbiologische Informationen für den Jäger*, edited by R.R. Hofmann, pp. 147-153. St. Gallen, Switzerland: Jagd & Hege Verlag.

Noakes, D.C.G., and E.K. Balon
1982. Life histories of tilapias: an evolutionary perspective. In *Biology and Culture of Tilapias*, edited by R.S.V. Pullin and R. Lowe-McConnell, pp. 61-83. Manila: ICLARM Conference Proceedings No. 7.

Neumann, A.
1968. Rehwild Population Hohenbucko. *Beitrage Zur Jagd und Wildforschung*, VI, pp. 93–101. Berlin, DDR: Deutsche Akademie der Landwirtschaftswissenschaften.

Otaosji, N.
No Developmental variation of the antlers of Japanese
date. deer at Nara Park.

Peterson, R.L.
1955. *North American Moose*. Toronto, Ontario: University of Toronto Press.

1974. A review of the general life history of moose. *Naturaliste Canadien*, 101:9-21.

Portmann, A.
1959. *Einfuhrung in die vergleichende Morphologie der Wirbeltiere*. (Second Edition). Basel: B. Schwabe.

Skal, O.
1982. *Jagdparadis Alaska*. 2nd Edition. Leopole Stocker Verlag.

Stanley, S.M.
1979. *Macroevolution. Pattern and Process*. San Francisco: W.H. Freeman.

Thenius, E., and H. Hofer
1960. *Stammesgeschichte der Säugetiere*. Berlin: Springer Verlag.

Ulenhaut, J.
1959. Bemerkungen zur Nevaustellung eines Trischen Rosenhirsch Skeletts. *Verhandlungen der Naturawissenschaften der Heimat*, 34:51-54.

Vogt, F.
1936. *Neue Wege der Hege*, Neumann-Neudamm.

1948. *Das Rotwild*. Vienna: Östereichischer Jagd-und Fischerei Verlag.

1951. *Das Rehwild*. Vienna: Österreichischer Jagd-und Fischerei Verlag.

Vrba, E.S.
1980. Evolution, species and fossils: how does life evolve. *South African Journal of Science* 76:61-84.

Waddington, D.H.
1957. *The Strategy of the Genes*. London: George Allan and Unwin.

1975. *The Evolution of the Evolutionist*. Ithaca, New York: Cornell University Press.

Walther, F.
1958. Zum Kampf- und Paarungsverhalten einiger Antilopen. *Zeitschrift für Tierpsychologie*, 15:340-380.

Wemmer, C.M.
1983. Systematic Position and Anatomical Traits (Chapter 2). In *The Biology and Management of an Extinct Species, Pere David's Deer*, edited by B.B. Beck and C.M. Wemmer, pp. 15–25. Park Ridge, New York: Noyes Publications.

Wemmer, C.M., L.R. Collins, B.B. Beck, and B. Rettberg
1983. The ethogram (Chapter 6). In *The Biology and Management of an Extinct Species, Pere David's deer*, edited by B.B. Beck and C.M. Wemmer, pp. 91-125. Park Ridge, New Jersey: Noyes Publications.

White, M.J.D.
1978. *Modes of Speciation*. San Francisco: W.H. Freeman.

Whitehead, G.K.
1972. *Deer of the World*. London: Constable.

Wilson, E.O.
1975. *Sociobiology*. Cambridge, Massachusetts: Belknap Press, Harvard Press.

Wolf, G.J.
1983. The relationship between age and antler development in Wapiti. In *Antler development in Cervidae*, edited by R.D. Brown, pp. 29–36. Kingsville, Texas: Ceasar Kleberg Wildlife Research Institute.

Appendix I.   Live weights, antler weights and production of antlermass per unit of metabolic weight.

Species	Live Weight kg	Antler Weight (both antlers)	Antler Weight g W$kg^{.75}$	Antler Weight g W$kg^{.1.35}$	Author
Cervus elaphus, red deer East Germany	134.4	4.9	124.0	6.6	Neumann, 1968
Cervus elaphus, red deer Germany, East Prussia	265	8.9	135.5	4.8	Kramer, 1963, p. 271
Cervus elaphus, red deer Germany, East Prussia	270	9–11.5	135.1–172.7	4.7–6.0	Kramer, 1963, p. 271
Cervus elaphus, red deer Germany, East Prussia	232	12.25	206.0	7.8	Linke, 1957, p. 13
Cervus elaphus (Rominten 1890–1898)	187.5 (69)	5.2	103	4.5	Frevert 1977
(Rominten 1899–1906)	180.5 (135)	5.95	121	5.35	Frevert 1977
Rominten 1907–1912)	178.0 (117)	6.77	139	6.20	Frevert 1977
Rominten (Medieval stag)	308	18.7	254	8.2	Frevert 1977
(largest Rominten stag)	238	11.7	193	7.22	Frevert 1977
(Rominten 1935–1942)	215	8.81 (64)	157	6.25	Frevert 1977
Cervus elaphus					
Vogt's experimental stags 6 yr.	261.5 (5)	12.07	186	6.58	Vogt 1948
7 yr.	245.4 (5)	11.56	186	6.87	Vogt 1948
8–9 yr.	241.4 (8)	11.95	195	7.26	Vogt 1948
10–11 yr.	218.8 (9)	12.17	214	8.44	Vogt 1948
Cervus elaphus, red deer Germany, Brandenburg	176	6.0	124.2	5.6	Linke, 1957, p. 89
Cervus elaphus, red deer Germany, East Prussia	216	7.5	133.1	5.3	Linke, 1957, p. 89
Cervus elaphus, red deer Germany (experimental)	212.5	14	251.8	10.1	Vogt, in Beninde 1937 p. 163, 167
Cervus elaphus, red deer Germany, Medieval	324.3–428.2	10–19.86	130.1–211	4.1–5.56	Kiessling, 1913, p 24, 43 Beninde 1937, p 165
Cervus elaphus, red deer Europe-West	150	7.5	174.8	8.7	Linke, 1957, p 89
Cervus elaphus, red deer Carpathian Mts.	270	9.0	135.0	4.7	Linke, 1957, p. 89
Cervus elaphus, red deer Caukasus Mt.	337	11.0	139.9	4.3	Linke, 1957, p. 89
Cervus elaphus, red deer stag, Crimea, USSR	296	10–11.5	151.0–161.2	4.6–5.3	Heptner et al. 1961
C. e. xanthopygos, Jzubr stag, Manchuria	170–250	7	126.9–148.6	4.1–6.8	Heptner et al. 1961

Species	Live Weight kg	Antler Weight (both antlers)	Antler Weight g Wkg.75	Antler Weight g Wkg.1.35	Author
C. e. bactrianus, Buchard stag,	130	5.5	142.9	7.7	Heptner et al. 1961
C. e. sibiricus, Wapiti Siberia, Altai Mountains	350	14	173.2	5.1	Linke, 1957, p. 88
C. e. sibiricus, Wapiti Siberia, Altai Mountains	250–300	7–20	111.3–277.4	4.1–9.1	Heptner et al. 1961
C. e. nelsoni, Wapiti Banff, Alberta, N. America	333	4–11 (x=8)	102.6	4.3	Flook, 1970
C. e. nelsoni, Wapiti North-West Alberta N. America	350	9.1–14.5[2]	112.4–179.2	3.3–5.33	Eben-Ebenau, R. (personal communication)
C. e. nelsoni Southern Alberta	350	16.5	204	6.0	Geist, V. unpublished
C. e. nelsoni, Wapiti Elk Island National Park Canada	378.2 (n=25)	7.2	84.0	2.4	Geist, V. W. Wishart, unpublished
C. e. nelsoni, Wapiti New Mexico	350	13.8–15.5	170–191	5.1–5.7	Wolf 1983
C. e. manitobensis, Wapiti Manitoba	478.6	15.29	149	3.74	Blood and Lovaas 1966
Cervus nippon hortulorum Silka deer, Manchuria	117–131	1.6–3.7	45.0–95.9	2.6–5.1	Heptner et al. 1961
C. n. nippon, Sika deer Japan	80	0.9–1.14	33.6–42.6	2.4–3.1	Otaosji (undated)
Dama dama, fallow deer Germany, East Prussia	87.5	3.0–3.5	104.9–110.8	7.2–8.36	Kramer, 1963, p. 308
Dama dama, fallow deer East Germany	58.6[3]	2.56	120.9	10.5	Mehlitz & Siefert 1974
Megaceros, Irish elk Ireland	575[4]	39.1	333	7.35	Gould, 1974, Owen 1846
Elaphurus davidonus, Pere Davids deer	172	5.9 (4.0–8.6) (n=103)	124 (85–181)	5.7 (3.9–8.25)	C. Wemmer, personal comm Wemmer 1983
Rusa unicolor, Sambar India	272	26–3.6[5]	38.8–53.7	1.3–1.9	Whitehead, 1972 p. 105, 106
Rusa unicolor, Sambar	197	4.0	76.1	3.2	R. L. Marchinton 1985
Rusa unicolor, Sambar	295	4.8	67.4	2.2	(personal communication)
Rusa timorensis, Rusa Java	160	3.1–4.8[5], 7[6]	68.9–106.7	3.3–5.1, 7.4	Hoogerwerf, 1970
Rucervus duvauceli, swamp deer, India	175	7.7	160	7.2	Whitehead, 1972, p. 120
Rucervus eldi, Eld's deer	105	3.38 (2.5–4.9) (n=21)	103 (76–149)	6.3 (4.7–9.1)	C. Wemmer, personal communication

Species	Live Weight kg	Antler Weight (both antlers)	Antler Weight $g\,Wkg^{.75}$	Antler Weight $g\,Wkg^{1.35}$	Author
Axis porcinus, hog deer India	40	0.4[5]	25.2	2.7	Whitehead, 1972, p. 115
Axis porcinus, hog deer Nepal	68	0.59	24.9	2.0	Sunquist, M. 1982 (personal communication)
Axis axis, spotted deer India	86	2.3[5]	81.4	5.6	Whitehead, 1972, p. 113
Preewalskium albirostris White-lipped deer, Tibet	230	12.0	203	7.8	Cai Guiguan, personal communication
Rangifer tarandus osborni, Osborn's Caribou, B.C.	180[7]	8.6	175.0	7.76	Geist, V. unpublished
Rangifer tarandus caribou, Woodland, Alberta	180	6.8–12.2 (n=4)	138–248	6.1–11.0	Eben-Ebenau, R. (personal communication)
Rangifer tarandus, reindeer, Eurasia	180	12	244.2	10.8	Heptner et al. 1961
Rangifer tarandus, reindeer, European	120–150	3–11	82.7–256.4	4.7–12.7	Herre 1956
Rangifer tarandus, reindeer, introduced to Pribilof Islands	180	16.8	342	15.1	Geist, V. unpublished
Odocoileus birginiunus, white-tailed deer, Alberta	87.1[9]	1.3	45.6	3.1	Geist, V. unpublished
Odocoileus virginianus, (captive) n=11 whitetailed deer	79.5 (55.5–101.4)	0.96 (.56–1.45)	35.9 (24.8–49.4)	2.6 (2.4–2.8)	K. V. Miller & J. J. Hamilton (personal communication)
Odocoileus virginianus (captive) same mature buck	78.2–86.4	1.3–1.5	51.3–52.6	3.5–3.8	R. L. Marchinton, (personal communication)
Odocoileus virginianus, white-tailed deer, Michigan	84.1	0.68	24.5	1.7	McCullough 1982
Odocoileus hemionus mule deer, Colorado	84.1	1.65	59.4	4.2	Anderson and Medin 1969
Odocoileus hemionus mule deer, Lesser Slave Lake, Alberta	110	2.1–3.5 (x=2.6, n=11)	61.8–103.0	3.7–6.1	Eben-Ebenau, R. (personal communication)
Capreolus capreolus, Roe deer, Germany, East Prussia	27	0.3–0.4	26.5–33.8	3.5–4.7	Kramer 1963
Capreolus capreolus, Roe deer, Germany	17.2–26.0	0.26–0.67	30.8–65.5	5.6–8.2	Bieger in V. Raesfeld 1956, p. 12, 27, 34
Blastocerus bezoarticus Pampas deer, Zoo Berlin	35	0.22–0.3	15.3–20.8	1.8–2.47	Fradrich, H. 1981 (personal communication)
Alces alces alces, moose Germany, East Prussia	513[10]	8.6	79.8	1.9	Kramer 1963 p 216
Alces alces alces, moose Germany, East Prussia	534	13	117	2.7	Kramer 1963 p 220
Alces alces alces, moose Germany, East Prussia	420–440	9.5	98.9–102.4	2.6–2.7	Kramer 1963 p 113

Species	Live Weight kg	Antler Weight (both antlers)	Antler Weight g Wkg$^{.75}$	Antler Weight g Wkg$^{.1.35}$	Author
Alces alces alces, moose Sweden	477	7.8–14.7[11]	76.4–144.0	1.9–3.6	Peterson 1955 p 94, Kramer 1963 p 222
Alces alces alces, moose West Siberia	518	18.6[12]	171.3	4.0	Heptner et al. 1961
Alces alces alces, moose Norway	600	15.0	124	2.7	von Koppy 1926
A. a. pfitzenmayeri East Siberia	600	20	165	3.6	Heptner et al. 1961
A. a. cameloides Manchuria	300	6	83.2	2.7	Heptner et al. 1961
A. a. andersoni British Columbia	450	14.5[13]	148.4	3.8	Geist, V. unpublished
A. a. andersoni Lesser Slave Lake, Alberta	542[14]	24	213.7	4.9	Eben-Ebenau, R. 1953 p 88
A. a. andersoni Lesser Slave Lake, Alberta	500	15.0–22.7	141.8–214.6	3.4–5.2	Eben-Ebenau, R. 1983 (personal communication)
A. a. andersoni Elk Island National Park, Alta	460.5 (n=23)	5.0–6.1	50.3–61.4	1.3–1.5	Geist & Wishart unpublished
A. a. gigas Alaska	565[15]	22.87 (n=145)	197.1	4.4	Skal 1982 p 146
A. a. gigas Alaska	600	35.83 (16)	296	6.36	Skal 1982
A. a. andersoni Ontario	492	14.0	134	3.25	Peterson 1955, 1974

The weights are those of the largest, mature trophy stags. The antler weights are with upper skull or reconstructed to that criterion. The body weights, where possible, are lean weights of rutting stags, unless stated otherwise. Antler weight is affected by drying (about 10%) but more importantly by habitat; some large antlers can be light and others of similar dimensions relatively heavy. Numbers in brackets refer to sample size or range of values.

1. The body weights for six exceedingly fat stags, shot 1713-1715 of Freiburg (southern Germany) between September 21 - October 5, just before the rut. The maximum antler weight is for the largest set of red deer antlers ever collected and found at the Moritzburg, near Dresden, Germany (DDR) (see Wagenknecht 1981, p. 383). This antler weight is given with a small skull plate and would have probably reached 21 kg with a whole skull.

2. Based on one shed antler weighing dry 16 kg from the Smoky River of Alberta. Courtesy R. Eben-Ebenhau, Slave Lake, Alberta.

3. Based on a large sample of fallow deer.

4. The body weight of *Megaceros* was estimated by various scaling techniques; the range of weights for old stags ranged probably from 460-700 kg, if the spread was similar to that found in recent deer, in which the lightest mature and old male is about 0.65 the weight of the largest. Antler weight is that given by Owen (1846) for a large head.

5. These are calculated weights, using linear dimensions of antlers and a density of 1.9 g per cm^3. I determined from photos that the first tine is $\frac{1}{3}$ the length of the beam, and the second tine is $\frac{1}{5}$.

6. Based on a large antler weighing 3.5 kg.

7. This is the reconstructed *lean* weight of a four-year old, large but not exceptional Osborn caribou from the Spuzisis

Plateau of Northern British Columbia, Canada. His fat weight was approximately 226 kg at the time of kill, before the rutting season.

8. This is the heaviest set of *Rangifer* antlers known. They come from a bull of an introduced herd in the Pribilof Islands, and is now in a private collection. It is also the heaviest *relative* antler weight of extant deer.

9. The post-rut weight of an old, unexceptional Alberta white-tailed buck.

10. I have listed the body weight and the corresponding antler weight of trophy bull moose from Europe; averages are from pooled weights.

11. These weights are those of top trophy bulls displayed at an exhibition of trophies.

12. This is the weight of a former world record European-West Siberian type moose.

13. This was the largest-antlered of some 250 bulls killed in 1958 in Wells Grya Park, British Columbia. The bull was 4.5 years old. The body weight is representative of large bulls from that area.

14. Here I corrected Eben-Ebenhau's figures by multiplying field dressed weight by 1.25, not 1.5.

15. This is a calculated weight for large Alaska Trophy bull moose. It was derived using linear measurements for large Alaska and Canadian bull moose (Peterson, 1955, p. 74). Former exceeded latter by 1.0426. This difference cubed is 1.133, or 13.3%. Three large Canadian bulls averaged 506 kg; Alaska bulls would thus weight 573 kg. Using skull length for scaling: 70 skull lengths recorded by Skal (1982) for Alaska trophy bulls exceeded those of the large Elk Island bull moose by 1.0642. The average lean weight of the Elk Island bulls was 460.5 kg; consequently, Alaska trophy bulls would weight $460.5 \times (1.0642)^3 = 555$ kg. My estimate is thus 565 kg for average, large trophy bulls.

16. This is the heaviest set of Alaska moose antlers on record and come from a former world record bull.

17. The body and antler weights appear to be representative of large, old bulls bordering on the trophy class.

Part II

Case Studies of Exotic Deer

HEMANTA RAJ MISHRA
and
CHRIS WEMMER
King Mahendra Trust for Nature Conservation
P.O. Box 3712
Babar Mahal
Kathmandu, Nepal

Conservation and Research Center
National Zoological Park
Front Royal, Virginia 22630
U.S.A

The Comparative Breeding Ecology of Four Cervids in Royal Chitwan National Park

ABSTRACT

Data on the reproduction of chital (*Axis axis*), hog deer (*Axis porcinus*), sambar (*Cervus unicolor*), and barking deer (*Muntiacus muntjak*) were collected year round during a three year period in the terai habitats of Royal Chitwan National Park, Nepal. The annual profile of the antler cycle is distinctive in each species, but hard antlers can be observed in all species every month of the year. The birth seasons differed in a similar fashion, but fawns were seen in nearly every month in only sambar and chital. Distinctive birth peaks were evident in all but barking deer. In hog deer and sambar the season of peak births coincides with the post-burn greensward (April–May) and the monsoon (June–July), respectively. Chital on the other hand have a birth peak in December–February, a period of low forage productivity. These and other aspects of seasonal reproduction in the four species are compared and discussed.

Introduction

Most cervids that have been studied in Europe and North America exhibit distinct breeding cycles (Severinghaus and Cheatum, 1956; Linsdale and Tomich, 1953; Verme, 1965; Guinness et al., 1971; Chapman and Chapman, 1975; Kucera, 1978; McCullough, 1979). In the temperate region for example, most deer rut in autumn, and fawns are born in the spring. This cycle has obvious survival benefits as environmental factors, particularly weather, are extreme between seasons (Sadleir, 1969). In contrast to the deer of Europe and North America very little is known about the breeding cycles of deer in southern Asia. Limited published information suggests that in some species breeding seasons are not consistent throughout the geographic range. Regional differences in climate and vegetation are believed to have resulted in these variations (Krishnan, 1959; Prater, 1965; Berwick, 1974). Eisenberg and Lockhart (1972) suggested that in Sri Lanka breeding of deer is synchronized to seasons of drought and rainfall and consequently to the availability of forage. Some confusion in the literature appears to have resulted from observations of Asian deer in zoological parks, particularly in Europe and America where most have been reported to breed throughout the year (Bedford and Marshall, 1972; Jarvis and Morris, 1962; Asdell, 1964; Crandall, 1964; Schaller, 1967; Miller, 1975). This study is the first long-term attempt to monitor breeding cycles, through all seasons in four species of South Asian deer in their natural environment. The species of concern are the chital or axis deer (*Axis axis*), the hog deer (*Axis porcinus*), the sambar (*Cervus unicolor*), and the Indian munjak (*Muntiacus muntjak*). In this paper we shall be concerned with answering the following questions: (1) What is the seasonal pattern of reproductive activity in males and females? and (2) what is the adaptive significance of the observed patterns between species? Field work commenced in Chitwan in late May 1978 and ended at the beginning of October 1981. This report is based on 40 months of field study concentrated in the Sauraha sector of the park.

Methods

Study Site

As detailed descriptions of the study site can be found elsewhere (Laurie, 1978; Sunquist, 1981; and Mishra, 1982) the following sketch covers only major aspects. Royal Chitwan National Park is situated in the vicinity of latitude 27.3 degrees North, and longitude 84.2 degrees East. It lies in a large river basin along the flood plains of the Rapti, Reu, and Narayani rivers in the inner terai of Nepal. The southern boundary contains various spurs of the Siwalik Hills, and reaches an elevation of about 800 m. The climate is sub-tropical with the southeast monsoon the dominant factor. Three seasons are discernible, a dry hot premonsoon from late February to May, a hot and humid monsoon season from June to September, and a cool dry post-monsoon season from October to January.

The vegetation is predominated by almost monotypic stands of sal (*Shorea robusta*) which occupy 70% of the park area. Riverine forest extends along river banks, water courses and islands in both the Narayani and Rapti rivers and occupies 7% of the park area. Grasslands occupy the remaining 23% of the park, and form diverse and complex communities of at least 40 species. Tall grass associations (*Themeda* and *Saccharum* spp.) attain heights of 6–8 m, while old village Khar-Jhaksi grassland (mainly *Imperata cylindrica*) ranges from 1–2 m. The grasslands are important seasonal food sources for nearly all ungulates in the park.

Data Collection

Observations were made while quietly cruising an established transect line (52.4 km) on elephant back. Deer sightings were recorded on printed data cards mostly between 6:00–10:00 hours and 15:00–19:00 hours. Sighting frequencies were greatest during the pre-monsoon months following the annual burn and harvest of grasses by villagers. This is a time of improved visibility when many ungulates are attracted to the greensward.

Seasonal aspects of the male reproductive cycle were defined by quantifying antler development, bellowing, and male-female interactions. Male deer seen during routine transect cruises were classified as having shed, velvet or hard antlers. Chital antlers were further classified according to their estimated size (Schaller, 1967; Sharatchandra and Gadgil, 1981; Miura, 1981) and the number of branches (Ables, 1974). Hard antlers were categorized as class 1 (unbranched spikes < 10 cm.), class 2 (branched antlers < 30 cm.), class 3 (branched antlers > 30 cm and < 60 cm), and class 4 (branched antlers > 60 cm.). Males with shed antlers were distinguished by the raw scar visible on the tops of their pedicels. New antler growth proceeds immediately, and is noticeable in early stages of development as a bulb-like bifurcation. These were termed "first fork antlers". Likewise, antlers with the second bifurcation were called "second-fork" antlers, and those with well developed brow and upper tines were classified as "fully developed" velvet antlers. Velvet "spikers" were also distinguished.

Rutting male chital emit a characteristic and distinctive bellow (Graf and Nichols, 1966; Schaller, 1967; Ables, 1974). Lydekker (1901) described it as a

Mishra and Wemmer

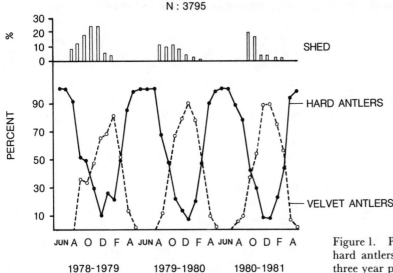

1978-1979   1979-1980   1980-1981

Figure 1.   Percent occurrence by month of shed, velvet and hard antlers in chital based on 3795 observations over a three year period (1979–1981).

peculiar moan, while Graf and Nichols (1966) described it as sounding like "y-o-o-o-w-w" or "h-h-o-u-u-h". We would describe it as a series of shrill, choked blasts suddenly forced out as if the animal was running out of breath. Records of bellows were enumerated from fixed locations. Between 5:00–21:00 hours on a total of seven days each month records were made of the date, time, bellowing bouts, and the number of elements per bout. The number of hours (16) and the number of days (7) were kept constant for all months so data could be compared. When cruising transects flehmen, tending of females, mounting or mount attempts were recorded as and when sighted. Size and state of antlers of the males in question were also noted.

The seasonal variation in the number of newly born fawns was considered indicative of the breeding cycle in females. The number of adult does and fawns seen along the transects was recorded and grouped by months. Coat color and relative body height were the main criteria used to distinguish fawns from older juveniles (see Eisenberg and Lockhart, 1972). Timing of births is difficult to determine precisely in the field as ungulates in general and cervids in particular hide their young immediately after birth (Pruitt, 1960; Espmark, 1964; McCullough, 1971; Lent, 1974). In chital introduced in Hawaii, the hiding phase was estimated to be 7–10 days (Graf and Nichols, 1966). In captive Reeve's muntjak (*Muntiacus reevesi*), it was estimated to last up to 4 weeks (Yahner, 1980). Since it is not known how long most deer in Asia hide their young, we assumed it unlikely to last more than 2 weeks. The age of fawns described hereafter was estimated to be less than about 30 days in chital, sambar and hog deer. Since it was difficult to distinguish between newly born fawns and older juveniles in barking deer, their

fawns were estimated to be younger than 3 months (Eisenberg and Lockhart, 1972).

Results

Chital

ANTLER PHENOLOGY

Between June 1978 and May 1981, a total of 3795 observations of male chital in different stages of antler development were made, and the numbers observed with shed, velvet and hard antlers in each month were standardized as percentage of the total seen in any specific month (Figure 1). The chital population started shedding their antlers in August and the last animals had shed by March. Both antlers were dropped more or less simultaneously. Only 7 animals were seen carrying one antler. A few animals (n = 47) appeared to be bleeding at the raw antler scar. Within 2 weeks of shedding a shiny knob-like outgrowth covered with fine hair was prominent. In the next 15-20 days a bulb like bifurcation developed on the antler surface and by December most chital had developed the second fork (Table 1). By February, most deer had developed a distinct brow tine and upper tine. The peak occurrence of velvet antlers was between December and February after which sightings of velvet antlers declined, and by May over 95% of the deer had hard antlers (Figure 1). The peak season of velvet was also the period when the sexes segregated and foraged separately (Mishra, 1982). It was also the time when most fawning took place. Similarly, the peak period of hard antlers coincided with the peak period when the sexes mixed, and there was a strong correlation between the percentage of males with hard antlers and frequency of mixed groups sighted (r_s = 0.957, P<.001). Sexes started to mix as soon as the antlers

Table 1. Chital stages of shed and velvet antler development in number and percent observed in each month (1980–1981)

Month	Total Number Classified	Shed N	Shed %	Spike N	Spike %	1st Fork N	1st Fork %	2nd Fork N	2nd Fork %	Fully Developed N	Fully Developed %
June	0	0	0	0	0	0	0	0	0	0	0
July	0	0	0	0	0	0	0	0	0	0	0
Aug.	25	14	56.0	0	0	10	40.0	1	4.0	0	0
Sept.	58	31	53.4	3	5.2	24	41.4	0	0	0	0
Oct.	73	26	35.6	2	2.8	29	39.7	13	17.8	3	4.1
Nov.	54	13	24.1	5	9.3	23	42.5	12	22.2	1	1.9
Dec.	59	2	3.4	9	15.3	11	18.6	31	52.5	5	10.2
Jan.	58	2	3.5	5	8.6	8	13.8	25	43.1	18	31.0
Feb.	230	7	3.0	42	18.3	33	14.3	54	23.5	94	40.9
Mar.	136	4	2.9	16	11.8	14	10.3	21	15.4	81	59.6
Apr.	10	0	0	0	0	0	0	2	20.0	8	80.0
May	2	0	0	0	0	0	0	0	0	2	100

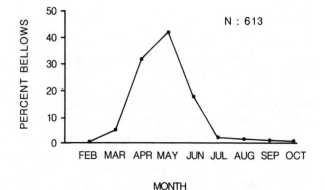

Figure 2. The monthly frequency of bellows by male chital based on 16 hour sampling periods seven days each month.

stripped velvet. Out of 869 hard antlers classified in 1980–1981, 19.2% were spike antlers, 27.7% estimated to be less than 30 cm, 28.6% estimated to be > 30<60 cm, and 24.5% were estimated to measure over 60 cm.

BELLOWING

Bellows of rutting males were heard only from February to September. The frequency of bellows reached a peak in May, then declined rapidly with the last bellow heard in September (Figure 2). This behavior has a marked diurnal pattern with peaks in early morning and late afternoon (Figure 3). The number of ele-

ments or bouts per rutting call ranged from 1 to 11 but most calls consisted of 4 elements (Figure 4). There was no apparent seasonal pattern in the number of elements per bellow bout though the delivery of the elements in bouts appeared to be more rapid in April and May.

MALE-FEMALE INTERACTIONS

A total of 174 male-female interactions were observed (Table 2).

TENDING

Tending behavior was observed in all the months except between November to January. Of the total of 93 observations, 79 were between March and June and the peak was reached in May (Table 2). Of these observations, 56 males (60.2%) had antlers between 30–60 cm; 7 (7.5%) had antlers estimated to be less than 30 cm, 5 (5.4%) were young bucks in spike antlers, and no chital in velvet were seen in the tending postures.

FLEHMEN

Except for one record in October all 33 observations were recorded between January and June. Most flehmen was observed in April (n = 11). Of the total observations, 26 males (78.8%) had antlers estimated to be over 60 cm in length; 5 (26.1%) had antlers estimated to be between 30–60 cm; 2 (6.1%) had antlers

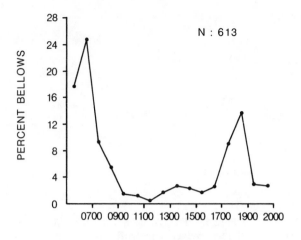

Figure 3. Partial diel rhythmicity of bellowing by male chital during the rutting period.

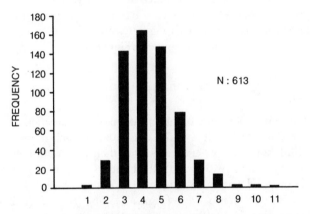

Figure 4. A frequency distribution of the number of elements composing the bellows of rutting chital.

estimated to be less than 30 cm, and none had spike or velvet antlers.

MOUNTS OR ATTEMPTS TO MOUNT

This behavior was not observed between October and January. Most males were seen mounting or attempting to mount females in May (Table 2). Of the 44 records 24 males (54.5%) had antlers estimated to be over 60 cm, 11 (25.0%) had antlers estimated to be 30–60 cm, 5 (11.4%) had less than 30 cm antlers; 3 (6.8%) had spike antlers, and one (2.3%) had fully developed velvet antlers.

COPULATION

Two copulations were recorded, both in May by males with antlers estimated to be over 60 cm.

Table 2. Monthly frequencies of male—female interactions in chital based on three years of data (1978–1981)

Months	Tending	Flehmen	Mount	Copulate
January	0	2	0	0
February	5	1	3	0
March	17	6	5	0
April	25	11	14	0
May	27	9	15	2
June	12	5	4	0
July	1	0	0	0
August	2	0	1	0
September	1	0	2	0
October	3	1	0	0
November	0	0	0	0
December	0	0	0	0
Totals	93	35	44	2

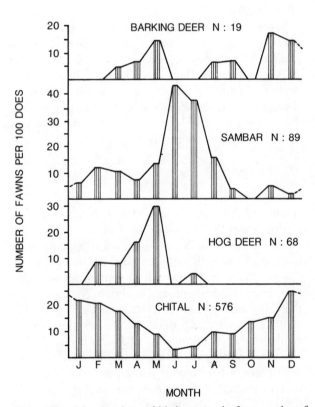

Figure 5. A comparison of birth season in four species of cervids in Royal Chitwan National Park (1979–1981).

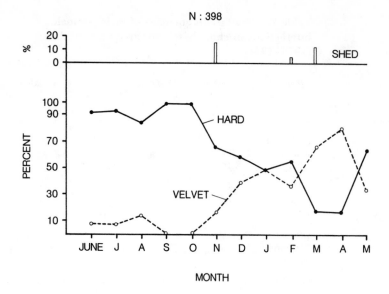

Figure 6. The hog deer antler cycle in percent of shed, velvet, and hard antlers observed in each month (1979–1981).

ANNUAL CYCLE OF FEMALES

Monthly sample sizes were not consistent so data were standardized as number of fawns per 100 does recorded by months.

Fawns were sighted in every month of the year. However, the ratio of fawns per 100 adult does increased from the lowest level of 2.8 in June to a peak of 24.9 in December and after January it started to decline (Figure 5). Thus despite year-round births, there was a distinct seasonal pattern of parturition. The main season of births was during the relatively cold and dry post-monsoon season.

The Hog Deer

ANTLER CYCLE

A total of 398 observations of hog deer bucks were recorded and the percentage of shed, velvet and hard antlers in each month was computed (Figure 6). Male hog deer were rather elusive, and it was difficult to observe them clearly enough to see new antler scars. One deer with shed antlers was seen in November and the rest were seen between February and March. Except for 6 animals all those with velvet antlers were sighted between the months of December and May. The peak occurrence of velvet was in April and the occurrence of hard antlers peaked in September–October when no deer in velvet were seen (Figure 6). The timing of antler development in hog deer was 2–3 months later than chital.

ANNUAL CYCLE OF FEMALES

A total of 68 fawns were recorded, and with the exception of one in July all were seen between February and May. The number of fawns per 100 does increased steadily from February and reached a peak in May after which there was a sharp decline. Fawning in hog deer was more synchronized than in chital, about 4 to 5 months difference existing between the peak periods of fawning in the two species (Figure 5).

The Sambar

ANTLER CYCLE

A total of 360 sambar observations were classified as percent shed, velvet and hard antler in each month. Chitwan sambar began shedding their antlers in February, and a few deer with shed antlers were seen until August. However, the highest percentage of antlerless males was seen in May (Figure 7). The percentage of deer in velvet increased from 11.9% in April, and reached a peak of 77.3% in August. Velvet antlers began to decline in September and by December–January over 90% of the animals were in hard antlers (Figure 7). The antler cycle of sambar was seasonally opposite that of chital. When most chital were in velvet (December–January), the majority of sambar carried hard antlers.

ANNUAL CYCLE OF FEMALES

Of 89 fawns observed, only 7 were seen between September and January. The number of fawns per 100 does increased from 2.2 in December to a peak of 42.8 in June, after which it declined to zero in October. As in the antler cycle, the fawning cycles in chital and sambar were also out of phase (Figure 5).

The Barking Deer

ANTLER CYCLE

A total of 248 barking deer observations were classified according to the state of the antlers (Figure 8). Because of its small size and the presence of long

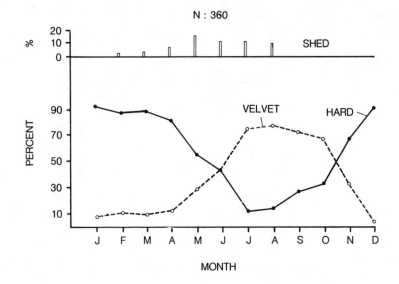

Figure 7. The sambar antler cycle in percent of shed, velvet, and hard antlers observed in each month (1979–1981).

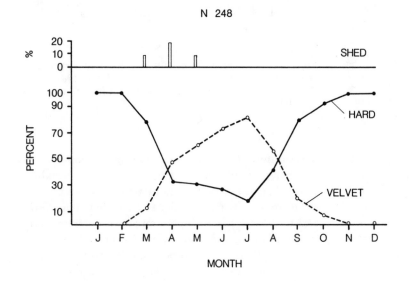

Figure 8. The barking deer antler cycle in percent of shed, velvet, and hard antlers observed in each month (1979–1981).

antler pedicels it was difficult to discern animals with recently shed antlers. Only 11 male deer were recorded in the anterless condition, all between the months of March and May. Animals with velvet antlers were seen in most months except from October to January. The peak velvet period was July when over 50% of the deer seen had velvet antlers. All deer seen between December and February had hard antlers (Figure 8).

ANNUAL CYCLE OF FEMALES

Only 19 barking deer fawns were seen as these small forest dwelling deer seldom leave cover with their young. The number of fawns per 100 does showed a peak in November with 2 smaller peaks in May and August–September (Figure 5).

Discussion

The antler cycle in chital indicates that the Chitwan population comes into rut sometime during the pre-monsoon season from March–May. The frequency of bellows also indicates that rut commences in February and reaches a peak in May. Male-female interactions indicate that most mating occurs in April and May just before the monsoon rains. A comparison of the mating season in Chitwan with those reported from elsewhere (Table 3) suggests similarities even in seasonally contrasting parts of the world. The annual cycle of male breeding activity in the exotic environment of Texas (Ables, 1974) and Hawaii (Graf and Nichols, 1966) is similar to that in Chitwan. The pattern is also similar to that seen in Kanha National

Table 3. A review of breeding seasons in indigenous and introduced populations of chital (*Axis axis*)

Source	Place	Peak Mating Period	Birth Season
Hodgson, 1847	N. India	Dec–Jan	Jun–Jul
Inverarity, 1895	N. India	Throughout the year	Throughout the year
Fletcher, 1911	S. India	Oct–Apr	—
Brander, 1982	Cent. India	Apr–May	October
Krishnan, 1959	S. India	Throughout the year	Throughout the year
Graf and Nichols, 1966	Hawaii, U.S.A.	Apr–Aug	Nov–Mar
Schaller, 1967	Khana, N.P., India	May	February
Berwick, 1974	Grier, India	Mar–May	Aug–Sept
Eisenberg and Lockhart, 1972	Wilpattu, N.P., Sri Lanka	Jan–Feb & Jun–Aug	Sept–Oct & Dec–Jan
Ables, 1974	Texas, U.S.A.	Mid-May	January
This study	Chitwan N.P., Nepal	Apr–May	Dec–Jan

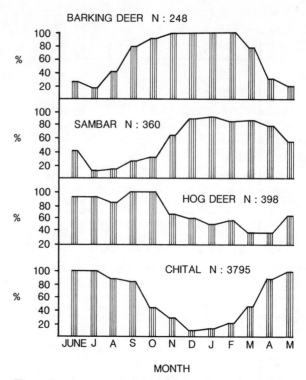

Figure 9. A comparison of antler cycles in four species of cervids in Royal Chitwan National Park (1979–1981). [Ordinate = percentage of males observed in hard antler each month.]

Park (Schaller, 1967) and the Gir Forest (Berwick, 1974) where climate, vegetation, and particularly rainfall contrasts with that of Chitwan. Eisenberg and Lockhart (1972) reported two peak periods of birth in Sri Lanka which coincided with the bimodal distribution of rainfall.

The main season of parturition in the Chitwan chital was during the post-monsoon months of December and January which is also similar to that in Texas and Hawaii (Ables, 1974; Graf and Nichols, 1966). Though some breeding occurred throughout the year, the chital of Chitwan exhibited a distinct seasonal breeding cycle.

In the past, some authors suggested that sambar retain their antlers for 2–4 years before casting (Fletcher, 1911; Lydekker, 1924), but we found no evidence of it in Chitwan and there is no evidence sup-

porting this view either in captive or wild populations in other parts of the world (Crandall, 1964; Schaller, 1967). The antler cycle of sambar in Chitwan is similar to that in Kanha National Park (Schaller, 1967) and to those reported by hunters from different parts of India during the colonial era (Jerdon, 1874; Baldwin, 1877; Russel, 1900; Stockley, 1913; Brander, 1923). In contrast to the chital, the rut and parturition of the sambar is six months out of phase with these events in chital.

In Chitwan, most hog deer come into rut in September–October and parturition occurred in April–May. This is similar to that reported in Corbett National Park in northeast India (De and Spillett, 1966) and Burma (U Yun Tin, 1967).

The breeding cycle of hog deer lies between the extreme differences in seasons of chital and sambar. It may be inferred from the antler cycle that hog deer continue to rut about 2–3 months after chital and commence rutting several months before sambar (Figure 9). Similarly there is a difference of 2–4 months in the parturition cycle of the hog deer and those of chital and sambar (Figure 5).

The antler cycle of barking deer was also highly seasonal, but parturition did not appear to be seasonal possibly because of inadequate data. The antler

Mishra and Wemmer

cycle observed in Chitwan is similar to those reported in captive or wild barking deer throughout the range (Dubost, 1971; Barrette, 1977). One peculiarity of this species is the apparent dissociation of the antler cycle with male reproductive activity (Barrette, 1977). In Sri Lanka, Barrette (1977) also found that there was no distinct fawning season. Thus it is questionable whether there is a synchronized rutting period. The barking vocalization was once regarded to indicate rut (Soaper, 1969), but recent studies in captivity failed to support this hypothesis (Yahner, 1980). Though the period of hard antlers of barking deer and sambar overlap, most barking deer retain their hard antlers when most sambar are in velvet. Similarly the period of hard antlers in barking deer overlaps the period when chital and hog deer are shedding or in velvet. This animal has smaller antlers than the larger species and also retains hard antlers longer (Figure 9), probably because it does not take long for the antlers to grow.

In the temperate region the effect of seasons on reproduction is obvious and pronounced. Most deer there rut in autumn, and most fawns are produced in spring when food is more abundant (Linsdale and Tomich, 1951; Southern, 1964; Taylor, 1956; Sadleir, 1969; Mitchell et al., 1977). The growth of antlers and consequently reproductive cycles coincide with the increase in day length (Goss, 1969 a and b; Lincoln, 1971; McDowell, 1970).

In tropical regions the annual cycle of rainfall is closely associated with forage production and the breeding cycles of many ungulates (Philipson, 1975; Eltringham, 1979; Delany and Happold, 1979). One of the main differences between temperate and tropical regions is that in higher latitudes winter is less productive because of shortage of sunlight and consequently food (Eltringham, 1979). But regardless of latitudinal differences, pregnancy and lactation add an extra burden to all ungulates and are times of maximum nutritional need for females (Sadleir, 1969). In contrast to day length, rainfall, particularly the onset and duration, is not as predictable. Thus some births in the tropics occur throughout the year, but the peak is reached at a time when fawn survival is optimal (DuPlessis, 1972; Skinner et al., 1973; Estes, 1976; Sekulic, 1978; Eltringham, 1979; Delany and Happold, 1979).

There seem to be two differences between the breeding cycles of the deer in Chitwan and those of Europe and North America. In the latter the period of breeding is discreet and more synchronized than in the deer of Chitwan. In moose (Alces alces) in British Columbia for example, Edwards and Ritcey (1958) reported that about 85% of pregnant females produced young in a ten day period. In the red deer (Cervus elaphus) in Scotland over two thirds of the calves were produced within 3 weeks (Guinness et al., 1978) and in roe deer (Capreolus capreolus) over 80% of the fawns are born within a month (Loudon, 1980). Sadleir (this volume) summarizes the literature on this topic. Though there is a distinct birth peak in Chitwan calving seasons there span a much longer period than in Europe and North America.

The other difference is the lack of seasonal uniformity in the breeding cycles of the four species of deer. Peak breeding periods are not the same in all these species. In this respect the deer of Chitwan are more similar to African ungulates where breeding seasons are often attenuated and some species have different seasonal birth peaks (Leuthold and Leuthold, 1975; Eltringham, 1979; Delany and Happold, 1979). There, some species conceive during decreasing photoperiod, some conceive when days are getting longer, and there are some in which breeding cycles are not correlated with day length (Spinage, 1973). Chital produce most of their young during the cool–dry season (December–January), and conceive when day length is increasing. Sambar on the other hand produce young in June–July during early monsoon, and conceive during increasing day length. The breeding cycle of hog deer is between these extremes.

Leuthold and Leuthold (1975) state that though rainfall in the tropics is often considered to be a causative factor governing reproductive cycle it often fails to explain why some species have restrictive breeding cycles and some breed throughout the year. Several factors may influence reproductive season in the deer of Chitwan. Understanding the mechanism underlying the differences requires more research on the availability and quality of forages taken by each species. Fawning generally coincides with the season when nutritious forage is available (Verme, 1965; Sadleir, 1969; McCullough, 1979; Picton, 1979).

The breeding cycle of the sambar appears to be in agreement with the hypothesis that the peak season of births coincides with the onset of rainfall as in many of the African ungulates (Delany and Happold, 1979; Eltringham, 1979). New growth of browse is more abundant during the monsoon than any other season of the year.

The main parturition season in hog deer coincides with the new growth of grasses following the burn. The history of fire as an ecological factor in Chitwan is not known, but it has been reported that man has burned grasslands in Asia for thousands of years (Bolton, 1975; Laurie, 1978) and there is considerable evidence of natural fires caused by lightning (Wharton, 1968; Ashton and Ashton, 1972; Kozlowski and Ahlgren, 1974). Assuming fire has been a component of the hog deer's environment, the fawning season coincides with the annual fire and the new growth of nutritious grasses (Kozlowski and Ahlgren, 1974; Afolayan and Fafunsho, 1978; Field, 1976). The breeding cycle of hog deer appears to fit the hypothesis that fawning coincides with the period when both quality and quantity of forage is highest.

Why is the fawning peak in chital out of phase with the monsoon rains or burning in contrast to the hog deer and sambar? Why do chital give birth at a time of year when food availability is apparently low? Chital not only graze and browse but also feed in association with monkeys, taking dropped leaves, petioles, flowers and fruits. The nutritive value of these foods is probably high, and it would be important to calculate how much chital rely on them. It may be that food obtained from monkeys compensates for the presumed low value of forage at this time of year. The necessary information is not available at present.

Another factor that might influence breeding seasons is the extent of monsoon flooding. In areas close to rivers, where most chital occur, extensive flooding can develop in hours. Blouch (1977) believed high rainfall to be important in the breeding seasonality of white-tailed deer in the llanos region of Colombia. However, if this were the only factor operating in Chitwan one would expect it to apply also to hog deer and sambar which utilize lowlying grassland and riverine forest respectively. Clearly there are other factors.

It is important to remember that natural selection probably operates not only on the time of births but on other parts of the reproductive cycle as well. It is known that the condition of female ungulates at the time of mating is important for successful fertilization and early embryo development (Sadlier, 1969). Verme (1965) reported that deer on a high plane of nutrition began breeding earlier than those on a low plane. In east Transvaal in South Africa, Hall-Martin et al (1975) found that unlike most African ungulates, the giraffe (*Giraffa camelopardalis*) did not reproduce to coincide with the most favorable season for calf survival. There, it was the time of mating that coincided with the seasonal abundance of forage. McGinnes and Downing (1977) examined ten years data on factors that affected the peak period of fawning in white-tailed deer in Virginia. They concluded that the physical condition of the doe at time of conception was the only factor that was strongly correlated with peak periods of fawning.

In Chitwan, most mating in chital appeared to take place during the pre-monsoon season when young grasses were abundant after the old crop was burnt. Presumably the females were then in better physical condition than at other times of the year. At present the exact significance of the chital's breeding season must remain an open question and it is certainly an area where future research would be fruitful.

Acknowledgments

This study would not have been possible without the generous support and personal interest of His Royal Highness Prince Gyanendra Bir Bikram Shah. Financial assistance was provided by His Majesty's Government of Nepal, the Smithsonian Institution, World Wildlife Fund-US, and the Friends of the National Zoo (FONZ). For their various contributions we thank D. Challinor, C. Coon, D. Heck, C. McDougal, T. H. Reed, R. Simons, J. L. D. Smith, M. and F. Sunquist, and I. R. Taylor. Sushma Mishra was indispensable to the success of the study. The dedication of all the tiger project shikaris and elephant men merit special note, but particularly Prem Bahadur Rai, Man Badahur Tamang, Vishnu Tamang, and the legendary Kancha Lama.

Literature Cited

Ables, E.D.
1974. The axis deer in Texas. *Caesar Kleberg Research Program and Texas A & M University.*

Afolayan, T.A., and M. Fafunsho
1978. Seasonal variation in protein content and the grazing of some tropical savanna grasses. *East African Wildlife Journal,* 16:97–104.

Asdell, S.
1964. *Patterns of mammalian reproduction.* Ithaca: Cornell University Press.

Ashton, P., and M. Ashton
1972. The quaternary era in Malesia. *Department of Geography Miscellaneous Series No. 13.* University of Hull, U.K.

Baldwin, J. H.
1877. *The large and small game of Bengal and the northwestern provinces of India.* London: Kegan Paul.

Barrette, C.
1977. Some aspects of the behaviour of muntjacs in Wilpattu National Park. *Mammalia,* 41:1–34.

Bedford, Duke of, and F. Marshall
1942. On the incidence of the breeding season in mammals after transference to a new latitude. *Proceedings of the Royal Society of London, Series B,* 130:396–399.

Berwick, S.H.
1974. The community of wild ruminants in the Gir forest ecosystem. Ph.D. Dissertation, Yale University.

Blouch, R.A.
1977. Breeding seasonality in a population of Colombian white-tailed deer (*Odocoileus virginianus gymnotis*). Ms. Thesis, College of Forest Resources, University of Washington, Seattle.

Bolton, M.
1975. Royal Chitwan National Park Management Plan (1975–1979). *Project Working Document No. 2.* National

Parks and Wildlife Conservation Project, Kathmandu.

Brander, A.
1982.   *Wild animals in central India.* Dehra Dun: Natraj Publishers.

Chapman, D., and N. Chapman
1975.   *Fallow Deer. Their history, distribution and biology.* Suffolk, U.K.: Terence Dalton Ltd.

Crandall, R.L.
1964.   *The management of wild mammals in captivity.* Chicago: University of Chicago Press.

De, R.C., and J.J. Spillett
1966.   A study of chital or spotted deer in Corbett National Park, Uttar Pradesh. *Journal of the Bombay Natural History Society,* 63:576–593.

Delany, M.J., and H.C.D. Happold
1979.   *Ecology of African Mammals.* London: Longmans.

Dubost, G.
1971.   Observation ethologiques sur le Muntjak (*Muntiacus muntjak* Zimmermann 1780 et *M. reevesi* Ogilby 1839) en captivite et semi-liberte. *Zeitschrift für Tierpsychologie,* 28:287–427.

DuPlessis, S.S.
1972.   Ecology of blesbok with special reference to productivity. *Wildlife Monograph,* 30:1–70.

Edwards, R.Y., and R.W. Ritcey
1958.   Reproduction in a moose population. *Journal of Wildlife Management,* 22:261–268.

Eisenberg, J.F., and M. Lockhart
1972.   An ecological reconnaissance of Wilpattu National Park, Ceylon. *Smithsonian Contributions to Zoology,* No. 101.

Eltringham, S.K.
1979.   *The Ecology and Conservation of Large African Mammals.* London: McMillan Press.

Espmark, Y.
1964.   Rutting behaviour in reindeer (*Rangifer tarandus* L.). *Animal Behaviour,* 12(1):159–63.

Estes, R.D.
1976.   The significance of breeding synchrony in the wildebeest. *East African Wildlife Journal,* 14:135–152.

Field, C.R.
1976.   Palatability factors and nutritive values of the food of buffaloes (*Syncerus caffer*) in Uganda. *East African Wildlife Journal,* 14:181–201.

Fletcher, W. F.
1911.   *Sport on the Nilgiris and in Wynaad.* London: MacMillan.

Goss, R.
1969a.   Photoperiodic control of antler cycle in deer:—(a) Phase shift and frequency changes. *Journal of Experimental Zoology,* 311–324.

1969b.   Photoperiodic control of antler cycle in deer:—(b) Alteration in amplitude. *Journal of Experimental Zoology,* 223–234.

Graf, W., and L. Nichols
1966.   The axis deer in Hawaii. *Journal of the Bombay Natural History Society,* 63:629–734.

Guinness, F.G., A. Lincoln, and R.V. Short
1971.   The reproductive cycle of female red deer (*Cervus elaphus* L.). *Journal of Reproduction and Fertility,* 27:427–438.

Guinness, F.E., R.M. Gibson, and R.H. Clutton-Brock
1978.   Calving times of red deer on Rhum. *Journal of Zoology,* 185:105–14.

Hall-Martin, A.J., J.D. Skinner, and J.M. Van Dyk
1975.   Reproduction in the giraffe in relation to some environmental factors. *East African Wildlife Journal,* 13:237–248.

Hodgson, B.
1847.   On various genra of the ruminants. *Journal of the Asiatic Society of Bengal,* 16:685.

Inverarity, J.
1895.   The chital or spotted deers. *Journal of the Bombay Natural History Society,* 9:481-485.

Jarvis, C., and D. Morris
1962.   The International Zoo Yearbook Vol. 3, London.

Jerdon, T.
1874.   *Mammals of India, a natural history of all the animals known to inhabit continental India.* London: J. Wheldon.

Kozlowski, T.T., and C.E. Ahlgren
1974.   *Fire and Ecosystems.* London: Academic Press.

Krishnan, M.
1959.   *The Mudumalai Wildlife Sanctuary.* Madras State Forest Department.

Kucera, T.E.
1978.   Social behaviour and breeding systems of the desert mule deer. *Journal of Mammalogy,* 59:463–476.

Laurie, W.A.
1978.   The ecology and behaviour of the greater one-horned rhinoceros. Ph.D. Dissertation, University of Cambridge.

Lent, P.C.
1974.   Mother-infant relationships in ungulates. In *The behaviour of ungulates and its relation to management,* edited by V. Geist and F. Walther, pp. 14–55. IUCN Publication, New Series No. 24.

Leuthold, W., and B.M. Leuthold
1975.   Temporal patterns of reproduction in ungulates of Tsavo National Park, Kenya. *East African Wildlife Journal,* 13:159–169.

Lincoln, G.A.
1971.   The seasonal reproductive changes in red deer stag (*Cervus elaphus*). *Journal of Zoology,* 163:105–123.

Linsdale, J.N., and P.Q. Tomich
1953.   *A herd of mule deer.* Berkeley, California: University of California Press.

Loudon, A.S.I.
1980.   The biology and management of roe deer in commercial forests. Ph. D. Dissertation, University of Edinburgh.

Lydekker, R.L.
1901.   *Mammals. Library of natural history 2.* New York: The Saalfield Publishing Company.

Lydekker, R.L.
1924.   *The game animals of India, Burma, Malaya, and Tibet.* London: Roland Ward Ltd.

McCullough, D.R.
1971.   The tule elk: its history, behavior and ecology. *University of California Publications in Zoology,* 88:1–191.

McCullough, D.R.
1979.   *The George Reserve Deer Herd. Population ecology of K-selected species.* Ann Arbor: University of Michigan Press.

McDowell, R.D.
1970.   Photoperiodism among breeding eastern white-tailed deer (*Odocoileus virginianus*). *Transactions of the Northeast Section, The Wildlife Society,* pp. 19–38.

McGinnes, B.S., and R.L. Downing
1977.   Factors affecting the peak of white-tailed deer fawning in Virginia. *Journal of Wildlife Management,* 41:715–719.

Miller, R.
1975.   Notes on the behaviour of hog deer in an enclosure. *Natural History Bulletin of the Siam Society,* 26:105–131.

Mishra, H.R.
1982.   A delicate balance, tigers, rhinoceros, tourists, and park management vs. the needs of the local people in Royal Chitwan National Park, Nepal. Paper presented to the Third World National Parks Congress. Bali, Indonesia. IUCN, Gland.

Mishra, H.R.
1982.   The ecology and behaviour of chital (*Axis axis*) in the Royal Chitwan National Park, Nepal (with comparative studies of hog deer (*Axis porcinus*), sambar (*Cervus unicolor*) and Barking deer (*Muntiacus muntjak*)). Ph.D. Dissertation, University of Edinburgh, U.K.

Mitchell, B., B.W. Staines, and D. Welch
1977.   *Ecology of red deer. A research review relevant to their management in Scotland.* Banchory: Institute of Terrestrial Ecology.

Miura, S.
1981.   Social behaviour of axis deer during the dry season in Guindy Sanctuary, Madras. *Journal of the Bombay Natural History Society,* 78:125–138.

Phillipson, J.
1975.   Rainfall, primary productivity and 'carrying capacity' of Tsavo National Park (East Kenya). *East African Wildlife Journal,* 13:171–201.

Picton, H.D.
1979.   A climate index and mule deer fawn survival in Montana. *International Journal of Biology,* 23:115–122.

Prater, S.
1965.   *The book of Indian animals.* Bombay: Bombay Natural History Society.

Pruitt, W.O.
1960.   Behaviour of the barren-ground caribou. *Journal of Mammalogy,* 42:550–551.

Russell, C.
1900.   *Bullet and shot in Indian forest, plain and hill.* London: W. Thacker and Co.

Sadleir, R.M.F.S.
1969.   *The ecology of reproduction in wild and domestic animals.* London: Methuen.

Sadleir, R.M.F.S.
This volume   Reproduction of female Cervidae.

Schaller, G.
1967.   *The deer and the tiger.* Chicago: University of Chicago Press.

Sekulic, R.
1978.   A note on interactions between the sable and the roan antelopes in Kenya. *Journal of Mammalogy,* 59:444–446.

Severinghaus, C., and E. Cheatum
1956.   Life and times of white-tailed deer. In *The deer of North America,* edited by W. Taylor, pp. 57–186. Washington, D.C.: Stackpole Company and The Wildlife Management Institute.

Sharatchandra, H.C., and M. Gadgil
1981.   On the time budget of different life history stages of chital (*Axis axis*). *Journal of the Bombay Natural History Society,* 75 (suppl.): 949–960.

Skinner, J.D., J.H.M. Vanzyl, and J.A.H. Heerden
1973.   The effect of season on reproduction in the black wildebeest and red hartebeest in South Africa. *Journal of Reproduction and Fertility Supplement,* 19:101–110.

Soaper, E.A.
1969.   *Muntjac. A study of these elusive Asiatic deer which colonized an English garden.* London: Longmans Green.

Southern, H.N.
1964.   *The handbook of British Mammals.* Oxford: Blackwell Scientific Publications.

Spinage, C.A.
1973.   The role of photoperiodism in the seasonal breeding of tropical African ungulates. *Mammal Review,* 3:71–84.

Stockley, V. M.

1913.   *Big game shooting in India, Burma, and Somaliland.*
London: H. Knox.

Sunquist, M.E.

1981.   The social organisation of tigers (*Panthera tigris*) in
Royal Chitwan National Park, Nepal. *Smithsonian
Contributions to Zoology*, No. 336.

1956.   *The deer of North America.* Washington, D.C.:
Stackpole Company and The Wildlife Management
Institute.

U. Yun Tin

1967.   *Wild animals of Burma.* Rangoon: Rangoon Gazette
Ltd.

Verme, L.J.

1965.   Reproduction studies on penned white-tailed deer.
Journal of Wildlife Management, 29:47–79.

Wharton, C.

1968.   Man, Fire and Wild Cattle in South East Asia. *Proceedings of the Tall Timbers Fire Ecology Conferences*,
8:107–167.

Yahner, R.H.

1980.   Barking in a primitive ungulate (*Muntiacus reevesi*).
Function and adaptiveness. *American Naturalist*,
16:157–177..PA

ERIC DINERSTEIN
Wildlife Science Group
College of Forest Resources AR-10
University of Washington
Seattle, Washington 98195

Deer, Plant Phenology, and Succession in the Lowland Forests of Nepal

ABSTRACT

The monsoonal lowland forests of South Asia are notably rich in the number of deer species. In the Royal Bardia Wildlife Reserve, Nepal, five cervids occurred sympatrically: barking deer (*Muntiacus muntjak*), hog deer (*Axis procinus*), chital (*Axis axis*), swamp deer (*Cervus duvauceli*), and sambar (*Cervus unicolor*). Chital, the most common species in Bardia, responded to seasonal changes in leaf and shoot development by shifting the grass and browse proportion in their diet and by relative time spent in each habitat type. Biotic and abiotic factors, most notably fire and the monsoon rains, triggered major changes in plant phenology which directly influenced deer forage abundance and quality. Fire, grazing, and flooding also arrest succession in grassland and savannah habitats that are critical for deer.

Biomass estimates of all deer species indicated that grasslands and successional forests supported more deer than did mature sal (*Shorea robusta*) forests. Deer forage production in continuous sal forest appears to be much lower than in successional habitats. In Bardia, as in many other reserves of this region, sal forests account for 50–70% of reserve land. Management efforts to enhance deer use in relatively sterile sal forest may include selective felling and burning to create patches of high forage production.

272

Introduction

Few areas of the world offer a more diverse array of deer species than do the monsoonal lowland forests of South Asia. As many as five species occur sympatrically in several of the wildlife reserves of this region. In the Royal Bardia Wildlife Reserve, Nepal, this assemblage includes: two small deer, the barking deer (*Munticaus muntjak*) and the hog deer (*Axis porcinus*); the intermediate-sized chital (*Axis axis*); and two large species, the swamp deer (*Cervus duvauceli*) and the sambar (*Cervus unicolor*). These species occupy a number of different habitat types ranging from tall grass flood plain to mature semi-deciduous forest (Dinerstein, 1980). Deer habitat use in South Asian forests is strongly influenced by the alternation of severe hot-dry periods and the monsoon. Human interference through burning, domestic cattle grazing, and clearing of the forest has also had a major impact on deer habitat. Such factors result in changes in the composition and distribution of plant communities, plant phenology, and ultimately, forage abundance and quality (Dinerstein, 1979a).

The primary purpose of this paper is to illustrate how habitat and diet selection by deer in monsoonal lowland forests are influenced by plant succession and phenological patterns. Most of my data relate to chital but other species are discussed where I have sufficient information. A secondary objective is to suggest ways in which these patterns can be manipulated in the interests of managing deer populations in South Asia. Sound management is required because deer as a group are the most important prey items for the endangered tiger (*Panthera tigris*) (Schaller, 1967; Sunquist, 1981; Tamang, 1982).

Study Area

The Royal Bardia Wildlife Reserve (hereafter referred to as Bardia) is located in the southwestern corner of Nepal at 81°20'E, 28° 35'N (Figure 1). The reserve lies within the terai zone, a thin flat strip of land skirting the outermost foothills of the Himalayas. The forests and grasslands of the terai were long regarded as some of the premier big game hunting areas of South Asia (Smythies, 1962). The 350 km² reserve is bordered on the west by the Gerwa (Karnali) River and on the east by the Babai River. The highest point in the reserve occurs along the crest of the Siwalik range which delineates the northern boundary of Bardia. The Siwaliks drop abruptly to the south, leaving much of the reserve at an elevation of about 300 m. Approximately 70% of the reserve is covered by relatively undisturbed mature forest; the remainder is composed of grasslands, savannahs, and successional forests. Portions of grasslands, savannahs, and forest

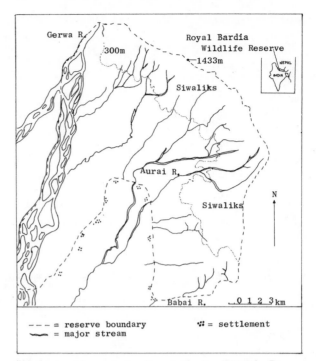

Figure 1. Map of the Royal Bardia Wildlife Reserve (KBWR), Nepal. Approximately 70% of the reserve is covered by mature sal forest; the remainder consists of grasslands and successional forests.

tracts adjacent to the reserve boundaries were previously cleared and cultivated or grazed by domestic cattle. By 1975, however, such activities had ceased. Shortly thereafter, the Bardia reserve was officially designated as a tiger sanctuary by His Majesty's Government in conjunction with the World Wildlife Fund's "Operation Tiger" project. A more detailed description of the Bardia reserve can be found in Dinerstein (1979a).

Climate

Rainfall and temperature patterns delimit the annual cycle into three distinct periods: a hot-dry season (mid-February–mid-June), the monsoon (mid-June–late September), and a cool-dry season (October–mid-February) (Figure 2). Nearly all of the precipitation occurs within the four month wet season. Occasionally, heavy premonsoon showers occur during May and early June. This is also the period of dramatic wind and lightning storms. High temperatures prevail from the late hot-dry season through the middle of the monsoon. The coolest temperatures of the year were recorded in December and January.

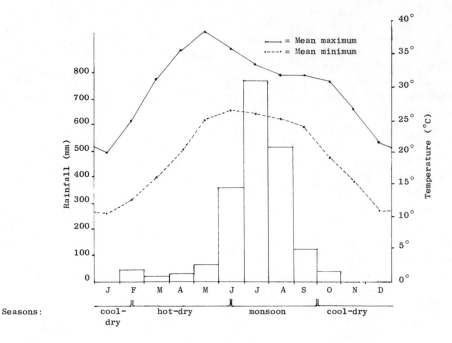

Figure 2. Climatic regime. Rainfall and temperature patterns separate the annual cycle into three distinct seasons.

Vegetation

The forests of the Bardia reserve have been classified as moist semi-deciduous forest (Stainton, 1972; Champion and Seth, 1968). Vegetation analysis of the six major vegetation types in the Bardia reserve is provided in Dinerstein (1979a). A brief summary of these types appears below.

Mature Forests

LOWLAND SAL FOREST

Shorea robusta (or 'sal' as it is known generically throughout South Asia) is the most abundant large tree in the reserve. Sal forest covers approximately 250 km^2 of the reserve in pure stands, along with a co-dominant canopy tree, *Terminalia alata*, or in mixed stands. Fourteen species of canopy trees and 23 species of understory trees have been recorded for this vegetation type. Two distinct layers appear to exist. Eighty-six percent of the tree species in the canopy and understory layer are deciduous. In some sal forest stands, the groundstory layer is primarily composed of woody shrubs and tree seedlings. Tall perennial grasses, such as *Thysanolaena maxima*, *Themeda* spp., and *Saccharum* spp., predominate in the understory of other types.

HILL SAL FOREST

Hill sal forest is restricted to the steep slopes of the south facing Siwalik ridge. Prominent species in this association are sal, *Terminalia alata*, and *Anogeissus lati-*

folia. Hill sal forest is more open than lowland sal forest and the trees are smaller. *Phoenix acaulis*, a palm, is a common understory plant. Along the crest of the Siwaliks is a forest dominated by chir pine (*pinus roxburghii*).

Successional Forests

Successional forests in the Bardia Reserve take several forms. The composition of these forests seems to be influenced by proximity to river banks, soil type, fire history, and grazing by both domestic and wild ungulates (Dinerstein, 1979a).

EARLY RIVERINE FOREST

This association is restricted to major water courses and flood plain islands. Early riverine forest is composed almost exclusively of two tree species, *Dalbergia sissoo* and *Acacia catechu*. Both species are tolerant of minor flooding and form the first seral stand of trees in this region. The understory vegetation is dominated by tall perennial grasses and a few shrub species. Disturbance, in the form of burning and flooding, occurs almost annually.

MOIST MIXED RIVERINE FOREST

This forest type is also associated with water courses but where flooding is less severe. Tree diversity is highest in this association with is canopy species and 23 understory species. A unique feature is the prominence of evergreen species; canopy coverage is almost

Dinerstein

unbroken as a result of the dominance of *Ficus racemosa* and *Syzygium cuminii*. *Bombax ceiba* occurs as a common emergent. The understory layer is dominated by the ubiquitous *Mallotus philippinensis*. Climbers are conspicuous, especially *Cissempelos pariera* and the spiny palm *Calamus tenuis*.

SECONDARY OPEN MIXED HARDWOOD ASSOCIATION

This forest type is a variant of the moist-mixed riverine forest. The main difference between the two is the much higher density of the shrub layer in the secondary open mixed hardwood forest.

Other Habitats

SAVANNAHS AND DERIVED GRASSLANDS

The difference between a savannah and a grassland in the Bardia reserve is associated with the degree of human interference that has occurred in the past. Where clearing once occurred and fires remain frequent, grasslands predominate as hot fires and shading by fast-growing grasses appear to retard seedling regeneration. Fire protection in one grassland area in the Bardia reserve (Lamkhole Phanta) led to the successful establishment of numerous *Terminalia alata* seedlings. Over 40 species of grasses and sedges have been identified in this habitat. The most common plants include tussock-forming perennials such as *Imperata cylindrica*, *Saccharum spontaneum*, *Erianthus ravennae*, and *Vetiveria zyzanoides*. Tree diversity is also high with over 30 species recorded. Most important are several members of the Rubiaceae (*Adina cordifolia*, *Mitragyna parviflora*, and *Xeromphis spinosa*) *Garuga pinnata*, and *Bombax ceiba*.

TALL GRASS FLOOD PLAIN

Along the banks of the Gerwa, Babai, and to a lesser extent, the Aurai River occur expanses of treeless tall grass flood plain associations. Most conspicuous are the shrub *Tamarix dioica* and tall (3–4 m) perennial grasses such as *Erianthus ravennae* and *Saccharum spontaneum*. Large portions of the areas covered by flood plain communities are inundated during the monsoon. Deposition of silt is often heavy along the river banks.

Methods

Data were collected in the Bardia reserve from June 1975 until July 1977. During the first year phenology transects were established in all of the community types described above. Exact locations of individual plants along the transects were marked. All plants along phenology transects were identified by comparing field collections with herbarium specimens at the Dept. of Medicinal Plants Herbarium, Ministry of Forests, Kathmandu. In the initial phase of this study I kept only casual records of phenological events. In the second year of the study (1976), I recorded phenological data on a weekly basis. I also augmented transect data with phenology observations from other parts of the reserve. Observations from ten tree platforms (machans), all located within transect trees, aided data collection on canopy species.

I collected data on 68 species of trees, 9 species of climbers (including vines and lianas), 21 species of shrubs, 16 species of forbs, 32 species of grasses, and 5 kinds of cultivated crops. I monitored tree phenology because observations by Schaller (1967) indicated that South Asian deer fed on tree leaves, flowers, and fruits when accessible. Moreover, seedlings and saplings of certain canopy species were heavily browsed by the ungulates in Bardia. The surprisingly low number of shrub and forb species included in this study is a reflection of the low diversity and density of these life forms relative to tall grass species in the groundstory layer of South Asian forests.

For nearly all trees, climbers, shrubs, forbs, and grasses, at least ten individuals/species were included in the analysis. Twenty-five individuals per species were examined weekly for several of the dominant tree, shrub, and grass species. The following phenological events were noted for woody plants: leaf flushing, leaves falling, leafless, flowering, and fruiting. Graminoid and forb phenology were divided into three categories: new shoots or leaves emerging, senescence/burned, and flowering. The criterion for determining a change in a phenological episode was if 25% of the individuals of a species in question shifted from one category to another over the course of the week. A more thorough description of sampling techniques used in phenology studies and vegetation analysis of deer habitat is presented elsewhere (Dinerstein, 1979a).

Most of the data collected on deer habitat use and food habits were obtained by direct observations from machans with the aid of binoculars. I also walked systematic ground transects through all habitats at weekly intervals to obtain additional data on deer habitat use and food habits. I estimated deer densities based on sample area counts from tree platforms and by counts from motor vehicles when deer concentrated on recently burned grasslands and savannahs. See Dinerstein (1979b, 1980) for more detailed descriptions of deer sampling methods employed during this study.

Results and Discussion

The results and discussion are presented in five parts. The first section provides a detailed account of the annual phenology of deer forage plants in the Bardia

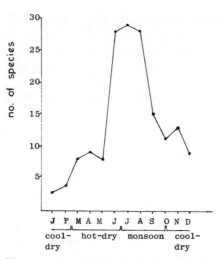

Figure 3. New leaf and shoot production of grass species.

nology data point to soil moisture and fire as important factors in the seasonal abundance of new leaf tissue (Figure 3). Eighty percent of the grass species studied become senescent during the cool dry season (Appendix I, List 1). New growth in early June is triggered by premonsoon showers (Dinerstein, 1979b). For example, in the last week of May only eight species of grasses produced new shoots. By the second week of June, however, 25 species (75% of those studied) had flushed new leaves.

Annual fires stimulate new growth in the grasslands of the Bardia reserve. Several abundant forage species, all tussock-forming perennials, respond to the annual burning regime by sending up new shoots. Within two weeks after a fire, green shoots of *Imperata cylindrica, Saccharum spontaneum, Vetiveria zyzanoides,* and *Erianthus ravennae* carpeted vast expanses of charred grasslands.

Forbs and Shrubs

Forbs and shrubs respond to environmental factors in a similar fashion, and data for these groups are therefore treated together (Figure 4, Appendix I, Lists 2 and 3. Like grasses, new growth in forbs and shrubs is stimulated by monsoon rains, and most species cease growth by the end of the monsoon period. Many forb and shrub species observed died back by January and remained dormant until the next rainy season. Shrub and forb phenology is also regulated by burning. Several shrubs produce new leaves after a light burn, but most forbs and a few shrubs are eliminated by hot fire.

Cultivated Crops

The southern boundary of the reserve is bordered by cultivation. When I discovered that deer frequently entered fields to feed on cultivated plants, I included five different crops in my weekly transects. Wheat and lentils are planted in the cool-dry season and harvested in the hot-dry period. Maize and rice are monsoon crops. Mustard is planted and harvested in the cool-dry season (Figure 5).

Trees

Of the 68 species of trees studied, 58 (85%) were deciduous (Figure 6). Leaf flushing was greatest in March, April, and May during the hottest, driest period of the year (Appendix I, List 4). The peak period of leaflessness occurs between the first week of February and the last week of April. Several forest types are predominantly leafless at different times of the year: early riverine forest (January), savannah (Jan–March), and sal forest (late March–April). In contrast, moist-mixed riverine forest is dominated by evergreen species.

reserve. These data are necessary for interpreting seasonal changes in deer diets and habitat use. The second section describes the response by chital and several other deer species to shifting patterns in forage availability.

The third section provides a model for explaining patterns of plant succession in Bardia and perhaps for other terai reserves. This is followed by a discussion of how the five deer species are distributed along the successional gradient. The last section focusses on the implications of deer habitat use for park management. The role of habitat manipulation in maintaining healthy deer populations is discussed. Alternatively, the effects of a preservationist policy on deer densities and prey availability for tigers is also considered.

Phenological Patterns

One myth popular among temperate-zone biologists is that tropical and subtropical regions of the world enjoy a continuous growing season (Stiles 1980). Climatic patterns in the terai zone of Nepal dispel this idea as it applies to subtropical monsoonal forests (Figure 2). Distinct phenological patterns emerge in response to the strongly seasonal nature of subtropical environments. Because of the number of plant species involved in this study, I treat them by category (i.e. grasses, shrubs, etc.). Detailed phenology data for each species can be found in the Appendices.

Phenology of Grasses

A unique feature of the natural vegetation of the terai is the contribution of tall and intermediate-sized grasses to the total plant biomass of the region. In the Bardia reserve several tall perennial species are conspicuous in almost all of the plant communities. Phe-

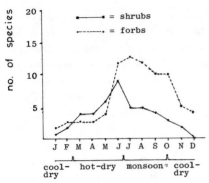

Figure 4.   Leaf inception for forb and shrub species.

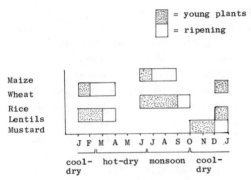

Figure 5.   Phenology of important crops cultivated around the reserve.

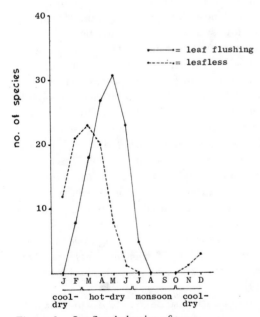

Figure 6.   Leafing behavior of trees.

A bimodal pattern in fruiting activity was observed (Figure 7). The first peak occurs in the cool-dry season (Dec–Jan) and the second occurs at the end of the hot-dry season and into the early monsoon (May–June). At least 14 tree species produce fleshy fruits that are eaten by deer (Dinerstein, 1979b).

Climbers

Leaf production in climbers is highest above the browse line of deer. However, leaves and fruits of climbers and trees are made accessible by the foraging activities of monkeys. Climbers are mostly evergreen; only two of the seven species exhibited marked leaf drop and flushing (Appendix I, List 5). Most species of climbers fruit during the cool-dry season.

Deer Responses to Changes in Phenological Events

Changes in leafing and fruiting patterns of plants affect deer in several important ways. Most apparent is the influence of plant phenology on forage quality and abundance. Seasonal changes in forage production would then influence both diet and habitat selection by deer. These changes, if predictable, might also be expected to exert strong selective pressure on reproductive schedules of deer. Leaf flushing of canopy species influences the thermoregulatory behavior of deer by modifying temperature and light levels on the forest floor. Finally, changes in the amount of vegetative growth in the understory layer affects the visual detection of predators and the amount of escape cover in a given habitat.

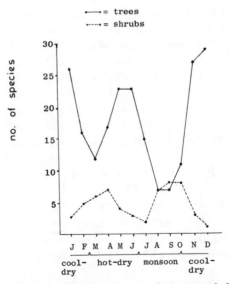

Figure 7.   Fruiting patterns for trees and shrubs.

Diet Selection by Deer and Forage Quality and Abundance

The dietary habitats of deer are influenced by morphology, two obvious factors being body size and bite size (Bell, 1971; Jarman, 1974; Geist, 1974; Hanley, 1980). Smaller deer species require more nutritious forage per unit of body weight per day than do larger cervids. In general, browse species are more nutritious and digestible than graminoids due to the thick cell walls and high silica content of the latter. Small deer can also be highly selective feeders because of small bite size. Thus, we might expect that in a community of deer such as in the Bardia reserve, the smallest species, barking deer (18 kg) and hog deer (45 kg), would be highly selective browsers and the intermediate-sized chital (60 kg) should consume mostly browse. The two largest deer (swamp deer—160 kg and samber—230 kg) would be grazers.

In reality the prediction is only partly correct. For example, hog deer must be grazers as radio-telemetry studies and numerous direct observations indicate that they are restricted to grasslands and savannahs in Chitawan National Park, Nepal (S. Dhungel, pers. comm.). My own observations of chital in the Bardia reserve (Dinerstein, 1979b) combined with Schaller's (1967) data from Kanha National Park, India, show that chital, while willing browsers, are mainly grazers. Sambar are most common in the Bardia reserve where the sal forest understory is dominated by woody vegetation and grasses are few. Food habits of barking deer and swamp deer seem to fit predictions about diet selection.

A foraging model that incorporates the ratio of rumen capacity to body weight might increase accuracy of predictions of deer diet and habitat selection in the terai. For example, a comparison of rumen volume/body size ratios might explain why hog deer live in grasslands and barking deer are restricted to forested habitat where browse and fruits are much more abundant. The hog deer, like the barking deer, is a small ruminant capable of foraging selectively. If browse and forbs are more digestible than grasses, then it seems likely that the small-bodied hog deer should occupy the same forested tracts as barking deer to seek out young leaves and fruits. I hypothesize that the high ratio of rumeno-reticular volume/body size in hog deer permits it to exploit grassland habitats because the large rumen volume allows a slower turnover time necessary for the breakdown of cell walls in grasses. In contrast, the small rumen to body size ratios of barking deer along with higher nutritional requirements restrict this species to forested habitat where fruits, leaves, flowers, and buds are more abundant.

The discrepancy between theory and observations in diet selection can also be attributed to the degree of opportunism exhibited by deer. Annual fires probably serve as important cues for shifting the proportion of browse and grasses in the diet. Grass shoot production, stimulated by burning, is more abundant and probably more nutritious than most browse. Within two weeks after a fire it was not uncommon to observe large herds of up to 80 chital grazing the new shoots. Much smaller groups of swamp deer and hog deer were also observed in these grasslands. Feeding observations indicate that in Bardia the shoots of *Imperata cylindrica, Saccharum spontaneum, Cynodon dactylon*, and *Vetiveria zyzanoides* provide the bulk of deer forage after fires in the hot-dry season and throughout the monsoon (Dinerstein 1979b). Some of these species become unpalatable to the smaller species of deer once growth has progressed beyond the shoot stage.

As the monsoon ends chital begin to include more browse in their diet. Several forb and shrub species common in sal forests are heavily browsed at this time. It appears that after October forage abundance declines considerably from the early monsoon peak. After the end of the growing season I frequently observed chital browsing the dried fallen leaves of at least five common tree species in the savannahs (*Bombax ceiba, Adina cordifolia, Randia dumetorum, Mitragyna parvifolia*, and *Holoptelia integrifolia*). Few quantitative data exist concerning the nutritional value of deer browse during the late cool-dry season in South Asian forests. Nevertheless, forage quality and abundance seems to be lowest at this time of year because of the scarcity of many new green shoots or young leaves.

There is some evidence that the quality of deer browse in South Asian forests improves considerably by February (Berwick, 1974). Photoperiod is probably the proximate cue for leaf flushing by trees and shrubs. Leaf inception by important browse plants in the Bardia reserve initiates a switch in the proportion of browse and grasses in the diet. As new browse becomes abundant, chital and nilgai, a large antelope (*Boselaphus tragocamelus*), seek out low branches, saplings, and seedlings of at least eight tree species and several shrubs. The trees most heavily browsed include *Xeromphis spinosa, Holoptelia integrifolia, Casearia tomentosa, Streblus asper, Terminalia alata, Gardenia turgida, Emblica officinalis*, and *Antidesma diandrum* (Dinerstein, 1979b).

Forage abundance also increases during the late hot-dry season and early monsoon because the common canopy tree species begin to fruit. This peak in fruit biomass attracts monkeys and, ultimately, deer. Schaller (1967) observed chital waiting under foraging monkey troops at four different tree species at Kanha National Park. Data from the Bardia reserve extends this feeding association to at least 21 different tree

Dinerstein

species (Dinerstein, 1979b). Chital, and to a lesser extent hog deer and barking deer, were frequently sighted feeding on the following plant parts dropped by monkeys: the large fleshy flowers of *Bombax ceiba* (February); the fruits of *Ficus racemosa* (April–July); the fruits of *Acacia catachu* and *Dalbergia sissoo* (November); and the fruits of *Syzigium cuminii* and *Schleichera oleosa* (July). Several of these species, especially *Ficus racemosa* produce large fruit crops. Barrette (this volume) suggests that small deer, such as barking deer, should be classified as arboreal feeders because a substantial portion of their diet (e.g. fruits, leaves of canopy species) consist of tree parts. My data on barking deer from the Bardia reserve attest to this phenomenon.

Crops are cultivated for ten months out of the year in the fields surrounding the reserve. Crop damage by ungulates, mainly nilgai and wild boar (*Sus scrofa*) but also from chital, can be substantial, especially to rice, lentils, and young mustard plants. With deer now protected by law from poachers, croplands offer lush forage without the need to remain constantly on the alert for large predators. Deer living close to agricultural areas feed on crops when natural forage is less available, and these foods may be very important.

Reproductive Seasonality of Deer and Plant Phenology

Deer in temperate latitudes restrict parturition to the months of mild weather and plentiful green forage production. Tropical deer from aseasonal regions, or where forage conditions remain adequate throughout the year, might be expected to show no seasonal pattern. Nevertheless, few tropical regions of the world lack at least some alternation of wet and dry periods. Moreover, tropical deer living in strongly seasonal habitats might exhibit a definite birth season in response to negative factors. For example, Blouch (this volume) attributed the reproductive seasonality of white-tailed deer (*Odocoileus virginianus gymnotis*) in the llanos region of Colombia to the effects of prolonged heavy rains on fawn survival.

Two peaks in production of new grass shoots occurred in the Bardia reserve, the first after the dry season fires (February) and the second after the start of the monsoon (June). The peak period for parturition in chital occurs in February (Dinerstein, 1980) coinciding with the flush of new shoots in the *Imperata* grasslands. A similar pattern for chital was observed in Chitawan National Park by Mishra and Wemmer (this volume). Without dry season fires, grass forage production in February would be inadequate and fawn survival extremely low. Because the standing crop of tall grasses is well cured by January, the probability of annual fires is high after this period. Fires set by the native Tharus, who for centuries have burned

the terai grasslands during the dry season, may be highly predictable. It is conceivable that this burning regime has been established for a long enough period for chital to synchronize parturition with dry season fires.

The congener of the chital, the hog deer, reproduces during the monsoon (Mishra and Wemmer, this volume). Because hog deer are restricted to grassland, it seems logical to ask why parturition is not synchronized with the dry season fires. One possibility may be that the chital feeds on the shoots of grasses in the burned grasslands but seeks daily cover in riverine forest. The hog deer, in contrast, seeks hiding cover in tall grassland, which is least abundant after the fires. Thus, predation on hog deer fawns might be much higher during the dry season than in the monsoon. The other deer species, with the exception of barking deer, reproduce during the monsoon peak. Barking deer, at least in Chitawan, show no seasonal pattern (Mishra, 1982).

Deer Responses to Changes in Shade Cover

Vertebrates and invertebrates rely on riverine forests as daytime and seasonal refugia in dry tropical forests during arid periods (Janzen and Schoener, 1968). In the Bardia reserve the increased use of moist-mixed riverine forest by deer during the hot-dry season is partly explained by the need for close access to surface water. Another attraction is the dense shade that this forest type offers during the hottest hours of the day. During the hot-dry season most trees are leafless or flushing new leaves. Two common evergreen trees, *Syzigium cuminii* and *Mallotus philippinensis*, with their dense umbrella-like crowns are sought out by deer in this forest type to reduce thermoregulatory costs.

Plant Succession in Monsoonal Terai Forests

Data from both tropical and temperate forests have challenged traditional views of forest succession as an orderly process leading to a stable climax community. In species-rich tropical forests, where most natural regeneration of canopy trees occurs in gaps and densities of individual species are low, a systematic pattern of community replacement does not occur.

Forest dynamics in much of South Asia are unknown or undescribed. The dynamics of sal forest and its associated species have received much attention because of the economic importance of these timber trees (Puri, 1960; Champion and Seth, 1968). Based upon a survey of the literature and over two years of observations in Bardia, I constructed a simplified model of forest dynamics (Figure 8). The purpose of this model is to arrange habitat types along a gradient

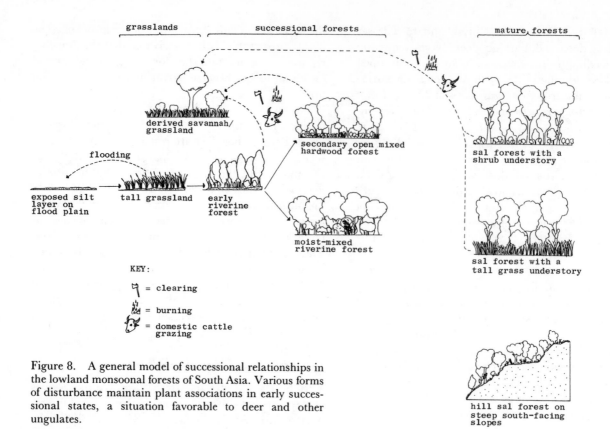

Figure 8. A general model of successional relationships in the lowland monsoonal forests of South Asia. Various forms of disturbance maintain plant associations in early successional states, a situation favorable to deer and other ungulates.

from seral associations to mature forest and to illustrate how the type, severity, and periodicity of disturbance can alter community structure and composition. Whereas this model is specific to Bardia, it probably has application to other reserves in the terai zone.

Seasonal flooding during the monsoon has a dramatic impact on vegetation. Few woody species in Bardia are able to survive where a dense grass cover remains inundated by water for extended periods. Viewed in this light, the tall grasslands distributed along the flood plains of major river systems in the terai are maintained by an annual "natural" disturbance; the derived savannah/grasslands located away from river courses were once forested and are maintained by fire and grazing.

Dalbergia sissoo and *Acacia catechu* are the first two tree species to colonize flood plain vegetation. Both species fix nitrogen and tolerate submersion of their roots. Moist-mixed riverine forest tends to be more common where the threat of flooding is less severe but where soild remain waterlogged during the monsoon. The secondary open mixed hardwood forest is common along rivers where soils are deeper and better drained than in riverine forest. This type often abuts mature sal forest. Sal forest is dominant away from the rivers

in the dry interior of the reserve. Regeneration of sal is high in Bardia, indicating that it is persistent even in the face of periodic fires. Where sal forests have been partially cleared, derived savannahs can be maintained through annual burning.

The effects of wild ungulates on vegetation structure and composition have been neglected by wildlife researchers in South Asia with the exception of elephant browsing in Sri Lanka (Mueller-Dombois, 1972). Selective browsing of tree seedlings by wild herbivores may have an important effect on which species reach the canopy layer and may explain the dominance of sal in Bardia. Sal is fire resistant and its seedlings may be much less palatable to deer and other herbivores than are the seedlings of other tree species.

Heavy grazing pressure by domestic livestock combined with annual fires may have arrested grassland succession in Bardia and in the Royal Chitawan National Park. The economically important thatch grass *Imperata cylindrica* was once dominant on old village sites within the reserves. Observations made in 1984 in Chitawan (10 years after domestic stock were removed from the park) suggest that in areas with a high water table and low grazing pressure, *Imperata cylindrica* grassland is replaced by a tall grass habitat.

Dinerstein

Table 1. Summary of deer observations in the major vegetation types in the Royal Karnali-Bardia Wildlife Reserve, Nepal, March 1976–May 1977

Vegetation type	Tall grass flood plain		Derived savannah/ grassland		Early riverine forest		Moist-mixed riverine forest		Secondary open mixed hardwood forest		Mature sal forest	
Species	n	G	n	G	n	G	n	G	n	G	n	G
Barking deer	0	0	6	6	0	0	7	7	7	7	23	21
Hog deer	17	9	21	13	1	1	0	0	9	5	6	2
Chital	38	10	5532	642	226	24	651	137	130	26	361	28
Swamp deer	0	0	19	4	7	1	5	1	0	0	0	0
Sambar	0	0	1	1	0	0	0	0	0	0	15	15

n = total number observed
G = number of groups observed

In sum, fire, grazing and flooding have had a major influence in altering the distribution of plant associations within the reserve. I suggest that without these factors, secondary forests, tall grasslands, and derived savannahs would cover a much smaller portion of the reserve than they do presently.

Deer Use of Successional and Mature Forests

I attempted to spend equal time estimating deer numbers in each vegetation type to infer trends in habitat use. Nevertheless, the data are subject to several biases. First, observability varied by habitat and season; in areas dominated by tall grass direct observations were often difficult. Second, results are biased against small secretive deer (hog deer, barking deer) and those species most active at night (sambar). Third, I ignored the use of croplands by cervids. I included track counts and pellet group counts as a way of compensating for the problems of poor visibility in certain habitats (Dinerstein, 1979b; 1980).

Chital, swamp deer, and hog deer were most commonly sighted in the first types where tall and intermediate-sized grasses dominated each habitat (Table 1). These species probably utilized tall grassland much more than indicated. Track counts along flood plains and data from other areas where hog deer and swamp deer are more common than in Bardia support this claim (C. Rice, pers. comm.; S. Dhungel, pers. comm.; Martin, 1978; Mishra, 1982). Sambar were rarely observed in secondary forests but were sighted frequently in mature sal forest. Sambar do feed in grasslands in Chitawan National Park (Mishra,

1982). Barking deer, never abundant anywhere, were most often sighted in secondary forests and in mature sal forest. Records of barking deer vocalizations indicate that they are most common in moist-mixed riverine forest. Although this paper deals strictly with cervids, it is noteworthy that nilgai, wild boar, rhinoceros (*Rhinoceros unicornis*), water buffalo (*Bubalis bubalis*), and blackbuck (*Antelope cervicapra*), like most deer, prefer grasslands and secondary forests to mature sal forest.

Biomass estimates for wild ungulates in South Asian habitats all reveal a common trend—values are always higher in more open habitats than in closed-canopy forest (Eisenberg and Seidensticker, 1976). Another interpretation is that biomass estimates are highest in habitats subjected to major disturbance (flooding and fires) and lowest in undisturbed mature forest (Dinerstein, 1980). In turn, production of deer forage is highly correlated with habitat disturbance in Bardia. For example, percent cover of preferred forage plants in the derived savannah/grasslands and in early riverine forest was 83.0% and 56.2%, respectively. In contrast, percent cover of preferred forage plants in the shrub understory of mature sal forest amounted to only 3.3% (Dinerstein, 1979a and unpublished data). These data further suggest the relative sterility of mature sal forest as deer habitat.

Management Implications

The indigenous people of the terai zone, the Tharus, have been manipulating deer habitat for centuries without access to game management texts. Tharus started fires to burn off the old dormant layer of grass and stimulate new growth during the hot-dry season when adequate forage was more difficult to procure for their domestic stock. Generally, burning took place after villagers obtained a sufficient quantity of tall grasses for thatching and cane frameworks (mainly *Imperata cylindrica, Saccharum spontaneum,* and *Erianthus ravennae*) and for making rope (*Ischaemum angustifolium*). The flush of tender green shoots benefitted both domestic stock and wild grazers. The cutting of timber for building construction opened up small patches of forest and increased the amount of edge habitat available to deer. Excavation of irrigation canals from a major river, through the jungle, and into the fields provided new sources of drinking water during the hot-dry season. In return, wild cervids along with wild boar provided an important protein source for subsistence farmers.

Now that national parks and wildlife reserves have been created from the remaining jungle areas of the terai, biologists have the opportunity to apply a more scientific and experimental approach to deer management. The rationale for such a program is obvious. Without human interference, the trend of the vegetation is from short grassland to tall grassland and from diverse successional forests to continuous mature forest. These trends, especially the shift from *Imperata* grasslands to tall elephant grasses result in lowered deer densities, particularly chital. Put another way, wildlife managers are faced with the paradox of managing weedy (r-selected) species in a predominantly mature (k-selected) forest type. Reliance on a strict policy of habitat preservation will insure that much of the habitat in sanctuaries dominated by sal forest, like Bardia, will remain underutilized by deer and their principal predators, tigers and leopards.

Basically, there are four important means of manipulating deer habitat in the terai: clearing patches of forest, water hole development, burning, and flooding. Of these, only seasonal flooding is beyond the control of managers. We can assume that the effects of flooding will increase in severity in the future as deforestation continues unchecked in the Himalayas (Reiger, 1976).

Many species of tropical mammals rely heavily on plants common to forest gaps as important sources of fruits, seeds, and green forage in otherwise mature forest (Fleming, 1979; Dinerstein, 1983). Perimeters of forest gaps are especially productive sites for deer food plants. It is common knowledge that one means of enhancing deer use is to increase the amount of edge habitat available. Selective cutting, if applied properly, could lead to increased deer use of unbroken sal forest by providing more opportunity for deer food plants to increase in dominance. One important factor is that clearings should be located close (within 2 km)

to a perennial source of surface water. Evidence from the Bardia reserve suggests that deer seldom use habitats greater than 2 km from available surface water (Dinerstein, 1979b). Another possibility would be to dig or enlarge existing water holes in dry sal forest adjacent to cleared patches.

Fire is a potentially valuable tool in managing deer habitat in Bardia. Unfortunately, only obvious short-term effects of fire on grazing conditions are understood whereas long-term trends are mainly speculative. This is partly because there are no data on fire history. In addition, no data exist on primary productivity, effects of grazing and browsing on plant composition, and nutritional content of the major forage grasses in various stages of growth. The effects of various burning regimes on grassland species composition are also unknown. For example, the grass *Imperata cylindrica,* a dominant species in disturbed South Asian grasslands, flowers and sets seed soon after fire. It has seeds well adapted for wind dispersal, it spreads by a tenacious rhizome, and appears to increase in cover under a regime of heavy grazing and burning. Management of grasslands in South Asia requires an experimental study to monitor long-term changes in species composition, and seasonal changes in forage biomass and quality as it affects wild herbivores. Ideally, such a program should include replicated treatment and control plots involving exclosures, simulated grazing, and burning.

The balance between preserving wildlife habitat and improving the lot of subsistence farmers is a tenuous one in South Asia. Prior to the establishment of wildlife sanctuaries, agriculturalists converted some of the prime wildlife habitat in the terai, alluvial grassland, into rice paddies. Now that most South Asian sanctuaries are strictly protected, local villagers are prohibited from continuing past land use practices and receive little direct economic benefit from conservation. Furthermore, present efforts to curb crop damage by wild ungulates are largely unsuccessful. Most South Asian wildlife sanctuaries are too remote to attract enough tourist dollars to compensate farmers for crop losses. The antipathy that many farmers express towards conservation efforts necessitated the deployment of armed guards to protect against further encroachment. Whereas this is a necessary, if unavoidable, short-term solution, a more permanent answer must be sought.

I propose a solution to the problem that ideally will benefit deer populations and local residents. Although continuous sal forest is unproductive as deer and tiger habitat, it does boast several important timber species. By selectively cutting trees to create gaps and mosaics of forests and grasslands, wildlife managers would improve forage availability for deer considerably and ultimately increase deer populations. This scheme could become an important element in rural development if revenues obtained from selective felling could be channeled directly into the local village economies. Alternatively, felled timber could be used directly in the construction of local schools, hospitals, bridges, and/or cottage industries.

I am not advocating a policy of selective cutting over entire sanctuaries; managers should instead designate certain areas as ecological reserves and others as experimental zones. Selective cutting in the experimental forests could begin as a pilot study and, if successful, could be conducted on a rotating basis. Because most South Asian wildlife managers were initially trained as foresters, this program could easily be implemented. In addition, villagers already rely on reserves as the sole source of thatching grass, thus setting a precedent for direct transfer of reserve forest products to locals (H. Mishra, unpubl. data). Limited grazing rights in marginal areas administered by parks and reserves might also win support of the villagers.

Those individuals familiar with problems of wildlife preservation in South Asia realize that without concurrent local development, conservation efforts rest on fragile underpinnings. Most South Asian reserves are basically islands of jungle surrounded by cultivation. Few reserves, I believe, will survive this century if they receive only the support of western conservationists and wealthy city-dwellers but lack the popular following of local peasant farmers.

Acknowledgments

This study was made possible by the joint cooperation of the Smithsonian/Peace Corps Environmental Program, Peace Corps/Nepal, and the National Parks and Wildlife Conservation Office (NPWCO), His Majesty's Government, Nepal. I gratefully acknowledge the support of J. Sherburne from Smithsonian, W. Weber and V. Miedema from the American Peace Corps, and H. Mishra from NPWCO. In Bardia, Warden K.M. Shrestha provided logistical support and use of the reserve vehicle for censusing deer. I sincerely thank G. Singh for his companionship, assistance, and advice. D. Clark, R. Taber, C. Wemmer, J. Fox, J. Lehmkuhl, and J. Zarnowitz offered many helpful comments to improve the manuscript.

Literature Cited

Bell, R.H.V.
1971.   A grazing ecosystem in the Serengeti. *Scientific American*, 225:86–93.

Berwick, S.H.
1974.   The community of wild ruminants in the Gir forest ecosystem, India. Ph.D. dissertation. Yale University, New Haven.

Blouch, R.A.
This Breeding seasonality in a population of Colombian volume white-tailed deer (*Odocoileus virginianus gymnotis*).

Champion, H.G., and S.K. Seth
1968.   *A revised survey of the forest types of India*. Delhi: Manager of Publications.

Dinerstein, E.
1979a.   An ecological survey of the Royal Karnali-Bardia Wildlife Reserve, Nepal. Part I: Vegetation, modifying factors, and successional relationships. *Biological Conservation*, 15:127–150.

1979b.   An ecological survey of the Royal Karnali-Bardia Wildlife Reserve, Nepal. Part II: Habitat/animal interactions. *Biological Conservation*, 16:265–300.

1980.   An ecological survey of the Royal Karnali-Bardia Wildlife Reserve, Nepal. Part III: Ungulate populations. *Biological Conservation*, 18:5–38.

1983.   Reproductive ecology of fruit bats and the seasonality of fruit production in a Costa Rican cloud forest. Ph.D. dissertation. University of Washington, Seattle.

Eisenberg, J.F., and M. Lockhart
1972.   An ecological reconnaissance of Wilpattu National Park, Ceylon. *Smithsonian Contributions to Zoology*, 101:1–118.

Eisenberg, J.F., and J. Seidensticker
1976.   Ungulates in southern Asia: A consideration of biomass estimates for selected habitats. *Biological Conservation*, 10:298–308.

Fleming, T.H.
1979.   Do tropical frugivores compete for food? *American Zoologist*, 19:1157–1172.

Frankie, G.W., H.G. Baker, and P.W. Opler
1974.   Comparative phenological studies of trees in tropical wet and dry forests in the lowlands of Costa Rica. *Journal of Ecology*, 62:881–919.

Geist, V.
1974.   On the relationships of social evolution and ecology in ungulates. *American Zoologist*, 14:205–220.

Hanley, T.A.
1980.   Nutritional constraints on food and habitat selection by sympatric ungulates. Ph.D. dissertation. University of Washington, Seattle.

Janzen, D.H., and T.W. Schoener
1968.   Differences in insect abundance and diversity between wetter and drier sites during a tropical dry season. *Ecology*, 49:96–110.

Jarman, P.J.
1974.   The social organization of antelope in relation to their ecology. *Behaviour,* 48:215–267.

Martin, C.
1978.   Status and ecology of the barasingha (*Cervus duvauceli branderi*) in Kanha National Park, India. *Journal of Bombay Natural History Society,* 74:61–132.

Mishra, H.R.
1982.   The ecology and behaviour of the chital (*Axis axis*) in the Royal Chitawan National Park, Nepal. Ph.D. dissertation. University of Edinburgh.

Mishra, H.R., and C. Wemmer
This   The comparative breeding ecology of four cervids in
volume Royal Chitwan National Park, Nepal.

Mueller-Dombois, D.
1972.   Crown distortion and elephant distribution in the woody vegetations of Ruhuna National Park, Ceylon. *Ecology,* 53:208–226.

Puri, G.S.
1960.   *Indian forest ecology.* New Delhi: Oxford Book and Stationery.

Schaller, G.B.
1967.   *The deer and the tiger.* Chicago: University of Chicago Press.

Smythies, E.A.
1974.   *Big game shooting in Nepal.* Calcutta: Thacker, Spink, and Co.

Stainton, J.D.A.
1972.   *Forests of Nepal.* London: John Murray.

Stiles, F.G.
1975.   Ecology, flowering phenology, and humming bird pollination of some Costa Rican *Heliconia* species. *Ecology,* 56:285–301.

Sunquist, M.E.
1981.   The social organization of tigers(*Panthera tigris*) in Royal Chitawan National Park, Nepal. *Smithsonian Contributions to Zoology,* 336:1–98.

Tamang, K.M.
1982.   The status of the tiger(*Panthera tigris tigris*) and its impact on principal prey populations in the Royal Chitawan National Park. Ph.D. dissertation. Michigan State University, East Lansing.

Appendix I.   List of species and their phenological behavior are provided below. Those species eaten by *Axis axis* and parts utilized are denoted in the following way:

g = grazed
b = leaves browsed
s = seedlings browsed (trees only)
f = flowers
fr = fruits
Jan. 3–Aug. 4 = phenological event occurred from the third week in January until the fourth week in August
DI = data incomplete

List 1. Phenological records for grasses

Species	part eaten	period from shoot expansion to senescence	flowering/ fruiting
Apluda autica	g	June 3–Nov. 1	Sept. 2–Nov. 1
Arundo donax	g	June 2–Feb. 2	Sept. 2–Nov. 1
Brachiaria sp.		June 2–Aug. 3	Aug. 3–Nov. 1
Chrysopogon aciculatus		June 2–Sept. 4	Aug. 3–Nov. 1
Coix lachryma-jobi		June 2–Sept. 4	Sept. 4–Nov. 1
Cynodon dactylon	g	Feb. 2–Jan. 1	Mar. 3–Nov. 1
Dactyloctenium aegypticus	g	June 4–Aug. 3	Aug. 1–Sept. 4
Dendrocalamus strictus	g	year-round	did not flower
Desmostachia bipinnata	g	Mar. 3–Jan. 1	Mar. 4–July 3
Digittaria sp.	g	June 1–Aug. 3	July 3–Nov. 4
Echinochloa colonum	g	June 2–Aug. 3	July 4–Nov. 2
Echinocloa sp.	g	June 2–Aug. 3	July 4–Nov. 4

Dinerstein

List 1. *Phenological records for grasses* (cont.)

Species	part eaten	period from shoot expansion to senescence	flowering/ fruiting
Eleusine indica		June 2–Aug. 4	July 4–Nov. 4
Eragrostis coerctata	g	June 2–Aug. 4	July 4–Nov. 3
Eragrostis unioloides	g	July 3–Aug. 3	Aug. 3–Nov. 3
Erianthus ravennae	g	Mar. 3–Jan. 1	Sept. 1–Oct. 1
Iaperata cylindrica	g	Mar. 1–Jan. 1	Mar. 2–July 3
Oryza sativa (rice)	g	June 3–Sept. 4	Sept. 4–Oct. 4
Panicum sp.	g	June 1–Aug. 3	July 3–Oct. 4
Paspalum distichum	g	June 2–Sept. 1	Aug. 3–Oct. 4
Paspalua scrobiculatum		June 2–Sept. 2	Aug. 3–Oct. 4
Polypogon aonospeliensis	g	Mar. 1–June 3	Mar. 4–June 3
Pseudopogonothera contortum	g	Aug. 1–Dec. 3	Oct. 1–Jan. 1
Saccharum benghalensis	g	June 2–Nov. 2	Oct. 3–Nov. 2
Saccharum spontaneum	g	Mar. 3–Jan. 1	Sept. 1–Oct. 4
Setaria glauca	g	June 2–Aug. 3	July 1–Oct. 1
Sporobolus diander	g	June 2–Aug. 3	July 1–Sept. 3
Theaeda sp.	g	June 4–Nov. 3	Aug. 3–Nov. 3
Thysanolaena maxima	g	June 2–Nov. 3	Aug. 3–Nov. 3
Triticum sativa (wheat)	g	Dec. 2–Feb. 3	Feb. 3–Apr. 1
Vetiveria zyzanoides	g	Apr. 2–Aug. 3	July 1–Oct. 4
Zea mays (corn)	g	June 2–July 4	July 4–Sept. 2

List 2. *Phenological records for forbs*

Species	part eaten	new leaves	dormant	flowering
Aegeratum conyzoides	b	Sept. 4–Nov. 2	Apr. 1–Sept. 4	Oct. 3–Apr. 2
Cucurligo orchidioides		May 4–July 3	Oct. 3–May 4	May 3–Sept. 4
Cynoglossum wallachii		June 2–July 3	Nov. 2–June 2	June 3–Sept. 4
Desmodium sp.		July 2–Aug. 3	Oct. 1–July 2	July 3–Oct. 2
Elopantus scaber	b	Oct. 1–Nov. 1	Jan. 1–Oct. 1	Oct. 2–Jan. 1
Euphorbia acaulis	b	June 1–Aug. 3	Jan. 1–May 3	Apr. 3–May 3
Euphorbia huerta		Mar. 4–July 3	Nov. 2–Mar. 4	Apr. 2–Nov. 2
Globba ramosa		June 2–July 1	Aug. 3–June 2	July 2–Aug. 3
Gnaphilium luteo-album		Mar. 2–July 3	Aug. 2–Mar. 2	Mar. 4–June 2
Majus sp.		June 2–Aug. 4	Nov. 2–June 2	Aug. 2–Nov. 2
Oxalis corniculata		Feb. 1–Mar. 3	Aug. 4–Jan. 3	Feb. 2–Mar. 3
Polygonum barbatum		Apr. 1–Apr. 4	Dec. 2–Apr. 2	Apr. 3–Dec. 2
Polygonum plebujum		Jan. 2–Feb. 1	July 2–Feb. 1	Feb. 2–July 2
Scoparia dulcis	b	July 2–July 4	Nov. 2–July 2	Aug. 1–Sept. 4

List 3. *Phenological records for shrubs*

Species	part eaten	leaf drop, leaflessness	leaf flushing	flowering	fruiting
Adhatoda vasica		evergreen		Dec. 3–Apr. 1	Feb. 3–May 3
Callicarpa macrophylla	b	Nov. 1–Mar. 3	Mar. 3–Apr. 2	June 3–Sept. 3	Sept. 3–Nov. 4
Callotropis gigantica		Nov. 1–Jan. 4	Jan. 4–Mar. 4	Feb. 1–June 1	May 3–July 1

List 3. Phenological records for shrubs (cont.)

Species	part eaten	leaf drop, leaflessness	leaf flushing	flowering	fruiting
Cassia tora		Oct. 3–May 4	May 3–July 3	Aug. 3–Oct. 2	Sept. 4–Nov. 3
Clerodendron viscosum	b	evergreen		Feb. 3–Apr. 4	Apr. 4–Jun. 4
Colebrookia oppositifolia		Mar. 4–Sept. 2	Sept. 2–Oct. 3	Jan. 1–Mar. 1	Mar. 1–July 1
Grewia sp.	b,fr	Jan. 1–Feb. 4	Feb. 4–Apr. 3	Apr. 1–June 1	May 3–July 1
Indigofera sp.		Dec. 3–May 3	May 3–June 3	July	DI
Leea robusta	fr	Nov. 4–May 3	May 3–June 3	May 4–Sept. 1	Sept. 1–Oct. 4
Moghania bracteata	b	Apr. 1–Sept. 4	Sept. 4–Nov. 4	Aug. 3–Dec. 1	Dec. 1–Apr. 3
Moghania stobilifera	b	Apr. 1–Sept. 4	Sept. 4–Nov. 4	Aug. 3–Oct. 3	Dec. 1–Apr. 3
Phoenix acaulis	b	DI	June 1–Aug. 3	Mar. 3–Apr. 2	Apr. 2–May 3
Pogostemon benghalensis	b	Mar. 4–Aug. 3	Aug. 2–Sept. 2	Jan. 3–Apr. 2	DI
Sida acuta		Jan. 1–June 1	June 1–Sept. 1	Oct. 1–Nov. 2	Nov. 2–Dec. 3
Sida rhombifolia	b	Jan. 1–June 1	June 1–Sept. 1	Oct. 1–Nov. 2	Nov. 2–Dec. 3
Urena lobata	b,fr	Nov. 3–July 3	July 3–Sept. 2	Sept. 4–Oct. 3	Oct. 3–Nov. 4
Woodfordia fruticosa	b	evergreen		Mar. 2–Apr. 4	Apr. 4–June 3
Zizyphus mauritiana	b,fr	Feb. 1–Mar. 4	Mar. 4–June 3	Apr. 4–June 3	Sept. 2–Feb. 4
Tamarix dioica		evergreen		Sept. 4–Oct. 4	Oct. 4–Nov. 3
Azanza lampas	b,fr	Dec. 3–May 4	May 4–June 4	Aug. 4–Sept. 2	Sept. 2–Oct. 4

List 4. Phenological records for trees

Species	part eaten	leaf drop, leaflessness	leaf flushing	flowering	fruiting
Acacia catechu	s,fr	Nov. 1–Apr. 3	Apr. 3–July 3	June 3–Aug. 3	Nov. 1–Feb. 1
Adina cordifolia	b,fr	Jan. 1–May 2	May 2–June 2	July 2–Aug. 3	Nov. 1–Feb. 1
Aegle marmelos*	s	Mar. 1–May 3	May 3–June 2	Mar. 3–May 3	Apr. 3–June 1
Albizia lebbek		Feb. 1–Apr. 1	Apr. 1–May 3	Apr. 3–May 2	Oct. 1–Dec. 4
Albizia odoratissima		evergreen	Mar. 4–May 3	Apr. 4–May 2	Oct. 3–Feb. 1
Albizia procera		evergreen?		June 4–Aug. 3	Oct. 3–Feb. 1
Alstonia scholaris	s	evergreen		Feb. 1–Mar. 4	May 2–June 4
Anogeissus latifolia		Dec. 2–Apr. 3	Apr. 3–June 3	June 3–July 2	Oct. 3–Dec. 4
Antidesma diandrum	s	Feb. 1–Apr. 1	Apr. 1–June 1	May 2–June 4	Dec. 1–Feb. 1
Bauhinia malabarica	b	DI	Mar. 3–May 4	Aug. 3–Oct. 1	Jan. 1–June 1
Bauhinia racemosa	fr	Jan. 1–Apr. 1	Apr. 1–May 4	Apr. 4–June 1	Oct. 3–Jan. 1
Bauhinia variegata		Jan. 1–May 1	May 1–June 1	Feb. 3–Apr. 3	June 4–Sept. 3
Bischofia javanica		Nov. 3–Feb. 1	Feb. 1–Apr. 1	Apr. 1–May 4	Nov. 1–Feb. 1
Bombax ceiba	b,f	Oct. 3–Mar. 3	Mar. 3–Apr. 3	Jan. 3–Mar. 3	Apr. 2–June 2
Buchanania latifolia		Feb. 3–May 3	May 3–June 2	May 3–June 2	DI
Butea monosperma		Jan. 4–Mar. 4	Mar. 4–Apr. 4	Feb. 4–Mar. 4	Mar. 4–May 2
Careya arborea		Mar. 1–May 3	May 3–June 2	Apr. 1–Apr. 3	Apr. 3–June 3
Carissa opaca		evergreen		Apr. 3–May 4	Nov. 4–Jan. 1
Casearia tomentosa	b	Dec. 3–Mar. 4	Mar. 4–Apr. 4	Apr. 3–May 3	June 1–Aug. 1
Cassia fistula		Apr. 3–May 3	May 3–June 2	May 2–Aug. 1	Nov. 1–Mar. 1
Toona ciliata		Nov. 1–Feb. 3	Feb. 3–Mar. 4	Apr. 3–May 3	June 1–Aug. 1
Cordia dichotoma	fr	DI	Mar. 1–May 1	Mar. 2–Apr. 4	May 1–July 1
Dalbergia sissoo	fr	Nov. 3–Feb. 2	Feb. 2–Apr. 2	Mar. 3–Apr. 3	Dec. 1–Feb. 3
Dillenia pentagyna		Jan. 2–June 3	June 3–July 2	Apr. 4–June 4	June 4–Sept. 1

Dinerstein

List 4. Phenological records for trees (cont.)

Species	part eaten	leaf drop, leaflessness	leaf flushing	flowering	fruiting
Diospyros tomentosa		DI	DI	Mar. 3–May 1	Nov. 1–Feb. 1
Ehretia laevis	s	Feb. 3–June 2	June 2–July 3	Mar. 3–Apr. 4	Nov. 3–Feb. 1
Emblica officinalis	s,fr	Jan. 1–Apr. 2	Apr. 2–May 3	Apr. 2–May 1	Oct. 3–Feb. 2
Ficus racemosa**	b,fr	Sept. 4–Apr. 1	Sept. 4–Apr. 1	—	Feb. 3–Jan. 1
Ficus hispida		DI	Feb. 1–Apr. 1	—	Jan.–Dec.
Ficus benghalensis	fr	DI	Mar. 1–May 1	—	Feb. 3–Apr. 3
Ficus religiosa	fr	DI	Feb. 1–May 1	—	Mar. 3–June 1
Gardinia turgida	s	DI	DI	Feb. 2–Apr. 3	Nov. 1–Jan. 4
Garuga pinnata	s,b	Oct. 4–May 1	May 1–June 1	Mar. 3–Apr. 3	Apr. 3–June 3
Glochidion velutinum		DI	DI	Feb. 3–Apr. 3	June 3–Aug. 3
Gmelina arborea		DI	Mar. 1–May 1	Mar. 1–Apr. 4	Apr. 4–July 1
Grewia elastica		DI	DI	Apr. 2–June 2	Sept. 1–Dec. 1
Grewia oppositifolia		DI	DI	Apr. 2–June 3	Oct. 2–Dec. 4
Holoptelia integrifolia	s,b	Jan. 1–Apr. 2	Apr. 2–June 3	Feb. 1–Mar. 3	Mar. 3–May 3
Hymenodictyon excelsum		Oct. 1–June 1	June 1–July 3	June 3–Aug. 3	Nov. 1–Jan. 4
Kydia calcina		Feb. 1–May 1	May 1–June 2	July 3–Sept. 3	Dec. 1–Mar. 1
Lagerstroemia parviflora		Nov. 2–Apr. 4	Apr. 4–June 3	May 2–June 4	Oct. 1–Jan. 2
Lannea coromandelica		Jan. 1–May 1	May 1–June 2	Mar. 2–Apr. 4	June 1–Aug. 1
Litsea monopetala		evergreen		Mar. 2–Apr. 4	July 2–Aug. 4
Macaranga sp.		Feb. 3–May 4	May 4–July 1	Aug. 1–Sept. 4	Nov. 1–Jan. 1
Mallotus philippinensis***	b,f	Mar. 3–May 2	May 2–July 1	Sept. 3–Nov. 2	Jan. 1–Apr. 2
Mangifera indica		evergreen		Feb. 4–Mar. 3	May 3–July 3
Madhuca latifolia	b,f	Feb. 1–May 1	May 1–May 4	Mar. 4–May 3	June 3–July 3
Miliusa velutina		DI	DI	Mar. 3–May 3	June 2–July 4
Mitragyna parvifolia	b	Jan. 1–Apr. 3	Apr. 3–Jun. 2	May 4–June 3	Nov. 3–Jan. 4
Murraya koenigii		Jan. 3–Mar. 3	Mar. 3–Apr. 3	Mar. 3–May 3	May 3–Aug. 1
Oroxylum indicum		Feb. 1–May 1	May 1–June 1	June 1–Aug. 1	Nov. 3–Feb. 1
Ougeinia oojeinensis		Feb. 1–Apr. 1	Apr. 1–May 2	Mar. 1–Apr. 4	May 2–June 4
Pinus roxburghii****		evergreen		Feb. 1–May 1	Apr. 1–June 1
Xeromphis spinosa	s,b	Feb. 2–Apr. 3	Apr. 3–June 3	Apr. 4–June 3	Nov. 1–Mar. 2
Xeromphis uliginosa	s,b	Feb. 2–Apr. 1	Apr. 1–May 1	Apr. 4–June 3	Nov. 1–Mar. 2
Schleichera oleosa	fr	Jan. 1–Feb. 1	Feb. 1–Apr. 1	Mar. 3–Apr. 3	Apr. 3–June 3
Salix tetrasperma		Feb. 4–Mar. 3	Mar. 3–Apr. 3	Mar. 3–Apr. 3	Apr. 3–June 3
Semecarpus anacardium	fr	Jan. 1–May 2	May 2–June 2	July 2–Aug. 1	Nov. 1–Feb. 2
Shorea robusta	b	Feb. 4–Apr. 3	Mar. 4–May 2	Mar. 4–May 2	May 2–July 3
Spondias pinnata		Nov. 1–May 1	May 1–June 1	Mar. 3–May 3	Nov. 1–Feb. 1
Sterculia villosa		Jan. 1–June 1	June 1–July 1	DI	DI
Streblus asper	s	evergreen	Mar. 1–Apr. 1	Mar. 1–Apr. 2	Apr. 2–June 2
Syzigium cuminii	b,fr	evergreen	Mar. 4–Apr. 3	Apr. 4–June 2	June 2–Sept. 2
Syzigium cerasoides		evergreen	May 1–June 1	Apr. 2–May 4	Aug. 1–Sept. 2
Terminalia alata	s	Mar. 3–June 2	June 2–July 2	June 4–Aug. 3	Jan. 4–Mar. 3
Terminalia chebula	fr	DI	Apr. 1–May 1	June 4–Aug. 3	Jan. 2–Mar. 3
Trewia nudiflora		Jan. 1–Feb. 3	Feb. 3–Apr. 1	Feb. 3–Apr. 3	Apr. 3–July 2
Zizyphus sp.	fr	Mar. 2–Apr. 1	Apr. 1–June 2	Apr. 4–June 3	DI
Bridelia retusa		Apr. 1–May 1	May 1–July 1	May 3–July 3	Oct. 3–Jan. 1

*A. marmelos flowers and fruits in alternate years.

**F. racemosa flowers and all Ficus flowering behavior could not be recorded.

***M. philippinensis is normally evergreen but showed marked leaf drop and flushing in 1976.

****P. roxburghii flowers and fruits in alternate years.

List 5. Phenological records for climbing species

Species	part eaten	leaf drop, leaflessness	leaf flushing	flowering	fruiting
Acacia pinnata		evergreen		June 3–Aug. 3	Nov. 3–Feb. 1
Bauhinia vahlii		Mar. 4–Apr. 2	Apr. 2–June 3	Apr. 4–June 4	Jan. 1–Feb. 4
Calamus tenuis	b	evergreen		Aug. 1–Aug. 4	Feb. 1–May 4
Cissempelos pariera		evergreen		July 1–Oct. 1	Oct. 1–Nov. 1
Cuscuta reflexa		(no leaves)		Sept. 3–Feb. 3	Feb. 3–Apr. 3
Ichnocarpus frutescens	b	evergreen		Aug. 3–Nov. 3	Dec. 3–Feb. 3
Milletia auriculata	s	evergreen		May 3–June 3	Nov. 3–Jan. 1
Smilax prolifera	b	evergreen		Aug. 1–Oct. 1	Dec. 1–Feb. 2
Butea parviflora	s	Apr. 1–Jun. 1	June 1–June 4	Sept. 3–Dec. 4	Feb. 3–Apr. 3

Dinerstein

CHOOMPOL NGAMPONGSAI
Department of Conservation
Kasetsart University
Bangkok 10900
Thailand

Habitat Use by the Sambar (*Cervus unicolor*) in Thailand: A Case Study for Khao-Yai National Park

ABSTRACT

A study of habitat use by the sambar (*Cervus unicolor*) was undertaken in Khao-Yai National Park, a famous sambar range in Thailand, from January to December 1976, and November 1979 to September 1980. The vegetative canopy-cover and the percentages of forage categories available and in the sambar's diet were determined in both grassland and forest habitats. Of the 72 vegetative species recorded in grassland, only 25 species were eaten by sambar. Forty-seven forest species were also eaten. Food preference calculations indicate that only seven species in the grassland and 21 species from the forest are preferred. *Imperata cylindrica* and *Neyraudia reynaudiana*, both weeds and widely distributed over shifting cultivation areas in tropical Asian countries, are highly preferred by sambar. Five forest species were highly preferred, accounting for 5.4% of the food species available, but 14% of the diet.

Population estimates from November 1979 to 1980 were 0.23, 0.13 and 0.95 deer per hectare for daylight, spotlight and pellet-group counts, respectively. Range conditions and trends as well as sambar management are discussed.

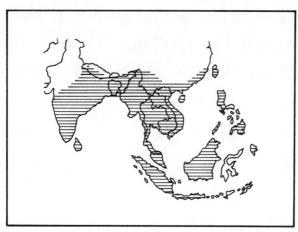

Figure 1. The distribution of the sambar (*Cervus unicolor*) in south Asia (based on available references).

Introduction

Thailand has a population of approximately 47 million or about 9 persons per square kilometer. Estimates of population growth rate vary from 2.2% to 3.0% per annum. It is predicted that it may rise to between 80 and 160 million by the middle of the 21st century. The ever-increasing human population results in decreased forest area and habitat for wildlife. Forest areas are now only 25.4% of Thailand's geographical area compared to 38.6% in 1973 (Wacharakitti et al., 1978). The sambar (*Cervus unicolor*) is found in all types of forested areas throughout the country (Figure 1), but preferred habitats are those portions of forest in close proximity to grasslands or secondary growth. An understanding of sambar habitat requirements, such as food, cover, water, and living space is needed for successful management of the species. Wildlife cannot be overlooked in Thailand nowadays because it is basic for economic, recreational, and aesthetic as well as ethical and scientific values. Until careful studies have been undertaken, habitat problems for Thailand's wildlife cannot be addressed.

Thailand is in the humid tropics under the influence of monsoon climatic conditions, and vast areas are well-covered with luxuriant forests. The forests of Thailand are varied owing to the composite nature of the country's topography, the considerable range of its latitude and longitudes, and its variation in temperature and precipitation (Smitinand, 1977). The two primary types of forest are evergreen and deciduous, but sambar are highly adaptable deer, found in a wide variety of habitats across south Asia (Figure 1). Khao-Yai National Park was selected as the study area because it contains several types of forests and is well know in Thailand as sambar habitat.

The specific study objectives were (a) to investigate the vegetative composition of grassland and forest habitat used by sambar, (b) to determine what plant foods are preferred by sambar on the range, and (c) to determine the number of plant species necessary in the habitat to sustain populations for sound management.

Though the sambar is a typical and widespread forest-dweller of southern Asia, little has been investigated of its biology. The following description is intended as general background on this large but little known ungulate. Sixteen subspecies of sambar have been described (see Whitehead, 1972; Grzimek, 1972) ranging from Ceylon through India to Burma, southern China, and Taiwan, south to Thailand, Malaysia, Sumatra, Borneo, and Celebes (Medway, 1969). The race in Thailand is *Cervus unicolor equinus*, Cuvier, 1823 (Lekagul and McNeely, 1977). Full-grown stags stand about 1.37 m at the shoulder and weigh about 227 kg. The coloration of both sexes is uniform light brown, with paler under parts. Stags are generally darker than hinds, approaching black or slaty gray in old males. The hair is long and coarse, and stags have a heavy ruff around the throat when mature (Thom, 1937; U Tun Yin, 1967). The first set of antlers are straight spikes grown at approximately one year of age. The second set has two tines, and the third and subsequent sets of antlers always have three tines (Medway, 1969). The antler-shedding period is from May to July and most antlers are cleaned of velvet in December (Thom, 1937). During the rutting season, old stags stalk about with erect tail, outstretched nuzzle, and everted face glands (Thom, 1937). At this time they are highly dangerous, especially in captivity. Grouping tendencies change in the course of the year, but details on social organization, use of space, and mating system are unknown. Each male fights for his territory and retains females which enter his area. After the mating season, stags disassociate with females and stay by themselves until the next rut. Most fawns are dropped during the rainy season. At Khao-Yai National Park, mating occurs in January and February, with most young being born during September and October. Sadleir (this volume) summarizes the scant information on female reproduction.

The sambar is essentially an animal of the more open deciduous forests and does not favor dense tree growth. According to Krishnan (1972:479) it is much more diurnal in its habits than is generally realized. The loud, alarm call of the sambar is a familiar sound of South Asian forests. Calling deer raise the tail to reveal the white underside, and both sexes stamp their

Ngampongsai

feet when suspicious of danger (Peacock, 1933; Bentley, 1976).

Methods

Grassland Community

Three grassland sites at Nhong-King, Morr-Singh-Toe and Nhong-Puck-Chee (700–900 m above sea level) were selected for intensive investigations. Square-meter plots were used to sample the grassland community. Plots were distributed regularly throughout the three sample-grassland areas. A species-area curve was applied to determine the number of plots needed to sample the forage species adequately. Braun-Blanquet's criterion (1932) was used; the sample was considered adequate when the species-area curve became approximately horizontal. Forty-eight, 43 and 45 plots were required respectively for Nhong-King, Moor-Singh-Toe and Nhong-Puck-Chee. Plots were spaced at 100 m intervals in lines 100 m apart. The line intercept method was used to determine the percentage of plant cover (Canfield, 1941).

Grasses and herbs were clipped at the mean grazing height observed for each species and placed in a plastic bag in order to estimate production and utilization (Brown, 1954; National Research Council, 1962). After weighing the fresh specimens, the grasses and herbs were oven dried at 75°C for 24 hours. Leafy-twigs were treated similarly but at 100°C. After cooling to room temperature, samples were weighed to the nearest 0.001 gm and moisture percentages computed.

All species of grasses, forbs, shrubs and trees present were identified for each plot. For woody plants, the number of leafy-twigs up to 2 m high, (the maximum browsing height of samber) were tallied by the twig-count method (Shafer, 1963).

Sambar Forest Foods

The twig-count method (Shafer, 1963) was also used on ten plots of 1 × 6 m to determine the amount of browsed and unbrowsed leafy twigs. Plots were laid in those portions of the forest in close proximity to grasslands. The original lengths of browsed twigs were obtained by comparing their twig diameters with those of unbrowsed leafy-twig specimens; 30–50 specimens of unbrowsed leafy-twigs were selected randomly from different plants to determine mean dried weights.

Food Preference Study

There are two important considerations in herbivore food habit studies : the percentage of the animal's diet which a plant species contributes, and the percentage of each forage which is cropped by the feeding animal (Papageorgiou, 1972). The dietary percentage indicates the principal food consumed. The percentage cropped illustrates the degree to which that species is chosen from among those available. If all forage species present were available in equal quantities, the composition of the animal's diet alone would indicate its food preferences. Such conditions, however, do not exist in nature. The formula proposed by Petrides (1975) was used to calculate a preference rating for each food plant. The ratio of the percentage in the diet to the percentage available yields a value which if greater than 1.00 indicates the relative degree of preference, and if under 1.00 illustrates the degree of unattractiveness. A ratio of 1.00 demonstrates that a species is eaten as it is encountered, being neither sought out nor neglected. The percentages used in the ratio were calculated from species' dry weights. In addition, a 12-day feeding trial was also conducted with a tame 3-year-old female sambar. Only the two most preferred forage foods were offered to the deer in order to determine the forage preference rank.

Population Study

In studies of wild herbivores, the relations between vegetation and animal population are of great importance. In this study, the pellet-group count, first described by Bennett et al. (1940) and modified later by Neff (1968), was used. Circular plots of 4.65 m^2 (50 ft^2), recommended by Smith (1968) as being the most economic and precise, were used. The number of plots needed in each sample size was obtained from pre-sample survey plots applying the formula used by Grieb (1958). Based on a pre-sample survey, 102, 147 and 73 sample plots were calculated as necessary at Nhong-King, Moor-Singh-Toe and Nhong-Puck-Chee, respectively. Plots were distributed over the entire study areas at each locality. The distance between plots was 20 m. All plots were cleared of pellet-groups before data were collected. The standard value of 12.0 pellet-groups per deer-day was used (Ngampongsai, 1977). Daylight (17:00–19:00) and spotlight (20:00–23:00) counts were also applied along the permanent 10 km road route.

Results and Discussion

Grassland Community

There were 46, 46 and 42 plant species identified for Nhong-King, Moor-Singh-Toe and Nhong-Puck-Chee respectively (Table 1). Grass and sedge species varied between 10 and 13 and forbs between 22 and 25. Herbaceous plants provided most ground cover. The vegetative canopy-cover differed at the three grassland sites (Figure 2). Grasses and sedges were most abundant at Moor-Singh-Toe (74.7%) and less so at Nhong-King and Nhong-Puck-Chee (55.3 and 40.2%

Table 1. Total and common forage species found in the grasslands, Khao-Yai National Park (July 1976)

Forage Species	Nhong-King	Moor-Singh Toe	Nhong-Puck Chee
Grass and sedges:			
Imperata cylindrica[a]	x	x	x
Carex indica[b]	x	x	x
Carex cruciata[b]	x	x	x
Ischaemum muticum[b]	x	x	x
Coelorachis glandulosa[b]	x	x	x
Cyperus sp.[b]	x		x
Neyraudia reynaudiana[a]	x	x	x
Panicum notatum	x	x	
Chrysopogon aciculatus	x	x	
Scirpus grossus[b]	x		x
Eragrostis capensis[b]	x	x	
Cyanodon dactylon	x		
Paspalum conjucatum[c]	x		
Cyperus digitatus			x
Fimbristylis trichoides		x	x
Forbs:			
Eupatorium odoratum[b]	x	x	x
Portulaca quadrifida	x	x	x
Erechtites hieracifolia	x	x	x
Pteris sp.	x	x	x
Hedyotis sp.	x	x	x
Adiantum sp.	x	x	x
Helicteres obtusa[b]	x	x	x
Utricularia aurea	x		
Ipomoea aquatica	x	x	
Ipomoea sp.[b]			x
Hygrophila erecta	x		
Portulaca sp.	x	x	x
Portulaca oleacea			x
Dioscorea stemonoides[b]	x	x	x
Vernonia elliptica[a]	x	x	x
Scoparia dulcis[b]	x	x	x
Spilanthes ocmella[b]	x	x	x
Alpinia sp.[a]	x	x	x
Polygonum chinense	x		
Costus speciosus[b]	x		
Mosses	x	x	x
Jussiaca suffruticosa	x		x

Table 1. (cont.)

Forage Species	Nhong-King	Moor-Singh Toe	Nhong-Puck Chee
Amaranthus gracilis	x		
Stachytarpheta indica	x		x
Euphorbia hirta	x		
Hygrophila minor	x		
Phyllanthus urinaria	x	x	
Commellina nudifolia		x	
Centella asiatica		x	
Parameria bartata		x	
Arisaema sp.		x	
Crotalaria elliptica		x	
Vernonia parishii[b]		x	
Alpinia oxymytra		x	
Hedyotis coronaria		x	
Hedyotis corymbosa		x	
Eryngium foetidum[b]			x
Blumea napifolia			x
Emilia sonchifolia			x
Ageratum conyzoides			x
Merremia gemella			x
Shrubs:			
Desmodium biarticulata[b]	x	x	x
Desmodium cephalotoides	x	x	x
Prismatomeris albidifolia	x		
Melastoma malabathricum	x	x	x
Ixora sp.		x	
Pandanus sp.		x	
Trees:			
Schima wallichii	x	x	
Cratoxylon formosum[a]	x	x	
Wrightia tomentosa[a]	x		x
Bridelia sp.[b]	x	x	x
Sapium baccatum		x	
Choerospondias axillaris		x	x
Altingia excelsa		x	
Trema orientalis			x
Hibicus macrophylla			x
Oroxylum indicum			x
Total: species	46	46	42
Common: species		31	29

[a]Preferred (P = 1.00 to 1.99)
[b]Neglected (P = <1.00)
[c]Highly preferred (P = >1.99)
(blank) avoided

Ngampongsai

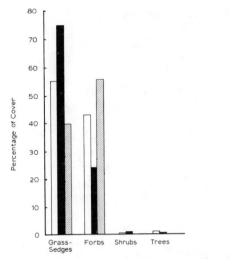

Figure 2. Vegetative canopy–cover at Nhong-King (open bars), Moor–Singh–Toe (solid bars), and Nhong–Puck–Chee (dotted bars) grasslands, Khao–Yai National Park, July 1976.

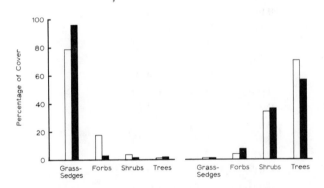

Figure 3. Percentages of forage categories available (open bars) and in the sambar's diet (solid bars) for (a) grasslands, January–September 1976, and (b) forests, January–December 1976, Khao–Yai National Park.

respectively). The percentages of cover for forbs were 43.0, 24.0 and 59.8 for Nhong-King, Moor-Singh-Toe and Nhong-Puck-Chee respectively.

Shrubs and trees were responsible for less cover percentage at all three sites, probably because of burning frequency. By dry weight, species available in the field were 79.4% grasses and sedges, 17.1% forbs, 2.9% shrubs, and 0.5% trees. Consumption of these respective categories was 96.1%, 2.4%, 0.6%, and 0.7% (Figure 3a).

Preferred Grassland Foods

Of 72 forage species found in the grasslands (Table 1), 25 were eaten by sambar (Table 2). Seven species, *Paspalum conjugatum*, *Wrightia tomentosa*, *Alpinia* sp., *Neyraudia reynaudiana*, *Veronia elliptica*, *Imperata cylindrica* and *Cratoxylon formosum*, were preferred foods. The seven preferred food species were low both in percentages of availability and diet compared to *Imperata cylindrica* and *Neyraudia reynaudiana* (Table 2). *Imperata* comprises 88.6% of the sambar's diet and 69.8% of the available forage. It was observed to be heavily grazed year round. *Imperata* and *Neyraudia* are both weeds in south and Southeast Asia where cultivation and old forest clearings are found. The dependence of sambar on these two weeds could be of ecological and economic significance. Sambar could be used possibly to control *Imperata*, or could be ranched along with cattle or other domestic stock. However, sambar prefer only new sprouts of *Imperata*.

Forest Forages

There are 47 species available of which 21 species were found to be preferred foods in the forest habitat (Table 3). The percentages of plants available were 0.4% grasses and sedges, 3.3% forbs, 33.8% shrubs, and 70.5% trees while the percentages of plant consumed were 0.4%, 7.3%, 36.3%, and 56.9% respectively (Figure 3b). *Carallia branchiata* and *Knema laurina* have food preference ratings exceeding 3.00. Five preferred food species had ratings over 2.00. These highly preferred species constituted only 5.4% of the food available, but accounted for 14.2% of the sambar's diet. Fourteen of the preferred species constituted only 47.8% of the animal's diet and 29.9% of the available food in the forest. Twenty-six species were rated as neglected food species. These form 62.8% of available food and 38.9% of the diets. *Lasianthus cyanocarpus*, *Catanopsis acuminatissima*, and *Melaleuca seutellatum* are the most important forest food species, contributing 21.3%, 7.2% and 6.1% of the sambar's diet, respectively.

When comparing the preferred food of grassland and forest habitats, grasslands have more forage

Table 2. Sambar food preference ratings for grassland forages, Khao-Yai National Park, January to September 1976

Forage Species	Forage Dry Weight (kg/ha) Available (A)	Removal (R)	Percentages Available (a)[a]	Diet (d)[a]	Removal (r)[a]	Preference Ratings (P)[a]
Paspalum conjugatum	0.247	0.200	0.20	0.04	80.97	2.00
Wrightia tomentosa[b]	2.666	1.556	0.21	0.34	58.36	1.62
Alpinia sp.	1.656	0.954	0.13	0.21	57.61	1.62
Neyraudia reynaudiana	26.173	14.289	2.04	3.10	54.59	1.52
Vernonia elliptica	9.400	4.700	0.47	1.02	50.00	1.38
Imperata sylindrica	895.617	409.041	69.77	88.61	45.67	1.22
Cratoxylon formosum[b]	3.432	1.471	0.28	0.32	42.86	1.14
Ischaemum muticum	17.992	5.785	1.40	1.25	32.15	0.89
Eryngium foetidum	0.008	0.002	0.0006	0.0004	25.00	0.67
Dioscorea stemonoides	0.360	0.080	0.03	0.02	22.22	0.67
Carex cruciata	48.787	9.638	3.80	2.09	19.76	0.55
Coelorachis glandulosa	2.205	0.377	0.16	0.08	18.62	0.50
Eragrostis capensis	1.546	0.274	0.12	0.06	17.72	0.50
Carex indica	9.135	1.492	0.71	0.32	16.33	0.45
Scirpus grossus	16.105	2.578	1.26	0.56	16.00	0.45
Helicteres obtusa	3.979	0.622	0.31	0.14	15.63	0.45
Cyperus sp.	0.127	0.018	0.01	0.004	14.17	0.40
Bridelia sp.	0.170	0.020	0.01	0.004	11.76	0.40
Spilanthes ocmella	33.767	4.422	2.63	0.96	13.10	0.37
Costus speciosus	0.165	0.015	0.01	0.003	9.09	0.30
Scoparia dulcis	0.525	0.054	0.04	0.01	10.29	0.25
Desmodium biarticulata	38.388	2.742	2.99	0.59	7.14	0.20
Vernonia parishii	0.841	0.060	0.07	0.01	7.13	0.14
Ipomoea sp.	0.068	0.004	0.01	0.001	5.88	0.10
Eupatorium odoratum	170.027	1.255	13.25	0.27	0.74	0.02
Total = S	1283.206	461.622	100.00	100.00	—	1.00

[a] $a = \dfrac{A}{SA} \times 100$; $d = \dfrac{R}{SR} \times 100$; $r = \dfrac{R}{A} \times 100$; $P = \dfrac{d}{a}$; S = Summation
[b] Grassland shrubs; all other species herbaceous

Table 3. Sambar food preference ratings for forest forages, Khao-Yai National Park, January to December 1976

Forage Species	Forage Dry Weight (kg/ha) Available (A)	Removal (R)	Percentages Available (a)[a]	Diet (d)[a]	Removal (r)[a]	Preference Ratings (P)[a]
Carallia brachiata	0.399	0.327	0.58	1.96	81.96	3.38
Knema laurina	0.247	0.186	0.35	1.11	75.30	3.17
Lithocarpus rodgerianus	0.110	0.074	0.16	0.44	67.27	2.75
Neolitsea zeylanica	0.068	0.045	0.10	0.27	66.18	2.70

Ngampongsai

Table 3. (cont.)

Forage Species	Forage Dry Weight (kg/ha)		Percentages			Preference Ratings (P)[a]
	Available (A)	Removal (R)	Available (a)[a]	Diet (d)[a]	Removal (r)[a]	
Eugenia sp.	0.535	0.333	0.78	1.99	63.67	2.55
Eugenia siamensis	1.072	0.655	1.58	3.32	61.10	2.48
Ficus sp.	1.321	0.759	1.94	4.54	57.46	2.34
Nephelium mutabile	0.983	0.480	1.45	2.87	48.83	1.98
Uvaria rufa	0.341	0.150	0.50	0.98	43.99	1.78
Melaleuca seutellatum	2.313	1.016	3.41	6.08	43.93	1.78
Hedyotis sp.	0.752	0.316	1.11	1.98	42.02	1.70
Lasianthus cyanocarpus	8.734	3.560	12.85	21.30	40.76	1.66
Lithocarpus eucalyptifolia	0.434	0.163	0.64	0.98	37.56	1.53
Castanopsis acuminatissima	3.220	1.201	4.47	7.19	37.30	1.52
Uncaria homomalla	0.209	0.078	0.31	0.47	37.32	1.52
Eugenia sp.	0.170	0.062	0.25	0.37	36.47	1.48
Murraya paniculata	0.098	0.033	0.14	0.20	33.67	1.34
Eugenia ripicola	1.857	0.521	2.73	3.12	28.06	1.42
Uvaria sp.	0.453	0.154	0.66	0.92	34.00	1.39
Styrax sp.	0.632	0.177	0.93	1.06	28.01	1.14
Podocarpus neriifolius	0.297	0.079	0.44	0.47	26.60	1.07
Uncaria sp.	0.656	0.146	0.97	0.87	22.26	0.94
Rourea stenopetala	0.332	0.609	0.49	0.41	20.78	0.84
Mangifera sylvatica	1.976	0.396	2.91	2.36	19.99	0.81
Ixora sp.	8.454	1.667	12.45	9.97	19.72	0.80
Carex cruciata	0.263	0.049	0.39	0.39	18.63	0.74
Symplocos laurina	0.724	0.133	1.07	0.80	18.37	0.74
Clausena excavata	3.819	0.687	5.62	4.11	18.00	0.73
Dioscorea bulbifera	2.020	0.343	2.97	2.05	16.98	0.69
Alpinia oxymytra	4.278	0.713	6.30	4.26	16.67	0.68
Linostoma thorelii	0.282	0.046	0.42	0.28	16.31	0.67
Cinnamomum subavenum	0.928	0.147	1.37	0.88	15.84	0.64
Desmos sp.	1.097	0.157	1.62	0.94	14.31	0.58
Memecylon ovatum	3.782	0.530	5.57	3.17	14.01	0.57
Ardisia arborescens	2.030	0.245	2.99	1.52	12.51	0.51
Gonocaryum lobbianum	0.883	0.110	1.30	0.66	12.46	0.51
Alpinia sp.	0.163	0.020	0.24	0.12	12.27	0.50
Fraxinus floribunda	0.478	0.056	0.70	0.34	11.72	0.49
Litsea verticellata	1.111	0.111	0.119	1.64	10.71	0.43
Camellia oleifera	1.195	0.121	1.76	0.72	10.13	0.41
Cinnamomum iners	1.519	0.146	2.24	0.87	9.61	0.39
Evodia gracilis	2.081	0.172	3.06	1.03	8.27	0.34
Aglaia odorata	0.196	0.016	0.29	0.10	8.16	0.34
Artabotrys harmandii	1.698	0.100	2.50	0.60	5.89	0.24
Jasminum sp.	0.904	0.047	1.33	0.28	5.20	0.21
Adiantum sp.	0.610	0.027	0.90	0.16	4.43	0.18
Litsea sebifera	2.206	0.076	3.25	0.46	3.45	0.14
Total = S	67.927	16.715	100.00	100.00		

[a] $a = \dfrac{A}{SA} \times 100$; $d = \dfrac{R}{SR} \times 100$; $r = \dfrac{R}{A} \times 100$; $p = \dfrac{d}{a}$; S = summation

Table 4. Dry-weight forages eaten by a 3-year old female sambar during a 12-day feeding trial (January 24, 1977) at Khao-Yai National Park, Thailand

Grass Species	Grams Offered	Grams Consumed	Percentages
Neyraudia reynaudiana	6,863.06	6,225.75	91.15
Imperata cylindrica	7,632.02	6,754.79	88.51
Totals	14,495.08	13,010.54	

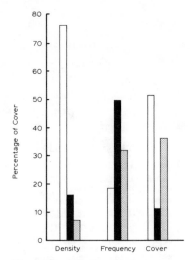

Figure 4. Density, frequency, and percentage cover of preferred (open bars), neglected (solid bars), and avoided (dotted bars) sambar foods on grasslands in Khao–Yai National Park, July 1976.

available per hectare. Rating values for the forest species indicate that sambar prefer forest species at least when the grassland species are absent. The sambars' ideal habitat in Khao-Yai is a mixture of grassland and forest. Whether sambar could survive on *Imperata* grasslands alone has not been investigated.

Feeding Trial

The captive sambar preferred *Neyraudia reynaudiana* to *Imperata cylindrica* (Table 4). The feeding trial response supports the relative food preference values determined on the wild grassland where 91% and 88% of *Neyraudia* and *Imperata* were consumed respectively.

Range Condition and Trend

Two indicators were used to appraise range condition and trend: (1) the degree of utilization of highly preferred forage species, and (2) the extent to which the more heavily utilized range species remained dominant in the plant community. Plant species having preference ratings over 1.00 were termed "decreasers" because of the effect of heavy grazing. Species rated below 1.00 were labeled "increasers". Those species which were not utilized as foods were classified as "avoided increasers". There were 4 grassland species (Table 2) and 7 forest plants on the study areas (Table 3) which were consumed in excess of the 50% level and these 11 species also were scarce plants in the community.

Grassland plot sample analysis in Khao-Yai revealed that "decreaser species" constituted 52% of the range, while 11% were "increasers" and 37% were "avoided-increasers" (Figure 4). No scarcity or overuse of preferred foods was noted. Density and frequency percentages for these categories were 76.5% and 18.2% for "decreasers"; 16.4% and 49.4% for "increasers", and 7.1% and 31.9% for "avoided increasers" respectively (Figure 4). There were no obvious signs in the study area of excessive utilization of forage species leading to range degradation.

Population Density

Estimated sambar densities during the 1976–1977 period were 0.02, 0.10 and 3.68 deer per hectare by daylight, spotlight and pellet-group counts, respectively (Table 5). The pellet-group counts yielded a very high and possibly inflated density estimate compared to daylight and spotlight counts in the same area. Pellet groups were often difficult to delineate, and sampling plots were not placed in the forest. To improve the accuracy of the estimate Ruangchan (1982) investigated sambar density in the same area by sampling plots both in the forest and grassland areas. A minimum of 10 associated pellets was the criterion to identify one pellet-group as recommended by Ngampongsai (1981). The sambar density thus estimated was only 0.95 deer per hectare (Table 5).

Table 5. Comparison of average sambar densities obtained from various methods from two investigators, Khao-Yai National Park, Thailand

	Deer/ha	
Types of Count	Ngamponsai, C. (1976–77)	Ruangchan, S. (1979–80)
Roadside Counts:		
Evening tallied	0.02	0.023
Spotlight surveys	0.10	0.13
Pellet-group counts	3.68	0.95

Results obtained from daylight and spotlight counts of both studies differed only slightly. The 0.95 deer per km² estimate seems to be a rather high density in natural range, but it is probably reasonably accurate since Khao-Yai Park is well protected.

Management Recommendations

Methods of managing sambar populations may differ depending on the type of habitat and form of land use. In protected areas where the primary objective is maintaining natural conditions, it is recommended that (1) habitat relations and population counts of sambar and other large mammals be recorded annually using the best reliable methods, and (2) attempts should be made to determine the extent to which sambar require forest cover and other habitat types to satisfy their basic living requirements. In addition, various forest species produce fruits used as food by sambar, and the importance of these fruit-bearing species for the deer and vice versa should be studied in a broader ecological sense.

In livestock grazing areas or regions of shifting agriculture the needs are somewhat different. Because sambar feed on *Imperata* grass, a well-known weed associated with shifting cultivation in tropical Asia, future investigations should attempt to determine whether sambar are more suitable for meat-production on range lands than domestic stock.

Specific objectives should include (1) determination of how *Imperata* grasslands should be ʼmanaged to maximize useful forage production and how sambar react to such sites, and (2) improved understanding of the effects of frequency and intensity of mowing and controlled burning in stimulating new production and energy cycling.

Acknowledgments

Special thanks are extended to the Kasetsart University for giving leave of absence. Without financial support from the Friends of the National Zoo for round trip travel expenses, I would certainly never have had the opportunity to attend the symposium and for this I am most grateful. Finally, my sincere appreciation and thanks also go to all colleagues who helped me in preparing the manuscript, and to Ms. Payao Na Bangcharg for her typing.

Literature Cited

Bennett, L.T., P.F., English and R. McCain
1940.   The study of deer populations by use of pellet-group counts. *Journal of Wildlife Management*, 4:398–403.

Bentley, A.
1976.   *An introduction to the deer of Australia.* Melbourne: Hawthorn Press Pte. Ltd.

Braun-Blanquet, J.
1932.   *Plant sociology.* (Trans. rev., ed. by G.D. Fuller and H.S. Conard). New York: McGraw-Hill Book Co.

Brown, D.
1954.   Methods of surveying and measuring vegetation. *Commonwealth Bureau of Pastures and Field Crops, Bulletin 42*, 223 pp.

Canfield, R.H.
1941.   Application of the line interception method in sampling range vegetation. *Journal of Forestry*, 39:388–394.

Grieb, J.R.
1958.   *Wildlife Statistics.* Colorado Game and Fish Department, 96 pp.

Grzimek, B.
1972.   *Grzimek's Animal Life Encyclopedia.* New York: Van Nostrand Reinhold Co.

Krishnan, M.
1972.   An ecological survey of the larger mammals of Penisular India. *Journal of the Bombay Natural History Society*, 69:479–499.

Lekagul, B., and J.A. McNeely
1977.   *Mammals of Thailand.* Kurusapha Ladprao Press.

Medway, L.
1969.   *The wild mammals of Malaya and off-shore islands including Singapore.* London: Oxford University Press.

National Research Council
1962.   Basic problems and techniques in range research. *Publication 890, National Academy of Science*, Washington, DC, 342 pp.

Neff, D.J.
1968.   The pellet group count techniques for big game trends, census, and distribution: a review. *Journal of Wildlife Management*, 32:597–614.

Ngampongsai, C.
1977.   Habitat relations of the Sambar (*Cervus unicolor*) in Khao-Yai National Park, Thailand, Ph.D. Thesis, Michigan State University, 115 pp.

Ngampongsai, C.
1981.   The application of pellet-group counts in estimating sambar population. *Proceedings of the 2nd Seminar on Wildlife of Thailand*, Volume 2, pp. 316–320.

Papageorgiou, N.
1972.   Food preference and survival of the agrimi (*Capra aegagrus cretensis*) on Crete. M.S. Thesis, Michigan State University, 48 pp.

Peacock, E.H.
1933.   *A game-book for Burma.* London: Witherby and Co.

Petrides, G.A.
1975. Principal foods versus preferred foods and their relations to stocking rate and range condition. *Biological Conservation*, 7:161–168.

Ruangchan, S.
1982. Study on sambar population and its group structure in Khao-Yai National Park, M.S. Thesis, Kasetsart University.

Sadleir, R.M.F.S.
This   Reproduction of female Cervidae.
volume

Shafer, E.L.
1963. The twig-count method for measuring hardwood deer browse. *Journal of Wildlife Management*, 27:428–437.

Smith, R.H.
1968. A comparison of several sizes of circular plots for estimating deer pellet-group density. *Journal of Wildlife Management*, 32:585–591.

Smitinand, T.
1977. Vegetation and ground cover of Thailand. *Technical paper No. 1, Department of Forestry and Biology, Kasetsart University*, 15 pp.

Thom, W.S.
1937. The Malayan or Burmese sambar. *Journal of the Bombay Natural History Society*, 39:309–319.

U Tun Yin
1967. *Wild mammals of Burma*. Rangoon: Rangoon Gazette Ltd.

Wacharakitti, S., P. Boonnorm, P. Saguantam, and A. Boonsher
1979. The assessment of forest areas from Landsat Imagery. *Forestry Research Bulletin No. 60, Faculty of Forestry, Bangkok*, 22 pp.

Whitehead, G.K.
1972. *Deer of the World*. London: Constable and Co., Ltd.

CLAUDE MARTIN
WWF-Switzerland
Postfach
8037 Zürich
Switzerland

Interspecific Relationships between Barasingha and Axis Deer in Kanha National Park, India, and Relevance to Management

ABSTRACT
The southern subspecies of barasingha (*C. duvauceli branderi*) has experienced a long and steady decline to critical numbers in its last stronghold in Kanha National Park in Central India. The barasingha in Kanha National Park is sympatric with the axis deer (*Axis axis*) which in the past years has increased to numbers above 10,000 within the area of barasingha occurrence. In this study the effects of common exploitation of grassland within the densely forested area has been analyzed. Barasingha and axis show a pronounced grass diet overlap from the point of view of species. Axis deer, however, are much more flexible and resort to browse when the grass cover becomes scarce in the dry season. Barasingha depend almost exclusively on grasses and suffer from competition for certain key species, particularly after burning. Grazing impact showed significant positive correlation with the dry open grassland type. Pellet frequencies of the two sympatric deer species showed decreasing correlation with increasing grass cover height. Tall grass areas promote segregation and reduce pressure. Park management succeeded in enlarging the park to include more and better grassland. Management was reviewed also. The barasingha population has increased considerably since then.

Introduction

The use of grassland areas by sympatric ungulates is often a complicated process and has been described as a function of the structure, mechanical properties and chemical composition of the herb layer. African ungulates have developed adaptations to available forage and exploit grasslands by grazing in succession according to morphology and body size (Lamprey, 1963; Gwynne and Bell, 1968). It has even been suggested that on East African savannahs grazing activity of the earlier species facilitates feeding of ungulate species later in succession (Bell, 1970). Such intricate relationship to avoid competition between grazing ungulates have not often been evaluated for ungulates in regions other than Africa. Schwartz and Ellis (1981), however, found similar size-related trends among bison, pronghorn and domestic species, but pointed out that forage quantity and quality strongly influenced forage use. Interspecies overlap seemed also dependent upon the recent evolutionary history where niche separation could develop. Other authors described competitive exploitation between sympatric deer species: Martinka (1968) and Krämer (1973) expected competitive exploitation between mule deer (*O. hemionus*) and white-tailed deer (*O. virginianus*) during shortage of important foods. Krausman (1978) on the other hand found significant differences between the diets of these two species in Big Bend National Park, Texas.

The question of competitive exploitation becomes crucial when rare or endangered species are involved. The southern subspecies of barasingha (*C. duvauceli branderi*) some years ago was on the verge of extinction. Its last population occurs in Kanha Natoinal Park in Central India, where it is sympatric with an abundant population of axis deer (*Ax. axis*), besides a number of less dominant ungulates. Both barasingha and axis are gregarious deer congregating on the open grassland areas of the park. It has been suggested that the two species compete with each other under scarce grassland conditions after extensive burns (Martin, 1977). Scarce habitat conditions have earlier led to drastic management measures to save the barasingha from extinction (Panwar, 1972; Martin and Huber, 1973). In this paper the data on grassland use is analyzed in view of the interspecific relationship between barasingha and axis deer prior to a revision of management in 1972. Recent population trends as a response to management are also discussed.

The Study Area

Kanha National Park is situated in the western part of the Maikal-Hills in Central India, at altitudes between 500 to 890 m. Below 610 m the sal tree (*Shorea robusta*) is predominant, locally it forms almost monotypic stands; the prevalent undergrowth is a medium-sized shrub, *Moghania congesta*. Above 610 m the forest is composed of about 50 tree species, and the main undergrowth is a bamboo species (*Dendrocalamus strictus*). The center of the western part of the park is formed by a large opening known as the Kanha Meadow. This meadow harbors most of the perennial watering places. The area is drained in the north by the Sulcum River and its tributaries. Along the wide valley of the Sulcum there are several other meadows. These openings were caused by former shifting cultivation of the local tribes. They have not been reoccupied by forest due to annual frosts and fires that keep sal seedlings from progressing. The vegetation on the meadows consists of more than 90 grass species; forbs are common only along forest edges and in the forest. Until the mid 1960s virtually the only suitable habitat available to the barasingha in the then Kanha National Park was the 6 km² Kanha Meadow. This area was totally burned each year during the cool season probably since 1902–1903 until management was reviewed in 1972. Regular burning altered the grass flora of Kanha Meadow to short grasses dominated by annual species (Martin and Huber, 1974).

All other sizeable open grassland areas were occupied by villages and their rice fields until the village Sonph north of the Kanha Meadow was translocated in 1969. Further grassland areas were added when the park boundary was extended to the south in 1970. In 1974, under Project Tiger, the Supkhar area was added to the park bringing its total area to 940 km².

Decline of Barasingha

In the early 1960s the barasingha population of the present Kanha National Park had dwindled from more than 3000 animals recorded in a Forest Department census in 1938 to less than 200. This population by then was the only known and confirmed population of *C. d. branderi* that remained in Central India. Schaller (1967) considered the southern subspecies of barasingha in danger of extinction, when he counted no more than 82 in 1964 and 55 in 1965. The Forest Department census figures for these years were somewhat higher but also hardly exceeded 100 animals (Figure 3). The very low fawning rate of 15/100 hinds determined by Schaller (1967) also pointed to the grave status of the Kanha population, and gave at least a superficial explanation for the alarming decline. The decline of *C. d. branderi* is to some extent paralleled by the decline of the more common northern subspecies *C. d. duvauceli* occurring in the alluvial plains at the foot of the Himalayas. But the decline of some of the northern subspecies populations can more clearly be attributed to loss of habitat (Singh, 1978 Schaaf, 1978).

A number of possible reasons for the decline of the Kanha population of *C.d. branderi* had been given by Schaller (1967). Brucellosis was mentioned because it causes abortion of the foetus which would have an effect on fawning rate. Brucellosis, however, seemed an unlikely cause for a steady decline that continued over decades. If disease was to be the cause one would expect oscillation of population figures. McDiarmid and Matthews (1974) also found that brucellosis was of little significance to deer.

Baiting of tigers in the Kanha Meadow, which was the core area of the barasingha's home range in the 1960s, caused a temporarily higher rate of mortality among the already depleted barasingha population (Panwar, 1972; 1978). Predation by tiger under natural conditions, however, was shown to have no relevant effect on the barasingha population size (Martin, 1977).

Methods

The evaluations presented in this paper are essentially based on data collected during a 2-year study carried out from April 1971 to April 1973. Additional and more recent information on population trends and dispersal were obtained from H.S. Panwar, Director, Project Tiger. More detailed information on methods used is given in Martin (1977).

Feeding Data

Indications on feeding habits of barasingha and axis deer are based on a large number of opportunistic observations. Identifications of grazed plants were made on the spot, immediately after the grazing animal(s) had been watched through binoculars. Identification of grasses was critical during their growing period. Grazed specimens were thus marked with aluminum tags and identified later.

Grass Cover Analysis

During the flowering periods of 1971 and 1972, specimens of all grasses and grass-like plant species occurring in the sal area were collected and identified. Identification of the specimens was made by the Indian Forest Research Institute in Dehra Dun, U.P. Excluding some rare species, a total of 81 grasses and grass-like plants were found in the study area. In October 1972, a plot method was used to sample the larger meadows within the study area. Plots were 10 square meters and circular. Plot centers were placed by pacing off compass lines in north-south and east-west direction at intervals of 200 steps. The total number of plots was 791, of which 456 fell in meadows. The following items were recorded:

(1) The five predominant grasses or grass-like plant species (if present) and the degree of their abundance (rank order).

(2) The principal grassland type, distinguished by the presence or absence of shade, and by high or low ground moisture as follows:
—Dry open (open grassland plains)
—Moist open (depressions, ravines)
—Dry shady (forest edges, beneath loose tree stands)
—Stream bed (often sandy, or with rocky outcrops)
Locations were identified as "moist" if the ground still had a swampy character in October, i.e. roughly one month after the end of the monsoon rains. Locations were considered shady if the plot was found to have more than 50% shade at noon.

(3) The grass height was measured with a board that was segmented every 5 cm, and read from a distance of 10 meters.

(4) Grazing incidence:
Low—none or one plant grazed
Medium—two to ten plants grazed
High—more than 10 to all plants grazed
The data collected in the 228 plots of the Kanha Meadow were used to compute a correlation matrix (Program BMD 02 D of the Health Science Computing Facility, UCLA) with 35 variables. It included the correlation among the occurrence of the 24 most common grass species and the four grassland types, the grass height and the grazing incidence. Partly, these variables were a priori interdependent.

Pellet Frequency Correlation

The distribution patterns of fecal pellets were checked to assess intensity of grassland use by barasingha and axis deer. A total of 84 plots were located in the study area meadows according to a stratified random design and were permanently marked with wooden pegs. Plots were 50 m² and circular. High pellet densities impeded the identification of pellet groups. Therefore single pellets were counted.

The first count was carried out from March 12–16, 1972. Consecutive counts were carried out on July 5–12, 1972 and March 8–13, 1973. Each time pellets were classified, counted and removed from the plot. *Durability of pellets:* Generally pellets dry up quickly and remain unaffected in open areas until the next monsoon, but they do not weather the second monsoon. Pellets dropped during a period of heavy rain may be washed away within the same monsoon season. Occasionally pellets were lost due to termite attack. Neither type of loss seemed to seriously affect the results of semiannual or even annual counts.

Table 1. Diet of barasingha and axis deer among the 24 most common grass species of the Kanha Meadow. Grass species are listed according to their occurrence in grassland types. Underlined signs indicate bulk food species.

Dry open	Barasingha	Axis
Bothriochloa odorata	<u>+</u>	<u>+</u>
Diandrochloa japonica	+	+
Digitaria stricta	+	+
Dimeria connivens	+	+
Eragrostiella bifaria		+
Eulalia trispicata	+	+
Heteropogon contortus	+	+
Mnesithea laevis	+	+
Pauicum austroasiaticum		+
Pseudopogonatherum contortum	+	+
Saccharum spontaneum	<u>+</u>	<u>+</u>
Schizachyrium brevifolium	+	
Setaria glauca	+	+
Themeda quadrivalvis	+	+
Themeda triandra	<u>+</u>	+
Moist open		
Eragrostis unioloides	+	+
Ischaemum indicum	+	
Ischaemum rugosum	+	
Iseilema prostratum	+	+
Narenga porphyrocoma	+	
Vetiveria zizanioides	+	+
Dry shady		
Apluda mutica	+	+
Bothriochloa odorata	<u>+</u>	<u>+</u>
Chionachne koenigii	+	
Themeda triandra	<u>+</u>	+
Stream bed		
Arthraxon quartinianus	+	+
Saccharum spontaneum	<u>+</u>	<u>+</u>
Vetiveria zizanioides	+	+

Species identification of pellets: The diameter of axis deer pellets vary from 6.5–9.0 mm, whereas barasingha pellets are always wider, even from fawns. Barasingha pellets are cylindrical in contrast to the pileate axis deer pellets. Axis pellets are usually dark brown to black when dry, whereas barasingha pellets are light brown. The shapes of pellets were fairly constant, except during the monsoon when deformed pellets also occurred. Occasionally pellets had to be disregarded due to difficulties in identification.

Correlation of pellet frequencies: Spearman Rank Correlation tests were used to test correlated occurrence of the two species' pellets in the sample plots.

Population Census

Since 1953 the Forest Department has carried out an annual wildlife census in mid-June using a standardized block count technique. Forest guards with aids are distributed in delineated sections of the park, where they count the wildlife between fixed hours on two consecutive days. The Forest Department's census gives a fair idea of the population size of the large gregarious herbivores. Determination of barasingha population size during the study period is described in Martin (1977).

Results

Feeding Habits and Diet Overlap

The diet of barasingha is almost exclusively composed of grasses. Very few observations of barasingha eating browse or fruit were made by Schaller (1967). Even bamboo, though gramineous and locally abundant is avoided. Riverine *Saccharum spontaneum*, *Bothriochloa adorata* and *Themeda triandra* formed the bulk of the barasingha's diet in the cool-dry season. A larger variety of grasses is fed upon during and after monsoon (Martin, 1977). Barasingha, however, feed on grasses in all four major grassland types (Table 1).

The diet of axis deer covers a very wide range of grasses as well as browse species. The latter include leaves from the trees, shrubs, vines and forbs. A number of fruits are also fed upon. Schaller (1967) identified 35 browse species eaten by axis deer at Kanha, which is an incomplete list. The bulk of the axis deer diet is still made up of grasses, but they rely more heavily on browse when the availability of grasses on open area is reduced. Axis deer exploit all grassland, but they prefer the dry open and dry shady types.

The diet spectrums of barasingha and axis deer include practically all common grasses of the Kanha Meadow (Table 1). On the species basis this suggests an almost total diet overlap of the common grasses. Barasingha and axis deer form mixed herds in all seasons except monsoon until December. This means

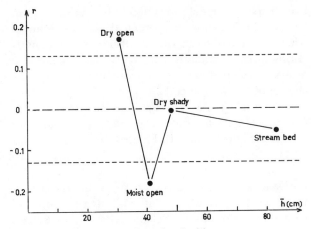

Figure 1.   Correlation of grazing incidence.

An analysis of fecal pellet distribution does not accurately reflect utilization patterns, but can show degree of visitation to different habitats by both species. A highly significant correlation ($P < 0.05$) was found in the occurrence of barasingha and axis pellets deposited during the dry season. This confirmed common utilization patterns by the two species during the season when food shortage prevailed in Kanha Meadow. Correlations in the occurrence of the two species pellets was less pronounced in the other seasons (Martin, 1977).

To test common use by the two species under different habitat conditions correlations of pellet frequencies were determined in four open areas differing in mean height of grass cover (Figure 2). Pellet frequencies in the sample plots were totaled to represent the deposition of one full year. There was a decreasing correlation of common pellet occurrence with increasing height of grass cover. The significant positive correlation of pellet occurrence of barasingha and axis deer in the short grass Kanha Meadow gives further evidence of competition in an area of food shortage. Tall grass on the other hand appears to promote the segregation of the two species.

Response to Management Measures

A very important improvement of the barasingha's range conditions was effected by the inclusion of additional grassland areas in the park just prior to this study. The Sonph village situated north of the Kanha Meadow was relocated in 1969, which released suitable grassland at a 10 km distance from the core area of the former population. Cattle grazing was also stopped in neighboring open areas. Schaller (1967) could not locate fawning barasingha, though he ob-

that a short competitive period of grassland use may occur during the cool and dry seasons when the nutritive content of the grass cover is low. Stomach content analysis would be necessary to yield more precise information on quantity and diet selectivity with respect to different parts of the same species. Culling would be necessary for representative samples but was not feasible.

Effects of Grazing on Grass Cover

Particularly severe grazing pressure was caused by axis deer on the few major perennial grass species upon which barasingha were subsisting during the dry season, i.e. *Bothriochloa odorata*, *Saccharum spontaneum* and *Themeda triandra*. Under the scarce habitat conditions as they prevailed in the Kanha Meadow these grasses were grazed down to earth. In the dry season after extnesive burns barasingha avoided grazing in dry open areas. At the end of the dry season some barasingha showed signs of malnutrition (Martin, 1977). Axis deer on the other hand continued grazing the stubbles of perennials or concentrated more on browse. But with the new sprouts in the early days of the monsoon season up to 2000 axis deer congregated again on Kanha Meadow. There is a significant high grazing impact in the dry open type. Grazing intensity decreases with increasing grass height (Figure 1). There is no significant correlation between high grazing impact and avoidance with dry shady and stream bed types of grassland. Only the moist open type shows a significant negative correlation with grazing impact, which is due to the more pronounced avoidance of this type by the most abundant grazer, axis deer.

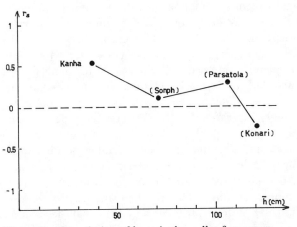

Figure 2.   Correlation of barasingha pellet frequences.

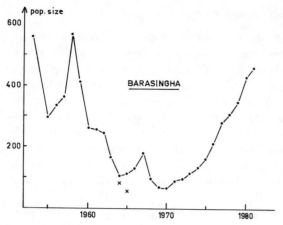

Figure 3.   Barasingha census figures.

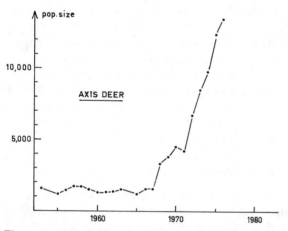

Figure 4.   Axis deer census figures.

served barasingha leaving Kanha Meadow during early monsoon and staying away through the fawning period from August–October. In 1971, however, the barasingha population adopted the northern meadows as monsoon range, and fawning was recorded there in tall grass areas. The reproductive success described as very low by Schaller (1967) in 1964–65 subsequently increased to 41.2 fawns per 100 hinds in 1972 and 36.1 per 100 in 1973. It was shown also that barasingha adapt to changes in food and water availability by seasonal movement between different open areas (Martin, 1974; 1977). To release grazing pressure in the Kanha Meadow a number of other management measures were undertaken resulting in part from this study. Those led to a discontinuation of total annual burning. The Kanha Meadow was subsequently protected from fires by fire-breaks for a number of years before returning to a system of three to

five years rotational burning. Other measures included the creation of perennial water resources which promoted the growth of tall grass areas. Panwar (1978) gives a comprehensive review of management measures carried out to enhance the barasingha's chance of survival since 1969.

The barasingha and axis deer populations have experienced somewhat differing courses during the past 30 years (Figures 3 and 4). Figures for axis deer which exclude the new areas of the park in the south and east are not available to me for the years following 1976. Barasingha census figures obtained by the Forest Department were consistent with figures obtained with other methods by Schaller (1967) and Martin (1977). Even if considerable systematic error is taken into consideration, there can be little doubt that barasingha and axis populations increased to a multiple of their respective sizes as at the end of the 1960s. The increase of the barasingha population began much more slowly than in the axis population.

As significant as the population increase is the dispersal of barasingha that went hand in hand with the increase. Whereas barasingha rutting was confined to the Kanha Meadow in 1972–73 and included the total population, rutting herds are now regularly observed in five additional open areas of the park (H. Panwar, pers. comm.). A distinct sub-population apparently has settled south of the Kanha Balaghat ridge (Figure 5).

Discussion

Barasingha and axis deer did not necessarily have a long common evolutionary history. Mani (1974) pointed out that the mammalian fauna of Central India is composed of elements from the humid tropical Indo-Chinese and Malayan subregions that intruded the area during the Tertiary. South Asian deer for the most part evolved from the forest living forms. Some like the barasingha or the brow-antlered deer (*C. eldi*)

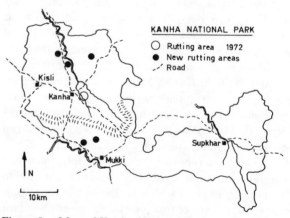

Figure 5.   Map of Kanha National Park.

adapted to the marshy grassland in the alluvial flood plains at the foot of the Himalayas. The northern subspecies of barasingha (*C. duvauceli branderi*) and the axis deer are still often allopatric. Thus during its post Tertiary colonization of Central India the barasingha confronted new physiographic conditions and new competitors as well. The Central Indian barasingha, however, remained dependent upon virtually an exclusive diet of grass. The fact that the graminivorous barasingha was at all able to colonize the Central Indian forests can be attributed to the rich grass flora typical of the undergrowth and openings in sal forest. The barasingha responds to pronounced seasonal differences of food and water availability by movement between areas.

There is no evidence for niche separation or feeding succession between barasingha and axis deer on Kanha Meadow as found by Bell (1970) for Serengeti ungulates. But the overlap of forage species does not give a final answer to the extent of diet overlap, because it was not possible to quantify diets or to distinguish between items of the same forage species.

The competitive exploitation of certain perennial key species such as *Bothriochloa odorata* or *Saccharum spontaneum* was evident from direct observation of grazing animals and the grazing impact on these species. However, the condition of the Kanha Meadow of the 1960s and early 1970s was not a natural one. First of all the barasingha were forced to remain in the area of Kanha Meadow, due to lack of other suitable habitat until 1969. By this they were exposed to competition with axis deer. And second, annual burning of the meadow and heavy grazing suppressed key perennial species of the barasingha diet.

Under these circumstances the barasingha was vulnerable to intense seasonal competition with axis deer because of its narrow dietary spectrum and limited flexibility of food selection. More generalized species like the axis deer are able to respond more flexibly to habitat changes, either natural or man-induced (Kurt, 1978).

Resource competition between sympatric deer species during the dry season, as inferred from the results of this paper, are comparable to competitive relations between sympatric wintering populations of *O. hemionus* and *O. virginianus* as described by Martinka (1968) and Krämer (1973).

The data presented in this paper suggests that the different grassland types are not equally subject to heavy grazing impact. Competitive exploitation by barasingha and axis deer is apparently severe on dry open grassland. This often fire-induced habitat receives additional impact from subsequently intensive grazing. Other types of grassland are under less severe pressure. Moist open grassland, for example, appears to be avoided by axis deer. Tall grass areas additionally promote segregation of the two species. A significant group size difference between barasingha groups in different cover types has already been described (Martin, 1977).

In conclusion, the more diverse grasslands available from the point of view of grass cover height, species composition and soil moisture, the greater the segregation is between the two sympatric deer species and the less stringent the competitive effect of axis deer on barasingha. The management measures applied to the barasingha habitat since 1969 undoubtedly followed the line of these conclusions. The Kanha population of *C. d. branderi* today is relatively safe, despite the drastic increase of axis deer (Figure 4). Today both species have larger populations and much wider distribution within the National Park.

Acknowledgments

This paper reports on work supported by the World Wildlife Fund under Project 702. I am indebted to the Forest Department of Madya Pradesh which offered free accomodations at Kanha as well as other support. I wish to thank in particular H.S. Panwar, presently Director Project Tiger, who provided me with recent information on size and dispersion of the barasingha population. Without his intelligence and forceful management the future of the barasingha in Kanha National Park would be very uncertain.

Literature Cited

Bell, R.H.V.
1970. The use of the herb layer by grazing ungulates in the Serengeti. In *Animal populations in relation to their food resources*, edited by A. Watson, pp. 111–123. Oxford and Edinburgh: Blackwell.

Gwynne, M.D., and R.H.V. Bell
1968. Selection of vegetation components by grazing ungulates in the Serengeti National Park. *Nature 220*, 390–393.

Krämer, A.
1973. Interspecific behaviour and dispersion of two sympatric deer species. *Journal of Wildlife Management*, 37(3):288–300.

Krausman, P.R.
1978. Forage relationships between two deer species in Big Bend National Park, Texas. *Journal of Wildlife Management*, 42(1):101–107.

Kurt, F.
1978. Socio-ecological organization and aspects of management in South Asian deer. *Proceedings of a Working Meeting of the Deer Specialist Group of the Survival Service Commission*, International Union for the Conservation of Nature, Morges, Switzerland. pp. 219–239.

Lamprey, H.F.
1963.   Ecological separation of the large mammal species in Tarangire Game Reserve Tanganyika. *East African Wildlife Journal*, 1:63–92.

Mani, M.S.
1974.   *Ecology and biogeography in India*. The Hague.

McDiarmid, A., and P.R. Matthews
1974.   Brucellosis in wildlife. *Veterinary Record*, June 15th, p. 559.

Martin, C.
1974.   Monsoon migrations of the barasingha (*C. d. branderi*) in Kanha National Park (India). *XI International Congress on Game Biology*, 305–314.

1977.   Status and ecology of the barasingha (*C. d. branderi*) in Kanha National Park (India). *Journal of the Bombay Natural History Society*, 74(1):60–132.

Martin, C., and M.L. Huber
1973.   Zur Grasflora des Kanha National Parkes. *Vierteljahresschrift der Naturforschenden Gesellschaft in Zürich*, 118:11–21.

Martinka, C.A.
1968.   Habitat relationships of white-tailed and mule deer in northern Montana. *Journal of Wildlife Management*, 32(3):558–565.

Panwar, H.S.
1972.   Management plan for Kanha Tiger Reserve. Unpublished mimeographed report, 166 pp.

1978.   Decline and restoration of the Central Indian barasingha (*C. d. branderi*). *Proceedings of the Working Meeting of the Deer Specialist Group of the Survival Service Commission*, International Union for the Conservation of Nature, pp. 143–158.

Schaller, G.B.
1967.   *The deer and the tiger*. Chicago: University of Chicago Press.

Schaaf, D.
1978.   Some aspects of the ecology of the swamp deer or barasingha (*C. d. duvauceli*) in Nepal. *Proceedings of the Working Meeting of the Deer Specialist Group of the Survival Service Commission*, International Union for the Conservation of Nature, pp. 65–86.

Schwartz, C.C., and J.E. Ellis
1981.   Feeding ecology and niche separation in some native and domestic ungulates on the shortgrass prairie. *Journal of Applied Ecology*, 18:343–353.

Singh, A.
1978.   The status of swamp deer (*C. d. duvauceli*) in the Dudhwa National Park. *Proceedings of the Working Meeting of the Deer Specialist Group of the Survival Service Commission*, International Union for the Conservation of Nature, pp. 132–142.

Martin

MICHAEL J.B. GREEN
Department of Applied Biology
Pembroke Street
Cambridge CB2 3DX
United Kingdom

Some Ecological Aspects of a Himalayan Population of Musk Deer

ABSTRACT

The ecology of the Himalayan musk deer (*Moschus chrysogaster*) was studied in the Kedarnath Sanctuary of the Garhwal Himalaya (India) from 1979 to 1981. The study area of 2.5 sq. km comprises evergreen oak and conifer forest, birch-rhododendron scrub and pasture. The climate is monsoonal, with a mean annual precipitation of 3,093 mm, and conditions are most severe during the three month period of snow-cover in winter. Musk deer were encountered 151 times for a total of 64 hours 23 minutes during 1521 hours of fieldwork. Only solitary musk deer were recorded, except once when two males were seen fighting. Musk deer tended to remain in dense cover during the day and to use open habitat at night, when they were more active. There was no evidence of any seasonal altitudinal movement but warmer aspects were probably preferred. The density of the study population at 3–4 animals per sq. km is lower than that of populations occurring in regions that experience less snow, suggesting that population density varies with the availability of food in winter. Data on reproduction and mortality are discussed in relation to investigations on Chinese and Russian populations of musk deer.

Introduction

The threatened status of the Himalayan musk deer first received international recognition in 1974 when the species became listed as "vulnerable" in the Red Data Book (IUCN). For over a century populations have been declining due to increasing demands for musk, a glandular secretion of the male animal. Musk is highly esteemed for its cosmetic and alleged medicinal properties and fetches up to U.S. $45,000 per kg on the international market (Green, in press). Although the secretion can be removed easily from the live animal (Flerov, 1952), hunters kill musk deer in order to excise the gland. The best musk and the greatest quantities are found in mature males, but hunting methods are indiscriminate of the age and sex of animals. The mean weight of a musk gland is 25 g (Green, in press). Between 1974 and 1980 the international trade in Himalayan musk was approximately 200 kg, which could equate to an annual slaughter of up to 32,000 musk deer (Green, in press). However, population estimates based on export statistics need to be treated cautiously because musk may be highly adulterated by the time it reaches the international market.

Typically, musk deer inhabit the upper forest and scrub levels between 2200 m and 4300 m (Schaller, 1977). Such vegetation is thinned or cleared in patches to meet local requirements for fuelwood and timber. Subsequent grazing by livestock inhibits regeneration. Even where the forest canopy is complete, its understory seldom remains intact.

A combination of these two pressures has considerably reduced populations throughout the species' Himalayan range, from Afghanistan through Pakistan, N. India and Nepal, to Burma and extending into parts of Tibet and southwest China. Although the size of the Himalayan population has not been estimated, its density drops most dramatically in a northwest direction along the main axis of the Himalaya. Thus, populations in Afghanistan, Pakistan and Kashmir are very sparse while those in Sikkim and Bhutan are believed to be least severely depleted (Green and Singh, 1981; Green, 1986).

In view of the absence of any sound ecological information which could have provided a basis for conserving musk deer, a three year project (No. 1328) was sponsored by World Wildlife Fund in collaboration with the Government of India. The project was based in Kedarnath Sanctuary, Uttar Pradesh, from 1979 until 1981.

This paper describes the study population, in terms of its density and structure, and includes a preliminary analysis of all encounters with musk deer in the study area.

The literature on musk deer taxonomy has been very confused. The earliest name given to the Himalayan musk deer is *Moschus chrysogaster* Hodgson 1839 but this changed to *Mos. moschiferus* Linnaeus 1758 after Flerov (1952). In recent reviews, Groves (1975) recognizes two species in the Himalaya while Grubb (1982) concludes that only a single species, *Mos. chrysogaster* is present.

Description of the Study Area

Kedarnath Sanctuary

The Kedarnath Sanctuary is situated in the Garhwal Himalaya, about 300 km northeast of Delhi (Figure 1). It encompasses an area of 967 sq. km. which ranges in altitude from 1160 m to 7068 m. In the north the sanctuary is bounded by a range of peaks, mostly over 6000 m, and in the south by the Mandal/ Okhimath road, which is closed in winter. The main valleys tend to run in a north-south direction so that all of the sanctuary is fully exposed to the summer monsoon.

Every summer some 80,000 pilgrims visit Kedarnath Temple, which is located at 3562 m to the northwest of the sanctuary. Throughout this season all but the most inaccessible alps are grazed by livestock. Before winter, when the sanctuary becomes snow-bound, tourists leave and local people return to their villages with their buffalo, goats and sheep.

Shokh Study Area

The study area was located at Shokh (3050 m), chosen on account of its southern aspect, year round water supply, relatively good access and presence of musk deer habitat. This site, at latitude 30°29'N and longitude 79°13'E, is just south of Tungnath Temple (3500 m) and overlooks the Mandal/Okhimath road (2800 m).

The study was confined to an area of 2.5 sq. km, bounded by two ridges which culminate in Chandrasila peak (3680 m) to the north and by the road to the south. A small area was chosen because deep snow limits mobility in winter. Although the ancient pilgrim route to the shrine at Tungnath passes through the study area, it is normally used by local villagers. Tourists prefer to use the new bridlepath at Chopta Chatti, just outside the study area.

In summer the Shokh pastures used to be periodically grazed by over 700 goats and sheep. Also bamboo and medicinal plants were removed from the area to meet local and commercial demands. Following the onset of the project, these practices within the study area were prohibited by the Divisional Forest Officer so as to prevent further deterioration of the

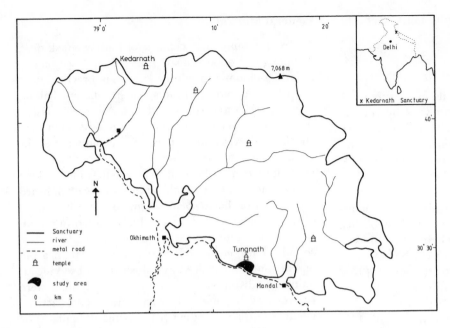

Figure 1. Map of Kedarnath Santuary showing the location of the study area.

Table 1. Monthly precipitation (mm) recorded at Shokh from 1 June 1979 to 24 December 1981

Year	Winter			Spring			Summer			Autumn			Annual
	J	F	M	A	M	J	J	A	S	O	N	D	
1979	—	—	—	—	—	538	775	930	90	42	12	71*	>2457
1980	69*	85*	57*	36	91	421	1064	805	413	47	8	24*	3120
1981	174*	68*	98*	94	175	325	1258	678	202	22	83	34*	>3180
Mean	122*	77*	78*	65	133	428	1032	804	235	37	35	47*	3093
%	3.9	2.5	2.5	2.1	4.3	13.8	33.4	26.0	7.6	1.2	1.1	1.5	99.9

*Precipitation fell as snow but was measured by its equivalent as rain.

Table 2. The mean daily maximum and minimum temperatures (°C) at Shokh, based on records from 11 March 1979 to 24 December 1981. N denotes sample size.

Mean	Winter			Spring			Summer			Autumn		
	J	F	M	A	M	J	J	A	S	O	N	D
Max	4.3	5.9	8.0	15.3	17.9	18.4	17.8	17.4	17.2	13.3	9.8	6.7
N	41	36	59	54	64	71	63	61	48	75	67	64
Min	−4.8	−3.6	−2.1	3.5	5.7	8.6	10.4	9.8	7.1	3.1	−0.2	−2.7
N	43	37	62	55	64	71	66	66	49	77	69	70

habitat and minimize disturbance to musk deer and other wild animals.

Climate

The southeasterly monsoon prevails from June until September. Its time of arrival can vary by several weeks but July and August tend to be the wettest months. Table 1 shows that the monsoon accounts for 80% of the mean annual precipitation (3093 mm). A further 10% falls as snow in winter between December and March.

Snow usually arrives late in December and remains in the study area until a month after the thaw begins in mid March. On exposed, level ground at Shokh, snow accumulates to a depth of 75 cm but often it exceeds 100 cm on forested, northern slopes. Elsewhere snow occasionally falls at altitudes as low as 1500 meters.

The lowest temperature (−10.5°C) was recorded in January and the highest (25.0°C) in May. Insolation is greatly reduced during the monsoon by perpetual cloud and mist so that field observations are almost impossible. Monthly mean temperatures are given in Table 2.

Vegetation

The vegetation of the Kedarnath Forest Division, within which occurs the sanctuary, is described by Agrawala (1973). The main vegetation types found in the study area are listed in Table 3. Owing to former use by man and livestock, a noticeable amount of the forest understory has been depleted. Within the temperate and subalpine zones, patches of grassland have developed as a result of being cleared for fuelwood and subsequently grazed by livestock. Also the pastures were burnt, probably every two or three years, in order to remove dominant tussock-forming grasses (e.g. *Danthonia cumminsii*) and allow more succulent herbs to emerge.

Mammals

Apart from musk deer, *Moschus chrysogaster*, other large mammals recorded in and around the study area include common langur (*Presbytis entellus**), fox (*Vulpes vulpes*), Himalayan black bear (*Selenarctos thibetanus**), Himalayan yellow-throated marten (*Martes flavigula*), leopard (*Panthera pardus*), snow leopard (*P. uncia*), wild boar (*Sus scrofa*), sambar (*Cervus unicolor**), Himalayan tahr (*Hemitragus jemlahicus**), serow (*Capricornis sumatraensis*) and goral (*Nemorhaedus goral*). Those species marked by an asterisk were not seen in the study area during the winter months.

General Methods

In order to maximize chances of finding musk deer, sampling was opportunistic rather than based on any strictly random procedure. It was impracticable to record the amount of time spent in different habitat types, in order to correct the data for observer bias, as distances between vegetation types were often very short. Whenever a musk deer was encountered in the study area details of its activity and habitat were recorded; thereafter the animal was watched for as long as possible. In dense jungle, animals were often heard but moved off before being seen. As disturbed musk deer sometimes called or seemingly stotted in alarm, their identification was based on these distinctive sounds. Thus, encounters varied from briefly hearing or watching a musk deer, as it flushed, to observing an animal, undisturbed, for several hours. Animals were recorded as "resting" when lying down and "active" whether feeding, standing (ruminating or vigilant) or travelling. If an animal was flushed its activity was registered as "unknown" unless indirect evidence enabled its former behavior to be determined. Among the habitat variables measured were altitude, aspect, slope and percentage cover with respect to tree canopy, shrub layer and ground layer. Altitude was measured to the nearest 10 m using an altimeter, aspect was estimated by eye on an eight point scale (N, NE, etc.) and slope was gauged in approximately 10° units (i.e. > 1°, > 10°, > 20° etc.) with the occasional use of a clinometer to check visual estimates. Cover values for the various vegetation layers were estimated over an area of approximately 10 m radius from the location of an animal according to the following scale: 0, > 1%, > 25%, > 50%, > 75%. Time was recorded in India standard time which is 13 minutes behind local time. Seasonal and diel changes in habitat use were examined using nonparametric statistics (Siegel, 1956), as was the relationship between activity and habitat use. The data were analyzed on the Cambridge University IBM 370/165 computer using the Statistical Analysis Systems package (Helwig and Council, 1978). All probability values are two-tailed. Where it is stated in the text that two samples are significantly different, this indicates a significant difference at the 0.05 level or at a higher level of significance.

A number of individuals were recognized on the basis of their sex and a knowledge of their ranging habits but animals were seldom seen closely and for long enough to identify individuals from characteristic markings. Whenever possible, animals were sexed from the presence or absence of tusks, which project to below the lower jaw in adult males. Age could be distinguished between juveniles and adults. A pair of

Table 3. Principal vegetation types within Shokh study area (2,700–3,680)

Vegetation Type	Approx. Altitude (m)	Dominant Species
Moist Temperate Zone		
Kharsu oak forest	2,700–3,300	*Quercus semecarpifolia*
Upper Oak/fir forest	2,700–3,200	*Abies pindrow*
Subalpine Zone		
Birch/Rhododendron scrub forest	3,100–3,500	*Betula utilis* with *Rhododendron campanulatum*
Alpine Zone		
Rhododendron scrub	3,350–3,500	*Rhododendron campanulatum*
Pasture	>3,500	Grasses and herbs

8 × 30 binoculars were always carried in the field; sometimes a zoom telescope (15× to 60×) mounted on a tripod proved useful. From October 1980 onwards an image intensifier (SS20 MkII by Rank Pullin Controls) was available for observing animal activity at night.

In spring and autumn a census of the study area was conducted by a silent drive method. The study area was subdivided into seven blocks, each of which was surveyed sequentially by up to 12 men placed at 30–50 m intervals. The men walked through the jungle, in line abreast, recording any animals seen. Also one or more men were positioned strategically above the forest level in order to coordinate the census, using a whistle, and to spot any animals which otherwise might have flushed undetected from the block. All blocks were surveyed, either in the early morning or late afternoon, within a two day period. Duplicate records, arising from the same animal being seen in several blocks, were minimized by conducting drives in directions which tended to flush animals out of the study area rather than into adjacent blocks.

Results

Habitat Preference

During 1521 hours of routine fieldwork musk deer were encountered on 151 occasions, 85 times in daytime and 66 times at night. Encounters at night were more frequent (1 per 3.7 h) than during the day (1 per 15.1 h). Only 83 of these records were used in the analysis of habitat use as the rest were biased due to deliberate searches for one individual.

The musk deer's association with altitude, aspect or angle of slope and cover, provided by trees, shrubs or herbs, was examined in relation to date, time and animal activity using the Kruskal-Wallis one-way analysis of variance by ranks. The year was divided into four seasons, as in Table 1, on the basis of the climatic regime, the 24 hour cycle was divided into six four hourly periods and activity was classified as active or resting. Observations were ranked in a single series for each variable and their ranks were summed by season, four hour period or type of activity and tested for heterogeneity between classes (Table 4).

As the Kruskal-Wallis analysis tests only for heterogeneity, a further analysis was carried out whereby variables for habitat use were correlated with date, time and activity by means of the Kendall rank correlation coefficient (Table 5). Activity was scored as one for resting and as two for active for the purposes of correlation. Time, date and aspect are periodic rather than linear by nature so correlations are based on the cosine and sine functions of these variables, measurements of which were converted to a scale of 360 degrees. Thus, for example, the 24 hour cycle is treated in terms of day or night by cos (time) and as a.m. or p.m. by sin (time). Day is negative and night is positive with respect to cos (time). Similarly, a.m. is positive and p.m. is negative with respect to the sine function (see Green, 1985).

The results of both methods are generally in agreement so reference will usually be confined to those of the Kruskal-Wallis analysis. Specific mention of correlations is limited to the few instances when a pattern, which was not shown to be significant by the Kruskal-Wallis test, was found to be significantly correlated with the appropriate cosine or sine model, the latter being the more sensitive of the two methods of analysis.

Table 4. Median values, with sample sizes in parentheses, of the musk deer's association with altitude, angle of slope, and various types of vegetation cover classified by a) seasons (df = 3), b) time of day (df = 5), and c) activity (df = 1). Values of X^2 are based on the Kruskal-Wallis Test.

Median:	Altitude (m)	Aspect[1]	Slope (°)	Tree Cover (%)	Shrub Cover (%)	Herb Cover (%)
a) Season						
Winter	3200 (17)	SW (16)	>30 (16)	0 (17)	>25 (16)	0 (13)
Spring	3200 (25)	SSW (25)	>30 (25)	0 (25)	> 1 (25)	>25 (22)
Summer	3260 (7)	S (7)	>30 (7)	0 (7)	> 1 (7)	>50 (7)
Autumn	3200 (34)	NW (33)	>30 (33)	0 (34)	>25 (32)	>50 (29)
X^2	1.75	na	0.67	0.58	3.00	26.46***
b) Time						
00–04	3350 (1)	NW (1)	>30 (1)	0 (1)	0 (1)	>75 (1)
04–08	3230 (27)	WNW (28)	>30 (26)	0 (27)	> 1 (26)	>50 (23)
08–12	3200 (28)	S (28)	>30 (28)	0 (28)	>25 (28)	>25 (23)
12–16	3140 (9)	WSW (9)	>30 (3)	>25 (9)	>25 (8)	>25 (8)
16–20	3170 (12)	SW (11)	>30 (11)	> 1 (12)	> 1 (11)	>25 (10)
20–24	3238 (6)	NW (6)	>30 (6)	0 (6)	0 (6)	75 (6)
X^2	11.28*	na	4.32	7.90	15.36**	9.40
c) Activity						
Resting	3200 (12)	S (12)	40 (12)	0 (12)	50 (12)	> 1 (12)
Active	3200 (12)	NW (12)	>30 (12)	0 (12)	> 1 (12)	>50 (12)
X^2	0.01	na	2.71	0.37	7.05**	4.08*

*$P < 0.05$; **$P < 0.01$; ***$P < 0.001$.

[1]The Kruskal-Wallis test is not applicable for aspect. Data refer to the most frequent aspect in each class.

Table 5. Correlation coefficients (tau) showing the relationship between the musk deer's association with altitude, aspect or angle of slope and various types of vegetation cover and the time of year, time of day and activity. N denotes sample size.

Variable	Altitude	Cos (aspect)	Sin (aspect)	Slope Angle	Tree Cover	Shrub Cover	Herb Cover
Cos (date)	−.083	.108	−.141	.088	.091	.098	−.260**
Sin (date)	−.002	−.076	.075	.054	.011	.105	−.362***
Cos (time)	.188	.106*	−.062	−.100	−.251**	−.401***	.205
Sin (time)	.187	−.078	−.147	.127	−.210	−.093	.084
N	83	81	81	81	83	80	71
Activity	−.016	.403*	−.168	−.340	.190	−.535**	.387*
N	24	24	24	24	24	24	24

*$P < 0.05$; **$P < 0.01$; ***$P < 0.001$.

Green

Altitude

The median altitude at which musk deer were encountered in the study area is similar for all seasons (Table 4a) and does not vary according to activity(Table 4c). There is no evidence to suggest that animals move to lower altitudes in winter, as is commonly believed by the local people of Garhwal and other Himalayan regions.

Musk deer frequented lower altitudes during the daytime than at night, this trend being significant (Table 4b). The pattern of daily altitudinal movement is indicative of the musk deer's use of forest or scrub during the day and of pastures at night, the latter habitat tending to occur at higher altitudes than the former.

Slope

The median angle of slope on which musk deer were encountered does not vary with season, time of day or activity (Table 4a-c). There is indirect evidence that the musk deer's association with slope is influenced by a preference for warmer aspects. Firstly, animals tended to frequent northern slopes at night and southern ones during the daytime, the correlation between cos (aspect) and cos (time) being significant (Table 5). Secondly, animals were more active on northern slopes whereas they rested more on southern slopes, as shown by the significant correlation between cos (aspect) and activity (Table 5). Northern slopes may be warmer at night because they are probably the more sheltered, due to the study area being bounded to the north by ridges and completely exposed to the south. Conversely, southern slopes are warmer than northern ones during the daytime when they receive more insolation.

Vegetation Cover

The musk deer's seasonal use of the different layers of the vegetation varies significantly only in the case of herb cover (Table 4a). Median values rise to a peak in summer and fall to zero with the arrival of snow in winter. This trend is attributed to the seasonal growth of the herb layer rather than to any seasonal changes in the musk deer's preference for herb cover.

Musk deer used most tree cover during the afternoon (Table 4b). This trend is significant, based on the correlations between use of tree cover and both cos (time) and sin (time), as given in Table 5. However, the higher altitudes in the study area are above the tree-line so the pattern of use of tree cover probably reflects the daily altitudinal movements of musk deer, described previously, rather than a need for tree cover during the afternoon.

Cover afforded by shrubs was important to musk deer during daylight hours but at night, under the cover of darkness, musk deer used the open pastures where, except in winter, more food was available (see Green, 1985). The use of more shrub cover during the daytime than at night is significant (Table 4b). Conversely, most herb cover was used at night (Table 4b), the correlation between use of herb cover and cos (time) being significant (Table 5).

The activity of musk deer is significantly related to their use of shrub cover and herb cover but not tree cover (Table 4c). Tree cover was zero in eleven out of twelve encounters with resting musk deer, emphasizing the relative unimportance of trees as a refuge during periods of inactivity. Shrubs, on the other hand, provided at least some cover on all twelve occasions that musk deer were encountered resting. The significant upward trend in herb cover with increasing activity is indicative of the musk deer's use of pastures for feeding purposes.

Population Size

The results of the population census undertaken each spring and autumn are given in Table 6. Estimates of population size based on autumn counts, which vary from four to six animals, are lower than those based on spring counts, which range between eight and ten animals. This seasonal difference is not significant in the case of combined spring (18) and autumn (10) totals for 1980 and 1981 (Binomial test: z = −1.32, P > 0.10). Nevertheless, the consistent trend of fewer musk deer being recorded in the autumn, compared with the spring, is probably of biological relevance and could be due to seasonal differences in ranging behavior. The autumn coincides with the rut, when musk deer may range more widely in order to re-establish or maintain claims to peripheral parts of their range (Bannikov et al., 1980). This may include cliffs and rocky outcrops, where musk deer tend to concentrate during the rut (Jackson, 1979). Thus, animals may be more scattered in their distribution or more concentrated in relatively inaccessible parts of their range during the autumn. A greater proportion of the population, therefore, is likely to be missed in this season. It is also possible that musk deer are more difficult to spot in the autumn due to the tall herb layer, particularly in open habitat.

It seems likely, therefore, that more accurate estimates of population size are obtained from spring than from autumn censuses. The density of the study population, based on spring counts, is estimated to have been 3–4 musk deer per sq. km. in 1980 and 1981.

Sex and Age Composition

Various data, although limited, suggest that the sex ratio of the study population was approximately 1:1.

Table 6. Numbers of musk deer recorded in the study area in 1979–81 using a silent drive method of census

Date	Adult			Juvenile	Total
	Male	Female	Unclassified		
October 1979	0	0	4	0	4
May 1980	2	2	6	0	10
October 1980	1	1	3	1	6
April 1981	1	1	6	0	8
October 1981	0	1	2	1	4
Total	4	5	21	2	32

For instance, males were recorded on four occasions and females on five occasions during censuses in 1980 and 1981 (Table 6). An equal number (three) of known females and males is further supporting evidence. Opportunistic sightings of males, on 13 occasions, and females, on 11 occasions, are also indicative of an even sex ratio.

Musk deer attain maturity within 18–24 months by which time they weigh 10–12 kg. In captivity up to 75% of this body weight is attained within six months of birth (Shaposhnikov, 1956; Green, 1985). Hence, juveniles were readily distinguished from adults only in the summer and autumn seasons. Out of a total of 14 musk deer counted in the autumn censuses of 1979–1981, two (14%) were juveniles (Table 6). Similarly, the proportion of juveniles is 13% based on opportunistic sightings of musk deer during routine field work. Juveniles were observed twice (6 October 1979, 29 July 1981) and adults on 13 occasions between July and October in 1979–81.

Reproduction

Single births are more common than twins in captive Himalayan musk deer (Table 7) but no births were witnessed during the present study, nor were any young or juvenile musk deer seen with their mothers. Adult females were observed on three occasions between June and September (23 July 1979, 17 June 1980, 17 June 1981) but never accompanied by offspring. One young musk deer, weighing 1.5 kg and so probably 1–2 weeks old, was brought to me on 11 June 1979 from just outside the study area, at Tungnath, where it had been found the previous day. It died within a few days of being caught. This single record, together with limited information concerning Himala-

yan musk deer born in captivity (Table 7), suggests that the season of births begins in June and extends for approximately seven weeks, until after mid-July. With a gestation period of 196–198 days (Table 7), copulation must occur between mid-November and the end of December.

At least four musk deer were born during the study period, based on records of juveniles. Three of these survived to at least an age of about three months, as inferred from the dates on which they were sighted and the fourth, mentioned below, died at about two months old.

Mortality

Only one musk deer is known to have died during the study period. This was a juvenile which was seen being attacked by a pair of yellow-throated martens on 31 August 1979 (A.N. Singh, pers. comm.). A similar event occurred in the nearby Valley of Flowers on 18 September 1980 when local people rescued a juvenile musk deer that had been chased to the point of exhaustion by yellow-throated martens. No carcasses or skulls of musk deer were found either in the study area or elsewhere in the sanctuary on any other occassion.

Group Size

Musk deer are essentially solitary, animals seldom being seen together. Of 123 observations of musk deer in the study area, 122 were of solitary animals and one was of two males. These sightings amounted to 3789 minutes of observation time. The observation of the two males only lasted for a few seconds, one male briefly chasing the other before retracing its tracks and moving out of sight. Only solitary animals were thought to have been present on a further 28 occasions, totalling 74 minutes, when musk deer were encountered but not actually seen. Also a solitary animal was recorded on the one occasion when the species was seen elsewhere in the Kedarnath Sanctuary.

Activity Pattern

Activity, based on 44 observations of musk deer, was recorded for a total of 2914 mintues, of which 59.1% were classified as resting and 40.9% as feeding or other activities. These percentages do not necessarily represent the amount of time that musk deer spent resting and feeding because my observation time was not evenly distributed throughout the 24 hour cycle.

The longest continuous observation of a musk deer lasted 408 minutes during which the animal alternated seven times between bouts of activity and resting. The maximum length of active and resting bouts is at least 84 min and 167 min, respectively, but the exact durations are unknown because observations

Table 7. Details of captive births of Himalayan musk deer in the Indian subcontinent

Location	Altitude m	Date of Birth	Gestation Days	Litter Size	Sex	Wt. g	Authority
Kathmandu Valley	1,300	June 1831	c.170	1	M	?	Hodgson, 1831
Kufri	2,760	June 1970	?	2*	?	?	Green, 1985
		17 June 1979	>169	1	F	c.1.0	Jain, 1980
Meroli	2,130	5 July 1981	196	1	M	0.6	Green, 1985
		17 July 1981	198	1*	F	0.6	Green, 1985
Kedarnath Sanctuary	2,600	29 June 1984	?	1	F	?	C.B. Singh, pers. comm.
		9 July 1984	?	1	F	?	C.B. Singh, pers. comm.

*Young that died within two weeks of birth

did not coincide with the beginning of respective bouts. Of eight complete records of active bouts, the mean duration is 41 minutes (range = 17–71 minutes) and that of 15 complete records of resting bouts is 58 minutes (range = 22–133 minutes). The difference between the means was not tested for statistical significance because observations were not independent. Nevertheless, the mean durations are compatible with the overall proportions of time spent active (41%) and resting (59%), as above.

A time-budget was constructed based on the total amount of time that musk deer spent active and resting within each four hour period of the 24 hour cycle. As this time-budget does not account for eighteen observations of activity of less than a minute's duration, the pattern of activity was also analyzed on the basis of the number of active and resting bouts for each four hour period. A bout represents a period of activity or rest of variable length lasting from only a few seconds, in the case of an animal that flushed immediately on being observed, to many minutes. If a bout spanned the division between four hour periods, it was scored for both.

The proportion of time spent active was maximal (59.0%) between 2400 h and 0400 h, thereafter dropping to a minimum level (23.3%) between 1200 h and 1600 h and subsequently rising (Figure 2a). A similar pattern of activity emerges from the analysis of activity bouts although it accentuates the diel trend and shows a peak in activity at 0400–0800 h rather than at 2400–0400 h (Figure 2b).

Discussion

In the absence of any long term study of the Himalayan musk deer most of the relevant scientific literature is based on studies of musk deer in China and Russia. The mean density of *Mos. moschiferus* in Russia is 0.6 animals per sq. km. Population density exceeds 1.4

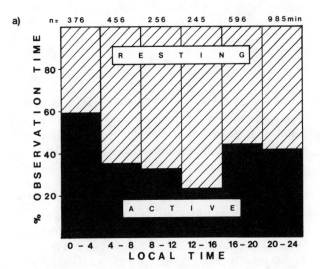

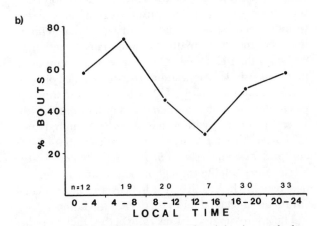

Figure 2. The 24 hour pattern of activity in musk deer based on a) the proportion of time that animals spent active and resting, and b) the proportion of bouts in which animals were active for each four-hour period.

Table 8. The mean litter size (l.s.) for different species of musk deer

Species -Region	Pop. Status	No. Preg. Females	No. Embryos/Offspring			Mean l.s.	Authority
			Triplet	Twin	Single		
Mos. moschiferus							
Yakutia	wild	9	0	6	3	1.7	Egorov, 1965
E. Sayan	wild	76	?	?	?	1.8	Lobanov, 1970
E. Sayan	wild	90	12	50	28	1.8	Bannikov *et al.*, 1980
Mos. berezovskii							
Szechuan	captive	12	0	2	10	1.2	Bista *et al.*, 1979
Szechuan	captive	204	1	137	59	1.6	Anon., 1974
Mos. chrysogaster (sifanicus)							
Quinghai	wild	12	0	2	10	1.2	Zheng and Pi, 1979
Himalaya	captive	7	0	1	6	1.1	Table 7

animals per sq. km. over 20% of the species' distribution and may reach 4–6 animals per sq. km. in good habitat (Bannikov, et al., 1980). By comparison, the density of the study population at 3–4 musk deer per sq. km. is above average. This suggests that the habitat is favorable and that poaching has been minimal, no doubt due to the protective influence of the nearby temple at Tungnath.

In the absence of poaching, food is likely to be the main factor limiting population density. Thus, the higher density of *Mos. chrysogaster* (5–6 animals per sq. km.) in Sagarmatha National Park of Nepal (Upreti, 1979), where the species also receives protection from the influence of monasteries in the region, may be due to more food being available during winter. This is likely because Sagarmatha National Park experiences less snow than Kedarnath Sanctuary, on account of its more easterly location. Similarly, the density of *Mos. moschiferus* in East Sayan, U.S.S.R., is 8.0–8.5 animals per sq. km. in a region where the depth of snow is 10–15 cm, compared with a maximum of 4 animals per sq. km. in a region where snow depth reaches 65–70 cm, and in some years 1.5–2.0 m (Lobanov, 1970). Herbs are available throughout the winter in the former region whereas arboreal lichens and mosses constitute the chief food for musk deer in the latter region.

The approximately 1:1 sex ratio of the study population is similar to that recorded in other populations, both captive and wild. The sex ratio at birth does not differ significantly from a 1:1 ratio in captive *Mos. berezovskii* ($X^2 = 0.62$, df = 1, P > 0.20), based on a sample of 11 male and 15 female fawns (Bista et al., 1979). Similarly, the proportion of males to females was 1:0.93 and 1:0.74 in two wild populations of *Mos. moschiferus* in East Sayan (Lobanov, 1970). Sample sizes are not specified but other data suggest that they are above 30 animals. Young of the year accounted for 17% and 24% of the populations, respectively. The recruitment rate was higher in the population that experienced more snow during winter. By comparison, the proportion of juveniles (13–14%) in the study population appears to be somewhat low, but this estimate may not be accurate because of the small sample size.

No information about twinning rates was obtained from the study population. The mean litter size is appreciably lower for *Mos. chrysogaster* (1.1) than for either *Mos. moschiferus* (1.7–1.8) or *Mos. berezovskii* (1.6–1.7) in both captive and wild populations (Table 8). Whether such differences are species specific or governed by environmental conditions is uncertain.

The young of all species of *Moschus* are usually born in May or June (Bannikov et al., 1980; Zheng and Pi, 1979; Green, 1985). There appears to be a trend of increasing length of gestation and birth weight with increasing size in species (Table 9). *Mos. berezovskii*, the smallest species, has the shortest gestation period and lowest birth weight. Conversely, *Mos. chrysogaster* is considered to be the largest species and has the longest gestation period and highest birth weight. Heavier birth weight in *Mos. chrysogaster* might be due to the lower mean litter size (Table 8).

Hodgson's record of "about 170 days" for the gestation period of *Mos. chrysogaster* appears to be exceptionally short compared with data from other sources (Table 9). It is based on the birth of a young musk

Green

Table 9. The range in the length of gestation and birth weight for different species of musk deer. Sample size is given in parentheses.

Species -Region	Pop. Status	Gestation Days	Birth Weight g	Authority
Mos. moschiferus				
Yakutia	wild	185–195 (?)	no data	Shaposhnikov, 1956
E. Sayan	wild	no data	635 (1)	Egorov, 1965
E. Sayan	wild	no data	460–500 (?)	Bannikov *et al.*, 1980
Mos. berezovskii				
Shensi	captive	178–189 (?)	no data	Zhang *et al.*, 1979
Szechuan	captive	179–187 (?)	350–558 (15)	Bista *et al.*, 1979
Szechuan+	captive	178–192 (?)	455–604 (?)	Anon., 1974
Mos. chrysogaster				
Quinghai	wild	no data	700–750 (2)*	Zheng, 1980
Himalaya	captive	c.170 (1)	no data	Hodgson, 1831
Himalaya	captive	196–198 (2)	600 (2)	Table 7

+ Provinces include Szechuan, Shensi and Anhui.

*Weight at three days old.

deer in captivity in June following mating in January, as witnessed by the keepers. Possibly, mating occurred earlier but was not noticed.

The term "hiders" has been used to describe ungulates in which the young conceal themselves in the period after their birth (Lent, 1974). It is a common phenomenon among cervids and also occurs in moschids. According to Bannikov et al. (1980), young musk deer remain in secluded locations up to the age of two months. Thereafter, lactation ceases as fawns begin to feed independently for themselves while following their mothers. Hodgson (1831) noted that a female disassociated herself from her offspring six weeks after birth. Young musk deer, therefore, soon adopt a solitary existence which is maintained throughout life. Although the lack of any sightings of mothers with their young in the present study suggests that the "following" phase is virtually absent, Dang (1968) saw females accompanied by young on a number of occasions between June and August.

It has already been mentioned that the young grow rapidly, attaining most of their body weight by the age of six months. As in the present study, Egorov (1965) was unable to distinguish between juvenile and adult musk deer after October or November. Musk deer usually become sexually mature by the age of about 18 months (Egorov, 1965; Lobanov, 1970) but females may be capable of reproducing in their first year (Hodgson, cited in Jerdon, 1867). Quite likely, females breed in their first year in populations that are subject to heavy hunting pressure (McNeely, 1973). No infor-

mation about the age of first reproduction or longevity was derived from the study population. The oldest animal in captivity at Kufri, Himachal Pradesh, was a male aged 14.5 years but, in China, captive musk deer have been known to live up to an age of 20 years (Zhang, 1983). Musk deer are less likely to live to such an age in the wild. Out of a total of 60 animals sampled from two populations in East Sayan, the average ages of musk deer were 3.0 years and 3.2 years, respectively. The oldest animal was a female aged nine years (Lobanov, 1970).

Mortality, due to either predation or disease, does not appear to have been high in the study population. No adults were known to have died during the study period but one out of four juveniles was killed by yellow-throated martens. Other evidence from scats indicates that leopard (*Panthera* spp.) and fox occasionally prey on musk deer (see Green, 1985). Similarly, Jackson (1977) found the remains of musk deer in only one of twelve snow leopard scats. Fox (*Vulpes* spp.), lynx (*Lynx lynx*), yellow-throated marten (*Martes flavigula*), wolf (*Canis lupus*) and wolverine (*Gulo gulo*) are probably the principal predators of the musk deer in China and Russia, although young rather than adult musk deer are also susceptible to predation by white-footed weasels (*Mustela altaica*) and eagles *Aquila* spp. (Zheng and Pi, 1979; Bannikov et al., 1980). The remains of musk deer have been found in up to 50% of lynx scats, in the Altai and East Sayan, and of wolverine scats, in eastern Siberia. In the latter region, musk deer account for 50% of the diet of the yellow-throated marten but this high level of predation does not exceed 8–12% of the musk deer population's annual production (Bannikov et al., 1980). Both lynx and wolverine are solitary hunters whereas the fox and yellow-throated marten hunt in pairs. In the Himalaya, the yellow-throated marten invariably hunts in pairs or small family groups, but the fox is almost certainly a solitary hunter (Green, 1981, unpublished data).

Diel and seasonal variations in the musk deer's use of habitat reflect the often conflicting needs for food, cover from predators, including man, and shelter from the elements. The analyses show that musk deer have adopted an optimal strategy by using the more exposed parts of their range (i.e. pastures) under the cover of darkness and taking refuge in cover provided by shrubs during the daytime. This strategy is modified in winter when the snow-covered pastures are not frequented at all except when travelling between different parts of the home range (see Green, 1985).

The importance of vegetation cover to musk deer is recognized by Bannikov et al. (1980) who maintain that lack of opportunities to escape, hide or take shelter is one reason for the migration of musk deer in autumn. With the onset of snow, which covers much of the low-lying vegetation, musk deer may move 12 km., or even 35 km., in some parts of Russia. Such distant movements, however, are uncommon in Russia because sufficient resources usually occur within the home range even in winter. In the present study there is no evidence of any seasonal movement; good cover is available throughout winter and food probably remains adequate (see Green, 1985).

Musk deer are often described as being crepuscular (Flerov, 1952; Xiang, 1974) or nocturnal (Bannikov et al., 1980). Information from the present study indicates that musk deer are more active at night than during the daytime and that they alternately feed and rest throughout the night. Such a polyphasic pattern of activity is typical for ruminants, in which the specialized ruminating routine precludes long periods of complete inactivity or activity (Leuthold, 1977).

A nocturnal pattern of activity is considered to be a feature of primitive artiodactyls (Dubost, 1975) and presumably reduces the risks of predation. Whether or not such behavior in musk deer has been influenced by the hunting and pastoral activities of man over many centuries is not known. The provision of adequate cover, however, is obviously of paramount importance for the future conservation and management of the species.

Acknowledgments

World Wildlife Project No. 1328 was set up following initiatives taken by Dr. C.W. Holloway and Mr. N.D. Jayal on behalf of the International Union for Conservation of Nature and Natural Resources and the Government of India, respectively, and formed part of IUCN's threatened deer programme. The study was wholeheartedly supported by Mr. V.B. Singh, Chief Wildlife Warden of Uttar Pradesh, and well backed up by Mr. A.K.C. Fernhout of WWF (International). I am very grateful to Drs. S.K. Eltringham and W.A. Laurie for helpful comments on various drafts of the manuscript, to Drs. D. Brown and N.W. Galwey for advice on statistical matters and to Mary, my wife, for assisting with the preparation of this paper.

Literature Cited

Agrawala, N.K.
1973. Working plan for the Kedarnath Forest Division 1972–73 to 1981–82. Naini Tal, Uttar Pradesh: Working Plans Circle.

Anonymous
1974. Feeding musk deer in captivity and collecting musk from the live animal. *Dongwuxue Zazhi*, 2:11–14.

Bannikov, A.G., S.K. Ustinov, and P.N. Lobanov
1980. *The musk deer Moschus moschiferus in the USSR.* Gland, Switzerland: International Union for Conservation of Nature and Natural Resources.

Bista, R.B., M.N. Shrestha, and B. Kattel
1979. Domestication of the dwarf musk deer (*Moschus berezovskii*) in China. Unpublished report. Kathmandu: National Parks and Wildlife Conservation Office.

Dang, H.
1968. Musk deer of the Himalaya. *Cheetal (Journal of the Wildlife Preservation Society of India, Dehra Dun),* 2(1):84–95.

Dubost, G.
1975. Le comportement du Chevrotain africain, *Hyemoschus aquaticus* Ogilby (Artiodactyla, Ruminantia). *Zeitschrift für Tierpsychologie,* 37:403–501.

Egorov, O.V.
1965. *Wild ungulates of Yakutia.* Moscow: Nauka. Translated from Russian by Israel Programme for Scientific Translations, Jerusalem.

Flerov, K.K.
1952. Musk deer and deer. In *Fauna of USSR. Mammals I.* pp. 14–45. Moscow and Leningrad: The Academy of Sciences of the USSR. Translated by Israel Programme for Scientific Translations, Jerusalem.

Green, M.J.B.
1981. A check-list and some notes concerning the mammals of the Langtang National Park, Nepal. *Journal of the Bombay Natural History Society,* 78:77–87.

Green, M.J.B.
1985. Aspects of the ecology of the Himalayan musk deer. Ph.D. thesis, University of Cambridge.

Green, M.J.B.
1986. The distribution, status and conservation of the Himalayan musk deer *Moschus chrysogaster*. *Biological Conservation*, 35:347-375.

Green, M.J.B.
In press. The musk trade, with particular reference to its impact on the Himalayan population of *Moschus chrysogaster*. In *Conservation in developing countries*. Bombay: Bombay Natural History Society.

Green, M.J.B., and A.N. Singh
1981. The ecology and conservation of the Himalayan musk deer. In *Wildlife in India*, edited by V.B. Saharia, pp. 173–190. New Delhi: Ministry of Agriculture.

Groves, C.P.
1975. The taxonomy of *Moschus* (Mammalia: Artiodactyla), with particular reference to the Indian region. *Journal of the Bombay Natural History Society*, 72:662–676.

Grubb, P.
1982. The systematics of Sino-Himalayan musk deer (*Moschus*) with particular reference to the species described by B.H. Hodgson. *Säugetierkundliche Mitteilungen*, 30:127–135.

Helwig, J.T., and K.A. Council
1978. *SAS users guide*. Raleigh, North Carolina: Statistical Analysis Systems Institute.

Hodgson, B.A.
1831. Contributions in natural history (the musk deer and *Cervus jarai*). *Gleanings in Science*, 3:320–324.

IUCN
1974. *Red Data Book*. I Mammalia. Morges, Switzerland: International Union for Conservation of Nature and Natural Resources.

Jackson, R.
1977. A report on wildlife and hunting in the Namlang (Langu) Valley of West Nepal. Unpublished report. Kathmandu: National Parks and Wildlife Conservation Office.

Jackson, R.
1979. Aboriginal hunting in West Nepal with reference to musk deer *Moschus moschiferus moschiferus* and snow leopard *Panthera uncia*. *Biological Conservation*, 16:63–72.

Jain, M.S.
1980. Observations on birth of a musk deer fawn. *Journal of the Bombay Natural History Society*, 77:497–498.

Jerdon, T.C.
1867. *The mammals of India: a natural history of all the animals known to inhabit continental India*. Roorkee, India: Thomason College Press.

Lent, P.C.
1974. Mother-infant relations in ungulates. In *The behaviour of ungulates and its relationship to management*, edited by V. Geist and F. Walther, pp. 14–55. Morges, Switzerland: International Union for Conservation of Nature and Natural Resources.

Leuthold, W.
1977. *African ungulates: a comparative review of their ethology and behavioural ecology*. Berlin: Springer-Verlag.

Lobanov, P.N.
1970. Characteristics of the distribution, structure and reproduction of the musk deer population in Eastern Sayan. *Ekologiya*, 6:94–99.

McNeely, J.
1973. Musk deer, kasturi. Unpublished report. Kathmandu: National Parks and Wildlife Conservation Office.

Schaller, G.B.
1977. *Mountain monarchs. Wild sheep and goats of the Himalaya*. Chicago and London: University of Chicago Press.

Shaposhnikov, F.D.
1956. Material on the ecology of the musk deer in the north-eastern Altai. *Zoologicicheskii Zhurnal*, 36:1084–1093.

Siegel, S.
1956. *Nonparametric statistics for the behavioural sciences*. New York: McGraw-Hill.

Upreti, B.N.
1979. Himalayan musk deer. *Journal of the Natural History Museum, Kathmandu*, 3:109–120.

Xiang, C.X.
1974. A study of the ecology of the musk deer and methods for its live capture in the Guangxi Zhuang People's Autonomous Region. *Dongwuxue Zazhi*, 2:9–10.

Zhang, B.
1983. Musk deer: their capture, domestication and care according to Chinese experience and methods. *Unasylva*, 35:16–24.

Zhang, B.L., F.M. Dheng, B.S. Li, D.X. Zhu, and S.W. Chen
1979. *The farming of musk deer*. Peking: Agriculture Publishing Company.

Zheng, S.W.
1980. The feeding and management of young wild musk deer. *The Protection and Use of Wildlife, China*, 1:22–23.

Zheng, S.W. and N.L. Pi
1979. A study of the ecology of *Moschus sifanicus*. *Acta Zoologica Sinica*, 25:176–186.

319

RALEIGH A. BLOUCH
and
SUMARYOTO ATMOSOEDIRDJO
World Wildlife Fund Indonesia Program
P.O. Box 133
Bogor, Indonesia

Directorate of Nature Conservation
Jl. Ir. H. Juanda 9
Bogor, Indonesia

Biology of the Bawean Deer and Prospects for Its Management

ABSTRACT

The rare and elusive Bawean deer (*Axis kuhli*) is endemic to Bawean Island, Indonesia, and was the subject of a two-year study to determine its biological requirements and formulate a plan for its management. Vegetation surveys and fecal pellet counts on permanent plots provided much of the data gathered. The current population was estimated at about 300, most of which are found in the western part of the island. Their prime habitat is secondary forest but recently burned grassy openings are heavily used in the dry season. Since they have been subjected to uncontrolled hunting for many generations they require habitats which provide good cover. A wildlife reserve was created to protect the species and its management policies include controlled burning of grassy openings plus thinning of teak plantations to encourage understory development.

Introduction

The Bawean deer (*Axis kuhli,* Müller and Schlegel, 1836) is endemic to the small Indonesian island of Bawean, giving it the most restricted range of any deer species in the world. In 1977 very little was known about the biology of the species, but it was classified as rare by the IUCN (1972) and it was feared that the wild population was declining. Therefore the Indonesian Directorate of Nature Conservation (PPA) aided by the World Wildlife Fund (WWF) sponsored a two-year study of the deer's ecology. The data gathered were used to plan a wildlife reserve on the island and to formulate management policies to ensure the continued existence of the species in its native habitat. Earlier publications (Blouch and Sumaryoto, 1978a, 1978b, 1979) have presented some of the results of this study; the present report will summarize the most important findings.

Methods

We employed a combination of indirect study methods since Bawean deer are extremely secretive and difficult to see. A total of 323 permanent circular plots of 20 m² each were randomly located from 10 to 50 m apart at three sites. Vegetation type and density, soil characteristics, and fire history were recorded on each plot. Every month for a year all plots were searched for fecal pellets of deer and wild pigs (*Sus verrucosus*). Tracks and evidence of feeding by these two species were also noted. Observations of captive Bawean deer at the Surabaya Zoo indicated that the defecation rate was similar for all sex and age classes at about 13 pellet groups per day.

On 38 occasions night-long watches were kept at six locations in the field near the permanent plots. Observations were recorded of all deer seen, heard vocalizing, or heard walking, and the data obtained were used to determine breeding seasonality and activity patterns. The season of births was determined by the rare instances when young fawns were encountered and by the appearance of small fecal pellets in the field.

Results and Discussion

Description of the Area

Bawean Island is located about 150 km north of Java. It is of volcanic origin, roughly circular in shape, with an average diameter of about 15 km and an area of some 200 km². The central region is mountainous with peaks from 400 to 646 m in altitude. The coastal area is primarily agricultural land and is characterized by low hills separated by broad valleys. Precipitation comes mostly during the northwest mon-

soon lasting from the end of October through March, and amounts to about 2,500 mm a year on the south coast.

Forests cover 4700 ha or about 23% of the island. Teak (*Tectona grandis*) plantations make up about 60% of the forested area. The remaining natural forests are confined to the steep sides and tops of the higher hills and mountains, often occurring as islands surrounded by teak. Planting of teak began about 40 years ago and, by 1954, Hoogerwerf (1966) noted that some hills were already entirely teak covered and that the Forestry Service was planting at an increasing rate. Most teak planting occurred 10 to 15 years ago with the last being done in 1975.

The human population on Bawean is dense and increasing rapidly. In 1954 there were 45,000 people (Hoogerwerf, 1966), by 1975 there were 62,000 (Blower, 1975), and in 1977 there were 70,000, mostly concentrated in the coastal belt. Principal occupations are fishing and farming, the main crops being rice, cassava, coconuts, and bananas. Livestock on the island consists of about 7000 cattle, 5000 goats and sheep, and a few hundred oxen and horses. These are tethered and allowed to graze near the villages.

Bawean deer and wild pigs are the only wild ungulates on the island. The deer have been subjected to uncontrolled hunting, probably since the island was settled over 500 years ago. Since the people are predominantly Muslim the wild pigs are not eaten, but they are sometimes killed as pests because of damage they cause to crops.

Status and Distribution

The Bawean deer ranks as one of the rarest animals in the world. The entire population is, and always has been, confined to Bawean Island. It is not known how the deer originally came to be on the island, but some think that the ancestors of the present population were hog deer (*Axis porcinus*) introduced by early European traders. It seems more likely that they are descended from one of the now extinct deer species, including *Axis oppenoorthi* and *A. lydekkeri*, of which fossils dating from the upper Pleistocene have been found in Java. At that time during periods of low sea levels Bawean and Java were connected by land. The closest surviving relatives of the Bawean deer are the hog deer of mainland Southeast Asia and the Calamian deer (*A. calamianensis*) found on the Calamian Islands in the Philippines (see also Groves and Grubb, this volume).

Bawean deer are small, an adult male averaging about 1400 mm total length, 315 mm hind foot length, and 650 mm height at the shoulder. They are lower at the shoulder than at the hip, giving them a crouched appearance. Each antler normally has three points

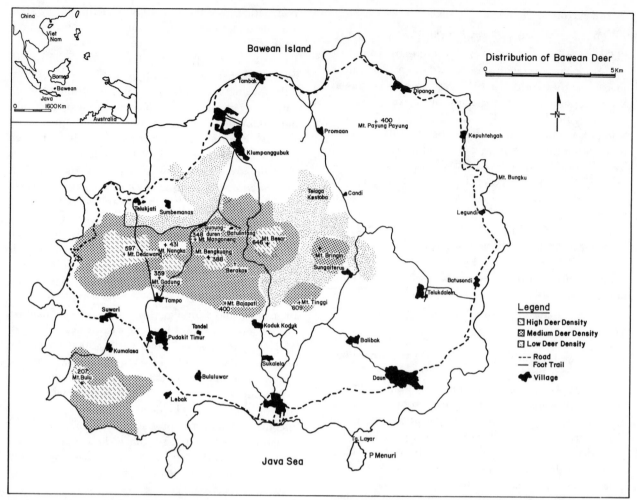

Figure 1. Distribution of Bawean deer.

consisting of a brow tine and a forked main beam; the longest main beam encountered measured 470 mm. Pelage is brown with a white throat and often some white around the eye. Fawns may occasionally have faint spots for a short time.

Large numbers of deer have never been reported on Bawean, although accounts from the nineteenth century indicate they were then fairly plentiful. By the turn of the century one observer stated, obviously incorrectly, that they had apparently been exterminated (Hoogerwerf, 1966). This situation follows the general trend on Java where deer numbers were drastically reduced by 1900 because of the increasing human population and the availability of firearms.

In 1916 the remaining mountain forests on Bawean (about 5000 ha) were set aside as protection forest, protecting them from being cut for shirting agriculture. Forests quickly regrew on abandoned clearings. Deer numbers increased in response to this improvement of the habitat, and in the years prior to World

War II were at a relatively high level in spite of continued uncontrolled hunting with firearms. During the Japanese occupation beginning in 1942 hunting was prohibited on Bawean. Whether or not it actually stopped, the deer population seems to have been in fairly good shape during the 1950s. Hoogerwerf (1966) reported that in 1954 there were enormous amounts of fallow land covered with secondary growth of young trees, shrubs, and herbs. He felt that the deer were not then very rare, but was alarmed at the rate of conversion of deer habitat to dry land agriculture.

During the 1960s hundreds of hectares of the remaining forests were cut and planted to teak with dire consequences for the deer population. Deer displaced from the cut forests were easy prey for hunters using nets and dogs. More importantly, the conversion of good habitat to the generally poor habitat provided by young teak plantations continued to adversely affect the deer population up to the present. A positive effect of the proliferation of teak plantations is that they

Blouch and Atmosoedirdjo

have maintained some type of forest cover on many areas that would otherwise have been converted to dry-land agriculture.

Sitwell (1970) and Blower (1975) both roughly estimated the deer population at about 500 after short visits to the island. While Sitwell thought that hunting was not intensive enough to damage the herd in 1969, six years later Blower reported heavy hunting pressure was causing the population to decline.

Today there are about 300 deer left on Bawean, although the actual number may be as low as 200 or as high as 400. To derive this figure we surveyed all deer range on the island by foot and, based on the data obtained from the pellet counts, estimated deer densities as high (11–15 deer/km²), medium (6–10 deer/km²), or low (1–5 deer/km²). Most deer are found in the natural forests in the western half of the island's mountainous central region (Figure 1). An isolated segment of the population is doing quite well in 25–30 year old teak plantations near the village of Kumalasa in the southwest corner of the island.

The deer are extremely shy, so they never venture far from dense cover and only rarely do they come near human habitations. They are usually found in the steepest and most rugged terrain within their restricted range. Occasionally a deer is sighted on the beach in the Kumalasa area or on the main road west of Mt. Dedawang, but it is safe to say that the vast majority of Bawean Islanders have never seen a Bawean deer.

Reproduction and Mortality

In the wild population most fawns are born between February and June, although occasional births may occur in other months. Assuming a gestation period of seven months, then most mating takes place from July to November. Bucks having hard antlers and assumed to be in breeding condition may be found at all times of the year.

The herd of more than 50 captive Bawean deer at the Surabaya Zoo produce fawns year round. The reason for the difference in breeding seasonality between captive and wild deer is not clear, but the artificial social conditions imposed by captivity may be responsible. At the zoo, deer of all sex-age classes are kept together in close quarters throughout the year, while deer in the wild are essentially solitary with bucks and does seeking each other only for purposes of mating.

Surabaya Zoo officials report that the Bawean deer there always give birth to single fawns. The increase in the population of these captive animals between 1972 and 1977 indicates that all adult and yearling females were producing fawns at a rate of about 1.3 per year, a figure achievable because in some years does give birth twice.

Since among wild deer the majority of births is confined to a five-month season the likelihood of any doe producing two fawns in a year is reduced, and therefore the productivity of wild deer is probably lower than that of captive deer. The incidence of twin births among wild deer seems to be very low, although former hunters report that they occasionally found a doe carrying twin fetuses.

Deer have no natural predators on the island other than large pythons (*Python reticulatus*). Since these snakes are not abundant it is certain that they have little effect on the deer population. Although wild pigs and long-tailed macaques (*Macaca fascicularis*) could perhaps kill young deer there is no evidence that they do so.

After our arrival on Bawean in 1977 there has been no further deer hunting. Currently the greatest cause of deer mortality is domestic dogs running wild in the forests. Of 11 dead deer examined between October 1977 and May 1979, nine were killed by dogs, one was a fawn found in a rice field and killed by people, and one adult doe died when it became entangled in roots and broke a leg. Gross examination of these animals revealed no evidence of diseases. As indicated by the condition of the bone marrow, all four adults examined showed adequate stores of body fat and all three fawns had little or no stored fat. No deer debilitated by malnutrition or deer mortalities due to starvation were encountered.

Killed by dogs were four adult males, two adult females, one yearling male, one female fawn, and one male fawn. The preponderance of adult males supports the contention of former hunters that these animals are the easiest to hunt.

Behavior

Bawean deer under natural conditions are essentially solitary. The only associations observed were of does with their fawns, of bucks in breeding condition following receptive does, or of two bucks interacting aggressively. Bucks in rut frequently challenge each other and at times fight with their antlers, especially if in the vicinity of a receptive doe.

Much communication is by means of vocalizations. Both bucks and does emit short, sharp barks, with those of the does generally being somewhat higher pitched. Up to 100 of these barks may be given in a series, though commonly one call consists of five or ten barks audible at up to 100 m.

At night a hidden man imitating this vocalization with a whistle can call both bucks and does up to within 20 m, although rarely will they emerge from cover. A deer being called in will generally bark in answer as it approaches. In addition, bucks in breeding condition will challenge by stamping their feet and

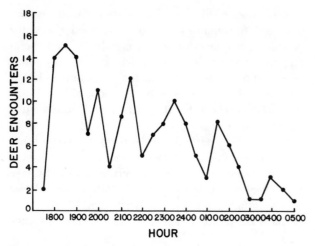

Figure 2. Nocturnal activity pattern of the Bawean deer. Deer encounters are total number of deer heard walking, seen, or heard vocalizing during 38 nights spent in six locations from Oct. 1977 to Sep. 1978.

snorting. Does often use this vocalization to locate their fawns if they have become separated. Fawns will answer with a high pitched squeak audible only for short distance. Unlike muntjac (*Muntiacus muntjak*) and hog deer (Miller, 1975), Bawean deer never bark when startled, preferring to slip away quietly if at all possible.

Bucks frequently rub the bark off small saplings with their antlers and this may serve as a means of visual communication, announcing their presence in an area to other deer. Captive deer commonly rub their preorbital glands against objects, and it may be supposed that this is a form of scent marking.

Bawean deer are predominantly nocturnal, spending the daylight hours resting in dense cover. Beginning just after dark at 1800 hours they emerge and are active intermittently throughout the night. Peaks of activity occur about every two hours with periods of rest in between (Figure 2). As the night progresses, activity becomes less intense and rest periods become longer until by sunrise most deer have retired for the day.

There are indications that for at least several days in succession a deer will return to the same general area of dense cover to hide during daylight. If approached by a man it will normally sit quietly until the man walks by or move away silently ahead of him. Thus deer are very seldom seen during the day, even by people who commonly walk through the forests. At night they move into more open forest areas or grasslands and cassava fields where, in addition to feeding, they court, challenge, fight, or mate.

One receives the impression that in areas of seemingly suitable deer habitat where wild pigs are especially numerous deer are few or absent. Although this hypothesis is not supported by a correlation analysis of track data gathered on permanent plots, nevertheless it bears keeping in mind, especially as numbers of pigs and deer can be expected to increase after establishment of the wildlife reserve. There is virtually no competition for food between these species, but it may be that there is some type of competition for space. If deer and pigs do not like to associate with each other it would be the deer that are displaced from an area rather than the pigs.

Food and Cover Requirements

Deer feeding was observed on 39 plant species. Forbs (15 species) and grass-like plants (14 species) make up the bulk of the diet. Browsing was observed on eight species of woody plants but is mostly confined to the young leaves and twigs of two species of *Ficus* and the vine known as rombok (*Merremia peltata*). In addition, the large drupe-like fruits of the trees *Irvingia malayana* and *Elaeocarpus glaber* are heavily fed on when in season.

Young growth of the much-maligned lalang grass (*Imperata cylindrica*) is an important food of the Bawean deer. It is eaten in large quantities not only because of its relative abundance, but also because it is preferred over most other grass species and is sought out by deer. The grasses *Paspalum conjugatum* and *Axonopus compressus* are probably at least as favored as young lalang although they are not as abundant. They have the advantage of being palatable at all stages of growth, whereas old lalang is not eaten at all.

Among the forbs, signs of feeding are most frequently seen on the vine-like fern *Lygodium circinnatum*. The young leaves and growing shoots of wild banana (*Musa*), *Tridax procumbens*, *Pericampylus glaucus*, and *Euphorbia geniculata* are also commonly eaten.

Suitable food species are widely dispersed and generally abundant throughout the deer range and at all times of the year. Even where deer feeding is heaviest, signs of browsing and grazing are seldom conspicuous and there is always palatable food remaining. Therefore food cannot be considered a limiting factor to the present deer population.

The presence of cover, that is, a brushy growth of woody plants less than about three meters tall, is the most important factor in determining good Bawean deer habitat. The cover on each of the permanent study plots was classified as none, light, medium, or dense, and deer use was judged by the number of fecal pellet groups found. Analysis of the data thus gathered indicated that on plots with no cover, deer use was very significantly less than one would expect to find if deer were using all cover densities at the same intensity ($X^2 = 18.06$; df = 1). In other words,

Blouch and Atmosoedirdjo

deer avoided habitats providing no cover. Deer showed no significant preference or aversion to areas classed as having light cover ($X^2 = 0.75$; df = 1). The preference deer showed for those plots with medium and heavy cover was highly significant ($X^2 = 8.91$; df = 1 and $X^2 = 7.03$; df = 1).

Presently a large amount of Bawean's forests consists of teak plantations with poor understories. The absence of cover in these areas is responsible for the low densities of deer they support and must be considered an important limiting factor of the deer population.

Habitat Preferences

The habitats sampled with permanent study plots were classified as eight types, and intensity of deer use of each type was estimated by the abundance of fecal pellet groups (Figure 3). Since pellets tended to be washed away by heavy rains, only counts were used that were made during months preceded by a month with less than 100 mm of precipitation. Thus, deer density estimates presented here are typical of habitat use during the dry season.

Secondary forest (19.2 deer/km²). This habitat type is by far the most preferred by Bawean deer. It is characterized by an overstory dominated by fast-growing secondary tree species such as *Ficus variegata*, *Macarange tanarius*, and *Anthocephalus indicus*. The understory is quite dense, made up of such species as *Leea indica*, *Ficus* spp., *Antidesma montanus*, and *Garcinia celebica*. Much of this habitat is found as patches within teak plantations where the teak planting failed. There are seldom fires within these forests.

Teak with understory (7.4 deer/km²). The species composition of this habitat is similar to secondary forest except that the overstory is dominated by teak. Also the understory is generally less dense because of occasional fires. The mixture of species in the overstory caused by the invasion of the teak plantation by other trees results in a reduction of the highly flammable litter created by dried teak leaves. As a result, fires are less frequent than in pure stands of teak and therefore a brushy understory is allowed to develop. This habitat provides the optimum combination of teak production, deer production, and watershed protection. Consequently, creation of this forest type should be the aim of teak plantation management on Bawean Island.

Primary forest (5.6 deer/km²). Old forests subject to little human disturbance and generally not easily accessible were included in this classification. Species composition of both the overstory and understory often varies greatly from one mountain to another. Common overstory trees include *Symplocos adenophylla*, *Eugenia lep-*

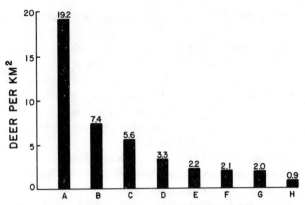

Figure 3.   Densities of Bawean deer in various habitats. A = Secondary forest; B = Teak with understory; C = Primary forest; D = Teak with grass; E = Brush; F = Rombok; G = Disturbed primary forest; H = Teak without understory.

idocarpa, *Dracontomelon mangiferum*, *Nauclea* sp., *Radermachera gigantea*, *Canerium asperum*, *Irgingia malayana*, *Calophyllum saigonense*, and *Persea rimose*. The understory contains reproduction of overstory trees plus such species as *Leea indica*, *Psychotria* spp., *Antidesma montanus*, *Memecylon floribundum*, *Petunga microcarpa*, and *Guioa diplopetala*. As a rule, deer cover is good in this habitat type but food species are rather scarce.

Teak with grass (3.3 deer/km²). These areas are usually less than three hectares in size under very sparse teak with lalang (*Imperata cylindrica*) as the dominant grass. Although the overall deer density on this habitat is relatively low, deer use during the first month after burning is very high. Pellet counts made on areas two weeks after they had been burned showed that during this period densities averaged 43.1 deer/km². This heavy use was accounted for by nocturnal feeding, mainly on the young lalang during the first week after the fire. The sedges *Scleria lithosperma* and *Fimbristylis dichotoma* were grazed to a lesser extent. By about five weeks after it has been burned an area is no longer attractive to deer.

Brush (2.2 deer/km²). This habitat is often found on poor, sandy soil and is characterized by a growth of woody plants less than three meters tall with no overstory. *Melastoma polyanthum* and *Eurya nitida* are the predominant shrubs. Deer densities are low here not only because food species are scarce, but also because the cover afforded, although dense, is usually too hot during the day to be comfortable for deer.

Rombok (2.1 deer/km²). Rombok (*Merremia peltata*) is a vine which typically forms a dense canopy, covering over young teak or secondary growth trees and often breaking them down by its weight. Although rombok is commonly eaten by deer, a habitat dominated by this species does not appear to support good deer densities. This is probably because there are usually few other species present under dense rombok and the ground is often quite bare of vegetation.

Disturbed primary forest (2.0 deer/km²). Old forests currently being disturbed by illegal cutting of live trees for timber and firewood are classed in this habitat type. Plant species are a mixture of those found in primary and secondary forest habitats. Since both cover and food species appear to be adequate, the low deer densities found here are probably due to the frequent presence of humans.

Teak without understory (0.9 deer/km²). The majority of this type is characterized by practically pure stands of dense teak less than 15 years old. Fires fueled by dry teak leaves occur almost every dry season causing a virtual absence of understory and ground cover. Severe erosion creates gullies to depths of two meters and, in many areas, has stripped away up to 15 cm of the forest floor, leaving teak roots exposed and causing windfalls. Not only does this habitat provide very little watershed protection, but also it is by far the least attractive to deer. This vegetation type covers extensive areas, so it is extremely important that management policies attempt to encourage the development of a healthy understory here.

Agricultural land. No pellet count plots were located in agricultural land so we have no estimate of the intensity of deer use in such areas. Frequently at night deer will enter fields bordering forests where they will sometimes eat young leaves of corn and cassava. Usually the damage caused is not extensive since the grasses and forbs growing in the fields seem to be at least as palatable as the crops. Species often fed on include *Brachiaria distachya, Paspalum conjugatum, Axonopus compressus, Euphorbia geniculata, Synedrella nodiflora, Merremia tridentata, M. umbellata,* and *Ipomoea obscura.*

Conclusion

Based on the findings of this study a 4500 ha wildlife reserve was created to conserve the Bawean deer and its habitat. Besides providing complete protection from hunting, reserve management policies include controlled burning of the grassy lalang openings, and thinning of teak plantations to encourage understory development. It can be expected that deer numbers will increase, perhaps eventually to the point where they could cause appreciable crop damage. In fact by 1981, after four years of protection from hunting, islanders reported that it was already becoming easier to observe deer because they were venturing farther from heavy cover. Reserve management policies may

have to be modified in the future if the deer population becomes too large.

On the other hand, when the entire wild population of a species is confined to an area as small as Bawean Island there is always the danger that an introduced disease could cause its extinction. Fortunately the Bawean deer has proven to be a prolific breeder in captivity, and there are at least 70 individuals in the Surabaya, Jakarta, and Singapore Zoos which could be made available for reintroduction to the island if necessary. Occasional young deer captured on Bawean are taken to the Surabaya Zoo to increase the genetic diversity of the captive herd there.

Acknowledgments

This study was produced through the cooperation of the Indonesian Directorate of Nature Conservation and the World Wildlife Fund Indonesia Program. All funds for the WWF projects involved (Projects 1329 and 1666) were provided by the Gerrits Foundation.

We especially appreciate the support we received in Bogor from WWF Representatives Mr. John Blower and Mr. Jeffrey McNeely. Our observations of captive deer were made possible with the help of Mr. Ki Soemali and Mr. Bambang Soehardjito of the Surabaya Zoo. Plant specimens were identified by Mr. Nedi of the Bogor Herbarium. Perhaps contributing most to the success of the project was the help we received from out friends and acquaintances on Bawean Island, particularly Mr. Halimi Fahmi and Mr. Zen.

Literature Cited

Blouch, R.A., and S. Atmosoedirdjo
1978a. Preliminary report on the status of the Bawean deer (*Axis kuhli*). In *Threatened Deer, Proceedings of a Working Meeting of the I.U.C.N. S.S.C Deer Specialist Group,* pp. 49–55. Morges: International Union for Conservation of Nature and Natural Resources.

1978b. An indirect approach to obtain Bawean deer population data. In *Proceedings of a Symposium on Wildlife Management in Southeast Asia,* pp. 93–97. Bogor, Indonesia: BIOTROP.

1979. *Proposed Bawean Island Wildlife Reserve Management Plan.* Republic of Indonesia, Bogor: The World Wildlife Fund Indonesia Programme for The Directorate of Nature Conservation.

Blower, J.H.
1975. Report on a visit to Pulau Bawean. *FAO Nature Conservation and Wildlife Management Project in Indonesia.* INS 72/013.

Hoogerwerf, A.

1966.   Notes on the Island of Bawean (Java Sea) with special reference to the birds. *Natural History Bulletin of the Siam Society,* 21:313–40.

International Union for Conservation of Nature and Natural Resources.

1972.   *Red Data Book, Vol. 1: Mammalia.* Morges.

Miller, R.

1975.   Notes on the behavior of hog deer in an enclosure. *Natural History Bulletin of the Siam Society,* 26:105–31.

Sitwell, N.

1970.   Bawean Island expedition. *Animals,* 12:389–93.

DENNIS C. TURNER
Ethology and Wildlife Research,
Institute of Zoology
University of Zürich-Irchel,
Zürich, Switzerland

Exploitation of Agricultural Areas by Roe Deer: Behavioral and Ecological Adaptations

ABSTRACT

Differences in time-budgeting by a roe deer population of various group sizes and in three sectors along an environmental gradient were investigated at a study site in eastern Switzerland. Both group size and sector significantly influenced the amount of time spent on a particular behavior (two-way ANOVAs with nested design). After marked animals were assigned to one of the three home sectors, their behavior was compared when in the home sector, when in a neighboring sector, and with that of animals from and in that neighboring sector. Animals from each sector were capable of changing their behavior to approach that of animals in a second sector. It was concluded that this population showed no evidence for a genetically-fixed "field deer" ecotype.

Introduction

It may seem odd that a report on roe deer (*Capreolus capreolus* L.) appears in this symposium section on little known species or populations in exotic habitats; the behavior and ecology of this species have been thoroughly investigated in Europe. Nonetheless, this study does concentrate on a population of roe deer in an "exotic" habitat, namely in an agricultural area of eastern Switzerland. Indeed it stresses adaptations in the behavior of these animals concomitant with the exploitation of field habitats.

Field-living roe deer have received little attention until recently, and opinions differ as to whether these animals represent a separate, even genetically-fixed ecotype apart from the more typical "forest" deer (Pielowski, 1981), or simply one of several forms of the same animal showing short-term adaptations in behavior to local environmental conditions (Stubbe and Passarge, 1979). The present study does not attempt to resolve this question in general, but does attempt an answer for one population inhabiting a field area.

In connection with recent studies on the behavior and ecology of this population (Geiger, 1980; Turner, 1978, 1979, 1980), we often asked ourselves if we were dealing with field deer and how applicable our results were for roe deer in general. Some characteristics of field deer, as summarized in the literature by Pielowski (op. cit.) and Stubbe and Passarge (op. cit.), were certainly visible in our population: true field deer remain in cultivated fields throughout the year and form aggregations of 10 to 30 (even up to 100) animals in fall and winter. Their diet consists largely of grains and crop plants.

Because of peculiarities in the habitat of our population we chose to analyze behavior along an environmental gradient; this might shed light on the degree to which our animals adapted their behavior to local conditions. Since the amount of time an animal devoted to a particular behavior had already proven itself an interesting, dependent variable (Turner, 1978, 1979, 1980), the present analysis continued along these lines.

Methods

General methods have been described in detail elsewhere (Turner, 1979); therefore, only essentials shall be repeated here.

Study Site and Population

The study site near the village of Zizers, Canton Grisons, Switzerland, covered ca. 200 ha of flat, agricultural cropland and a small wooded area to the north (Figure 1). Between 50 and 80 deer inhabited this area, depending on the time of year and hunting

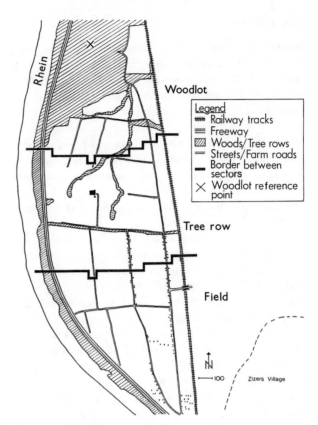

Figure 1. The Zizers study site.

pressure. About 50% of the animals were individually marked at any one time during the study.

Artificial border lines were used to divide the site along the environmental gradient, woodlot/tree row/field. Using a reference point in the woodlot, I divided the study site into 3 sectors: an area < 800 m away from this point; an area between 800 and 1600 m away from this point; and an area > 1600 m away from the reference point (Figure 1). The northern-most area, henceforth called the woodlot sector, was characterized by the proximity of the only stand of trees available to the population. This middle area (tree row sector) contained long relatively dense hedgerows and windrows. Isolated trees offered little protective cover in the field sector though they were planted in rows along the farm roads.

All land at the study site not covered by woods or hedgerows was cultivated and planted with typical crop species or pastures. The amount of protective cover therefore varied from sector to sector and with season: permanent, year-round cover was only available to the deer in the woodlot and tree row sectors. The cover offered by crop fields in all sectors increased from spring to summer, then disappeared with the fall harvest (Turner, 1979).

Data Collection

Behavioral samples were taken from a car driving through the study site once each 2 hours over the entire day (census duration $\simeq$ 1.5 hours). The behavior of focal animals was recorded continuously on tape usually for 1 minute (range 0.75–1.5 minutes). Behavior elements were defined in an ethogram, in which five elements constituted about 90% of the animal's *active* time (Turner, 1979). These five behaviours—feeds, orients, social behavior, moves ($\simeq$ searches for food) and walks—are analyzed in the present study. Resting behavior (lying) was analyzed separately from active behavior.

The number of the sampled animal (if marked), the number of other animals within its sight and 50 m (group size > 1), and its location on a 1:5000 scale map with a superimposed 50 × 50 m coordinate system, were registered. Data were collected during 978 field hours between April 1976 and August 1977, and have been partially analyzed and reported elsewhere (Turner, 1979, 1980). In spite of proven differences between time-budgets of animals in different age-sex classes and between five different phases of the year, samples from both sexes were pooled (excluding those from fawns) and analyzed separately for spring and summer (April through August, 1976 and 1977) and for fall and winter (October 1976 through March 1977).* This division of the year corresponds roughly to a "less social" (territorial), and a "more social" (aggregating) period in the life of the Zizers deer. A total of 4506 behavioral samples were available for testing the effects of group size and sector on time budgeting during the two periods (an average of 167 samples per cell).

Statistical Analyses

The Effect of Group Size and Sector on Time-budgeting by Active Animals

For each of the five behavioral elements separately, two-way ANOVAs were conducted to test the effect of group size (in classes) and sector on the mean time spent per minute on a particular behavior. Since significant interactions between the effects of group size and sector appeared, a nested design was utilized in conjunction with a regression approach. In additional one-way ANOVAs, the effect of sector on time-budgeting by single animals was analyzed. Differences between the grand means for single and group animals were compared by Behrens-Fisher tets.

*The differences between sexes, age-classes and the five phases were generally less pronounced than differences found between group sizes and sectors. Adding sex-age as an independent variable in the present analysis would have reduced the observations per cell too greatly for a meaningful analysis.

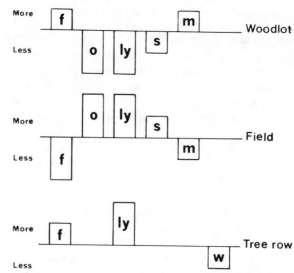

Figure 2. A qualitative illustration of the effect of sector on time-budgeting; horizontal lines represent means for the entire population. The height or depth of a bar indicates direction and consistency of a significant result over time. Bars of double height or depth were drawn whenever at least two significant test results were found, one in each yearly period and both (or all) in the same direction. (For each behavior four tests were run: one on single animals and one on group animals in both yearly periods). Unit bars represent one significant result in one period.

The Effect of Group Size and Sector on Resting Behavior

The proportion of animals seen that were lying was taken as an indication of resting behavior and compared for different groups sizes and between sectors. It was assumed that the number of lying animals per cell was binomially distributed; the probability of lying consisted of an additive effect for group size, sector and their interaction. To analyze these data, the Weighted Least Squares method of Grizzle, Starmer and Koch (cited in Forthofer and Lehnen, 1981) was utilized.

Determination of Home Ranges and Home Ranges Sector

After it was demonstrated that sector had a significant effect on the time budget of animals in the population, I asked whether animals from one sector showed the same time budget when sampled in a second sector. To answer this, it was first necessary to determine the home ranges of marked animals. For those individuals for which at least 10 map points were available, the weighted center and borders of a theoretical ellipse were calculated, assuming the samples were from a two-dimensional normal distribution of points. The ellipse theoretically enclosed 95% of the sample points and was defined as the home range of an animal. The approximations of home ranges by the 95%

ellipses were fairly accurate; the observed percentages of points within these outer borders were 96.0% (spring and summer, 1977) and 96.2% (fall and winter, spring and summer, 1977). Lastly, the home sector of an individual was determined (Figure 2). If the weighted center of a range and more than 50% of the observed core points (within a 75% ellipse) for that animal were found in the same sector, that individual was called a woodlot (or tree row, or field) animal.

Comparison of Time Budgets Over All Marked Animals When in the Home Sector and in a Neighboring Sector

Mean time spent on a behavior by *all* individuals from and in one home sector was compared with time spent on the same behavior 1) by all animals from the same home sector when in a neighboring sector, and 2) by animals from and in that neighboring sector. For each behavior separately, this was accomplished by one-way ANOVAs with contrasts; the contrasts (see Figure 3a under Results) were tested for significance using either the pooled-variance-estimates or separate-variance-estimates and Behrens-Fisher tests, when residual variances were not homogeneous. For resting behavior, the proportions of animals lying were compared by Chi-Square tests.

Non-parametric Tests for Changes in the Behavior of Individuals When They Were Observed in a Neighboring Sector

In a last series of tests, the mean values *per* individual were compared. Of particular interest were the comparisons of behavior in two sectors for those individuals sampled in *both* sectors (paired Wilcoxen-tests). Means per individual in the two home sectors were also compared by Wilcoxon-tests, but again using values from all individuals in the respective home sector (see Figure 3b).

Assessment of Adaptability in Behavior

By comparing the behavior of animals from one home sector with that of animals from the same home sector when in a neighboring sector, an assessment of their adaptability to the new sector could be made. This assessment was made *qualitatively*, but based on three, two-way statistical comparisons (see Figure 4). Prerequisite for consideration of the three comparisons on any one behavior was a statistically significant difference in time spent on a behavior between the animals of two sectors when in their home sectors (see Appendices I and II). Cases for and against adaptability were tabulated twice: once using test results from the contrasts over all marked animals (Appendix I), and over using non-parametric results where means *per* individual were utilized and paired tests for changes

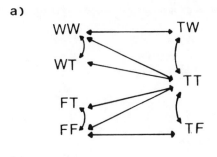

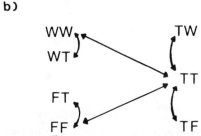

Figure 3. Two-way comparisons made to test for behavior differences: a) tests run using mean values of *all* marked animals (contrasts from one-way ANOVAs); b) the non-parametric comparisons using mean values *per* individual. The first letter of a pair indicates animal origin (home sector); the second letter, its location during the behavioral sample. W=woodlot; T=tree row; F=field.

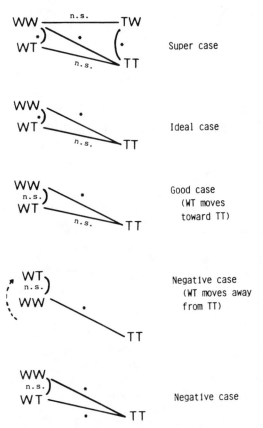

Figure 4. Interpretation of the three, two-way comparisons to assess behavioral adaptability (see text and Figure 3).

Table 1. Effect of group size on time-budgeting by active deer in Spring and Summer[1]

Behavior	$\bar{X}$-Time spent (sec) per minute by deer in groups	Difference in sec to $\bar{X}$-time spent by single animals	Difference to average for deer in groups for group size:		
			2 Deer	3–4 Deer	5+ Deer
feeds	21.9	−1.3	−3.6***	−1.5	5.1***
orients	17.1	7.3***	−0.1	0.9	−0.8
social behavior	8.2	−6.1***	4.0***	0.0	−4.0***
moves	5.2	−0.9**	−0.3	0.0	0.4
walks	3.5	2.4***	0.3	0.3	−0.5

[1] Levels of significance indicated: not significant (n.s.); trend (+), $0.05 \leqq p\ 0.1$; *, $p < 0.05$; **, $p < 0.01$; ***, $p < 0.001$

Table 2. Effect of group size on time-budgeting by active deer in Fall and Winter

Behavior	$\bar{X}$-Time spent (sec) per minute by deer in groups	Difference in sec to $\bar{X}$-time spent by single animals	Difference to average for deer in groups for group size:			
			2 Deer	3–4 Deer	5–9 Deer	10+ Deer
feeds	22.3	−6.9	−9.8***	2.4	3.1+	4.3*
orients	19.0	7.4+	8.4**	0.1	−1.6	−6.8***
social behavior	4.2	−0.6	−1.1	−0.8	0.7	1.2
moves	5.5	−3.8***	−1.6*	0.1	−0.1	1.7*
walks	4.1	5.0*	3.3*	−0.6	−1.5*	−1.3+

Table 3. Effect of group size (a) and sector (b) on "resting behavior"

a)

Season	$p(lying)$ singles	$p(lying)$ group	Group size					
			1	2	3–4	5+	5–9	10+
Spring and Summer	5.5%	16.5%	−11.0***	−5.0***	−1.8	6.8***	—	—
Fall and Winter	19.7%	32.2%	−12.5*	−10.0*	−2.0	—	2.6	9.4**

b)

Season	Test data	$p(lying)$	Sector		
			Woodlot	Tree row	Field
Spring and Summer	single animals	5.5% ***↘	0.8	−0.7	−0.1
	group animals	16.5% ↗	−7.1***	3.4**	3.7*
Fall and Winter	single animals	19.7% *↘	−15.7*	10.3	5.3
	group animals	32.2% ↗	−12.6***	4.4*	8.2**

Table 4. Effect of sector on time-budgeting by active deer in Spring and Summer

Behavior	Test data	$\bar{X}$-Time spent (sec) per minute and significant differences	Sector		
			Woodlot	Tree row	Field
feeds	single animals	20.6	−0.3	1.9+	−1.6
	group animals	21.9	2.0+	2.0*	−4.1***
orients	single animals	24.4 ⟍***	−1.2	−1.0	2.3+
	group animals	17.1 ⟋	−3.3***	−0.5	3.9***
social behavior	single animals	2.0 ⟍***	0.9	0.0	−0.9+
	group animals	8.2 ⟋	0.5	−1.0	0.5
moves	single animals	4.2 ⟍**	−0.4	0.0	0.4
	group animals	5.2 ⟋	−0.3	−0.1	0.4
walks	single animals	5.9 ⟍***	0.3	−1.3*	1.0
	group animals	3.5 ⟋	−0.5	0.0	0.5

Table 5. Effect of sector on time-budgeting by active deer in Fall and Winter

Behavior	Test data	$\bar{X}$-Time spent (sec) per minute and significant differences	Sector		
			Woodlot	Tree row	Field
feeds	single animals	15.5	10.6*	4.9	−15.5+
	group animals	22.3	6.2***	1.5	− 7.7***
orients	single animals	26.3 ⟍+	−8.9	0.5	8.4
	group animals	19.0 ⟋	−6.1***	0.4	5.7**
social behavior	single animals	3.7	2.3	1.3	− 3.7
	group animals	4.2	−1.9**	−0.3	2.2*
moves	single animals	1.8 ⟍***	1.3+	0.4	− 1.8
	group animals	5.5 ⟋	1.9**	−0.8+	− 1.1*
walks	single animals	9.0 ⟍*	−4.9	−7.2	12.1
	group animals	4.1 ⟋	0.0	0.1	− 0.1

in the behavior of the same marked animals in two sectors were conducted (Appendix II).

Results
The Effect of Group Size on Time-Budgeting

In larger groups more time was devoted to feeding, less time for social behaviors (Table 1). In spring and summer no significant differences were found between different group sizes in time spent orienting, moving (searching for food) or walking. However, comparison of means of animals in all group sizes with means of all single animals yielded significant differences for each behavior except feeds.

Larger groups spent more time in fall and winter feeding and moving, and less time orienting and walking (Table 2). The amount of social behavior was apparently independent of group size. Single animals spent significantly less time moving than animals in groups (of all sizes), but significantly more time walking and somewhat more time orienting.

With respect to resting behavior, single animals were less often seen lying than animals in groups, and the probability of lying increased with increasing group size (Table 3a). Although this was true for both periods, the group effect may have been somewhat stronger in fall and winter.

The Effect of Sector on Time Budgeting

During spring and summer, sector had no effect on the resting behavior of single animals (Table 3b). In general, animals in the woodlot sector were less often seen lying, and animals in the tree row and field sectors were more often seen lying, during both periods and regardless of whether alone or in groups.

Animals sampled in the *field sector* spent less time feeding (significant only for animals in groups) and more time orienting (significant for animals in groups, tendency by single animals) (Table 4). Animals sampled in the *tree row sector* spent more time feeding (group samples significant, tendency by single animals), and single animals devoted significantly less time to walking. Animals sampled in the *woodlot sector* spent less time orienting (significant only for animals in groups) and somewhat more time feeding (only a tendency for animals in groups).

Animals sampled in the *woodlot sector* devoted more of their active time to feeding (both as single animals and in groups) and less to orienting (only significant for animals sampled in groups) (Table 5). Samples from groups in this sector also showed significantly less social behavior and more time moving. Single animals also spent slightly more time moving.

Animals sampled in the *field sector*, on the other hand, devoted less time to feeding and more time to orienting, although significant differences were only found in animals sampled within groups (Table 5). These animals also spent significantly more time on social behavior (only in group samples) and less time moving (significant only for group samples).

No significant differences in grand mean values appeared in the data from *tree row* samples.

Figure 2 qualitatively illustrates the effect of sector found on all behaviors. The mirror image between results from the woodlot sector and from the field sector cannot be overlooked. Results from the tree row sector show little divergence from mean population values, except for resting behavior where test results are similar to those from the field sector. These patterns will be discussed below.

Assessment of Adaptability in Behavior

Various two-way comparisons were made (Figure 3). The prerequisite that animals differed significantly between sectors in time devoted to moving, walking and social behavior was not met; therefore, only the behaviors feeds, orients and rests are considered.

The use of three, two-way statistical comparisons [from Appendix I (ANOVA contrasts) or Appendix II (Non-parametric tests)] for the qualitative assessment of adaptability is illustrated in Figure 4. The "super case" for adaptability in behavior would have re-

Table 6. Cases for (+) adaptability in time budget using mean values over all individuals

Animals from	In sector	Spring and Summer			Fall and Winter		
		feeds	orients	rests	feeds	orients	rests
W	T	∅	∅	∅	+	+	−
F	T	+	∅	∅	+	∅	+
T	W	∅	∅	∅	−	−	+
T	F	−	∅	∅	+	∅	−

Table 7. Cases for (+) adaptability in time budget using mean values per marked individuals

Animals from	In sector	Fall and Winter		
		feeds	orients	rests
W	T	+	+	+
F	T	+	∅	∅
T	W	+	+	+
T	F	−	∅	∅

quired three significant differences out of five comparisons; this was neither expected, nor found. Two combinations of results were assumed to speak for adaptability; two cases, against adaptability. Both "ideal" and "good" cases for adaptability were found (as well as negative cases), but because of the qualitative nature of this distinction, both were tallied simply as cases favoring (+) the behavioral adaptability hypothesis.

From mean values over all animals, seven cases speaking for adaptability were found—at least one for animals from each sector. Five cases speaking against the adaptability hypothesis were found (Table 6). Generally, more comparisons could be made in fall and winter than in spring and summer, i.e. the differences between behavior in home sectors were more frequent or larger at this time of year.

A summary of results from the non-parametric comparisons using mean values *per* individual appears in Table 7. Here no comparisons could be assessed in spring and summer. A total of seven cases (at least one for animals from each sector) spoke for the adaptability hypothesis and only one case spoke against it.

Turner

Discussion

Group Size

Generally, the larger the group, the more time an individual devoted to feeding during both periods of the year. Either the animals gathered at particularly good feeding places and the "groups" were rather passive aggregations, or the animals actively sought out other individuals, perhaps benefitting from foraging in groups. I suspect the former interpretation applies during the spring and summer, and the latter, during fall and winter. During spring and summer, normally the less social, territorial time of year, the larger groups showed significantly less social behavior in spite of the proximity of four or more animals. The significantly high value for a group size of two was certainly due to doe-fawn and doe-buck associations during the rut. Time devoted to moving (searching for food between bites) and walking from one place to another did not vary with group size, even though differences were found between single and group animals.

In fall and winter on the other hand large groups spent greater time moving and less time walking than small groups. Single animals moved (i.e. searched for food) significantly less than animals in groups, and this difference was probably greater in fall and winter than in spring and summer. Single animals walked significantly more than group animals, and again this difference was probably greater in fall and winter. Additionally, there was no significant difference between the time single or group animals devoted to social behavior in fall and winter, as opposed to spring and summer. "Social behavior" of single animals consisted largely of orienting toward other animals or groups. Single animals oriented more toward other animals in fall and winter than in spring and summer; singletons and small groups also walked more at that time. Larger groups spent more time feeding and searching for food, and less time walking. Amount of social behavior did not vary with group size in fall and winter, but decreased with group size in spring and summer. I interpret this combination of results as an indication of more social behavior in large groups during fall and winter than in summer and spring, and therefore, that groups in fall and winter were more than passive aggregations.

This was supported by the data on time spent orienting: during both periods of the year singletons spent more time surveying their surroundings than group members. However, only during fall and winter did group size have a significant effect on orienting: the larger the group, the less time spent orienting per sample. Evidently during this period when protective cover was at a minimum, the animals either exploited

Figure 5. Typical scenes from fall and winter: Single animals spend more time walking (above), presumably to join animals in groups (below), which feed more and orient less.

each other as cover (Geist, 1974) or relied on each other as sentinels (Figure 5).

In both periods, the probability that the sampled animal was lying increased with increasing group size. The differences between single animals and group animals, or single animals and those in groups of various sizes, may have been greater in fall and winter than in spring and summer, but these were not statistically examined. I suspect that those animals lying in groups during spring and summer were from different age-sex classes (e.g., yearlings, or several does with offspring) than those lying together during fall and winter (e.g. animals from all classes), but this has not been analyzed yet.

Sector

Animals sampled in the woodlot sector rested less often than those from the tree row and field sectors, which exhibited similar resting levels. This difference had little to do with the probability of seeing, or overseeing an animal (resting) in the woodlot; they were never protocolled in the woodlot itself, but in open fields in this sector or on the field-woods border. They were probably animals which lived in the woods, came into the fields to feed, and returned to rest in the seclusion of the woods.

Data on their behavior when active in the open supported this idea. Woodlot animals spent more active time per minute feeding, particularly in fall and winter when they moved more in search of food. I expected them to spend more time orienting—to be more cautious—than animals in other sectors, when outside of their usual cover. Instead they oriented fewer seconds per minute than the other animals. Perhaps they were more cautious on the forest edge before entering the open areas to feed intensively. During fall and winter, groups of woodlot deer also showed less social behavior, again interpreted as favoring time for feeding when exposed.

Animals in the tree row sector exhibited intermediate time budgets. Resting behavior resembled that of field animals in that neither disappeared into cover to rest as often as the woodlot-animals did. (Tree row animals did, however, often lie on the edges of hedgerows.) They spent somewhat less time walking, which may reflect the central location of their cover.

Animals in the field sector devoted less of their time to feeding than those animals in the other two sectors. As Table 8 indicates, this was not due to differences in food abundance or availability between the sectors. The most preferred vegetation types in Zizers were the pastures, and amount of time spent feeding does not correlate well with the abundance of deer per sector.

I suspect that the main factor affecting behavior in the field sector was its lack of cover, reflected in the highest amounts of time spent orienting. The field sector was also the closest of the three to the village of Zizers and certainly that most often visited by pedestrians and cross-country skiers. Less time spent feeding there was certainly related to the amount of time the animals needed to survey their surroundings. The higher rates of social behavior in groups in fall and winter, and only then, were probably due to disturbance-related changes in group size and composition.

Assessment of Adaptability

Interestingly, most differences in time-budget behavior between sectors were found in fall and winter, when differences in environmental conditions between sectors—especially the amount of cover—were greatest. Although leniently defined and qualitatively assessed, enough cases speaking for adaptability in the behavior of Zizers deer were found to conclude that our study animals were *not* "field deer" in the classic sense. Most supportive of this conclusion were the findings that 1) marked individuals *changed* their behavior in a neighboring sector, and 2) animals from all three sectors, including the *field* sector, were capable of making such changes.

This does not exclude the possibility that some animals in the Zizers population were, at the time of this study, evolving into the field ecotype. Unfortunately, due to increasing disturbances and the marks of civilization at this study site, we may never see the outcome of such evolutionary processes. On the other hand, roe deer show remarkable ability to colonize new habitats and the Swiss population in general is certainly not endangered (see Turner et al., in this volume); in time we may indeed be able to locate the field ecotype within our borders.

Acknowledgments

This research project was financially supported by the Swiss National Science Foundation (Grants 3.788.76 and 3.511.79) and Canton of Zürich, which is gratefully acknowledged. Travel funds to attend the symposium were also provided by FONZ. The Hunting Administration of the Canton Grisons, the hunters of Section Calanda (BKPJV) and the village officials of Zizers are thanked for their support. Ch. Geiger allowed a preview of his dissertation data on social organization of these deer, which was appreciated. Dr. H. Rüst and A. Leibacher provided much statistical advice and solved computer-programming problems. Jeanine Stocker and Cécile Ganz helped enormously in preparing the manuscript, while my wife, Heidi, was thoughtfully patient during the past few months.

Table 8. Percentage of sector area covered by pastures

	Spring + Summer	*Fall + Winter*
Woodlot	10	25
Tree row	24	51
Field	21	34

Literature Cited

Forthofer, R.N., and R.G. Lehnen
1981. Public Program Analysis. Belmont, California: Lifetime Learning Publications.

Geiger, Ch.
1980. Bestandesschätzung und Populationsdynamik beim Rehwild in den Zizerser Feldern, Kt. Graubünden. *Feld, Wald, Wasser,* 8(4):19–21.

Turner

Geist, V.

1974. On the relationship of social evolution and ecology in ungulates. *American Zoologist*, 14:205–220.

Pielowski, Z.

1981. Das Feldreh—eine Bereicherung der Wildtierfauna unserer Feldreviere. *Jagd und Hege*, 3(Mai 1981):14–15.

Stubbe, C., and H. Passarge

1979. *Das Rehwild*. Berlin: Verlag J. Neumann-Neudamm.

Turner, D.C.

1978. Aktivitätsmuster freilebender Rehe im Verlauf des Frühjahrs: optimale Ausnützung der Tageszeit. *Revue Suisse de Zoologie*, 85(4):710–718.

1979. An analysis of time-budgeting by roe deer (*Capreolus capreolus*) in an agricultural area. *Behaviour*, 71(3-4):246–290.

1980. A multi-variate analysis of roe deer (*Capreolus capreolus*) population activity. *Revue Suisse de Zoologie*, 87(4):991–1002.

Appendix I. Comparisons made to assess adaptability: sample sizes, means (over *all* marked individuals) and levels of significance[1]

a) Spring and Summer

		WW — TT[2]	WW[3] — WT	TT — WT	TT — TW	WW — TW
n		111 369	25		67	
feeds	x̄	19.5 n.s. 21.7	∅[4]	∅	∅	∅
orients	x̄	19.7 n.s. 20.6	∅	∅	∅	∅
rests[5]	%	11.3 n.s. 13.0	∅	∅	∅	∅
n		212 700	51		121	
		FF — TT	FF — FT	TT — FT	TT — TF	FF — TF
n		180 369	49		21	
feeds	x̄	18.6 * 21.7	18.6 n.s. 21.6	21.7 n.s. 21.6	21.7 + 29.1	18.6 ** 29.1
orients	x̄	22.4 n.s. 20.6	∅	∅	∅	∅
rests	%	12.5 n.s. 13.0	∅	∅	∅	∅
n		392 700	92		52	

b) Fall and Winter

		WW — TT	WW — WT	TT — WT	TT — TW	WW — TW
n		66 156	11		16	
feeds	x̄	33.1 ** 25.3	33.1 n.s. 31.2	25.3 n.s. 31.2	25.3 n.s. 24.8	33.1 n.s. 24.8
orients	x̄	10.4 *** 18.3	10.4 n.s. 18.1	18.3 n.s. 18.1	18.3 n.s. 17.5	10.4 * 17.5
rests	%	20.8 ** 37.9	20.8 *** 61.8	37.9 ** 61.8	37.9 + 19.0	20.8 n.s. 19.0
n		101 314	34		21	
		FF — TT	FF — FT	TT — FT	TT — TF	FF — TF
n		61 156	57		19	
feeds	x̄	19.6 * 25.3	19.6 n.s. 23.8	25.3 n.s. 23.8	25.3 + 17.6	19.6 n.s. 17.6
orients	x̄	19.1 n.s. 18.3	∅	∅	∅	∅
rests	%	48.3 * 37.9	48.3 + 36.9	37.9 n.s. 36.9	37.9 n.s. 27.3	48.3 + 27.3
n		174 314	103		22	

[1] L.S.: not significant (n.s.); trend (+), $0.05 \leqq p < 0.1$; *, $p < 0.05$; **, $p < 0.01$; ***, $p < 0.001$

[2] WW — : first letter of a pair indicates animal origin, second letter, its location; W = Woodlot, T = Tree row, F = Field; dash indicates the comparison made

[3] Sample sizes are indicated only once for each condition

[4] ∅ = comparison not allowed (see text)

[5] Whereas means for feeds and orients are in sec/min, rests is given as percentage lying out of n samples below

Appendix II. Assessment of adaptability using mean values *per* marked individual: Levels of significance under "a" are from Wilcoxon tests on data from all individuals; levels shown under "b" are from Paired-Wilcoxon tests using mean values from individuals sampled in both sectors (numbers of such individuals given in parentheses).[1]

		a	b			
		WW — TT — FF	WW — WT	FF—FT	TT — TW	TT — TF
Spring and Summer						
feeds	x̄	18.2 n.s. 21.5 n.s. 19.0	∅	∅	∅	∅
orients	x̄	21.2 n.s. 22.9 n.s. 23.4	∅	∅	∅	∅
rests	%	7.9 n.s. 11.1 n.s. 12.7	∅	∅	∅	∅
Fall and Winter						
feeds	x̄	33.5 * 25.2 * 19.0	32.5 n.s. 31.9(4)	19.0 * 23.4(6)	25.4 n.s. 27.9(8)	23.7 n.s. 28.3(5)
orients	x̄	10.1 ** 18.2 n.s. 17.3	9.5 n.s. 19.5(4)	∅	17.1 n.s. 13.9(8)	∅
rests	%	19.1 ** 40.0 n.s. 47.3	24.1 n.s. 53.4(4)	∅	39.5 + 17.7(12)†	∅

[1]Symbols same as in Appendix I

†p = 0.052

RALEIGH A. BLOUCH
World Wildlife Fund Indonesia Program
P.O. Box 133
Bogor, Indonesia

Reproductive Seasonality of the White-tailed Deer on the Colombian Llanos

ABSTRACT   Breeding condition was examined in 48 white-tailed deer (*Odocoileus virginianus gymnotis*) collected on the plains of eastern Colombia. Estimated birth dates indicate a fawning season from September through March with an apparent peak in December. During the corresponding period of conceptions, most bucks had polished antlers. However, bucks with polished antlers were encountered throughout the year. It is hypothesized that the reproductive seasonality of these deer is caused by the adverse effects of prolonged heavy rains on fawn survival.

Introduction

Breeding seasonality among tropical ungulates has received some attention from zoologists. Cervids of temperate zones exhibit a high degree of reproductive synchrony, which insures that parturition will occur early in the period of optimum forage quality. In contrast, tropical and subtropical deer tend to have extended sexual seasons and may breed at any time of the year (Amoroso and Marshall, 1960). Schaller (1967) reported that two neighboring chital (*Axis axis*) populations in India had different breeding seasons, and Hershkovitz (1972) concluded that the periodicity of breeding among neotropical deer is probably highly localized. Tropical goats and cattle often show breeding cycles related to the rainy season (Fraser, 1968), which may vary over short distances. Similarly, Talbot et al. (1965) stated that in Africa the breeding cycles of many ungulates are related to the rainy seasons, with periods of rut and production of young occurring at the time of year when optimum nutrition is most likely to be available. On the other hand, Dasmann and Mossman (1962a) found that in Rhodesia there was no obvious synchronization of breeding between different ungulates, some species producing young during the rainy season, others during the dry season, and still others year round. The peak of lambing among impala (*Aepyceros melampus*) in various parts of southern Africa varies over a five month period, probably because of local differences in climate and plant phenology (Dasmann and Mossman, 1962b).

Among mammals generally, births occur in a season that provides optimum conditions for the survival and growth of the young (Bullough, 1961). Furthermore, indigenous ungulates normally do not breed at times which would result in births taking place during seasons of severe weather (Fraser, 1968). In other words the timing of birth is controlled by multiple of environmental factors, including avoidance of lethal conditions as well as conditions favoring higher survival. Presumably, then, the apparent differences in breeding seasons reported for tropical and subtropical ungulates will be found to stem from ecological differences between populations.

The present report deals with seasonal breeding in the white-tailed deer (*Odocoileus virginianus*), particularly the tropical race *gymnotis*. In Mexico, McCabe and Leopold (1951) found that the fawning season of the Sonora whitetail (*O. v. couesi*) commenced shortly after the onset of the rainy season when the plants were at or near their peak of annual growth. Klein (1982), without mentioning seasonal rainfall patterns, reported that for *O.v. nelsoni* in Honduras 13 of 14 estimated parturition dates were from January to June. The reproductive biology of the tropical lowland race native to South America (*O. v. gymnotis* Wieg-

mann, 1833) is known mainly through the work of Brokx in the Venezuelan llanos (plains). He found that reproduction occurred throughout the year. Subsequently I was able to study the reproductive ecology of this deer in the llanos of Colombia, a region of considerably higher rainfall. This report compares the patterns of seasonal reproduction of the Colombian and Venezuelan deer and suggests an ecological cause for the observed differences.

The study area, El Tuparro wildlife reserve, is administered by the Colombian Agency for the Development of Renewable Natural Resources (INDERENA), and comprises some 492,000 hectares bordered by the rivers Orinoco, Tomo, and Tuparro in the eastern part of the Comisería of Vichada. It lies between five and six degrees north latitude at elevations varying between 75 and 250 meters above sea level. Consequently the climate is tropical, with a mean annual temperature of about 28° C. Daily variations in temperature are greater than the difference between mean temperatures of the warmest and coolest months. Snow (1975) reported an average yearly rainfall of 2249 mm over a 16 year period at Puerto Ayacucho, Venezuela, a town about 50 km north of the reserve. Data from this station are representative of conditions in the dryer, eastern part of El Tuparro. A well defined dry season occurs from December into March. Due to the deep channels of the rivers and streams, flooding of the savanna during the rainy season is not extensive.

Approximately 85% of the reserve consists of tall bunch-grass savanna as defined by Beard (1953). The remainder is primarily semi-evergreen gallery forest along the rivers and streams. Beard (1953) and Blydenstein (1967) have described the vegetation of llanos areas similar to El Tuparro.

The reserve is located in one of the few extensive areas of neotropical savanna to remain undisturbed by the effects of modern man. Prior to the arrival of INDERENA in 1971 the land was unsettled except for three fishermen's huts near the Orinoco River. The area has never been used for agriculture or grazing or domestic stock. Following ancient custom, nomadic Indians of the Cuiba and Guahibo tribes pass through the reserve on their rounds of subsistence hunting, fishing, and gathering. As they have done for centuries, these Indians set fires which burn virtually all the savanna each dry season.

Methods

Reproductive data used for this report consist of observations of lactation, pregnancy, and condition of antlers from 48 white-tailed deer collected year-round in or near the reserve. From November 1970 until my arrival at El Tuparro in December 1972, INDERENA

Table 1. Breeding condition of 16 adult doe Colombian white-tailed deer (*O. v. gymnotis*) and antler condition of 24 adult and yearling bucks collected from 1967 to 1975 (A = adult; Y = yearling)

| | | *Does* | | *Bucks* | | |
		Lactating	Pregnant	Antlerless	Velvet	Polished
December	Dry	1		1A 2Y	1A	
January	Dry			1Y		1A
February	Dry				2A	
March	Dry	4	1		1Y	3A 1Y
April	Rainy	4			2A	
May	Rainy	1			1A 1Y	
June	Rainy					
July	Rainy		1		1A	
August	Rainy		1		2A	
September	Rainy		1	1Y		
October	Rainy		2		1A	
November	Rainy				1A	1Y

personnel collected 11 bucks (six adults, four yearlings, and one fawn) and 13 does (10 adults, one yearling, and two fawns). Between my arrival and July 1975 I added to the sample 16 bucks (nine adults, four yearlings, and three fawns) and five does (four adults and one fawn). This material is stored in the collection of INDERENA in Bogotá. In addition, I used material from two adult does and one adult buck collected in March 1967 about 50 km north of the reserve and housed in the collection of the National University in Bogotá.

I determined the ages of five fetuses by physical development (Armstrong, 1950) and of 11 deer 15 months old or younger by tooth eruption and replacement (Brokx, 1972b). A gestation period of 200 days was assumed. Since the method used for aging fetuses was developed for northern races of white-tailed deer which are considerably larger than *gymnotis*, ages of late term fetuses were estimated based on physical characteristics other than crown-rump length. From the ages of the 16 young deer and fetuses, birth dates were estimated to the nearest month.

Results

Sixteen does over two years of age were collected. Of these, 10 were lactating and six were pregnant (Table 1). None was simultaneously visibly pregnant and lactating. Five of six pregnant does collected were carrying single fetuses and one carried twins, for a fetal rate of 1.17. The low incidence of multiple births was confirmed in field observations of does with young

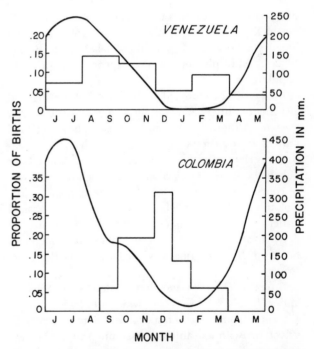

Figure 1. Curves of annual precipitation patterns and histograms of *O. v. gymnotis* births in the llanos of Colombia and Venezuela. Colombian data based on 16 birth dates estimated in the present study and precipitation records from Puerto Ayacucho, Venezuela (Snow 1976). Venezuelan data modified from Brokx (1972a) and based on 58 estimated birth dates and precipitation records from near Calabozo, Venezuela.

fawns. None of the three female fawns and one yearling collected showed signs of having bred. There was no evidence of does breeding more than once per season.

Fawning was found to occur through a seven-month period from September to March with a peak in December (Figure 1). The corresponding period of mating activity extends from March through September.

The antler cycle of the bucks is less well defined. Animals with polished antlers may be encountered at any time of year (Table 1). However, all five adult bucks with growing antlers or without antlers were collected during months not associated with mating activity, and nine of 11 adults with polished antlers (82%) were collected during the mating season. The antler cycle in yearlings appears to be less defined than in older deer.

Discussion

Since births in the Tuparro deer population are restricted to a seven-month period, it can be inferred that it is a highly unlikely occurrence for a doe to breed more than once per season. This is in marked contrast to the situation in Venezuela, only about 400 km to the north, where the does are polyestrus and breed year round, often while still lactating (Brokx, 1972c). Multiple births are uncommon in both populations.

Brokx (1972a) concluded that periodic casting and growing of antlers is definitely a characteristic of *O. v. gymnotis*. Although individual bucks can have polished antlers at any time of year, he noted that antler seasons overlap in such a way that peak numbers have polished antlers during months in which the majority of conceptions occur. A similar pattern exists in the Colombian deer, but whereas in Venezuela polished antlers were mainly characteristic of bucks during the dry season, in Colombia the highest proportion of bucks in this condition was encountered in the rainy season.

Brokx (1972a) found that males with polished antlers had larger testes with wider tubules containing a greater abundance of spermatozoa than bucks in velvet or without antlers. Assuming that polished antlers indicate spermatogenesis, it was interesting to note that three of 11 adult and yearling males (27%) had polished antlers during the period October through February, although no conceptions were detected during these months. It is hypothesized that the lack of breeding between October and February is due to an absence of ovulating does.

Schaller (1967) thought it possible that the onset of the rut among chital in India may have been influenced by the presence of nutritious green forage. In El

Tuparro, the does begin conceiving and the majority of the bucks attain polished antlers during March, coincidental with the first rains of the season and the consequent burst of vegetative growth. However, I postulate that breeding seasonality of the Tuparro white-tailed deer is not primarily related to yearly nutritional variations but is in fact caused by the adverse effects of heavy rains on fawn survival.

Soaking severely degrades the insulation value of an ungulate's pelage and also increases body heat loss by evaporation. In India, Minett (1947) exposed sheep to rain showers and recorded an average decrease in body temperature of 1.0° C. In tests with infant caribou, a metabolic increase due to wet pelage was equivalant to that caused by a lowering of the atmospheric temperature by 10° C (Hart et al., 1961). Besides causing direct energy costs to the animal, soaking by heavy rains may increase the incidence of disease. Minett (1947) suggested that the prevalence of certain diseases of domestic stock during the monsoon in India may be associated with the chilling resulting from rainfall. Pneumonia is commonly the primary cause of mortality among infant lambs exposed to the weather in the United States (Venkatachalam et al., 1949; Safford and Hoversland, 1960).

Homeothermic mechanisms are not developed in newborn mammals (Brody, 1945), so neonates are highly vulnerable to adverse environmental conditions. Body temperature in young water buffalo (Minett, 1947) and metabolic rate in infant caribou (Hart et al, 1961) have been shown to be more susceptible to environmental variations than in older animals of the same species.

Tropical mammals have a very small range of temperature tolerance; that is, their critical temperatures are very close to their normal body temperatures. Metabolic rates increase rapidly when environmental temperatures fall below these critical temperatures (Scholander et al., 1950).

Consequently it is reasonable to expect that the survival of newborn fawns of a tropical race of white-tailed deer will be adversely affected by long periods of heavy rain. The El Tuparro whitetail population has a breeding season in which no births occur during the months having more than about 250 mm of rain. These rains are substantially heavier than those in the Venezuelan llanos studied by Brokx, where white-tailed fawns are indeed born and survive during the rainy season. A comparison of rainfall and fawning patterns is given in Figure 1.

The hypothesis that the reproductive seasons of tropical ungulates are locally influenced by the adverse effects of the rainy season appears to be supported by these data for the neotropical white-tailed deer. It seems to merit study as a more general relationship in the ecology of tropical ungulate populations.

Acknowledgments

The field work for this study was done as part of a cooperative effort between the Peace Corps and IN-DERENA. I am grateful to Dr. Jorge Hernández-Camacho of INDERENA for much help while I was in Colombia. Dr. Peter A. Brokx kindly made available unpublished information from Venezuela, and Prof. Richard D. Taber of the University of Washington provided many suggestions for the improvement of the manuscript.

Literature Cited

Amoroso, E.C., and F.H.A. Marshall
1960. External factors in sexual periodicity. In *Marshall's Physiology of Reproduction*, Volume 1 Part 2, edited by A.S. Parkes, pp. 707–800. London: Longmans Green and Co. Ltd.

Armstrong, Ruth A.
1950. Fetal development of the northern white-tailed deer (*Odocoileus virginianus borealis* Miller). *American Midland Naturalist*, 43:650–666.

Beard, J.S.
1953. The savanna vegetation of northern tropical America. *Ecological Monograph*, 23:149–215.

Blydenstein, J.
1967. Tropical savanna vegetation of the llanos of Colombia. *Ecology*, 48:1-15.

Brody, S.
1945. *Bioenergetics and growth*. New York: Hafner Press.

Brokx, P.A.
1972a. A study of the biology of Venezuelan white-tailed deer (*Odocoileus virginianus gymnotis* Wiegmann, 1833), with a hypothesis on the origin of South American cervids. Ph.D. dissertation. Canada: University of Waterloo.

1972b. Age determination of Venezuelan white-tailed deer. *Journal of Wildlife Management*, 36:1060–1067.

1972c. Ovarian composition and aspects of the reproductive physiology of Venezuelan white-tailed deer (*Odocoileus virginianus gymnotis*). *Journal of Mammalogy*, 53:760–772.

Bullough, W.S.
1961. *Vertebrate Reproductive Cycles*. Norwich: Jarrold and Sons.

Dasmann, R.F., and A.S. Mossman
1962a. Reproduction in some ungulates in southern Rhodesia. *Journal of Mammalogy*, 43:553–537.

1962b. Population studies of impala in southern Rhodesia. *Journal of Mammalogy*, 43:375–395.

Fraser, A.F.
1968. *Reproductive Behaviour in Ungulates*. London and New York: Academic Press.

Hart, J.S., O. Heroux, W.H. Cottle, and C.A. Mills
1961. The influence of climate on metabolic and thermal responses of infant caribou. *Canadian Journal of Zoology*, 39:845–856.

Hershkovitz, P.
1972. The recent mammals of the neotropical region: a zoogeographic and ecological review. In *Evolution, Mammals, and Southern Continents*, edited by A. Keast, F.C. Erk, and B. Glass, pp. 311-431. Albany: State University of New York Press.

Klein, E.H.
1982. Phenology of breeding and antler growth in white-tailed deer in Honduras. *Journal of Wildlife Management*, 46:826–829.

McCabe, R.A., and A.S. Leopold
1951. Breeding season of the Sonora white-tailed deer. *Journal of Wildlife Management*, 15:433–434.

Minett, F.C.
1947. Effects of artificial showers, natural rain, and wallowing on the body temperatures of animals. *Journal of Animal Science*, 6:35–49.

Safford, J.W., and A.S. Hoversland
1960. A study of lamb mortality in a western range flock; I. Autopsy findings on 1051 lambs. *Journal of Animal Science*, 19:265–273.

Schaller, G.B.
1967. *The Deer and the Tiger. A Study of Wildlife in India*. Chicago and London: University of Chicago Press.

Scholander, P.F., R. Hock, V. Walters, F. Johnson, and L. Irving
1950. Heat regulation in some arctic and tropical mammals and birds. *Biological Bulletin*, 99:237–258.

Snow, J.W.
1976. The climate of northern South America. In *World Survey of Climatology*, Vol. 12: *Climates of Central and South America*, edited by W. Schwerdtfeger, pp. 259–379. Amsterdam, Oxford, and New York: Elsevier Scientific Publishing Company.

Talbot, L.M., W.J.A. Payne, H.P. Ledger, L.D. Verdcourt, and M.H. Talbot
1965. The meat production potential of wild animals in Africa. *Technical Communication, Commonwealth Bureau of Animal Breeding and Genetics No. 16,*.

Venkatachalam, G., R.H. Nelson, F. Thorp, Jr., R.W. Luecke, and M.L. Gray
1949. Causes and certain factors affecting lamb mortality. *Journal of Animal Science*, 8:392-397.

W. V. BRANAN
and
R. L. MARCHINTON
Florida Defenders of the Environment
102 West Third Avenue
Tallahassee, Florida 32303

School of Forest Resources
University of Georgia
Athens, Georgia

Reproductive Ecology of White-tailed and Red Brocket Deer in Suriname

ABSTRACT

Deer of Suriname were studied from June 1980 through January 1982. Red brockets were found to occur throughout the interior forests of Suriname, at a density of approximately 1 per square kilometer. Average age of harvested animals was 2.4 years, with 41% of individuals in older age classes (3 years and above). The sex ratio approached 1:1. Two of 18 collected fetuses were twins while all others were singletons. Fawning occurred over at least an 8 month period centered in December and January during the shorter wet season. Breeding activity peaked during the long wet season. Antler and breeding cycles were apparently 1 year in length. Weights of testes and epididymides of mature bucks showed little change throughout the year and were not related to antler condition. The quantity of spermatazoa in the epididymides did not seem related to antler condition.

White-tailed deer were restricted to a 10-km-wide band of marshes bordering the Atlantic Ocean and to grassland savannas on the Surinam-Brazil border. Along the coast, the dry season was severe, and densities appeared not to exceed 1 or 2 deer per square kilometer. Our observations suggested that breeding and fawning periods were similar to the red brocket's in the interior. We observed twinning as well as follicular activity in both ovaries during the same cycle. The antler cycle appeared to be 1 year in length, with a peak of casting in October-November.

Introduction

The Foundation for Nature Preservation in Suriname, STINASU, invited the University of Georgia to conduct a field study of Suriname deer. Three deer species occur in Suriname, including the red brocket deer, *Mazama americana americana* (Erxleben, 1777), brown brocket deer, *M. gouazoubira nemorivagus* (F. Cuvier, 1817), and white-tailed deer, which are either *Odocoileus virginianus gymnotis* (Wiegmann, 1833) of Venezuela and Guyana, *O. v. cariacou* (Boddaert, 1785) of French Guiana (Hershkovitz, 1948; Husson, 1978), or intergrades between these two geographically defined subspecies. All deer in Suriname are in the subfamily *Odocoileinae*. Our project was the first modern study of either the brockets or whitetails in Suriname. The reproductive information presented here represents a part of our results.

Deer of northern South America have been studied or discussed by Allen (1915), Tate (1939), Simpson (1941), Hershkovitz (1948, 1958, 1969, 1972), Walsh and Gannon (1967), Brokx (1972), Whitehead (1972), Handley (1976), Husson (1978), Klein (1982), Blouch (this volume) and others. Antler and fawning seasonality interested early naturalists, who often speculated that fawns were born in all months and antlers were carried for years. For example, Hershkovitz (1958) reported that no cyclical rhythm of rutting, fawning, antler shedding, or molting had yet been observed in white-tailed deer of the Neotropical region. More recently, Hershkovitz (1972) stated that in South America the season of rut in white-tailed deer varies according to locality. Brokx's (1972) study in Venezuela indicated that whitetails cast antlers annually, and there was a peak of casting. He speculated that white-tailed deer can reproduce at any time of the year, although most fawning occurred in the wet season. Blouch (this volume) reported that whitetails in Columbia fawned more often in the dry season, avoiding the adverse effects of prolonged heavy rains on fawn survival. Klein (1982) reported that his observations on white-tailed deer in Honduras suggested some population synchrony in antler growth as well as a broad distribution of parturition dates between January and June.

Study Area

Suriname is located from 1°30′ to 6°00′ north latitude, in northeastern South America, and is bordered by the Atlantic Ocean, French Guiana, Brazil, and Guyana. It is about the size of the state of Georgia (163,265 sq. km.), and is mostly wilderness. Temperatures average 27°C, with day to night temperature variations exceeding seasonal variations, and photoperiod changing less than 1 hour over the year.

Table 1. Meteorological environment of tropical Suriname as compared to temperate Georgia, USA

	Suriname (north)	Georgia (central)
Latitude	4 to 6 N	34 N
Photoperiod shifts	1 hr	8 hr
Normal monthly rainfall	8 to 33 cm	7 to 13 cm
Yearly rainfall	220 cm coast drier	125 cm
Normal temperature extremes	20 to 36 C	− 12 to +40 C

However, Suriname is not necessarily less seasonal than temperate regions since there is a distinct rainfall cycle, with rainfall (at Paramaribo) varying from 8 to 33 cm per month (Table 1).

Methods

We were able to collect and/or examine 126 red brockets and 29 white-tailed deer, with the cooperation of several local hunters, from June 1980 through January 1982 (8 brown brockets were also obtained). Most brockets were taken by nightlighting from autos, or in the daytime while swimming rivers to escape hunting dogs. White-tailed deer were usually taken by daytime or spotlight stalking.

Our methods were adapted from those currently used by deer management biologists in the United States. Population densities were estimated from track count indices (Tyson, 1959), and by spotlight counts (Progulske and Duerre, 1964). Approximately 400 hours were spent night hunting and spotlight counting for brockets along heavily hunted and unhunted forest roadways and by walking through various forest areas. Seventy-five hours were devoted to spotlight hunting for white-tailed deer in marshes, swamps and along rivers and beaches.

Year classes of both the brockets and white-tailed deer were estimated from eruption and wear of the molariform teeth, following methods developed by Severinghaus (1949) for white-tailed deer in the United States. We believe that this is a reasonable method for Suriname white-tailed deer based on (1) our observation that premolar 4 (3rd tooth in molariform row) of a captive white-tailed deer was replaced when that female was known to be 18 months of age, (2) if a white-tailed deer was judged to be 18 months old based on tooth replacement, it would generally be judged 18 months based on tooth wear, and (3) Brokx (1972) found that the method was reasonably accurate for determining ages of white-tailed deer in Venezuela. Because there are no published criteria to determine the age of red brockets, this species presented a special problem. We elected to use Severinghaus' formula, since (1) the molariform tooth eruption and replacement sequence is similar to that of white-tailed deer, and (2) red brockets that were judged equivalent to 18 months due to replacement of premolar 4 were also judged equivalent to 18 months according to tooth wear. We were unable to find any brockets of known age to validate these criteria.

Fetal ages of both the brockets and white-tailed deer were determined primarily by the developmental characteristics reported for North American white-tailed deer by Armstrong (1950), supplemented by hind-foot length, total length, crown-rump length, and weight of each fetus. Fetal ages were back-dated and fore-dated to determine breeding and fawning dates. We assumed a 200-day gestation period for white-tailed deer, which is equivalent to that of North American Odocoileinae. This is supported by Sanchez (in Husson, 1978) and was used by Brokx (1972). Gestation of a red brocket at the Bronx Zoo, in New York, was reported to be 218 days (M. C. MacNamara, pers. comm., also see Thomas, 1974). Recognition of recently formed corpora lutea, enlarged uteri, young fawns, and doe-fawn track groups reinforced our projected breeding and fawning seasons.

Ovaries were removed, placed in 10% formalin, and later measured, sagitally sliced every 3 mm, and inspected for presence of luteal glands. Testes and epididymides were removed, weighed, measured, and preserved in 10% formalin. Three 5-micron sections from several epididymides were prepared using standard histological techniques and stained with hematoxylin and eosin. Sperm densities were compared by counting systematically selected 1 mm × 1 mm fields at 450-power magnification.

Due to small sample sizes, data from throughout the country were pooled by species. Consequently, local variations of cyclic phenomena, such as fawning and antler casting, may have been obscured.

Results

Red Brocket Deer

Red brockets occurred at a density of approximately 1 per square kilometer throughout the interior forest, which covers 85% of Suriname. Red brockets are the largest of the 4 extant brocket species, occasionally growing to 55 kg in Suriname, and a 65-kg buck (whole unbled carcass) was weighed (using our scales) by a cooperating hunter near Baboenhol. This is a greater weight than previously published for this species. The sex-age profile of hunter-killed red brockets (Figure 1) indicated a nearly even sex ratio,

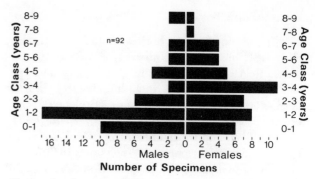

Figure 1. Sex-age profile of harvested Suriname red brocket deer, indicating a 49:51 (M:F) sex ratio with 41% above 2 years of age.

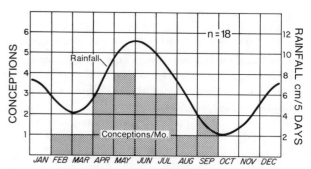

Figure 2. Rainfall cycle and projected breeding season of Suriname red brocket deer, based on backdating of fetuses. Most conceptions occurred during the longer wet season.

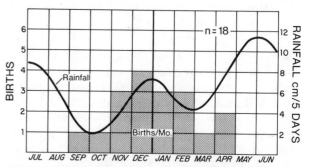

Figure 3. Rainfall cycle and projected fawning season of Suriname red brocket deer, based on foredating of fetuses. Most births centered around the shorter wet season.

Branan and Marchinton

an average age of 2.4 years, and a substantial proportion of individuals in the upper age classes.

BREEDING AND FAWNING

Seventeen pregnant does were examined. The youngest was estimated to have been 13 months old at breeding. Only one doe carried twins, suggesting that twinning occurs in less than 10% of red brocket pregnancies. The birth weight of a brocket fawn, which lived 4 days after being delivered caesarian, was 2325 g. The productivity of red brockets is low compared to temperate white-tailed deer.

Based on our examination of fetuses, red brocket breeding occurred from February through September, with most occurring during the longer wet season (Figure 2). The data indicated a definable, although very broad, fawning season, which peaked November through February (Figure 3) during the shorter wet season. Some fawns are dropped over a longer period, including at least September through April.

RUT AND ANTLER CYCLE

Testes and epididymides of young bucks began rapid weight increases between 8 and 12 months of age, revealing the onset of puberty (Figure 4). This occurred when the total skull length (greatest distance from anterior of premaxillaries to posterior border of occipital condyles) reached approximately 197 cm (Figure 5). Adult testis and epididymis size was reached by about 17 months. The youngest buck examined that had polished antlers (1 cm antler length) was estimated to be 8 months old, and had a testis-epididymis weight (average) of 13 g. Weights of the testes and epididymides of mature bucks (17 months and older) indicated no synchronized change in size through the year nor any obvious difference that could be related to antler condition (Figure 6). The lowest testis-epididymis weight for an individual above 30 months of age (22 g) was only slightly smaller than the largest (26 g), indicating that once the testes and epididymides reach maximum size, little seasonal weight changes occur. This phenomenon is contrary to the large seasonal weight variation reported for deer in temperate regions (Illige, 1951; Lambiase et al., 1972; Chapman and Chapman, 1975; Mirarchi et al., 1977a; Mirarchi et al., 1977b) and suggests that testosterone levels and spermatogenesis in individual bucks do not undergo great cyclic variations in equatorial regions.

Cross sections of the epididymides from two velvet-antlered adult bucks revealed spermatazoan densities averaging 192 and 255 per mm while three adult bucks with polished antlers had spermatazoan densities of 174, 212 and 258 per mm, further indicating that

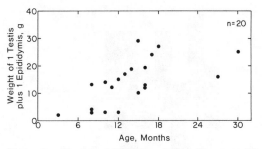

Figure 4. Testis-epididymis weights of harvested Suriname red brocket bucks vs age, as determined from Severinghaus' formula for northern white-tailed deer (see methods). Testis-epididymis apparently began increasing between 7 and 12 months of age.

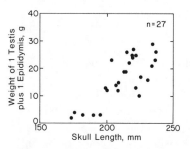

Figure 5. Testis-epididymis weights of harvested Suriname red brocket bucks vs total length of skull. Note that individuals with skulls shorter than 197 mm have testis-epididymis weights of less than 4 g.

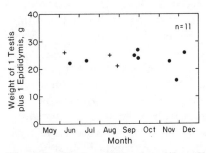

Figure 6. Testis-epididymis weights of harvested Suriname red brocket bucks vs month. The + symbol indicates bucks in velvet antlers. All bucks were 17 months or older, assuming Severinghaus's formula is correct for red brockets. Note that weights showed little change throughout the year, and were not related to antler condition.

bucks in velvet have adequate numbers of spermatazoa to breed successfully. Several other velvet-antlered bucks also revealed considerable spermatazoa in the epididymides, although postmortem deterioration prevented their precise quantification. Three bucks estimated to be 10, 11, and 12 months old had no spermatazoa in the epididymides, while spermatazoa were present in two 15-month and one 16-

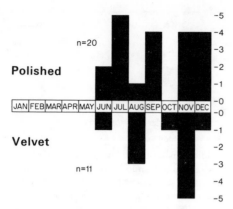

Figure 7. Antler condition of harvested Suriname red brocket bucks, 1-year and older, by month. No samples were obtained January through April.

month-old bucks, indicating that sexual maturity is attained shortly after 1 year of age.

Eleven of the 31 (35%) red brocket bucks that were 1-year or older when collected were in velvet (Figure 7). This suggests a 1-year antler cycle, as the North American Odocoilinae, which are known to be on a 1-year cycle, spend about 40% of the year in velvet. An alternative hypothesis, which we do not favor, is that bucks hold their antlers for an indefinite period of time, and the 35% in velvet is merely coincidental. We were unable to observe any captive male red brockets to determine antler cycle. However, three years observation of one captive brown brocket showed that this individual cast antlers in June or July on a 1-year cycle.

Some bucks were found to be in velvet throughout our collecting period, even after we omitted individuals below 1.5 years of age. This, along with the data on testes-epididymides weights, suggested that breeding was more 'year-round' than the data from the does indicated. We found, however, that the highest ratio of polished to velvet antlers occurred from May through July, which is near the middle of the breeding peak estimated from fetal development.

White-tailed Deer

White-tailed deer primarily inhabit coastal marshes and swamps, usually within 10 km of the ocean. We weighed a 55-kg buck, and believe that some deer on Suriname coastal marshes reach at least 60 kg. A second habitat, which we studied for only 1 week, was Sipawilini Savanna on the Surinam-Brazil border. The coastal and Sipawilini populations were 450 km apart and probably have been separated since the decline of grassland savanna areas following the last ice age. Brokx (1972) suggested that the Sipawilini

population may be linked more closely to the Venezuelan populations than to the coastal Suriname population. White-tailed deer habitats appeared to overlap those of the brockets' only along their margins.

Track counts and observations suggested coastal deer population densities of about 1 or 2 deer per square kilometer. This contrasts with typical densities in the southeastern United States of 6 to 15 deer per square kilometer. Deer and tracks were occasionally observed near the ocean, even on beaches (where breezes deter mosquitoes), but during the long dry season none were seen within 3 km of the ocean. We consider this the most severe stress period, and assume that white-tailed deer migrate farther inland in search of succulent forage. On Sipawilini savanna, we estimated less than 1 deer per square kilometer. The average age of the coastal deer examined was 1.9 years (Figure 8).

BREEDING AND FAWNING

Results of ovarian examination are presented in Table 2. Doe 002 apparently experienced estrus at about 11 months of age, but was first bred in her next cycle at 1 year. Doe 021 was nursing a 2-month-old fawn (020, also taken), and showed no corpora lutea or large follicles in either ovary, indicating that the corpora lutea had fully regressed since parturition, and that follicle maturation did not occur immediately postpartum. Doe 024 had a large corpus luteum in each ovary (6.0 mm, 6.5 mm dia.); thus, ovulation occurred in both ovaries during the same cycle.

Two of the three white-tailed deer fetuses collected were twins, conceived when doe 096 was about 20 months of age. Our data on fetuses, fawns, and lactating does indicated that Suriname white-tailed deer fawns were dropped from at least September through February. We cannot rule out year-round fawning, but suspect that fawn survival would be low during the dry season.

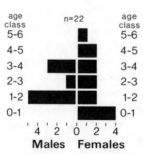

Figure 8. Sex-age profile of harvested Suriname coastal white-tailed deer.

Branan and Marchinton

Table 2. Ovarian characteristics in relation to age for several red brocket and white-tailed does

Deer number	Age[a]	Collection date	Ovary dimensions[b]			Corpora lutea (CL) dimensions		Comments
			Length	Width	Thickness	Length	Width	
Red brocket deer								
019	5.5 yr	1 Nov	14.9	9.5	8.4	5.1	5.1	CL present in each ovary indicated both ovaries were active during same cycle.
			18.2	11.8	8.8	5.5	5.5	
036	3.0 yr	27 Nov	12.2	9.2	6.9	absent		Only one ovary collected.
093	3.0 yr	27 Jul	15.5	10.6	9.0	7.2	9.0	67-day-old fetus in utero.
			12.0	11.5	5.5	absent		
114	4.0 yr	3 Sep	14.4	11.1	6.9	8.1	9.6	133-day-old fetus in utero. Only one ovary collected.
132	2.0 yr	26 Oct	17.4	10.9	6.3	6.5	8.6	46-day-old fetus in utero.
			13.6	11.8	5.5	absent		
White-tailed deer								
002	1.0 yr	9 Aug	15.7	8.7	7.6	6.0	6.0	Apparently pregnant although uterus not visibly enlarged; regressing CL in second ovary suggested first ovulation at 11 months but apparently not bred during first cycle.
			11.1	8.0	5.7	2.0	2.0	
020	2 months	9 Nov	10.5	5.0	3.9	absent		
			10.2	6.6	4.4	absent		
021	5.5 yr	9 Nov	17.2	12.3	12.0	absent		Uterus enlarged but regressing 2 months after birth of a fawn (020); lack of CL suggested no post-partum estrus.
			12.3	10.0	7.1	absent		
024	4.5 yr	13 Nov	13.2	10.5	7.7	6.5	6.5	Uterus enlarged; apparently in early pregnancy; CL in each ovary indicated both active in same cycle.
			16.4	11.2	8.7	6.0	6.0	
096	2.0 yr	30 Jul	14.7	13.9	5.5	7.5	8.0	90-day-old twins in utero; 2 CL present in one ovary. Only one ovary collected.
						6.0	7.9	

a) Ages estimated to half-year classes
b) All measurements in millimeters

We observed 3 separately maintained captive white-tailed bucks for 2 years. Through these observations, and talks with each deer's owners, we accumulated records on 14 antler cycles. All 3 deer annually cast in October or November, and began growing new antlers immediately. All 3 deer cast antlers about 2 weeks later in 1981 than they had in 1980. Our observations of 9 hunter-killed bucks from the coastal habitat, however, indicated that antler casting occurred as early as June, and we could not rule out the possibility that some antlers were cast in any month. The 3 captive white-tailed bucks had visibly larger neck girths and were more aggressive at times when in polished antler. In fact, most coastal hunters in Suriname erroneously believe that two types of white-tailed deer exist—one in which the bucks have enlarged necks and a more common one with smaller necks. The fact that all three captive bucks which we observed were in antler synchrony strengthens our hypothesis that there was a limited amount of white-tailed deer breeding synchrony.

Discussion

There is much confusion about the extent to which tropical deer express seasonality of reproductive phenomena. Field studies are limited and results seem to vary greatly among localities as well as species. Observations of tropical deer maintained in zoos located in temperate environments often indicate no definable annual patterns. This should be expected, however, since deer that have been moved to totally different environments (temperature, rainfall, photoperiod) may be unable to respond to the proximate stimuli which influence the initiation of velvet shedding, antler casting, or breeding.

The results of our study in Suriname indicated that antler cycles were 1 year in length, but antler condition was rather weakly synchronized with breeding, especially among the red brockets (Table 3). Other indications of reproductive readiness (e.g., testes weights) for individual male brockets did not show much annual variation. In spite of this, most red brocket and white-tailed does in our sample conceived during half of the year, and fawns were primarily born during the other half. The long fawning season peaks after the two driest months of the year (September and October), and few fawns were dropped during these two months. By the time these dry months come again, the youngest fawns are several months old.

The fact that there are reproductive seasons in the tropics, and that they vary among localities, is not especially surprising when one examines some of the environmental pressures presumed to be exerted on deer at various latitudes. In the arctic and extreme temperate latitudes, for example, windchill and deep snows severely affect fawn survival, and the timing of the fawn drop is critical. The breeding season for does is relatively short and bucks need to retain reproductive capability for only two or three months to be capable of breeding all does. At these latitudes, the photoperiod cycle is pronounced and serves as the proximate factor upon which deer synchronize annual cycles. As one moves to lower temperate latitudes, harsh winter conditions exert less effect upon fawn survival, and reproductive success is influenced by local and sometimes more subtle phenomena. The timing of reproductive events thus becomes less synchronized throughout a given latitude.

In the tropics, warm temperatures prevail year-round at lower elevations, and deer are subjected to different selective regimes. Relatively local monsoons or droughts probably become important factors limiting fawn survival. Photoperiod, which is nearly constant, may be largely (or wholly) replaced as the proximate cycle-regulating factor by a complex of locally variable phenomena including rainfall.

The general adaptive strategy for deer of all latitudes is one in which does drop their fawns near the beginning of the time most favorable for ultimate fawn survival, or after any particularly unfavorable condition has passed. In Suriname, rainfall may be the dominant weather factor, but it varies from year to year in onset, intensity, and duration. In the absence of a pronounced, regular, benign fawning season, a broader breeding season favors overall fawn survival. Does in the population enter estrus over a major portion of the year. As a result, bucks must retain their reproductive capability for a major portion of the year in order to pass on their genetic information through a greater number of fawns.

Table 3. Breeding and antler cycles of Suriname red brocket and white-tailed deer as compared to white-tailed deer in temperate Georgia, USA. Information in parentheses is based on limited data.

	Red brocket	White-tailed deer	
	Suriname	Suriname	Georgia
Breeding	Apr–Oct	(Apr–Oct)	Nov–Dec
Fawning	Sep–Apr	(Sep–Apr)	Jun–Jul
Antler cycle	(1 year)	1 year	1 year
Antler casting peak	not clear	(Oct–Nov)	March
Casting synchrony	weak	(fair)	strong

Branan and Marchinton

Acknowledgments

We thank the National Science Foundation Division of International Programs, the World Wildlife Fund Netherlands Appeal Project 1623, the University of Georgia School of Forest Resources, and the University of Georgia Research Foundation for financial assistance. Hank Reichart, Director, the Foundation for Nature Preservation in Suriname (STINASU), the University of Suriname Faculty of Natural Resources, especially A. E. Van Dijk, and the Suriname Ministry of Agriculture Forest Service, especially F. L. Baal, provided valuable cooperation in Suriname. E. E. Provost and S. L. Jones assisted with the examination of reproductive tracts. T. D. Atkeson, J. Glasser, P. E. Hale, W. M. Lentz, and A. S. Johnson assisted with critical reading of the manuscript.

Literature Cited

Allen, J.A.
1915. Notes on American deer of the genus Mazama. *Bulletin of the American Museum of Natural History,* 34:521–553.

Armstrong, R. A.
1950. Fetal development of the northern white-tailed deer. *American Midland Naturalist,* 43:650–666.

Blouch, R. A.
1987. Reproductive seasonality of the white-tailed deer on the Colombian llanos. This volume.

Brokx, P.
1972. A study of the biology of Venezuelan white-tailed deer (*Odocoileus virginianus gymnotis* Wiegmann, 1883), with a hypothesis on the origin of South American cervids. Unpublished Ph.D. thesis, University of Waterloo.

Chapman, D. and N. Chapman
1975. *Fallow Deer.* Lavenham: Terence Dalton Limited.

Handley, C. O.
1976. Mammals of the Smithsonian Venezuelan project. *Brigham Young University Science Bulletin, Biological Series* 20(5):61–62.

Hershkovitz, P.
1948. The technical name of the Virginia deer with a list of the South American forms. *Proceedings of the Biological Society of Washington* 61:41–48.

1958. The metatarsal glands in white-tailed deer and related forms in the neotropical region. *Mammalia,* 22:537-546.

1969. The evolution of mammals on southern continents. VI. The recent mammals of the Neotropical region: zoogeographic and ecological review. *Quarterly Review of Biology,* 44:1–70.

1972. The recent mammals of the neotropical region: a zoogeographic and ecological review. In *Evolution, Mammals, and Southern Continents,* edited by A. Keast, F.C. Erk, and B. Glass, pp. 311–431. Albany: State University of New York Press.

Husson, A. M..
1978. *The mammals of Suriname.* Leiden: E. J. Brill.

Illige, D.
1951. An analysis of the reproductive pattern of whitetail deer in South Texas. *Journal of Mammalogy,* 32:411–421.

Klein, E. H.
1982. Phenology of breeding and antler growth in white-tailed deer in Honduras. *Journal of Wildlife Management,* 46:826–829.

Lambiase, J. T., R. P. Amann, and J. S. Lindzey
1972. Aspects of reproductive physiology of male white-tailed deer. *Journal of Wildlife Management,* 36:868–875.

Mirarchi, R. E., P. F. Scanlon, and R. L. Kirkpatrick
1977a. Annual changes in spermatazoan production and associated organs of white-tailed deer. *Journal of Wildlife Management,* 41:92–99.

Mirarchi, R. E., P. F. Scanlon, R. L. Kirkpatrick, and C. B. Schreck
1977b. Androgen levels and antler development in captive and wild white-tailed deer. *Journal of Wildlife Management,* 41:178–183.

Progulske, D. R., and D. C. Duerre
1964. Factors influencing spotlighting counts of deer. *Journal of Wildlife Management,* 28:27–34.

Severinghaus, C. W.
1949. Tooth development and wear as a criterion of age in white-tailed deer. *Journal of Wildlife Management,* 13:195–216.

Simpson, G. G.
1941. Vernacular names of South American mammals. *Journal of Mammalogy,* 22:1–17.

Tate, G. H. H.
1939. The mammals of the Guiana region. *Bulletin of the American Museum of Natural History,* 76:151–229.

Thomas, W. D.
1974. Observations on captive brockets. *International Zoo Yearbook,* 15:77–78.

Tyson E. L.
1959. A deer drive vs. track census. *Transactions of the North American Wildlife Conference,* 24:457–464.

Walsh, J., and R. Gannon
1967. *Time is short and the water rises.* New York: Dutton.

Whitehead, G. K.
1972. *Deer of the world.* London: Constable.

WILLIAM D. ELDRIDGE,
MARK M. MACNAMARA
and
NICOLAS V. PACHECO

U.S. Fish and Wildlife Service
1011 E. Tudor Road
Anchorage, Alaska 99507

New York Zoological Society
The Zoological Park
185th Street and Southern Boulevard
Bronx, NY 10460

Corporacion Nacional Forestal
Correo Entre Lagos
Casilla 22
Osorno, Chile

Activity Patterns and Habitat Utilization of Pudus (*Pudu puda*) in South-Central Chile

ABSTRACT

Pudu activity patterns, habitat utilization and food habits were studied in southcentral Chile on the basis of seven radio-collared animals monitored from one to 19 months (85–3, 130 hours). Pudu were active day and night with rest periods lasting 2–5 hours; greatest activity occurred in the early morning, late afternoon and evening, and late evening. Activity was less on calm sunny days than windy days, but variation among pudus and between days was considerable. Pudu survive in highly disturbed mature and secondary forests. Home ranges were 16–26 ha in area and contained preferred trails and resting areas. Habitat composition differed between home ranges with quila being most utilized, most probably as cover. Matoral and forest are used more than expected on the basis of availability. There was no evidence of migration. A variety of food plants are used, but few are preferred. Herbaceous vegetation is most utilized in the 0-20 cm stratum, and ferns, vines and trees are most important foods in the 20–200 cm stratum. A wide variety of exotic species was also utilized as food.

Introduction

The pudu (*Pudu puda*) is a small forest deer, weighing less than 15 kg. Although listed as an endangered species (U.S. Gov., 1982), Miller et al. (1983) suggest that "inadequately known" is more appropriate terminology. Formerly, pudus were widely distributed in Chile and extended into similar habitat in the western ranges of the Patagonian sub-region of Argentina. The range extended from about 35° S latitude along the Andean foothills and coastal range of Chile to 49° S latitude (Figure 1) (Miller et al., 1973; Miller and Rottmann, 1976). The pudu is a lowland deer and is not found on slopes above 1700 m, probably due to snow depths (Miller et al., 1973).

Miller et al. (1973) report that although more than 5 million ha of pudu habitat remain in Chile, and the present population probably numbers in the thousands, the pudus' range has diminished considerably with increasing incursions and habitat destruction by

Figure 1.   Range of *Pudu puda* in Chile and location of the study area.

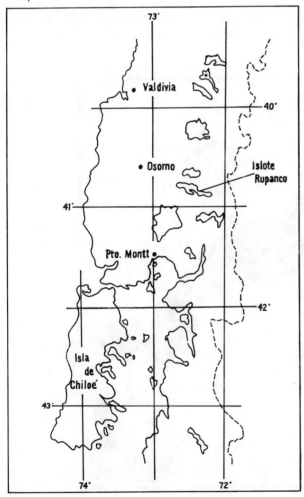

man. Hershkovitz (1982) summarized the primarily anecdotal life history information on pudus. To our knowledge, no intensive field work has been done on wild pudus and little is known concerning their biology, ecology, food habits, behavior and social system.

The objectives of this study were to determine activity patterns, habitat use, and food utilization of pudus in their natural habitat. The study was initiated in 1975 and continued until June 1980.

Study Area

The study area consisted of a peninsula, called "Islote", and an island in Lago Rupanco, the province of Osorno, in the lake district of south-central Chile. The lake is located at the base of the Andes 175 m above sea level, at 40° 52.5′ S latitude and 72° 24.5′ W longitude (Figure 1). The areas of the peninsula and island are approximately 1200 and 130 ha respectively. The peninsula is approximately 10 km long with a ridge 415 m in elevation running two thirds of its length (Figure 2). The peninsula, the primary study area, is a Fauna Reserve of the Corporacion Nacional Forestal (CONAF) where access is restricted to the public and domestic animals. The peninsula was the site of a study on the ecological impact of European red deer (*Cervus elaphus*) and fallow deer (*Dama dama*), which were introduced in small numbers (Ramirez et al., 1981; Eldridge et al., 1980; Ramirez and Godoy, 1981; and Heitzer and Ramirez, 1980). The island was privately owned and supported a high population of red and fallow deer during the study. Pudu were permanent residents on the peninsula and sporadically visited the island in low numbers.

Physical Environment

Climate is characterized by high annual precipitation with mild, wet winters and short, dry summers and is classified as an oceanic west coast climate with a mild Mediterranean influence (Thomasson, 1963). The mean annual total precipitation for 21 years at Lago Rupanco was 1.894 m of which 37% occurred in winter and 12% in summer (Almeyda and Saez, 1958). The mean annual temperature in Osorno, approximately 90 km to the east, is 12.5°C with a range of 5° to 25°C (Di Castri and Hajek, 1976). During the study, light snow fell at lake level on two occasions, melting within a few hours. Above altitudes of 1000 m in southcentral Chile much of the winter precipitation is snow, and altitudes greater than 2000 m are perpetually snow covered.

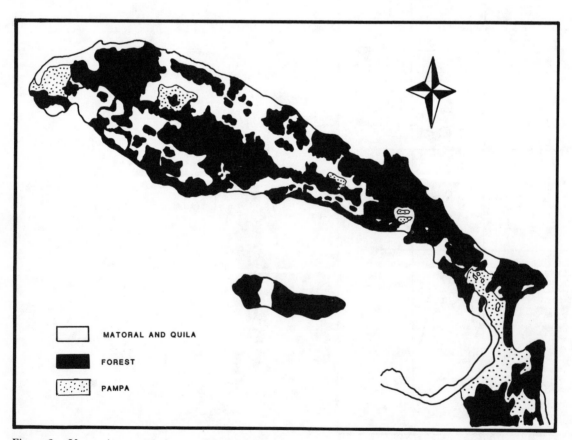

MATORAL AND QUILA

FOREST

PAMPA

Figure 2.   Vegetation associations on Islote Rupanco.

354   Eldridge, MacNamara, and Pacheco

The soils are deep, somewhat acidic (pH = 5.2), rich in organic material (16%) with a high capacity for phosphorus fixation (Weinberger, 1971), nutrient poor, and subject to erosion (Ramirez et al., 1981).

Vegetation

The vegetation of the Chilean Lake District, the primary pudu habitat, has been described by various authors (Brun, 1975; Oberdofer, 1960; Schmithusen, 1956; Thomasson, 1963; Quintanilla, 1974). Schmithusen (1956) classified the region encompassing the study area as temperate evergreen rain forest and summer-green deciduous forest. Veblen and Ashton (1978; p. 151) state that "the temperate evergreen rain forests are comprised of broad-leafed evergreen trees rich in species and displaying a luxuriant development of epiphytes and lianas. The summer-green deciduous forest is less rich in species." Ramirez et al. (1981) described three primary vegetation associations on the peninsula Islote: forest, shrub, and pampas.

Forest Association. Three forest sociophytological units, identified by Oberdorfer (1960), were present on Islote (Ramirez et al., 1981): 1) the *Lapageno-Aextoiconetum* unit, called the Olvillo Forest, was dominant on Islote; 2) the *Larelia-Weinmannietum* unit only prospered on the highest points of the peninsula; and 3) the *Dombeyo-Eucryphietum* unit was sparsely represented along the lakeshore (Figure 3).

The Olivillo forest is typical of the "Valdivian Rainforest" occurring continuously from Concepcion to Chiloe (Ramirez et al., 1981). It is a multi-stratified, evergreen forest dominated by olivillo trees (*Aextoxicon punctatum*), which reach heights of 30 m and have a dense canopy impeding light penetration. Other common canopy species include *Eucriphia cordioflia* and *Laurelia philippiana*. A secondary tree stratum exists, followed by a sparsely represented shrub layer and a lush herbaceous layer (Ramirez et al., 1981). Variations of this general structure are common depending on the degree to which the canopy has been opened by man-made or natural causes. The three forest sociophytological units comprised 56% of the vegetative cover on Islote (Figure 2).

Shrub Association. Shrub formations are secondary communities formed after the destruction of the native forest. There are two clearly distinguishable sociophytological units in this association, which we call "matoral" and "quila." Matoral is dominated by trees and shrubs and has been classified by Oberdorfer (1960) as the *Rhapithumno-Aristoletietum* community. Herbs, vines and ferns are abundant in this community, and the number of species is high compared to the quila community.

Quila, dominated by bamboo species, is not diverse due to the dense cover and impenetrable growth of bamboo. The herbaceous layer is almost absent in thick stands, which are common. Variations of this community occur depending on humidity and age of the stand. More humid and less dense stands can support a rich variety of other plant species and are inter-

Figure 3. Relative location of vegetation communities on Islote Rupanco.

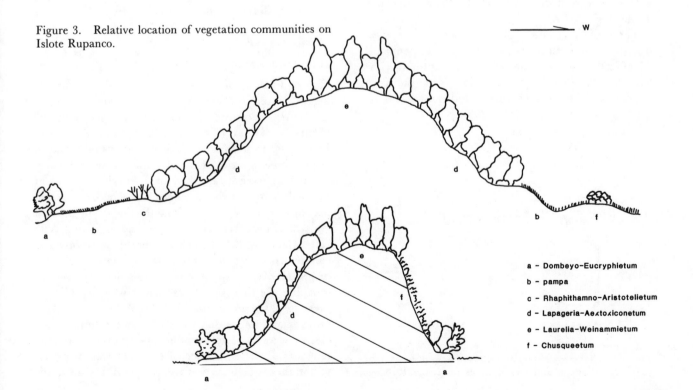

a – Dombeyo-Eucryphietum
b – pampa
c – Rhaphithamno-Aristotelietum
d – Lapageria-Aextoxiconetum
e – Laurelia-Weinammietum
f – Chusqueetum

mediate in successional stage between the typical, thick bamboo community and the matoral community. Oberdorfer (1960) recognized three vegetation groups called *Chusquetum* (Figure 3) with modifiers. The shrub association, including quila and matoral, comprised 31% of the vegetative cover on Islote (Figure 2).

Pampa Association. This association results from complete destruction of native forest combined with continuous intervention by man. It consists almost exclusively of grasses and herbaceous species, most of which have been introduced from Europe. This association comprised 12% of the vegetative cover on Islote (Figure 2).

Species lists, importance values, and a discussion of the vegetation of the peninsula communities are presented in detail by Ramirez and Godoy (1981) and in part by Ramirez et al. (1981) and Heitzer and Ramirez (1980). The successional relationships of the primary associations and communities are presented in Figure 4.

Methods

Telemetry Observations

Seven pudus were fitted with radio transmitter collars. Observation periods for the seven pudus ranged from approximately 85 hours in one month to 3,130 hours over 19 months. For the last pudu, a Rustrak strip-chart recorder was used to monitor activity when an observer was not present. Sexes and ages of pudus with radios, and dates of monitoring, are listed in Table 1.

Three of four radio-monitored pudus were introduced to the existing population on the peninsula. The fourth was a resident adult male captured with a leg-snare modified to prevent injury. One pudu was introduced to the island. Introduced pudus were ob-

Table 1. Age, sex, observation time, and home range of pudus with radios

Pudu #	Age–Sex	Observation Dates	Total Hours	Home Range (Ha)
1	Ad female	6/78 to 10/78	382	23.6
2	Yr female	9/77 to 12/77	322	16.5
3	Ad female	9/76 to 11/76	830	10.2[a]
4	Ad male	11/78 to 5/80	3,124	25.5
5	Yr male	12/75 to 1/76	206	26.1
B	Yr female	2/76 to 3/76	103	—
C	Ad male	6/76 to 6/76	85	—

[a]Introduced to the island

tained from local residents shortly after capture, except No. 5, which was a yearling male born in captivity. They were maintained in an enclosure up to two weeks to monitor health until release.

Radio-collared pudus were located and monitored with a hand-held three-element Yagi antenna. Fixes were assigned by triangulation (Heezen and Tester, 1967). Activities for pudus No. 1–4 were categorized as moving, non-moving and slightly moving. Activities for pudus No. 5–7 were classified as non-moving and moving. Slightly moving referred to a slightly varying radio signal but no change in location. Activities were recorded by date, time, habitat type and weather conditions. Habitat was divided into four categories: forest, pasture, quila, matoral.

Habitat Analysis

PUDU HOME RANGES

Home ranges of pudus were determined by connecting the outermost telemetry fixes. Vegetation within the home range was measured by a series of techniques based on height strata. Beginning approximately 50 m from an outside boundary of a pudu's home range, a series of parallel line-transects of varying length were established at approximately 50 m intervals across the home range. The length of the line occupied by all plants touching the line in the 20–200 cm stratum was recorded by species and habitat type (after Canfield, 1941). To characterize sub-canopy and canopy cover we measured the diameter-at-breast-height (DBH) of all woody plants taller than two m touching the line. Quadrats (1 m²) were established every 10–20 m on alternating sides of the line for sampling vegetation within the 0–20 cm stratum. Cover classes were used to estimate plant cover (Daubenmire, 1968). The number of stems of woody plants within these quadrats was also recorded. Plant species

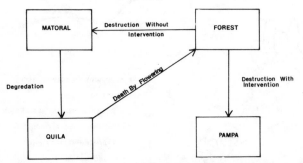

Figure 4. Successional relationships among primary vegetation associations and communities on Islote Rupanco.

Eldridge, MacNamara, and Pacheco

were treated separately and then grouped as trees, shrubs, vines and epiphytes, ferns, mosses, grass-likes, and bamboo.

PUDUS WITHOUT RADIOS

Two methods were used to quantify habitat use by wild pudus on the peninsula: 1) all pudu tracks and sightings of pudus within each major habitat type were recorded; and 2) vegetation was sampled surrounding fresh evidence of browsing by pudus. In the track index, we recorded fresh tracks, estimated number of pudus involved, and the habitat in which they occurred. In the second method, habitat was analyzed by using a 5 × 5 m quadrat centered over the freshly utilized browse. Cover classes and DBH were used to measure vegetation in the 20–200 cm and the 200+ cm strata, respectively. Two 50 × 100 cm plots, located in opposite corners of the 5 × 5 m quadrat, were used to determine cover class for all species, and number of stems of woody species, in the 0–20 cm stratum.

Food Habits

PLANTS UTILIZED BY PUDUS WITH RADIOS

Food habits data were collected in spring and summer for pudus 1, 2 and 4. For vegetation in the 20–200 cm stratum, the cms of transect line touched by a plant were multiplied by the height of the plant as well as the percentage available to eat, and the estimated percentage browsed. These values were summed by plant species and by plant groups and converted to percentage index of food eaten. Percentage classes used for cover analysis were also used for the estimation of percent available to eat and percent browsed.

A similar method was used for plants within the 0–20 cm height stratum except a cover class of 1 m² quadrats was used, rather than centimeters of a line transect. In this stratum 100% of all plants was available to be eaten.

PLANT UTILIZATION BY PUDUS WITHOUT RADIOS

To avoid disturbing pudus with radios an intensive browse analysis focussed on pudus living in unstudied home ranges. Pudu browsing in forest and matoral throughout the peninsula was studied by using the 5 × 5 m quadrats, centered around fresh evidence of pudu browsing, discussed above. Cover class and the estimated percentage browsed were determined for the shrub stratum in 5 × 5 m quadrats by the methods described above. Two 50 × 100 cm quadrats were used to measure these parameters in the herb stratum.

Food habits of recently captured pudus were observed in enclosures in matoral/pampa on Islote and the island. Direct observation of bites per plant spe-

cies was used in pampa, as well as utilization percentage of 1 m² quadrats. Browsed plant tips were counted for plants within the 20–200 cm stratum as an independent measure of utilization but this was not practical in the 0–20 cm stratum. It was feasible in the more intensely utilized enclosures.

Ivlev's Selectivity Coefficient (Ivlev, 1961) was used to determine a relative preference rating of plants eaten in three pudu home ranges and browse plots throughout Islote as follows:

$$\text{Selectivity Coefficient} = \frac{\% \text{ eaten} - \% \text{ cover}}{\% \text{ eaten} + \% \text{ cover}}$$

Resulting values range from -1.0 to $+1.0$ and indicate a relative preference among species or plant groups, with the most positive being the most preferred species. These values were calculated for plant species and plant groups by habitat.

Results and Discussion

Activity Patterns

The proportions of time in which pudus were active, resting and partially active are presented in Table 2. If partially active and active categories are combined, periods of activity ranged from 55 to 66%. Although some of the activities classified as partially active probably resulted from grooming and ruminating while resting, based on direct observations we think feeding in one location (which made movements difficult to detect) was the primary activity in this category. Therefore, we feel that the best way to analyze the data is by combining the partially active and active categories.

Chi-square analysis revealed highly significant differences among the seven pudus in the proportion of

Table 2. Active and resting percentages by Pudu

Pudu No.	Active (%)	Partially Active (%)	Resting (%)	N (hrs)
1	60.8	5.8	33.5	382
2	55.9	4.6	39.5	322
3	51.6	1.2	47.2	830
4	43.2	11.5	45.2	3,124
A	51.1	—	48.9	206
B	54.6	—	45.4	103
C	52.2	—	47.8	185
	47.7	7.7	44.7	Total 5,152
		55.3[a]		

[a]Combined active and partially active values

Table 3. Differences[a] in active and resting percentages among pudus

Pudu No.	Active	Resting
1	4.57	−4.57
2	1.41	−1.41
3	−1.67	1.67
4	−0.96	0.96
5	−1.30	1.30
B	−0.18	0.18
C	−0.95	0.96

[a]The tabular adjusted residuals (Everitt, 1977) are measures of deviation from expected values. + = preference, − = avoidance. Critical values are 1.96 ($P < 0.05$), 2.58 ($P < 0.01$).

Table 4. Activity percentages and differences[a] among seasons for Pudu 4

Season (months)	Active (%) residual[a]	Resting (%) residual[a]	N (hrs)
Fall (3, 4, 5)[b]	52.8	47.2	1084
	−12.01[a]	12.00[a]	
Winter (6, 7, 8)	54.5	45.5	650
	−1.00	1.00	
Spring (9, 10, 11)	51.5	48.5	616
	−14.09	14.09	
Summer (12, 1, 2)	60.2	39.8	772
	27.19	−27.19	

[a]The tabular adjusted residuals (Everitt, 1977) are measures of deviation from expected values. + = preference, − = avoidance. Critical values are 1.96 ($P < 0.05$), 2.58 ($P < 0.01$).
[b]Month numbers, January = 1.

Table 5. Maximum and minimum ranges for % activity in a 24-hour period beginning at 12:00 noon

	Pudu 4 (N = 20)		Pudu 2 (N = 1)		Pudu 3 (N = 4)	
	A	R	A	R	A	R
Minimum	29	32	56	43	44	33
Maximum	67	62	—	—	67	55

A = active
R = resting

time in which they were resting and active. Subsequent analysis of cell residuals (Everitt, 1977) showed that this variation was due to a significant deviation in behavior by pudu one, which was active 65% of the time (Table 3).

SEASONAL ACTIVITY PATTERNS

Sufficient data for analyzing seasonal differences was available only for pudu 4, the resident adult male captured on the peninsula. Chi-square analysis revealed significant differences in activities among seasons. This pudu was more active than inactive during all seasons. However, analysis of residuals (Everitt, 1977) revealed that it was less active during fall and spring, and more active during summer, than expected (Table 4). We expected a high active percentage during the fall breeding season, but it did not occur.

DAILY ACTIVITY PATTERNS

Results of 25, 24-hour activity periods for three pudus (Table 5) revealed that considerable variation in 24-hour periods existed and it is difficult to characterize a typical day for a pudu (Figure 5). Pudus were active day and night and rarely pursued any one activity for more than two to three hours at a time, and often less. The pudus' dramatic reaction to disturbances by humans, dogs and predators could have contributed to the variability in daily activity patterns.

A chi-square test and subsequent analysis of residuals (Everitt, 1977) of activities of four pudus by hour groups revealed significant differences among pudus and among hour groups in the proportion of time classified as active or resting (Table 6). Pudus appear to have resting periods during mid-day and active periods during late afternoon and evening and early morning. Although the results suggest that pudus are more nocturnal than diurnal there was pronounced variation in activity among pudus between days.

ACTIVITY PATTERNS AND WEATHER

Weather conditions were coded into the following six classifications: sunny-calm, rainy-calm, cloudy-calm, sunny-windy, rainy-windy and cloudy-windy. A chi-square test and analysis of residuals (Everitt, 1977) revealed significant differences in activity patterns among weather groups (Table 7). Each pudu was significantly less active on sunny-calm cays and was more active than expected on sunny-windy days.

Because pudus lead a secretive life in dense cover, the effect of sun and rain on pudus may not be as apparent compared with species that are more directly exposed to the elements. In captivity some

Eldridge, MacNamara, and Pacheco

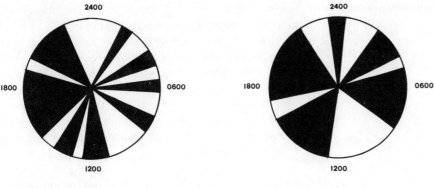

Figure 5. Examples of 24-hour activity patterns for two pudus.

| ACTIVE |
| RESTING |

Table 6.   Differences[a] in activities by hour groups by Pudu

Hour Group	Pudu 1		Pudu 2		Pudu 3		Pudu 4	
	A	R	A	R	A	R	A	R
0400–0700	12.0	−12.0	−4.0	4.7	−2.7	2.8	− 3.5	3.5
0800–1000	− 7.8	7.8	− .6	.8	9.2	−9.7	−25.3	25.3
1200–1500	−22.7	22.8	−2.4	2.8	−5.3	5.5	− 8.0	8.0
1600–1900	−11.4	11.4	−1.5	1.8	−5.1	5.4	− 5.1	5.1
2000–2300	29.5	−29.5	−4.8	5.7	3.9	−4.0	15.3	−15.3
2400–0300	8.4	− 8.4	−1.6	1.9	− .0	.0	6.9	− 6.9

[a]The tabular adjusted residuals are measures of deviation from expected values. + = preference, − = avoidance. Critical values are 1.96 (P < 0.05) 2.58 (P < 0.01).
A = active (partially active and active categories combined)
R = resting

Table 7.   Differences[a] in activities by weather groups

Weather	Pudu 1		Pudu 2		Pudu 3	
Weather	Active	Resting	Active	Resting	Active	Resting
Sunny, calm	−15.4	15.4	−2.3	2.3	− 2.4	2.4
Sunny, windy	2.8	− 2.8	2.3	−2.3	2.4	− 2.4
Rain, calm	18.0	−18.0			− 3.9	3.9
Rain, wind	− 9.1	9.1			−34.0	−34.0
Cloudy, calm	− 1.3	1.3			−12.5	12.5
Cloudy, wind	− 3.9	3.9			− 8.3	8.3

[a]The tabular adjusted residuals are measures of deviation from expected values. + = preference, − = avoidance. Critical values are 1.96 (P < 0.05) 2.58 (P < 0.01).

Table 8. Percent cover of major habitat types for pudu home ranges

	Forest	Matoral	Quila	Pampa
Pudu 1	15	19	61	5
Pudu 2	29	10	61	—
Pudu 3	12	28	55	5
Pudu 4	8	14	78	—
Pudu 5	33	12	47	8
X̄ + sd	19 ± 11	17 ± 7	60 ± 11	4 ± 3

pudus are intolerant of heat (Junge, 1966; E. Francani, pers. com.) and this might explain the reduced activity of our pudus on sunny-calm days. The results might also be explained by the wariness of pudus which could cause them to rest when they might be most easily seen or heard by predators.

ACTIVITY PATTERNS BY HABITAT TYPE

Considerable variation existed between home ranges in the percentages of each habitat type but quila was dominant in all (Table 8). A chi-square test revealed significant differences in activities by habitat type based on use versus availability. A subsequent analysis of residuals (Everitt, 1977, Table 9) revealed that although quila was the most utilized habitat, it was not preferred for any activity by any pudu and was used significantly less than expected for each activity by all pudus except pudu 2 where the resting value was within expected limits. Pampa, which occurred in the home range of two pudus on the peninsula, was also used significantly less than expected. Forest and matoral, comprising less than one-third of the cover in any home range, were used significantly more than expected for each activity by each pudu. Results were

similar when partially active and active categories were combined or considered separately.

Although pudus fed on quila, we suspect that traveling comprised disproportionately more time in quila than other habitats. Quila is typically poor in diversity and availability of food species. Forest, matoral and pampa support a large variety of food species. Food availability is probably an important reason why pudus were significantly more active than expected in forest and matoral.

The high percentage of quila in the pudus' home ranges and the small percentage of pampa are probably explained by their respective value as escape cover. Bamboo, which dominates quila, sprouts from a central area and droops to the ground, which provides innumerable natural "tunnels" at ground level. Pudus are able to move through this habitat at nearly full speed, while larger animals are impeded. Although a variety of food sources is available in pampas, pudus appear easily preyed on in this habitat (most of the locally caught pudus were first sighted in pampa). The low activity value for pampa may also be due to the difficulty of obtaining "fixes" in pampa due to its proximity to other habitats and due to the likelihood that pudus use pampa primarily at night becaue of predation. Obtaining "fixes" in small areas of pampa at night was difficult.

A problem common to all the pudu home ranges, particularly in quila, was obtaining location fixes without disturbing the animal. For example, a pudu might select a small patch of quila in a forested area to rest but the observer could not determine if the pudu was in the quila or the forest nearby without disturbing the animal. When disturbed the activity patterns and habitat use of that pudu were disrupted for at least the rest of the day.

During data collection we thought that pudus were selecting quila for resting, either in large tracts or small patches in other habitats, but our results did not verify this.

Table 9. Differences[a] in activities by habitat by pudu

Activity	Forest Pudu			Matoral Pudu			Quila Pudu			Pampa Pudu		
	1	2	4	1	2	4	1	2	4	1	2	4
Active	63.2	15.6	2.0	54.5	19.6	156.2	−92.5	−45.6	−135.8	−110.3	−17.2	—
Partially active	28.3	10.3	20.6	11.6	21.7	29.7	−30.9	−13.1	− 88.9	− 40.3	−43.2	—
Resting	43.8	12.8	21.3	17.2	11.3	89.6	−47.1	− 5.3	− 37.0	− 50.1	−62.2	—

[a]The tabular adjusted residuals (Everitt, 1977) are measures of deviation from expected values. + = preference, − = avoidance. Critical values are 1.96 (P < 0.05) 2.58 (P < 0.01).

Eldridge, MacNamara, and Pacheco

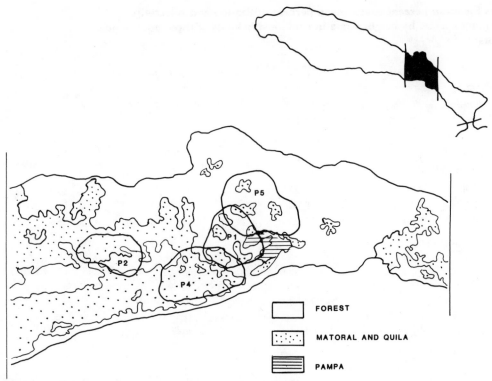

Figure 6. Home ranges of pudus 1,2,4, and 5 on Islote Rupanco.

FOREST

MATORAL AND QUILA

PAMPA

Movements within a Home Range

The sizes of pudu home ranges (Table 1) are maximum values, representing the most distant "fixes". We rarely mapped movements consecutively from point to point because it was difficult to follow pudus in the tangled bamboo and because of our concern over disturbance. However, it was clear that movements of individual pudus varied greatly on a daily basis. Pudus appeared to have trail systems, usually under bamboo or dense vegetation, that were regularly used between the numerous feeding and resting areas.

Each home range was used by at least one other pudu on occasion, and tracks indicated they occasionally moved together or followed one another. Home ranges of radio-collared pudus introduced to Islote overlapped the home range of the resident adult male, during different periods of time (Figure 6). It is possible that pudus, particularly males and females, occupy overlapping home ranges, and that disputes arise only when the animals meet on shared territory.

The home range of the adult female introduced to the island was smaller (10 ha) than those of the introduced or resident pudus on the peninsula. The high population of exotic deer virtually eliminated shrub and herbaceous strata on the island, and this restricted pudu activity to an area denied to exotic deer

Table 10. Differences[a] in habitat types among pudu home ranges

	Habitat			
	Forest	Matoral	Quila	Pampa
Pudu 1	−1.14	1.39	−0.33	0.75
Pudu 2	1.44	− .82	−0.10	−1.36
Pudu 4	−2.94	− .01	3.15	−1.80
Pudu 5	2.77	− .03	−2.79	2.22

[a]The tabular adjusted residuals are measures of deviation from expected values. + = preference, − = avoidance. Critical values are 1.96 ($P < 0.05$), 2.58 ($P < 0.01$).

by fences and steep slopes. Thus pudu did not venture into areas occupied by exotics after initial wanderings on the island.

Habitat Analysis

The primary purpose of the habitat analysis was to describe the habitat within the home ranges of pudus with radios. Within forest, quila and matoral 175 plant species were divided into 7 primary plant groups (trees, shrubs etc.). Numbers of species were

Table 11. Highest values for mean percent cover, mean percent utilization and selectivity coefficients of important plant species by height strata in combined habitats of three pudu home ranges and all browse plots

Plant Species	$\bar{X}$ % Cover			$\bar{X}$ % Utilization		$\bar{X}$ Preference*	
	over 2m	20–200	0–20	20–200	0–20	20–200	0–20
Trees							
Aextoxicon punctatum	45.25	2.50	3.00	5.81			
Rhaphithamnus spinosus	16.50	4.25		10.67		.56	.10
Laurelia philippiana	13.80	4.75		1.25			
Eucryphia cordifolia	5.80			2.00			
Aristotelia chilensis	8.10	1.00		8.25		.64	
Myrceugenia planipes		2.00					
Persea lingue						.75	
Shrubs							
Fuchsia magellanica	2.10						
Rubus constrictus				18.50		.80	
Bamboo							
Chusquea quila		65.25		2.00		−.70**	−.31**
Ferns							
Hypolepsis rugusule						.47	
Polystichum chilensis				3.75		.49	
Blechnum microphyllum				1.25		.22	
Blechnum astatum						.49	
Blechnum chilense		.75		12.75			
Blechnum blechnoides		1.50		6.00	6.25	.49	
Blechnum auriculatum		1.00	2.00	1.75	1.26		
Herbs							
Oxalis rocea						.74	
Luzuriaga erecta					3.25		.55
Luzuriaga radicans		2.00	13.67	3.25	30.33	.58	.40
Leptocarpha sifrilaris				3.00			
Nertera granadensis			13.69		31.66		.48
Pilea elliptica					.67		
Prunella vulgaris					.68		
Arrhenatherum elatius					1.32		
Pilea elegans			8.25				
Leptostigma arnottianum					.66		
Plantago lanceolata					3.75		
Vines							
Boquila trifoliata				1.75	3.50		.70
Pseudopanax valdiviense		2.25	6.67				
Hydrangea integerrima				6.25	3.25		.26
Mitraria coccinea				1.75	1.25	.75	.37
Moss							
Unknown species			4.12				

*Ivlev's Selectivity Coefficient: +1 = preference; −1 = avoidance
**included for comparison

Eldridge, MacNamara, and Pacheco

highest in the lower plant strata. Species richness varied with habitat type depending on age of stand, disturbance and humidity.

Although quila dominated all home ranges (Table 8), a chi-square analysis and subsequent analysis of residuals (Everitt, 1977) revealed significant differences in habitat composition among home ranges (Table 10). There was less forest and more quila than expected in the home range of the resident adult male. The home range of the introduced yearling male had more forest and pampa, and less quila, than expected.

In the canopy stratum (over 2m), trees were the dominant plant group in forest and matoral (65–95% total cover), followed by shrubs (5–3% total cover), for all home ranges and browse plots. Common canopy species dominated home ranges including *A. punctatum* and *L. philipiana*, *E. cordifolia* and *R. spinosus* (Table 11). The canopy stratum was not measured in quila, where trees occurred sparsely as remnants of the destroyed forest. Species richness was low in the canopy stratum for all habitats, ranging from 10 to 13.

Cover of major plant groups in the shrub stratum (20–200 cm) was variable among home ranges (Table 12). Trees dominated the shrub stratum in forests and matoral, followed by bamboo and vines in pudu home ranges and browse plots. Bamboo dominated in quila and when all habitats were combined (Table 12). Species richness was lowest in quila (12–26) but considerable variation existed in this habitat among pudus. Important species in the shrub stratum included *C. quila*, *A. punctatum*, *L. philipiana*, *Pseudopanax valdiviense*, and *R. spinosus* (Table 11).

Herbs dominated all habitat types in the herbaceous stratum (0–20cm), followed by ferns or vines with grass-like plants common in matoral (Table 12). Important species in the herb stratum included *N. granadensis*, *L. radicans*, *B. blechnoides*, and *Picea elegans*, and seedlings of *A. punctatum* (Table 11).

Food Habits

SHRUB STRATUM

After measuring the height, cover (or line intercept) and percent available of individual plants to the pudu as food, the estimated percentage browsed was summed by species, by plant group (trees, shrubs,

Table 12. Mean percent cover of major plant groups in four pudu home ranges by plant height strata, habitat type, and all habitats combined ($\bar{X} \pm$ sd)

Plant Group	Forest		Matoral	
	0–20 cm	20–200 cm	0–20 cm	20–200 cm
Trees	8.00 ± 8.12	36.50 ± 7.18	5.50 ± 3.11	33.25 ± 13.96
Shrubs	1.25 ± 1.26	4.00 ± 2.83	3.50 ± 3.42	9.25 ± 6.29
Bamboo	0	23.50 ± 15.67	0.75 ± 0.96	16.50 ± 25.21
Herbs	55.75 ± 13.37	11.50 ± 12.51	50.75 ± 19.17	11.25 ± 5.62
Vines	16.25 ± 7.09	15.75 ± 9.36	3.25 ± 3.77	8.75 ± 5.25
Ferns	7.75 ± 2.06	6.00 ± 5.72	10.00 ± 4.97	18.50 ± 6.19
Mosses	6.25 ± 4.86	0	10.50 ± 19.67	0
Grass-likes	3.00 ± 2.71	3.00 ± 4.08	16.50 ± 7.19	5.00 ± 2.58

Plant Group	Quila		Combined Habitats	
	0–20 cm	20–200 cm	0–20 cm	20–200 cm
Trees	12.00 ± 8.54	6.00 ± 6.92	4.67 ± 1.53	20.75 ± 14.68
Shrubs	0.67 ± 1.15	3.00 ± 3.46	1.33 ± 1.53	4.50 ± 2.89
Bamboo	0	86.00 ± 11.79	0.33 ± 0.58	66.67 ± 18.23
Herbs	55.00 ± 4.00	1.67 ± 1.15	57.67 ± 9.48	8.50 ± 11.79
Vines	13.00 ± 4.36	0.67 ± 0.58	10.33 ± 5.86	7.00 ± 6.00
Ferns	7.00 ± 8.19	3.00 ± 4.36	9.33 ± 1.53	6.00 ± 1.41
Mosses	11.00 ± 8.72	0	8.33 ± 4.04	0
Grass-likes	1.33 ± 2.31	1.33 ± 1.53	3.33 ± 1.53	2.75 ± 4.19

Table 13. Percent food utilization by habitat and height strata for pudu home ranges and browse plots

Habitat	0–20 cm Pudu 1	4	2	Browse Plots	20–200 cm Pudu 1	4	2	Browse Plots
Forest	42	72	55	31	39	35	58	38
Matoral	36	8	45	69	57	45	42	62
Quila	22	20			4	20		

etc.) and by habitat type for each height stratum. The summation by habitat type indicates in which habitat most of the feeding occurred, and these data are presented in Table 13. Because of the different techniques utilized, direct comparison between height strata is not possible. However, evidence of browsing was more apparent in forest and matoral than quila for each pudu. Pudus utilized matoral substantially more for feeding than forests in browse plots, which had equal samples from each habitat (Table 13).

The most utilized plant group in the shrub stratum (20–200cm) differed among pudus. Ferns, trees, and shrubs were most utilized in forests, matoral, quila and all habitats combined (Table 14). Shrubs were the most preferred plant group in all habitats combined (Table 14) and each habitat except quila, where trees were most preferred. Vines and herbs were also important in some habitats for individual pudus. Bamboo was least preferred in all habitats. Generally, 60 to 80% of the species available were utilized in each habitat. The five species most utilized by each pudu accounted for 65–100% of all utilization in each habitat. Considering cover and preference, the most important food species to pudus in the shrub stratum for combined habitats were *B. blechnoides*, *B. chilensis*, *R. constrictus*, *R. spinosus*, *H. intergenea*, and *L. radicans* (Table 11). Generally, the important food species also ranked high in importance values for each habitat on Islote (Ramirez et al., 1981).

Browsed plant tips were also counted in the shrub stratum as an independent measure of utilization (Table 14). Although percentages were similar to those based on estimates, trees and ferns exchanged positions as the most utilized group.

Table 14. Mean percent food utilization of major plant groups determined from pudu home ranges and browse plots ($\bar{X} \pm$ sd)

(20–200cm) Plant group	Forest	Matoral	Quila	All habitats combined	All habitats combined*
Trees	27.05 ± 11.12	28.00 ± 16.39	18.05 ± 7.78	23.05 ± 05.80	30.21 ± 6.25
Shrubs	19.00 ± 22.00	15.00 ± 12.49	2.50 ± 3.54	22.75 ± 13.67	15.36 ± 9.67
Bamboo	4.50 ± 4.43	1.25 ± 0.96	27.00 ± 42.51	3.50 ± 3.41	2.03 ± 3.21
Herbs	10.25 ± 11.98	17.00 ± 10.03	0.50 ± 0.71	9.50 ± 10.01	19.45 ± 8.22
Vines	17.25 ± 24.30	3.50 ± 3.11	19.00 ± 26.87	10.50 ± 11.56	10.28 ± 9.45
Ferns	20.25 ± 16.88	32.75 ± 14.36	13.00 ± 18.30	24.00 ± 13.47	22.46 ± 11.46
Grass-likes	2.00 ± 3.37	3.25 ± 2.63	6.00 ± 8.49	3.50 ± 2.65	2.75 ± 2.34

(0–20cm) Plant group	Forest	Matoral	Quila	All habitats combined	
Trees	3.00 ± 2.94	2.75 ± 2.21	9.00 ± 12.73	3.00 ± 4.57	
Shrubs	0.25 ± 0.50	1.25 ± 0.96	0	0.75 ± 0.50	
Bamboo	0.25 ± 0.50	0	0	0.25 ± 0.50	
Herbs	72.25 ± 14.13	66.50 ± 28.10	63.00 ± 22.62	81.75 ± 11.59	
Vines	14.25 ± 10.81	2.75 ± 2.75	17.50 ± 24.75	8.75 ± 6.55	
Ferns	8.50 ± 7.14	21.25 ± 19.82	11.00 ± 9.90	9.25 ± 2.87	
Grass-likes	0.75 ± 0.50	5.50 ± 6.19	0	1.75 ± 1.25	
Moss	0	0	0	0	

*Determined from numbers of plant points browsed

Eldridge, MacNamara, and Pacheco

Table 15. Mean food preference ranking of major plant groups for combined habitats by height strata for four pudus and all browse plots

Plant Group	0–20 cm	20–200cm
Trees	4.15[a] (5)[b]	3.78 (4)
Shrubs	4.00 (4)	1.36 (1)
Bamboo	4.67 (6)	5.61 (6)
Herbs	1.76 (1)	3.64 (3)
Vines	2.83 (3)	3.78 (4)
Ferns	2.00 (2)	2.85 (2)
Grass-likes	4.81 (7)	4.78 (5)
Mosses	5.27 (8)	—

[a] 1 = most preferred; 6 = least preferred
[b] Rank of means

Table 16. Most utilized (%) pampa species by captive pudus during late spring and early summer

Plant Species	Nov. 15 (N = 15)[a]	Feb. 20 (N = 15)[a]	Importance value rank[b]
Trees, Shrubs			
Aristotelia chilensis	3	4	46
Fuchsia magellanica	4	2	—
Rhaphithamnus spinosus	2	2	—
Rubus constrictus	16	12	4
Herbs, Ferns, Grasses			
Holcus lanatus	8	9	3
Dactylis glomerata	8	25	7
Plantago lanceolata	12	11	5
Lotus uliginosus	18	15	2
Blechnum chilense	4	4	9
Prunella vulgaris	10	6	8
Trifolium repens	9	3	24
Total Percent	94	82	
% Species utilization	69	89	

[a] 1 m² quadrats
[b] Rank of 72 species (Ramirez and Godoy [1981])

HERB STRATUM

In the herbaceous stratum (0–20cm) herbs, then ferns or vines, were the most utilized plant group in all habitats (Table 14). Use of moss was not detected, grass-like plants and shrubs were of minor importance, and bamboo was generally unavailable in this stratum. Depending on habitat and home range, from 25–79% of the available plant species were utilized by individual pudus. The five most utilized species, which varied among pudus, comprised from 68 to 100% of total utilization in each habitat.

Herbs and vines, followed by ferns, were the most preferred plant groups in all habitats in this stratum (Table 15). Mosses and grasses were least preferred. Junge (1966) also reported a dislike for grasses and sedges among pudus. Considering cover and preference, the most important food species to pudus in the 0–20 cm stratum were *L. radicans*, *B. blechnoides*, *N. granadensis*, and *L. erecta* (Table 11).

PAMPA

Utilization of pampa vegetation was determined from wild pudus in enclosures on Islote and the island. The primarily exotic pampa vegetation consisted of 72 species of grasses, herbs and woody plants (Ramirez and Godoy, 1981). The introduced raspberry, *R. constrictus*, is considered a plague in southcentral Chile because it quickly dominates pampas without continuous intervention by man. With the removal of domestic stock and humans from Islote, *R. constrictus* rapidly expanded on pampas during the study. Many of the introduced species common to pampas were annuals, perennials or deciduous. Some, such as grasses and *R. constrictus*, lost all green material during winter. However, many of the herbs provided green material throughout the year and were readily utilized by pudus.

Although difficult to measure, we attempted to determine relative importance of pampa species to pudus based on percent cover and estimated utilization from the m² plots in enclosures (Table 16). Less than one-half of the species recorded on Islote by Ramirez and Godoy (1981) were recorded in the enclosures, but the common dominant species were present. Herbaceous species important to pudus included *Plantago lanceolata*, *Lotus uliginosus* and *Dactylus glomerata*. Preference for *Plantago* by pudus was also reported by Junge (1966). Although our data are limited, late summer and late spring variations in use of pampa vegetation did not appear important, except in a few species (Table 16). Certain species common in the exclosure were obviously avoided, including *Juncus aragrostis* and certain sedges. These species are also avoided by domestic stock and apparently have little

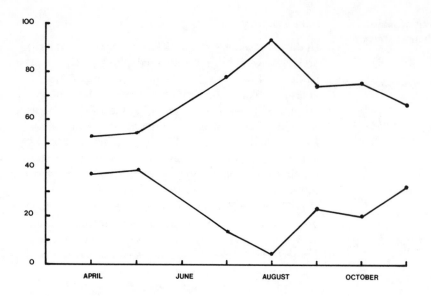

Figure 7. Utilization of pampa species and *Rubus constrictus* by captive pudus from number of bites per plant species.

forage value. Young bamboo plants, not present in the island enclosure, were planted in pampa along with several common tree species. Nearly all the planted young tree species were killed through browsing or more often, antler scraping, but the bamboo sprouts were virtually untouched. Bamboo in the enclosure on Islote was utilized in minor amounts.

The importance of *R. constrictus* to pudus in other habitats has been indicated, and also was apparent in pampa where captive pudus rapidly established a browse line on it. Because it is deciduous, marked differences in its utilization occur among seasons. Observations of a feeding captive adult male over eight months, based on numbers of bites per plant species, indicated a switch to other, primarily herbaceous, pampa vegetation when *R. constrictus* was unavailable (Fig. 7).

The importance of pampa vegetation to pudus varied with individual captive animals. Some appeared to utilize herbaceous vegetation and *R. constrictus* almost entirely, using other habitats only for resting. Others spent considerably more time in matoral within the exclosure.

Antler Rubbing and Bark Scraping

Antler rubs and bark scrapes from teeth were observed throughout Islote and the exclosures. We analyzed both together because we know from captive observations that they often occurred together and are difficult to distinguish. Of the 20–200 cm height stratum browse plants, trees had the highest frequency of use in all habitats, followed by shrubs; vines, ferns, bamboo and other sturdy vegetation were also utilized in low percentages (Table 17).

Damage to plants ranged from light to severe; the

Table 17. Frequency percentage of antler damage or scraping (with teeth) of the most utilized plant species by habitat in browse plots (20–200 cm strata)

Plant Species	Combined Habitats (n = 235)	Forest (n = 111)	Matoral (n = 124)
Trees	69	85	55
Rhaphithamnus spinosus	17	32	3
Eucryphia cordifolia	14	19	10
Aristotelia chilensis	12	3	19
Embothrium coccineus	4	0	7
Laurelia sempervirens	3	7	0
Laurelia philippiana	3	2	4
Shrubs	18	8	27
Fuchsia magellanica	6	4	9
Corynabutilon uitifolium	5	0	9
Rubus constrictus	4	0	7
Ferns	4	2	6
Blechnum chilense	3	1	5
Number of species utilized	35	28	25

Eldridge, MacNamara, and Pacheco

latter often caused death of the plant. Most damage occurred in the 20–75 cm height range. Although frequency of damage generally occurred in proportion to availability, certain species were preferred: *E. cordifolia*, *L. philippiana*, *R. spinosus* and *A. chilensis*. *L. philippiana* was also preferred for antler rubbing by exotic deer (Ramirez et al., 1981), probably due to its strong odor.

Discussion

Habitat Utilization

Analysis of pudu habitat in the diverse rain forest presented numerous problems, including the sample size of pudu home ranges. Variability in habitat utilization appears common in pudus. Based on observations on Islote and throughout south central Chile it is clear that pudus are found in a variety of habitats, from relatively undisturbed mature forests to totally altered habitats.

In analyzing our data we assumed that introduced pudus selected home ranges typical of resident pudus. It is possible that introduced pudus were forced to accept less desirable habitats by resident pudus but we had no way of measuring such an effect. In captivity, both males and females are highly territorial, often killing pudus newly introduced to an established group. However, we suspect that territoriality was not a significant or unnatural factor in our study because:

1) Islote became a reserve shortly before the study after years of disturbance by humans and dogs, grazing of domestic stock, and logging, which would have reduced the pudu population. This was confirmed by steadily increasing pudu track sightings after the area became a reserve (Courtin et al., 1980). All domestic stock and human disturbance were removed for the study, providing undisturbed habitat previously unavailable which would allow for expansion of the population.

2) The pudu population on Islote was relatively isolated because of the narrow "neck" of the peninsula (Figure 2). Humans, domestic dogs, and extensive pampa surrounding the entrance would inhibit natural immigration and lessen the likelihood of over-saturation from introduced animals.

3) Natural predation by pumas (*Felis concolor araucanus*) probably kept populations below saturation. Pumas entered Islote on two occasions during the study, remaining for extended periods and raising three cubs. We estimated that in 249 days one adult puma removed a minimum of 30 pudus from Islote, and frequency of track sightings dropped dramatically (Courtin et al. 1980).

4) Based on captive observations and observations of wild pudus and tracks (Table 18), it is evident that

Table 18. Percentage of fresh pudu tracks by habitat and size of pudu group

| Habitat | No. of Pudus in group (n = 707) | | | | |
	1	2	3[a]	4	Total
Forest	19	5	2	1	27
Matoral	27	15	10	1	53
Quila	12	1	2	—	15
Pasture	5	—	—	—	5
Total	63	21	14	2	100

[a]Tracks may have been made by two pudus walking along the same trail twice.

pudus do not form herds and rarely if ever occur in groups larger than three. Yearling pudus are forced to establish new territories when expelled by adults. We suspect that these pudus wander until a home range is established, probably in a manner similar to our introduced animals.

5) Pudus are commonly forced to re-establish or emigrate due to natural habitat changes. Bamboo, the dominant component of quila, flowers at 18–20 year intervals (Ramirez et al. 1981). Upon flowering, the entire stand dies rapidly, permitting successional developments (Figure 4). Natural fires also force emigration.

6) The pudus that were introduced to Islote were captured in normal habitat within a few kilometers of the study area.

Our results and others (Ramirez et al. 1981) indicate that the disturbed vegetation communities on Islote are typical of south–central Chile. Pudus have adapted to highly disturbed forests, and although this does not ensure maintenance of high population levels, it is clear that pudus are not dependent on mature forests for all their needs. We believe this adaptability evolved in habitats that were constantly changing due to three kinds of natural events: 1) South–central Chile is tectonically one of the most active areas in the world (Veblen and Ashton, 1978). Forested slopes are regularly cleared during earthquakes, permitting successional developments similar to those resulting from man-made destruction (Veblen and Ashton, 1978). As we have shown, many colonizing plant species are preferred foods of pudu. 2) Dramatic habitat changes are regularly brought about by the flowering of bamboo; and 3) blow-downs are common, resulting from periodic high mountain winds and shallow root systems typical of many canopy species.

We believe pudus could survive even in severely disturbed habitats, such as pampa with some protective cover, except the high predation in these habitats by puma and patagonia fox (*Dusicyon grisseus*), and humans and domestic dogs, and diseases and parasites associated with domestic stock and dogs. Pudus are vulnerable to certain parasites. Diaz et al. (1977) reported that *Cysticerces teniucollis* was observed in large numbers in each of eight pudus examined, including five from our study area. Because the domestic dog is an uncontrolled and widespread intermediate host for this parasite, it poses a serious indirect threat to pudus throughout the range of human occupancy.

Habitat Analysis

Certain aspects of pudu habitat were not analyzed and their importance to pudus can only be surmised. Relief ranged from relatively level, rolling terrain to steep slopes (60°) with rocky outcrops. We do not know if pudus prefer moderate slopes and more level terrain but are forced to utilize steeper slopes because of man's activities. In addition, fallen trees were common throughout Islote, including pudu home ranges. When considered as a vegetation class they occupied from 5 to 15% of the four pudu home ranges in the 20–200 cm stratum. Trunks provide support for numerous vines utilized by pudus. Pudus also walked on fallen trunks to reach preferred browse species, but we do not know if this was common. One pudu was observed utilizing a hollow log for shelter during a severe rainstorm.

There were several problems in the analysis of habitats. 1) Composition of plant species in quila varied substantially among home ranges. Food availability in quila in the home range of the adult resident male was much higher than that of pudu one, making comparison difficult. 2) Transitional areas between habitats, particularly quila and matoral, were difficult to classify. 3) Bamboo and vines were difficult components of pudu habitat to measure. Dense bamboo often had a high cover percent reflecting thick stems as much as leaves. Vine cover was difficult to measure because vine species grew profusely along the forest floor, in trees, shrubs, bamboo and on other vines as well as some ferns. We think vines may have been under-represented as a plant group in the study.

Food Habits

Five aspects of food utilization must be addressed in considering our results: 1) detectability of utilization, 2) seasonal variation in food habits, 3) utilization of pampa vegetation, 4) relative use of herbaceous and shrub strata, and 5) influence of other herbivores.

When utilizing browse estimates or counts, we assumed that use of all plant groups or species was equally detectable. This is probably an invalid assumption, particularly with a small animal like pudu. Herbaceous vegetation was probably underestimated in this study because browsing of small leaves, particularly when completely removed, was difficult to determine. Use of mosses, while probably low, was also difficult to determine. Use of ferns was relatively easy to detect, and therefore may have been over-estimated. These biases might be avoided by use of stomach contents (which was impractical), exclosures (which may not show detectable differences), and fecal analysis (which was attempted but not completed).

Analysis of food habits was conducted during spring and summer when both evergreen and deciduous species were available. We did not address fall and winter food habits, although utilization of the predominantly evergreen native species is probably similar throughout the year. The degree of seasonal variation probably depends on the importance of deciduous, annual and perennial species in the diet, and this undoubtedly varies greatly among pudus depending on availability.

The utilization of pampas by pudus was not determined in this study primarily because it was a minor part of the home ranges of radio-collared pudus. Yet it is evident from our observations on Islote and elsewhere in Chile that pudus commonly use this habitat type. Although observations of captive pudus provide insight into the species most utilized by pudus, we do not know the relative importance of pampa to other habitats as a food source.

We did not attempt to determine relative use of the herb (0–20 cm) stratum and shrub (20–200 cm) stratum and do not know which is most important to pudus, although we suspect the lower stratum is used most. Different techniques used in the two strata precluded comparison.

When measuring pudu food utilization we assumed that all browsing was by pudus and not other herbivores. Becaue few other herbivores were present in Islote during the study we think this is a valid assumption. Potential competitors included the European red deer (10 to 50 animals), fallow deer (1 to 2 animals), and the European hare (*Lepus europeaus*). Each species utilized pampa habitat and surrounding forests generally away from pudu home ranges (Eldridge et al., 1980). Only rarely did these species enter a pudu's home range; so we think the impact on our results, if any, was minor.

Acknowledgments

We thank Dr. Jurgenn Rottmann, Juan G. Ahrntz, and Sergio Courtin L., of the Corporacion Nacional Forestal, Chile, for their enthusiastic support. We thank Drs. Goetz Shurholz, Sterling Miller, Kenneth Raedeke, and Richard Taber for their support and advice. We thank Dr. Dirk Derksen, Dr. Curt Freese, and Melvin Monson of the Fish and Wildlife Service for their approval of the project. We are indebted to Drs. Carlos Ramirez and Roberto Godoy, Universidad Austral, Chile, for their invaluable assistance in plant identification and analysis. Dr. Fredrick Meyer of the U.S. National Arboretum was also helpful. We are particularly indebted to Debbie Amos for her timely assistance in computer programming and statistical analysis. Colleen Handel and Greg Konkle provided valuable programming assistance. We thank John Trapp and Dr. Kenneth Raedeke for critical review of the manuscript. We thank Robert Hawkins, Wildlife Materials Inc., for his assistance in developing an effective radio collar for pudus. We are indebted to the World Wildlife Fund and the New York Zoological Society for funding the project.

We thank the late Helmut and Helly Schilling for enthusiastically providing a study area and logistical support. We owe our thanks to Manuel Pacheco and his family for voluntary assistance, whenever it was needed, in often difficult field conditions. Finally, we thank Connie Dod for her technical assistance in developing figures, and her support throughout the project.

Literature Cited

Almeyda, A.E., and F. Saez S.
1958.   Recoplacion de datos climaticos de Chile y mapas sinopticos respectivos. *Ministerio de Agricultura*. 195 pp.

Brun, R.
1975.   Estructura y potencialided de distintos tipos de bosque nativo en el sur de Chile. *Bosque (Valdivia, Chile)*, 1:6–17.

Canfield, R.
1941.   Application of the line interception method in sampling range vegetation. *Journal of Forestry*, 39:338–394.

Courtin, S.L., N.V. Pacheco, and W.D. Eldridge
1980.   Observaciones de alimentacion, movimentos y preferencias de habitat del puma, en el Islote Pupanco. *Medio Ambiente (Valdivia, Chile)*, 4(2):50–55.

Craighead, J.J., F.C. Craighead, Jr., L. Rugg, and B.W. O'Gara
1973.   Home ranges and activity patterns of non-migratory elk of the Madison drainage herd, as determined by biotelemetry. *Wildlife Monograph, No. 33*. 50 pp.

Daubenmire, R.
1968.   *Plant Communities*. New York, Evanston, and London: Harper & Row.

Diaz, C., H. Rioseco, and V. Cubillos
1978.   Prospeccion y patologia del parasitismo en cervidos autoctonus y exoticos en el sur de Chile. *Boletin Chileno de Parasitologia*, 32:86–89.

Di Castri, F., and Hajek, E.
1976.   Bioclimatologia do Chile. *Viccerectoria Academia de la Universidad Catolica de Chile*, 128 pp.

Everitt, B.S.
1977.   *The Analysis of Contigency Tables*. New York: John J. Wiley and Sons, Inc.

Eldridge, W.D., and N.V. Pacheco
1977.   Capacidades y limitaciones del uso de radiotelemetria en Ciervos en Chile. *Medio Ambiente*, 2:147–148.

Eldridge, W.D., N.V. Pacheco, and S.L. Courtin
1980.   Preferencia de habitat y patrones de actividad del ciervo rojo exotico en el Sur de Chile. *Medio Ambiente*, 4:56–74.

Heezen, K.L., and J.R. Tester
1967.   Evaluation of radio-tracking by triangulation with special reference to deer movements. *Journal of Wildlife Management*, 31:124–141.

Hertzer, R. and C. Ramirez
1980.   El impacto del ciervo rojo sobre la vegetacion del Islote Rupanco (Osorno, Chile). *Medio Ambiente*, 4(2):75–81.

Hershkovitz, P.
1982.   Neotropical Deer (Cervidae) Part 1. Pudus, Genus *Pudu* Gray. *Fieldiana, Zoology*. New Series, No. 11, 86 pp.

Heusser, C.J.
1974.   Vegetation and climate of the southern Chilean Lake District during and since the last interglaciation. *Quarternary Research*, 4:290–315.

Ivlev, V.S.
1961.   *Experimental Ecology of the Feeding of Fishes*. New Haven: Yale University Press.

Junge, C.
1966.   Pudu (*Pudu pudu*) at Chillan Viejo Zoo. *International Zoo Yearbook*, 6:263–264.

Kohls, G.M.
1969.   *Ixodes taglei* n. sp. (Acarina:Ixodidae) a parasite of the deer, *Pudu pudu* (M.) in Chile. *Journal of Medical Entomology*, 6(3):280–283.

Miller, S.D., J. Rottmann, K.J. Raedeke, and R.D. Taber
1983.   Endangered Mammals of Chile: Status and Conservation. *Biological Conservation*, 25:335–352.

Miller, S.D., J. Rottmann, and R.D. Taber
1973.   Dwindling and endangered ungulates of Chile: Vicuna, Lama, Hippocamelus, and Pudu. *Transac-*

tions of the North American Wildlife and Natural Resource Conference, 38:55–68.

Miller, S.D., and J. Rottman
1976.   Guia para el reconocimento de mamiferos Chilenos. Apartado Expedicion a Chile Lord Cochrane, Santiago.

Oberdorfer, E.
1960.   Pflanzensoziologishe Studien in Chile - Ein Vergleich mit Europa. *Flora et Vegetatio Mund.,* 2:1–208.

Pisano, E.
1956.   Esqueme de clasificacion de las comunidades de vegetales de Chile. *Agronomia,* 230–33.

Quintanilla, V.
1974.   La representacion cartografica preliminar de la vegetacion chilena - Un ensayo fitoecologico del Sur de Chile. *Vicerrectoria Academica de la Universidad Catolia de Valparaiso.* 73 pp.

Ramirez, C., R. Godoy, W.D. Eldridge, and N.V. Pacheco
1981.   Impacto ecológico del ciervo rojo sobre el bosque de Olivillo en Osorno, Chile. *Anales del Museo de Historia Natural de Valparaiso,* 14:195–210.

Ramirez, C., and R. Godoy
1981.   Impacto del ciervo rojo Europeo en la flora y vegetacion del Islote, Rupanco, Osorno - Chile. Informe final. Instituto de Botanica Universidad Austral de Chile. Valdivia. 143 pp.

Schmithuesen, J.
1956.   Die raumliche Ordnung der chilenischen Vegetation. *Bonner geographische Abhandlungen,* 17:1–86.

Thomasson, K.
1963.   Araucanian Lakes: Plankton studies in north patagonia with notes on terretrial vegetation. *Acta Phytogrophica Suecica,* 47:1–139.

U.S. Government
1982.   50 CFR. Endangered and threatened wildlife and plants. 17.11, 68 p.

Veblen, T.T., and D.H. Ashton
1978.   Catostrophic influences on the vegetation of the Valdivian Andes, Chile. *Vegetatio,* 36:149–167.

Wikum, D., and G.E. Shanholtzer
1978.   Application of the Braum-Blanquet Cover-Abundance scale for vegetation analysis in land development studies. *Environmental Management,* 2:323–329.

Eldridge, MacNamara, and Pacheco

MARK MACNAMARA
and
WILLIAM ELDRIDGE

New York Zoological Society
Bronx, New York 10460

U.S.D.I.,
Fish and Wildlife Service
1011 East Tudor Road
Anchorage, Alaska
99503

Behavior and Reproduction in Captive Pudu (*Pudu puda*) and Red Brocket (*Mazama americana*), a Descriptive and Comparative Analysis

ABSTRACT

The behavior of solitary and group living pudu (*Pudu puda*) and red brocket (*Mazama americana*) was studied for 546 hours in captivity at the Isla Victoria Breeding Center, Nahuel Huapi National Park, Argentina, and the New York Zoological Park. Deer were observed in home enclosures and in unfamiliar enclosures with or without fresh conspecific urine and feces. Forty behavior patterns were recorded and described, and reproduction in the wild and in captivity is briefly reviewed. The behavior of these two species resembles that of most other cervids, but several patterns are unique to each species. The communication repertory of pudu and brocket includes primarily visual and olfactory patterns, and both share a suite of behavioral characteristics with other small solitary forest ruminants.

Introduction

The small, solitary forest ruminants are the least known members of three families of artiodactyls: the Tragulidae, Bovidae and Cervidae. They include such diverse groups as the chevrotains, *Tragulus* and *Hyemoschus* the duikers, *Cephalophus* and morphologically conservative deer such as the muntjacs, *Muntiacus* tufted deer, *Elaphodus cephalophus* Chinese water deer, *Hydropotes inermis* brocket deer, *Mazama* and pudus, *Pudu*, and exhibit a combination of features that Geist (1971) has termed the "duiker syndrome," Barrette (1975) calls this group of similar but unrelated species the small, solitary forest ruminants (SSFRs). All species that exhibit this adaptive syndrome are small and found in tropical and temperate regions of Asia, Africa and South America.

Mammals, more than any other vertebrates, communicate through two channels that are relatively difficult to study: olfactory and tactile. SSFRs are especially difficult to study in the field because they are also nocturnal/crepuscular, and live in dense habitats in generally remote regions of the world. Only recently, have a few significant studies on SSFRs become available (see Barrette, 1975 and 1977; Dubost, 1968; and Waser, 1975). The last three decades have seen a wealth of ethological studies of mammals, both in nature and in the laboratory. The majority of these studies have concentrated on the more social species, especially primates and gregarious ungulates, and few have been done on SSFRs, leaving a large gap in the knowledge of these species (Barrette, this volume).

Though both pudu and brocket are considered solitary, breeding and care of the young compel them to be at least minimally sociable (Eisenberg, 1966). Many mammalian species go far beyond that minimum, exhibiting elaborate social systems (Eisenberg, 1966). "The social behavior of a species comprises responses to other individuals that ensure a particular pattern of dispersion of the population in space and successful pairing" (Crook and Gartlan, 1966).

This study is a contribution to the knowledge of the behavior of the red brocket deer, *Mazama americana*, and the southern pudu, *Pudu puda*, two small cervids whose ethology is virtually unknown. The primary goal of the study was to describe and compare the behavior patterns and the intraspecific communication systems of these two species.

Background

The literature on free-living brocket and pudu is almost entirely anecdotal and repetitive. The information it provides on the biology of wild pudu and brocket can be summarized briefly as follows:

Pudu

The two species of pudu (*P. puda* and *P. mephistopheles*) are among the smallest of the world's deer, weighing about 9 kg. and standing about 38 cm. high at the shoulder. They have a disjunct range, consisting of the Valdivian Forests of Chile and Argentina (*P. puda*) and the montane paramos of Peru, Columbia and Ecuador (*P. mephistopheles*) (Miller et al., 1973).

The range of the southern pudu, *P. puda*, in Chile extends from the province of Aysén in both primary and coastal mountain ranges. Pudus are also found on the islands of Mocha, Chiloe and others, and isolated populations probably exist in the Andes from the province of Curico southward (Miller et al., 1973). Habitat types similar to those in Chile are found only in the western ranges of the Patagonian subregion (A. Tarak, pers. comm.).

The climate over much of pudu range, particularly the southern half, is characterized by high annual precipitation (2 to 4 meters), mild wet winters, short dry summers, and is classified in the Koppen System as an oceanic west coast climate with a mild Mediterranean influence (Thomasson, 1963). Above altitudes of 1000 meters, much of the winter precipitation is in the form of snow, and altitudes greater than 2000 meters are perpetually snow covered. *P. puda* is found in temperate forests from sea level to about 1700 m. and forages for fruits and succulent sprouts (Miller et al., 1973). Much of its range falls into an area known as the Chilean and Argentine lake district, and the vegetation regions are classified as temperate evergreen rain forests and summer-green deciduous forest. The same area is broadly classified as Northern and Southern Valdivian rain forest by Veblen and Ashton (1978), who report that the temperate rain forest is composed of broad-leaved evergreen trees, among which *Nothofagus dombeyi* predominates. The summer-green deciduous forest is characterized by the deciduous *N. oblique* or *N. alpina*, as well as evergreen trees such as *Laurelia sempervirens* and *Persea lingue*.

Observations by Greer (1965), Osgood (1943) and Wetterberg (1972) indicate that pudu utilize habitats ranging from relatively dry, rocky sites to wet, marshy areas but are sighted infrequently in the highly disturbed central valley and are now restricted to more suitable habitat in the Andean and coastal range foothills.

In the wild, pudu or their tracks are generally seen solitarily or in pairs. Occasionally numerous pudu tracks can be seen, indicating that several pudu may use one area, but not necessarily at the same time (Eldridge et al., this volume).

Male pudu bear antlers which are short and unbranched, and at least in temperate zones, they are

MacNamara and Eldridge

Table 1. Sex, identification, birth date, and origin of study animals

Red Brocket *Mazama americana*

Sex:	Identification:	Birth Date:	Death Date:	Origin:
Male	Group 1 670689	(Arrived N.Y.Z.S. 8-28-67)	10-24-80	Wild Caught: Costa Rica
Female	Group 1 00.694	(Arrived N.Y.Z.S. 6-27-68)	1-18-79	Wild Caught: Costa Rica
Male	Group 1 76120I	7/9/76	—	Born N.Y.Z.P.
Female	Group 2 680695	12/15/68	12/13/79	Born N.Y.Z.P.
Male	Group 2 00.692 W/W	9/7/69	—	Born N.Y.Z.P.
Female	Group 2 751790	9/24/75	—	Born N.Y.Z.P.
Male	Single 731119	12/5/73	5/10/77	Born N.Y.Z.P.
Female	Single 761208	7/20/76	—	Born N.Y.Z.P.

Pudu *Pudu pudu*

Sex:	Identification:	Birth Date:	Death Date:	Origin:
Male	Blue/White	? Adult 1978	—	Born Isla Victoria
Male	Red/White	11-78	—	Born Isla Victoria
Female	White/White	? Adult 1978	—	Born Isla Victoria
Female	Yellow/White	? Adult 1978	—	Born Isla Victoria
Female	Green/White	? Adult 1978	—	Born Isla Victoria

grown and shed annually (Vanoli, 1967; Hick, 1969; Hershkovitz, 1982). In the regions surrounding Osorno, Chile, antlers are dropped in mid-July and are regrown and cleaned of velvet by mid-November, with rut taking place in April, May and June.

Brocket

The brockets, *Mazama,* are similar to pudus, but their form is more typically deer-like, slender-legged and light-bodied. There are four species of brocket: the red, *M. americana* the brown, *M. gouazoubira* the little red, *M. rufina* and the dwarf, *M. chunyi.* The red brocket is found in every South American and Central American country, except Chile, and is consequently the best-known member of the genus and the topic of this investigation. It has been reported to breed throughout the year, but most frequently in July, August and September, which generally coincides with the winter dry season (Gardner, 1971; Whitehead, 1972). Branan (1982, this volume) reports births for red brocket in Suriname during January through April and October through December.

The unbranched antlers are shed at any time of the year, but may be carried longer than a year. The annual antler cycle is governed by levels of male sex hormones in the blood; which in temperate regions, wax and wane seasonally in response to day length (Goss, 1983). In the tropics, where there is less photoperiodic variation, some deer shed antlers sporadically. A transition zone from temperate to tropical antler seasonality may occur at latitudes 10° to 18°

(Goss, 1983). Brocket at the Bronx Zoo breed both when antlers are hard and in velvet, similar to the Indian muntjac, *Muntiacus muntjak* (Barrette, 1977).

Red brockets range from sea level to 3900 m. (Hershkovitz, 1959) and are usually referred to as forest dwellers. However, they frequently invade crop land at night (Osgood, 1912). According to Gardner (1971), they have small, individual ranges, usually circle in a space of a kilometer when hunted, and are considered diurnal and solitary. Pearson (1951) reports that he never saw more than one at a time or the tracks of more than one animal in a place.

Methods

At the beginning of the study in 1977 there were nine brockets at the Bronx Zoo and six pudu at the Isla Victoria pudu breeding center in Nahuel Huapi National Park, Argentina. Between 1977 and 1981, eleven brocket and five pudu died. Table 1 presents the personal history information of the brockets and pudu that were observed.

Animal Enclosures

Pudu

Captive pudu are housed at the Isla Victoria breeding center, consisting of ten solid wooden walled, interconnecting enclosures with an eight-meter-high observation tower, a small food storage area, and a nursery for hand rearing young. Two large pens (10 m. × 30 m.) are used primarily for behavioral observations;

Table 2. Number and percentage (in parentheses) of the eleven most common behavior patterns exhibited by individually housed pudu and brocket under three different cage conditions; 1 = familiar cage; 2 = unfamiliar cage; 3 = unfamiliar cage recently occupied and scent marked by unfamiliar conspecific

| Behavior | Pudu | | | | | | Brocket | | | | | |
| | 1 | | 2 | | 3 | | 1 | | 2 | | 3 | |
	Male	Female	Male	Female	Male	Female	Male	Female	Male	Female	Male	Female
Defecate	12 (3.0)	33 (15.6)	15 (6.9)	49 (16.1)	155 (27.9)	120 (25.1)	50 (25.8)	45 (28.3)	313 (31.4)	174 (34.4)	677 (37.3)	429 (38.5)
Urinate	24 (6.0)	16 (7.6)	32 (14.6)	27 (8.9)	50 (9.0)	56 (11.7)	15 (7.7)	16 (10.1)	141 (14.1)	73 (14.4)	167 (9.2)	115 (10.3)
Smell Feces	15 (3.8)	26 (12.3)	33 (15.1)	46 (15.1)	85 (15.3)	57 (11.9)	25 (12.9)	34 (21.4)	81 (8.1)	127 (25.1)	245 (13.5)	171 (15.3)
Smell Urine	7 (1.8)	11 (5.2)	16 (7.3)	15 (4.9)	71 (12.8)	23 (4.8)	9 (4.6)	13 (8.2)	69 (6.9)	52 (10.3)	66 (3.6)	98 (8.8)
Bite and Lick Object	38 (9.5)	13 (6.2)	14 (6.4)	56 (18.4)	61 (11.0)	48 (10.0)	10 (5.2)	23 (14.5)	70 (7.0)	9 (1.8)	135 (7.4)	0
Forehead Rub	15 (3.8)	0	41 (18.7)	2 (0.7)	10 (1.8)	33 (6.9)	20 (10.3)	0	137 (13.7)	10 (2.0)	85 (4.7)	50 (4.5)
Antler Rub	6 (1.5)	—	17 (7.8)	—	21 (3.8)	—	0	—	0	—	51 (2.8)	—
Paw Ground	0	0	0	0	0	4 (0.8)	0	0	0	0	0	0
Flehmen	4 (1.0)	0	6 (2.7)	0	41 (7.4)	11 (23)	35 (18.0)	3 (1.9)	65 (6.5)	26 (5.1)	367 (20.2)	93 (8.3)
Preorbital Mark	2 (0.5)	0	6 (2.7)	0	23 (4.2)	7 (1.5)	—	—	—	—	—	—
Self Groom	276 (69.2)	112 (53.1)	39 (17.8)	110 (36.1)	38 (6.9)	120 (25.1)	30 (15.5)	25 (15.7)	121 (12.1)	35 (6.9)	24 (1.3)	159 (14.3)
Total	399	211	219	305	555	479	194	159	997	506	1,817	1,115

four 5 m. × 5 m. pens house breeding pairs and are used for behavioral observations; and four small stalls (2.5 m. × 5 m.) are isolation areas for pregnant females, surplus males, or newly-arrived animals. The enclosures contain soil substrates with native grasses and shrubs, and a small "box" shelter for protection during inclement weather (MacNamara, 1981). Early in 1982, the breeding facility was enlarged and an additional ten enclosures were added to accomodate the growing population.

Brocket

Brockets are maintained at the South American Exhibit complex in five interconnecting, indoor enclosures, 4 m. × 4 m. All indoor enclosures connect with four adjacent outdoor pens measuring 15 m. × 12 m. Several animals are exhibited to the public in a 200-square-meter exhibit. All brockets are kept indoors from November to April in cages with concrete floors, solid metal or brick walls, and cage fronts of wire mesh (5 cm × 5 cm.). All cages are bedded with hay or straw. During the summer months, the animals have access to the outdoor corrals which have a sand and rock substrate and are surrounded with two-meter-high wooden walls. The area for public exhibition is enclosed with a two-meter-high concrete wall, has a soil substrate, and is heavily planted with shrubs and small trees. At all times, each group is visually separated from all others by solid partitions.

Behavior Recording Methods

In 1977, I observed two groups of brockets and two single individuals at the Zoo for 350 hours in 219 days. Group I consisted of four animals—two males (M

670689, M 761201) and two females (F 00.694 and F 771030). Group II consisted of one male (M 00.692) and two females (F 680695 and F 751790). The single individuals were (731119) and (761208). In 1978 and 1979 during two one-month visits to Isla Victoria, I observed one group of pudu for 196 hours. The group consisted of two males (M Blue/White, M Red/White) and three females (F White/White, F Yellow/White and F Green/White). During this time, I familiarized myself with and recorded the frequency of the 40 social behavior patterns of each species (5837 observations in pudu; 7371 in brocket (Table 3)). Over 1000 black and white and color 35 mm photographs were taken, using 50–200 mm. lenses. I attempted to record everything the animal did, used binoculars when needed, and wrote observations in notebooks. I also observed individual behavior patterns during 30-minute sampling periods under three different environmental conditions. Behavior descriptions of individually-housed animals are based on 150 observation hours of four male and four female brocket and 150 hours of observation on two male and two female pudu. In order to simulate a more natural and varied environment, individuals were observed in a familiar, or "home" enclosure, an unfamiliar enclosure that was clean of urine and feces from conspecifics, and an unfamiliar enclosure recently inhabited by a conspecific animal and containing feces and urine. Eleven behavior patterns were recorded and quantified (Table 2).

Ethogram

Behavior Patterns of Solitary Living Animals

The individual behaviors described below are included under three categories: maintenance, object-

MacNamara and Eldridge

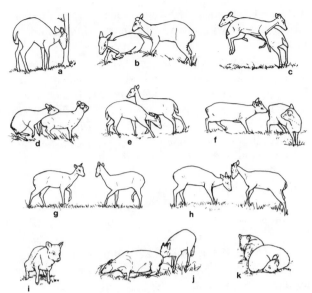

Figure 1. Some behavior patterns of red brocket deer (*Mazama americana*) and pudu (*Pudu puda*) (drawings based on photographs). (a) Forehead rubbing (FR) by a male brocket, (b) A female brocket pawing the back of (PB) of a reclining female, (c) Jump parallel (JP), male brocket in foreground, female behind. (d) Place head on rump (PHR) by a male pudu, (e) poke with antlers (PA) by a male brocket to a female, (F) Rump sniffing (RS) by a male to a female pudu, (g) Broadside display (BD), male brocket at left, female at right, (h) Head high (HH), in a male brocket (right), and Head low (HL) in the animal to the left, (i) Urination (U) posture of a female pudu, (j) Crouching (C) in a female pudu (left) in response to rump sniffing (RS) by a male, (k) the loose curl sleeping posture of two pudu.

oriented contact patterns and scent marking, but the categories are not mutually exclusive. For example, maintenance behaviors such as defecation or forehead rubbing are also included in the scent marking category. Biting, licking and scraping an object with the lower incisors is included as an investigative behavior but may also serve to mark objects and is often performed with scent marking behaviors. Also, some individual behaviors may be performed in a social context when in the presence of a conspecific animal or group.

MAINTENANCE BEHAVIOR

Resting and sleeping: Pudu and brocket assume similar postures when lying down and resting or sleeping. They rest in a loose curl (Hassenberg, 1965) where the long axis of the body is bent into a semicircle (Figure 1k). The dorsoventral axis of the body is oriented in the vertical plane, and the animal then bears most of its weight on its hind feet, forefeet and rostrum. This position is typical of fawns. In the stretch position on the other hand the long axis of the body is more or less straight. The front feet are often tucked under the body, but sometimes may extend in front of the ani-

mal. This posture exposes more body surface and apparently permits the animal to radiate excess body heat. Deep sleep is rare among the Cervidae (Barrette, 1975). Pudu and brocket occasionally fell asleep, but always less than a minute at any given time.

Both species often rest in a standing position, remaining motionless, staring straight ahead, and with the head in an upward, relaxed position, and the legs straight.

Walking, foraging and investigating: The importance of olfaction in pudus and brockets becomes obvious after watching individuals move about their enclosures. Both species constantly sniff the ground, objects, and the walls of their enclosures. Unless they are moving rapidly from one place to another, their nose is kept at or below shoulder level and they frequently stop to sample the environment by sniffing, licking, biting or chewing objects. Singly-housed pudu and brocket spent 56.5% and 27.9% of the time respectively investigating the environment while moving about the enclosure. During these active periods, the deer continuously *lick* and *bite objects* (pudu, BO: M 113, F 117; brocket, BO: M 215, F 32). BO was similar in both species, was usually preceded by nasal contact; the object was licked until visibly wet, and was sniffed and scraped with the lower incisors. Parts of the face, forehead and antlers were often rubbed on the same spot. Frequently marked areas became worn and visibly different from other areas in the environment. Both sexes of each species often perform *flehmen* after smelling or licking an object, the ground, or their own or a conspecific animal's urine or feces (pudu, F: M 51, F 11; brocket, F: m 567, F 122). BO and F both increase dramatically when individuals are placed in an unfamiliar environment or one recently occupied by conspecifics (Table 2). When not following a well-worn path both species walk in a zig-zag fashion and frequently sniff, which probably improves the chances of finding scattered food items and scent spots. Both species also forage intermittently as they explore their enclosure. Pudu frequently rear on their hind legs to eat leaves of fruit beyond reach and in this posture bend over shrubs or bamboo to feed on the leaves. M. Rumboll (pers. comm.) reports he has seen pudu actually "climbing" stalks of bamboo and foraging for leaves while completely off the ground. Brocket deer were never seen to rear on their hind legs while foraging.

Comfort Movements: Like other cervids, pudus and brockets lick and comb their fur with their incisors, scratch with their hind hooves, and shake their head and bodies. Both species often vigorously scratch the inside of their ears with their hind hooves and stretch with one hind leg extended backward. Neither species was seen to wallow in dust or mud but would often rub their necks and heads against trees or other objects in their enclosure. All of these behaviors were included in *self-grooming* (pudu, SG: M 353, F 342; brocket, SG: M 175, F 219).

Forehead rubbing (FR) (Figure 1a) and *antler rubbing* (AR) may be considered comfort movements but are described more fully as object-oriented contact behaviors. Both males and females rubbed objects and parts of their bodies with their foreheads. Males often alternated rubbing with their foreheads and rubbing with their antlers. Males rub objects with their antlers in all stages of growth, even during early growth when velvet antlers are small (< 2 cm.). Antler rubbing consists of up and down movements of the head while pressing them against an object. In most cases, the anterior and medial sides and tips of the antlers are rubbed; the antler is less frequently hooked around an object to rub the lateral and posterior surfaces.

Elimination Postures: Elimination postures of pudu and brocket are similar and differ little from Barrette's (1975) description of elimination postures in muntjac. When defecating abundantly, both species do so in the posture characteristic of their sex. Male pudu and brocket assume an inconspicuous posture, hind legs slightly extended out and backward and the tail up. Females of both species crouch slightly and lift the tail when defecating. During urination, males of both species stretch the hind legs out and squat slightly. Females of both species assume an exaggerated squat occasionally touching the ground, similar to the posture of a female dog (Figure 1i). Both pudu and brocket employ several methods to deposit scents on objects. They *bite, lick* and *scrape objects* with their lower incisors (BO), *rub objects* with their foreheads (FR) and/or antlers (AR), *paw the ground* (PG), and *deposit feces* (D) *and urine* (U) on the ground. In addition, pudu *rub the face and preorbital glands* on objects (PM), but brockets which lack preorbital glands were never seen rubbing objects with this part of the face.

Males and females of both species bite, lick and scrape objects in their enclosures as described earlier. Most contact sites were between 45 cm. and 60 cm. above the ground and were conspicuous, and the same spot was used frequently. Individuals moved about their enclosures and paused at specific contact spots, usually trees, fence posts, or corners or edges of wooden or metal shelters. Many spots became well worn and stained from the constant rubbing, scraping and licking. On several occasions, brocket and pudu mouthed and chewed fallen twigs and branches. Often, BO was combined with FR and AR and was usually alternated. Forehead rubbing was slow and gentle while exploring a new enclosure. Forehead rubbing became vigorous in both sexes during agonistic interactions with unfamiliar individuals, and objects were rubbed rapidly, and sometimes forcefully struck

with the forehead. One female brocket, when excited, struck a post with such force that a thud could be heard.

All males were observed antler rubbing. Individuals in hard antler always AR when placed in an unfamiliar or scent-marked cage, and the behavior appeared to serve a marking function. Exploring males moved slowly around an enclosure, and methodically smelled, licked and rubbed fence posts, trees, and corners of shelters with the forehead and antlers. Antler rubbing usually was directed to well-worn rubbing spots. Both species thrashed bushes, grass or hay, and one male of each species frequently stabbed hay or mowed grass and carried it around on its head. AR in brockets occasionally became vigorous, and one individual (M 670689) gored a stump, pressing hard enough to mark the wood and broke off a piece of antler in the process.

Pawing the ground was rarely observed in individually-housed pudu and never was observed in individually-housed brocket. PG was only seen in one female pudu (F Black/Yellow) on entering a strange cage. (See "Behavior patterns of animals living in groups" for a full description.)

Forehead rub (pudu, FR: M 22, F 0; brocket, FR: M 596, F 37), as described in a previous section, occurred in both species but was not observed in female pudu. Volkman and Ralls (1973) also described this behavior in captive red brockets and suggested it is a means of scent deposition by the sudoriferous glands in the forehead. The presence of these glands has been confirmed by W. Branan (pers. comm.). Unlike these authors I observed both sexes to FR, including males in velvet.

Pudu males FR infrequently, and this is usually a part of AR or PM.

Antler rub (pudu AR: M 74: brocket, AR: M 439) occurred in bouts consisting of one to 25 vertical strokes. At times, AR becomes very vigorous, and objects are gored with enough force to dent the wood. Pudu males stripped the bark of small saplings in their enclosure during the rutting season.

Brocket males rubbed objects when antlers were in all stages of growth, even when they were less than 2 cm. long and in velvet.

Preorbital marking occurred only in the pudu (PM: M 31, F 7). In this species of pudu, the preorbital glands are large, the external opening conspicuous, and the lacrimal fossa correspondingly deep (Hershkovitz, 1982). In marking with preorbital glands, an animal went to an object it seemed to recognize, sniffed and sometimes licked it, and then carefully brought its cheek and opened preorbital glands close to the area, applied its face and brushed the gland on it lightly. Usually, conspicuous objects were marked at the ani-

MacNamara and Eldridge

mal's shoulder level or higher (e.g., branches, fence posts, and corners of their shelters). Occasionally, they stretched to mark areas several centimeters above their head. After marking the area was sniffed and licked while the gland was open, and the process was repeated up to nine times. Preorbital glands were also opened during dominance displays, courtship and when alarmed, disturbed or entering a new enclosure. When investigating a new enclosure or unfamiliar conspecific the preoribtal glands were opened and closed in a pulsating rhythm, but object marking did not take place.

Behavior Patterns of Animals Living in Groups

SCENT MARKING AND OBJECT-ORIENTED PATTERNS

(1) *Pawing the Ground* (PG): Males and females of both species pawed the ground by repeatedly striking and pulling the forefoot sharply across the substrate, digging into the soil and sometimes uprooting grass.

Pudu (of both sexes) were observed to PG when investigating a new and unfamiliar area. A dominant female would PG near and occasionally strike a prone female in an attempt to displace it. Dominant males would PG while staring at males or females before aggressive encounters. One male (Blue/White) pawed the ground violently, tore up clumps of grass and alternately thrashed the ground with his antlers while standing a few feet in front of a female.

PG was performed by male brocket deer before and during agonistic encounters. Both sexes would PG when investigating new areas or unfamiliar objects.

PG is associated with agonistic behavior in both species but may also be a form of scent marking. The interdigital glands in the forefeet of *Mazama* and *Pudu* are deep and associated with a well-developed saccule (Flerov, 1952; Hershkovitz, 1958).

(2) *Forehead Rub* (FR): The front of the head between the eyes and antlers in males and the base of the ears in females was pressed and moved vertically up and down against objects. FR occurs in both species but was not observed in female pudu.

Pudu males FR infrequently (FR: M 22). It was always associated with investigating a new area or an object previously marked by itself or a conspecific. FR was usually combined with antler rubbing or preorbital marking.

(3) *Antler Rub* (AR): AR consisted of vertical head movements while pressing the antlers against an object.

Pudu AR only in hard antler or when cleaning off velvet.

During agonistic encounters with males or females AR became more vigorous, and trees, gate posts, or shelters were attacked with antlers. Male 670689

would vigorously AR and gore objects when approached by an observer. If the observer remained in the area, he would eventually attempt to gore his cage mates. While cleaning the animals' exhibit, a keeper was punctured in the shin and knocked down by this male.

(4) *Thrash* (T): Thrashing consists of swinging the head from side to side and forcefully striking the ground or vegetation with the head or antlers. T occurred in the males of both species and was performed once by female brocket 751790. This was an aggressive animal that forehead rubbed prior to agonistic encounters; in one case, she thrashed a small shrub.

Males usually thrashed in view of other animals in the enclosure during threat displays or agonistic encounters; 81% of all thrashing recorded by male pudu and 95% of all thrashing by male brocket occurred during agonistic encounters or dominance displays.

(5) *Bite and Lick Object* (BO): BO was done in the presence of conspecifics or alone and was seen primarily during investigation of new areas and objects, or objects that had been previously licked. The behavior may be a type of scent marking, but it does not seem to have any other social significance. It was generally ignored by cagemates.

(6) *Preorbital Mark* (PM): PM undoubtedly serves to scent mark certain areas, and both sexes frequently alternated marking an object with sniffing, licking and flehmen. It was also combined with FR, AR, BO and object aggression.

(7) *Stamp with Forefeet* (SFF): Both species struck the ground sharply and alternately with the front feet or with both feet simultaneously. Though often performed in the presence of conspecifics generally SFF was not directed to group members. It appeared most often when alarmed, when a strange object was encountered, or when exploring an unfamiliar environment.

SFF may deposit interdigital scent. Both pudu and brocket possess interdigital glands, but the presence of scent following SFF has not been confirmed.

(8) *Urination* (U), and (9) *Defecation* (D): Deposition of urine and feces is considered scent marking. Both occur in the presence of other individuals, and the specific postures described earlier may have communicative value. Alvarez, et al. (1975) suggested that defecation and tail posture in fallow deer, *Dama dama*, may serve as a signal of alarm. As described previously, both pudu and brocket urinate and defecate large quantities in typical postures and sparingly with minimal postural adjustments while walking. This behavior probably spreads urine and fecal scent over a larger area. Both species sniffed dung piles and urine spots, often performed flehmen, and would U and D on the same spot. Pudu visit the same areas and defecate in one or two spots, which, if not disturbed, form

large piles of dung (latrines). Brockets, unlike pudu, did not defecate in latrines. Males of both species were attracted to females urinating in a squatting position, and smelled and licked the ano-genital area, and performed flehmen.

Companion-Oriented Patterns

NON-CONTACT INVESTIGATIVE PATTERNS

(10) *Follow* (F): Adult and young males F females and other males while foraging or investigation a new enclosure. Followers slowly walked a meter or more behind a conspecific, and often smelled and licked objects, and marked areas contacted by the individual being followed. Flehmen was often observed during F, and urine and feces were deposited in the same spots used by the individual being followed. Females generally F other females and rarely males. When a female was in estrus, F became more intense and led to chasing and eventually courtship behavior.

(11) *Force up Without Contact* (FU): Dominant males and females FU subordinate individuals that are bedded down. The dominant animal slowly approached, stood close by (usually less than 30 cm.) and stared at the reclining individual who got up, avoided eye contact, and moved away, and was often followed. Barrette (1975) frequently observed muntjacs being chased from their beds (506 observations), usually by more dominant individuals. Both males and females were forced up and out of their resting places by either males or females.

(12) *Smell Urine* (SU), and (13) *Smell Feces* (SF): When walking, foraging or investigating, each sex of both species SU and SF when urine or fecal pellets were encountered.

Pudu males, while following females, stopped to SU and SF, flehmen, sometimes D and/or U, and then walked rapidly to catch up to the female who was moving away. The dominant male pudu (Blue/White) was observed to SU and SF more than any other individual in the group and usually when following a female, or when visiting a frequently used marked latrine. All three females would SF and SU from each other and the two males in the group.

Brocket females rarely SU and were only observed to SF at large dung piles. Brocket male 670689 followed female 00.694 and SU 32 times and SF 15 times prior to courtship and successful breeding. Male brockets smelled fecal deposits 314 times, of which 82% were less than 30 minutes old and 18% that were older than 30 minutes.

Submissive Patterns

(14) *Withdrawal* (W): Depending on circumstances, both species walked, trotted, ran or bounded away in response to an approaching individual. When chased hard or frightened, subordinate animals crouched low and attempted to crawl behind or under any available shelter to escape.

When unreceptive to approaching males, female pudu crouched low to the ground and remained motionless or crawled away in this posture. Subordinate female pudu ran from dominant females until exhausted and then crouched or lay flat against the ground. Males were never observed to crawl, but young males would lie down flat when frightened.

Subordinate brockets did not crawl away from approaching individuals but would run and attempt to hide when frightened by an approaching animal.

(15) *Lying Down Flat* (LDF): This is the most extreme form of submission. The legs were folded under the body, which was pressed against the ground; the head and neck were extended horizontally, with the nose pointing straight ahead and the chin resting on the ground. LDF was often observed in young or subordinate animals when approached by a dominant animal or when exhausted after a chase. This behavior was also seen in infant pudu when frightened. One three-day-old pudu fawn standing next to its mother dropped to the LDF position when I entered the enclosure. The mother ran away, and the fawn remained motionless in the middle of the corral. LDF was assumed from a standing position or a crouched position. As a dominant animal approached, the subordinate animal often tried to be inconspicuous by first crouching and then lowering itself closer to the ground in the LDF position.

(16) *Crouch* (CR) (Figure 1j): This is a submissive posture in which the inferior animal remained motionless when approached by a dominant animal. During CR, the tail was down and often tightly tucked between the hind legs. Male brockets were never observed to CR, and females would CR only when approached by dominant females. Female pudu, however, frequently CR when approached by males and females.

(17) *Submissive Stand* (SS): This behavior was seen in both species and consisted of a lowered head and slightly crouched posture while remaining motionless and avoiding eye contact. It was the mildest form of submission and usually preceded the more submissive CR, LDF or withdrawal.

Aggressive and Threat Patterns

(18) *Antler Pointing* (AP): Antler pointing is usually interpreted as a threat behavior and is found in most antlered cervids (e.g., Geist, 1966; Schaller, 1967; McCullough, 1969; Barrette, 1975; Wemmer et al., 1983). Males directed AP to either sex by facing the oppo-

nent, lowering the head, and pointing antlers in the opponent's direction. Pudu and brocket AP more frequently toward males than females and this usually preceded violent body contact. The individual pointed its antlers at conspecifics while approaching or standing while the recipient withdrew in response or stood motionless until the opponent approached. Brocket male 670689 AP males 75% and females 25% of the time. Pudu male (Blue/White) AP only males (Red/White) and always preceding an agonistic encounter.

(19) *Head High* (HH) (Figure 1h, right): During HH, the animal remained motionless with legs stiffly erect and the body at maximum height. The head is held erect with the nose pointing slightly upward. HH occurs in both species (more commonly in brocket), in both sexes, and was seen in both single sex and mixed sex encounters. HH was usually performed close to and facing an opponent and generally during initial encounters. Brockets stood perpendicular to and with the head held directly over the opponent's back. This pattern often preceded foreleg kick or rearing on hind legs and jumping.

(20) *Head Low* (HL) (Figure 1h, left): During HL, the animal remained motionless with legs stiffly erect and body at maximum height. The head was held lower than the horizontal body axis with the nose pointing forward and parallel with the ground. HL appears to be an intention movement to butt or poke an opponent and often preceded an aggressive interaction.

(21) *Broadside Display* (BD) (Figure 1b): This is a common display pattern in hoofed animals that consists of a lateral presentation and may be interpreted as a means of blocking another's path (lateral T-position) (Walther, 1984) or as an initiation of fighting from a lateral position. The BD combines a broadside orientation with exaggerated posturing, the erection of hair and special positions of tails, ears, and horns or antlers. During a BD, pudu arched their backs, placed their front feet back under the body and shifted their weight to the hind legs. The tail was held horizontal to the ground while the ears were either vertically erect or pointed slightly forward. The preorbital glands were open and sometimes pulsating. Brocket also strongly arched their backs and straightened their legs and feet, apparently to maximize their height. The tail was often held erect and was arched and clamped tightly over the back. The head was held high or low. When two brockets BD simultaneously, they assumed a parallel or reverse parallel orientation to each other. Often two displaying animals slowly circled each other in a stiff-legged gait while maintaining a parallel position. The pudu were not observed to mutually BD.

(22) *Standing Parallel* (SP), and (23) *Jumping Parallel*

(JP) (Figure 1c): These behavior patterns were observed only in brocket deer. They were mutual, precontact behaviors that often preceded aggressive interactions. SP occurred when two animals stood within a meter of each other. Body orientation was head to head or the reverse parallel position and the posture was erect on stiff legs, with the head held high and the nose pointed forward or slightly upward. Remaining parallel, one or both animals would rear up on the hind legs. The animals circled each other alternately walking, jumping, but making no contact. If neither animal withdrew, JP usually became more violent, and the deer began to jump toward one another, struck with their feet and body and also tried to jump over each other, while lashing out with their fore and hind feet.

(24) *Chase* (C): Dominant pudu or brocket chased subordinates at a full run many times around an enclosure. During the chase, both animals were silent or made squeaking sounds and panted loudly. The chaser generally moved more slowly in a smaller radius, and thereby forced the subordinate to run faster and further. When the pursued animal tired, it panted and salivated, and attempted to hide and occasionally made a squealing sound. While chasing, pudu performed two behavior patterns not observed in brocket.

(25) *Strike with Forefeet* (SWF): Rising up on the hind legs and striking an opponent that was attempting to withdraw, and (26) *Attempt to Bite* (AB): Chasing with mouth open and trying to bite an opponent when it was within a meter.

The remaining six patterns were agonistic, involved violent contact, and thus were potentially damaging. These six contact patterns preceded or occurred during fights, or preceded retreat (=W) of a subordinate.

(27) *Chest on Back* (CB): Seen only in pudu, one animal placed a foreleg over the back of its opponent and with its chest on the opponent's back, forced it to withdraw or lie down.

(28) *Poke with Nose* (PN): During an agonistic encounter, both pudu and brocket males and pudu females poked subordinates with the nose, occasionally lifting the animal off its feet. PN was directed toward both sexes.

(29) *Poke with Antlers* (PA) (Figure 1e): Males also poked subordinates with their antlers, usually in the side or rump. PA varied in intensity from a harmless slow, gentle push with the antler tips to a rapid, sometimes damaging jab. PA was directed toward both subordinate males and females.

(30) *Butt* (B): Bumping the head against the body or head of an opponent was observed primarily during female-female interactions. B was seen once in a brocket male and was not observed in male pudu.

(31) *Paw Back* (PB) (Figure 1b): Dominant animals

violently struck the backside and rump of prone subordinates with the forefeet. Usually seen during aggressive encounters, PB forced the subordinate up and away from the aggressor.

(32) *Bite* (Bi): Male and female pudu and female brocket bit the rump, sides and sometimes the midback region when chasing or forcing a subordinate out of a resting posture.

(33) *Fighting* (F): Fighting was complex and consisted of a series of elements seen only during violent agonistic interaction that were often damaging to both individuals. Numerous fights were recorded on film and a complete analysis of fighting behavior will be given elsewhere. Fighting generally occurred between unfamiliar individuals or between familiar animals only when they were introduced to a strange environment or enclosure marked by unfamiliar conspecific animals. Males and females of both species jumped and kicked with the forelegs and slammed their heads into the bodies of opponents. Fights between males of both species included jumping and kicking, thrashing with the forelegs, chasing and antler-to-antler contact. One pudu male was gored in the left foreleg during a fight. No brocket males were gored, but numerous scrapes around the head and neck were inflicted from antlers. Female pudu were never observed to fight with adult males and were always submissive or ignored them. However, they were very aggressive toward other females and young males (less than one year) and chased, bit, kicked and pawed the backs of subordinate individuals. Female brocket fought with females, as well as males. Fighting opponents chased each other, jumped at and over one another, and kicked and thrashed with all four feet. After the fight, the dominant animal walked about the enclosure while the subordinate withdrew, and lay down and attempted to hide.

Sexual Patterns

(34) *Low Stretch* (LS): The low stretch consisted of several elements, and was directed only by males to females. In a LS approach, the male walked rapidly toward a female, usually from behind with his neck at or below the horizontal position, nose forward, and tongue flicking in and out of his mouth. Sometimes squealing sounds were produced. As male pudu got closer to the female the pace became slower; he then assumed a crouched position and slinked toward the female with neck extended upward and nose pointed straight ahead toward the rump of the female. Brocket approached females in a similar fashion but did not lower their bodies or slink. They walked rapidly and slightly lowered the head to the same level as the female's rump.

(35) *Tongue Flick* (TF): Tongue flicking was seen in both species and consisted of rapidly moving the tongue in and out of the mouth when the head was pointed toward the female. TF was only seen in sexually interested males when following a female in LS or when standing near a female.

(36) *Rump Sniff* (RS) (Figure 1f and j): Males and females of both species smelled the rump and perianal region of conspecifics.

(37) *Vulva Lick* (VL): Males VL when following or standing close to a female that appeared to be in estrus and did not withdraw. VL often stimulated the female to urinate.

(38) *Taste Urine* (TU): While the female urinated, the male placed his nose and tongue in the urine to taste it.

(39) *Flehmen* (F): Males usually performed flehmen in response to urine. F was usually performed by males during sexual encounters, but was observed in both sexes during investigation of new environments or individuals.

(40) *Place Head on Rump* (PHR) (Figure 1e): If a female was near estrus, the male often placed his head on the female's rump or back after VL and F. PHR is equivalent to what Barrette (1975, 1977) termed chin, which occurs in many cervids (Kurt, 1968; McCullough, 1969; Wemmer et al., 1983). PHR often occurred before mounting; the female usually walked away from the male, and PHR was repeated. This behavior was seen only in males and was observed more frequently in pudu than brocket.

(41) *Attempt Mount* (AM): The male stood up on his hind legs and attempted to straddle the female with the front legs. The female either withdrew or crouched and prevented a successful mount.

(42) *Mount* (M): The correct posture just prior to and during copulation. The penis was extended and the male's weight was supported by the female and his hind legs.

Investigative Contact

(43) *Sniff, Lick Head* (SLH): Smelling and licking the head (face, antlers, ears and neck) was often a mutual behavior and occurred nose to nose or when two individuals were standing next to each other.

(44) *Sniff, Lick Body* (SLB): Sniffing and licking all other parts of the body (legs, sides, belly and tail).

Reproduction

Brocket

According to Walker (1975), Asdell (1964), and Dansie and Wince (1970), brocket deer are aseasonal breeders and young are born throughout the year. Of 38 births at the Bronx Zoo (See Table 3) young have been born

Table 3. Distribution of births of captive pudu at Isla Victoria, Nahuel Huapi National Park, Argentina, and brocket at New York Zoological Park, Bronx, New York

MONTH:	Jan.	Feb.	March	April	May	June	July	August	Sept.	Oct.	Nov.	Dec.	TOTAL:
Brocket Births:	2	1	3	2	2	3	7	3	5	1	4	5	38
Pudu Births:	4	2	0	0	0	0	0	0	0	1	8	7	22

Table 4. Electro-ejaculated semen characteristics of a red brocket (I.D. No. 781001) at the Bronx Zoo

Date	Age Year	Volume of Semen Collected (ml)	Motility %	Status[1] 0–5	Sperm[2] X 10⁹/ml	% Normal[3]
Dec.	2	0.1	50	4	0.2	93
Nov.	3	0.8	70	4		88
Feb.	4	0.3	75	5	3.2	92
April	4	0.9	70	5	1.3	91
May	4	0.6	80	5		
June	4	1.0	80	5	0.8	92
July	4	0.8	80	5		91

1. Forward progression—5 equals the fastest forward movement
2. Concentration (sperm/ml)
3. % Normal sperm

Excerpted from: Stover, et al., 1984

in every month of the year. Field reports indicate spring and summer births. Murie (1932) recorded an apparently full-term fetus from a female shot on April 1 in Guatemala. Dalquest (1953) reported a single embryo on May 19 in Mexico, and Miller (1930) a near full-term fetus in July in the Mato Grosso. Working in Peru, Gardner (1971) stated that breeding occurs throughout the year, and does and fawns are found in almost any month. However, he stated that the most concentrated mating activity is in July, August and September, generally coinciding with the winter dry season. The greatest number of young fawns was found in February, March and April. This coincides with the observed period of most concentrated rut (July–September). The gestation period ranges from 222 to 228 days.

The number of young per birth is given as two by Goodwin (1946) in Costa Rica. However, Dubost (1968) and Asdel (1964) state that only one fawn is born. According to Lydekker (1898), Walker (1975), Whitehead (1972), one or two may be born, but twins

are rare. All 37 births at the Bronx Zoo have been single.

At the Bronx Zoo, breeding has been observed in all seasons. Males do not show any seasonal rut and irregularly shed and regrow antlers, in some cases, retaining a pair of hard antlers for over a year. Males are also capable of breeding females when in either "hard" or "soft" antler. Semen samples collected from male 781001 by electroejaculation (Table 4) during seven months of the year contained normal sperm in all samples (Stover, et al., 1984).

Pudu

In the wild, the majority of fawns are born between November and January, coinciding with the spring of the southern hemisphere, after a gestation of about seven months (202–233 days) (Hershkovitz, 1982). A fall rut in April, May and June corresponds to the November through January births. Antlers are shed and regrown seasonally each year. Neumeyer (in

Schmidt, 1944) reports six births in Neuquén, Argentina, from November through January. Two births in the Osorno-Llanquihue region of Chile, recorded by Vanoli (1967), occurred in November and December. Hershkovitz (1982) lists eighteen births in Western European zoos that occurred in eight different months, with eleven occurring in May. At the Isla Victoria breeding facility, twenty-two births occurred in the austral spring and summer months (Table 3).

Three females arriving at the Bronx Zoo in April, 1983, from Santiago, Chile, produced young in November and December of the same year and in March of the following year.

Discussion

Deer were observed in familiar and unfamiliar enclosures in order to simulate natural conditions, and as expected the frequency of most behavior patterns in both species greatly increased when the animals moved into the unfamiliar enclosure, self grooming was the exception; it decreased or increased only slightly (Table 2).

In a familiar enclosure, both pudu and brocket were less active and spent most of the time resting, foraging, ruminating or grooming. Grooming was the most common behavior pattern exhibited by pudu under familiar conditions. In males and females 69.2% and 53.1% of all behavior patterns were grooming patterns. Investigative behaviors, such as smelling urine and feces, and biting and licking objects, were infrequent and were exhibited during foraging activity. Marking behaviors were also infrequent; defecation and urination constituted only 3% and 6% of the total patterns observed for males and 15.6% and 7.6% for females in their "home" or familiar cage. Under these conditions, urination and defecation were normal, complete evacuations, performed in the typical elimination posture and thus were considered maintenance behaviors. When in an unfamiliar cage previously occupied and marked by conspecifics, investigative and marking behaviors increased dramatically. Under these conditions urination and defecation were considered forms of marking behavior; the frequency was increased and the deposit was sparing after investigation of marks left by conspecifics. In male pudu, defecation became the most common behavior pattern under these conditions and occurred as many as 155 times. Other forms of marking, such as antler rub and preorbital mark, also increased when in an unfamiliar cage.

Brocket behaved similarly to pudu as they moved from their home area into an unfamiliar enclosure. However, defecation rates and urination rates were more frequent in brocket than in pudu under condi-

tion 3 (Table 2). Male brockets defecated 677 times during 25 hours of observation in a cage marked by conspecifics. These feces were generally not well formed pellets but small, yellowish-colored pasty blobs. Forehead rubbing was a frequent marking pattern, occurring 35 times in males and 50 times in females.

Table 5 presents behaviors that are associated with social encounters and interactions with the environment. The first nine of the 44 patterns listed are directed toward the environment, may serve to mark objects or redirect aggression. Alternatively, they may function simply as maintenance behaviors. Marking the environment usually advertises an animal's presence, sex or social status. In deer, these patterns include wallowing, use of dung piles, marking of objects with glandular secretions, scraping the ground or objects with feet, teeth or antlers, and specialized urination.

Pawing the ground is common in artiodactyls (Walther, 1984). Cervids generally paw and scrape the ground before wallowing or when smelling a conspecific's urine or feces. Wallowing preceded by pawing the ground occurs in *Alces* and *Cervus*. Most cervids, however, do not wallow. In most deer object aggression, such as antler rubbing and thrashing vegetation, is strongly associated with pawing the ground. Both pudu and brocket paw the ground most frequently when encountering a strange individual or unfamiliar environment and this behavior is often associated with object aggression, although as mentioned previously, PG may also function as a form of scent marking.

The glands used for object marking in cervids are most commonly located on the head, such as the subauricular glands of pronghorn, frontal glands of roe deer, sudoriferous glands of the forehead of black-tailed deer (Quay and Muller-Schwarze, 1970) and brocket deer (W. Branan, pers. comm.), and preorbital glands in nearly all cervids, including pudu (see Muller-Schwarze, this volume). According to Walther (1984), only the males of certain cervids mark with preorbital glands. Pudu differ in that both male and female rub objects with their preorbital glands.

Although antler rubbing, thrashing and stamping with the forefeet may leave olfactory and visual marks in the environment, they are often associated with object aggression. Biting and licking objects as seen in brocket and pudu may also function to deposit scent or evaluate marks left by other individuals. Robin (1979) observed that eating sometimes occurs in connection with object marking, and that animals took marked or unmarked objects in their mouths, hastily chewed them, and swallowed or spit them out. Saliva is a secretion available to all ungulates but has not

MacNamara and Eldridge

Table 5. Number and percentage (in parentheses) of behavior patterns observed in captive groups of pudu and brocket

Behavior:	Pudu: Male:		Pudu: Female:		Brocket: Male:		Brocket: Female:	
Paw Groud	16	(0.5)	10	(0.4)	36	(0.7)	18	(0.9)
Forehead Rub	22	(0.6)	0		596	(11.2)	37	(1.8)
Antler Rub	74	(2.1)	—		439	(8.3)	—	
Thrash	26	(0.7)	—		19	(0.4)	1	(0.1)
Bite Object	126	(3.6)	71	(3.1)	212	(4.0)	57	(2.8)
Preorbital Mark	42	(1.2)	28	(1.2)	—		—	
Stamp with Front Feet	12	(0.3)	30	(1.3)	7	(0.1)	18	(0.9)
Urinate	297	(8.5)	236	(10.1)	315	(5.9)	306	(14.9)
Defecate	576	(16.4)	320	(13.8)	795	(15.0)	389	(18.9)
Follow	268	(7.6)	52	(2.2)	123	(2.3)	20	(1.0)
Force Up Without Contact	29	(0.8)	9	(0.4)	10	(0.2)	17	(0.8)
Smell Urine	116	(3.3)	96	(4.1)	121	(2.3)	21	(1.0)
Smell Feces	121	(3.5)	91	(3.9)	314	(5.9)	56	(2.7)
Withdraw	267	(7.6)	452	(19.4)	204	(3.8)	213	(10.3)
Lie Down Flat	34	(1.0)	68	(2.9)	38	(0.7)	37	(1.8)
Crouch	19	(0.5)	102	(4.4)	0		18	(0.9)
Submissive Stand	16	(0.5)	61	(2.6)	6	(0.1)	19	(0.9)
Antler Point	8	(0.2)	—		29	(0.6)	—	
Head High	29	(0.8)	35	(1.5)	142	(2.7)	63	(3.1)
Head Low	15	(0.5)	4	(0.2)	58	(1.1)	17	(0.8)
Broadside Display	17	(0.5)	8	(0.4)	97	(1.8)	41	(2.0)
Stand Parallel	0		0		5	(0.1)	6	(0.3)
Jump Parallel	0		0		8	(0.2)	24	(1.2)
Chase	218	(6.2)	159	(6.8)	215	(4.1)	153	(7.4)
Strike With Forefeet	62	(1.8)	93	(4.0)	13	(0.3)	21	(1.0)
Attempt to Bite	12	(0.3)	29	(1.3)	0		0	
Chest on Back	45	(1.3)	16	(0.7)	0		0	
Poke With Nose	49	(1.4)	34	(1.5)	6	(0.1)	0	
Poke With Antler	23	(0.7)	—		41	(0.8)	—	
Butt	0		8	(0.4)	1		6	(0.3)
Paw Back	6	(0.2)	40	(1.7)	7	(0.1)	13	(0.6)
Bite	10	(0.3)	4	(0.2)	0		2	(0.1)
Fight	7	(0.2)	12	(0.6)	8	(0.1)	6	(0.3)
Low Stretch	39	(1.1)	0		16	(0.2)	0	
Tongue Flick	97	(2.8)	6	(0.3)	127	(2.4)	23	(1.2)
Rump Sniff	106	(3.0)	23	(1.0)	103	(1.9)	39	(1.9)
Vulva Lick	94	(2.7)	—		126	(2.4)	—	
Taste Urine	30	(0.9)	4	(0.2)	10	(0.2)	0	
Flehmen	83	(2.4)	7	(0.3)	378	(7.1)	20	(1.0)
Place Head on Rump	128	(3.7)	0		5	(0.1)	0	
Attempt Mount	103	(2.9)	0		40	(0.8)	6	(0.3)
Mount	22	(0.6)	0		75	(1.4)	0	
Sniff, Lick Head	63	(1.8)	70	(3.0)	282	(5.3)	238	(11.6)
Sniff, Lick Body	183	(5.2)	149	(6.4)	284	(5.4)	155	(7.5)
Total Number of Patterns:	3,510		2,327		5,311		2,060	
Number of Pattern Types:	40		31		39		31	

been shown to be used for environmental marking in most species (Walther, 1984), although Beuerle (1975) described saliva marking in wild boar (*Sus scrofa*).

Marking with excrement is widespread among mammals, but its communicative value is not always clear. Since urination and defecation are normal physiological processes, they can only be considered to have communicative importance when conspecifics react to them or when an animal deposits feces and urine in definite locations or when the process is performed in a specialized way. According to Walther (1984), cervids usually do not use feces or urine as a special means of marking. However, in both pudu and brocket, defecation and urination occur frequently in both individually-housed and group-living captive individuals (Tables 2 and 5). Pudu resemble muntjac (Barrette, 1975) and musk deer (Frädrich, 1966) which also form localized dung piles in producing a specialized feces when encountering a conspecific's marks.

During social interactions, four types of submissive behavior were observed. Withdrawal is the most common form of submission in both pudu and brocket and is generally performed by inferior individuals avoiding a dominant animal and usually results in the termination of an interaction unless followed or chased by the dominant animal. In contrast to withdrawal, the remaining three submissive patterns are displays that enable an inferior animal to remain in the presence of a dominant animal despite its aggressiveness. Lying down flat and crouching are the most extreme forms of submission observed in pudu and brocket and are the opposite of dominance or threat displays and indicate the acceptance of the inferior role. Both patterns, however, may be more common in captive than free-ranging animals due to the inability to escape from dominating animals. Submissive standing was observed in both species and is the mildest form of submission. Occasionally, however, it preceded aggression. The lowered head and outstretched neck of the subordinate animal afforded good position for defense against attack.

The four submissive patterns are often done in response to one or more of the sixteen aggressive patterns that were observed. Of the sixteen patterns, nine involve direct and sometimes violent body contact.

Use of the antlers and associated displays in pudu and brocket resemble those of other cervids. The broadside display (BD) seen in male and female pudu and brocket is very similar and resembles BD found in other cervids. However, several patterns are unique. Head High (HH) for example is a common aggressive pattern in deer which precedes antler contact and combat. In brocket, however, head high (HH) frequently precedes aggressive jumps at an opponent.

HH also precedes fighting in pudu, but jumping at an opponent is rarely seen. Rather the animal attempts to put its chest on the back of the opponent. HH in males may function to display the antlers and is interpreted as an antler display for many other species of cervid (Walther, 1984). Muntjacs are an interesting exception among the cervids and have no "head high" threat and do not rear on the hind legs and strike with the forefeet (Barrette, 1975).

Brocket, but not pudu, were observed to mutually BD in a parallel or a reverse parallel position and would begin circling, always keeping their flanks toward each other. The mutual BD was sometimes preceded by or followed by standing parallel (SP) or jumping parallel (JP). These patterns are non-contact patterns that function to intimidate an opponent without overt fighting. However, if neither animal withdraws, the circling and jumping intensifies and usually results in a violent interaction.

Chasing was the most commonly observed aggressive pattern in both species. The pursued individual would attempt to withdraw by running and hiding and avoid any contact with pursuer. During a chase, pudu, but not brocket, were observed to try to strike with the forefeet and attempt to bite the withdrawing animal. Six other agonistic behaviors observed involved violent contact and preceded a fight or withdrawal of a subordinate or actually occurred during a fight.

In pudu and brocket, as in many other cervids, a sexual encounter usually develops up to a point where the female urinates and the male tests the urine by tasting it, presumably to determine the female's reproductive condition. If the female is not receptive, the encounter usually ends, or an aggressive interaction results from violation of the female's individual space by the approaching male. If a female is in estrus, however, sexual activity continues to copulation.

Sexual encounters often start with the male approaching and sniffing, and licking the female's genital area. Many ungulates and most cervid males approach females in a low stretch posture. This is the case in *Muntiacus* (Barrette, 1975), *Alces*, *Odocoileus* (Geist, 1963), *Axis* (Schaller, 1967), *Rangifer* (Pruitt, 1960), *Capreolus* (Kurt, 1968), *Cervus elaphus* (Geist, 1966), and *Elaphurus* (Wemmer et al., 1983).

Pudu approach females in the low stretch similar to other deer. However, unlike most other species, as the male pudu gets close to the female, his pace becomes slower, he lowers his body in an exaggerated crouching position with belly almost touching the ground, and he slinks forward with neck and head extended pointing upward toward the female's rump. Like other cervids male brockets approach rapidly and lower the head slightly to the level of the female's rump.

MacNamara and Eldridge

Courtship behavior in male pudu and brocket includes a number of patterns which probably assess the receptivity of the female, such as rump sniff, vulva lick, taste urine and flehmen. All of these behaviors are typically seen during sexual encounters, but also take place during investigation of strange individuals or investigation of unfamiliar environments. Females rump sniff males and other females. If a female appears to be receptive, the male generally follows her closely and may perform any of the following patterns in various combinations prior to actual copulations: place head on rump, foreleg kick (not observed in brocket), tongue flick and attempt mount. When males place head on the rump or attempt a mount, the female either withdraws or stands and allows copulation to occur. Placing head on rump is equivalent to what Barrette (1975) terms chin, which occurs in many cervids (Kurt, 1968; McCullough, 1969). A detailed analysis of courtship in pudu and brocket will be given in a later paper.

In summary, the courtship and estrous behavior of brocket and pudu resembles that of most other cervids. However, male pudu exhibit a pronounced submissive crouch while approaching females regardless of reproductive condition.

Literature Cited

Alvarez, F., F. Braza, and A. Norzagaray
1975. The use of the rump patch in the fallow deer (*Dama dama*). *Behaviour*, 56:298–308.

Asdell, A.A.
1964. *Patterns of mammalian reproduction*. 2nd Edition. London: Constable and Company.

Barrette, C.
1975. Social behavior of muntjacs. Unpublished Ph.D. dissertation, University of Calgary, Canada, 234 pp.

1977. The social behavior of captive muntjacs, *Muntiacus reevesi* (Ogilby 1939). *Zeitschrift für Tierpsychologie*, 43:188–213.

1987. The comparative behavior and ecology of chevrotains, musk deer, and morphologically conservative deer. This volume.

Beuerle, W.
1975. Freilanduntersuchungen zum Kampf-und Sexualverhalten des europäischen Wildschweines (*Sus scrofa* L.). *Zeitschrift für Tierpsychologie*, 39:211–258.

Burckhardt, D.
1958. Observations sur la vie sociale du Cerf (*Cervus elaphus*) an Parc National Suisse. *Mammalia*, 22:226–243.

Crook, J.H., and S.S. Gartlan
1966. Evolution of primate societies. *Nature* (London), 210:1200–1230.

Dalquest, W.W.
1953. Mammals of the Mexican State of San Luis Potosi. *Louisiana State University Studies, Biological Series*, 1:1–229.

Dansie, O.
1970. *Muntjac*. Leed, England: The British Deer Society.

Dubost, G.
1968b. Les niches écologiques des forêts tropicales sudaméricaines et africaines, sources de convergences remarquables entre ronqeurs et artiodactyles. *Terre et Vie*, 22:3–28.

Eisenberg, J.F.
1966. The social organization of mammals. *Handbuch der Zoologie*, 8(39):1–92.

Eldridge, W., M. MacNamara, and N. Pacheco
This volume. Activity patterns and habitat utilization of pudus (*Pudu puda*).

Flerov, K.K.
1952. *Fauna of the U.S.S.R., Mammals, Musk Deer and Deer* (Volume 1, No. 2). Academy of Sciences of the U.S.S.R. Israel Program of Scientific Translations.

Frädrich, H.
1966. Einige Verhaltensbeobachtungen am Moschustier (*Moschus moschiferus* L.) *Zoologische Garten*, 33:65–78.

Gardner, A.L.
1971. Postpartum estrus in a red brocket deer, *Mazama americana*, from Peru. *Journal of Mammalogy*, 52(3):623–624.

Geist, V.
1963. On the behavior of the North American moose (*Alces alces andersoni*, Peterson 1950) in British Columbia. *Behaviour*, 20(3–4):377–416.

1966. Ethological observations on some North American cervids. *Zoologische Beiträge* (N.F.), 2:219–250.

1971. The relation of social evolution and dispersal in Old World deer during the Pleistocene. *Quarternary Research*, 1:283–315.

Greer, J.K.
1965. Mammals of Malleco Province, Chile. *Publication of Michigan State University, Museum of Biology Series*, 3:49–152.

Hassenberg, L.
1965. *Ruhe und Schlaf bei Säugetieren*. Wittenberg Lutherstadt: Ziemsen.

Hershkovitz, P.
1958. The metatarsal glands in white-tailed deer and related forms of the neotropical region. *Mammalia*, 22:537–546.

1959. A new species of South American brocket, genus *Mazama* (Cervidae). *Proceedings of the Biological Society of Washington*, 72:93–96.

1982. Neotropical deer (Cervidae) Part I Pudus, Genus *Pudu* Gray. *Fieldiana Zoology*, New Series, No. 11:1–86.

Hick, U.
1969. Successful raising of a pudu *Pudu pudu* at Cologne Zoo. *International Zoo Yearbook*, 9:110–112.

Kurt, F.
1968. *Das Sozialverhalten des Rehes Capreolus capreolus L., eine Feldstudie.* Mammalia Depicta. Hamburg and Berlin: Paul Parey Verlag.

Lydekker, R.
1898. *The deer of all lands: A history of the family Cervidae living and extinct.* London: Rowland Ward Ltd.

MacNamara, M.
1981. Project pudu. *Oryx*, 16:185–186.

McCullough, D.R.
1969. The tule elk, its history, behavior and ecology. *University of California Publications in Zoology*, 88:1–209.

Miller, F.W.
1930. Mammals from southern Mato Grosso. *Journal of Mammalogy*, 11:10–22.

Miller, S., J. Rottmann, and R.D. Taber
1973. Dwindling and endangered ungulates of Chile: *Vicugna, Lama, Hippocamelus* and *Pudu. Transactions of the North American Wildlife andNatural Resources Conference*, 38:55-68.

Muller-Schwarze, D.
1987. Evolution of cervid olfactory communication. This volume.

Müller-Using, D., and R. Schloeth
1967. Das Verhalten der Hirsche (Cervidae). *Handbuch der Zoologie*, 8 Band, 43 Lieferung, 10(28):1–60.

Murie, A.
1932. Mammals from Guatemala and British Honduras. *Miscellaneous Publications of the Museum of Zoology, University of Michigan*, 26:1–30.

Osgood, W.H.
1912. Mammals from Western Venezuela and Eastern Colombia. *Field Museum of Natural History Publication No. 155*, Zoological Series, Vol. 10(5):33–66.

1943. The mammals of Chile. *Field Museum of Zoology Series*, 30(542):1–268.

Pearson, O.P.
1951. Mammals in the highlands of Southern Peru. *Bulletin of the Museum of Comparative Zoology*, 106:115–174.

Pruitt, W.O.
1960. Behavior of the Barren-Ground Caribou. *Biological Publication of the University of Alaska*, No. 3:1–44.

Quay, W.B., and D. Muller-Schwarze
1970. Functional histology of integumentory glandular regions in black-tailed deer (*Odocoileus hemionus columbianus*). *Journal of Mammalogy*, 51:675–694.

Robin, N.P.
1979. *Zum Verhalten des Kleinkantschils (Tragulus javanicus,* Osbeck 1765). Zürich: Juris.

Schaller, G.B.
1967. *The deer and the tiger.* Chicago: University of Chicago Press.

Schmidt, H.
1944. *Argentinische Säugetiere.* Buenos Aires: Imprenta Mercier.

Stover, J., W.K. Westom, and M.C. Patterson
1984. Comparative semen analysis of thirteen species of Artiodactyla at the New York Zoological Park. *Proceedings of the 26th International Symposium of Diseases of Zoo and Wild Animals.* Brno, Czechoslovakia, pp. 73–81.

Struhsaker, T.T.
1967. Behavior of elk (*Cervus canadensis*) during the rut. *Zeitschrift für Tierpsychologie*, 24:80–114.

Thomasson, K.
1963. Araucanian Lakes: Plankton Studies in North Patagonia with notes on terrestrial vegetation. *Acta Phytogeographica Suecica*, 47:1–139.

Vanoli, T.
1967. Beobachtungen an Pudus, *Mazama pudu* (Molina, 1782). *Säugetierkundliche Mitteilungen*, 15:155–163.

Veblen, T.T., and D.H. Ashton
1978. Catastrophic influences on the vegetation of the Valdivian Andes, Chile. *Vegetatio*, 36(3):149–167.

Volkman, N., and K. Ralls
1973. Scent marking in the red brocket, *Mazama americana. Zoologica*, 58:55–57.

Walker, E.P.
1975. *Mammals of the World.* 3rd Edition. Baltimore: The Johns Hopkins Press.

Walther, F.R.
1984. *Communication and Expression in Hoofed Mammals.* Bloomington: Indiana University Press.

Waser, P.
1975. Spatial associations in a "solitary" ungulate; the bushbuck *Tragelaphus scriptus* (Pallas). *Zeitschrift für Tierpsychologie*, 37:24–36.

Wemmer, C., L.R. Collins, B.B. Beck, and B. Leja
1983. Ethogram (Chapter 8) in *The biology and management of an extinct species. Pere David's deer*, edited by B. Beck and C. Wemmer, pp. 91–125. Park Ridge, New Jersey: Noyes Publications.

Wetterberg, G.B.
1972.   Pudu in a Chilean National Park. *Oryx,* 11(5):347–351.

Whitehead, G.K.
1972.   *Deer of the World.* London: Constable and Company.

JUAN R. MERKT
Department of Zoology and Institute of Animal Resource
Ecology
University of British Columbia
Vancouver, B.C. Canada
V6T 1W5

Reproductive Seasonality and Grouping Patterns of the North Andean Deer or Taruca (*Hippocamelus antisensis*) in Southern Peru

ABSTRACT

During a study on the ecology and behavior of the North Andean deer or taruca (*Hippocamelus antisensis*) in southern Peru, I collected information on the deer's reproductive cycle and grouping patterns. Tarucas bred seasonally. Most small fawns were observed towards the end of the rainy season between February and April; mating was most common in June, during the dry season; and antler-shedding in males occurred in September/October, at the onset of the rainy season. The deer occupied open, mountainous terrain and lived in social groups. Solitary animals were uncommon, though males tended to be more solitary and formed smaller groups than did females. Mixed-sex aggregations were largest and most common throughout the year, except during the fawning period. The seasonal grouping patterns of tarucas resemble those of some mountain Caprinae.

Introduction

The North Andean deer or taruca (*Hippocamelus antisensis*) is a medium-sized deer inhabiting the high Andes between northern Argentina and Chile and northern Peru (Cabrera, 1961; Grimwood, 1969; I.U.C.N., 1982). A description of external characteristics of the deer can be found in Pearson (1951), Roe and Rees (1976), Walker (1964), and Whitehead (1972).

Tarucas are currently categorized as "vulnerable" (I.U.C.N., 1982) but no systematic surveys of the species have been carried out to ascertain their present status. Information on their biology and ecology is sketchy, speculative, and in some cases full of anecdotal or contradictory accounts (Roe, 1974). That is not surprising because *Hippocamelus* has never been the subject of comprehensive field studies.

In 1980 and 1981 I carried out a study on the ecology and behavior of tarucas in southern Peru. The purposes of the study were: 1) to describe and quantify the reproductive cycle, social structure, behavior, and activity patterns of the taruca; 2) to describe and quantify seasonal and daily patterns of distribution of the deer within the ecological range of the study area and; 3) to compare the habitat distribution of *Hippocamelus* with that of other ungulates of the area. In this paper I present the first results of this study and concentrate on some aspects of the reproductive cycle and seasonal grouping patterns of *Hippocamelus antisensis*. A fuller report detailing the social organization of the taruca is presented elsewhere (Merkt, 1985). As did Roe and Rees (1976) I have adopted the common name taruca, the correct local name used in Peru for the species, to distinguish it from the huemul (*H. bisulcus*) presently found in central and southern Chile and neighboring areas of Argentina.

Materials and Methods

Study Area

This study was carried out at La Raya (about 14°30′S, 70°58′W) in southern Peru (Figure 1). This site is accessible, has a relatively large deer population, and has a large and well equipped research and range management station, the Centro Nacional de Camelidos Sudamericanos. My observations were made within the station's 120 km² area, though the main study area was limited to about 75 km². The region is part of the Puna, a treeless, high Andean formation dominated by perennial bunch grasses. Here, the eastern and central cordilleras of the Andes come together forming a "knot" at the divide between the Amazon and Lake Titicaca basins, and the terrain is very rugged with steep-sided mountains surrounding a broad main valley and smaller side valleys.

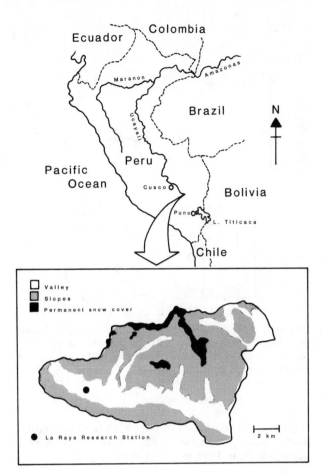

Figure 1. Map of Peru and the study area at La Raya.

Rocky outcrops or permanent ice fields cover most of the upper slopes and mountain tops. Within the altitudinal range of the study area (4070 to 5470 m) three ecological zones occur: Paramo Subalpino (subalpine meadow), Tundra Alpina (alpine tundra), and Nival (glacial) (O.N.E.R.N., 1965).

The vegetation consists mainly of tall bunchgrasses (*Festuca, Stipa,* and *Calamagrostis* spp) which give cover to smaller graminoids, forbs, mosses, and lichens. Marshy vegetation, dominated by *Distichia muscoides,* is common along the well-irrigated valley bottoms and on some slopes where water filters out from the melting glaciers. Shrubs (*Senecio, Baccharis* spp) are largely absent, except in a few sites along the upper limit of the vegetation.

The climate in the highlands of southern Peru has been described by O.N.E.R.N. (1965), Pearson (1951), and Troll (1968). Annual precipitation of about 900 mm is strongly seasonal, with a wet season in October through April and a dry season in May through Sep-

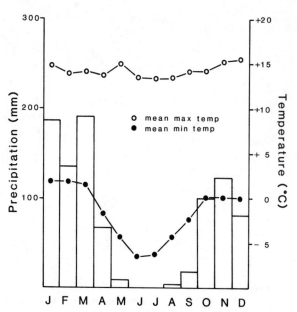

Figure 2. Mean monthly precipitation (mm), and mean maximum and minimum temperatures (°C) at La Raya. Means were estimated from 1980 and 1981 daily records. Precipitation is shown by bars.

Table 1. Mean number of days with freezing night temperatures (≤ 0°C) at La Raya, Peru. Means were estimated from 1980 and 1981 daily records.

Month	Number of days with night frosts
January	5
February	4
March	5
April	26
May	31
June	30
July	31
August	30
September	23
October	17
November	13
December	16

tember (Figure 2). Most of this precipitation is in the form of rain or hail (below 4,800 m) and snow or hail (above 4,800 m).

Both the altitude and the precipitation regime greatly influence temperature patterns in these tropical highlands. Mean annual temperatures range from 6°C at 4,100 m to 0°C above 4,800 m (O.N.E.R.N., 1965) and fluctuate little with season. Large diurnal fluctuations do occur. The intense solar radiation at these elevations results in relatively warm days and cold nights. This is especially true during the dry season, a time of clear skies and heavy night frosts (Table 1). During the rainy season, diurnal fluctuations in temperature are less marked. Night temperatures are usually above freezing but days tend to be cold because of overcast skies. Figure 2 shows mean monthly maximum and minimum temperatures at La Raya.

The main human activity at La Raya involves research and management of the alpaca (*Lama pacos*). Over 5000 alpacas are maintained in herds averaging 340 animals. The station also supports about 400 llamas (*Lama glama*) and a few domestic sheep, cattle, and horses. Most of the highland pastures of Peru are used for extensive alpaca grazing, but unlike La Raya, these lands are community owned and in some areas domestic sheep outnumber alpacas. Beside *Hippocamelus*, large wild mammals include the vicuña (*Lama vicugna*), the Andean fox (*Dusicyon culpaeus andinus*), the mountain cat (*Felis colocolo*), and the occasional cougar (*Felis concolor*). Among small mammals, wild guinea pigs (*Cavia tschudii*), and mountain viscachas (*Lagidium peruanum*) are common in restricted areas. Also present are the grison (*Grison* sp), the skunk (*Conepatus rex*), and about 6 species of small rodents of which *Akodon* and *Phyllotis* spp are the most common (Peggy Stern, pers. comm.).

Study Animals and Data Acquisition

Field work began in November 1980 and ended in December 1981, though some preliminary observations were made between August and October 1980. The area was covered on horseback, and tarucas were observed mainly from regular search paths and lookout points. Weather and time permitting, groups were observed for as long as they remained in sight with the aid of binoculars and a 20–45× spotting scope. All observations were made in daylight between 0500 and 1800 hrs. Tarucas were observed at distances of 30 to 1500 m, though most observations were within a range of 100–1,000 m.

Animals were classified into 5 broad age/sex classes: adult males, adult females, yearling males, yearling females, and fawns. Adult males were distinguished by their large body size, large antlers (rear tine up to twice the ear length), long rostrum, and

Females   **Males**

Figure 3. Facial markings of eight known individuals. Also note antler shapes in adult males.

thick neck. Adult females were smaller than adult males, lacked antlers, and had long rostra but thin necks. Yearlings, with short rostra and thin necks, were smaller than adult males and females. Though most yearling males had only a pair of short spikes, some had forked antlers. Fawns were distinguished by their small size and their unspotted dark grey coats. About a month after birth, however, fawns started to acquire the sandy-brown pelage characteristic of older animals.

I was eventually able to identify specific individuals by the markings on their heads and, in the case of males, also by the size and shape of their antlers. Figure 3 illustrates the facial patterns and antlers of selected known individuals.

Once a group was located, I recorded the presence of any known individual, the number and classes of deer within the group, their activities at 5-min intervals, any behavioral interaction between two animals, and a range of environmental variables at the beginning, end, and every hour during the observation period. Throughout the study I conducted 175 observation periods ranging from less than 5-min to 8-hrs in duration. On average observations lasted approximately 1 hour. Since deer density was relatively low (about 1.2 animals/km²) groups were found widely apart, and it was rare to have more than one group in sight. However, if a group being monitored changed in size and/or composition (because of animals joining or leaving the group) it was treated as a new group. Thus, I had 208 group sightings which included 310 observations of adult males, 500 of adult females, 264 of yearlings, and 112 of fawns. In addition, I observed 19 groups whose composition could not be determined for age/sex classes.

Data Analysis

Data from 1980 and 1981 showed the same pattern and, unless otherwise specified, have been combined. Sample sizes were small in some months, and all group data have been pooled into 2-month periods. From July 1981 on, I could not distinguish yearling females born in 1980 from adult females. Yearling males, however, were distinguished as such until the end of the study in December 1981. Fawns born in early 1981 were considered yearlings from September 1981 on or, if males, when they grew their first set of antlers.

Results

Tarucas were observed between 4100 and 5200 m elevation mainly on mountain slopes, especially near rock outcrops, or on mountain tops. The deer were non-migratory and used year-round home ranges.

Reproduction

Here I consider only three events related to reproduction: 1) fawning (births), determined by the relative number of fawn sightings; 2) mating activity, defined by the frequency and nature of male/female interactions; and 3) the antler cycle in males.

To estimate the relative number of fawns born per month I used the number of fawn sightings/100 adult females. I distinguished small fawns from older fawns by pelage color and sized relative to their mother's. In 1981, fawns appeared between February and April, with a sharp peak in March, late in the rainy season (Figure 4). About 83% of all small fawn sightings (29/35) occurred between 20 February and 31 March.

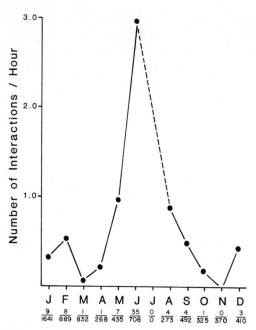

Figure 4. Relative number of small fawns (<1 month old) expressed as fawn sightings per 100 adult females. November sightings correspond to 1980 only, the remaining to 1981.

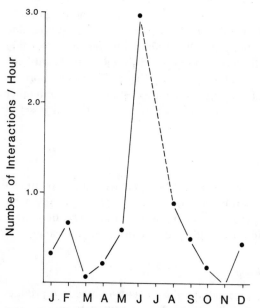

Figure 5. Number of adult male/female interactions per hour of observation. Only observations of 5-min or longer have been included. Ratios represent number of interactions over total monthly observation time (in min). No data were obtained in July. Data from 1980 and 1981 have been combined.

These "birth" dates, however, are likely to be biased, and peak number of births may have occurred earlier in February (see below). Only 2 fawns were observed in November 1980, outside the main fawning season.

In the analysis of male/female interactions, only observations of 5-min or longer were used. A male/female interaction was defined as any sequence of behavioral displays or contact behaviors between adult sexes. They usually were initiated by a male approaching a female and were often ended by the female moving away or by the male mounting the female. A total of 70 interactions were recorded during 64 observation periods totaling 107 hrs. 51 min.

The highest number of interactions took place in June in the middle of the dry season (Figure 5). The number of interactions was lowest in March and April when both sexes were most segregated. Male/female interactions were also rare in October and November when males had dropped their antlers (see below).

The proportion of male/female interactions that led to mounting was also highest in June (Figure 6). Most of the time I could not distinguish between successful and attempted mounts. The former might also have been relatively more frequent in June. Although I did not have any observation periods of 5-min or longer during July, breeding may have continued into July. All males were in velvet (Figure 6).

Extrapolation from peak of mating activity in June to peak of relative number of sightings of small fawns in March gives an approximate gestation period of 270 days. This figure is among the highest of any cervids (see Sadleir, this volume; Eisenberg, 1981: Appendix 4). The most likely explanation is that births actually occurred before taruca fawns were first observed. In most cervids, young remain hidden for some time after birth (De Vos, 1967; Lent, 1974). From evidence presented elsewhere (Merkt, 1985), I estimate peak number of births in February, with the birth season extending from January to March. This correction yields an approximate gestation period of 240 days, a figure more compatible with those known for other deer.

Data on antler condition was based on 453 male sightings (adults and yearlings pooled together). The antler cycle was highly synchronized and seasonal (Figure 7). The proportion of males with clean antlers increased from 30% in January to 100% in May, though all adult males had already shed the velvet in February. During the dry season, when mating activity was most intense (Figures 5 and 6), all males had clean antlers (Figure 7). By September males were dropping antlers, and some new antlers were in velvet. By December all males were in velvet (Figure 7).

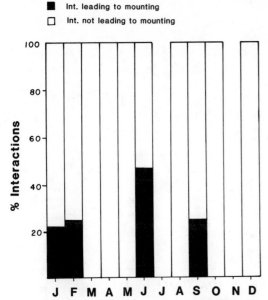

Figure 6. Percentage of adult male/female interactions that led and did not lead to mounting of females by males. No data were obtained in July and no interactions occurred in November. Data from 1980 and 1981 have been combined.

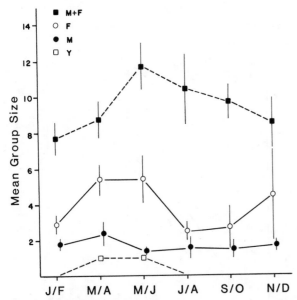

Figure 7. Percentage of males (adults and yearlings pooled together) with no antlers (NA), antlers in velvet (V), or antlers free of velvet (NV). n = number of male sightings. Data from 1980 and 1981 have been combined.

In summary, 94% of births occurred towards the end of the rainy season; mating took place during the driest months; and antler shedding in males was observed during the onset of the rainy season. Therefore, the reproductive cycle in *Hippocamelus antisensis* is markedly associated with seasonal climatic patterns.

Grouping Patterns

Mean group size for the entire study was 6.4 (±0.36 SE) deer, and groups ranged from 1 to 31 animals. Mean size varied little seasonally but was consistently smaller (5.0–5.3 deer) just prior to and during fawning (January–April) and larger (7.3–7.6 deer) during the rest of the year (Table 2).

Groups were classed into 3 group-types of various age/sex compositions (Table 3). Mixed groups contained both adult males and adult females and also included yearlings and/or fawns most of the time (Table 4). Male groups consisted of one or more adult males and rarely included yearlings of either sex. Fawns never occurred in male groups (Table 4). Female groups contained one or more adult females and often included fawns and/or yearlings (Table 4). Yearlings never associated to form all-yearling groups.

Table 2. Mean group size of *Hippocamelus antisensis* at La Raya throughout the year. Data from 1980 and 1981 have been combined and pooled into 2-month periods.

Month	Mean size (± SE)	Number of groups
January/February	5.3 (± 0.60)	61
March/April	5.0 (± 0.59)	43
May/June	7.4 (± 0.89)	57
July/August	7.3 (± 1.50)	20
September/October	7.3 (± 1.01)	21
November/December	7.6 (± 1.16)	26

Table 3. Group types of *Hippocamelus antisensis* encountered at La Raya between August 1980 and December 1981*

Group type	$\bar{X}$ (± SE)	% (n)
Mixed groups	9.5 (± 0.54)	52.9 (108)
Male groups	1.8 (± 0.21)	22.5 (46)
Female groups	4.2 (± 0.46)	24.5 (50)

*Only groups of known composition are included.

Table 4. Total number of groups of *Hippocamelus antisensis* with and without young (yearlings and fawns pooled together) for the entire study

Group type	Groups with young	Groups without young
Mixed groups	81	26
Male groups	4*	42
Female groups	28	22

*These groups contained no fawns.

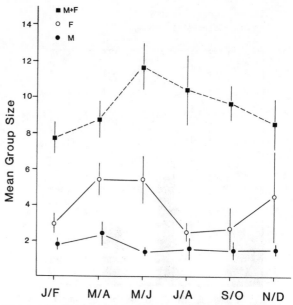

Figure 8. Mean size of mixed-sex (M+F), female (F), and male (M) groups. Vertical lines represent ± SE. Data from 1980 and 1981 have been combined and pooled into 2-month periods.

I consider four aspects of grouping patterns: 1) the mean size of the four group-types during the year; 2) changes in the proportions of group-types over the year; 3) the age-sex distribution of individual deer among the different group-types; and 4) the temporal stability of these groups.

Mixed groups were by far the largest throughout the year though they were relatively smaller ($\bar{x} = 7.7$–8.8 deer) before and during fawning (January–April) and larger ($\bar{x} = 10.4$–11.7 deer) during the dry season (May–August) when mating took place (Figure 8). On average mixed groups consisted of 2.4 adult males, 3.9 adult females, and, if present, 2.8 young (fawns and yearlings pooled together).

Male groups were very stable in size and consisted mainly of 1 solitary male or 2 adult males (Figure 8). The largest male group contained 5 adult males. Yearlings of either sex occurred with adult males only on four occasions between January and April. Female groups were relatively larger ($\bar{x} = 5.4$ deer) during and after fawning (March–June) and smaller ($\bar{x} = 2.5$–4.5 deer) during the rest of the year (Figure 8). On average they consisted of 2.5 females and, if present, 3.2 young (fawns and yearlings pooled together). All observations of yearlings unaccompanied by adults occurred between March and June; in all cases, yearlings were solitary (Figure 8).

Mixed groups were present year-round and, with the exception of January–April, were the most common group-type (Figure 9). The low proportion of mixed groups before and during fawning was associated with a slight increase in the proportion of male groups and a marked increase in the proportion of female groups. After fawning, mixed groups became progressively more common and by November/December, when all males had dropped their antlers or were in velvet, almost 80% of all groups were mixed.

The manner in which different sex/age classes associated with different group-types varied seasonally (Figures 10–15). Adult males spent most of the time in

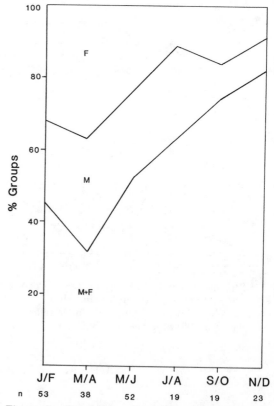

Figure 9. Percentage of mixed-sex (M+F), male (M), female (F) groups. n = number of groups. Data from 1980 and 1981 have been combined and pooled into 2-month periods.

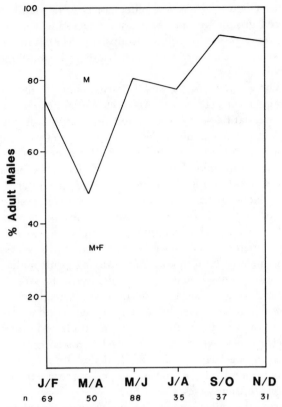

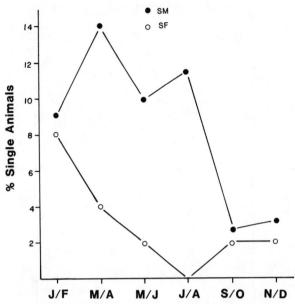

Figure 12. Percentage of single adult males (SM) and adult females (SF). Single females accompanied by their fawns have been included. Data from 1980 and 1981 have been combined and pooled into 2-month periods.

Figure 10. Relative number of adult males in mixed-sex (M+F) and male (M) groups. n = number of male sightings. Data from 1980 and 1981 have been combined and pooled into 2-month periods.

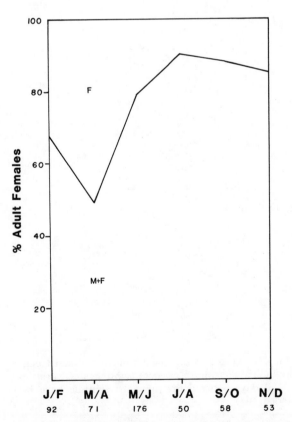

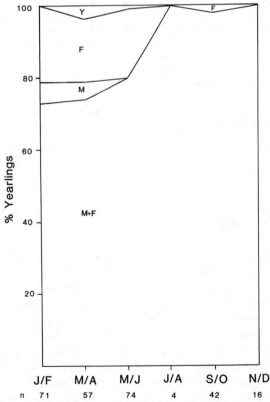

Figure 13. Relative number of yearlings (males and females pooled together) in mixed-sex (M+F), male (M), and female (F) groups. n = number of yearling sightings. Data from 1980 and 1981 have been combined and pooled into 2-month periods. (y = lone yearlings.)

Figure 11. Relative number of adult females in mixed-sex (M+F) and female (F) groups. n = number of female sightings. Data from 1980 and 1981 have been combined and pooled into 2-month periods.

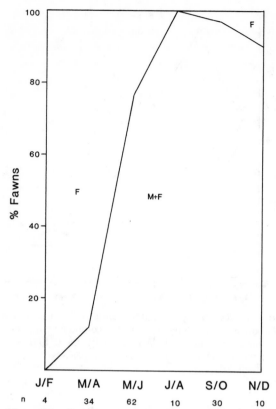

Figure 14. Relative number of fawns in mixed-sex (M+F) and female (F) groups. Although fawns born in early 1981 were considered yearlings from September 1981 on, I have included them here between September and December to show the yearly association pattern of this class. n = number of fawn sightings. Data from 1980 and 1981 have been combined and pooled into 2-month periods.

mixed groups, except during fawning, when more than 50% of them were found in male groups. The pattern for adult females was similar to that of adult males. They spent most of the time in mixed groups, except during fawning, when 50% of them were associated with their fawns or other females.

Both adult males and females were associated in mixed groups or with animals of their own sex throughout the year. Solitary animals were infrequently observed. Adult males, however, were solitary more often than adult females (Figure 12). The proportion of single males was above 9% between January and August, and reached a peak of 14% in March/ April during fawning. Only 3% of all adult males were found solitary between September and December, during antler shedding and growth. During most of the year single females (accompanied or not by their fawns) were extremely rare. Only immediately prior to fawning did the proportion of solitary females increase to 8%.

Most yearlings remained in mixed groups throughout the year (Figure 13). Young fawns were observed exclusively in female groups between February and

April (Figure 14). A few older fawns were found in mixed groups in April when some lactating females began to return to mixed groups. By May/June almost all fawns were with their mothers in the large mixed groups.

The occurrence of small fawns only in female groups from February to April, clearly indicates that *all* pregnant females segregated from mixed groups and thus from adult males. No female groups were observed in December 1980 or 1981. Females began to segregate in mid–January, when 6 female groups (29% of all groups in this month) were encountered. Some lactating females were first seen in mixed groups in early April. These group observations and the records of two known pregnant females indicate that sexual segregation may have lasted from 5 to 10 weeks.

A different pattern was found among adult males. Records of known males (5 of which were the largest males during the study) indicate that although up to 50% of adult male sightings during the fawning season were in male groups, some rejoined mixed groups several times, while others rarely left mixed groups. This finding suggests that adult males do not move away from mixed-sex groups; rather, pregnant females segregate themselves.

From the analysis so far, it is not clear how stable or "cohesive" the various types of groups described were at different times of the year. A measure of relative stability can be obtained by comparing changes in

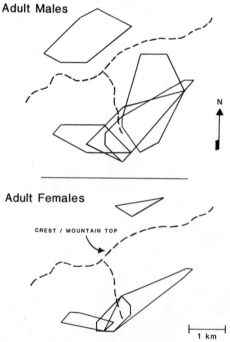

Figure 15. Locations of known adult males and females. Only individuals with 5 or more sightings and with more than 30 days between first and last sighting have been included.

Table 5. Changes in group size/composition within observation periods. Only observations of 30 minutes or longer have been included.

Group-type	Total number observations	Number of changes per observation/hour
Female	10	0.02
Male	12	0.02
Mixed-sex	43	0.01

Table 6. Number of sightings of known individuals and number of *different* groups in which the former were found. Only animals with 5 or more sightings are included. Mean time-span between first and last sighting was 135 days. Mean time-span between sightings was 15 days.

Class	No. animals	Total sightings	Total no. of different groups
Adult males	8	80	74
Adult females	4	27	27

group size and composition within observation periods with longer term changes obtained from data on known individuals.

On the whole, all group types remained very stable in size and composition within observation periods (Table 5) both during and outside the fawning season. Even large groups (9–18 animals) retained their identity during observations that lasted up to 6 hours. This suggests that tarucas formed cohesive social aggregations at least during daily activities.

Data on known individuals, however, indicate that specific groups did not remain stable over several days. Known adult males and females were both observed to be in groups of different size or composition on almost all occasions in which these individuals were identified (Table 6).

Locational data from these known animals indicate that both sexes remained in particular areas during the study (Figure 15) and strongly suggest that adults have year–round home ranges, though seasonal shifts in habitat use are marked (Merkt, 1985). This resulted in different animals associating with particular individuals or groups but not with others within the study area. It appears that although particular groups were not stable on a long-term basis, different individuals seemed to be part of larger "sub-population" units.

To summarize, tarucas displayed a strong tendency to form social groupings throughout the year. Solitary animals were infrequent. Group size and structure, however, changed seasonally and these changes were highly correlated with the reproductive cycle of the deer. Mixed-sex groups were the largest and most common, except during the fawning season when smaller single-sex groups were more frequent. At this time, all pregnant females (and perhaps some barren females as well) were completely segregated from mixed-sex groups. Although adult males were frequently seen in male groups during this period, data on known individuals indicate that male groups are transient. My observations strongly suggest that pregnant females move away from and subsequently avoid, contact with male or mixed groups. Finally, the seasonal groupings of tarucas are neither random aggregations of individuals nor stable social units. Both sexes formed short-term cohesive social groups while foraging and engaging in other activities during the day but did not aggregate always with the same individuals on a longer-term basis. Although unstable, these groups were comprised of individuals who remained in restricted areas year-round. Thus, these "open" groups appeared to be subsets of larger and perhaps more stable sub-population units.

Discussion

Reproductive Cycle

Tarucas breed seasonally in an area characterized by marked seasonal fluctuations in the environment. Mating occurs during the driest months (in winter); antler shedding in males, during the onset of the rainy season (in spring); and fawning, towards the end of the rainy season (in late summer/fall).

The sparse information available for this species in other locations in southern Peru is consistent with my findings. Pearson (1951) examined six specimens from Arequipa and Puno in December. Three adult males had their antlers in velvet and one young male had short spike antlers and lacked the last molars. Pearson did not mention if the latter also had antlers in velvet. The remaining two were pregnant females. From the size of one fetus (410 mm), he estimated birth in February or March. Whitehead (1972) claimed that the rut in Peru occurs between June and August and Roe and Rees (1976) recorded instances of courtship and mounting behavior during their observations between 8 June and 15 June in Puno. They noted that all adult males had antlers free of velvet. Although they observed no small fawns, some older fawns may have been mistaken for yearling females. During a preliminary study of tarucas in Pampa Galeras (15°40′S, 74°40′W), Ayacucho, between 24 February and 20

June 1980, I observed fawns in April. I was unable, however, to find deer in March. In the course of making 20 group observations in this location, I observed only one instance of mounting behavior on 17 May. I could not find any deer in June. All males had clear antlers throughout the study.

The relationship between breeding cycles and seasonal environments is well documented for many ungulates in northern latitudes (e.g. Anderson, 1981; Bunnell, 1982; Chapman and Feldhamer, 1982; Schaller, 1977) where seasonal breeding presumably occurs in response to periodic fluctuations in food availability (Bunnell, 1982; Geist, 1974a). The climatic patterns in northern latitudes, however, are different from those in tropical highlands (Troll, 1968) and the differences may explain why the timing of reproductive events in *Hippocamelus antisensis* differs from that in northern latitude ungulates.

Temperate climates are characterized by seasonal variation in day length and temperature. This pattern results in most young being born during the spring and early summer, a period of rapid plant growth. The onset and length of the birth season in any particular location is related to the duration and predictability of this plant-growing season (Bunnell, 1982).

On the other hand, in tropical highlands climate is characterized by large diurnal fluctuations in temperature and season is influenced by summer rains; there are almost no changes in day length throughout the year. Drought and subzero night temperatures in the winter limit the growing season to one part of the year (Troll, 1968). During the dry winter months most areas are devoid of green vegetation and many annual forbs and small grasses disappear. At the onset of the wet season (in spring) increasing rains bring moisture to the dried-out soils, but the still persistent night frosts (see Table 1) result in a slow recovery of the vegetation. Although I made no attempt to monitor plant phenology, my observations indicate that plant growth at La Raya reaches its peak sometime in February/March. This time appears to be best suited for birth in *Hippocamelus*.

The vicuña (*Lama vicugna*) is the only other local wild ungulate living as high as the taruca. It too has a restricted breeding season in southern Peru and gives birth to young between February and April (Franklin, 1974), with a peak of births in March (Koford, 1957; pers. obs.). Another wild ungulate comparable in size to *Hippocamelus* that inhabits tropical highlands is the Walia ibex (*Capra ibex walie*). It is found in the Simien Mountains of Ethiopia, at about the same latitude as La Raya but north from the equator. Seasons are thus reversed. Although Walia ibexes breed throughout the entire year, they have distinct rutting and birth peaks (Nievergelt, 1974, 1981). Births are most common in

September/October, at the end of the rainy season, and this time coincides with greater availability of fresh food (Nievergelt, 1974). The fact that Walia ibexes can breed year-round presumably reflects the more constant environmental conditions existent in the Simien Mountains. Ibexes are found at an average elevation of 3,390 m (Nievergelt, 1974) which is lower than that for *Hippocamelus* at La Raya (above 4100 m). Although the Simien Mountains have a well-defined rainy season (from May to September/October) and large diurnal temperature fluctuations (mean temperature remains fairly constant throughout the year), mean minimum temperatures never drop below 0°C and even absolute minimum temperatures never fall below -2.5°C (Nievergelt, 1981; Table 1). The result is that newly grown vegetation is available year-round (Nievergelt, 1974).

I conclude that the breeding cycle in *Hippocamelus* is strongly seasonal and is determined by the precipitation and temperature patterns characteristic of southern Peru. A quantitative study of the effects of rainfall and temperature on plant growth and a comparison of taruca breeding cycles under different climatic conditions are needed to test this hypothesis. Differing environmental conditions seem to exist within the geographic range of *Hippocamelus antisensis*. Tarucas have been reported in a number of high Andean habitats ranging from more equatorial environments in La Libertad (about 8° S), Peru, to more temperate latitudes in Catamarca (about 28° S), Argentina; and from wetter and more constant climate of the eastern Andean slopes to drier and more unpredictable environments of the western slopes of the Andes (I.U.C.N., 1982). My observations of two fawns outside the main fawning season at La Raya, suggest that tarucas could breed at other times of the year and thus be able to adapt to local conditions within their entire range.

Grouping Patterns

At La Raya tarucas live in open habitat and are gregarious. The largest group I observed consisted of 31 animals although groups of over 40 deer have been reported occasionally by personnel of La Raya Research Station.

Information on the distribution of tarucas suggests that they live in open country throughout their range (I.U.C.N., 1982; Jungius, 1974; Pearson, 1951; Roe and Rees, 1976; Whitehead, 1972), and zoo-archaeological findings indicate that natives have hunted tarucas in the high Andes since at least 6,000 years B.C. (Wheeler, 1982). Grimwood's (1969) claim that the distribution of *Hippocamelus antisensis* is determined by the availability of *Polylepis* forests seems unfounded (Roe, 1974; Roe and Rees, 1976; pers. obs.).

Data on group size elsewhere are meager, but they suggest that tarucas are also gregarious in other locations. Jungius (1974) observed some solitary males and groups of 3 to 13 animals in rugged terrain above timberline in northwestern Bolivia and Pearson (1951) found tarucas in groups of 2 to 8 animals among grassy hills interspersed by rugged rock outcroppings in southern Peru. Roe and Rees (1976) observed six groups ranging from 3 to 14 deer in the same type of habitat in southern Peru. From their data (Table 1, p. 726) I computed a mean group size of 6.8 ($\pm$ 1.58 SE) deer. In Pampa Galeras, Ayacucho, I found tarucas at very low densities (approx. 0.3 deer/km^2) occupying the same mountainous, open terrain. Group size ranged from 1 to 11 animals, but mean size was somewhat lower ($\bar{x}$ = 2.65 $\pm$0.55 SE) than it was at La Raya ($\bar{x}$ = 5.8 $\pm$0.49 SE) for the same months.

The relationship between group size and habitat has been extensively examined for African ungulates and has led to development of a general model. According to Estes (1974), Geist (1974b), Jarman (1974), and Leuthold (1977) ungulate species or populations occupying open habitats live in social groups, whereas those inhabiting dense bush or forest tend to live singly or in very small groups. Groups in open habitat presumably form in response to greater availability and more even distribution of food resources and to predation pressures derived from their conspicuousness in open terrain. Although this model was developed mainly for African bovids, it seems to apply to cervids as well (Clutton-Brock et al., 1982; Eisenberg, 1981; Hirth, 1977; Maublanc et al., 1985; Takatsuki, 1983).

As predicted by the above model, the social structure of *Hippocamelus antisensis* differs from that of its closest relative, the Chilean huemul (*H. bisulcus*). In the Nevados de Chillan and Rio Claro areas, Povilitis (1978, 1983) found huemuls mainly in dense shrub or forest habitats at elevations between 1,450 and 1,700 m. Mean group size was very small (mean = 1.6 animals) and huemuls were seen singly or in adult male-female pairs with or without young. Another close relative of *Hippocamelus*, the white-tailed deer (*Odocoileus virginianus*), lives in a variety of habitats, but tends to form large social groups only in open habitats (Hirth, 1977). Similar phenomena have been observed in roe deer, *Capreolus capreolus* (Maublanc et al., 1985), and sika deer, *Cervus nippon* (Takatsuki, 1983).

Although the general tendency of tarucas to form social aggregations can be explained by the above model, a closer examination of the habitat is required to explain seasonal changes in social structure of the species. Unlike most seasonal breeding cervids, where males and females rarely intermix outside of the mating season (Clutton-Brock et al., 1982; De Vos et al., 1967; Hirth, 1977), tarucas form mixed-sex groups nearly all year. Thus, sexual segregation in *Hippocamelus* is confined to the birth season. During this period, there are marked sexual differences in habitat use (Merkt, 1985). A major factor influencing habitat segregation of the sexes in tarucas appears to be predation risk to fawns (Merkt, 1985).

Tarucas are unique among cervids but resemble some mountain Caprinae in social organization and habitat utilization. The use of restricted and localized areas by tarucas year-round may have facilitated the formation of mixed-sex groups outside of the mating season. Although more detailed information is needed for comparisons across species of mountain Caprinae, some evidence suggest that *Capra* species are more restricted in their year-round movements and use a more specialized habitat than do *Ovis* species (Schaller, 1977). In contrast to goats, *Ovis* species show a marked sexual segregation nearly all year (Geist, 1971; Schaller, 1977). Thus, tarucas resemble goats more than sheep in habitat use and social structure.

Acknowledgments

I wish to thank Dr. William E. Rees for support, advice, and encouragement throughout the study, and Drs. Fred L. Bunnell, A.R.E. Sinclair, and J.N.M. Smith for advice and reviewing this manuscript. I extend my sincere gratitude to Dr. Fred Bunnell for his general guidance during analysis of my data and for making possible my participation in this cervid symposium.

During my stay in Peru, many people and several institutions made this study possible. I am deeply indebted to Dr. Alberto Sato, Director, Instituto Veterinario de Investigaciones Tropicales y de Alture (I.V.I.T.A.), Universidad National Mayor de San Marcos, Lima, for kindly allowing me to work at La Raya Station, Cusco. I am most thankful to Dr. Julio Sumar, Coordinador Tecnico, I.V.I.T.A., and all his colleagues at La Raya for giving me their friendship and invaluable material support. Ing. Juan Alpaca, Administrador de La Raya, Ministerio de Agricultura, was also most helpful and supportive. Sr. Renato Marin provided advice and helpful information on tarucas in the Cusco area. Domingo Jara was an excellent guide and, along with other personnel from I.V.I.T.A. and Ministerio de Agricultura, assisted me in the field on many occasions. I am most grateful to Peggy Stern for her friendship and encouragement, and for her generous help many times during my study.

For field support during a preliminary study at the

Vicuña National Reserve in Pampa Galeras, Ayacucho, I thank Dr. Antonio Brack, former Director of the Vicuña Project in Peru, and Dr. Rudolf Hofmann, former Head of the German Mission for Technical Cooperation at the Reserve. I also thank Dr. Marc Dourojeanni, former Director General of the Direccion General Forestal y de Fauna, Ministerio de Agricultura, Lima, for giving me full moral support and helpful information during the initial stages of the study.

My deepest thanks go to my relatives in Lima and Cusco, especially William and Luisa Leonard, for their more than generous hospitality during my stay in Peru.

Finally, I wish to thank very especially Marie Ladouceur for going out of her way to type several drafts of this manuscript.

This work was partially funded by the Faculty of Graduate Studies and the School of Community and Regional Planning at the University of British Columbia, B.C., Canada.

Literature Cited

Anderson, A.E.
1981. Morphological and physiological characteristics. In *Mule and Black-tailed Deer of North America*, compiled and edited by O.C. Wallmo, pp. 27–97. Lincoln: University of Nebraska Press.

Bunnell, F.L.
1982. The lambing period of mountain sheep: synthesis, hypotheses, and tests. *Canadian Journal of Zoology*, 60:1–14.

Cabrera, A.
1961. Catalogo de los Mamiferos de America del Sur. *Revista del Museo Argentino de Ciencias Naturales "Bernardino Rivadavia". Ciencias Zoologia*, 4(2):308–732.

Chapman, J.A., and G.A. Feldhamer (eds.)
1982. *Wild Mammals of North America: Biology, Management, and Economics.* Baltimore: Johns Hopkins University Press.

Clutton-Brock, T.H., F.E. Guinness, and S.D. Albon
1982. *Red Deer: Behavior and Ecology of Two Sexes.* Chicago: University of Chicago Press.

De Vos, A., P. Brokx, and V. Geist
1967. A review of social behavior of the North American cervids during the reproductive period. *American Midland Naturalist*, 77:390–417.

Eisenberg, J.F.
1981. *The Mammalian Radiations: An Analysis of Trends in Evolution, Adaptation, and Behavior.* Chicago: University of Chicago Press.

Estes, R.D.
1974. Social organization of the African Bovidae. In *The Behavior of Ungulates and its relation to Management*, edited by V. Geist and F. Walther, pp. 166–205. Morges: IUCN.

Franklin, W.L.
1974. The social behavior of the vicuña. In *The Behavior of Ungulates and its Relation to Management*, edited by V. Geist and F. Walther, pp. 477–487. Morges: IUCN.

Geist, V.
1971. *Mountain Sheep: A Study in Behavior and Evolution.* Chicago: University of Chicago Press.
1974a. On the relationship of ecology and behavior in the evolution of ungulates: theoretical considerations. In *The Behavior of Ungulates and its Relation to Management*, edited by V. Geist and F. Walther, pp. 235–246. Morges: IUCN.
1974b. On the relationship of social evolution and ecology in ungulates. *American Zoologist*, 14:205–220.

Grimwood, I.R.
1969. Notes on the distribution and status of some Peruvian mammals. *Special Publications, American Committees for International Wildlife Protection, and New York Zoological Society, Bronx, N.Y.*, 21:1–86.

Hirth, D.H.
1977. Social behavior of white-tailed deer in relation to habitat. *Wildlife Monograph*, 53:1–55.

I.U.C.N.
1982. Mammal Red Data Book, Part 1. *International Union for the Conservation of Nature and Natural Resources (I.U.C.N.). Gland: IUCN Publications.*

Jarman, P.J.
1974. The social organization of antelope in relation to their ecology. *Behaviour*, 48:215–267.

Jungius, H.
1974. Beobachtungen am Weisswedelhirsch und anderen Cerviden in Bolivien. *Zeitschrift für Säugetierkunde*, 39:373–383.

Koford, C.B.
1957. The vicuña and the puna. *Ecological Monographs*, 27:153–219.

Lent, P.C.
1974. Mother-infant relationships in ungulates. In *Behavior of Ungulates and Its Relation to Management*, *edited by V. Geist and F. Walther, pp. 14–55. Morges: IUCN.*

Leuthold, W.
1977. *African ungulates: a comparative review of their ethology and behavioral ecology.* Zoophysiology and Ecology, Volume 8. Berlin: Springer-Verlag.

Maublanc, M.L., E. Bideau, and J.P. Vincent
1985. Donnees preliminaires sur la tendance gregaire chez le chevreuil (*Capreolus capreolus*) en milieu ouvert, durant l'automne et l'hiver; comparaison avec le milieu forestier. *Mammalia*, 49:3–11.

Merkt, J.R.
1985.   Social Structure of Andean Deer (*Hippocamelus anti-sensis*) in Southern Peru. M.Sc. Thesis. University of British Columbia, Vancouver, Canada.

Nievergelt, B.
1974.   A comparison of rutting behavior and grouping in the Ethiopian and Alpine ibex. In *The Behavior of Ungulates and its Relation to Management*, edited by V. Geist and F. Walther, pp. 324–340. Morges: IUCN.

1981.   *Ibexes in an African Environment*. Ecological Studies Volume 40. Berlin: Springer-Verlag.

O.N.E.R.N.
1965.   Programa de inventario y evaluacion de los recursos naturales del Departamento de Puno, Sector de Prioridad 1. Oficina Nacional de Evaluacion de Recursos Natruales (O.N.E.R.N.), Lima, Peru.

Pearson, O.P.
1951.   Mammals in the highlands of southern Peru. *Bulletin of the Museum of Comparative Zoology*, 106:116–174.

Povilitis, A.
1978.   The Chilean huemul project: a case history. In *Threatened Deer*, pp. 109–128. Morges: IUCN.

1983.   Social organization and mating strategy of the huemul (*Hippocamelus bisulcus*). *Journal of Mammalogy*, 64:156–158.

Roe, N.A.
1974.   Information collected from literature on the ecology and behavior of the cervid genera *Mazama, Pudu,* and *Hippocamelus*. University of British Columbia. Unpublished manuscript.

Roe, N.A., and W.E. Rees
1976.   Preliminary observations of the taruca (*Hippocamelus antisensis:* Cervidae) in southern Peru. *Journal of Mammalogy*, 57:722–730.

Schaller, G.B.
1967.   *The Deer and the Tiger*. Chicago: University of Chicago Press.

1977.   *Mountain Monarchs: Wild Sheep and Goats of the Himalaya*. Chicago: University of Chicago Press.

Takatsuki, S.
1983.   Group size of sika deer in relation to habitat type on Kinkazan Island. *Japanese Journal of Ecology*, 33:419-425.

Troll, C.
1968.   The cordilleras of the tropical Americas: aspects of climatic, phytogeographical, and agrarian ecology. In *Geo-ecology of the Mountainous Regions of the Tropical Americas*, edited by C. Troll, pp. 15-56. Bonn: Dummlers Verlag.

Wheeler, J.C.
1984.   On the origin and early development of Camelid pastoralism in the Andes. In *Animals and Archaeology, Herders and Their Flocks*, Volume 3, edited by J. Clutton-Brock and C. Grigson, pp. 395–410. Fourth International Conference of Archaeozoology. Oxford, British Archaeol. Rep. (in press).

Whitehead, G.K.
1972.   *Deer of the World*. London: Constable.

J.E. JACKSON
and
ALFREDO LANGGUTH

Instituto Nacional de Tecnologia Agropecuario
Estación Experimental Agropecuaria San Luis
Casilla de Dorreo N° 17, 5730 Villa Mercedes
San Luis, Argentina

Departemento do Biologia CCEN
Campus Universitario-UFPb
58000 Joao Pessoa
Paraiba, Brasil

Ecology and Status of the Pampas Deer in the Argentinian Pampas and Uruguay

ABSTRACT

The past and present status of the pampas deer (*Ozotoceros bezoarticus*) in the Argentinian pampas and Uruguay is discussed, together with the reasons for its decline and the chances for its recovery. The once extremely abundant native cervid populations have been decimated by the effects of man's direct and indirect activities—overhunting, habitat change, competition with livestock, and disease. Only one thousand *Ozotoceros* are estimated to survive in Uruguay and some 400 in the pampas. Habitat is described, together with aspects of breeding, antler cycle, hard size and composition and behavior.

Introduction

The pampas deer (*Ozotoceros bezoarticus*) is considered the most elegant of all South American cervids. Its exact size and color vary geographically. Adult males are slightly larger than females, standing about 70 cm at the shoulder and weighing around 25 kg. The coat is smooth and short-haired with white or creamish underparts, inside the ears, sides of the muzzle and around the eyes. The tail is of medium length (15 cm). No marked difference exists between summer and winter pelage. Notable features include two whorls of hair —one situated towards the base of the neck and the other over the shoulders—although their exact position demonstrates considerable individual variation. The branched antlers are of moderate size, classically bearing three points each —a brow tine and a simple upper bifurcation. More detailed descriptions are given in Cabrera and Yepes (1940), and Whitehead (1972).

Pampas deer have a strong pungent smell, characteristic of the species, that resembles concentrated human sweat. Darwin (1839) remarked on its "overpowering strong and offensive odour" which could be detected half a mile downwind of a herd. The odor is strongest in bucks, especially during the rut, but is easily noted at a distance all year. The interdigital glands of the rear feet produce the exudate responsible for this scent (Cahalane, 1939). These and other cutaneous glands are described by Langguth and Jackson (1980).

Hershkovitz (1958) reviewed the nomenclature for the pampas deer. In this paper, *Ozotoceros* Ameghino,

1891 is preferred to *Blastoceros* L. to clearly distinguish between this and the marsh deer (*Blastoceros dichotomus*) and because it is the most frequently used scientific term for pampas deer. The true systematic status of this and many other South American Cervidae is debatable (Kraglievich, 1932; Cabrera, 1941; Haltenorth, 1963). Most recently Bianchini and Delupi (1979) proposed its inclusion in the genus *Odocoileus* Rafinesque, 1832. Groves and Grubb (this volume) briefly review the systematic relationships of *Ozotoceros* and other South American Odocoileini.

On the basis of coat color and cranial morphology, Cabrera (1943) recognized three subspecies:

(a) *O. b. bezoarticus* whose natural range includes eastern and central Brasil south of Amazonia between the plateau of Mato Grosso and the Upper Río San Francisco, and from there southwards to the State of Río Grande do Sul and the Republic of Uruguay.

(b) *O. b. leucogaster*'s traditional habitat is southwestern Brasil (southern Mato Grosso), southeast Bolivia, Paraguay and northern Argentina.

(c) *O. b. celer* is the southernmost form, whose distribution embraced the entire pampas region (Figure 1).

Coat color varies considerably within surviving populations in Uruguay and Argentina. Cabrera (1943) studied only few individuals from scattered localities. The question of subspeciation in pampas deer could be profitably reviewed according to current taxonomic criteria.

Past Status

Pampas deer once lived throughout the natural grasslands of eastern South America situated between latitudes 5°–40°S. Due to man's direct and indirect activities, this ungulate has suffered a substantial reduction in both numbers and distribution pattern across much of its former range (Jungius, 1976). Of the three races, this process is particularly marked in the austral or Argentinian form *O. b. celer*, which is recognized as the continent's rarest deer (Holloway, 1975). Although noting that population densities were low and declining, Jungius (1976) did not consider *O. b. bezoarticus* or *leucogaster* to be endangered, but a fuller survey is urgently needed to determine their actual status.

Reports of explorers and pioneer settlers and place names and folklore, clearly demonstrate that this deer abounded in the virgin pampas during the 18th and 19th centuries. Cabrera (1943) records that *celer* still roamed in great numbers throughout these grasslands until 1900, yet today it is on the brink of extinction.

This cervid's original range across the grassland biotope matched that of the sparse nomadic Indian tribes who hunted it on foot using bolsadoras, bows

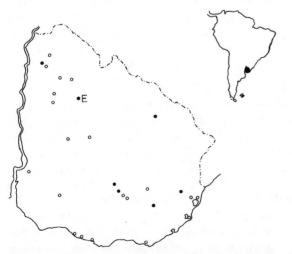

Figure 1. Pampas deer (*Ozotoceros bezoarticus*) distribution in Uruguay. E = El Tapado, open circles = past sites, black circles = present sites.

and arrows, and lances. Their existence and lifestyle depended on this species, much as the plains Indians of North America relied on bison for their survival.

With the arrival of the Spaniards the pampas started to change. During the 17th and 18th centuries, the descendants of introduced cattle and horses multiplied. The Indians became expert horsemen, and both they and the immigrants exploited the feral livestock. At the trade's peak around 1780, some 800,000 hides were exported annually. The feral stock practically died out due to overcropping, and the demand for skins was increasingly filled by exploitation of the vast deer population.

Until a century ago, much of the pampas was still under Indian domination and the habitats were not greatly altered by the low cattle and horse stocking rates. In 1879, General Roca's campaign terminated the traditional Indian lifestyle and led to the colonization of the pampas. The appearance of roads, railways and fences, a massive influx of settlers and the effects of the introduction of diverse livestock systems changed extensive tracts of virgin ecosystems.

Nowadays the entire pampas is dedicated to food production. Excepting lagoons and small pockets of agriculturally marginal land, practically no large areas of native grassland remain.

The recent history of *Ozotoceros* in the neighboring Republic of Uruguay mirrors that of the Argentinian pampas. Their decline over the past two hundred years can be appreciated from Figure 2, which is based on documentary evidence, personal visits, and reliable data from local people. Most reports indicate that the large scale disappearance occurred since the late 1800s.

In summary, over–exploitation for hides, food and sport, habitat destruction, and competition with domestic livestock were major reasons for the decline of the pampas deer. Daguerre (1970) for example calculated the trade in pelts from 1860–70 as totalling over two million, and official hunting statistics note that in 1880, 61,401 pampas deer skins were shipped from the port of Buenos Aires. According to popular belief, certain diseases of livestock, notably foot and mouth disease, and various gut parasites have periodically decimated pampas deer, but no adequate study of disease impact was ever done, and the evidence is circumstantial. It is no coincidence that the few locations where pampas deer still survive represent virtually the last habitats that have escaped intense human influence and remain almost natural.

Present Status

By 1976 the distribution of *O. b. celer* had been reduced to only a few sites (Figure 2). Jungius (1976) also

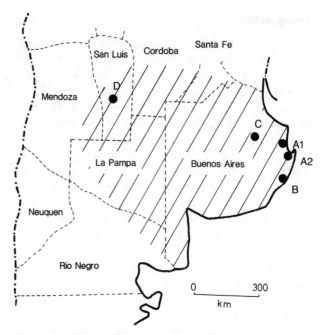

Figure 2. Distribution of *Ozotoceros bezoarticus celer* in the 19th century and in 1976. A = Bahia Samborombón (1= Samborombón, 2 = Campos Del Tuyú), B = Punta Médanos, C = La Corona, D = San Luis.

recorded a small population near Miramar which is believed to be the Punta Médanos herd near Pinamar. The total stock was put at 110–125.

Reassessment of stocks and the results of protection give the 1982 populations as: (a) Bahía Samborombón 90 (Samborombón 60; Campos del Tuyú 30); (b) Punta Médanos 3; (c) La Corona 15; (d) San Luis 300; total 418.

We estimated the group on El Tapado in Uruguay at 500 head, but the other populations are considerably smaller, varying between 10–200 animals. From all the information amassed we put the total of pampas deer remaining in Uruguay at about one thousand.

Conservation

The history of active conservation of *O. b. celer* dates from the mid 1960s, but unheeded calls to save this deer were made far earlier (Anon, 1884; Saenz, 1930; Marelli, 1944; Giai, 1945).

In Argentina and Uruguay direct responsibility for wildlife rests with the provinces. In Buenos Aires, the establishment of a captive breeding unit was considered the only practical means of preventing the subspecies extinction. Between 1967–69, four rescue operations took place in Samborombón to obtain stock for a breeding nucleus. As a result, 16 specimens were successfully introduced into an enclosure at La

Jackson and Langguth

Corona whilst at least 25 animals perished as a direct consequence of the capture. Since then the herd has had a checkered history. A policy of minimal management was adopted and deer numbers there have not increased.

In 1975, H. Jungius of World Wildlife Fund toured South America to carry out a survey for the IUCN Deer Specialist Group. As a result of that visit, IUCN/WWF project 1303 was launched in 1976 to provide the basis for sound conservation of *O. b. celer*. The original intention was to study the ecology of the population prior to making conservation plans. However, the plight of the population was assessed as so grim that immediate action was taken to remedy the most pressing problems and prevent extinction of dwindling stocks. When the international input ended in late 1979, a number of important measures had been taken, including the establishment of a private wardened reserve of 3500 ha with a 400 ha buffer zone in Campos del Tuyú.

Antipoaching steps instigated in Samborombón resulted in a rapid recuperation of numbers and a commitment to create a wardened provincial coastal sanctuary of 9,000 ha (Table 1). As numbers in the Bahía de Samborombón rise, natural recolonization to adjacent off-reserve zones can be expected. To maximize gene flow translocations of pure *O. b. celer* should be done ensuring that reintroduction maxims are strictly adhered to. Reintroduction to new sites should be technically feasible, but suitable habitats must be secured and protected.

The future of the captive breeding venture at La Corona is difficult to predict. It started in 1968/69 with 17 animals; a decade later (May 1978) there were 22. Most recent estimates are 15. No deer have been removed for restocking and no introductions of young stock have taken place. Recommendations for improved breeding success (Jackson, 1978) were rejected.

To concentrate on immediate conservation steps, much of the original ambitious research program proposed by IUCN/WWF 1303 had to be shelved. A sound working knowledge of the deer and its habitats was amassed, but in both the Argentinian pampas and Uruguay basic studies must be resumed for improved management in the future.

Ecology

Reliable scientific data on the ecology of pampas deer are scanty. The information presented here originates from our visits to all known pampas populations and to El Tapado in Uruguay. Observations were collected on foot, horseback, and from vehicles, boats and light aircraft. A total of 316 days were spent in the field in Argentina and 7 in Uruguay. The present findings are far from exhaustive, but it is vital to report any information, however, on this endangered deer.

Habitat

The pampas deer formerly occupied a wide selection of open habitats as reflected in the diversity of sites where they still survive.

Bahía de Samborombón. The narrow fringe of saltmarsh extending some 120 km along the western edge of the Río de la Plata estuary, represents one of the few remaining natural ecosystems in the otherwise highly agricultural province of Buenos Aires. This zone, sculptured by daily and periodic tidal inundation, comprises a mosaic of meandering creeks, drainage canals, lagoons and marismas. Stands of taller grasses and sedges with copses of low trees grow on the few islets of higher ground. Access to the area is treacherous – and sufficiently difficult to ensure that some deer survived there despite substantial poaching pressure. The land is of minimal agricultural value or interest at present although cattle are increasingly invading to utilize the sparse amount of palatable grazing.

Two geographically distinct units persist nowadays–Samborombón and Campos del Tuyú–at either end of the Bahía.

Punta Médanos. This is a relict of mature sand dunes, lying between the Atlantic and the agricultural hinterland. The remainder of the once extensive dune belt that stretched for some 250 km has been almost entirely subject to afforestation and tourist exploitation.

La Corona. This captive group at this site occurs within a 28 ha of what was formerly short grass cattle pasture with a central lagoon.

San Luis. On the western edge of its original range, *O.*

Table 1. Numbers of pampas deer spotted in standardized aerial censuses in Bahia Samborombón, before and after introducing antipoaching measures in late 1976

Date	Total Seen
September 75	9
July 76	14
January 78	23
May 78	29
July 78	22
August 78	27
October 78	37
March 79	33
April 79	27
August 79	44

b. celer still lives in south-central San Luis. The inhabited areas are near natural, semi-arid tussock grassland with large rolling fixed dunes and small copses of thorn scrub. These areas were never overgrazed by cattle, and contain remote zones with difficult or restricted access to man. Hunting by the sparse human population is discouraged by the landowners of nearby estancias. The annual rainfall (400–500 mm) is concentrated in the summer months, with low vegetative production in the dry winter months. Temperatures are extreme with absolute summer maximums of 40° and winter minimums of −15°.

Uruguay. Most populations there now are in rolling hilly areas, dominated by temperate grasslands, dissected by streams and small valleys, and interrupted by rocky outcrops and ridges. Apart from scattered plantations, *Eucalyptus* windbreaks or riverside spinnies, the zone is treeless and the land largely devoted to extensive sheep and cattle rearing.

Group Size and Composition

Even when more numerous, pampas deer lived in small mixed herds, rarely exceeding five or six individuals (Cabrera and Yepes, 1940). They continue to do so today (Figure 3), and in the open short grassland of El Tapado, they are scattered in small groups across the plains. The herds are fluid in both size and composition, and bucks in particular, move freely

from one group to another in all seasons. The mother-fawn bond appears strong with the young staying with the dam until at least a year old. Bucks mix with does all year and there is no evident habitat partitioning according to sex or age. Heavily gravid females and those with tiny fawns lead a more solitary existence and the fawn does not follow the mother until about six weeks of age. Larger aggregations form on common feeding grounds such as burnt patches, but enter and leave the spot as smaller units.

No marked regular daily or seasonal movements were noted. Where they are not harrassed and climatic conditions are favorable, pampas deer feed at intervals throughout daylight hours.

Fuller details on ethology will be published, but basically the behavioral repertoire of *O. b. celer* closely parallels that of the white-tailed deer (*Odocoileus virginianus*).

Rut

Reproductive activity was witnessed, although infrequently, over the period December–February. High daytime temperatures and insect activity in this season restrict cervid activity to nighttime. Sparring was seen between males in hard antler, bouts often being between nonequals with the smaller one initiating them. True fights were rare and were distinguished from sparring in that the winner pursued the loser afterwards. There was no indication of harem formation or the establishment of territories or stands. One or more bucks harried estrous does across large distances. Additional information on behavior was summarized by Jackson (1985).

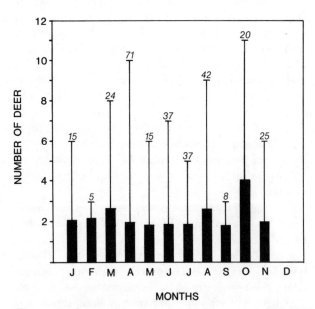

Figure 3. Seasonal breakdown of pampas deer herd size during the study period. Black bars = mean group size; lines = maximum group size; numbers = number of groups seen. Data combined for two areas: Bahia Samborombón (188 groups) and San Luis (111 groups). No data available for December.

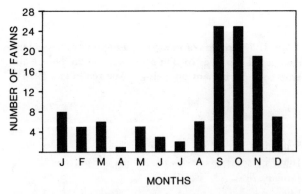

Figure 4. Seasonal distribution of 112 pampas deer births. Data commbined from four areas: Samborombón (n = 43), Punta Médanos (n = 3), La Corona (n = 19), and San Luis (n = 48).

Jackson and Langguth

Births

Pampas deer are spotted at birth, with the general coat color more chestnut than in older fawns. The dappled pelage is lost when about one month old. Only singletons were seen and twins have never been reported.

Dates of birth were estimated by sightings of neonates, or heavily gravid does, maternal behavior, or extrapolating back from the size and characteristics of fawns.

The data in Figure 4 suggest that births are not strictly seasonal in the province of Buenos Aires but occurred more frequently in spring and summer. This is confirmed by other authors (Cabrera and Yepes, 1940; Bianchini and Perez, 1972b). In San Luis, with marked seasonal changes in climate, the bulk of the young are spring-born (September–November) al-though odd ones are dropped in other months too. In Uruguay, our observations revealed that births are synchronized, the vast majority being spring-born.

Antler Cycle

The state of the antlers was noted during all visits to wild herds. In the captive unit, adult males could be distinguished individually and their progress monitored. The results for La Corona (Table 2), indicate that the majority are in hard antler from November–December through to July. In the Bahía de Samborombón, including Campos del Tuyú, antlers were cast about July, and were cleaned of velvet by the end of the year (Table 3). Bianchini and Perez (1972a) concluded that in La Corona and Campos del Tuyú, shedding takes place between June and September, younger animals being the first to lose their antlers.

Table 2. Antler cycle of pampas deer in La Corona captive herd

										Date										
		1976							1977										1978	
	Oct.	Nov.	Dec.	Jan.	Feb.	Mar.	Apr.	May	Jun.	Jul.	Aug.	Sep.	Oct.	Nov.	Dec.	Jan.	Feb.	Mar.	Apr.
Total known Adults present	7	7	7	8	8	8	8	7	7	7	6	6	6	6	6	6	5	5	5
Total known Adults seen	7	7	7	8	8	8	7	7	7	7	5	6	6	6	2	5	5	4	2
No. recently Cast	0	0	0	0	0	0	0	0	1	0	3	0	0	0	0	0	0	0	0
No. in Velvet	7	7	2	2	1	1	0	0	0	1	1	6	5	3	1	0	0	0	0
No. in herd Antler	0	0	5	6	7	7	7	7	6	6	1	0	1	3	1	5	5	4	2
No. visits	2	6	4	8	7	6	12	10	14	8	5	5	4	4	1	5	5	1	1

Table 3. Number of adult pampas deer seen in various phases of the antler cycle in Bahía Samborombón

Stage of cycle	Month												
	Jan.	Feb.	Mar.	Apr.	May	Jun.	Jul.	Aug.	Sep.	Oct.	Nov.	Dec.	Total
Recently cast	0	0	0	0	0	0	8	1	0	0	0	0	9
Velvet	0	1	0	0	0	0	0	13	5	14	9	0	42
Hard antler	9	1	10	8	8	0	7	0	0	0	1	0	44
Undetermined	0	0	1	2	0	0	0	5	2	1	1	0	12
Total	9	2	11	10	8	0	15	19	7	15	11	0	107

During October, November and December, all deer were in velvet which was stripped by late January or early February. The current findings suggest that the major events in the antler cycle were about one month ahead of those observed by the authors cited above.

In San Luis observations were discontinuous but suggested a cycle similar to that of the eastern populations of *O. b. celer*, being perhaps slightly earlier with the antlers cast in June–July. Five bucks seen in February were all in hard antler. In June, five were in hard antler, one had recently cast, one had one antler left and one cast, and five were in the early stage of regrowth. By September, all 14 adult males seen were in velvet with the antlers about two thirds grown.

In El Tapado, Uruguay, bucks spotted in January were all in hard antler. In May, 37 adult males were observed—34 in hard antler, two with one antler just cast, and one animal showing the initial stage of regrowth. By September, all 70 males screened were in velvet with the antlers nearly fully grown.

Like roe deer (*Capreolus capreolus*), male fawns grew small antlers or "buttons" during their first year, a feature not previously documented for the pampas deer. Comparative data on a population at La Travesía (Jackson, 1986) are in general agreement with these findings.

Conclusions

Ozotoceros bezoarticus was once the principal large mammalian herbivores in the extensive grasslands of the pampas and Uruguay. Both areas have undergone rapid, recent radical, and irreversible changes. Only in the last 100 years has most of the *O. b. celer* range been incorporated into intensive agricultural production. Existing habitats could probably be manipulated to favor deer populations but criteria on how to do so are wanting.

Although some conservation success has been achieved with *O. b. celer*, the situation of the species in both the pampas and Uruguay is still precarious. Their last refuges are threatened, some poaching continues despite legal protection, and daily contact with livestock increases the risk of disease transfer and competition. The success of captive breeding has been minimal and a major policy change is required if it is to function properly.

More studies of pampas deer ecology are urgently called for to provide a biological basis for a successful pampas deer recovery. These requirements must harmonize with the local socio-economic and conservation climate if they are to work.

Literature Cited

Anderson, R.
1978.   *Gold on Four Feet*. Melbourne, Anderson and Associates.

Anonymous
1884.   Letter to editor. *La Campana*, 4 September 1984.

Bianchini, J.J., and J.C.L. Perez
1972a.   El comportamiento de *Ozotoceros bezoarticus celer* Cabrera en cautiverio. *Acta zoológica Lilloana*, 29:5–16.

1972b.   Informe sobre la situación del ciervo de las pampas *Ozotoceros bezoarticus celer* Cabrera 1943 en la Provincia de Buenos Aires. *Acta Zoológica Lilloana*, 29:149–157.

1972b.   Informe sobre la situación del ciervo de las pampas *Ozotoceros bezoarticus celer* Cabrera 1943 en la Provincia de Buenos Aires. *Acta Zoológica Lilloana*, 29:149–157.

Cabrera, A.
1941.   Cranial and dental characters of some South American Cervidae. *Field Museum of Natural History*, Zoological Series, 17:125–235.

1943.   Sobre la sistemática del venado y su variación individual y geográfica. *Revista del Musso de La Plata*, Tomo III, Sección Zoología 5–41.

Cabrera, A., and J. Yepes
1940.   *Los mamíferos Sudamericanos*. Buenos Aires, Companía Argentina de Editores.

Cahalane, V.H.
1939.   Deer of the world. *National Geographic Magazine*, 76:463–510.

Deguerre, J.B.
1970.   El venado o ciervo de las Pampas. *Diana*, 363:20–24.

Darwin, C.
1839.   *Narrative of the Surveying Voyages of His Majesty's Ships, Adventure and Beagle, between the Years 1826 and 1836, Describing Their Examination of the Southern Shores of South America, and the Beagle's Circumnavigation of the Globe*. London: Henry Colburn.

Giai, A.G.
1945.   Venados y gamas. Buenos Aires, *La Prensa*, 19 de agosto de 1945.

Grimwood, I., and T. Whitmore.
1978.   Report to IUCN on conservation in South America. Unpublished.

Haltenorth, T.
1963.   Klassifikation der Säugetiere: Artiodactyla. *Handbuch der Zoologie* Volume 8, Part 1, Contribution 18; 1–167.

Jackson and Langguth

Hershkovitz, P.

1958.   The metatarsal glands in white-tailed deer and re-
         lated forms of the Neotropical region. *Mammalia*
         22:537–546.

Holloway, C.

1975.   Threatened deer of the World: Research and conser-
         vation projects under the IUCN Programme. *Deer,*
         3:428–433.

Jackson, J.E.

1978.   Observaciones y recommendaciones sobre el futuro
         del rebaño de *Ozotoceros bezoarticus celer* en la estancia
         La Corona. Unpublished report, IUCN, 14 pp.

1985.   Behavioural observations on the Argentinian pam-
         pas deer (*Ozotoceros bezoarticus celer*, Cabrera, 1943).
         Zeitschrift für Säugetierkunde, 50:107–116.

1986.   Antler cycle in pampas deer (*Ozotoceros bezoarticus*)
         from San Luis, Argentina. *Journal of Mammalogy,*
         67(1):173–176.

Jungius, H.

1976.   Status and distribution of threatened deer species in
         South America. In *World Wildlife Yearbook 1975–76,*
         pp. 203–217. Morges, Switzerland: World Wildlife
         Fund.

Kraglievich, L.

1932.   Contribución al conocimiento de los ciervos fósiles
         del Uruguay. *Anales del Museo Nacional de Historia
         Natural de Montevideo,* Serie 2:355–438.

Langguth, A., and J. Jackson.

1980.   Cutaneous scent glands in pampas deer *Blactoceros
         bezoarticus* (L., 1758). *Zeitschrift für Säugetierkunde,*
         45:82–90.

MacDonagh, E.J.

1940.   La etología del venado en al Tuyú. *Notas del Museo de
         la Plata* Tomo V, Zoología N° 33:49–68.

Marelli, C.A.

1944.   La protección del ciervo de las pampas o gama en
         las provincias de Buenos Aires y Santiago del Es-
         tero. *El Campo* año 29, 338:52–58.

McDiarmid, A.

1978.   Threatened deer—disease implications, field work
         and management. In *Threatened Deer, Proceedings on
         the Working Meeting of the Deer Specialist Group of the
         Survival Service Commission,* edited by G.K. White-
         head, pp. 364–378. Morges, International Union for
         the Conservation of Nature.

Saenz, J.P.

1930.   La Fauna argentina: el venado. *La Nación* 5 January
         1930:28–29.

Whitehead, G.K.

1972.   *Deer of the World.* London: Constable.

KENT H. REDFORD
Museum of Comparative Zoology
Harvard University
Cambridge, Massachusetts 02138
and
Department of Zoological Research
National Zoological Park
Smithsonian Institution
Washington, DC 20008

The Pampas Deer (*Ozotoceros bezoarticus*) in Central Brazil

ABSTRACT

This paper reports data on group size, group composition, birth season and antler cycles for a population of the pampas deer, (*Ozotoceros bezoarticus bezoarticus*) in central Brazil. The average group size from 422 groups was 1.36 with 54% of the groups composed of a single animal and 26.8% of two animals. For 388 groups in which all animals were sexed the sex ratio was 1 : 1.29. All male groups comprised 31.8% of the total sightings as compared with 36.5% for all female groups. The largest group observed was eight.

The antler cycle was not tightly synchronized and stags in velvet were seen during at least four months of the year. Births also were not tightly synchronized and the birth season apparently extends from July to December with a peak in October and November. Consequently males in rutting condition may be present most of the year.

The data from this population are compared with those from Uruguayan, Argentinian and captive populations of *Ozotoceros*.

Introduction

The pampas deer *Ozotoceros* with one species and three subspecies is the least known of the six genera of deer found in South America. At the time of European colonization *O. bezoarticus* was probably found in most of the open grassy areas south of the Amazon basin, east of the Andes and north of Patagonia (Carvalho, 1973). It was extensively hunted by some Argentinian Indians whose livelihood depended on this species (Jackson and Langguth, this volume). With the arrival of Europeans and horses, guns, livestock and large-scale agriculture pampas deer numbers dropped greatly and its current range has shrunk vastly with at least one of the three subspecies in grave danger of extinction (Jackson and Langguth, this volume). *Ozotoceros* is listed as endangered (Honacki et al., 1982).

Data on these deer are vital for developing a conservation program and urgent steps must be taken before suitable *Ozotoceros* habitat has completely disappeared. Information on *Ozotoceros* is also of great theoretical interest because of their southerly distribution. Few cervids occur as far south as the pampas deer. Consequently, the data from these animals could be used to test hypotheses on the effects of latitude on cervid reproductive biology. Many of these hypotheses have been developed using the data available for tropical and northern hemisphere deer thereby eliminating a way of testing them. Hopefully the data presented in this and Jackson and Langguth's (this volume) paper will stimulate extensive research on the beautiful, and vanishing, pampas deer.

Methods

This paper provides data on group size, group composition, and antler cycles for the northern subspecies of pampas deer, *Ozotoceros bezoarticus bezoarticus* (Cabrera, 1943) which has not been studied and is threatened over much of its range by complete loss of suitable habitat. Deer were observed in 131,000 hectare Emas National Park, Brazil located in the far western portion of the state of Goias (18°19'S and 52°45'E). Emas Park consists of approximately 60% grassland which grades into cerrado (scrubby savanna vegetation). The park is located on the watershed between the LaPlata and Amazon River basins and is drained by two small rivers which support narrow gallery forests along their banks. The open grassy areas are thickly dotted with termit mounds, principally those of *Cornitermes cumulans*. The climate is highly seasonal with a hot rainless season lasting from April to mid-September. At this time grass fires burn much of central Brazil and the park is almost completely burned at least once every several years. The

cooler wet season during which about 1500 mm of rain falls, begins in December and lasts through April.

Incidental observations of *Ozotoceros* were made during a study of the feeding ecology of the giant anteater, *Myrmecophaga tridactyla,* which spanned the dry season of 1980 and 1981. Data gathered in the field were combined with unpublished reports filed by two groups who had visited the Park (Schaller and Duplaix-Hall, 1975; Pereira et al., 1981), information from the Brasilia Zoo (Monteira Lima, pers. comm.) and data from the literature.

Results and Discussion

Deer were never observed in the gallery forest and only rarely in the more closed cerrado habitats, but preferred open rolling hills. In areas which had not burned the grass could reach three meters and deer were invisible. However, such tall grass was rare in the park and the deer could easily be seen moving and feeding in areas of short grass. Recently burned areas were favored by *Ozotoceros* and deer were commonly seen feeding and drinking in wet grassy areas bordering gallery forests and in open areas at the springheads which fed the two rivers.

A total of 422 groups of *Ozotoceros* were recorded of which 203 were observed April to October 1980 and September to October 1981 (this paper) and 219 of which were observed August to September 1978 (Pereira et al., 1981). The average group size of these combined observations was 1.36 with 54% of the groups being composed of a single animal (Table 1). Jackson and Langguth (this volume) reported 43.8% of their 299 groups as consisting of single animals with an

Table 1. Group size and composition in *Ozotoceros bezoarticus* in Emas National Park, Brazil

Group size	♂♂	♀♀	Mixed (including with young)	Unsexed	Total	%
1	107	99	0	22	228	54.0
2	22	47	38	6	113	26.8
3	2	6	28	2	38	9.0
4	1	2	16	3	22	5.2
5	2	0	9	0	11	2.6
6	0	0	5	1	6	1.4
7	0	0	3	0	3	.7
8	0	0	1	0	1	.2
Σ	134	154	100	34	422	

average group size of 2.19. In Emas single males were seen only slightly more frequently than single females.

Groups of two animals were seen 113 times (26.8%) as compared with Jackson and Langguth's figure of 28.8%. Of the Emas groups the majority (75.2%) were two females with young. The 38 observations of groups of three (9%) were also composed primarily of females with young (73.7%). Groups greater than two were seen much less frequently and only 21 of 422 groups were larger than four. The largest group seen in Emas Park was eight, an observation also made by Schaller and Duplaix-Hall (1975). This contrasts with Jackson and Langguth who reported one group of 11 and seven groups (out of 299 total) eight and larger.

Schaller and Duplaix-Halls' (1975) report of only 22% (of 210 tallied) single sightings as probably due to their survey being conducted during October to November, further into the birth season when more females would be expected to be accompanied by fawns or when the fawns had come out of hiding. Jackson and Langguth report fawns as accompanying their mothers after six weeks of age. The data reported in this paper were obtained primarily from the end of the dry season and the first weeks of the wet season. Seasonal variation in group size is apparent from the park staffs' reports of herds of up to 50 deer during the height of the wet season. Such a pattern is not seen when examining Jackson and Langguth's data from Argentina and Uruguay: in these areas average group size remains between 1.75 and 3.1 throughout the year with no strong seasonal trends. Further research may clarify this point.

Of 388 groups for which the sex of all members was determined for all group members there were 262 males, 338 females and 14 young: a sex ratio of 1 : 1.29. These figures yield 97.7% adults which is much higher than the 85% calculated by Schaller and Duplaix-Hall (1975). They commented on the low percentage of yearlings (6% of 169 deer) which they attributed to poor survival of the previous year's fawn crop. Only 13.6% of the females were observed with fawns —less than the 20% reported by Schaller and Duplaix-Hall (1975) although this might be expected because of the later timing of their survey.

All male groups comprised 31.8% of the 422 total sightings of which 79.9% were single males and 20.1% multiple male groups. The largest all male group observed had five stags, three of which were in velvet and two in hard antler. All female groups were 36.5% of the total, 64.3% of which were single females and 35.7% multiple females. The largest female group contained four animals.

These groups larger than two usually consisted of both females and males. Mixed sex groups comprised 18.9% of the sample with 91 males, 119 females and 14 young. Thirty-six percent of the 58 groups comprised of only adults had more females than males, 24% had more males and 27.9% had an equal sex ratio. The most common group size was three (34.5%) followed by two (29.3%). The largest group recorded was eight and consisted of three males and five females.

The beginnings of antler pedicel growth in male *Ozotoceros* has been observed as early as 15 days (Monterio Lima pers. comm.) though Frädrich (1981) reports it beginning about three months. These are probably the "antler buttons" referred to by Jackson and Langguth (this volume). The general pattern appears to be for one year old males to have spike antlers, two year olds to have a total of four tines and males two years and older to have six tines, although Frädrich (1981) reports that animals in a high nutritional plane can skip the four tine stage. Stags apparently begin growing a new set of antlers as soon as the old one has been shed (Frädrich, pers. comm.).

No buck with more than six tines was observed in Emas Park; however, some six point males had considerably heavier antlers than others, an observation also made by Frädrich (1981). There is apparently a thickening of antlers through most of the life of a stag. In Uruguay Jackson et al. (1980) reported six points to be normal with accessory spikes not uncommon. They also found one dead nine pointer. Of 89 stags surveyed in the Park, 48 had six tines, 31 had four tines, one had three tines and nine had two tines. Only one broken antler was observed.

Frädrich (1981) working on captive *Ozotoceros* from Paraguay in the West Berlin Zoo reported no fixed rutting season though he observed an annual antler cycle in which antlers were dropped in December and January. Whitehead (1972) reporting on an unidentified population of pampas deer stated that antlers were shed in May though some bucks kept their racks a month or two longer. Jackson and Langguth (this volume) reporting on two Argentinian populations stated that between January and July over 85% of the stags were observed in hard antler and from August to November 70% of the stags were in velvet.

In the Brasilia Zoo in 1978 one male's antlers were observed in velvet in June (Monteiro Lima, pers. comm.), while the first velvet in Emas Park was observed in early July (a group of three males, all in velvet). In September 1981 of 34 bucks counted in the Park, 15 were in velvet and 19 in hard antler; these included two, four and six tined bucks. Small groups of males containing both velvet and hard antlered males were frequently observed.

Ozotoceros always gives birth to a single fawn, although one female in Emas Park was observed with two similar-sized young. The fawns are spotted at birth which apparently takes place in open grassland.

Frädrich (1981) states that twins are rare in captivity and that the gestation is a little longer than seven months with females giving birth every ten months. Whitehead (1972) reports that most fawns are born in September and November though births have been reported from almost all months. In the Argentinian pampas births were reported in all 12 months though 62% of 112 births took place in the months September through November.

In the Brasilia Zoo five births were recorded in August, October and November of three years. In Emas Park the first fawn in 1980 was observed on October 12th and on September 16th in 1981. No fawns were observed in May through August but at the beginning of observations in April 1980 two fawns were seen. No observations were made from October to April though Schaller and Duplaix-Hall (1975) observed 15 fawns during their six day survey which took place October 30th to November 4th. Their conclusion was that there was an extended birth season from about late July to December with a peak in October and November. However, if the sighting of two fawns in April was normal it could be that the birth season lasts from August to April, again with a peak in October–November. This would agree to a large extent with the findings from Argentina where 90.5% of the recorded births occurred from August to April (Jackson and Langguth, this volume).

Discussion

If this extended birth season exists, with a gestation of about seven months, conceptions would take place from December through September. The fact that bucks were in hard rack at least from April through November and many were in velvet during the peak of the birthing season would indicate that rutting behavior in Emas Park takes place during a large proportion of the year. This suggestion is strengthened by Frädrich's (1981) observation that there is no fixed rutting season in his West Berlin animals, Whitehead's (1972) statement that births were observed in all months in a southerly population of *Ozotoceros* and Jackson and Langguth's (this volume) observation of rutting behavior in all months.

Additionally, in the Argentinian population at Samborombón 20.9% of the births took place seven months after only 2.3% of the stags were in hard rack. And, as mentioned before, 62% of the births were concentrated in three months while the incidence of stags in hard antler was fairly evenly distributed across six or seven months. If male fertility is positively related to antler hardness then these data indicate that some stags were responsible for a highly disproportionate number of fawns. However, it is pos-

sible that *Ozotoceros* stags, like muntjacs (*Muntiacus muntjac* and *M. reevesi*) can be fertile while their antlers are still in velvet (Barrette, 1977a).

The existence of a well delineated rutting and birth season is well known in north temperate populations of such deer as *Odocoileus virginianus* and *Cervus elaphus*. In contrast, cervids inhabiting monsoon tropical areas such as *Asix axis* are known to have both rutting and birthing periods that last throughout the year, often with distinct seasonal peaks (Schaller, 1967; Mishra and Wemmer, this volume). In this respect *Ozotoceros* is much more like *Axis* than *Odocoileus* despite its distribution in the southerly high latitudes. Also like chital, pampas deer have a marked increase in number of births associated with the rains. The timing and extent of this peak can vary markedly between populations as has been elegantly shown by Schaller (1967) for barasingha.

The population of *Ozotoceros b. bezoarticus* in Emas Park, estimated by Schaller and Duplaix-Hall at about 1000 animals, appears to be a healthy one. However, with soybean fields and cattle ranches surrounding the park, it has become an isolated population. With most of the grassland of South America threatened with or already altered by large scale farming and ranching, Emas Park represents an unmatched, very fragile, place to study pampas deer and other endangered fauna of this vanishing habitat.

Acknowledgments

I would like to thank the Brazilian Institute of Forestry Development for permission to work in Emas Park and Heber Silva de Oliveira, the Director, for assistance in the Park. The Organization of American States, National Geographic, Friends of the National Zoo, Harvard University and Sigma Xi provided funding for my research. G. Schuerholz, G. Schaller, H. Frädrich and Raimundo David Monteiro Lima provided unpublished information for which I am very grateful. This paper was greatly improved by the criticism of H. Frädrich, J. Jackson, K. Kranz, J. Eisenberg and particularly C. Wemmer.

Literature Cited

Barrette, C.
1977a. Some aspects of the behaviour of muntjacs in Wilpattu National Park. *Mammalia*, 41:1–34.

Carvalho, C.T.
1973. O veado campeiro (Mammalia, Cervidae). Secretario Estado dos Negócios da Agricula Coordenador Pesquisas Recurcos Naturais. *Instituto Florestal Boletin técnico* No. 7.

Frädrich, H.
1981.   Beobachtungen am Pampashirsch, *Blastoceros bezoar-ticus* (L., 1758) *Zoologische Garten*, 51:7–32.

Honacki, H.J., K.E. Kinman, and J.W. Koeppl (eds.)
1982.   *Mammal Species of the World*. Allen Press: Lawrence.

Jackson, J., P. Landa, and A. Langguth
1980.   Pampas deer in Uruguay. *Oryx*, 15:267–272.

Jackson, J.E., and A. Langguth
This   Ecology and status of the pampas deer (*Ozotoceros*
volume *bezoarticus*) in the Argentian Pampas and Uruguay.

Mishra, H.R., and C.M. Wemmer
This   The comparative breeding ecology of four cervids in
volume Royal Chitwan National Park, Nepal.

Pereira, S.M., G. Schuerholz, and E.K. Bastos
1981.   Parque Nacional das Emas. Apêndice ao Plano de
         Manejo (Trabalho de campo). Unpubl. report.

Schaller, G.B.
1967.   *The Deer and the Tiger*. Chicago: University of
         Chicago Press.

Schaller, G.B., and N. Duplaix-Hall
1975.   Notes on the large mammals of Parque Nacional das
         Emas. Unpublished report. IBDF Proc. no.
         004370/75.

Whitehead, G.K.
1972.   *Deer of the World*. New York: Viking Press.

Part III

Management in the Wild and in Captivity

DANNY C. WHARTON
New York Zoological Park
Bronx Park
Bronx, New York 10460

Captive Management of the Large Malayan Chevrotain (*Tragulus napu*) at New York Zoological Park

ABSTRACT

This article contains a description of diet, housing, breeding, health management and handling techniques for a captive collection of *Tragulus napu*, the larger Malayan chevrotain (or mouse deer). A note on genetic management is included in reference to the fact that this collection is descended from a single pair of animals imported in 1961. Growth and development of inbred versus outbred young are discussed.

Introduction

All tragulid species have been maintained in captivity in various zoos throughout the world, including the three species of the genus, *Tragulus javanicus, meminna* and *napu,* as well as *Hyemoschus aquaticus* (Crandall, 1964). However, only *Tragulus javanicus* and *napu,* the Malayan species, have so far proven adaptable enough to be bred in significant numbers in captivity (Olney, 1984).

From 1904 to 1926, six specimens of *Tragulus* (including one specimen of *meminna*—the Indian chevrotain) were received at New York Zoological Park (Bronx Zoo) (Crandall, 1964). Although one animal lived almost three years, the record for these captive animals was not good. Even as late as 1964 when Crandall's *Management of Wild Mammals in Captivity* was published, the four years and eight months longevity record set in 1909 by a London specimen of the greater Malayan chevrotain (*Tragulus napu*) in 1909 was still standing. Crandall himself (1964) notes: "...in spite of the fact that most of the Asiatic chevrotains that reach zoological gardens are handreared, perfectly tame animals, they never have become firmly established." He would be surprised today to know that several of the New York specimens he referred to in the same text (then only recently acquired) would live longer than 14 years. The single pair of *Tragulus napu* acquired in 1961 eventually produced 16 young and over 175 descendants to date. Thirty of these are living in several collections in the United States, the majority of specimens still residing at the Bronx Zoo (Figure 1).

No one can say for certain why tragulids did so poorly in captivity in New York and elsewhere before the arrival of the 1961 pair. Since then, the lesser Malayan chevrotain (*T. javanicus*) has also done well in captivity, both in Europe and Asia. The 1982 Census of Rare Animals in Captivity (Olney, 1984) shows 56 specimens total, over half of which were captive born. The purpose of this report is to summarize aspects of management practiced at the Bronx Zoo, with the single species *Tragulus napu.*

Diet

One might suspect diet as a major factor in the success of modern collections. Again, Crandall (1964) reports markedly different diets for the animals received 1904–1926 as opposed to those received in 1961. The earlier diet of mostly leaves, fruits, and roots is conspicuously low in protein, diced bread being its major source. Later diets are relatively high in protein.

The current daily ration per chevrotain consists of approximately 75 grams sweet potato, 75 grams carrot, 50 grams hydroponically grown grass (oats, rye,

Figure 1. The large Malayan chevrotain, *Tragulus napu*; a descendent of a pair of animals imported to the U.S. in 1961.

barley), ½ cup Blue Seal brand "Herbi Mix" (fortified grain mixture), and 3 monkey chow biscuits. To this diet is added 0.3 ml multiple vitamin drops (pet drops) sprinkled on vegetables.

Monkey chow is a highly nutritious biscuit and is fed to a number of non-primates as a sort of nutritional insurance. It assays at 15% protein and includes the whole array of vitamin and mineral supplements. The fortified grain mixture assays at 16% protein.

Rabbit salt blocks were provided in the past, but when provided lately they have been largely ignored. The grain ration, however, does contain salt.

Information on diet in the wild is sparse. Lekagul and McNeely (1977) suggest that *javanicus* feeds on shoots, grass, wild fruits, buds and young leaves.

Housing

There are 30 specimens of *Tragulus napu* at New York Zoological Park. All but five of these are housed off-exhibit in the basements of the Primate House and Lion House. The cages measure approximately 1 m × 1 m × 1 m, and are kept in rows with shift doors connecting the units. Cages constructed of wood with hardware cloth fronts are raised one m off the floor on wooden legs. Metal pans hold food and water and the floor is covered with about 2 cm of shavings which are changed daily.

The animals on exhibit are kept in a glass-fronted enclosure of similar dimensions. Some rock work and wooden logs are also provided in addition to the standard food and water pans.

The most important factor we have had to consider in housing this species is their penchant for injuring themselves in sudden bursts of panic. By providing cages of small dimensions, the animals are unable to build up a great deal of velocity during these moments of panic. While they still bounce off walls from time to time, they usually do so without serious injury in these cages.

Animals on exhibit are exposed to glass-tapping by the public, but generally they become placid and seldom react violently to novel stimuli.

Normally a single pair and one offspring are the maximum number of chevrotains housed together. A breeding pair is usually given access to two cages and are shifted together in one cage only during cleaning. In the past, one male, two or three females and their offspring were successfully housed together in the same caging (F. Casella, pers. comm.). However, increased nervousness and unrest are seen when more than two adults are kept in the same cage. Compatible mother-adult daughter pairs are prone to permanent upset upon the introduction of a male to their space. Offspring have on occasion been left with the parents for over a year when the pair fails to produce another youngster. However, adult males usually pursue and often cause injury to young of either sex when they reach approximately six months of age.

Twelve hours of white fluorescent light are alternated with twelve hours of dark most of the time in the off-exhibit areas in the Lion House basement. Lighting is often altered from this regimen for the benefit of other species. Also, heat lamps on other species from time to time provide at least some light during the dark hours. The light switch in the Primate House basement malfunctioned in 1980 leaving the animals in constant, 24 hours of light per day for several months. All of these variations in lighting appear to have occurred without ill effect.

Handling

Hands-on restraint is avoided as severe back, leg and hip injuries can occur when the animals try to free themselves from the handler's grasp. Males may also injure the handler by slashing with the "tusks" or protruding canines. Moves are best accomplished by allowing the specimen to become accustomed to a small, windowless crate so that simply closing the door is all that is necessary to contain the animal prior to moving.

Until recently, ear tattooing for identification was performed on the day the young animal was separated from its parents. Now, it is delayed until a more critical need for handling arises, or is done at one or two weeks of age when there is much less resistance to handling.

When handling must be performed (e.g., medical treatment), the chevrotain is seized as quickly as possible and clutched to the handler's chest with both arms pinning the animal's legs and body in firm restraint. Return of the animal to its cage is best accomplished by swift release in order to minimize the chances for struggle and injury.

Breeding

Prospective mates are usually housed separately in adjoining cages for at least several days and introduced by simply opening the shift door. In most cases, the animals spend the next 3 or 4 hours investigating each other (ano-genital sniffing, nose-tongue contact around the face). In some cases, the introduction incites sudden panic. If panic continues the animals are separated and reintroduced a few days later. If no panic is observed within the first hour, the pair usually settles down together without incident.

Animals that have had mating experience are generally less problematic upon introduction to a new mate. Young chevrotains, particularly those that have lived in isolation for several weeks or months, are the most difficult to introduce, especially when both animals are young and accustomed to isolation. We usually attempt to pair young chevrotains immediately upon separation from parents (with older, experienced animals where possible). Separation from parents is usually accomplished at around five months of age, right at (or just prior to) the birth of the next young. It should be noted that older young are tolerated quite well by the post-partum mothers.

Post-partum estrus is the rule in the Malayan chevrotain (Davis, 1965; Cadigan, 1972), and in our collection copulation is most often observed on the day of parturition. In observing the New York collection in the early 1960s, Davis (1965) noted copulation in one pair only 85 minutes after parturition. Pregnancy frequently results from these post-partum matings. Under ideal circumstances, a female will regularly reproduce every 5 months (152–155 days; Davis, 1965). Since 1961, only one set of twins has occurred in over 175 births. Both fetuses were stillborn. When post-partum copulation does not occur or result in pregnancy, estrus reoccurs 14 days later (Ralls, Barasch, Minkowski, 1975).

Davis (1965) reported that two chevrotain fawns produced by the original (and presumably unrelated) founders of the New York collection weighed 371 and 379 grams. Weights taken since 1979 indicate that virtually no fawns weigh as much as these first two. Weights of 250–325 grams are considered good and weights of 225 grams are not uncommon. Low birth weights are often related to neonatal mortality. Small fawns are given every chance to settle in quietly with their mothers by separating the male as soon after the birth as possible. This eliminates several hours of courtship and mating that would otherwise take place. We usually give the fawn a month or two to become established before reintroducing the male. This results in birth intervals of seven months or more, but we still see five month intervals, indicating that mating often occurs before the new birth has been noticed. An excellent description of sexual behavior in *T. napu* may be found in Ralls, et al. (1975).

Chevrotain fawns are routinely given a multiple vitamin injection at birth, and a heat lamp is provided in one corner. Weights are taken daily for the first three days and every other day for the remainder of the first week. Loss of up to 10 grams between days one and two is not unusual. Continued loss at this rate indicates that the fawn has not yet commenced nursing. Under normal circumstances, fawns either weigh more on day three than day two, or at least exhibit little or no additional weight loss. By day four, weight gain accelerates in the normal fawn and usually the fawn continues growth without interruption until adult size is reached at about 6 months. Time-lapse video tape recordings of one fawn made by MacNamara and Kalina (1981) showed that nursing frequency increased from 13 times on day one to 29 times before day six. After day five, nursing decreased to a low of three times on day nine. Intake of solid food may have been sufficient to cause the decreased demand for milk. Nursing probably continues until 3 months of age (Davis, 1965).

Adult size is reached by six months, but the skeleton continues to ossify and males do not show the large, protruding canines until 10 months of age at the earliest. They continue to grow throughout life, although they are broken off accidently from time to time and, as a result, seldom exceed 5–7 cm in length.

Female chevrotains can attain sexual maturity as early as 4.5 months, as demonstrated by one female which gave birth at 9.5 months of age (Davis, 1965). A male was observed copulating at 135 days of age (Davis, 1965), but with a female that bred with a mature male at the same time. In any case, the female apparently did not conceive until about 14 days later as indicated by the birth interval of 172 days. Breeding was not observed during the cycle that resulted in pregnancy; however, both males were still housed with her at the time (F. Casella, pers. comm.). Another male (811113) experienced a spontaneous ejaculation at 128 days of age while being tattooed in the right ear. Microscopic examination of the ejaculate showed it to be seminal plasma only, lacking in sperm cells (J. Stover, pers. comm.). When the male

was a little over 10 months of age his mate aborted a 75 gram fetus. We might guess, from the size of the premature fetus, that it was conceived when the sire was around 7 months of age.

It should be noted that handrearing of *T. napu* has been mostly unsuccessful; however, most attempts have been with fawns that have not nursed and have continued to lose weight in the presence of a live, healthy dam. Since this occurs with experienced as well as inexperienced dams, we suspect that the fawns may lack the proper interest and/or ability to feed.

Genetic Management

Needless to say, genetic management of a population descended from a single pair is a great concern. Ideally, one should introduce additional specimens from the wild and discontinue the inbreeding necessary under the present circumstances. Further importation has so far proved to be difficult: (1) in finding a practical source of the species and (2) planning for lengthy, multiple quarantines of relatively delicate animals. Nonetheless, we are pursuing importation in order to assure this species a better foothold in western zoological gardens. The original pair produced 16 offspring, thirteen of which not only survived to weaning, but lived for years afterward—one reaching an age of 14 years and seven others living at least 10 years. This might indicate that a non-inbred population of *Tragulus napu* would be relatively easy to propagate. The current, inbred population exhibits lower birth weights and lower neonatal viability. We also suspect our females achieve delayed sexual maturity, but other aspects of our management preclude objective analysis (e.g., young females are not always housed with a mature, proven male).

On the positive side, the inbred population still exhibits good fertility. Few animals have proven to be non-breeders and a supply of young (albeit frail) are produced regularly.

Six of the original pair's offspring have descendants in the current collection. Pedigree data of a fairly reliable nature is available on each specimen and pairings are still possible which yield offspring with inbreeding coefficients lower than .30. The majority of matings are made on a maximum avoidance of inbreeding basis (see Wright, 1969). Individuals with the highest inbreeding coefficients often produce young with the lowest. The highly inbred animals are less likely to represent all possible lines and are therefore more available for the "outcrossing" that is possible within this context.

Health Management

Several health problems have been identified in *T. napu* in the New York collection (E. Dolensek, pers.

comm.). These include a polyarthritis, pneumonia, an upper respiratory problem seen in connection with a frothy nasal exudate, and opacity and ulceration of the eyes in neonates.

The upper respiratory problem has not been a significant concern since the installation of a humidifier in the Primate House basement area. A minimal humidity of 80% appears to be a requirement for this species' well-being.

Eye lesions generally clear up as the neonate grows. We are not certain whether this clearing is spontaneous, or a result of Vitamin E, A, and selenium provided in the routine injection given to all neonates. It appears that heat lamps and vitamin injections have been factors responsible for increased survival of the more fragile, inbred young now produced.

Products mentioned in the text:

Blue Seal Herbi Mix
Manufactured by H.K. Webster Co. Inc.,
Lawrence, MA

Monkey Chow
Manufactured by Ralston-Purina
Checkerboard Square
St. Louis, MO 63188

Pet Drops
Manufactured by Upjohn
Kalamazoo, MI

Literature Cited

Cadigan, F.C.
1972. Brief report on copulatory and perinatal behavior of the lesser Malayan Mouse deer (*T. javanicus*). *Malayan Nature Journal*, 25:112–116.

Casella, F.
1963. Personal notes on observation of *T. napu* (September 16). Unpublished.

Crandall, L.S.
1964. *Management of Wild Mammals in Captivity*. Chicago: University of Chicago Press.

Davis, J.
1965. A preliminary report of the reproductive behavior of the small (sic) Malayan Chevrotain. *International Zoo Yearbook*, 5:42–44.

Lekagul, B., and J. McNeely
1977. *Mammals of Thailand*. Bangkok: Kurusapha Ladpra Press, Sahakarnbhat Company.

MacNamara, M., and J. Kalina
1981. Time-lapse video tape recording as a tool in behavioral studies. *International Zoo Yearbook*, 21:207–209.

Olney, P.J.
1981. Census of rare animals in captivity in 1980. *International Zoo Yearbook*, 21:383.

Ralls, K., C. Barasch, and K. Minkowski
1975. Behavior of captive mouse deer, *Tragulus napu*. *Zeitschrift für Tierpsychologie*, 37:356–378.

Wright, S.
1969. *The Theory of Gene Frequencies*. Vol. II. Chicago: University of Chicago Press.

HANS FRÄDRICH
Zoologischer Garten Berlin
Hardenbergplatz 8
D-1000 Berlin 30
West Germany

The Husbandry of Tropical and Temperate Cervids in the West Berlin Zoo

ABSTRACT

The deer collection of the Berlin Zoo presently comprises 21 species and subspecies, some of them seldom found in captivity. Details are given on housing, feeding and general management (incompatibility of stags, negative effects of handrearing, problems resulting from an unbalanced sex ratio). Although some of the tropical species were imported into Europe long ago they continue to reproduce year round. Males of these species follow an individual rather than a seasonal antler cycle; they are fertile throughout the year regardless of the stage of antler development. Brocket and marsh deer show a tendency to wear the same set of antlers much longer than other deer. Post-partum estrus in tropical deer seems to be more frequent than previously believed. Description of a muntjac hybrid (*M. muntjak* × *M. reevesi*) is also included.

History

Deer have always played a very important role in the 138-year-old history of the Berlin Zoo. For a long period of time they were better represented than any other family of large mammals, and by the turn of the century about 35 varieties —including some hybrids—were to be found in the collection. This number will never be reached again as we do not have the facilities to house them properly. In the old days space was even more limited. The animals—mainly single stags or pairs—lived side by side in long and narrow barred enclosures. This museum-like display made breeding very difficult but was a considerable attraction to taxonomists and trophy hunters since it enabled them to compare museum specimens with living animals, and to observe antlers and antler development in a variety of species. Of the many interesting species found at that time some are worth mentioning: North Andean deer, *H. antisensis* (1889–1902, 1931–1941, Figure 1h), marsh deer, *B. dichotomus* (1896, 1900–1094, 1940, Figure 1i), pampas deer, *Ozot. bezoarticus* (1900–1916), Bawean deer, *Axis kuhli* (1901), Schomburgk's deer, *C. schomburgki* (1862–1877, 1899–1911 – the last specimen of its kind in a zoo, Figure 1a), Kashmir deer, *C. elaphus hanglu (1905–1914)*, Barbary deer, *C. elaphus barbarus* (1899–1915, 1926–1940), Sardinian red deer, *C. elaphus corsicanus* (1901–1914, 1929–1940, Figure 1g), and Persian fallow deer, *C. mesopotamica* (1900–1903). In others, namely Southeast Asian species like the Prince Alfred's deer, *C. mariannus alfredi* (1910–1938, Figure 1b) good breeding results were achieved for many years. None of these groups, including the North Andean Deer which had given birth to at least 6 males and 6 females within 10 years survived World War II (Frädrich, 1978). Except for the Schomburgk's deer, extinct since 1938, all other species still exist in the wild but most of them are struggling for survival and are found in zoos—if at all—in very small numbers only. In view of their precarious status the question arises—what has happened to the rich material of former times? Most specimens, sent to museums, are still preserved as skins or skeletons, a number of photographs exists (Figure 1), and some basic biological information was published in miscellaneous papers. This seems to be little, and yet it is more than was normally done in those days.

One of the main tasks of a modern zoo is education; another is breeding. Both require space. The concept of an overall comprehensive collection was partially abandoned already in the early 1930s in favor of more naturalistic displays of deer groups instead of single specimens. Even today we are keeping 21 species and subspecies of deer totaling about 120 individuals, but the process of reduction, resulting in specialization, is likely to continue in the future, because of the lack of space a typical city zoo now faces (Frädrich, 1980).

Housing

In European zoos wild cattle and antelope from warmer countries are traditionally housed in solid well-heated buildings, but stables for deer have always been rather simple from the technical point of view. After a period of acclimatization most cervids, even if imported from tropical regions, prove to be quite hardy in cold weather. They remain outdoors for many hours during the daytime even when temperatures are below freezing, and they rarely suffer frostbitten ears or tails as long as they have access to their shelters. Stables for tropical deer are heated by electric radiators in the winter, guaranteeing temperatures above freezing. These precautions have to be taken not only for the grey brocket, *Maz. gouazoubira*, and marsh deer, *B. dichotomus*, both of which are nonseasonal breeders and in our experience are more sensitive to cold than the others (Figure 2), but also for all species with no fixed breeding season, like axis deer (*Axis axis*), hog deer (*Axis porcinus*), rusa deer (*C. timorensis*), muntjacs and tropical pampas deer. They give birth in winter as well as summer months (Figures 2 and 3), and without heated shelters their young might easily succumb to frost, snow or cold rain. An interesting case is the Eld's or brow-antlered deer (*Cervus eldi thamin*). Even though it does have a fixed reproductive cycle the rut is so late in the year that in northern latitudes most of their young are born in the early winter (Blakeslee et al., 1979). This species, which has been kept in Europe and the US already in the second or even third generation, did not shift its breeding season to periods of mild weather in its new environment (see Figure 3). The barasingha (*Cervus duvauceli*) on the other hand, gives birth predominantly in fair weather months, but late births can be adversely affected by winter weather. On the other hand, Southern pudus (*P. puda*) are perfectly able to adjust within one or two years to the climatic conditions of the northern hemisphere, both in antler cycle and reproductive behavior (Frädrich, 1974), a phenomenon also known of red deer, *C. elaphus*, brought from Europe to southern South America or New Zealand (Whitehead, 1972).

The outdoor enclosures are relatively small, varying in size from 75 to 900 square meters. Most of them consist of sandy natural ground, others have a harder surface with interspersed sandy areas, allowing the deer to rest comfortably. Drainage is excellent, thus we do not have any serious problems with endoparasites. Shade, very important to the Northern and Southern pudu and for musk deer as well, is provided

Figure 1. A montage of little–known deer, many of which were exhibited at the Berlin Zoo in bygone days. (a) This Schomburgk's deer (*Cervus schomburgki*), caught in 1897 on the Korat plains of Thailand, was acquired by the German Mr. Bethge, Director of the Siamese Railways, and was given by him to the Berlin Zoo, where it lived – the last specimen of its kind in captivity – from July 29, 1899 until September 7, 1911, photo by Berlin Zoo. (b) Prince Alfred's deer (*Cervus mariannus alfredi*): virtually nothing is known of the present distribution of this deer from the Philippines, photo by Berlin Zoo. (c) The rusa deer (*Cervus timorensis*) from the Moluccas (Indonesia), photo by Berlin Zoo. (d) The small Philippine sambar (*Cervus mariannus*), photo by Berlin Zoo. (e) Thamin or Burmese brow-antlered deer (*Cervus eldi thamin*), this specimen of unknown origin, photo by Berlin Zoo. (f) Musk deer (*Moschus* spp.) have virtually disappeared from Western zoos, photo by Berlin Zoo. (g) The short-legged Sardinian red der (*Cervus elaphus corsicanus*) – threatened with extinction, photo by Berlin Zoo. (h) North Andean deer (*Hippocamelus antisensis*), photo by Berlin Zoo. (i) Marsh deer (*Blastocerus dichotomus*), photo by Hans Frädrich. (j) Southern pudus (*Pudu puda*), photo by Fred Kleinschmidt. (k) Northern pudus (*Pudu mephistopheles*), photo by Reiner Baumann.

Frädrich

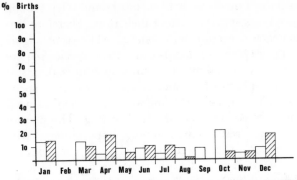

Figure 2.   Monthly distribution of births at the Berlin Zoo of two South American aseasonal breeders. Clear bars = grey brocket (*Mazama gouazoubira*), n = 24; Cross-hatched bars = pampus deer (*Ozotoceros bezoarticus*), n = 21.

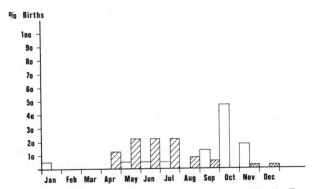

Figure 3.   Monthly distribution of births at the Berlin Zoo of two Asian deer exhibiting loosely synchronized breeding seasons. Clear bars = Eld's or Burmese brow-antlered deer (*Cervus eldi thamin*), n = 21; cross-hatched bars = barasingha (*Cervus duvauceli*), n = 32.

by a number of trees and bushes, the trunks of which are protected from nibbling and rubbing of the antlers. To facilitate the rubbing off of velvet stags are provided with pine branches, "planted" vertically and replaced from time to time. These branches also serve as cover, hiding the animals from the visitors' view. In most enclosures there are facilities for the newborn young where they can hide (tree trunks, wooden racks protecting live trees). This proves especially useful when older fawns are still in the group since they tend to disturb the newborn just by their curiosity. Where there are no moats (210 cm deep, 150 cm wide at the base and 510 cm on top), we use fences which are 180 cm high, for even the smallest species, when startled, may show a considerable ability to jump. For smaller species moats are less well suited than for bigger ones.

Feeding

Feeding of grazers like barasingha (*C. duvauceli*), axis and red deer generally is not problematical, but on occasion troubles do arise with some of the browsing species. Roe deer, mule and white-tailed deer, brockets, pudus and, to a lesser degree, muntjacs need an extremely varied diet throughout the year. In addition to the basic food, consisting of rolled oats, crushed corn, white bread, pellets (developed for dairy cattle) and good quality hay, they receive many kinds of fruits and vegetables according to the season. This diet is supplemented with mineral salt, linseed and regularly by aromatic tea leaves. Twigs of willow, maple, birth and others are given whenever obtainable. We have been forced to refrain from keeping moose because we are unable to supply them with the large amount of browse they require.

During the winter some of the more delicate deer are fed small portions of leaves which we deep-freeze mainly for certain leaf-eating monkeys. In spite of all our efforts with regard to a balanced diet we sometimes observe physical deterioration of nursing females. This applies mainly to those browsers in which twins are frequent. During lactation, roe, mule and white-tailed deer therefore need special attention. Gewalt (1966) reports on captive deer having occasionally eaten live and dead birds as well as meat. Although meat and eggs are readily accepted by some deer as they are by duikers (*Cephalophus*) we do not think it necessary to supply them with animal protein. Repeated cases of cannibalism in rusa deer, *C. timorensis*, in which a male killed and partially ate even a 10-day-old young, have to be attributed more to behavioral defects than to an inadequate diet.

Social Problems

The aggressiveness of male cervids from temperate zones usually does not permit the keeping of several adult stags with the females during the rutting period. Therefore younger males are removed from the herd at the end of their second year; the extremely incompatible Chinese water deer (*Hydropotes inermis*) are separated at an even earlier age. Male tropical deer are more tolerant because of their individual antler cycles, but as younger stags they seem to suffer psychically from adult males at least in smaller enclosures, so it is advisable to remove them annually at a given time. Often the lack of rivalry among equal stags leads to an increasing aggressiveness which then may be directed toward the females, causing panic and sometimes casualties among them. Heavy logs that can be rolled over but not thrown may distract the stags for some time but are not an overall remedy to this problem.

"Toys" of this kind do not work in smaller species carrying spike-like weapons. Stags wearing large spreading antlers can be prevented from persecuting females by a barrier of wooden posts having gaps narrow enough for the females but not the stags to slip through. Specimens proven to persecute their females to a critical extent are immobilized to have their antlers sawn off. At first, the removal of the weapons is a shock to the animal, but it nearly always quickly recovers psychically and is perfectly able not only to regain its former social rank, but also to resume normal sexual activity. The latter observation has been disputed, but from our experience we do not know of a single case where an animal treated in that way became unfit for breeding. The sight of a stag wearing antler stumps is admittedly not very appealing to the public, so whenever possible we try to avoid this procedure. Muntjacs are the only deer in which several fully grown males can be kept together with the females in an extremely limited space. This is quite astonishing as *Muntiacus* is clearly not a very social species (Barrette, 1977a). Although we never experienced serious fighting among the males, females are likely to suffer in this situation from the permanent stress; they become nervous and intimidated and show a clear tendency to neglect their young.

Pregnant females belonging to the more nervous species like Eld's deer, marsh deer and pampas deer usually are separated from the group in order to give them privacy when birth-giving and during the first weeks of nursing. This method helps to quickly establish a strong mother-child relationship which certainly is an advantage when they become reintegrated into a larger group after some weeks.

Hand-rearing is not so much a technical problem as a general one. We decide each time according to circumstances on how to proceed when a young is born in poor condition or rejected by its mother. If the animal belongs to a common species in most cases we refrain from the time-consuming procedure of hand-rearing as we understand this sort of natural selection to be in the interest of maintaining a healthy stock. As a substitute for the mother's milk we use exclusively the milk of domestic goats. We keep a number of goats just for that purpose, and have successfully used goats as foster mothers for newborn marsh deer which obstinately refused to take the bottle. In most cases hand-reared fawns develop well, and even animals that were runts at birth may reach normal size and weight. Bottle-feeding, however, quite often leads to defects in behavior. Hand-reared stags may refuse to mate as adults, and therefore become useless for breeding programs. Females, put into a group when independant, may become pregnant, but having never learned to fight with conspecifics they are suppressed

again and again by herd members and often remain social outcasts throughout their lives. Therefore it is somehow contradictory to bottle-feed fawns belonging to rarer species of deer because these species require especially careful management to guarantee their survival as physically fit and behaviorally normal specimens. Yet for the time being we cannot afford to avoid the risks connected with hand-rearing. The present veterinary restrictions regarding importation of wild ruminants from certain developing countries in Southeast Asia and Latin America are likely to be tightened further on the international scale, and consequently captive stock of rare deer is now extremely valuable since it will be hardly possible to replace losses or add wild-caught specimens.

Breeding Season and Antler Cycle

In the temperate and cold regions of Eurasia and North America antler and reproductive cycles of cervids are controlled by photoperiod. European deer kept in European zoos mate and give birth at the same general time as their wild relatives, thus showing that optimal feeding throughout the year has no effect on seasonal breeding. Whereas rutting and parturition are restricted to a few well-defined months in deer from northern latitudes, things are different in a tropical environment. Although breeding there may be determined by various ecological factors, notably the dry and rainy season, several tropical species are known to give birth at any time of the year (see Sadleir, this volume). Some deer inhabiting the lowland regions of tropical South America show a tendency to wear the same set of antlers much longer than a year (Bubenik, 1966). Although there is a lack of precise and detailed information from the wild we have been able to confirm this unusual phenomenon in our zoo. A *Maz. gouazoubira*, about 8 years old, shed his antlers on December 16, 1966, keeping the new spikes until his death on August 30, 1969. Data on captive *B. dichotomus* just collected indicate that stags of breeding age and in excellent health may wear an antler set up to 21 months. If male fertility were only dependent on the presence of hard antlers, these stags would be able to mate successfully for a long period of time, which also would result in a prolonged period of parturition if females were fertile year round. In others, namely some of the Southeast Asian species, i.e., rusa deer (*Cervus timorensis*) and, hog deer (*Axis porcinus*), stags undergo a regular yearly antler cycle, but it is more an individual rather than a seasonal one, so that in a given population all stages of antler development may be seen at the same time. Theoretically one could hypothesize that in a gregarious species the widespread distribution of birth dates is due only to stags

Frädrich

with hard antlers which then successively become involved in mating. Such clear interdependence is, however, unlikely to exist. In nearly all cases shown in our records only one male was involved in breeding and yet the young were born in almost any month of the year. Barrette's statement (1977b), that muntjacs are perfectly able to successfully mate while still in velvet, therefore does not only apply to this genus but to brockets (*Mazama* spp.), marsh deer (*Blastocerus dichotomus*), and tropical pampas deer (*Ozotocerus bezoarticus*) as well. The females of all these species hence must be polyestrus throughout the year.

Post-partum Estrus and Twins

Another striking feature of at least some tropical deer is the post-partum estrus. It occurred repeatedly in our *M. muntjak*, and that not only in females having experienced stillbirths or having lost their fawns, but also in specimens rearing their young. The average birth interval was 241 days (n = 60) (gestation period 210 days, n = 40, range = 205–215). Lactation therefore does not inhibit ovarian activity, and consequently females may be pregnant almost continuously. An immediate post-partum estrus was also found in *B. dichotomus*. A female, whose fawn was taken away on its second day, was observed mating two days after parturition and gave birth to another calf 271 days later. This birth interval must be identical with the so far unknown gestation period of this species. As the post-partum estrus has also been found in *Maz. americana* (Gardner, 1971) this phenomenon is likely to be more common in tropical deer than previously believed. It might prove particularly adaptive for smaller species (including *Tragulus*), suffering from heavy predation and therefore needing a high reproduction rate.

In this context it should be mentioned that twins, on the other hand, are extremely rare in deer originating from warmer regions. Neither in muntjacs nor in any of the neotropical species in our zoo did we record even a single case of twinning, and it is reported also that the otherwise multiparous white-tailed deer in warmer climate usually gives birth to a single young (Crandall, 1964). Only in barasingha deer did we once record twins, and of course it is very often noted in Chinese water deer which, however, can hardly be classified as a tropical species.

Sex Ratio

A review of the births that have occurred during the last 20 years in some of our more prolific groups clearly shows to what an extent a zoo may have to deal with the problem of supernumerary males. Although the figures are not statistically significant, only in barasingha deer were more females than males born (6%, n = 32). An approximate 1:1 sex ratio was found in pampas deer (n = 21), Manchurian sika (n = 44), sambar (n = 32) and Indian muntjac (n = 71). Males exceeded females by 16% in *Maz. gouazoubira* (n = 24), by 14% in Burmese Eld's deer (n = 21), by 20% in Reeve's muntjac (n = 55), by 9% in axis deer (n = 51), and by 4% in hog deer (n = 62). Juvenile mortality affected both sexes equally. However, many less males are needed for breeding programs, and surplus male stock has to be disposed of one way or the other. Culling is a common practice for deer that are well established in our collections, but rarer species of course cannot be treated that way. As it is not desirable to keep these deer just in pairs the establishment of all-male groups will probably be necessary in the future. In the long run these groups may serve as a gene reservoir which may be utilized whenever necessary. (A sperm bank would be equally helpful but for the time being artificial insemination in zoo animals is still in a very early and tentative stage.) It is our policy to send surplus young of rarer species to other places as soon as our own breeding group is adequately stocked. These transactions, usually based on breeding loan agreements, are mainly carried out on a national rather than international scale, because they enable us to easily acquire specimens we might need again in the future. The risk involved in overseas transports with veterinary restrictions and the prolonged quarantine periods are necessary but unfortunate obstacles that are difficult to overcome. This is also true for some recommendations made by studbook keepers: although useful in principle, in the case of ruminants they are sometimes hard to follow.

In spite of all the difficulties mentioned, even a zoo with limited space is able to become an important supplier to other institutions. It should also serve as a place for comparative studies, namely of those cervids which are difficult to observe in the wild. We recently started an extensive program of genetic studies in our zoo. In this context it may be worth mentioning that just for that purpose we tried to obtain muntjac hybrids. Whereas an Indian female (*M. muntjak*) which lived in a group of Reeve's muntjacs (*M. reevesi*) for more than two years did not become pregnant, a Reeve's female did conceive when put together with Indian males. Thus on October 8, 1980, a male hybrid was born and raised, followed on September 8, 1981 by a stillborn young and on March 19, 1982 by a premature-born male. Regarding the surprising difference in the number of chromosomes (*M. muntjak* with only 6, *M. reevesi* with 46), as found by Wurster and Atkins (1972) and confirmed by Neitzel (1979, 1982) in our zoo, this strange creature, which looks like a small

Indian except for the head, is of considerable interest. It is most unlikely that it will prove to be fertile.

Many species of deer have vanished completely from zoo collections during recent decades or have become very rare (Figure 1). The uniformity of the captive stock is regrettable since many of the less conspicuous smaller species are not very well known. As long as it is not too late these species should receive more intensive study and expanded breeding.

Literature Cited

Barrette, C.
1977a. Fighting behavior of muntjac and the evolution of antlers. *Evolution*, 31, 1:169–176.

1977b. Some aspects of the behaviour of muntjacs in Wilpattu National Park. *Mammalia*, 41, 1:1–34.

Blakeslee, C.K., G.R. Clifford, and K. Ralls
1979. Behavior and reproduction of captive brow-antlered deer, *Cervus eldi thamin* (Thomas, 1918). *Säugetierkundliche Mitteilungen*, 29:114–127.

Bubenik, A.
1966. *Das Geweih*. Hamburg and Berlin: Paul Parey.

Crandall, L.S.
1964. *The management of wild mammals in captivity*. Chicago and London: The University of Chicago Press.

Frädrich, H.
1974. Notizen über seltener gehaltene Cerviden, Teil II. *Zoologische Garten* 45, 1:67–77.

1978. Bemerkungen über Nord-Andenhirsche (*Hippocamelus antisiensis*) im Berliner Zoo. *Bongo*, 2:81–88.

1980. Breeding endangered cervids in captivity. *International Zoo Yearbook*, 20:80–89.

Gardner, A.L.
1971. Postpartum oestrus in a red brocket deer, *Mazama americana*, from Peru. *Journal of Mammalogy*, 42:623–624.

Gewalt, W.
1966. Hirsche und Antilopen fressen Tauben an. *Zeitschrift für Säugetierkunde*, 31:407–409.

Neitzel, H.
1979. Chromosomenevolution in der Familie der Hirsche (*Cervidae*). *Bongo*, 3:27–38.

1982. Karyotypenevolution und deren Bedeutung für den Speciations-prozess der Cerviden (*Cervidae; Artiodactyla; Mammalia*). Ph.D. Dissertation, Freie Universität Berlin.

Whitehead, G.K.
1972. *Deer of the world*. London: Constable.

Wurster, D.H., and N.B. Atkins
1972. Muntjac chromosomes: a new karyotype for *Muntiacus muntjak*. *Experientia*, 28:972–973.

CHARLES T. ROBBINS,
OLAV T. OFTEDAL
and
KATHERINE I. O'ROURKE

Wildlife Biology Program
Washington State University
Pullman, Washington 99164

Department of Zoological Research
National Zoological Park
Washington, DC 20008

Department of Veterinary Microbiology and Pathology
Washington State University
Pullman, Washington 99164

Lactation, Early Nutrition, and Hand-Rearing of Wild Ungulates, with Special Reference to Deer

ABSTRACT   Cervid milks contain 19–26% dry matter, 6–11% fat, 6–10% protein, 3–5% sugar, and 1.1–2.0% ash. When compared at peak lactation, cervid milks are all reasonably similar in gross composition and more concentrated than domestic bovid milks. Ingestion of colostrum and immunoglobulin absorption are essential for neonatal survival. Both the duration and number of suckling bouts decrease during lactation in maternal-raised cervids as the rate of milk removal from the udder increases. Recommendations for hand-rearing are given with the recognition that far more research is needed to understand lactation and growth in cervids.

Introduction

Lactation has long been of interest to cervid biologists attempting to elucidate life history patterns in deer. While the behaviorist and ecologist have long quantified various parameters of cervid lactation, major progress in understanding the transfer of nutrients and passive immunity from the mother to the neonate has been more recent. The advent of isotope methods for measuring milk consumption by maternal-nursed fawns (MacFarlane et al., 1969; Holleman et al., 1975), the development and application of electrophoretic and coagulation tests to quantitate milk and serum immunoglobulins (O'Rourke and Satterfield, 1981; Parkinson et al., 1982), and the application of evolutionary theory to all aspects of reproductive biology have stimulated lactation research. Milk production imposes a large and sustained energy and nutrient demand on the lactating female. The cost and success of reproduction is a function of both prenatal and postnatal transfer of nutrients and immune system elements to the young, but the quantitative contribution of postnatal transfers is far greater than prenatal transfers in cervids.

Detailed knowledge of normal nutrient intakes, disease and immune processes, and growth of maternal-

Table 1. Published reports on the gross composition of cervid milks[1]

Species	References	Number of Milk Samples	Lactation Stage (days postpartum)
Alces alces (Moose, European elk)	Kaestli (in Ben Shaul, 1962)	1	0?
	Borg (in Ben Shaul, 1962)	1	45?
	Ivanova, 1965	15	15
	Cook et al. 1970b	2	45– 85?
	Franzmann et al., 1975	20	4– 90?
Capreolus capreolus (Roe deer)	Borg (in Ben Shaul, 1962)	1	60?
Cervus elaphus (Red deer, North American elk)	Borg (in Ben Shaul, 1962)	1	2
	Ben Shaul, 1962	?	?
	Arman et al., 1974	101	0–261
	Krzywinski et al., 1980	15	0–286
	Robbins et al., 1981	84	7– 84
Cervus nippon (Sika deer)	Ben Shaul, 1962	?	?
Dama dama (Fallow deer)	Jenness and Sloan, 1970 (Jenness, pers. comm.)	1	60– 90
Odocoileus hemionus (Black-tailed and mule deer)	Browman and Sears, 1955	1	28
	Kitts et al., 1956	1	28
	Jenness and Sloan, 1970	1	?
	Mueller and Sadleir, 1977	60?	7–240
Odocoileus virginianus (White-tailed deer)	Murphy, 1960	1	21
	Silver, 1961	4	1–150?
	Ben Shaul, 1962	?	?
	Youatt et al., 1965	34	1– 21
	Jenness and Sloan, 1970 (Jenness, pers. comm.)	2	25?
Rangifer tarandus (Reindeer and caribou)	Werenskiold, 1895	2	60–110?
	Aschaffenberg et al., 1962	2	3–100
	Berge, 1963	13	50–100?
	Hatcher et al., 1967	2	0– 3
	Luhtala et al., 1968	47	25–100
	Luick et al., 1974	5	21–140

[1]Reported values converted to days postpartum for comparative purposes. Where only date of sampling is reported, approximate stage of lactation in days is calculated from usual parturition dates for the species.

Robbins, Oftedal, and O'Rourke

nursed cervids is required to evaluate and improve the hand-rearing of deer. Diarrhea, poor growth, and death are recurrent reminders of our inadequate knowledge of lactation. Published articles stress successful attempts while failures are seldom reported. The trial-and-error- process commonly used in hand-rearing orphaned neonates is rarely conducted in controlled circumstances that would allow firm conclusions to be drawn about the causes of success or failure. Fastidious attention to sanitation, liberal use of antibiotics and supplements, and early introduction of solid foods may have allowed young to survive on formulas that are far from optimal.

In this paper we briefly review available data on lactation, early nutrition, and the transfer of passive immunity in deer and offer comments on hand-rearing. We have focused on understanding the natural lactation process from which future improvement in hand-rearing must develop. Information on other un-gulates is included for comparative purposes and to illustrate comments that probably apply to cervids as well.

Milk Composition

Milk is a complex secretory fluid containing lipids in emulsion, proteins in colloidal dispersion, and various organic and inorganic constituents in aqueous solution (Ling et al., 1961; Jenness, 1974; Johnson, 1974). Interspecific differences occur not only in the relative proportions of the major nutrient categories (water, fat, protein, sugar and ash), but also in the specific components within each category. Knowledge of the detailed constituents of milk is restricted to a few domesticated species and humans. Among ruminants the domesticated bovids have been well studied, but rather little is known about cervid milks.

The earliest analyses of reindeer milk stem from 19th century Norway (Werenskiold, 1895), but most

Table 2. The gross composition of cervid milks at mid or peak lactation, with comparative data from some bovids

Species	Lactation Stage (days after birth)	Number of Samples	Dry Matter	Fat	Protein[1]	Sugar[2]	Ash	References
Cervidae								
Alces alces	> 2	15	21.5	10.0	8.4	3.0	1.5	Ivanova, 1965
	4–90	20	24.5	5.8	10.3	—	2.0	Franzmann et al., 1975
Cervus elaphus	3–31	'6	21.1	8.5	7.1[3]	4.5	1.4[4]	Arman et al., 1974
	5–77	6	22.1	9.4	6.2[3]	4.9	1.1	Krzywinski et al., 1980
	14–77	28	19.0	6.7	5.7	4.2	1.3	Robbins et al., 1981
Odocoileus hemionus	14–35	12	—	12.6	7.2[5]	4.8	1.4[5]	Mueller and Sadleir, 1977
Odocoileus virginianus	21–28	4+	22.5	7.7	8.2	4.6	1.5	Compilation[6]
Rangifer tarandus	21–30	6	26.3	10.9	9.5	3.4	1.3	Luhtala et al., 1968
								Luick et al., 1974
Bovidae								
Bos taurus	"Mature"	2000+	12.4	3.7	3.2[3]	4.6	0.7	Compilation[7]
Bubalis bubalis	30	42	16.8	6.5	4.3	4.9	0.8[8]	Eltawil et al., 1976
Oreamnos americanus	15–45	11	21.3	8.1	6.4	4.3	0.9	Robbins and Stevens, 1981
Ovis aries	14–35	194+	18.2	7.1	5.0	4.9	0.8	Compilation[9]
Ovis dalli	21–42	4	22.9	9.5	7.2	5.3	0.9	Cook et al., 1970a
Taurotragus oryx	30–60	11	21.9	9.9	6.3	4.4	1.1	Treus and Kravchenko, 1968

[1]Crude protein (total nitrogen × 6.38) unless otherwise noted.

[2]Values obtained by difference excluded.

[3]True protein (protein nitrogen × 6.38).

[4]Ash value from Ben Shaul (1962).

[5]Protein determined by dye-binding; ash value from Kitts et al. (1956).

[6]Mean values calculated from references in Table 1.

[7]Macy et al. (1953).

[8]Ash value from compilation by Laxminarayana and Dastur (1968).

[9]Oftedal (1981).

studies of cervid milks have occurred in the past few decades (Table 1). Data of at least a fragmentary nature exist for 8 cervid species (Table 2). Systematic studies encompassing most of the lactation period have been conducted in 3 species: red deer and North American elk, *C. elaphus* (Arman et al., 1974; Krzywinski et al., 1980; Robbins et al., 1981), black-tailed deer, *O. hemionus columbianus* (Mueller and Sadleir, 1977), and reindeer-caribou, *R. tarandus* (Luhtala et al., 1968; Luick et al., 1974). Virtually nothing is known about the milks of the smaller and tropical deer. Given these limitations of the data base, the generalizations about cervid milks made herein must be considered tentative.

Deer appear typical of ruminants in that milk composition is a function of lactation stage. Both the initial secretion (colostrum) and late lactation milk tend to be higher in dry matter, fat, and protein than milk produced during the middle or peak of lactation (Hatcher et al., 1967; Luhtala et al., 1968; Arman et al., 1974; Luick et al., 1974; Mueller and Sadleir, 1977; Robbins et al., 1981). The progressive rise in dry matter, fat, and protein in late lactation is especially pronounced in *Rangifer* (Luick et al., 1974). Sugar or lactose has declined in late lactation in reindeer and black-tailed deer, but remained relatively constant in *C. elaphus* (Luick et al., 1974; Mueller and Sadleir, 1977; Arman et al., 1974; Robbins et al., 1981).

In view of compositional changes that occur over the course of lactation, interspecific comparisons are most appropriate at equivalent postpartal periods. Reports on cervid milks that include few samples or provide insufficient information on sampling time are difficult to evaluate. For example, the values reported by Ben Shaul (1962) for *C. elaphus, C. nippon,* and *O. virginianus* are uniformly high in dry matter (34–36%), fat (19.0–19.7%), and protein (10.3–12.4%) and probably comprise colostral or late lactation samples, but no sampling information is given. The single sample of *Dama dama* milk was collected rather late in lactation (2–3 months postpartum, R. Jenness pers. comm.). Many reports and references to *Rangifer* milk are biased by the preponderance of late lactation samples, and thus overemphasize the high levels of dry matter, fat, and protein that occur in this period.

Mean values for peak lactation milk can be extracted from studies of 5 cervid species (Table 2). For comparison, representative values for a few bovids have also been included. Cervid milks appear to contain about 19–26% dry matter, 6–11% fat, 6–10% protein, 3–5% sugar and 1.1–2.0% ash. *Rangifer* milk at this time is only slightly higher in dry matter, fat, and protein than most of the other cervids studied. The apparent difference in fat content between *O. hemionus* and *O. virginianus* is surprising and may re-

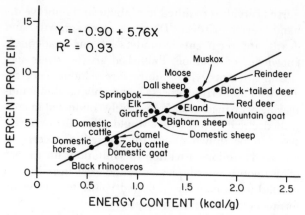

Figure 1. Milk protein and energy concentrations in ungulate milk (Kitts et al., 1956; Tener, 1956; Chen et al., 1965; Gregory et al., 1965; Treus and Kravchenko, 1968; Baker et al., 1970; Cook et al., 1970a; Van Zyl et al., 1970; Arman et al., 1974; Luick et al., 1974; Franzmann et al., 1975; Hall-Martin et al., 1977; Mueller and Sadleir, 1977; Krzywinski et al., 1980; Robbins et al., 1981; Robbins and Stevens, 1981). When energy values were not reported, caloric equivalents of 9.25 kcal/g of fat, 5.85 kcal/g of protein, and 3.69 kcal/g of lactose were used (Overman and Gaines, 1933).

flect sampling bias rather than true interspecific differences. In some ruminants fat content rises several fold during the course of milking such that the degree of mammary emptying achieved during milking and the degree to which the mammaries may have been emptied by suckling young prior to milking may influence analytical results. Sampling bias may partly explain the disparate fat values reported for *A. alces* (Table 2). While all deer studied produce milks that are decidedly more concentrated than cow's (*Bos taurus*) milk, the milks of many wild bovids are quite similar in gross composition to cervid milks (Table 2, Figure 1). Ungulate milks generally show 3 groupings relative to their dry matter, fat, protein, and energy content: (1) the dilute Perissodactyla milks, (2) concentrated wild cervid and bovid milks, and (3) intermediate domestic camelid and bovid milks (Figure 1). There is no obvious correlation of milk composition to either cervid body size or habitat. Admittedly, the limited number of cervid species examined thus far are all north temperate deer of moderate to large body size, however.

The whey proteins in deer milks are apparently analogous to alpha-lactalbumin, beta-lactoglobulin, and other whey proteins found in cow's milk (Lyster et al., 1966; McDougal and Stewart, 1976). The fats of cervid milks are similar to cow's milk in containing high levels of palmitic, stearic, oleic, and myristic acids along with smaller amounts of short chain fatty acids (Luhtala et al., 1968; Cook et al., 1970b; Glass et al., 1971; Glass and Jenness, 1971; Krzywinski et al.,

Robbins, Oftedal, and O'Rourke

Table 3. Mineral content of wild ungulate milk relative to domestic cow's milk (Treus and Kravchenko, 1968; Baker et al., 1970; Cook et al., 1970a,b; Van Zyl and Wehmeyer, 1970; Arman et al., 1974; Luick et al., 1974; Hall-Martin et al., 1977; Vorherr, 1978; Krzywinski et al., 1980; Lonnerdal et al., 1981).

Species	Stage of Lactation	Number of Samples	Total Milk Ash % of Dry Matter	% of Fresh Milk	g/100 kcal	Ca	P	Na	K	Mg	Fe	Cl	Cu	Zn
BOVIDAE														
Caprinae														
Dall sheep	Middle	4	4.1	0.94	0.71	25.6	16.3	6.6	8.3	1.6	0.1	—	—	—
Muskox	Late	5	4.4	1.20	0.81	24.4	12.6	3.6	9.0	2.4	0.1	—	—	—
Other bovids														
Black wildebeest	Late	2	5.0	1.00	0.74	22.1	7.6	8.2	11.5	2.1	0.01	—	0.009	—
Eland	Middle	24	5.0	1.10	0.76	24.3	16.4	5.1	11.5	2.5	0.01	—	0.004	—
Springbok	Complete	26	5.0	1.10	0.75	23.7	15.5	4.5	10.9	2.8	0.02	—	0.004	—
CERVIDAE														
Moose	Middle to Late	2	6.4	1.60	1.08	22.4	17.3	9.8	5.1	1.6	0.50	—	—	—
Red deer	Middle	11	5.4	1.14	0.72	23.4	18.0	4.1	10.8	2.2	—	6.4	—	—
Reindeer	Middle	11	4.9	1.30	0.54	24.6	19.2	3.8	11.0	1.3	≤0.05	4.8	—	0.08
GIRAFFIDAE														
Giraffe	Middle to Late	7	5.0	0.86	0.78	7.8	11.9	4.4	10.5	0.6	0.02	—	0.002	0.06
Means for milk of wild artiodactyls (± 1 S.D.)			5.0 ±0.6	1.16 0.20	0.76 0.14	22.0 5.4	15.0 3.6	5.6 2.2	9.8 2.1	1.9 0.7	— —	5.6 1.1	0.005 0.003	0.07 0.01
Domestic cow	Mature milk		5.6	0.73	1.03	17.9	16.5	8.0	20.0	1.6	0.01	14.8	0.002	0.06

1980). Lactose is the predominant sugar, but other unidentified sugars have been observed (Jenness et al., 1964).

The milks of cervids and other wild ungulates contain far more ash per unit of fresh milk than does cow's milk (Table 3). However, when the ash is compared to either milk dry matter or energy content, the milks of wild ungulates generally provide less ash than does cow's milk. The relative concentrations of several of the minerals, such as calcium, phosphorus, magnesium, and zinc, are similar to that occurring in the ash of cow's milk. However, sodium, potassium, and chloride are markedly less concentrated in the milk ash of wild ungulates than in the ash of cow's milk, while iron and copper can range up to 50 times more concentrated in the ash of wild ungulate milk than in cow's milk. These differences must be viewed with caution since many of the analyses are based on exceedingly small sample sizes; several of the ash values even within a species vary by 10 to 15 fold (Van Zyl and Wehmeyer, 1970; e.g. copper), and few of the reports are from similar stages of lactation.

Milk and Dry Feed Intake

The immediate ingestion of milk and the gradual, although increasing, use of solid feeds is essential for the

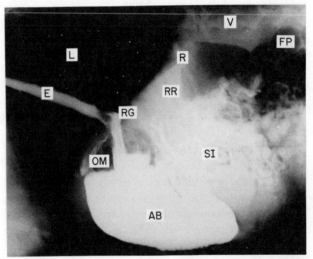

Figure 2. Radiograph of the passage of a milk-contrast medium consumed by a bottle-fed, three week old elk calf. The mixture consumed approximately 20-30 minutes prior to the radiograph exposure can be seen as it moves into the small intestine. Structures indicated are the esophagus (E), reticular groove (RG), Omasum (OM), abomasum (AB), small intestine (SI), rumen-reticulum (RR), fecal pellets forming in the large intestine (FP), lungs (L), ribs (R), and vertebral column (V).

survival and growth of neonatal cervids. Milk ingestion and the necessary functional development of the rumen-reticulum for digesting solid feed provide complex evolutionary and physiological problems for cervids. Although solid food characteristic of the adult cervid diet passes from the esophagus into the rumen-reticulum, milk must not enter the first two stomach compartments where an explosive lactic acid fermentation would occur, but must pass directly to the true stomach or abomasum.

The reticular groove, a bi-lipped muscular channel passing along the reticular wall between the esophageal and omasal orifices, closes reflexively as milk passes down the esophagus and shunts milk directly into the abomasum while by-passing the rumen-reticulum (Figure 2). The reticular groove functions irrespective of whether milk is consumed from the teat, bottle, or bucket (Matthews and Kilgour, 1980). The rumen-reticulum bypass is essential for the absorption of colostral immunoglobulins which would be readily degraded by rumen bacteria. More importantly, the normal protease enzyme activity in the neonatal abomasum and small intestine must be temporarily suppressed during the first several hours of life when the small intestine is permeable to intact immunoglobulins. Protease suppression includes a delay in the production of stomach acid and the incorporation of enzyme inhibitors, notably of trypsin, in colostrum (Thivend et al., 1980).

The ingestion of colostrum is the crucial immunologic event in the survival of the neonatal ruminant. Ruminants have low immunoglobulin concentrations at birth since there is neither transplacental transfer of immunoglobulins from the dam's serum nor exposure to infectious organisms *in utero* to stimulate the fetal immune system. Passive immunity is acquired by ingestion and absorption of intact immunoglobulins from the maternal colostrum during the first 24 hours after birth (Brambell, 1970). Failure to absorb adequate amounts of maternal antibody often results in neonatal septicemia or diarrhea and is associated with increased mortality in domestic and wild ruminant species (McGuire et al., 1976, 1977; Sawyer et al., 1977; Parkinson et al., 1982).

Passive transfer of maternal antibody in nondomestic ruminants, particularly cervids, has been evaluated by several methods. Total serum protein is easily measured with a hand held refractometer. Since the uptake of maternal antibody increases the total serum protein concentration in the neonate, the difference between pre-suckle and post-suckle values is a measure of passive transfer of antibody (Parkinson et al., 1982). If pre- and post-suckle samples are not available, gamma globulins (primarily immunoglobulins) can be quantitated by serum protein electrophoresis.

While this test can be performed on samples of nondomestic ruminant serum without species-specific standards (Trindle et al., 1978; O'Rourke and Satterfield, 1981), technical expertise and costly equipment are required. Single radial immunodiffusion is a precipitation test in agar gel containing antiserum to the immunoglobulin to be measured. IgGl, the immunoglobulin class transferred in the serum, can be precisely quantitated in domestic species for which antisera and standards are available. An adaptation of this test using commercially available bovine reagents for quantitation of IgGl in *C. elaphus* serum has been described (O'Rourke et al., 1982).

Antibody levels of neonates in field situations are more conveniently estimated with one of the rapid serum tests described for domestic ruminants. The zinc sulfate test is based on the relative increase in turbidity of the reagent when serum is added (McEwan et al., 1970). The test is read visually or spectrophotometrically. Since the test is sensitive to species differences (Parkinson et al., 1982) as well as changes in temperature, pH, hemolysis and CO_2 uptake, the test is quantitatively most accurate when the neonate sample is compared to standardized serum for each species. If species-specific standards are not available, a pool of normal adult serum can be used. A 24 hour old neonate should have nearly the same immunoglobulin value as the dam (Youatt et al., 1965) and a sample with less than 25% of the adult value may be considered hypogammaglobulinemic (Satterfield and O'Rourke, 1981).

The glutaraldehyde test is based on coagulation of serum by the reagent (Tennant et al, 1979). When a 10% glutaraldehyde reagent is used, the test detects gamma globulin levels in three ranges—less than 0.4 g/dl serum, more than 0.6 g/dl, and the intermediate range of 0.4–0.6 g/dl. In a survey of 103 samples from 26 species of nondomestic ruminants, the glutarldehyde test accurately identified neonates with less than 0.4 g/dl (O'Rourke and Satterfield, 1981). In a second study in which gamma globulin concentrations were not determined, the test result was a reliable predictor of neonate survival in wild ruminants (Duffelmeyer, 1981). A major drawback to the use of the 10% glutaraldehyde test is its inability to detect partial failures of passive transfer, i.e., those animals that receive suboptimal amounts of colostrum. For example, mule deer with less than 1.4 g/dl gamma globulin had high mortality rates even though those animals with at least 0.6 g/dl had positive glutaraldehyde tests (Parkinson et al., 1982). A modification of the glutaraldehyde test has recently been developed to detect higher gamma globulin levels than 0.6 (O'Rourke et al., 1982).

The catabolism of maternally derived immu-

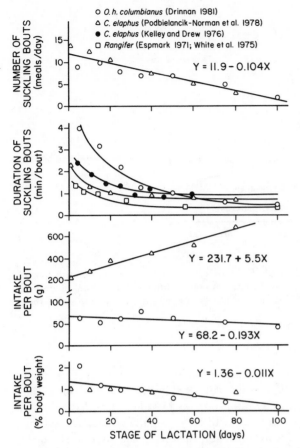

Figure 3. Daily nursing bout characteristics in captive black-tailed deer and *C. elaphus* and captive and free-ranging *Rangifer* during the first 3 months of lactation. The points are means extracted from figures presented by the original authors and are not individual observations.

in 10 hours of observation at 8–9 days of age, or approximately 10 times in 24 hours if the frequency remained unchanged during the rest of the day. However, the number of daily nursing bouts of captive red deer observed by Bubenik (1965) and Kelley and Drew (1976) in early lactation were approximately one-half those observed in the above studies. The number of nursing bouts and their duration decrease as lactation progresses (Lent, 1974). The mean duration of suckling bouts in captive and free-ranging *C. elaphus* agrees quite closely (Johnson, 1951, 0.5–1.75 minutes; McCullough, 1969, 0.25–2.0 minutes). The similarity between suckling bout duration in captive and free-ranging *C. elaphus* and *Rangifer* (White et al., 1975) suggests that at least some of the nursing parameters are not affected by captivity.

Because of the decrease in both the number and duration of suckling bouts, the total daily nursing time decreases in both black-tailed deer and *C. elaphus* from approximately 30 minutes during the first few days to 2 to 3 minutes by 90 days of age (Figure 4). The reduction in total nursing time as daily milk in-

noglobulins during the first 2 months is usually more rapid than the production of antibody by the fawn, resulting in an overall decrease in serum immunoglobulins. Gamma globulin levels fell from 1.9 g/dl on day 1 to 0.66 on day 21 in white-tailed deer (Youatt et al., 1965) and from 1.55 g/dl on day 7 to 0.9 on day 21 in mule deer (Trindle et al., 1978). This decrease in immunoglobulin concentration is only one factor in survival during the first few months since protection from infectious disease depends on the concentration of antibody specific for antigens in the environment, the number and virulence of the infectious organisms, and husbandry conditions.

Nursing behavior, milk intake, and dry feed intake also change during lactation. For example, captive maternal-raised black-tailed deer and North American *C. elaphus* neonates nurse from 10 to 15 times per day in distinguishable nursing bouts during the first several days of life (Figure 3). Similarly, captive red deer observed by Arman et al. (1974) nursed 4 times

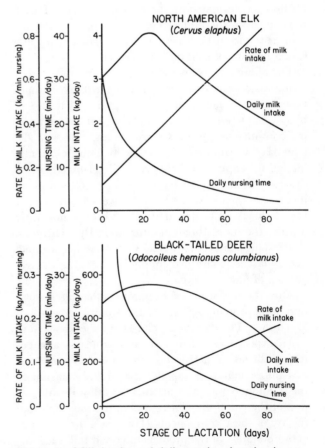

Figure 4. Milk intake and daily nursing duration in captive, maternal-nursed black-tailed deer and *C. elaphus* during the first three months of lactation (Podbielancik-Norman et al., 1978; Robbins et al., 1981; Drinnan, 1981).

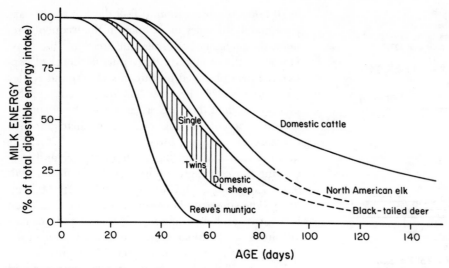

Figure 5. The shift from milk to solid food for several artiodactyla neonates nursed by well-fed mothers (Joyce and Rattray, 1970; Yahner, 1978; Sadleir, 1980; Bailey and Lawson, 1981; Robbins et al., 1981). The line for the Reeve's muntjac is based upon Yahner's observation of frequent grazing by two weeks of age and weaning by eight weeks.

take is increasing during early lactation is accomplished by dramatically increasing the rate of milk removal from the udder. The rate of milk intake increases 6 fold in both deer and *C. elaphus* during the first 3 months of lactation (Figure 4).

The relative intake per nursing bout in captive, maternal-raised black-tailed deer and *C. elaphus* is maximum in early lactation and ranges from 1 to 2% of body weight (Figure 3). The absolute intake per nursing bout increases in *C. elaphus* from an average of 220 g on day 1 to almost 700 g on day 90. Thus, total milk intake in captive *C. elaphus* is determined by a decrease in the frequency of nursing bouts and an increase in the intake per bout. Conversely, intake per bout in black-tailed deer does not change significantly during the first three months (60±11g, Drinnan, 1981). Thus, total milk intake in captive black-tailed deer is largely controlled simply by changing the frequency of nursing bouts.

After the initial period of immunoglobulin absorption, milk proteins are digested in a more conventional manner. The caseins precipitate in the abomasum when exposed to gastric acid and proteases and entrap milk fat. Whereas non-casein (whey) proteins and milk sugar pass rapidly from the abomasum to the small intestine following suckling, slow disintegration of the casein-fat clot results in the more gradual release of these components (Hill et al., 1970). Since about 80–90% of the proteins in cervid milks are casein (Arman et al., 1974; Luick et al., 1974; Jenness, 1974; Krzywinski et al., 1980), the formation of a gastric clot is undoubtedly a normal part of milk digestion. Even though fawns suckle infrequently, the re-

lease of fat and protein from the abomasum to the small intestine is probably more or less continuous.

The weaning process in young, well-fed cervids is quite gradual with only insignificant amounts of solid food consumed during the first 3 to 4 weeks of life (Figure 5). Milk intake generally peaks during this time (White et al., 1975; Sadleir, 1980; Robbins et al., 1981). The subsequent reduction in milk intake and the simultaneous functional development of the rumen due to fermentation of solid food provide the

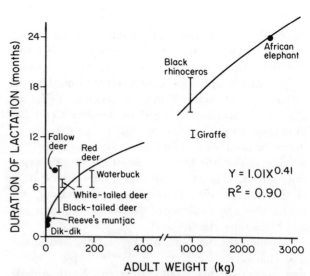

Figure 6. The duration of ungulate lactation as a function of maternal weight (Aschaffenburg et al., 1961; Gregory et al., 1965; Laws, 1969; Spinage, 1969; Hendrichs and Hendrichs, 1970; Hall-Martin et al., 1977; Jackson, 1977; Scanlon and Urbston, 1978; Yahner, 1978; Krzywinski et al., 1980; Poché, 1980; Sadleir, 1980).

Robbins, Oftedal, and O'Rourke

stimulus and basis for increasing solid feed intake. Restrictions to milk intake, such as the reduced intake of twin versus single sheep (Figure 5), can markedly increase the rate at which dry feed is consumed by the neonate (Muller-Schwarze et al., 1982). Although larger species tend to have longer lactation periods (Figure 6), there is insufficient data to determine to what extent the longer neonatal dependence in larger species is due to a slower initial intake of dry feed, a slower rate at which dry feed replaces milk once dry feed begins being consumed, or simply a prolonged tail to the lactation cycle in which milk is playing a very minimal nutritional role.

Hand-Rearing

Although cervids normally exhibit appropriate maternal behavior, neonates are often hand-reared to produce tractable experimental or display animals. Hand-rearing of even precocial cervids can be difficult due to nutritional and disease problems. Feeding practices must to a large extent be determined by the objectives and constraints on each hand-rearing effort. Survival, growth rates, general health, adult size, long-term reproductive success, and economic and personnel limitations are probably the most common criteria or constraints. In response to the extremely low growth rates and high mortality reported in many hand-rearing programs, Robbins et al. (1981) suggested that we should ultimately be capable of hand-rearing neonates with growth rates and health equal to those infants being maternal-nursed. It is certainly conceivable that lower rates of milk intake, correspondingly slower growth rates, but a more rapid shift to a more economical solid diet will ultimately be the method of choice as tempered by the effects of early nutrition on health and subsequent adult reproductive success of body size. Although Geist (1971) has suggested a close link in wild ungulates between early nutrition and adult reproductive success and behavior, well controlled studies defining the extent to which early milk intake and growth can be reduced without compromising adult size, behavior, and reproductive success are needed.

Because of the inability of cervid neonates to correctly control milk intake when hand-reared, the nutritionist must first estimate an appropriate milk feeding schedule. Fawns left to consume milk *ad libitum* invariably develop diarrhea and, if prolonged, may die. Milk feeding levels for hand-reared neonates can be predicted by summing individual maintenance and production requirements and interacting these with milk and dry feed composition, the efficiency of nutrient metabolism, and intake control mechanisms (Brody and Nisbet, 1938; Moen, 1973; Robbins and Moen, 1975; Odtedal, 1981). While agreement between observed and predicted intakes of maternal-nursed neonates is often quite good when using the factorial approach to estimate intake, the number of assumptions inherent in the estimates for wild ungulates is large. The balancing nature of different errors may be as accountable for the current agreement between observed and predicted values as is a precise understanding of all facets of the lactation and growth processes.

Necessary milk intake can also be predicted from interspecific regressions developed from observations of maternal-raised neonates (Oftedal, 1981; Robbins et al., 1981). Intake of milk nutrients at the peak of lactation in a wide range of mammalian species is described by the following equations:

$$Y_{kcal/day} = 226W_{kg}^{0.837} \qquad \text{(energy)}$$

$$Y_{g/day} = 10.6W_{kg}^{0.83} \qquad \text{(protein)}$$

where W is neonatal weight at peak lactation (Oftedal, 1981). For example, the observed energy intake in North American *C. elaphus* at peak lactation (4770 kcal/day) agrees quite closely with the predicted value of 4726 at 21 days of lactation. However, when the same equation is used to estimate intake on day 1, the predicted (2912 kcal/day) and observed (3544) values become more disparate, although probably acceptable for many hand-rearing programs.

Milk energy intake can also be predicted from the equation developed by Robbins et al. (1981) from data on 6 ruminant species.

$$\ln X = \frac{Y - 0.0671}{0.0225}$$

where Y is the average rate of gain per unit of mean body weight during the first month (kg/day/mean body weight) and X is the mean milk intake in Mcal/day/unit of mean body weight during the first month. However, when the mean milk intake from the above equation is multiplied by the age specific body weight, milk intake is underestimated during the first 2 weeks and subsequently overestimated during the remaining 2 weeks of the first month (Figure 7). If the above corrections are generally appropriate for cervids and the average decay slopes for the cervid lactation curve (Robbins et al., 1981) are applied after the peak is reached at approximately 21 days, observed and predicted milk intake functions agree quite closely (Figure 8). Once solid food begins to be consumed in significant amounts, weaning can occur quite rapidly in hand-rearing efforts by more rapidly decreasing the amount of milk fed so as to force an increased consumption of solid food.

The following hand-rearing practices are recommended as applying generally to cervids:

1. The neonate should not be removed prior to the

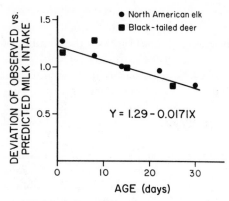

Figure 7. Comparison between the measured milk intake in maternal-nursed cervids (Sadleir, 1980; Robbins et al., 1981) during the first month and that predicted using the milk energy regressions of Robbins et al. (1981).

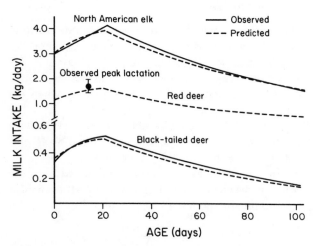

Figure 8. Comparison between the measured milk intakes in *C. elaphus* and black-tailed deer and that predicted using the equations of Robbins et al. (1981) and the corrections in Figure 7 as summarized in the text (Arman et la., 1974; Sadleir, 1980; Robbins et al., 1981). Only the peak milk production in red deer is given because of the tremendous variation between individuals.

time when significant colostral immunoglobulins have been absorbed. The transfer and absorption of immunoglobulins is maximum during the first 12 hours and virtually ceases by 24 hours. For those cervid neonates in which immunoglobulin transfer is suspect due to time of maternal-neonate separation or a history of poor neonate survival, appropriate immunoglobulin tests should be conducted. If the neonate is hypogammaglobulinemic, either frozen colostrum should be given orally if the neonate is less than 24 hours old and/or serum from adult animals injected parenterally if intestinal closure has already occurred (Satterfield and O'Rourke, 1981). While species-specific

colostrum is preferred, colostrum from other species may be used although the donors' immunoglobulin supply should have a high titer of antibodies specific for the diseases likely to be encountered by the neonate. For example, mule deer and Eld's deer can absorb globulins from cow colostrum (Duffelmeyer, 1981; Parkinson et al., 1982), but the protection provided by heterologous proteins has yet to be determined. The benefits of immunoglobulin transfer far outweigh the potential risks of antigenic reactions to foreign proteins and almost certain death if antibody concentrations are inadequate.

2. Both overfeeding and drastic underfeeding should be avoided. Overfeeding results when handlers fail to recognize that cervid neonates are capable of consuming milk far in excess of healthy norms. However, starvation as the cure for overfeeding is equally repugnant. Milk intake at any given meal should not exceed 3 to 4% of body weight, and frequent small feedings should be encouraged.

3. Milk formulas should simulate maternal milk composition as far as possible. While dilute formulas, such as cow's milk, can be used, their consumption requires the feeding of approximately double the volume if energy and nutrient deliveries are to be comparable to maternal-raised neonates. The feeding of such large volumes of lactose-rich milk may predispose neonates to diarrhea. The protein of any milk replacer should either be casein or a similar protein capable of forming an effective clot in the abomasum.

4. Hand-reared neonates should be given access to dirt, or iron dextran solutions be injected if domestic ungulate milks are used. Domestic ruminant milks are notoriously low in iron (Blaxter et al., 1957). Geophagia is commonly observed in young ungulates, and it can be an important means of meeting iron requirements (Underwood, 1977). For example, maternal-raised elk and white-tailed deer neonates consumed soil by day 5 and 7, respectively (Jacobsen, 1973; Podbielancik-Norman et al., 1978) with the elk consuming 84 g of soil ash/day by 21 days of age. Iron injections are preferred to supplementing the milk directly since other mineral deficiencies (notably phosphorus) can be produced by iron precipitation. Most commercial milk replacers do contain added iron such that continued supplementation is unnecessary when these formulas are used.

5. Selenium should be injected as soon as the neonate is obtained in those geographical areas where soil and vegetation selenium levels are considered inadequate for domestic livestock.

6. All neonates should be stimulated to defecate and urinate at each feeding until they are observed eliminating voluntarily.

Robbins, Oftedal, and O'Rourke

Conclusions

Many additional studies on behavior, nutrition, and disease are needed if we are to understand lactation and early growth of wild ungulate neonates. Our current understanding of this exciting and challenging area is elementary at best.

Literature Cited

Arman, P., R.N.B. Kay, E.D. Goodall, and G.A.M. Sharman
1974.   The composition and yield of milk from captive red deer (*Cervus elaphus* L.). *Journal of Reproduction and Fertility*, 37:67–84.

Aschaffenburg, R., M.E. Gregory, S.J. Rowland, and S.Y. Thompson
1961.   The composition of the milk of the African Black rhinoceros (*Diceros binornis;* Lin.). *Proceedings of the Zoological Society of London*, 137:475–479.

Aschaffenburg, R., M.E. Gregory, S.K. Kon, S.J. Rowland and S.Y. Thompson
1962.   The composition of the milk of the reindeer. *Journal of Dairy Research*, 29:325–328.

Bailey, C.B., and J.E. Lawson
1981.   Estimated water and forage intakes in nursing range calves. *Canadian Journal of Animal Science*, 61:415–421.

Baker, B.E., H.W. Cook, and J.J. Teal
1970.   Muskox (*Ovibos moschatus*) milk. I. Gross composition, fatty acid, and mineral constitution. *Canadian Journal of Zoology*, 48:1345–1347.

Ben Shaul, D.M.
1962.   The composition of the milk of wild animals. *International Zoo Yearbook*, 4:333–342.

Berge, S.
1963.   Protein/fat in milk from different species of domestic animals. *Acta Agricultura Scandinavica*, 13:220–226.

Blaxter, K.L., G.A.M. Sharman, and A.M. MacDonald
1957.   Iron deficiency anemia in calves. *British Journal on Nutrition*, 11:234–246.

Browman, L.G. and H.S. Sears
1955.   Mule deer milk. *Journal of Mammalogy*, 36:473–474.

Brambell, F.R.
1970.   *The transmission of passive immunity from mother to young.* New York: Elsevier Publishing.

Brody, S., and R. Nisbet
1938.   Growth and development. XLVII. A comparison of the amounts and energetic efficiencies of milk production in rat and dairy cow. *Missouri Agriculture Experiment Station Research Bulletin,,* 285:1–30.

Bubenik, A.B.
1965.   Beitrag zur Geburtskunde und zu den Mutter-Kind-Beziehungen des Reh—(*Capreolus capreolus* L.)

und Rotwildes (*Cervus elaphus* L.). *Zeitschrift fur Säugetierkunde*, 30:65–128.

Chen, E.C.H., D.A. Blood, and B.E. Baker
1965.   Rocky Mountain bighorn sheep (*Ovis canadensis canadensis*) milk. *Canadian Journal of Zoology*, 43:885–888.

Cook, H.W., A.M. Pearson, N.M. Simmons, and B.E. Baker
1970a. Dall sheep (*Ovis dalli dalli*) milk. 1. Effects of stage of lactation on the composition of the milk. *Canadian Journal of Zoology*, 48:629–633.

Cook, H.W., R.A. Rausch, and B.E. Baker
1970b. Moose (*Alces alces*) milk. Gross composition, fatty acid, and mineral constitution. *Canadian Journal of Zoology*, 48:213–215.

Drinnan, R.L.
1981.   A quantitative analysis of the feeding behavior of suckling black-tailed deer (*Odocoileus hemionus columbianus*). M.S. Thesis, Simon Fraser University, Burnaby, Canada.

Duffelmeyer, J.
1981.   Use of the glutaraldehyde method for detection of gamma globulin in young ungulates at the Bronx Zoo. *Proceedings of the 1st Annual Meeting of the American Association on Zoo Techniques*, Seattle, Washington, 1:95–112.

Eltawil, E.A., S.A. Moukhtar, E.S. Galat, and E.S. Khishin
1976.   Factors affecting the production and composition of Egyptian buffalo milk. *Tropical Animal Health and Production*, 8:115–121.

Espamrk, Y.
1971.   Mother-young relationship and ontogeny of behavior in reindeer (*Rangifer tarandus* L.). *Zeitschrift für Tierpsychologie*, 29:42–81.

Franzmann, A.W., P.D. Arneson, and D.E. Ullrey
1975.   Composition of milk from Alaskan moose in relation to other North American wild ruminants. *Journal of Zoo Animal Medicine*, 6:12–14.

Geist, V.
1971.   *Mountain sheep: A study in behavior and evolution.* Chicago: University of Chicago Press.

Glass, R.L., and R. Jenness
1971.   Comparative biochemical studies of milk. VI. Constituent fatty acids of milk fats of additional species. *Comparative Biochemistry and Physiology*, 38B:353–359.

Glass, R.L., H.A. Troolin, and R. Jenness
1971.   Comparative biochemical studies of milks. IV. Constituent fatty acids of milk fat. *Comparative Biochemistry and Physiology*, 22:415–425.

Gregory, M.E., S.J. Rowland, S.Y. Thompson, and V.M. Kon
1965.   Changes during lactation in the composition of the

milk of the African black rhinoceros (*Diceros bicornis*). *Proceedings of the Zoological Society of London,* 145:327–333.

Hall-Martin, A.J., J.D. Skinner, and A. Smith
1977. Observations on lactation and milk composition of the giraffe *Giraffa camelopardalis. South African Journal of Wildlife Research,* 7:67–71.

Hatcher, V.B., D.H. McEwan, and B.E. Baker
1967. Caribou milk. 1. Barren-ground caribou (*Rangifer tarandus gorenlandicus*): gross composition, fat and protein constitution. *Canadian Journal of Zoology,* 45:1101–1106.

Hendrichs, H., and U. Hendrichs
1970. *Freilandsuntersuchungen zur Okologie und Ethologie der Zwerg-Antilope Madoqua (Rhynchotragus) kirkii Gunther, 1880.* München: R. Piper and Company, Verlag.

Hill, K.J., D.E. Noakes, and R.A. Lowe
1970. Gastric digestive physiology of the calf and the piglet. In *Physiology of digestion and metabolism in the ruminant,* edited by A.T. Phillipson, pp. 166–179. Newcastle: Oriel Press.

Holleman, D.F., R.G. White, and J.R. Luick
1975. New isotope method for estimating milk intake and yield. *Journal of Dairy Science,* 58:1814–1821.

Ivonova, G.M.
1965. Chemical composition and nutritive value of elks' milk. *Dairy Science Abstract,* 27:556.

Jackson, J.
1977. The duration of lactation in New Forest fallow deer (*Dama dama*). *Journal of Zoology,* 183:542–543.

Jackson, R.M., M. White, and F.F. Knowlton
1972. Activity patterns of young white-tailed deer fawns in south Texas. *Ecology,* 53:262–270.

Jacobsen, N.K.
1973. Physiology, behavior, and thermal transactions of white-tailed deer. Ph.D. Thesis, Cornell University, Ithaca, New York.

Jenness, R., E.A. Regehr, and R.E. Sloan
1964. Comparative biochemical studies of milks. II. Dialyzable carbohydrates. *Comparative Biochemistry and Physiology,* 13:339–352.

Jenness, R., and R.E. Sloan
1970. The composition of milks of various species: A review. *Dairy Science Abstract,* 32:599–612.

Jenness, R.
1974. The composition of milk. In *Lactation: A comprehensive treatise,* edited by B.L. Larson and V.R. Smith, pp. 3-107. New York: Academic Press.

Johnson, A.H.
1974. The composition of milk. In *Fundamentals of dairy chemistry,* edited by B.H. Webb, A.H. Johnson, and J.A. Alford, pp. 1-57. Westport, Connecticut: AVI Publishing.

Johnson, D.E.
1951. Biology of the elk calf, *Cervus canadensis nelsoni. Journal of Wildlife Management,* 15:396–410.

Joyce, J.P., and P.V. Rattray
1970. The intake and utilization of milk and grass by lambs. *Proceedings of the New Zealand Society of Animal Productivity,* 30:94–105.

Kelly, R.W. and K.R. Drew
1976. Shelter seeking and suckling behavior of the red deer calf (*Cervus elaphus*) in a farmed situation. *Applied Animal Ethology,* 2:101–111.

Kitts, W.D., I. McT. Cowan, J. Bandy, and A.J. Wood
1956. The immediate post-natal growth in the Columbian black-tailed deer in relation to the composition of the milk of the doe. *Journal of Wildlife Management,* 20:212–214.

Krzywinski, A., K. Krzywinska, J. Kisza, A. Roskosz, and A. Kruk
1980. Milk composition, lactation and the artificial rearing of red deer. *Acta Theriologica,* 25:341–347.

Laws, R.M.
1969. Aspects of reproduction in the African elephant, *Loxodonta africana. Journal of Reproduction and Fertility Supplement,* 6:193–217.

Laxminarayana, H., and N.N. Dastur
1968. Buffaloes' milk and milk products. Part 1. *Dairy Science Abstract,* 30:177–186.

Lent, P.C.
1974. Mother-infant relationships in ungulates. In *Behavior of ungulates and its relation to management,* edited by V. Geist and F. Walther, pp. 14-55. Morges, Switzerland: International Union for the Conservation of Nature and Natural Resources.

Ling, E.R., S.K. Kon, and J.W.G. Porter
1961. The composition of milk and the nutritive value of its components. In *Milk: the mammary gland and its secretion,* edited by S.K. Kon and A.T. Cowie, pp. 195-263. New York: Academic Press.

Lonnerdal, B., C.L. Keen, and L.S. Hurley
1981. Iron, copper, zinc, and manganese in milk. *Annual Review of Nutrition,* 1:149–174.

Luhtala, A., A. Rautiainen, and M. Antila
1968. Die Zusammensetzung der finnischen Rentiermilch. *Suomen Kemistilehti B.,* 41:6–9.

Lyster, R.L.J., R. Jenness, N.I. Phillips, and R.E. Sloan
1966. Comparative biochemical studies of milks. III. Immunoelectrophoretic comparisons of milk proteins of the artiodactyla. *Comparative Biochemistry and Physiology,* 17:967–971.

Luick, J.R., R.G. White, A.M. Gau, and R. Jenness
1974. Compositional changes in the milk secreted by grazing reindeer. I. Gross composition and ash. *Journal of Dairy Science,* 57:1325–1333.

Robbins, Oftedal, and O'Rourke

Macy, I.G., H.J. Kelley, and R.E. Sloan
1953. *The composition of milks*. Natural Resource County Publication 254. Washington, D.C.: National Academy of Science.

Matthews, L.R., and R. Kilgour
1980. Learning and associated factors in ruminant feeding behavior. In *Digestive physiology and metabolism in ruminants*, edited by Y. Ruckenbusch and P. Thivend, pp. 123-144. Lancaster, England: MTP Press, Ltd.

McDougall, E.I., and J.L. Stewart
1976. The whey proteins of the milk of red deer (*Cervus elaphus* L.). A homologue of bovine B-lactoglobulin. *Biochemistry Journal*, 153:647–655.

McEwan, A.D., E.W. Fisher, I.E. Selman, and W.J. Penhale
1970. A turbidity test for the estimation of immunoglobulin levels in neonatal calf serum. *Clinica Chimica Acta*, 27:155–163.

McCullough, D.R.
1969. The Tule elk: Its history, behavior, and ecology. *University of California Publication on Zoology*, 88:1–209.

McGuire, T.C., N.E. Pfeiffer, J.M. Weikel, and R.C. Bartsch
1976. Failure of colostral immunoglobulin transfer in calves dying from infectious disease. *Journal of the Americam Veterinary Medical Association*, 169:713–718.

McGuire, T.C., T.B. Crawford, and A.L. Hallowell
1977. Failure of colostral immunoglobulin transfer as an explanation for most infections and deaths in neonatal foals. *Journal of the American Veterinary Medical Association*, 170:1302–1304.

Moen, A.N.
1973. *Wildlife ecology: An analytical approach*. San Francisco: W.H. Freeman and Company.

Mueller, C.C., and R.M.F.S. Sadleir
1977. Changes in the nutrient composition of milk of black-tailed deer during lactation. *Journal of Mammalogy*, 58:421–423.

Muller-Schwarze, D., B. Stagge, and C. Muller-Schwarze
1982. Play behavior: Persistence, decrease, and energetic compensation during food shortage in deer fawns. *Science*, 215:85–87.

Murphy, D.A.
1960. Rearing and breeding white-tailed fawns in captivity. *Journal of Wildlife Management*, 24:439–441.

Oftedal, O.T.
1981. Milk, protein and energy intakes of suckling mammalian young: A comparative study. Ph.D. Thesis, Cornell Univ., Ithaca, New York.

O'Rourke, K.I., and W.C. Satterfield
1981. Glutaraldehyde coagulation test for detection of hypogammaglobulinemia in neonatal nondomestic ruminants. *Journal of American Veterinary Medical Association*, 179:1144–1146.

O'Rourke, K.I., T.C. McGuire, and C.T. Robbins
1982. Manuscript in prep.

Overman, O.R., and W.L. Gaines
1933. Milk-energy formulas for various breeds of cattle. *Journal of Agricultural Research*, 46:1109–1120.

Parkinson, D.E., R.P. Ellis, and L.D. Lewis
1982. Colostrum deficiency in mule deer fawns: Identification, treatment and influence on neonatal mortality. *Journal of Wildlife Discussion*, 18:17–28.

Poché, R.M.
1980. Elephant management in Africa. *Wildlife Society Bulletin*, 8:199–207.

Podbielancik-Norman, R.S., W.D. Norman, C.T. Robbins, and E.D. Mould
1978. Nursing behavior and general activity patterns of captive elk. Unpublished manuscript, Washington State Univ., Pullman.

Robbins, C.T., and A.N. Moen
1975. Milk consumption and weight gain of white-tailed deer. *Journal of Wildlife Management*, 39:355–360.

Robbins, C.T., R.S. Podbielancik-Norman, D.L. Wilson, and E.D. Mould
1981. Growth and nutrient consumption of elk calves compared to other ungulate species. *Journal of Wildlife Management*, 45:172–186.

Robbins, C.T., and V. Stevens
1981. Mountain goat milk composition. Unpublished manuscript, Washington State University, Pullman.

Sadleir, R.M.F.S.
1980. Energy and protein intake in relation to growth of suckling black-tailed deer fawns. *Canadian Journal of Zoology*, 58:1347–1354.

Satterfield, W.C., and K.I. O'Rourke
1981. Management of hypogammaglobulinemic neonatal nondomestic hoofed stock. *Journal of the American Veterinary Medical Association*, 179:1147–1149.

Sawyer, M., C.H. Willadsen, and B.I. Osburn
1977. Passive transfer of colostral immunoglobulins from ewe to lamb and its influence on neonatal mortality. *Journal of the American Veterinary Medical Association*, 171:1255–1259.

Scanlon, P.F., and D.F. Urbston
1978. Persistence of lactation in white-tailed deer. *Journal of Wildlife Management*, 42:196–197.

Silver, H.
1961. Deer milk compared with substitute milk for fawns. *Journal of Wildlife Management*, 25:66–70.

Spinage, C.A.
1969. Naturalistic observations on the reproductive and maternal behaviour of the Uganda defassa waterbuck. *Zeitschrift für Tierpsychologie*, 26:39–47.

Tener, J.S.
1956.   Gross composition of musk-ox milk. *Canadian Journal of Zoology*, 34:569–571.

Tennant, B., B.H. Baldwin, R.K. Braun, N.L. Norcross, and M. Sandholm
1979.   Use of the glutaraldehyde coagulation test for detection of hypogammaglobulinemia in neonatal calves. *Journal of the American Veterinary Medical Association*, 174:848–853.

Thivend, P., R. Tooullec, and P. Guilloteau
1980.   Digestive adaptation in the preruminant. In *Digestive physiology and metabolism in ruminants*, edited by Y. Ruckebusch and P. Thivend, pp. 561-585. Lancaster, England: MTP Press, Ltd.

Treus, V., and D. Kravchenko
1968.   Methods of rearing and economic utilization of eland in the Askaniya-Nova Zoological Park. *Symposia of the Zoological Society of London*, 21:395–411.

Trindle, B.D., L.D. Lewis, and L.H. Lauerman
1978.   Evaluation of stress and its effects on the immune system of hand-reared mule deer fawns (*Odocoileus hemionus*). *Journal of Wildlife Discussion*, 14:523–537.

Underwood, E.J.
1977.   *Trace elements in human and animal nutrition*. New York: Academic Press.

Van Zyl, J.H.M., and A.S. Wehmeyer
1970.   The composition of the milk of the springbok (*Antidorcas marsupialis*), eland (*Taurotragus oryx*) and wildebeest (*Connochaetes gnou*). *Zoologica Africana*, 5:131–133.

Vorherr, H.
1978.   Human lactation and breast feeding. In *Lactation*, Vol. IV, edited by B.L. Larson, pp. 181-280. New York: Academic Press.

Werenskiold, F.
1895.   Rensdyrmelk. *Tidsskrift for det Norske Landbrug*, 2:372–375.

White, R.G., B.R. Thomson, T. Skogland, S.J. Person, D.E. Russell, D.F. Holleman, and J.R. Luick
1975.   Ecology of caribou at Prudhoe Bay Alaska. In *Ecological investigations of the tundra biome in the Prudhoe Bay Region*, edited by J. Brown, pp. 151-201. Fairbanks: University of Alaska Biological Paper No. 2.

Yahner, R.H.
1978.   Some features of mother-young relationships in Reeve's muntjac (*Muntiacus reevesi*). *Applied Animal Ethology*, 4:379–388.

Youatt, W.C., L.J. Verme, and D.E. Ullrey
1965.   Composition of milk and blood in nursing white-tailed does and blood composition of their fawns. *Journal of Wildlife Management*, 29:79–84.

Robbins, Oftedal, and O'Rourke

ANDRZEJ KRZYWIŃSKY
Institute of Genetics and Animal Breeding
Polish Academy of Sciences
Popielno
12-222 Wejsuny
Poland

Artificial Insemination and Embryo Transfer in Deer: Applying These Methods for Propagating Endangered Species

ABSTRACT

In 1977 at the Working Meeting of the SSC Deer Specialist Group a motion was made to organize a sperm bank of rare deer for artificial insemination. In 1977 at Popielno three red deer calves were born following artificial insemination with frozen semen. They were the first wild ruminants in the world obtained by this method. Experiments continue on red deer as well as other deer species. From 1975 to 1982 semen was collected, frozen, and stored from 15 red deer, two moose and one roe. Attempts were also made to freeze semen collected post mortem from the epididymides. Red deer semen exhibits seasonal changes in consistency, appearance and biochemistry. In 1981 work was begun on embryo transfer using four donor and four recipient red deer hinds. Prostaglandins were used for estrous synchronization, and various doses of PMSG were given to stimulate superovulation. The findings suggest that embryo transfer has considerable potential for preserving rare species and subspecies of deer, and shows promise for conservation biology in its capacity to quickly increase population size for captive propagation and reintroduction programs.

Introduction

As civilization has developed more and more animal species are endangered with extinction. Of the living 37 species and perhaps 200 subspecies of deer as many as 29 are listed in the Red Data Book of the IUCN. Nineteen of these are very rare species. Many deer of northern India, Tibet and China are drastically reduced in numbers compared to the beginning of the 20th century (Whitehead, 1978). The main reason for the decline in the wild of many Asiatic deer has been merciless hunting for velvet. The Schomburgk's deer (*Cervus schomburgki*) for example was once found in great numbers in the lowlands of Thailand, but by the middle of the 19th century it was rare. Although bred in captivity the last Schomburgk's deer died in the Berlin Zoo in 1911, while the last animal in the wild was shot in 1938 (Frädrich, 1980). The breeding of rare and endangered deer involves small numbers of individuals that are often separated by great distances. This creates many difficulties such as inbreeding and the threat of disease or catastrophe. Crossbreeding with other related species or subspecies can also occur, as happened in the rare Kerama sika deer (*Cervus nippon keramae*), Persian fallow deer (*Dama dama mesopotamica*) and Formosan sika deer (*Cervus nippon taiouanus*).

Freezing semen for insemination and embryos for implantation may be useful methods for protecting captive populations of rare species of deer from extinction. In 1977 at the Working Meeting of the Survival Service Commission's Deer Specialist Group (Longview, Washington) many aspects of protecting rare deer were discussed. The need for a semen bank was put forward as one method of protection (Whitehead, 1978). Much work has been done on collecting semen from deer using electroejaculation (Seager, 1977; Bierschwal, et al., 1968; Jaczewski and Morstin, 1973), but this method usually resulted in poor quality semen not suitable for freezing and insemination. Furthermore, electroejaculation was often stressful to the animals. Research on collecting semen from red deer (*Cervus elaphus*) has been carried out for several years in Popielno, Poland. Various methods of semen collection using the artificial vagina (AV) have been developed (Krzywiński, 1979a) and adopted for use with exotic species (Wemmer and Portillo, 1983). The AV makes it possible to collect semen not only from tame individuals, but also from a certain number of wild animals.

It is known that ejaculates can be collected from some males throughout the entire year, but during antler growth there is a complete lack of spermatozoa (Krzywiński, 1979 a,b). Semen collection with a hand held AV can be done only with very tame animals, which have strong sexual instincts. Semen collection is easier to accomplish using an artificial hindquarters, attached to a very tame, trained female. Some males even react positively to a dummy (stuffed hind). The behavior of red deer stags during semen collection using a dummy has been described in detail (Krzywiński and Bobek, 1984).

In 1977, after artificial insemination with previously frozen semen, three red deer calves were born (Krzywiński, 1979a). These fawns were the first wild ruminants in the world to be obtained in this way.

In addition to semen collection using an AV attempts have also been made to collect semen post mortem from male red deer and moose (Krzywiński, 1981). Apart from creating a bank of frozen semen, breeding rare deer species can also probably be done by embryo transfer. In some domestic animals this method is already almost routine (Betterridge, 1981) and recently embryo transfer has been accomplished from bongo to eland antelope (Dresser et al., 1984, 1984, 1985), from gaur to a domestic Holstein cow (Stover et al., 1981; Stover and Evans, 1984), and from a Grant's zebra to a domestic quarter horse (Foster and Bennett, 1984). Within-species embryo transfer has also been accomplished in Barbados sheep (Oosterhuis and Durrant, 1981) and the common marmoset (Summers and Wenhnick, 1984). The greatest benefit of embryo transfer is it makes possible a greater number of young from a given number of females. Frozen embryos can also be stored for future use.

While relatively little research has been carried out on wild animals the significance of embryo transfer technology for the future has already been stressed (Polge, 1978; Wildt et al. in press). Recent results indicate that a recipient can be different subspecies or even a different species than the donor. Embryo transfer may be a practical aid for preventing extinction by bolstering captive propagation for reintroducing rare deer to the wild. Of course, perfecting these techniques requires thorough knowledge of the biology of reproduction of the animals to be used.

Methods

Experimental Animals

Until 1979 about 30 to 40 red deer were kept on the deer farm in Popielno in ten 50×20 m or 25×20 m enclosures. In order to expand the research program another deer farm was then built near Popielno in the Piska Forest. The main purpose of the research was to continue deer insemination studies. Apart from red deer (ca 50 animals) there are several moose (*Alces alces*), several roe deer (*Capreolus capreolus*), one Pere David's stag (*Elaphurus davidianus*), and one sika stag (*Cervus nippon*). The farm covers about 80 hectares,

Krzywinsky

Figure 1. Semen collection from moose bull using an artificial hindquarters attached to a cow (photographed by A. Stachurski).

including about 50 ha of primarily pine forest, 15 ha of old reed plantation, 3 ha of pasture, and a small amount of swamp land.

The entire area is divided into three smaller enclosures—a 10 ha winter enclosure for moose and roe deer, a 20 ha winter enclosure for red deer, and a 50 ha summer enclosure for all animals. Four 0.5 ha enclosures are used to separate females for determining and synchronizing estrus, as well as for semen collection of males.

Red deer were fed a concentrate in winter, but received only a small amount of feed concentrate in the summer. Moose received branches and bark of various trees, dry leaves, hay of leaves, carrots and beets.

Animals were hand-reared for taming (Krzywiński, et al., 1980). Special attention was paid to hand-rearing females to be used as teaser hinds. These females underwent special training with harnesses and the artificial hindquarters (Figure 1).

Methods of Semen Collection

Several variants were developed to collect semen using an AV. The AV was (a) installed in the deer-skin artificial hindquarters which was fixed to a hind (Figure 1) (Krzywiński, 1976; Krzywinski and Jaczewski, 1978), (b) installed in a stuffed hind, or (c) hand-held by an attendant during mounting by the stag. Initially an AV was used that had a special "membrane collector" (Krzywiński, 1976) inserted inside. In 1979 a new type of AV using a metal container was developed for deer. Several sizes were made depending on the species of deer. These AVs were used when the semen was collected for freezing since temperature could be controlled and then diluted. During antler growth when ejaculates are liquid, an AV with a membrane collector or even a shortened rubber AV used for cattle was sufficient.

Freezing Semen

Semen was diluted with the following: glycerolated fructose-yolk-citrate extender, milk extender or DTH. Semen was frozen either in pellets on dry ice or in nitrogen vapor, and transferred to liquid nitrogen.

Detection of Estrus in Hinds

Estrus was detected with the use of vasectomized males. Everyday before feeding during the rutting season, vasectomized males were herded into corrals with females. Estrus was checked three times daily when synchronizing hormones were used for embryonic transfer purposes.

Preparation for Embryo Transfer

Estrous synchronization was performed with 1.0 ml Estrumate and then 750 to 1750 i.u. PMSG. Embryo transfer was done at the Department of Animal Reproduction and A.I., Institute of Zootechnics, Balice, Kraków. Anesthesia was administered using 2% Rompun and Combelen.

Artificial Insemination in Hinds

Hinds in estrus were placed in individual pens and immobilized with succinylcholine chloride. Insemination was always done with the animal lying on its side using a speculum and insemination pipettes used for cattle. One or two semen pellets were placed in an ampule containing 1-2 ml physiological saline solution (0.9%) which had previously been warmed by hand. The second pellet was added about 1 minute after the first one. It was attempted to place the semen in the cervix, but it was not always possible due to the inappropriate size of the insemination pipettes. In such cases the semen was deposited intravaginally.

Results

Semen Collection from Red Deer Stags

From 1975 to 1982 15 red deer stags were trained for semen collection. The number of ejaculates collected from individual males by various methods differed. The greatest number of ejaculates was collected from stag 43; a total of 98 ejaculates was collected from October 1975 to November 1980. After October 1980 semen continued to be collected from this stag by Prof. Jaczewski. This stag was very tame and also had strong sexual instincts which made it possible to collect semen using every method, even during antler growth. Most stags during this time did not show sexual activity. In 1979 seven stags were hand reared for future semen collection. Annual changes of red deer semen and antler cycle are summarized in Figure 2.

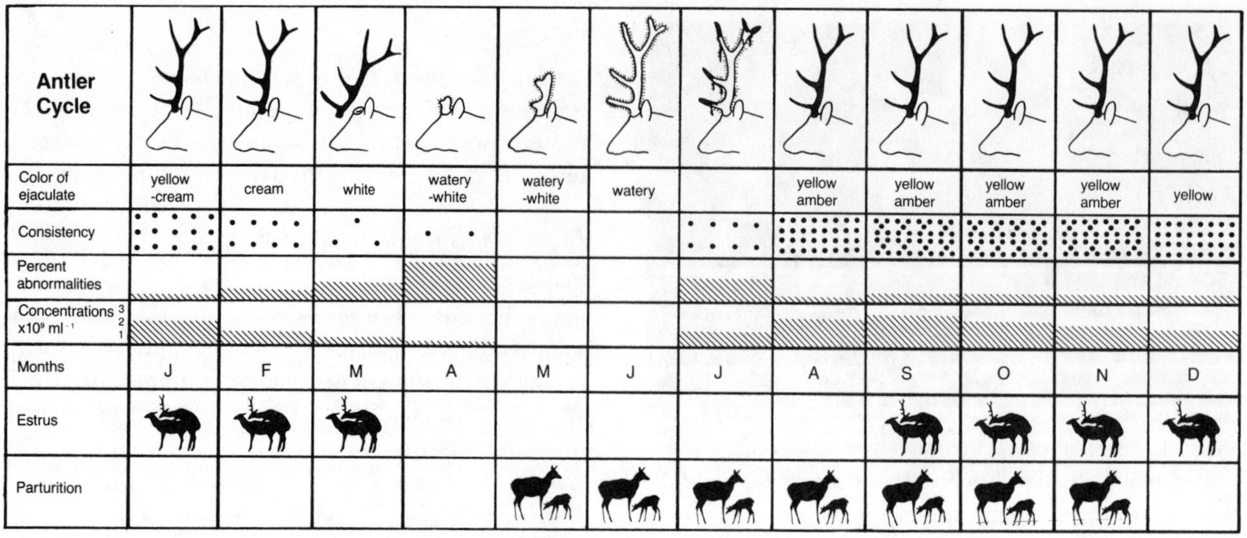

Figure 2. Annual changes in semen characteristics, antler phenology, and female reproductive seasonality in red deer (*Cervus elaphus*).

Semen Collection from Moose Bulls

Bull no. 2, who was hand reared in 1978, was very gentle. The first ejaculate from this moose was collected in 1980. A young male moose (no. 4, born 1979) was used as a teaser after being given 0.5 ml 10% Rompun intramuscularly. Semen was collected with an artificial vagina held in the hand. This AV was an adaptation of one usually used for cattle. An ejaculatory thrust occurred during the third mounting. Traces of a small amount of yellow semen with the consistency of thin honey were seen on the sides of the container in the AV. Since bull no. 2 was shot accidently in October 1981, attempts were made to collect semen from the bull no. 4. Since this bull was not as tame as the previous one, and aggressive during the rut, semen was collected with an artificial hindquarters attached to a cow (no. 6, born 1980) (see Figure 1). This cow had been taught to be led with a halter and reigns. The AV was constructed by the author and was similar to that used for red deer except that it was larger. On 17th and 19th October 1981 two ejaculates were collected. Behavior of moose bulls during semen collection was similar to red deer. It appears that young male moose may be used as teasers but they should be maintained in a separate enclosure at other times.

Semen Collection from Roe Buck

On 7 October 1980 an artificial hindquarters was fixed to a female roe deer (no. 6) after being given 0.5 ml 5% Rompun. Buck no. 25 was led into the same enclosure. After several very rapid mountings a copulation occurred. A small amount of semen was found on the sides of the rubber AV and some spermatozoa were seen under the microscope.

Freezing of Semen

Twenty three ejaculates were frozen from red deer stags collected by AV. Nine of the best ejaculates were stored in the semen bank. Attempts at freezing semen collected post mortem from moose and red deer were also made (Krzywiński, 1981).

Reccurrence of Estrus in Hinds and Artificial Insemination

The length of the estrous cycle was 18.7 days ± 1.7 (Krzywiński and Jaczewski, 1978). Twelve red deer hinds were artificially inseminated. Two frozen ejaculates from stag no. 43 obtained on 1 October and 2 December 1976 were used for artificial insemination. The first ejaculate contained 20–30% motile cells after thawing, while the second one contained a little over 50% motile cells. Three hinds gave birth to normal healthy fawns following insemination: the female was born after 232 days of gestation and two males were born following 231 and 235 day gestations.

Preliminary Experiments with Embryo Transfer in Red Deer

Twelve hinds kept in four 0.5 ha enclosures were used for the experiments. After determining the estrous cycle by using vasectomized males 8 hinds having similar estrous cycles were retained for the experiment. Four hinds were used as donors and four as recipients. Prostaglandin (1 ml/hind) was given to synchronize estrus. There was definite estrus in the 4 recipients.

Figure 3. Estrous behaviour of red deer females after treatment of prostaglandin (photographed by A. Krzywiński).

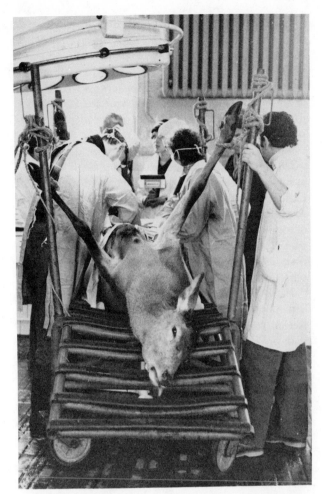

Figure 4. Flushing of the uterine horn with Dulbecco solution to obtain the embryo. Position of the animal during surgery (photographed by A. Turczański).

Several times the other hinds mounted hind no. 11, which is rarely observed during normal estrus (Figure 3). In the hinds prepared as donors by injections of prostaglandin and PMSG there were pronounced signs of estrus in hind no. 27, and moderate signs were shown by hind no. 10. The animals were to be operated on 14th and 15th December in the Institute of Zootechnics in Balice (500 km from Popielno). The animals arrived at Balice two days later, however, and it was decided to operate only on three donor hinds (Figure 4). No ovulation occurred in the hind that received the largest dose of PMSG 1750 i.u. In the hind which received 1200 i.u. PMSG there was only one corpus luteum. The hind which received the smallest dose of PMSG 750 i.u. was not operated on due to the delay in reaching Balice. In July she was found to be pregnant.

Discussion

The AI experiments carried out on red deer demonstrate that it is possible to collect semen with an AV, to freeze it, and to successfully impregnate females leading to normal birth. Fifteen red deer males were trained for semen collection. The methods developed make it possible to collect semen routinely in spite of large individual differences in behavior. It is possible to collect semen from stags that are either very tame or even aggressive towards people, as well as those that are more wary. An AV held in the hand can be used only with some very tame males. Such animals, of course, must be hand reared. It is important to train for semen collection at a young age in those animals that are not aggressive. Semen collection using a dummy (stuffed hind) appears to be relatively easy. It does not require earlier preparation of the animal and can be used without difficulty in zoos.

One advantage is safety for the people involved. It is also possible to improve semen collection by building into the dummy the insulation needed for maintaining constant temperature. One drawback, however, is that not all animals react positively to the dummy. This phenomenon is known in domestic animals (Wierzbowski, 1959). Use of the artificial hind quarter is time consuming since it requires hand rearing and training the teaser hind to be led with a halter and reins. Initial attempts to collect semen from moose and roe deer show that methods used for red deer are also effective.

A knowledge of the annual spermatogenic cycle is necessary in order to collect semen when sperm density and motility are maximum. Until now our knowledge of these factors was incomplete and based on testes histology from post mortem studies (Lincoln, 1971).

Our preliminary research also shows that deer semen can be successfully frozen for insemination, but insemination is somewhat more complicated than in domestic animals since it requires anesthesia of the animal. In this experiment the percent of pregnant hinds was rather low (25%); however, it should be possible to improve insemination success with the use of better equipment, and by determining the optimal time of insemination and the proper deposition of semen.

The creation of semen banks of rare deer species would make it possible to breed even small groups of animals scattered throughout the world. This could reduce the inbreeding which often occurs in zoos where group size is frequently small. The introduction of unrelated animals is often hampered because transport of adult animals is quite difficult, transportation costs are high, there is a risk of death during transport, and there may also be a need for quarantine.

Banks of frozen embryos might prove to be more expedient technological resources than frozen semen. Recent research on embryo transfer in domestic animals has yielded excellent results. In 1980 in North America alone there were 16,000 embryo transfers in cattle (Betteridge, 1977). It is possible to obtain as many as 50 embryos yearly from one cow (Seidel, 1981), but the greatest advantage of the method for captive propagation is the acceleration of population growth using many dams and sires. The positive results achieved in domestic animals should make us optimistic that similar results can be obtained with rare species. It should be stressed that this branch of research in wild animals is still in its infancy (Polge, 1978). In the case of extinct taxa it would be possible to transfer embryos into common closely related species. Allen (pers. comm.), for example, was successful in transferring a horse embryo into a female donkey and vice versa, and normal young developed in both cases.

Embryo transfer seems to be clearly possible when done between species that give fertile offspring such as mufflon and domestic sheep (Bunch, et al., 1977). Active programs in exotic animal embryo transfer are being pursued at a number of American and at least one European zoo.

In the case of deer, for example, for embryos of rare subspecies such as hangul (*Cervus elaphus hanglu*), Yarkand deer (*C. e. yarkandensis*), Bactrian deer (*C. e. bactrainus*), Corsican red deer (*C. e. corsicanus*) recipients could be the females of the common red deer (*C. e. hippoelaphus*). For the rare Persian fallow deer (*Dama dama mesopotamica*) the female of the common fallow deer (*Dama dama dama*) could be used, while for the rare Kerama sika deer (*Cervus nippon keramae*), Formosan sika deer (*C. n. taiouanus*) or Dybowski's sika deer (*C. n. hortulorum*) could be used. The evidence at hand on a number of exotic ungulates suggests that red deer (*Cervus elaphus*) could be a recipient for other genera such as Pere David's deer (*Elaphurus davidianus*), and axis deer (*Axis axis*), etc., but future research must determine the taxonomic limits of compatibility in the absense of other obstacles such as behavioral and body size differences. Even if embryo transfer is possible only within species, it would be possible to employ the method in 16 of the 29 species and subspecies listed in the Red Data Book. While there are political and economic constraints embryo transfer is a promising alternative for quickly increasing populations of rare species and subspecies. The freezing of embryos and their storage in banks is a means of ensuring the survival of forms threatened with extinction.

Acknowledgments

Experiments on embryo transfer were made in cooperation with the Department of Physiology and Artificial Insemination of the Institute of Zootechnics in Balice. I would like to thank Prof. S. Wierzbowski for valuable advice and Dr. Wierzchoś for consultation and for performing the operation. These studies were carried out within the Institute of Zootechnics, Project 09.S.S.

Literature Cited

Betteridge, K.J.
1977.   Embryo transfer in farm animals. *Canadian Department of Agriculture, Monograph No. 16.*

Bierschwal, C.J., E.C. Mather, C.E. Marzin, D.A. Murphy, and L.J. Korschgen
1968.   Collection of deer semen by electro-ejaculation. *International Congress of Animal Reproduction and Artificial Insemination, Paris,* 2:1001–1004.

Bunch, T.D., W.C. Foote, and B. Whitaker
1977.   Interspecies ovum transfer to propagate wild sheep. *Journal of Wildlife Management,* 41:726–730.

Dresser, B., C. Pope, L. Kramer, G. Kuehn, R. Dahlhausen, E. Maruska, B. Reece, and W. Thomas
1985.   Birth of bongo antelope (*Tragelaphus euryceros*) to eland antelope (*Tragelaphus oryx*) and cryopreservation of bongo embryos. *Therigenology,* 23:190 (abstract).

1984.   Nonsurgical embryo recovery and successful interspecies embryo transfer from bongo (*Tragelaphus euryceros*) to eland (*Taurotragus oryx*). *Proceedings of the American Association of Zoo Veterinarians,* 1980:180.

Dresser, B., C. Pope, L. Kramer, G. Kuehn, R. Dahlhausen, and W. Thomas
1984.   Superovulation of bongo antelop (*Tragelaphus euryceros*) and interspecies embryo transfer to African eland (*Tragelaphus oryx*). *Theriogenology,* 21:232 (abstract).

Durrant, B., and K. Benirschke
1981.　Embryo transfer in exotic animals. *Theriogenology,* 15:77–83.

Foster, W., and S. Bennett.
1984.　Non-surgical embryo transfer between a Grant's zebra and domestic quarter horse: a tool for conservation. *Proceedings of the American Association of Zoo Veterinarians,* 1984:181.

Frädrich, H.
1980.　Breeding endangered cervids in captivity. *International Zoo Yearbook,* 20:80–89.

Gray, A.P.
1972.　*Mammalian Hybrids.* Edinburgh: Commonwealth Agricultural Bureaux.

Jaczewski, Z., and J. Morstin
1973.　Collection of the semen of the red deer by electroejaculation. *Pr. Materialy Zootechniczne,* 3:83–86.

Krzywiński, A.
1976.　Collection of red deer semen with the artificial vagina. *Eighth International Congress of Animal Reproduction and Artificial Insemination, Kraków,* 4:1002–1005.

Krzywiński, A.
1979a.　Sztuczna inseminacja jelenia szlachetnego, *Cervus elaphus* L. Ph.D. Dissertation, Institute of Genetics and Animal Breeding, Polish Academy of Sciences.

Krzywiński, A.
1979b.　Further observations on collection and freezing of semen and artificial insemination in red deer (*Cervus elaphus* L.). *International Scientific Symposium Kraków-Mogilany,* 1977:118–127.

Krzywiński, A.
1981.　Freezing of post mortem collected semen from moose and red deer. *Acta Theriologica,* 26:424–426.

Krzywiński, A., and B. Bobek
1984.　Semen collection from red deer males with a dummy. *Acta Zoologica Fennica,* 171:175–178.

Krzywiński, A., and Z. Jaczewski
1978.　Observations on the artificial breeding of red deer. *Symposium of the Zoological Society of London,* 43:271–287.

Krzywiński, A., K. Krzywiński, J. Kisza, A. Roskosz, and A. Kruk
1980.　Milk composition, lactation and the artificial rearing of red deer. *Acta Theriologica,* 25:341–347.

Lincoln, G.A.
1971.　The seasonal reproductive changes in the red deer stag (*Cervus elaphus*). *Journal of Zoology,* 163:105–123.

Oosterhuis, J., and B. Durrant.
1981.　Embryo collection and transfer in Barbados sheep. *Proceedings of the American Association of Zoo Veterinarians,* 1981:124.

Polge, C.
1978.　Embryo transfer and embryo preservation. *Symposium of the Zoological Society of London,* 43:303–316.

Seager, S.W.J.
1977.　Artificial insemination of non-primates. *Symposium on the Artificial Breeding of Non-domestic Animals (London),* Abstract: 10.

Seidel, G.
1981.　Superovulation and embryo transfer in cattle. *Science,* 211:351–358.

Stover, J., and J. Evans.
1984.　Interspecies embryo transfer from gaur (*Bos gaurus*) to domestic Holstein cattle (*Bos taurus*) at the New York Zoological Park. *Proceedings of the Tenth International Congress on Animal Reproduction and Artificial Insemination,* 2:243–245.

Stover, J., J. Evans, and E. Dolensek
1981.　Interspecies embryo transfer from the gaur to domestic Holstein. *Proceedings of the American Association of Zoo Veterinarians,* 1981:122.

Summers, P., and C. Wennick
1984.　Embryo transfer in the common marmoset monkey (*Callithrix jacchus*). *Proceedings of the Tenth International Congress on Animal Reproduction and Artificial Insemination,* 2:245–246.

Wemmer, C., and T.P. Portillo
1983.　Towards semen collection of exotic ungulates using non-electric methods. *Proceedings of the Annual Conference of the American Association of Zoological Parks and Aquariums,* 195–202.

Whitehead, G.K.
1978.　Captive breeding as a practical aid to preventing extinction, and providing animals for reintroduction. *Proceedings of the Working Meeting of the Deer Specialist Group of the Survival Service Commission, International Union for the Conservation of Nature,* pp. 353–363.

Whitehead, G.K.
1981.　Captive breeding as a practical aid to preventing extinction, and providing animals for re-introduction. *Deer,* 7–21.

Wierzbowski, S.
1959.　Odruchy plciowe ogierów. *Roczniki Nauk Rolniczych Kraków,* 73-B-4:753–788.

R.W. KELLY,
P.F. FENNESSY,
G.H. MOORE,
K.R. DREW,
and
A.R. BRAY
Invermay Agricultural Research Centre
Ministry of Agriculture and Fisheries
Private Bag
Mosgiel, New Zealand

Management, Nutrition, and Reproductive Performance of Farmed Deer in New Zealand

ABSTRACT Deer farming in New Zealand commenced in the late 1960s using animals captured from the feral population. The two principal species farmed are red deer (*Cervus elaphus*) and fallow deer (*Dama dama*), with an estimated total of 200,000 deer farmed by the end of 1982. The paper describes aspects of farming red deer. Techniques, including grazing management and velvet antler removal are reported. The growth of red deer has a seasonal pattern related to appetite and there is a potential to produce high yields of carcass meat per hectare. Observational data indicate that velvet antler production and hind fertility are associated with animal liveweight. Studies on mating management indicate that harem formation and dominance relationships between stags have important implications on intensive farms, and that a stag is capable of successfully mating at least 50 hinds in a season.

Introduction

All deer in New Zealand originate from introduced animals, commencing in 1851 with the liberation of red deer (*Cervus elaphus*). Today there are six species of feral deer viz. red deer, wapiti (*C. elaphus nelsoni*), fallow deer (*Dama dama*), sika deer (*C. nippon*), whitetail (*Odocoileus virginianus*), sambar (*C. unicolor*) and rusa (*C. timorensis*). For these the number of recorded liberations varies from over 220 for red deer to eight for rusa deer (Harris, 1974). Due to no indigenous predators or competitors and legislated protection, feral populations were readily established. Red deer are the most numerous and widespread, being found throughout New Zealand's forested and tussock land, followed in numbers by several widely separated herds of fallow deer and one large herd of wapiti. These three types of deer, and primarily red deer, form the basis of the New Zealand deer farming industry.

Establishment of Deer Farming

Rapid proliferation of feral populations in the early 1900s led to deer competing with sheep and cattle farming, and widespread damage to natural vegetation. As a result protective legislation was removed, and a government deer control program initiated in 1931. In 1956 the New Zealand Forest Service became responsible for the control of noxious animals, and professional cullers were employed to shoot deer as a means of control and eradication. Up to 1967 more than one million deer were killed on official government operations (Whitehead, 1972).

Commercial exploitation of deer began in the late 1950s with the export to West Germany of venison recovered from feral animals, made possible by the game-food market in that country that allowed the sale of meat such as venison without any preslaughter animal inspection. With a rapid increase in value of exported venison in the late 1960s (Drew, 1976a) there was a marked increase in shooting activities, to the extent that helicopters became the usual means from which the animals were shot and carcasses transported to game packing houses (Challies, 1974). The effects of hunting have led to a decrease in numbers of feral animals, an improvement in their condition, less browsing pressure on vegetation and a change in the distribution of the feral deer away from areas of easy access for hunting (Challies, 1977).

The experience gained by people in running some deer extensively (Pinney and Kilgariff, 1976), a slump in world beef prices in the mid 1970s, removal of inhibitory legislation for deer farming, development of capture and management techniques (Brookes, 1976; Wallis and Faulks, 1976) and the high prices for velvet

antler (up to $NZ286 per kilogram) and live animals (up to $NZ3200 each) in the late 1970s have all contributed to a rapid development of deer farming as an industry in the last decade. Whereas there was an estimated 7000 deer held on registered farms in 1975 (Drew, 1976b), in mid 1980 there were approximately 104,000 (Gladden, 1981), and it is anticipated that by the end of 1982 200,000 will be farmed, of which about 170,000 will be red deer.

The basis for management practices adopted on the early deer farms relied on observations of the behavior of wild animals together with much trial and error. With the development of a deer research facility at Invermay Agricultural Research Center in 1973, and work commenced in 1966 at the Rowett Research Institute in Scotland (Blaxter, et al., 1974, p. 77), there has been a considerable accumulation of knowledge on the performance of farmed red deer. This paper reports aspects of applied research and farming experience as it relates to the management, nutrition and reproductive performance of farmed red deer in New Zealand. The main productive end points of deer farming are velvet antler from the stag, and production of animals for slaughter (venison) or sale to other farms. Velvet antler is sold to eastern Asian countries, particularly Korea, where it is used in traditional medicine. Saleable by-products include hides, tails, eyeteeth, penis and sinews.

Management

The general approach of the New Zealand farmer, of which more than 2000 run deer (herd sizes ranging from a few animals to several thousand), has been to extend management practices used in sheep and cattle farming to the deer farm. In fact many deer herds are run as an alternative enterprise on part of established sheep or cattle farms. As a consequence, whereas some activities tolerate the unique behavior of deer, much of the time their gregarious nature is utilized to impose established farming practices. Annual management involves separation of younger stock from the main adult herd to allow them to be preferentially fed, and separation of the sexes to facilitate velvet harvesting in the spring-summer period and to control mating. The following outlines specific points related to the construction and management of deer farms in New Zealand.

Fences, Layout and Yards

Perimeter fences are usually 2m high, made of 13 wire high tensile netting with 150 or 300 mm wide gaps. Tanalised pine posts are spaced at a maximum of 4.9 m apart to comply with regulations. Present costs of erecting these fences are about $NZ6–7/m.

Cheaper subdivision fences are used, but 2 m high fences are required to keep stags separated from and between mating groups. For grazing control of young stock from weaning (3 or 6 months old) to 15 months of age, 1 m high sheep netting with a top or outrigger electric wire is adequate. Temporary electric fences at 60–70 cents/m are widely used for break feeding herds on pasture. One "hot" wire can contain some herds, but when availability of pasture is restricted 4 "hot" wires spaced from about 15 cm to 130 cm high are necessary.

The general layouts of paddocks, topographical considerations aside, are invariably centered on a system for yarding deer. Wing fences towards gate-ways and a flowing system of lane-ways (a most essential feature for control in yarding fractious deer) are generally used. Aids to moving deer vary from dogs to the use of horses, vehicles or helicopters. Scrim or a blanket held between two people, providing a visual barrier, has been found to be useful in moving deer up or down a lane-way for yarding.

The designs of yards vary but contain the following essential features:—
(a) Indirect approach of the yarding race
(b) Yard walls close boarded or solid
(c) 2.25 m high walls
(d) No sharp corners or projections
(e) Darkened pen for handling

Recently mechanical crushes have been developed to assist in the restraint of deer particularly for disease testing and velvet antler removal.

Acclimatization of Deer

Generalizations of the method of deer farm management in New Zealand are not easily made. This is due to the wide difference between the behavior of highly sensitive and easily exciteable recently captured feral deer compared with the almost cheeky tameness of some farm bred animals. High death rates due mainly to post capture myopathy have been recorded in recently captured feral deer, particularly those caught by helicopter techniques. Factors which reduce such losses include placing the captured deer temporarily in dark pens immediately after capture and releasing them after several days into paddocks with a few tamer deer and a small amount of cover to hide with minimal disturbance.

The quietening of deer for farming has largely resulted from hand feeding supplements, the weaning of calves from wilder hinds, culling the wilder animals and by permitting deer to become accustomed to paddock, laneway and yard systems on the farm by leaving gates open to allow voluntary familiarization rather than movements forced by humans.

Separation of Age/Sex Classes

Generally stags and hinds are kept separated by fences except for the period of mating (the rut). Separating stags from the breeding hinds is necessary to avoid disturbing calving groups when yarding the stags for velveting.

Calves are usually weaned at 3 months of age, before the rut, as a matter of convenience to allow easier implementation of a drenching program for control of the lungworm (*Dictylocaulus viviparus*) and gastrointestinal nematodes (Mason, 1977). However, on extensive farms with large paddocks it may be impractical to yard hinds with calves for early weaning. Instead, weaning occurs in winter when hinds and calves can be easily enticed off the high blocks into smaller paddocks using supplementary feeds.

Yearlings at 13 months of age need separation by sex to avoid bossing and mounting by males, and to allow preferential feeding of the females to ensure good reproductive performance (see section on Reproduction).

Velvet Antler Production and Removal from Stags

Observational data indicate that velvet antler production is associated with liveweight and age of the stag (Figure 1). For every 1 kg liveweight difference the weight of velvet produced changes by about 0.01 kg.

Animal protection organizations have questioned the indignity and methods of removing growing antlers in the velvet from stags. However, practical experience and observations dictate that unless

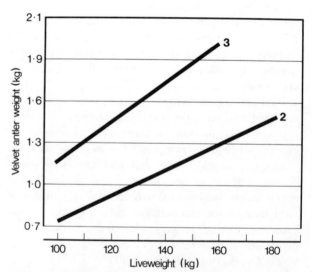

Figure 1. Relationship between velvet antler weight (Y) and liveweight (LW) of 2 and 3 year old stags. Values in kg.
1. $Y_2 = 0.009$ LW—0.18, r = 0.53** (LW = 27 months old, pre-rut).
2. $Y_3 = 0.014$ LW—0.25, r = 0.60*** (LW = 2.5 years old, mid winter).

Kelly, Fennessy, Moore, Drew, and Bray

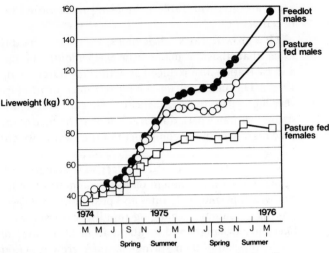

Figure 2. Growth of red deer from 3 to 27 months of age (from Drew, 1976b).

antlers are removed from stags on farms they are likely to injure humans, other deer and damage fences. Irrespective of the high commercial value of velvet antler it is far easier and safer for man and deer to remove antlers in velvet before they have become hardened and pointed (Moore and Searle, 1980).

In New Zealand legislation requires that stags must be given an adequate degree of analgesia prior to velvet antler removal. The tranquilizer most commonly used is xylazine hydrochloride (Rompun, Bayer) at doses between 30–60 mg/100 kg liveweight, which works far more effectively when the stags are held in darkened pens. About 15 minutes after Rompun injection, local anaesthetic (2% xylocaine) is administered on either side of the head to the infratrochlear and zygomaticotemporal nerves (Adam, 1979). A tourniquet is then applied around the pedicles and the velvet antlers sawn off about 1 cm above the coronet. Once removed the velvet antlers are hung upside down (to avoid blood loss) and allowed to cool before sealing in plastic bags for freezing. Farmers sell the frozen velvet antlers to agents of processing plants where they are dried prior to export.

Nutrition and Growth

A knowledge of potential rates of growth and nutritional requirements is vital in any attempt to maximize the production from farmed deer. It is important that animals for slaughter attain their slaughter weight as quickly as possible in the particular conditions, while for breeding stock it is imperative that they are ready to breed successfully as young as possi-

ble. The importance of liveweight in velvet antler production has already been mentioned. Therefore, from the beginning nutritional studies have formed an important part of the research program at Invermay.

Young Animals

In order to maximize the efficiency of production, farm animals must be fed to permit high rates of growth at times when they have the capacity for such growth. The red deer is no exception—the periods of high potential growth are during the first few months of life and during the following spring–summer. To maintain high rates of milk production and consequently high rates of growth of suckling calves it is imperative that a high quality pasture be offered throughout lactation. Formerly at the Invermay deer farm, pastures were allowed to grow rank to provide for cover for the young calves. Such pastures are of low quality and the consequences for milk production of the hind and growth of the calf were considerable. Pasture growth control improved pasture quality, and contributed to increasing weaning weights of calves from about 35 kg to 50 kg at 100 days of age. However, shelter for calves should not be neglected; this may be provided by rough patches of long grass produced by temporarily fencing off small areas from grazing, or by scrub areas in calving paddocks.

Growth potential was measured initially with young stags from 6–27 months of age fed on high quality diet *ad libitum* in a feedlot. The growth of these animals was compared with other stags and hinds grazing pasture from 3–27 months of age (Figure 2).

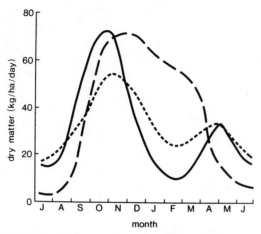

Figure 3. Seasonal pattern of pasture production at 3 sites in New Zealand (from Molley, 1980).

Growth rate of the pasture feed animals was less than their potential as revealed by the feedlot study. However, a seasonal pattern of growth was evident in both the pasture-fed and in the feedlot stags even though the latter were fed to appetite. The seasonal nature of feed intake and growth has been confirmed in many subsequent studies (Fennessy, 1982).

The New Zealand farming system is generally based on the grazing of high quality ryegrass-white clover pastures that have rapid growth in the spring-summer period (Figure 3). Therefore for an efficient utilization of the pasture, grazing systems must be organized to utilize the feed grown during this time. For this reason, studies sought to provide basic data on the potential production from young deer under intensive systems of grazing. A knowledge of sex differences in growth rates and the effects of castration were considered important. The results of grazing trials performed over the spring–summer period in three

years are given in Table 1. Stocking rates varied between years.

The growth rates of females were considerably lower than those of males from 9–15 months of age, and castration also reduced growth rates (Drew et al., 1978). The potential for young red deer to produce very high yields of carcass meat per hectare during the spring–summer period is largely a consequence of the very high lean tissue component of the gain in weight (Table 2).

Prior to 1982 few farmed red deer were slaughtered, but with the establishment of deer slaughtering premises which permit both ante- and post-mortem inspection the situation is changing rapidly. Most stags are likely to be slaughtered at about 15 or 26 months of age at the end of their spring–summer growth period while a few of the better performing stags in terms of weight gain and velvet antler production (and temperament) will be retained.

Adult Animals

Typical patterns of liveweight change of farmed red deer are shown in Figure 4. The adult stag exhibits a very marked cyclical pattern of weight change during the year. In the spring–summer the stag gains considerable weight, of which a very high proportion is fat (Figure 5). Also, the rapid weight gain just prior to the rut is probably due to increased water retention in the carcass tissues under the influence of testosterone. In this respect the water: protein ratio of several muscles and of the whole carcass was much higher in entire than in castrate stags slaughtered just prior to the rut (Tan and Fennessy, 1981). The high weight gains of the spring–summer are followed by a dramatic weight loss during the rut where weight losses of up to 32% have been recorded for stags during a two month period, even when the stag has not been used for breeding ($\bar{x} = 13.6\%$, SE = 1.4, n = 27). The patterns

Table 1. Liveweight gain and estimated production of carcass meat from red deer on first class grazing land at Invermay during the September to February period (deer aged 9–14 months)[1]

| Year | Days | Liveweight gain (g/day) | | | All animals | |
		Males	Castrates	Females	Liveweight gain (kg/ha)	Carcass gain (kg/ha)
1974/5	145	258	—	153	803	482
1975/6	171	244	211	—	1219	731
1976/7	170	226	—	—	1193	716

[1]K.R. Drew (unpublished)

Table 2. Components of carcass gain in stags between September and March (spring-summer)[1]

Age	Carcass gain (kg)	Carcass chemical fat gain (kg)	% of carcass gain as chemical fat
Yearling	26.4	3.8	14
2 years old	21.5	5.0	23
Aged (5–6 years old)	33.9	21.5	63

[1]Drew & Suttie (1982)

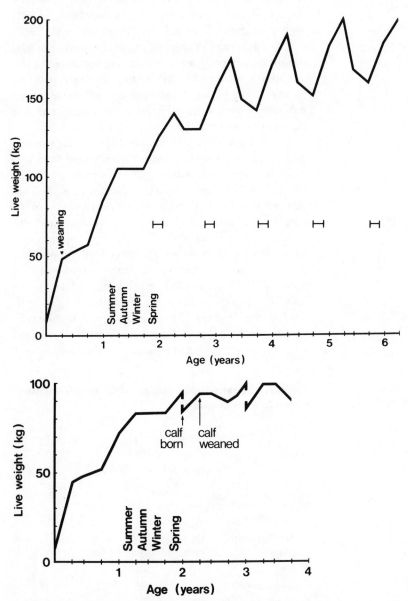

Figure 4. The liveweight pattern of farmed stags (a) and hinds (b), ⊢⊣ designates the period of velvet antler growth, calves are weaned at about 100 days of age (from Fennessy et al., 1981).

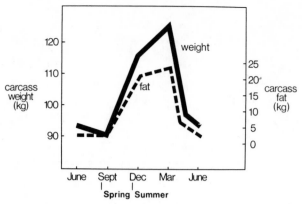

Figure 5. The pattern of change in carcass weight and carcass chemical fat in aged stags through the spring–summer period (from Drew and Suttie, 1982).

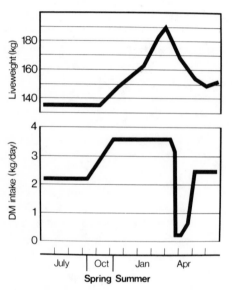

Figure 6. The patterns of feed intake and liveweight gain for a stag aged 2.5 to 3.5 years, and fed to appetite indoors (from Fennessy, 1982).

of weight changes of grazing stags are similar to those recorded in penned stags fed to appetite indoors. The typical pattern of feed intake and weight change for such a stag is shown in Figure 6. Observations on stags in mating groups during the peak phase of the rut indicate that grazing activity is low, comprising less than 10% of activities recorded at 5 minute intervals during the day (A.R. Bray, unpublished). Following the period of very low feed intake during the rut, intake increases and weight tends to stabilize for the winter period. The post-rut live-weight can also be maintained in stags outdoors so long as they are fed *ad libitum*. However, because of environmental influences coupled with a very low level of body energy reserves, the actual feed required by the stag may be up to 50% higher outdoors than indoors (Fennessy et al., 1981).

The adult hind (Figure 4b) can be expected to gain weight in late pregnancy and during lactation; in this situation some weight loss can be tolerated during the winter. If the plane of nutrition is inadequate to permit weight gain during lactation then weight should be maintained over the winter period.

To the casual observer it may appear that the seasonal nature of growth of farmed deer would fit in well with the pattern of pasture growth as outlined in Figure 3. However, two important factors must be considered: the very high relative feed requirement of the stag during winter and the high requirement of the lactating hind in summer. The energy requirements by season for the various age classes of red deer are given in Table 3. The stag's winter requirement is about 27% of its annual requirement while for the hind, the period of lactation amounts to 43% of its annual requirement. These aspects are highly relevant to the New Zealand pastoral system since during winter, pasture growth is severely limited by climatic

Table 3. Metabolizable energy (ME)[1] requirements of red deer by season

Season	Autumn	Winter	Spring	Summer
(days)	65	100	100	100
	Me requirement (MJ ME/day)			
Stags				
3–15 months	16	20	27	26
15–27 months	24	28	32	30
Older	20	34	40	38
Hinds				
3–15 months	15	18	22	21
Older	22	23	24	47

[1]The ME requirements have been derived on the basis of the liveweight changes shown in Figures 4a and 4b, Fennessy, et al. (1981).

Kelly, Fennessy, Moore, Drew, and Bray

conditions while during summer, pasture growth is not always reliable being very dependent on moisture supply. Such patterns of feed demand mean that the New Zealand deer farmer must become highly skilled as a manager of both his animals and the pasture.

Reproduction

The seasonal breeding of red deer has a pattern of mating (the rut) in autumn (April) and calving in summer (late November–December) following a 233 day gestation. Observations during the rut indicate an intensive period of activity of about three weeks when most hinds conceive, which is confirmed by calving records showing that the majority of hinds calve over a period of less than a month (Kelly and Moore, 1977; Bray and Kelly, 1979).

Performance about Mating

In the stag, sperm are first detectable in the epididymis at about 14 months of age. However, the majority of deer farmers do not use stags until they are at least 27 months of age, partly as it allows measurements on growth and velvet production to aid selection decisions.

In adult stags in late summer there is rapid hypertrophy of neck muscles, development of a rutting odor and increased aggressiveness towards other stags and man. The majority of adult stags commence roaring in the month (March) before the onset of the hinds' breeding season. These changes are associated with a marked increase in plasma testosterone concentrations (Kelly et al., 1980).

Stags, which almost without exception have had their antlers removed in the velvet stage, are joined with hinds at any time in the three weeks prior to the expected onset of the breeding season of the hinds. Harem formation activities by the stags commence immediately on joining with the hinds. Observations of harem sizes in the feral population, and information from Scotland (Blaxter et al., 1974), led most of the early deer farmers to join animals at a stag:hind ratio of about 1:10 (range 1:5 to 1:28 for 7 deer farms). However, records from a single sire joining at Invermay in 1975 showed that a stag successfully mated 32 of 35 hinds, with 31 being pregnant to the first mating. This, together with other observations where one stag in multi-stag groups was noted to be dominant during most of the rut, resulted in studies on commercial herds to test the effect of numbers of stags and hinds per herd on mating behavior and subsequent calving performance (Bary and Kelly, 1979). Sizes of herds ranged from 1–12 stags and 15–196 hinds, run in paddocks of 10 ha or less.

The results from this work can be summarized as

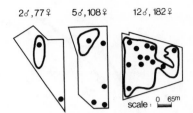

Figure 7. Stag and hind dispersion in 3 herds at the peak of the rut. (•) stag location, solid line describes perimeter of herd (Bray and Kelly, unpublished).

follows. In nine herds in which 2–5 stags were present (mean number of hinds/herd = 112, range 15–196), a single stag in each herd maintained a harem (consisting of nearly all hinds), and performed all of the observed mating. Stag:hind ratios clearly did not reflect mating loads of each stag. Signs of sexual exhaustion (high mount:serve ratio) of the dominant stag were recorded in some herds with more than 100 hinds. The ability of the stag to maintain control of the majority of hinds was reduced in herds of more than 5 stags; in the extreme situation no stag was able to maintain a harem in a herd containing 12 stags and 182 hinds. Typical animal dispersion during mating is shown in Figure 7. Nevertheless, in the herd of 12 stags one stag still performed the majority of observed services and was dominant in aggressive interactions with other stags. The dominant stag was usually, but not always, the oldest and largest of the stags joined with the hinds. Calving performances related to mating observations indicated that some stags sired at least 73 calves in one season, and that fewer stags could be successfully used than the 1:10 ratio (Figure 8). However, the observation of sexual exhaustion in

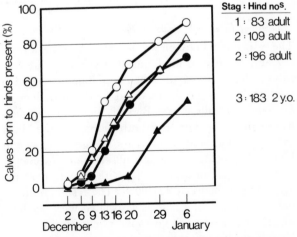

Figure 8. Cumulative calving performances of 4 herds on one commercial farm, 1978 (from Bray and Kelly, 1979).

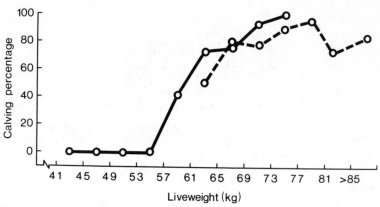

Figure 9. Calving performances of 2 year old hinds related to liveweight (4 kg grouping, n ≥10 per group) at the previous rut.
(--) Invermay, 1975–1980, n = 130.
(—) From Hamilton and Blaxter (1980), n = 177.

stags maintaining harems of over 100 hinds and in one herd of 77 hinds resulted in the conservative recommendation to farmers that if deer are to be mated in small paddocks the number of hinds should be limited to 50 per paddock for single-sire joining. If much larger numbers are present then large numbers of stags should be used to limit harem formation and spread the mating load. The dominant stag should be replaced at least after three weeks of mating, particularly in single-sire herds. These practices will limit the effect of any stag infertility on calving percentages, and will allow genetic progress to be made by the use of selected sires and identification of their progeny.

In larger paddocks, the area over which a single stag can exert an influence is reduced. More stags form harems, and so the effect of individual animals on the herds' reproductive performance is reduced.

Influence of Liveweight on Hind Fertility

The association between liveweight at the time of mating and fertility of hinds, aged 2 years or older at calving, for Invermay deer has been found to be similar to the relationship reported for farmed deer in Scotland (Hamilton and Blaxter, 1980) at common liveweights. The data from both sources for the hinds calving performance at 2 years of age is shown in Figure 9. In older hinds our observations extend to mating weights of over 110 kg, with calving percentages ranging between 90–100%. The results indicate that the fertility of a hind is associated with her liveweight at mating, with no apparent effects of age (see Hamilton, this volume).

Performance at Calving

Despite the initial experience of high calf losses (27%) when hinds were run at high stocking rates (22 hinds/ha) in small paddocks (<1.3 ha) during the establishment of the Invermay deer farm (Kelly and Whateley, 1975), in subsequent years herds at Invermay have had average calf mortality rates of 11% (range 2–21%). On 97 commercial properties the average calf mortality rate in 1980/81 was 8.2% (Asher et al., 1981). High mortality rates have occurred in herds of 2 year old hinds when nutrition has been poor in late pregnancy, or where experimental management has disturbed animals during calving.

Individual hind-calf identification is difficult if not impossible for the large scale deer farmer due to the small number of suckling periods during the day and their short duration (Kelly and Drew, 1976). However, with small numbers of animals observation of hind-calf pairing following a period of several hours' separation has been used to establish hind-calf relationships. On a herd basis udder inspection at 2½ months after the commencement of calving has proven to be an accurate method of recording the number of calves born and reared to a herd, as twinning is an exceptionally rare phenomena in red deer, and it also provides reasonable information on the number of calf mortalities (60–100% accurate). Recently, the use of the marked udder method (Davis et al., 1981) has proven useful following calving in a single herd for separating groups of hinds and their progeny post calving.

Kelly, Fennessy, Moore, Drew, and Bray

There are two basic limitations to commercial production influenced by the reproductive performance of red deer. Firstly being a monotocous species, calving percentages on the farm will rarely exceed 95%. Secondly, with calving not occurring until late November–December, much of the period of peak pasture production in spring (Figure 3) cannot be utilized for calf growth prior to their first winter.

An attempt to induce multiple calving in red deer was made in 1976 using 10 hinds older than 27 months of age. To synchronize estrus progestagen impregnated intravaginal sponges were used, followed by intramuscular injection of 1000 i.u. of pregnant mares' serum gonadotrophin (PMSG) on day 14 of the subsequent estrous cycle.

Treatment with PMSG induced ovulation rates varying from 1–12 per hind, mean value = 4.4. Only 3 hinds calved to the PMSG ovulation (ovulation rates of 3, 6, 6) all having a single calf. Measurements of peripheral progesterone concentrations in 4 barren superovulated hinds (≥3 corpora lutea, Kelly et al., 1982) suggest that pregnancy may have been established but that embryonic mortality occurred in the early stages. It is quite likely that the potential for multiple pregnancies in red deer is markedly limited by the average of only 8 maternal caruncles (range 4–12 per hind, n = 49) available for placental attachment. The possibility of increasing reproductive rates through the forementioned technique therefore appears remote.

Techniques to advance the onset of the breeding season are currently under investigation. Progestagen treatment together with PMSG induced estrus approximately 3–4 weeks earlier than the normal time of onset in 8 of 9 hinds (89%). Eight of these, on the basis of mating records, conceived to mating at that estrus.

Conclusion

Although now firmly established in New Zealand as a profitable form of livestock production, the farming of deer is still developing rapidly and many aspects of production need investigation. On the research side for example, there is a lack of estimates of genetic parameters. Livestock production records are now being systematically kept on many farms and this performance recording could assist in the selection of herd sires. The New Zealand velvet antler industry will increasingly concentrate on improving the size and quality of the product through selection, and cross-breeding with wapiti. Improvement in antler production through better feeding and management is

not simple and until current research into the mechanism of antler growth is complete little further progress is likely.

The processing of farmed deer through licensed slaughter premises is a very recent development and much has yet to be learned about the effects of pre- and post-slaughter treatment of the animal and carcass on venison quality. Detailed venison market research has been intensified with the development of range reared game meat and the industry is demonstrating confidence in its future.

Despite large fluctuations in the value of live animals and velvet over the past five years, deer still remain a more profitable form of land use than conventional livestock systems in New Zealand (Ritchie and Giles, 1981). Deer farming has certainly become an established part of New Zealand agriculture.

Acknowledgments

The authors gratefully acknowledge the assistance of technical staff of the Nutrition and Animal Production Sections at the Invermay Agricultural Research Center in the conduct of these studies, and the deer farmers who have been involved in the off-station research. The Friends of the National Zoo provided generous financial assistance to enable R.W. Kelly to attend the Conference.

Literature Cited

Adams, J.L.
1979.   Innervation and blood supply of the antler pedicle of the red deer. *New Zealand Veterinary Journal*, 27:200–201.

Asher, G.W., J.L. Adam, T. Reid, and M. Langridge
1981.   Reproductive performance of red deer in the Northern North Island region. In *Agricultural Research Division Annual Report, N.Z. Ministry of Agriculture and Fisheries*, pp. 43–44.

Blaxter, K.L., R.N.B. Kay, G.A.M. Sharman, J.M.M. Cunningham, and W.J. Hamilton
1974.   *Farming the Red Deer*. Edinburgh, Scotland: HMSO.

Bray, A.R., and R.W. Kelly
1979.   Mating management and reproductive activity of intensively farmed red deer. *Proceedings of the New Zealand Society of Animal Production*, 39:94–99.

Brookes, R.A.
1976.   Deer trapping and herd management. In *Deer Farming in New Zealand, Progress and Prospects*, edited by K.R. Drew and M.F. McDonald, pp 5–8. New Zealand Society of Animal Production Occasional Publication No. 5.

Challies, C.N.

1974. Use of helicopters in the New Zealand commercial venison industry. *East African Agriculture and Forestry Journal*, 39:376–380.

Challies, C.N.

1977. Effects of commercial hunting on red deer densities in the Arawata Valley, South Westland, 1972–76. *New Zealand Journal of Forestry Sciences*, 7:263–273.

Davis, G.H., T.R. Wallis, and A.R. Bary

1981. Marked udder method (MUM)—a technique for identifying the progeny of ewes where identification at birth is not practicable. *Proceedings of the New Zealand Society of Animal Production*, 41:229–232.

Drew, K.R.

1976a. The farming of red deer in New Zealand. *World Review of Animal Production*, 12:49–60.

Drew, K.R.

1976b. Deer Farming. *Proceedings of the Ruakura Farmers Conference*, 27:53– 57.

Drew, K.R., P.F. Fennessy, and G.J. Greer

1978. The growth and carcass characteristics of entire and castrate red stags. *Proceedings of the New Zealand Society of Animal Production*, 38:142–144.

Drew, K.R., and J.M. Suttie

1982. Quality meat from farmed deer. *Proceedings of the New Zealand Deer Farmers Association Annual Conference, No. 7*, Technical Addresses pp. 39–47.

Fennessy, P.S.

1982. Nutrition and growth: In *The Farming of Deer, World Trends and Modern Techniques*, edited by D. Yerex, pp. 105–114. Wellington, New Zealand: Agricultural Promotion Associates Ltd.

Fennessy, P.F., G.H. Moore, and I.D. Corson

1981. Energy requirements of red deer. *Proceedings of the New Zealand Society of Animal Production*, 41:167–173.

Gladden, N.

1981. Deer—Population and health survey 1980. *Aglink* FPP259. Media Services, Ministry of Agriculture and Fisheries, Wellington, New Zealand.

Hamilton, W.J., and K.L. Blaxter

1980. Reproduction in farmed red deer. 1. Hind and stag fertility. *Journal of Agricultural Science, Cambridge*, 95:261–273.

Harris, L.H.

1974. A Hunting Guide to Introduced Wild Animals of New Zealand. *New Zealand Forest Service Information Series*, No. 64. Wellington, New Zealand: Government Printer.

Kelly, R.W., and K.R. Drew

1976. The behaviour and growth of deer in improved pastures. In *Deer Farming in New Zealand, Progress and Prospects*, edited by K.R. Drew and M.F. McDonald, pp. 20–25. New Zealand Society of Animal Production Occasional Publication No. 5.

Kelly, R.W., K.P. McNatty, G.H. Moore, D. Ross, and M. Gibb

1982. Plasma concentrations of LH, prolactin, oestradiol and progesterone in female red deer (*Cervus elaphus*) during pregnancy. *Journal of Reproduction and Fertility*, 64:475–483.

Kelly, R.W., and G.H. Moore

1977. Reproductive performance in farmed red deer. *New Zealand Agricultural Sciences*, 11:179–181.

Kelly, R.W., G.H. Moore, and K.R. Drew

1980. Characteristics of red deer (*Cervus elaphus L.*) related to their performance as farmed animals. *Proceedings of the Australian Society of Animal Production*, 13:198–201.

Kelly, R.W., and J.A. Whateley

1975. Observations on the calving of red deer (*Cervus elaphus*) run in confined areas. *Applied Animal Ethology*, 1:293–300.

Mason, P.C.

1977. Gastrointestinal parasitism in red deer. *New Zealand Agricultural Sciences*, 11:182–183.

Molley, L.F.

1980. Land alone endures. Land use and the role of research. Discussion paper No. 3. pp. 33, *New Zealand Department of Scientific and Industrial Research*, Wellington, New Zealand.

Moore, G.H., and A.K. Searle

1980. Removal of velvet antler from farmed red deer. *Proceedings of the 4th Annual Conference of the Animal Science Technicians Association of New Zealand*.

Pinney, B., and P. Kilgariff

1976. Handling deer under extensive conditions. In *Deer Farming in New Zealand, Progress and Prospects*, edited by K.R. Drew and M.F. McDonald, pp. 9–14. New Zealand Society of Animal Production Occasional Publication No. 5.

Ritchie, J.M.W., and K.H. Giles

1981. Deer—Economics red deer farming. *Aglink* FPP250. Media Services, Ministry of Agriculture and Fisheries, Wellington, New Zealand.

Tan, G.Y., and P.F. Fennessy

1981. The effect of castration on some muscles of red deer. *New Zealand Journal of Agricultural Research*, 24:1–3.

Wallace, T., and J. Faulks

1976. Live deer capture by helicopter. In *Deer Farming in New Zealand, Progress and Prospects*, edited by K.R. Drew and M.F. McDonald, pp. 2–4. New Zealand Society of Animal Production Occasional Publication No. 5.

Whitehead, G.K.

1972. *Deer of the World*. New York: Viking Press.

W.J. HAMILTON
Hill Farming Research Organisation
Glensaugh Research Station
Laurencekirk
Scotland AB3 1HB

Farming Red Deer (*Cervus elaphus*)—Some Aspects of Research and Development in Scotland and Their Implications for the Management of the Deer and the Pastoral Resources

ABSTRACT

On heather dominant pastures in northeast Scotland, stocking levels of more than 2 hind grazing equivalents (H.E.) ha^{-1} caused changes to occur in the floristic composition of the sward. The problems of farming red deer on such resources with potentially high levels of plant utilisation, such that overgrazing, mechanical damage and soil erosion can occur are discussed. Resource management in winter snow conditions and the importance of shelter within each enclosure are also discussed. A stock carrying capacity of 1 H.E. ha^{-1} is suggested as reasonable for the resource and for the performance of the animal.

The breeding performance of the hinds varied according to the level of nutrition during the first winter of life. Hind liveweight at the rut was related to calf birth weight, calf growth rate and time of calving. Calf mortality was heaviest post weaning and reached 12% of calves weaned. Adult mortality was 1.8%. Stag performance was such that one stag mated successfully with 28 hinds so that they all calved in a 20 day period. Longevity and fertility are discussed—all 42 eleven-year-old hinds at Glensaugh produced calves in their eleventh year with birth weights of 8.5 kg for stags and 7.7 kg for hinds.

The number of supporting animals for a 100 hind breeding stock where the calves are removed at weaning was given so that each breeding hind maintained required 1.5 ha of resource.

Introduction

Red deer are indigenous to Scotland and currently occupy some 3.14 million hectares (Red Deer Commission 1979) or some 40% of the total land area. Although wild deer are common on the sheep grazings in the Highland area, much of the land held exclusively for deer, and where the highest densities occur, is of high relief amplitude and is unsuitable for forestry or agricultural use.

From an estimated population of 255,000 red deer (Red Deer Commission, 1979) at an overall stocking rate of 0.12 ha^{-1}, some 40,000 animals are culled annually, representing a venison output of 1800 tons or 0.573 kg ha^{-1}.

During the mid 1960s an excellent market for venison had developed in Western Europe and by 1969 the price offered to the Scottish sporting estates had trebled to 47 pence/kg dead carcass weight (d.c.w.). Prices paid to farmers for lamb produced on similar recourses at that time was 38 pence/kg d.c.w.

This economic differential was sufficiently significant to promote an investigation to establish whether it was feasible to farm this animal, and to determine whether the farming of red deer could be an economically viable proposition on hill and upland pastoral resources.

Early in 1970 an area of heather (*Calluna vulgaris*) clad hill land on the Glensaugh Research Station was allocated to the Red Deer Farming Research Project and was enclosed with a deer fence.

This paper will consider the results of some of the work carried out at Glensaugh by the Hill Farming Research Organisation and the Rowett Research Institute, and the implications of these in relation to the management of the animal and the pastures.

The Land Resources

The Glensaugh deer farm lies in the eastern foothills of the Grampian Mountains some 200 km inland from the east coast, on land which rises from 180 m to 430 m altitude. The primary resources used for the project have already been described in some detail (Blaxter et al., 1974).

The soils vary from fluvial gravels in the valley bottoms, supporting grassland (*Festuca* spp) communities, to colluvial and humus iron podzols on the lower slopes, bearing heather dominant and bracken (*Pteridium aquilinum*) dominant vegetation, in association with bent grasses (*Agrostis* spp.). On the higher slopes on peaty podzols, heather cover is usually 85 to 90% and is associated with blaeberry (*Viccinium myrtillus*) and tufted hair grass (*Deschampsia flexuosa*). The hill tops and high plateaus are covered with a deep blanket bog peat where heather is co-dominant with sheathing cotton grass (*Eriophorum vaginatum*).

Traditionally, land resources of this kind are used for sheep production systems, wild red deer range, or for the breeding and management of red grouse (*Lagopus lagopus scoticus*). In more recent times large areas have been afforested.

In terms of the ruminant animal, this resource has a low nutritional status. The digestibility of the dry matter (D.M.) of current season's shoots of heather varies from 60% in June to 50% in September, and 40% over the winter period January to March (Hill Farming Research Organisation, 1979). Even in summer, heather alone, mainly because of low voluntary intakes, provides little more than the maintenance requirements for body weight in a grazing sheep (Milne et al., 1978). The relative quality of a heather dominant pasture as a grazing resource is judged by the amount of the more highly digestible *Agrostis-Festuca* communities present, and their dispersal throughout the pasture. The higher the proportion and the more widely dispersed the better the pasture is deemed to be. Studies of the diet selection by deer grazing similar resources (Staines, 1970; Colquhoun, 1971) indicate that deer select a mixed grass-heather diet throughout the year with grass predominating in summer. The amount of herbage eaten by deer when fed on all heather diet is much less than when fed on grass/heather mixtures (Milne et al., 1978). In comparative studies with sheep, Milne et al. (1977) demonstrated that red deer can eat twice as much digestible organic matter as sheep when fed poor quality roughages in winter and spring, and were able to digest their higher intakes to the same extent as the sheep. These results suggest that red deer are very well suited to utilise these poor quality heather dominant hill pastures. Deer also appear to fit the ecosystem rather well if one assumes that their greatest energy requirement is during late pregnancy and early lactation. In late May, June and July the quality of the herbage on the resource is at its best. At Glensaugh 63% of all calves born on the farm were born during the first twenty days of June (Hamilton and Blaxter, 1980). The seasonal appetite cycle, a distinctive pattern of food intake (Blaxter et al., 1974; Milne et al., 1978) with considerably reduced intakes in the winter months, must be an advantage in biological and economical terms. Supplementary feed inputs to livestock systems are likely to be less where the peak energy requirements of the animal coincide with the period of maximum growth of the primary resource.

When red deer are kept on heather dominant grazings throughout the year, the main objective of management will likely be to retain the status quo as regards the composition of the vegetation, or at most,

Hamilton

accept a slow change to *Agrostis-Festuca* grassland in areas where soil conditions promote this plant succession. The level of stocking on a resource of this type will determine the degree of herbage utilisation and hence the stability of the sward. The removal of 60% of the current season's shoots of heather does not affect shoot production in the following year, but removal of 80% reduces production by half, and heavy autumn grazing is particularly damaging to the plant (Grant et al., 1978). In recent studies (Grant et al., 1981) of the responses of heather dominant vegetation to controlled grazing by red deer, stocking rates ranged from 1.0 to 2.5 hind equivalents (H.E.) ha^{-1} (Blaxter et al., 1974). Heather utilisation levels as measured from the pastures ranged from 25 to 60% of current season's shoot production. Similar values of production utilisation were calculated from the stocking rate, liveweight and intake data. The primary plant production from resources of this type is estimated to be 2000 to 2500 kg D.M. ha^{-1} (Hill Farming Research Organisation, 1979) with a seasonal variation of up to 25% (Miller, 1966). Over the four year period of study, floristic changes only occurred on the heather dominant areas. Old heather was less able to withstand grazing than was young heather and heather cover was reduced in areas where the stocking rate was consistently above 2 H.E. ha^{-1}.

The height of the heather sward rarely impedes access by deer to the grazings, but frequently does to hill sheep on systems where burning is infrequent and where utilisation levels are commonly 5–15%, which allow the plant to grow vigorously. On sheep grazings, burning off the heather, on average every 10 years, is required to maintain a good proportion of young vigorous stands of less than 300 mm in height. Current season's shoots from young heather plants have been shown to be more nutritious than those from old heather (Grant and Hunter, 1968). Where pastures are stocked with red deer and utilisation levels of 40 to 50% are achieved, burning frequency will be reduced if the height of the standing crop is the main criterion. However, age is related to quality and level of production, and it is likely that heather grazed by deer to this extent will require regular burning, and the burned areas will require protection from overgrazing until regeneration is complete.

During the winter months in deep snow conditions, farmed deer are fed hay to maintenance requirements, and as the snow melts the deer eat less hay and graze the exposed heather. The snow melts on the lower slopes first and the areas adjacent to the hay feeding points rapidly become overgrazed, and tracked by the trampling of the deer. In situations of this kind it is best in the interests of preserving the recourse to confine the deer to a small enclosure on a freely drained site and only allow access to the hill pastures when snow cover is less than 30%. It would also be wise to disperse the stock over the entire farm area to ensure an equal degree of grazing pressure throughout.

Mechanical damage of the herbage from trampling along fence-lines can be severe and in some situations where soil erosion has followed, has led to the total collapse of the fence. Two electrified wires, one at 300 mm and the other 1000 mm from the ground, and both held by offset brackets some 450 mm from the fence, have reduced fence walking and have maintained a stable soil and vegetation structure along the fence-line.

Severe overgrazing has also occurred in situations where the area of naturally sheltered pasture within an enclosure is too small in relation to the total area of the paddock. In cold and windy conditions deer congregate and graze in the sheltered areas to the ultimate destruction of the heather. Allowances related to stocking rate and grazing management should be made when planning the layout of enclosures, so that adequate sheltered areas are provided within the system.

When farming red deer on these heather dominant resources on year round grazing systems with such potentially high levels of pasture utilisation, careful control of the stocking rates and the seasonal grazing pressures are essential. Experiences at Glensaugh suggest that on better quality resources on the humus iron soils, stocking rates of about 1 H.E. ha^{-1} would appear to be consistent with the maintenance of the character of the resource and the provision of an adequate pasture for the animal. Co-dominant *Calluna/Eriophorum* vegetation on the deep peat areas with annual production levels of 1450 to 1700 kg D.M. ha^{-1} (HFRO, 1979) is particularly useful for grazing in the early spring before calving, but has a much lower stock carrying capacity.

Animal Production

Hind Growth and Performance

The foundation stocks of red deer for the research project were purchased as calves from Scottish sporting estates. They were caught at one to three days old, and reared artificially in pens on ewe milk substitute, barley based concentrates, and dried grass (Hamilton, 1974; Blaxter et al., 1974). In due course the naturally reared offspring from these animals were retained for the breeding herd. Weaning of calves occurred mostly in September each year, when calves were put on to the hill pastures, fed a concentrate supplement daily, and offered hay *ad libitum* in severe weather conditions.

The amount of concentrate fed over the winter

period had a marked effect on the growth rates of the cohorts (Hamilton and Blaxter, 1981; Blaxter et al., 1981). Feed level inputs to groups of calves were 0.45, 0.57, 0.68, 0.91 and 1.0 kg/hd/day, of a barley based concentrate.

The mean daily live-weight gains for the hind calf groups ranged from 25 g/hd/day to 80 g/hd/day, over the 210 day winter period. At the end of April concentrate feeding was stopped, and the calves were summered on the heather dominant pastures. Over the 155 day period to September, daily liveweight gains ranged from 55 g/hd/day to 146 g/hd/day with considerable seasonal variations.

The mean 15 month liveweights of the cohorts, prior to grouping with the stags for the rut, varied from 49 to 74 kg. From the subsequent growth rate data for these cohorts, the equilibrium weight for mature Glensaugh hinds on hill pasture was calculated to be 81.5 kg.

An analyis of the calving records for these cohorts for the years 1973 to 1978 (Hamilton and Blaxter, 1980) showed that the fertility of a hind was related to her body weight at the rut in September/October. Hinds weighing 52 kg or less will not calve at all. The probability of a 60 kg hind calving was 0.49 and that for an 80 kg hind was 0.91. Increasing the 15 month liveweight of a hind, from 60 kg to 90 kg, doubles the number of calves weaned and increases the liveweight of calves weaned by 160%. The reproductive response to a 15 month liveweight increases with age. A 10 kg increase, from 60 kg to 70 kg liveweight, results in an increase in the calf crop from 29/100 hinds at 27 months 40 47/100 hinds by 111 months. The weight of the hind at the rut was also shown to be significantly related to the birth weight of her calf in the following June, and to the growth rate of the calf to weaning in September when three months of age (Blaxter and Hamilton, 1980). An increase of 20 kg in hind liveweight, from 60 kg to 80 kg at the rut, resulted in an increase of 1 kg in the birth weight of the calf and an increase in growth rate to weaning of 10 to 14%. The mean daily growth rates of the calves born to these cohorts from birth to wean varied from 173±16 g/day to 270±3 g/day with considerable seasonal fluctuations. Hind liveweight at the rut was also related to time of birth, small hinds calve later than large hinds so that for every additional 4 kg of liveweight, calving was one day earlier (Hamilton and Blaxter, 1980). Early calves enjoy a longer growing season and are heavier at weaning in the autumn.

Calf mortality was found to be related to the weight of the calf at birth (Blaxter and Hamilton, 1980), being 100% for calves weighing 4 kg or less, and declining to 5% for calves weighing 6 kg to 7 kg.

Mortality rises to 13% for calves of 8 kg to 9 kg and is 28% for those over 9 kg. The overall perinatal and postnatal mortality of calves was minimal at hind weights of 75–85 kg. The death rate in adult animals over 15 months of age was found to be 1.8% per annum.

These results suggest, therefore, that in order to maximise the production from a stock of breeding hinds on poor quality hill resources, one should select for recruitment to the herd those hind calves which are born early in the season, and are between 7 and 8 kg at birth. These calves should have had good summer growth rates to reach 38 to 45 kg at weaning in September. Thereafter, if they have to winter on the hill pastures, they should receive a minimum of 1 kg/hd/day of a good quality concentrate. The summer pasture should be adequate to allow a minimum growth rate of 100 g/day in which case 15 month weight should then be about 70-75 kg.

In subsequent years, to maintain high levels of production, those hinds whose liveweights are below equilibrium weight in September would be best separated and given preferential treatment in groups according to their liveweight deficit. They could be placed on the best of the pastures on the farm and, if necessary, fed a concentrate supplement during the rut to help them regain their body weight status.

Stag Growth and Performance

A study of the growth of stags, reared under the same conditions and on identical nutritional regimes as the hinds discussed previously, has shown that the daily gain of the stags was 35% greater than the hinds over the first winter period (Hamilton and Blaxter, 1981). This initial gain had been reduced at 15 months to 16% and then diverged again so that at 87 months, stags were some 69% heavier than hinds. The 15 month weights for the stag cohorts ranged from 52 kg to 94 kg and the equilibrium weight was calculated to be 154 kg.

The rutting performance of stags used for breeding over the period was assessed (Hamilton and Blaxter, 1980). There were no differences in fertility between matched groups of hinds exposed to one or two stags and the results of running 60 hinds with three stags were similar. One stag successfully mated 28 out of 30 in his group, most of which calved within a 20 day period. Under hill farming conditions, a ratio of one mature stag per 25 hinds would seem reasonable to provide some insurance against possible accidents causing injury or death, and in the larger herds, a degree of selection, and an opportunity to replace stags during the rut. Stags were joined with the hind groups during the first week in October each year.

Calves were mostly weaned in late September. Some of the hinds had stopped lactating by this time although there were seasonal differences. Leaving calves with their lactating dams during the rut had no effect on the fertility of the hinds (Hamilton and Blaxter, 1980). However, if calves are left out on the hill during the rut they can be subjected to very severe weather conditions before the herd is gathered from the hill in mid November. By this time the quality of the herbage available to those calves will have declined considerably. This period in the life of a calf, from September to the end of November, is a period of high potential growth. Calves weaned on to a barley based concentrate and fed *ad libitum* attained growth rates of 330 g and 250 g per hd/day for stags and hinds respectively (Blaxter et al., 1974). Stag calves left on the hill with their dams during this period of the rut in 1974 and 1975 gained an average 120 g/day. During the 'bad weather' rut of 1976, stag calf growth rate was an average 53 g/day.

Although it is possible to feed calves out on the grazings over the winter period and achieve good growth rates and 15 month weights prior to slaughter, there is a considerable economic cost for winter feed. Calf losses in October–November can be as high as 12% of all calves weaned (Blaxter et al., 1981).

The current cost of wintering deer calves on a high plane of nutrition is £37 per head and if liveweights averaging 78 kg were obtained for stags at 16 months the saleable carcass in skin would amount to some 58% or 45 kg. The current price varies from £1.32/kg = £59.40 in skin to £2.40/kg for dressed butchers' carcass killing out at 50% and worth £80.70. Weaned four month old suckled calves are currently selling for £50 to £65 per head in October for growing on to slaughter weight on arable grass pastures. Producing weaned suckled calves for sale in the autumn is probably the most attractive system of management for hill land resources of this type. The productive life of a breeding hind will no doubt vary according to the environment in which she is kept, but we can now state with some confidence that a farmer can expect at least 10 calf crops before having to cull from the herd. The Glensaugh hinds born in 1971 all (42) produced calves in their eleventh year, their 10th calf crop. Calf birth weights were 8.5 kg for stags and 7.7 kg for hinds.

In a suckled calf production system on a good quality heather dominant pasture where the vegetation cover is some 75% heather dominant, the remainder being wet flush vegetation with communities of *Agrostis-Festuca/Deschampsia* and associated species, the stocking rate as discussed earlier would be of the order of one H.E. ha⁻¹.

For a 100 hind breeding herd on a 4 month old suckled calf production system the resource requirement would be:—

100 breeding hinds in regular ages	100 H.E./annum
15 calves retained for breeding (13h + 2s)	11 H.E./annum
6 adult breeding stags	6 H.E./annum
85 calves for 3.5 months	3 H.E./annum
	120 H.E./annum

An area of 120 hectares of resource is required to support 100 breeding hinds, the stags and the young stock. However, to this must be added an allowance for reductions in yield during dry seasons of say 20% and 5% for that area burned and unproductive, giving a total of 150 ha of resource—or 1.5 ha per breeding hind maintained.

This figure is no more than a useful guide to prospective farmers considering farming deer on heather dominant pastures, the quality of which vary considerably. It does, however, provide a base upon which to make an economic assessment of a proposed farming enterprise on such resources and would only require minor adjustments in either direction to fit most situations.

Literature Cited

Blaxter, K.L., A.W. Boyne, and W.J. Hamilton
1981. Reproduction in farmed red deer. 3. Hind growth and mortality. *Journal of Agricultural Science*, Cambridge, 96:115–128.

Blaxter, K.L., R.N.B. Kay, G.A.M. Sharman, J.M.M. Cunningham, and W.J. Hamilton
1974. *Farming the Red Deer*. Edinburgh: Department of Agriculture and Fisheries for Scotland: H.M.S.O.

Blaxter, K.L., and W.J. Hamilton
1980. Reproduction in farmed red deer. 2. Calf growth and mortality. *Journal of Agriculture Science*, Cambridge, 95:275–284.

Colquhoun, I.R.
1971. The grazing ecology of red deer and blackface sheep in Perthshire, Scotland. Ph.D. dissertation, University of Edinburgh.

Grant, S.A., G.T. Bartram, W.I.C. Lamb, and J.A. Milne
1978. Effects of season and level of grazing on the utilisation of heather by sheep. 1. Responses of the sward. *Journal of the British Grassland Society*, 33:289–300.

Grant, Sheila A., W.J. Hamilton, and C. Soutar
1981. The responses of heather dominated vegetation in north east Scotland to grazing by red deer. *Journal of Ecology*, 69:189–204.

Grant, Sheila A., and R.F. Hunter

1968a. Interactions of grazing and burning on heather moors and their implications in heather management. *Journal of the British Grassland Society*, 23:285–293.

Hamilton, W.J.

1974. *The artificial rearing of red deer calves to provide a domesticated stock*. Edinburgh: Scottish Agricultural Industries.

Hamilton, W.J., and K.L. Blaxter

1980. Reproduction in farmed red deer. 1. Hind and stag fertility. *Journal of Agricultural Science*, Cambridge, 95:261–273.

1981. Growth of red deer stags under farm conditions. *Journal of Agricultural Science*, Cambridge, 97:329–334.

Hill Farming Research Organisation

1979. *Science and Hill Farming. Twenty-five years of work at the Hill Farming Research Organisation. 1954–1979*. Penicuik, Edinburgh: Hill Farming Research Organisation.

Miller, G.R.

1966. 12th Progress Report, Nature Conservancy Unit, Grouse, Moorland Ecology.

Milne, J.A., J.C. MacRae, A.M. Spence, and S. Wilson

1976. Intake and digestion of hill-land vegetation by the red deer and the sheep. *Nature*, 263:763.

1978. A comparison of the voluntary intake and digestion of a range of forages at different times of the year by the sheep and the red deer (*Cervus elaphus*). *British Journal of Nutrition*, 40:347–357.

Staines, B.W.

1970. The management and dispersion of a red deer population in Glen Dye, Kincardineshire. Ph.D. dissertation, University of Aberdeen.

THOMAS J. FOOSE
AAZPA Conservation Coordinator
ISIS Office
Minnesota Zoological Garden
Apple Valley, Minnesota 55124

A Strategic View of the History, Status, and Prospects of Cervids in Captivity

ABSTRACT   Captive propagation and research is becoming an increasingly important component of conservation strategies for endangered wildlife including many cervids. Thus it is relevant to consider the history, status, and prospects for the family Cervidae in captivity using available data from IZY, ISIS and Studbooks.

Quantitative data of any significance on captive populations of cervids is available for only the last decade. Data adequate for population analysis and management are only now becoming available.

To assess the capacity of zoos to propagate and maintain viable populations of cervids, a survey of existing numbers by species is presented. These numbers are then used as a crude assessment of the total captive habitat apparently available for cervids of different "captive ecologies." By postulating several possible population sizes for genetic and demographic viability, it is possible to estimate how many taxa could be maintained with existing space and resources.

Genetic and demographic management of cervid populations in captivity is also discussed. No cervid is yet being managed as a biological population in captivity, although much groundwork has occurred.

The need for a strategic approach to cervids in captivity relative to other ungulates is emphasized, as is the desirability of interactive management of wild and captive populations for species preservation.

467

Table 1. Status of cervid species in captivity. A tabulation of the numbers of cervids by species according to data in the two major sources, ISIS and IZY. Also indicated is the number of institutions maintaining the species. For those species not reported as currently in zoos by either ISIS or IZY, there is an indication if either source ever recorded the species.

Species	ISIS (31-12-85)		IZY (1-1-82)		Previously in captivity*
	Specimens	Facilities	Specimens	Facilities	
Moschus moschiferus	1/0 = 1	1	2/2 = 4	3	—
Moschus berezovskii	—	—	—	—	—
chrysogaster	—	—	—	—	—
sifanicus	—	—	—	—	—
Elaphodus cephalophus	0	0	—	—	Yes
Muntiacus crinifrons	2/1 = 3	2	3/3 = 6	1	—
feae	0	0	0/1 = 1	1	—
muntjac	7/9 = 16	3	—	—	—
reevesi	140/202/22 = 364	50	—	—	—
rooseveltorum	0	0	—	—	No Mention
Cervus albirostris	0	0	3/4 = 7	1	—
axis	120/195/7 = 322	26	—	—	—
dama	75/129/17 = 221	29	—	—	—
duvauceli	57/105/11 = 173	14	121/179/19 = 319	27	—
elaphus	72/171/14 = 257	45	—	—	—
eldi	48/68/2 = 118	7	81/90/17 = 188	16	—
mariannus	0/2 = 2	1	—	—	—
mesopotamicus	0	0	10/15 = 25	3	—
nippon	95/169/10 = 274	29	—	—	—
porcinus	5/9 = 14	5	—	—	—
timorensis	4/9 = 13	1	—	—	—
unicolor	13/23 = 36	3	—	—	—
Elaphurus davidionus	66/109/3 = 178	18	352/621/106 = 1079	106	—
Alces alces	13/12/1 = 26	8	—	—	—
Ozotoceros bezoarticus	5/6 = 11	2	10/14 = 24	8	—
Blastocerus dichotomus	2/4 = 6	1	4/1 = 5	4	—
Capreolus capreolus	5/7 = 12	2	—	—	—
Hippocamelus antisiensis	0	0	—	—	Yes
bisulcus	0	0	—	—	Yes
Hydropotes inermis	24/20 = 44	6	—	—	—
Mazama americana	18/27 = 45	12	—	—	—
gouazoubira	0/1 = 1	1	—	—	—
rufina	0	0	—	—	Yes
chunyi	0	0	—	—	No Mention
Odocoileus hemionus	19/19/2 = 40	9	—	—	—
virginianus	85/164/27 = 276	42	—	—	—
Pudu mephistopheles	0	0	—	—	Yes
pudu	10/11 = 21	3	22/24 = 46	6	—
Rangifer tarandus	52/90 = 142	24	—	—	—

*Crandall (1964) or I.Z.Y.

Foose

Introduction

As the world's wildlands are diminished and fragmented at an ever accelerating rate, captive populations become increasingly important for the survival of many species, particularly the mega-mammals. Moreover, captivity can provide not only sanctuary against extinction, but also the opportunity for research that is difficult or impossible with wild populations, but that may contribute to their survival. Therefore, it seems appropriate that a major symposium on the Cervidae should consider the history, status, and prospects for the entire family in captivity.

Unfortunately, the systematic compilation of data requisite for this kind of quantitative survey does not enjoy a long tradition in "zoodom" collectively. While a number of institutions have maintained excellent records even from the last century, the concept of comprehensive compilation for all species in captivity is relatively recent and not yet fully realized.

International Zoo Yearbook (IZY) has collected and published data on various taxa considered rare or endangered since 1961 (Jarvis, 1961–1968; Lucas, 1969–1971; Lucas and Duplaix-Hall, 1972; Duplaix-Hall, 1973–1975; Olney, 1976–1984). More recently, the International Species Inventory System (ISIS) (Seal et al., 1977; Flesness et al., 1982) has attempted, taxonomically and informationally, more comprehensive collection of data. The most recent inventories of each census are presented in Table 1. However, each of these two enterprises is afflicted by different but very significant limitations.

IZY considers only rare and endangered forms for most of its survey and restricts data to simple counts of specimens by taxon, sex, institution, and captive/wild origin. Data are collected on reproduction for more taxa by *IZY*, but again the data are merely enumerations. The latest volume of *IZY* (Olney, 1984) presents inventory data on 14 species (for four of which only selected subspecies are included) and reproduction results on 24 species, differentiating numerous subspecies thereof (Table 6).

ISIS is more ambitious in the amount and nature of data it compiles. Vital statistics (individual identification, sex, birth dates, death dates, parentage, and location histories) are currently registered in the computer for 13 genera, 26 species, and 69 subspecies of cervids (Flesness et al., 1986). These more extensive data are essential for the genetic and demographic analysis and management of captive cervids. However, ISIS data are limited by the extent of membership participation in both time and space. Collection of data commenced in 1974. Thus, very little historical data before the mid-1970s are included. Moreover, participation is still geographically dominated by North American institutions, although re-

Table 2. Studbooks for cervids. The five species of cervids for which International Studbooks are maintained.

Cervus duvauceli	*Barasingha*	Dr. D. Schaaf (Atlanta)
Cervus eldi	*Eld's Deer*	Prof. J. Doumenge (Paris)
Elaphurus davidianus	*Pere David's Deer*	Dr. V. Manton (Whipsnade)
Ozotoceros bezoarticus	*Pampas Deer*	Dr. H. Frädrich (West Berlin)
Pudu puda	*Pudu*	C. Kruyhoft (Antwerp)

cruitment in Europe, Australia, and Latin America has been growing steadily. Currently, ISIS receives data from about 215 institutions.

For selected species, the most comprehensive sources of information are Official Studbooks. There are now Studbooks maintained on 5 of the 37 cervid species being recognized for this analysis (Table 2). The Studbook on Pere David's Deer (*Elaphurus davidianus*) is the oldest but actually, in published form, is only a register. Populational management requires more detailed information on birth dates, death dates, and parentage of individual animals.

History

Because the nature of this analysis is quantitative and the amount of data is so limited, consideration of history will be restricted to a relatively recent and superficial survey. Table 1 is a compendium on the occurrence of cervids in captivity as documented by *IZY*, ISIS, and/or Crandall (1964). Of the 37 extant species of cervids, 27 are represented in existing collections. Of the other 10 species, 5 are not recorded by *IZY* or Crandall (1964) as having appeared in captivity in this century: *Moschus berezovskii, M. chrysogaster, M. sifanicus, Muntiacus rooseveltorum, and Mazama chunyi.*

The dearth of quantitative historical data is indicated by Table 3 which incorporates all forms for which 10 continuous years of census data have been located for captive collections in the only known source, *IZY*. In another year or two, ISIS will, of course, be able to provide such data for more species but few institutions.

There is hope on the horizon for this disappointing situation. Dan Wharton (New York Zoological Society) and Marvin Jones (Zoological Society of San Diego) are now collecting data on cervids and other families for publication in "A History of Ungulates in Captivity," which should vastly improve our knowledge in this area.

Table 3. Captive cervids for which there are 10 years of census data published. The population sizes of cervids in captivity for those species for which IZY reports ten continuous years of data.

Species	1971	1972	1973	1974	1975	1976	1977	1978	1979	1980	1981	1982
Moschus mochiferus	9	2	12	6	3	5	9	15	7	15	4	4
Cervus (dama) mesopotamicus	14	15	8	15	9	10	17	12	20	23	27	25
Cervus (porcinus) kuhli	4	7	?	15	31	36	55	64	64	86	100	83
Cervus duvauceli	124	128	134	149	158	159	180	215	245	263	291	319
Cervus elaphus bactrianus	39	38	35	40	40	42	43	38	57	49	54	42
Cervus eldi eldi	32	27	29	38	25	31	49	37	16	28	42	61
siamensis	10	18	8	9	7	6	3	3	2	3	2	3
thamin	37	43	57	65	65	69	71	89	82	111	101	124
Elaphurus davidianus	550	600	641	640	726	777	813	873	801	986	992	1079
Blastocerus dichotomus	2	6	1	8	5	1	3	2	2	4	6	5
Ozotoceros bezoarticus	6	2	5	4	4	5	9	18	18	18	22	24
Pudu pudu	16	19	23	33	29	30	29	30	34	39	42	46

Based on "Census of Rare Animals in Captivity" in *International Zoo Yearbook*, Volumes 12–23

UNGULATE GENERA

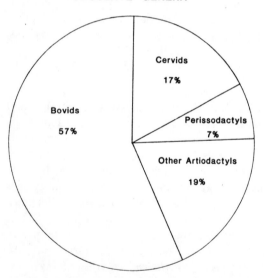

Figure 1. Ungulate Genera. A diagram illustrating the relative percentage of ungulate genera in the Bovidae, the Cervidae, other Artiodactyla families, and the Perissodactyla.

Status and Prospects

Of greater significance than the history are the current status and even more, the prospects or potential for maintaining cervids in captivity. In particular, there is a need for strategic assessment and allocation of the limited captive habitat for achievement of various objectives, the most critical being sanctuary for endangered forms. There, thus, will be an attempt to place the Cervidae in perspective relative to other ungulates and captive capacities.

Taxonomically, cervids represent 17% of the genera of ungulates (Figure 1). Depending on the classification, there are about 15 genera, 40 species, and 205 subspecies recognized (Honacki et al., 1982; Seal and Makey, 1974; Groves and Grubb, this volume). Of these taxa, 31 forms are cited by the IUCN Red Data Book as being in some stage of endangerment in the wild (Jane Thornback, IUCN Species Conservation Monitoring Unit, personal communication) (Table 4).

In captivity, the relative status of the entire family can be considered quantitatively only for those institutions participating in ISIS. Ungulates (Artiodactyla and Perissodactyla) currently constitute 37.5% of the approximately 38,000 living mammal specimens registered in ISIS (Figure 2). Indeed, the Artiodactyla, Perissodactyla, Primates, and Carnivora (excluding the pinnipeds) comprise 85% of all mammals in ISIS institutions, an abundance far in excess of their proportional representation among all mammalian taxa. However, among the ungulates, the number of cervid species being maintained by ISIS participants

Foose

Table 4.   Cervid species and subspecies listed in the IUCN Red Data Book. Status codes are: E = Endangered; V = Vulnerable; R = Rare; I = Indeterminable; O = Out of Danger (?).

Taxon	Status	Taxon	Status
Moschus moschiferus moschiferus	V	*Cervus elaphus corsicanus*	E
Muntiacus crinifrons	I	*wallichi*	E
feae	E	*barbarus*	E
Dama mesopotamica *	E	*hanglu*	E
Axis kuhli **	R	*yarkandensis*	E
Axis calamianensis **	V	*bactrianus*	E
Cervus duvauceli	E	*macneilli*	I
Cervus eldi eldi	E	*nannodes*	O
siamensis	E	*Odocoileus virgianus clavium*	R
Cervus nippon taiouanus	E	*leucurus*	O
keramae	E	*Odocoileus hemionus cerrosensis*	R
mandarinensis	E	*Hippocamelus antisensis*	V
grassianus	E	*bisulcus*	E
kopschi	E	*Blastocerus dichotomus*	V
Cervus albirostris	I	*Ozotoceros bezoarticus celar*	E
		Pudu mephistophiles	I

*considered *Cervus mesopotamicus* by ISIS; **considered *Cervus (=Axis) porcinus calamianensis* and *C. (=Axis) porcinus kuhli* by ISIS and ASC.

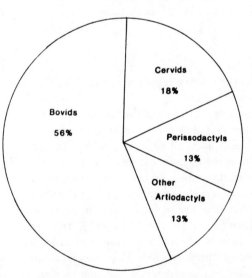

MAMMAL SPECIMENS IN ISIS

Ungulates 37%

Other Mammals 15%

Primates 29%

Carnivores 19%

UNGULATE SPECIMENS IN ISIS

Cervids 18%

Bovids 56%

Perissodactyls 13%

Other Artiodactyls 13%

Figure 2.   Two diagrams. The first illustrating the relative percentage of mammal specimens representing ungulates, primates, carnivores, and other mammals reported alive in ISIS participating zoos. The second diagram depicts the relative percentage of ungulate specimens representing the Bovidae, the Cervidae, other Artiodactyla families, and the Perissodactyla reported alive in ISIS participating zoos.

Table 5. Ungulate taxa in captivity. A tabulation by family of ungulate genera (abbreviated "Gen." or "G"), species ("Sp." or "S"), and subspecies ("Subsp." or "SS") that are: extant, cited in the IUCN Red Data Book; maintained in facilities participating in ISIS; and cited in the IUCN Red Data Book and are reported in zoos by ISIS and/or IZY.

| Family | Taxa extant | | | Taxa cited in Red Data Book | | | Taxa in ISIS facilities | | | Red Data Book taxa | | | | | |
| | | | | | | | | | | In ISIS | | | In IZY | | |
	Gen.	Sp.	Subsp.	G	S	SS	G	S	SS	G	S	SS	G	S	SS
Cervidae	15	37	205	8	18	35	13	26	69	5	8	8	4	11	14
Tragulidae	2	4	60	0	0	0	1	1	2	0	0	0	0	0	0
Antilocapridae	1	1	5	1	1	2	1	1	3	1	1	0	1	1	0
Bovidae	51	127	486	22	38	60	36	80	161	19	26	26	20	28	27
Cattle	4	12	26	3	9	18	4	9	19	3	6	8	3	5	5
Sheep/Goats	11	26	112	5	8	15	9	8	36	4	3	5	5	6	9
Antelope	36	89	348	14	21	27	23	53	106	12	17	13	12	17	13
Camelidae	3	6	7	2	2	2	4	5	7	2	2	2	1	1	1
Giraffidae	2	2	10	0	0	0	2	2	7	0	0	0	0	0	0
Suidae	5	8	78	2	2	5	3	3	4	0	0	0	2	2	2
Tayassuidae	2	3	20	1	1	1	1	2	7	0	0	0	0	0	0
Equidae	1	8	21	1	5	9	1	7	12	1	5	7	1	5	7
Tapiridae	1	4	7	1	3	3	1	4	5	1	3	3	1	3	3
Rhinocerotidae	4	5	9+	4	5	8	3	3	4	3	3	3	3	3	3
Hippopotamidae	2	2	5	1	1	2	2	2	5	1	1	1	1	1	1
Total	89	207	914	43	76	127	68	136	286	33	49	50	34	55	58

closely reflects the relative representation of this family at the generic level.

Table 5 indicates the status of the Cervidae in relation to other families of ungulates in ISIS institutions and with less adequacy, all captive facilities. In particular, the status of endangered forms is presented. Table 6 contains the same kind of data in terms of the various genera of Cervidae. Some interesting phenomena are the predominance of *Cervus* and the dearth of South American forms. (It should be noted that for almost every species, the ISIS inventory includes a category of unspecified species. This category has been enumerated as a subspecies in the counts of this taxonomic level in Tables 5 and 6. While some may object to this convention, these specimens are occupying a distinct taxon at least in the records. Moreover, in many cases, a zoo subspecies has probably already evolved.)

If taxa are to be maintained viably in captivity, they must be managed as biological populations, particularly if the purpose is propagation and preservation of endangered forms. Indeed, many believe the primary mission of zoos is now to provide sanctuary for endangered species.

Unfortunately, even with scientific and coordinated management, the capacity of zoos and aquariums for populations large enough to be viable is very limited in relation to the great and growing number of species requiring sanctuary in captivity. Muckenhirn (1981) for AAZPA member institutions and Conway (1986) for zoos worldwide have attempted to assess the amount of "captive habitat" (space and resources) available for captive populations and propagation. Approximately 47,000 "mammal spaces" were recorded in AAZPA facilities by Muckenhirn's report, while Conway estimated a total of 181,462 "mammal spaces" in all the mainstream zoos of the world. Both reports emphasize the finite capacity of "zoos," considering the sizes of the populations that must be maintained for viability.

Thus, selection of species becomes a process of assigning priorities for allocation of the space and resources available in zoos. For genetic reasons, captive populations should be as large as possible (Soulé,

Foose

Table 6. Cervid taxa in captivity. A tabulation by genera of cervid species (abbreviated "S") and subspecies ("SS") that are: extant; cited in the IUCN Red Data Book; maintained in facilities participating in ISIS; and cited in the IUCN Red Data Book and reported in zoos by ISIS and/or IZY.

| Genus | Taxa extant | | Taxa cited in Red Data Book | | Taxa in ISIS facilities | | Red Data Book taxa | | | |
| | | | | | | | In ISIS | | In IZY | |
	Species	Subspecies	S	SS	S	SS	S	SS	S	SS
Moschus	4	8	1	1	1	1	1	1	1	1
Elaphodus	1	3	0	0	0	0	0	0	0	0
Muntiacus	5	19	2	2	3	6	1	1	2	2
Cervus	10	64	7	20	10	28	4	5	7	10
Elaphurus	1	1	0	0	1	1	0	0	0	0
Alces	1	7	0	0	1	3	0	0	0	0
Ozotoceros	1	3	1	1	1	2	0	0	0	0
Blastocerus	1	1	1	1	1	1	1	1	1	1
Capreolus	1	3	0	0	1	2	0	0	0	0
Hippocamelus	2	2	2	2	0	0	0	0	0	0
Hydropotes	1	2	0	0	1	2	0	0	0	0
Mazama	4	30	0	0	2	5	0	0	0	0
Odocoileus	2	50	2	3	2	11	1	1	0	0
Pudu	2	3	1	1	1	1	0	0	0	0
Rangifer	1	9	0	0	1	6	0	0	0	0
Total 15	37	205	17	31	26	69	8	9	11	14

1980; Frankel and Soulé, 1981). But there are many species competing for this space (Foose, 1981a and b). Thus, capacity must be a compromise between maintaining large populations for genetic diversity and demographic stability and providing sanctuary for as many species as possible. Strategic selection of species would, therefore, seem to require: assessment of the space and resources that are available in zoos; ascertainment of what species are in need of sanctuary; allocation of the captive habitat optimally. The Species Survival Plan (SSP) of the AAZPA is attempting to provide guidance for such strategic selection.

Tables 7 through 10 are an attempt to apply this type of analysis to the cervids, both in relation to other ungulates and within the Cervidae itself. Tables 7 and 8 consider ISIS institutions. Tables 9 and 10, more speculatively, attempt to consider all captive facilities. Perry and Kibbee (1974) and Muckenhirn (1981) have previously performed similar types of analyses at grosser levels for captive populations.

Each of the tables states the number of taxa (genera, species, and subspecies) extant as well as those cited in the IUCN Red Data Book. Thereafter is a crude measure of the capacity of the captive facilities considered, provided by the number of specimens of various taxa currently being maintained. It is being assumed that the present populations represent approximately both the space and the resources available for these types of animals.

For each species and category, there is then a calculation of the number of taxa that could be accommodated in the habitat estimated for the ISIS institutions if the population of each form has to be maintained at one of three minimal sizes (100, 250, or 500) for genetic and demographic viability. These population sizes cover the range of several hundreds now being recommended as minimum viable population (MVP) numbers for large mammal taxa in captivity by population biologists, considering reasonable genetic and demographic objectives and problems (Soulé et al. 1986). The specific MVP for any taxon will depend upon: the genetic objectives (how much diversity is to be preserved for what period of time) and the biology of the species (generation time under

Table 7. Apparent capacity of ISIS facilities for ungulates. A tabulation of the number of specimens in each ungulate family reported to be in ISIS participating zoos. Also indicated is the number of taxa that could be accommodated for each ungulate family if the population of each taxon is maintained by management at one of three levels (100, 250, or 500 animals) for genetic and demographic reasons. The resultant figures in the last three columns of the table are obtained by dividing the total number of specimens maintained by the indicated population level (100, 250, 500).

Family	Taxa extant			Taxa cited in Red Data Book			Specimens in ISIS 31-21-85	Taxa maintainable if population		
	Genera	Species	Subspecies	G	S	SS		100	250	500
Cervidae	15	37	205	8	18	35	2,617	26	10	5
Tragulidae	2	4	60	0	0	0	51	0	0	0
Antilocapridae	1	1	5	1	1	2	93	1	0	0
Bovidae	51	127	486	22	38	60	8,066	81	32	16
Cattle	4	12	26	3	9	18	1,053	10	4	2
Sheep/Goats	11	26	112	5	8	15	1.992	20	8	4
Antelope	36	89	348	14	21	27	5,021	50	20	10
Camelidae	3	6	7	2	2	2	891	9	4	2
Giraffidae	2	2	10	0	0	0	337	3	1	0
Suidae	5	8	78	2	2	5	45	0	0	0
Tayassuidae	2	3	20	1	1	1	148	1	0	0
Equidae	1	8	21	1	5	9	1,430	14	6	3
Tapiridae	1	4	7	1	3	3	165	1	0	0
Rhinocerotidae	4	5	9+	4	5	8	269	2	1	0
Hippopotamidae	2	2	5	1	1	2	185	2	1	0
Total	89	207	914	43	76	127	14,297	143	57	28

the management regime and the social dynamics which will determine the total number of animals that must be maintained to achieve some genetically effective population size which in turn governs how rapidly genetic diversity is lost). For rough overall estimates of the capacity of captive facilities for ungulates and/or cervids, the 250 level of minimal population is probably the most generally relevant. The estimates for all captive facilities are based either on Studbooks or on simple but, hopefully, plausible extrapolations using multiples of ISIS populations or *IZY* reproduction.

Admittedly, there are defects in this type of analysis. One problem is that there is incomplete information on the numbers of various taxa being maintained. Only for those institutions participating in ISIS and/or for those species surveyed by *IZY* or Studbooks is there even an estimate. Moreover, this kind of analysis considers only quantity, not quality of habitat. It is fallacious to consider that the species as categorized are really interchangeable in their captive ecologies (i.e., requirements for facilities and resources).

Nevertheless, despite all its defects, this analysis does, in my opinion, provide an informative, if rough, picture of the situation for cervids in captivity. Patently, not all taxa, even those presently endangered, could be maintained in populations large enough to be viable in the facilities that appear available. There will have to be choices.

There may be hope for ameliorating this rather inadequate situation by expanding captive facilities in two ways. One is territorial expansion. Zoos are developing larger and more naturalistic facilities, such as the Conservation and Research Center of the National Zoological Park, the San Diego Wild Animal Park, and the St. Catherine's Island of the New York Zoological Society. Further, zoos can develop cooperative programs with private facilities possessing large tracts of land and sincere commitment to conservation. The AAZPA, through its Species Survival Plan (Foose, 1982), is attempting such cooperative ventures with some exotic animal ranches in Texas. With these types of programs, a convergence and integration of both

Table 8. Apparent capacity of ISIS facilities for cervids. A tabulation of the number of specimens in each cervid genus reported to be in zoos participating in ISIS. Also indicated is the number of taxa that could be accommodated for each genus if the population of each taxon is maintained at one of three levels (100, 250, or 500) for genetic and demographic reasons. The resultant figures in the last three columns are obtained by dividing the total number of specimens maintained by the indicated population level (100, 250, 500).

Genus	Taxa extant		Taxa cited in Red Data Book		Specimens in ISIS 31-12-85	Taxa maintainable if population		
	Species	Subspecies	Species	Subspecies		100	250	500
Moschus	4	8	1	1	1	0	0	0
Elaphodus	1	3	0	0	0	0	0	0
Muntiacus	5	19	2	2	383	4	1	0
Cervus	10	64	7	22	1,430	14	6	3
Elaphurus	1	1	1	1	178	2	1	0
Alces	1	7	0	0	26	0	0	0
Ozotoceros	1	3	1	1	11	0	0	0
Blastocerus	1	1	1	1	6	0	0	0
Capreolus	1	3	0	0	12	0	0	0
Hippocamelus	2	2	2	2	0	0	0	0
Hydropotes	1	2	0	0	44	0	0	0
Mazama	4	30	0	0	46	0	0	0
Odocoileus	2	50	2	3	316	3	1	0
Pudu	2	3	1	2	21	0	0	0
Rangifer	1	9	0	0	142	1	0	0
Total 15	37	205	18	35	2,474	25	10	5

captive and wild populations into a strategy to preserve species seems all the more plausible. Indeed, Texas has already become the surrogate habitat for feral populations of many exotic species of cervids (Table 11).

The other is technological expansion through development of cryogenic preservation of gametes in conjunction with artificial insemination, embryo transfers, etc. These techniques, if perfected, may reduce the actual number of animals that must be maintained to achieve specified effective population sizes for genetic viability.

Genetic and Demographic Status and Prospects

Viable programs to propagate and preserve cervids in captivity will require genetic and demographic management. There will be no attempt in this paper to discuss in detail the components of such programs. For further information on genetic and demographic analysis and management of captive populations, spe-

cifically cervids, the reader is referred to Ralls et al. (1979), Foose and Foose (1982) and Wemmer (1976). An additional paper of relevance, although ostensibly considering wild populations of moose (*Alces alces*) and white-tailed deer (*Odocoileus virginianus*), is Ryman et al. (1981).

No cervid is yet being managed optimally as a population in captivity, although some attempts are in progress. Through an analysis of *IZY* records, Pinder and Barkham (1978) have identified species they consider to be self-sufficient in captivity. Two of the species they cite are barasingha (*Cervus duvauceli*) and Pere David's deer (*Elaphurus davidianus*). However, even if these two species are self-sufficient, the viability or vitality of these populations in an evolutionary sense may be problematic.

It now appears that all surviving Pere David's deer may have descended from 3 animals imported into Europe at the end of the last century (Marvin Jones, personal communication). All barasingha in North America track back, by paper trials, to no more than

Table 9. Estimated capacity of captive facilities for ungulates. A tabulation very similar to Table 7, except that there has been an attempt to extrapolate to all captive facilities, not just zoos participating in ISIS. Thus the "Estimate of total captive habitat" is the number of specimens reported worldwide in zoos by studbooks or IZY or where these sources are not available through extrapolation by multiplying ISIS figures by a factor of 3 (except in the case of Suidae, where instead the number reported bred by IZY is multiplied by a factor of 10, because of the depauperate representation of this family in North America collections due to USDA regulations).

| Family | Taxa extant | | | Taxa cited in Red Data Book | | | Estimate of total captive habitat | Taxa maintainable if population | | | |
	Genera	Species	Subspecies	G	S	SS		100	250	500	1000
Cervidae	15	37	205	9	18	35	7,851	78	31	16	8
Tragulidae	2	4	60	0	0	0	153	1	0	0	0
Antilocapridae	1	1	5	1	1	2	279	3	1	0	0
Bovidae	51	127	486	22	38	60	24,198	242	97	48	24
Cattle	4	12	26	3	9	18	3,159	26	11	5	3
Sheep/Goats	11	26	112	5	8	15	5,976	50	20	10	5
Antelope	36	89	348	14	21	27	15,063	129	51	26	13
Camelidae	3	6	7	2	2	2	2,673	27	11	5	3
Giraffidae	2	2	10	0	0	0	1,011	10	4	2	1
Suidae	5	8	78	2	2	5	1,350	13	5	3	1
Tayassuidae	2	3	20	1	1	1	444	4	2	1	0
Equidae	1	8	21	1	5	9	4,290	43	17	8	4
Tapiridae	1	4	7	1	3	3	495	5	2	1	0
Rhinocerotidae	4	5	9+	4	5	8	807	8	3	2	1
Hippopotamidae	2	2	5	1	1	2	555	5	2	1	0
Total	89	207	914	44	76	127	44,106	441	176	88	44

seven founders. There is reason to believe the European collections of barasingha do not enjoy a much larger base of founders. Consequently, the genetic diversity contained in these populations may be quite limited. It is not evident if these populations will eventually be subject to inbreeding depression that will ultimately cause their extinction. Some authors (Whitehead, 1978) have contended that in the case of the Pere David's deer, the species has successfully passed through a genetic bottleneck and now is in a state of benign homozygosity. Results of studies to demonstrate inbreeding depression have been inconclusive (Ralls et al., 1979; Foose, 1982). Electrophoretic examination has failed to reveal any polymorphism in this species (Ryder at al., 1981).

However, even if Pere David's deer is "safe" from inbreeding, it may be a genetic mummy. If as many conservationists believe the primary and ultimate purpose of captive propagation is to provide a reservoir of the wild gene pool for eventual reestablishment in their endemic ecosystems, the elimination of inbreeding depression by production of super-homozygotes will not be enough (Templeton and Read, 1984). It's not the semblance of a species but the diversity of its genes that should be preserved so the evolutionary potential of the species is not lost (Soulé, 1980; Frankel and Soulé, 1981).

It is too late to obtain any more founder stock for Pere David's deer, but not for other species like the barasingha. Even for Pere David's deer, it is not too late to manage the population to preserve what diversity might remain.

This is the objective of the Species Survival Plan (SSP). The SSP is a response to the need for better organization and significant improvement of the efforts to propagate endangered species in captivity as part of the global strategy to preserve the wildlife of the planet. Indeed, in the future, captive and wild populations will increasingly have to interact if species are to be preserved. One species of cervid, the barasingha (*Cervus duvauceli*), has already been designated for an SSP program. Another species, Eld's deer (*Cer-*

Foose

Table 10. Estimated capacity of captive facilities for cervids. A very similar tabulation to Table 8 by extrapolated to all captive facilities worldwide. Numbers represent: the IZY inventory where available; the ISIS census for *Odocoileus*; otherwise 3× the ISIS population, except in the case of *Capreolus* (10× ISIS) and *Hydropotes* (5× ISIS).

	Taxa extant		*Taxa cited in Red Data Book*		*Estimate of total captive habitat*	*Taxa maintainable if population*			
Genus	*Species*	*Subspecies*	*Species*	*Subspecies*		*100*	*250*	*500*	*1000*
Moschus	4	8	1	1	15	0	0	0	0
Elaphodus	1	3	0	0	0	0	0	0	0
Muntiacus	5	19	2	2	1,149	11	4	2	1
Cervus	13	64	7	22	4,290	43	17	8	4
Elaphurus	1	1	1	1	1,079	11	4	2	1
Alces	1	7	0	0	78	1	0	0	0
Ozotoceros	1	3	1	1	33	0	0	0	0
Blastocerus	1	1	1	1	18	0	0	0	0
Capreolus	1	3	0	0	120	5	2	0	1
Hippocamelus	2	2	2	2	0	0	0	0	0
Hydropotes	1	2	0	0	230	5	2	1	0
Mazama	4	30	0	0	138	1	1	0	0
Odocoileus	2	50	2	3	316	9	4	2	1
Pudu	2	3	1	2	63	0	0	0	0
Rangifer	1	9	0	0	426	4	2	1	0
Total	37	205	18	35	7,955	79	32	16	8

vus eldi), has not yet been designated but a program for populational management is being organized by the National, New York, Miami, and San Diego Zoos, in consultation with the SSP. Hopefully, these endeavors

Table 11. 1979 census of exotic cervids feral in Texas. A tabulation by species of the numbers of exotic cervids estimated to be free-ranging in Texas. Texas Department of Parks and Wildlife (1985).

Muntiacus muntjac	3
Cervus axis	38,035
canadensis	1,597
dama	10,507
duvauceli	226
elaphus	730
nippon	7,972
unicolor	36
canadensis × *elaphus*	500
Elaphurus davidianus	16

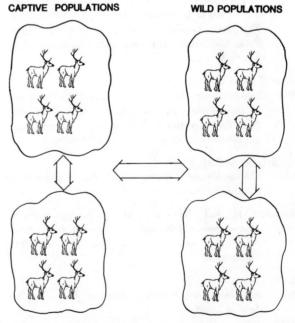

Figure 3. A schematic diagram of a conservation strategy for cervids that incorporates both wild and captive populations that are interactively managed for species preservation.

can contribute to an integrated strategy to preserve the Cervidae through interactive management of wild and captive populations (Figure 3).

Literature Cited

Conway, W.
1986.   The practical difficulties and financial implications of endangered species breeding programs. *International Zoo Yearbook*, 24. In press.

Crandall, L.
1964.   *Management of Wild Mammals in Captivity.* Chicago: University of Chicago Press.

Duplaix-Hall, N.
1973.   *International Zoo Yearbook*, 13. London: Zoological Society of London.

1974.   *International Zoo Yearbook*, 14. London: Zoological Society of London.

1975.   *International Zoo Yearbook*, 15. London: Zoological Society of London.

Flessness, N., and Grahn and K. Hastings
1982.   Species Distribution Report of International Species Inventory System (ISIS). Apple Valley, Minnesota: International Species Inventory System.

Foose, T.
1982.   An update on the Species Survival Plan (SSP) of the AAZAP. *Proceedings of the 1981 AAZPA Annual Conference*, pp. 8–16. Wheeling, West Virginia: American Association of Zoological Parks and Aquariums.

1983.   The relevance of captive populations to the conservation of biological diversity. In *Genetics and Conservation*, edited by C. Schonewald-Cox, S. Chambers, B. MacBryde, and L. Thomas, pp. 374-401. Menlo Park, California: The Benjamin/Cummings Publishing Company.

Foose, T., and E. Foose
1982.   Demographic and genetic status and management. In *Biology and Management of an Extinct Species, Pere David's Deer*, edited by B. Beck and C. Wemmer, pp. 133-186.   Park Ridge, N.J.: Noyes Publishers.

Frankel, O., and M. Soulé
1981.   *Conservation and Evolution.* Cambridge: University of Cambridge Press.

Honacki, J.H., K.E. Kinman, and J.W. Koeppl (editors)
1981.   *Mammal Species of the World*. Lawrence, Kansas: Allen Press, Inc. and the Association of Systematics Collections.

Jarvis, C. (editor)
1961.   *International Zoo Yearbook*, 1. London: Zoological Society of London.

1962.   *International Zoo Yearbook*, 2. London: Zoological Society of London.

1963.   *International Zoo Yearbook*, 3. London: Zoological Society of London.

1964.   *International Zoo Yearbook*, 4. London: Zoological Society of London.

1965.   *International Zoo Yearbook*, 5. London: Zoological Society of London.

1966.   *International Zoo Yearbook*, 6. London: Zoological Society of London.

1967.   *International Zoo Yearbook*, 7. London: Zoological Society of London.

1968.   *International Zoo Yearbook*, 8. London: Zoological Society of London.

Lucas, J. (editor)
1969.   *International Zoo Yearbook*, 9. London: Zoological Society of London.

1970.   *International Zoo Yearbook*, 10. London: Zoological Society of London.

1971.   *International Zoo Yearbook*, 11. London: Zoological Society of London.

Lucas, J.; and N. Duplaix-Hall (editors)
1972.   *International Zoo Yearbook*, 12. London: Zoological Society of London.

Muckenhirn, N.
1981.   The role of zoological parks and aquariums in captive propagation of rare and endangered species. Special Report to the AAZPA. Wheeling, West Virginia: American Association of Zoological Parks and Aquariums.

Olney, P. (editor)
1976.   *International Zoo Yearbook*, 16. London: Zoological Society of London.

1977.   *International Zoo Yearbook*, 17. London: Zoological Society of London.

1978.   *International Zoo Yearbook*, 18. London: Zoological Society of London.

1979.   *International Zoo Yearbook*, 19. London: Zoological Society of London.

1980.   *International Zoo Yearbook*, 20. London: Zoological Society of London.

1981.   *International Zoo Yearbook*, 21. London: Zoological Society of London.

1982.   *International Zoo Yearbook*, 22. London: Zoological Society of London.

1984.   *International Zoo Yearbook*, 23. London: Zoological Society of London.

Perry, J., and P. Kibbee
1974.   The capacity of American zoos. *International Zoo Yearbook*, 14:240–247.

Pinder, N., and J. Barkham
1978. An assessment of the contribution of captive breeding to the conservation of rare mammals. *Biological Conservation*, 13:187–245.

Ralls, K., K. Bruegger, and J. Ballou
1979. Inbreeding and juvenile mortality in small populations of ungulates. *Science*, 206:1001–1003.

Ryman, N., R. Baccus, C. Rutlerwall, and M. Smith
1981. Effective population size, generation interval, and potential loss of genetic viability in game species under different hunting regimes. *Oikos*, 26:257–266.

Ryder, O., P. Brisbin, A. Bowling, and E. Wedemeyer
1981. Monitoring genetic variation in endangered species. *Proceedings of the Second International Congress on Systematics and Evolutionary Biology*, edited by G. Scudder and J. Raveal, pp. 417–424. Pittsburgh, Pennsylvania: Hunt Institute for Botanical Documentation.

Seal, U., and Makey D.
1974. *ISIS* Mammalian Taxonomic Directory. Apple Valley, Minnesota: International Species Inventory System.

Seal, U., D. Makey, D. Bridgewater, L. Simmons, and L. Murtfeldt
1977. ISIS: A computerized record system for management of wild animals in captivity. *International Zoo Yearbook*, 17:68–70.

Soulé, M.
1980. Thresholds for survival: Maintaining fitness and evolutionary potential. In *Conservation Biology*. edited by M. Soulé and B. Wilcox, pp. 151–169. Sunderland, Massachusetts: Sinauer.

Soulé, M., W. Conway, T. Foose, and Gilpin
1986   The milennium ark: how long the voyage, how many staterooms, how many passengers? *Zoobiology*, 5(2):101–113.

Templeton, A., and B. Read
1984. Factors eliminating inbreeding depression in a captive herd of Speke's Gazelle (*Gazella spekei*). *Zoobiology*, 3(3): 177–199.

Wemmer, C.
1976. A long range breeding program for endangered ungulates at Front Royal. *Proceedings of the American Association for the Advancement of Science* Boston, Massachusetts: A.A.A.S.

Whitehead, G.K. (editor)
1978. *Threatened Deer, Proceedings of the Working Meeting of the Deer Specialist Group of the Survival Service Commission.* Morges, Switzerland: International Union for the Conservation of Nature.

U.S. SEAL
and
M. BUSH
Bldg. 49, Rm. 207
V.A. Medical Center
54th St. & 48th Ave., S.
Minneapolis, Minnesota 55417

Department of Animal Health
National Zoological Park
Smithsonian Institution
Washington, DC 20009

Capture and Chemical Immobilization of Cervids

ABSTRACT

Cervids have been held in captivity for thousands of years. Drugs for immobilization and capture of adult animals were introduced in 1953. Thousands of cervids have since been immobilized for management and treatment of captive animals and for capture of free ranging animals. Available data from the literature and unpublished data from zoos have been collected to provide a summary of dosage information. The drugs used have characteristic short-term effects on the physiology, metabolism, and serum hormone concentrations of cervids which must be considered in the collection and interpretation of clinical, metabolic, and reproductive data from these immobilized animals. Available evidence suggests that manually restrained or succinylcholine immobilized cervids respond with increased secretion of adrenal corticosteroids and progesterone as well as with changes in hematology indicative of splenic contraction, and with increased serum levels of muscle enzymes. Serum progesterone levels characteristic of pregnancy can be obtained in males and anestrous females confounding the use of these data for diagnosis of reproductive state. Anesthetized animals yield more nearly normal values.

Introduction

The demeanor of deer, both captive and free ranging, requires that they be restrained while samples are collected, measurements made, treatments administered, or equipment attached. Restraint of captive animals may be accomplished manually or with chutes but for many species and circumstances these procedures carry a high risk to the animals and personnel and may be very labor intensive. The advantages of a quiet or unconscious animal for procedures has stimulated a continuing study of injectable chemical immobilizing agents in the search for the ideal injectable anesthetic (Denny and Gill, 1970; Ericksen, 1968, 1978; Green, 1963; Hubbell, 1965; Hugie, 1977; Jenkins et al., 1961; Kitchen, 1966; Lanphear, 1963; Rosen and Bischoff, 1952; Short, 1969; Siglin, 1965; Talbot and Lamprey, 1961; Thomas, 1961; Wright, 1963). The capture and restraint of free ranging wild cervids poses additional problems including unfavorable environmental conditions, difficulty of access or trapping and drug administration, running or struggling during the excitement phase response to the drugs, unknown condition of the animal, variable recovery times, and post-recovery depression of function.

The management need for intensive data on local populations and the scientific value of ecological, demographic, genetic, and physiological information on individual animals in a population has motivated testing in wild species of a wide range of drugs available from human medicine and veterinary drugs developed for application to domestic species. Much information, not repeated here, is available on the capture, restraint, immobilization, and handling of free ranging and captive wild animals (Harthoorn, 1965; Harthoorn, 1976; Taber and Cowan, 1969; Fowler, 1978; Fowler et al., 1978; Nielsen et al., 1982; Nielsen, 1982; Hebert and McFetridge, 1982; Klös and Lange, 1980) and should be consulted.

This review summarizes much of the available published literature on the chemical immobilization of cervids and several other ungulate families and also includes unpublished data from about 20 zoos on some species for which there are no other available data. Data are presented indicating that the injectable immobilizing agents have characteristic effects on hematology, serum chemistries, and serum hormones which can influence the interpretation of these assays. There are several genera for which little or no information has been found (Tragulidae, Moschidae, *Pudu*, *Hippocamelus*, *Blastocerus*, *Ozotocerus*, and *Elaphodus*) and would be welcome. There is evidently a need for a careful study of several genera and species in captivity (*Hydropotes*, *Capreolus*, *Mazama*, and *Muntiacus*) to improve our ability to handle them. Patterns of dosage for the most useful drugs in cervids are evident and provide guidance for application to species as yet unstudied in the wild.

Drugs Used as Immobilizing Agents in Cervids

We have found about 200 references to 17 injectable drugs tested as immobilizing agents in cervids. In addition, barbiturates and inhalation anesthetics have been used for surgical procedures in many species (Trindle and Lewis, 1978; Wolf et al., 1965). The majority of the references are for etorphine, xylazine, or succinylcholine used in moose (*Alces*), elk or red deer (*Cervus elaphus*), and white-tailed deer or mule deer (*Odocoileus*).

The drugs used for immobilization have included a ganglionic stimulating agent (nicotine), neuromuscular blocking agents (gallamine, curare, succinylcholine, suxemethonium), centrally acting agents (tranquilizers, narcotics, and hypnotics), and anesthetics (dissociative drugs). Gases and barbiturates have been used after restraint.

Neuromuscular Blockers

The neuromuscular blocking agents act by interruption of transmission of the nerve impulse at the skeletal neuromuscular junction (Tavenor, 1971). They are classified in two groups. The depolarizing agents (succinylcholine) depolarize the membrane in the same manner as acetylcholine but more persistently. This results in a brief period of firing (muscular fasciculation), followed by neuromuscular paralysis. Removal depends upon esterase action. The competitive agents (d-tubocurarine and gallamine) combine with cholinoceptive sites at the post junctional membrane and block the transmitter action of acetylcholine. They produce motor weakness but no fasciculations. They are removed by redistribution, liver metabolism, and excretion.

A competitive neuromuscular blocking agent, gallamine triethyliodide (Flaxedil), was the first injectable agent described for immobilization of a cervid (Hall et al., 1953). These workers also described a gun and darts for delivery of the drugs. No further reports were found of the use of gallamine presumably because of its narrow safety margin and the limited efficacy of the antidote (edrophonium chloride or Tensilon).

Ganglionic Stimulation

The ganglionic stimulating drug (Gilman et al., 1980), nicotine (as the salicylate), was favored briefly for immobilization of *Odocoileus* (Behrend, 1965; Crockford et al., 1957a & b, Fuert et al., 1958; Hamilton undated, Jenkins et al., 1955; and Montgomery, 1961) and *Alces* (Rausch and Ritcey, 1961). The use of nicotine was quickly abandoned in published work because of its narrow margin of safety and the many adverse effects associated with its stimulatory properties. The drug is still distributed and is used by conservation officers in some states. This needs to be discouraged.

Miscellaneous Agents

Trials were reported of reserpine (Cowan et al., 1962), ethyl isobutrazine (Howe, 1966; Day, 1969), paraldehyde and curare (Hall et al., 1953) in *Odocoileus*, and of suxethonium, a succinylcholine derivative, in red deer (*Cervus e. elaphus*) (Jewell and Lowe, 1965; Jewell et al., 1965). A device for electrical anesthesia, the Taser, has been tested in several cervid species (Jessup et al., 1981) but there have been no further reports of its use.

Anesthetics

Anesthetics perhaps act by stabilization of neuronal membranes with a consequent decrease in amount of transmitter released by the nerve impulse and also an action on post-synaptic receptors. They produce: analgesia or loss of pain sense, unconsciousness, delirium or excitement, conditions allowing surgery (stable respiration, loss of reflexes, and muscular relaxation), and respiratory paralysis. They act upon the cerebrospinal axis at all levels. Possible mechanisms of action include: (a) failure of brain to receive impulses from sensory stimulation, (b) failure of arriving sensory impulses to be stored in brain centers, and (c) failure of arriving sensory impulses to produce "affect" or "awareness".

The dissociative anesthetics (Corssen and Domino, 1966; Corssen et al., 1968; Winters et al., 1972; Beck, 1972; Beck, 1974) were developed to provide drugs with analgesic and amnesic properties but with retention of major reflexes. The first of the series widely used in wild animals was phencyclidine (Dean et al., 1973; Seal and Erickson, 1969). It was removed from the market as the result of drug abuse legislation. Ketamine was the next member of the series and it is widely used today (Beck, 1974). Its use in cervids has greatly increased in combination with xylazine (Clarke and Hall, 1969; Jones, 1972; Jarofke, 1980). The combination provides more rapid induction and relaxation, in contrast to the hypertonicity experienced with ketamine alone, and post-recovery tranquilization or depression. The third member of the series, CI-744, is a 1:1 combination of tiletamine hydrochloride (CI-634) and a diazepionone tranquilizer (CI-716) (Gray et al., 1974; Franzmann and Arneson, 1974). Only ketamine is currently available commercially.

Centrally Acting Drugs

TRANQUILIZERS

This class includes the phenothiazines, benzodiazepines, and butyrophenones. Examples are promazine, acepromazine, diazepam, droperidol (Sadove et al., 1971), and azaperone. Effects are to reduce anxiety, produce psychomotor slowing, emotional quieting and affective indifference or the neuroleptic syndrome (O'Neil et al., 1972; White et al., 1982). They may have a sedative effect. They are synergistic with and prolong the effects of hypnotic or narcotic drugs. Phenothiazines lower convulsive threshold, but have a strong antiemetic effect. Many are retained for a long time (Moss and Clarke, 1977; Weir and Sanford, 1969). They act by blocking release and uptake of neurotransmitters.

Their effects in combinations with immobilizing drugs are: sedative, antiarrhythmic effects on heart, antihistaminic with protection against pulmonary edema, antiemetic, and additional respiratory depression. They may decrease blood pressure and disrupt temperature regulation (especially the phenothiazines). Termination of activity occurs by physical redistribution, metabolic degradation, and renal excretion.

Phenothiazine tranquilizers which have been used in cervids include chloropromazine (Cowan et al., 1962; Day, 1969); acepromazine alone (Cowan et al., 1962) and in combination with etorphine in the preparation "Immobilon" (McKean and Magonigle, 1978); promazine primarily in combination with phencyclidine (Seal and Erickson, 1969; Seal et al., 1970; Seal et al., 1972; Wesson et al., 1979b) or with ketamine (Seal et al., 1983); propionylpromazine (Jones, 1972) and triflupromazine (Coggins, 1975; Dean et al., 1973) in combinations with narcotics.

A benzodiazepine derivative, diazepam (Valium), has been used orally (Done et al., 1975; Heuschele, 1960; Ratcliffe, 1962; Thomas et al., 1967; Pusateri et al., Hawkins et al., 1967; and Murray, 1965) and by injection in *Odocoileus*, *Dama*, *Axis*, *Cervus nippon*, and *Antilocapra*. Used alone, large doses are required for sufficient quieting to allow handling of nervous animals. It is not satisfactory for capture. Sedated animals are ataxic, may become bloated, and receive aggression from untreated bucks. Similar aggression towards white-tailed deer (*Odocoileus*) immobilized with succinylcholine was noted by Scanlon et al. (1977). Intravenous administration of diazepam to a hypertonic immobilized animal can provide relaxation. There is a single report of the use of another derivative (RO-5-3448) added in feed for tranquilization of *Odocoileus* (Wesson et al., 1979b).

This class includes the barbiturates, chloral hydrate, and xylazine. They produce drowsiness and are general depressants. They reduce oxygen consumption in all tissues. Effects range from mild sedation to coma. They do not produce analgesia and may be used for surgical anesthesia but require addition of an analgesic drug. They depress respiration and are prone to produce laryngospasm. Removal depends upon drug-metabolizing enzyme systems in liver.

Xylazine is a non-narcotic sedative analgesic (Bauditz, 1972; Lindau and Gorgas; Savarie, 1976). It is a specific alpha$_2$-adrenergic agonist but may have other receptor activity. Xylazine is capable of sedating ungulates and carnivores at high doses (Gauckler and Kraus, 1970; Goltenboth and Klos; Smuts, 1973), however, many animals may overcome this sedation if stimulated. Its primary use is to potentiate cyclohehane and narcotic anesthetics (Harrington, 1974; Hime and Jones, 1970). Xylazine has been reported to depress respiration, gut motility, and body temperature. It can also produce a profound hyperglycemia followed by glycosuria and polyuria (Brockman, 1981: Custer et al.; Knight, 1980). The effects of xylazine can be antagonized by either yohimbine or tolazoline. It is available in 20 and 100 mg/ml injectable solutions.

NARCOTICS

This class includes the opioid anesthetics, morphine and the related derivatives etorphine, fentanyl, carfentanyl (Alford et al., 1974; King and Klingel, 1965; Robinson and Sedgwick, 1974). They act upon the central nervous system and bowel. They produce: analgesia which can occur without loss of consciousness, drowsiness, change in mood, neural clouding, depressed respiration (by decreasing sensitivity to CO_2), constriction of pupil, decrease in propulsive contractions in bowel, and activation of chemoreceptor trigger zone in medulla to produce nausea. Their mechanism of action is to combine with specific receptors in the brain and other tissues to prevent release or uptake of neurotransmitters. They are metabolized in the liver. Antagonists, some with agonistic activity, are available for etorphine and fentanyl. They include diprenorphine, naloxone, and naltrexone. The narcotics in use with cervids are etorphine and fentanyl (Novack et al., 1978; McClain and Hug, 1980). A new fentanyl derivative (R 33799) is currently undergoing field testing (Hofmeyr, 1977; De Vos, 1978). It is water soluble, may be prepared in concentrated solution, and is slightly more potent than etorphine in some species. Fentanyl, usually in combination with xylazine or a tranquilizer, is used as an alternative to etorphine and may provide a wider safety margin in some species (Jones, 1972; York, 1975; Haigh et al., 1977b; Skjonsberg and Westhaver, 1978). It is extensively used in New Zealand, Canada, and Africa but is not available commercially in a usable form for cervids in the USA.

Stages of Anesthesia

The sequence of events occurring during the immobilization of cervids can be characterized in terms of the sequence occurring with increasing depth of anesthesia. (Harthoorn, 1976; Fowler, 1978b; Gilman et al., 1980). The depth of anesthesia is traditionally divided into 4 stages each with characteristic signs. (A) Analgesia with loss of consciousness. (B) Delirium with excitement and involuntary activity, increased muscle tone, hypertension, tachycardia, vomiting or retching, defecation and urination, irregular breathing, and susceptibility to reflex respiratory arrest. (C) Surgical planes with increasing depth: 1. Regular abdominal and thoracic respiration with roving eyes; 2. Shallower respiration and fixed eyeballs; 3. Increased abdominal respiration with less thoracic respiration; 4. Intracostal paralysis; 5. Stopping of all respiration; (D) Respiratory paralysis–followed by cardiac arrest and circulatory failure and death.

Table 1. Approximately progressive signs of chemical immobilization or anesthesia in cervids using injectable anesthetic drugs

Slight behavioral changes	Straddle legged stance
Lowering of eyelids	Down but able to rise spontaneously
Relaxed tail	Down but able to rise if stimulated
Penis relaxed	Down but unable to rise—head up
Standing (not moving)	Down but unable to rise—head down
Moving away from other animals	Lateral recumbency
Lowered head, standing	Spontaneous movements present
Increased salivation	Movement reflex present
Abnormal behavior	Respiratory reflex—rectal stretching
Aimless walking	Pedal reflex
Agitated walking and running	Swallowing reflex
Hackney gait	Corneal reflex
Ataxia	Palpebral reflex

Table 2. Induction times for moose immobilized with (H+) or without (H−) hyaluronidase added to fentanyl and xylazine

	H+ Injection site		H− Injection site	
	Optimal (A)	Suboptimal (B)	Optimal (C)	Suboptimal (D)
N	36	22	30	16
Mean (min)	6.38	14.86	10.08	11.78
SD	2.47	4.40	4.58	5.16

Statistical analysis of differences: (1) A vs C—P < 0.001; (2) A + B vs C + D—not significant; (3) A vs B—P < 0.001; (4) C vs D—not significant; (5) B vs C—P < 0.001.
Data from Haigh, 1979.

The patterns and sequence of response of cervids to immobilization have been described in detail and may include signs and symptoms in approximately the sequence presented in Table 1.

Modifiers of Response to Drugs

Drug Delivery

Partial delivery may occur because of a powder charge failure, spraying of drug during firing, bouncing of the dart, and freezing of drugs in the syringe. We used barbed needles on our darts in rifles and pistols to prevent bounces and assist recovery of the darts in free-ranging animals. The optimal sites of injection (Thomas and Marburger, 1964) are heavily muscled areas such as the haunch and shoulder which are well vascularized and allow rapid absorption (Table 2). Penetration below fat layers is essential and depends

upon the use of appropriate length needles. Induction time can easily be doubled by partial delivery into fat. Absorption of drugs appears to be facilitated by the addition of hyaluronidase to the drug mixture when used with either fentanyl and xylazine or succinylcholine (Tables 2 and 3).

Recent Drug History

Many of the drugs used for immobilization induce the enzymes for their metabolism in liver. Therefore serial druggings may require more drug to achieve the same effect. This effect will diminish if a week or longer interval occurs between treatments. Care must also be taken if other drugs have been used in the animals recently. Some of the drugs for treatment of parasites inhibit esterases that hydrolyse succinylcholine and will prolong its action. The same is true for some insecticides.

Normal Life History Events

Sex effects on drug dosages required for immobilization in the Cervidae appear to be primarily a function of body weight, but bucks in rut for Pere David's deer are more sensitive to the depressive action of xylazine. We have found captive white-tailed bucks early in rut to require more drug when either phencyclidine or ketamine are used. These animals are in very good nutritional condition which may not be the case for free-ranging animals. We found that twice daily manual restraint of white-tailed does reduced their activity levels during estrus, but did not affect the ability of the buck to detect heat and to achieve conception. Capture of pregnant wild moose (Alces) with succinylcholine appeared to yield a 50% reduction in calves observed in the group in the spring (Ballard et al., 1981). Capture with etorphine produced no increase in calf mortality. A study of the menstrual cycle

Table 3. Effects of succinylacholine chloride (Anectine) and Hyaluronidase (Wydase) administered to trapped adult Alaskan moose within the Kenai Moose Research Center (MRC) Enclosure, July 1, 1969, to May 1, 1974 (sample size in parentheses)

	Anectine		Anectine + Wydase	
	Male	Female	Male	Female
Induction Time (min)				
Mean	9.4(26)	10.2(79)	6.4(38)	6.6(110)
Pooled Mean	10.0(105)		6.5(148)	
Time Immobilized (min)				
Mean	21.5(25)	24.2(78)	25.6(32)	29.9(98)
Pooled Mean	23.5(103)		28.8(130)	

Adapted from Franzmann et al., 1974.

Seal and Bush

Table 4. Variation in the dosage rate of succinylcholine effective in immobilizing captive white-tailed deer injected intramuscularly by Cap-Chur projectile syringe (data from Jacobson et al., 1976)

Month	N	Dosage rate (mg/kg) Mean	SE	Latency period (min) Mean	SE	Immobilization period (min) Mean	SE
1971							
Sep	3	0.249	0.010	4.7	0.67	16.7	2.60
Oct	8	0.240	0.007	3.8	0.71	16.6	1.42
Nov	4	0.246	0.004	4.9	0.51	17.2	2.02
Dec	17	0.216	0.005	5.7	0.55	18.1	1.09
1972							
Jan	15	0.203	0.007	3.6	0.21	21.8	1.74
Feb	7	0.149	0.003	4.2	0.53	22.8	3.88
Mar	6	0.157	0.013	5.0	0.90	13.7	2.12
Apr	5	0.196	0.013	4.6	0.68	19.2	0.37
May	7	0.202	0.007	4.4	0.72	16.6	1.53
Jun	7	0.224	0.013	4.6	0.97	15.1	2.01
Jul	6	0.230	0.007	4.0	0.75	15.1	1.94
Aug	5	0.234	0.101	4.7	0.40	16.0	1.64
Sep	12	0.248	0.006	5.3	0.41	15.1	0.97
Oct	6	0.250	0.010	5.0	0.92	14.9	1.38
Nov	6	0.248	0.007	4.8	0.64	16.7	3.83
Dec	8	0.224	0.007	3.9	0.59	21.5	2.10

Table 5. pH and blood gas data from excited and calm Pere David's deer

Assay	Excited $\bar{x}$	SE	Calm $\bar{x}$	SE	$P <$
Number	5		11		
Induction Time	13	3.3	7.1	0.67	0.01
Respiratory rate (min)	58	11	11	3.5	0.01
Heart rate (min)	92	9.1	59	2.6	0.01
pH	7.46	.09	7.33	0.03	NS
PCO_2 (mm Hg)	11.8	2.27	41.6	2.09	0.01
PO_2 (mm Hg)	101	2.56	48	5.28	0.01
Bicarbonate (mEq/L)	7.4	0.24	21	1.12	0.01
Body temperature corrected data					
Number	3		5		
Rectal temp. (C)	42.2	0.83	39.6	0.23	0.01
pH	7.50	0.06	7.25	0.04	0.01
PCO_2 (mm Hg)	11	2.2	47	3.4	0.01
PO_2 (mm Hg)	151	10.3	51	6.5	0.01
Bicarbonate (mEq/L)	8.0	0.5	20	2.3	0.01

Adapted from Smeller et al., 1976.

in rhesus monkeys concluded that daily use did not alter cycle length or serum hormone levels. It did reduce the incidence of anovulatory cycles, an effect attributed to a reduction of the stress of handling (Channing et al., 1977). Seasonal effects have been carefully documented for succinylcholine in white-tailed deer with lower doses necessary in winter (Jacobsen et al., 1976) (Table 4).

State of the Animal

The data on Pere David's deer in different collections indicate a difference in the duration of depression following immobilization. Data on red deer in Scotland suggest that animals from Rhum are more sensitive to xylazine than the mainland animals (Fletcher, 1974).

The Siberian subspecies of roe deer (*Capreolus*) appears to require 4–6 mg of etorphine for immobilization whereas the European form requires 0.5–1.2 mg. Moose and elk have also been observed to require less succinylcholine in the winter for capture (Skjonsberg and Westhaver, 1978).

Nutritionally depleted animals may need only ½ to ⅓ of the drug doses necessary for comparable well-fed animals. This may be reflected in an increased acute mortality rate with the use of succinylcholine, and with all drugs or the stress of capture a higher incidence of acute and delayed capture myopathy and death may occur. Starved sambar will succumb to doses of succinylcholine as small as 6–8 mg. Nutritional depletion may also be reflected in prolonged recovery times with the use of xylazine and the dissociative anesthetics. Diseased animals are frequently also nutritionally depleted (cachexia) and are immobilized with smaller doses of drugs and have prolonged recovery times. Animals with acute trauma will usually require a full drug dosage for immobilization and may be more difficult to subdue as the result of the stimulation associated with the injury.

Excitement of Pere David's deer prior to immobilization increases induction time, respiratory rate, heart rate and body temperature (Table 5) (Smeller et al., 1976). Blood gas changes also reflected the level of excitement. Rectal temperatures in moose measured shortly after immobilization provided an index of the state of excitement (Franzmann et al., 1975). Blood glucose levels increased in proportion to excitement and rectal temperature. They may serve as another means of stratification of samples or animals for data analysis (Table 6). Maintenance of white-tailed deer under etorphine and xylazine anesthesia yielded sta-

Table 6. Blood chemistry values for assays related to adult female rectal temperature class in moose (sample size in parentheses)

Blood values	Rectal Temperature Class				
	1(30)	2(200)	3(200)	4(75)	5(29)
Glucose mg/dl	118	132	142	152	172
LDH mU/dl	278	314	335	353	382
Albumin g/dl	4.72	4.51	4.51	4.36	4.27
Globulin g/dl	2.52	3.00	2.99	3.08	3.24
Alpha 1 g/dl	0.28	0.37	0.34	0.37	0.41
Alpha 2 g/dl	0.46	0.57	0.57	0.56	0.61
Beta g/dl	0.61	0.73	0.73	0.74	0.79
Gamma g/dl	1.18	1.40	1.36	1.40	1.44

Data are from Franzmann and LeResche, 1978.

Table 7. Effects of etorphine HCL and xylazine on venous blood gas values of eight white-tailed deer during time of immobilization

Time post-injection (min)	pH	PCO_2 (mm Hg)	PO_2 (mm Hg)	HCO_3 (mEq/L)	Deer
10	7.35	46.33	32.00	24.87	3 bucks
15	7.28	46.50	27.50	21.55	4 fawns
25	7.35	46.50	31.50	25.10	2 bucks
35	7.30	49.00	32.00	23.50	1 buck
50	7.32	44.50	31.50	22.22	4 fawns

Data are from Presidente et al., 1973.

Table 8. Drug effects on blood assays of adult white-tailed bucks sampled in March

Assay	Restraint		Drugs		$P <$
	$\bar{x}$	SE	$\bar{x}$	SE	
Number	20		19		
Testosterone ng/dl	22.6	1.7	11.1	1.1	.0001
Glucose mg/dl	187	9.4	161	9.4	.0001
Cortisol ug/dl	5.7	0.5	0.3	0.2	.0001
Progesterone ng/ml	1.51	0.2	.28	.05	.0001
Hemoglobin g/dl	20.8	1.2	15.3	0.3	.0001
Hematocrit vol %	51.7	0.6	37.4	0.8	.0001
Red cells 106/ul	16.7	0.2	12.3	0.3	.0001

No effects were observed on thyroxine, urea, MCV, MCHC, and WBC. U.S. Seal unpublished data.

ble blood pH and gas values (Presidente et al., 1973) (Table 7). Thus these studies indicate that drug immobilized animals do not develop acidosis as a result of the drugs.

Excitement associated with restraint (Wesson et al., 1979 a, b, c) appears to increase the serum concentrations of cortisol, testosterone and progesterone in white-tailed bucks (Table 8). The levels of progesterone achieved with physical restraint in bucks, fawns, castrate does, and nonpregnant does were frequently greater than 2 ng/ml and values of 5 ng/ml have been observed (Wesson et al., 1979b, Seal et al., 1983; Plotka et al., 1983). The adrenal gland appears to be the source of this progesterone. The use of serum samples collected from restrained white-tailed deer for measurement of progesterone to infer the presence of an active corpus luteum or pregnancy may be invalid. It would be desirable to determine if this magnitude of secretion of adrenal progesterone in response to restraint occurs in other cervids. The biological significance of this secretion also deserves study.

Physiological Effects of Immobilization

Restraint

Manual restraint of cervids for examination or collection of samples has the appeal of not introducing the hazards of drugs and a recovery process. However, capture myopathy has been reported in pronghorns and elk captured without the use of drugs (Chalmers and Barrett, 1977; Lewis et al., 1977). Captive, untamed white-tailed deer handled without drugs exhibit multiple signs of acute excitement including increased body temperature, heart rate, respiration, increased adrenocortical secretion, splenic contraction with changes in hematology, increased blood glucose, glucagon, growth hormone, endorphins, muscle enzymes, and nonesterified fatty acids (Table 9) (Seal et al., 1972; Wesson et al., 1979a,b,c; Seal et al., 1981). The effects of manual restraint are persistent (Figures 1–3), with elevated levels of enzymes and changes in hematology evident one week later (Seal et al., 1981).

Chemical

Tame animals have minimal changes in blood values with blood drawing or immobilization (Mautz et al., 1980). Separation of post-restraint effects from possible direct effects of the drugs requires the use of tame animals, collection of multiple serial samples from drugged animals to allow the acute effects of the immobilization to subside, and experiments directed at identification of each drug's effects. Trapping and handling of white-tailed deer results in bruises which are sufficient to account for the acute and persistent increases in muscle enzymes observed.

Seal and Bush

Table 9. Short-term effects of phencyclidine and promazine on hematology and blood chemistry of eight pregnant adult white-tailed deer

Assay (units)	Restraint		Postdrugs	
	$\bar{x}$	SD	$\bar{x}$	SD
Serum Protein (g/dl)	5.7	0.7	4.9	0.4*
	128	26	142	32**
SGOT (KU)	18.6	2.5	15.8	2.7*
Hemoglobin (g/dl)	13.3	1.7	11.3	1.7*
Erythrocyte Count (106/ul)	49	5.7	42	6.9*
	37	3.6	37	3.1
Hematocrit (vol.%)	37	1.0	37	0.7
MCV (fl)	2120	700	1500	470*
MCHC (g/dl)	230	35	192	33*
Leukocyte Count (103/ul)	50	19	101	36*
	144	6.0	142	3.0
Fibrinogen (mg/dl)	4.3	0.3	4.6	0.5
CPK (IU)	9.8	0.5	9.7	0.7
Sodium (mEq/l)	6.7	1.0	4.9	0.9
Potassium (mEq/l)	66	7	85	5*
Calcium (mg/dl)				
Phosphorus (mg/dl)				
Cholesterol (mg/dl)				

Adapted from Seal et al., 1981. *Significant difference, * P < 0.01, ** P < 0.05. The animals were handled by restraint from a crate for the first sample, given the drugs, and another sample collected 45 minutes later.

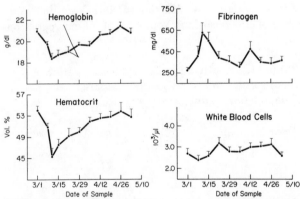

Figure 1. A group of 8 pregnant does were handled weekly by manual restraint to collect undrugged baseline blood samples. The values in each graph of each figure are plotted as means and standard errors. Collectively the data in all 3 figures indicate that handling produced an increase in adrenocortical activity, in acute phase reactants, and in serum levels of tissue enzymes suggestive of tissue damage or membrane leakage. This handling effect was particularly marked during the first 4 weeks and then the animals appeared to be less profoundly affected physiologically by the procedures. These data reinforce the observation that serum progesterone of adrenal origin may provide misleading results particularly in samples collected from undrugged animals. This figure provides data on hemoglobin, hematocrit, white blood cells, and fibrinogen.

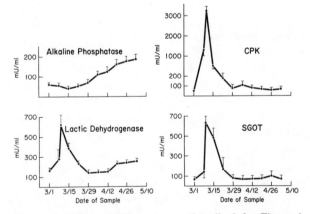

Figure 2. The conditions are as described for Figure 1. Data on alkaline phosphatase, lactic dehydrogenase, creatine phosphokinase, and serum glutamic-oxalacetic transaminase are provided in this figure.

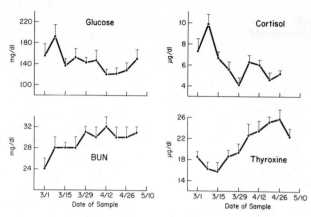

Figure 3. The conditions are as for Figure 1. Data on serum glucose, serum urea nitrogen, cortisol, and thyroxine are shown in these graphs.

Table 10. Effects of an opiate and naloxone on serum levels of pituitary hormones in man.

Hormone	Enkephalin	Naloxone
ACTH	—	+
LH	—	+
FSH	(−)	(+)
TSH	(+)	NC
GH	+	NC
PRL	+	NC
AVP	?	+
Cortisol	—	+

Adapted from Morley, 1981.

Each drug has a characteristic spectrum of effects. The narcotics (Table 10) increase the secretion of thyroid stimulating hormone, growth hormone, and prolactin and decrease the secretion of ACTH, LH, perhaps FSH, and of cortisol. This means that pituitary hormone data on samples obtained from animals immobilized with etorphine or fentanyl cannot be taken as representative of baseline levels. Xylazine increases blood glucose, serum urea, and glucagon and decreases the secretion of insulin, ACTH and cortisol (Knight, 1980). It probably affects the secretion of other pituitary hormones as well. Xylazine produces a diuresis and glycosuria (Thurmon et al., 1978) that can lead to a mistaken diagnosis of diabetes. Ketamine increases blood glucose and in prolonged anesthesia inhibits spontaneous surges of LH secretion, however, it does not appear to affect prolactin secretion in rats (Meltzer et al., 1978), the estrous cycle in white-tailed deer (Plotka et al., 1982) or the menstrual cycle in rhesus monkeys (Channing et al., 1977).

Complications of Immobilization

The most commonly encountered complications of immobilization in cervids are hyperthermia, hypertonicity and tremors, respiratory depression and arrest, vomiting with occasional aspiration, trauma, hypothermia in cold weather, capture myopathy, and death. Bloating is rarely reported and little evidence has been found for metabolic acidosis (Smeller et al., 1976; Presidente et al., 1973) in contrast to reports for African ungulates (Harthoorn and Van der Walt, 1974; Harthoorn and Young, 1974). One report has

Table 11. Results of serum chemistries from a moose with capture myopathy compared with data from 5 control adult female moose

Factor	Hours after Capture			Controls	
	0	22	46	$\bar{x}$	S.D.
Na (mEq/l)	141.5	140.5	139.5	139.7	3.66
K (mEq/l)	4.6	3.3	2.5	4.6	0.19
CL (mEq/l)	89	82	79	93	2.0
Ca (mg/dl)	10.0	7.7	7.6	9.9	1.12
P (mg/dl)	1.6	0.8	1.1	2.3	0.62
Mg (mg/dl)	2.6	3.4	2.3	2.8	1.1
BUN (mg/dl)	6	28	31	9	2.1
Creatinine (mg/dl)	1.9	2.8	2.8	2.0	0.16
CPK (IU/dl)	2.4	1640	2065	8.8	3.4
GOT (IU/dl)	53	2130	3670	61	12.4

Adapted from Haigh et al., 1977.

Seal and Bush

Table 12. Rectal temperature and capture associated deaths in white-tailed deer

Temperatures	Captured	Deaths
Celsius	M/F	
37.2 − 39.9	10/8	0/0
40.0 − 41.8	8/6	1/4

These does were captured in March in Minnesota (Seal et al., 1978).

described a possible adverse effect of succinylcholine on pregnancy in moose (Ballard and Tobey, 1981). Delayed deaths of wild-caught and released radio-tagged animals has been described for caribou (Fuller and Keith, 1981).

Capture myopathy (Harthoorn and Young, 1874; Harthoorn, 1977; Harthoorn, 1980; Hebert and Cowan, 1971) has been described in pronghorns (Chalmers and Barrett, 1977), moose (Table 11) (Haigh et al., 1977a), elk (Lewis et al., 1977), and white-tailed deer (Kocan et al., 1980; Wobeser et al., 1976). We observed a high rate of mortality in white-tailed does in one winter (Table 12) and followups on several of these animals showed a similar picture. The basis for this disorder has not been established in cervids. Xylazine suppresses gut motility (Cook and Kane, 1980) and produces a disruption of temperature regulation (Young, 1979) which usually is not of significance under the conditions of controlled ambient temperature as in zoos, but can be a significant cause of complications in very cold or hot weather. Xylazine may also produce prolonged depression (8 - 24 hours) unless reversed with yohimbine or tolazoline.

Methods of Access and Drug Delivery

Access

This is the most expensive part of the animal capture process when full accounting of vehicles and personnel hours is made. The comment is frequently made that narcotics such as M-99 cannot be used because of cost. However, this must be balanced against the cost of failed immobilizations, acute and delayed mortality rates, induction time, ease of working with the animal while immobilized, control of the anesthesia, and time spent monitoring recovery.

Methods of access for capture that have been recorded include stalking, blinds, cannon and drop netting (Hawkins et al., 1968; Hawkins et al., 1979) drives, herding, land vehicles, animal transport (horses and elephants), and helicopters (individual animals and herding). Partial cost and time data have

been presented for removal of white-tailed deer (Table 13) from a reservation and for techniques used to mark moose (Table 14). Various trapping and driving procedures appear most efficient for large numbers of animals. Helicopters have been effective for herding or hazing of animals into traps and for location and capture of individual animals in difficult terrain or distributed over large areas. We have estimated the cost of helicopter time, drugs, and supplies at 250 to 300 dollars per animal for collection of individual animals. This does not include the personnel costs which would be about 45 to 90 minutes per animal for 1 or 2 people at a minimum.

Access to captive animals may include preparations such as removal of food and water, separation or isolation from other members of a group, and choice of time and approach to minimize excitement. The com-

Table 13. Relative effciency of deer removal techniques used at the NASA Plum Brook Station, 1973–77

Method	Deer	Manhours/deer	Mortality
	N	Mean Hours	%
Public hunts	1330(a)	1.8	100.0
Box traps	2035	2.8	2.1
Professional removal	284	3.0	100.0
Immobilization drugs	44	4.1	13.6
Rocket nets	17	6.9	23.5
Scientific collections	453	8.5	100.0

(a) This figure does not include an estimated 232(14.9%) fatally crippled and lost animals.

Data are from Palmer et al., 1980.

Table 14. Comparison of techniques used to mark moose in Laurentide Provincial Park

Technique	Moose tagged	Days/moose	Moose/day(max)	Cost/moose
	N	Mean	Max.	$
Automatic device	505(a)	20.0	?	40(b)
In enclosure	16	1.7	2	500
Electric fence	0			
Helicopter	56	0.3(c)	9(c)	150
Snowmobile	35	1.0	5	110
Boat	31	1.6	4	100

(a) Number of distributed collars.

(b) Estimated from number of distributed collars.

(c) Five flying hours are considered as 1 day.

Data are from Roussel and Pichette, 1974.

mon hazards of immobilization of captive cervids appear to be vomiting and regurgitation, hyperthermia from hyperactivity and hypertonicity, trauma from running into obstacles and fences, and generalized excitement and escape behavior in other members of a group. We also find it helpful to cover the eyes of restrained or partially immobilized animals being handled. Loud noises serve to stimulate animals immobilized with ketamine.

Drug Delivery

Modes of delivery of drugs range from shooting darts with powder charged guns from helicopters to hand syringes for animals captured in nets or caught up and restrained (Jones, 1976; Liscinsky ey al., 1969; Lovett and Hill, 1977; Short and King, 1963). When guns or pistols are being used we have found it essential to use barbed needles on the dart syringes to assure that the dart is retained long enough for delivery of the drugs. This is important for minimizing the rate of failed shots and time lost observing an animal for drug effects. Use of barbs increases the recovery rate of the syringes. It is not economical to spend time searching for syringes particularly in a helicopter operation. Blowguns are useful for captive animals (Barnard and Dobbs, 1980; Fletcher, 1980; Warren et al., 1979). They reduce the noise and the impact trauma associated with drug delivery. Impact trauma always occurs with darts delivered from either a rifle or pistol. The delivery of the drug by powder-driven charges in the metal darts also produces trauma in the muscle which makes the use of clean or sterile darts essential to avoid infections at the injection site (Bush and Gray, 1972). This wound is vulnerable to infection and routinely requires treatment. The effective range of the blowgun is perhaps 10 meters. Care must be taken with the use of narcotics in blowgun syringes to avoid contamination of the mouthpiece and to protect against sprays. We find jabsticks useful for delivering drugs to closely confined animals in pens, cages, traps, and nets.

Reported Drug Dosages by Taxon

The dosage information presented here has been derived from published data, several published tabulations (Heck and Rivenburg, 1972; Jarofke, 1980; Jones, 1972) and unpublished data from 20 zoos. The tabulations may be considered guidelines only since no details or indication of morbidity or mortalities were presented. The zoo data were submitted as photocopies of actual records which has allowed us to gain an impression of the actual course of the individual immobilizations and has permitted a tabulation of complications encountered including mortalities. We

have placed the detailed data into computer data files which can be updated on a continuing basis. We would be pleased to receive additional data, especially on poorly represented taxa, to allow periodic updates for people interested in cervid immobilization. The data are presented separately for animals in captive collections and free-ranging wild animals.

Tragulidae

No data have been reported for wild animals. Captive animals have been handled by restraint. Administration of nitrous oxide and halothane by face mask to a restrained animal was successful.

Moschidae

No data have been reported for wild animals. One captive adult female was successfully immobilized by M. Green (pers. comm.) in an Indian zoo with 10 mg of ketamine and 5 mg of xylazine. It went down in 15 minutes and recovered.

Antilocapridae

Pronghorns have been captured in groups by herding with helicopters into traps and then using manual restraint (Chalmers and Barrett, 1977; Seal and Hoskinson, 1978). Capture myopathy has been reported as a cause of death in about 5% of animals captured with these techniques (Chalmers and Barrett, 1977). Application of succinylcholine to pronghorn immobilization was not successful (Amstrup and Segerstrom, 1981). Trials in 46 animals yielded 34 failures, 11 immobilized, and 5 deaths. Several animals required resuscitation. Induction time was dose dependent but the margin of safety was very narrow. Twenty-six pronghorns were selcctively captured by darting from helicopters using etorphine with either xylazine or acepromazine (Table 15) (Autenrieth et al., 1981). The survival rate was 81%. Mean induction times ranged from 7 to 20 minutes and recovery times from 1.4 to 9.3 minutes. A 3-fold dose of the antagonist is recommended administered by both i.m. and i.v. routes. The use of oral baits containing either diazepam or promazine was not successful for capture of wild pronghorns (Pusateri et al., 1982).

Cervidae

Hydropotes: No data have been reported for wild animals. Recommendations of Jones (1972) are M-99 0.06 mg/kg with acepromazine 0.25 mg/kg with no details. M. Cranfield (pers. comm.) used 60 mg of ketamine and 20–30 mg of xylazine in adults. Detailed records were available from a zoo for 4 animals weighing 19 to 30 pounds. M-99 alone (0.5

Table 15. Observational data, vital statistics, and drug dosages used in tranquilizing pronghorn antelope (*Antilocapra americana*)

Variable	Mature Male			Mature Female			Immatures		
	Mean	S.D.	N	Mean	S.D.	N	Mean	S.D.	N
Induction minutes	20.4	13.5	11	14.1	5.0	9	7.0	2.6	6
Resp. rate	146	25.9	10	135	28.2	9	146	22.1	6
Heart rate	170	23.5	7	174	55.6	9	198	55.6	6
Rectal temp. C	42.4	1.3	11	42.7	0.9	9	42.2	0.5	6
Body wgt. kg	53(a)	2.3	11	45(a)	4.0	9	37(a)	7.5	6
M99 mg/kg	0.11	0.04	11	0.10	0.02	9	0.15	0.02	6
Xylazine mg/kg	1.21	0.58	5	1.06		1	1.10		2
Acepromaz. mg/kg	0.08		3	0.11	0.01	8	0.09		4
M50-50 mg/kg	0.32	0.12	11	0.32	0.08	9	0.44	0.11	6
Recovery minutes	3.2	2.6	10	1.4	0.7	9	9.3	8.7	6

(a) Estimated weight.

Data are from Autenrieth et al., 1981.

mg/8.6 kg, 2 year old female) was ineffective with the animal down in 6 minutes and up in 1.5 minutes. Injection of M-99 0.5 mg/10 kg with 10 mg xylazine put an animal down in 6 minutes with relaxation and it came up in 2 minutes after M-50/50 injection. Ketamine alone at 200 and 400 mg initial doses (13.5 and 9 kg females respectively) was ineffective and required i.m. and i.v. supplementation. The animals were hypertonic and salivated. Recovery was prolonged in the lighter animal. The use of a tranquilizer with the immobilizing drug appears essential.

Capreolus: No data have been reported for wild animals. Jarofke (1980) suggests 0.5 to 1.0 mg/kg xylazine for sedation and 1.5 to 3.0 mg/kg for immobilization. Schultze et al. (1976) indicate, on the basis of 97 trials, that 3 mg/kg of xylazine is only a rough guide with more drug frequently being needed. Full recovery requires 4 to 5 hours. No complications were observed. Heck and Rivenburg (1972) indicated differences in adult doses of M-99 (mg/animal) for the European form with 1.2 mg for males and 0.5 mg for females. The Siberian form required 6.0 mg for males and 4.5 mg for females.

Alces: Recorded experience with capture and movement of moose extends back at least 100 years in North America (Pimlott and Carberry, 1958). Overall mortality in these operations averaged 1 death for 2 animals moved. Many of the deaths were delayed and infections were common. The advent of drugs has greatly reduced mortality with wild capture (Skjonsberg and Westhaver, 1978; LeResche et al., 1974). Drugs used include nicotine (Rausch and Ritcey, 1961), succinylcholine (Bergerud et al., 1964; Nielson

Table 16. Successful immobilizations of 107 Shiras moose using succinylcholine chloride

Age-Class	N M/F	Dose (mg)	Induct. (min ± S.E.)		Duration (min ± S.E.)		Depth of Immobil.*	
							Opt	Exc
June 16—Feb 14								
Adult	4/0	18–20	6	1.7	29	5.4	2	2
	27/16	15–17	9	3.5	25	6.6	42	1
	5/7	12–14	10	2.0	22	5.2	9	
Sub-	2/1	15–17	13	1.2	28	9.4		3
Adult	4/6	12–14	9	3.3	27	3.3	9	1
Calves	1/0	12–14	6		30			1
Feb 15—June 15								
Adult	0/3	15–17	9	2.0	31	10.4	1	2
	4/17	12–14	10	3.4	26	5.6	20	1
	0/1	9–11	5		29			
Sub-	1/0	12–14	7		55			1
Adult	3/1	9–11	8	6.0	25	9.1	4	

Data taken from Houston, 1969.

*Opt = Optimal, Exc = Excessive.

and Shaw, 1967; Houston, 1969; Franzmann and Arneson, 1974; Ballard and Tobey, 1981), M-99 (Houston, 1970; Franzmann and Arneson, 1974; Roussel and Patenaude, 1975; Haigh et al., 1977b; Franzmann and LeResche, 1978; Gasaway et al., 1978; Smith and Franzmann, 1979; Lynch and Hanson, 1981), phencyclidine (Lynch, 1978), and fentanyl (Haigh et al., 1977b; Haigh, 1979).

Mean induction time with succinylcholine varied between 6 and 10 minutes in 107 moose. The dose range was 12 to 20 mg per animal in adult males. Down time varied between 22 and 29 minutes with shorter times at the lower doses (Table 16). Lower doses were required in the winter months (Nielson and Shaw, 1967; Houston, 1969). Twelve animals were considered excessively immobilized and 87 were optimal. Addition of hyaluronidase to the drug in the syringe shortened induction time about 33% and increased down time about 15%, Table 2 (Franzmann and Arneson, 1974). A similar decrease in induction time was observed with addition of hyaluronidase to a mixture of fentanyl and xylazine (Table 2) (Haigh, 1979). The failure rate in capture of moose with succinylcholine was about 25% and 11 animals required artificial resuscitation (Houston, 1969). Reported mortality rates with succinylcholine were 11/42 (Bergerud et al., 1964), 2/119 (Houston, 1969) in animals stalked on foot or from vehicles, and 5/97 (Nielson and Shaw, 1967) using helicopters in the winter. Use of succinylcholine in pregnant moose cows appeared to increase fetal mortality by 50% whereas M-99 had no effect (Ballard and Tobey, 1981).

A trial in 5 animals with CI-744 yielded such variable induction times (1 to 42 minutes) and long recovery times that it was not tested further in a field situation (Franzmann and Arneson, 1974).

Etorphine alone was used in Canada for immobilization of 118 moose with 10 deaths (Tables 17 and 18) (Lynch and Hanson, 1981). Doses ranged from 5–7 mg. Unbaited pagewire traps were used to trap 104 of the moose and 12 were darted from a helicopter. Induction time averaged 15 minutes and recovery time was 1.9 with i.v. or 11.6 minutes with i.m. administration. Induction times were the same for animals darted from the helicopter or on the ground. Heart rates, respiration and body temperature were elevated in the drugged animals.

Etorphine with xylazine was used on 105 moose in Alaska (Gasaway et al., 1978) with 26 in August, 22 in October, and 57 in April. The 4 deaths occurred in August, 3 of which were in 9 animals receiving 7 mg M-99 and 400 mg xylazine. This was the highest dose of xylazine used. There were 9 failures of darts which hit animals. At least 4 were due failures of the dart system. The routine dose developed for free-ranging

Table 17. Reaction parameters of 118 M99 immobilized moose

Reaction	N	$\bar{x}$	S.E.	Range
First effect, min.	74	9.9	1.1	2–11
Induction, min.	101	15.0	1.4	3–44
Recovery, min.				
I. V M50–50	79	1.9	0.1	1–6
I. M. M50–50	7	11.6	2.8	4–25
Heart rate/min.	38	96.7	8.7	56–162
Respiration rate/min.	48	57.0	8.0	11–128
Rectal temp. C	23	41.5	8.5	39.4–42.8

Note: The reversing agent, M50–50, was administered at twice the dosage of M99. Data are from Lynch and Hanson, 1981.

Table 18. Capture mortality in 118 M99 immobilized moose

Method	Number		Mortality (%)
	Darted	Died	
Trap	104	7	6.7
Helicopter	12	3	25.0
Free-ranging	2	0	0
Totals	118	10	8.5

Data are from Lynch and Hansen, 1981.

Alaskan moose weighing 450–640 kg was 7 mg M-99 and 300 mg xylazine for immobilization and 20 mg of M-50/50 for reversal. The cost of the procedure with these drugs was cheaper than with succinylcholine because of reduced helicopter time per moose immobilized and fewer darts lost. This was the result of more consistent immobilization and shorter distance traveled.

Doses recommended for captive moose are 4.0 to 5.5 mg M-99 plus 0.1 mg/kg of acepromazine (Jones, 1972), 0.01 mg/kg of M-99 with 0.3 mg/kg of xylazine (Jones, 1972), 5–7 mg of M-99 per animal or 1.5 mg/kg of xylazine for immobilization (Jarofke, 1980), and 0.5 mg/kg of xylazine for sedation (Jarofke, 1980). *Pudu:* There are no data for wild animals. The only dose for captive animals (Jones, 1972) was 0.06 mg/kg M-99 plus 0.25 mg/kg of acepromazine. *Mazama:* There are no data for wild animals. Data on 11 immobilizations of *M. americana* in one zoo are available. The animals were estimated to weigh 30 pounds. Ketamine at 150 mg followed with another at

Table 19. Response times of captive white-tailed deer after intramuscular injections of xylazine

Dosage or stress status of deer	First reaction			Induction time			Recovery time		
	N	Mean	S.D.	N	Mean	S.D.	N	Mean	S.D.
mg/kg									
0.89–1.49	14	1.93	0.77	10	4.60	2.74	9	136	75
1.50–2.49	32	2.06	0.77	32	5.76	4.74	31	195	101
2.50–3.49	5	1.70	0.65	4	4.19	2.12	4	232	54
3.50–8.00	5	1.15	0.28	5	3.15	2.13	5	299	97
Stress status									
Wild, just trapped	33	1.67	0.65	34	3.84	2.18	33	190	111
Semi-tame captive	11	2.43	0.83	7	4.82	2.59	5	207	66
Wild, kept quiet for 6—48 hrs.	12	2.08	0.76	10	9.85	6.29	9	221	86
All deer	56	1.91	0.76	51	5.15	4.08	49	198	101

Data are adapted from Roughton, 1975.

80 mg was used in one instance with success. M-99 was given i.v. at doses ranging from 0.6 to 1.0 mg in 10 instances. The drug was diluted 5-fold for i.v. administration in 4 recent cases. Antidote, M-50/50, was given at twice the dose of M-99 i.v. There were no deaths or difficulties in recovery.

Hippocamelus, Blastocerus, and *Ozotoceros*: There are no data available for either wild or captive animals of these three genera.

Odocoileus: Extensive data are available for both species in the wild and in captivity (Skjonsberg and Westhaver, 1978). The literature on *O. virginianus* is reviewed in Wesson et al. (1979a,b,c) and Seal et al. (1981). Drugs used include succinylcholine (Pistey and Wright, 1959 & 1961; Cowan et al., 1962; Allen, 1970; Wesson et al., 1974; Jacobsen et al., 1976; Palmer et al., 1980) which is being tested for bow hunting (Anderson, 1961; Causey et al., 1978; Gutierrez et al., 1979), nicotine (Jenkins et al., 1955; Crockford et al., 1957a,b; Fuert et al., 1958; Hamilton, undated; Montgomery, 1961; Behrend, 1965), phencyclidine (Seal and Erickson, 1969; Seal et al., 1972; Dean et al., 1973; Seal et al., 1978; Seal et al., 1981), CI-744 (Gray et al., 1974), ketamine (Beck, 1974; Seal et al., 1983), etorphine (Wallach et al., 1967; Woolf, 1970, 1974; Woolf et al, 1974; Presidente et al., 1973; Presnell et al., 1973; Mautz et al., 1980), xylazine (Table 19) (York and Huggins, 1972; Schmidl, 1974; Roughton, 1975; Mautz et al., 1980), gas anesthesia (Wolff et al., 1965), and oral tranquilizers (Murray, 1965; Thomas et al., 1967).

Drugs used in *O. hemionus* include succinylcholine (Boyd, 1962; Cowan et al., 1962; Nordan et al., 1962; Pearson et al., 1963; Day et al., 1965; Miller, 1968; Sauer et al., 1969), phencyclidine (Day et al., 1965; Denney, 1965; Dean et al., 1973), ketamine (Richter, 1977), etorphine (Heck and Rivenburg, 1972; Jarofke, 1980), and gas anesthesia (Trindle and Lewis, 1978).

Field capture of these deer can be accomplished with a combination of 2 mg/kg of phencyclidine and 0.5–1.0 mg/kg of xylazine or 5–8 mg/kg of ketamine and 0.5–2.0 mg/kg of xylazine or 0.05 mg/kg of etorphine and 0.5 mg/kg of xylazine. Depression can be prolonged and temperature regulation is disrupted by xylazine. It is essential to follow body temperature and take corrective action with either hypo- or hyperthermia. We use 5 mg/kg of ketamine and 2 mg/kg of promazine for trapped animals since the duration of depression is short, the dose can easily be supplemented, and the disruption of temperature regulation is minimal. Similar doses can be given intravenously to restrained animals for rapid effect. Rarely, respiratory arrest occurs which can be relieved by several compressions of the chest. We have had approximately 1 death per 1000 immobilizations by this method. It is important to supplement the dosages as needed for longer procedures to minimize struggling since this will elevate body temperatures and increase the risk of broken bones.

Rangifer: Bergerud et al. (1964) used succinylcholine for the capture of Newfoundland caribou. Etorphine was used for wild capture of woodland caribou (Laisher, 1972) either as M-99 which contains 1 mg/ml of etorphine or as Immobilon which contains 10 mg/ml of acepromazine and 2.45 mg/ml of etorphine (Table 20) (Fuller and Keith, 1981). Animals hazed

Table 20. Etorphine immobilization of 25 woodland caribou in NE Alberta during November to April

	Survived (18)	Died (7)	
	Mean	Mean	P <
Etorphine dose, mg/100kg	4.5	5.1	NS
Hazing time, min.	6.1	13.0	0.03
Immobilization time, min.	12.3	22.7	0.01
Handling time, min.	25.7	39.1	0.02
Diprenorphine dose, mg/100kg	9.8	9.8	NS
Recovery time, min.	7.8	9.2	NS

Adapted from Fuller and Keith, 1981.

into position were darted by a man on the ground. The effective dose of etorphine was 4.5 mg/100 kg. Induction time of surviving animals was about 12 minutes and recovery time after antidote was about 8 minutes. Seven of 25 animals captured died, of which 6 deaths were delayed up to one week. Significant differences noted between Immobilon and M-99 were shorter recovery time (3.2 vs 11.2 minutes) and lower respiration rate (12.7 vs 37.2 per minute) with Immobilon.

Suggested doses for captive animals are 1.5 mg/kg of xylazine or 3.2 to 5 mg/animal of M-99 for immobilization and 0.5 mg/kg of xylazine for sedation (Jarofke, 1980), 3.2 and 4.5 mg/animal for female and male caribou respectively and 5 mg for adult male domesticated reindeer (Heck and Rivenburg, 1972), and 0.8 to 1.2 mg/kg for sedation of reindeer (Jones, 1972).

Elaphodus: No data are available for wild or captive animals.

Muntiacus: No data are available for wild animals. Zoo animal data are available for animals designated *M. muntjak* and *M. reevesi*. Suggested doses for captive animals are 0.06 mg/kg etorphine plus acepromazine 0.25 mg/kg (Jones, 1972), 1.6 mg etorphine for adult *M. muntjak* (Heck and Rivenburg, 1972), 0.8 mg etorphine for adult male *M. reevesi* (Heck and Rivenburg, 1972), and 60–70 mg ketamine plus 25–30 mg xylazine for adults (M. Cranfield, pers. comm.). Detailed data were received for 71 immobilizations from 4 zoos including 46 from NZP. Reported body weights ranged from 5 to 21 kg with most between 9 and 14 kg. Overall, we have the impression that these animals are difficult to smoothly immobilize. There have been many changes of drugs and dosages, restraint is frequently required, vomiting has been noted on 5 occasions, and 2 losses occurred. Slow re-

covery was reported with the mixture of etorphine and xylazine in 3 of 4 animals. Xylazine alone at doses of 30 to 60 mg required restraint to handle the animals. Use of diazepam alone at 12 to 30 mg required restraint. Ketamine plus xylazine at doses inducing rapid relaxation produced respiratory depression leading to the use of lower doses requiring restraint. CI-744 was used with satisfactory results in 9 of 13 animals at 25 to 60 mg per animal. Overall, satisfactory results have been obtained in only 50—60% of immobilizations. It is notable that most animals have been injected by hand syringe suggesting a significant level of excitement prior to any drug effects.

Dama: Data are available for captive animals free-ranging in paddocks and confined to small spaces. Heck and Rivenburg (1972) indicate 2.4 mg M-99 for adult males and females. Jones (1972) recommends 0.03 mg/kg etorphine plus 0.5 to 1.0 mg/kg xylazine and notes that acepromazine with etorphine provides insufficient sedation. Jarofke (1980) lists 1–2 mg/kg xylazine for sedation. Kilde and Klein (1973) used 4.5 mg/kg of xylazine to immobilize 2 animals. M. Cranfield (pers. comm.) notes that fallow deer have tremors and hypertonicity with either etorphine or fentanyl. He used 3 mg of M-99 plus 75–100 mg of xylazine or 25–30 mg of fentanyl and 25–30 mg xylazine and then administers 20 mg/45 kg of doxipram immediately to reverse respiratory depression. A cast of fatal malignant hyperthermia following use of an etorphine-xylazine mixture has been described (Pertz and Sundberg, 1978) and note was made of 3 animals dying with Immobilon (Chapman, 1973). Sedation of fallow deer in stalls or paddocks has been achieved with diazepam in food at doses of 30 to 70 mg/kg (Heuschele, 1960; Thomas et al., 1967; Done et al., 1975; Geiger, 1976) although Geiger reported he had to dart the animals with an additional 4 mg/kg of xylazine to allow handling and transport. Scanlon (1973) in 18 attempts on 11 animals successfully immobilized 10 with succinylcholine. One female died. Effective doses ranged from 0.105 to 0.220 mg/kg. Ineffective doses ranged from 0.088 to 0.220 mg/kg. Immobilization time averaged 7.2 minutes and ranged from 2 to 22 minutes. Smooth immobilization and good relaxation are difficult to achieve in this species.

Axis: Data are available for captive *A. porcinus* and wild and captive *A. axis*. No data are available for *A. kuhli* or *A. calamianensis*. Heck and Rivenburg (1972) used 1.6 mg M-99 for adult and 0.25 mg for 5 month-old *A. porcinus*. Jones (1972) lists 0.04 to 0.06 mg/kg of etorphine plus 0.2 to 0.25 mg/kg of acepromazine for *Axis spp.* and notes that xylazine in combination gave better relaxation but recovery was prolonged. Jarofke (1980) lists 0.5 to 1.5 mg of M-99 or 3 to 4 mg/kg of xylazine to immobilize *A. porcinus* and 1–2 mg/kg of

Seal and Bush

xylazine to sedate. Xylazine at 1 and 1.8 mg/kg was used for sedation of 2 animals (Sutherland and Hodgkin, 1974). One zoo reported 53 immobilizations over 7 years with 3 deaths. M-99 was used alone 51 times in doses ranging from 1–3.5 mg for adult animals. The higher doses were used in the last 2 years of the series.

We used 400 mg CI-744 or 200 mg ketamine plus 100 mg xylazine, or 3 mg M-99 for immobilization of wild *A. axis* in India with no losses (Sinha, 1976; Nair, 1977).

Elaphurus: There are no data for wild Pere David's deer but extensive data are available for captive animals in stalls and open meadows (Smeller et al., 1976; Bush, 1982). Heck and Rivenburg (1972) list 5.0 mg M-99 for adult males. Jones (1972) lists 0.02 mg/kg of etorphine plus 0.1 mg/kg of acepromazine and notes that use of xylazine in combination with etorphine causes a prolonged depression. Jarofke (1980) lists 0.3 to 0.5 mg/kg of xylazine for sedation and 0.5 to 1.0 mg/kg for immobilization. Bush (1982) used etorphine at 0.008 mg/kg (range 0.003–0.015) plus xylazine at 0.1 mg/kg (range 0.045–0.2) in 88 procedures with no losses. The average induction time was 13 (3–33) minutes. Body temperatures ranged from 100.5 to 109 F. The animals responded to antidote in 1 to 4 minutes but were stuporous for 4–12 hours. No arousal was obtained by treatment with doxapram. Adult males in rut were even more sensitive to depression with xylazine and were given only 15 mg with 1.8 to 2.3 mg of M-99 for effect. The results of 36 immobilizations of animals in another collection with only M-99 indicated doses of 3.5 to 6 mg/animal for adults and 2–4 mg in yearlings. The doubled dose of M-99 required appears to be a significant difference between animals in the 2 lineages or a reflection of their extreme sensitivity to xylazine in the combination. This phenomenon may parallel that with *C. elaphus* from Rhum which are 20–40 times more sensitive to xylazine than the mainland animals (Fletcher, 1974).

Cervus: There are not data available for *C. alfredi, mariannus,* or *albirostris*. Extensive data are available for wild and captive *elaphus* ssp. and captive *nippon* ssp. There are limited data for wild and captive *unicolor* and *duvauceli* and for captive *eldi* and *timorensis*.

C. timorensis: Jones (1972) lists 0.04 to 0.06 mg/kg plus 0.2 to 0.25 mg/kg of acepromazine for immobilization.

C. eldi: No data were found in the literature. One zoo reported 7 experiences using 2–3.5 mg of M-99 with no losses. Acepromazine, 5 mg, was added one time. NZP has recorded 122 experiences in 16 individuals with 1 death. Two animals have been immobilized 30 times each with 5 to 30 mg xylazine followed by 50 to 125 mg of ketamine for treatments with satisfactory results. CI-744 was used on 20 occasions in doses of 25

to 250 mg depending on weight. A combination of 0.7 mg M-99 and 10–30 mg xylazine has been used in 8 individuals with poor results about 50% of the time.

C. duvauceli: Heck and Rivenburg (1972) list 3.2 to 4.0 mg of M-99 with excellent results. M. Cranfield (pers. comm.) reports 2.0 to 2.5 mg M-99 plus 50 to 80 mg of xylazine for immobilization. Jones (1972) lists 0.015 mg/kg of etorphine plus 0.5 to 1.0 mg/kg of xylazine for immobilization and indicates that acepromazine does not provide adequate relaxation. One zoo reports 3–4 mg M-99 for 6 adults and 1.5 to 2.5 mg for 5 young animals. A combination of 3–4 mg of acepromazine was used with 2–2.5 mg M-99 in 3 of the young animals.

C. unicolor: One zoo reports use of 3 to 5 mg of M-99 in 10 animals with no losses. Another 4 animals were given 3 mg of acepromazine with the M-99. Capture of 5 wild animals in India was accomplished with 5 mg of M-99 in combination with 25–50 mg of xylazine. Induction time averaged 9 minutes but the animals moved up to 1 km.

C. nippon: Three subspecies of this species are treated separately in captive populations. These are *C. n. nippon* or Japanese sika, *C. n. dybowskii* or Dybowski sika and *C. n. taiounannus* or Formosan sika. Heck and Rivenburg (1972) list 2.2 to 3 mg M-99 for *nippon*, 2.8 to 3.5 for *dybowskii*, and 2.0 to 2.5 for *taiounannus*. Jones (1972) lists 0.04 to 0.06 km/kg etorphine plus 0.2 to 0.25 mg/kg of acepromazine for the species. Jarofke (1980) lists 2–3 mg per animal of M-99 or 3–4 mg/kg of xylazine for immobilization of *nippon* and 2 mg/kg of xylazine for sedation. He lists 3–3.5 mg M-99 or 3–4 mg/kg of xylazine or 2.5 mg/kg xylazine plus 1.2 mg/kg of ketamine for immobilization of *dybowskii* and 2 mg/kg of xylazine for sedation.

One zoo reported 108 experiences with *taiounannus* with no losses reported. Between 1974–7, 76 animals were given 0.5 to 1.5 mg M-99 with adults receiving the high dose. During 1980, 17 adult animals were given 2.0 to 2.5 mg M-99. During 1981 10 animals were given 1–2 mg M-99 and 2–3 mg of acepromazine and 10 animals were given 0.5 to 1.5 mg of M-99.

C. elaphus: There are multiple named races of this species in the immobilization literature. The major ones are the red deer and the wapiti or elk. Free-ranging animals have been captured or immobilized after trapping with etorphine (Coggins, 1975; Woolf et al., 1973), phencyclidine (Denney, 1965), succinylcholine (Flook et al., 1962; Harper, 1965; Jewell and Lowe, 1965; Jewell et al., 1965; Pedersen and Pedersen, 1975). Effective doses of succinylcholine for elk range from 10–20 mg, (Table 21) (Harper, 1965; Skjonsberg and Westhaver, 1978). Induction times range from 3 to 15 minutes and some animals fail to go down. Recovery times range from 10 to 20 minutes. It was noted

Table 21. Location of injection of 50 mg/cc succinylcholine chloride and associated latent period and duration of paralysis of Roosevelt elk on the Millicoma area (averages shown in parentheses)

Location of Drug Injection	N	Dosage (mg)	Induction (min)	Duration of paralysis (min)
Hip	91	8–30(14)	1–15(6)	14–122(43)
Shoulder	24	10–20(14)	3–10(5)	27–119(51)
Back	10	10–25(15)	3–12(6)	22–105(44)
Paunch	12	10–20(13)	6–20(12)	19–60(33)
Neck	5	10–20(15)	4–7(5)	28–40(33)
Lower leg, feet, udder	6	10–20(14)	3–10(7)	18–100(46)

Data are from Harper, 1965.

that a smaller dose was required in the winter, about 10 mg, than in the summer—about 20 mg (Skjonsberg and Westhaver, 1978). A similar seasonal dependence has been reported for white-tailed deer and moose. Etorphine in combination with 20 mg triflupromazine was used to immobilize 52 elk trapped during the summer in Oregon (Table 22) (Coggins, 1975). Doses ranged from 0.017 to 0.045 mg/kg of etorphine based upon estimated weights. No deaths were reported. The mean induction time ranged from 13 to 21 minutes and the mean recovery time after administration of M50-50 was 1.2 minutes (Table 23). There was no followup for delayed effects.

Xylazine has been used for sedation of captive elk and red deer (Thurmon et al., 1972; Fletcher, 1974) with the observation that different populations of red deer can differ 40 fold in their sensitivity (Fletcher, 1974). Also additional anesthetic was required for procedures on the elk. Etorphine was used for surgery in an elk (Woolf and Swart, 1970). Heck and Rivenburg (1972) list 1.0 to 2.8 mg M-99 for red deer and 3.2 to

4.0 mg for elk. Jarofke (1980) lists 3.5–4.0 mg M-99 or 3–4 mg xylazine for immobilization of elk and 1–2 mg xylazine for sedation. He lists 1 mg/kg xylazine plus 5 mg/kg ketamine or 1–2.8 mg of M-99 or 3–4 mg of xylazine for immobilization of red deer. He listed 1–2 mg/kg of xylazine or 5 mg/kg of ketamine for sedation of red deer. Jones (1972) listed 0.02 mg/kg of etorphine plus 0.1 mg/kg of acepromazine for immobilization of the species. He notes that xylazine in combination with etorphine provides better sedation but prolongs recovery.

One zoo reported use of 2.5–3.0 mg M-99 in 10 4–6 month old Tule elk with induction times of 5–10 minutes and no problems. Three adults were put down with 3 mg. A zoo reported 27 immobilizations of Roosevelt elk using M-99 at 5–6 mg for adults, 1.3–3.5 mg for yearlings, and 1.5–2.5 mg for juveniles. No fatalities were recorded.

Summary and Conclusions

The data for this survey of immobilization of the Cervidae were drawn from the literature, data submitted by zoos and zoo veterinarians, and from our own records.

We believe that it would be useful for veterinarians and cervid biologists to agree upon a standard set of data items to be collected as animals are immobilized. This would allow pooling and comparisons of records to detect significant trends such as sex, seasonal, excitement, and genetic effects. The data items which we believe are a necessary minimum are: ambient temperature, purpose of anesthesia, age (estimated if necessary as young, juvenile, or adult), body weight (taken after immobilization if possible), sex, state of animal (calm, active, excited, chased—with duration of chase prior to drug administration), drugs and dosages, site of administration, time of administration using a 24 hour clock, time when the animal goes down (induction time), additional drugs given, name, dose, and time of antagonist, time the animal rises to

Table 22. Sex, age, and mean drug dosages used to immobilize 52 Rocky Mountain elk

Age-class	N	M99 (mg)	Mean induction time (min)	M50–50 (mg)	Mean reversal time (min)
Adult F	18	6.5(5–7)*	21(10–35)	13(10–14)	1.1 (0.7–4.0)
Yearling F	16	4(3–7)	14(3–28)	7.9(4–14)	1.6 (0.5–11)
Yearling M	18	4.7(3–8)	12.6(6–39)	8.3(4–10)	1.1 (0.5–2)

*Range in parentheses. Data are from Coggins, 1975.

Table 23. Average induction times for groups of deer successfully immobilized with etorphine hydrochloride

Category	*N*	*Induction time (min:sec.)** *Minimum*	*Maximum*	*Mean*
Free-ranging	14	1:10	4:20	2:24
Captive, hand inj.	15	0:50	20:45	4:55
Captive, dart inj.	12	5:00	18:00	10:05

*Time in minutes and seconds to either recumbency or hand capture.
Data from Woolf, 1970.

ANTHESTHIA RECORD WORKSHEET FOR N.Z.P. ANIMAL HEALTH

SPECIES____/13 ACC. NUMBER____/6 DATE__/__/__/8 (MM DD YY)

AGE (Yrs)____/2 (NB,NN,J,AD,AG,U) Weight (Kg)____/4 Actual or Estimate____/1

SEX____/1 (M,F,U) ANIMAL/GROUP____/2 (PR,H_AV, C_RP,RD,MR,PP,MT,ED,IS)

PURPOSE OF ANESTHESIA ____/2 (MG,TN,RX,SR,PM,D?,CS,ES,EU) STATUS____/1 (D,C,A,E.S)

HEALTH____/1 (N,D,T,U) FASTED____/1(Y,N,U)

DRUG I____/3 (M99,CAR,KET,SER,ROM,ACE,PRO,VAL,SC,744,H,N) DOSE I (mg) ____/4

DRUG II____/3 Dose II(mg)____/4 Route____/1 (D,P,S,B,V,O,T,A) RESULTS____/1 (N,P,F,S,E)

DRUG SUPPLEMENT____/3 DOSE SUPPLEMENT (mg)____/4 ROUTE____/1

ANTAGONIST (mg)____/5 (M 00.0 mg)

COMPLICATIONS____/4 (SAlivation, COnvulsion, Death, SHock, Vomit, Aspriation, CYanosis, Respir/Arrest, ≥____Temp ≤____Temp ≥____HR, ≤____HR Cardic/Arrest, ≥____Respir ≤____Respir, Multiple-see-comments-)

TEMP (C)____/4 HEART RATE/MIN____/3 RESPIRATION RATE/MIN____/3

COMMENTS____/150

METHOD OF DRUG ADMINISTRATION

TIME OF ADMINISTRATION

INITIAL SIGN OF DRUG EFFECT

ONSET OF RESTRAINT/ANESTHESIA

END OF RESTRAINT/ANESTHESIA

TIME OF ANTAGONIST (name/mgs)

ANIMAL NORMAL AGAIN

CONCURRENT DRUG GIVEN

SIGNED DATE

SI-3425
1-4-82

Figure 4. A sample anesthesia record work sheet used by the N.Z.P. Animal Health Department.

feet, complications, body temperature, and overall impression of the effectiveness of the event. A useful excitement scale is that of Franzmann and Thorne (1970) and Franzmann et al. (1975). A data form of the type used at the National Zoological Park may serve as an example (Figure 4).

We may expect continuing improvements in techniques of chemical immobilization of the Cervidae (and other wild animals) with the development and testing of an antagonist for xylazine (yohimbine), the expanded availability and use of new water soluble potent derivatives of the opioid fentanyl (carfentanyl), the development and testing of water soluble benzodiazepine tranquilizers related to diazepam (midazolam), and the preparation for testing of the separate enantiomers of ketamine, currently available only as the racemic mixture.

Literature Cited

Alford, B.T., R.L. Burkhart, L., and W.P. Johnson.
1974. Etorphine and diprenorphine as immobilizing and reversing agents in captive and free-ranging mammals. *Journal American Veterinary Medical Association,* 154:701–705.

Allen, T.J.
1970. Immobilization of white-tailed deer with succinylcholine chloride and hyaluronidase. *Journal of Wildlife Management,* 34:207–209.

Amstrup, S.C., and T.B. Segerstrom
1981. Immobilizing free-ranging pronghorns with powdered succinylcholine chloride. *Journal of Wildlife Management,* 45:741–745.

Anderson, C.F.
1961. Anesthetizing deer by arrow. *Journal of Wildlife Management,* 25:202–203.

Autenrieth, R.E., G.L. Copeland, and T.D. Reynolds
1981. Capturing pronghorn using a helicopter and etorphine hydrochloride. *Wildlife Society Bulletin,* 9:314–319.

Ballard, W.B., and R.W. Tobey
1981. Decreased calf production of moose immobilized with anectine administered from helicopter. *Wildlife Society Bulletin,* 9:207–209.

Barnard, S.M., and J.S. Dobbs
1980. A handmade blowgun dart: its preparation and application in a zoological park. *Journal of the American Veterinary Medical Association,* 177:955–953.

Bauditz, R.
1972. Sedation, immobilization and anesthesia with Rompun in captive and free-living wild animals. *Veterinary Medical Review,* 3:204–226.

Beck, C.C.
1972. Chemical restraint of exotic species. *Journal of Zoo Animal Medicine,* 3:3–8.

Beck, C.C.
1974. Ketamine anesthesia. *Journal of Zoo Animal Medicine*, 5:6.

Behrend, D.F.
1965. Notes on field immobilization of white-tailed deer with nicotine. *Journal of Wildlife Management*, 29:889–890.

Bergerud, A.T., A. Butt, H.L. Russell, and H. Whalen
1964. Immobilization of Newfoundland caribou and moose with succinylcholine chloride and cap-chur equipment. *Journal of Wildlife Management*, 28:49–53.

Boyd, R.J.
1962. Succinylcholine chloride for immobilization of Colorado mule deer. *Journal of Wildlife Management*, 26:332–333.

Brockman, R.P.
1981. Effect of xylazine on plasma glucose, glucagon, and insulin concentrations in sheep. *Research Veterinary Science*, 30:383–384.

Bush, M., and C.W. Gray
1972. Sterilization of projectile syringes. *Journal of the American Veterinary Medical Association*, 161:672–673.

Bush, M.
1982. Chemical immobilization. In *Biology and management of an extinct species, Pere David's deer*. Edited by B. Beck and C. Wemmer, pp. 36-38. Park Ridge, New Jersey: Noyes Publications.

Causey, K., J.E. Kennamer, J. Logan, and J.J. Chapman, Jr.
1978. Bowhunting white-tailed deer with succinylcholine chloride-treated arrows. *Wildlife Society Bulletin*, 6:142–145.

Chalmers, G.A., and M.W. Barrett
1977. Capture myopathy in pronghorns in Alberta, Canada. *Journal of the American Veterinary Medical Association*, 171:918–923.

Channing, C.P., S. Fowler, B. Engel, and K. Vitek
1977. Failure of daily injections of ketamine HCL to adversely alter menstrual cycle length, blood estrogen, and progesterone levels in the Rhesus monkey. *Proceedings of the Society of Experimental Biology and Medicine*, 155:615–619.

Chapman, D.
1973. Immobilon and deer. *Veterinary Record*, 92:711.

Clarke, K.W., and L.W. Hall
1969. Xylazine—a new sedative for horses and cattle. *Veterinary Record*, 85:512–517.

Coggins, V.L.
1975. Immobilization of Rocky Mountain elk with M99. *Journal of Wildlife Management*, 39:814–816.

Cook, C.S., and K.K. Kane
1980. Apparent suppression of gastrointestinal motility due to xylazine–a comparative study. *Journal of Zoo Animal Medicine*, 11:46–48.

Corssen, G., and E.F. Domino
1966. Dissociative anesthesia: further pharmacologic studies and first clinical experience with phencyclidine derivative CI-581. *Anesthesia and Analgesia*, 45:29–40.

Corssen, G., M. Miyasaka, and E.F. Domino
1968. Changing concepts in pain control during surgery: dissociative anesthesia with CI-581: a progress report. *Anesthesia and Analgesia*, 47:746–759.

Cowan, I. Mct., A.J. Wood, and H.C. Nordan
1962. Studies in the tranquilization and immobilization of deer (*Odocoileus*). *Canadian Journal of Comparative Medicine*, 26:57–61.

Crockford, J.A., F.A. Hayes, J.H. Jenkins, and S.D. Feurt
1957a. Nicotine salicylate for capturing deer. *Journal of Wildlife Management*, 21:213–220.

1957b. Field application of nicotine salicylate for capturing deer. *Transactions of the North American Wildlife Conference*, 22:579.

Custer, R., L. Kramer, S. Kennedy, and M. Bush
1977. Hematologic effects of xylazine when used for restraint of Bactrian camels. *Journal American Veterinary Medical Association*, 171:899–901.

Day, J.
1969. Drug use for capturing and restraining animals. *Abstract of the Arizona Game and Fish Department*, 4.

Day, G.I., R.F. Dyson, and F.H. Landeen
1965. A portable resuscitator for use on large game animals. *Journal of Wildlife Management*, 29:511–515.

Dean, R., W.W. Hines, and D.C. Church
1973. Immobilizing free-ranging and captive deer with phencyclidine hydrochloride. *Journal of Wildlife Management*, 37:82–86.

Denney, R.N., and R.B. Gill
1970. Annotated bibliography on mammal immobilization with drugs. *Colorado Division of Game, Fish and Parks Special Report* 15. 27 pp.

Denney, R.N.
1965. Immobilization and tranquilization studies on Colorado deer and elk. *Colorado Game, Fish and Parks Department Job Completion Report, W-38-R-18*. Part I:5–22.

DeVos, V.
1978. Immobilization of free-ranging wild animals using a new drug. *Veterinary Record*, 103:64–68.

Done, S.H., P. Lees, O. Dansie, and L.W. Watkins
1975. Sedation and restraint of fallow deer with diazepam. *British Veterinary Journal*, 131:545–548.

Ericksen, E.
1968. Sedation and anesthesia of zoo animals. *Nordisk Veterinaermedicin*, 20:657–679.

Eriksen, E.
1978. Medicamentous immobilization and capture of wild animals and deer. Copenhagen, Denmark. *Kongelige*

Veterinaer. og Landbohojskole. 198 pp. ISBN 87-871-5136-7.

Fletcher, J.
1974. Hypersensitivity of an isolated population of red deer (*Cervus elaphus*) to xylazine. *Veterinary Record*, 94:85–86.

Fletcher, K.C.
1980. Needle reinforcement of butane powered darts. *Journal of Zoo Animal Medicine*, 11:44–46.

Flook, D.R., J.R. Robertson, O.R. Hermanrude, and H.K. Buechner
1962. Succinylcholine chloride for immobilization of North American elk. *Journal of Wildlife Management*, 26:334–336.

Fowler, M.E.
1978a. *Restraint and handling of wild and domestic animals*. Ames, Iowa: Iowa State University Press.

Fowler, M.E. Editor-in-chief
1978b. *Zoo and wild animal medicine*. Philadelphia, Pa.: W. B. Saunders Company.

Franzmann, A.W., and E.T. Thorne
1970. Physiologic values in wild bighorn sheep (*Ovis canadensis canadensis*) at capture, after handling, and after captivity. *Journal American Veterinary Medical Association*, 157:647–650.

Franzmann, A.W. and P.D. Arneson
1974. Immobilization of Alaskan moose. *Journal of Zoo Animal Medicine*, 5:26–32.

Franzmann, A.W., A. Flynn, and P.D. Arneson
1975. Serum corticoid levels relative to handling stress in Alaskan moose. *Canadian Journal of Zoology*, 53:1424–1426.

Franzmann, A.W., and R.E. LeResche
1978. Alaskan moose blood studies with emphasis on condition evaluation. *Journal of Wildlife Management*, 42:334–351.

Fuert, S.D., J.H. Jenkins, F.A. Hayes, and J.A. Crockford
1958. Pharmacology and Toxicology of nicotine with special reference to species variation. *Science*, 127:1054–1058.

Fuller, T.K., and L.B. Keith
1981. Immobilization of Woodland caribou with etorphine. *Journal of Wildlife Management*, 45:745–748.

Gasaway, LW. C., A.W. Franzmann, and J.B. Faro
1978. Immobilizing Moose with a mixture of etorphine and xylazine hydrochloride. *Journal of Wildlife Management*, 42:686–690.

Gauckler, A. and M. Kraus
1970. Zur Immobilisierung von Wildwiederkauern mit xylazine (Bay BA 1470). *Zoologische Garten*, 38:37–46.

Geiger, G.
1976. Combination of Rompun (xylazine) and Valium (diazepam) for the immobilization of fallow deer. *Praktische Tierarzt*, 57:830–833.

Gilman, A.G., L.S. Goodman, and A. Gilman (eds)
1980. *The pharmacological basis of therapeutics*. New York: Macmillan Publishing Company.

Goltenboth, R. and H.G. Klos
1970. Application of Rompun for the immobilization of zoo animals. *Berliner Muenchener Tierarztliche Wochenschrift*, 83:147–151.

Gray, C.W., M. Bush, and C.C. Beck
1974. Clinical experience using CI-744 in chemical restraint and anesthesia of exotic specimens. *Journal of Zoo Animal Medicine*, 5:12–21.

Green, H.
1963. New technique for using the Cap-Chur gun. *Journal of Wildlife Management*, 27:292–296.

Guinness, F., G.A. Lincoln, and R.V. Short
1971. The reproductive cycle of the female red deer, *Cervus elaphus* L. *Journal of Reproduction and Fertility*, 27:427–438.

Gutierrez, R.J., R.A. Howard, Jr., and D.J. Decker
1979. 'In My Opinion"—hunting ethics, self-limitation, and the role of succinylcholine chloride in bowhunting. *Wildlife Society Bulletin*, 7:170–172.

Haigh, J.C.
1979. Hyaluronidase as an adjunct in an immobilizing mixture for moose. *Journal of the American Veterinary Medical Association*, 175:916–917.

Haigh, J.C., R.R. Stewart, G. Wobeser, and P.S. MacWilliams
1977a. Capture myopathy in moose. *Journal of the American Veterinary Medical Association*, 171:924–926.

Haigh, J.C., R. Stewart, R. Frokjer, and T. Hauge
1977b. Capture of moose with fentanyl and xylazine. *Journal of Zoo Animal Medicine* , 8(3):22-29.

Hall, T.C., E.B. Taft, W.H. Baker, and J.C. Aub
1953. A preliminary report on the use of flaxedil to produce paralysis in the white-tailed deer. *Journal of Wildlife Management*, 17:516–520.

Hamilton, R.
No date. Capture of deer in Indiana with nicotine salicylate. *Research Report of the Indiana Department of Conservation*.

Harper, J.A.
1965. Immobilization of Roosevelt elk by succinylcholine chloride. *Journal of Wildlife Management*, 29:339–345.

Harrington, R.
1974. Immobilon-Rompun in deer. *Veterinary Record*, 94:362.

Harthoorn, A.M.
1980.   Exercise as a necessary preliminary to disturbance, restraint or handling of captive wild animals. *Communication—Pretoria.*

Harthoorn, A.M.
1965.   Application of pharmacological and physiological principles in restraint of wild animals. *Wildlife Monograph, No. 14.* 78 pp.

Harthoorn, A.M., and K. Van der Walt
1974.   Physiological aspects of forced exercise in wild ungulates with special reference to (so-called) overstraining disease. 1. Acid-base balance and pO^2 levels in Blesbok (*Damaliscus dorcas phillipsi*). *Journal of the South African Wildlife Management Association,* 4:25–28.

Harthoorn, A.M., and E. Young
1974.   A relationship between acid-base balance and capture myopathy in zebra (*Equus burchelli*) and an apparent therapy. *Veterinary Record,* 95:337–342.

Harthoorn, A.M.
1976.   *The Chemical Capture of Animals.* London: Bailliere Tindall.

Harthoorn, A.M.
1977.   Problems relating to capture. *Animal Regulation Studies,* 1:23–46.

Hawkins, R.E., D.C. Autry, and W.D. Klimstra
1967.   Comparison of methods used to capture white-tailed deer. *Journal of Wildlife Management,* 31:460–464.

Hawkins, R.E., L.D. Martoglio, and G.F. Montgomery
1968.   Cannon-netting deer. *Journal of Wildlife Management,* 32:191–195.

Hawkins, R.E., W.D. Klimstra, L.W. Lamely, and D.C. Autry
1979.   A new remote capture method for free-ranging deer. *Journal of Mammalogy,* 51:392–394.

Heck, H., and E. Rivenburg
1972.   Dosages of M99 used on hoofed mammals at Catskill Game Farm. *Zoologische Garten N.F.,* 42:282–287.

Hebert, D.M., and I. McT. Cowan
1971.   White muscle disease in the mountain goat. *Journal of Wildlife Management,* 35:752–756.

Hebert, D. M., and R.J. McFetridge
1982.   *Chemical immobilization of North American game animals.* Edmonton, Alberta: Alberta Energy and Natural Resources.

Heuschele, W.P.
1960.   Immobilization of captive wild animals with succinyl choline using the projectile type syringe. *International Zoo Yearbook,* 2:308-309.

Hime, J.M. and D.M. Jones
1970.   The use if xylazine in captive wild animals. *International Symposium on Diseases of Zoo Animals,* 11:2–5.

Hofmeyr, J.W.
1977.   The introduction of R 33799 in game immobilization procedures. Ms. 8pp.

Houston, D.B.
1969.   Immobilization of the Shiras moose. *Journal of Wildlife Management,* 33:534–537.

Howe, D.L.
1966.   Investigation of tranquilizing, anesthetizing and immobilizing drugs when used on game animals. *Wyoming Job Completion Report FW-3-R-13,* WP9-J3W. 15pp.

Hubbell, G.L.
1965.   Capture and restraint of zoo animals. *Journal American Veterinary Medical Association,* 147:1044–1048.

Hugie, R.D.
1977.   Use of chemical restraints in handling wildlife. *Parks,* 2:19–22.

Jacobsen, N.K., S.P. Armstrong, and A.N. Moen
1976.   Seasonal variation in succinylcholine immobilization of captive white-tailed deer. *Journal of Wildlife Management,* 40:447–453.

Jarofke, D.
1980.   Cervidae. In *Handbook of Zoo Medicine.* Edited by H.G. Klös, and E. M. Lang, pp. 233-247. New York: Van Nostrand Reinhold Company.

Jessup, D.A., J.W. Foster, and W.E. Clark
1982.   An electronic means of immobilizing deer: Taser. *California Veterinarian,* 36(1):31-34.

Jenkins, J.G., F.A. Hayes, S.D. Feurt, and J.A.. Crockford
1961.   A new method for the live capture of canines with applications to rabies control. *American Journal of Public Health,* 51:902–908.

Jenkins, J.H., S.D. Feurt, F.A. Hayes, and J.A. Crockford
1955.   A preliminary report on the use of drugs for capturing deer. *Proceedings of the Southeast Game and Fish Commission,* 9:41.

Jewell, P.A., and V.P.W. Lowe
1965.   A trial with the projectile-syringe rifle to capture wild red deer on Rhum. *Journal of Zoology,* 146:272–277.

Jewell, P.A., P. Keen, and E.H. Tong
1965.   The use of the muscle relaxant suxethonium to immobilize captive animals with the projectile syringe rifle. *Journal of Zoology,* 146:263–271.

Jones, D.M.
1972.   The use of drugs for immobilization, capture and translocation of non-domestic animals. *Veterinary Annual,* 13:320–351.

Jones, D.M.
1976.   An assessment of weapons and projectile syringes used for capturing mammals. *Veterinary Record,* 99:250–253.

Kilde, A.M., and L.V. Klein
1973. Restraint of two fallow deer with xylazine. *Journal of Zoo Animal Medicine*, 4:21.

King, J.M., and H. Klingel
1965. The use of the oripavine derivative M99 for the restraint of equine animals and its antagonism with the related compound M285. *Research Veterinary Science*, 6:447.

Kitchen, H.
1966. Handling and restraint in deer and other wild animals. *Laboratory Animal Digest*, 4:3–7.

Kloppel, G.
1969. Zur Immobilisation von Zoo- und Wildtieren. *Kleintier-Praxis*, 14:203–207.

Klös, H.G. and E.M. Lang
1980. *Handbook of Zoo Medicine*. New York: Van Nostrand Reinhold Company.

Knight, A.P.
1980. Xylazine. *Journal of thw American Veterinary Medical Association*, 176:454–455.

Kocan, A.A., T.R. Thedford, B.L. Glenn, M.G. Shaw, and R.W. Wood
1980. Myopathy associated with immobilization in captive white-tailed deer. *Journal of the American Veterinary Medical Association*, 177:879–881.

Laisher,
1972. Anesthesia of reindeer. *Veterinariya*, 5:76–78.

Lanphear, P.R.
1963. Tranquilization and immobilization of wild animals. *Journal of the American Veterinary Medical Association*, 142:1126–1129.

LeResche, R.E., U.S. Seal, P.D. Karns, and A.W. Franzmann
1974. A review of blood chemistry of moose and other cervidae, with emphasis on nutritional assessment. *Nature Canada*, Ottawa, 101:263–290.

Lewis, R.J., G.A. Chalmers, M.W. Barrett, and R. Bhatnagar
1977. Capture myopathy in elk in Alberta, Canada: A report of three cases. *Journal of the American Veterinary Medical Association*, 171:927–932.

Lindau, K.H., and M. Gorgas
1969. Versuche mit Bay VA 1470. *Intnational Symposium on the Diseases of Zoo Animals*. 11:135–137.

Liscinsky, S.A., G.P. Howard and R.B. Waldeisen
1969. A new device for injecting powdered drugs. *Journal of Wildlife Management*, 33:1037–1038.

Lovett, J.W., and E.P. Hill
1977. A transmitter syringe for recovery of immobilized deer. *Journal of Wildlife Management*, 41:313–315.

Lynch, G.M. and Hanson, J.A.
1981. Use of etorphine to immobilize moose. *Journal of Wildlife Management*, 45:981–985.

Mautz, W.W., R.P. Davison, D.E. Boardman, and H. Silver
1980. Blood serum analysis of chemically and physically restrained white-tailed deer. *Journal of Wildlife Management*, 44:343–351.

McClain, D.A. and C.C. Hug
1980. Intravenous fentanyl kinetics. *Clinical Pharmacology and Therapeutics*, 28:106–114.

McKean, T.A., and B. Magonigle
1978. The effect of immobilization with M-99 plus acepromazine on physiological parameters of domestic goats. *Journal of Wildlife Management*, 42:176–179.

Meltzer, H.Y., D. Stanisic, M. Simonovic, and V.S. Fang
1978. Ketamine as an anesthetic for obtaining plasma for rat prolactin assays. *Proceedings of the Society for Experimental Biology and Medicine*, 159:12–15.

Miller, F.L.
1968. Immobilization of free-ranging black-tailed deer with succinylcholine chloride. *Journal of Wildlife Management*, 32:195–197.

Montgomery, G.G.
1961. A modification of the nicotine dart capture method. *Journal of Wildlife Management*, 25:101–102.

Morley, J.E.
1981. The endocrinology of the opiates and opioid peptides. *Metabolism*, 30:195–209.

Moss, M.S., and E.G.C. Clarke
1977. A review of drug "clearance times" in racehorses. *Equine Veterinary Journal*, 9:53–56.

Murray, R.E.
1965. Tranquilizing techniques for capturing deer. *Proceedings of the 15th Annual Conference of the Southeast Association of Game Fish Commission*, pp.4–15.

Nair, N.R.
1977. The art of scientific immobilisation of animals. *Indian Forester*, 103:64–79.

Nielsen, L.
1982. *Chemical immobilization in urban animal control work*. Milwaukee, Wisconsin: Wisconsin Humane Society, Inc.

Nielsen, L., J.C. Haigh, and M.E. Fowler. Editors
1982. *Chemical immobilization of North American wildlife*. Milwaukee, Wisconsin: Wisconsin Humane Society, Inc.

Nielson, A.E. and W.M. Shaw
1967. A helicopter dart technique for capturing moose. *Proceedings of the Western Association of Game and Fish Commission*, 47:182–199.

Nordan, H.C., A.J. Wood, and I.McT. Cowan
1962. Further studies on the immobilization of deer with succinylcholine. *Canadian Journal of Comparative Medicine and Veterinary Science*, 26:246–248.

Novack, G.D., J.L. Bullock, and J.H. Eisele
1978.   Fentanyl: Cumulative effects and development of short-term tolerance. *Neuropharmacology,* 17:77–82.

O'Neil, A., A.P. Winnie, M.E. Zadigian, and V.J. Collins
1972.   Premedication for ketamine anesthesia: Phase 1: The "classic" drugs. *Anesthetics and Analgesics Current Research,* 51:475–482.

Palmer, D.T., D.A. Andrews, R.O. Winters, and J.W. Francis
1980.   Removal techniques to control an enclosed deer herd. *Wildlife Society Bulletin,* 8:29–33.

Pearson, H.A., A.D. Smith, and P.J. Urness
1963.   Effects of succinylcholine chloride on mule deer. *Journal of Wildlife Management,* 27:297–299.

Pedersen, R.J., and A.A. Pedersen
1975.   Blood chemistry and hematology of elk. *Journal of Wildlife Management,* 39:617–620.

Pertz, C., and J.P. Sundberg
1978.   Malignant hyperthermia induced by etorphine and xylazine in a fallow deer. *Journal American Veterinary Medical Association,* 173:1243.

Pimlott, D.G., and LW.J. Carberry
1958.   North American moose transplantations and handling techniques. *Journal of Wildlife Management,* 22:51–62.

Pistey, W.R., and J.F. Wright
1961.   The immobilization of captive wild animals with succinylcholine. *Canadian Journal of Comparative Medicine and Veterinary Science,* 25:59–68.

Pistey, W.R., and J.R. Wright
1959.   Immobilisation and capture of wild animals with succinylcholine. *Veterinary Medicine,* 54:446-449.

Plotka, E.D., U.S. Seal, L.J. Verme, and J.J. Ozoga
1982.   Reproductive steroids in the white-tailed deer (*Odocoileus virginianus borealis*). IV. Origin of progesterone during pregnancy. *Biology of Reproduction,* 26:258-262.

1983.   The adrenal gland in white-tailed deer: a significant source of progesterone. *Journal of Wildlife Management,* 47:38-44.

Presidente, P.J.A., J.H. Lumsden, D.R. Presnell, W.A. Rapley, and B.M. McCraw
1973.   Combination of etorphine and xylazine in captive white-tailed deer: II. Effects on hematologic, serum biochemical and blood gas values. *Journal of Wildlife Disease,* 9:342–348.

Presnell, K.R., P.J.S. Presidente, and W.A. Rapley
1973.   Combination of etorphine and xylazine in captive white-tailed deer: I. Sedative and immobilization properties. *Journal of Wildlife Disease,* 9:236–341.

Pusateri, F.M., C.P. Hibler, and T.M. Pojar
1982.   Oral administration of diazepam and promazine hydrochloride to immobilize pronghorn. *Journal of Wildlife Disease,* 18:9–16.

Ratcliffe, H.L.
1962.   Diazepam (tranimal) as a tranquilizer for zoo animals. *Report of the Penrose Research Laboratory, Zoological Society of Philadelphia,* pp. 10–13.

Rausch, R.A., and R.W. Ritcey
1961.   Narcosis of moose with nicotine. *Journal of Wildlife Management,* 25:326–328.

Richter, A.G.
1977.   Ketamine-xylazine immobilization of a mule deer. *Journal of the American Veterinary Medicine Association,* 171(9):987.

Robinson, P.T., and C.J. Sedgwick
1974.   Comment on M99 insert's drug dosage information. *Journal of Zoo Animal Medicine,* 6:7.

Rosen, M.N. and A.I. Bischoff
1952.   The relation of hematology to condition in California deer. *Transactions of the North American Wildlife Conference,* 17:482–495.

Roughton, R.D.
1975.   Xylazine as an immobilizing agent for captive white-tailed deer. *Journal of the American Veterinary Medical Association,* 167:574–576.

Roussel, Y.E., and R. Patenaude
1975.   Some physiological effects of M99 etorphine on immobilized free-ranging moose. *Journal of Wildlife Management,* 39:634–636.

Roussel, Y.E., and C. Pichette
1974.   Comparison of techniques used to restrain and mark moose. *Journal of Wildlife Management,* 38:783–788.

Sadove, M.S., S. Hatano, B. Zahed, T. Redlin, P. Arastounejad, and R. Roman
1971.   Clinical study of droperidol in the prevention of the side effects of ketamine anesthesia: A preliminary report. *Anesthetics and Analgesics Current Research,* 50:388–393.

Sauer, B.W., H.A. Gorman, and R.J. Boyd
1969.   A new technique for restraining mule deer. *Journal of the American Veterinary Medical Association,* 155:1080–1084.

Savarie, P.J.
1976.   Pharmacological review of chemicals used for the capture of animals. *Proceedings of the Vertebrate Pest Control Conference,* 7:178–184.

Scanlon, P.F.
1973.   Observations on the immobilization of fallow deer with powdered succinylcholine chloride injected by dart. *Veterinary Record,* 93:396–398.

Scanlon, P.F., R.E. Mirachi, and J.A. Wesson, III
1977.   Aggression toward immobilized white-tailed deer by other deer and elk. *Wildlife Society Bulletin,* 5:193–194.

Schultze, H., J. Werner, H. Breustedt
1976.   Unsatisfactory results with xylazine (Rompun) for the immobilization of roe deer. *Praktische Tierarzt,* 57:833–835.

Schmidl, J.A.
1974. Experimental use of Rompun in the exotic species. *Journal of Zoo Animal Medicine,* 5:8–10.

Seal, U.S., J.J. Ozoga, A.W. Erickson, and L.F. Verme
1972. Effects of immobilization on blood analyses of white-tailed deer. *Journal of Wildlife Management,* 36:1034–1040.

Seal, U.S., and A.W. Erickson
1969. Hematology, blood chemistry and protein polymorphisms in the white-tailed deer (*Odocoileus virginianus*). *Comparative Biochemistry and Physiology,* 30:695–713.

Seal, U.S., and A.W. Erickson
1969. Immobilization of carnivora and other mammals with phencyclidine and promazine. *Federation Proceedings,* 28:1410–1419.

Seal, U.S., A.W. Erickson, and J.G. Mayo
1970. Drug immobilisation of the Carnivora. *International Zoo Yearbook,* 10:157–170.

Seal, U.S., M.E. Nelson, L.D. Mech, and R.L. Hoskinson
1978. Metabolic indicators of habitat differences in four Minnesota deer populations. *Journal of Wildlife Management,* 42:746–754.

Seal, U.S. and R.L. Hoskinson
1978. Metabolic indicators of habitat condition and capture stress in pronghorns. *Journal of Wildlife Management,* 42:755-763.

Seal, U.S., L.J. Verme, and J.J. Ozoga
1981. Physiologic values. In *Diseases and parasites of white-tailed deer,* edited by W.R. Davidson, pp 23–26. Tallahassee, Florida: Tall timbers Research Station.

Seal, U.S., L.J. Verme, J.J. Ozoga, and E.D. Plotka
1983. Metabolic and endocrine responses of deer to increasing population density. *Journal of Wildlife Management,* 47.

Short, C.E., and J.M. King
1963. The design of a crossbow for immobilization of wild animals. *Veterinary Record,* 76:628–630.

Short, C.E.
1969. Anesthesia, sedation and chemical restraint in wild and domestic animals. *Bulletin of the Wildlife Disease Association,* 5:307–310.

Siglin, R.J.
1965. Movements and capture techniques. A literature review of mule deer. *Colorado Department of Game, Fish and Parks and Colorado Cooperative Wildlife Research Unit Special Report No. 4,* 39pp.

Sinha, S.K.
1976. Drug immobilization trials on free-living Indian wild animals. *Cheetal,* 17:29–54.

Skjonsberg, T., and A. Westhaver
1978. A study in the chemical immobilization of animals with suggestions for application in Canada's national parks. *Unpublished Working Paper,* 82 pp.

Smeller, J., M. Bush, and U.S. Seal
1976. Observations on immobilization of Pere David's deer. *Journal American Veterinary Medical Association,* 169:890–893.

Smith, C.A., and A.W. Franzmann
1979. Productivity and physiology of Yakutat Forelands moose. *Alaska Department of Fish and Game. Pittman-Robertson Final Report* W-17-10 and W-17-11. 18 pp.

Smuts, G.L.
1973. Xylazine hydrochloride (Rompun) and the new retractable-barbed dart ("drop-out" dart) for the capture of some nervous and aggressive antelope species. *Koedoe,* 16:159–173.

Sutherland, C., and J. Hodgkin
1974. Tranquilizing deer. *Veterinary Record,* 95:71.

Taber, R.D. and I. McT. Cowan
1969. Capturing and marking wild animals. In *Wildlife Management Techniques,* edited by R.H. Giles, pp. 277–318. Washington, D.C.: The Wildlife Society.

Talbot, L.M., and H.F. Lamprey
1961. Immobilization of free-ranging East African ungulates with succinylcholine chloride. *Journal of Wildlife Management,* 25:303–310.

Tavernor, W.D.
1971. Muscle relaxants. In *Textbook of Veterinary Anesthesia,* edited by L.R. Soma, pp. 111-120. Baltimore, Maryland: The Williams and Wilkins Company.

Thomas, J.W., R.M. Robinson, and R.G. Marburger
1967. Diazepam in the capture and handling of cervids. *Journal of Wildlife Management,* 31:686–692.

Thomas, J.W., and R.G. Marburger
1964. Mortality in deer shot in the thoracic area with the Cap-Chur gun. *Journal of Wildlife Management,* 28:173–175.

Thomas, W.D.
1961. Chemical immobilization of wild animals. *Journal of the American Veterinary Medical Association,* 138:263–265.

Thurmon, J.C., D.R. Nelson, and J.O. Mozier
1972. A preliminary report on the sedative effect of Bay VA 1470 in elk (*Cervus c. canadensis*). *Journal of Zoo Animal Medicine,* 3:9–14.

Thurmon, J.C., D.R. Nelson, S.M. Hartsfield, and C.A. Rumore
1978. Effects of xylazine hydrochloride on urine of cattle. *Australian Veterinary Journal,* 54:178–180.

Trindle, B.D., and L.D. Lewis
1978. Methoxyflurane anesthesia in mule deer (*Odocoileus hemionus*) fawns. *Journal of Wildlife Diseases,* 14:519–522.

Wallach, J.D., R. Frueh, and M. Lentz
1967. The use of M-99 as an immobilizing and analgesic agent in captive wild animals. *Journal of the American Veterinary Medical Association,* 151:870–876.

Warren, R.J., N.L. Schauer, J.T. Jones, P.F. Scanlon, and R.L. Kirkpatrick
1979. A modified blow-gun syringe for remote injection of captive wildlife. *Journal of Wildlife Disease*, 15:537–541.

Weir, J.J., and J. Sanford
1969. Metabolism and excretion of promazine by the horse. *Journal of Pharmacology and Pharmaceutics*, 21:169–175.

Wesson, J.A. III, P.F. Scanlon, R.L. Kirkpatrick, and H.S. Mosby
1979a. Influence of the time of sampling after death on blood measurements of the white-tailed deer. *Canadian Journal of Zoology*, 57:777–926.

1979b. Influence of chemical immobilization and physical restraint on packed cell volume, total protein, glucose, and blood urea nitrogen in blood of white-tailed deer. *Canadian Journal of Zoology*, 57:756–767.

Wesson, J.A. III, P.F. Scanlon, R.L. Kirkpatrick, H.S. Mosby, and R.L. Butcher
1979c. Influence of chemical immobilization and physical restraint on steroid hormone levels in blood of white-tailed deer. *Canadian Journal of Zoology*, 57:768–776.

Wesson, J.A., P.F. Scanlon, R.E. Mirachi
1974. Immobilization of white-tailed deer with succinylcholine chloride: Success rate, reactions of deer and some physiological effects. *Proceedings of the 28th Annual Conference of the Southeast Association of Game and Fish Commission*, 28:500–506.

White, P.F., W.L. Way, and A.J. Trevor
1982. Ketamine - its pharmacology and therapeutic uses. *Anesthesiology*, 56:119-136.

Winters, W.D., T. Ferrar-Allado, C. Guzman-Flores, and M. Alcaraz
1972. The cataleptic state induced by ketamine: A review of the neuropharmacology of anesthesia. *Neuropharmacology*, 11:303–315.

Wobeser, G., J.E.C. Bellamy, B.G. Boysen, P.S. MacWilliams, and W. Runge
1976. Myopathy and myoglobinuria in a wild white-tailed deer. *Journal of the American Veterinary Medical Association*, 169:971–974.

Wolff, W.A., R.W. Davis, and W.V. Lumb
1965. Chloral hydrate-halothane-nitrous oxide anesthesia in deer. *Journal of the American Veterinary Medical Association*, 147:1099–1101.

Woolf, A.
1974. Recovery of M99 immobilized white-tailed deer and wapiti using low dosages of M50-50. *Journal of Zoo Animal Medicine*, 5:18.

Woolf, A.
1970. Immobilization of captive and free-ranging white-tailed deer (*Odocoileus virginianus*) with etorphine hydrochloride. *Journal of the American Veterinary Medical Association*, 157:636–640.

Woolf, A., H.R. Hays, W.B. Allen, Jr., and J. Swart
1973. Immobilization of wild ungulates with etorphine HCL. *Journal of Zoo Animal Medicine*, 4:16–19.

Woolf, A., and J.H. Swart
1970. Etorphine hydrochloride: anesthetic for surgery on an elk (*Cervus canadensis nelsoni*). *Journal of the American Veterinary Medical Association*, 157:641–642.

Wright, J.F.
1963. Chemical restraint of exotic animals in a disease regulatory program. *Canadian Journal of Comparative Medicine and Veterinary Science*, 27:13–16.

York, W., and K. Huggins
1972. Rompun (Bay VA 1470). *Journal of Zoo Animal Medicine*, 3:15–17.

York, W.
1975. Fentanyl citrate for wild animal capture. *Journal of Zoo Animal Medicine*, 6:14–15.

Young, P.L.
1979. The effect of xylazine on the body temperature of cattle. *Australian Veterinary Journal*, 55:442.

ERHARD UECKERMANN
Forschungsstelle für Jagdkunde und
Wildschadenverhütung des Landes
Nordrhein-Westfalen
Forsthaus Hardt,
5300 Bonn 3

Managing German Red Deer (*Cervus elaphus* L.) Populations

ABSTRACT

The Federal Republic of Germany has the second largest population of red deer in Europe, estimated at 85,000 animals and distributed in isolated pockets of varying size. While game was protected in medieval Europe it was not until 1898 that population management was first proposed by von Raesfeld. Current management of red deer evolved from his system of selective shooting ("Hege mit der Büchse") which was established in part as national game law in 1934. A year later game bag statistics were instituted to survey the cull. The objectives of management are the establishment of game in all suitable habitats, regulation of oversized populations, and qualitative enhancement of game through selective shooting. Hunting authorities operate on county and state levels, and the hunting territory (Revier) is the basic management unit. The operators of the hunting territory must submit population estimates and harvest plans to county authorities for approval. Trophy quality is a primary criterion for regulating age distribution of stags, but in both sexes body size, physical condition and health are factors which determine selective cull. Determination of density limits, population characteristics, habitat quality, and forest protection are discussed.

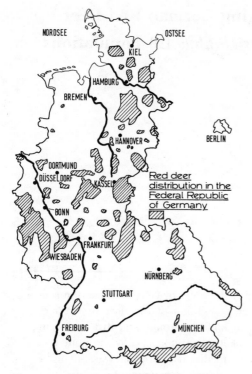

Figure 1. Distribution of red deer (cross-hatched areas) in the Federal Republic of Germany, 1980.

Table 1. Estimated red deer populations in European countries as of 1982 based on various sources (personal communication and in literature)

Country	Population
Scotland	270,000–280,000
Austria	180,000
Federal Republic of Germany	85,000
German Democratic Republic	60,000
Poland	60,000
Czechoslovakia	43,000
Hungary	38,000
France	36,000
Yugoslavia	30,000
Spain	25,000
Norway	25,000
Switzerland	20,000
Great Britain except Scotland	20,000
Bulgaria	13,000
Belgium	5,000
Denmark	4,000
The Netherlands	1,500
Sweden	1,500

Distribution and Population Size of Red Deer in Europe

The annual game bag has been recorded in Germany since 1935. The current population is estimated at 85,000 animals and is distributed in isolated pockets of varying size over most of the Federal Republic of Germany (Figure 1). In spite of its large human population (247 inhabitants/km²) and level of industrialization, the Federal Republic of Germany is second only to Austria in the density of large game mammals (Table 2). Table 1 gives information about the estimated totals of the populations in some European countries, and Figure 2 sketches the distribution of red deer in Europe.

Population information does not exist for all European countries, but the total European population is estimated at one million animals. The most abundant European game species is the roe deer with a population estimated at 6 million. The red deer holds second position followed by moose.

The annual harvest of red deer in the Federal Republic of Germany has gradually increased over the past 25 years (Figure 3). The highest cull was yielded in the hunting-year 1977/78, that is, 33,439 animals. That year there was also an attempt to reduce the overall populations, and apparently it succeeded, for the total harvest was decreased during subsequent years.

The red deer population of the FRG has probably reached its maximum since it now occupies all areas in which its existence is believed tolerable in the views of forestry and agriculture. For Europe altogether, however, some further increases in the red deer population are expected.

History of Red Deer in Germany

There is evidence that red deer occupied Europe since the turn of the Pliocene to the Pleistocene, i.e., about 1

Table 2. European countries with high densities of cloven-hoofed game

Country	Cloven-hoofed Game Density Per Km²	Human Inhabitants Per Km²
Austria	9.4	90
Federal Republic of Germany	6.7	247
German Democratic Republic	5.0	155
Czechoslovakia	3.0	118
Hungary	2.7	114

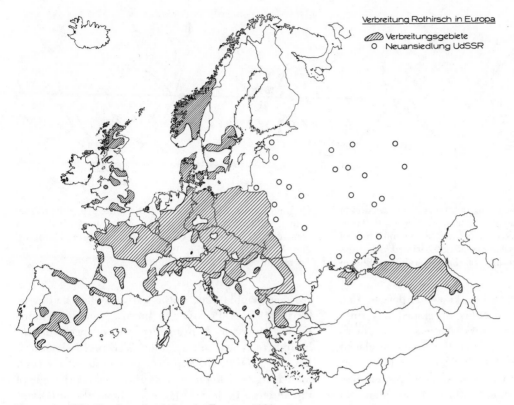

Verbreitung Rothirsch in Europa
⬚ Verbreitungsgebiete
O Neuansiedlung UdSSR

Figure 2.   Distribution of red deer in Europe, 1980.

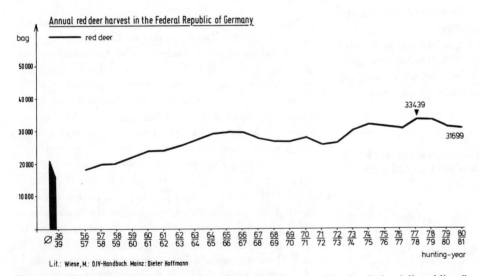

Figure 3.   Development of the number of red deer harvested in the Federal Republic of Germany from hunting-year 1956/57 to 1980/81.

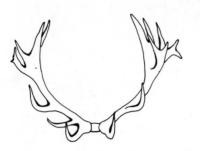  

Figure 4a.   Uneven twenty-four pointer of the collection of Schloss Moritzburg in Saxony, 18.86 kg according to Mandel, 1961. b.   Uneven sixty-six pointer of the collection of Schloss Moritzburg. c.   Antlers of the best red deer stag taken from a hunting-ground of the Federal Republic of Germany since 1945; weight of the antlers 9.13 kg, 225.9 points. (Based on photographs in "Das Waidwerk in Deutschland", edited by G. von Lettow-Vorbeck, Hamburg and Berlin: Paul Parey, 1963.)

million years ago. The earliest known antlers had no crowns, but displayed strongly developed bay tines and a crosswise terminal fork. Antlers with crowns have been found at least since the first interglacial period (Beninde, 1937). Antlers from several hundred years ago are smaller than those found in present day Germany. The best known medieval collections of antlers are in the castles of Moritzburg in Saxony (Figure 4a) and Erbach in the Odenwald. The maximum weight of red deer antlers of the 17th and 18th centuries was 18.86 kg, and the maximum number of points was 66 (Mandel, 1961) (Figure 4b). During the feudal period red deer populations were large, but game was managed without consideration of habitat damage. The revolution of 1848 temporarily gave hunting permission to everybody, and within a short time this brought about a far-reaching destruction of red deer populations. But as early as 1850 the largest German states, Prussia and Bavaria, only gave hunting permission for hunting territories of specified minimum size. The result was today's keepered-shoot-system (Reviersystem). Red deer populations have been increasing continuously since then, as has the size of the antlers (Table 3). Figure 4c shows the antlers of the best red deer stag taken in the FRG since 1945.

The Hunting Establishment, Management, and Regulation

The beginnings of red deer population management go back to von Raesfeld who in 1898 already advocated "Hege mit der Büchse" (selective shooting), in his monograph "Red Deer." Many of his considerations were established as national game-law on July 3, 1934. Universal regulations were established for a game harvest plan and hunting quotas for large game, except wild boar. In 1935 game-bag statistics were instituted to survey the cull.

After 1934 special hunting authorities were instated that operate on county and state levels. Population estimates and resulting harvest plans have to be submitted to the county authorities by the operators of each hunting-territory. Harvest plans are approved by a committee for the 12 months (1 April to 31 March) of the "hunting-year." The harvest plan for hinds is differentiated by age, and the plan for stags is differentiated by age and quality classes. The cull has to follow these plans, and is checked by the county authorities at trophy shows in which the antler and lower jaws of all killed stags must be exhibited. The aim of this harvest plan system was the establishment of game populations in all suitable habitats, the regulation of oversized populations, and the qualitative enhancement of the game through selective shooting.

In the early days harvest plans put too much em-

Table 3.   Best German red deer stags at the world hunting exhibitions of Budapest 1971 and Plovdiv 1981

	World Hunting Exhibition	Year Taken	Weight of Antlers in Kg	Score
Federal Republic of Germany	Budapest	1959	9.13	225.90
German Democratic Republic	Budapest	1969	9.86	225.85
Federal Republic of Germany	Plovdiv	1973	7.59	211.91
German Democratic Republic	Plovdiv	1979	11.00	232.60

Figure 5. Bark stripping damage to spruce done in summer.

Figure 6. Print of red deer stags fraying a tree, from Petrus de Crescentiis, 1583.

phasis on a rather unrestricted increase of game populations through "Hege" management (Raesfeld, 1898). After 1945 this led to the establishment of the new term "game population management" (Ueckermann 1956). Similar plans for a new system of population management in the DDR were published by Wagenknecht in 1965.

Management Measures

Management of red deer populations includes maintenance of optimum feeding conditions in hunting territories, and reduction of local populations to prevent damage to forest plantations.

Motives for Game Population Management

Twenty-nine percent of the FRG is covered by forest. These forests are classified as: 42.5% spruce and other conifer, 27% pine and larch, 23% beech and other deciduous trees, and 7.5% oak. Ninety-five percent of the forests are timber forests.

Spruce and beech are seldom intermingled with other trees. The intensive management of the forests

increases deer damage. Where the density of game is high, damage can be severe. Bark stripping is the most serious damage caused by red deer (Figure 5). Red deer strip the bark of standing trees in winter as well as in summer, and fungi then infect the wood and destroy it. In a spruce-forest with severe bark stripping damage a loss of about 10% of the forest is estimated. Bark stripping has been witnessed since the Middle Ages as a natural behavior of red deer. In the "Hausvaterbuch" (pater familias book) of Petrus de Crescentiis bark stripping is discussed as an emergency-food in winter and as sign aiding hunters to find red deer stags. The extent of bark stripping damage depends on the condition of the habitat and the density of game populations (Figure 6) (Ueckermann, 1960). Browsing damage is also caused by red deer—forest plants are eaten up to a height of about 1.5 m. Like bark damage, browsing occurs in summer and winter, and certain species of trees are preferred. Others like the birch are less attractive. Fraying damage caused by thrashing trees, boughs, or shrubs with the antlers is far less important. Petrus de Crescentiis in the 16th century also mentioned this, and used it as an indicator for estimating the size of the antlers from the height of the damage (Figure 7). Crop damage by red deer is also possible, but this is not a problem at present.

Red deer incur the most damage to trees in Europe, followed by moose, European bison, roe deer, sika deer, fallow deer, and mouflon. Control of red deer populations therefore is necessary, the aim being a tolerable density of game, which, calculated from the extent of bark stripping, should be 1.5 to 2.5 animals per 100 ha. Where improvement of feeding conditions

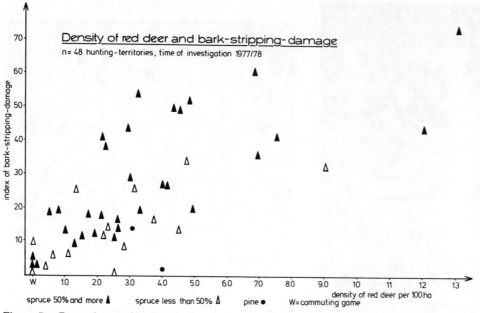

Figure 7. Dependency of bark stripping damage on the density of game in 48 hunting-territories in Northrhine-Westphalia.

is undertaken, up to 4 animals per 100 ha are tolerable.

Many species of large game suffer losses from vehicular traffic. Red deer are less affected: the casualty figure is only 2.7% relative to the annual bag (Ueckermann, 1964).

Red deer must also be managed for hunting interests, which in the FRG are strongly aimed at gaining mature trophies. That requires an age distribution corresponding to the pyramidal age distribution of normal populations. The cull is prescribed for sexes and age classes on this basis. The objective, also grounded in federal game-law, is to preserve red deer as a game species living in freedom in the FRG wherever habitat makes this tenable.

Game Population Management

Evaluation of Hunting-Territory Location

The density and value of red deer to the hunter are influenced by the habitat. A characterization of habitat has been useful long since for the determination of a tolerable density of game. The first proposal concerning red deer habitat can be found in Hartig (1877).

In 1951 a grading system for the quality of roe deer habitats was devised (Ueckermann, 1951). The amount of edge, the size of pastures, the quality of soil, and the composition of forests were evaluated, graded, and combined in a score ranging between 40 and 100. An optimal population density is suggested

according to the score of the habitat. When these scores were used for the evaluation of red deer habitat, and compared with the average weights of adult hinds, no significant correlation resulted. This can be explained by the fact that red deer populations in the FRG show genetic differences derived from hybridizations, and that many populations have been isolated for a long time (Ueckermann, 1955; Oloff, 1965; Kleymann and Bergmann, 1976).

Density of Game

A distinction is necessary between a population density that is economically tolerable, and a density that is of optimal biotic impact. A higher density of game is possible if economic considerations for forestry are ignored, and a certain amount of damage is allowed. The economically tolerable density of game is mainly determined by the extent of bark stripping damage (Figure 6). In the absence of supplemental feeding, a biotic density of 5 animals per 100 ha can be supported. If winter feeding is implemented, a maximum biotic density of 10 animals per 100 ha is possible. Intensive feeding throughout the year renders a density of >20 animals per 100 ha possible.

Economically tolerable game density is established for major districts by averaging kill data from areas within the district. The district is differentiated into central and peripheral areas in order to deal with differences in population density. Tolerable densities of game are fixed by state and county hunting au-

Table 4. Tolerable densities of game (red deer, fallow deer, and roe deer) proposed for habitats of differing quality in the Federal Republic of Germany (from Ueckermann, 1960)

Game Species	Habitat Quality	Habitat Evaluation	Tolerable Density of Game per 100 Ha	
			Economic	Biotic
Red Deer	Poor	40–55	1.5	—
	Average	56–70	2.0	—
	Good	>71	2.5	—
Fallow Deer	Poor	40–55	3	—
	Average	56–70	6	—
	Good	>71	10	—
Roe Deer	Poor	40–55	3	7
		46–50	4	8
		51–55	5	9
		56–60	6	10
	Average	61–65	7	11
		66–70	8	12
		71–75	9	13
	Good	76–80	10	14
		81–85	11	15

thorities and are considered within the framework of game harvest planning. Populations of other species of game are also considered in establishing the value (Table 4). The populations are settled up in the ratio of 1:1. Table 4 contains proposed tolerable densities of red deer, fallow deer, and roe deer (Ueckermann, 1960).

The desired density of game is related to the spring population size. Population estimates are made by the hunting tenants from counts at winter feeding stations or from track counts after fresh snowfall. Red deer populations often were underestimated in the past (Reulecke, 1980). Game keepers may have made intentional mistakes to evade orders for the reduction of their herds. There are also cases of overestimated populations in order to achieve higher culls (Ueckermann et al., 1974). Population estimates can be controlled by the county hunting authorities through back-calculation with the actual cull numbers.

Red deer populations as well as other populations of game will probably be dealt with more statistically in the future than at present. First, the number of hunters and people interested in hunting is increasing, leading to many more observations of game; second, attempts are being made to improve habitats in which game is thought to be tolerable, and to fix a tolerable density of red deer population. The development of the hunting-territories will therefore improve, i.e., infrastructure such as stalking-trails, high-seats, and pastures. All of this will lead to an improved knowledge of game populations.

Population Growth

Population increase is defined as the annual ratio of increase of red deer killed by hunters. It is usually stated as a percentage value of the number of red deer hinds including yearlings existing on April 1. The increase is about 65 to 70% of the hinds existing on April 1. The increase is about 80% in adult hinds, i.e., animals able to calve (Ueckermann, 1960; Schröder, 1974). The annual increase of the red deer population taken by hunters is fixed by the game harvest plan.

Sex Ratio

The objective of managing roe deer and red deer populations is to maintain a sex ratio of 1:1 which approximates the sex ratio at birth. Generally, however, a higher cull is reported of female than male game. In spite of the fact that there is no biological reason for this the higher proportion of female red deer is included among statistics (Ueckermann et al., 1976). Many hunters are believed to evade the game harvest plan by shooting more stags than hinds and reporting them as hinds, thus pretending to fulfill the demands of the game harvest plan. To prevent false reports federal game-law can require proof, i.e., the intact carcass has to be shown to the hunting-authority or its delegate.

Optimum Age

The theoretical age distribution is oriented at the optimum trophy age of stags, i.e., maximum antler size which is reached at 10 or more years of age. Age distribution pyramids are constructed that slightly exceed the age of best trophy production (Figure 8). The

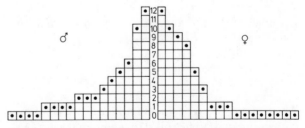

Figure 8.   Normal age distribution of a red deer population on April 1, sex ratio 1:1, total population on April 1 (spring population) 100 animals, increase 70%, zero-age group (expected increase), animals to be taken.

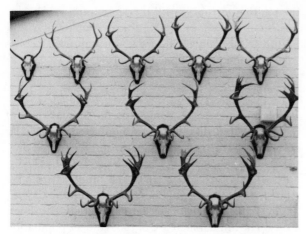

Figure 9. Series of cast antlers of a German red deer stag from the first to the tenth head. The stag was taken at the age of 12; at the eighth head the maximum score of 208 was reached.

Table 5. Age and sex structure of the red deer harvest

Age Groups	Percentage to be Culled
Males	
Male Fawns	20
Stags (1–3 yrs.)	45
Stags (4–9 yrs.)	20
Stags (10 yrs.)	15
Females	
Hind Calves	45
Hearsts	20
Adult Hinds	35

maximum life expectancy of red deer is about 20 years, and stags display the largest antlers between 8 and 14 years of age (Figure 9).

Age of red deer in the field is estimated from body shape and size of antlers. More important, however, is the personal knowledge of individual deer starting at birth. This is possible because the relatively small number of red deer are managed by a large number of hunters, who spend a great deal of time in the field. Age estimates of living individuals are evaluated after the cull by checking the condition of the cheek teeth.

Age Distribution

The age distribution is determined by the number of animals, the optimum age, the sex ratio, and the desired rate of increase. Figure 8 displays the age distribution of a theoretical, perfectly structured red deer population consisting of 100 animals with an optimum age of 12 years and a projected successful production by 70% of the hinds living on April 1. The rate of increase is 35 animals per year. This number is rounded off to the next even number, divided in half, and added to the zero-age groups on both sides of the age pyramid. If the actual age distribution approximates the theoretical desired age structure, each year's increase is utilized as the annual cull.

Structure of the Harvest

The boxes of the age pyramid marked by a point indicate the animals to be culled to maintain the age pyramid (Figure 8). This results in a percentage calculation of the harvest, related to male and female game (Table 5). We have in the example male fawns; red

deer stags, 1 year old to 3 years old; red deer stags, 4 years old to 9 years old; and red deer stags 10 years old and older; in the females we have hind calves, i.e., 1 year old animals, and hinds 2 years and older.

The shooting tenant must report the actual age distribution in his population. The county hunting authorities have to license the cull which must conform to the above regulations (Table 5).

Selective Cull

In the old days the hereditary qualities of red deer populations were improved by "Hege mit der Büchse", e.g., shooting of all weak and disabled individuals. Today "selective harvests" are strictly oriented at age classes, and in each class the weaker individuals are shot. "Weaker" animals are determined almost exclusively by the character of the trophy. Figure 10 illustrates which antler sets are classified as defective in 2-year-old red deer (i.e., "deer of the second head").

A selective harvest based on body size and condition is also attempted with females.

Management Districts

Red deer can migrate over long distances and cross several hunting territories. Therefore, for several decades management combined several territories into a management district which in most cases is fixed by the hunting authorities for continuous red deer populations.

Hunting Area Planning

This term implies the determination of red deer populations and the establishment of a tolerable density of game for a given area. Culling is carried out in areas

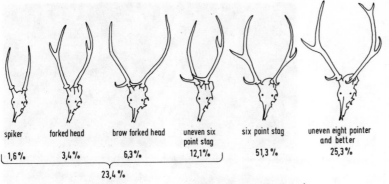

spiker   forked head   brow forked head   uneven six point stag   six point stag   uneven eight pointer and better

1,6 %   3,4 %   6,3 %   12,1 %   51,3 %   25,3 %

23,4 %

Developement of red deer antlers 2nd head
93 trophieshows till 1981/82
n = 1757

Figure 10. Types of development of the antlers of red deer "stags of the second head" (2 year old stags).

where game are not regarded as tolerable (Ueckermann, 1980).

Improvement of Grazing Conditions

The existing investigations show that bark stripping damage and browsing damage can be reduced effectively by improving grazing conditions. If measures are taken to improve grazing conditions, the tolerable density of red deer can be increased by about 1.5 animals per 100 ha. Planting grazing areas and winter feeding are the main measures for improving feeding conditions. Since the habitats differ, the development of a conceptual model based on natural conditions and requirements was developed to deal with differences between areas and habitats (Ueckermann and Scholz, 1981). Planting permanent grazing areas and feeding red deer in winter, for example, is considered a useful improvement of upland habitats and areas with a high percentage of spruce. Figure 11 illustrates an ideal network of grazing areas on a hunting-territory before and after planning. Grazing areas generally do not exceed 0.5 ha and are secluded so that game can graze during daylight hours, especially in forest districts with high human recreation value. Grazing area requirements are calculated on the basis of resident game populations, that is, an area of 0.1 ha is estimated to be the average requirement of one red deer.

In most places the period of feeding in winter is established by state law. Feeding is usually carried out from November 1 to the middle of April. In former years shooting tenants often fed game just as a lure during the rutting season. This led to legally established restrictions of the winter feeding period. The ration of feed given is 50% to 75% of the daily requirement per individual. The rations consist of lush feed in the form of rapes or silage, hay, and a small

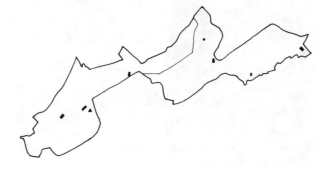

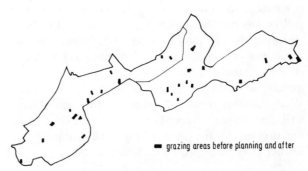

■ grazing areas before planning and after

Figure 11. Planning of grazing areas for a red deer hunting-territory, above grazing areas before planning, below ideal distribution after planning.

Figure 12. Plastic wrappers around a beech to prevent bark stripping damage.

Figure 13. Spruce treated with a plane-iron in order to prevent bark stripping damage.

percentage of concentrated commercially produced pellets. Decentralized feeding is the rule on the plains and uplands, i.e., food for only 10–15 animals is laid out at one feeding place. In high mountains (> 1000 m elevation) fewer feeding sites are used and consequently assemblages gather of up to 100 red deer. Winter feeding results in a distinct reduction of bark stripping damage. Special additives to the feeds have not proven effective in reducing bark stripping any further (Ueckermann, 1971; Hofmann, 1980).

Technical Precautions

Technical precautions have been used in Germany since the last century to prevent forest damage by red deer and other game species. The Federal Republic of Germany produces more chemicals than any other European country for preventing wildlife damage to crops and forests; about 1000 tons are being produced per year. Ninety percent of them are browsing repellents. However, in recent years progress has not been made in developing more sophisticated techniques, as sales of chemicals and instruments have not been particularly successful.

Measures to reduce game damage to forests are expensive, and amount to 80% of all costs to protect forests. The costs per ha are about 10 DM.

Protective measures can be classed into protection of areas and protection of single trees. Protection of areas is carried out by fencing. Fences must be 1.9 m high to keep red deer out. The amount of fencing is limited in order to compromise the interests of hunting and forestry. If the red deer populations are limited too, cultivated areas can provide game with very fair grazing conditions.

Protection of single trees is only possible by preventing browsing, bark stripping, and fraying damage. Browsing damage in winter is almost exclusively prevented by chemicals. Chemical treatment in November protects the plants until the beginning of the spring growing period. According to the plant protection law of 1968, chemicals for the prevention of game damage may be put on the market only if officially permitted, i.e., they must be proven harmless to plants and animals.

Depending on the tree species bark stripping damage is prevented by chemicals, mechanical-bio-

Ueckermann

logical methods, and mechanical protection. Broad-leaf trees are protected by chemicals or by mechanical means in the form of plastic wrappers (Figure 12). Spruce is protected against bark stripping almost exclusively by mechanical-biological devices, that is, by scraping-irons and plane-irons (Figure 13).

Fraying damage can be prevented by mechanical arrangements, but in practice protective measures against fraying damage by red deer are not necessary because trees are so seldom damaged this way (Ueckermann, 1981).

Outlook

Red deer now occupy all areas in the Federal Republic of Germany in which their presence does not conflict with other human interests. Further enlargement of red deer range is not desirable. Local reductions of red deer populations are necessary because of damage to trees and crops. The culling plan specifies removal by age, antler quality, and weight. In most cases optimum size of the trophy is the objective of regulating the age distribution (Drechsler, 1980). Measures for improving grazing conditions should be intensified to create resting areas for game as compensation for disturbances by people seeking recreation in the forest, and to improve conditions for hunting.

Literature Cited

Beninde, J.
1937. *Zur Naturgeschichte des Rothirsches.* Leipzig: Schöps.

1940. Die Fremdblutkreuzung (sog. Blutauffrischung) beim deutschen Rotwild. *Zeitschrift für Jagdkunde.*

Briedermann, L.
1979. Hinweise zur Organisation und Durchführung der Bonitierung unserer Jagdgebiete. *Unsere Jagd,* 29:328–330.

Bubenik, A.
1970. Klassische Hege—klassischer Irrtum? *Die Pirsch,* 22:90–99.

Corbet, G.B.
1978. *The Mammals of the Palaearctic Region: a taxonomic review.* London and Ithaca: British Museum (Natural History) and Cornell University Press.

Crescentiis, P. de
1583. *New Feldt und Ackerbau.* Franckfurt am Mayn.

Dreschsler, H.
1980. Über die Geweihbildung bei Rothirschen im "Rotwildring Harz" in den Jahren 1959–1978. *Zeitschrift für Jagdwissenschaft,* 26:207–209.

Georgii, B., and W. Schröder
1980. Radiotelemetrisch gemessene Aktivität weiblichen Rotwildes (*Cervus elaphus* L.). *Zeitschrift für Jagdwissenschaft,* 24:9–23.

Hartig, G.L.
1877. Lehrbuch für Jäger und für die welche es werden wollen. 2. Band, 10. Aufl. Stuttgart.

Hofmann, R.R.
1980. Anwendung wildbiologischer Forschungsergebnisse in der Bewirtschaftung von Reh- und Rotwild. *Wien: Tagungsbericht Wald und Wild,* herausgegeben vom Forschungsinstitut für Wildtierkunde der Veterinärmedizinischen Universität Wien, 201–222.

Kleyman, M., and F. Bergmann
1976a. Beiträge zur Kenntnis der Infrastrukturen beim Rotwild. Teil 1: Zur Entwicklung und gegenwärtigen Situation der Rotwildbestände in der BRD. *Zeitschrift für Jagdwissenschaft,* 22:20–28.

1976b. Beiträge zur Kenntnis der Infrastrukturen beim Rotwild. Teil 2: Erste Versuche zur Klärung der genetischen Struktur von Rotwildpopulationen anhand von Serumprotein—Polymorphismen. *Zeitschrift für Jagdwissenschaft,* 22:28–35.

1976c. Beiträge zur Kenntnis der Infrastrukturen beim Rotwild. Teil 3: Zur genetischen Struktur von Rotwildpopulationen anhand von Blutgruppen-vergleichsuntersuchungen. *Zeitschrift für Jagdwissenschaft,* 22:121–134.

Mandel, G.
1961. Moritzburg. *Wild und Hund,* 64:177–179.

Neumann, A.
1963. Wilddichte und Winteräsung (Bonitierung von Rotwildgebieten nach der reduzierten Winteräsungskapazität in Kiefernrevieren) Beiträge zur Jagd- und Wildforschung. *Tagungsberichte* Nr. 61, Deutsche Akademie der Landwirtschaftswissenschaften zu Berlin, 69–79.

Oloff, H.-B.
1965. Der Rotwildbestand im Pfälzer Wald. *Zeitschrift für Jagdwissenschaft,* 11:1–54.

Raesfeld, F.V.
1898. *Das Rotwild.* Berlin: Paul Parey.

Reulecke, K.
1980. Rotwildring Harz—Bilanz eines Versuchs, Rotwild zu hegen und Forstwirtschaft zu treiben. *Wien: Tagungsbericht Wald und Wild,* herausgegeben vom Forschungsinstitut für Wildtierkunde der Veterinärmedizinischen Universität Wien, 96–110.

Schröder, W.
1974. Untersuchungen zur Vermehrung des Rotwildes im Harz. *Wild und Hund,* 77:6–8.

1980. Raum- und Zeitverhalten des Rothirsches, Gesichtspunkte für das Rothirschmanagement. *Wien: Tagungsbericht Wald und Wild,* herausgegeben vom Forschungsinstitut für Wildtierkunde der Veterinärmedizinischen Universität Wien, 20–34.

Ueckermann, E.

1951. *Die Einwirkung des Standortes auf Körpergewicht und Gehörnbildung des Waldrehes.* Hannover Münden: Dissertation Forstliche Fakultät.

1955. Ein Erklärungsversuch der bei Rotwild in Westdeutschland anzutreffenden Unterschiede im Körpergewicht. *Zeitschrift für Jagdwissenschaft,* 1:92–98.

1956. *Das Damwild.* Hamburg und Berlin: Paul Parey.

1960. *Wildstandsbewirtschaftung und Wildschadenverhütung beim Rotwild.* Hamburg und Berlin: Paul Parey.

1964. Erhebung über die Wildverluste durch den Strassenverkehr und die Verkehrsunfälle durch Wild. *Zeitschrift für Jagdwissenschaft,* 10:142–168.

1971. *Die Fütterung des Schalenwildes.* 2. Aufl. Hamburg und Berlin: Paul Parey.

1980. Abgrenzung der Rotwildvorkommen und Festlegung der wirtschaftlich tragbaren Wilddichte dargestellt am Beispiel des Landes Nordrhein-Westfalen—Ein Beitrag zur Jagdlichen Raumordnung. *Wien: Tagungsbericht Wald und Wild,* Herausgegeben vom Forschungsinstitut für Wildtierkunde der Veterinärmedizinischen Universität Wien, 283–305.

1981. *Die Wildschadenverhütung in Wald und Feld.* 4. Aufl., Hamburg und Berlin: Paul Parey.

Ueckermann, E., and G. Goepel

1973. Die Auswirkung der Massnahmen zur Wildstandsbewirtschaftung beim Rotwild im Lande Rheinland-Pfalz auf die Bestandesentwicklung, Abschusserfüllung, Abschussgliederung, Geweihqualität und die Wildschadenssituation in den Jagdjahren 1960/61 bis 1971/72. *Zeitschrift für Jagdwissenschaft,* 19:25–56.

Ueckermann, E., J. Zander, H. Scholz, and D. Lülfing

1974. Durchführung und Auswirkung der Massnahmen zur Wildstandsbewirtschaftung beim Rotwild im Lande Nordrhein-Westfalen. *Zeitschrift für Jagdwissenschaft,* 20:13–39.

Ueckermann, E., G. Goepel, J. unter Mitarbeit von Zander, H. Scholz, and D. Lülfing

1975. Die Auswirkung der zunehmenden Innanspruchnahme des Waldes durch die erholungsuchende Bevölkerung auf das Verhalten des Wildes und die Bejagungsmöglichkeit der Wildbestände. *Zeitschrift für Jagdwissenschaft,* 21:50–63.

Ueckermann, E., J. Zander, H. Scholz, and D. Lülfing

1977. Die Auswirkung der Winterfütterung auf den Schälumfang des Rotwildes und den Verbissumfang des Rot- und Rehwildes in dem Rotwildversuchsrevier Hochgewälds-Unterwald/Eifel. *Zeitschrift für Jagdwissenschaft,* 23:153–162.

Ueckermann, E. and H. Scholz

1981. *Wildäsungsflächen, Planung, Anlage, Pflege.* 2. Aufl. Hamburg und Berlin: Paul Parey.

Vorreyer, F. and Drechsler, H.

1966. Mehr alte Hirsche. *Zeitschrift für Jagdwissenschaft,* 12:161–172.

Wagenknecht, E.

1965. *Bewirtschaftung unserer Schalenwildbestände.* Berlin: VEB Deutscher Landwirtschaftsverlag.

1981. *Rotwild.* Berlin: VEB Deutscher Landwirtschaftsverlag.

ALBERT W. FRANZMANN
and
CHARLES C. SCHWARTZ
Alaska Department of Fish and Game
Moose Research Center
P.O. Box 3150
Soldotna, Alaska

Management of North American Moose Populations

ABSTRACT

An assessment of moose (*A. alces*) management in North America is provided with emphasis on the changing balance between the biological information base with social and economic forces. The importance of research in building an information base is emphasized and the evolution of moose research through three stages (discovery and recognition, assessment, and prediction) is outlined as they relate to the evolution of management. The impact of the Pitman-Robertson Act and technological development during the post World War II period on the information base was significant.

However, changes were occurring in demands upon the resource such as non-harvest use, land tenure changes and subsistence priorities which altered management procedures and formalized the management planning process. Moose have had a history of population eruptions resulting from events which produce seral vegetation such as fire, land clearing, and forestry practices. This information has allowed integration of these and other practices favoring seral vegetation into active moose management programs. The challenge to the management biologist today is greater than ever with increased demands upon the moose resource, yet harvest management remains a major management tool as we enter the 1980s.

Background (Pre Pitman-Robertson Act)

The key word in the title of this presentation is management and its definition must be considered before attempting an assessment of moose (*A. alces*) management in North America. Webster defines management as a judicious use of means to accomplish an end. This broad definition places emphasis on a goal or objective. We can thereby understand how wildlife management, and in this case moose management, has been subject to both praise and condemnation depending on the goals a person or group perceives to be valid. The limitations to achieving various goals are basically biological, economic and social. An assessment of moose management in North America becomes an assessment of a balance, often tenuous, between the biological information base and the demands placed upon the resource through social and economic spheres of interest. A perspective of current moose management requires a view of both the evolution of the information base and demands upon the species and its habitat.

Research to provide an information base for management has been an evolutionary process with three stages: (1) discovery and recognition, (2) assessment, and (3) prediction. In North America we have passed through the discovery and recognition phase and are generally into the assessment phase. Unfortunately, not much of the total effort today is in the prediction stage even though the potential exists.

The information base began with the first sightings of moose in North America and then progressed slowly. Early work was primarily descriptive (Audubon and Bachman, 1951; Powell, 1855; King, 1866; Grant, 1902; Hornaday, 1904; Merrill, 1920; and Seton, 1927). At this time, our information base for management was practically nil. Nevertheless, it was apparent to early observers that market hunting and exploitation were detrimental and laws were passed to protect moose. For example, moose seasons as far west as Montana were closed in 1897 and did not reopen until 1945 (Mussehl and Howell, 1971). Moose were given total protection for a period of 5 years beginning in 1893 in Minnesota (Moyle, 1965). Other conservation programs were initiated during this era, such as trapping and transplanting animals and establishing game preserves with wardens to oversee them to protect the wildlife resource. Schmidt (1978) extensively reviewed early management of big game animals in North America and noted that most of man's effects on big game were incidental or, if intentional showed little forethought.

Background (Post Pitman-Robertson Act)

The major impact on the information base for moose, and all wildlife in the United States, was the Federal Aid in Wildlife Restoration (Pitman-Robertson) Act of 1937. This act earmarked funds for a special excise tax on sporting arms and ammunition for wildlife restoration and primarily directed our management efforts toward improving our knowledge about wildlife through research. From that time forward understanding rapidly expanded, aided also by the corresponding technological boom. It is not in the realm of this paper to provide an update on the specifics comprising our present knowledge about moose. This information is available in review form (Peterson, 1955; Bedard, 1975; Franzmann, 1978; 1981), through annual proceedings of the North American Moose Conference workshop and wildlife journals. It is necessary, however, to illustrate in general terms how the evolving information base balanced by resource demands was applied to North American moose management in the post Pitman-Robertson Act period.

Moose are the largest living cervid, and the Alaskan subspecies in the largest of the genus. In North America, moose inhabit the boreal forest from the Arctic Ocean to the Rocky Mountains of Colorado, Utah and Wyoming and across the northern tier of the contiguous states and provinces from the Atlantic to the Pacific oceans.

Adult female moose weigh from 350 to 550 kg and are smaller than males that weigh from 450 to 700 kg. Moose may live to over 20 years and in good habitat both sexes may reproduce at 16 months, thereby having great reproductive potential. Calves weigh 11 to 16 kg at birth in late May and early June and will grow rapidly their first summer to attain weights of 125 to 175 kg by October. The breeding season or rut occurs from mid-September to mid-October and cows generally produce single calves following approximately a 240 day gestation period. However, twinning does occur and the rate is related to the quality of habitat.

Moose are considered a seral species, in that they generally prefer sub-climax type habitats which may result from such events as forest fire, changes in riparian habitat due to flooding, land clearing associated with homesteading and construction, forestry practices favoring deciduous browse regrowth, climatic changes favoring browse availability and production, and habitat rehabilitation directed toward moose production. Moose respond to productive seral habitats by increasing their productivity (higher twinning rates, increased yearling conception, pregnancy rates approaching 100%, strong viable calves), and if mortality factors (winter severity, predation, harvest, accidents and disease) are minimized dramatic population increases occur. Conversely, when the forces are reversed rapid declines are experienced. Management procedures have been directed toward maximizing positive and minimizing negative forces.

Managers were benefitted in their attempts to maximize moose numbers by forces beyond their control such as forestry practices, land clearing and wildfires. Much information was gained about moose biology by studying and observing the effects that these forces had upon populations. This information was used to develop mechanical browse rehabilitation and prescribed burning procedures. Another force beneficial to moose productivity was the broad scale predator control programs in the United States during the 1940s and 1950s and until recently in many areas in Canada; these forces were extremely beneficial to many populations. Nevertheless, the efficiency of management procedures to maximize moose numbers depended upon the quality of the information base regarding the specific moose population and the political financial support generated by public demand. By the late 1960s the technology was adequate to effectively maximize moose productivity in some North American moose populations given political and financial support. Nevertheless, managers were seldom given this support due, in part, to changing public demands.

Up through the 1960s the demands on the moose resource were primarily from the hunting segment of the public. Therefore, management of moose through that period was directed toward producing moose for the harvest. The most widely applied management regimens were related to regulating harvest. Populations were monitored by aerial surveys (Timmermann, 1974) and harvest was managed accordingly, depending upon goals established for a population. Harvest management included adjusting methods and means of harvest, season lengths, access restrictions, sex and age rstrictions, temporal and spatial restrictions, and permit or registration hunts.

Background (Post Earth Day)

During the late 1960s, a new public was generating demands. An "ecological awareness" movement was born on Earth Day. The political force generated by the movement was well funded and represented in state, provincial, and national governments of the United States and Canada. Anti-hunting and anti-gun forces joined the ranks and political pressure mounted. The pressure was primarily to preserve resources and oppose their use. Regardless of one's interest, it was apparent that new pressures were developing through the 1970s that would influence the management of moose resources by redirecting goals and objectives. More emphasis would be placed upon the "non-consumptive" or "non-harvest" use of the moose.

Another public force that would influence demands on the moose resource and influence management options was surfacing during the 1970s. Subsistence use of wildlife resources by Native Americans is not a new phenomenon, but received general public awareness with passage of various legislative acts at the national and state level (Alaska Native Land Claim Settlement Act of 1971, Marine Mammals Protection Act of 1972, Alaska Subsistence Law of 1978, Alaska Lands Act of 1980). These laws recognized subsistence use and in some instances gave priority to subsistence use of wildlife resources. The Alaska Native Land Claims Settlement Act also altered land tenure by removing some public lands to private ownership and the Alaska Lands Act reclassified some public lands and dictated how they were to be used and managed. Similar legislation is pending in Canada and with the majority of North American moose populations in Alaska and Canada, management options for the future have been redirected and altered by legislation through public demands.

Cumming (1974) outlined the evolution of moose managment in Ontario as: (1) protection from suspected over-exploitation; (2) development of some limited use; (3) increased use of an underdeveloped resource; (4) sustained yield and optimum use of the resource; and (5) recreational and economic benefit to the people. This outline accommodates events in most regions of North America and depicts the changing demands upon the moose resource into the 1970s. His last category, recreational and economic benefits to the people, should perhaps be exemplified by the major recent public forces of ecological awareness, subsistence and changing land tenure.

The State of Alaska game management policies may be used as an example of how management goals have reflected to the changing demands. In 1973, a set of policy statements were published (Alaska Department of Fish and Game, 1973a):

> The Alaska Department of Fish and Game recognizes the Constitutional mandate of the State of Alaska to manage moose on the sustained yield principle for the benefit of the resource and the people of the state, and also recognizes that national interests must be considered. The Department recognized the singular importance of maintaining suitable habitat for moose, and advocates the development and implementation of comprehensive resource use planning. The Department recognizes that there are many uses of moose, that present priorities may not be the priorities of the future, and that management plans must consider all uses. In many areas of the state, recreation is the most important use of moose. Recreational uses include: sport hunting in its various forms; observation, both incidental to other activities and as the primary objectives; and wilderness experience, which includes the aesthetic rewards of being aware of or observing

moose in natural interactions with their environment. The Department recognizes its responsibility to provide for all these uses in its management plans, and holds that they are generally compatible. Sport hunting with the gathering of meat as an important consideration has traditionally been the dominant use of moose in Alaska. This use will be encouraged in most areas, and salvaging of all edible meat will remain a condition of taking moose. In many areas, moose will be managed to provide maximum recreational opportunity. This concept recognized the value of the opportunity to be selective in hunting, to enjoy uncrowded hunting conditions, to make use of remote areas, and to enjoy various other eperiences which enhance wildlife-oriented activities. In selected areas with highly developed access and intensive hunter use, or where the human population is partially dependent upon moose for food, moose will be managed for the maximum sustained yield of animals. Management techniques may include harvest of moose of all sexes and ages, liberal seasons and bag limits, access improvement, and habitat manipulations. Certain areas of the state will be managed to provide hunting opportunities of the highest aesthetic quality. Management techniques may include, but not be limited to, regulation of access, regulation of sex, age, and antler size and conformations of animals taken, and population manipulation. The Department will encourage recreational observation of moose through public information and education, and will provide for such activities in its management plans. Although hunting is generally considered compatible with recreational observation of moose, certain areas exceptionally suited to viewing moose as the primary objective may be zoned in time or space to restrict hunting in favor of observation of moose in their most natural population and social structure. The Department will manage moose to provide sustained yields of animals for humans and for wild carnivore populations that depend upon them for food. Whenever substantial conflicts arise between humans and predators over the use of moose, the predator population will be managed to minimize such conflicts. A few areas may be reserved for scientific studies where moose populations and/or habitat can be manipulated. The Department recognizes that responsible moose management must be based on scientific knowledge.

Other statements were included in the policy statements which addressed some specific problems. The policy statements were revised and expanded by the Department and endorsed by the Alaska Board of Game in 1980 and are included in Appendix I. Also in 1973, the Alaska Department of Fish and Game published a compendium on Alaska's wildlife and habitats (Alaska Department of Fish and Game 1973b). This book contained maps of the entire state and delineated the distribution of all species including moose. Seasonal concentration areas for moose were also depicted. Comprehensive species and land-use planning had begun.

By 1976, a set of draft proposals for Alaska wildlife management plans were produced. These statewide plans superimposed upon the distribution maps for each species various management goals for that area. Many areas corresponded to established Game Management Units and Subunits, but in some cases goals were prescribed for much smaller areas. The 6 basic goals and their interpretation are:

1. *To provide an opportunity to view, photograph and enjoy wildlife*. This goal recognizes the great values of being able to see wildlife in a context not necessarily related to actual taking, and emphasizes yield in terms of aesthetic values. There are important areas where the combination of wildlife abundance, unique opportunity and human access result in this use accruing the maximum benefit to people. Emphasis on viewing and photographing may exclude all other uses. However, other uses, including hunting, may be allowed if compatible.

2. *To provide for optimum harvest*. This goal emphasizes yield of animals for human use. Within this goal are accomodated the needs for domestic utilization, especially by rural residents, but also by recreational hunters primarily interested in meat; commercial harvests—and situations involving maintenance of wildlife populations at specified levels. Aesthetic quality of experience and production of trophy animals may be compromised.

3. *To provide the greatest opportunity to participate in hunting*. This goal recognizes the recreational values of hunting and emphasizes the freedom of opportunity for all citizens to participate. In this case, the opportunity to participate is deemed more important than success or standards of quality of experience.

4. *To provide the opportunity to hunt under aesthetically pleasing conditions*. This goal emphasizes the quality of the hunting experience. To achieve this goal, it may require limiting the number of people who may participate, as well as the means used to take game. Criteria for such areas include natural or wilderness character of the land, low hunter densities, and emphasis on hunting without the aid of motorized vehicles.

5. *To provide an opportunity to take large animals*. This goal emphasizes the opportunity for hunters to take large animals. To accomplish this goal will usually mean

Franzmann and Schwartz

that participation of hunters will be limited, and the population manipulated to produce the maximum number of large animals.

6. *To provide an opportunity for scientific and educational study.* This goal recognizes the desirability and need to provide for scientific and educational use of wildlife to achieve a scientific basis for evaluating management options. Such management requires setting aside areas solely for this purpose, but in most cases, this use is compatible with other uses.

These plans were not designed as exclusionary, but designated priority when goals conflict. Also planning was not conceived as a one-time effort. Rather it must be continuous and flexible based upon a balance between the information base and social as well as economic pressures. The Alaska management plans, as we depicted, have already received a major direction change with passage of the Alaska Subsistence Law of 1978 which recognized subsistence use and gave it top priority. Information based on poulations research will force reassessment of our goals and the economic climate will permit or disallow certain options.

We have based our example on Alaska's experience; however, each state and province has had similar experiences. None are exactly the same, but we cannot outline the experiences of each.

Present Status

Today, moose managers in North America must address new and diverse objectives and goals brought about by changing social and economic forces. The biological information base for moose management must expand to adapt to these new objectives. Planning is an integral part of implementing new objectives, but planning without knowledge of the resource is not sufficient. Research efforts must be given the highest priority because proper moose management will increasingly require more intensive management of smaller populations in which only small margins of error are allowable. Greater precision will be required to manage under these circumstances, and the better the manager is informed, the greater will be the chances of meeting the objectives.

Land tenure changes, reclassification of lands, and impacts of development will weigh heavily on the ability to implement management programs outlined by the planning process. In Alaska and Canada today these changes are so rapid and the forces influencing planning so diverse that planning is often thwarted. Moose poulations basically rely on available habitat, and maintaining and/or creating moose habitat will remain the managers' highest priority. Today's manager is often left with this single objective while the more definitive planning process takes place. The battle is often one of convincing the people who represent various demands on the resource that no measures will be meaningful for retaining healthy moose populations, if adequate habitat is not available.

Regulation of harvest remains a primary tool in North American moose management in spite of changing demands. This was emphasized during a workshop session at the 1981 North American Moose Conference and Workshop (summary published in *Alces*, 1981). States and provinces represented were: Alaska; Alberta, British Columbia, Maine, Manitoba, Minnesota, New Brunswick, Newfoundland, Northwest Territories, Nova Scotia, Ontario, Quebec, Saskatchewan, and Yukon Territories. These jurisdictions represent nearly all North American moose range. The survey indicated the total estimate of moose hunters was 400,000 with a harvest in 1979–80 of 68,850 moose. For comparison, Sweden and Norway estimate 235,000 hunters with a harvest in 1979–80 of 135,000 moose. Harvest quotas were established using methods including aerial census data, sex and age classifications, harvest data, mail and personal hunter surveys, population trends, population modelling, and range condition. No jurisdiction used just a single method.

All but one province adjust their quotas annually. Five jurisdictions (Alaska, British Columbia, Manitoba, Newfoundland and Saskatchewan) employed a form of sex-age specific licensing (bulls, bull-calves, calves, yearling bulls, bulls with certain antler development). In all jurisdictions except Alberta, Northwest Territories, Quebec, and Yukon Territories, some form of lottery is held to determine licensee in at least one part of the state or province.

Compulsory registration is required for successful hunters in Alaska, Maine, Minnesota, New Brunswick, Newfoundland, Northwest Territories, Nova Scotia, and Quebec. All others are on a voluntary basis. Hunter safety courses are required in British Columbia, Manitoba, Newfoundland, Nova Scotia, Ontario, Saskatchewan, and Quebec.

The difference in moose harvests in North America (68,850) versus Norway and Sweden (135,000) is largely due to the intensive forestry industry in Scandinavia which has benefitted moose populations because forestry and moose management were closely integrated and both countries lack major predators of moose. The potential to emulate this productivity is present in many areas of North America, but the social and economic forces have not provided the demand. The demands in North America are increasing toward non-harvest use of resources and the climate to produce moose at levels reached in Scandinavia may not occur.

Controversy has always followed wildlife resource management even when the management objective was simply to maximize moose numbers. Today, the manager must satisfy many more demands and controversy will be a fact of life for that person. The salvation for the manager is to be fortified with a strong information base; with it he or she can live with the controversy, but without it he or she will be a victim of it.

Literature Cited

Alaska Department of Fish and Game
1973a. *Alaska Game Management Policies.* Juneau: Alaska Department Fish and Game. 64 pp.

1973b. *Alaska's Wildlife and Habitat.* Juneau: Alaska Department Fish and Game. 144 pp; 563 maps.

Audubon, J.J., and J. Bachman
1851. *The Viviparous Quadrupeds of North America*, Vol. 2. New York: V.G. Audubon. 334 pp.

Bedard, J.
1975. *Alces; moose ecology.* Quebec Les Presses de Universite Laval. 741 pp.

Cumming, H.G.
1974. Moose management in Ontario from 1948 to 1973. *Naturaliste Canadiene,* 101:673–687.

Franzmann, A.W.
1978. Moose. In *Big Game of North America; Ecology and Management,* edited by J.L. Schmidt and D.L. Gilvert, pp. 61–81. Washington, D.C.: Wildlife Management Institute.

1981. *Alces alces.* Mammalian Species No. 154. American Society of Mammalogists. 7 pp.

Grant, M.
1902. Moose. *New York Forest, Fish and Game Commission Report* No. 7, pp. 225–238.

Hornaday, W.T.
1904. *The American Natural History.* New York: Charles Scribner's Sons.

King, W.R.
1866. *The Sportsman and Naturalist in Canada.* London: Hurst and Blackett.

Merrill, S.
1920. *The Moose Book,* 2nd ed. New York: E.P. Dutton and Company, New York.

Moyle, J.B.
1965. *Big Game in Minnesota.* St. Paul: Minnesota Department of Conservation Technical Bulletin. No. 9.

Mussehl, T.W., and F.W. Howell
1971. *Game Management in Montana.* Helena: Montana Fish and Game Department.

Peterson, R.L.
1955. *North American Moose.* Toronto: University of Toronto Press.

Powell, J.E.
1855. "Untitled letter regarding moose in Maine." *Proceedings of the Philadelphia Academy of Natural Science,* 7:343–344.

Schmidt, J.L.
1978. Early management: intentional or otherwise. In *Big Game of North America: Ecology and Management,* edited by J.L. Schmidt and D.L. Gilbert, pp. 257–270. Washington, D.C.: Wildlife Management Institute.

Seton, E.T.
1927. *Lives of Game Animals,* Vol. 3. New York: Doubleday Doran.

Timmermann, H.R.
1974. Moose inventory methods: a review. *Naturaliste Canadiene,* 101:615–629.

Franzmann and Schwartz

FRANK L. MILLER
Canadian Wildlife Service
Western and Northern Region
#1000, 9942—108 Street
Edmonton, Alberta, T5K 2J5
Canada

Management of Barren-Ground Caribou (*Rangifer tarandus groenlandicus*) in Canada

ABSTRACT

Barren-ground caribou (*Rangifer tarandus groenlandicus*) range over 2,000,000 km^2 of tundra and taiga in northcentral mainland Canada and 500,000 km^2 on the tundras of arctic islands. Current numbers are estimated at about 500,000. Use of the barren-ground caribou resource was totally unregulated until the 1950s. Range-wide aerial surveys in 1949 and 1955 suggested that a caribou crisis existed—where there was thought to be millions there were only hundreds of thousands. Population surveys made prior to 1967 lacked quantitative measures of confidence. Most population surveys made between 1967 and 1976 had large 95% confidence intervals, but surveys since 1977 have improved. The accuracies of harvest data collection to date are unknown. A wolf poisoning program was carried out from 1951 to the early 1960s, but the benefit to caribou was never measured. Since 1977 total herd size has been extrapolated from the population estimates obtained during caribou calving ground surveys, plus herd sex and age composition obtained in the fall rutting period. A fixed value of 1.25 is used to adjust for observer bias. Currently, less than 5% of the hunters are restricted in their annual take of barren-ground caribou. All Dene, Inuit, and Metis are in practice exempt from caribou hunting regulations; although only the Dene have this right by treaty. The crux of caribou management remains the same in Canada after 33 years: the caribou managers have no control over the primary users—the native peoples. Without such control effective management is impossible.

Introduction

This paper deals with the management of these barren-ground caribou (*Rangifer tarandus groenlandicus*) that occur in northcentral mainland Canada. These caribou live in discrete herds or populations that migrate seasonally, often for several hundreds of kilometers, between winter and summer ranges. Their migratory and gregarious nature is manifested in some of the most spectacular sights in the natural world. It is not, however, just the migratory nature of these caribou nor their gregarious nature that generates the massed thousands of animals which impose a unique management approach. Equally important is the huge expanse of their ranges and the ancient but rapidly changing relationship with the humans on those ranges.

The management agencies are the governments of the Northwest Territories (NWT) and the provinces of Manitoba and Saskatchewan. Currently the Canadian Wildlife Service (CWS), a federal wildlife agency, uses its expertise in caribou biology to research problem areas and advise those management agencies.

The caribou users are the Eskimos (Inuit) north of the treeline; and Cree, Chipewyan and Dogrib Indians (Dene) south of the treeline, and a relatively small number of Metis and people of European descent. Archaeological studies reveal a close relationship between man and caribou extending back 7000 years (Gordon, 1975). A change in that old relationship between caribou and primitive hunters to one between caribou and modern hunters has been compressed into a few decades of this century.

That shift from nomadic scattered bands of hunters depending on primitive weapons to hunters based in settlements, travelling by snowmachine, motor powered canoes, or aircraft and armed with high-power rifles is one of the greatest factors in caribou management. Although the late 19th century saw the beginning of these changes in hunting patterns, it was after the Second World War when the momentum of change accelerated. Accompanying these changes was a sharp increase in population growth of native groups because of markedly reduced death rates. In addition, the compelling pace of oil, gas and mineral development is further changing the lives of the migratory barren-ground caribou and the caribou users.

Study Area

Caribou ranges

The study area in this review includes all of the ranges of the Canadian form of barren-ground caribou in Canada (Figure 1). Those caribou range over 2,000,000 km² of tundra and taiga in north–central mainland Canada within the NWT and northern por-

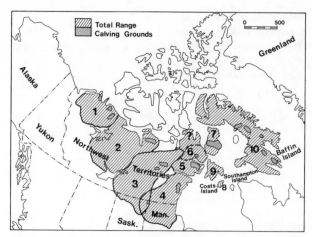

Figure 1. Ranges of migratory barren-ground caribou (*Rangifer tarandus groenlandicus*) herds in north–central Canada: (1) Bluenose, (2) Bathurst, (3) Beverly, (4) Kaminuriak, (5) Lorillard, (6) Wager Bay, (7) Melville Peninsula, (8) Coats Island, (9) Southampton Island, and (10) Baffin Island.

tions of the provinces of Manitoba and Saskatchewan. Although tundra and taiga ranges are used in winter, summering occurs mainly on the tundra with midsummer migrations of some herds penetrating into the taiga. All calving grounds are on tundra areas that are traditional to each herd and are not shared by other herds.

Canadian barren-ground caribou also occur on tundra ranges of Baffin Island (495,000 km²), which lies in arctic waters between Canada and Greenland; and on tundra ranges of Coats Island (800 km²) and Southampton Island (43,000 km²) in the waters of northern Hudson Bay.

Tundra is synonymous with barren ground and is the vast treeless area of high latitudes with continuous permafrost in the subsoil. Taiga is the northern circumpolar boreal forest and in Canada includes both the forest-tundra and the northwestern transition sections of the boreal forest (Rowe, 1959). Much of the entire range is covered with bogs, muskegs, ponds, streams and lakes, and water covers 36% of the total landmass and up to 60% in some areas (Kelsall, 1968).

The tundra is carpeted with mosses, lichens, sedges, grasses, dwarfed woody plants and herbaceous flowering plants. Vegetation is lush in low areas, scant in higher drier areas (Kelsall, 1968). Dwarfed black spruce (*Picea mariana*), white spruce (*P. glauca*), tamarack (*Larix laricina*), jack pine (*Pinus banksiana*), birches (*Betula* spp.), aspen (*Populus tremuloides*), poplar (*P. balsamifera*), alders (*Alnus* spp.) and willows (*Salix* spp.) grow on the forest-tundra.

The forested portion of the study area, corresponding generally with the caribou winter range, is open boreal forest, with black spruce mostly dominant inland. White spruce dominate sites with better soils or drainage, tamarack is often dominant on the more northern sites, and jack pine on burned or drier sandy sites. Birches, aspen, poplar, alders and willows are sometimes locally dominant.

The winters are severe and prolonged, springs cool and wet, summers relatively dry and moderate. Winter temperatures are consistently below −29°C and often dip to −40°C. The mean annual minimum temperature is −46°C, and the lowest recorded temperature is −51°C (Kelsall, 1968). The mean annual maximum temperature is 27°C. Mean annual precipitation is 30–41 cm on the winter range and 15–30 cm on the summer range (Kelsall, 1968). The mean annual total snowfall on the winter range is 102–127 cm, the mean annual maximum depth of snow is 51–76 cm (Kelsall, 1968).

Caribou herds

A herd of caribou are defined as an aggregation of caribou that remains together for at least a major portion of the year and in which all breeding females share an affinity for specific calving grounds not used by females of other herds. If the herd experiences only a minor interchange of animals (10%) with other herds over the long term it could also be called a population. Such is the case for the Kaminuriak and Beverly herds (Miller and Robertson, 1976; Parker, 1972b) and most likely for the Bathurst and Bluenose herds.

Calef (1979) gave the population status of barren-ground caribou in the NWT, which represented essentially all *R. t. groenlandicus* in Canada in 1977. He concluded that there were about 509,000 barren-ground caribou in seven major herds (Table 1).

However, only the Kaminuriak, Beverly, Bathurst and Bluenose herds have in that order been intensively studied, and thus their numbers, distributions and discreteness are relatively well known. Those herds have received attention because they are the most heavily utilized by native hunters and thus the most economically important. The status and discreteness of the Lorillard, Wager Bay and Melville Peninsula herds on the mainland and the Baffin Island herd(s) are not known and they remain virtually unstudied. A resident herd of barren-ground caribou exists on Coats Island. It appears to fluctuate greatly every several years due to winter die-offs and numbers of caribou on the island can range from several hundreds to several thousands. Currently, the herd is in a low phase and numbers about 1000 animals or less. Southampton Island has a resident herd of barren-ground caribou, introduced there in 1967, which currently numbers about 1500 animals. Southampton Is-

Table 1. Estimated numbers of migratory barren-ground caribou (*Rangifer tarandus groenlandicus*) in seven major herds on northcentral mainland Canada

| Caribou herd[a] | Estimates | | | |
	size[b]	year	size[c]	year
Bluenose	90,000	(1975)	36,000	(1981)
Bathurst	150,000	(1977)	90,000	(1980)
Beverly	131,000[d]	(1978)	105,000	(1980)
Kaminuriak	44,000	(1977)	38,000	(1980)
Lorillard	17,000	(1976)		
Wager Bay	12,000	(1976)		
Melville Peninsula	52,000	(1976)		

[a]Baffin Island population estimates at 20,000 in 1974 (Calef 1979).
[b]From Calef (1979).
[c]Personal communication from A. Gunn, Northwest Territories Wildlife Service.
[d]Personal communication from D. C. Heard, Northwest Territories Wildlife Service.

land once had many caribou but they were greatly reduced by the 1930s, apparently due to overhunting, and wiped out by the 1950s.

All herds of barren-ground caribou are restricted to tundra ranges in the NWT—except the Kaminuriak, Beverly, Bathurst and Bluenose herds (Figure 1). Those four herds have taiga wintering ranges and sometimes move in and out of the taiga while on midsummer migrations. Only caribou of the Kaminuriak and Beverly herds traditionally wintered south of the NWT in northern Manitoba (Kaminuriak) and Saskatchewan (Beverly). However, since the early 1970s relatively few of the Kaminuriak caribou have wintered in Manitoba. The Beverly herd still retains its tradition of wintering in the south–central taiga of the NWT and northern Saskatchewan.

Methods

The management of caribou falls into two phases; first, the techniques to collect the management data, and second, the practices used to implement management decisions.

That a large proportion of the barren-ground caribou's life-cycle is spent in the open, either on frozen lakes or north of the treeline usually in large concentrations, encourages the estimation of population size from aerial counts.

Estimation of population size

The first attempt to estimate caribou numbers was made during the winters of 1948–49 and 1949–50. The aerial surveys employed direct counts along non-systematic linear transects of variable widths over mainly forested areas supplemented by oblique photography of large groups of animals. A second attempt to count all the mainland herds in 1955 used systemically spaced transects over taiga and tundra in late winter and spring. From 1955 to 1958, various parts of the caribou ranges were surveyed using the same approach of systematic but non-stratified transects. The next range-wide aerial survey in 1967 was over tundra ranges and concentrated on the spring migration of the three western herds. Total counts, systematic stratified transects and aerial photography of large groups were combined to derive estimates of the size of each population.

Past field observations and ear-tagging studies had suggested that the caribou populations could be identified on the basis of the calving grounds that they traditionally returned to every year. Thus, in 1965, 1966 and 1967, aerial surveys were flown over calving grounds as suggested. The calving ground of the Bathurst herd was delimited by unsystematic flights and then surveyed by non-stratified strip transects. In 1968 emphasis shifted to delimitation of the calving ground by systematic transects, followed by a random block survey on the Kaminuriak Herd (Parker, 1972a). Until 1977 random blocks (41.4 km^2) were used on the other calving grounds which had been surveyed at sporadic intervals.

In 1977 and subsequently, D. Heard, NWT Wildlife Service (NWTWS), refined and standardized the survey of the calving grounds. The area is flown three times: (1) non-systematic flights delimiting the calving ground boundaries; (2) systematic strip transects establishing the caribou densities for stratification with survey coverage allocated according to relative densities of the caribou; and (3) surveying the individual strata. Aircraft altitude and transect width are standardized at 122 m agl and 0.4 km, respectively.

Surveys of the caribou on the calving grounds are used as an index to the number of breeding females in a population (on the assumption that all breeding females of each herd have separate calving grounds and return to the same ones annually). The proportion of breeding females is extrapolated to the total population. Although the caribou on the calving grounds are mostly breeding females, yearlings, sub-adults and non-pregnant females accompany the breeding females from the winter ranges. Ground counts of cows with or without distended udders are used to enumerate the proportions of breeding and non-breeding females as soon as possible after the aerial surveys are flown.

The extrapolation of the calving ground population to an estimate of total population must use the proportion of breeding females in the total population. The only data available are based on a relatively large sample obtained from a collection of caribou from the Kaminuriak herd in 1966–1968: 69% of all cows >1 years of age. The data, supported by results from Alaska and Newfoundland, have been applied to many surveys conducted since 1968. The second factor required to extrapolate a calving ground population to a total population estimate is the proportion of cows over 1 year of age in the population obtained by ground sex and age segregation counts for each herd during the rut.

The problem of observer error is inherent in any survey technique. To compensate for observer error, since 1977 the NWTWS has consistently applied a 25% correction factor to aerial surveys. In addition, in some years the calving grounds may be completely or partially snow-covered which has a pronounced effect on the visibility of caribou to aerial observers. The timing of the surveys must coincide with the peak of calving so that the caribou will be dispersed in small groups; however, variations in the peak of calving can confound the survey timing. The observers may then be trying to estimate numbers in groups of hundreds of caribou. In high density areas, decisions as to which side of the transect boundary the caribou are on add to the errors inherent in the method. Movements of the caribou between strata can confound estimates as the calving ground surveys usually take several days to complete and poor weather frequently intervenes.

The magnitude of the observer errors has not been measured directly, but comparisons of visual counts with counts from high level (457–762 m agl) photography are possible. In 1980, stereo photography counts (1:4000 scale) were compared with visual countings. The comparisons were repeated in 1982 on the Bathurst and Beverly calving grounds.

Estimation of Population Parameters

Productivity. The best data on age-specific fertility of caribou cows were obtained from fetal counts in 545 cows shot between April 1966 and July 1968 from the Kaminuriak herd. Samples were also obtained from the Beverly herd in the late 1950s and early 1980s, but sample sizes were small. The annual return of all pregnant cows and most non-pregnant cows to the calving grounds is an opportunity to monitor productivity. Counts from the ground classify cows with or without distended udders as the udder remains distended 7–14 days even after a calf is lost.

Natural mortality. Caribou one year of age or less is the only age class that is morphologically readily recognizable in the field throughout the entire year. Comparisons of cow-calf ratios after calving and in late winter are measures of first-year mortality. Because most calves are born within a few days of each other, the assignment to age is simplified when describing the age structure of a population.

The cow-calf ratio during the rut and late winter is obtained by counting the caribou found on frozen lakes. In the fall, the prime bulls may be recognized by their large size and antlers, and white mane, whereas young bulls (2–3 years old) and cows have to be distinguished by the presence or absence of a vulva patch or penis sheath. In late winter, distinguishing young bulls and cows is difficult as the bleached long hairs of the winter pelage can mask the external genitalia. At that time, most cows have retained their antlers but a small proportion of cows are genetically bald and some young bulls have not yet shed their antlers. The shortened face profile and small body size distinguish the calves of the year.

Natural mortality of cohorts older than 1 year is indirectly deduced from the proportion of 1 year olds entering the population, from the estimated human kill and from changes in population size determined from successive estimates based on calving ground surveys. Additionally, some estimates of natural mortality were obtained from ear-tag returns of Beverly and Kaminuriak caribou, and from a life-table constructed from 943 Kaminuriak caribou, collected 1966–1968.

Human Kill of Caribou

From 1948 until 1978, natives in the NWT obtained General Hunting licenses (GHL) on an annual basis, and were required to provide oral accounts of yearly game kills to the licensing authority at renewal time. In 1978 the GHL became a permanent (life-long) issue to eligible hunters and new approaches to obtaining caribou kill data were initiated. Harvest statistics are currently collected by several methods from native hunters throughout the NWT.

In the Baffin Region the Baffin Region Inuit Association (BRIA) has collected all harvest data under contract since January 1980. They use a calendar on which hunters record their kills, and the information is then collected monthly by a settlement monitor.

In the Keewatin Region caribou harvest data are collected by monthly interviews with active hunters in six of the settlements and coordinated by the regional biologist. Baker Lake is currently (1981–82) the exception—because of the socio-political climate there, a monthly best guess is provided by the wildlife officer from personal observations and conversations with the hunters.

In the Fort Smith Region the estimates of caribou harvests that had been made by the wildlife officers were replaced in 1980 by personal or telephone surveys. Those surveys are coordinated by the regional biologist. When resources allow, check stations are set up on winter roads through areas that receive heavy hunting pressures.

In the Inuvik Region estimates of monthly kills of caribou obtained from interviews, personal observations and hearsay are made by wildlife officers in some settlements and by local monitors under contract in other settlements. Data from settlements without wildlife officers are provided by the local Hunters and Trappers Association (HTA) or from visits by wildlife officers. The caribou harvest statistics are coordinated by the Regional Resource Development Officer.

Distribution Studies

The separate winter and summer ranges and distances of hundreds of kilometers traversed by the caribou during their annual cycle led to considerable emphasis on mapping the distribution of the caribou in the 1950s and 1960s. From 1959 to the early 1970s, the aerial searches to describe distribution were supplemented by information from marked caribou.

In marking caribou, advantage is taken of the caribou's gregarious behaviour at rivers and lakes in the summer. The caribou tend to be in large groups and swim across lakes or rivers at certain traditional sites. The swimming caribou are easily caught from a large canoe and either ear-tags or collars are attached.

A method of capturing caribou in late winter was to drive them into nets set along their trails in the trees in deep snow adjacent to lakes. Using this method radio neck collars were attached to caribou in 1970 and the animals were followed to the calving grounds and post-calving areas.

Other Studies

In the late 1950s studies were made of the reproductive biology of the caribou, with general observations on behavior and movements. A more detailed and wider-ranging research program was initiated in 1966 by CWS. The program included the necropsies on 943 caribou of the Kaminuriak herd and 56 caribou of the Beverly herd which was a bench mark in the collection of reproductive, growth and sex-age data. The caribou's relationship with range and snow conditions was also studied, as were numbers, survey methods and distributions.

The Kaminuriak program was the first comprehensive research program on barren-ground caribou in Canada, and most efforts since then have focused on monitoring population size and composition. Oil, gas and mineral developments have raised concerns about the effects of development on caribou and as a consequence research into caribou behaviour and movements on winter ranges and calving areas was initiated in the early 1980s.

In cooperation with native hunters, data have been collected since 1980 on reproduction, fat condition and range use on the winter ranges of the Beverly herd, partly because of concern over the impact of forest fires. Current studies are emphasizing forage selection and use, snow conditions and forage availability. In vitro-digestibility techniques, rumen analysis and feeding crater examinations are used along with descriptions of range use and snow conditions.

The causes of calf mortality and the rates of calf survival in the Beverly herd are being described in 1980–83 to evaluate the need and timing for a wolf control program. The carcasses located on the calving grounds are examined to ascertain mortality factors. In addition, cow-calf ratios are monitored on the calving ground, during the rut and late winter.

Management Practices

The need to manage the barren-ground caribou results from detected declines in the numbers of barrenground caribou without equivalent declines in the real or asserted requirement by natives for caribou. All of the management pactices are thus generated to attempt to halt or reverse declines in the numbers of caribou.

Restriction of Hunting

Regulation of hunting is potentially the most effective and sensitive management tool that the caribou managers can use, but in practice it is the most contentious and currently of almost no importance. Most efforts in the past have tried to extoll the conservation ethic through education and regulation, but this ethic has been almost non-existant in the past hunting practices of caribou hunters. At present in NWT, Big Game License Holders are allowed two caribou per year. There is no general hunting season for non-natives (except registered trappers) in Manitoba or Saskatchewan. GHL holders in the NWT and Indians and Metis in Manitoba and Saskatchewan are essentially unrestricted in their kill. The importance of land access to wintering caribou is recognized by the NWT Game Ordinance which in effect regulates against hunting along one highway, and on one access road to mines on the winter range of the Bathurst herd. Only the reintroduced caribou population on Southampton Island has a restricted harvest controlled by issue of 50 tags.

The sale or bartering of caribou meat is legal only between GHL holders, except for caribou meat taken under a commercial license. Commercial tags are only issued in limited numbers on Baffin Island and Coats Island and have the intent of allowing NWT institu-

tions and hotels to be legally supplied with caribou meat. The sale or bartering of caribou meat is not legal in Manitoba or Saskatchewan.

It is illegal under the NWT Game Ordinance to feed caribou meat to dogs in or within 8 km of a settlement, or to shoot caribou within 12 h of being positioned by an aircraft. Such regulations have a negligible effect on controlling the kill of caribou because they are ignored by the hunters and not enforced by wildlife officers.

Predator Control

Wolf control was instigated in the early 1950s as a short-term effort to reduce the caribou decline. Large baits of 9–45 kg of meat (usually caribou) were impregnated with strychnine pellets and frozen into lakes on occupied caribou winter ranges. By the winter of 1955–56 baits were used on most caribou winter ranges and the effort continued at that level until 1960. Efforts were considerably reduced by 1964 and ended by 1970.

Range Control and Protection

The effects of forest fires on the quality and quantity of winter ranges have been questioned repeatedly. Studies in the 1960s attempted to quantify the range composition and biomass in various aged stands, and to describe caribou diets from feeding craters and rumen analyses.

More recently, concerns of native peoples and fire control personnel have caused a resurgence of interest in caribou and forest fires. However, lacking firm conclusion about the deleterious effects of fire on caribou winter ranges, fire management has been somewhat desultory.

In the late 1970s it was suggested by native hunters that oil, gas and mining exploration activities interfered with the access of caribou to some areas of their ranges. One outcome of these concerns was a series of Land Use regulations to close the calving grounds of the Beverly and Kaminuriak herds to mining exploration while the caribou were using the area. Additionally, the areas of rivers and lakes traditionally used as crossings by the caribou of the Beverly and Kaminuriak herds were closed within 8 km to industrial exploration.

Results

Techniques

POPULATION SIZE

The 1948–49 estimate of the number of barren-ground caribou was only a rough approximation because of the methodology employed (Banfield, 1954). Banfield's estimate of 668,000 caribou suggested a decline from one to several million (Banfield, 1957) guessed at earlier. A range-wide estimate in 1955 of 270,000 animals indicated that the decline had continued (Kelsall, 1968). A re-analysis of the 1955 data (Parker, 1971) suggested that an estimate of 390,500 was more likely. A decade later (1968) a survey with a greater degree of precision gave an estimate of 385,500 (Thomas, 1969).

Population estimates subsequent to 1967 were for individual herds, but until the method was standardized to a calving ground survey in 1977, comparisons of surveys are hindered by differences among the methods. In some cases re-analysis of the raw data has lead to adjusted estimates.

The comparisons of population estimates and of numbers of breeding cows on the calving grounds of individual herds during the 1970s and 1980s found a decline in each of the Kaminuriak, Beverly and Bathurst herds, and stability in the Bluenose herd. The preliminary result from aerial surveys in June 1982 does not support the trend for a decline in the Kaminuriak herd, but the significance of single surveys compared to trends remains unknown. The only comparison of high altitude photography with a visual survey (on the Bathurst calving ground in 1980) suggests the observer bias correction factor of 25% is insufficient (D. Heard, pers. comm.). More data are required, however, before the applicability of that result can be tested and extended to other calving ground surveys.

Population Parameters

Productivity. Dauphiné (1976) found that in the Kaminuriak herd no calves had ovulated (n=12), but 57% (n=7) of the 18 month old caribou, 80% (n=20) of the 30 month old cows and 96% of the 3+ year old cows (n=55) had ovulated. Fetuses occurred in 2% (n=57) of the yearlings, 48% of 2 year olds (n=69) and 90% of the 3+ year old cows (n=280). Dauphiné noted that embryonic and fetal mortality were rare and that the major cause of reproductive failure in 1+ year old caribou was failure to conceive after ovulation.

The high productivity of 3+ year old caribou as described by Dauphiné (1976) is also borne out by estimations of the proportions of breeding females to all females over 1 year of age on the calving grounds. In June 1978, 1980 and 1982 the proportions of breeding females (cows with distended udders) on the Beverly calving grounds were 81.1%, 73.5% and 80.0%.

Mortality

Reported estimates of mortality of caribou aged 1 year or less were mostly unreliable before 1977 (information from 1967 and 1968 were exceptions). Lack of information about survey methodology employed and the failure to adjust for adult-female mortality in calculating calf:cow ratios reduced the value of those earlier ratios. Recent figures for the Beverly herd (1976–1981) suggest that calf survival was 30–40% from June to April. Calf mortality is usually highest on the calving grounds and on the winter ranges in response to variations in predation and weather.

The average mortalities for all age groups of females and males (aged 1–10 years) were calculated to be 21% and 27%, respectively, from a life-table based on a sample from the Kaminuriak herd (Miller, 1974). However, the estimates of natural mortality extrapolated from herd recruitment, total population change and human kill are considerably lower and, for the Kaminuriak herd, average only 7%. On the other hand, tag returns from 7.2% of the 7463 Beverly caribou tagged between 1960 and 1973 suggest average annual mortality of 21% in the 1960s and 1970s.

Human Kill of Caribou

Caribou Harvest Data Prior to 1978

In the NWT, accuracy and completeness of the annual harvest ledgers were determined mainly by the effort made by the different licensers. The general consensus of NWTWS personnel during the period was that the harvest ledgers were inaccurate and unreliable. Harvest estimates could vary by as much as 100% depending on the method of estimation that was used. In addition, ledgers for over a decade of harvest (1952–53 to 1963–64) are now missing. Harvest information from Manitoba and Saskatchewan consisted of fragmentary collections by game officers and some biologists and served only as minimal estimates of unknown confidence.

If we do not have an accurate measure of hunter kill in a herd, we cannot obtain a good estimate of natural mortality. Thus, we cannot use data on natural mortality and recruitment to get a good estimate of the allowable sustainable annual harvest of the herd. All of those associated calculations are only as good as the poorest value used. Therefore, inaccurate hunter kill data mean inaccuracies of unknown magnitude in subsequent estimates of population size and dynamics. For instance, while GHL returns for Baker Lake, NWT, stated that the caribou harvest was 1,078 in 1976–77, hunter interviews suggested that it was 4,100 (Interdisciplinary Systems, 1978; Dickinson and Herman, 1980). Those two estimates of the native kill of caribou by Baker Lake hunters varied by 400%, which makes both values suspect.

In general the percentages of native hunters reporting their caribou hunting success in the NWT dropped drastically from 1970–71 to 1976–77 and has remained that way, seemingly, because of differences between native hunters and caribou managers. For example, the proportion of native hunters reporting their kill of caribou ranged from 62% to 88% in 1970–71 and dropped to 13% to 49% in 1976–77, the information based on a sample of seven Inuit (NWT) and Dene (Saskatchewan) settlements that hunt the Beverly herd. The year to year accuracies of harvest statistics prior to 1978 were not known and never will be. In a sense, it is all academic because no meaningful management action for caribou occurred in Canada during the 1970s.

Caribou Harvest Data After 1978

Baffin Region. There are high expectations for the calendar method because there is considerable native involvement. However, the system is not without flaws. Shortcomings result from (1) data being lost or not recorded for various time periods because settlement monitors lost interest in collecting the information; (2) some hunters being afraid the data will be used against them; (3) the NWTWS not having control over the length of the project because most of the funding comes from elsewhere; and (4) the NWTWS having no agreement with the contractor, the Baffin Region Inuit Association, which insures access to the data.

Keewatin Region. The system suffers from (1) data gaps caused by staff turnovers, annual leave and prolonged vacancies; (2) difficulty in finding an impartial resident to collect the data; (3) no collection of data from outpost camps; and (4) the collected data remaining questionable because there is, especially at Baker Lake, a lack of trust on the part of many native hunters. The Keewatin Inuit Association (KIA) has negotiated a harvest collection contract in 1981 similar to BRIA's contract for collections of harvest data but the results have not yet been seen.

Fort Smith Region. The methods being used for collection of caribou harvest data have just been initiated and they have not been evaluated within the region. They will, however, most likely suffer from some or all of the shortcomings listed for the Baffin and Keewatin regions.

Inuvik Region. The approaches used to obtain caribou harvest data in this region mainly suffer from staff workloads and vacancies and, also to some extent, from the previously listed shortcomings in the other three regions.

In summary, the accuracy of harvest data to date is virtually unknown. Thus, the data are unacceptable for the management of large migratory herds of barren-ground caribou that can withstand annual harvests of only 2 to 5% over the long term. Conclusions drawn from such data lack confidence.

Distribution Studies

A key result of the distribution surveys of the 1950s and 1960s and the ear-tag returns was the realization that herds annually returned to traditional calving grounds. During range-wide survey in 1967 Thomas (1969) followed the herds from the winter ranges toward their respective calving grounds. He (Thomas, 1969) subsequently named the four major herds after a prominent lake or waterbody near where they calved.

Between 1959 and 1970 and in 1979, 7,463 caribou were marked from the Beverly herd, 2,551 from the Kaminuriak herd and 608 from the Bathurst herd. Subsequently, the ear-tags and collars were returned by hunters at the rate of 7.2% for the Beverly herd, 6.4% for the Kaminuriak herd and 5.4% for the Bathurst herd. The program of tagging and collaring was discontinued on the mainland in part because of strong opposition from native hunters.

Comparisons of distributions of the Beverly, Bathurst and Kaminuriak herds in the 1950s, 1960s and 1970s are hampered by the irregularity of what were mostly, only partial surveys of the winter ranges. Too often the distribution information was a by-product of other objectives, densities were not objectively measured and only parts of the ranges were covered.

The occupancy patterns on the winter ranges appear to be changed in the late 1970s from that seen previously, with the changes particularly evident for the Kaminuriak herd. A large segment of that herd used to winter in the taiga of northern Manitoba, but has not been abundant there since the early 1970s. Also, the extreme southward and westward movements of the Beverly herd in the 1940s and 1950s were not repeated in the 1960s and 1970s, creating the impression of a smaller winter range. The winter range of any one herd is that area used at any time in the past. Within the entire winter range, there are apparent shifts in the occupancy pattern (e.g., Kelsall, 1968): an area will be used for several years and then the caribou stop using it. The reality of this apparent shift and the reasons have not been pursued in any study.

Other Studies

The investigations that contributed most of the data necessary for management were the detailed studies of the Kaminuriak herd in 1966–70 (e.g., Parker, 1972a; Miller, 1974; Dauphiné and McClure, 1974; Miller and Broughton, 1974; Dauphiné, 1976; and Miller, 1976). Those studies supplemented earlier work, especially the demographic data on productivity, age and sex composition. Those data suggested that range quality was not a limiting factor, although snow influenced forage availability and mortality. Other contributions of the Kaminuriak studies were improvements in capture methods (Miller, et al., 1971), population surveys (Parker, 1972a) and specific techniques such as estimating the age of caribou (Miller, 1972; Miller and McClure, 1973).

Management Practices

Restriction of Hunting

It is not possible to determine whether the educational efforts and minor regulation changes from the 1940s to 1960s had much effect on reducing the hunting of caribou. Probably the prime determinants of hunting practices were the dramatic social changes, especially the coalescing of nomadic hunting groups into settlements, the provision of wage-earning jobs and the capability of using store-bought foods, clothing and other goods.

Since the 1960s, the increasing articulation of the doubts of the native users about the ability or right of the territorial government to manage caribou has further eroded any evaluation of the effectiveness of the educational approach and the minor regulatory restrictions.

Essentially there are seven classes of hunters that utilize migratory barren-ground caribou: (1) "Treaty Indians" (Dene); (2) "Non-status Indians" (Indians without a treaty or individuals that have lost their status); (3) "Metis" (people of Indian and usually European mixed ancestry); (4) "Inuit" (Eskimos); (5) "Resident sport meat hunters" (non-native); (6) "Non-resident sport hunters" (Canadians or landed immigrants); and (7) "Alien non-resident sport hunters" (foreign nationals).

Theoretically, only treaty Indians are exempt from hunting regulations under the "British North American Act" and other individual treaties. However, in reality there has been practically no enforcement of laws or regulations regarding seasons and bag limits on caribou, when the offenders were non-status Indians, Metic, or Inuit. Also, enforcement of caribou hunting regulations in the vast, remote areas of caribou ranges has been at such low levels that resident meat hunters, native and non-native alike, can and do violate game laws with little fear of being caught and even less fear of being convicted. In practice the only people that have been restricted in their taking of caribou have been the non-resident and alien sport hunters and some law abiding resident sport or meat hunters. Therefore, the existing laws and regulations regarding the taking, possession and uses of caribou have been of only limited value in caribou management.

Currently, socio-political attitudes in northern Canada make it even less likely that any of the first four classes of caribou hunters will be restricted in their taking of caribou, unless it is through acts of self-restraint. The hiring of native game officers may work some hardships on resident game offenders, but the remoteness and vastness of the caribou ranges and the small size and immobility of enforcement staffs allow game violaters to continue their practices largely unhampered. Such illegal killing of caribou is unlikely to stop in the near future as both natives and long time non-native residents believe they have a right to unlimited use of caribou as a source of fresh meat.

Thus, attempts at educating caribou hunters on the need for conservation of the caribou resource have been unsuccessful. Many older hunters continue the old practices of excessive killing of caribou when the meat is no longer necessary for their survival, and many younger hunters kill in excess, apparently disregarding the future of the resource and the generations of hunters to come.

Predator Control

Kelsall (1968) believed that the wolf poisoning program from 1951 into the 1960s reduced wolf numbers. It is unclear whether the reduction in wolf numbers had any even short-term marked effect on the caribou populations. However, as noted by Kelsall (1968) the killing of 6,890 wolves on winter ranges in the NWT alone between 1952 and 1961 most likely gave thousands of caribou at least temporary salvation. The figures for recruitment of caribou on the western ranges during the peak years of wolf control (1957–1961) were relatively high (19.5%). In the 1970s, a figure of 10% was accepted by NWTWS as a likely average of recruitment for the Kaminuriak and Beverly herds. The improved recruitment during control may have been due to factors other than wolf control.

Artificial Stocking

The only restocking of previous range with barren-ground caribou occurred in the summer of 1967. Forty-eight caribou (26 adult females, 12 adult males, and 10 calves) from Coats Island in Hudson Bay were immobilized with drugs and transplanted by aircraft to Southampton Island, about 150 km to the north. Subsequent information on the success of the reintroduction is fragmentary, but aerial searches in 1981 suggest that the introduced herd numbers over 1,400 animals (C. Gates, pers. comm.). Restocking efforts are not practical on an extensive range basis to meet user demands for long-term sustained harvests. Therefore, restocking can be considered only as a useful management practice in special situations—such as establishing discrete island populations.

Under current and foreseeable levels of caribou management it is unlikely that any meaningful use of range controls or protection will be used on caribou ranges. Studies done in Canada during the 1960s led to the conclusion that forest fires on caribou winter ranges had extensive detrimental impacts on the forage supply and, thus, on caribou numbers (Scotter, 1964, 1967; Kelsall, 1968). Then in the 1970s some researchers drew a totally opposite conclusion and believed that forest fires were both beneficial and necessary to provide the heterogeneous forage supply needed by caribou (Bergerud, 1974; Johnson and Rowe, 1975; Miller, 1976).

New studies of the impact of forest fires on caribou winter ranges were initiated in 1982 by CWS and NWTWS researchers. Whether forest fires are good or bad for caribou remains debatable. However, there is no doubt that too much burning of winter ranges in too short a time would be detrimental. Therefore, when annual rates of forest fires increase markedly, protective action should be taken. Forest fire control is likely to be the only form of range protection that is possible, with the exception of more stringent Land Use regulations, which it may be possible to impose within the near future.

Land Use regulations have been in effect since the late 1970s to restrict the levels and kinds of activities on the traditional calving grounds and post-calving areas of the Kaminuriak and Beverly herds. The regulation of the areas came about because the Inuit of Baker Lake, NWT, pressed their belief through a federal court that mining exploration activities (and caribou biologists activities) were disturbing the caribou and causing them to leave their normal ranges. As a consequence, companies, biologists and other parties wishing to travel and work within the restricted areas between 15 May and 31 July of each year must obtain a release from the responsible Land Use Inspector, if their activities would be subject to Land Use regulations.

Mining companies interested in exploring an area under Land Use regulations oppose these restrictions and are in the process of "fighting" for changes that would allow them to work without hinderance. Such changes would also make the regulations essentially meaningless. However, in view of the looming North American energy crisis and the current economical situation in Canada, it is unlikely that conservation of the caribou resource will be foremost in the minds of decision makers. Caribou biologists currently see the native hunters as both the decimators and possible saviours of the barren-ground caribou in Canada. Only the political strength of the native peoples of northern Canada can ultimately save the caribou resource; that is, if they first accept the need for the conservation of the caribou.

Discussion

The phrase "living streams" is an apt description for the spectacle of the massed migrations of the barren-ground caribou. The sight of thousands of caribou and the realization of the low human population isolated in a few scattered settlements can deceive one as to the critical need for caribou management. In the eyes of present day hunters, the fact that they have long coexisted with the caribou and that there are still seemingly hundreds of thousands of caribou obscure the need to manage the caribou. Tragically, on the ground the difference between 1000s and 10s of 1000s is not obvious. The hunters have lost sight of what coexistence meant in practice and how far it is removed from the situation today.

Before the invasion of European culture in the North, Indians and inland Eskimoes either had to move to the caribou or wait for them at traditional sites such as water crossings. With bow and arrows, spears and ingenious traps they could kill and cache caribou to survive until the caribou again returned to their hunting areas. If the caribou did not return, the people had to find them or starve. However, the advent of the rifle in the North, followed by an active fur trade between Europeans and natives allowed many natives to alter their lifestyles. But freedom from total dependency on caribou brought a new dependency on store goods, especially rifles and ammunition which made hunting much easier but required more hunting and trapping to acquire them. A vigorous trade in caribou meat and hides was developed by the fur traders and whalers with the natives, and the native's relationship with the caribou changed forever. The killing of caribou by Europeans and natives increased markedly and resulted in the declines seen since the 1930s.

Even though the concentration of people into settlements and the availability of store bought goods reduced the number of caribou killed, the populations of the Indians and Inuit who utilize the caribou have steadily increased. Even as the number of caribou needed per family of four has dropped from about the 250 caribou (Lawrie 1948) to about 2–5 per person in the early 1980s, the number of people has increased by about 4% per year. Extrapolation of populations of native peoples in the NWT to the year 2000 exceeds 50,000 (Fuller and Hubert, 1981). In addition, the increased cost of owning and operating snowmobiles and a "back to the land" movement has fostered a resurgence of dog teams, which are usually fed caribou meat. Paralleling the increase in native populations, there is an increasing awareness of their cultural uniqueness and ties with the land. A measure of this is the NWTWS's Outpost Program which supports families returning to live off the land. In 1982, support was offered to 1400+ people in 154 camps outside the settlements.

Caribou can still be seen by thousands and they continue to migrate along traditional routes, even close to settlements. However, the general pattern of reduced numbers of breeding females on the calving grounds of three of the four major mainland herds between 1977 and 1982 warns of population declines, and the need for management.

Barren-ground caribou populations have characteristics that facilitate management. Current data describe the populations as relatively distinct and discrete which makes for well defined management units. Their gregariousness, use of open habitat and traditional areas means that large samples of population parameters such as calf survival, productivity, sex ratio, numbers of breeding females and total population can be readily obtained, given adequate funds and personnel. The quality and quantity of summer or winter range are not generally considered to be limiting populations. Also there is no evidence that endemic diseases such as brucellosis, benoitosis and parasites are factors in population dynamics. The reproductive rate is relatively fixed as twinning in the wild is unknown, and there is no evidence of shifts in the age of breeding. Variations in calf and adult survival are the most important parameters in population dynamics, which suggest that management by control of hunter kill and predation should be effective and sensitive. The most important non-human predator is the wolf; however, for ecological and economical reasons, wolf control is only a short-term emergency tool to give reduced caribou populations a breathing space. The concentration of the caribou users into relatively small settlements, almost all of which have a wildlife officer stationed there, should facilitate both the counting of caribou killed and the enforcement of any regulations, if the native hunters cooperate.

The failure of federal, provincial or territorial jurisdictions to manage caribou is their failure to regulate the kill of caribou by humans. The complex reasons for that failure are interwoven with threads from history, cultural conflicts and politics. Briefly, the apprehension and misunderstandings about the need to collect hunter kill statistics have over the decades spilled over and have led to most native users' rejecting the need to manage caribou.

The theme of this paper is how caribou lend themselves to effective management but are not managed. It has dealt with the four herds that migrate between the taiga and tundra. Those herds may have subpopulations that normally winter in the taiga although some may stay on the tundra in most years. There are other lesser little known populations of barren-ground caribou that remain year-round on the tundra. Along the arctic mainland coast, on the peninsulas of Boothia and Melville south to Baker Lake and on Baffin Island there are caribou whose numbers, population discreteness and status are an enigma. Their relatively low levels of human use (except some Baffin herd) and location in the most isolated areas of the NWT, where poor weather prevails most of the time and rough terrain is ubiquitous, explain our ignorance of them.

Even against a background of conflict over who owns and has rights to the wildlife and the increasing use of wildlife as a pawn in Land Claims negotiations, there are signs of hope. In spring 1982, the federal, provincial and territorial governments joined with representives of the caribou users to sign an agreement and establish a Caribou Management Road for the Beverly and Kaminuriak herds. Only through such cooperative efforts, and through real involvement of the users in management programs, will the years of mistrust be eroded.

The crux of barren-ground caribou management in Canada remains the same after 33 years, that is, managers have no control over the primary users of the resource—the native peoples. Without such control effective management is impossible.

Acknowledgments

Much of the data in this paper and not otherwise referenced came from personal communications with Dr. A. Gunn, NWTWS, regarding material in NWTWS files or unpublished reports authored by L. Allison, G.W. Calef, D.C.M. Elliott, A. Gunn, D.C. Heard, and L.W. Kale; or from proceedings of the Federal-Provincial-Territorial Caribou Technical Committee. I am most grateful to Dr. A. Gunn, NWTWS, for her assistance and I fully acknowledge that without that information I could not have compiled much of the foregoing material, and that any distortion of the facts is my sole responsibility. I thank Drs. W.E. Stevens and D.C. Thomas, CWS, for critically reading earlier versions of the manuscript.

Literature Cited

Banfield, A.W.F.
1954. Preliminary investigation of the barren-ground caribou. *Canadian Wildlife Service Management Bulletin*, Serial 1, No. 10A. 79 pp.
1957. The plight of the barren-ground caribou. *Oryx*, 4:5–20.

Bergerud, A.T.
1974. Decline of caribou in North America following settlement. *Journal of Wildlife Management,* 38:757–770.

Calef, G.W.
1978. Population status of caribou in the Northwest Territories. In *Parameters of caribou population ecology in Alaska,* edited by D.R. Klein and R.G. White, pp. 9–16. Proceedings of the Symposium and Workshop on Biological Papers of the University of Alaska, Special Report No. 3.

Dauphiné, T.C., Jr.
1976. Biology of the Kaminuriak population of barrenground caribou. Part 4: Growth, reproduction, and energy reserves. *Canadian Wildlife Services Report,* Serial No. 38. 71 pp.

Dauphiné, T.C., Jr., and R.L. McClure
1974. Synchronous mating in Canadian barren-ground caribou. *Journal of Wildlife Management,* 38:54–66.

Dickinson, D.M., and T.B. Herman
1980. Management of some terrestrial mammals in the Northwest Territories of sustained yields. *Science Advisors Board of the Northwest Territories,* Yellowknife. Report No. 4. 71 pp.

Fuller, W.A., and B.A. Hubert
1981. Fish, fur and game in the Northwest Territories: Some problems of, and prospects for, increased harvests. In *Renewable resources and the economy of the North.* Proceedings of the First International Symposium on renewable resources and the economy of the North, edited by M.M.R. Freeman, pp. 12–29. Banff, Alberta, Canada.

Gordon, B.H.C.
1975. Of men and herds in barrenland prehistory. *National Museum of Man Mercury Series of Archeological Survey of Canada,* Paper No. 28. 541 pp.

Interdisciplinary Systems Limited
1978. Effects of exploration and development in the Baker Lake area. Volume One: *Study Report Prepared for the Department of Indian Affairs and Northern Development,* Ottawa. 309 pp.

Johnson, E.A., and J.S. Rowe
1975. Fire in the subarctic wintering ground of the Beverly caribou herd. *American Midland Naturalist,* 94:1–14.

Kelsall, J.P.
1968. The migratory barren-ground caribou of Canada. *Canadian Wildlife Service Monograph,* No. 3, Ottawa. 340 pp.

Lawrie, A.H.
1948. Barren-ground caribou survey, Keewatin. *Canadian Wildlife Service Report* C873 Ms.

Miller, D.R.
1974. Seasonal changes in the feeding behavior of barrenground caribou on the Taiga winter range. In *The behavior of ungulates and its relation to management,* edited by V. Geist and F. Walters, pp. 744–755. Vol. 2. IUCN New Serial Publication No. 24. Morges, Switzerland.

Miller, D.R., and J.D. Robertson
1967. Results of tagging caribou at Little Duck Lake, Manitoba. *Journal of Wildlife Management,* 31:150–159.

Miller, F.L.
1972. Eruption and attrition of mandibular teeth in barren-ground caribou. *Journal of Wildlife Management,* 36:606–612.

Miller, F.L., D.R. Behrend, and G.D. Tessier
1971. Live capture of barren-ground caribou with tangle nets. *Transactions of the North East Section of the Wildlife Society,* 28:83–90.

Miller, F.L., and E. Broughton
1974. Calf mortality on the calving ground of Kaminuriak caribou. *Canadian Wildlife Service Report,* Serial No. 26, 26 pp.

Miller, F.L., and R.L. McClure
1973. Determining age and sex of barren-ground caribou from dental variables. *Transactions of the North East Section of the Wildlife Society,* 30:79–100.

Parker, G.R.
1971. Trends in the population of barren-ground caribou. Part 1: Total numbers, mortality, recruitment, and seasonal distribution. *Canadian Wildlife Service Report,* Serial No. 20, 95 pp.

Parker, G.R.
1972b. Distribution of barren-ground caribou harvest in northcentral Canada. *Canadian Wildlife Service Occasional Paper,* No. 15, 20 pp.

Rowe, J.S.
1959. Forest regions of Canada. *Department of Northern Affairs Natural Resources, Forestry Branch,* Bulletin 123:1–71.

Scotter, G.W.
1964. Effects of forest fires on the winter range of barrenground caribou in northern Saskatchewan. *Canadian Wildlife Service Wildlife Management Bulletin,* Serial 1, No. 18. 111 pp.

Scotter, G.W.
1967. Effects of fire on barren-ground caribou and their forest habitat in northern Canada. *Transactions of the North American Wildlife Natural Resources Conference,* 31:246–259.

Thomas, D.C.
1969. Population estimates of barren-ground caribou March to May, 1967. *Canadian Wildlife Service Report,* Serial No. 9, 44 pp.

Miller

DALE R. MCCULLOUGH
Department of Forestry and Resource Management
145 Mulford Hall
University of California, Berkeley
Berkeley, California 94720

The Theory and Management of *Odocoileus* Populations

ABSTRACT

Deer of the genus *Odocoileus* are the most important wild ungulates in North America in both numbers and economic value. A pluralistic society however has placed conflicting demands on the wildlife manager to be all things to all people. The tradeoffs of deer population management are low residual populations yielding high recruitment rates, intermediate residual populations yielding intermediate recruitment rates, or high residual populations yielding low, zero, or even negative recruitment rates. Which of these situations is desireable depends on the goals of the management program. The traditional logistic model is not sound for managing populations of k–selected mammals such as *Odocoileus*. A deterministic model based on productivity and potential yield curves for mule and white-tailed deer is presented to predict population responses to various exploitation rates, assuming hunting to be the only source of mortality. In these k–selected species relatively small changes in reproductive potential have relatively large impacts on maximum sustained yield (MSY) towards K, and any shift in that direction leads to greater susceptibility to over–exploitation. Deterministic predictions are discussed, as well as influences and effects of residual population, stochasticity, and functional refugia.

Introduction

The genus *Odocoileus* consists of two living species which are confined to North, Central, and northern South America. The white-tailed deer, *O. virginianus*, which is generally an eastern species, extends south into South America, but contains some western representatives that extend virtually to the Pacific Coast in Oregon. A number of subspecies (or races) have been named, but variation is typically clinal in nature, and the boundaries between subspecies are arbitrary. The mule deer, *O. hemionus*, is largely a western species that extends from southeastern Alaska southward into western Mexico. It usually occupies more xeric environments than the white-tailed deer. It has a number of named subspecies that are characterized by discontinuities in characters due to partial barriers to gene flow created by deserts and mountain chains. The black-tailed deer (*O. h. columbianus* and *O. h. sitkensis*) of the Pacific Coast, for example, is easily distinguished from the typical mule deer type.

Because of their wide distribution and adaptation to sub-climax vegetation types, these deer are the most important ungulates in North America in both numbers and economic value. Hundreds of thousands of hunters pursue deer in legal seasons each fall, and unknown (but appreciable) numbers of poachers year round. In many areas deer are responsible for damages to gardens, crops, and forest regeneration. Thousands are struck by cars each year causing expensive repair bills, human injuries, and occasionally deaths and, invariably, death of the deer. Deer have high aesthetic values.

Never have the challenges facing the deer manager been greater than they are today. A pluralistic society has placed conflicting demands on the profession to be all things to all people. Protectionists and antihunting groups want the population to be unhunted, while hunters believe the population can be harvested for recreational sport. This circumstance means that no longer can the efforts of the management agencies be directed at single goals.

My research on population dynamics of deer populations has been conducted to blur the distinctions between the meanings of theory and management. Experimental manipulations of population size have been done to test the full range of densities so that functional relationships between deer numbers and their resources can be established for any given density. Management is thereby enabled to select specific manipulations to satisfy the goals and desires of whatever user group or groups a given program is directed. Furthermore, the consequences of single use decisions on other use groups can be predicted and tradeoff strategies developed.

The presentation will begin with simplified relationships, in order to illustrate the basic responses of deer populations to exploitation, and proceed to complexity that is more akin to what one faces in the real world. I hasten to add, lest I create false expectations, that the problem of real world management in all of its differing circumstances is far beyond the current state of the art.

What I propose to do is present a conceptual framework and rationale for attacking the problem, along with evidence from the George Reserve white-tailed deer herd in southern Michigan that this approach can work (McCullough, 1979), and has worked since the population had to be managed successfully to conduct the necessary experiments. I allude to current research on black-tailed deer at Hopland Field Station in California that is designed to demonstrate that the approach can usefully be employed in a more complex environment, where the manager is confronted by uncontrollable variables such as natural predators and drought.

Productivity

The basis of yield, on a sustained program, is recruitment. Because deer are K-selected (i.e., large, long-lived animals with low reproductive rates and high parental investment in offspring over long parental care periods), their recruitment shows strong density dependent effects. Thus, high recruitment rates usually are realized at low population densities, and these rates decline as population size increases because of intraspecific competition for food. Usually in deer the competition is not based on the amount of forage consumed, but rather the quality of forage consumed. The problem is not finding enough vegetation to fill the rumen (deer dying of malnutrition usually have full rumens), but the net energy and nutrient balance possible on the diet obtained. If the better plant parts of the most digestible species are readily available, the net gain can be put to growth and reproduction. If the net balance is zero, the intake has had to be used for replacement and maintenance at the expense of foregoing growth and reproduction. If the net balance is negative, the loss has to come from the body mass, and this condition cannot be sustained for long or death by starvation will result.

The tradeoffs of deer population management, therefore, are that one can have low residual populations yielding high recruitment rates, intermediate residual populations yielding intermediate rates, or high residual populations yielding low, zero, or at times, negative recruitment rates. Which of these cases is most desirable depends upon the goals of the management program.

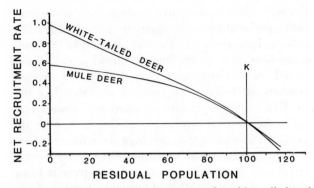

Figure 1. Net recruitment rate curves for white-tailed and mule deer. Curve for white-tailed deer from the George Reserve and mule deer estimated as described in the text. K is standaridzed at 100 and numbers can be read as percentages.

Most human ventures involve obtaining the highest product yield, and analogous thinking leads deer population managers to tend towards programs that give the maximum sustainable yield (MSY) of deer. This approach is resisted by people who want no deer to be killed for philosophical reasons. The latter may be satisfied by live deer removed and transplanted to other suitable but unoccupied habitat, but this assumes that there is empty habitat available. None of the above approaches to deer management is liable to satisfy the people suffering economic losses, for they want to have the lowest residual deer population with the lowest net recruitment.

Recruitment rate and productivity curves are shown in Figure 1 based on the George Reserve deer herd for white-tailed deer (McCullough, 1979) and estimated for the mule deer for which similar data are lacking. The latter estimate is based on published life table parameters, reproductive rates by age, and some general models for age of first reproduction that I have developed. While the absolute values may be somewhat in error, the relative values, as compared to white-tailed deer, should be reasonable. To equalize the comparison, K is set to 100, and the numerical values can be read directly as percentages.

In general, the mule deer is a more K-selected species than the white-tailed deer. It has a later mean age of first reproduction and greater longevity as far as can be determined by existing data. Under ideal food conditions, white-tailed deer females can reach embryo rates of greater than 1.0, and twins (and even triplets) have been recorded (Haugen, 1975; McCullough, 1979). The highest embryo rate I have found reported for mule deer fawns was 0.3 (3 of 10 fawn females) reported by Robinette et al. (1973) for a captive herd of mule deer. Single cases of fawn preg-

nancies have been reported from the wild (Jensen and Robinette, 1955; Thomas and Smith, 1973; Nellis et al., 1976) but Connelly (1981c) stated they are rare. Similarly, mule deer female fawns that become pregnant are reported by Robinette to exceed 41 kg in body weight, while for white-tailed deer of the George Reserve, the weight of conception runs about 36 kg and Severinghaus and Cheatum reported a fawn that was pregnant that weighed only 22 kg. Pregnancy rates reported for white-tailed deer usually exceed those of mule deer, but there seems to be little difference in rates between the two species for $\geq$ 2 year old females. For example, comparison of reproductive rates given by Severinghaus and Cheatum (1956) and those I observed for variable densities of white-tailed deer on the George Reserve (McCullough, 1979) with reproductive rates of the mule and black-tailed deer reviewed by Robinette et al. (1977) shows similar ranges of variation. Therefore, the maximum rate of reproduction for the mule deer in Figure 1 was based upon a reproductive rate of 0.3 for fawn females, and comparable rates to white-tailed deer for older females.

Longevity, another correlate of K-selection, is longer in mule deer than in white-tailed deer. The oldest deer I obtained on the George Reserve were 12.5 years (McCullough, 1979) and these values are typical of other studies of eastern white-tailed deer. From a sample of almost 2000 deer in northern Michigan, only one reached 14 years (Ozoga, 1969). Conversely Robinette reported a 19-year-old mule deer in Utah, and a number of black-tailed deer jaws collected at Hopland Field Station by William Longhurst and Guy Connelly exceeded 12 years. Records of old age in captivity of white-tailed deer (Severinghaus and Cheatum, 1956) are generally lower than those of black-tailed deer (Cowan, 1956) and mule deer (Robinette et al., 1977).

Based on the net recruitment curves of mule and white-tailed deer, productivity (and potential yield) curves can be derived (Figure 2). These can be used as

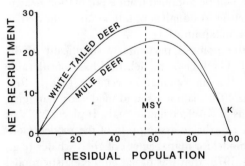

Figure 2. Net recruitment numbers (productivity) for white-tailed deer and mule deer depending upon residual population size.

deterministic models to predict the response of the two species to various exploitation rates, assuming hunting is the only source of traumatic mortality (McCullough, 1979:85). Clearly this is an unreasonable assumption in most cases where predators and other directly inducing mortality factors are present. But it is useful to first illustrate the simple case before dealing with the complex. We will also assume that the desired kill can be achieved exactly, another unrealistic assumption in the real world.

MSY, of course, is the maximum value at the peak of the productivity parabola. It can be seen that the white-tailed deer exceeds the mule deer under equivalent conditions. For white-tailed deer MSY is 33% of the residual population plus recruitment while for mule deer it is 27%. Since maximum longevity does not play a role in heavily exploited populations, it should be noted that this effect is due to the greater reproductive capacity of the white-tailed deer, and particularly the early age of sexual maturity. As emphasized by Cole (1954), Lewontin (1965) and others, age at first reproduction is a dominant variable in evolution of rate of population increase.

Furthermore, the point on the curve where MSY occurs for white-tailed deer is to the left of that of the mule deer. For white-tailed deer, MSY occurs at residual populations that are 56% of K while for mule deer they ate 63% of K. This shift also is a consequence of age at first reproduction (McCullough, unpublished data) with the degree of the shift to the right correlated with increasing delay of age of sexual maturity. Fowler (1981) presented a theoretical model to account for this shift, and reviewed the literature for evidence to support the conclusion. Chapman (1981) reached similar conclusions about marine mammals.

The practical consequences of this shift are many. First, species that are more K-selected will have greater shifts and will support lower rates of exploitation. They have less resilience in the form of density dependent reproduction adjustment. They are more easily over-exploited whether by intent or ignorance. Second, MSY will be obtained from a population near to K; i.e., denser residual populations are required to sustain the maximum take.

The latter point is particularly significant in the real world. The logistic model, that has considerable heuristic value in population ecology (May, 1976, May et al., 1979), is not a sound model for managing populations of K-selected mammals. It places MSY at 50% of K as a basic assumption of the model. Consider the model for management of great whales (e.g., see Norris, 1978) that was based on the logistic model adopted by the International Whaling Commission (IWC) as recently as 1974. Great whales have delays in first reproduction of about 4–6 years (Allen, 1974;

Lockyer, 1972) as compared to the 2 years of the mule deer and would have productivity curves with MSY substantially shifted to the right of that of the mule deer. Managed by the logistic model, great whales would be greatly overexploited long before they reached MSY based on 50% of K. Doubtless this model had little to do with devastation of whale stocks given the political process of decision-making by the IWC. But, in any event, it is long since time to abandon the logistic model, at least for the management of K-selected mammals. Fortunately, progress is being made, and recently MSY of porpoises was set at 65–80% of K (Smith, 1979).

The important message is that relatively little difference in reproductive potential has a relatively great impact on the shift of MSY towards K, and any shift in that direction leads to greater susceptibility to overexploitation. Mule deer populations underwent a general decline throughout much of the western U.S. in the late 1960s and early 1970s (Workman and Low, 1976; Connelly, 1981a). To what extent this was due to overhunting was strongly debated, but certainly it contributed in some populations, although deficient as a general explanation (Connelly, 1981a). Yet, one wonders if the exploitation rates sustained on the well-studied white-tailed deer populations (including the George Reserve herd) were not extrapolated to mule deer populations where similar studies were sporadic and incomplete. The results on mule deer from the National Bison Range in Montana reported by Connelly (1981b) are probably the most complete to date, and were geared to removal of annual increment rather than to attempt to manipulate annual increment through compensatory responses to density. To my knowledge, the experiments I am currently conducting on population manipulation of the black-tailed deer herd at Hopland Field Station in California are the first systematic attempts to address this question.

Deterministic Predictions

It is important to note that any point on the x axis of Figure 2 can be a stable equilibrium point (except, of course, values so low that fertilization doesn't occur or inbreeding depression occurs) provided the correct removals are taken. Note, further, that a given removal can stabilize the population at two different points on the productivity curve, one on the left descending arm of the parabola and one on the right descending arm. This relationship explains why sometimes populations that are stable at a low level may increase to a much higher level where they are once again stable, and vice versa. If a mortality factor that is fairly constant is holding the population at a low level, and is released for a brief period, then reinstated, the popu-

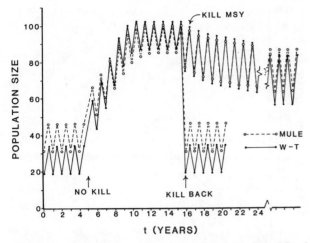

Figure 3. Simulations with a deterministic model of fixed kills on white-tailed and mule deer populations. Initial kill is 15, which is at equilibrium on the left arm of the productivity curve (Figure 2). Note higher residual population in mule deer. In year 5, no kill is taken, and a kill of 15 is resumed thereafter. The populations grow to the equilibrium point on the right arm of the parabola. In year 16, the populations are killed back to the equilibrium point for a kill of 15 (below) or MSY is killed (above).

lation will grow to the other side of the parabola and come to balance. If the population is then reduced to a low level by a change in a mortality factor that substantially reduced the population, a balance at the left arm of the parabola may be reestablished.

This situation can be simulated with the deterministic model. Figure 3 illustrates the two equilibrium points, and the management approaches thus made possible. Since a given kill of 15 animals per year will stabilize the white-tailed deer population at a residual of 19 or 88 and the mule deer at 31 or 86, which is the desirable residual will depend upon the objective of the program. If it is a sport hunting program, and deer hunters want to have a high population to be assured that the population is not being overexploited, the kill of 15 should be taken from the higher residual population. If the purpose of the program is to reduce the number of deer-car collisions (or crop damage, or other negative aspect of the deer herd) the lower residual population would be preferred. The size of the kill is equal in both cases, and each population equilibrium is sustainable (however, as will be discussed below, the equilibrium on the right is far more easily achieved in practice). Because the kill in one case comes from pre-hunt populations of 34 and 46 for white-tailed and mule deer, respectively, and 103 and 101 in the other, the hunter effort to achieve the given kill will not be the same. Because of their cryptic be-

havior, catch per unit effort under most hunting circumstances is density dependent. Thus, under most conditions, the average deer taken from a low population will require greater effort than the average deer from a high population. Although the kill of 15 was selected arbitrarily, any other size of fixed kill has equilibrium points on both arms of the parabola except MSY, which has a single point at the peak of the parabola.

Behavior rules for the models can be stated to predict population responses to any given fixed kill or change in fixed kill depending upon the residual population at the start. It is most convenient (although certainly not required) to assume that the time order is recruit, then kill, because this mimics the order usually followed in the real world. Thus, the residual population is equivalent to the posthunt population, which gives birth to offspring in spring or summer (potential new recruits), part of which survive to fall (recruits) and are subject to hunting in fall seasons.

The rules are as follows:
1. If a fixed kill exceeds MSY, continuing the fixed kill will lead to population extinction no matter what the residual population.
2. If the residual population is on the left arm of the parabola or at the residual population that yields MSY, a fixed removal equal to recruitment will stabilize the population at that residual.
3. If the residual population is on the left arm of the parabola, and the fixed kill exceeds the recruitment, the population will be driven to extinction. If the recruitment exceeds the kill, the residual population will grow to the balance point on the right arm of the parabola for that fixed kill.
4. If the residual population is on the right arm of the parabola, and if the kill exceeds the recruitment at the residual population (but is less than MSY, see 1 above), the residual population will decline to the balance point for that fixed kill on the right arm of the parabola. If the kill is less than the recruitment, the residual population will grow to the balance point nearer to K.

Kill by Sex and Age

The manipulation of sex and age in harvests involves complexities that are beyond the scope of this paper (see McCullough, 1979, 1982). The major points, however, are as follows. Deer populations are relatively insensitive to variation in sex and age selectivity, and rather large deviations from random selection are necessary to cause departure from mean population responses to density. The mule deer, because of its lower reproductive rate, is slightly more sensitive to age and sex manipulation than the white-tailed deer.

The most common deviation, bucks-only hunting, results in residual populations that are nearly at K. Bucks-only hunting cannot produce MSY of bucks. Obtaining MSY of both bucks-only and total population requires removal of both sexes in proportion to their presence in the population. Thus, in terms of high yield management, there is no advantage to being selective for sex or age in the kill.

Influence of Exploitation on Residual Population

Because density dependent recruitment rates go up as the size of the kill of deer increases, many deer biologists have assumed that there was total compensation. This is untrue for K-selected species, as I have shown for the George Reserve white-tailed deer population (McCullough, 1979). Management for MSY results in a decline in the residual population over what it is at K, and in most cases, the prehunt population declines as well. This accounts for much of the failure of communication between deer hunters and managers, where the former's point of reference is the number of deer "in the field" (i.e., residual population) while the latter's is game in the bag. Thus, hunters have called heavy antlerless kills disastrous because they have reduced the size of the deer population, while managers have considered them successful because they result in high, sustainable harvests.

The relationship between size of kill and residual population can be most easily comprehended by a stock-recruitment graph, where residual population is the stock. Both x and y axes must have the same scale so that any value on one axis is correlated with the same value on the other by a 45° line (i.e., the slope, b = 1; line A, Figure 4). The productivity curve (Figure 2) can then be plotted above the 45° line, which has been done in Figure 4 for white-tailed and mule deer. Because sustainable kill is based on recruitment, at any given residual population on the x-axis, the distance below the 45° line is the number of animals in the residual population, and the distance above the 45° line to the recruitment curve is the number of animals recruited. To stabilize the population at that residual population, the kill must be the same number as the number of recruits. Therefore, for stability at any given value of residual population, the height of the recruitment curve represents the prehunt population, the distance from the recruitment curve and the 45° line the size of the required kill, and distance from the 45° line to the zero intercept of the y-axis the residual population size.

From Figure 4 it can be seen that at MSY, the residual population is only 56% of K for the white-tailed deer, and 63% for mule deer. For both species,

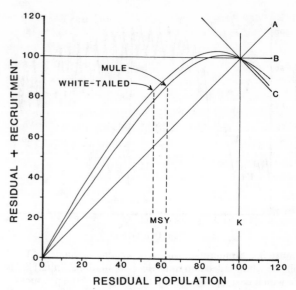

Figure 4. Stock recruitment model for white-tailed and mule deer. See text for further explanation.

prehunt populations at MSY are less than K, although at moderate kills, the prehunt populations are greater than K (i.e., the recruitment curve exceeds the horizontal line B, that intercepts K). The fact that the white-tailed deer exceeds the mule deer again reflects the relative difference in reproductive rate of the two species.

The high kill and relatively low residual population that prevail under management for MSY understandably give pause to hunters, who characteristically are conservative and concerned about the size of the population in the field. Because they have the intuitively appealing belief that high populations are necessary to support high kills (which they do on a one-time basis), they oppose the non-intuitive actual condition that it is relatively low populations that sustain continuous high kills (McCullough, 1979).

Population Stability and Residual Population Size

Earlier discussion pointed up the relative instability of the population on the left arm of the productivity parabola (Figure 2). At a given residual population if there is overexploitation (i.e., the kill exceeds the recruitment) the population will be driven to extinction, whereas if it is underexploited (kill is less than recruitment), the residual population will grow to the balance point on the right arm of the parabola. The only way to stabilize the residual population on the left arm of MSY is to exactly remove the recruitment. While, in theory, this sounds easy, in practice it is nearly impossible, because methods of assessing the necessary parameters to achieve this end are woefully inadequate.

Conversely, achieving stability on the right arm of the parabola at a given residual population is relatively easy because of the self-correcting behavior of the population. Thus, if the recruitment at a given residual population is exceeded by the kill, the lowered residual population results in a higher recruitment that tends to push the population upwards towards the original residual population. If kill continues to exceed recruitment, so long as it is less than MSY, a new balance point between kill, recruitment, and residual population will be reached. If the kill is less than the recruitment, the increased residual population will recruit fewer individuals, which will tend to return it to the original residual population if the original kill is taken in future years. If too few are killed consistently, a new balance of kill and recruitment at a higher residual population will be reached.

What this means, in practical terms, is that management of populations at residual population sizes on the right arm of the productivity parabola is resilient and forgiving of mistakes. The density dependent responses of the population tend to correct, and adjacent balance points are reached so long as the residual population is not near that yielding MSY. If near MSY, the possibility of accidentally reducing the residual population to the left of MSY is greater.

There are further practical considerations to this relationship. It is easier to interpose a management program designed to achieve MSY starting from a residual population near K because of the resilience of the population to exploitation. A basic strategy of gradually increasing the kill and monitoring the population response includes little risk, and the information gained can be used in a practical model based on empirical data from the population in question.

It is virtually impossible to predict where MSY will be by projecting from data obtained while residual populations are still on the left arm of the parabola. This situation may occur because the population has been overexploited in the past, new habitat has been created (e.g., a large fire in deer range) and in cases of introduction or reintroduction of populations into empty habitat. Estimations of population parameters and measurements of vegetation have more or less large sampling error, and are not as sensitive as the population responses. The changes at MSY are subtle, and usually the residual population needs to be rather higher before one can be sure that the right arm of the parabola has been reached because of sampling error. There are problems with time lags also (see time lag section) and parameter values may be inflated over equilibrium values. Under conditions of easy censusing and high accuracy (e.g., in openland species), one might do fairly well in tracking population parameters, and management can be more precise. With cryptic species such as deer, it is unrealistic to expect precision in management, and a larger margin of error is a prudent part of the management program. As previously noted, residual populations on the left arm of the parabola are unforgiving of mistakes of overexploitation. Underexploitation leads to growth of the population to the right arm of the parabola. It is usually preferable to not exploit the population until it is on the right arm of the parabola.

Functional Refugia

An exception to the conclusion that populations are easily overexploited and driven to extinction if the residual population is on the left arm of the productivity parabola is the presence of a functional refuge. This may take any of a number of forms, including a legally designated refuge. A functional refuge is defined here as an area, or circumstance, that protects the residual population from further exploitation once it declines below a certain size. Functional refugia include physical and spacial attributes such as large, unroaded areas where access is difficult, and impassable or impenetrable habitats where deer are protected. They also include human traits such as lack of hunting skills or motivation. Hunters may not be willing to continue to hunt if low deer population size discourages them and results in their perceiving their chances of success as being too low. Similarly, human attitudes about deer, such as the resistance of many hunters to shooting females, may result in a functional refuge for a given sex/age class. Finally, hunting regulations may have the characteristics of a refuge. Protecting given sex/age classes, restrictions on equipment, specified hunting hours, setting bag limits (which removes skilled hunters and retains unskilled ones), prohibiting baiting, and restricting use of dogs all provide functional refugia.

The influence of refugia on population responses is shown in Figure 5. In essence, the area on the left arm of the productivity parabola is a sanctuary, and

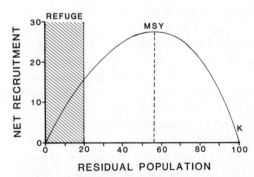

Figure 5. Net recruitment (productivity) curve for white-tailed deer with a functional refuge at 20 animals.

whereas the residual population can be reduced readily by overexploitation to this point, further reduction is constrained. This is the usual situation with control of problem wildlife where populations are fairly readily reduced to some point, and beyond which it is difficult or impossible to reduce them further. It also explains why eradication, often the most desirable goal, is so seldom achieved, and control is accepted even though it requires continuous (and expensive) input.

Time Lags

There are two main kinds of time lags, programmatic and trophic level. Programmatic time lags, which are non-destructive, are traceable to the shift in relationship of kill to recruitment and related shift in residual population with a change in management. It is the time it takes to move from one equilibrium at a given kill to another with a change in kill. Figure 3 illustrates this kind of lag which occurred with shifting kills to move from the balance point of kill of 15 per year on the left arm of the productivity curve to the balance point for the same kill on the right arm. The time involved in the lag depends upon the magnitude of change in kill and on which arm on the parabola the initial residual population was. Thus, a change in kill from 15 to 10 per year made at the residual population balance point on the left arm would have a long lag while the same change made at the residual population balance point on the right arm would be short. Conversely, shifting from a kill of 15 per year to 20 per year would result in a short lag starting from either balance point. The new equilibrium would be reached quickly if the residual population was on the right arm, and extinction (a highly stable balance point!) would occur rapidly if on the left arm. These lags cause relatively little problem, because they are usually short, encompassed in the model, and, therefore, are predictable.

Because productivity curves are based on equilibrium values over a range of residual populations from O to K, they encompass only population responses that do not result in lowering K by vegetation damage; i.e., exceeding the resilience of the vegetation to maintain a steady state relationship with the browsing/grazing pressure. Equilibrium overshoots are incomplete in that they occur seasonally when the residual population plus recruitment exceed K, but the subtraction of the kill reduced the population below K. For purposes of designation, these overshoots can be called non-destructive overshoots as opposed to cases where vegetation destruction occurs. Destructive "overshoot", where rapid population growth results in a population size greater than K, results in vegetation damage, and lowering of K.

The tendency of a population to produce either kind of overshoot is related to its reproductive potential with more r-selected species prone to greater overshoot than more K-selected species. If the relationship between recruitment rate and residual population is linear, as with the logistic model, then the tendency of a population to overshoot can be expressed by the numerical value of the y-intercept (i.e., where x = 0). Y-intercept values of 0 to 1 do not overshoot, values of 1 to 2 overshoot and oscillate dampening out to K, and values greater than 2 overshoot and oscillate with greater amplitude until extinction occurs (McCullough, 1979). I have proposed that K-selected species can be defined as those with y-intercepts of ≤ 2 since these populations tend to track K, surely the significant point about a species being K-selected.

However, as pointed out earlier, the logistic model is unrealistic for large, K-selected mammals which have non-linear relationships of recruitment rate to residual populations. And, different subspecies or populations of even the same species may have somewhat different shapes. All of these cases are easily solved graphically by a stock recruitment graph (Figure 4). If any part of the recruitment curve exceeds the horizontal line (b = 0; line B) but does not exceed the line perpendicular to the 45° line (i.e., b = −1; line C, Figure 4) that population will overshoot and, with decreasing oscillations, dampen out to K. Both the white-tailed and mule deer curves show this relationship, and corresponding population growth curves for the two species are shown in Figure 6. A recruitment curve that exceeded line C would oscillate erratically, as is typical with r-selected species. Note that these

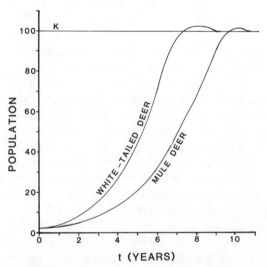

Figure 6. Deterministic population growth curves for white-tailed and mule deer. White-tailed deer reach K in 8 years while mule deer require 10 years because of lower reproductive rate.

McCullough

growth curves are based on mean productivity values, and are non-destructive by definition.

Destructive overshoots are also more likely the greater the recruitment rate of the species in question. However, nearly all species of ungulates have the capacity to produce destructive overshoots under certain circumstances. Destructive overshoots present problems of unpredictability because they deviate from equilibrium values. Residual populations exceed K, not just seasonally or temporarily as in non-destructive overshoot, but yearlong. Since K is, by definition, the maximum population size that can be supported on a sustained basis, residual populations greater than K exceed the capacity of the vegetation to sustain continued browsing/grazing, and changes in the vegetation result in even less capacity to support browsing/grazing. That is, K itself is reduced.

Destructive overshoot occurs in situations where artificially low population sizes result in "accumulation" of resources in a living, dynamic sense. (Note, however, that vegetation damage can occur under other circumstances; see stochasticity below). These include cases where populations have been heavily over-exploited, new habitat has been created, or introductions to favorable habitat have occurred.

A key point is that the deviation of population response from the equilibrium values of a productivity curve occurs not at K, but at the inflection point of the S-shaped population growth curve upon the equilibrium productivity curve (Figure 7). The inflection point in Figure 7 corresponds to the residual popula-

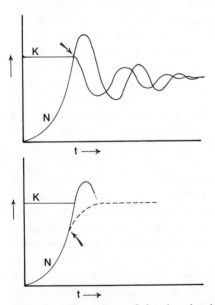

Figure 7. Two views of the time lag in destructive overshoot. Arrows on the curves indicate the beginning of the time lag. Top: Time lag as commonly conceived. Bottom: Time lag as suggested by the George Reserve white-tailed deer overshoot.

tion size that gives MSY for the white-tailed deer in Figure 2. Figure 7 shows the destructive overshoot curve for the George Reserve white-tailed deer population that comes from an experiment I am currently conducting. This population was purposefully overexploited to reduce it to a residual population size of 10 in 1974–75. The population was not exploited at all in the following 4 years to allow unimpeded population growth. Population growth, if adjusted for different starting sizes, virtually duplicated the growth of the original introduction of 6 animals in 1928, a much celebrated example of deer population growth in a favorable environment (McCullough, 1982). The population reached an estimated 212 in 1980–81, which greatly exceeds the equilibrium of K of 176 (McCullough, 1979).

The amount of damage to the vegetation in a destructive overshoot depends upon by how much and how long the residual population exceeds the equilibrium curve. Typically, the damage to the vegetation precedes the decline in the deer population so that the lagged population drives the vegetation to even lower capacity. A pronounced population "crash" is usually required to bring the residual population below the depressed K, and allow vegetative recovery to occur.

On the George Reserve, the population growth following the original introduction overshot and caused damage to the vegetation, which was gradually brought under control by shooting. However, vegetative responses remained depressed until the population was reduced to a residual of about 80, as evidenced by the continuous recruitments below the equilibrium values (McCullough, 1979, 1984). However, when the population was held below 80 for several years, the vegetation recovered and recruitment rates increased to the equilibrium values.

In the current overshoot experiment damage to the vegetation is not being allowed because shooting is being used to reduce the seasonal population, which exceeds K following recruitment, to a residual population below K (130 animals). The purpose of the experiment is to show that the overshoot is traceable to an "accumulation" of food resources and, that as the accumulation is used up, the size of the kill that is required to bring the residual population to 130 subsides over time from a value greatly above the equilibrium value to the equilibrium value. Thus, the initial kill in the first year required to bring the population down to 130 was 82, and in subsequent years it is predicted that this will drop to an average of 43, the mean productivity curve equilibrium number.

Stochasticity

Up to this point the productivity curve in Figure 2 has been treated largely as an invariable function in a

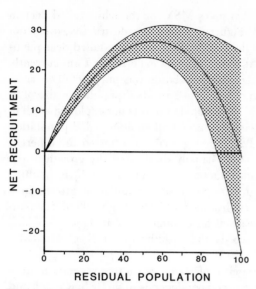

Figure 8. Net recruitment (productivity) curve with 95 percent confidence limits based on the George Reserve white-tailed deer population.

deterministic fashion. This artifice was useful for purposes of illustration. But, at this point, it is necessary to recognize that the productivity curve is the mean value with variance on either side due to good and poor years and other stochastic events, including chance. Variation from the mean values has consequences that require modification of some of the earlier conclusions based on the mean values.

The confidence bounds on the productivity curve (Figure 8) are narrow on the left end of the curve, and broaden out as one moves to the right towards K (McCullough, 1979). In practical terms this means that variation from the mean value is less when residual populations are small, and greater as one nears K. This relationship influences population behavior relative to population density with predictability being most reliable at low densities and least at high densities.

A previous conclusion was that the left arm of the productivity parabola inherently was rather unstable. Addition of stochasticity results in even greater instability. Thus, one cannot simply determine the mean number of recruits, and kill that number of animals. One needs to determine the exact number of animals recruited in a given year, and remove that number. Assume that the mean number of recruits is 15 at a residual population on the left arm of the parabola. If for white-tailed deer in a given year the variation is 17 recruits, and only 15 animals are killed, an increase in the residual population from 19 to 21 results. Because this higher residual population has a higher mean recruitment (17 versus 15), an equal

stochastic variation in the opposite direction in the following year will be required to bring the residual population back to the initial residual population. This may occur occasionally, but is improbable to be maintained for long.

The same is true if a low recruitment value occurs, and fewer than 15 are recruited while 15 are killed. A deviation of recruitment to the high side would be required to bring the residual population back to the initial value.

Furthermore, deviations between years may be in the same direction, which further increases the unlikelihood of a stable balance. Thus, in all cases where the recruitment cannot be measured exactly and removed exactly, the population will either grow to the balance point on the right arm of the parabola, or go to extinction. The direction will depend on whether by chance the recruitment was high or low in the first year. Given stochasticity, the importance of functional refugia takes on even greater meaning in preventing extinctions.

The same problem pertains to management at MSY for overexploitation, but not underexploitation. If higher than mean recruitments occur and mean recruitment is killed (by definition, MSY) the residual population will increase. Because the residual population will be on the right arm of the parabola, decreasing recruitment will tend to reduce the residual population back towards that at MSY. However, if recruitment is below the mean, and the mean recruitment is killed, the residual population will be shifted to the left arm of the parabola, where lower mean recruitment occurs. Just as with the examples on the left arm of the productivity parabola, variation in the opposite direction will be required to prevent subsequent extinction (assuming no refugium). Therefore, continued removal of mean MSY from a stochastically varying recruitment will sooner or later lead to extinction.

Simulations with the George Reserve deer model showed that the fixed kill had to be reduced from the mean MSY recruitment of 49 to 46 to avoid extinction if recruitment were stochastic. If the kill is stochastic as well, the fixed kill must be reduced even further to 43 (McCullough, 1979).

More conservative management of residual populations further on the right arm of the productivity parabola are quite stable. Because recruitment is compensatory, stochastic variation in recruitment is subsequently corrected, and the residual population tends to return to the balance point of mean recruitment and mean kill.

However, a different kind of problem develops if no kill is taken. The residual population grows to K where the confidence bounds are broad (Figure 8) and, hence, deviations from the mean recruitment (zero) greatest. Variance in the high side results in residual populations that exceed K. Thus, overshoot can occur, particularly if more than one good year occurs in a row which forces the residual population upward. When the average or poor year follows, a high residual population must subsist on a diminished resource base, and vegetation destruction is highly likely.

It can be seen that protection of a population from hunting, which is tantamount to managing for residual populations at K, results in an inherently unstable situation, although extinction is unlikely given the wide range of density dependent adjustment that is possible. Natural fluctuations are greater at K than they are for residual populations reduced by hunting (McCullough, 1979). Large fluctuations are more likely to cause vegetation damage and reduction of K. Catastrophies, the devastation of the population by the periodic occurrence of the extreme case (e.g., the 20 year winter) are more likely.

However, it should be noted that high population fluctuations at K are not universal, since they are caused by variation in the environment. Thus, in highly variable environments, population fluctuations at K are extreme, while in highly stable and predictable environments a stable equilibrium of residual populations may well occur. Therefore, vegetation damage by unhunted populations of deer is not inevitable; for stable environments, equilibrium between residual populations at K and vegetation can be maintained. Also, in extreme environments where bad years are frequent (as for example at the northern extremes of the deer range where severe winters are frequent), the population may be reduced so frequently that it seldom or never reaches K, and it may be continually expanding from low levels with few density dependent effects. Similar patterns may hold for other extreme environments, for example, deep snow in mountainous regions, and drought in xeric areas.

In extreme environments, natural fluctuations may entirely overshadow density dependent effects. In terms of productivity curves, what this means is that either seasonal extremes force the residual population to the left arm of the parabola and K is unchanged (as with hard winters in the northern fringes of the range) or that K itself is fluctuating wildly (as is typical of desert conditions).

Both environmental variance and the frequency distribution of good and poor years influence the precision of management that is possible and the management strategy that should be applied. Figure 9 shows diagrammatically various environmental variations assuming that there are not sequences or cyclic

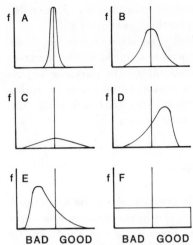

Figure 9. Schematic diagrams of the frequency distributions of good and bad years in different environments. A, leptokurtic frequency distribution, highly stable environment. B, normal frequency distribution, moderately stable environment. C, platykurtic frequency distribution, highly unstable environment. D, right-skewed frequency distribution, usually moderately stable, good environment, with occasional bad years. E, left-skewed frequency distribution, usually moderately stable, poor environment, with occasional good years. F, random frequency distribution, highly unstable environment.

patterns. Figure 9A shows a leptokurtic distribution of good and bad years that is exhibited by stable environments. Density effects are predominant in population behavior and management can be precise for any program goal. Figure 9B shows a normal distribution where environmental variation is greater than in 9A, but still relatively small and does not overshadow density effects. Thus management can be based on density, but the margin allowed for error needs to be greater. Figure 9C shows the platykurtic distribution of a highly variable environment. Environmental variation will overshadow density effects, and management must be *ad hoc* to continually adjusting to the driving variable, the uncontrollable variation in the environment. Figure 9D shows a skewed distribution where most years are good, but an occasional bad year occurs. Density effects are predominant except for the occasional severe year. Management strategy is basically precise and based on density dependent population behavior, but periodic *ad hoc* adjustments are required to adjust for the extreme year. Figure 9E shows the distribution where most years are poor with occasional good years occurring. This situation is typical of many deserts. Management should be based on the model poor year, with density dependent population behavior practiced, but with a wide margin of error. Occasionally good years can be taken advantage of on an *ad hoc* basis. Random environments (Figure 9F) behave like the platykurtic ones (Figure 9C).

If the good and bad years show sequencing or especially cycles (predictable sequences), the manager may be able to switch strategies by pursuing aggressive programs with narrower margins of error during good periods, and conservative ones with wide margins of error during poor periods.

Natural Predators

There is considerable question about the role of predators in the dynamics of deer populations. Elsewhere I have reviewed the literature about predation on deer, and argued that vulnerability of prey was the key element in coexistence of predator and prey (McCullough, 1979). Whatever the merits of that argument, it can be stated categorically that the presence of healthy populations of deer on the North American continent when European man arrived was evidence of some density-related factor that allowed coexistence of deer and their predators over hundreds of thousands of years.

It is of great practical concern to us whether a deer is killed by a predator, or an accident, or a human factor, for the share available to each is diminished. But it must be remembered that to the surviving deer population only the fact of an individual's removal is important, not the cause. One less female in the population is one less female whatever the cause of its demise. Therefore, the consequences of density to the survivors is the same, and can be expressed by productivity curves such as Figure 2 where the residual population is that remaining after those killed by natural predators and humans have been removed. In this sense, the cause of the mortality is irrelevant; only the number is important.

While in terms of the residual population, the number of individuals killed is strictly additive for natural predators and human kills, the capability to make kills is probably not, given that there is strong evidence that both hunting success of predators and humans is dependent on the density of prey (McCullough, 1979). Selectivity for sex and age is different, but as previously noted, the density dependent response of deer populations is rather insensitive to deviations in age and sex composition.

It is extremely difficult to measure the number of deer taken by predators, and practically, it is not necessary. One can establish the empirical relationship of recruitment rate to human hunting kill starting from a deer population that is near K with a given small human kill and an unknown natural predator kill. One would want to stabilize whatever predator control effort one was making so that changes in that variable did not introduce noise into the system.

By increasing the human kill in small increments, the functional relationship between recruitment, residual population, and human kill could be established. In effect, this would show what was available for a human kill given the unknown natural predator kill. If the human take came at the expense of predator kill (i.e., was substitutive), the empirical productivity curve would have a steep right arm. If human take and natural predator take were largely additive, the right arm would be shallower. Steepness or shallowness can be judged somewhat by comparing the observed empirical curve to the expected curve with the absence of natural predators, such as Figure 2. Since in essence, the human kill is being taken "after" the predators have taken their share, the functional relationship of deer density to predator success is already integrated into the empirical model. Similarly because the human take is based on that "left over" from the natural predator kill, management of the human kill for no more than MSY will mean that MSY for the actual population including both predator and human kills will not be exceeded. Of course, this approach assumes that the deer population is to the right of MSY, and that initially the deer population was actually sustaining both the natural predator and human kill.

This approach is currently being taken with the density experiment I am conducting on the Hopland Field Station black-tailed deer population. Coyotes take an unknown portion (mainly fawns) of the population that I am not optimistic about being able to measure directly. Nevertheless, it should be possible to determine MSY for the human take, and, by difference, approximate what must be going to other causes including coyote predation.

Habitat Manipulation

Deer are usually categorized as subclimax adapted species (Leopold, 1950; Taylor, 1956) and over most of their range this is true. Nevertheless, this generalization should not obscure the fact that in some situations, particularly on the xeric extremes of the distribution of both species, they occupy climax stages. In general, deer populations were favored by the extensive modifications of climax vegetation with settlement by European man, beginning in the east on a large scale in the 1700s and extending to the west in the 1800s. Concomitant unregulated hunting reduced deer populations to low levels and resulted in extirpation of deer from much of their range by the turn of the 20th century. With the extensive creation of favorable habitat, and effective legal protection by the

1930s, deer populations built up to unprecedented levels, peaking in most areas in the late 1940s or early 1950s. Successional progression has reduced deer habitat since that period and deer are on a long-term decline. Long-term oscillations in deer populations might be expected to continue given the synchronization of forest growth cycles and slow vegetation change in the xeric, non-forested, ranges of the west. However, intensive forest management, and artificial manipulation of both forest and non-forest vegetation have resulted in short rotations. This, plus the great natural heterogeneity of vegetation with differing successional rates promises to result in an approximate steady state sometime in the future. The long-term future of deer populations looks promising. One of the things modern man is very good at is destruction of climax vegetation. And, in contrast to climax-adapted ungulates that are likely to be more and more restricted to reserves, deer are likely to remain broadly distributed and live in close proximity to humans.

Deer can be benefitted readily by habitat manipulation over most of their range, and there can be no question that habitat management is the keystone to continuing high populations. Yet, because habitat management changes K, it causes difficulties with population modeling and management. In principle, adjusting models for creation and loss of K is simple. Simply change the slopes of the recruitment rate curves (Figure 1). In practice, this is extremely difficult, because of the problem of determining K by measurements on vegetation. Although there are a plethora of methods, so far no one has succeeded in deriving reliable estimates of K, even for domestic stock in relatively simple vegetation. Consider that the productivity curve in Figure 2 is the deer population's complex integration of plant species composition, palatability, digestibility, and seasonal availability in a heterogeneous environment, typically composed of a mosaic of vegetation types, and one begins to comprehend the task that confronts the person embarking on an estimation of K from measurements of vegetation.

As previously noted, estimating MSY and K on an expanding population is virtually impossible until the residual population yielding MSY (right arm of the productivity curve) is exceeded, and exceeded by sufficient amount to be separable from sampling error. Overshoot time lags greatly complicate the problem because they produce population responses that exceed the equilibrium values. Indeed, the overshoot experiment currently being conducted on the George Reserve is motivated partly by the need for a strategy of coping with overshoot that brings population parameters to equilibrium values without destructive effects on the vegetation, and reduced K.

Loss of K through loss of habitat because of successional change is somewhat more manageable because it typically occurs more slowly. If the population is being managed for MSY there is serious risk of over-exploitation, beause the productivity curve is being lowered and shifted to the left as K shifts to the left. If the population is being managed more conservatively on the right arm of the productivity curve, it will compensate for excessive kills, and lowering equilibrium values with loss of K has a reasonable probability of being discovered through monitoring of the residual population and shifts in the population parameters.

In cases where the successional period of the vegetation is very short, precise population management is likely impossible. For example, the advantages to deer in manipulating the California chaparral type are short-lived (Taber and Dasmann, 1958).

Obviously there is much to be gained by management for habitat steady states where habitat is created at the same rate it is lost. Such states may not be achievable because of uneven flows of forest products and operating budgets, to mention only a couple of problems. Thus the blessings of being able to rather readily create favorable deer habitat may be enjoyed at the cost of loss of precision in population management. Net benefit must be considered. It is pointless to invest in creation of new habitat if the population has to be managed so conservatively as to give yields no better than could be achieved by more precise management of the existing population. It is not an immutable rule that more deer is better.

Management Decisions

From the above discussion, the general management programs for given objectives can be outlined. If the objective of the program is to minimize deer-car collisions or crop damage, heavy harvests of either sex and any age will be required to maintain low residual populations. If a functional refuge is present in the system, liberal regulations can be framed, and the refuge used to constrain the lower limit of the residual population. If no refuge is present, and a continuing deer population is desired, careful monitoring will be required to maintain the specified population by *ad hoc* adjustments of kill, because management on the right arm of productivity curves is so unstable.

If the goal of the program is to maximize the harvest, the population can be managed for either sex, any age, to residual populations somewhat above MSY. This area of the productivity curve is quite stable and self-correcting for management errors or environmental variation. Obtaining MSY would require much more precise monitoring of the population, and *ad hoc* adjustments for environmental variability from year to year. Relatively low residual populations result from this management system.

If the goal of the program is a high residual population then total protection can be implemented. In extremely stable environments, this may result in stable residual populations, but in fluctuating environments variation in residual populations that exceed K cause considerable risk of vegetation damage. *Ad hoc* kills may remove this risk if they are feasible. Bucks-only hunting results in residual populations that are very near K and harvests that are minimal. Populations managed like this are prone to similar instabilities as totally protected populations.

Programs of harvest that are intermediate to the above represent tradeoffs between single goals. Pursuing single goals will satisfy certain user groups and anger others. Tradeoffs, depending on where they are made, will more or less satisfy or anger the various interest groups. Whether balances of this kind will result in mutual satisfaction or mutual dissatisfaction is hard to say. Given the completely different philosophical views of hunters and protectionists tradeoffs between these groups seem unlikely to be mutually satisfactory. But development of productivity curves will form the basis for meeting management goals of various kinds, and reduce the uncertainty of the program the manager elects to pursue.

Acknowledgments

The research on the George Reserve, upon which most of this paper is based and which is continuing at present, was supported by NSF grants GB-28822X, GB-41139, GB-41139/7300787, and DEB 79-11534. Studies at Hopland Field Station are supported by the California Agricultural Experiment Station. I am indebted to the administrators of these areas for their support and cooperation: Theodore Hubbell, Nelson Hairston, (late) Donald Tinkle, Robert Storer, Francis Evans, Richard Alexander, and Al Murphy. My thanks to the many research assistants and other graduate students who assisted with the work: Dennis King, Dennis Bromley, Fred Samson, Bruce Coblentz, Michael Collopy, David Hirth, David Kitchen, (late) John P. Clark, (late) Jim Feist, Edwin Chinn, Yvette McCullough, John Bissonette, Steve Newhouse, John Wehausen, Peter Flanagan, Terry Bowyer, Eve Kunen, Mike Fairchild, Bill Carmen, Audrey Goldsmith, Gregg Miller, Tom Kucera, John Simon, Paul Beier, Jenny Dusheck, Nick Menzies, Chris Byrne, and James Edelson.

Literature Cited

Allen, K.R.
1974. Recruitment to whale stocks. In *The whale problem: a status report*, edited by W.E. Schevill, pp. 352–358. Cambridge: Harvard University Press.

Chapman, D.G.
1981. Evaluation of marine mammal population models. In *Dynamics of large mammal populations*, edited by C.W. Fowler and T.D. Smith, pp. 277–296. New York, NY: John Wiley and Sons.

Cole, L.E.
1954. The population consequences of life history phenomena. *Quarterly Review of Biology*, 29:103–137.

Connelly, G.E.
1981a. Trends in populations and harvests. In *Mule and black-tailed deer of North America*, edited by O.C. Wallmo, pp. 225–243. Washington, D.C.: Wildlife Management Institute, and Lincoln, Nebraska: University of Nebraska Press.

1981b. Limiting factors and population regulation. In *Mule and black-tailed deer of North America*, edited by O.C. Wallmo, pp. 245–285. Washington, D.C.: Wildlife Management Institute, and Lincoln, Nebraska: University of Nebraska Press.

1981c. Assessing populations. In *Mule and black-tailed deer of North America*, edited by O.C. Wallmo, pp. 287–345. Washington, D.C.: Wildlife Management Institute, and Lincoln, Nebraska: University of Nebraska Press.

Cowan, I. McT.
1956. Life and times of the coast black-tailed deer. In *The deer of North America*, edited by W.P. Taylor, pp. 523–617. Harrisburg, Pennsylvania: Stackpole Co., and Washington, D.C.: Wildlife Management Institute.

Fowler, C.W.
1981. Density dependence as related to life history strategy. *Ecology*, 62:601–610.

Haugen, A.O.
1975. Reproductive performance of white-tailed deer in Iowa. *Journal of Mammalogy*, 56:151–159.

Jensen, W., and W.L. Robinette
1955. A high reproductive rate for Rocky Mountain mule deer (*Odocoileus h. hemionus*). *Journal of Wildlife Management*, 19:503.

Leopold, A.S.
1950. Deer in relation to plant succession. *Transactions of the North American Wildlife and Natural Resources Conference*, 15:571–580.

Lockyer, C.H.
1972. The age at sexual maturity of the southern fin whale (*Balaenoptera physalus*) using annual layer counts in the ear plug. *Conseil Permanent International pour l'Exploration du la Mer. Journal du Conseil*, 34:276–294.

Lewontin, R.C.
1965.   Selection for colonizing ability. In *The genetics of colonizing species*, edited by H.G. Baker and G.L. Stebbins, pp. 77–91. New York: Academic Press.

May, R.M., ed.
1976.   *Theoretical ecology*. Philadelphia: W.B. Saunders Co.

May, R.M., J.R. Beddington, C.W. Clark, S.J. Holt, and R.M. Laws
1979.   Management of multispecies fisheries. *Science*, 205:267–277.

McCullough, D.R.
1979.   *The George Reserve deer herd: population ecology of a K-selected species*. Ann Arbor: University of Michigan Press.

1982.   Population growth rate of the George Reserve deer herd. *Journal of Wildlife Management*, 46:1079–1083.

1984.   Managing white-tailed deer populations: lessons from the George Reserve. In *The white-tailed deer of North America*, edited by L.K. Hall, pp. 211–242. Washington, D.C.: Wildlife Management Institute.

Nellis, C.H., J.L. Thiessen, and C.A. Prentice
1976.   Pregnant fawn and quintuplet mule deer. *Journal of Wildlife Management*, 40:795–796.

Norris, K.S.
1978.   Marine mammals and man. In *Wildlife and America, Council on Environmental Quality*, edited by H.P. Brokaw, pp. 320–328. Washington, D.C.: U.S. Fish and Wildlife Service and National Oceanic and Atmospheric Administration.

Ozoga, J.J.
1969.   Some longevity records for female white-tailed deer in northern Michigan. *Journal of Wildlife Management*, 33:1027–1028.

Robinette, W.L., C.H. Baer, R.E. Pillmore, and C.E. Knittle
1973.   Effects of nutritional change on captive mule deer. *Journal of Wildlife Management*, 37:312–326.

Robinette, W.L., N.V. Hancock, and D.A. Jones
1977.   The Oak Creek mule deer herd in Utah. *Utah Division of Wildlife Publications*, pp. 77–15.

Severinghaus, C.W., and E.L. Cheatum
1956.   Life and times of the white-tailed deer. In *The deer of North America*, edited by W.P. Taylor, pp. 57–331. Harrisburg, Pennsylvania: Stackpole Co., and Washington, D.C.: Wildlife Management Institute.

Smith, T., ed.
1979.   Report of the status of porpoise stocks workshop. Southwest Fisheries Center Administrative Report LJ-79-41. 120 pp.

Taber, R.D., and R.F. Dasmann
1958.   The black-tailed deer of the chaparral. *California Department of Fish and Game, Bulletin 8*, 163 pp.

Taylor, W.P., ed.
1956.   *The deer of North America*. Harrisburg, Pennsylvania: Stackpole Co., and Washington, D.C.: Wildlife Management Institute, 668 pp.

Thomas, D.C., and I.D. Smith
1973.   Reproduction in a wild black-tailed deer fawn. *Journal of Mammalogy*, 54:302–303.

Workman, G.W., and J.B. Low, eds.
1976.   Mule deer decline in the west. *Utah State University, College of Natural Resources, and Agricultural Experimental Station*, 134 pp.

DENNIS C. TURNER,
CHRISTIAN GEIGER
and
HANSJÖRG BLANKENHORN

Ethology and Wildlife Research,
Institute of Zoology,
University of Zürich,
Zürich, Switzerland

Project Leader,
Swiss Ornithological Station,
Sempach, Switzerland

Federal Game Commissioner,
Federal Forestry Office,
Laupenstrasse 20, Berne, Switzerland

Factors to Consider in Future Roe Deer Management in Switzerland

ABSTRACT   New estimates of the total Swiss roe deer (*Capreolus capreolus*) population in spring were made based on 1) the assumption that all losses were to be replaced each year and calculation of the numbers of animals required to replace those losses, and 2) density estimates for different regions and the forested area in each region. Federal statistics on losses to the hunt and all other causes between 1968 and 1980 were analyzed. Original federal estimates indicated a growth, then a decline in population size to ca. 100,000 animals in 1980. The new estimates and data on losses yielded values between 150,000 and 180,000 animals in spring, and show a population stabilization at these levels. Given levels of forest damage and indications of weight changes in the deer, this stabilization probably occurred at unacceptably high levels. Assuming certain management goals, a reduction of the roe deer population to levels adapted to local conditions is recommended.

Introduction

Estimates of population size for forest-dwelling species are burdened by relatively large margins of error; for the secretive roe deer (*Capreolus capreolus*), this margin of error may lie between 150 and 300% (Gossow, 1976). For many years, the Game Commissioner's Section within the Swiss Federal Forestry Office in Berne has tallied estimates of roe deer numbers provided by the hunting season and on numbers of deaths due to other causes, again as reported by the cantons.

Although the public has access to these yearly reports, an analysis of the long range data has never been published. On the other hand, one often hears that total population estimates are too conservative, and foresters report increasing levels of damage within some wooded areas. As newly installed Federal Game Commissioner, H.J. Blankenhorn was particularly interested in the above mentioned problems and promoted the analysis of data available from his office for 1968 through 1980.

We asked the following questions for this analysis:

1) Using data available on total annual population losses, what is the resulting population size estimate, assuming demographic characteristics known from the literature and simple replacement of losses without change in population size.

2) Based on reported density estimates and the total forested area in Switzerland, what is the resulting population size estimate and how does this estimate compare with that above?

3) What can be learned from the numbers of deaths to causes other than the hunt, and in particular, are there any indications here of population growth, decline or stabilization?

4) What are the consequences of answers to the above questions for future roe deer management decisions in Switzerland?

Methods

Original data provided by the Game Commissioner's Section and utilized here are presented in Appendices II-IV. Since most results were obtained either by combining various columns in these appendices and/or graphically presenting the original numbers or the combined values, we shall limit our discussion here to the methods utilized to reach new population estimates.

Population Estimates Based on Loss-Replacement

The method used to estimate the total spring population in Switzerland is presented in detail in Appendix I. To reach our estimate, we assumed no change in total population size from year to year, i.e., that total

registered losses due to the hunt and all other causes simply were to be replaced by young animals. We then asked what fawn production would be required just to replace that year's losses in the following spring, assuming a low fawn mortality (25% by the next spring) and a "high" fawn mortality (50% by the next spring). Both rates are within the range of reported values (Ellenberg, 1978; Geiger, 1980; Kurt, 1977; Wandeler, 1976); if non-representative, then it is the higher rate (50%) which may be underestimated.

We then calculated the number of does needed in order to produce those numbers of fawns, first assuming a high fawning rate of two fawns per doe (giving a lower number of does required), then a lower fawning rate of 1.5 fawns per doe. Again these values are consistent with those reported in the literature (Borg, 1970; Ellenberg, op.cit.; Merten, 1980; Sägesser and Kurt, 1966; Strandgaard, 1972; Wandeler op.cit.).

Given the number of does required, we estimated the number of bucks in the population assuming a sex ratio of 1:2 (male:female) among animals older that 1.5 years. Although this ratio seems quite biased, it is biased in favor of a *lower* buck population (and therefore, lower total population) and consistent with adult ratios reported in the literature for populations where hunting pressure on bucks is higher than on does. Ellenberg (op.cit.) reviewed this literature and found adult male:female ratios between 1:1.5 and 1:2.

We defined yearlings simply as the replacment of losses from the previous year, with exception of the calculation for 1968, the first year. Here, we assumed losses were the same in 1967 and 1968.

Four spring population estimates could be calculated, two lower and two upper estimates, depending on which combination of assumptions one chose (Appendix I). We decided to average the two middle estimates, and henceforth, this average is reported as the "replaced-loss" estimate.

Population Size Based on Reported Densities and Total Forested Area

The total area of Switzerland covered by forests is 1,117,900 ha, and this area can readily be divided into different regions depending on elevation, climate, forest composition, etc. (see Appendix IV). Naturally, one would expect different roe deer densities in forests of these regions. Although no one study has examined these differences, we were able to obtain a first approximation of densities from various Swiss field studies, extrapolations from similar European habitats, and personal observations (CG) (Bramley, 1970; Geiger, 1980; Hartmann, 1973; Kleiber, 1973; Mueller, 1972; Pfister, 1976; Robin, 1974; Stubbe amd Passarge,

1979). The density values which were utilized for the different regions of Switzerland were:

Midlands	30 deer/100 ha forest (excluding fawns)
Jura	14
Prealpine	21
Alpine	10
Southern Switzerland	7

For each region the number of deer was estimated by multiplying density × forested area, and a total Swiss population estimate was secured by adding all of these values.

Results

Population Size Based on Loss-Replacement

There is divergence between the original Federal Forestry Office population estimates and our estimates based on simple replacement of losses each year for the years 1968 through 1980 (Figure 1). Both curves indicate a population increase from 1968 until 1976, and 1978. The original estimate indicates a reduction after 1976, our estimate indicates a possible stabilization in total population size in 1977–1978. Henceforth, only the population estimate based on loss-replacement will be graphically portrayed.

Increasing numbers of animals were shot each year from 1970 to 1977, but the curve levels off thereafter (Figure 2). This trend is reflected in both the curve for total losses and for population size, based on loss-replacement. However, the curve for all other deaths also seems to stabilize after slowly increasing to 1977. This becomes most evident when one plots losses successively from year to year against estimated population size (Figure 3).

It appears that the Swiss roe deer population has stabilized; if one accepts our assumptions, then simple replacement of losses requires a spring population size of ca. 150,000 animals.

Population Size Based on Density Estimates

The significance of the numbers of deer indicated for each region of Switzerland and total spring population based on density estimates and areas covered by forest will be discussed below (Table 1).

Deaths to Other Causes

Total population losses *excluding* those animals shot and hit by vehicles are plotted in Figure 4. (The reason for excluding losses to vehicles will soon become evident.) The peaks for 1970 and 1977 deserve closer attention, and will be discussed in connection with Figure 5.

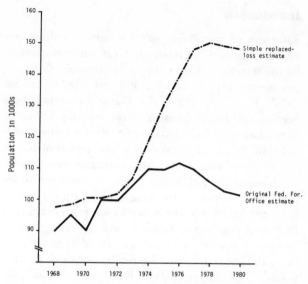

Figure 1. Yearly population estimates from 1968 to 1980 based on tallies by Berne and replaced losses (see text and Appendix I).

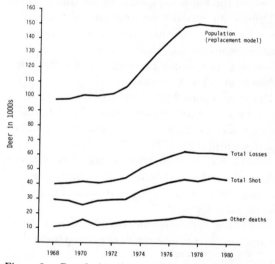

Figure 2. Population size, total losses and those losses broken down into animals shot and deaths due to all other causes for each year.

Table 1. Regional and total population estimates based on reported densities

Region	Numbers estimated
Midlands	71,670
Jura	27,818
Prealpine	39,984
Alpine	35,830
Southern Switzerland	9,212
Σ	184,514

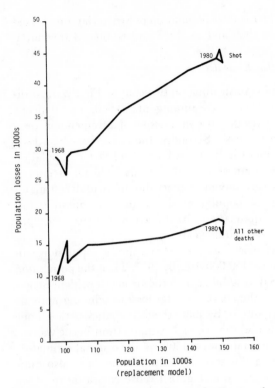

Figure 3. Population losses due to the hunt and all other causes plotted for each year consecutively against population size.

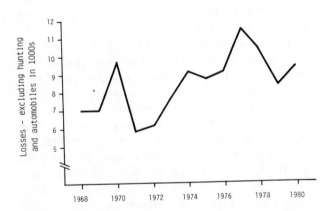

Figure 4. Population losses each year excluding those to the hunt and deer hit by vehicles.

The same losses have also been broken down by cause of death (Figure 5). The peaks evident in Figure 4 are most visible in the curve for deaths due to old age, malnutrition and/or disease. Deaths due to farm machines, almost excusively fawns, rise sharply to 1976 and appear to fall as sharply thereafter. Natural accidents follow a similar, though less pronounced trend. The curves for both deer killed by dogs and for

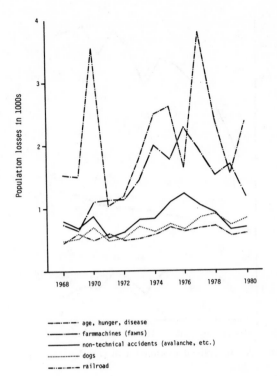

-.-.-.- age, hunger, disease
.... farmmachines (fawns)
―――― non-technical accidents (avalanche, etc.)
·········· dogs
-··-··-··- railroad

Figure 5. Yearly losses broken down by cause of death when known.

animals hit by trains show slight, but relatively constant increases to 1978, then either decline or stabilize.

Lastly, we treat losses to vehicular traffic (Figure 6). As can be seen in the middle curve, the number of registered vehicles in Switzerland rose steadily each year between 1968 and 1980. As one would expect, the number of deer/car accidents also rises, but appears to approach a plateau (upper curve). Indeed, the number of losses when corrected for number of registered vehicles may have declined in the last few years (lower curve).

Discussion

In this section, we shall first examine population losses to causes other than the hunt; then the various population estimates and indications of stabilization will be discussed. Lastly, we shall mention the consequences of our report for future roe deer management decisions in Switzerland.

Losses to Causes Other Than The Hunt

The interpretation of loss-curves in Figure 5 is based on our knowledge of environmental changes between 1968 and 1980. The two main peaks in losses due to old age, malnutrition and/or disease are obviously re-

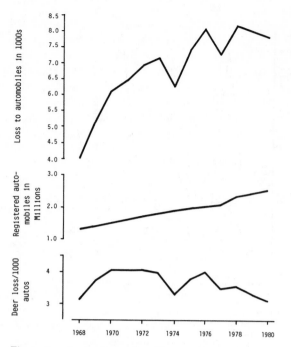

Figure 6.   An analysis of accidents with vehicles over time.

lated to hard, long winters. The rise and probably the fall in the curve for deaths due to farm machinery reflect the increased mechanization of Swiss farms and changes in the number and, therefore, timing of pasture cuts. The curve for natural accidents may also correlate with the hard winters, but generally rises and falls with the reported population growth and decline (Fed. For. Office), or stabilization (our estimate). Likewise, the curves for losses to dogs and to train traffic increase slowly with the population increase, then cease to rise in the last three years. Train traffic, based on track-kilometers, did not appreciably change during these 13 years.

In spite of steadily increasing numbers of registered vehicles, losses to vehicles (Figure 6) seem to have reached a plateau. During the same period, kilometers of paved road only increased from ca. 62,000 to 65,000; before being opened to the public, new stretches of freeway are always enclosed by deer fences. We suspect that the increase in losses is more directly related to the increase in vehicles, than in road kilometers. Interestingly, the number of deer deaths per 1000 vehicles decreased over the last few years. Whether this is due to the increased application of deer-protective measures (e.g., reflectors on tree trunks near streets, warning signs for drivers), or basic changes in the behavior of deer toward roads cannot be determined from these data.

In summary, non-hunting factors are strongly indicated as determinants of population trends, and in-

deed the roe deer population of Switzerland increased between 1968 and ca. 1977 and stabilized thereafter.

Population Estimates

Figure 1 is misleading on two counts. Firstly, the ordinate is broken (beginning at 90,000, not 0 deer), which gives the false impression of a tremendous population increase. Secondly, the curve based on loss-replacement indicates a larger and faster population increase than seen in the original official estimates. This is certainly an artifact due to a) underestimates of original population size with concomitantly low hunting quotas, and b) the rapid increase in quotas during the middle years.

Nevertheless, we arrived at a spring population estimate of ca. 150,000 deer by 1977. Then the population appeared to stabilize with the strongest evidence coming from the curve for total losses excluding animals shot (Figure 3). By 1980, the discrepancy between our estimate and the original estimate from Berne was ca. 50,000 animals, or ca. 150% of the original estimate*.

Judging the accuracy of our estimate is also difficult. The curve in Figure 1 represents a mean; if we assume conditions that lead to an absolute minimal spring population size (d+h+j in Appendix I) we arrive at an estimate of ca. 127,000 deer, still 25–30,000 more than the original estimate. On the other hand, if one assumes conditions leading to the highest estimates (g+i+j), the result is a total spring population of ca. 180,000 animals, which is fairly close to the estimate based on densities (184,500).

We are aware of the pitfalls of using density estimates and total forested area to calculate population size. Various factors influence roe deer density including forest composition and structure, contiguous area of a tree stand, length and structure of forest perimeter, adjacent areas and their structure, elevation and conditions of snow cover, local hunting pressure, disturbances, etc. Although dividing Switzerland into the standard regions utilized by geographers, botanists, and zoologists eliminates some of these problems, others remain. Also, density estimates from field studies of roe deer may be somewhat higher than average densities for a region, since researchers tend to select "good" deer areas for their studies. Nonetheless, we wanted to present a second population estimate, based on a totally different method than loss-replacement. Since the maximal estimate from the loss-replacement calculation and the estimate based on densities and forested area are fairly close, we conclude

*At this point, the cantonal hunting inspectors' offices are to be complimented. Although underestimated, the margin of error is at the lower end of errors reported by Gossow (1976).

Turner, Geiger, and Blankenhorn

that spring population size in Switzerland has probably not exceeded ca. 180,000 deer.

It was theoretically possible to check whether the population could have stabilized at the level of 150,000 animals; to do this we averaged loss-values between 1977 and 1980, inserted these into the equation in Appendix I, and calculated yearly losses required to hold the population size constant at ca. 150,000 animals. We followed the development of required losses for six further years and found that 1) on the average, ca. 4500 additional losses were required to hold the population size constant, and 2) the required additional losses oscillated around and converged on this figure over time.

In addition to the ca. 17,700 deaths reported to other causes, it is undeniable that another 4,500 could escape notice. Unnoticed deaths would have increased the number of losses to be replaced each year in our calculations, and raised the population size estimates above 150,000. Likewise, our simple model was based on no population growth, in spite of reports to the contrary. If growth had been considered, again the total estimate would have increased. Therefore, our estimate of 150,000 animals in spring may indeed be conservative. We conclude that roe deer population size in Switzerland has stabilized, most probably between 150,000 and 180,000 animals in spring.

Consequences for Future Management Decisions in Switzerland

Before we make any general recommendations, it is important to realize that Switzerland, with its diverse landscape, offers differing conditions for the development of roe deer populations; these conditions should always be considered. Nonetheless, three points must be stressed: 1) the general underestimation of real population size, which probably varies in degree depending on habitat and region; 2) the apparent stabilization of population size at the higher levels; and 3) forest damage. There can be no doubt that in some areas of Switzerland a natural rejuvenation of well-adapted, pristine forests is next to impossible without specific protective measures, e.g., fences or chemical treatment (Schweiz. Forstverein, 1974). Simultaneously, unpublished reports show at least a tendency toward reduction in average weights of animals shot in some areas over the past few decades (Hauser, 1973; Hunting Inspectors' Offices of Berne and Thurgau, pers. comm.); this is indicative of overpopulation and overexploitation of resources. Additionally, various man-made changes in the environment have increasingly concentrated the deer population: land-reclamation; elimination of hedgerows; the planting of large monocultures; the growth of cities, suburbs and villages, etc. This con-

centration of animals is naturally accompanied by higher browsing levels in and around forests.

These developments are projected to continue into the future, and force us to recommend the reduction of the roe deer population in some areas of Switzerland, if one values the goals of natural rejuvenation of forests (with acceptable levels of protective measures) and a roe deer population in good condition.

We have indicated a stabilization of the population, which, given the above mentioned goals, occurred at too high a level. But the fact that a stabilization is in progress opens the door to more effective application of culling methods to lower the population. Here the hunters of Switzerland will play an important role. The task now is to inform both the responsible persons in the federal and cantonal governments and the hunters of these findings and to see that action is taken. To effectively reduce the population, the hunting pressure on does and younger animals should be increased above past levels. It is also imperative that the results of such measures be continuously monitored and adapted to local conditions. The opportunities for cooperation between hunting authorities, hunters and forestry officials are many, and would be enhanced by an appropriate public information campaign.

Acknowledgments

A special debt of thanks is due to A. Volken, Game Commissioner's Section, Federal Forestry Office, who has laboriously prepared the statistics on population losses over many years. The numbers tallied were regularly reported to Berne by the hunting inspectors' offices of each canton and represent a tremendous amount of work by their employees; this is gratefully acknowledged. We thank the cantonal offices of Berne and Thurgau for providing unpublished information on deer weights over the past few decades. Jeanine Stocker and Cécile Ganze, Ethology and Wildlife Research, Institute of Zoology, University of Zürich, contributed greatly to the realization of this manuscript. The Swiss National Science Foundation (Grant No. 3.511.79) and Friends of the National Zoo provided travel funds, which are gratefully acknowledged.

Literature Cited

Borg, K.
1970. On mortality and reproduction of roe deer in Sweden during the period 1948–1969. *Viltrevy*, 7:121–149.

Bramley, P.S.
1970. Numbers and social behavior of roe deer (*C. capreolus*) in a Dorset wood. Ph.D. Thesis, University of Aberdeen.

Ellenberg, H.
1978. Zur Populationsökologie des Rehes (*Capreolus capreolus* L., Cervidae) in Mitteleuropa. *Spixiana* (Supplement), 2:1–211.

Geiger, C.
1980. Bestandesschätzung und Populationsdynamik beim Rehwild in den Zizerser Feldern, Kt. Graubünden. *Feld, Wald, Wasser*, 8:19–21.

Gossow, H.
1976. *Wildökologie: Begriffe, Methoden, Ergebnisse, Konsequenzen*. München: BLV Verlagsgesellschaft.

Hartmann, D.
1973. Struktur und Verteilung einer Rehpopulation (*C. capreolus* L.) vor und nach einem Reduktionsabschuss. Ph.D. Thesis, University of Zürich.

Hauser, J.
1973. Konstitutionsmessung am Rehwild/Vergleich von Daten der letzten 20 Jahre. Semesterarbeit, University of Zürich.

Kleiber, H.
1973. Biotopansprüche und Wohnraumgrössen individuell markierter Rehe (*C. capreolus* L.) im Revier Staffelfach. Thesis, University of Zurich.

Kurt, F.
1977. *Wildtiere in der Kulturlandschaft*. Zürich: Eugen Rentsch Verlag.

Mertens, C.
1980. Rehkitz-Geburten im Gehege. *Feld, Wald, Wasser*, 8(10):22–24.

Mueller, K.
1972. Zur Oekologie der Liegezonen und Aufzuchtszonen des Rehwildes. Ph.D. Thesis, University of Zürich.

Pfister, H.P.
1976. Oekologische Inventarisation im Raume des projektierten Rangier-Bahnhofes Olten-Daeniken. Contracted Impact Statement, University of Zürich.

Robin, K.
1974. Räumliche Verschiebungen und Angaben zur Wohnraumgrösse von Rehen (*C. capreolus* L.) in einem Gebiet der St. Galler Voralpen. Ph.D. Thesis, University of Zürich.

Saegesser, H., and F. Kurt
1966. Ueber die Setzzeit 1965 beim Reh. *Mitteilungen der Gesselschaft für Naturforschung Bern, Neue Folge*, 23:21–38.

Schweizerischer Forstverein
1974. Bericht über die Wildschaden Frage. Wildschadenkommission des Schweizerischen Forstvereins, März 1974.

Strandgaard, H.
1972. An investigation of corpora lutea, embryonic development, and time of birth of roe deer, *Capreolus capreolus*, in Denmark. *Danish Review of Game Biology*, 6:1–22.

Stubbe, C., and H. Passarge
1979. *Das Rehwild*. Berlin: Verlag J. Neumann-Neudamm.

Wandeler, A.
1975. Die Fortpflanzungsleistung des Rehes (*Capreolus capreolus* L.) im Berner Mittelland. *Jahrbuch des Naturhistorischen Museums Bern*, 5:245–301.

Appendix I. Method used to estimate spring population based on simple loss-replacement

Loss to be replaced: a[1]

Required fawn production	♀♀ - needed to produce fawns	♂♂ - population[6] > 1 ½ Yr.	Yearlings[7]	Estimates
b[2]	$d^4 - f^5$	h	j	Min. d+h+j Min. f+h+j
c[3]	$e^4 - g^5$	i	j	Max. e+i+j Max. g+i+j

$$\text{Population estimate} = \frac{(f+h+j) + (e+i+j)}{2}$$

[1] a = total registered losses (hunting + all other causes)
[2] b = a/0.75; assuming 25% fawn mortality to next fawning
[3] c = a/0.50; assuming 50% fawn mortality to next fawning
[4] d = b/2, e = c/2; assuming 2 fawns born/ ♀
[5] f = b/1.5, g = c/1.5; assuming 1.5 fawns born/ ♀
[6] h = (d+f)/4, i = (e+g)/4; assuming sex ratio of 1 ♂ : 2 ♀♀
[7] j = replaced-loss from previous year

Appendix II. Statistics provided by the Swiss Federal Forestry Office, Berne: estimated total population, numbers shot, registered losses to all other causes and total population losses

Year	Population estimate[1]	Numbers shot				All other losses[2]	Total loss
		Bucks	Does	Fawns	Total		
1968	90,000	14,088	12,520	2,419	29,027	11,089	40,116
1969	95,000	13,900	11,283	3,244	28,427	12,266	40,693
1970	90,000	12,501	9,997	3,613	26,111	15,778	41,889
1971	100,000	13,841	10,490	4,501	28,832	12,307	41,139
1972	100,000	14,161	10,718	4,643	29,522	13,114	42,636
1973	105,000	14,176	11,049	4,861	30,086	14,947	45,033
1974	110,000	15,837	13,725	6,383	35,945	15,364	51,309
1975	110,000	16,968	15,593	6,816	39,377	16,168	55,545
1976	112,000	19,068	15,703	7,486	42,257	17,176	59,433
1977	110,000	18,874	16,934	8,172	43,980	18,767	62,747
1978	106,000	18,823	16,454	8,024	43,301	18,400	61,701
1979	103,000	19,762	17,406	8,283	45,451	16,365	61,816
1980	102,000	19,294	16,835	7,829	43,958	17,279	61,237

[1]Original Fed. For. Office estimate; see text for explanation.
[2]See Appendix III for a breakdown by cause of death.

Appendix III. Causes of death (excluding hunting) and numbers of cases reported, provided by the Swiss Federal Forestry Office, Berne

Year	Age, hunger, disease	Automobiles	Train traffic	Non-tech. accidents[1]	Hunting wounds[2]	Dogs	Chemicals	Farm machines[3]	Unknown	Total
1968	1,527	4,023	458	798	606	486	21	749	2,421	11,089
1969	1,506	5,203	591	683	559	518	19	653	2,534	12,266
1970	3,558	6,104	495	889	382	712	11	1,105	2,522	15,778
1971	1,044	6,459	605	537	436	484	15	1,131	1,596	12,307
1972	1,178	6,950	497	626	503	529	42	1,139	1,650	13,114
1973	1,758	7,186	530	822	482	723	25	1,439	1,982	14,947
1974	2,499	6,272	585	832	609	631	10	2,018	1,908	15,364
1975	2,621	7,439	703	1,097	685	751	18	1,791	2,063	16,168
1976	1,620	8,088	630	1,235	668	662	6	2,286	1,981	17,176
1977	3,815	7,311	692	1,060	681	850	7	1,928	2,423	18,767
1978	2,447	8,222	721	926	716	916	6	1,529	2,917	18,400
1979	1,530	8,045	568	663	751	731	3	1,696	2,378	16,365
1980	2,405	7,888	603	689	764	840	12	1,179	2,899	17,279

[1]Non-technical accidents include avalanches, fallen trees, etc.
[2]Not included in hunting statistics by Berne.
[3]Almost exclusively fawns.

Appendix IV. Further data provided by federal offices in Berne and utilized for calculations in the text.

a) Area covered by forest

Region of Switzerland	Forested area in Hectares
Swiss Midlands	238,900
Jura	198,700
Prealpine	190,400
Alpine	358,300
Southern Switzerland	131,600
Total	1,117,900 ha

b) Registered vehicles in Switzerland

1968	1'303'065
1969	1'414'883
1970	1'525'036
1971	1'610'134
1972	1'719'001
1973	1'822'096
1974	1'899'511
1975	1'973'726
1976	2'044'372
1977	2'116'341
1978	2'342'598
1979	2'456'767
1980	2'564'926

Turner, Geiger, and Blankenhorn

A.S.I. LOUDON
Department of Forestry and Natural Resources
Edinburgh University
Edinburgh EH9 3JU, Scotland

The Influence of Forest Habitat Structure on Growth, Body Size and Reproduction in Roe Deer (*Capreolus capreolus* L.)

ABSTRACT

Roe deer populations are generally considered to be regulated by the social and territorial behavior of resident breeding animals. Two hypotheses have been proposed to explain the relationship between reproductive rate and population density. In one, reproductive rate is independent of density due to the buffering effect of territorial behavior; in the other, reproductive rate is density dependent, high density populations having lower reproductive rates because of increased competition for food or high levels of social strife. These hypotheses are examined for roe populations living in upland spruce forests in northern Britain. It is shown that ovulation rate in roe is crucially dependent upon body weight which in turn is dependent on forest habitat. Maternal body weight has an important influence on kid body weight and on kid fat reserves. Thus, populations with large body weights are characterized by high kid survival. High density roe populations (>20 deer/100 ha) have much higher reproductive rates than low density (>12 deer/100 ha) populations. These data are discussed in relationship to the habitat stability of forests inhabited by roe deer.

Introduction

The roe deer is the smallest of the five deer species indigenous to Europe. The animal is thought to have originated in Eurasia but is now found in all European countries with the exception of Ireland. In the early nineteenth century, the roe deer was very reduced in range in many countries (Prior, 1968; Cederlund, 1981) due to heavy hunting pressure and forest clearance. Recently, there has been a significant increase in the range of roe deer throughout Europe. Some authors (e.g., Ahlen, 1965) have suggested that the increase has been due to the removal of predatory animals and the development of effective game legislation, but there is little doubt that the key factor determining the success of roe has been the development of extensive commercial forests throughout Europe. In these forests, roe frequently cause serious damage to commercial crops of young trees. Attempts to alleviate this damage by sport-shooting or heavy culling by professional hunters have generally been ineffective in reducing damage levels.

Numerous attempts have been made on estates and forests throughout Europe to improve antler quality and body size by selective shooting. While a number of authors have described regional variations in body size and antler quality (e.g., Bubenik, 1959), there is no evidence that these differences can be attributed to the system of management. Klein and Strandgaard (1972) compared reproductive performance (based on corpora lutea counts) in four study areas in Denmark and concluded that there was no correlation between body size and ovulation rate for these populations. Surprisingly, this study showed that populations in areas of low soil fertility had high average body weights compared with those in areas of high soil fertility; differences in chemical composition of the rumen contents were, however, insignificant.

In south Scotland and northeast England, large areas of upland sheepwalk have been afforested since the end of the war. Regional variations in soil fertility are slight and differences between forests in the growth rates of the main tree species planted (*Picea sitchensis*) are small. These forests thus form a very large area of an almost pure monoculture of Sitka spruce planted at different times since the war. Currently, large numbers of roe deer are shot each year as part of a damage control operation by the Forestry Commission. This study describes an investigation into the effects of forest age structure on body size and reproductive rates in roe populations.

Methods

Twelve forests in northeast England and south Scotland were studied, seven in Scotland and five in England (see Table 1). In all of these forests, rangers were employed to shoot deer and culling rates were generally similar to those in other state forests. In all, data from the winter cull of females (October 22 - February 28) were collected for three years from October 1977 to February 1980. Rangers were asked to record the eviscerated weight of all deer shot as well as collect lower jaws and reproductive tracts from all

Table 1. The 12 study forests in south Scotland and northeast England

	Forest	Area (ha)	No. rangers	Deer cull 1977/78	1978/79
1	Ae	6291	2	107	210
2	Craik	4943	1	106	106
3	Elibank	4105	1	80	77
4	Glentress	3959	2	122	77
5	Moffat	10630	3	237	305
6	Newcastleton	3759	1	115	179
7	Wanchope	8048	2	207	267
8	Falstone	13267	3	219	160
9	Kielder	10159	3	244	190
10	Redesdale	5009	1	67	132
11	Hamsterley	3895	1	64	—
12	Wark	11528	2	329	229
	Totals	85,593	22	1897	1932

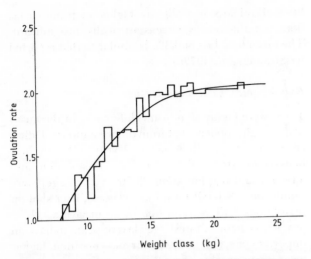

Figure 1. The relationship between weight class and ovulation rate for roe culled in 1977-79. The transformed data are described by the relationship P=1-exp (-0.1709, W-10.7) where P is the probability of a roe doe twinning (n=421). Data have been divided into 0.45 kg (1 lb.) weight classes.

females including kids. The kidneys plus all associated perirenal fat were removed from deer shot in forests 1, 4, 6 and 7 in 1978/79. In addition to providing samples, rangers recorded details of other deer present in the group at the time of shooting including other adult females, adult males and kids at foot. In the case of groups containing only one adult female in which that female was culled, the number of kids at foot was used to calculate and index twinning rate and kid survival for females of different weight classes. Finally, rangers provided information on the forest type within which the deer was shot. Plantations were classified into the following categories: 1. Newly established plantation, <15 years of age; 2. Trees 15-25

years of age; 3. 25+ years; 4. Felled and replanted site <15 years of age within an existing forest.

Corpora lutea were counted by cross-sectioning the ovaries and if present, fetuses were counted after the uterine horns had been cut longitudinally. Fat content of the perirenal area was assessed on a dry matter basis to the nearest gram. Animals were aged by examining the pattern of tooth eruption until two years of age, and thereafter by tooth section.

Results

Body Weight and Fertility

The relationship between eviscerated body weight and ovulation rate (number of corpora lutea) is shown in Figure 1. Despite variations in fertility between weight classes, the trend for ovulation rate to increase with body weight is clear, the data being fitted by the relationship P = 1-exp (-0.1709, W-10.7), where P is the probability of a roe doe producing more than one corpus luteum (Figure 1). Failure to ovulate is uncommon in roe populations in this area; over a two year period, only seven females out of a sample of 421 had no corpus luteum present. The data in Figure 1 suggest that animals with a clean weight of more than 18 kg (25.46 kg live weight) had greater than 90% probability of producing two or more corpora lutea.

Data were analyzed by age-class for primiparous, two-year-old and three-year-old females and the differences in slopes and intercepts were compared by analysis of variance and co-variance (Snedecor and Cochran, 1967). Differences in fertility between age classes were slight. The intercept of primiparous does was significantly higher than for older females, but there were no significant differences between two-year-old and older females (Table 2). The lower fertil-

Table 2. Comparisons of ovulation rate for females shot in 1977–1978 against log of body weight for different age classes and population types. Standard errors and computed values for slopes and intercepts were compared by analysis of variance and covariance.

					Probability level	
	n	Correlation Coefficient	Intercept	Slope	Intercept	Slope
Habitat						
Trees <15 years old	213	0.9812	10.156	0.1998	NS	NS
Trees >25 years old	197	0.9314	10.940	0.1722		
Age						
Yearlings	188	0.8966	11.236	0.2142	0.05	NS
2 year old +	233	0.9108	10.562	0.1462		
2 year	111	0.9046	10.721	0.1648	NS	NS
3 year +	122	0.8372	10.219	0.1799		

Table 3. An estimate of fetal loss for breeding females culled in 1977/78 and 1978/79

Age	Number of corpora lutea	Number of fetuses	Fetal Loss %	N
1	1.36	1.25	9.9	78
2	1.77	1.68	5.1	47
3	1.86	1.71	8.0	62
4	1.78	1.67	6.2	39
5+	1.82	1.73	5.0	46
			6.84	

ity of the primiparous doe was almost certainly due to very low twinning rates in light-weight females. This had the effect of increasing the slope and the intercept; when all weight classes below 14 kg for the primiparous does were removed, differences between ages in fertility were slight. There was no evidence, based on limited data, that fertility declined in relationship to body weight for animals of three years of age or more.

Ovulation Rate and Fetal Loss

Counts of corpora lutea may give an accurate indication of ovulation rate but assessment of fetal loss is complicated because roe exhibit the phenomenon of delayed implantation. For much of the period of the winter cull, embryos remain unimplanted and thus comparisons of ovulation rate with fetal counts are only possible when fetuses are visible to the naked eye (Table 3). Generally, there was a close correlation between the number of fetuses and number of corpora

lutea. Fetal loss was slightly higher in primiparous does but differences were statistically insignificant. The mean fetal loss of 8.3% is similar to that reported by Strandgaard (1972a).

Body Weight, Condition and Habitat

There were highly significant differences in the mean body weights of deer shot from different forests. Differences in mean adult weights (2 years old or more) between forests 5 and 7 (<15 year old plantation) and forests 1 and 6 (plantation 25-50 years of age) were significant (P<0.001 for all age classes), deer shot on plantations <15 years of age being on average 12% heavier. Generally, forest age class appears to have an important effect on body weight and condition, higher mean body weights and fat reserves occurring in roe shot on forest plantations of less than 15 years of age (Table 4). Canopy closure at approximately 15 years of age appears to have a marked effect on body weight and condition of resident roe populations. Females from young plantation stages had reached adult weights by 18 months of age; females in closed canopy habitat were lighter and had not reached adult weight at the same age. Although samples were obtained at discrete time intervals and it was not possible to compare growth rates between habitats, it must be assumed that deer on young plantations grow faster and achieve adult body weight more quickly than deer in mature stages of forest development with a high proportion of closed canopy habitat.

A number of kids shot in closed canopy habitat had no detectable kidney fat, and the mean fat values for deer in these forests were over three times lower than for kids in forest plantations of less than 15 years of age (Table 4). Many kids of these plantations had fat reserves in excess of those recorded for adults in closed

Table 4. Mean clean weights and kidney fat reserves of roe deer on young newly afforested habitat (trees <15 years of age) and from closed canopy habitat where more than 80% of the trees are ≥25 years of age

Age	0	1	2	3	4	5+	Forest
Mean weight (kg)	13.6	16.3	16.6	16.2	16.1	17.4	
Mean kidney fat (g)	28.2	84.6	91.7	56.8	72.9	85.9	<15 yrs
N	47	29	32	12	14	19	

Age	0	1	2	3	4	5	
Mean weight (kg)	10.2	12.9	13.6	13.8	13.7	14.1	
Mean kidney fat (g)	8.4	21.6	34.6	41.7	44.6	40.5	≥25 yrs
N	58	37	21	14	8	12	

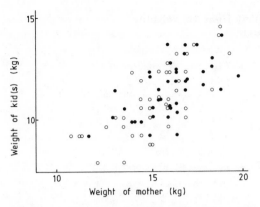

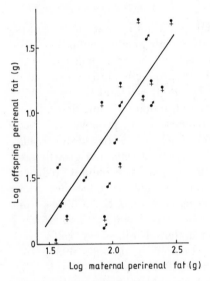

Figure 2. Maternal and kid weights for complete family groups shot in 1978 over the period October 22 - February 28. Twin kids (solid circles) do not differ significantly in weight from singletons (open circles) for a given weight class of mother.

Figure 3. The scaling of kidney fat reserves of roe deer and their offspring for family groups shot at Moffat forest. Fat reserves of male kids do not differ significantly from the fat reserves of female kids.

canopy habitat. The difference in fat reserves between the two habitat types was significant for all age classes (P<0.01). Kid weights correlated well with maternal weights both between and within forest habitats (Figure 2) and there was no significant difference in the weights of kids shot as singletons or twins. In forests 1 and 5, a number of complete family groups were shot and it was thus possible to compare the fat reserves of the mother and kid (Figure 3). Kid fat reserves scaled log linearly with maternal fat reserves. There was no significant difference in the slope for deer shot on plantations of <15 years of age.

An index of the kid loss was calculated from a comparison of the number of kids at foot with the expected number based on the relationship between ovulation rate and body weight. In general, lightweight females had fewer than the expected number of kids at foot in the winter, and females of 10-13 kg weight (after evisceration) appeared to have less than half of the expected number of offspring at foot (Table 5). Heavier weight classes on the other hand (16-19 kg) had a considerably lower loss index; of six animals culled with body weights greater than 20 kg, all had twins at foot. Between forests, there was a good correlation between adult fertility (based on mean corpora lutea counts) and the average number of kids at foot. Forests 5,2 and 7 with high doe fertility had a greater proportion of kids at foot in the winter cull than forests with intrinsically low fertility (i.e., forests 8,9 and 1; Figure 4).

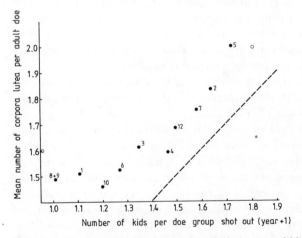

Figure 4. The relationship between ovulation rate and kid survival to the first winter. Data from twelve forests (listed in Table 1). Open symbols are from two Danish populations described in Klein and Strandgaard (1972). Dashed intercept indicates 100% survival from ovulation to six months of age.

Table 5. Kid losses of breeding females in relation to weight class (data from Ae, Falstone, Kielder, Moffat, Newcastleton, Redesdale, Wark and Wanchope forests)

Weight class	Kidding rate*	N. does	N. kids	Ratio	Loss (%)	N. primiparous ♀♀
10–11	0.98	7	1	0.14	85.7	7
12–13	1.48	28	19	0.68	54.2	22
14–15	1.64	39	52	1.33	18.5	28
16–17	1.81	87	137	1.57	12.7	50
18–19	1.90	21	37	1.76	6.8	13
20–21	1.93	4	8	2.0	0	1
22+	1.94	2	4	2.0	0	0
Totals		178	258			121

*From $P = 1 - \exp(-0.1709(W - 10.7))$ and assuming a mean fetal loss of 8.3% from Table 3.

Discussion

Body Weight

The data presented show very clearly that for roe populations in upland conifer plantations in south Scotland, there was a close relationship between body weight and ovulation rate. One unexpected feature of these data is that both ovulation rate and fetal loss appear to be independent of age, primiparous does having lower fertility primarily on account of their lighter weights rather than age. In this study, comparisons were made of winter weights with ovulation rate and therefore can only serve as a general guide to body weight at the time of the rut in July or August. In the case of primiparous does, this is likely to be an especial problem since such animals on poor quality habitats may continue growth for longer than animals living in newly afforested plantation habitat. This may explain why the slope of ovulation rate versus age is steeper for yearling than adult does.

The age structure of the forest was clearly of considerable importance in determining the reproductive rates of resident deer. Fertility was higher in young stages of forest development, differences in fertility being attributed to differences in weight. Prior (1968) has suggested that in southern England, forest age structure has an important influence on reproductive performance of roe populations and in *Odocoileus*, a number of authors have suggested that logging and fire have important effects on nutrition (Klein, 1970; Robinson, 1958) and body size (Einarsen, 1964).

Several studies have shown that body size is an important determinant of ovulation rate in deer. Hamilton and Blaxter (1980) showed that for a population of red deer hinds maintained on a hill farm in northeast Scotland, the probability of conception is dependent on weight (and not age) at the time of the rut. In wild red deer, lightweight populations with slow maturation rates living on poor quality range are characterized by low reproductive rates (reviewed by Mitchell et al., 1977). Body size and fat reserves are clearly interrelated and in domestic ungulates, fat reserves increase allometrically in proportion to body size (Seebeck, 1968; Black, 1974). In wild deer, high fertility, early puberty and accelerated growth rates are associated with the quality of habitat (red deer, Challies, 1974; Staines, 1978; white-tailed deer, Cheatum and Severinghaus, 1950; Klein, 1964), while recent work on red deer has shown that habitat was a profound effect on maternal milk yield, calf growth and hind fertility (Loudon et al., 1983, 1984). In a recent analysis, Drew (1985) has shown that for captive red deer, body weight and not age determines total carcass fats.

In roe deer, fat reserves scale allometrically with body weight (Loudon, unpublished) and since large body weight females had on average larger kids at foot, it may be inferred that maternal milk yield and kid growth over the first summer of life are closely correlated with body condition and habitat quality. High body weight female roe are thus characterized by high fertility, larger than average offspring and the offspring have higher survival rates than those born to light weight females. These differences can be attributed to habitat—in this case, the age structure of the forest.

Population Density, Reproductive Rate and Habitat

Watson (1967) established three criteria which should be met if social behavior is considered to limit breeding density: 1. There must be a surplus of non-breeding animals; 2. Animals are prevented from holding territories and breeding by the established holders; and 3. Non-breeders are capable of taking a territory and breeding if given the chance. In a series of removal experiments, Bramley (1970a, b) demonstrated that in the case of roe bucks territorial behavior did indeed limit the breeding density of males and a number of other studies on roe populations have confirmed these results (Strandgaard, 1972b; Ellenberg, 1978; Loudon, 1979a).

There are relatively few published studies in which data on mean bulk territory size and population density are quoted (Figure 5). In general, the relationship between territory size and population density is nonlinear. One interpretation of these data is that at high densities, roe bucks resist further encroachment and the lower limit to mean territory size is set by mutual intolerance, or the "elasticity" of the territory (Huxley, 1934; Zimmermann, 1971). One clear implication is that breeding sex ratio also shifts with density, being biased in favor of females at high densities. Ellenberg's (1978) study is of particular interest, since the population was enclosed and emigration prevented. Mean territory sizes declined with increasing population density (Figure 5), but breeding sex ratio was heavily biased towards females (2.6 females: 1 male). This compares with data from populations in which emigration occurred and breeding sex ratio was less biased towards females (1.85:1, S. England, Bramley, 1970b; Loudon, 1978; 2:1, Denmark, Strandgaard, 1972b).

In Klein and Strandgaard's (1972) comparison of four populations in different areas of Denmark, the authors concluded that body size was inversely correlated with density, being greater at low densities because of reduced stress and social interaction rather than competition for food. On the basis of a small sample size, the authors suggested that reproductive rate was independent of density. Data presented here contradict that conclusion. In this study, there were substantial differences in reproductive performance, growth rate, body size and body condition between different populations, these differences being attributable to the effect of habitat, principally the age of the forest plantation. Reliable density data for these populations are not available, but limited sampling over a few habitats suggests that population density is maximal (>25 deer/100 ha) on the youngest stage of forest development and declines to <5 deer/100 ha with canopy closure (Loudon, 1979b, 1982). If these figures are of general application within these forest types, it follows that population density may be positively correlated with reproductive performance and roe populations may differ from the general trend in cervids for an increase in density to be associated with a decline in reproductive performance (e.g., white-tailed deer, McCullough, 1979; red deer, Mitchell et al., 1979). The principal reason for these differences may lie in the profound effect that the territorial and social behavior of roe deer has in regulating breeding population density. It will be of considerable interest to see whether woodland populations of red deer conform to the same trend.

Forest structure is known to be crucial to deer populations and many authors have drawn attention to the need for more detailed information on the effect of forest habitat on the density and reproductive performance of deer (Koring and Gossow, 1979; Dzieciolowski, 1979; Ueckermann, 1957). However, management of roe is still dominated by traditional concepts from hunting literature. The data presented here were based on material collected from populations living in a comparatively uniform habitat of similar soil quality, the main habitat variable being the age of the tree. While there are good reasons for caution in extrapolating these findings to other forest types and climates, they do indicate that habitat has a profound effect on roe reproductive rates. Such information should be gathered for other forest habitats and used to develop management models based on biological data.

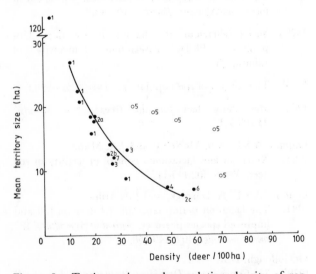

Figure 5. Territory size and population density of roe. Data from: 1, Bobek, 1977; 2a,c, Loudon, 1979a; 2b, Loudon, upland young plantation, unpublished; 3, Strandgaard, 1972b; 4, Bramley, 1972a; 5, Ellenberg, 1978; 6, Klein and Strandgaard, 1972; 7, Prior, 1968. Open symbols (5) are for the enclosed population studied by Ellenberg, 1978.

Acknowledgments

Much of the data presented here was collected by forest rangers in southern Scotland and northeast England. Their cooperation throughout the project is gratefully acknowledged. The students of Edinburgh University assisted in drive counting roe populations in spruce populations, and I am grateful for their help. Dr. R. Muetzelfeldt provided statistical advice and Dr. P. Jones kindly read through an earlier draft of the paper. The work is financially supported by the Forestry Commission.

Literature Cited

Ahlen, I.
1965.   Studies on the red deer in Scandinavia. III Ecological investigations. *Viltrevy*, 3:177-37.

Black, J.L.
1974.   Manipulation of body composition through nutrition. *Proceedings of the Australian Society of Animal Production*, 10:211-218.

Bobek, B.
1977.   Summer food as the factor limiting roe deer population size. *Nature*, 268:47-49.

Bramley, P.S.
1970a. Numbers and social behavior of roe deer in a Dorset wood. Unpublished Ph.D. thesis, University of Aberdeen.

1970b. Territoriality and reproductive behaviour of red deer. *Journal of Reproductive Fertility*, Supplement 11:43-70.

Bubenik, A.B.
1959.   Ein Beitrag zum Problem der Rehwildgehege. *Deutsche Jaeger - Zeitung*, 25:255.

Cederlund, G.
1981.   Some aspects of roe deer (*Capreolus capreolus*) winter ecology in Sweden. Doctoral dissertation, University of Stockholm.

Challies, C.N.
1974.   Trends in red deer (*Cervus elaphus*) populations in Westland forests. *Proceedings of the New Zealand Ecological Society*, 21:45-50.

Cheatum, E.L. and C.W. Severinghaus
1950.   Variations in fertility of white-tailed deer related to range conditions. *Transactions of the North American Wildlife Conference*, 15:170-190.

Drew, K.R.
1985.   Meat production from farmed deer. In *Biology of Deer Production*, edited by P. Fennessy and K.R. Drew, pp. 285-290. Proceedings of the International Conference held at Dunedin, New Zealand, 13-18 February 1983. Royal Society of New Zealand, Bulletin 22.

Dzieciolowski, R.
1979.   Structure and spatial organization of deer populations. *Acta Theriologica* 24, 1:3-21.

Einarsen, A.S.
1946.   Crude protein determination of deer foods as applied to management technique. *Transactions of the North American Wildlife Conference*, 11:309-312.

Ellenberg, H.
1978.   The population ecology of roe deer in Central Europe. *Spixiana*, Supplement 2, Munich.

Hamilton, W.J. and K.L. Blaxter
1980.   Reproduction in farmed red deer. 1. Hind and stag fertility. *Journal of Agricultural Science*, Cambridge, 95:261-273.

Huxley, J.
1934.   A natural experiment on the territorial instinct. *British Birds*, 27:270-277.

Klein, D.R.
1970.   Food selection by North American deer and their response to over-utilization of preferred plant species. In *Animal populations in relation to their food resources*, edited by A. Watson, pp. 25-46. British Ecological Society Symposium, 10. Edinburgh: Blackwell Scientific Publications.

Klein, D.R., and H. Strandgaard
1972.   Factors affecting growth and body size of red deer. *Journal of Wildlife Management*, 36:64-72.

Koenig, E., and H. Gossow
1979.   Even–aged plantations as a habitat for deer in central Europe. In *The ecology of even-aged forest plantations*, edited by E.D. Ford, D.C. Malcolm, and J. Atterson, pp. 429–451. International Union of Forest Research Organizations Meeting, Edinburgh, September 1978.

Loudon, A.S.I.
1978.   The control of roe deer populations: a problem in forest managment. *Forestry*, 51: 73-83.

1979a. Social behaviour and habitat in roe deer. Unpublished Ph.D. dissertation, University of Edinburgh.

1979b. The control of roe populations. *Deer*, 4:515-520.

1982.   Too many deer for the trees?. *New Scientist*, 93:708-711.

Loudon, A.S.I., A.S. McNeilly, and J.A. Milne
1983.   Nutrition and lactational control of fertility in red deer. *Nature* 302:145-147.

Loudon, A.S.I., A. Darrock, and J.A. Milne
1984.   The lactation performance of red deer on hill and improved species pastures. *Journal of Agricultural Science, Cambridge*, 102: 149-158.

McCullough, D.R.
1979.   *The George Reserve Deer Herd. Population Ecology of a K Selected Species*. Ann Arbor, Michigan: University of Michigan Press.

Mitchell, B., B.W. Staines, and D. Welch
1977. *Ecology of Red Deer*. Banchory: Institute of Terrestrial Ecology, Natural Environment Research Council.

Prior, R.
1968. *The Roe Deer of Cranborne Chase: an Ecological Survey*. Oxford: Oxford University Press.

Robinson, D.J.
1958. Forestry and wildlife relationship in Vancouver Island. *Forestry Chronicle*, 34:31-36.

Seebeck, R.M.
1968. Developmental studies of body composition. *Animal Breeding Extracts*, 36:167-181.

Snedecor, G.W. and W.G. Cochran
1967. *Statistical Methods*. Ames, Iowa: Iowa State University Press.

Staines, B.W.
1978. The dynamics and performance of a declining population of red deer (*Cervus elaphus*). *Journal of Zoology*, 184:403-419.

Strandgaard, H.
1972a. An investigation of corpora luea, embryonic development, and time of birth of roe deer (*Capreolus capreolus*) in Denmark. *Danish Review of Game Biology*, 6:7.

1972b. The roe deer *Capreolus capreolus*) population at Kalø and the factors regulating its size. *Danish Review of Game Biology*, 7:1–205.

Ueckermann, E.
1957. *Wildstandsbewirtschaftung und Wildschadenverhütung beim Rehwild*. Wirtschafts-und Forstverlage Euting - Hamburg und Berlin: Paul Parey. K.G. Neuwied.

Watson, A.
1967. Population control by territorial behaviour in Red Grouse. *Nature*, 202:506-507.

Zimmerman, J.L.
1971. The territory and its density dependent effect in *Spiza americana*. *Auk*, 88:591-612.

RICHARD D. TABER
and
KENNETH J. RAEDEKE

College of Forest Resources AR-10
University of Washington
Seattle, WA 98195

The Management of *Cervus* in North America

ABSTRACT

Elk management has the same three objectives as management of any other renewable living resource: to maintain genetic diversity; to maximize human benefits from the resource; and to keep conflicts between the existence and use of the resource and other human values within tolerable limits.

North American elk populations once numbered perhaps 10,000,000, distributed coast-to-coast, from southern Canada into Mexico, in the races (from east to west) *canadensis, manitobensis, nelsoni, merriami, nannodes,* and *roosevelti.* Now, *merriami* is extinct, but replaced by *nelsoni,* and *canadensis* is of uncertain status.

Reduction to about 90,000 or about 1% of original stocks by 1900, elk have since increased to about 500,000 as a result of transplantation, dispersal, and regulated harvest, under the control of state and provincial wildlife agencies. Harvest is by recreational hunting by licensed sportsmen, with financial support of regulatory agencies being related to license sales. Use of elk meat is for human food; commercial use of elk or elk parts is largely forbidden. The annual harvest is about 100,000 elk.

Elk habitat now consists largely of forest and forest-range lands, both public and private. It suffers from both diminution (i.e., encroachment of incompatible land uses) and deterioration (i.e., increase of competing land uses), partially off-set by winter-range purchase and beginnings of integrated renewable resource management on public lands. Private land managers, with no prospects for financial return under the free-hunting system, have no incentive to manage elk other than for minimization of crop damage. The exceptions are Texas and Indian

Reservations, where access is controlled by the land manager, and hunting-access fees can be charged.

In national parks and refuges, where hunting is not allowed, and the aboriginal wolf is absent, elk may be controlled by over-population, undernutrition, and climatic stress, with attendant pressures on the carrying capacity of the habitat.

Continuation of current trends, and meeting of current needs, will result in better base data for elk harvest management, better integration of elk with other natural resources in the management of public lands, local increases in the carrying capacity of elk habitat, and continued habitat losses to uses incompatible with elk survival.

Introduction

This report concerns the native populations of *Cervus elaphus* in North America, and their management. The term *management* implies that we will view elk, at least in part, as living resources for human use, and that we will consider human cultures and activities as they affect or relate to elk.

As a natural resource, a mosaic of elk populations has both non-renewable and renewable aspects. Genetic heterogeneity is non-renewable in the common case that the living animals uniquely capable of transmitting certain genes must continue to live and reproduce if those genes are to endure; elimination of a race eliminates a resource. As a renewable resource, an elk population is capable of producing as rich a multitude of goods and services as humans desire. That different human groups may have different, and conflicting desires, is one of the themes of this report.

The management of any living renewable resource has three broad objectives:

(1) To preserve genetic heterogeneiety. This includes the conservation of extant taxa, and the avoidance of new selective pressures resulting in diminished genetic heterogeneity.

(2) To use the resource efficiently for current and long term human needs.

(3) To reduce conflicts between competing uses of the resource and between use of the resource with other human values to currently tolerable levels.

Elk, like humans, are relatively recent immigrants to North America from Eurasia. They moved into their present North American range during the Pleistocene, some 100,000 years ago (Bryant and Maser, 1982). Subsequently they spread through the temperate parts of the continent from coast to coast, from southern Canada into temperate Mexico. They were especially abundant over much of the tall-grass prairie and its forest ecotones and in the forest openings and edges of the eastern flank of the Rockies. Aboriginal

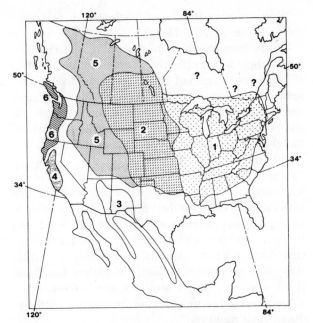

Figure 1. Original distribution of 1. Eastern elk (*C. e. canadensis*). 2. Manitoban elk (*C. e. manitobensis*). 3. Merriam elk (*C. e. merriami*). 4. Tule elk (*C. e. nannodes*). 5. Rocky Mountain elk (*C. e. nelsoni*). and 6. Roosevelt elk (*C. e. roosevelti*), based on available records. (Reproduced with permission from "Elk of North America: Ecology and Management" (Thomas and Toweill, editors, 1982), Wildlife Management Institute and Stackpole Books.)

numbers have been estimated to be about ten million (Seton, 1927).

Six races have been identified (distributed from east to west): *canadensis, manitobensis, nelsoni, merriami, nannodes,* and *roosevelti* (Figure 1). The race *merriami*, which comprised the southwestern extremity of elk distribution, is now extinct, wiped out by over-hunting in the days of European settlement. The race *canadensis*, which was widespread, though at probably low densities, over the eastern half of the continent, may well also be extinct for the same reasons, but possibly some survive in Ontario (Bryant and Maser, 1982).

European settlement had a catastrophic impact on North American elk populations. The pioneers and settlers of European heritage brought with them a material need for the meat and hides that the elk could provide, both for domestic use and trade, and cultural beliefs that encouraged their free exploitation of the elk as a resource. The biblical injunction was plain, in Genesis (9):

"And God blessed Noah and his sons, and said unto them, Be fruitful, and multiply, and replenish the earth."

"And the fear of you and the dread of you shall be upon every beast of the earth . . ., into your hand they are delivered."

"Every moving thing that liveth shall be meat for you . . ." (Anon. 1892:13–14).

On the frontier, where the remaining elk were to be found, there was no effective restraint on the freedom of humans to hunt and kill elk for any purpose, personal or economic. There was some of the feeling, deeply rooted in human traditions, that meat should not be wasted. This colors the account of a winter slaughter in Iowa (Bryant and Maser, 1982).

"In the severe weather of winter they were often driven to seek shelter and food in the vicinity of the settlements. At such times the people, not satisfied with killing enough for their present need, mercilessly engaged in an exterminating butchery. Rendered bold by their extremity, the elk were easily dispatched by such implements as axes and corn-knives. For years they were so numerous that the settlers could kill them whenever they desired to, but several severe winters and indiscriminate slaughters soon greatly reduced their numbers."

Elk Population Management

As a wave of settlement swept over North America in the nineteenth century a philosophy of free hunting prevailed. Legal ownership of wildlife (in the U.S.) was held in common by the citizens of each state. Game was important as food, and could also be sold. Firearms, increasingly effective and less expensive as the industrial revolution progressed, were universally distributed. Numbers of big game animals, such as elk, dropped precipitously.

Observers differed in their reaction to the obvious diminution of wildlife. Some felt that it was the inevitable accompaniment of the spread of civilization. Others, more fully aware that wildlife and civilization were successfully co-existing in Europe, groped for ways of reducing hunting pressure on remnant surviving wildlife populations.

An early success was the establishment of Yellowstone Park in 1872. Although the initial legislation was not sufficient to protect the elk and other game from hide-hunters, this first U.S. National Park became a focal point for public coneren, and the principle of full wildlife protection in National Parks crystallized over the next two decades. The elk in the Yellowstone region soon responded to protection and began to increase.

Some were trapped as early as 1892 for shipment to zoos, and a decade or so later shipments began to be made to points all over the continent, for release in the wild. At present there are still large numbers of elk available but little need for further transplantation.

The race *nelsoni* was preserved by Yellowstone Na-

tional Park. The race *roosevelti* which survived as a heavily persecuted population in the rainforest of the Olympic Peninsula in Washington, was protected by the establishment of the Olympic National Monument in 1909. Eventually this monument, in expanded form, became the present Olympic National Park.

In the early 1900s battle-lines were being drawn between two schools of wildlife conservation in North America, and the conflict was especially violent in the United States. One school attributed the real and continuing decline of wildlife populations to over-shooting, and demanded the establishment of game refuges, in which there would be no hunting whatsoever, and long periods of full protection for certain vulnerable species, including most big game. We may call this the preservationist school. Their philosophy prevailed in the establishment of parks and refuges.

The opposing school freely agreed on the basic problem: over-hunting. However, it did not believe that hunting could be stopped. After all, there were millions of well-armed citizens who were, in common, the legal owners of the game, and who were, in general, firmly convinced of their right to pursue it when and where they wished and dispose of it as they saw fit. So this second school, which we will call the conservationist school, cast about for an effective approach. This, as it developed, consisted of gradually bringing the millions of hunters under a measure of control through simple regulations, and means of enforcing these regulations.

Licenses to hunt (and fish) were legislated in states and provinces, even, at first, in some smaller governmental units such as counties. The resulting revenue, in the U.S., was used directly to fund state enforcement agencies (Departments of Fish and Game). In Canada, although license fees were not used directly to fund provincial regulatory agencies, the agencies' annual budgets tended to parallel license income.

The most acceptable hunting regulations for the majority were those whose thrust was "fair shares for all," and which gave first consideration to the use of game as food for the hunter and his family. Among such regulations were restrictions on weapons and methods, a limit on the daily or seasonal bag per hunter, and the elimination of any commercial use of game species such as elk.

The U.S. sporting arms and ammunition industry obviously had a stake in the perpetuation of large numbers of hunter-clients, and by extension, in the restoration and maintenance of the largest possible stocks of game. This industry, from the earliest days of the present century, has provided continuous financial and political support for the conservationist school of elk management.

Taber and Raedeke

These developments stung some active preservationists. William Hornaday, Director of the New York Zoological Park, a man well versed in wildlife biology and welfare, articulated his distress (1913: preface):

"I have been shocked by the accumulation of evidence showing that all over our country and Canada fully nine-tenths of our protective laws have practically been dictated by the killers of the game, and that in all save a very few instances the hunters have been exceedingly careful to provide "open seasons" for slaughter, as long as any game remains to kill."

And later (p. 69) in the same volume:

"It seems to be natural for the minds of men who live in America in the haunts of big game to drift into the idea that the wild game around them is all theirs. Very few of them recognize that every other man, woman and child in a given state or province has vested rights in its wild game."

At the very time that Hornaday was expressing these sentiments, organized groups of hunters were raising funds to bring elk for stocking their local areas from the increasing Yellowstone National Park (and adjacent National Elk Refuge) populations. By rail and truck, during the first decades of this century, elk of the race *nelsoni* were released in regions from which they had been extirpated and others that were originally (and sometimes still) inhabited by the other native races.

Such scattered efforts were gradually brought together in organized state and provincial programs of elk management. Early activities focussed on control of hunters who did not abide by the regulations (poachers) and on predatory animals. Many states closed the hunting season for elk temporarily and offered bounties for the control of cougars. Wolves had already been eliminated from most of the U.S.

Elk management measures of restocking, harvest management (including total protection at times), and predator control were accompanied by a general increase in elk populations. As elk increased it became apparent that license sales were not generating enough revenue to address such emerging management problems as crop damage alleviation, and reduction of winter mortality. At the same time, there was a tendency of some state legislatures, hard pressed for revenue in the Depression years, to divert license monies for non-wildlife purposes.

The two needs, to keep license revenue for wildlife uses, and to augment it with additional funds, were met with a single remedy in the U.S. A federal excise tax on sporting arms and ammunition provided monies that were disbursed to the states, provided that their use of license revenue conformed to federal standards. This improved state wildlife funding tightened the bond between the license-buying public and the state regulatory agency, a political relationship that could consequently be expected to be stronger in the U.S. than in Canada.

As elk became still more numerous, complaints about elk damage to private lands increased. Most large elk populations, by World War II, summered in forested mountains in the western half of the continent, and descended in the early winter in response to increasing snow depth. The extent of the down-slope movement was proportional to the severity of the winter. At the same time, however, the lower slopes were commonly used for domestic livestock, particularly cattle grazing, and the stream bottoms were cultivated for hay production, for winter cattle food. In regions more favorable for agriculture, fields were fenced and cultivated, orchards were established, and the like. Elk moving downslope in the winter, then, became more and more likely to find their winter forage depleted by summer cattle grazing or to find haystacks or orchards, which they severely damaged in their search for food.

Managerial response to problems of this sort has included:

—financial compensation to the landowner for elk damage.

—purchase of important elk winter range.

—fencing to keep elk out of former areas of damage.

—feeding, to hold elk up-slope from potential damage areas.

—late-season controlled hunts, to reduce damaging populations and drive the survivors up-slope.

Parallel with these specific damage control measures has been the development of overall elk management programs. These have been characterized by the division of the state or province into elk management units. With each unit there are typically different land ownerships and uses but only one pattern of elk hunting regulations.

It is principally through variations in the hunting regulations that the state or province attempts to achieve its objectives with regard to elk management, which are:

—to maximize the satisfaction of the hunting public.

—to maximize the productivity of the elk population.

—to keep damage by elk within tolerable limits.

Success in attaining these objectives may be measured in the increasing sales of hunting licenses, and decreasing complaints of damage.

Satisfaction of the hunting public is envisioned to include access to elk habitat for hunting, success in finding and harvesting elk, and a perception that the regulatory process is open to sportsmen input. At the same time it is coming to be recognized that access, carried to an extreme, leads to the crowding and dissatisfaction of hunters. Experimental closure of roads to motor vehicles during the hunting season has been successful in reducing the perception of crowding, but it is obvious that even a fully-stocked habitat has finite limits. Among efforts to relieve hunter-congestion are week-day openings, multiple openings for different groups of hunters, limitation of hunters to primitive weapons, notably bows or muzzle-loading rifles, and limiting total hunter numbers through some form of lottery. All of these are reasonably acceptable and effective.

The dimension of hunter satisfaction that is termed hunter-success is measurable, since it is the legal kill per hundred individual hunters per year. For elk it has been found to vary from almost 100 (for certain limited hunts) down to almost zero. Potter (1982), in an analysis of elk hunting on U.S. National Forest lands, found that about 6 percent hunter success was sufficient to bring the hunters back another year, but that below that point the number of hunters declined.

For North American elk management, elk productivity means the production of elk, rather than the production of mature trophy bulls, since the average license-buying sportsman is satisfied with the opportunity to bag an elk of any age or sex. Management of elk productivity, then, should ideally operate through control of the herd size after hunting, to balance it with available winter forage, and control of age and sex structure of the population to assure successful reproduction. In real life, unfortunately, reliable data on either population size or forage availability is largely lacking. Computer models using field data, currently popular, produce results of uncertain validity because of the low quality of that data. Rule-of-thumb management decisions are the most common:—take only antlered bulls when you want the population to grow; also take antlerless elk (calves and cows) in limited numbers to stabilize the population at the current level; take all elk more liberally to reduce the populations.

Since one bull can breed many cows, and since some bulls are capable of breeding at one-and-a-half years, it would seem a straightforward matter to harvest bulls heavily after the October breeding season, allowing all antlered individuals (i.e., those 1.5 years and older) to be taken. This would permit the bull calves to survive for another year, become yearlings, and breed. But only some, not all yearling bulls, are capable of effective breeding. Selections in such a heavily harvested population, would be for early sexual maturation, presumably accompanied by reduction in skeletal size. Thus there would be a new set of

selective pressures in place of those under which elk evolved to their present form.

In addition, if yearling bulls are not capable of inseminating all cows in their first estrus, some cows will conceive following their second or later estrus, and will give birth after the optimal time has passed, with reduced prospects for calf survival.

In actual practice, the states with the most heavily harvested elk populations recognize the need for some adult bull escapement, and aim for a post-hunt sex ratio of at least six antlered bulls per 100 antlerless elk. This can be achieved by control of hunter numbers, or facility of access, or by stipulating that, in order to be legal game, a bull must exhibit more than one antler point on a side. This last approach, however, has its flaws. If the requirement is for two or three points per side, the better-developed yearlings, which carry such antlers, will be taken, while the poorer specimens, carrying only spikes, will survive. If the requirement is for four points per side, bulls will generally not become legal game until they are two-and-a-half years old, and the yearling bull population, perfectly acceptable to hunters, will be protected from hunting. It would seem that for current North American condiions it would be more successful, in terms of managerial objectives, to control the breeding bull segment by control of hunter number or access rather than by declaring spikes illegal game.

It is reasonable to suppose that a heavy cropping of males by hunters will improve the winter foraging prospects for the cows, by lessening potential male competition. However, there is an increasing amount of evidence that bulls and cows feed in different areas during the winter and especially during the last two critical months before calf-drop. But if bull-cow competition is negligible, cow-cow competition certainly can occur.

The increase in elk populations that has apparently occurred in North America demonstrates a measure of success in management of the female, or productive component. Females exhibit biological changes as they age: their leadership tendencies grow stronger and their reproductive potential grow weaker. Exploitation of the female portion of the population through hunting tends to reduce life expectation. This increases the average productivity per surviving female and weakens the attachment of an elk group to a particular set of home-range traditions, as embodied in the habits of their old lead cow—" . . . herself of the long neck" as Darling said. It would seem probable, then, that a moderate amount of cow-harvesting would promote the spread of elk through an increased rate of productivity and a weakening of specific home-range bonds. The increase of elk kill from the 1930s to the 1970s, which has taken place while cow-harvests

Taber and Raedeke

have been going on, may be due to any or all of three factors: increasing productivity due to younger average cow age; increasing spread, colonization, and therefore forage base due to weaker ties to tradition; and/or annually harvesting a larger proportion of the base population each year.

A fourth factor is weather. Recent decades have experienced few really severe winters. However, in the northern extremity of the natural elk distribution, in Canada, severe winters in the 1968–1971 period probably contributed to a steep decline in elk numbers, as reflected in a declining kill until the most recent few years, in which there has been an upturn (Figure 2).

It is possible, through the employment of simulation models of elk populations, to assess the degree to which a hypothetical population could withstand an ever-increasing rate of harvest without itself declining. As more harvest pressure is applied productivity will rise, for reasons mentioned above, and a greater harvest will be realized year after year—up to a point.

It is probable that the long-continued rise in annual elk harvest (Figure 3) is due to the interaction of all three factors—increased hunting pressure and proportional take, increased population productivity, and spread of elk populations. For each of these the manager, unfortunately, can obtain only partial glimpses of what is actually happening in the population.

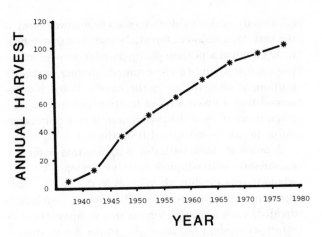

Figure 3. Annual legal elk harvest (in thousands of elk) in North America. Yearly variations were smoothed by calculating annual average harvest in five year intervals.

Hunting pressure has risen, he can surmise, when there are more hunters and a lower rate of hunter success. Increased population productivity should be reflected in the winter ratios of bulls : cows : calves that most state and provincial wildlife agencies obtain. And the spread of elk is shown by their colonization of new winter ranges and their increased appearance in the outskirts of human settlement. But information of this sort is not sufficient for a quantitative assessment of how much each of these factors has contributed to an increased annual harvest.

Determining the annual legal harvest is not easy, because in North America the licensed hunter is ordinarily not restricted to one particular hunting area, but can go to one or another at will, within the state or province for which he holds a hunting license. Various sampling schemes include use of checking stations at which hunters leaving the hunting area report. In most cases, however, the hunting region is so large, and road access is so unrestricted that many hunters are never checked. Personal interviews of hunters in the field, too, are hampered by the thin distribution of hunters over huge areas, so that it is expensive to obtain a sufficient sample for a reliable harvest estimate. Cost considerations have driven most agencies to mail surveys. Some, such as Colorado, have used a systematic telephone interview with success (Mohler and Toweill, 1982). Generally speaking, each state or province uses its own system of estimating the annual legal elk harvest within its own borders, and there is no independent assessment of the precision or accuracy of any of the annual estimates. Therefore the various harvest estimates must be taken with a degree of faith.

It is from these annual harvest estimates, of uncertain validity, that the elk managers work back toward a total population estimate, since elk cannot be count-

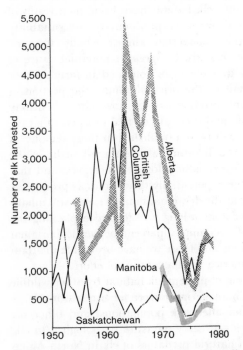

Figure 2. Elk harvest in some Canadian provinces, 1950-1979. (Reproduced with permission from "Elk of North America: Ecology and Management" (Thomas and Toweill, editors, 1982), Wildlife Management Institute and Stackpole Books).

ed directly with any degree of accuracy over most of the vast, mountainous, forested range that they inhabit. Even when a portion of the population winters below the forest, and can be counted, another, unknown portion, winters higher in the woods. But if it is assumed that a given level of hunting pressure takes a given proportion of the population, then a population estimate can be calculated from the kill.

A major problem with this system is that while it is reasonably well adapted to large regions, such as whole states, it is difficult to apply to the smaller management units into which each state or province is divided, since a hunter, who is free to hunt where he wants, often does not know the proper designation of the unit within which he bagged his elk.

Washington State has recently addressed this problem, by requiring each elk hunter to choose one only of several elk hunting regions. This will provide better information on both hunter numbers and harvest by region.

The future may well hold a problem of another sort. As long as there is only one consumptive user, the licensed elk hunter, accurate estimates of harvest may not be necessary for adequate management decisions. But with a resurgence of claims to fishing and hunting rights by Native Americans a legal philosophy of resource allocation has arisen, and allocation requires reliable enumeration.

Potter (1982:546) provides some background for this development:

"The legal questions involved in on-reservation hunting generally have been settled. States have no jurisdiction over wildlife and hunting on Indian reservations. Ceded lands and off-reservation hunting are the chief sources of conflict."

"Ceded lands are those lands originally comprising the territory of Indian tribes. On signing treaties, the Indian ceded these lands to the United States, while reservations were retained by or granted to the tribes. After treaties were signed, many Indians continued their custom of hunting on their usual territory, including ceded lands without challenge. The initial problems arose when ceded lands became a part of a state admitted to the union. The states took a more possessive attitude on the premise that statehood transferred sovereignty of ceded land to the newly created state. In other words, Indians practicing the same customs as before statehood were considered in violation of the state's authority." (Potter, 1982:546).

Over recent decades the relations between Native Americans and the states within which they hunt elk have moved toward clarification, but a complete resolution has not, at this writing, been achieved. Briefly, it has been ruled that " . . . while Indians are not considered totally exempt from state regulations off

reservation, the burden is on the state to prove that regulations are necessary for resource preservation . . . (and) that the state can regulate Indian hunting and fishing only if conservation cannot be achieved by other means, such as restricting non-Indian hunting and fishing" (Potter 1982:546).

While there has not, as yet, been a court ruling as demanding as the Boldt decision applied to elk populations, it appears that such a ruling is a possibility for the future. The successful allocation of the harvestable elk to two (or more) contending groups would require a much more accurate knowledge of elk populations on the part of the regulatory agencies than they now appear to have. Meeting this need would require the development of new or improved techniques of population enumeration and assessment. This would have its costs, but the data generated would be of quality more appropriate for the elk population management simulation models that have recently been developed than that now routinely available to elk managers.

Elk Habitat

Several elements enter the consideration of elk habitat: the pre-emption of former or potential habitat by non-compatible uses; the effects of other wildlife populations on actual and potential elk population; and the integration of other more or less compatible land uses with the aims of elk management.

A glance at the map (Figure 1) will show that vast areas of former elk habitat have been, as a result of their potential biological productivity and suitability for cultivation, converted almost wholly to agricultural use. Elk are too great a potential cause of agricultural damage to be tolerated in farmland, so well over half of the original range, the portion of highest plant productivity, is now almost entirely devoid of elk, and there are no real prospects that elk populations will be re-established in these regions. If we make a rough estimate that three-fourths of the original elk range is now lost to other uses, and that this lost range is potentially three times as productive of elk forage as the dry, mountainous range still inhabited, we have gone a long way toward explaining the difference of over ninety percent between aboriginal elk populations and those we have been able to attain in North America with a century of effort.

The sharing of present elk habitat by other wildlife species is of managerial concern for two reasons: large predators can affect elk populations; and other big game species can carry parasites pathological to elk.

The main natural predators of elk in North America are the wolf, the cougar, and the two bears, black and brown. The wolf was eliminated from present elk range in the U.S. by 1920, and Canadian populations were also suppressed, though not as completely. The

Taber and Raedeke

cougar was subject to bounty over most elk range, in the U.S., until fairly recent years.

An increasing public sympathy for large predators has emerged over the past two decades, in North America, as a part of a general concern for the preservation of the diversity of life. This has led to passage of legislation for the protection of endangered forms on a national and international scale. The plains wolf, listed as an endangered form, is now covered by full legal protection in the elk ranges of the Northern Rocky Mountains in the U.S., but there are as yet few wolves there. In contrast, the coastal wolf, found on Vancouver Island, is currently abundant. Its depredations on deer and elk, on the one hand, and a large measure of public sympathy, on the other, have presented the provincial regulatory agency with a knotty managerial problem. Similar problems will occur if and when wolves ever become abundant again on elk range in the U.S.

While the severe reduction of wolf populations was considered necessary during the early days, for the protection of livestock, the cougar was controlled mainly because of its predation on game. Even such a staunch animal-lover as Hornaday had scant sympathy, in 1914, for this large carnivore (1914, 140):

"The Mountain Lion of the west, known to us as puma or cougar, . . . is a destructive, dangerous, and intolerable pest. Wherever it is found it is fearfully destructive to deer and young elk and it must be hunted down and destroyed regardless of cost . . ."

Wildlife agencies considered cougar control a matter of high priority, offering bounties and providing full-time lion control agents. The fewer cougar eating game, it was reasoned, the more game for the license-buyer. Gradually, however, public sympathy, and the political support that it engenders, eliminated the subsidized persecution of the cougar. For example in Washington State, a bounty was offered for the killing of cougars from 1905 to 1960. From 1961 to 1965 the cougar was listed as a non-bountied predator. In 1966 the cougar became a game species, with a limit of one per licensed hunter per year, and that is its status still. The result is an apparent increase in cougar range and numbers.

Bear predation of elk is focused largely on calves, both newborn and during early spring before they have regained their strength. Its relative importance for elk management is currently becoming better understood as the biological facts become better known. Where bears are abundant the potential for a significant reduction in elk herd productivity exists. The same may be said for wolf predation and cougar predation as well, though the elk they kill may be older. Until recently, predators have been severely controlled throughout most elk ranges; their current increase may abviously lead to increased impacts on elk populations, and hence elk management. But elk predation has been subject to relatively little investigations, so the elk manager has insufficient grounds on which to base managerial decisions concerning it. All that can be said at present is that predation on North American elk will probably be greater in the next half-century than it was in the last one.

Elk are susceptible to two nematode parasites of native deer. The meningeal worm (*Paraelaphostrongylus tenuis*) of white-tailed deer in the eastern U.S. poses a hazard for elk described by Kistner et al. (1982: 210):

"Naturally occurring disease from the parasite is rare in white-tailed deer (Eckroade et al., 1970; Prestwood, 1970), but this parasite is devastating to other North American Cervids . . . attempts to reintroduce elk into eastern United States probably are doomed to ultimate failure since this parasite is found in white-tailed deer from Georgia to Maine and westward to Oklahoma and eastern Texas . . .. Also, translocation of infected eastern white-tailed deer to western states and establishment there of the meningeal worm would be devastating to western cervids."

The arterial worm (*Eleophora schneideri*) of western North America is also of concern in elk management, as indicated by Kistner et al. (1982: 207):

"Arterial worms coevolved with mule deer and possibly moose, and disease in these hosts is uncommon (Hibler and Adcock, 1971; Worley, 1975) . . . the parasite is a major pathogen in Rocky Mountain elk . . . clinical cases have been reported from Arizona, Colorado, New Mexico, and Wyoming . . . with high populations of mule deer and/or horseflies elk numbers can be limited severely."

The integration of elk management with other more-or-less compatible uses of the land is a large topic that can only be high-lighted here.

There are extensive public lands in the present range of North American elk. In addition, especially in the U.S., there is much land in private ownership. These private lands, in general, are treated like public lands with respect to elk management. That is, the owner has no right to the elk beyond those of any other citizen, and hunter access is not controlled. Exceptions include the state of Texas, which has strong trespass laws and little public land, and Indian Reservations, which are controlled completely by the respective tribes.

Elk management on the extensive public and associated private lands has consisted largely of population restoration and harvest control, as has been discussed. On a smaller scale, purchases have been made with state wildlife funds of some important elk winter ranges. Now, rising land values have largely precluded much more land purchase, and concern for elk habitat is focussed on maintaining the quantity and enhancing the quality of present habitat.

The quantity of elk habitat is continually being reduced by such noncompatible uses as road and reservoir construction, winter sports development, mining and human settlement. The loss of range to incompatible uses has been partially off-set by the land purchases mentioned above, but the major future challenge will be to pursue the integrated management of renewable resources on public lands, set forth in such recent legislation as the 1976 National Renewable Resources Planning Act, which directs the U.S. Forest Service to integrate wildlife needs with those of other renewable resources such as timber and grazing. The successful pursuit of these integrated-use objectives with regard to elk management will require substantially more reliable information on elk and elk habitat than is now available. Many good studies have been made on a small scale, but the large-scale experimental work that would yield reliable predictions on the scale of a forest or game management unit, the scale at which management is actually practiced, has not been undertaken. The reasons are that it is difficult and hence expensive, and that the managers have not considered it of high priority in relation to their other needs. However, the trends noted earlier suggest a need for more accurate monitoring of elk populations and harvests. Now, the requirement for integration of elk with other resources management on public lands will also call for more accurate monitoring of elk populations. This, in turn, will permit the controlled investigation of the effects of experimental habitat manipulation, and so lead to the development of a body of reliable data on which to base managerial decisions.

Some public lands are managed not for productivity but for other objectives:—the National Park lands provide a prime example. In extent, they constitute only a small proportion of total elk habitat. But several characteristics make them important in the whole matrix of continental elk management: many national parks support elk populations; national park objectives in elk management are not aimed toward elk production and harvest but toward an integration of elk populations with other elements in a natural landscape; and the Native Americans and large mammalian predators that once helped stabilize elk populations no longer do so, particularly in the U.S. The result has been a tendency for elk, which are generalized and adaptable, to increase and put pressure on their own habitat, which is shared by other plant and animal species. This has posed a management problem, for which two different solutions have been devised. One is the direct control of elk populations by shooting. Since recreational hunting is generally forbidden in the national parks of North America, this shooting has been carried out by agency professionals. This periodic culling is the common practice in Canada. In the U.S. it has been practiced, but its perceived unfavorable public reception has led to the development of an alternative solution to the problem. This has been to view signs of heavy habitat use—i.e., changes in plant composition, reduction in plant vigor, increases in soil exposure, increases in accelerated soil erosion and the like—as representing a "Zootic disclimax" rather than "elk damage."

Currently, however, National Park biologists recognize that elk populations can become so large that they should somehow be controlled (Houston, 1980). Present practice is to attempt to achieve this control through state-administered recreational hunting of these populations if and when they are driven beyond park boundaries by deep snows.

Literature Cited

Anonymous
1892.   *The Holy Bible*. Philadelphia: John C. Winston and Co.

Bryant, L.D., and C. Maser
1982.   Classification and distribution. In *Elk of North America: Ecology and Management*, edited by J.W. Thomas and D.E. Toweill, pp. 1–60. Washington, D.C.: Wildlife Management Institute and Stackpole Books.

Eckroade, R.J., G.M. ZuRhein, and B.M. Levy
1970.   Meningeal worm invasion of the brain of a naturally infected white-tailed deer. *Journal of Wildlife Discussion*, 6:430–436.

Hibler, C.P., and J.L. Adcock
1971.   Elaeophorosis. In *Parasites and Diseases of Wild Mammals*, edited by J.W. Davis and R.C. Anderson, pp. 262–278. Ames: Iowa State Univ. Press.

Hornaday, W.T.
1913.   *Our Vanishing Wildlife*. New York: New York Zoological Society and Charles Schribner's Sons.

Houston, D.B.
1980.   The northern Yellowstone elk-winter distribution and management. In *North American Elk: Ecology, Behavior and Management*, edited by M.S. Boyce and L.D. Hayden-Wing, pp. 263–272. Laramie: University of Wyoming.

Kistner, T.P., K.R. Greer, D.E. Worley, and O.A. Brunetti
1982.   Diseases and parasites. In *Elk of North America: Ecology and Management*, edited by J.W. Thomas and D.E. Toweill, pp. 181–218. Washington, D.C.: Wildlife Management Institute and Stackpole Books.

Taber and Raedeke

Mohler, L.L., and D.E. Toweill

1982.   Regulated elk populations and hunter harvests. In
        Elk of North America: Ecology and Management, edited
        by J.W. Thomas and D.E. Toweill, pp. 561–598.
        Washington, D.C.: The Wildlife Management In-
        stitute and Stackpole Books.

Potter, D.R.

1982.   Recreational use of elk. In *Elk of North American:
        Ecology and Management*, edited by J.W. Thomas and
        D.E. Toweill, pp. 509–560. Washington, D.C.: The
        Wildlife Management Institute and Stackpole
        Books.

Prestwood, A.K.

1970.   Neurologic disease in a white-tailed deer massively
        infected with meningeal worms. *Journal of Wildlife
        Discussion*, 6:84–86.

Worley, P.E.

1975.   Observations on epizootiology and distribution of
        Elaeophora schneideri in Montana Ruminants. *Journal
        of Wildlife Discussion*, 11:486–488.